UNITED STATES ARMY IN WORLD WAR II

The Technical Services

THE SIGNAL CORPS: THE OUTCOME
(Mid-1943 Through 1945)

by

George Raynor Thompson
and
Dixie R. Harris

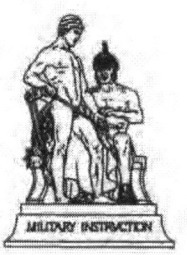

CENTER OF MILITARY HISTORY

UNITED STATES ARMY

WASHINGTON, D.C., 1991

UNITED STATES ARMY IN WORLD WAR II

Stetson Conn, General Editor

Advisory Committee
(As of 1 July 1964)

Fred C. Cole
Washington & Lee University

Lt. Gen. August Schomburg
Industrial College of the Armed Forces

James A. Field, Jr.
Swarthmore College

Maj. Gen. Hugh M. Exton
U.S. Continental Army Command

Earl Pomeroy
University of Oregon

Brig. Gen. Ward S. Ryan
U.S. Army War College

Theodore Ropp
Duke University

Brig. Gen. Elias C. Townsend
U.S. Army Command and General Staff College

Lt. Col. Thomas E. Griess
United States Military Academy

Office of the Chief of Military History

Brig. Gen. Hal C. Pattison, Chief of Military History

Chief Historian

Chief, Histories Division

Chief, Editorial and Graphics Division

Editor in Chief

Stetson Conn

Col. Albert W. Jones

Col. Walter B. McKenzie

Joseph R. Friedman

. . . to Those Who Served

Foreword

With this volume Dr. Thompson and Mrs. Harris conclude the story of U.S. Army Signal Corps operations in World War II. *The Outcome* is largely a success story, as it picks up in 1943 and carries on past V–J Day. Of all the technical services, the Signal Corps was least prepared for war in 1941. But by mid-war the Corps was operating efficiently at home and all over the world. Even so, there were always difficulties to be overcome. Further, other agencies conducted feuds and raids. The Army Air Forces, though using Signal Corps equipment through the end of the war, was never satisfied with it.

The authors have told the story with candor. The point of view is that of the Signal Corps, but the range of subject matter should prove interesting and instructive to military men and to students of both technology and public administration.

Washington, D.C.
1 July 1964

HAL C. PATTISON
Brigadier General, USA
Chief of Military History

Authors

George Raynor Thompson, coauthor of *The Signal Corps: The Test,* published in this series in 1957, has an A.B. degree from Harvard College and a Ph.D. degree from Princeton University. In 1942 he was a Carnegie Research Fellow of The Johns Hopkins University in the history of Graeco-Roman science. From 1943 to 1946 he was an officer in the Office of the Chief of Naval Communications. He joined the staff of the historical office of the Signal Corps in 1947, becoming its chief in 1952. He has provided operation research services in the U.S. Army Strategic Communications Command since 1962.

Dixie R. Harris, after receiving an A.B. degree from Ohio State University, studied law for four years and was admitted to the bar of Ohio in 1938. From 1942 to 1944 she was employed by the Signal Corps Publications Agency at Wright Field, Ohio. From 1945 to 1947 she served with the historical section of the Office of the Chief Signal Officer, and in 1949 she joined the staff of the Signal Corps section of the Office of the Chief of Military History. She became assistant chief of the Signal Corps historical office in 1952 and is coauthor of the present volume's predecessor, *The Signal Corps: The Test.*

Preface

With this volume, third and last in the Signal Corps subseries, the authors close the book on the history of the Corps in World War II. They close it to the extent that they hereby complete the account as published in the UNITED STATES ARMY IN WORLD WAR II histories. But they hope that this volume, subtitled *The Outcome,* together with its predecessors, *The Emergency,* to Pearl Harbor Day, and *The Test,* to mid-1943, may open up to the military specialist, and to the general reader as well, new vistas of significance in the immense and complex scene of signal communications and electronics in World War II.

The Signal Corps: The Outcome, continuing the chronological treatment generally followed throughout this subseries, depicts the entire activity of the Corps at home and overseas to V–J Day. The volume is in all respects a sequel to *The Signal Corps: The Test,* wherein the authors had carried the story to mid-1943. At that point in time, the Signal Corps' struggle to obtain better control over communications throughout the Army had reached a crisis in the Washington headquarters. Or rather the Corps was just subsiding, not altogether happily, from that crisis, by 1 July 1943. In the field, in North Africa, the Signal Corps had just passed its first great combat test of the war.

Thereafter, as Signal Corps troops, equipment, and doctrine continued to meet further tests in one field of combat after another around the world, commanders increasingly realized the unprecedented scope of signal communications. They recognized that they had to have far more communications and electronics, on a larger scale and in a greater variety, than they had ever expected to require. In all theaters the outcome of Signal Corps efforts to anticipate and meet Army needs became increasingly evident. The soundness, the validity of these efforts stood revealed in the unfailing maintenance of vital command and control throughout the U.S. Army in its World War II operations.

Hence in this volume the authors have recounted in some detail Signal Corps activities in each theater overseas. The theater account occupies the first half of the book, the remainder being devoted to major activities that centered in the Office of the Chief Signal Officer and to a number of special activities such as world-wide strategic communications, electronic warfare, and signal security and intelligence. Greater justice might have been done to signals overseas had an entire volume been devoted solely to their recounting. But this was not possible within the confines of the chronological format and within the limitations of the three volumes allotted to the Signal Corps subseries.

The Signal Corps: The Outcome is the work of two authors. They collaborated closely on the over-all treatment of the book. They jointly researched and wrote Chapters I and XI. The other chapters are the work of the one or the other, as follows: Mrs. Harris, Chapters II, III, IV, V, XII, XIII, XVI, and XVII; Dr. Thompson, Chapters VI, VII, VIII, IX, X, XIV, XV, XVIII, and XIX. The research and writing were accomplished almost entirely within the Signal Corps since 1952, in which year the original organization pursuing the World War II history of the Corps, the Signal Section of the War Department Historical Division, transferred from the General Staff into the Signal Corps.

The authors owe much to the many who have enabled the completion of this book, beginning with four Chief Signal Officers (Maj. Gen. George I. Back (Ret.), Lt. Gen. James D. O'Connell (Ret.), Maj. Gen. Ralph T. Nelson (Ret.), and Maj. Gen. Earle F. Cook (Ret.)), whose terms of office extended in some degree over the years when this volume was being prepared. Their support and interest were unfailing. Thanks are also due to the many Signal Corps officers who read the manuscript. As participants in the events described, they provided the authors with insights and understanding that gave greater meaning to the paper records. Grateful appreciation is tendered to Mrs. Helen Sawka, Mrs. Gladys Newsome, and Mrs. Marion McKnight, the three typists who accomplished in succession in this office their essential portion of the task with faithful care and effort.

In the Office of the Chief of Military History, Dr. John Miller, jr., the Deputy Chief Historian, with valuable suggestions and assistance from the Chief Historian, Dr. Stetson Conn, supervised and guided the revision of the text. Miss Ruth Stout, Chief of the Editorial Branch, OCMH, began the editing of *The Outcome*, evincing the same high professionalism and devotion that marked her contributions to both predecessor volumes of the Signal Corps subseries. Although she had not completed her work when she died suddenly in January 1962, the guidelines she had laid down enabled her colleagues to carry the job through. Special thanks are extended to the photographic editor, Ruth Alexandra Phillips, who selected the illustrations. The authors alone, however, are responsible for interpretations made and conclusions drawn in the volume and for any errors of omission or commission.

Washington, D.C.   GEORGE RAYNOR THOMPSON
1 July 1964   DIXIE R. HARRIS

Contents

Tables

Illustrations

All illustrations are from the files of the Department of Defense.

THE SIGNAL CORPS: THE OUTCOME

CHAPTER I

Looking Toward the Theaters of Combat

By the middle of 1943 the United States was heavily involved in total war. The civilian population had become accustomed to a changed mode of life. All were by now familiar with job freezes, bond drives, security restrictions, travel congestion, and interminable waits in long queues to obtain rationing stamps or to expend them for the commodities needed daily, so essential yet now so scarce. At many points the means and purposes of everyday commerce and civilian manufacture had become identical with those of the armed forces. The second great world war of the twentieth century was far from concluded, though nearing the end of its fourth year. For the United States, many months of uneasy isolation and tentative intervention before Pearl Harbor had terminated in a sudden plunge over the brink. The nation had experienced in its first eighteen months of war a brief period of confused impotence, a slightly longer period of desperate defeats, a slow growth of confidence, then a concentration upon offensives and a demonstration of the capacity to win. In mid-1943 the war was being carried to the enemy.

Japan, by many the most hated, still remained, despite losses at Midway and in the south and southwest Pacific, a successful conqueror in large regions of Asia, Indonesia, and Oceania. Germany, the strongest and by many others the most hated, had lost heavily in Africa and had withdrawn. Though also continuing to lose ground in the Soviet Union, the Germans stubbornly resisted the Russians and remained a formidable foe. Strategy on the Allied western front was being directed against the weakest of the triune enemy, Italy, which, having lost its possessions in Africa, was soon to lose Sicily and be forced into a surrender. Against Italy, a large Allied logistical build-up was being prepared, first against Sicily, followed by landings at Salerno and Anzio and drives up the Italian mainland. A second, more powerful build-up was to be aimed at captive France. This build-up was of the most various, comprehensive, and exhaustive sort. By itself alone, it demanded enough to strain the hearts of millions.

Such was the view of the war in mid-1943 as seen from the zone of interior, where the supplies were being assembled and additional troops marshaled for movement to the theaters. It was a war deeply joined, but far from concluded. It was a balance in which the weight of American matériel and men must tip in favor of the Allies. To this end all the planning, training, and supplying agencies of the Allies were engaged. Among them the U.S. Army Signal Corps stood at its maximum of numbers and responsibilities. Nearly 26,000 officers and 290,000 enlisted men wore the crossed flag

GENERAL INGLES

insignia of the Signal Corps. More than 60,000 civilians worked in Signal Corps offices and installations.[1] The budget at this time totaled five billion dollars. The entire Army-Navy budget stood at a hundred billion. In other words, of each dollar used from this vast sum, the Signal Corps spent a nickel.[2] To convert this money into trained troops fully equipped to carry out signal assignments and to support these troops in the theaters of combat was a task that faced the incoming Chief Signal Officer, Maj. Gen. Harry C. Ingles.

Signal Corps Organization and Status, Mid-1943

General Ingles and His Team

The abrupt change of leadership by which General Ingles replaced Maj. Gen. Dawson Olmstead in June 1943 brought about a number of changes in the Signal Corps structure.[3] General Ingles was an able and experienced officer, generally regarded particularly competent as a "staff man." After his graduation from the United States Military Academy in

GENERAL CODE

1914 (a classmate of Lt. Gen. Brehon B. Somervell, under whom he would now serve), his Army assignments had given him a wide variety of field and staff experiences. He had served in a number of important Signal Corps assignments—as a department director at the Signal Corps School, as a member of the Signal Corps Board, as a battalion commander, as division signal officer in the Philippines. In a broader area, he had spent four years on the War Department General Staff (G–3) and another four as an instructor at the Command and General Staff School. In Panama in 1941–42 he served Lt. Gen. Frank M. Andrews as Chief of Staff, Caribbean Defense Command, and in early 1943 he became Deputy Commander, United States Forces in Europe.[4]

---

[1] (1) As of 30 June 1943, the exact figures according to The Adjutant General's Office were 25,874 commissioned officers and 288,159 enlisted men. Not included in this compilation are warrant officers and Waacs with Signal Corps installations. TAG, Strength of the Army (STM–30), 30 Jun 43. (2) Civilian Personnel, 16 Jan 53, prepared by Amanda Tichenor, in Theodore Whiting, Statistics, Table CP–4. Draft MS in OCMH files.

[2] Proceedings of Board to Investigate Communications, Tab P, p. 11, Testimony of Maj Gen Dawson Olmstead. AG 311 (5–10–43) (1) Bulky Pkg, Army RG 207.03 Job A50–55.

[3] For an account of the change and underlying reasons, see George Raynor Thompson, Dixie R. Harris, Pauline M. Oakes, and Dulany Terrett, The Signal Corps: The Test (December 1941 to July 1943), UNITED STATES ARMY IN WORLD WAR II (Washington, 1957), pp. 560ff.

[4] (1) Biographical Sketch, Who's Who in the Signal Corps. SigC Hist Sec file. (2) The New CSigO, SigC Tech Info Ltr 20 (Jul 43), p. 5.

As Assistant Chief Signal Officer, Maj. Gen. James A. Code, Jr., the only high-ranking Signal Corps officer to serve continuously in the same position throughout the war, provided the continuity important to policy matters and administration.[5] One of the Signal Corps' outstanding younger officers, Code had been ordered to Washington from the field in 1941 at the insistence of the General Staff, at a time when the Army's high command was something less than satisfied with the Signal Corps' performance. General Code was responsible for many of the administrative innovations that had sparked the Signal Corps' successful struggle to cope with the exigencies of war. For example, he shaped up the Signal Corps Control Division, which was established in late 1941. Later, the other technical services and the Army Service Forces (ASF) headquarters organized similar control divisions.[6] Code

General Colton

also inaugurated the Office of the Chief Signal Officer (OCSigO) expediting section, which had labored valiantly to boost production in 1942, and the patent section, which had broken the patent license bottleneck obstructing electronic production.[7] During Ingles' tenure, as during Olmstead's, Code continued to exert a great deal of behind-the-scenes influence.

General Ingles exercised the prerogative of an incoming chief and reorganized his office, streamlining it along functional lines. It was time for modifications. The extreme pressures of the first eighteen months of war had brought many new duties to the Signal Corps. To handle each new function, a new section or branch had been grafted onto the parent

[5] Code's title was Deputy Chief Signal Officer until December 1942, when he became the Assistant Chief Signal Officer and Col. Carroll O. Bickelhaupt was named Deputy Chief Signal Officer. In June 1943 the position of Deputy Chief Signal Officer was abolished. See SigC Administrative Log, 1939–45, OCSigO Orgn Chart 16–a, 30 Mar 42, thru Chart 26, 12 Jul 43. SigC Hist Sec file.

[6] (1) Dr. Courtney R. Hall, Staff Functions and Staff Agencies, Office of the Chief Signal Officer (1945), and The Development of the Office of the Chief Signal Officer, 1917–15 August 1945 (1945), SigC Hist Monographs D–3 and D–1, pp. 14–42 and 116–17, 150, respectively. SigC Hist Sec file. (2) CSigO, Annual Report, Fiscal Year 1942, p. 31. (3) Dulany Terrett, *The Signal Corps: The Emergency (To December 1941)*, UNITED STATES ARMY IN WORLD WAR II (Washington, 1956), p. 297. For Code's own account of the Control Division, see "Organization," *Radio News*, vol. 31, No. 2 (February, 1944), an issue devoted entirely to the Signal Corps, p. 90.

In June 1942 ASF was called the Services of Supply. The Services of Supply became ASF in March 1943. In this volume the designation ASF is used throughout.

[7] (1) Hall, Dev of OCSigO, p. 140. (2) CSigO, Annual Rpt, FY 43, p. 397.

organization. That organization by mid-1943 had sprouted so many offshoots that they overburdened the main forked trunk, namely, since September 1942, the Signal Supply Services and the Signal Operating Services. Two of the Signal Corps' ablest specialist officers, Maj. Gen. Roger B. Colton and Brig. Gen. Frank E. Stoner, headed the Signal Supply Services and Signal Operating Services, respectively.[8] Colton was an experienced officer who had specialized in electronics engineering and research. Stoner was a communications system specialist. But each of the two structures had spread too far to function with complete efficiency. The Signal Supply Services embraced not only all the divisions handling the entire field of supply—requirements, facilities, procurement, production, distribution, inspection, stock control, international aid, and so on—but also research, development, engineering, and maintenance activities. The Signal Operating Services was equally diversified. Its responsibilities included the great Army Command and Administrative Network (ACAN) communications system as well as activities relating to signal security and to military training and organization, but not civilian personnel and training matters. These last were attached to the Executive Office.[9]

General Ingles drew a sharp line between staff and operating functions. One of his first concerns became the formation of a true staff division. The Directorate of Planning, a small section attached to the Executive Office, had per-

formed some of this work, but much of it had been carried on by branches at the operating level. On 9 July 1943, Ingles consolidated these branches with the Office of the Planning Director to form the Operations Division.[10] Eventually this division contained seven branches: Theaters, Intelligence, Logistics Planning, Communication Coordination, Operational Research, Communications Liaison, and Special Planning. It was redesignated the Plans and Operations Division.[11] For the rest of the war, this division acted as the OCSigO general headquarters staff, handling all the planning and co-ordination concerned with tactical and strategic matters. Two other staff sections that had been attached to the Executive Office became full-fledged staff units—the Legal Division and the Fiscal Division.[12]

Late in 1942, General Olmstead had created the Operational Research Group composed of civilian scientific personnel headed by Dr. William L. Everitt of Ohio State University. Everitt was a distinguished electrical engineer, a former president of the Institute of Radio Engineering, and had also taught at Cornell University, the University of Michigan, and Ohio State University.[13] As principal scientific adviser to the Chief Signal Officer, Dr. Everitt contributed studies and suggested new applications and methods of approach on many important subjects, particularly in the field of radar. By late

[8] CSigO, Annual Rpt, FY 43, pp. 2off.

[9] SigC Admin Log, 1939–45, OCSigO Orgn Chart 18, 30 Sep 43, and Chart 25, 1 Jun 43. For definition of ACAN and discussion of the wartime ACAN system, see below pp. 580ff.

[10] Code had proposed this solution eighteen months earlier. See Memo, DCSigO to CSigO, 23 Mar 42. EO DCSigO file.

[11] CSigO, Annual Rpt, FY 44, pp. 84–85.

[12] (1) SigC Admin Log, 1939–45, OCSigO Orgn Chart 25, p. 85, and Chart 27, p. 94. (2) CSigO, Annual Rpt, FY 44, pp. 21–23.

[13] Hall, Staff Functions and Staff Agencies of OCSigO, pp. 91ff.

Dr. EVERITT

1944 the operational research activities had become so important and so diverse that the unit became a separate box on the organizational charts under the name Operational Research Staff.[14]

General Ingles chopped the operating segments of his office into functional compartments, making each a "service." In so doing, he split General Colton's Signal Supply Services into two elements, separating procurement and distribution from research and development. General Stoner's Signal Operating Services was likewise divided, all personnel matters, both military and civilian, being brought together in one organizational unit and communications operations forming another. Designated Engineering and Technical, Procurement and Distribution,

Personnel and Training, and Army Communications, respectively, these organizations together with Army Pictorial, which had enjoyed service status all along, henceforth comprised the operating services.[15] The arrangement was logical and workable; it endured beyond the end of the war and into the postwar years.[16]

Supplying a World-wide Operation

General Ingles' reorganization reflected especially his concern for supply activities. In this area, he agreed with many others, a major deficiency had long existed.[17] His predecessor, General Olmstead, had felt that "supply begins with research and development."[18] The Signal Corps, engrossed in perfecting its equipment, had not given equal attention to expanding its wartime production effort. In its own ranks, the Signal Corps had very few officer specialists in

[14] SigC Admin Log, 1939–45, OCSigO Orgn Chart 31, 1 Jan 45.

[15] SigC Admin Log, 1939–45, OCSigO Orgn Chart 26, 12 Jul 43; Chart 27, 15 Aug 43; Chart 30, 16 May 44.

[16] With a few minor changes in names and functions and redesignations of "services" as "divisions." See, for example, SigC Admin Log, 1946–56, OCSigO Orgn Charts, 15 Nov 46, 6 Dec 52, and 1 May 55.

[17] (1) Capt Charles R. Novick, The Story of Supply in the Signal Corps in World War II, pt. IV, Distribution (1945), SigC Hist Monograph B–1d, p. 9. SigC Hist Sec file. (2) Thompson, Harris, *et al.,* *The Test, passim.* (3) Memo, DCSigO (Code) for CSigO (Olmstead), 10 Sep 42. EO DCSigO file.

[18] Proceedings of Bd to Investigate Com., Tab P, p. 6.
  The British had already walked the same path. When the Ministry of Supply was formed a few months after Britain entered the war, the organization included research and development as well as supply. The differences in these two functions dictated a reorganization early in 1942 that placed production under one chief and R&D under another. R. F. H. Nalder, *The History of British Army Signals in the Second World War* (London: Royal Signals Institution, 1953), pp. 118, 122.

supply matters.[19] Yet by mid-1943 the war had reached the stage where production was of paramount importance. Whether the Signal Corps supply organization should have been separated from research and development earlier was a question that now became academic. General Colton, a top research engineer, was given much credit for "maintaining and pushing radar" in the Signal Corps laboratories during the trying period from 1939 to 1943.[20] It was Colton, many persons inside and outside the Signal Corps declared, whose foresight and daring had turned Signal Corps research toward the electronic projects that were paying such handsome dividends in battle.[21] Releasing him from his supply duties, General Ingles now left him free to try to resolve electronic engineering problems that, it was hoped, would keep the United States ahead of the enemy. The whole area of supply, the Chief Signal Officer made the responsibility of Maj. Gen. William H. Harrison.[22]

Harrison was a former vice-president of the American Telephone and Telegraph Company. Since 1940 he had been intimately connected with the defense

GENERAL HARRISON

and war effort, first as director of the Construction Division of the National Defense Council, later as chief of the Shipbuilding, Construction and Supplies Branch of the Office of Production Management, and later still as director of the Production Division of the War Production Board. In June 1942 Harrison had joined the staff of General Somervell, the commanding general of the ASF. In April 1943, Somervell had placed him in charge of the Army Pictorial Service during its brief existence as an ASF agency before it was returned to Signal Corps control. Recognizing the urgency of the Signal Corps needs and Harrison's unique qualifications for the job, Somervell agreed to release him.[23] For its part,

[19] MS Comment, Brig Gen Alfred M. Shearer, SigC (Ret.), former DCSigO ETOUSA, Jul 59.

[20] Interv, SigC Hist Sec with Col Rex Van Den Corput, former Dir SigC Radar Lab and CO SCGSA, 16 Feb 49. SigC Hist Sec file.
Colton had followed Col. William R. Blair as Director of Signal Corps Laboratories in 1938. In the 1930's Blair developed the Army's first radar, the searchlight control set, SCR-268, for which he received on 20 September 1957 important patent rights (U.S. Patent 2,803,819).

[21] Intervs, SigC Hist Sec with (1) Col Albert F. Cassevant, CO Evans Sig Lab, 10 Feb 50; (2) Dr. Edward L. Bowles, former Sp Consultant to SW Henry L. Stimson, 21 Nov 57; (3) Maj Gen Alfred W. Marriner, former Dir Air Com, WDGS, 13 Feb 50.

[22] SigC Admin Log, 1939-45, OCSigO Orgn Chart 26, 1 Jul 43.

[23] General Code instructed his executive officer to "have a notation made that only with the concurrence of the Commanding General, Army Service Forces, would General Harrison be assigned to supply activities." Log entry, 6 Jul 43. DCSigO folder, 1942-45, SigC Hist Sec file.

the Signal Corps was happy to have a man of such wide supply and procurement experience, and of national prestige.

Harrison's newly organized Procurement and Distribution (P&D) Service at first consisted of 2 divisions and 7 branches, but soon its growth overshadowed the other Signal Corps services. By May 1944, it comprised 4 divisions — Requirements, Production, Procurement, Distribution — and 16 branches. Its staff responsibility extended over an impressive array of field agencies: 3 procurement districts and 2 procurement offices; 14 depots; the Storage and Issue Agency; the Inspection Agency and 5 associated inspection zones; the Stock Numbering Agency and 3 branch offices; 5 production field offices; 2 price adjustment offices; and the Cost Analysis Agency and its 3 field offices.[24]

On taking over the P&D Service, Harrison warned Ingles not to expect satisfactory operations for at least ninety days.[25] He spent his first few weeks probing for weaknesses in the Signal Corps supply structure. He conferred repeatedly with his staffs, studied charts and graphs, and then set out on visits to the most important field agencies as well as to the nineteen principal manufacturers who produced 60 percent of all Signal Corps items of equipment. Harrison found a number of things that needed attention: a growing shortage of labor;

ineffectual production follow-up and service to contractors; and a "distressing situation" in records, which prevented an accurate measure of the volume of procurement needs. He planned further decentralization of operations, and especially hoped to develop better yardsticks to measure performance and results.[26]

During the summer of 1943 the business of procuring, storing, packing, issuing, shipping, maintaining, repairing, and replacing signal equipment occupied the largest place in the Signal Corps schedule. Thousands were engaged in it, both at home and abroad, as civilians and as soldiers. An axis extending between Washington and Philadelphia contained most of the administrative supply bureaus of the Corps. Upon this axis turned most of the operating elements in signal supply. Thus an electronic supply realm was created in which each organizational element took its place and lent its energy toward the total global effort.

The effort was twofold. Primarily, as the period of America's active participation in the European invasion drew near, it was directed toward amassing literally mountains of signal equipment and

---

[24] SigC Admin Log, 1939–45, OCSigO Orgn Chart 30, 14 May 44.

[25] Memo, Harrison for Ingles, 1 Sep 43, sub: P&D Sv. SigC DS (Harrison) Orgn P&D Sv. This subject file is one of more than one hundred personal file folders maintained by Harrison, not Dewey-decimal numbered. Hereafter referred to as SigC DS (Harrison) with file subject cited.

[26] (1) Memo, CG Chicago Sig Depot for Ingles, 24 Jul 43, no sub. (2) Memo, Harrison for Ingles, 13 Aug 43, sub: SNA. (3) OCSigO R&W Action 3, ACSigO to Chief P&D Sv, 7 Sep 43, sub: Proposed Change in Orgn, and Incl 1, Memo, Harrison for Ingles, 7 Sep 43, sub: P&D Sv, Rqmts Br. (4) Memo, Contl Div OCSigO for CSigO, 22 Sep 43, sub: Co-ordination of Cost Analysis Activities With Those of Price Adjustment, Contract Renegotiation, Price Analysis, and Price Policy Cmte. (5) Memo, Chief P&D Sv for CO's Proc Dists, Dirs of Inspec Agency, and Divs of P&D Sv, 3 Apr 44, sub: Establishment of SigC Prod Fld Ofs. (6) Incl 1, Statement of Orgn of OCSigO, par. 10, P&D Sv, with Memo, CSigO for Dirs of Staff Divs, et al., 1 Jan 44, sub: Functional Responsibilities. All in SigC DS (Harrison) Orgn P&D Sv.

getting the items into the hands of troops. This was supply in terms of quantity. A secondary but very vigorous effort could be expressed in terms of quality. It was concentrated on ways of improving existing procedures—for example, better marking methods for easier identification of package contents; increased mechanization in warehousing for faster movement of supplies; elimination of unnecessary paperwork in requisitioning; and improvement in methods of forecasting deliveries. In matters of contracting, every attempt was being made to assure that spare parts, maintenance supplies, power supplies, and instruction literature were all delivered at the same time as the primary equipment. These efforts were closely tied to the research and development emphasis on standardization and maintenance.

Research and Development
Oriented Toward Immediate
Theater Needs

Before mid-1943 research, in advance of the other activities under the Signal Corps, had reached and passed the point of trial, most notably in the case of mobile ground radar and of mobile FM (frequency modulation) radio. Research must always precede the test product, and development must attend the tests of the product before standardization, contracting, and mass supply begin. Research and development were therefore the most remote of the Signal Corps' principal tasks. Operations were the most immediate. Operations took the Corps into World War II at every moment of the day; success or failure became instantly apparent. Supply paid off almost as directly. In training, the separation

from the test of battle was much longer. In research and development, the distance became so great that for the work to be of value, the researchers had to anticipate the course of events by years. To some extent the scientific efforts of the belligerents continued to be bent upon a war two, three, or ten years in the future. To a greater extent engineering was now tied to the immediacies of field reports.

What if the enemy's scientists were ahead? This was the question that drove researchers to close every gap possible and shorten the lapse of time between the blueprint and the battlefield.[27] Suppose that all enemy equipment was as good as the best that had been captured in North Africa. Suppose, even more alarmingly, that, inasmuch as Africa was an outlying theater, an Allied attack upon the European mainland would bring out unheard-of equipment, long since perfected and held in reserve. The Wuerzburg radar was a better gun director than any radar the Allies possessed in the field in 1943.[28] There were disturbing rumors of superweapons, of rocket bombs. Current development, therefore, had to reach the field in half the time, or a tenth the time once thought necessary. Thus midway in the war, at a point that still was only the opening stage of an intense campaign, research and development activity simul-

---

[27] CSigO, Annual Rpt, FY 44, pp. 188ff, 208.
[28] The Germans had possessed the Wuerzburg, *Flakmessgerat* 39-T, since 1940. Radiating on medium-length waves at about 500 megacycles, it was accurate to a degree not surpassed until the Americans used the SCR-584 to direct antiaircraft guns at Anzio early in 1944. (1) "German Radar," *Radar* (May, 1944), p. 6. SigC Hist Sec file. (2) James P. Baxter 3d, *Scientists Against Time* (Boston: Little, Brown and Company, 1946), p. 145.

taneously reflected the past, the present, and the future.

Upon which, present or future, should the laboratories now place the more stress? Should they divert the bulk of their time into long-term developments or into improvements for immediate application? These questions the ASF settled soon after General Ingles came to the helm and the build-up for the invasion of Normandy began: emphasize what is needed now, or in the next few months. There was even considerable reduction in laboratory personnel, at ASF orders, during the summer of 1943. Then, in December, General Colton ordered all the laboratories to concentrate on practical matters that would help the troops in the field directly. He pointed the efforts of both the Signal Corps Aircraft Signal Agency (SCASA), at Dayton, Ohio, and the Signal Corps Ground Signal Agency (SCGSA), at Fort Monmouth, New Jersey, toward the support of major military actions that he knew would come in the European theater within six months. He listed, in order of importance, procurement and issue control lists, maintenance lists, and maintenance equipment. These he followed with additional matters of maintenance and instruction, which had to be stressed and accomplished with dispatch, even if it meant taking engineers off research jobs. Moisture-proofing techniques would have to be improved. Depot instructions would have to be compiled and issued, as would technical bulletins and informational material of all kinds pertaining to Signal Corps equipment. The laboratories turned their men toward the heavy practical program, which was intended to lend all possible support to the operations of

GENERAL MATEJKA

Signal Corps men and equipment on the fields of combat. The program had to be completed by the winter of 1944.[29]

The Peak of Training

General Ingles' creation of the Personnel and Training Service followed the pattern of the ASF headquarters in consolidating all military and civilian personnel functions under one unit.[30] The chief of the new service was Brig. Gen. Jerry V. Matejka, just returned from the North African Theater of Operations, United States Army (NATOUSA), where he had been the chief signal officer at Allied Force Headquarters

[29] Ltrs, Colton, Chief E&T Sv, to CO SCGSA, 18 Dec 43, and to CO SCASA, 18 Dec 43, sub: Rev Work Prog. SigC 413.44 Gen 15 (RB-2135). For further details, see below, pp. 427ff.
[30] CSigO, Annual Rpt, FY 44, p. 455.

(AFHQ) since September 1942. Before that he had served the Signal Corps cause effectively in the European theater, first as a special observer beginning in 1940, and then on the staff of the successor organizations, Special Observer Group (SPOBS), United States Army Forces in the British Isles, and the European Theater of Operations, United States Army (ETOUSA).[31]

Matejka took control of the Signal Corps training activities at their peak. By the summer of 1943 Signal Corps training was reasonably well synchronized with the intake of men and the overseas demands. Month after month, thousands of newly drafted men, technician students, specialist students, officer candidates, and officers went into the mill unfamiliar with Signal intricacies and came out knowledgeable and ready for duty. It was another version of supply. From beginning to end the school process tried to achieve the most efficient standardized products in specialized categories of a wide variety.

Specialist training activity reached its highest point in the summer of 1943. On 30 June some 47,000 Signal Corps soldiers were enrolled in Signal Corps training installations, plus 10,000 Army Air Forces (AAF) students and another 10,000 from the other arms and services.[32] An all-time peak enrollment in the Officers School (officers studying advanced communications subjects) came at the end of July, when 2,817 students were enrolled.[33] The officer candidate school, on the other hand, reached its peak enrollment some months earlier, in 1942, and thereafter showed a steady decline.[34]

During the fiscal year that ended 30 June 1943, 16,087 officers had completed Signal courses and 134,359 enlisted men had gone through the various schools, as follows:

Type	Number
Service schools	46,441
Replacement training centers	44,363
Unit training centers	10,301
Supply depots	2,626
Civilian schools	28,863
Other institutions	1,765
Total	134,359

Not only were Signal Corps men trained in these institutions, but between 1942 and 1944 a large number of men from the other arms and services received communications instruction. Such students numbered in all about 75,000, of whom some 14,000 went through the Signal Corps replacement training centers, 2,100 officers and 33,000 enlisted men completed courses in Signal Corps schools, and about 1,050 officers and 25,000 enlisted men studied in civilian schools teaching Signal Corps courses.

In mid-1943 Signal Corps replacement training centers and specialists' schools were in operation at Fort Monmouth, New Jersey; Camp Crowder, Missouri; and Camp Kohler, California. Camp Crowder also housed a unit training center. Radar training was concentrated at the Southern Signal Corps School,

[31] See account of Matejka and the Signal Section, AFHQ, in Thompson, Harris, et al., The Test, pp. 343ff., 363ff.

[32] CSigO, Annual Rpt, FY 44, p. 472.

[33] Capt Frederick Reinstein, Study of Signal Corps Officer Schooling, 1939-44 (1944), SigC Hist Monograph C-7, 32ff. SigC Hist Sec file.

[34] Capt Frederick Reinstein, Training Study of the Signal Corps Officers' Candidate School (1944), SigC Hist Monograph C-6, app. A, Tab D, OCS Enrollment and Graduates by Months, Jul 41-Jun 44. SigC Hist Sec file.

Camp Murphy, Florida, and photographic training at the Signal Corps Photographic Center at Long Island City, New York. Signal Corps depots were conducting supply courses; Signal Corps officers were enrolled in advanced radar courses at Harvard University and the Massachusetts Institute of Technology (MIT); cryptographic training was going on at Arlington Hall and at Vint Hill Farms Station in Virginia; and courses at scores of vocational and plant schools and colleges throughout the United States and in British military schools in the United Kingdom were preparing Signal Corps officers and enlisted men for their varied military communications missions.[35]

The production of phenomenal communications devices, new tactical doctrines, and combat experience exerted strong influence on school courses. Emphasis shifted from individual instruction to teamwork for both enlisted men and officers. The requirements for officers, as well as for enlisted specialists, were changing from the earlier patterns. In the summer of 1943 officer cadres for division signal companies, in high demand in the earlier months of the war, were a drug on the market. The Army Ground Forces (AGF), overstrength, began to use their own officers to staff divisions and no longer looked to the Signal Corps for cadres.[36] On the other hand, officers for supply assignments were needed badly, for mounting production was filling the depots and warehouses in the theaters faster than the meager supply staffs could handle the stock. A supply course scheduled to begin at Fort Monmouth on 1 July 1943 had to be deferred almost a month because the prospective students were hurried off to Europe, without benefit of training, to fill urgent supply needs.[37]

Notwithstanding faults still inherent in the rigidity of a Signal Corps troop structure that demanded flexibility, and despite the difficulty of laying down stable school plans in a fluid situation, all training agencies were making progress in intensive instruction on a broadening scale. The necessity of providing large numbers of Signal Corps men for duty with the Army Air Forces created by itself more diversity of training than had existed altogether at the outset of war. For a time the disparate Army Air Forces and the Signal Corps, with interests as opposite as they were identical, collaborated in training for a new circumstance of war. For the new Aircraft Warning Service (AWS), for example, the Signal Corps trained AAF men and the AAF trained Signal Corps men.[38]

Increasingly, through 1943 and into 1944, all training policy was shaped

[35] For an account of training facilities and activities from 30 June 1943 to the end of the war, see below, pp. 507ff.

[36] (1) R&W Action 1, Lt Col Duncan Hodges, Mil Pers Br OCSigO, to Mil Tng Br, 17 Jun 43, sub: Off Cadre Pers. SigC 352 Ft. Monmouth 3, May–Jul 43. (2) Ltr, CSigO to Comdt ESCS Ft. Monmouth, 25 Jun 43, sub: Discontinuance of Off Cadre Pers Tng. SigC 353 Ft. Monmouth 2 (RTC), Jun–Jul 43.

[37] (1) R&W Action 1, Maj James A. Wadsworth, Sig Sup Sv to Mil Tng Br, 24 Jun 43, sub: Tng Sig SupO's for Overseas Assignment. (2) Ltr, Col Louis Cansler, Actg Dir Sig Troops Div, Offs Advanced Prog. Both in SigC 353, Ft. Monmouth 2 (RTC), Jun–Jul 43.

[38] The Signal Corps School at Camp Murphy devoted itself to individual training of radarmen for the AAF. The AAF's three signal aviation unit training centers at Drew Field, Tampa, Florida, Pinedale, California, and Langley Field, Virginia, were established in co-operation with the Signal Corps to prepare Signal Corps units for field service with the AAF.

toward readying as many men as possible for shipment overseas as quickly as possible.[39] Many moved out from eastern ports toward Sicily and points in Italy. Almost as many were funneled into the build-up for the invasion of Normandy. To meet European demands, many men were being brought back from the Alaskan Department and the Northwest Service Command, by this time a military backwater.[40] In the sprawling Pacific areas other Signal Corps men were thinly strewn.

The field of combat on which Signal Corps manpower and training plans met their test was as diverse as it was extensive. Each area taught new lessons, proved or exploded old theories.

The Signal Corps Mission in the Theater of Operations

Duties and Doctrine

The Signal Corps, like the other technical services, served the Army in a special way. The commodity it handled is less obvious than food or clothing, less spectacular than bridge building, and less gratefully received than medical care. Modern communications involve for the most part electronic means. Electronic phenomena are generally not visible; to many they are mysterious and yet to all they are so familiar as to be taken for granted. Thus communications are seldom mentioned in official dispatches or noted in historians' accounts unless they fail. It is the absence of good communications rather than their presence that makes news.[41]

As the Army's communications agency, the Signal Corps had specific duties in the field. Spelled out by regulations (as of 1943), these duties included the installation, maintenance, and operation of all signal communications within armies; within army, armored, and cavalry corps; and within infantry, cavalry, motorized, and armored divisions. They included provision of the communications required at the headquarters of each of these units for their respective army, corps, and division troops and installations, and for communicating with the next lower and adjacent headquarters.[42]

The principles of signal operations in the field were not new. They followed well-established signal doctrine, as it had been practiced in the United States

[39] For a general discussion of training of nondivisional units 1942-45, see Robert R. Palmer, Bell I. Wiley, and William R. Keast, *The Procurement and Training of Ground Combat Troops,* UNITED STATES ARMY IN WORLD WAR II (Washington, 1948), pp. 499-560.

[40] Memo, Maj Sidney Shelley, O/C Unit Tng Sec Mil Tng Br, for file, 22 Jan 44, sub: Pers Required for Unit Activations. SigC 353 Gen MT-269.

[41] Maj. Gen. Horace H. Fuller, the commander of the 41st Division in SWPA, told Lt. Col. Irwin C. Stoll, the division signal officer, "The chief of staff and myself have a limited knowledge of Signal Corps equipment. . . . When the signal communications function properly, as we expect they will, expect no praise, but should they fail, expect plenty of hell." Lt Col Irwin C. Stoll, Div SigO 41st Div, A Chronological History of Signal Corps Operations of the Sunset Division in the Southwest Pacific Theater of War, p. 2. SCIA file 71 Stoll Rpts. This is one of a group of miscellaneous folders from Plans and Operations Branch, Office of the Chief Signal Officer, containing intelligence reports, observers' reports, and other important documents, which were turned over to the Signal Corps Intelligence Agency (SCIA) after World War II. (See Bibliographical Note, below.)

[42] AR 105-15, Field Signal Communication, 1 Aug 42 and Change 2, 11 Jun 43.

Army for many years.[43] Nevertheless, the application of these principles to the sort of warfare that was being waged in this most nearly global of all wars demanded the creation of many new techniques. In a number of aspects, this war differed from any other in which the Signal Corps had participated. World War I, for example, had been a conflict involving static situations—trench warfare—where wire lines and telephones served as the primary means of communication. There had been no invasions of enemy-held coast lines. There had been but one overseas theater for the U.S. Army in World War I—France. There the Signal Corps, American Expeditionary Forces, had received a single primary mission—the transmission of communications from the rear and all the way to the front. This mission entailed two classes of duties. They were the construction, operation, and maintenance of the general system of communications—that is, the network of lines wherever U.S. units were located—and communication by all possible means between and within the units in combat.[44] The Signal Corps in World War I controlled all combat communications, except those for the field artillery. That was a long step from the headquarters signal needs of the Army in the Civil War, when the Corps came into being.

In World War I it was thought at first that an infantry division could be served by a field signal battalion of 3 companies (wire, radio, and outpost),

each numbering 75 men. When it was found that a single infantry regiment needed a 66-man signal platoon, the total number of men for the signal outpost company was increased from 75 to 280. This increase provided a signal platoon of an officer and 65 signal soldiers for assignment to each regiment of infantry. This was for trench warfare conditions. Fewer, it was thought, would be needed for open warfare. The exact opposite proved to be the case. "The increase of the outpost company was the first expression of the needs of the American forces for more signal communications."[45]

Shorn of its control over combat signals by the reorganization of the Army in 1920, the Signal Corps nonetheless continued during the postwar years to disagree with the general trend of high-level War Department thinking on the question of the extent of signal communications the Army needed. More, much more, would be needed, the Signal Corps was convinced, in any future war. And so it proved. The pressure for more signal communications grew intense as World War II progressed. The pressure came from War Department headquarters, from headquarters in every theater, from every lesser headquarters down the chain of command, from every airplane pilot and tank commander, and finally from every patrol and platoon demanding its portable wire or radio equipment.

In the years between the two world

---

[43] See FM 24–5, 19 Oct 42, the basic manual on signal communication, and pertinent manuals in the "11," or Signal Corps series.

[44] (1) Col C. F. Martin, Hist Sec, Army War College, Signal Communications in World War I, Aug 42, p. 2. SigC Hist Sec file. (2) Terrett, *The Emergency*, pp. 23–24.

[45] (1) Rpt of Col Parker Hitt, SigO First Army AEF, contained in CSigO, Annual Rpt, 1919, p. 359–60. (2) Martin, Sig Com in World War I, pp. 9–10. (3) *Historical Sketch of the Signal Corps (1860–1941)*, Eastern SigC Schs Pamphlet 32 (Ft. Monmouth, 1942), p. 82.

wars, maneuvers had served in a limited way as testing grounds for new theories, new types of equipment, and new troop organizations. But no maneuver, however brilliantly conceived and executed, could substitute for the unlimited experience gained in actual battle. By mid-1943, the Signal Corps was confirming and perfecting in battle signal communications techniques that were applicable to the changed conditions of a complex, fast-moving, highly technological war. And although control of combat communications was no longer a part of the Signal Corps mission as it had been in World War I, the Signal Corps still provided signal doctrine and signal equipment down to every last army communicator.

To fulfill their mission, Signal Corps radiomen and wiremen built networks of wire lines and radio circuits over continents and oceans to reach the theaters of war. In the theaters they wove these vital nets over beaches, mountains, rivers, and plains so as to serve the troops in combat. The Signal Corps' statutory mission was twofold: as a service and as a combat arm, a distinction shared only by the Corps of Engineers.[46]

The signal organizations followed no standard pattern in the various theaters of war in World War II. This was to be expected, for there was in fact no such thing as a "standard" theater. In a theater such as Europe, with its large land masses, extensive road nets, numerous airfields, and commercial means of communications, the theater signal officer

could take maximum advantage of existing and newly constructed long-line telephone and telegraph communications with all their ramifications. The Pacific theater, on the other hand, was characterized generally by large water areas and comparatively small land areas. Long-line wire circuits were almost nonexistent; radio circuits of all types had to be used to the maximum. In addition, large-scale joint operations with naval and air commanders were the order of the day.[47]

Thus no single type of signal organization could be made to fit all possible theater situations. Flexibility remained the basic doctrine in good signal planning and operation. In order to grasp what the Signal Corps did in the theaters and to measure its degree of success in accomplishing its mission, one must first comprehend the general principles that governed all World War II theater signal organizations.

Signal Officers in a Theater of Operations

On the staff of every higher combat organization—theater, army group, army, corps, division—a signal officer served with Signal Corps troops under his oper-

---

[46] Congress first officially recognized the Signal Corps' status as a combat arm by Section 2, Act of June 4, 1920 (41 Statutes 759), popularly known as the Allison or National Defense Act, *Military Laws of the United States* (annotated), 1939, pages 26, 45.

[47] Maj Mandel N. Goldstein, A Type Theater Signal Office (Pacific), 1948, Sig Sch Monograph, p. 1. The Sig Sch Libr, Ft. Monmouth. (For a discussion of the Signal School monographs, see Bibliographical Note.) See also among these monographs, Maj Ralph W. Bergman, Planning and Policy Making (At Theater Signal Section), 1950; Maj Albert Redman, Jr., Signal Communications Within a Theater of Operations, 1953; Capt Collins L. Cochran, Signal Planning at the Theater Level, 1950; Maj Forrest V. Diehl, Theater Chief Signal Officers Communication Responsibilities, 1948; Capt Samuel M. Beem, Organization and Responsibilities of the Headquarters Signal Officer in the Combined Headquarters, 1950.

ational control. The duties of these officers were essentially the same, varying only in degree of responsibility according to the size of the organization they served and its peculiarities of mission, location, or structure.

As a staff officer, the signal officer headed a special staff section, the signal section. He provided the commander and his staff members with information and technical advice concerning the condition, capabilities, and requirements of communications. He submitted his estimates and plans drawn up to support military operations directly to the commander or his chief of staff. And as the commander, so far as training and tactical employment of all Signal Corps troops assigned to serve his headquarters were concerned, he implemented his plans. Thus he served in a dual capacity —as a staff officer and as a commander of troops. The two functions, though lodged in the same individual, were separate and distinct. Furthermore, his command function was dual (operations and supply).[48] The more clearly the commander realized the distinctions and dualities of the Signal Corps mission, the less he subordinated his signal officer to reporting through a single staff section such as G–4 instead of directly to him or his chief of staff, and the more efficient his signal operation became. In some World War II theaters the staff organizations and procedures tended to hamper the efficiency with which the signal officers could discharge their duties; in others the commanders granted their signal officers the utmost authority.[49]

To assist him, the signal officer had a staff of Signal Corps officers trained in various specialties—frequency experts, radio experts, experts in wire, supply, planning, administration, and the like. Around these officers the signal section or division was built and the organization expanded. A typical theater signal organization might include sections for administration and personnel, supply, training, photography, liaison, security and intelligence, requirements, long lines, traffic, and a headquarters signal office. If such a theater signal organization was a combined activity incorporating Allied personnel, as was the Signal Division of Supreme Headquarters, Allied Expeditionary Force (SHAEF), additional sections might be required to take care of special Allied needs and complexities. For a smaller organization the signal officer's staff office was of course much less elaborate.

The signal officer promulgated signal policies and procedures as a part of the over-all headquarters standing operating procedures or, in many cases, as separate signal documents. A signal communication SOP provided standard basic plans and procedures to be followed in establishing the communications systems essential to the control of all operations of the army in the field. The signal

---

[48] (1) Report of Proceedings of War Department Board of Officers to Review the Signal Communications Doctrine of the Army, 1947, Tab G, Detailed Discussion and Findings, p. 7. Often cited in other publications as Reeder Report, copy in SigC 676, The Sig Com Doctrine of the Army, 1947. (2) AFSC Lecture C–1, Employment of Communications in the Army, Tab 9, pt. II, p. 1. SigC OP 352 AFSC Rpts, vol. 6, 1948–49. (See Bibliographical Note.) (3) Field Manuals cited in n. 43, above.

[49] (1) USFET, Gen Bd Rpt, Study 112, Signal Corps Personnel, Training, and Command and Administrative Structure, pp. 14–16 and apps. 5 and 6. (Hereafter referred to as USFET Gen Bd Rpt, with study number, title, and page cited.) (2) See below, pp. 239ff.

officer also prepared signal operation instructions and standing signal instructions, which were distributed to all army components. The SOI's contained technical information that was subject to frequent change for security or other reasons—call signs, radio frequencies, authenticator codes, visual and sound signals, and so on. The SSI's set forth signal policy and provided technical guidance to signal operating troops.[50]

Signal officers at all levels, beginning at the theater level, issued these various documents. At each echelon, they were based on those received from the next superior echelon, but modified to meet the specific needs of the command. All of them taken together constituted the co-ordinating and integrating element of signal communications that made it possible for a commander of thousands or even millions of men to exercise control over the operations of his troops in World War II.

Relationships Between the Signal Officer and the Commander

The position of the signal officer resembled that of a general staff officer much more closely than did that of any other special staff officer.[51] In a number of ways the relationship between a commander and his signal officer was unusual and close, especially in the field of planning. That this should be so was quite natural. In fact, it was essential.

Since the execution of command is almost wholly dependent upon signal communications, the control of troop operations rested very heavily upon the technical skill and professional integrity of the signal officer. A commander that recognized the value of his communications assigned a good signal officer and trusted his judgment. The commander could thus more easily decide such tactical questions, for example, as whether to leave communications behind, sacrificing them temporarily for the sake of a fast advance, or to delay the advance until communications had been brought up and made ready. "How can you weigh the value of communications if you don't know their employment in war?" a Navy officer queried an Armed Forces Staff College audience in 1949, seeking to emphasize that commanders must improve their comprehension of military communications. "Napoleon once said he owed his success to being a few minutes early," this officer recounted. "Communications may be able to give you those few minutes."[52]

General Ingles put the same idea in different words. Communications, he said, constituted the weapon placed in the hands of the commander to accomplish his mission, just as a rifle placed in the hands of an infantryman was the weapon for the accomplishment of the infantryman's mission. "We all think it right and proper that the infantryman should be well trained in the use of his weapons," said Ingles. "It is, therefore, not at all unreasonable that we should expect the commander and his staff to be

---

[50] (1) FM 100–11, Jul 48, pp. 89ff. (2) MS Comment, P&P Div OCSigO, Jul 59. (3) AFSC Lecture C–1, Employment of Com in the Army, Tab 9, pt. II, pp. 2–3.

[51] Rpt of Proceedings of WD Bd of Officers to Review the Sig Com Doctrine of the Army, 1947, Tab G, p. 7.

[52] AFSC Lecture C–2, Employment of Communications in the Navy, Tab 4, p. 8. SigC OP 352 AFSC Rpts, vol. 6, 1948–49.

trained in the use of their weapons." [53]

Another important decision which the commander had to make involved timing. Communications at headquarters needed to be installed and ready before the commander made his moves. This called for realization on his part that his communications facilities were so important that if necessary he should wait upon them. General Ingles illustrated his point with an incident involving Lt. Gen. Courtney H. Hodges, First Army commander, and his signal officer, Col. Grant A. Williams. "A few months ago," said Ingles, "I spent a couple of days at his [Hodges'] headquarters . . . then near Chauny . . . soon to move to Charleroi. . . . I asked General Hodges when he expected to move to Charleroi. He replied, 'I do not know. I never move anywhere until Williams tells me I can.'" [54]

Communications required the expenditure of considerable amounts of time, manpower, and transportation. A commander willing to recognize that fact could have virtually anything he wanted in the way of communications facilities. But, "communications, contrary to the apparent conception of some commanders and many staff officers, is not an item of issue to be shipped by transport, requisitioned on a Form 445, and issued from depots." [55]

The Importance of Signal Planning

In no other field was the relationship between the signal officer and the commander closer than in the area of planning. Planning constituted a large part of the theater signal mission. "The most important single function," some officers called it. [56] Signal planning involved more than determining how many wire or radio circuits were needed to provide communications among military headquarters in a given area. Signal planning affected every member of the general staff and many members of the special staff. The concern of G–1 for personnel matters, G–2 for intelligence and signal communications security, G–3 for operations and countermeasures, and G–4 for supply and administration all required a heavy expenditure of signal communications planning. In a combined operation other services and Allied nations multiplied the need for signal communications. [57] The most de-

[53] Gen Ingles, CSigO, Lecture Before Army-Navy Staff College, 19 Mar 45. SigC Hist Sec file.

[54] Speaking of Navy practices in these matters, General Ingles added in his lecture, "I am informed that Admiral Nimitz did not move his headquarters from Pearl Harbor to Guam until he was advised by his communications officer that the communications system at Guam was established." Ingles, Lecture Before Army-Navy Staff College, 19 Mar 45.

[55] Col. David P. Gibbs, "The Commanders Communications," *The Army Combat Forces Journal,* vol. 5, No. 7 (February, 1955), p. 48. Colonel Gibbs (subsequently major general), son of Maj. Gen. George S. Gibbs, who was the ninth Chief Signal Officer of the U.S. Army, from 1928 to 1931, was himself appointed as the twentieth Chief Signal Officer on 1 July 1963.

The twentieth Chief Signal Officer was also the last. A reorganization, effective 1 March 1964, eliminated the Signal Corps as a separate organization of the Army, just as the Chemical, Ordnance, and Quartermaster organizations had been removed in extensive reorganizations two years earlier. General Gibbs become head of the Office of the Chief of Communications-Electronics (OCCE), a staff activity under the Deputy Chief of Staff for Operations. At the same time, the major task of operating Army strategic communications worldwide was assigned to the U.S. Army Strategic Communications Command, a new field command (headed by Maj. Gen Richard J. Meyer) directly under the Army Chief of Staff.

[56] Goldstein, A Type Theater Sig Of (Pac), p. 8.

[57] Cochran, Sig Plng at the Theater Level, pp. 2–3.

tailed instructions had to be issued. There were of course the normal signal problems of radio systems organization, frequency allocation, wire systems organization, locations of installations, siting of mutual interference devices, cryptography, signal supply, and maintenance. Allied participation created many other problems arising from variations in signal communication practices and procedures among the signal services of different nations and among the different services of the same nation. All had to be resolved since electronic phenomena recognize no geographical boundaries and yield allegiance to no single jurisdiction.

In moments of frustration signal officers sometimes suggested that their tables of organization and equipment (TOE's) ought to include a mind-reading section equipped with crystal balls, Ouija boards, magic wands and potions, and magicians' caps.[58] Such suggestions grew out of the unfortunate fact that too frequently planners took no account of signals. Too often commands that would in fact require extensive signal communications drew up plans and went ahead with their implementation without consulting or even informing the signal officer.[59] Often the situation arose because the using arm, service, or agency lacked knowledge of the capabilities and limitations of signal communications means.[60]

Control Over Signal Supply

Another important function of the unit signal officer was his control of, and responsibility for, supply and maintenance of signal equipment for the troops assigned or attached to the headquarters. This included direct operating control of the signal depots, signal sections of general depots, and signal dumps within the command, and the control of all signal repair and maintenance facilities. Such control was a unique attribute enjoyed by no other signal or communications officer in the armed forces of the nations engaged in World War II. The reasons for giving U.S. Army signal officers this control were eminently practical. In the first place, the success of communications depended upon the ready availability of equipment and its state of repair. Equipment items always had to be near the place they were to be used at the time they were needed.[61] The diversity and complexity of signal communications equipment created many difficulties of handling and identification for supply men not trained in signal matters. It made good sense on all counts to give signal officers control of their own supply matters.

Control over his supply enabled a signal officer to maintain pools of signal supplies for immediate replenishment and to expand signal systems with utmost rapidity. The War Department board of officers appointed after the war to review the communications doctrine of the Army singled out control of supplies as one of the characteristics that "made the U.S. signal communication more successful and more responsive to

---

[58] AFHQ CSigO Monthly Bull, Jul 44, final page of app. A. SigC Hist Sec file. (See Bibliographical Note.)

[59] USFET Gen Bd Rpt No. 111, Signal Corps Operations, pp. 27-32.

[60] "The telephone companies in America have spoiled the non-technical military commanders. They are used to good service and make no distinction between Keokuk and Tombouctou." MS Comment, Maj Gen Frank E. Stoner (Ret.), Jul 59.

[61] FM 100-11, Jul 48, pp. 19-21, 74-75, 88-89.

demand than the signal communication of any other army. . . ." [62] This feature of United States Army organization drew the envy of all Allied signal officers during World War II.[63] The British Director of Signals thought so highly of the American system that in 1944 he pressed for its adoption for the Royal Signals. The costliness in manpower prevented the British from adopting the plan midway of the war, but it was urged as a postwar policy.[64]

Direct control of his own supply permitted the signal officer to make the most effective use of equipment in any given situation. "The most effective use" might mean handing over critically needed items to another service or to an ally. As a matter of fact, signal officers frequently did give signal equipment to the British, to the U.S. Navy, and to the Air Forces, particularly in the Mediterranean theater. Again, control of supply permitted signal officers in the theaters to set up training programs much quicker and more easily.[65]

Supporting Combat Signals

"In modern warfare no commander can exercise control over more than a mere handful of men by his physical presence." [66] In the final analysis, the ground battles of World War II were fought by small combat units—squads, platoons, companies—in contact with the enemy all along a wide front. Often each unit fought semi-independently, in terrain and amid circumstances peculiar to that particular struggle. The outcome of the larger battles resulted from the cumulative effort of innumerable small unit actions. Yet throughout the entire massive, sprawling effort of myriads of men on many miles of battlefield there had to exist intelligence and control. This control extended upward through a permanent chain of command linking squad, platoon, company, battalion, regiment, division, corps, army, and army group. And all of it, all the way to the top and down to the forward platoon sergeant or squad leader, was accomplished by the technical means that the Signal Corps supplied in order to extend the human voice or to carry the symbols of speech by which men convey information or give commands.[67]

The portable radios, the hand-laid wire and portable switchboards that combat soldiers carried and artillery observers employed, the vehicular radios and heavy-duty wire equipment and teletypewriters in battalion and regimental headquarters were all developed, procured, and distributed by the Signal Corps. But the men who operated the equipment below division level were the soldiers of the using units, on the principle established after World War

---

[62] Rpt of Proceedings of WD Bd of Officers to Review the Sig Com Doctrine of the Army, 1947, Tab G, p. 8. Signal and AGF officers queried by the board overwhelmingly indorsed the system, 66 to 11 and 60 to 3, respectively (Tab E, p. 15).

[63] AFSC Lecture C-1, Employment of Com in the Army, Tab 9, pt. II, p. 1.

[64] Nalder, *The History of British Army Signals in the Second World War*, pp. 322–24. General Nalder said, "For the future, however, it seems clear that Signals should establish their own base depots and be entirely responsible for all handling from the docks forward."

[65] (1) Interv, SigC Hist Sec with Brig Gen Terence J. Tully (Ret.), former DCSigO AFHQ, 22 Aug 59. SigC Hist Sec file. (2) See below, pp. 29–30.

[66] FM 100-11, Jul 48, p. 1.

[67] AFSC Lecture O-1, The United States Army, Tab 1, pt. I, p. 4. SigC OP 352 AFSC Rpts, vol. 5, 1948–49. See also vol. 9, Tab 42.

I that unity of command must be observed, and that there must be no specialist troops not under the commander's control below the division level. The necessities of combat put the control over the communication means of command firmly in the hands of the fighting men themselves. A measure of the increase in the use of communication means in World War II is the increase in the numbers of men who served at least part time as communicators in combat units. About 4 or 5 percent in 1941, the number more than doubled by 1945. In the infantry division, 2,400 men, or about 12.6 percent, were engaged in communications work.[68]

These combat communicators made much use of their short-range radios, particularly of the FM variety, which the U.S. Army alone possessed in World War II. They were the SCR–300 walkie-talkie, the infantry and armored force vehicular sets in the 500 series, and the artillery sets in the 600 series. "In one Infantry division," explained battalion radioman T/4 Paul L. Zens, a veteran of the Siegfried Line fighting late in the war, "we had a minimum of 81 SCR–300 radios operating on 18 frequencies and more than 150 sets in the 600 series on about 40 frequencies. I *know*," Zens emphasized, "the war in Europe would have lasted longer if we hadn't had FM on our side. We were able to shoot fast and effectively because we could get information quickly and accurately by voice, on FM."[69]

The Signal Corps units themselves, composed of Signal Corps troops under Signal Corps officers who served in the field army from the division level up, did not in World War II constitute an especially large percentage. In a typical field army having three corps, each containing three infantry divisions and one armored division, the Signal Corps troops were about 3.4 percent of the total force. In addition to the division signal companies and the corps signal battalions, Signal Corps troops in a typical field army included a headquarters signal service company, a signal operations battalion furnishing communications at the army command posts, one or more construction battalions making telephone cable and wire installations down to corps level and back to army rear, one or more signal radio intelligence companies, a pigeon company, and a signal photographic company. Finally, there were the signal repair company and the signal depot company, which tended to the supply and maintenance functions of the field army.[70] These troops often were augmented by special detachments in various categories and, in the later stages of the war, by various cellular teams.

The division signal company had grown from 232 in 1940 to 322 by March 1942. In the reorganization of the AGF tables in March 1943, the division signal company was cut nearly a third, to 226 men, by eliminating truck drivers from the tables of organization and equipment (their duties being assigned to other specialists) and

---

[68] AFSC Lecture C–1, Employment of Com in the Army, Tab 9, p. 3.

[69] Paul L. Zens, "A GI's Report on Lower-Band FM—A Veteran Radio Operator's Experience with FM under Battle Conditions," *FM and Television*, vol. VI, No. 1 (January, 1946), p. 21. See also below, pp. 491–92.

[70] (1) AR 105–15. (2) MS Comments (a) Col Williams and (b) U.S. Army Sig Sup Agency, Jul 59. (3) AFSC Lecture C–1, Employment of Com in the Army, Tab 9, p. 3.

by the transfer of the radio intelligence (RI) platoon to the corps after it had been decided that radio intelligence was properly a corps function.[71] This action brought vehement objections from some theater commanders, who protested that the reduction in the division signal company was so completely at variance with all combat experience as to prove entirely impractical.[72]

Throughout the campaigns in Sicily and Italy the scarcity of signal troops at all levels worried the field commanders.[73] As a matter of fact, few signal companies in NATOUSA were reorganized under the new tables. Fifth Army's signal officer, Brig. Gen. Richard B. Moran, said flatly that divisions in the theater could not be provided with satisfactory signal service under the prescribed organization, which he described as "totally inadequate." Division signal companies, he reported in November 1943, were operating under the 1942 tables and, he added, ". . . in nearly every case even this strength has had to be increased." [74] By one strategem or another—special authorizations, organization of new units from pool personnel,

and so on—the theater succeeded in providing the communications service deemed essential. "In order to fight this war a minimum number of men are needed," said Moran. "It doesn't matter how many are in a unit if the total number may be had. If units are reduced in size, more units are required, thus increasing overhead." [75]

Similarly, in the European theater, First Army never recognized the AGF reorganization of the division signal company. In fact, according to Colonel Williams, First Army's division signal companies always contained close to four hundred men. Each corps had a radio intelligence company, not a platoon. And in early 1945, after the Battle of the Bulge, First Army's signal troops in nearly all categories were augmented some 10 percent by the assignment of cellular teams.[76]

The Development of the Cellular Plan of Unit Organization

Even before war began, Signal Corps training officers were engaged in a vigorous and vocal attempt to obtain more flexibility in the organization of signal units.[77] The existing Signal TOE's seemed neat and precise on paper—a signal company for a division, a signal battalion for a corps or a field army. Unfortunately the needs of war did not fit this classic pattern. Task forces, reinforced divisions, and other unorthodox units fought the early engagements of World War II. Each required special

[71] Kent Roberts Greenfield, Robert R. Palmer, and Bell I. Wiley, *The Organization of Ground Combat Troops,* UNITED STATES ARMY IN WORLD WAR II (Washington, 1947), p. 310.

[72] See, for example, Sig Sec AFHQ, History of the Signal Section Allied Force Headquarters, 24 July 1942–10 November 1945 (1945) (hereafter cited as Hist Sig Sec AFHQ), p. 58. SigC Hist Sec file. This 184-page document contains detailed accounts of Signal Section activities for the period covered, divided into five chronological parts and supplemented by appendixes covering special histories of the Wire, Supply, Radio, and Photographic Divisions of the Signal Section, AFHQ.

[73] See below, pp. 51–52, 60ff.

[74] Ltr, Gen Moran, SigO Fifth Army, to Hodges, Third Army, 12 Nov 43, sub: Answers to Questions Regarding Sig Com, Fifth Army. SCIA file 104 Fifth Army.

[75] Ltr, SigO Fifth Army to DCSigO AFHQ, 1 Feb 44. SCIA file 104 Fifth Army.

[76] MS Comment, Williams, Jul 59.

[77] Thompson, Harris, et al., *The Test,* pp. 35–36.

groupings of Signal Corps men, equipment, and communications installations tailored to fit the situation. Many remote stations or small headquarters did not need the entire signal service company they were entitled to, only a detachment. On the other hand, in the Pacific a "type" signal battalion was not big enough to furnish the necessary communications for a corps operating in thick jungle growth.[78] The Signal Corps therefore resorted to special tables and organized experimental units. Continuing to press for more flexible standard tables of organization, the War Plans Division of the Office of the Chief Signal Officer by February 1942 had presented recommended revisions to every single one of the existing T/O's.[79]

The Signal Corps, dissatisfied with such makeshift arrangements, took bits and pieces of existing tables and fitted them together in a new cellular-type T/O that provided a pool of trained detachments for transfer to foreign service as required.[80] A fixed station company of 12 detachments (16 officers, 259 enlisted men) was organized under the new table of organization as a part of the 15th Signal Service Regiment at Fort Monmouth, and additional detachments were organized in September 1942 at Camp Beale, California.[81]

The Signal Corps won strong support for its views on unit flexibility from the signal officers of ground force units. The Chief Signal Officer encouraged unit commanders to treat "type" organization tables only as guides, altering and adapting them to fit a given tactical requirement or situation. Newly created tables, designed for flexibility, made their appearance throughout 1942. For example, 11–367, published early in 1942 for the signal photo company was extremely flexible.[82] In June, three additional cellular-type team training organizations were authorized at Camp Crowder.[83] The 823d Signal Wire Operations Service Company, the 824th Fixed Radio Station Company, and the 825th Signal Repair Company all trained teams in the specialties indicated by the company designations and furnished them as required for small installations at overseas points.[84]

Possibly no signal task was more exacting or required more kinds of signal specialists than aircraft warning duty. Yet the tactical situations under which aircraft warning troops were used varied greatly. On 1 July 1942 a new TOE 11–400 was issued. The Signal Corps said of it that it is:

. . . designed to replace those T/O's for all aircraft warning units below the size of a regiment. It is a flexible table . . . providing . . . for almost any situation involving a

---

[78] Capt Wilson G. Burden, Signal Corps Enlisted Administration, OCSigO Mil Pers Tng Study, p. 46. SigC Hist Sec file. The following material is based on this study except where otherwise noted.

[79] SigC Tech Info Ltr 3 (Feb 42), p. 39.

[80] Ibid. This table of organization became T/O 11–187, published 12 February 1942.

[81] (1) An. 5, 1st Ind, TAG to CSigO, 18 Feb 42, to OCSigO Mil Tng Br Study, History of Unit Training, Signal Corps Units, 7 December 1941–1 December, 1945. SigC Hist Sec file. (2) Memo, CSigO for Plans Div SOS, 28 Sep 42, sub: Constitution and Activation of Certain Sig Fixed Radio Station Dets. SigC 320.2, T/O, Jan 42–Sep 42 (MT–22). The Signal Fixed Radio Station Company was redesignated the 822d Signal Fixed Radio Station Company on 7 October 1942. AG 320.2 (10–5–42) OB–I–SP–M.

[82] SigC Tech Info Ltr 7 (Jun 42), pp. 41–43.

[83] AG 320.2 (6–7–42) MR–M–GN, 22 Jun 42, sub: Orgn of SigC Units in Jul 42.

[84] Hist of Unit Tng, SigC Units, 7 Dec 41–1 Dec 45, p. 11.

task force. The usual functions . . . are subdivided in such a manner as to provide sections and teams that may be added to provide any number of radars and special ground observation posts, complete with the necessary plotting board and administrative personnel to meet the tactical situation for which the organization is intended.

A company or a battalion could be made up of any combination of units from among headquarters; reporting platoons; radar operating, plotting board, radar maintenance, message center, radio, wire, telegraphic, ground observer radio, and telephone teams; and medical and mess personnel.[85]

The new aircraft warning organizations and the teams being furnished by the team training organization at Camp Crowder proved spectacularly successful. Through the late summer of 1942 the Signal Corps pressed for permission to set up additional training organizations based on a cellular TOE. The Army Service Forces and the Chief Signal Officer bombarded each other's offices with correspondence suggesting plans and counterplans. On 2 September Brig. Gen. LeRoy Lutes, then Chief of Operations, ASF, wrote to General Olmstead, then Chief Signal Officer, suggesting that a typical signal service company or battalion be developed for training purposes and to serve as a reservoir of trained signal teams. "It is believed," wrote Lutes, "that a single type unit . . . would be easier to administer. . . ."[86] But Signal Corps tasks were too varied to squeeze all of the teams into one organization. It would be possible, the Chief Signal Officer said in his

reply, to fit all the units into two organizations—a signal special unit training battalion and a signal construction and operations training battalion.[87] This proposition won approval. On 25 January 1943, the 847th and 848th Signal Training Battalions were formally constituted at Camp Crowder.[88] Their authorized strength totaled 41 officers, 1,244 enlisted men and 61 officers, 1,418 enlisted men, respectively. Their function was to train units for overseas duty. Their organization was based upon the building block principle, that is, parts of existing tables were grouped together to fill the needs for specialized teams.[89]

The change in training structure constituted a long step toward flexibility and maximum utilization of personnel. Still it did not go far enough. Something more than a revamping of the old tables of organization was required. It is important to emphasize that, up to this point, *cellular* had meant merely taking parts of existing tables and fitting them together in new combinations. There existed no broad authority to create entirely new organizations from a single table. In other words, the effort so far was a remodeling job. What the Signal Corps really needed was a completely new and modern blueprint.

In its search for better organization of units the Signal Corps did not stand alone. The whole Army in late 1942 sought some solution toward flexibility and economy in the use of manpower

---

[85] Burden, SigC Enlisted Admin, p. 53.

[86] Memo, ACofS for Opns SOS (ASF) for CSigO, 2 Sep 42, sub: Establishment of SigC Tng Units. SigC SPSMT 320.2 Gen 3, 1942.

[87] Memo, CSigO for CG SOS OPD, 1 Oct 42, sub: Establishment of SigC Tng Units. SigC SPSMT 320.2 Gen 3, 1942.

[88] AG 320.2 (1-11-43) OB-1-SP-M, 14 Jan 43, sub: Constitution, Activation and Orgn of Sig Tng Units.

[89] Burden, SigC Enlisted Admin, pp. 48-49.

and equipment.[90] Late in December the Chief of Staff, General George C. Marshall, had written to ASF and AGF suggesting among other things that the existing organization of service troops was wasteful, especially in the numerous cases in which small groups or units were required for small missions. "It seems to me that we should have these service units so set up that we can put together composite battalions, composite regiments, and composite brigades. . . ." [91] Essentially, this was precisely what the Signal Corps had been saying in relation to signal units.

Thus in July 1943 when the new Chief Signal Officer, General Ingles, proposed a sweeping reorganization of the bulk of all Signal Corps training units, he was asking for something almost sure to be approved. Ingles wanted new tables of organization to provide for all needed types and sizes of cellular signal service teams, as determined by past experience, present demands, and estimated future requirements from all theaters of operations. He proposed that each cellular team, whether requested individually or as a component of a complete cellular signal service organization, be equipped with its appropriate table of equipment immediately after being authorized for a theater. Men and equipment would be shipped together to their destination. Ingles' also asked for a bulk allotment to the Signal Corps of enough men to permit him to continue training in step

with theater requirements and to provide constant replenishment of training pool personnel as trained teams were withdrawn.[92] Anticipating the prompt approval that the ASF gave, the Signal Corps had prepared a new TOE 11–500, which, when it was issued, was backdated to 1 July 1943. It was based upon the 1942 TOE 11–400 for aircraft warning units.[93]

In the opinion of Signal Corps training officers, the new TOE 11–500 was nearly perfect. It provided for fifty-four types of cellular teams, then believed to be all that were necessary to organize Signal units for any mission.[94] Teams bore 2-letter designations, which indicated roughly their size and mission. For example, EF meant a 16-man radio link team, while a 5-man photographic laboratory unit bore the designation FB, and GD identified a 3-position switchboard team of 34 men.[95] Putting teams together in various groupings provided an infinite number of combinations.

The cellular plan met the one supreme test of any plan—it worked. In fact it worked so well that the other technical services soon adopted it. Nonetheless, throughout the war the Signal Corps, the original proponent of the cellular plan of organizational structure, remained its largest user. By mid-1945, near the end of the war, the number

[90] Memo, WDGS G–3 for CG SOS, 12 Jan 43, sub: Reorgn of Sv Units, Tab 4, ASF Mobilization Div Study, Troop Units Activated by the ASF for Overseas Use. OCMH files.

[91] Memo, Gen Marshall for Lt Gen Lesley J. McNair, Gen Somervell, and Brig Gen Idwal H. Edwards, 29 Dec 42. WDGS 302.2/5773.

[92] Memo, CSigO for CG ASF, 10 Jul 43, sub: Sig Units Provided in Troop Basis 1943. SigC 320.2 Troop Basis, Jan 43–Dec 43 (MT–135).

[93] Burden, SigC Enlisted Admin, p. 52.

[94] Experience in 1944 and 1945 brought many more new teams into being.

[95] TOE 11–500, Signal Service Organization, 1 Jul 43. Later editions changed these figures—in the 22 September 1944 issue an EF team contained 26 men; an FB team, 25. TOE 11–500, 22 Sep 44.

of Signal Corps cellular teams organized under TOE 11–500 had increased to 116. Proposals to add even more teams were under consideration when the war ended. By contrast the Quartermaster Corps, the second largest user of cellular teams, had 86 such units. The Transportation Corps had 74; the Corps of Engineers, 72; the Medical Department, 61; Corps of Military Police, 46; the Ordnance Department, 40; the Chemical Warfare Service, 26. In addition there were 12 composite teams used by all services.[96]

Some teams organized under TOE 11–500 numbered only 2 men, whereas others numbered as many as 9,591 men. Small or large, they served on specialized tactical missions and under varying field conditions with an efficiency and economy that would have been quite impossible to attain under the prewar organization. The great majority of TOE 11–500 teams served as one cell of a composite team designed to perform a specific signal task. For example, cellular radio, message center, messenger, wire operations, and wire construction teams together provided a composite group capable of furnishing communications for a service area or a small headquarters. The beauty of this arrangement was that, as the headquarters grew or contracted, teams could be added or subtracted to meet the requirements exactly without duplication or loss of economy.[97] By the middle of 1945, 55.8 percent of all ASF Signal

Corps troops had been organized under the cellular plan.[98]

Summary

The topics in this chapter are touched only lightly and do not by any means cover all the signal problems and responsibilities in a theater of operations. Nor should they be taken as fixed signal doctrine; signal doctrine changed to meet the changing conditions of warfare. Neither can it be said that this was the way it was done in every theater in World War II; each theater presented its own unique conditions.

Nevertheless the responsibilities set forth do represent some of the basic problems that the Signal Corps faced in the theater. The record of what was done in World War II in the area of signal communications can serve as a guide to understanding and charting new ideas. The principal facts that must be understood are that signal communications serve the commander; that they are flexible and varied; that each of the means and systems is a part of a larger intricate system that covers the whole of the theater and links it with the zone of interior; and that in these years of conflict, mid-1943 to September 1945, the Signal Corps came close to achieving the goal of all communicators—a thoroughly integrated system. North Africa had provided the initial testing ground.[99] The early campaigns in the Pacific and the campaigns in Sicily and Italy taught additional lessons. All of them came to fruition in the great invasion of France in June 1944.

---

[96] CSigO, Annual Rpt, FY 45, p. 607.

[97] Capt Mac C. Eversole, Capabilities, Limitations, and Employment of Table of Organization and Equipment 11–500 Radio and Radar Teams (1951), Sig Sch Monograph, p. 20. The Sig Sch Libr, Ft. Monmouth.

[98] CSigO, Annual Rpt, FY 45, p. 608.

[99] See Thompson, Harris, et al., The Test, pp. 353–86.

CHAPTER II

The Signal Corps in Sicily and Italy

In the weeks that followed the end of the Tunisia Campaign in May 1943, the Allied command in the Mediterranean reorganized for new operations in Sicily and Italy. At the same time, U.S. headquarters staffs pored over the voluminous reports of "lessons learned" in the North African fighting. The Signal Corps had done well in North Africa, despite a fair share of initial mistakes and preliminary fumbles. Signal Corps doctrine and organization had proved equal to the test. Signal equipment, almost without exception, had proved to be excellent. Most important of all from the Signal Corps point of view, the North African campaign had again demonstrated the importance of military communications of the modern army.[1] Army-wide acceptance of this fact significantly influenced all other campaigns to the end of the war.

The Signal Section, AFHQ

During the first three months of operations in North Africa, that area was officially part of the European Theater of Operations. The North African Theater of Operations (NATO) was created on 4 February 1943. At the same time, responsibility for the supply, personnel, and administration of U.S. units, which had been vested in the European Theater of Operations, United States Army, passed to the newly activated North African Theater of Operations, United States Army. The communications zone supply organization, Services of Supply (SOS) NATOUSA, was established on 15 February.[2] The highest command in the theater, the inter-Allied, unified Allied Force Headquarters, controlled all ground, air, naval, and service operations in the theater.

A thoroughly integrated British-American staff of communications experts served both the Signal Section of AFHQ, organized in 1942, and the corresponding NATOUSA Signal Section, set up in May 1943. The Signal Corps' General Matejka was designated chief signal officer in both commands.[3]

In July 1943, the top communications position in the theater passed from American to British hands. The able and experienced General Matejka left for the United States to head the Personnel and Training Service in the Office of the Chief Signal Officer in Washington. An equally able and experienced

---

[1] George F. Howe, *Northwest Africa: Seizing the Initiative in the West,* UNITED STATES ARMY IN WORLD WAR II (Washington, 1957), pp. 669–77.

For an account of the Signal Corps in the Tunisia Campaign, see Thompson, Harris, *et al., The Test,* pp. 352–86.

[2] NATOUSA GO 1, 4 Feb 43; NATOUSA GO 6, 14 Feb 43.

[3] Hist, Sig Sec AFHQ, p. 24.

British officer, Maj. Gen. Leslie B. Nicholls, succeeded him. Nicholls' deputy was an American, Col. Terence J. Tully. Colonel Tully had served as the task force signal officer for the landings in the Oran area in North Africa and as the II Corps signal officer throughout the Tunisia Campaign. The assistant deputy signal officer of AFHQ was another American, Col. Rex W. Minckler.[4]

The Chief Signal Officer, AFHQ, served as adviser to the Allied Commander in Chief on all signal matters and as co-ordinator of signal policy throughout the theater. The Signal Section maintained contact with signal officers of all subordinate units on technical and administrative matters; estimated requirements for signal supplies (both tactical and fixed plant), exclusive of those necessary for unit equipment maintenance; supervised the installation, maintenance, and operation of the theater signal system, including the AFHQ message center; handled codes and ciphers; and examined enemy signal equipment and supervised signal intelligence matters.[5] This last was a signal function in the U.S. Army only, since in the British Army it was handled by intelligence officers.

A Combined Signal Board, operating in AFHQ, devoted its attention primarily to the control of submarine cable and commercial radio facilities. Radio frequency allocation, a function ordinarily charged to a combined signal board, was delegated to the Radio Division, Signal Section, without reference to the board. Similarly, the Signal Intelligence Section handled field radio procedures, combined cipher procedures, and combined security procedures.[6]

By the time the Tunisia Campaign ended in May 1943, the Signal Section, AFHQ, was a bustling outfit well able to carry out its part of the theater mission.[7] Three signal service regiments, the 2623d, 2624th, and 2625th, operated the extensive theater communications facilities at the Atlantic Base Section in Casablanca, at the Mediterranean Base Section in Oran, and at the AFHQ in Algiers, respectively. The first two Women's Army Corps (WAC) groups had arrived in the theater in February and in April. From among these women, later organized as the 6666th and 6667th WAC Service Companies, the Signal Section obtained a limited number to take over various secretarial duties, act as telephone operators, and perform numerous Signal Center tasks, all of which they accomplished with a high degree of efficiency.[8] The Signal Section had to wait until September before its own WAC communications company arrived.[9]

By mid-1943 the theater communications system embraced all of the modern means of electrical transmission. Submarine cables linked Gibraltar, Casablanca, and Algiers, and carried an immense amount of traffic. Landline teletypewriter facilities were expanding rapidly. Radio circuits, however, were still the backbone of the system. Circuits to Washington, London, and Cairo, established during the early days of the

[4] *Ibid.*, p. 51, Fig 3, Orgn Chart, 16 Nov 43.

[5] *Ibid.*, p. 7.

[6] *Ibid.*, p. 29.

[7] For an account of Signal Corps activities in North Africa before mid-1943, see Thompson, Harris, *et al., The Test*, pp. 337–86.

[8] (1) Hist, Sig Sec AFHQ, p. 26. (2) MS Comment, CD&O Div OCSigO, Jul 59.

[9] See below, p. 68.

North African campaign, constituted the basic means of intertheater communication, although within the theater itself the choice lay among any number of communications facilities.[10]

One of the most important programs initiated by signal planners at AFHQ was already well under way. This was the training program. Without it the demand that developed later for signal specialists to serve the various operations supported from AFHQ–NATOUSA almost certainly could not have been met. The need for a continuous signal training program became evident very early. Men were arriving from the United States without adequate training, too often taken from schools and training centers before they had finished their courses in order to fill urgent overseas requisitions.[11] At the same time, as field commanders became increasingly conscious of the importance of signal communications and more aware of what good communications could do for them, the standards of proficiency they demanded of their signal troops rose proportionately. A further schooling need sprang from the nature of the integrated command, where even the best-trained men, British as well as American, had to be taught the combined signal procedures essential to Allied operations. Futhermore, since French Army units were to be equipped with United States signal gear, French signalmen had to learn how to use it.[12]

To meet all these training needs the Signal Corps organized a school company within the 2624th Signal Service Regiment at Oran and included several French-speaking instructors on the staff. Students attended from all over the theater. At the Signal Center, British and American instructors organized classes to acquaint communications troops of both nations with the intricacies of combined signal procedures. Later these rather informal classes developed into full-time schools. The schools also furnished message center technicians for numerous operations. The acute shortage of trained cryptographic and maintenance personnel in the theater forced the 849th Signal Intelligence Service to open two schools at its headquarters near Algiers in early 1943. From these beginnings evolved the extensive theater signal training program that, in one guise or another, continued until the end of the war. The importance of this program merits emphasis. Through it, the theater itself readied thousands of signal specialists—specialists who became urgently needed during the course of the long Italian campaign, the move of AFHQ to Italy in July 1944, and the invasion of southern France in August of that year.[13] The Signal Corps was the only technical service to conduct a permanent school in the theater. Other services, including the Ordnance Department and the Corps of Engineers, wished to establish similar schools but found themselves thwarted

---

[10] Hist, Sig Sec AFHQ, pp. 29–30, 82.

[11] Thompson, Harris, et al., The Test, pp. 321–22.

[12] For a detailed discussion of French rearmament, see Marcel Vigneras, Rearming the French, UNITED STATES ARMY IN WORLD WAR II (Washington, 1957).

[13] (1) Hist, Sig Sec AFHQ, pp. 27, 34, 62. (2) Hq MTOUSA, Logistical History of NATOUSA-MTOUSA, 11 August 1942–30 November 1945, prepared by Officers of G–4 Div and Spec Staff Sec under direction of Col. Creswell G. Blakeney (Naples, Italy: Via Ponti Rossi, 1946), p. 255.

for want of equipment and by the War Department policy of refusing shipment of items for such special projects. In this regard, the signal officer's control over his own signal supply allocation proved its worth.[14]

Supply responsibilities of SOS NAT-OUSA, whose signal officer was Col. Harold S. Miller, included control of all base section operations and responsibility for developing local supply sources.[15] But issue of controlled items (that is, items in critically short supply, which in fact meant most signal items except unit T/E equipment, maintenance, and supply items) was an AFHQ responsibility.[16]

Planning for future operations, initially a function of the Combined Signal Board, came to be an important part of the AFHQ Signal Section's duties. A Planning Division had been set up late in 1942, with a Signal Corps officer, Maj. James P. Scurlock, as its chief. Allied decisions made during the inter-Allied conference at Casablanca in January 1943 set the stage for developing HUSKY, the operation plan for the invasion of Sicily. General Dwight D. Eisenhower immediately established Force 141, a planning headquarters in Algiers under General Sir Harold R. L. G. Alexander. Force 141 moved to the Ecole Normale at La Bouzaréa in mid-February.[17] In the Ecole Normale and in AFHQ proper, at conference after conference, Signal Corps members of the planning staffs ground out signal plans, amended, revised, and perfected them down to the last detail.

The Sicily Campaign

Among those who labored over the HUSKY signal plans was the man who was responsible for executing them, Col. Elton F. Hammond, Lt. Gen. George S. Patton, Jr.'s, Seventh Army signal officer. Hammond had been told to prepare estimates of the numbers of signal troops and quantities of signal equipment necessary to support the American contingent of four infantry divisions, one armored division, and one airborne infantry division.[18]

Plans and Preparations

Until the Allied invasion fleet sailed on 1 July, Hammond and his staff worked without respite. The Seventh Army (until D-day designated Force 343, comprising the I Armored Corps, reinforced) contained the 1st, 3d, 9th, and 45th Infantry Divisions, the 82d Airborne Division, and the 2d Armored Division. The assault echelon would include the II Corps (SHARK FORCE), Lt. Gen. Omar N. Bradley commanding, and the 3d Division (Joss Force), Maj. Gen. Lucian K. Trus-

---

[14] (1) Hist, Sig Sec AFHQ, pp. 27, 34, 62. (2) Interv, SigC Hist Sec with Tully, 22 Aug 58.

[15] Signal items procured through local sources in North Africa included copper wire, lead-covered cable, glass insulators, and telephone poles. For details, see below, pp. 364–65.

[16] Hist, Sig Sec AFHQ, pp. 41–42.

[17] When HUSKY was launched on 10 July, Force 141 was redesignated 15th Army Group.

[18] (1) *Report of Operations of the United States Seventh Army in the Sicilian Campaign, 10 July–17 August 1943* (Palermo, Sicily: Staff, Seventh Army, 1943) (hereafter referred to as *Seventh Army Rpt, Sicilian Campaign*), p. M–1. (2) Hq Seventh Army, SigO Rpt, Signal Corps Participation in the Sicilian Campaign, 22 Feb–20 Aug 43 (hereafter referred to as SigC Participation in the Sicilian Campaign). SCIA file 23 Tully Rpts 2. (See Bibliographical Note.)

cott, Jr., commanding. The II Corps would be composed of most of the 1st Division (subtask force DIME), the 45th Division (subtask force CENT), plus Ranger and engineer battalions and supporting troops. Paratroops of the 82d Airborne Division would be dropped ahead of the landing forces. A floating reserve (KOOL Force) would include most of the 2d Armored Division, plus the 18th Regimental Combat Team.[19] Hammond estimated that to furnish communications for these forces he would need an armored signal battalion, a signal service battalion, a construction battalion, 2 signal battalions, 4 signal companies (special), 2 depot companies, and 1 each repair, port service, radio intelligence, and pigeon companies, plus 8 units from signal photographic companies. This list did not include signal troops for Air Forces or divisional units. The estimate differed in a number of particulars from the troops he actually received. It was possible to furnish him with only 3 detachments of a signal repair company rather than a whole company, 1 depot company instead of 2, and 4 photographic units instead of 8. The signal service battalion, the construction battalion, and the pigeon company were cut from the list entirely, but he received a bonus with the assignment of a signal operations company that he had not asked for. The signal troops available by D-day

totaled nearly 9,000, including divisional and AAF units: 6,744 officers and men serving ground force units and 2,208 with the air arm.[20]

Preinvasion signal training presented difficulties. Much of the initial planning was finished before the end of the Tunisia Campaign in May; after that troop units assembled in training areas all the way from Casablanca to Bizerte, 1,100 air-line miles away. Rapid communication between these scattered units became a major problem that Hammond solved by a network of direct telephone lines, plus teletypewriter circuits at some points, radio links at others, radio command and administrative networks, scheduled motor courier service on a 700-mile daily route, and air courier service on a 2,260-mile daily schedule.[21] Many of the signal units lacked combat experience. Most of the men of the 1st, 3d, and 9th Signal Companies, the 71st and 72d Signal Companies (Special), the 286th Signal Company (Composite), the 53d Signal Battalion, and the 128th Signal Radio Intelligence Company had seen service in North Africa. The other signal units involved either had come directly from the United States or had served in the communications zone during the Tunisia Cam-

[19] Seventh Army Rpt, Sicilian Campaign, pp. A 6–7. The signal officers of the assault forces were Lt. Col. Grant A. Williams, II Corps, SHARK; Lt. Col. Henry J. Hort, 45th Division, CENT; Lt. Col. George Pickett, 1st Division, DIME; Lt. Col. James F. Brooke, 3d Division, Joss; and Maj. Carmon L. Clay, 2d Armored Division, KOOL. Ibid., an. 10, Sig Com Plan, sec. III, p. d–17.

[20] (1) Seventh Army Rpt, Sicilian Campaign, p. M–1. (2) SigC Participation in the Sicilian Campaign, pp. 8–9. (3) SigC Info Ltr 31 (Jun 44), p. 19. (4) Capt Sidney L. Jackson, Tactical Communication in World War II: Signal Communication in the Sicilian Campaign (1945), SigC Hist Monograph E–3b, p. 3. SigC Hist Sec file.

[21] (1) Seventh Army Rpt, Sicilian Campaign, pp. A–4, M–2. (2) SigC Participation in the Sicilian Campaign, pp. 10–11. (3) Col. Elton F. Hammond, "Signals for Patton," Signals, II, No. 1 (September–October, 1947), 7–8. (4) Jackson, Sig Com in the Sicilian Campaign, pp. 6–7.

paign. What was worse, about 25 percent of the men in many of the units were replacements who had had no signal specialist training at all.[22]

A further complication was a change in radio procedures ordered by AFHQ that made it necessary to train all radio operators in the British Link-Sign procedure, a method by which radio operators could identify each other with scant likelihood of revealing their identity to enemy listeners.[23] Because of the great distance between units only a limited number of men from each unit was able to attend the two one-day courses offered. The graduates then carried the instruction back to their teammates. Other special schools conducted in preparation for the invasion taught cadres of soldiers how to install, operate, and maintain Signal Corps carrier equipment and gave instruction in the British speech-plus-simplex and speech-plus-duplex equipment.[24]

Hoping to equip all units fully with all items on the tables of basic allowances and to provide maintenance for the first twenty-one days, Hammond requested an initial store of 19,220 tons of signal equipment. This quantity totaled one-sixth of all the signal supplies used in the entire operation, an unusually heavy proportion for initial stockage.[25] Twenty-nine requisitions went forward to the United States; sixty-three were processed in the North African theater. There was need for much special equipment, and a good deal of it had to be improvised. Hammond particularly wanted some SCR–299's specially mounted in moistureproof houses in 2½-ton amphibious trucks (Dukws), which could operate offshore in the surf or on land. By sailing date, he had twelve of them.

Getting enough waterproof bags was a constant source of trouble. Much of the signal equipment had to be specially packed to prevent damage from the rough handling sure to be encountered on the beaches. Storage and issue sections of the 206th Signal Depot Company were attached to each of the subtask forces to handle and care for signal supplies. In general, the forces would each carry a 21-day supply with them, with an added 15-day reserve packed and held in readiness in North Africa for an emergency. All other supplies could be counted on to arrive from the United States on scheduled shipments. As soon as possible after landing, a Signal Corps depot would be established to receive, store, and issue incoming supplies.

Communications and Equipment

The improvement in communications during the assault phase in Sicily showed that the lessons of North Africa had been studiously applied. Even so, there

[22] (1) *Seventh Army Rpt, Sicilian Campaign*, p. M–2. (2) SigC Participation in the Sicilian Campaign, p. 11.

[23] MS Comment, Dr. Bowles (former science adviser to SW), Jul 59.

[24] (1) *Seventh Army Rpt, Sicilian Campaign*, p. M–2. (2) SigC Participation in the Sicilian Campaign, p. 11. Colonel Williams, II Corps signal officer, heartily disliked the Link-Sign procedure, but rated the speech-plus-simplex and speech-plus-duplex equipment "very good." MS Comment, Williams, Jul 59.

[25] (1) *Seventh Army Rpt, Sicilian Campaign*, p. M–2. (2) SigC Participation in the Sicilian Campaign, p. 10. (3) Hammond, "Signals for Patton," *Signals*, II, No. 1, p. 8. (4) Hq Seventh Army, Notes on the Sicilian Campaign. SCIA 23.

were signal errors, especially in air operations: lack of good identification, which led to the tragic downing of troop carrier planes by friendly naval and anti-aircraft gunners; poor determination of paratroop drop zones, with paratroopers descending miles from their intended goals.[26] But communications over the beaches were much improved.

Special communications ships at sea assured that there would be no such breakdowns as occurred in TORCH, when the U.S. headquarters ship, the cruiser *Augusta*, fired her guns and the shock knocked out her improvised Army radio equipment.[27] Only one communications ship off Sicily, the *Ancon*, had been specially designed for her task.[28] On the others, unfortunately, communications had to be crowded into makeshift quarters, and operations suffered accordingly. The radio operators, the message center and code clerks, and the war room staff were badly cramped for space. Radio stations were scattered in widely separated places on the ship. This made it difficult to control operations, limited the number of channels that could be provided, and slowed up the clearing of radio messages.[29] Afterwards, the Army

Air Forces spoke bitterly of the shipboard communications arrangement, saying that the problem of mutual transmitter interference was so great that the use of one ship to mount circuits for all three services was an impossible arrangement.[30] Nevertheless, though their radio quarters were crowded and inconvenient, all headquarters ships maintained their appointed channels.

Radio sets were much better waterproofed this time. Units had done their own packing, placing their equipment items in waterproof bags. Only a small percentage of items suffered from sea water, although some damage occurred because of careless handling in the haste of landing. Some radio sets, for example those of the British 5th Division, had been packed in waterproof bags for four weeks before the invasion. Meanwhile condensation and sweating inside the bags rendered the radios ineffective until they had a chance to dry.[31] In general the radios of the U.S. signal troops worked well. Mounting the SCR-299's in Dukws proved to be an especially happy innovation. Inclosed in box huts similar to HO-17 and powered by two small PE-75's rather than by the usual large trailer-mounted PE-95, they and their amphibious transport proved "remarkably successful," according to 15th Army Group headquarters. "In some

---

[26] For paratroop actions, see (1) "Troops by Air," *Radar*, No. 3 (June 30, 1944), p. 24; (2) Omar N. Bradley, *A Soldier's Story* (New York: Henry Holt and Company, Inc., 1951), pp. 126–27, 132–34.

[27] Thompson, Harris, *et al.*, *The Test*, p. 359.

[28] Vice Admiral G. C. Towner, USN, "Communications for Command Control in an Amphibious Assault," *Signals*, XIV, No. 8 (April, 1960), 61.

The *Ancon* was the Navy's first "floating radio station." Other American headquarters and communications ships in the Sicilian invasion were the USS *Monrovia*, the USS *Orizaba*, the USS *Biscayne*, and the USS *Samuel Chase*.

[29] (1) *Seventh Army Rpt, Sicilian Campaign*, pp. M-2, -3. (2) SigC Participation in the

Sicilian Campaign, pp. 14–15. (3) Seventh Army, Notes on the Sicilian Campaign, p. 4. (4) Hq, 15th AGp, Notes on Sig Com of U.S. Troops in Opn HUSKY, Oct 43, pp. 2–3. SCIA file Rpts-Notes-Info, etc., on Sig Opns.

[30] Incl, Rpt of Opn HUSKY, with Ltr, AAF Northwest African Air Force to CG AAF, 21 Aug 43, sub: Transmittal. SigC AC 676 HUSKY Opn.

[31] (1) *Seventh Army Rpt, Sicilian Campaign*, p. M-2. (2) SigC Participation in the Sicilian Campaign, p. 13. (3) Notes on Sig Com of U.S. Troops in Opn HUSKY, p. 3.

instances, they got ashore eight hours earlier than other vehicles on the same craft and were placed in operation immediately." [32] Two Dukw-mounted SCR–299's landed at the wrong beach, put to sea, and cruised six miles to the II Corps command post.[33]

Among the smaller radios, both the older AM (amplitude modulation) sets such as the 193, the 284, the 511, and the new FM sets of the 500 and 600 series served well, with the 600's, especially SCR–609 and SCR–610, coming to the fore as excellent for amphibious work. The first radios ashore, according to the signal plan, were the small hand-carried SCR–536's, and the guidon set, SCR–511, one or the other of which every company commander was expected to carry. (Actually the 511 was used effectively between company and battalion; the 536 between company and platoon.) The Germans were intrigued by the SCR–536, some of which they captured in Sicily. They described it as "extremely effective"; its light weight, small size, efficiency, and range made it "ideal equipment for forward observers and companies." [34] Navy beach signal teams carried the FM artillery set SCR–609. Other troops used 284's and 610's to set up traffic control and regimental combat team and shore regimental command nets. Vehicular sets

followed, chief of which were the 299's and the old reliable 193's mounted in jeeps.

Everywhere they were used, the FM radios served outstandingly.[35] For example, the command net of the units of the Joss Force centered in an SCR–608 aboard the headquarters command ship, the USS *Biscayne*. Its operators, using the ten channels its pushbuttons provided, communicated with SCR–610's located in the command posts of each infantry regiment, of each assault battalion, and of the division artillery. The SCR–608 could call up any of these 610's, of whose two channels one was tuned to the control set aboard the *Biscayne*, the other to the common division frequency.[36]

Among the units of KOOL Force, an unofficial FM command net proved useful, employing armored force radios of the standard 500 type. An SCR–509 aboard the *Orizaba*, headquarters ship of KOOL Force, opened for business at 0800 on 10 July. The net took in the headquarters of Combat Command B, 1st Armored Division; the headquarters of the 18th Regimental Combat Team; the headquarters of the 142d Armored Signal Company aboard an LST (landing ship, tank); and the beachmaster. Five reserve SCR–509's were held aboard the *Orizaba* to be doled out as staff parties went ashore. This improvised net

[32] (1) Notes on Sig Com of U.S. Troops in Opn HUSKY, Oct 43, pp. 5–6. (2) The Dukw-Mounted Radio Set SCR–299–( ), SigC Tech Info Ltr 29 (Apr 44), pp 25–28.

[33] Of Dir Intel ASF, Intel Rpt, Statistical Data Based on Operation of II Corps in Sicily. SCIA 111 ODI Rpts.

[34] General der Panzertruppen Walther Fried, *The Fighting of the 29th Panzer Grenadier Division in Sicily* (Neustadt, Germany, 18 November 1947), translated by 2d Lt. Kurt Byrd, Hist Div SSUSA, pp. 30–32.

[35] (1) Jackson, Tactical Com in World War II, pt. II, Sig Com in the Sicilian Campaign, pp. 45–46. (2) Notes on Sig Com of U.S. Troops in Opn HUSKY, Oct 43, p. 6. (3) Ltr, Maj W. H. Crook, SigC, to DCSigO, 24 Jul 43, sub: Sig Com in Sicily. Sicily folder, SigC Hist Sec file. For favorable comment on the 600 series of FM sets in amphibious operations, see the Sicily folder, *passim*.

[36] Jackson, Tactical Com in World War II, pt. II, p. 65.

SCR–511 IN USE AT A HILLTOP COMMAND POST, IN SICILY

proved highly dependable and flexible—"priceless," Maj. Carmon L. Clay, the signal officer of the 2d Armored Division called it—since it became the sole means of communication for the command of KOOL and for the control of beach activities and unloading as the reserve units began landing. Before midnight the entire headquarters staff was ashore, albeit scattered, since landing craft did not always arrive at the designated beaches. However, the FM radio net kept everyone in contact. Further, the net remained the only means of communication on the

following day, 11 July. On the 12th a German tank threat was reported over the net, and a company of tanks of the 67th Armored Regiment landed and repulsed the enemy.[37]

Supply in Sicily

During the 38-day campaign, the signal supply system functioned effec-

[37] (1) Incl, Hq 2d Armd Div, Div SigO, Rpt of Opn HUSKY, pt. I, pp. 1–2, with Ltr, Hammond, SigO Seventh Army, to CSigO, 11 Oct 43, sub: Transmittal of Rpts. Sicily folder. (2) Jackson, Tactical Com in World War II, pt. II, p. 69.

tively, despite initial difficulties in establishing dumps. Signal supply planning on the whole had been sound, though wire and dry batteries were in short supply because the troops advanced much more rapidly than anyone had expected and used up their initial supply of wire quickly. There were some tight moments in the first three days of fighting, for the assault troops had brought in only sixty miles of assault wire and needed more than twice that amount.[38] The shortage of both wire and batteries remained acute until additional quantities arrived by convoy on the fourth day.[39] The 3d Division averted a similar shortage of wire only by instituting the most extensive salvage measures, such as sending troops out to recover every scrap of used wire from places where it was no longer needed. On one occasion, the division supply officer sent a truck on a 200-mile round trip to pick up a fresh supply of wire from the nearest dump.[40] As for radios, the 1st Division reported that only the unceasing efforts of the repairmen of the detachment from the 177th Signal Repair Company kept them going.[41] There was a universal complaint over the lack of spare parts kits supposed to be packed with the radios, as well as a short-

age of parts for the SCR–299's and for the mine detectors, SCR–625's.

Nevertheless, supply generally was far better organized than it had been for the North African campaign. Initially, in the assault phase, signal supplies went into signal dumps, one for each of the subtask forces, controlled by the subtask force signal officer and operated by the storage and issue sections of the 206th Signal Depot Company. As the invasion progressed and control of all units reverted to the Army, the old supply dumps closed and new ones opened closer to the advancing troops they served. The three repair units of the 177th Signal Repair Company were detached from their original assignment to the assault divisions and assigned to the storage and issue sections of the depot company, an arrangement that worked admirably. From AFHQ, Colonel Tully reported to General Ingles: "We mounted the Sicilian campaign very successfully, and it was said that this particular group of signal units was the best-equipped that ever went into combat." [42] On 27 July, the Palermo Signal Supply Depot opened in a captured Italian engineer depot. Since the engineers had communications responsibility in the Italian Army, the engineer depot housed large quantities of usable signal items, which Colonel Hammond's signal troops at once took over and started issuing along with American equipment.[43]

---

[38] Incl, Rpt Opn HUSKY, with Ltr, AAG to CG AAF, 21 Aug 43, sub: Transmittal. SigC AC 676 HUSKY Opn.

[39] (1) Historical Report of the 1st Signal Company, 8 August 1943. SigC Hist Sec file. (2) Incl, Ltr, 2d Lt Fred E. Parker, Sig SupO, to SigO Seventh Army, 23 Aug 43, sub: Lessons Learned From Opn HUSKY, with Ltr, Hammond to CSigO, 11 Oct 43. Sicily folder.

[40] Ltr, Gen Truscott, Hq 3d Inf Div, to CO Seventh Army, 26 Aug 43, sub: Rpt of Sig Com, Opn HUSKY. Sicily folder.

[41] Hist Rpt of the 1st Sig Co, 8 Aug 43.

[42] (1) Ltr, Sig SupO Seventh Army to SigO Seventh Army, 20 Aug 43, sub: Hist of Sig Sup in Sicily. Sicily folder. (2) Ltr, Tully, DCSigO AFHQ, to CSigO, 11 Sep 43. SCIA file 23 Tully Rpts 1.

[43] Seventh Army Rpt, Sicilian Campaign, p. M–17.

Photography

Four photographic units, two each from the 196th and 163d Signal Photographic Companies, accompanied the invading force into Sicily. Each unit consisted of one officer cameraman and six enlisted cameramen.[44] Actual photographic coverage began some thirty days before the invasion date when the cameramen made a complete pictorial record of the vast preparations then under way. The primary purpose was to furnish scenes to be used for a projected full-length feature film on the invasion, but as it turned out they were widely used for other purposes. Newsreel companies used the films extensively to demonstrate to audiences the thoroughness with which the Army prepared for an invasion. The War Department Bureau of Public Relations characterized the film as "magnificent" and rated it "the most perfect war coverage in the photographic medium seen during this war." [45]

All together, thirty-eight Army combat photographers covered the campaign. Thirty-two of them were attached to various tactical units, and six men, specially assigned, were under the direct control of Seventh Army. The men assigned directly to Seventh Army proved highly effective because they could be shifted about whenever and wherever their services were required. Once again,

as in North Africa, the advantages of a flexible organization were demonstrated.[46] Two cameramen volunteered for duty with the 82d Airborne Division. One of them was assigned to a glider unit, but the other found himself attached to the 505th Parachute Infantry. Although he had never made a parachute jump before, he dropped with the unit behind the enemy lines on the night of 9–10 July.

During the period 10 July to 31 August, Signal Corps photographers sent the War Department 3,200 still pictures, 56,500 feet of 35-mm. negative, and 1,650 feet of 16-mm. picture Kodachrome. The War Department Board of Review, judging the material "extremely interesting," forwarded an official commendation to the Seventh Army for the "prompt and efficient" manner in which photographic coverage of the campaign was handled.[47]

*New Types of Signal Units
in Sicily*

New units and services appeared in Sicily, for example, the SIAM service, SIAM standing for *signal information and monitoring.* This was an outgrowth of the British J service, as developed in the British Eighth Army in North Africa.[48] A friendly radio intercept

[44] (1) *Seventh Army Rpt, Sicilian Campaign,* p. M–14. (2) SigC Participation in the Sicilian Campaign, app. D to Sig Opns Plan, p. 47.

[45] (1) *Seventh Army Rpt, Sicilian Campaign,* p. M–14. (2) Ltr, Chief Pictorial Br WD BPR to ACofS G–2 AFHQ, 31 Jul 43, sub: Film Rcd of Invasion Rehearsal. Copy in SigC Participation in the Sicilian Campaign, p. 124.

[46] See Thompson, Harris, *et al., The Test,* p. 401.

[47] (1) Ltr, AG NATO to CG Seventh Army, 15 Sep 43, sub: Photographs. Copy in SigC Participation in the Sicilian Campaign, p. 122. (2) *Seventh Army Rpt, Sicilian Campaign,* p. M–14.

[48] See Thompson, Harris, *et al., The Test,* p. 537. The letters SIAM originally stood for *staff information and monitoring,* but quickly became, in American usage, *signal information and monitoring.* The latter meaning is used throughout this volume.

service, J was designed to monitor radio traffic between front-line units and to report what it overheard to higher headquarters. Thus staff officers might learn the current situation touching their own troops much more quickly than they could hope to be notified through routine reports sent up through normal channels. Since the J service could not listen to all radio nets of the front-line units at the same time, it was supplemented by the "phantom" service—a system wherein liaison officers obtained information from listening to radios of regiment, division, and corps staffs and transmitted it to higher headquarters. During the Tunisia Campaign, the United States II Corps as well as the British First and Eighth Armies had used improvised units for staff monitoring, but, in May 1943, the theater commander asked Washington to activate signal information and monitoring companies on the basis of one per army.[49] In the meantime, for HUSKY, the Americans borrowed two British J officers and drew upon the 1st and 3d Divisions' radio intelligence platoons for personnel.

As the American forces developed the J service, it served two purposes: to inform higher commands of the state of operations in forward units, and to provide information concerning abuses in security and procedure. The SIAM or J service in Sicily appears to have operated faithfully but rather unevenly, as could be expected from the makeshift arrangement. Most of the emphasis was placed on monitoring for security infractions, and numerous breaches were

detected and reported.[50] Apparently Seventh Army made little use of the other half of the J function.[51] In fact Colonel Williams of II Corps did not use it at all, feeling that "entirely erroneous concepts were obtained from eavesdropping and from the reports of inexperienced, irresponsible liaison officers."[52] Nevertheless, at the close of the campaign the 15th Army Group thought well enough of the results achieved to go on record as strongly in favor of the formation of special units constituting a SIAM service, to be separate from the radio intelligence units.[53]

Another new development was one whose seeds went back to the North African campaign. Runners, motorcycle messengers, and automobile couriers had long attended every signal center. But airplanes provided the swiftest means. In North Africa the Air Dispatch Letter Service had utilized small field artillery liaison planes and sometimes larger planes lent by the Air Forces for the convenience of corps and army message centers. This pioneer air dispatch system proved so valuable that thereafter it was used in campaigns throughout the war.[54] At the close of the campaign in Sicily, Colonel Hammond urged that "Piper cubs or equivalent light planes, with

---

[49] Ltr, Asst AG Hq NATO to TAG, 19 May 43, sub: Sig Monitoring Co. SigC IS 321 Sig Monitoring Co.

[50] (1) *Seventh Army Rpt, Sicilian Campaign,* p. M–14. (2) SigC Participation in the Sicilian Campaign, pp. 116–18. (3) Opn Rpt, 3151st SIAM Co (A Typical SIAM Company), p. 1. Opn Rpts RG 207 Admin 572–C.

[51] A tactical situation involving armored units deploying on a wide front offers more opportunities for exploiting J information. Hq Fifth Army SigO, Tentative Operation and Training Manual for the Signal Information and Monitoring Service, p. 4. SigC Hist Sec file.

[52] MS Comment, Williams, Jul 59.

[53] Notes on Sig Com of U.S. Troops in Opn HUSKY, p. 6.

[54] Interv, SigC Hist Sec with Tully, 22 Aug 58.

operation and maintenance personnel, must be provided the Signal Corps for army and corps messenger or courier service on the basis of six for army headquarters and three for corps headquarters." AFHQ agreed but added that helicopters would be even better because they could land on dirt roads and very small fields in nearly any sort of weather.[55]

Still another very new type of Signal Corps unit in Sicily was the 2650th Radio Relay Station Company, or rather two detachments of it. The company had already existed a few brief months, since the first of the year, as Company D of the 829th Signal Service Battalion. Company D, 829th Signal Service Battalion, with a crew of civilian engineers from the Fort Monmouth laboratories, had rendered a valuable service installing and operating the Army's first very high frequency (VHF) radio relay system, improvised from FM Motorola police sets that provided an excellent single-channel teletypewriter circuit, over the mountaintops from Algiers to Tunisia.[56]

In March 1943 the distinctive contribution of Company D had received recognition with a change of name to the 2650th Radio Relay Station Company. In midyear, while some detachments went to Sicily, others extended

the Algiers-Tunis channel over a 40-mile hop to Cape Bon, a 60-mile jump thence to the small isle of Pantelleria, thence a tremendous leap of about 150 miles to the British fortress island, Malta. In Sicily the detachments erected a station atop Cape Gallo, near Palermo, where to their surprise they found intact a German radio relay set of the decimeter type. They then installed another station located diagonally across the triangular island, at Mt. Laura, near the British sector headquarters at Syracuse.[57]

Plans originally called for Company E of the 829th Signal Service Battalion to furnish pigeon communications for HUSKY; thus two elements of the same battalion would have supplied simultaneously in Sicily one of the oldest and one of the newest modes of communication. Because of a scarcity of air transport for pigeoneers, no pigeons were used in Sicily. Colonel Hammond later stated that pigeons could have been used to great advantage in many instances. Units sent into the mountains to clear enemy points of resistance were out of communication with their parent organizations for as long as twenty-four hours, under radio silence to achieve surprise. In such cases pigeon messengers might have served well.[58]

Wire Communications

Mountaintop radio proved to be the only effective way of using FM after the

[55] (1) Hq Seventh Army, annex to Notes on the Sicilian Campaign, p. 11. SCIA 23. (2) Notes on Sig Com of U.S. Troops in Opn HUSKY, Oct 43, p. 5.

Capt. Henry N. Blanchard, Jr., commander of the 9th Infantry Division signal company, urged either a Piper Cub or helicopter for every division message center. Ltr, Blanchard to CG Seventh Army, Attn: SigO, 2 Sep 43, sub: Studies T/BA. Sicily folder.

[56] (1) See Thompson, Harris, et al., The Test, p. 372. (2) Interv, SigC Hist Sec with Capt Oliver D. Perkins and Joseph H. Durrer, Jan 45. SigC Hist Sec file.

[57] (1) Interv, SigC Hist Sec with Perkins and Durrer, Jan 45. (2) History of Company D, 829th Signal Service Battalion, sec. H, pp. 5–6, in the personal files of 1st Lt R. W. Reed, SigC. (3) Seventh Army Rpt, Sicilian Campaign, p. M-9.

[58] Seventh Army Rpt, Sicilian Campaign, p. M-13.

STRINGING WIRE *beside the Messina road.*

Allies drove into the interior of Sicily, for the high hills cut off VHF radiations and reduced the effectiveness of AM radio as well.[59] Wire and cable, therefore, became all the more important and an increasing problem in ratio to the speed of the pursuit. Throughout the campaign wire and cable, either single circuit lines or carrier, whenever carrier techniques could be applied to increase the traffic capacity, received heavy use. Commercial wire lines in Sicily were not extensive, and those that existed were badly damaged. Rehabilitating them was time consuming, but it had to be done on a large scale.

Shortages and unusually severe sabotage added to the troubles imposed by the unexpectedly heavy demand.[60]

Signal troops of the 3d Infantry Division endured a grueling test in the third phase of the campaign, during the advance from San Stefano to Messina. The division met determined German resistance on a narrow coastal road backed by mountains. The road along the coast offered a natural wire axis, but the route lay under interdicting artillery fire and was subject to the hazards of demolitions and numerous German mine fields laid at strategic points. Previous pole lines were utterly demolished. The wire crews laid their wire on the ground. The 2½-ton trucks the wiremen ordinarily used would have hopelessly blocked traffic on the narrow road, so the men payed out the wire from small ¼-ton trucks at first and fought a constant battle to maintain the line despite the ravages of enemy shellfire and the damage inflicted by friendly vehicles.

Soon the operation developed into a series of enveloping movements, a regiment at a time struggling over mountainous terrain impassable to any vehicle, where even pack animals could travel only with the greatest difficulty. Signalmen crept over the rocky, trackless mountainside, laying the wire by hand— a 5-mile stretch at San Fratello and a 20-mile line from San Marco to Mirto to Naso. Where mules could go, they carried the wire; where they could not, the men carried it. For the fifteen miles from St. Angelo di Brolo to Patti, they laid two lines of W–130 over terrain devoid of trails. One 6-mile stretch of

---

[59] Notes on Sig Com of U.S. Troops in Opn HUSKY, p. 6.

[60] (1) *Seventh Army Rpt, Sicilian Campaign,* p. M–5. (2) SigC Participation in the Sicilian Campaign, pp. 89–90.

Field Wire Along a Mule Trail in the Mountainous Capua Area, Italy

line on a narrow winding road from the coastal road to San Marco took a nightmarish twenty-four hours to lay; the route was under constant shellfire and was being used by three battalions of artillery.[61] Infantrymen, groping their way forward in darkness, often broke the precious wire by using it as a guideline.[62]

General Truscott, commanding the 3d Division, also had words of praise for the radio operators. He said that on one occasion, when the infantry occupied a hill position where no vehicle could follow, the officer and operators in charge of an SCR–193 in a ¼-ton truck "displayed extraordinary courage in continuing to operate the set from an exposed position on the flat ground outside the main lines." [63]

Colonel Williams, signal officer of the II Corps, later wrote of his wire problems. "The Sicilian campaign was more in the nature of a horse race," he said. "We moved the Corps CP fourteen times in thirty-eight days." He had heard meanwhile that the Signal Corps was developing an entirely new duplex, multichannel radio relay system (it would reach the field early in 1944 as AN/TRC–1, 3, and 4). "While we were moving so fast through the mountains

with practically no wire lines," Williams wrote to Col. James D. O'Connell in the Washington headquarters, "I certainly wished I had something like the radio carrier equipment you are working on. I had visualized such a system . . . but had no idea you had progressed so much along those lines." [64]

The Army would have to wait a few months for this tremendously important development, and meanwhile spiral-four field cable filled the gap. Hardly anyone felt entirely satisfied with this first spiral-four (it would be greatly improved by the time of the Normandy invasion), but it was the best wire available for corps use.[65] The II Corps' 53d Signal Battalion installed hundreds of miles of spiral-four in Sicily—in fact some 1,500 miles of wire lines of all kinds as the men kept up with the ground forces. In the five weeks of rapid combat that drove the Germans completely out of Sicily by late August, the Signal Corps men with the II Corps maintained wire contacts with all the units except for one division that ran ahead and was out of reach for two days, except by radio.[66]

As the troops pressed from Palermo to Messina, signalmen encountered

---

[61] Ltr, Truscott, Hq 3d Inf Div, to CG Seventh Army, 26 Aug 43, sub: Rpt of Sig Com, Opn Husky. Sicily folder.

[62] "We repeatedly stumbled into the wrong ravines trying to keep hold of our only guide, the thin phone wire laid along the ground from rendezvous to C.P. [command post]." Franklyn A. Johnson (formerly a 1st Division second lieutenant commanding a platoon on Mount Pellegrino in Aug 43), One More Hill (New York: Funk and Wagnalls Co., 1949), p. 111.

[63] Ltr, Truscott, Hq 3d Inf Div, to CG Seventh Army, 26 Aug 43, sub: Rpt of Sig Com, Opn Husky. Sicily folder.

[64] (1) Ltr, Williams, SigO II Corps, to O'Connell, OCSigO, 29 Oct 43. SCIA file 45 Misc, European Theater, N Through R, folder 1. (2) MS Comment, Dr. Harold A. Zahl and Amory H. Waite, U.S. Army Signal Research and Development Laboratories (USASRDL), Ft. Monmouth, Jul 59.

[65] (1) Ltr, Williams to O'Connell, 29 Oct 43. (2) MS Comment, Williams, Jul 59. (3) Hq AFHQ, Report of Lessons Learned in Operation Husky (Sig Sec). (4) Extract, par. 21 of Ltr, SigO Seventh Army to DCSigO AFHQ, in Ltr, DCSigO AFHQ to CSigO Fifth Army, 23 Aug 43. Sicily folder.

[66] Rpt, Williams, Hq II Corps SigO, 24 Aug 43, sub: Sig Com. SCIA file 124 (2000–3) Lessons and Rpts of Opns.

another formidable obstacle. The retreating enemy had placed mines liberally along the pole line route and the
railroad right of way, which the wire
lines usually followed. As a result of
earlier experience in the North African
campaign, special signal teams had been
trained to find and remove the deadly
devices. These teams rendered invaluable service in Sicily and Italy. Their
weapons were mine detectors, SCR–
625, developed by the National Defense
Research Committee (NDRC) at the
request of the Corps of Engineers, but
procured, stored, and issued by the
Signal Corps.[67] The SCR–625 was very
effective in detecting metallic mines,
but in the latter stages of the campaign
signalmen encountered a number of
wooden mines and at least one plastic
mine.[68] Experienced men using the SCR
–625 could usually detect the wooden
mines because of the nails used to construct them, but nonmetallic plastic
mines were obviously going to demand
a new kind of detector.[69]

By 17 August, the last organized German and Italian resistance had been
cleared from Sicily. Colonel Hammond
summed up a few statistics. His signal
troops had rehabilitated a total of
2,457 circuit miles of wire (950 miles
figured in pole line miles, 4,916 in
wire miles). AGF signalmen alone had
installed 1,800 miles of spiral-four cable.

In 42 days, radio operators had handled
8,303 incoming and outgoing radio messages constituting 885,943 word groups.[70]

A greater satisfaction lay in the general evaluation of Signal doctrine and
Signal methods as reflected in the performance of the troops and the equipment. By this yardstick, Signal Corps
participation in the campaign was a
success that augured well for the greater
campaigns to come.

The Italian Campaign

While the campaign in Sicily was in
progress, the United States Fifth Army
was readying its troops and perfecting
its plans for launching an assault on the
Italian mainland. Fifth Army had been
activated on 5 January 1943, at Oujda,
Morocco, under the command of Lt.
Gen. Mark W. Clark. It comprised initially the major elements of battle-wise
United States Army troops that had been
assigned to the Western and Center Task
Forces in the North African invasion.
Months of training and planning, which
had to be revised many times as the
tactical situation changed, culminated
on 9 September when Fifth Army undertook AVALANCHE, the operation aimed
at seizing the port of Naples. For the
invasion, Fifth Army consisted of the
U.S. VI Corps and the British 10 Corps,
striking simultaneously at points around
Salerno, south of Naples. The mission
of 10 Corps was to seize Salerno, the
Monte Corvino airdrome, and passes
northwest of Salerno, while VI Corps
was to secure the high ground covering
the Salerno plain. The operations were

---

[67] (1) Baxter, *Scientists Against Time*, pp. 100ff.
(2) James J. Cerruti, Historical Narrative of the
Philadelphia Signal Corps Procurement District
(1945), III, 622–26 (hereafter cited as Hist, PSCPD).
SigC Hist Sec file. (3) MS Comment, Lt. Gen James
D. O'Connell (Ret.), former CSigO, Jul 59.
[68] Seventh Army, Notes on the Sicilian Campaign, pp. 13, 21.
[69] Plastic Mine Detector AN/PRS–1 went into
production early in 1944. Cerruti, Hist, PSCPD,
p. 624.

[70] (1) *Seventh Army Rpt, Sicilian Campaign*,
p. M–9. (2) SigC Participation in the Sicilian
Campaign, p. 111.

to be supported by British and U.S. naval task forces, and by the U.S. XII Air Support Command.[71]

Under supervision of 15th Army Group, Clark's signal officer, General Moran, and his staff had prepared a signal plan much like the one used successfully in Sicily. It provided for communications at every stage—in convoy, on a command ship during the initial stages of the assault, for shore communications, for air communications, and progressively for tactical and administrative links as the assault waves landed and began consolidating their positions.[72]

Once again the *Ancon* would serve as Army headquarters ship, with Navy radio transmitters and receivers set up to work Army circuits, operated by a detachment of twelve men of the 63d Signal Battalion, together with a detachment of 7 British cipher experts.[73] Additional Signal Corps troops aboard other ships in the convoy and slated to land on D-day included a 64-man detachment of the 74th Signal Company to furnish shore communications for the shore battalion and for the engineer shore regiment headquarters; a 25-man detachment of the 812th Signal Port Service Company to provide for initial storage and issue of signal supplies; 40 officers and men of the 57th Signal Battalion to handle communications initially for the VI Corps; and the 36th Signal Company, which served the 36th

GENERAL MORAN

Infantry Division. There was also a 12-man photographic detachment of the 2625th Signal Service Regiment to furnish a pictorial record of the assault; a public relations detachment outfitted with a Dukw-mounted radio set; and 14 men of a SIAM unit to cover signal information and monitoring.[74]

Assault Communications at Salerno

When already three days at sea, and while converging upon the Gulf of

---

[71] (1) Fifth Army GO 1, 5 Jan 43. (2) Fifth Army Hist, I, 25–28.

[72] Hq Fifth Army, Sig an. 6 to FO 1, sec. II, Mission and Signal Plan. There is a copy in folder entitled Italy, SigC Hist Sec file.

[73] *Ibid.* Command post of the VI Corps afloat was the USS *Funston*; of the 10 Corps, H.M.S. *Hilary*; of the 36th Division, USS *Samuel Chase.*

[74] (1) Fifth Army, Signal Section Unit History, Month of September 1943 (hereafter referred to as Fifth Army, Sig Sec Hist, with date cited). SigC Hist Sec file. (2) Typical SIAM Co (3151st SIAM Co), pp. 2–6. (3) Hq Fifth Army, Sig an. 6 to FO 1, app. A, Enumeration of SigC Troops. (4) Hq 15th AGp, Report of Visit to Fifth Army Units, 23–28 September 1943 (Col Kerineth F. Zitzman), 30 Sept 43 (hereafter cited as Zitzman Rpt).

Salerno, the convoy ships' radios picked up General Eisenhower's announcement of the end of hostilities with Italy. Italy's withdrawal from the war was a boost to troop morale, but it left the AVALANCHE mission unchanged. On board the convoy vessels, all radios maintained silence except for one receiver that stood continuous watch on channel A–8, over which came hourly intelligence reports from 15th Army Group headquarters in Bizerte and from the photoreconnaissance unit at La Marsa airfield in Tunis. Shortly before midnight on the night of 8 September the moon went down, and in the ensuing darkness the first assault waves left the convoy vessels standing some twelve miles off the beaches to avoid the mine fields.[75]

The Germans were not caught by surprise. As the first assault waves reached the beach, enemy artillery, mortar, and machine gun fire began to rake the landing areas. German resistance was far heavier than it had been at the invasion of Sicily. The 36th Division was pinned to the beaches for several hours before it was able to struggle inland. The men, coming to the beaches almost unprotected, had no time to handle communications equipment with care and patience. Signal equipment losses for the division ran high.[76]

While the convoy was still at sea, each man of the 36th Signal Company had been thoroughly briefed in his particular duty. The company landed its sections in the order of their immediate utility in relation to the entire assault plan—first the radio teams, then the construction platoon, the telephone and telegraph section, the message center section, and finally the headquarters group. Since radio circuits are the first links to serve an assault force, the men from the radio section landed with the first assault waves, making their way up the beach with their SCR–536's, the "handie-talkies." Radio reconnaissance jeeps with long-range, mobile SCR–193 sets mounted in them provided the first communications with VI Corps headquarters at sea, with reconnaissance elements of the landed force, and in division and Fifth Army nets. Amphibious 2½-ton trucks, Dukws, carrying complete SCR–499 radio stations, kept communications linked between ships and shore during landing operations, and later on drove ashore to extend VI Corps communications to points off the Continent.[77] In the early morning darkness, members of radio teams often became separated, and as a result many teams were unable to operate.[78] Until 1000, six and a half hours after the first landings had begun, communication between divisions and their subordinate units remained practically impossible. Corps and division signal officers felt that not enough communications equipment was loaded to land early. Shortly thereafter, the situation improved slightly, but many unit commanders continued to resort to messengers, who

---

[75] (1) Fifth Army Hist, 1, 30–32. (2) Fifth Army, Sig Sec Hist, Sep 43, pp. 2–3.

[76] (1) Fifth Army, Sig Sec Hist, Sep 43. (2) Maj Arvo N. Niemi, Sig SupO, Fifth Army, Rpt to SigO Fifth Army, 6 Oct 43, sub: History of Signal Supply in Italy for AVALANCHE (U.S.) (hereafter cited as Niemi Rpt). Italy folder, SigC Hist Sec file. (3) Hq NATOUSA, Tng Memo 3, Lessons from the Italian Campaign, 10 Mar 44, pp. 17–18.

[77] Consolidated History of Signal Corps (36th Signal Company), pp. 1–2. ETOUSA Sig Sec Admin 572–A, Opns Rpt folder.

[78] Fifth Army Hist, I, 32.

SCR-625's Sweeping Italian Beach for Teller Mines

scuttled about in jeeps and small boats.[79]

An 18-man detail from the 36th Signal Company patrolled the beaches on D-day to receive the reconnaissance cars, jeeps, and other vehicles so necessary to the signal work at hand. The construction teams of the 36th came in with the regiments, and, since only one wire-laying vehicle was ashore at this crucial point, the men borrowed infantry jeeps to bring up the wire across the rutted, mine-strewn roads. Under almost constant enemy artillery fire, they strung 90 miles of wire the first day, connecting lines from the regimental command posts to the division command post. The telephone and telegraph section, which followed the construction teams, brought ashore just enough equipment for the first installations—4 switchboards, 15 telephones, 3 miles of assault wire, $1\frac{1}{2}$ miles of field wire, 6 telegraph sets, and 3 reels. By midnight the men had in operation a switching central and locals to all landed units.[80]

Signal supplies, which must be brought up quickly in any assault, be-

[79] (1) Hq NATOUSA, Tng Memo 3, Lessons from the Italian Campaign, 10 Mar 44, pp 17-18. (2) Zitzman Rpt.

[80] Consolidated Hist of SigC (36th Sig Co), p. 3.

gan to be discharged on the beaches about 1000 in such quantity that the 25 men assigned to the storage and issue platoon of the 812th Signal Port Service Company were barely able to keep up with the work of handling them. The men split into two groups and established two signal dumps on two different beaches about a half mile inland. By 1500, considerably earlier than expected, they were able to start issuing replacement items to troops who had lost their equipment in either the landings or the drive inland. Since the beaches were mined and further protected by wire entanglements, the first calls were for mine detectors, radios, and wire cutters. A little later, as the troops began consolidating their positions, they started asking for switchboards. Fortunately, neither of the signal dumps was bombed, but a significant quantity of signal supplies was lost aboard the Liberty ship *Gerhard*, which the enemy bombed and sank in the bay.[81]

On board the *Ancon*, the common message center used by both Army and Navy worked very well. Communications afloat proved most satisfactory, and co-operation between the two services was "perfect."[82] By pooling the cipher machines of the two services, the men were able to handle all the encoding work quickly and efficiently. All Army circuits aboard the *Ancon* opened at H-hour on D-day and established contact with all stations within a few hours. The *Ancon* herself had a narrow

escape in Salerno harbor, earning the nickname *Lucky*. German bombers sought her out for special attention. But though they dropped bombs near enough to cause some damage, they failed to sink the ship.[83]

In the late afternoon of D-day, Allied officers went ashore to seek a suitable site for Fifth Army's command post, and on the following day General Moran's deputy signal officer, Lt. Col. Francis E. Kidwell, arranged for the 63d Signal Battalion troops, Dukw-mounted radios, and communications, message center, and code room equipment to be put ashore.[84]

Good communications were a necessity, especially in the Salerno area, because the American and British elements of the Fifth Army had landed on widely separated beaches. Lt. Col. Frederick C. Lough, commander of the 63d Signal Battalion, succeeded in establishing communications between the two forces when his men piloted one of the radio Dukws over the battle-torn roads almost to the enemy's lines and there made contact with the British headquarters. The position of the 63d soon became precarious, along with those of the British 10 Corps on its left flank and other elements of the American VI Corps on its right. The Germans launched a fierce attack. Soon officers informed Colonel Lough that all the Allied forces were pulling back. With only four headquarters radios ashore,

---

[81] (1) Niemi Rpt. (2) Ltr, SigO Fifth Army to DSigO AFHQ, 26 Sep 43, with extracts from Ltr, Tully to Ingles, 17 Oct 43. Italy folder, SigC Hist Sec file. (3) Zitzman Rpt.

[82] Zitzman Rpt.

[83] Interv, SigC Hist Sec with Capt Edwin F. Erickson, CO 1st Sig Det aboard *Ancon*, 20 Nov 44. Erickson told of two British cipher experts, aboard the *Ancon*, who understood German and who eavesdropped on an enemy radio message that gave the exact location of the headquarters ship and ordered that she be sunk at any cost.

[84] Fifth Army, Sig Sec Hist, Sep 43, pp. 5–7.

Lough knew that to pull back meant shutting down communications, so he moved the sets back one at a time in order to keep the circuits open. It took all of that night and most of the next day to stagger the movement of the sets and still keep operating, but Lough managed it without losing any of his equipment.[85]

The Germans in their drive very nearly succeeded in splitting open the junction between the British and American corps. They drove a deep wedge between the two positions, leaving a narrow corridor along the sea just four miles wide. Fortunately the 63d had brought with it from Africa eight motorcycles, and Pvt. Leonard E. Revier and Pvt. Walter H. Gray volunteered to maintain a perilous messenger service between the two spearheads. Over terrain no jeeps could negotiate, they drove day and night around dangerous roadblocks, demolitions, and detours. Their route, twisting and turning, totaled some fifty miles down from the American areas toward the sea, skirting the coast line for the length of the narrow corridor almost along the water's edge, and then continuing up to the British area. "We had to make time," Revier said, "in order to get back in time to start out again. I got up to 60 once, when that whistling 88 struck barely 40 yards behind me." [86]

Other signalmen hastened to open additional channels of communication between the two forward prongs of the assaulting forces, bringing up wire to supplement and replace radio, in the traditional signal communications pattern. The 2d Platoon of Company A, 63d Signal Battalion, a wire construction platoon, landed at Paestum and unloaded its gear in a vineyard. Most of the men in this group of "tough linemen" were former employees of the Bell Telephone Company. Their commanding officer, Lt. Edward L. Haynes, was a former noncom who had spent most of his prewar duty with the 1st Cavalry and 2d Armored Divisions. Their first mission was to install spiral-four cable to the British 10 Corps, which had landed at Salerno, some fifteen miles to the north.[87] Haynes, assisted by T/Sgts. Robert Mosley and Lawrence Savage, went out to lay the lines. For fifteen miles over rocky hills and strange country, under the very noses of the Germans, they laid the precious thread of wire, working in and out of slit trenches by day and by the light of bomb flares at night. "That was just the beginning of our job, not the end," said crew chief Sgt. William E. Black. "They fought a stiff battle over our line and cut it almost as fast as we could repair it—almost, but not quite." [88]

Thus, first radio, then wire linked together the Allied spearheads. A group of twelve linemen from the 2d Platoon was sent out to rehabilitate a circuit of open wire and underground cable between the two armies in an area still occupied by the Germans. Their first night out they bivouacked in a railroad station where a long enemy ammuni-

---

[85] (1) 2d Lt Edwin E. Dowell, 6654th Sig Msg Ctr Co, Untitled Narr, p. 2. SCIA file, 105/4, 105/5, 105/6, from 1/10/43 to 4/1/44, Col Tully, Pers. (2) Interv, SigC Hist Sec with Col Lough (CO 63d Sig Bn), 5 Oct 44. SigC Hist Sec file.

[86] (1) Interv, SigC Hist Sec with Lough, 5 Oct 44. (2) Dowell, Untitled Narr, p. 3.

[87] Capt Stanley R. Livingston, Signal Corps Linemen in Combat, p. 2. SigC 319.7 SigC Combat Narrs, item 7, SigC Hist Sec file.

[88] Dowell, Untitled Narr, p. 3.

tion train sat on a siding. However, the lieutenant in charge became uneasy and moved his men out ahead of schedule to a position about a mile away. They had just settled down in their new position when the whole train blew up with a mighty roar. As the signalmen traveled on through the area, the local population cheered them, sometimes identifying them as British, sometimes as Americans. When they returned to Fifth Army after accomplishing their mission, they encountered an engineer outfit "complete with cameras, PIO [Public Information Office] men, and broad smiles, officially meeting our British allies." [89]

By the end of September 1943, with the plains of Salerno under firm control, the Fifth Army moved on Naples. Communications to the rear were fast consolidating. There were in operation seventeen radio transmitters and four telephone centrals: one 3-position TC-2 serving the beach area at Paestum, a TC-2 at the headquarters command post, and BD-96's at the rear echelon and at Battipaglia. Army switchboards were serving 118 local subscribers. A TC-3 teletype switchboard at the command post provided teletype service to the U.S. VI and the British 10 Corps. Spiral-four with carrier equipment was operating between VI Corps command post and the 3d Division. Already traffic processed through the code rooms and transmitted by radio and teletype had built up to an average of 23,000 code groups per day, straining the available cipher machines to the utmost. The ADLS, utilizing two cub airplanes, was operating on regular schedules. The

SIAM, or J service, was producing good results, and the 117th and 128th Radio Intelligence Companies were at work intercepting and studying enemy messages. A photographic laboratory arrived and set up for business. The separate radio channel and Dukw-mounted equipment for public relations proved to be particularly fortunate. They not only provided rapid means for the transmission of news, they also took a considerable load off the tactical means of communication. General Moran reported that "the PRO and correspondents without exception have been quite lavish in their praise of the manner in which press traffic has been handled." [90]

Signal Problems in the Autumn and Winter

The fierce Italian campaign was just beginning in that autumn of 1943, to continue long and sharp up the whole length of the peninsula. By the time the Volturno phase began on 12–13 October, more signal troops had arrived. The 71st Signal Company (Special) and the remaining troops of the 63d Signal Battalion went to work operating the message center, code room, switchboard, and radios of the Fifth Army command post. The 51st Signal Battalion crossed from Sicily and was assigned to signal operations in the Fifth Army rear echelon. The 229th Signal Operation Company was assigned to install and operate the message center and switchboard at Maddaloni, the switchboard at

---

[89] Livingston, SigC Linemen in Combat, p. 2.

[90] (1) Fifth Army, Sig Sec Hist, Sep 43. (2) Ltrs, "Dick" (Moran) to Tully, AFHQ, 26 Sep, 28 Sep, and 1 Oct 43, no sub. SCIA file 104 Fifth Army. (3) Ltr, Brig Gen Moran (Ret.) to Dr. George Raynor Thompson, 25 May 58.

Avellino, and the carrier installations at Portici and Salerno. The 212th Signal Depot Company went to Santa Maria to open Signal Depot No. 65.[91]

The rehabilitation of existing wire systems soon put a heavy strain on the limited number of signal troops. Except for one fortunate find, an underground cable along the railroad from Paestum to Pontecargano, practically all wire facilities had been thoroughly wrecked by the retreating Germans. "There are no wire lines left by the Boche," General Moran wrote Colonel Tully at AFHQ on 31 October. "Everything has to be constructed. We are doing all right on poles, crossarms, and insulators, but there isn't a foot of copper other than what we can salvage in short lengths. . . ."[92] Rapid repair of the underground cable system along Fifth Army's main route of advance was vital in order to relieve the strain on other means of communication. George Keith, a British expert who had helped construct the Italian underground cable system before the war, lent his expert knowledge in the reconstruction job.[93]

The AFHQ Signal Section assisted Fifth Army to the utmost. Several weeks before the invasion, Colonel Tully attached two officers from the AFHQ Wire Division to Army headquarters along with other officers from the Signal Section to form the AFHQ advanced group for Italy. The group landed on D plus 3. A month later, after Naples was taken, the group moved to that city. Working close behind Fifth Army, AFHQ signal detachments began the build-up of the main arterial truck line arrangements throughout Italy, rehabilitating fixed plant equipment and tying it into AFHQ nets. The work of the AFHQ detachments proved extremely valuable. Fifth Army signal combat elements, free of worry over communications to the rear, could concentrate entirely on the advance north. Meanwhile the AFHQ control points moved steadily behind the army, preparing for the move of AFHQ to Italy.[94]

General Moran's supply plan had provided for expected battle losses of an average of 10-percent excess for a 30-day period. Except for wire, which was being consumed in greater quantities than had been expected, there were no shortages in signal supply. During October 798 tons of signal equipment were issued, but wire of all kinds was in short supply, and a few types of radios were scarce. A little later a shortage of spare parts for power units developed, and the repair units found themselves unable to repair many of the unserviceable units on hand because of a lack of parts.[95]

As the campaign progressed supply problems eased. General Moran's system of complete inspection and overhaul given all signal items turned in by troops substantially reduced the demands for new equipment. Moran placed repair units at depots under control of depot

[91] (1) Fifth Army, Sig Sec Hist, Oct 43, p. 1. (2) Ltr, Moran to Tully, 1 Oct 43. SCIA file 104 Fifth Army.

[92] Ltr, Moran to Tully, 31 Oct 43. SCIA file 104 Fifth Army.

[93] Ltr, Moran to Thompson, 25 May 58.

[94] (1) Hist, Sig Sec AFHQ, pp. 98, 111, and app. E, Hist Rpt of Wire Div, p. 8. (2) Interv, SigC Hist Sec with Tully, 22 Aug 58.

[95] (1) Niemi Rpt. (2) Ltr, Maj Edwin O. Earl, Sig Off ExecO, to SigO SOS NATOUSA, 30 Jan 44, sub: Sig Sup Matters, Fifth Army. SCIA file, unnumbered, Rpts Misc North African Theater, S Through Z, folder 1.

commanders, who augmented the repair labor force by hiring Italian civilians.[96]

Equipment shortages could be remedied far more easily than shortages in skilled men, and personnel problems plagued Moran throughout the campaign. The 63d Signal Battalion was spread thin. A battalion, according to the tables, was supposed to operate three of the big long-distance SCR-299 radio sets, but Colonel Lough, the commander of the 63d, reported that at one time he had seventeen of the sets in almost continuous operation. That really meant continuous operation, he said, twenty-four hours a day.[97]

Signal officers in North Africa, Sicily, and Italy often felt that staff planning in Washington, especially at the War Department level, was unrealistic, not yet fully aware of the actual communications needs of such a war as World War II was proving to be. Time after time General Moran in Fifth Army and Colonel Tully at AFHQ improvised methods and services to fit the occasion.[98] For example, Moran organized thoroughly unorthodox wire salvage companies, the bulk of personnel made up

of former Italian soldiers, together with a few key Fifth Army signalmen. These companies recovered the wire that signal troops had no time to salvage in the heat of the campaign. Immediately in the wake of the advancing troops, the salvage companies gathered up the abandoned wire, took it to depots, tested it, and repaired it. Theirs was a valuable service not provided for in any table of organization.[99]

Within a week after the landings at Salerno, Moran had begun asking Tully to alleviate his serious problem of personnel replacement. He had to obtain at once twenty-four radio operators for the VI Corps, he wrote, even if he had to strip other organizations such as the 1st Armored Division. "Last night," he reported, "six men allegedly radio operators came in. One was an infantryman with no communication training, one was a barber, and the others had only basic radio operator training. Please get some help on this matter." [100] At the very time that Moran was writing there were only fifteen signal replacements within the entire theater to support demands originated by signal units totaling well over 20,000 men.[101]

Colonel Tully and Maj. Gen. Walter Bedell Smith, chief of staff of AFHQ,

---

[96] (1) SCIA file 104 Fifth Army, *passim*. (2) Ltr, Moran to Thompson, 25 May 58.

[97] Interv, SigC Hist Sec with Lough, 5 Oct 44.

[98] Moran had to improvise the following services among others: SIAM; special field artillery radio net; special commanders' radio nets in corps and divisions; tactical reconnaissance and photographic reconnaissance broadcast systems; special radio circuits for press dispatches to the United States and the United Kingdom; special teletype circuits for the exclusive use of the supply system and the military intelligence system; special requirements for Office of Strategic Services, Allied Military Government, and Special Services. Ltr, Moran to Hodges, Third Army, San Antonio, Tex., 12 Nov 43, sub: Answers to Questions Regarding Sig Com, Fifth Army. SCIA file 23 Tully Rpts 3.

[99] (1) Ltr, Moran to Thompson, 25 May 58. (2) Ltr, Tully to O'Connell, OCSigO, 17 Dec 43. SCIA file, unnumbered, Rpts-Notes-Info, etc., on Sig Opns.

[100] Ltr, Moran to Tully, 17 Sep 43. SCIA file 104 Fifth Army. "This was the personnel replacement system—to which Signals had violently and repeatedly objected—in operation! The replacements were being made by personnel 'experts' who seemed to think that a radio operator was a radio operator, regardless of whether he was to operate a simple regimental set or a complex fixed plant station." MS Comment, Tully, 22 Aug 58.

[101] Hist, Sig Sec AFHQ, p. 60.

worked hard to secure more men. Tully asked G–3, G–4, and Operations Division in the War Department General Staff for 4,000 Signal Corps men and 1,000 Wacs, or at least a bare minimum of 2,000 men and several WAC companies. "We are heading for a breakdown in communications," he wrote, ". . . We have reached the breaking point insofar as signal personnel is concerned." Even so, he drew a blank. "Our troop requirement studies," he soon informed Moran, "have been completely turned down by the War Department." [102] Tully could do only one other thing, namely close down less needed signal stations in the theater and assign the men to Moran, even if it meant robbing other organizations. He thus robbed General Patton's Seventh Army of his prized 1st Armored Signal Battalion over the General's violent objection. Patton protested to General Smith that "such important portions of its [Seventh Army's] staff as a signal battalion should remain with it." Tully's rebuttal to Smith pointed out that there was an acute shortage of signal units, that the 1st Armored Signal Battalion was the only unit not previously committed, and that therefore it must be made available for Italy. This extreme action grew out of Moran's warning of 13 November—"the matter of signal troops is becoming so serious that if help is not forthcoming soon, something must give. . . . Lord help us if we should sustain serious battle losses." [103]

Serious losses were indeed sustained. In that winter of 1943–44, in the teeth of strenuous opposition, linemen waded and swam across the mountain torrents in order to establish communications. Field reports described the procedure. Signal Corps crewmen tied a length of wire or cable around a volunteer's waist, bade him good luck, and tried to cover his crossing with fire support. Once over, the swimmer had to dig in and withstand whatever resistance the enemy provided, then set up for business, when the gunfire lessened, so that communications might be established with the forward units.[104] In support of VI Corps in the fighting at the Volturno, wire-stringing crews had to accomplish their task several times.

In the Calore sector alone, three crossings were necessary in order to keep the 45th Division in touch with corps headquarters. The difficulty, of course, rose principally from the fact that there were no bridges over which the reel carts and jeeps could roll, or from the fact that the engineer-built bridges were in priority use by the infantry. Ordinarily, the crews went approximately three hundred yards upstream from the main crossing, where, as in the 34th Division sector, there was only a light ponton bridge. This, the river, and the single, narrow, one-way road of approach were all under heavy attack from the air. A mitigation, though, was the appearance of improved spiral-four cable, which immediately became invaluable in these

[102] Ltr, Tully to Moran, 2 Nov 43. SCIA file 104 Fifth Army.

[103] (1) Ltr, Patton to Smith, 22 Nov 43. (2) Memo, Tully for Smith, 24 Nov 43. Both in SCIA file, 105/4, 105/5, 105/6, from 1/10/43 to 4/1/44, Col Tully Pers. (3) Ltr, Moran to Tully, 13 Nov 43. SCIA file 104 Fifth Army.

[104] (1) Organizational History of the 34th Signal Company, November 1943. 334–SIG–0.3 (1850) Nov 43. (2) Maj. Gen. Harry C. Ingles, CSigO, "Telephones Are in the Fight, on Every Battleground," *Bell Telephone Magazine*, XXIII, No. 1 (1944), 75. (3) CSigO, Annual Rpt, FY 44, pp. 13–14.

As winter approached, the Fifth Army drew near the Cassino corridor.[106] The problems of maintaining communications increased in direct proportion to the worsening weather and terrain. The Italian mountains, passively as cold, unyielding, hard, and dangerous as the active German enemy, resisted wire stringing, radios, and any communication device that had to be moved on wheels. No longer could linemen, for example, work from standard military vehicles specially designed for the work. Instead they had to resort to mules, carts, jeeps, and even bicycles, or, most frequently of all, were obliged to unroll huge spools of wire or cable by hand. "We have 20 men per regiment who just carry wire and do practically nothing else," one divisional chief of staff reported. Battalions frequently had twenty miles of wire in operation at a time, and their tables of organization allowed them just about half as many men as they needed. "For seven men to lay that much wire and then maintain it in these mountains," protested a communications officer of the 179th Infantry, "is just too much." [107]

The radiomen were beset with equal woes. Weeks earlier, AFHQ had asked Washington to search warehouses for any old pack radios SCR–179 and SCR–203, designed to be slung like saddlebags

Signal Repairman Tests *telephone wire in the Italian mountains.*

Volturno crossings. Captured German cable supplemented the allowance, and thus during the first night attempt each battalion had enough cable to string two sets on each boat trip. The lines went quickly out of use under enemy fire, however, and with daylight the German machine gunners controlled the banks. Radio took over, and meanwhile the men grimly repaired the cables. By late afternoon, telephone communication was open again.[105]

Crossing of the River Volturno—Com Aspect. Unit Hist file, SGBN–57–0.3.0 (24095) Master. (2) Hq NATOUSA, Tng Memo 3, Lessons from the Italian Campaign, 10 Mar 44, pp. 55–56.

[106] For a general report of this segment of the Italian campaign, see *Fifth Army at the Winter Line (15 November 1943–15 January 1944),* AMERICAN FORCES IN ACTION (Washington, 1945).

[107] (1) Fifth Army Hist, II, 55–56; III, 47, 60. (2) Hq NATOUSA, Tng Memo 3, Lessons from the Italian Campaign, 10 Mar 44, pp. 67–69. (3) WD BPR Press Release, 2 Mar 44.

[105] (1) Ltr, Lt Col Richard J. Meyer, CO 57th Sig Bn, to CG VI Corps, 29 Oct 43, sub: Rpt on

across a mule's back, and to ship them at once.[108] Once used by the cavalry, these ancient sets were warmly welcomed by the troops in Italy, who made utmost use of them. Primitive fighting conditions could put a premium value on what otherwise seemed antique equipment and transport alike. Pigeons, too, won renewed respect in the mountains, carrying as many as three hundred messages a week at some headquarters.[109]

Most of the carrying of signal equipment of all sorts fell to the soldiers. Hills, ridges, and peaks in all directions interfered with transmission, especially at the higher, line-of-sight frequencies. The standard short-range infantry radio was the SCR–284. Supposedly portable, its components, broken down for hand carrying, remained grievously heavy. Transporting the sets over rough terrain often damaged them, whether they were the ponderous 284 or the smaller guidon set, the SCR–511. Besides, men who could have been employed for better purposes had to serve solely as bearers. In addition, carrying the 511 bestowed a special hazard, for "the Germans keep a sharp lookout for radio antennas and shell every one they see."[110]

During the bitter and bloody fighting along the Winter Line, Signal Corps cameras did their best to record the action. The 163d Signal Photographic Company, which had been assigned to Fifth Army in September, arrived at Naples in mid-November. Col. Melvin E. Gillette, AFHQ photographic officer, had reported to Fifth Army about a month earlier as army photographic officer to plan photographic coverage of the campaign. A second assignment for Gillette, by direct War Department order, was the planning of a feature film on the Italian campaign.[111]

After the arrival of the 163d in Italy, Gillette was able to reorganize Fifth Army's photographic services to provide greater flexibility and efficiency. He assigned two 3-man photographic teams (a motion picture cameraman, a still photographer, and a jeep driver) to each active front-line division area, with an officer at division headquarters to coordinate their work. Gillette controlled all the teams from army headquarters, with the help of assistants at each corps headquarters. A regular courier service visited the teams daily, collecting exposed film and carrying forward supplies and equipment. The great advantage of the organization lay in its extreme flexibility. Teams could be moved quickly from one area to another as battle action shifted, without the necessity of going through command channels. In fact, the organization worked so well that it was used in the Mediterranean theater to the end of the war.[112] Sharing the dangers of the forward areas with the other combat troops, the photographers took their share of losses.[113]

Additional writers and directors arrived to help on the feature film. In early December Capt. John Huston, 1st Lt. Jules Buck, and an 8-man camera

[108] Ltr, Tully to Moran, 30 Oct 43. SCIA file 104 Fifth Army.

[109] AFHQ CSigO Monthly Bull, Apr 44, pp. 13–15, and Aug 44, p. 9.

[110] Ltr, CG AGF to CG's Army Ground Comds, 2 May 44, sub: Observers' Notes on the Italian Campaign, 13 Dec 43–10 Mar 44. SCIA file 46 Misc Observers' Rpts, folder 3.

[111] Hist, Sig Sec AFHQ, app. B, Hist Rpt of Photo Div, pp. 7–8.

[112] Ibid., p. 8.

[113] Ibid., p. 10.

crew arrived in Italy to film a special battle picture that was to depict one infantry unit in action, as representative of many. Working in the mountains to the south of Cassino, the photographers attached themselves to the 143d Infantry, then battling fiercely to gain a foothold on Mount Sammucro, towering high above the strategic town of San Pietro.[114] Captain Huston's task was to tell the story of one battle as completely as possible. The feature film he produced, eventually released under the title *The Battle of San Pietro*, caught the bloody destruction, the magnificent heroism, and the costliness of the fight. "On one occasion the men were totally without ammunition and fought with their hands and with rocks," Huston related. "Patrols would go out with the absolute certainty that there was no chance of their returning . . . men jumped the barbed wire in vain attempts to reach enemy strongpoints and, tossing grenades through narrow gun openings, met their death. This valley area [below Mount Sammucro] became known . . . as the Valley of Death." [115]

Operation SHINGLE

The 15th Army Group's long-term strategy for the capture of Rome had been planned well before the actions along the Winter Line began. Part of the planning involved an amphibious operation by Fifth Army south of Rome. This plan, Operation SHINGLE, originally scheduled for late 1943, had to be abandoned temporarily, principally for lack of landing craft. The second SHINGLE plan was decided upon on Christmas Eve, 1943. In SHINGLE, the U.S. VI Corps would make an amphibious landing in the rear of the enemy lines at Anzio, on the western coast of Italy, about thirty miles south of Rome. In support of Anzio, the British 10 Corps and the U.S. II Corps would assault the Gustav Line.[116]

The Anzio landing on 22 January 1944 progressed quietly and well. Fierce fighting came later. The signal pattern for amphibious invasions was now well established: equipment was waterproofed; vehicular SCR–299's, 193's, and 399's were so loaded on the landing craft that they would be among the first ashore; FM radios such as the SCR–609's were on hand for ship-shore communications; and special communications ships were available. The communications ship for the VI Corps was the USS *Biscayne*.[117] The ship for the 3d Division was an LST, but it received slight use as a communications headquarters since the division command post was so quickly set up ashore. At Anzio American troops first used in combat the new SCR–300, the first FM radio for the in-

---

[114] For an account of the struggle for Mount Sammucro and the village of San Pietro, see *Fifth Army at the Winter Line*, pp. 48–67.

[115] Interv, SigC Hist Sec with Huston, APS, 23 Mar 44.

For examples of the highly commendatory reviews that greeted public release of the film, see *The Nation*, CLX (May 26, 1945), 608; *Time*, XLV (May 21, 1945), 94, 96; *The New Yorker*, XXI (July 21, 1945), 30; The New York *Times*, July 14, 1945, II, 1:8.

[116] Martin Blumenson, *Anzio. The Gamble That Failed* (Philadelphia, New York: J. B. Lippincott Company, 1963), and by the same author, Salerno to Cassino, a forthcoming volume in the series UNITED STATES ARMY IN WORLD WAR II.

[117] Incl 2, Hq VI Corps Of of SigO, Com in the Anzio Beachhead, 20 Mar 44, to Ltr, Actg DCSigO AFHQ to CSigO, 15 May 44, sub: Rpts on Sig Com Anzio Beachhead and Opn SHINGLE. SigC OP 370.2 Rpt folder 3 Gen, 13 Jun–Jul 44.

UNDERGROUND SWITCHBOARD, NETTUNO

fantry. It was the "most successful instrument yet devised for amphibious communication," declared Lt. Col. Jesse F. Thomas, signal officer of the 3d Division. "Its range and reliability met or exceeded every expectation, and established it as the most valuable item of radio equipment in the Division."[118] It had great virtues, especially in its relatively light weight, about 40 pounds, compared with the components of the SCR-609 and 610, which totaled about 175 pounds and required the labors of three men to carry and operate. A Signal Corps officer who served as communications officer with the 4th Ranger Battalion, 1st Lt. Herbert Avedon, was especially enthusiastic about the SCR-300's batteries, the weak point in any portable radio set. They were "exceptionally fine," he said, and added that, though they were rated for but 24 hours, he had used them successfully up to 40 hours.[119]

Signal troops arriving in the Anzio-Nettuno area found many serviceable commercial and military wire facilities, which they quickly restored to service. During the first week when there was practically no enemy opposition, signalmen strung aerial circuits of spiral four cable to all the major combat units. This was good standard practice for an offensive plan, and up to this time the men had experienced only offensive action.

But the situation changed suddenly. The Germans rushed units down from the north and pinned the assaulting forces to the narrow beachhead with intensive artillery fire and incessant bombings. The signal wire plan had to change quickly to a defensive concept. All the open wire circuits, which at first had looked so useful and so easily rehabilitated, became useless.[120] Fortunately, just then someone discovered a complex system of tunnels, and all signal installations went deep underground. Those serving VI Corps holed up in mid-February in a series of dripping-wet wine cellars forty feet under the town of Nettuno.[121]

Meanwhile the quantity of wire necessary to maintain communications increased sharply. Enemy artillery fire repeatedly cut the wires, and bombing and shelling frequently knocked out command posts.[122] The 57th Signal Battalion laid many alternate wire lines; when an enemy shell cut 20 of the 40 main VI Corps circuits, the alternate routes sufficed to maintain communications to all divisions. The men ploughed in their wire lines, using Italian farm plows when they could not get the Signal Corps wire plow LC-61.[123] The signal battalion wire chief with an infantry division reported that his outfit laid more wire at Anzio than anywhere

[118] Incl, Ltr, Thomas, SigO 3d Div, to CG 3d Inf Div, 5 Feb 44, sub: Rpt of Opns 22–31 Jan 44, with Ltr, SigO Fifth Army to CSigO's, Allied Central Mediterranean Force AFHQ, et al., 17 Feb 44, sub: Rpt on Com Opn SHINGLE. SCIA file 110, To CSigO Washington, item 57.
[119] Memo, Sgt Richard H. Larsh, Intel and Security Div, for the O/C, 3 May 44, sub: Tech Intel (SigC), p. 1. SCIA file 45 Misc Rpts.

[120] (1) Summary of Lessons Learned in Operation SHINGLE, sec. 4, Wire Communications in a Defensive Situation, AFHQ, CSigO Monthly Bull, Apr 44, p. 26. (2) Incl 2, Com in the Anzio Beachhead, 20 Mar 44, p. 9.
[121] Incl 1, Ltr, Lough, CO 63d Sig Bn, to SigO Fifth Army, 14 Feb 44, sub: Visit to Anzio Beachhead, with Ltr, Tully to Ingles, 12 Mar 44. SCIA file 110, To CSigO Washington, item 50.
[122] Fifth Army Hist, IV, 163.
[123] (1) Ltr, Lough to SigO Fifth Army, 14 Feb 44. (2) Fifth Army Hist, IV, 163.

in North Africa or Sicily. "Twice our CP was blasted over our heads," he related, "and although we finally resorted to using double lines and radio, we had a hard time keeping communications open."[124] As a matter of fact, the heretofore unprecedented expenditure of wire created a serious supply problem. During March and April, emergency shipments of wire W–110 had to be rushed to Anzio from both the North African bases and the zone of interior.[125]

Now the men of the armored force, whose FM radios of the 500 series had been the envy of infantrymen, in turn envied the latter their new FM walkie-talkie, SCR–300. The signal officer of the 1st Armored Division begged Tully (who had just been promoted to brigadier general) for a radio like the SCR–300 for his patrol men. Theoretically, he wrote, when his men went on reconnaissance they rode down the road in light tanks, or in armored or scout cars. That was the theory, but it was not the practice here, where enemy gunfire raked the roads. "The patrols," he wrote, "walk, creep, or crawl, dragging a bulky SCR–509 and praying that they make no noise."[126]

It was during the critical first three weeks of February 1944 that the Signal Corps' new gun-laying radar, the SCR–584, came to Anzio and almost miraculously enabled the Americans to turn back the German bombers. In the week beginning 16 February, the German Air Force launched its strongest sustained air attack in that area as part of the all-out offensive designed to obliterate the beachhead. The German ace Dietrich Peltz, who had directed the mass air raids on London, was in charge. In seven days Peltz launched 89 separate attacks, employing on the second day alone no less than 172 planes. Cleverly, he used every possible strategem and deception device to confuse the radars, shelling with heavy guns to drive the defending gunners to cover, and jamming. The jamming especially was very effective, and there was evidence that the Germans had learned the frequencies that the American radars employed. Window, those small strips of metallic paper that blinded the radars, also appeared.[127]

At this critical moment an urgent call went to Algiers for the new, superior SCR–584's and SCR–545's, which could not be jammed by window as could the older SCR–268's. Within 48 hours, under intense pressure, crews were assembled and taught the rudiments of operation of the new gun-layers. By 24 February, the first SCR–584's were in place. That night a flight of 12 Junkers 88's appeared in close formation, dropping window. Forty-eight American guns, firing at the unseen targets by radar, caught them at close range and dropped 5 of the 12 with the first salvo. The remaining 7 jettisoned their bombs and fled. From that time on, enemy high-level night attacks diminished sharply. Encouraged, the American gunners began using the 584's and 545's, even by daylight, with growing success. By the end of March they had destroyed 22

[124] Quoted in Ingles, "Telephones Are in the Fight on Every Battleground," *Bell Telephone Magazine*, XXIII, No. 1, 69–92.

[125] Hist, Sig Sec AFHQ, p. 97.

[126] Ltr, Williams, Div SigO 1st Armd Div, to Tully, 27 Feb 44. SCIA file Rpts-Notes-Info, etc., on Sig Opns.

[127] Fifth Army Hist, IV, 172–73.

CAMOUFLAGED SCR–584 RADAR AND IFF (RIGHT) BESIDE A CEMETERY IN ITALY

unseen planes at extreme range with radar, and probably 24 more.[128]

Meanwhile, men of the 265th Signal Radio Relay Station Company brought their FM Motorola police radios to Italy. They had already set up radio relay channels in the Salerno area, extending them to Naples when that city fell to the Allies in October. Anzio was a thorn in the enemy's side, an Allied pocket far up the coast and isolated except by sea, until the radio relay company set up a station there and made contact with Naples. The Signal Corps men located their sets on the highest points in the area so that they were able to throw a channel completely over enemy territory from VI Corps at Anzio to Fifth Army headquarters near Naples. Communications over the channel were even better than a wire line could have provided, for no hazards of roadside traffic or sabotage could touch it. Messages flashed between the installations at 20,000 groups per day. The radio re-

[128] (1) *Ibid.*, p. 173 (2) Incl, Opn of SCR–584 at Anzio, with Ltr, Lt Col Arthur W. Warner, Air Defense Div SHAEF, APO 757, to Lt Col Norman L. Winter, OCSigO, 14 Jun 44. SigC 413.44 SCR–584 No. 13 (RB–2298). (3) Incl, Ltr, Maj Harris T. Richards, SigC, RadarO AA Sec AFHQ, to M.GG., AA&CD Sec AFHQ, 2 Apr 44, sub: Tech and Tactical Opn of the SCR–584 in the Anzio-Nettuno Bridgehead, with Ltr, Colton to CSigO, 7 Apr 44, same sub. SigC 413.44 No. 12 (RB–2297). (4) "What Happened at the Anzio Beachhead," *Radar*, No. 4 (August 20, 1944), pp. 29–34. SigC Hist Sec file.

lay became the main reliance between Anzio and Headquarters, Fifth Army, at Presenzano.[129]

The Liberation of Rome

The winter campaign in Italy was hard, costly, and in many ways frustrating. The stubborn German defense in the Cassino area and the counterattacks at Anzio dashed Allied hopes for an early penetration of the German positions. Static warfare continued in Italy until May 1944, while a major regrouping of the Allied armies took place, which relieved Fifth Army of responsibility for the Cassino sector, leaving it only Anzio and a narrow strip between the Liri River and the sea.[130]

The troops had earned the respite and rest period that nearly all units enjoyed during April. Yet rest for a division often meant none for the signalmen, who must keep communications installations operating normally. The message center section of the 34th Signal Company, for example, worked harder than ever during the month. It handled 5,921 outgoing and relay messages. The messengers drove 9,000 miles.[131]

There was a theater-wide shortage of signal troops, a shortage that General Ingles, the Chief Signal Officer, had predicted several months earlier. By mid-December 1943, the various theaters had piled up requests for 28,000 Signal Corps enlisted men for overseas duty alone, but Signal Corps plans and operations officers in Washington had been unable to persuade Operations Division, WDGS, to authorize more than 11,000. This did not include any T/O units that were a part of the AGF or the AAF. Ingles, writing to Tully, said, "The signal personnel which we must use in major operations in about six months has not yet been even authorized, and consequently not even inducted. If we were given these men tomorrow, we could not now have them properly trained for the service that is to be expected of them." [132]

There were too few men, too few replacements. The 51st and 53d Signal Battalions, through rotation, had already lost many men who would not be replaced for months. The shortage of replacements had already forced the "cannibalization" of various signal units —that is, stripping men from one unit and reducing it to skeleton strength in order to fill out another. It was admittedly a shortsighted policy that lowered efficiency all around, but it was the only practical solution at the time.[133]

Furthermore, over a period of months in late 1943 and early 1944, the War Department began publishing new tables of organization that in general cut down the number of troops in all signal organizations, in direct conflict with the

---

[129] (1) Hist of Co D, 829th Sig Sv Bn, sec. H, pp. 7–8. (2) Maj. Gen. William S. Rumbough, "Radio Relay, the War's Great Development in Signal Communications," *Military Review*, XXVI, No. 2 (May, 1946), 3. (Reprinted, but without illustrations or diagrams, in *Signals*, III, No. 5 (May–June, 1949), 30–34.) (Hereafter cited as Rumbough, "Radio Relay," *Military Review*, XXVI, No. 2.) (3) AGF Equip Review Bd, Preliminary Study, sec. XVIII, Communications Equipment, par. 89c, Apr 45. (4) Fifth Army Review Bd Rpt, Preliminary Study, sec. XVII, par. 89a, 12 Jun 45.

[130] Fifth Army Hist, V, 2.

[131] Orgn Hist, 34th Sig Co, Apr 44. 334–SIG–0.3 (1850) Apr 44.

[132] Ltr, Ingles, CSigO, to Tully, 14 Dec 43. SCIA file 110, To CSigO Washington, item 73.

[133] Hist, Sig Sec AFHQ, p. 60.

strong recommendations of the theater. General Moran of Fifth Army and General Tully at AFHQ were unhappy over the new table of organization for the corps signal battalion, for example. The new TOE 11–15, published 10 December 1943, reduced signal personnel for the battalion by some 12 percent. It was at almost complete variance with the recommendations AFHQ had sent to the War Department at the end of the Tunisia Campaign — recommendations born of battle experience and almost unanimously supported by signal officers who had had combat experience in North Africa. Maj. Gen. Alfred M. Gruenther, Chief of Staff, Fifth Army, and Maj. Gen. Geoffrey T. Keyes, commanding general of II Corps, agreed with General Moran that the new TOE would be highly detrimental to the operating efficiency and morale of the units. They stressed the fact that, throughout the campaigns to date, signal communications had been excellent, or better than excellent, under the old tables of organization. They believed that the new tables, on the contrary, would "likely insure such a lowering of con.._.nications efficiency as to cause a real failure under pressure." [134]

There may have been excellent reasons for the new tables, but to the men in the field, trying to give the sort of communications service required, the situation must have seemed ridiculous, or even worse, maddening. That is how it appeared to General Tully, who continued to be an outspoken opponent of the new tables, writing in June 1944:

We have literally spent more time squabbling with G–1 over these matters than . . . on planning future operations or fighting the enemy. From either a signal or practical viewpoint the whole matter has reached the superlative of being ridiculous. We have a clean cut case of a theater commander being given a directive by the War Department to put into effect certain Signal Corps reorganization which everyone in the field knows won't work.

General Tully most disliked "those marvelous products," TOE 11–15 (Corps Signal Battalion) and TOE 11–25 (Light Construction Battalion), but he also criticized the TOE's for the signal company, the heavy construction company, the army signal battalion, the radar repair maintenance team for ground forces, and cellular units.[135] Other theater signal officers in other areas echoed his complaints.[136]

General Tully's personnel problems continued throughout the Italian campaign. Some of them concerned quality of signal troops, not quantity. In April he wrote ". . . we are becoming acutely aware of the fact that we have many bodies, but very few of the highly trained specialists required for some of these large headquarters installations . . . we have definitely reached the bottom of the barrel and . . . the matter is becoming critical in from four to five different specialities." [137] Aside from registering the most vigorous protests, official as well as unofficial, there was little that theater officers could do to alter the ordained patterns of TOE's

[134] Ltr, Tully to CG NATOUSA, 23 Feb 44, sub: Reorgn of Sig Units, Fifth Army. SCIA file 104 Fifth Army.

[135] Ltr, Tully to Ingles, 18 Jun 44. SCIA file 110, To CSigO Washington, item 34.
[136] See, for example, USFET Gen Bd Rpt 112, pp. 6–7.
[137] Ltr, Tully to Moran, 11 Apr 44. SCIA file 104 Fifth Army.

and the methods of allotting specialist troops. Skyrocketing demands for signal troops put unremitting pressure on the theater signal schools. By mid-1944 the replacement problems of the theater had grown so acute that they had become the subject of serious dispute between the theater and the War Department, which had conducted two separate investigations of the matter early in 1944.[138] On 28 May, NATOUSA activated the Replacement Command, and the signal school was assigned to it.[139]

Despite the serious shortages of signal troops, the quality of communication service provided Fifth Army brought praise from its commander, General Clark. Clark thought especially highly of his signal officer, General Moran. Writing to General Colton in Washington to comment on the excellence of his signal equipment ("I am happy to say that it has been excellent—no case has come to my attention in which a serious interruption to signal communication has occurred due to equipment failure"), he added his appraisal of General Moran.

I can not write without telling you what a splendid job General Moran has done with the Fifth Army. Despite the worst type of combat conditions, particularly during the days immediately following our invasion in the Gulf of Salerno, General Moran and the Signal Section provided excellent communications for the Fifth Army. The quality of his work has been consistently superior and I am extremely grateful that General Moran has been the Signal Officer for Fifth Army. I cannot say too much in praise of what he has done.[140]

On 11 May 1944 the U.S. Fifth and the British Eighth Armies launched coordinated offensives in Italy. Spearheaded by initial successes of the French Expeditionary Corps (FEC) in breaking through the Gustav Line, the offensive soon gained momentum all along the front. British and Polish troops encircled Cassino. Cassino, the objective for which so much Allied and enemy blood and toil had been spent through bitter months, fell at last on 17 May. The reinforced Anzio forces broke out of the beachhead, where they had been contained for four months, and pushed on to a junction with Allied columns advancing from the south. Anzio and Cassino, place names grown familiar to millions of Americans, gave way to new names in the news—Santa Maria Infante, Itri, Minturno, Cisterna, and Velletri. Forced out of one defense after another, the Germans retreated northward. By the first week in June, the Fifth Army stood at the gates of Rome.[141]

Maintaining proper communications during the race to Rome was a taxing business. The signal officer of VI Corps, for example, described his problems during the period as "vicious." The VI Corps was heavily reinforced with artillery, two British divisions, and one U.S. armored division, almost doubling the normal signal load for a corps signal battalion.[142] The facilities of the corps

---

[138] History of the Replacement Training Command, North African Theater of Operations, June–September 1944. Opns Rpts 95–RCL–0.3 (18190) M.

[139] See History of the Replacement Training Command, through 1945, for accounts of signal school activities to the end of the war.

[140] App. 2 to Summ Rpt of Visit . . . to ETO, 5 Feb–24 Apr 44, Ltr, CG Fifth Army to Colton, Chief E&T Sv OCSigO, 28 Apr 44. SigC OP 370.2 Rpt folder 3 Gen, 13 Jun–8 Jul 44.

[141] Fifth Army Hist, V, *passim.*

[142] Report on Signal Communications, VI Corps, in AGF Bd Rpt, AFHQ–NATO (G–3 Sec), 26 Jul 44.

signal battalion were strained to the limit.

The breakout from the Anzio beachhead brought an abrupt change from the completely static signal situation, and the signal facilities had to be quickly transformed from underground to overhead construction. Several days before the breakout, the corps battalion set up a "battle" command post in an ancient castle in advance of the initial command posts. Here activity centered around the "war room," where G-2 and G-3 duty officers, the air officer, the artillery officer, and a G-4 traffic representative had desks. Signal troops installed direct wire for the air officer to his radio station, which was in contact with aircraft; a direct line for the artillery officer to the corps artillery S-3; two teletype locals in the clerks' room to transmit and receive tactical messages; and interconnected phones for the commanding general and his chief of staff. Numerous radio nets operated from the advance CP—a link to Fifth Army advance command post; one to VI Corps main command post; two command nets to divisions; one corps net for engineers and other corps troops; a liaison net linking the corps commander, artillery commander, and tank destroyer commander, with a fourth channel for any staff officer on reconnaissance. At the main CP other radio nets operated to the Fifth Army main CP, to the photo-reconnaissance unit, and to the VI Corps advance command post.[143]

Forty-eight hours after the breakout, enemy resistance on the eastern flank gave way, and the movement of division command posts started. Signal construc-

tion teams pushed ahead, building lines ahead of the division command posts so that lines could be in when the users arrived at the new locations. But the fortunes of war sometimes cancel out even the best-calculated plans. Three days after the breakout, the axis of advance shifted about 90 degrees, and the advantage of getting wire ahead of the advancing troops was wiped out. New lines had to be laid hurriedly along the new axis.

German resistance began to collapse. All units started moving rapidly, six to twenty miles a day. Wire construction speeded up. Where trees were available, the signal troops suspended spiral-four cable overhead; otherwise, they laid it on the ground like field wire—a necessary extravagance, for the costly cable was thus exposed to the ravages of vehicles and marching men. To save construction, the signalmen set up switching centrals close to one or more divisions. On the day Rome fell, the VI Corps command post moved to a point a few miles south of the city; that same night a reconnaissance party crossed the Tiber to pick out a new spot. By noon the next day all essential signal installations were in place and operating at the new location.[144]

This was the story of communications in the VI Corps, duplicated on a greater or smaller scale by every signal unit in the theater. The 36th Signal Company, serving the 36th Infantry Division of VI Corps, found its wire teams attacked by enemy patrols on more than one occasion. Radio and motor messenger service supplemented wire in the swift

---

[143] Ibid.

[144] (1) Ibid. (2) Com in the VI Corps, SigC Tech Info Ltr 35 (Oct 44), pp. 8–9. (3) Interv, SigC Hist Sec with Lough, 5 Oct 44.

advance. The radio section of the 36th Signal Company, hampered by hills and rugged terrain, resorted to an innovation that presaged important advances in communications equipment in postwar years. The men had been using SCR–193 sets with an intervening relay set to communicate with the division observation post and lower units. Now they went a step further, putting the small radiotelephone sets SCR–300 into use with relay arrangements for voice communication also. Not ordinarily used in division signal work, the SCR–300 nevertheless served well in the unusual situation.[145]

On 2 June an advance detachment of the 36th Signal Company moved to a new division command post in Velletri, which had been bypassed by the U.S. troops. The enemy, still in the area, laid down a withering fire, wounding a number of signalmen. Moving to still another location, a series of dugouts against a hill, the men found themselves targets for snipers firing directly into the positions. Then the Signal Corps men were called out to pursue and capture the snipers. Shellfire during the impasse at Velletri damaged the wire lines so severely that all sections of the signal company went on wire duty to help the construction company lay and maintain lines.[146] On 4 June the division wire supply gave out, and orders went out to abandon all wire as the regiments raced northward. Radio and motor messenger service temporarily became not only the principal means of communication, but indeed the only ones. More wire came forward, but the advance outran the ability of the construction section to lay anything but the most essential circuits. Like the 36th, the 34th Signal Company found it impossible to maintain communications and recover wire, too. The 34th laid nearly 400 miles of wire during the month of June but had time to recover only 125 miles of it as the units moved on.[147]

The dearth of signal troops, particularly wire construction men, placed a heavy burden on all the infantry and artillery units and the division signal companies, the II Corps reported. Construction teams of the 88th Signal Company worked night and day to keep lines available to the regiments, but the regiments moved so often that the lines, though available, were seldom used. It was impossible to keep all agencies of communication working all the time, but always some means was available.[148] The corps signal battalion, despite its own full schedule of duties, lent a hand to the hard-pressed units. Less than forty-eight hours after II Corps' attack started along the sea on 11 May, with the U.S. 85th and 88th Divisions abreast, all the linemen of the 338th Infantry of the 88th Division were exhausted, and the corps signal battalion sent twelve of its linemen to help out for three days. It also lent two complete wire teams to the 88th Division for a week in the action near Minturno, and, while the 88th was at Fondi, the corps signal battalion laid all of its internal wire in the rear of the division advance command post. At Scauri it laid sections of the division wire axis for both the 85th and the 88th. The corps signal battalion furnished the headquarters battery of II Corps with two light

[145] Consolidated Hist of SigC (36th Sig Co), p. 11.
[146] Ibid., pp. 11–12.

[147] Orgn Hist, 34th Sig Co, Jun 44. 334–SIG–0.3 (1850), Jun 44.
[148] History of the 88th Signal Company, May 1944. 338–SIG–0.3 (9792) Master, Feb–Dec 44.

construction teams whenever it was in combat. The corps signal officer voiced a strong plea for the inclusion of more linemen in all infantry, artillery, and division signal companies.[149]

Construction elements from six signal battalions worked to extend the main army open wire axis during the march on Rome. Fifth Army signal units used up 2,020 tons of signal equipment during the month of May alone, including 5,400 miles of assault wire and 14,800 miles of field wire. The message center at Fifth Army headquarters handled on an average 560 messages and 2,600 packets a day, while cryptographic traffic averaged 40,000 groups daily during the month. Pigeons, operating out of 28 lofts at 15 locations scattered over the entire army front, carried 1,810 messages. All together, in one month signal troops of the Fifth Army rebuilt more than 100 miles of main overhead line comprising 10 circuits from the Garigliano River area to Rome, built a connecting line to Anzio, with laterals connecting the Fifth and Eighth Armies, and managed to maintain wire communications to corps headquarters and the many army installations along the route.[150]

As always when an army started moving ahead very quickly, radio communications came into heavy use during the race to Rome. Radio intelligence platoons provided much essential information. The VI Corps G–2 called the work of the radio intelligence platoon "outstanding" and stated that information received from that source was second only to that from battle reconnaissance.[151] In II Corps, Col. Kenneth F. Zitzman, the signal officer, reported his radio intelligence unit "gave us excellent results . . . very worthwhile."[152] The fluid situation that rapidly developed also proved the worth of the SIAM service. When the heavy communications load was thrown on radio, many persons, some of them high-ranking officers who should have known better, used radio without considering its security vulnerability. Constant monitoring of friendly nets by SIAM enabled swift corrective action to be taken.[153]

The SIAM unit, as mentioned earlier, was at first an improvised outfit. On 16 February 1944 NATOUSA had authorized Fifth Army to organize a provisional SIAM company, the 6689th Signal Monitoring Company (Provisional).[154] When the drive for Rome began, the company had 3 corps platoons, 4 division platoons, and 5 liaison officers to cover an army of 3 corps and 13 divisions. Four of the officers worked directly with the division platoons, and the fifth was on duty with the French Expeditionary Corps troops.[155]

In the second half of its mission, providing staffs of divisions, corps, and army with prompt tactical information, SIAM also proved to be of considerable

---

[149] Hq AFHQ Sig Sec, Summary of Signal Lessons Learned by Signal and Communication Units of Fifth Army During the Italian Campaign, app. B to sec. I. Copy in AFHQ, CSigO Monthly Bull, Aug 44, pp. 13–16.

[150] AFHQ, CSigO Monthly Bull, Jul 44, p. 8.

[151] Rpt on Sig Com, VI Corps, in AGF Bd Rpt, AFHQ–NATO, 26 Jul 44.

[152] Observations on Sig Com Within II Corps, 11 May–25 May 44, Italy folder.

[153] Hq Fifth Army, Rpt on Lessons Learned in Italian Campaign (Sig Sec), p. 16.

[154] (1) SIAM Manual, Tentative Operation and Training Manual for Signal Information and Monitoring Company. SigC Hist Sec file. (2) Typical SIAM Co (3151st SIAM Co), p. 5.

[155] Typical SIAM Co (3151st SIAM Co), p. 6.

WIRING THE ROYAL PALACE, CASERTA

value.[156] In the rapid advance, forward commanders were unable to keep timely information flowing back through normal channels. The information gathered by SIAM in several cases kept front-line units from being shelled by friendly artillery. In another instance, SIAM information saved a company of tanks from being ambushed by enemy antitank guns. The SIAM service also provided divisions with most of their early information as to the location of flanking units and progress being made on other sectors of the front.[157] Officers of the SIAM service were always careful to inform G–3 that the information provided was unconfirmed, but actually it proved to be so accurate that it soon began to be accepted as official. It was not only accurate, it was timely, arriving anywhere from three hours to three days ahead of news through the regular information channels.

Meanwhile, during the summer, the War Department, approved the TOE's

[156] Hq Fifth Army, Rpt of Lessons Learned in the Italian Campaign (Sig Sec), p. 16.

[157] Ltr, Maj Roy E. Dial, Sig IntelO Fifth Army, to Lt Thomas J. Finn, Jr., 1 Oct 44. SigC OP 370.2 Rpt folder 4 Gen, 13 Jul–30 Dec 44.

submitted by Fifth Army for a SIAM company (TOE 11-875), and in July NATOUSA ordered Fifth Army to activate the 3151st SIAM Company. Immediately upon activation, it was assigned to Seventh Army for the invasion of southern France. In September NATOUSA ordered the activation of the 3326th SIAM Company for Fifth Army. The experienced men of the old provisional company (the 6689th) went with the 3151st to France. Only a cadre remained with Fifth Army, and the ranks of the new 3326th were filled out with men from antiaircraft artillery (AAA) battalions, replacement pool troops, and unit spares.[158]

Fifth Army did not delay in Rome, the first of the Axis capitals to fall. Much of Italy was still unconquered. Formidable natural barriers such as the Arno River lay ahead and, beyond them, the well-fortified Gothic Line in the Apennines. Though the Germans fell back in haste, they maintained good order, fighting persistent delaying actions, mining nearly every road and gully. City by city the Allied armies advanced, increasingly hampered as much by the lengthening supply lines as by the skillful German resistance. The Fifth Army took the seaport of Leghorn in mid-July and Pisa late in the month. The British Eighth Army entered Florence in early August. Exhausted by nearly four months of steady fighting, the armies halted at the Arno River. They had outrun their supply lines, and the Fifth Army had been greatly weakened by the loss of nine full infantry divisions and the equivalent of a tenth to Seventh Army for the invasion

of southern France. Rest, regrouping, and reorganization were necessary.[159]

Signal Planning for the Move of AFHQ to Italy

As the fighting moved further up the boot of Italy, the problems of supply and operational control forced AFHQ and NATOUSA to move from their location in Algiers to a point in Italy closer to the armies. The Royal Palace at Caserta, a 1,200-room, 6-story structure located twenty miles north of Naples, appeared to be the most likely spot for the new headquarters. Within this huge pile of masonry—dating from 1752 and having walls eighteen inches thick—signal personnel had to prepare a communications system to serve fifteen thousand persons —a formidable assignment. Seeking to get an early start, a small group of Signal Corps staff officers headed by Col. Emil Lenzner went to Caserta in October 1943 to look things over and to select a satisfactory area for the Signal Section in the palace.

Until June 1944, when the move finally was decided upon, signal planning staffs lived in a perpetual state of tension as the move was definitely scheduled and then just as definitely postponed time after time. New construction would proceed furiously while the move was "on," only to be discontinued and in some cases dismantled when new plans were made to conform to the changing tactical situation. For example, when the move seemed imminent, the 296th Signal Installation Company installed a multi-

_____

[158] *Ibid.*

[159] Fifth Army Hist, VI, *passim,* and VII, 2-3. For an account of invasion of southern France, see below, pp. 128ff.

ple switchboard in the palace. Construction crews worked around the clock, stopping work only two hours per day to grease and oil the digger equipment. Abruptly the move was canceled. Signal crews stopped work on the radio cables and removed most of the switchboard. Then they reinstalled it, and 15th Army Group, not AFHQ, moved into the palace. Six months later, in June 1944, it was finally determined that AFHQ would move into the palace after all. The 15th Army Group moved out to Rome, and signal crews started AFHQ installations once again. When AFHQ finally moved in, during July, every staff section found at least one telephone installed in its new office.[160]

The move of a large headquarters is a complex and massive operation. Given plenty of time and plenty of personnel and equipment, any competent signal officer can manage the communications details so smoothly that the headquarters he serves will scarcely know that a move has been made. Under wartime conditions, however, there is never enough time, and the difficulties imposed by a scarcity of men and equipment are compounded by the overriding necessities of maintaining security and keeping the echelons of command in continuous, unbroken touch with subordinate levels. In spite of all obstacles, the move of AFHQ on 20 July was so smooth that, insofar as communications were concerned, only the Signal Section, AFHQ, realized the amount of time, effort, and planning involved.

AFHQ started shifting units between the 2623d and 2625th Signal Service Regiments in September 1943 in order to make up two operating organizations to provide AFHQ communications concurrently at Algiers and at Caserta during the move. The 2623d moved from Casablanca (where the Atlantic Base Section activities were declining as the fighting front moved on) to Algiers and by December had its initial detachment operating in Caserta. The 2625th remained in Algiers as the rear echelon, systematically transferring its units to the 2623d in Italy as activities in Algiers dwindled. The three WAC headquarters companies arrived in the theater during this period, and a number of women from the communications platoons took over some of the communications duties at Oran and Algiers, a circumstance that permitted the shift to go on at an accelerated pace. In November the first entire WAC signal company, the 6715th WAC Communications Company (Provisional), arrived at Algiers.[161] Highly trained in communications techniques, these women were assigned as code and cipher clerks, as high-speed radio operators, to positions in traffic control, and in the message centers and other communications specialities. The Signal Corps was highly pleased with the superior performance of these women, who, according to General Tully, did everything well.[162]

---

[161] At first attached to the 2623d Signal Service Regiment, the 6715th eventually became a part of the 2629th WAC Battalion, which was organized to administer all Wacs in the Mediterranean theater except those with Fifth Army and the Air Forces. Hist, Sig Sec AFHQ, pp. 60, 120.

[162] (1) Interv, SigC Hist Sec with Tully, 22 Aug 58. (2) Hist, Sig Sec AFHQ, pp. 60, 83, 85. (3) Mattie B. Treadwell. *The Women's Army Corps*, UNITED STATES ARMY IN WORLD WAR II (Washington, 1954), pp. 318–21, 365.

---

[160] Hist, Sig Sec AFHQ, p. 104.

The business of dismantling installations in North Africa and moving signal equipment to Italy, while maintaining communications at both places, required the most exact planning and co-ordination. Meanwhile training activities mushroomed. Besides the scheduled move of AFHQ, the impending operation in southern France and the continuing need for more signal troops in the Italian campaign also clearly demonstrated the necessity for ever greater output from signal schools. A school for training telephone operators opened at Ecole Professionelle, another at Ecole Normale turned out specialists in teletype operations and procedures, a third at the 982d Signal Service area taught radio operators, and a fourth trained men in teletype maintenance.[163]

Providing radio facilities for the two headquarters brought feverish activity to the radio division. Beginning in May, and through the weeks right up to the moving date, some signal troops shifted circuits from Algiers to Caserta, where other crews were rushing new transmitter and receiver sites to completion. One troublesome complication arose. Preliminary planning for the impending operations of Seventh Army in southern France had called for radio control circuits to center at Algiers, and the Signal Section had already installed special circuits for the Office of Strategic Services and the Navy. Accordingly, the AFHQ terminals were allowed to remain at Algiers, with control exercised at Caserta. Other problems involved allocating new frequencies to permit AFHQ circuits to operate from the new location, and carefully co-ordinating the new frequencies with those of other theaters. There were new signal instructions and new diagrams to issue. Finally, there were additional circuits to establish, both radioteletype and telephoto. All this was done, not without problems for the Signal Section, but at least without major inconvenience to the using headquarters.[164] At no time during the move from North Africa to Italy was AFHQ out of contact with the nerve centers of the globe.[165]

In Caserta, the Signal Section enjoyed a well-equipped plant capable of handling a maximum of 1,000,000 groups and 7,000 messages daily. But traffic did not approach this figure until late in the Italian campaign, on 21 April 1945, when it reached 857,304 groups.[166] In fact, for a time after the move, traffic fell from the approximately 600,000 groups averaged in the latter part of the stay at Algiers to about 500,000—the natural consequence of the move and the closer association with many of the major headquarters.[167]

By the middle of August the AFHQ switchboard at Caserta contained 930 local lines and 140 local trunks and about 40 long distance trunks. The long-distance switchboard in Naples, which controlled all long lines in the area held by Allied forces, handled some 8,500 calls a day on ten positions.[168]

---

[163] (1) Hist, Sig Sec AFHQ, pp. 60–62. (2) Maj Edward E. Moran. Unit Training of Signal Troops in a Theater of Operations (21 Jul 49), Sig Sch Monograph, *passim*. The Sig Sch Libr, Ft. Monmouth.

[164] Hist, Sig Sec AFHQ, pp. 74–79.
[165] AFHQ, CSigO Monthly Bull, Sep 44, p. 1.
[166] Hist, Sig Sec AFHQ, p. 138.
[167] Ltr, Tully to Ingles, 12 Aug 44. SCIA file 110, to CSigO Washington, item 15.
[168] *Ibid.*

*Signal Techniques Along
the Gothic Line*

The fall campaign in Italy, which
broke the vaunted Gothic Line, began
in mid-August. The British Eighth Army
struck along the Adriatic; when the
Germans pulled reserves out of the
Gothic Line defenses to meet the British,
General Clark's Fifth Army attacked
through the mountains north of Florence
toward Bologna. One week's bloody
fighting in September rendered the main
line of German defenses useless. Heavy
casualties, torrential rains that trapped
vehicles in a sea of mud, and mounting
enemy opposition brought the tired
armies to a halt once more, just short of
Bologna, at the end of October.[169]

To prevent the enemy from finding
out that the 88th Infantry Division was
being withdrawn from the front lines in
August, the 88th Signal Company set up
an elaborate deception. The radio section kept a full division command net in
operation for ten days after the move had
been completed, transmitting dummy
traffic.[170]

The assault on the enemy's Apennine
stronghold turned into a worse nightmare for the signal troops than the dash
to Rome had been. It was a campaign
against the weather no less than against
the Germans. Almost constant rains in
September and October turned the roads
into quagmires. Bulldozers and tank
traffic cut the wire lines to ribbons. The
88th Signal Company, bivouacked in a
muddy field at the edge of a river, moved
into the town of Castel del Rio but
hastily moved out again when it found

that the German artillerymen considered
the town an excellent target. Tired of
working in knee-deep mud, the men
moved their switchboard to a better location; the next day enemy artillery laid
a direct hit on the spot just vacated. The
85th Signal Company had to abandon its
wire-laying 2½-ton trucks in favor of
½-ton vehicles that could negotiate the
perilous mountain roads over which the
circuits to the regiments were laid. When
the rains came, wheeled vehicles yielded
to pack mules on the slippery trails. But
even the mules could not long endure
the ordeal, and the men not only carried
the wire but laid it by hand. Since engineer units were widening and rerouting
roads, Signal Corps troops patrolled the
wire lines constantly to guard against
damage to the lines and to repair the
breaks that inevitably occurred. In some
areas almost entirely devoid of roads or
trails of any sort, troops and mule teams
used the wire as guidelines, especially at
night. One regiment reported that its
troops actually used wire lines to pull
themselves up the steep cliffs.[171]

When the autumn rains changed to
winter ice and snow, turning the front
quiescent, many an isolated unit resorted
to pigeon messengers to maintain contact. Mountainous terrain was not kind
to wire and radio communication, but
pigeons were not intimidated. The 209th
Signal Pigeon Company, which had been
activated in August at Cecina, Italy, delivered the birds by pack mule at night.
Beyond the static lines American patrols

---

[169] Fifth Army Hist, VII, 183–87.
[170] Hist, 88th Sig Co, Aug 44. 388–SIG–0.3 (9792)
Master, Feb–Dec 44.

[171] (1) Gothic Line Com, SigC Tech Info Ltr 42
(May 45), pp. 14–15. (2) Operations Report of the
85th Signal Company, September and October 1944.
385–SIG–0.3 (48366), Sep and Oct 44. (3) History,
88th Sig Co, Sep–Oct 44. 388–Sig–0.3 (9792) Master,
Feb–Dec 44. (4) Orgn History, 34th Sig Co, Sep
and Oct 44. 334–SIG–0.3 (1850), Sep and Oct 44.

probed ceaselessly. One such patrol deep in enemy territory, beset by enemy action, and running out of food, blankets, and medical supplies for its wounded men, sent back an urgent call for help by pigeon messenger. In a few hours parachutes dropped the needed supplies to the patrol.[172]

Far into partisan territory now, the armies worked tirelessly with the Italian partisans. Pigeons were particularly valuable to the partisans. They sewed the birds into their coat pockets, hid them beneath their jackets, or used the pigeon vest the troops of the 209th Signal Pigeon Company had devised. The birds carried back messages and overlay maps that disclosed much valuable information concerning enemy gun positions, concentration areas, and troop movements. Such partnerships between partisans and pigeons operated profitably to Bologna and as far north as Modena. By the end of December 1944, the birds had carried 10,423 messages. Until the armies jumped off in the swift spring offensive in April 1945, the 209th operated from 18 to 20 lofts all along the line. Since pigeons need time to become settled in their lofts at new locations and cannot adapt themselves to a fast moving army, from April 1945 until V–E Day the lofts operated through the II Corps headquarters message center to the rear.[173]

Throughout the winter, Fifth Army troops envied the Germans ensconced in the rich and comfortable Po Valley. True, Allied air attacks had punished the German transport severely, but more than twenty enemy divisions still held much of Italy's best industrial region and the approaches to the Alps. Fifth Army troops trained, regrouped, and brought up supplies for the spring offensive. On 16 December, Truscott (now a lieutenant general) took command of Fifth Army, General Clark assuming command of 15th Army Group.[174] Truscott's signal officer was Colonel Zitzman, formerly assigned to 15th Army Group and later II Corps' signal officer.[175] General Moran subsequently went to Austria to become the signal officer of the newly formed Headquarters, United States Forces in Austria.

During the comparative quiet of the winter, some signal units got their first allotments of new types of signal equipment. The 141st Armored Signal Company, for example, received the tape facsimile equipment RC–28 in November 1944. At first they operated the facsimile only on wire lines, but, finding that it created too much signal interference, they switched to radio operation, which worked very well.[176] The 34th Signal Company got six SCR–506 sets in February 1945 to replace the old SCR–193 sets that the division had used ever since it came overseas in 1942.[177]

Before the spring campaign began in April, division radio units initiated an elaborate program of deception designed to make the enemy believe that the entire II Corps was moving over to join

---

[172] History of the 209th Signal Pigeon Company, 15 July–December 1944, and 1 January–9 May 1945. SGCO–209–0.1 (20145).

[173] *Ibid.*

[174] Fifth Army Hist, VIII, 2. For some months during 1944, 15th Army Group was designated as Allied Armies in Italy.

[175] Fifth Army Hq, GO 186, 18 Dec 44.

[176] Historical Record of the 141st Armored Signal Company, November 1944. Opns Rpt 601–SIG–0.3 (1397) Master.

[177] Orgn Hist, 34th Sig Co, Feb 45. 334–SIG–0.3 (1850), Feb 45.

Eighth Army on the right. A dummy command post was set up at Forli in the Eighth Army area, while IV Corps set up a similar dummy post in the II Corps area. For ten days while some fighting units maintained radio silence, the dummy command posts received dummy messages, the real headquarters handling all communications by wire. Artillery batteries involved in the mythical move went off the air and fired their missions by telephone. Meanwhile, the 88th Division operators opened a dummy radio net in the Eighth Army zone, continuing until II Corps actually began its attack.[178]

The Closing Months of the Campaign

When the offensive got under way and the regiments started racing north, the division signal companies once more found themselves strained to the utmost. The 141st Armored Signal Company in particular found it almost impossible to keep up with the fast-traveling 1st Armored Division. But by this time it was an old story to the seasoned signal units. The wire teams worked night and day extending wire lines but accepted the situation philosophically if, in spite of their best efforts, the lines arrived too late to be of any use. They laid wire, the backbone of the communications system, if at all possible. If there was not enough time or if wire failed, radio filled the breach. If a regiment got out of range of the radio station in the command post, a relay team hurried out at once to set up a relay station to link up the too-distant

stations. Command posts became one-day affairs, one closing while another was being prepared. Message center sections packed their cipher machines and other essential equipment so that all could be used in the vans without unloading. The supply and repair sections moved almost as often as the command posts, keeping a flow of signal supplies moving forward and radios and vehicles operating at maximum efficiency.[179]

Apparently German strategy had been based to a large extent upon the assumption that even if Fifth Army broke out of the mountains and the first defenses south of the Po, it would have to stop at the Po to bring up supplies before resuming the offensive. Such was not the case. Supply proved to be so well organized and effective that Fifth Army units had no need to halt. Instead, they scrambled over the Po (crossing when and where they could) to pursue the disorganized German armies.[180] Soon the enemy retreat turned into a rout. The whole enemy front became a fluid and disorganized welter of wrecked equipment, blown-up roads and bridges, and bands of bewildered soldiers ripe for surrender. American Signal Corps units advancing north found the picture of war suddenly changing. The road networks became good; cheering crowds of Italian civilians lined the streets of hamlets and villages; sullen, disheartened groups of German prisoners of war streamed toward the rear under guard. But there were still snipers in the bypassed places,

[178] (1) Fifth Army Hist, IX, 26. (2) *19 Days From the Apennines to the Alps* (Milan, Italy: 1945), a popular history of the Po Valley Campaign, pp. 26–27.

[179] (1) Hist Rcd, 141st Armd Sig Co, Apr 45. (2) Orgn Hist, 34th Sig Co, Apr 45. 334–SIG–0.3 (1850) Apr 45. (3) Opns Rpt, 85th Sig Co, Apr 45. 385–SIG–0.3 (48366) Apr 45. (4) Hist, 88th Sig Co, Apr 45. 388–SIG–0.3 (9792) Master, Jan–Jun, Aug–Dec 45.

[180] Fifth Army Hist, IX, 109, 125.

occasional strafing planes, and artillery fire.[181]

On 2 May 1945, all German forces in Italy and western Austria surrendered to the Allies unconditionally. Signal Corps men monitoring German radio picked up the broadcasts sent in the clear from Bolzano ordering German soldiers in Italy to cease firing. Signal Corps circuits flashed the news to the world.[182] The campaign in Italy was over. Six days later came the German surrender in Berlin. The European phase of the war was ended. But to the soldiers of the Fifth Army, who had fought so long and so bitterly, it was hard to believe. It began to seem like the truth to the signal troops when they started turning in their excess equipment—wire reels, which they had used so often for laying wire from mule back in the rugged Apennines, pack mounts for radio sets SCR–284, and other special items of warfare not needed for occupation duties.[183] With the surrender of Germany, the primary mission of AFHQ—to defeat and destroy the Axis armies in North Africa and southern Europe—was accomplished. To be sure, important tasks remained. The Signal Section of AFHQ still faced problems incident to the occupation of conquered territory; the reorganization and equipping of troops scheduled for shipment to the Pacific; the demobilization of surplus units; and the liquidation of fixed plant equipment and surplus supplies.[184]

In Italy alone at the war's end, the combined military telephone and teletypewriter network contained 2,209 open wire route miles and 1,750 cable route miles, with 78,499 telephone circuit miles in use, and 43,013 teletype circuit miles. Telephone switchboard lines numbered 10,654, exclusive of the tactical headquarters boards and boards of less than 50 lines. In addition, 9,393 dial telephone lines served the various military headquarters through civilian dial telephone exchanges. The military teletype network consisted of 144 switchboard positions serving 849 individual teletype machines.[185]

The signal history of the Mediterranean was a long series of "firsts." Over the whole vast area from Casablanca to the Alps, the techniques of signal communication were tested and perfected. The bitter tests and lessons of North Africa, Sicily, and Italy helped win other Allied victories. Signal experiences in the Mediterranean influenced the course of the campaign in Europe so greatly that it would be difficult to point to a single aspect of communications planning or operations that did not take its cue from the Mediterranean.

Undoubtedly, from the Signal Corps point of view the most important result of the Mediterranean campaigns was the increased respect for signals and the upgrading of their importance in the eyes of combat commanders. As an AGF board report put it, "We are more dependent today upon mechanical means of communications for control of fighting units, and personnel to operate them than ever

[181] Hist, 88th Sig Co, Apr 45.

[182] (1) *19 Days From the Apennines to the Alps.* (2) Hist Rcd, 141st Armd Sig Co, Apr 45.

[183] Opns Rpt, 85th Sig Co, May 45. 385–SIG–0.3 (48366) May 45.

[184] For details concerning these matters, see: (1) Hist, Sig Sec AFHQ, pp. 164–84; (2) Hq NATOUSA OCSigO, Status of Signal Corps Activities, MTOUSA, 30 Jun 45. SCIA file, unnumbered, Mediterranean Theater folder 5.

[185] (1) Com in Italy. Opns Overseas folder, SigC Hist Sec file. (2) Hist, Sig Sec AFHQ, app. E, Wire Div, *passim.*

before in our history as an army." [186] went on to Europe. Their experience
From the Mediterranean many of the top with signal communications as the in-
division, corps, and army commanders strument of command in the Mediterranean influenced decisively the shape
and importance of Signal Corps participation in the European Theater of
Operations.

[186] Ist Ind, AGF Bd, AFHQ–NATO, 31 Jul 44, on
Ltr, Hq AGF to President, AGF Bd, AFHQ, sub:
Recommendations for Com Equip in the Inf Regi-
ment. Copy in Italy folder, SigC Hist Sec file.

CHAPTER III

The Signal Corps in the ETO
to Mid-1944

The Allied landings in Normandy on 6 June 1944 climaxed long months of planning and concentrated supply effort. The first build-up of men and equipment in England for a cross-Channel attack against the Continent had been drained away to North Africa in late 1942, and it had been necessary to build again. It took a great deal of time to construct and develop a system of depots, equip the invading forces, and plan an adequate communications network. Thousands of signal details had to be co-ordinated, integrated, and perfected.

Signal Corps preparations for the invasion rested principally in the hands of the signal staffs of two separate headquarters. In their disparate yet intermingled relationships and functions, these headquarters staffs typified the dual function of the Signal Corps as a supply service and as a highly specialized technical service invaluable to the exercise of command.[1] The Signal Service of the European Theater of Operations of the United States Army was concerned primarily with matters of supply and administration for the U.S. Army in Europe, whereas the Signal Section of the Supreme Headquarters Allied Expedi-

tionary Force was responsible primarily for signal matters as they applied to the integration of British and American forces and to the tactical and strategic control of those forces. This distinction greatly oversimplifies what were actually very complex, confused, and often bitterly contested areas of responsibility.[2] And it does not take into account the numerous subordinate or co-ordinate organizations that existed in the theater or the loss or addition of functions from time to time. Nevertheless, with due allowance for such factors, the signal responsibilities of the theater did divide roughly into the two areas noted.

The signal organizations of both ETO-USA and SHAEF owed much to their predecessor organizations in the United Kingdom, the Special Observer Group, which dated from mid-1941, and its successor, the United States Army Forces in the British Isles. The signal officer of both SPOBS and USAFBI was Colonel Matejka.[3] Matejka's energetic efforts established the Signal Corps as "probably the first of the technical services to ac-

---

[1] Thompson, Harris, et al., The Test, pp. 491-93.

[2] For a detailed discussion of command problems, organization, and planning in ETO, see Roland G. Ruppenthal, Logistical Support of the Armies, Volume I, UNITED STATES ARMY IN WORLD WAR II (Washington, 1953), Chapter V.

[3] Thompson, Harris, et al., The Test, pp. 339-40, 343-44.

quire practical working experience in the United Kingdom." [4] Seven days after his arrival in late May 1941, Colonel Matejka conferred with Col. Courtenay W. Fladgate, Deputy Director Signals, British War Ministry, and inaugurated a co-operative relationship that proved to be exceedingly valuable.[5] In the months that followed, Matejka visited various British communications installations and the General Post Office (GPO) Telecommunications Division, which controlled telegraph and telephone facilities in England; arranged details for the accommodation of Electronics Training Group (ETG) students from the United States to be trained in British schools and installations; and made many valuable contacts with British officers and officials.[6] By the time the United States entered the war, the Signal Corps had already established informal relationships and working arrangements with the British that paid handsome dividends later.

Invasion Plans and Preparations

The Signal Service, ETOUSA SOS

ETOUSA was the top American headquarters in the theater, but it occupied

GENERAL RUMBOUGH

a peculiar position as almost purely an administrative and supply headquarters. Throughout 1942 and 1943 its functions and those of the theater Services of Supply were difficult to separate or define. Under a succession of arrangements, Brig. Gen. William S. Rumbough doubled as the theater's chief signal officer on the special staff of the theater commander and as SOS chief signal officer on the special staff of Maj. Gen. John C. H. Lee, theater SOS commander. After the establishment early in 1944 of SHAEF as the Allied command responsible for directing operations, the ETOUSA and SOS staffs were combined on 17 January into a single ETOUSA SOS staff serving under General Lee. The ETOUSA SOS organization was the one U.S.

---

[4] Ruppenthal, *Logistical Support of the Armies, I,* 50.

[5] Sig Sv, Hq ETOUSA, Hist Rpt, OCSigO, vol. I, Activation to D–day, pp. 13–20, Admin 574. The document cited, together with Signal Service, Headquarters ETOUSA, Historical Report, Office of the Chief Signal Officer, Volume II, D–day to V–E Day, and separately bound Appendixes A and B to Volume II file Administrative No. 575–A (hereafter cited as ETOUSA Rpt, with volume and page numbers noted) comprise the basic records on which much of the material in the chapters recounting Signal Corps operations in the ETO is based.

[6] ETOUSA Rpt, I, 15–19.

organization not under the command control of SHAEF, though it remained under General Eisenhower as U.S. theater commander. While the theater chiefs of services remained available to the theater commander for direct consultation, they were specifically placed under the supervision of General Lee in his capacity as deputy theater commander for supply and administration as well as commanding general of SOS.[7] The complicated command structure in the theater left the theater responsibilities of the chief signal officer clear and unchanged through the various reorganizations, but it did create problems as to the precise manner and exact channels for accomplishing his mission.[8]

Essentially, the mission of the chief signal officer in the ETO was to provide communications for the Army while the build-up was in progress, to supply signal equipment for all the installations and headquarters and for the troops of the invading army, to arrange for the equipment required for fixed signal installations on the Continent in the wake of the invasion, and to keep replenishing the supply of signal equipment throughout the period of operation.[9] Stated thus, it constituted a large order. Yet this outline of the mission does not begin to suggest the complexities and problems with which Rumbough contended throughout the campaign.

General Rumbough and his initial staff arrived in England in June 1942, when ETOUSA was first activated.[10] Since the chiefs of the technical services were to operate under the Commanding General, SOS, General Rumbough moved to Cheltenham when General Lee established SOS headquarters there in July. Matejka remained in London as the Signal Corps representative at the theater headquarters.[11] When Matejka became chief signal officer of AFHQ in North Africa late in 1942, Col. Reginald P. Lyman took over the London office, serving in that capacity until he became signal officer of the newly organized 1st United States Army Group (FUSAG) in October 1943. Meanwhile General Rumbough and his staff at Cheltenham were free to concentrate upon the important SOS matters incident to the troop build-up in the United Kingdom: signal supply, provision of communications for incoming troops and for SOS and other U.S. headquarters installations, and signal plans and training for American units, which were beginning to arrive in considerable numbers. This organizational arrangement lasted until 21 March 1943, when the signal sections of Headquarters, ETO, and Headquarters, SOS, were merged.[12]

Even then, Rumbough maintained offices both in London and at Cheltenham—offices designated as the Basic Planning Echelon and the Operations Echelon, respectively. The senior officer in each echelon, Colonel Lyman in London and Col. Alfred M. Shearer at Cheltenham, served as deputy chief signal

[7] Organization of Theater Signal Personnel in ETO, Tab B, Memo, Col Murray D. Harris, ExecO OCSigO Hq ETOUSA, for Code, 5 Mar 45, sub: Orgn of Hq ETOUSA and Responsibilities of the CSigO. SigC 370.2 ETO (app. D) 1942–45, SigC Central files.

[8] (1) Ibid. (2) Ruppenthal, Logistical Support of the Armies, I, 201.

[9] ETOUSA Rpt, I, 4–5.

[10] Thompson, Harris, et al., The Test, p. 339.

[11] (1) Hq ETOUSA GO 19, 20 Jul 42, sec. I, Organization of Hq ETOUSA and Hq SOS ETOUSA. (2) ETOUSA Rpt, I, 21.

[12] Hq ETOUSA GO 16, 21 Mar 43.

officers.[13] On 1 April General Rumbough transferred his principal office from Cheltenham to London and in October concentrated in London all signal duties except supply and administrative responsibilities primarily associated with U.K. operations. In July Colonel Shearer became deputy chief signal officer for ETOUSA and SOS, a position he held until the war in Europe ended.[14] The final organizational rearrangement in January 1944 [15] simplified the channels of command for all the technical service chiefs, including the chief signal officer.[16]

The SOS headquarters organization in Europe followed the headquarters pattern in Washington. The United Kingdom was divided into zones for the receipt of cargo and into base sections for administration. The base sections, roughly comparable to the old corps areas in the zone of interior, possessed "virtually complete control over personnel and depot operations," but the technical services chiefs retained "technical control" of their services in the base sections through representatives on the base section staffs.[17] The base section commander controlled personnel and installations within his area, administered the depots, allotted space in them, and stored and issued the supplies. He was responsible also for maintenance and salvage operations. The chiefs of the services exercised their technical supervision by maintaining approved stock levels, requisitioning and purchasing the supplies, and outlining and supervising the various procedural policies.[18]

The American forces in England increased rapidly in the first six months of 1942. Soon their headquarters occupied not only the main portion of the building at 20 Grosvenor Square, London, in which it was housed originally, but also several other nearby buildings.[19] Each required its own telephone switchboard and interconnecting trunk lines. By October 1942 American forces in the vicinity of Grosvenor Square were using four switchboards, which handled 12,000 calls per day; one-third of these required interswitchboard trunking, which seriously impaired the efficiency of the system. Meanwhile ETOUSA officers searched for new quarters for the badly overcrowded signal center. The subbasement of the Selfridge department store annex, a nearly bombproof steel and concrete structure on Duke Street, offered enough space to accommodate both the Army and the Navy communications centers. *Nearly bombproof* in this case meant safe from anything but a direct bomb hit. On 19 December the signal center moved to the Duke Street location. About the same time that construction started on the Duke Street center (with a new central switchboard among other refinements), the British Government offered a section of a public air raid shelter that was nearing completion.

[13] Sig Sv ETOUSA, Historical Report of Personnel, Signal Service SOS-ETOUSA, Jul 42–Jun 43, p. 41. Admin 301.

[14] (1) *Ibid.*, pp. 14, 30, 53. (2) ETOUSA Rpt, I, 21.

[15] Hq ETOUSA GO 5, 17 Jan 44.

[16] (1) ETOUSA CSigO Off Memo 282, sub: Orgn of OCSigO, COMZ, 18 Dec 44. SCIA file European Theater folder 6. (2) Orgn of Theater Sig Pers in ETO, Tab B, Memo, Harris for Code, 5 Mar 45. (3) Interv, SigC Hist Sec with Maj Gen William S. Rumbough, 6 Jul 56.

[17] Ruppenthal, *Logistical Support of the Armies*, I, 170.

[18] ETOUSA Rpt, I, 52–53.

[19] For an account of the early days of ETOUSA, see Thompson, Harris, *et al.*, *The Test*, pp. 312–14.

The shelter, a series of tunnels one hundred feet under the Goodge Street underground station, offered a completely bombproof location. Here the British GPO and the Signal Service, ETOUSA, installed an emergency communications center, housing Army and Navy message centers and equipment rooms, the GPO radio, the British code room, and an emergency switchboard. The center was completed in March 1943.[20]

The signal center and the entire communications system serving the various United States Army headquarters grew to amazing proportions. The Signal Service, ETOUSA, made use of the existing British communications system as much as possible. The British GPO also furnished large quantities of telephone and teletypewriter materials. By D-day, 980 telephone switchboards and 15 teletypewriter switchboards served the various headquarters in the British Isles. The telephone switchboards had more than 1,200 positions. That is to say, more than 1,200 telephone operators sat at the 980 boards, endlessly plugging and unplugging the connections to 32,000 telephones. The same number of telephones could service an American city the size of prewar Spokane, Albany, Duluth, or Chattanooga. An average of 8,500,000 calls a month went over the system.[21] A network of 300 teletypewriter machines connected U.S. installations in England, Wales, Scotland, and Northern Ireland.

Extensive as the wire system was, a few well-placed bombs or a bit of careful sabotage might well have created havoc. To guard against such a contingency, the Signal Service installed emergency radio nets. The stations, though labeled *emergency,* operated constantly since, had they been left inactive until an emergency arose, their sudden appearance on the air would have told the enemy that a communications emergency did indeed exist. The stations were therefore on the air all the time, and, except for persons with a reason to know, none could tell whether the messages transmitted were real or dummy traffic.[22]

Many messages are too bulky, too secret, or of a nature that makes it physically impossible to transmit them by electrical means. For these, the Signal Service, ETOUSA, organized and operated a GHQ messenger service. It began in 1942 when a few men with several small trucks organized a local delivery service. Within a year the duty required the services of the whole 979th Motor Messenger Company. By train, motor vehicle, boat, and airplane, the messengers hurried about, traveling as many as 375,000 miles monthly to the ports, the base commands, and the many headquarters. In May 1944, on the eve of the invasion, the messenger service carried 2,904,298 messages.[23]

[20] (1) Historical Record of the Construction of the Duke Street Signal Center, 1942. Admin 578. (2) Historical Record of the Construction of the Signal Center Operational Headquarters 1943. Admin 580. (3) Hq ETOUSA, History of the Signal Center, Feb 42–Jan 44. 314.7 History Sig Ctr ETOUSA, Feb 42–Jan 44.

[21] (1) ETOUSA Rpt, I, 5. (2) Com Div, Monthly Activity Rpt (May 44). Admin 576.

[22] ETOUSA Rpt, I, 6.

[23] (1) Sig Sv ETOUSA Com Div, Monthly Activity Rpt Through Jul 44. Admin 576. (2) ETOUSA Rpt, I. 34–37.
The 979th Motor Messenger Company was attached to the 810th Signal Service Battalion, the first such unit activated, whose primary mission was to operate all static signal installations in the Communications Zone, ETO. Hq SOS ETO OCSigO, Current Info Ltr, I, No. 4 (Apr 44), 25. SigC Hist Sec file.

To broadcast entertainment and educational programs to the American troops in the United Kingdom, the Signal Service installed a network of fifty low-powered transmitting stations. Operated by the Special Services Division and the Office of War Information (OWI), this American Forces Network supplied the troops with a steady diet of music and information.[24]

As the invasion date drew near, ETO-USA signalmen rushed additional radio facilities to completion to serve the needs of the tactical forces. They installed a 40-kilowatt single sideband transmitter at Lingfield, Surrey, and the receiver station at Swanley Junction, Essex. These facilities provided one voice and three radioteletypewriter channels to the United States. The U.S. terminal was operated by the Long Lines Department, American Telephone and Telegraph Company. For operation with AFHQ in Caserta, a 1-kilowatt station was constructed. Two 50-kilowatt power units were installed for use in the event of loss of commercial power. In May the Signal Corps built a central radio control room to control all radio stations within the United Kingdom. The center was equipped with broadcast and facsimile transmission facilities. Late in the month, signalmen completed antrac VHF (radio relay) stations at Middle Wallop and on the Isle of Wight. These would provide cross-Channel facilities between the U.S. First Army on the far shore and the IX Tactical Air Command at Middle Wallop. Multichannel connections were installed to the London GHQ that would permit General Eisenhower and Field Marshal Sir Bernard L. Mont-

gomery to speak directly to Headquarters, First U.S. Army (FUSA), in France. Facsimile adapters were connected to each set of this circuit to permit the transmission and reception of reconnaissance photographs in support of FUSA. Still another radio station, one of 3 kilowatts, was built to provide high-speed International Morse, facsimile, and broadcast facilities to the Continent.[25]

The heavy task of providing signal equipment for all the using units in the ETO fell to the Supply Division, ETO-USA. This division, through its various branches, planned the ETO signal supply program; received, stored, accounted for, issued, and shipped or delivered all signal property in the United Kingdom (except certain Air Forces items and photographic supplies); installed, maintained, repaired, and salvaged signal equipment; and procured or purchased signal items furnished by Allied governments through the reciprocal aid program in the European area.[26]

The story of the Supply Division's struggles to fulfill its mission is one of "trial, hard work, and constant perseverance." [27] From the first small group of supply officers who journeyed from London to Cheltenham in July 1942 to put the signal supply service into operation, all but one man went to Africa in the winter of 1942 or moved up to key positions on the signal staff or in the base sections.[28] Before July 1942, the only

---

[24] ETOUSA Rpt, I, 6.

[25] (1) ETOUSA Rpt, I, 38. (2) See also account of SHAEF communications and radio relay installation below, pp. 87–88, 104ff. (3) MS Comment, Amory H. Waite, USASRDL, Jul 59.

[26] ETOUSA Rpt, I, 40–41.

[27] Ibid., p. 62.

[28] By April 1944, the Signal Supply Service at Cheltenham numbered 85 officers and warrant officers, 222 enlisted men, and 51 civilians. Ibid., p. 40.

signal depot in the theater had been the one at Carrickfergus, Northern Ireland, operated by the 203d Signal Depot Company.[29] That month five new signal depots opened. The 204th Signal Depot Company, spread thin, operated all of them until 1943, when the 208th and 216th Signal Depot Companies arrived in the theater to share the work.[30] By December 1943 the Signal Corps had eleven depots—nine were section depots and two were branch depots.

There were signal sections at G–16, Wem, midway between Birmingham and Liverpool; at G–18, Sudbury, northwest of Birmingham; G–22, Moreton-on-Lugg, 30 miles northwest of Gloucester; G–25, Ashchurch, 8 miles north of Cheltenham; G–40, Barry, 7 miles southwest of Cardiff; G–45, Thatcham, southwest of Reading; G–47, Westbury, 21 miles southeast of Bristol; and G–50, Taunton, 45 miles southwest of Bristol. G–55, Lockerly (Salisbury), was added to the list soon after the first of the year. The two branch depots were S–800, Bury St. Edmonds, 27 miles northwest of Ipswich; and S–810, Crossgar, 18 miles southeast of Belfast, Northern Ireland.[31]

Still another signal depot activity embraced the base repair shop at Depot O

–640, the main Ordnance depot at Tidworth, which installed radio sets in tanks and armored vehicles. In December 1943, the Signal Corps set up a storage and issue section at Tidworth to work more closely with Ordnance. Ordnance allotted the Signal Corps 30,000 square feet of space to store and issue the vehicular radio sets. All together, the Signal Corps by early 1944 had 600,000 square feet of covered storage space, almost 1,000,000 square feet of open space, and was handling approximately 2,500 tons of signal equipment and supplies each week.[32]

As in the United States, the signal depots in the United Kingdom specialized to some extent. For example, Sudbury handled common items of signal equipment for the AAF; Wem and Barry stockpiled operational supplies; Moreton-on-Lugg stored and distributed bulk table of basic allowances (T/BA) equipment shipped in advance of troops; and Thatcham stored project equipment for fixed installations, such as pole line equipment, radio plants, and communications systems.[33]

Until May 1943, troops and equipment were shipped to the theater at the same time, organizational equipment being force marked. This arrangement was never popular with supply men. Troops sailed on transports; equipment was loaded on slower cargo vessels. Thus the time and place of arrivals of troops and equipment varied widely, and marrying up the troops and their organizational equipment meant expending an inordi-

[29] History of the Signal Corps in ETO, p. 22, draft copy. Working file, 314.7 Mil Histories, vol. 2, Sig Sv, ETOUSA.
For account of Carrickfergus depot, see Thompson, Harris, et al., The Test, pp. 104–05.
[30] Ibid.
[31] (1) Report of Signal Supply Service Survey, ETOUSA, 1943, Tab 9, List of SOS Depots ETO Which Have Sig Secs and Sig Depots, 20 Dec 43. SigC AC 400.112 Sig Sup Survey of ETOUSA, 22 Sep –22 Dec 43. (2) ETOUSA Rpt, I, 60. (3) Sig Sup Div, Hq ETOUSA–SOS, 1st ed., Historical Summary of Activities, 28 Jul 43. Admin 572.
In the numerical designations for the depots, G stood for general, S for signal.

[32] Hist, SigC in ETO, p. 53.
[33] Hist Summ of Activities, Sig Sup Div, Hq ETOUSA SOS, 28 Jul 43.

nate amount of time and effort.[34] Some-times the delay was so great that equipment marked for one unit had to be given to another unit in order to avoid loss of valuable training time. At times some units received two issues while others got none. In any case, since the Signal Corps did not handle directly the organizational equipment records for the various units, it became virtually impossible for the Signal Supply Division to ascertain at all times just what items were in the theater, which units had their organizational equipment, and what items a unit needed to complete its equipment list.[35]

In mid-May 1943, the entire supply picture brightened with the introduction of the "bulk shipment" plan.[36] Under the new system, organizational equipment was shipped in bulk a month in advance of the troops for whom it was intended, according to the over-all troop basis for the period. In general the new plan worked very well. The base section signal officer was alerted ahead of time as to just which units were coming, the date of their arrival, and where they would be stationed. When a unit's advance party arrived, each signal officer received requisitions showing him just where to go to collect the equipment for his unit. Ideally, by the time a division had been in England a week, it would have 90 percent of its equipment, and in two or three weeks it would have 98 percent of it, all that it was likely to receive since there were always on Signal Corps

tables a few items of newly developed equipment that had not yet been manufactured.[37]

Throughout the war, in nearly every theater, signal supply officers complained bitterly about the War Department policy permitting newly standardized items to appear on TOE's months before they were actually available even in limited quantities. The Signal Corps tried to overcome the irritating problem by keeping the overseas commands informed in advance as to just what new items were planned and when they would be available.[38] In the ETO, theater instructions specified that newly standardized items should not be requisitioned or reported as shortages, but the ruling was almost impossible to enforce and still more difficult to explain to the various G-4's. The most plausible explanation for including such items in the first place was the requirement that they must be listed on current TOE's before funds could be obligated to procure the items.[39]

Although the advance shipment plan simplified supply distribution, for a time it operated to deplete the meager maintenance stocks in the United Kingdom. Stocks were just beginning to recover from the inroads made to fill equipment shortages for units destined for North Africa in late 1942. In September 1943 a theater cable to Washington warned that, of all equipment in the ETO, Signal Corps items were the most critical

[34] USFET Gen Bd Rpt, Study 110, Signal Supply, Repair, and Maintenance, p. 8.

[35] Hist, SigC in ETO, p. 47.

[36] AG Ltr, sub: Standard Procedure for Shipment of Equip and Sups to the U.K. AG 400.22 (16 May 43), OB–S–SPDD–M.

[37] Interv, SigC Hist Sec with Rumbough, 20 Feb 45.

[38] OCSigO Ser No. 48, Memo for Dirs of Staff Divs, Chiefs of Operating Svs, and Dir Off Sv Div, OCSigO, and CO's of Fld Activities, 26 Apr 45, sub: Sup of Newly Standardized Items to Overseas Comds, SigC OT 400 Sup Plan ETO.

[39] USFET Gen Bd Rpt, Study 110, pp. 9–10.

since they were not arriving in accordance with the shipment plan contemplated by the War Department, and depot stocks were virtually exhausted.[40]

Meanwhile, in the zone of interior the commanding general of the Air Service Command (ASC) at Patterson Field, Ohio, charged that large stocks of Signal Corps ground equipment had been built up in the United Kingdom and that issues of ground signal equipment items for units ordered into the United Kingdom ought to be greatly reduced. He added that such a reduction would permit the Signal Corps to catch up on the production of critical items that were behind schedule.[41] Presumably he had in mind production of signal items for the Army Air Forces.

The Chief Signal Officer at once sent two officers, Col. Byron A. Falk and Lt. Col. Caleb Orr, to the ETO to make a firsthand survey.[42] Falk and Orr spent three months checking depot stocks, records, and methods. Their survey covered controlled and critical items used by the AGF and the AAF as well as other important classes of items in short supply in the theater. The officers also visited troop units, both air and ground, to find out what signal items the troops had. Their findings indicated that the theater records were accurate, the back-order system excellent, and the requirements correctly computed. In fact, Orr reported that the system of

record keeping in the ETO was better than that of any supply system he had surveyed in the United States. Yet the records of the New York Port of Embarkation (NYPOE) showed large quantities of signal material shipped to the ETO for which there was no accounting. Theater supply men blamed this almost wholly upon the diversion of supplies to North Africa. During that campaign, many ships loaded with cargo that NYPOE records showed as having been received in the British Isles, actually were diverted to North Africa in midvoyage.[43]

Signal supply matters improved as a result of the Falk-Orr report. The NYPOE agreed to accept the accuracy of the theater monthly status reports and to fill requisitions without editing as quickly as material became available. Within two months, stocks on hand in the theater increased rapidly, although part of the rapid rise resulted from War Department action elevating the theater to the highest possible priority.[44]

"Operational project" planning received special attention during 1943 and early 1944. Operational projects provided advance procurement information months before a specific operation was mounted so that the required material could be manufactured and shipped. Ordinary tables of equipment were tailored for average situations. They did not cover such items as construction material for housing, port and dock facilities, fixed plant communications

---

[40] ETOUSA Rpt, I, 45.

[41] Incl 1, Ltr, Sig Off Hq ASC, Patterson Fld, Ohio, to CSigO, 22 Jul 43, with Rpt on Sig Sup Survey of ETOUSA, 20 Dec 43. SigC AC 400.112 Sig Sup Survey of ETOUSA, 22 Sep–20 Dec 43.

[42] Memo, CSigO for CG ASF, 13 Aug 43, sub: Equip for Units Ordered to the U.K., and 1st Ind, CG ASF to CSigO, 17 Aug 43. SigC 475 Gen 2, Aug–Dec 43.

[43] (1) Rpt, Sig Sup Sv Survey of ETOUSA, 20 Dec 43, pp. 28–29. (2) ETOUSA Rpt, I, 45 and 56. (3) Ltr, ACSigO to CG Patterson Fld, 8 Feb 44, sub: Equip for Units Ordered to the U.K. SigC EO Equip 44.

[44] ETOUSA Rpt, I, 46.

equipment, and many other kinds of material needed in vast quantities. Procuring such special equipment took a long time, often eighteen to twenty-four months. Yet supply planning officers could not estimate the materials needed for a given operation until the operational plan was in existence, and operational planning lagged notoriously. Actually, the War Department itself did not inaugurate the operational project system until the summer of 1943.[45]

The Signal Service, ETOUSA, set up a Projects Division, which soon broadened its scope of activity to become the Plans Division.[46] Typical Signal Corps projects included provision for all the fixed wire plant and equipment in the advanced theater of operations; material to install and maintain a communications system for railroad control in the continental operation; enough signal equipment to last from D-day through D plus 240 for the Corps of Engineers, for the Chemical Warfare Service, for the Ordnance Department, and for the Army Air Forces; radio equipment for the signal intelligence service network; a pool of 1,000 FM SCR–610 radios as insurance against enemy AM jamming during the assault phase; and many others. Operational projects provided (over and above T/BA allotments) thousands of miles of assault wire; public address systems for beach operations; waterproof bags for vehicular and portable radio sets; teletypewriters by the hundreds; package-type carrier telephone apparatus; a whole wire communication system for the Tactical Air Force; mine detectors; cryptographic

material; telephone central-office sets for six major signal centers; complete radio stations; and stockpiles of many, many other things.[47]

Special jobs fell to the Chief Signal Officer, ETOUSA. Many of them, such as the operation of the photographic service, were very important. Combat photography, one of the more glamorous duties, was only one phase of the photographic mission. The Army Pictorial Division, established in the theater headquarters in June 1942, soon grew to a size comparable to many independent agencies. It operated service laboratories, a supply section, a motor pool, a carpenter shop, a camera maintenance and repair shop, training facilities, a photographic news bureau, base section training film libraries, and other special services. During the two years of preparation for the invasion, the Army Pictorial Division turned out 85,000 negatives and 1,300,000 still picture prints. It also found, to its dismay, that the U.S. Army was filled with amateur photographers, whose pictures all had to be censored to be sure that they did not innocently reveal military secrets. To accomplish the censoring job, the Army Pictorial Division perforce had to process the films. By April 1944 the Signal Corps, in an average week, was processing 7,000 rolls of amateur film and making 70,000 prints. V-mail, too, was a Signal Corps responsibility or, rather, that portion of it that required photographic service. The Signal Corps used the British Kodak plant to capacity and processed the surplus itself. By D-day the volume of outgoing V-mail letters rose to 13,000,000 monthly. Approxi-

[45] WD Cir 220, 20 Sep 43.
[46] Sig Sv ETO, History of the Plans Division, p. 1. Admin 304.

[47] Sig Sv ETO, Hist, Plans Div, app. C, Summ of SigC Projs.

mately the same number was received in the theater.[48]

ETOUSA's signal responsibilities ranged over such divergent matters as exercising operational control of signal intelligence and reworking the electrical systems of jeeps to make it possible for the military police to install two-way radios. This last was a vital necessity in a London jam-packed with pleasure-bent American GI's on passes. ETOUSA's personnel included crystal-grinding teams to grind the millions of crystals needed for the thousands of radio sets stockpiled for the invasion and Wacs to take charge of many communications duties. General Rumbough wanted Wacs even if getting them meant cutting down on the number of enlisted men available for signal duty in the theater.[49] The Signal Corps arranged for pigeons (53 lofts, 4,500 pigeons, furnished by the British) and for floating telephone poles to the Continent; it was also concerned with the supply of batteries to the armies, and with the supply of spare parts.[50]

WACS OPERATING A RADIO-TELEPHOTO *transmitter in England.*

The Signal Division, SHAEF

By early 1943, signal officers on the staffs of various organizations already in the theater—ETOUSA, Naval Forces in Europe (COMNAVEU), and the British Admiralty, War Office, and Air Ministry—had already done a great deal of valuable spadework.[51] A plan had been developed for the full use of communications facilities existing within the United Kingdom. For example, communications posts and radio stations had been built along the southern coast of England as part of the British Defense Telecommunications Network (DTN).[52] Thus, a good deal of preliminary signal planning was already under way by 26 April 1943 when a combined British and American staff charged with framing a basic plan for the invasion began work at Norfolk House in St. James Square, London, under the Chief of Staff to the Supreme Allied Commander.

[48] ETOUSA Rpt, I, 82–94.

[49] Log entry, 17 Jan 44, CSigO Diary. SigC 313 Rcds–Diaries, I, Sig Sv ETOUSA.

[50] Log entries, 22 Jan, 25 Jan, 9 Apr, 16 Apr.

[51] (1) Report of Signal Division, SHAEF, Opn OVERLORD (hereafter cited as OVERLORD Rpt), I, 2. (2) Brig Lionel H. Harris, *Signal Venture* (Aldershot, England: Gale & Polden, 1951), p. 179.

[52] (1) Brig. Gen. Francis H. Lanahan, Jr., "Signal Planning for the Invasion," *Signals*, I, No. 3, (January–February, 1947), 34. (2) Brig. Gen. Francis H. Lanahan, Jr., "Build-Up for Battle," *Signals*, I, No. 1 (September-October, 1946), 19–20.

General Eisenhower was appointed
Supreme Commander on 14 January
1944, and COSSAC became Supreme
Headquarters, Allied Expeditionary
Force. A British signal officer, Maj. Gen.
C. H. H. Vulliamy, headed the SHAEF
Signal Division. His deputy was Brig.
Gen. Francis H. Lanahan, Jr., of the U.S.
Army Signal Corps. Roughly half of the
division personnel were British and half
were American.[53] Similarly, the signal
units that provided the communications
for SHAEF were divided between the
two allies. The 5th Headquarters Signals was British; the 3118th Signal Service Battalion, American. For the important message center duty with the
3118th, the Theaters Branch of the OC-
SigO in Washington selected experienced men from the 17th Signal Service
Company, the unit that operated the War
Department's own message center in the
Pentagon.[54]

From 11 August 1943 until General
Vulliamy arrived on 26 October, General Lanahan acted as the Chief Signal
Officer, SHAEF. Lanahan would in fact
become the Chief Signal Officer, SHAEF,
in March 1945, when Vulliamy departed
for India. Lanahan had already organized the Signal Division, which by early
1944 included many prominent Signal
Corps officers.[55] The Signal Division was
made up of British and American Army
officers only, there being too few competent communications planning officers
on the Air and Navy staffs, either British
or American, to spare any for full-time

GENERAL LANAHAN

work with the SHAEF Signal Division.
Yet the signal plan for the invasion had
to be fully co-ordinated among the
services; indeed, it had to be co-ordinated as no other signal scheme had ever
been. A multitude of items of organization and procedure awaited clarification.
"Communications by their very nature
cannot be kept in water-tight compartments, and act independently within
each service." [56] The Combined Signal
Board (CSB) was set up in October
1943 to accomplish the necessary high-
level co-ordination. With General Vulliamy serving as the chairman, the board
brought together signal officers of the
Allied navies, the Allied air forces,
ETOUSA, the 21 Army Group, and 1st
Army Group.[57] The CSB did, in fact,

[53] OVERLORD Rpt, I, 6.

[54] (1) CSigO, Annual Rpt, FY 44, pp. 102–03. (2)
Interv, SigC Hist Sec with Col William D. Hamlin,
Nov 44. SigC Hist Sec file.

[55] (1) OVERLORD Rpt, II, an. B, p. 59. (2) Harris,
Signal Venture, p. 244. (3) Interv, SigC Hist Sec
with Hamlin.

[56] Harris, *Signal Venture*, pp. 185–86.
[57] OVERLORD Rpt, I, 6–7.

provide a satisfactory solution. General Lanahan described it as outstanding for its "spirit of co-operation and willingness to compromise." [58]

Communications for SHAEF, both for its own headquarters and for connections to other commands, soon consumed enormous facilities, taking over telephone and telegraph circuits of the General Post Office and adding new circuits, especially radio to Washington. One of the main problems, when telegraph and telephone requirements first came under consideration in August 1943, was to find a bombproof site large enough to accommodate the SHAEF signal center. The British Air Ministry agreed to provide underground accommodations, and considerable work was done at the site before the Air Ministry reversed its decision. Wire facilities serving Headquarters, ETOUSA, were already installed in the south end of a tunnel of the underground railway station at Goodge Street, and the SHAEF signal center found a home in the north end of the tunnel. The GPO installed a 16-position switchboard, four positions of which were modified for use as a cross-Channel VHF radio switchboard, and a 70-line teleprinter switchboard connected to various headquarters and service organizations. [59]

SHAEF grew so fast that not all of its staff could be accommodated at Norfolk House. By January 1944, part of the Signal Division spilled over into a makeshift building at Portland Court, twenty minutes away, and for a time signal planning suffered because of the separation of that staff. Resumption of German bombings in late winter forced SHAEF to move out of London altogether. The new location at Bushy Park, Teddington, near Hampton Court, on the southwest edge of greater London, brought all the Signal Division together again in March. [60] Bushy Park was already headquarters for the U.S. Eighth Air Force, which made its switchboard (code name WIDEWING) available to SHAEF until other facilities could be installed. The WIDEWING camp grew "incredibly quickly, using collapsible hutting which they [the Americans] seemed to be able to fit together to provide any size or shape of building required," commented Brigadier Lionel H. Harris, a British member of the Signal Division and chief of its Telecommunications Section. [61] He added that the signal offices were more substantial and better protected from blast, a fortunate circumstance since otherwise they would have been flattened instead of merely bent, later on, by the near miss of a flying bomb.

SHAEF telephone facilities at Bushy Park at first were a 20-position board. By May the 20 operators had increased to 30. There were 24 teleprinters. Additional line facilities connected wireless links that could be brought under remote control either from the Goodge Street North signal center or from Bushy Park. A conference telephone system served the meteorological staffs of the combined services—the British Admiralty, the Air Ministry, the Allied Naval Expeditionary Force, Allied Expeditionary Air Force (AEAF), and SHAEF—by way of the Goodge Street center. Private wires connected the SHAEF

[58] Lanahan, "Signal Planning for the Invasion," *Signals*, I, No. 3, 34.

[59] OVERLORD Rpt, I, 6-13.

[60] *Ibid.*

[61] Harris, *Signal Venture*, p. 182.

War Room with each of the British and American air forces.[62]

SHAEF was plentifully supplied with radio facilities. They included the use of existing War Office, Air Ministry, and Admiralty circuits to Algiers and GPO channels to Washington.[63] Manual and automatic wireless rooms were installed both at the Bushy Park and Goodge Street North signal centers. There were transmitting stations at Lingfield and Wimbledon Common, and a receiving station at Eyenesford, south of London, with remote control lines terminating at Goodge Street North. Emergency control facilities at the signal centers at Goodge Street South (the emergency signal center for ETOUSA) and at Duke Street (the normal signal center for ETOUSA) gave assurance that SHAEF stations could be controlled from these centers if necessary.[64] Radioteletype-writer and radiotelephone circuits from SHAEF to AFHQ at Algiers and a radio-teletypewriter circuit from SHAEF to AFHQ at Caserta opened shortly before D-day. The U.S. Strategic Air Force already had in use a radioteletypewriter conference system that enabled typed conferences to be held with Washington and with Algiers, and the system was made available to SHAEF. Traffic facilities for the press were also readied before D-day.[65]

Some of the more important decisions of the CSB standardized the time basis and time expressions in messages throughout the theater; ordained a simple single-call procedure for all ground force radio communications; established telephone priorities; assigned cross-Channel cable and VHF radio circuits; and allocated radio frequencies. Time after time the members met to deal with problems concerning wire and cable, radio and radar, siting procedures, security and countermeasures, radio ships and cable ships, air and boat messenger service, codes and ciphers, air warnings, signal troops, training, communications for the assault forces, for the navies, for the air fleets, and for the press, speech scramblers for telephone talk, and much more besides.[66] Fortunately, by then a great fund of information had accumulated from experience in operations in North Africa, Sicily, Italy, and on the islands of the Pacific. In retrospect, signal planners were describing North Africa as "a small dress rehearsal for the great undertaking that was to follow." [67] The scale of communications for OVERLORD was perhaps twenty-five times greater than it had been for TORCH.

Of the many tasks confronting the signal planners, the most difficult was to evolve a workable plan of frequency allocation. It is never easy to develop an effective system to meet the needs of a large force—naval, air, ground, and service—in a combined operation. The difficulties multiply when several nations are concerned, for there are differences in types of transmission and frequency bands of the transmitters to consider. A minor mitigation in OVERLORD lay in the

[62] OVERLORD Rpt, I, 13 and app. B to NEPTUNE, Sig Instrs, pt. II, an. P. (2) Harris, Signal Venture, pp. 184–85.

[63] Harris, Signal Venture, pp. 184–85.

[64] OVERLORD Rpt, I, 20.

[65] OVERLORD Rpt, I, 21, and app. F to NEPTUNE, Sig Instrs, II, an. P. (2) Harris, Signal Venture, pp. 184–85.

[66] OVERLORD Rpt, I, 7, and II, 343–585.

[67] Lanahan, "Build-Up for Battle," Signals, I, No. 1, 19–20.

fact that the two nations involved spoke a common language and employed common procedures. An existing British system furnished the basis for the plan ultimately adopted.[68]

Invasion plans called for a concentration of about 90,000 transmitters within a limited area of land, sea, and sky. Complicating the allocation problem further were the rapidly increasing numbers of new radar devices, the many radios and radars used by the bombing and fighter defense forces, the powerful radio and radar jamming transmitters, and the radio and radar navigational aids of both air and sea craft. The CSB set aside the frequencies that the British Government required to meet its minimum needs, earmarked certain other frequencies serving essential war purposes, and then allotted frequencies in blocks based upon a study of bids submitted by the prospective users.[69] As expected, the using forces bid for several times as many frequencies as were available. The frequencies most in demand lay in the crowded high-frequency bands. In fact, the Radio Frequency Committee of the CSB received 3,300 requests for channels between 1.5 and 8 megacycles from the 6 major services and from no less than 27 contributing agencies, including the press and psychological warfare. The frequencies between 2 and 8 megacycles were overbid 400 percent, and in the 2- to 5-megacycle band the bids amounted to seven times the number the spectrum could provide.[70] Working out

a means of providing thousands of frequency packets, or channels, within tight limits without chaotic interference was a feat bordering upon the impossible. Brigadier Harris described the job as "rather like taking two selected octaves of a piano and putting in as many notes as was possible, without adjacent ones being so closely alike as to be indistinguishable."[71] General Lanahan, too, fell back on musical comparisons—frequency allocation, he said, would yield either orchestration in the air, or cacophony. "We were attempting to assemble the greatest ether orchestra in history, and the planning would determine whether the orchestra produced music and messages, or chaos and confusion."[72]

If the plan were to work, all commands would have to practice maximum economy in sharing their frequencies and in employing only the minimum power output at the transmitters. By December 1943 the Radio Frequency Committee of the CSB had agreed upon a tentative allocation, and the grinding of the necessary myriads of crystals began. But by February 1944 it became apparent that the AEAF required more frequencies. Over the strenuous objection of General Vulliamy and the signal staff,[73] the committee took frequencies from the ground forces and reduced the already narrow separation of channels in the 1- to 5-megacycle band from five

---

[68] USFET Gen Bd Rpt, Study 111, Signal Corps Operations, p. 1.

[69] Ibid.

[70] (1) USFET Gen Bd Rpt, Study 111, p. 2. (2) Harris, Signal Venture, pp. 187–88. (3) Maj. Gen.

Francis H. Lanahan, Jr., "Radio for OVERLORD," Signals, I, No. 4 (March–April, 1947), 49–50. (4) Lanahan, "Build-Up for Battle," Signals, I, No. 1, pp. 19–20. (5) Lanahan, "Signal Planning for the Invasion," Signals, I, No. 3, 32–36.

[71] Harris, Signal Venture, pp. 187–88.

[72] Lanahan, "Radio for OVERLORD," Signals, I, No. 4, 49–50.

[73] MS Comment in Ltr, Lanahan to Thompson, SigC Hist Div, 31 Oct 57. SigC Hist Div file.

kilocycles to four. That meant grinding more crystals, and on extremely short notice, for it was 10 May when the revised frequency allocation list was issued. But in this specialty the Signal Corps had become proficient, even to the point where what had once been a most exacting laboratory technique was now transported into the field, and mobile crystal grinding teams were at hand. The task of providing crystals by the thousands, meticulously prepared, emphasized the one drawback to their use. Nevertheless, the American decision to use crystal-controlled mobile FM radio greatly simplified the job of frequency control in the jam-packed spectrum of sky over Europe from D-day on.

By D-day the Signal Division of SHAEF had laboriously turned out twenty-one signal instructions, section by section, complete with appendixes, charts, maps, and equipment lists galore.[74] The signal instructions assigned responsibilities and laid down policies in general and in detail. Codes and ciphers furnished one example. The Combined Assault Code was to be used for all messages between headquarters engaged in an initial landing operation; the Combined Field Code, for all combined traffic where no other combined cipher was held; the Combined Strip Cipher, to supplement the Combined Cipher Machine. However, for the great bulk of heavy headquarters traffic, the Combined Cipher Machine system would assure secrecy on teletypewriter circuits, whether wire or radio. There were also joint and intraservice codes

and ciphers, special purpose codes and ciphers (a radiotelephone code called Slidex, a map reference code, an air support control code, an air warning code, and so on) with rules for their use, together with many details on their security and on action to be taken if a system were compromised.

The now universally employed cipher machines, both British and American, formed the basis of the cipher systems of the Allies.[75] The traffic loads, totaling astronomical numbers of words or 5-letter cipher groups, could have been dispatched efficiently in no other way. In the weeks just before the invasion, ETOUSA headquarters traffic climbed to a daily average of from 1.5 million to 2 million groups.[76] Such a mass of words could not have been enciphered and deciphered by hand, by cryptographic clerks converting letter by letter using such slow, arduous devices as strip boards, unless great delay could be tolerated and unless very large numbers of message center personnel could be provided. Of course neither could the one be tolerated nor the other provided. The automatic cipher machine was the solution. Moreover, it was much more secure, as well as mechanically precise. The German Radio Intelligence Service—the counterpart of the U.S. Signal Intelligence Service—admitted, after prolonged efforts to crack the Allied machine cipher systems, that they were unbreakable. German cryptanalysts succeeded, of course, in breaking many less secure systems, such as the Haglin, or M–209, though the individ-

---

[74] The whole occupies nearly two hundred pages in Operation OVERLORD Report, II, 157–342.

[75] (1) OVERLORD Rpt, I, 39, and II, 221–29. (2) Harris, *Signal Venture*, pp. 190–91.

[76] Lanahan, "Build-Up for Battle," *Signals*, I, No. 1, 20.

ual intercepts could generally not be read for some hours or days, quite enough time when temporary concealment was all the Allies expected. The Slidex code had been broken soon after the Germans first intercepted the traffic during maneuvers in southern England in March 1944.[77]

Speed and mass were the key words in the Army message centers in those greatest of all signal preparations to date. Mass communication was in fact the goal, commensurate with the total wars of the 20th century. The Allies readied huge quantities of short- and medium-range radio sets, of wire-line stores for combat use by battalions, companies, and platoons. There were tens of thousands of sets waterproofed, their batteries fresh and fully charged; hundreds of thousands of miles of assault and field wire, enough for the 5 divisions by land and the 3 by air in the D-day assault, enough for the 16 divisions that would be in Normandy within five days, enough for the million men who would be ashore in three weeks, enough and plenty to spare for the losses in battle.[78] But the focus of SHAEF signal planning centered on the massive traffic loads of the headquarters

—the millions of words telephoned and teletyped, whether by wire or by radio, or by both integrated into one system—accomplished even in the fleeting conditions of a military camp and as handily as in the well-established civilian communications system of a large modern metropolis.

Large armies on Normandy beachheads would require heavy duty communications lines back to England, and that meant, traditionally, submarine cable, and now more recently, radio channels in VHF. There were also, of course, numbers of Morse HF radio stations set up for headquarters use, but each station provided only one channel. Multichannel facilities had to be obtained The British provided cable and cable ships and also most of the initial supply of VHF radio. A number of British AM multichannel VHF systems were readied on the Isle of Wight to link up with companion sets whose crews followed hard upon the assault troops to the high ground beyond the GOLD and JUNO Beaches. Meanwhile, British cable ships stood by to unreel their coils between Southbourne and the Normandy beach near Longues as soon as the enemy could be pushed back and the sea lanes swept free of mines.[79]

A very important contribution to SHAEF signal planning derived from the signal staffs of the U.S. 1st Army Group and the British 21 Army Group. FUSAG was organized in October 1943.[80] Its signal officer was Colonel Lyman until April 1944, when Col. Gar-

[77] (1) A.D.I. (K) Rpt No. 407/1945, G.A.F. Signals Intelligence in the War, VI, The Breaking of Allied Cyphers in the West. SigC Hist Sec file, German Sigs Intel. (2) Hist Div EuCom, Foreign Mil Studies Br, Communication Project (MS # P-038k), pp. 67 and 108. OCMH files.

The Germans likewise used automatic cipher machines with their radioteletypewriter traffic, calling the devices "G-Secret" machines, or "Sawfish." Hist Div EuCom, Opns Hist Br, OKH (MS # P-041k), pp. 32, 38. OCMH files.

[78] Figures in part from Roger W. Shugg and Maj. H. A. DeWeerd, World War II: A Concise History (Washington: The Infantry Journal Press, 1946), pp. 298-99.

[79] (1) Harris, Signal Venture, pp. 177-78. (2) OVERLORD Rpt, III, 655-56.

[80] Hq ETOUSA GO 74, 16 Oct 43, Activation of Headquarters First Army Group.

land C. Black was assigned.[81] Since
FUSAG was expected to remain non-
operational until enough American
forces reached the Continent to put an
additional American field army into
operation, the principal planning burden for the early stages of the invasion
actually rested with the U.S. First Army.
A battle-hardened group of thirty-eight
officers, drawn from the old II Corps
of the North African campaign, comprised the heart of the FUSA staff.
Among them was the hard-driving signal officer, Colonel Williams.[82] In the
winter of 1943–44 Colonel Williams
learned during a visit from General
Colton, chief of research and development activities in the Office of the Chief
Signal Officer in Washington, that the
new FM multichannel radio relay, or
antrac, system was ready.[83]

This was exciting news. Colonel Williams of course was familiar with the
radio relay that the Signal Corps had

used earlier in the Mediterranean operations. That nonstandard equipment,
improvised from Motorola FM police
radios, had provided only a single circuit. The Signal Corps' new AN/TRC–3
and 4 sets provided for speech circuits
or four teletypewriter circuits for each
speech channel as desired. The new
sets could also transmit pictures and
sketches by means of facsimile equipment and could be connected directly
into the telephone and teletypewriter
circuits at either end.[84]

With General Bradley's quick authorization, Colonel Williams immediately
requisitioned all the antrac equipment
that the Signal Corps could have ready
by mid-1944: about twenty-one 100-
mile radio carrier systems, each consisting of 2 terminal sets and 3 intermediate relay sets to be placed 25 miles
apart, plus 100-percent backup spares.
He hoped to use the antrac to parallel
his wire systems from First Army to
rear echelon, to each corps, to lateral
armies, and to the air support command.[85]

In March 1944 the Signal Corps
shipped several complete 100-mile AN/
TRC–1, 3, and 4 systems, with spare parts
and auxiliary operating components, to
the United Kingdom. No one in the
theater knew how to assemble or operate the sets. The 980th Signal Service
Company, specially trained on antrac
equipment in the United States, had

---

[81] In April 1944, the Signal Section of FUSAG
comprised 156 officers and men. Hist, Sig Sec 12th
AGp, 19 Oct 43–12 May 45. 99/12–31.0 (31695)
Hist, Sig Sec 12th AGp.

[82] First U.S. Army, *Report of Operations, 20
October 1943–1 August 1944,* 7 vols. (Washington,
1945) (hereafter referred to as FUSA, *Rpt of Opns,
20 Oct 43 –1 Aug 44*). The Signal Section report is
contained in Book VI, Annex 12. The second printed report of FUSA covers the period 1
August 1944 to 22 February 1945, and the Signal
Section report is contained in Book III, Annex 8.

[83] Ltr, Col Grant A. Williams (Ret.), to Thomp-
son, SigC Hist Div, 24 Oct 57. SigC Hist Sec file.
This letter is one of a series dated 14, 24, and 31
Oct 57, hereafter referred to as Ltr, Williams to
Thompson, with date cited.

The word antrac commonly used by the Signal
Corps derived from the sets' official nomenclature,
AN/TRC–1, 3, or 4. For an account of antrac, or
radio relay, development, see below, pp. 494ff.,
and Thompson, Harris, *et al., The Test,* pp.
234ff., 371ff.

[84] (1) Rumbough, "Radio Relay," *Military Review,* XXVI, No. 2, 3. (2) MS Comment, Waite,
USASRDL, Jul 49.

[85] Ltr, Williams to Thompson, 24 Oct 57.

Later in the campaign, as more antrac equipment became available, it was used from each First
Army corps to at least three of the corps' divisions.

not yet arrived in the ETO. In April the Signal Corps dispatched two of its civilian laboratory engineers as technical observers to introduce the equipment in the theater, help install it, and train operators for it. "Observers" was a misnomer. Amory H. Waite and Victor J. Colaguori, assigned to the Technical Liaison Division of the Chief Signal Officer, ETOUSA, at once went to work under Colonel Williams and his supply officer, Lt. Col. Elmer L. Littell.[86]

First Waite and Calaguori had to find the sets. Several had gone to the bottom en route. The remaining sets, in lots of 188 boxes per set, were scattered in various supply dumps and warehouses from London to Wales. Once the sets were located, the engineers began assembling them and instructing officers and men in their use, which was complex, demanding a knowledge of carrier telephone and telegraph principles as well as those of VHF radio. Day and night the components of antrac—carrier terminals, both telephone and telegraph, facsimile, VHF antennas, coaxial cable, and power supplies—were their meat and drink. Waite and Colaguori worked ceaselessly with the 175th Signal Repair Company's officers and men (Capt. Herman E. Gabel, 1st Lts. Haynes and Keremetsis, T/Sgts. Richard Fullerton and George Wright, and others) who volunteered their time every night after the daily routine of the signal repair company to work till three or four in the morning. When the equipment assemblage of the first system

was completed, Waite and Colaguori gave short training courses to men of the 17th Signal Operations Battalion, FUSA, and to signalmen of FUSA's V, VII, and XIX Corps, demonstrating and giving detailed instruction to officers and men who soon would be depending upon it to a degree few communications men had hitherto dreamed.[87]

As the invasion date drew near, First Army's G-2 sought Colonel Williams' advice on the problem of getting aerial reconnaissance photographs from the beach to the headquarters of the IX Tactical Air Command at Middle Wallop, England, to help the airmen flying support missions.[88] The signal officer of the IX Tactical Air Command was Colonel Garland, with whom General Rumbough bracketed Colonel Williams for credit in inaugurating antrac in the

---

[86] Colaguori was one of the engineers who had helped install the original radio relay Motorola police sets in North Africa.

[87] (1) Tech Observers Amory H. Waite and Victor J. Colaguori, Report on the Combat Use of Radio Sets AN/TRC-1, 3, 4, and 8 in ETO, 1 May–11 October 1944, pp. 1–22 (hereafter cited as Waite-Colaguori Rpt). SigC 370.2 Rpt on . . . , 1 May –11 Oct 44. (2) Interv, SigC Hist Sec with Waite, 17 Feb 45. SigC Hist Sec file. (3) Ltr, Rumbough, CSigO ETOUSA, to CSigO, 2 Jul 44, and Incl 1, Rpt, First Army VHF Cross Channel Circuit, 1 Jul 44. SigC OP 370.2 Gen, 13 Jul–30 Dec 44 (Rpt folder 4). (4) ETOUSA Rpt, II, app. A (2), First Army Very High Frequency Cross Channel Circuit, pp. 7–13. (5) MS Comment, Waite, Jul 59.
Waite and Colaguori exemplified the idea of the new equipment introductory detachment (NEID), whose need was becoming ever more pressing as new and newer equipment appeared in the theaters. A NEID of 110 officers and 140 enlisted men took form under the Engineering and Technical Service, OCSigO, and provided teams that traveled on temporary duty to the theaters of war both to introduce new equipment and to bring back reports upon its performance. CSigO, Annual Rpt, FY 45, p. 249.

[88] Rumbough, "Radio Relay," *Military Review*, XXVI, No. 2, 3.

ETO. Williams had been assigned a squadron of twenty-one light liaison aircraft for messenger work, but they could not be equipped with IFF (identification, friend or foe) radar recognition equipment, and without it Williams was afraid to let them fly the English Channel. Antrac, of course, could transmit facsimile pictures. But would the radiations, planned only for 25-mile jumps, be able to span the eighty-three miles to the far shore? Waite said he believed they could. One facsimile channel and an emergency circuit into Combined Headquarters at Portsmouth would suffice at first, to be followed by multichannel operation as soon as possible.

With a deadline of four hours in which to draft complete plans for the installation and get the project under way, engineers from ETOUSA's Technical Liaison and Communications Divisions met on the Isle of Wight with British officers from the Royal Corps of Signals to pick a site. Waite and Colaguori feared that the signal might fade somewhat, since line-of-sight to the Normandy shore was not possible. The radiations would have to bend considerably over the curvature of the earth, even though the installations would be on high ground. The civilian engineers had made tests over a longer path in a comparable location in Maine with excellent results, but the fact that this circuit was to be General Eisenhower's only telephone link to FUSA made careful decisions necessary. One terminal set they placed on a hill near Middle Wallop. The pivotal relay assemblage was readied for St. Catherine's Hill on the Isle of Wight, with one receiver-transmitter pair facing north toward Middle

Wallop, the other pair facing southeast toward France.[89]

In his supply planning, Colonel Williams asked for a much greater quantity of signal items than the usual "type" field army would require. The initial assault into Normandy would be made without the benefit of the normal army supply system installations close in the rear; for weeks First Army might have to depend on the supplies it carried with it. In any event, Williams had learned in Sicily that a campaign in which a rapid breakout developed swallowed up signal supplies at a rate enormously greater than War Department calculations allowed.[90]

Washington supply officers were in fact appalled at First Army's signal list, not so much by the quantity as by the nature of the items requested. Almost all were in short supply. For example, from one list of 70 items, 29 were in the "critical" category, 9 were "most critical," and 12 were "practically nonexistent." Eventually Williams got most of what he asked for. First Army's signal equipment ran to 4,400 tons, whereas U.S. armies following in First Army's wake used about 3,300 tons.[91]

Signal Corps troops for the invasion constituted, all in all, the largest gathering of signalmen yet assembled for combat. FUSA's Signal Corps men alone totaled 13,420 men, including three joint assault signal companies (JASCO's), the recently devised units containing both Army and Navy com-

---

[89] (1) ETOUSA Rpt, II, app. A(2), pp. 7–13. (2) Waite-Colaguori Rpt. (3) Ltr, Williams to Thompson, 24 Oct 47. (4) MS Comment, Waite, Jul 59.
[90] Ltr, Williams to Thompson, 14 Oct 57.
[91] Log entries, 22, 24, and 25 Jan 44, CSigO Diary. SigC 313 Rcds–Diaries, I, Sig Sv ETOUSA.

municators.[92] Besides these troops, the FUSA list included 11 division signal companies, 2 of them airborne and 2 serving with armored divisions; 3 signal battalions; a signal operations battalion and a signal operations company; 3 construction battalions and 2 separate construction companies; a photographic company; a repair company; a depot company; a radio intelligence company; a pigeon company; and a number of smaller detachments, some American and some British.[93] Among these were traffic analysis units, an air liaison squadron, a signal intelligence supply unit, and an enemy equipment intelligence service (EEIS) detachment.[94] In addition, the troop list included three companies designated as signal service companies that actually were special units to perform signal intelligence functions at corps level. These troops Colonel Williams asked for because his North African and Sicilian experience

had convinced him of the urgent need for them, even though War Department tables did not provide for such units. He received them only after "endless wrangling and arguing." [95]

The Invasion

As the vessels bearing thousands of Allied troops moved out into the channel on the night of 5–6 June 1944, complete radio silence blanketed the armada. While the ships proceeded in darkness over the sea, huge air fleets of the troop carrier commands flew in the inky blackness overhead. But the blackness was as daylight to the eyes of radar. An American microwave early warning (MEW) radar at Start Point in Devon viewed the whole panorama of the invasion through the night.[96]

Radar for the Airborne Assault

From the electronics point of view, the assault of the 82d and 101st Airborne Divisions in advance of the VII Corps landings on UTAH Beach was very successful.[97] This was true even though many of the paratroopers were widely scattered in the drops. The mishaps resulted from circumstances having noth-

---

[92] The joint assault signal company provided shore party communications, shore fire control, and air liaison, requiring communications men well-trained, familiar with joint procedures and the complicated signal plan as well as with the organization and functions of both the landing force and the naval elements of the joint force. Lt. Col. Hubert D. Thomte, Staff Study Signal Communications for Beach Operations, Comd and Gen Staff College, Ft. Leavenworth, Kansas, 5 Apr 48. SigC OP Sig Com for Beach Opns, 1948. See also below, pp. 231ff.

[93] FUSA, Rpt of Opns, 20 Oct 43–1 Aug 44, bk. VI, an. 12, pp. 13–14.

[94] The EEIS team had the mission of discovering, assessing, and selecting items of enemy equipment to ship home for further study. Until mid-1943, the term EEIS meant Enemy Equipment Identification Service. (1) Maj. Franklin M. Davis, Jr., "Technical Intelligence and the Signal Corps," Signals, III, No. 6 (July–August, 1949), pp. 19–26. (2) Capt Chester A. Hall, Jr., Signal Corps Technical Intelligence, A Brief History, 1940–1948 (1949), SCTC Monograph, Camp Gordon, Ga., pp. 8–24. SigC Hist Sec file.

[95] Ltr, Williams to Thompson, 31 Oct 57.

[96] "Something Big Was On," Radar, No. 4 (August 20, 1944), pp. 2, 35. SigC Hist Sec file.

[97] (1) Gordon A. Harrison, Cross-Channel Attack, UNITED STATES ARMY IN WORLD WAR II (Washington, 1951), pp. 278–300. (2) UTAH Beach to Cherbourg (6 June–27 June 1944), AMERICAN FORCES IN ACTION (Washington, 1947), pp. 14–42. These two sources describe in excellent detail the airborne landings and the combat action of the units involved, but give almost no information concerning the electronic equipment used in the drops.

ing to do with the electronic devices employed; all performed well.

Five and one-half hours before the beach assault began, a score of Pathfinder planes from the IX Troop Carrier Command flew to Normandy guided by British Gee navigational aids and using ASV (air-to-surface vessel) radars, such as the SCR–717, to scan the terrain below.[98] Aboard the Pathfinders were paratroopers carrying Eureka beacons, AN/PPN–1, and signal lights to mark the designated drop zones to guide the troop carriers that would come after them. Cloud and fog obscured the landscape; not even the trained Pathfinders could locate all of the exact areas chosen for the drops.[99] The paratroopers drifted to earth in the Normandy fields and orchards, set out the light signals, and switched on their Eurekas. In two zones west of the Merderet River, Pathfinder teams found enemy units disturbingly near. The Americans dared show no lights; the Eurekas had to suffice.[100]

Half an hour later the great fleets of the Troop Carrier Command approached, their Rebeccas (AN/APN–2's) interrogating and receiving pulsed responses from the Eurekas on the ground, guiding the pilots to the drop zones. Enemy flak over Normandy had dispersed the troop carriers' tight formations; the main drops were generally scattered, but the carriers hit three drop zones exactly. Of 800 planes, only 20 were lost. Of the 512 aircraft and gliders that followed in successive waves, bearing additional troops, weapons, vehicles, and medical and signal units, only 8 were lost.[101] Ninety-five percent of all airborne troops dropped used information from the AN/APN–2 beacons; 25 percent dropped guided by radar alone, with no help at all from signal lights.[102] Afterward the top commanders agreed that "the principal causes of the dispersed drop pattern were cloud formations, flak and faulty navigation by some of the pilots."[103]

Despite the fact that, to the consternation of Signal Corps supply officers and installation crews, neither maintenance parts nor test sets IE–56 had arrived in England before D-day, all the American Rebecca-Eureka radar beacons had functioned properly. They emitted their responses as the Rebecca interrogators aboard the carrier planes approached within twenty miles. Only one Rebecca failed, AAF reported. Nor did the enemy jam the sets. If he had, the Allies would have been prepared with an alternate device employing microwaves since the Pathfinder troops carried down with

[98] For the story of Signal Corps development of the SCR–717 and other wartime radars and radio items of equipment, see Thompson, Harris, et al., The Test, Chapters III, VIII, and IX.

[99] (1) Wesley Frank Craven and James Lea Cate, eds., "The Army Air Forces in World War II," vol. III, Europe: ARGUMENT to V–E Day (Chicago: University of Chicago Press, 1951), pp. 188–89. (2) UTAH Beach to Cherbourg, p. 14. (3) Report by the Supreme Commander to the Combined Chiefs of Staff on the Operations in Europe of the Allied Expeditionary Force, 6 June 1944–8 May 1945 (hereafter cited as SCAEF Rpt), p. 23.

[100] Craven and Cate, eds., Europe: ARGUMENT to V–E Day, p. 188.

[101] FUSA, Rpt of Opns, 20 Oct 43–1 Aug 44, bk. VI, an. 12, p. 44.

[102] Incl, Rpt, CSigO, ETOUSA, Use of Radar in the Invasion of the Cherbourg Peninsula, 13 Jun 44, with Ltr, Actg Dir Tech Ln Div OCSigO ETOUSA to CSigO, 14 Jun 44, sub: Rebecca-Eureka Equipment. SCIA file Misc, European Theater, N–R folder 1.

[103] (1) FUSA, Rpt of Opns, 20 Oct 43–1 Aug 44, p. 119. (2) SCAEF Rpt, p. 23.

them a number of the very new radar beacons, AN/UPW. These were similar to Eurekas but operated on much higher frequencies in the S, or 10-centimeter, band, which responded to the radiations of the standard AI (airborne interception) and ASV microwave radars and gave visible indication on their oscilloscopes, just as the Eurekas did for the Rebeccas at much lower frequencies. As the carrier fleets came over the ground beacons, they flew at 500 to 600 feet elevation, determined by the low-level radar altimeter, AN/APN-1, and their paratroopers chuted into the darkness with a dropping accuracy of approximately plus or minus 400 yards. All together, it was by far a much better drop than previous ventures, in Sicily for example. It was the radar devices that made the difference in Normandy.[104]

The first Signal Corps troops to land in France were 28 men of the 101st Airborne Signal Company, who jumped with the division headquarters group and troops of the 3d Battalion of the 501st Parachute Infantry in the early morning darkness.[105] Of the 28, 21 dropped in the designated zone; the other 7, some

25 miles distant.[106] The men recovered only 4 of the 27 equipment bundles dropped; in them were 2 radios. The signalmen fought as infantrymen with the elements of the 501st, who marched on Pouppeville and captured it.[107]

Meanwhile other signalmen of the 101st also were engaged in combat. Making their preparations for the invasion, the men had remodeled one of the powerful long-range SCR-499's, mounting it in a 1/4-ton trailer, which could be towed by a jeep.[108] With the radio set crowded into one glider and the jeep into another, the men took off in the first flight of gliders from England. Four miles from the take-off point, the glider containing the jeep and its crew dropped. The other glider got away safely and landed under enemy fire. The signalmen unloaded the radio, hailed a passing jeep, and towed the set to the spot at Hiesville designated as division headquarters. They arrived while the men who had preceded them were fighting at Pouppeville. About 1800, the men got through to England with their first radio contact.[109] This SCR-499 did yeoman duty on D-day and for the rest of the first week of the invasion, serving the two airborne divisions as their link to England.

[104] (1) Baxter, *Scientists Against Time*, p. 87. (2) *SCAEF Rpt, 6 Jun 44–8 May 45*, p. 23. (3) Memo, Lt Col George F. Metcalf, Chief Electronics Div OCSigO, for Dir ARL, 3 Jul 44, sub: Visit to ETO. SCIA file European Theater folder 1–a. (4) Ltr, Maj Gen Robert W. Harper, ACofAS Tng, to CG I Troop Carrier Comd Stout Fld Indianapolis, Ind., sub: Use of Radar in Assault on France. AAG 413.44–AI Radar. (5) "Troops by Air," *Radar*, No. 3, pp. 24–29. (6) FUSA, *Rpt of Opns, 20 Oct 43–1 Aug 44*, bk. VI, an. 12, p. 44. (7) Rpt, CSigO ETOUSA, Use of Radar in the Invasion of the Cherbourg Peninsula, 13 Jun 44.

[105] AAR, 101st Airborne Sig Co, Report Normandy, 6 June–12 July 1944. Opns Rpt 3101–SIG-0.3.

[106] These seven joined other soldiers and fought their way through enemy territory toward the assembly area near Hiesville. Five of them made it on D plus 5; 2 were lost.

[107] (1) AAR, 101st Airborne Sig Co, Rpt Normandy. (2) Harrison, *Cross-Channel Attack*, pp. 283ff.

[108] The SCR-499 was the air-transportable version of the remarkably successful SCR-299, a complete vehicular radio station for communication between corps and division. SCR-499 components could be packed in crates of various sizes for air transport.

[109] AAR, 101st Airborne Sig Co, Rpt Normandy, p. 2.

The 82d Airborne Signal Company, dropping by parachute with the troops of the 82d Airborne Division at various locations in the vicinity of Ste. Mère-Eglise or coming in by glider, lost many men and much equipment. The radio section was seriously hampered—out of 6 high-powered sets sent into the combat zone, only one survived glider crash landings. Likewise, out of 13 low-powered sets brought in, only one was usable. In the first few days, a small wire platoon of 13 men struggled heroically to provide wire communications to 4 regiments and 20-odd organizations and attached units, besides operating switchboards at division headquarters. The magnitude of the task can be measured by the fact that a wire platoon serving a 3-regiment division ordinarily numbered 94 officers and men.[110]

Radio Countermeasures for the Invasion

Not all the Allied radio and radar emanations on the night preceding D-day were intended to direct and co-ordinate the operations of the invaders. A very considerable proportion of them sought to blind or deceive the enemy's eyes of radar and to deafen or deceive his ears of radio. It was especially necessary to jam his radars—in effect, to blind him during the crucial hours before the Allies established a beachhead. German confidence in *Festung Europa* rested heavily upon radar sets. The enemy had erected hundreds, of a dozen types, along the coasts, especially of course along the beaches facing England

from Dieppe to the tip of the Cherbourg peninsula. On one stretch the Germans had concentrated so many sets that there was one for each mile and a half of coast line.[111]

On the Allies' side of the Channel, radio countermeasure (RCM) plans, both to strike blind all radars in areas where the attack was coming and to create the appearance of a major attack where in fact only small deceptive forces were to operate, had long occupied the Allies. The planning required the most extensive co-operative action—British, American, Army, Navy. Through it all the Signal Corps played an important part, especially toward furnishing Signal Corps equipment, whatever the craft in which it was mounted or whatever the service responsible for operating it.[112] In the RCM planning for the invasion of Normandy, the British had predominated, "in view of the greater operational experience and resources of the RAF and to a lesser extent of the RN," as a British report put it.[113] American plans generally conformed to British proposals.

---

[110] Diary, 82d Airborne Sig Co, NEPTUNE Operations, 6 June–15 July 1944. Opns Rpt 382–Sig–0.3 (20178) Master.

[111] *Electronics Warfare, A Report on Radar Countermeasures,* released by the Jt Bd of Scientific Info Policy for OSRD, War and Navy Depts, revised 19 Oct 45 (Washington, 1945) (hereafter cited as *Electronics Warfare*), p. 18.

[112] E.g., AN/APQ–2, or Rug, which the Signal Corps had developed and produced for the Army Air Forces, was assigned in quantities to the Navy for use by the combined fleets in the invasion of the Continent, since it was "the only equipment available for use against the German Coastal Watch radars lining the European Coast." This set had first proved its value in mid-1943 during the invasion of Sicily. CSigO, Annual Rpt, FY 44, p. 322.

[113] Rpt No. JM/14 (2), Report on Electronics Countermeasures in Operation OVERLORD (hereafter cited as Rpt JM/14 (2)), pt. II, RCM Policy, Plng and Orgn, 22 Jul 44, sec. II, par. (24). SCIA file.

Jammers, both British and American, of many sizes and types, were marshaled to make utmost use of their capabilities. A thorough effort had already been made to bomb or shoot up all enemy stations, but not all the efforts of Ferret planes, photo missions, and espionage could pinpoint each of the many enemy radars for the bombers' attention. For the invasion, therefore, Allied planes and ships carrying RCM equipment sought to jam every enemy radar station that had escaped destruction. During the night before D-day, eight Royal Air Force craft and four American B–17's patrolled high over the south coast of England and the northwest French coast, operating Mandrel spot jammers (AN/APT–3's) tuned to the low frequencies of the enemy search radars, blinding them so that they could not see the vast air armadas forming over England and heading toward Normandy.

At H minus 7, before the leading elements of the invasion fleet came within range of German sea search detectors ashore, Allied shipborne radar jammers were switched on to blind the German scopes. When within range of enemy artillery on the beaches, the Allied crews retuned their jammers, moving from the frequencies of German search sets to the frequencies of their gun-laying radars, so as to disrupt radar-aided artillery fire against the invading ships. According to plan, some 240 low-power sets (AN/APQ–2's, or Rugs) aboard light landing craft formed the inshore screen. Offshore, 60 medium-power RCM sets operated from mine sweepers and destroyers. At sea, aboard cruisers and battleships, 120 high-power jammers added their bit to the electronic screen. This was the RCM onslaught, along

the main front from the sea, up to H-hour itself. Thereafter, certain ships were appointed to take over RCM control, their specialized crews listening for enemy radar and directing the jamming of it, using care not to interfere with the Allies' own radars, set up by this time on the beaches to watch for enemy planes and then direct gunfire. There was little jamming from land. England was too far away, except for basing the tremendous Tuba, or ground Cigar, one of which, set up near Brighton, was prepared to transmit in the 38- to 42-megacycle band with sufficient power to jam German aircraft communications across the Channel. There were available for the same purpose some airborne Cigar sets as well. The Allies also used some airborne jammers against the German long-range search Freyas.[114]

The invasion RCM was not by any means wholly direct jamming along the invasion front. A very valuable portion was deceptive radar measures staged in areas where there was to be no invasion. Radar, though a most potent weapon, could not only be jammed into blinded uselessness, but, ironically, could also be converted into a dangerous liability. RCM could be made deceptive, so manipulated as to produce target indications on an enemy's scope that would lead him into thinking large attacking forces were coming where there were none. Toward this end two diversions of a few ships and aircraft equipped to

[114] (1) Ibid., sec. 3, par. 27, sec. 4, par. 30, and an. N, app. B. (2) CSigO, Annual Rpt, FY 44 p. 321. (3) Joseph Reither, The Use of Radio and Radar Equipment by the AAF, 1939–45, AAF Hist Monograph, p. 149 of photostat copy in SigC Hist Sec file. (4) "Jamming on D Day; How It Upset Jerry's Radar Front," Radar, No. 6 (November 15, 1944), pp. 10–11. SigC Hist Sec file.

perpetrate RCM deception moved out—
one from Dover toward Calais and the
other from Newhaven toward Boulogne.
Their jammers, together with quantities
of aluminum foil (Chaff) dropped from
low-flying planes, gave the impression of
a huge fleet. Further plausibility was
lent by a few launches towing balloons
that carried radar reflectors. Some of the
diversion vessels also carried sonic equipment, another electronic innovation
in World War II. Sonic equipment consisted of nothing more than stentorian
loud-speakers, powered by large amplifiers and made articulate by record
players, whose records or recorded tape
emitted sounds that gave every indication of an approaching armada. In the
sky the British employed Moonshine,
metal foil kitelike reflectors that, when
towed or released by a few aircraft,
gave a radar picture of swarms of invading warplanes. All this RCM feint
worked especially well on the eastern
flank, causing the enemy to fire on the
fake armada and to send out E-boats on
the surface and fighter planes in the
air. As the German fighters circled vainly
in the night sky above Calais, wasting
valuable time and energy, the real invasion moved, free from air attack at
least, onto the invasion beaches from
SWORD to OMAHA. Thereafter, the RCM
offensive did not have to be maintained
as long or as intensely as planned, for
enemy resistance in the realms of air
and radar fast fell away.[115]

Communication on the Beaches

Troops of the U.S. V Corps landed on
OMAHA Beach on D-day meeting the fire
of the German 352d Division. Losses of
equipment were heavy. The 116th Infantry lost three-quarters of its radio sets
that morning, destroyed or waterlogged,
and command control suffered proportionately in that sector.[116] The 2d
Platoon of the 294th Joint Assault Signal
Company landed with elements of the
37th Engineer Combat Battalion at
OMAHA Beach during the first hour of
the assault. These signalmen, well
trained in amphibious operations, were
capable of carrying more than average
loads of equipment safely, but their vehicles were unloaded in deep water where
they had stalled and were hit by enemy
fire. Nevertheless, the men managed to
get most of their hand-carried items
ashore and turned them over to infantry troops and shore fire control parties
that had lost their communications
equipment in the fury and tumult of the
landings. With the remaining wire
equipment and salvaged bits of wire
picked up from the beaches, the JASCO
men, still under fire, set up a skeletal
wire system. This was the only communications system on the beach until noon
of D-day, when the 1st and 3d Platoons
landed, bringing with them enough
equipment to replace some of the losses
suffered by the 2d Platoon. A detachment
of the 293d Joint Assault Signal Company, which followed the 294th ashore,

---

[115] (1) *Electronics Warfare*, p. 20. (2) Rpt No.
JM/14 (2), 22 Jul 44, pt. II, sec. III, pars. 27 and
28, sec. 4, pars. 29 and 30; also Rpt No. JM/14
(4), pt. IV, 12 Aug 44, sec. VII. (3) "Radar Countermeasures," *The Engineer*, CLXXX, No. 4691
(December 7, 1945), 460–61.
There was also an extensive radio deception
program in the Calais-Boulogne area. See Winston

S. Churchill, "The Second World War," vol. V,
Closing the Ring (Boston: Houghton Mifflin Co.,
1951), p. 596.
[116] For an account of the over-all action on the
invasion beaches, see Harrison, *Cross-Channel Attack*, especially Chapter VIII.

lost one-third of its vehicles and half of its radio equipment when a shell struck the landing craft while it was still 350 yards offshore. Soon after landing, the men had a wire communications net under way (their D-day mission was to provide each element of the 6th Engineer Special Brigade with communications) and had established radio contact with the 116th Regimental Combat Team (RCT) by means of an SCR–300. At UTAH Beach, where the going was easier, the 286th Joint Assault Signal Company got ashore quickly and soon had wire communications functioning satisfactorily. The failure to get an SCR–193 ashore, however, left a gap in radio communication between the shore and the VII Corps' headquarters ship, the USS *Bayfield*, a gap the Navy fortunately plugged.[117]

During the initial assaults, the congestion in the water and on the beaches forced the abandonment of a plan for the JASCO's to lay field wire between headquarters ships and the troops on the beach; therefore radio became of the utmost importance.[118] However, the JASCO's spread their wire networks from 500 yards to a mile along the shore of the Cotentin peninsula and extended them from 5 to 12 miles inland. The biggest problem was to connect the forces on OMAHA and UTAH Beaches,

which was done initially by radio link, then by laying spiral-four cable.

The 1st Signal Company, serving the 1st Infantry Division, was divided into six main groups for separate loadings on separate ships. The first group of four officers and seventy-five men, landing at H plus 90, met heavy mortar, artillery, and machine gun fire and set up its first radio sets less than five feet from the water's edge. The sets communicated successfully with the regimental headquarters ashore and the division headquarters afloat. Later, when the machine gun nests had been cleared, the wire teams began laying their lines.[119]

According to the signal plan, an advance detachment of the 56th Signal Battalion attached to the 1st Infantry Division was to go ashore on OMAHA Beach at noon on D-day to install and operate V Corps' headquarters communications. However, only one wire team got ashore on schedule. The men faced a formidable task, more burdensome still because the wire team of the 29th Infantry Division had also failed to get ashore. There was little to work with; constant and heavy enemy fire harassed the men. They managed to install and maintain wire communications for both divisions and the beach—three point-to-point circuits that they kept in operation with a fair degree of success. No switchboard was available until the afternoon of D plus 1 when the rest of the advance detachment finally got ashore.[120]

Near evening on D-day the signal

[117] (1) FUSA *Rpt of Opns, 20 Oct 43–1 Aug 44,* bk. VI, an. 12, p. 16. (2) Col. Grant A. Williams, "First Army's ETO Signal Operations," *Signals,* II, No. 4 (March–April, 1948), 5–11. (3) OMAHA Beach. Folder No. 38, SigC Hist Sec file. (4) History of the 295th Joint Assault Signal Company, 1944. SGCO–294–0.1 (16389) Master. (5) Hist Sec ETOUSA, Opn Rpt, NEPTUNE, OMAHA Beach, 26 February–26 June 1944, Provisional Engineer Special Brigade Group, pp. 289–320.

[118] Williams, "First Army's ETO Signal Operations," *Signals,* II, No. 4, pp. 5–11.

[119] (1) AAR, 1st Sig Co, Jun–Dec 44. 301–SIG–0.3 (4873) M. (2) Hist Rpt, 1st Sig Co, 1 Jun–30 Jun 44. OP 370.2 Rpt folder 4 Gen, 13 Jul–30 Dec 44.

[120] FUSA, Sig Sv Hist Rcd, sec. V, p. 13. SCIA file European Theater folder 11-a.

officer of the 29th Division, Lt. Col. Gordon B. Cauble, and his signal headquarters detachment landed from an LCVP (landing craft, vehicle and personnel). They carried ashore two SCR–609's. As yet no communications net had been established on the battle-swept beach. The Signal Corps men of the 29th Division had been scattered aboard various vessels and were unable to follow their signal plan. Cauble and his men set up their 609's at the division command post in a rock quarry several hundred feet back from the beach. While running in a wire from a telephone line just laid on the beach, they succeeded in making radio contacts with a number of other adjacent units. "But it was D plus 2 before we really got our planned communication system established," Cauble later said. And even after they had located themselves in the cellar of a nearby chateau and after equipment and men began to accrue, communications remained a nightmare until American troops slackened the pace of their drive inland and wire lines caught up with them. "Wire communication was excellent by the fifth day," according to Cauble, "and after that, radio was not used in the higher echelons." [121]

At UTAH Beach, VII Corps communications lay in the capable hands of the veteran 50th Signal Battalion.[122] The battalion came ashore with the early waves of infantry at H plus 90. Of the various radio, message center, and wire teams, the forward section of the message center platoon under Lt. Alexius H. McAtee probably encountered the most frustrations. Prematurely landed in water so deep that most of their equipment was washed away, the men struggled ashore through heavy shelling and began operations as best they could. Battalion message center teams processed radio messages by flashlight throughout the night and in the morning initiated a "hitch-hike" messenger service to the 1st Engineer Special Brigade, since all message center vehicles had been washed away in landing.[123] Other advance elements of the 50th promptly set up radio communications for VII Corps headquarters and from corps to the 4th Infantry Division, the 82d and 101st Airborne Divisions, the Ninth Air Force, and the headquarters ships lying offshore.

Soon after H-hour, British and American ground radars went ashore. The American sets were LW's (light warning) such as the SCR–602's, SLC's (searchlight control) such as the SCR–268's, and the microwave sets such as the gun layer SCR–584.[124] They later included the huge 60-ton MEW radar, one of which landed on D plus 10. On the American beaches the initial air defense system included both American and British radars—at OMAHA, for example, a British GCI (ground controlled interception radar) and LW's of the American 555th Signal Aircraft Warning Battalion. They began landing late in the afternoon of D-day amid the litter on

---

[121] Interv, SigC Hist Sec with Cauble, 5 Jan 45. SigC Hist Sec file.

[122] The 50th Signal Battalion's overseas duty predated Pearl Harbor. It went to Iceland in September 1941 for two years, then moved to England late in 1943.

[123] History of the 50th Signal Battalion, September 1941–May 1945. SG BN 50-0 (27904) 207.03.

[124] Thirty-nine SCR–584's reached Normandy on D-day. "The SCR–584 Earns Its Keep," *Radar*, No. 5 (September 30, 1944), p. 3.

the sands while mortar and small arms fire continued to wound many of the men and severely damage some of the vehicles. The men moved the equipment over the beach and into the shelter of a draw east of St. Laurent-sur-Mer. By early the next morning the 555th Signal Aircraft Warning Battalion had its LW radars on the air and was reporting aircraft.[125] The few German planes that attacked the beaches found a hot and ready welcome.

All the radars were well prepared for the landings, however wild the surf and high the tide. One SCR–584 trailer van, which had failed to reach land, was discovered completely waterproof and airtight floating in the Channel. Towed to land and opened, it was found dry and ready to operate.[126] The 215th Signal Depot Company dried out, repaired, and reissued another set recovered from a sunken landing craft.[127]

Thus, despite all obstacles, men and equipment reached the beaches and beyond. The various networks rapidly went into operation: army, corps, and division command and point-to-point radio nets; regimental combat team radioteletypewriter and wire teletypewriter nets; separate telephone, teletypewriter, and radio nets for army and corps radio intelligence companies, including circuits to the G–2 of the headquarters served, and a cross-Channel net used jointly by the army company and the

Signal Intelligence Service, ETOUSA. Naval signal detachments established a beachmaster's boat control net and a beach net. During the assault the station on the FUSA headquarters ship entered two 21 Army Group command nets and established three FUSA command nets. The first of these included the corps headquarters and the Plymouth Signal Center; the second, an antiaircraft brigade and miscellaneous FUSA units; and the third, three engineer special brigades. Naval shore fire control nets also were in operation during the assault landings and till as late as the battle near Carentan and during the attack on Cherbourg. Forward troops made excellent use of FM radio. There were some disappointments, however. For example, the invasion plans had called for forty-four public address systems for use in the beach landings, but none had been received by 5 June and only sixteen were en route.[128]

Except in the worst of the battle-swept sectors, OMAHA communications were remarkably good. Radios and radars, large and small, got ashore and into operation without serious difficulties other than those imposed by the enemy. Radio frequencies were kept well in hand, with one exception. A powerful transmitter broke in upon the high frequency bands soon after D-day and caused considerable consternation. When it was found to be a commercial Press Wireless station broadcasting from the U.S. sector directly to New York, a suitable frequency was assigned to it.[129]

[125] Col. E. Blair Garland, "Radar in ETO Air–Ground Operations," *Signals*, III, No. 4 (March–April), 1949), p. 9.

[126] Harold Berman, SCEL, "The SCR–584: A Hard Hitting Radar Set," *Signals*, I, No. 2 (November–December, 1946), p. 41. For details of packaging these radars, see below, p. 424.

[127] MS Comment, Williams, Jul 59.

[128] CM–IN 3954–5, Jun 44, CG USASOS in British Isles to WD. SigC file, Hist of Proc of Beach Landing Public Address Systems AN/UIQ–1 DCSigO file.

[129] For details, see below, p. 110.

All together in the month of June, eighty-five complaints of interference in HF radio channels came to the Signal Division of SHAEF. All were corrected except three, whose sources of interference could not be discovered.[130] All in all the tremendously complex frequency plan for OVERLORD had succeeded well.

As in every invasion in the ETO since TORCH, communications ships played a basic role. Aboard the FUSA headquarters ship, the USS *Achernar*, a 50-man contingent from the 6th Signal Center Team and the 17th Signal Operations Battalion handled the communications center. The USS *Bayfield* served as the headquarters ship for VII Corps. Also present was the "Lucky" *Ancon*, overhauled after her brush with German bombs off Salerno.[131] The ship provided the communications headquarters of the V Corps under signal officer Col. Haskell H. Cleaves. Radio nets aboard these headquarters ships furnished communications between echelons of FUSA headquarters, both afloat and ashore in the initial days, as well as communications back to the army rear echelon in England.[132] The headquarters ships hovered off the beaches for five days until the command post of FUSA was safely in operation. Then the men who had operated the centers disembarked and reported for duty to the 17th Signal Operations Battalion.

The lodgment in Normandy secure, cable connections with England became established. Brigadier Harris and his American deputy, Col. William C. Henry of the Signal Corps, presided over the laying of the first cable from Southbourne, England, to the Normandy beach near Longues, a task completed on 10 June. The second cable, started soon after and parallel to the first, encountered ill fortune when the British cable ship *Monarch* was shot up by enemy gunfire on D plus 8. A Signal Corps photographer aboard her had been photographing the operation but his film was lost in the riddled chart room. By 17 June a second cable spanned the Channel and, with the aid of the first, assured large-scale communications. Hardly had the two vital lines been completed when ships dragging their anchors fouled and snapped both cables during the great storm of 20 June (D plus 14). Not till 24 June and 28 June were the broken ends of the first and second cables, respectively, picked up, miles of new cable spliced in, and the circuits restored.[133]

Radio Relay

Meanwhile, both the British and the American version of the new and tremendously significant innovation, multichannel radio relay, maintained heavy traffic loads. The equipment had been installed and put into operation much sooner than the cables. Moreover, it remained unaffected by the vagaries of the storms and hazards of the sea.

The American version of the equip-

---

[130] (1) Harris, *Signal Venture*, p. 201. (2) Lanahan, "Radio for OVERLORD," *Signals*, I, No. 4, p. 52. and "Signal Planning for the Invasion," *Signals*, I, No. 3, p. 36.

[131] See above, p. 47.

[132] (1) FUSA, *Rpt of Opns, 20 Oct 43–1 Aug 44*, bk. VI, an. 12, p. 16. (2) First Army Signal Section Historical Record, ETO, sec. I, pp. 9–12. SCIA file European Theater folder 11–a.

[133] (1) OVERLORD Rpt, III, 602, and chart, p. 655. (2) Harris, *Signal Venture*, pp. 202–05. (3) MS Comment, Waite, Jul 59.

ment—the antracs—performed with spectacular success. Among the many persons who waited out the first anxious hours of the invasion were the two civilian engineers, Waite and Colaguori. Some days earlier, it had been determined that one of the civilians "would have the rather doubtful privilege of going into France on D-day or shortly thereafter. A coin was tossed, two out of three, and Mr. Colaguori won." As Colaguori prepared his equipment and truck and drove to the docks, officers and men of ETOUSA's Technical Liaison Division helped Waite with the installation on the Isle of Wight, atop the hill called St. Catherine's. On St. Catherine's crest the British (and U.S. Navy, using British AM sets) had already placed the several terminals of the British VHF radio links intended to reach the British GOLD and JUNO Beaches.

On the rounded grassy summit of St. Catherine's stand the ruins of an ancient tower. A watchtower centuries old, it had witnessed signals before, for it had been used as a station for signaling the approach of enemy ships, including, on one renowned occasion, the Spanish Armada. More recently, the ruins had served as a landfall for the German air fleets. Now, as a final touch in this mixture of the hoary remote and fantastic new, the Signal Corps men installed the paraphernalia of the first antrac in Europe.

On D-day Waite and members of the 98oth Signal Company, specially trained on the AN/TRC–4 and newly arrived in the United Kingdom, began a long and anxious watch. "We could see the ships by the hundreds heading for France at our very feet almost," said Waite, "and others coming back . . . shell fire and bomb explosions were always audible and at night the distant red flashes. . . . One day passed, and then another. A British circuit came in first, much to my regret since I naturally wanted our boys to land first."

Fighting was heaviest at OMAHA. Colaguori, embarked on an LST with a unit of the engineers, could not get ashore throughout D-day. That night he succeeded, but it was many hours more before he could advance four hundred yards to the bluffs, where the fighting continued hotly.

Back on St. Catherine's hill, the Signal Corps men waited and worried. For seventy-two anxious hours they had no word from any American unit. Then at last, fourteen minutes past one o'clock on the afternoon of 8 June, they saw the indicator rise on the receiver meter, adjusted their equipment, and heard with complete clarity: "Hello, B for Bobbie; this is V for Victor." Waite, as soon as he could answer, replied with strict propriety, according to SOP: "Hello, V for Victor; this is B for Bobbie." Then with less propriety, "Where in hell have you been?" "What d'ya mean where have we been?" expostulated Colaguori at OMAHA Beach, "We've been through hell," punctuated by the nearby explosion of a German 88 shell, which the listeners in England heard clearly. Exchange of messages then began. Late that afternoon the first facsimile transmission passed over the complete length of the 125-mile relay from Middle Wallop to OMAHA Beach. Three or four days later, the headquarters of the First U.S. Army went ashore with carrier equipment, which immediately used the full potential of the antrac link as a

FIRST ANTRAC STATION IN EUROPE, ON ST. CATHERINE'S HILL, ISLE OF WIGHT

4-channel carrier system.[134] Scores and hundreds would follow as the demand for antracs reached a crescendo.

Lt. Col. John Hessel, formerly a civilian engineer at the Laboratories, now in Signal Corps uniform and serving in the Technical Liaison Division, Office of the Chief Signal Officer, ETOUSA, wrote triumphantly to a fellow engineer officer, Maj. William S. Marks, Jr., who was still serving in the Monmouth laboratories:

You will be glad to know that Victor went with Colonel Williams at a very early date and that cross-channel communication was established on the AN/TRC–1 on D plus 2 at 1314 hours. . . . The circuit has been in continuous operation without fading except for two periods of not more than one minute each. The general opinion seems to be that this is the most reliable cross-channel circuit yet put into operation.

These remarks bore a 14 June date. A continuation, dated 20 June, adds: "Information has just been received that Colonel Williams has been decorated by General Bradley for the conspicuous success of his communications. The last report received is that the circuit is still on 24-hour-per-day operation and carrying capacity traffic with no failure and no breakdown." [135]

---

[134] (1) Waite-Colaguori Rpt. (2) MS Comment, Waite, Jul 59.

[135] Ltr, Hessel to Marks, Camp Coles Sig Lab, 14 Jun 44. SigC 413.44, AN/TRC–1, 1943-45 (ET-2534).
"Waite and Colaguori both received Bronze Stars but much later." MS Comment, Waite, Jul 59.

The British sets on St. Catherine's worked well except during the warm parts of the day, when they faded out because of their AM characteristics. The American FM gear, on the other hand, did not lose modulation when signal strength weakened a bit during the midday hours. At such times, the American set provided cueing for the British to their installations at Caen.[136]

Facsimile transmission, too, received high praise. Photo reconnaissance planes took the pictures and flew them back to Middle Wallop for developing and identifying. Seven minutes after they were put on the facsimile machine on the Middle Wallop antrac, they had been received on OMAHA Beach and were being rushed to the gun control officer. The gunners had a continuing picture of enemy gun emplacements, tanks, and other targets concealed behind hedgerows, buildings, and terrain. Facsimile equipment transmitted typewritten material, line drawings, and photographs with equal ease.[137]

General Rumbough greeted the antracs enthusiastically. "This operation," he reported to General Ingles, "marks an important milestone in military radio communication. Tactical field radio equipment has been successfully integrated with wire line and terminal equipment to form a system comparable in reliability and traffic capacity to all-wire systems."[138]

Pigeons also landed on D-day, about five hundred of them. They were used to carry ammunition status reports, undeveloped film, and emergency messages. Communications by other means were so good, however, that the pigeon messengers were not used extensively.[139]

Communications for the Press

"Press communications," said General Lanahan, "is one of the most difficult problems facing an Army involved in modern mobile warfare." [140] Arrangements for press communications had occupied a large place in SHAEF signal planning, especially since it was well understood that President Franklin D. Roosevelt took a personal interest in communications for the press. To bolster the planning, Lanahan had obtained the services of Col. David Sarnoff, in civil life the president of RCA, to head the SHAEF section dealing with communications facilities for public relations matters.[141]

The generally unsatisfactory arrangements for press communications in the North African invasion clearly indicated

[136] MS Comment, Waite, Jul 59.

[137] (1) *Ibid.* (2) Waite–Colaguori Rpt, p. 29.

[138] Ltr, Rumbough to CSigO, 2 Jul 44, sub: VHF Radio Com. SCIA file 4 Rumbough Rpts folder 2. "Radio relay equipment," General Rumbough later declared in retrospect, "is a revolutionary development in communication." In fact, radio relay alone preserved communications on more than one occasion, when wire could not keep pace during

the onrush of American armies in Europe. Rumbough, "Radio Relay," *Military Review*, XXVI, No. 2, pp. 3–12, *passim.*

[139] (1) Ltr, 1st Lt Thomas H. Spencer, Comdg 2d Platoon (Sep) 280th Sig Pigeon Co, to SigO 12th AGp, 27 Jul 44, sub: Transmittal of Pigeon Rpt, and Incl, Use of Pigeons in the Invasion of France. SCIA file European Theater folder 1–a. (2) Pigeons on D-day, SigC Tech Info Ltr 43 (Jun 45), p. 17.

[140] Lanahan, "Signal Planning for the Invasion," *Signals*, I, No. 3, p. 36. "Press communications" included communications for press copy, live and recorded voice broadcasts, still and motion pictures, and service messages concerning these matters.

[141] Ltr, Lanahan to Col Roscoe C. Huggins, 31 Oct 57.

that a better plan must be provided for OVERLORD. In North Africa, the special broadcasting detachment organized to expedite press traffic back to the United States had been unable to perform its mission satisfactorily. The group of ten officers and twenty enlisted men was too small and, lacking its own communications equipment, had to depend on other organizations to handle the traffic. As a result, traffic was delayed, sometimes as long ·as several days.[142]

For OVERLORD, SHAEF on 29 December 1943 activated the provisional 6808th Publicity and Psychological Warfare Service Battalion.[143] Its mission, in addition to handling psychological warfare matters, was to house, feed, transport, and provide communications for the small army of war correspondents accredited to the U.S. armies for the operation.[144] The battalion was made up of hand-picked men from units already in the theater, plus specially selected personnel sent from the United States. Mobile radio broadcasting companies, originally called signal combat propaganda companies, were absorbed by the battalion. On 8 March 1944 the battalion was reorganized under TOE 30–46 as the 72d Publicity Service Battalion.[145]

A communications platoon of 106 men was provided in order to operate a one-kilowatt radio station and its associated terminal equipment, which would provide circuits to England, from which point the traffic would be relayed to the United States over commercial channels. Divided into four teams—a group of 15 men for each of the two American armies, First and Third, another group of 33 to remain in London, and a fourth team of 43 men assigned to 1st U.S. Army Group (later to 12th Army Group) —the platoon was slated to handle all press traffic for the U.S. armies on the Continent during the first sixty days of the operation. Two selected commercial companies, Press Wireless and Mackay Radio and Telegraph, would then establish circuits from the Continent direct to the United States.[146] Press Wireless was to become operational on D plus 60; Mackay, on D plus 90.

Press Wireless men and equipment landed in England a month before D-day, and Mackay crews arrived on the scene two weeks later. Press Wireless had brought along not only a 15-kilowatt transmitter but also a spare 400-watt transmitter just in case it might be needed to key the larger transmitter remotely. Meanwhile, Lt. Col. James B. Smith, the Signal Corps officer who served as communications officer of the Publicity and Psychological Warfare Section of FUSAG, was eaten up by worry—his 1-kilowatt transmitter (SCR–399) and its associated equipment had not arrived. Without it, the 72d Publicity Service Battalion would be helpless to move the press traffic according to plan. When he confided his worries to the Press Wireless crew, they offered him the use of their spare 400-watt transmitter until his SCR–399 arrived.[147]

---

[142] Lt Col James B. Smith, Communications for the Press (1950), Sig Sch Monograph. The Sig Sch Libr, Ft. Monmouth, p. 4.

[143] Hq ETOUSA, GO 99.

[144] (1) 12th AGp Report of Operations, XIV, 26–36. (2) Smith, Com for the Press, p. 4.

[145] 12th AGp, Rpt of Opns, XIV, 27–28.

[146] (1) SHAEF, NEPTUNE, Sig Instrs, pt. I, sec. XIX, item 8, par. 2. (2) Smith, Com for the Press, p. 5.

[147] The SCR–399 actually did arrive two days before D-day.

Smith countered by asking if the Press Wireless organization would be willing to take their 400-watt transmitter to France and operate it directly to the United States, if such an arrangement could be made. The Press Wireless men "jumped at the chance to give it a try." [148] They believed that their transmitter could reach the United States directly and that it would be able to operate for as long as two hours a day. After that, they thought, it could easily work back to England, from whence traffic could be relayed.

Smith set about "selling" his somewhat unorthodox plan. Journeying to Bristol to confer with First Army's Colonel Williams, Smith explained the plan and added that he would require some additional items of signal equipment to complete the station. Colonel Williams had only one question— Would it work? Assured that it would, he agreed and ordered his supply officer to give Smith the needed items to complete the station. They were in Smith's hands that same day. [149]

At higher headquarters, Smith encountered more scepticism. Many officers were of the opinion that the arrangement would not work. Then the problem of frequencies arose. A SHAEF frequency assignment officer agreed to wire the United States asking for a frequency assignment for the Press Wireless transmitter, and two days later a message from the United States arrived assigning the frequencies. Unfortunately, in his letter to SHAEF asking for the frequency assignment, Smith had neglected to mention that it was for a

commercial circuit, and SHAEF assumed that the circuit was to be operated by the Army. Thus the frequencies assigned were not commercial. [150]

Certainly no news event in history created more interest than the official announcement on 6 June 1944 of the Allied invasion of Normandy. While the world waited anxiously for news, the twenty-seven selected war correspondents who had accompanied the First Army struggled to get their dispatches written, approved by the censors, and sent. [151] In the American sector, the press radio circuits proved a sad disappointment. Six men of the communications platoon from the 72d Publicity Service Battalion landed about H plus 8. They carried with them a British 76 set, which they were to operate back to the base group in England until such time as the rest of the men could land with their SCR–399. The British set proved unsatisfactory for this purpose. [152] Furthermore, the scheduled Navy dispatch boat courier service to take press dispatches back to England failed to materialize until a week after D-day. For the first five days the airplanes and ships evacuating the wounded carried press copy back to the United Kingdom. [153] In addition, the Army carried a limited amount of press traffic over its operational circuits.

The Press Wireless transmitter was landed on the beaches of Normandy, in the First Army sector, on D plus

---

[148] Smith, Com for the Press, p. 7.
[149] Ibid.

[150] Ibid., p. 8.
[151] For an informal account of the problems of the military with war correspondents in general, see Col. Barney Oldfield, *Never A Shot in Anger* (New York: Duell, Sloan and Pearce, 1956).
[152] 12th AGp, Rpt of Opns, XIV, 103.
[153] Ibid., p. 47.

6. Testing out the equipment, the Press Wireless crew sent out the prearranged call letters—SWIF (Somewhere in France)—using none of the four frequencies that had been assigned for the circuit, but rather another commercial frequency that the company had used in transmitting from Paris to the United States before the war. To the amazement of all the technicians who had doubted that the 400-watt transmitter could span the ocean effectively, the Press Wireless receiving station in Long Island, New York, responded immediately, reporting perfect reception.[154]

Meanwhile Colonel Williams was under siege from the frustrated war correspondents, who demanded the use of Army circuits to file their press copy since the facilities the Army had provided for the press had not proved usable. Williams "did not propose to bog down (his) circuits to England with thousands of words of press material."[155] Since he was not authorized to permit Press Wireless to begin operating until SHAEF gave the word, pressure built up. Finally, after consulting G–2, who assured him that anything passed by G–2 censors could be sent, Williams told the Press Wireless team to go ahead. Press copy started streaming direct to the United States.

At SHAEF consternation reigned. Not only had the press transmitter opened without official sanction, it was also operating on an unauthorized frequency. Unable to get an official explanation, SHAEF sent a peremptory order to First Army to close down the

transmitter. Williams complied.[156] Then, in his own words, "All hell broke loose on my head." Eventually the furious complaints of all the news agencies and their correspondents carried the day, and the Press Wireless transmitter was permitted to begin operation again. As it turned out, transmission was good for sixteen hours a day rather than the two hours a day originally thought possible. As the SHAEF Signal Section ruefully remarked in a staff study prepared some months after the incident, "Although no known harm was done [by the unauthorized transmission] the potential danger of such occurrences to operations was great."[157]

On D plus 16, the powerful SCR–399 originally intended for the 72d Publicity Service Battalion arrived on the Continent and at once established contact with the United Kingdom. This circuit could have handled a maximum of 600,000 words daily, but it was used very little. For one thing, "the PRO was unaware of the establishment of the circuit or the capacity of traffic it might have handled."[158] For another, the commercial medium of transmission, more familiar to the newsmen, was transmitting directly to the United States. For the first ten days even the British press correspondents filed their copy with Press Wireless, which transmitted it to the United States and then back to the United Kingdom. After that the military established a teleprinter circuit from the beachhead back to the 72d's

[154] (1) Smith, Com for the Press, p. 12. (2) Oldfield, Never A Shot in Anger, p. 88.

[155] Ltr, Williams to Huggins, 31 Oct 57.

[156] (1) Ibid. (2) Incl 2, SHAEF, Sig Sec Staff Study, Press Communications, Oct 44, with Ltr, Lanahan, SigO SHAEF, to Ingles, CSigO, 8 Dec 44. SCIA file European Theater folder 6.

[157] Incl 2, SHAEF, Staff Study, Press Com, Oct 44.

[158] 12th AGp, Rpt of Opns, XIV, 103.

AEF Public Relations Activities, SHAEF Headquarters. *Technicians operate a record player (above) during an overseas broadcast. Newsmen at work in an improvised press wireless room (below).*

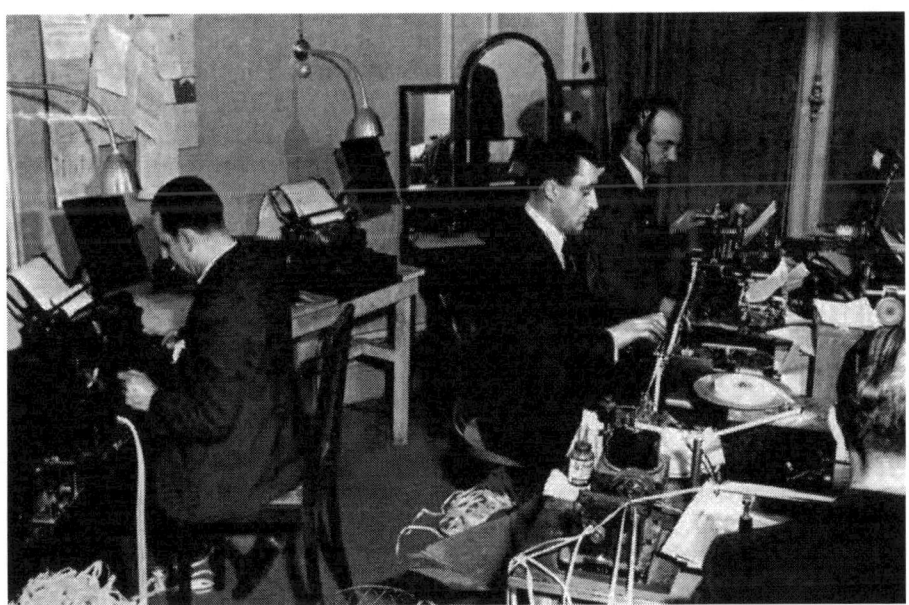

base group in London to permit the British correspondents to send their dispatches to London by direct circuit. Another SCR–399, modified for voice broadcast to London, received fairly heavy use since it provided the only means available for this purpose.

When Third Army became operational, in August 1944, it too demanded a direct press circuit back to the United States. The Mackay commercial service provided this circuit. The 2d Army Group Communications Team had accompanied Third Army to the Continent, bringing along an SCR–399 for transmitting press copy to London. When the breakout came, Third Army began moving so fast that there was no possibility of putting in a teleprinter circuit from Third Army headquarters back to London. Thus the SCR–399 became the only means of getting press copy direct to London.[159]

Photography

On D-day the combat photographers' movie and still picture cameras covered every facet of the landings. The cameramen of FUSA's 165th Signal Photographic Company were mostly photographic specialists who had received their training at the Academy of Motion Picture Arts and Sciences in Los Angeles. The company commander, Capt. Herman Wall, had spent months preceding D-day training his men for the part they were to play in the invasion. He had arranged to send back early photographs of the invasion by carrier pigeon, and three boxes of birds accompanied the photographers who embarked early

on the morning of D-day in an LCVP. The first pictures Wall sent back to England by carrier pigeon in the early morning hours. About 1030, as his craft approached the beach, he released a second bird carrying other negatives of the approach. About 1130 the LCVP beached, and the men started ashore. For nearly an hour Wall and his men photographed activities on their section of the landing area. Then, as they started down the beach in another direction, Wall was hit and badly wounded. For nearly three hours Wall and other wounded men lay in the field of fire where no one could come to their assistance. Finally a Dukw maneuvered close enough to permit men to risk coming in to get the wounded. Aboard a British boat, the men received medical attention. A section of Wall's leg that was badly mutilated had to be amputated.[160]

The Leica camera Wall had been using still hung about his neck. A ship's officer removed it, but Wall protested vigorously, insisting that the exposed film it contained was extremely important and that he could not be separated from the film until it was delivered safely into the hands of the proper authorities. In his own words: "In fact, I created such a fuss that the camera, with film, was returned." The next day an Army Pictorial Service representative picked up the film from the hospital in England where Wall was being treated. When the film was processed, it contained thirty-five perfect negatives of excellent quality, the first to be re-

---

[159] *Ibid.*, p. 104.

[160] (1) Opns Rpt, 165th Sig Photo Co, Sig Sv Hq ETOUSA. Admin 572–C. (2) Hq ETOUSA OCSigO, Current Info Ltr (Jul 44), pp. 36–39. SigC Hist Sec file.

INVASION PICTURE TAKEN BY CAPTAIN WALL

ceived of the actual landings. Within a few hours they were on their way to Washington by radiophoto transmission.[161]

Detachment P of the 290th Signal Photographic Company hit OMAHA Beach with the 5th Engineers Special Brigade. Lt. George Steck, his two enlisted still photographers, and two motion picture cameramen started their

photographic record as dawn broke on D-day. The first assault wave had already left the ship in the predawn darkness, but the photographers dared not use even a single flash bulb lest it alert the German defenders on shore. When daylight came, they started grinding out their invasion picture record, photographing the engineers waiting to go into battle. Their cameras caught the poignant vignettes of war—men checking their equipment, men saying goodbye to their friends, and the first casualties being brought back to the ship.

---

[161] *Ibid.*

Capt. Wall was later awarded the Distinguished Service Cross. Hq ETOUSA OCSigO, Current Info Ltr (Sep 44), p. 30.

First came five half-drowned crewmen from a tank that had been sunk going in with the first assault wave. Then the wounded from the beach started coming back. The boats carrying them were unloaded, then filled with the men going in with the second assault wave. The photographers climbed down into one of the pitching LCT's [162] (landing craft, tank).

It was late afternoon before the Germans were driven far enough back to let the engineers begin their work. Cruising in through a mine field, the LCT landed and the cameramen started taking their pictures—of German 88's hitting the water, casting up huge plumes of spray; of medical corpsmen working ceaselessly administering aid to the wounded; of men who had been killed even before they reached the shore; of the first groups of German prisoners; of the American soldiers methodically working their way forward toward the enemy. When night fell, the photographers captioned their pictures and sought a boat going to England, a boat to carry these first films back.[163]

When morning came, it was possible to see the first threads of the great cocoon that was the beachhead taking shape. Amid the scenes of destruction there was also purposeful activity— LCT's being unloaded, roads being built, bulldozers busy everywhere. By midafternoon the unfolding drama of the beachhead being cleared and transformed into a supply base was emerging. Beach track was being laid and the multitude of German mines were being cleared away. Boats of every sort, crammed with supplies, were coming to the beaches. Communications were being set up. The backbreaking work of the supply forces, the long and tedious job of consolidation, had begun.[164]

[162] Hq ETOUSA OCSigO, Current Info Ltr (Sep 44), pp. 18–19.

[163] *Ibid.*, p. 20.
[164] *Ibid.*, pp. 21–22.

CHAPTER IV

The Signal Corps in the ETO
to V–E Day—I

The initial assault on the Normandy beaches gained the Allies a tenuous toehold. Afterward came six weeks of bitter fighting as they struggled for room in which to build up a force large enough to exploit their potential material superiority.[1] The Germans fought tenaciously to contain the beachhead. They were aided by a freakish turn of exceptionally bad weather that not only seriously hampered efforts to land supplies across the beaches but also cut down the effectiveness of Allied air superiority. At the same time, the Allies benefited by the persistence with which the German command, convinced in part by Allied electronic deception, clung to the belief that the Pas-de-Calais area constituted the real point of invasion, with Normandy but a diversion.[2] One important element of this deception involved teams of the 3103d Signal Service Battalion, set up in southeast England. The radio net they simulated completely deceived the Germans,

making them think that an American army of three divisions was readying to invade France by way of the Pas-de-Calais, as captured German radio intelligence reports and maps later proved.[3]

In the initial lodgment and build-up in Normandy, as in the continued "threat" to the Pas-de-Calais area, the Signal Corps played its part. The Signal tasks were extremely varied. This account can underscore only a minute fraction of the signal work in the ETO, and it must be understood that what is not discussed contributed no less to the successful outcome than that which has been chosen as typical, or as unique.

Signal Techniques With the Armies

Expanding and Extending Communications

Within a week of D-day, radio, wire, and teleprinter circuits provided reliable communications links for all headquarters and all army echelons. First Army construction teams had begun to replace their hastily laid field wire with

[1] Forrest C. Pogue, *The Supreme Command,* UNITED STATES ARMY IN WORLD WAR II (Washington, 1954), pp. 170–91.

[2] General Eisenhower reported, "I cannot overemphasize the decisive value of this most successful threat, which paid important dividends, both at the time of the assault and during the operations of the two succeeding months." *SCAEF Rpt,* p. 27.

[3] (1) Capt Robert C. Doctor, Cover Plan and Signal Deception (Theater), World War II (1950), Sig Sch Monograph, p. 14. The Sig Sch Libr, Ft. Monmouth. (2) 12th AGp, Rpt of Opns, XI (Sig), 155–56, 178.

spiral-four cable and were swarming over the commercial lines leading to Cherbourg, rehabilitating and readying communications for that port city, once it should be captured. By mid-July this work engaged all the construction units in the theater—the 32d, 35th, and 40th Signal Construction Battalions and the 255th and 257th Signal Construction Companies.[4] A communications control office manned by the signal operations officers of the 17th Signal Operations Battalion and the 32d and 35th Signal Construction Battalions kept in constant touch with all phases of the signal work. These officers were empowered to reroute circuits, patch out defective facilities, and transfer troops when necessary to maintain communications. The radio nets handled 20,000 groups daily from 26 June to 24 July.[5]

Cherbourg fell on 27 June. An advance detachment of two officers and ten enlisted men of the 297th Signal Installation Company moved in at once to start repairs on the badly damaged Cherbourg exchange of the French Postes Télégraphes et Téléphones (PTT). Laboring sixteen hours a day, the men succeeded in finishing temporary repairs by 10 July, when they turned the job over to the 3111th Signal Service Battalion to complete the work and establish a permanent installation.

Within a day or two, a makeshift message center and a properly secured crypto room were operating. Cherbourg rapidly became an important communications center.[6]

While the British Second Army pinned down enemy strength around Caen, the U.S. First Army pivoted south after the fall of Cherbourg, attacking toward St. Lô. Two weeks of bloody fighting by the 29th Division yielded the vital railroad center on 19 July and unlocked the gateway out of Normandy.[7]

The first weeks of operations brought new developments at the FUSA headquarters level. At each location, complete communications had to be established between headquarters and all essential tactical units. Initially, the Signal Corps set up its telephone and teletypewriter centrals in tents, in deference to General Bradley's wish that his entire command post be under canvas.[8] In mid-July, when 12th Army Group became operational and General Bradley assumed command, General Hodges became FUSA's commander.[9] Hodges preferred his command post to be located indoors. Moving exceedingly heavy and bulky Signal Corps equipment into buildings built several centuries before Signal Corps equipment was invented proved difficult. When the men tried to shove it through doors or windows, it usually got hopelessly stuck.

---

[4] The 40th Signal Construction Battalion was one of several Negro units in the ETO that performed outstandingly, and earned high praise from Rumbough and from its own officers. (1) Capt Frederick Reinstein, Study of Signal Corps Unit Training, 1942–44 (1945), SigC Hist Monograph C–10, pp. 20–21. SigC Hist Sec file. (2) Interv, SigC Hist Sec with Col George F. Westerman (former CO Hq Co 40th Sig Const Bn), 21 Jun 58.

[5] FUSA, Rpt of Opns, 20 Oct 43–1 Aug 44, bk. VI, an. 12, pp. 18–20.

[6] Opns Rpt folder, Cherbourg Campaign, pp. 12–13. ETOUSA Sig Sec, Admin 572–E.

[7] For a detailed account, see Martin Blumenson, Breakout and Pursuit, UNITED STATES ARMY IN WORLD WAR II (Washington, 1961), pp. 79–182.

[8] Ltr, Williams to Thompson, 31 Oct 57.

[9] (1) Hq ETOUSA GO 73, 14 Jul 44. (2) Hq 12th AGp GO 1, 14 Jul 44. Both in Sig Sec 12th AGp Hist.

In any event, Colonel Williams had to prepare for a rapid advance once FUSA broke out of the beachhead. Completely mobile communications centers would be needed. He had the men of the 175th Signal Repair Company and the 215th Signal Depot Company install the telephone switchboard and main frame in 10-ton ordnance vans that Col. John B. Medaris, FUSA's ordnance officer, provided. When in operation, the two vans were lined up tailgate to tailgate with the backs open. The quartermaster officer, Col. Andrew T. McNamara, furnished canvas covers that could be laced around the two van bodies to keep out rain and permit operation under blackout conditions. The electronic equipment—the army switchboard and teleprinter switchboard, the reperforator equipment and the teleprinters, the highly secret enciphering equipment and the auxiliary equipment —everything not already in self-contained vans went into repair trucks, vans, or specially built shelters in cargo trucks. The men also built duplicate sets so that one could be installed and operating in a new command post before the army commander left his old one. Previously, all of Williams' carrier equipment associated with the radio relay had been installed in vehicles.[10]

When the breakout came and FUSA began moving rapidly, the mobile communications centers stood ready to accompany either tactical headquarters or main headquarters. FUSA's command post moves became virtually painless, considering the complexity of such an operation. Colonel Williams would se-

lect the next command post forward and would move his stand-by communications control to that point while the duplicate equipment was still in operation at the old post. Usually General Hodges and his section chiefs seized the opportunity afforded by a command post move to visit the front lines or to inspect depots and other installations. As Hodges had remarked, "I never move anywhere until Williams tells me I can." Ten or twelve hours later, the communications equipment would be set up at the new site, local extension telephones installed to the various staff sections of the army headquarters, trunk lines to the old command post to the rear spliced through, and everything ready for business at the new site. At the height of the rush across France and Belgium, FUSA's command post moved on an average of every four days.[11]

Since FUSA was the only American army to take part in the landings and initial combat on the Continent, it contained some of the best-trained and most experienced signal units. In general throughout the campaign, most of FUSA's signal operations progressed with remarkable smoothness. As FUSA pressed inland, wire assumed the principal communications load.[12] FUSA used all types of wire circuits—field wire, spiral-four, rapid pole line, British multiairline, open wire line, and commercial open line and underground cable

---

[10] (1) Williams, "First Army's ETO Signal Operations," *Signals*, II, No. 4, 11. (2) Ltr, Williams to Thompson, 31 Oct 57.

[11] Ltr, Williams to Thompson, 31 Oct 57. Commented Williams, "When FUSA closed out operations at the end of the war in Europe and we tried to move both sets of headquarters equipment at the same time, I suddenly discovered that the 17th Signal Operations Battalion had more vehicles than it had men!" MS Comment, Williams, Jul 59.

[12] See below, p. 124.

555TH SIGNAL AIR UNIT *spotting enemy planes somewhere in France.*

facilities. FUSA wire crews were so busy with urgent combat needs that they had no time until after the fall of Aachen to rehabilitate their first large commercial repeater station.[13]

Colonel Williams described FUSA's radio intelligence service as "very efficient from the very first day." The members of the traffic analysis units, some of the most intelligent men in the Army, performed particularly well. FUSA's army and corps radio intelligence companies possessed their own telephone, teletypewriter, and radio nets, and the army unit (the 113th Signal Radio Intelligence Company) was

in a cross-Channel net with the Signal Intelligence Service, ETOUSA.[14]

Strict attention to signal repair work kept FUSA signal maintenance to a minimum. As for supply, Williams had few complaints, describing it as "almost beyond reproach."[15] FUSA's photographic service, supplied by the 165th Signal Photographic Company, provided assignment units to each corps and division. The 165th became something of a legend in the theater; its photographers suffered more casualties and garnered more decorations than the men of any other Signal Corps unit in the ETO.[16]

One communications problem never solved to Colonel Williams' complete satisfaction was close-support communications between tanks and infantry.[17] The Signal Corps tried putting microphones and telephones on the rear of tanks, connected with the tank interphone system through holes drilled in the armor. This proved unsatisfactory because an infantryman could not keep up with the tank and still protect himself in those crucial combat situations when he needed communications most desperately. Trying another approach, Signal adapted SCR–510's, portable vehicular radio sets that would work on tank radio frequencies, altering the sets so that they could be carried on soldiers' backs. But the 510 weighed twenty-seven

---

[13] (1) FUSA, *Rpt of Opns,* 20 *Oct 43–Aug 44,* bk. VI, an. 12, *passim.* (2) Williams, "First Army's ETO Signal Operations," *Signals,* II, No. 4, pp. 8–9.

[14] (1) Williams, "First Army's ETO Signal Operations," *Signals,* II, No. 4, p. 11. (2) ETOUSA Rpt, pp. 106–08.

[15] Williams, "First Army's ETO Signal Operations," *Signals,* II, No. 4, p. 11. For a less favorable view, see remarks of Col. Elmer L. Littell, Williams' supply officer, below, pp. 147, 150.

[16] (1) CSigO, Annual Rpt, FY 45, p. 23. (2) MS Comment, Williams, Jul 59.

[17] For a discussion of the general problems of tank-infantry co-ordination in Normandy, see Blumenson, *Breakout and Pursuit.*

pounds—"When the going got rough, the foot soldiers simply abandoned them." [18] Finally, just before the Ardennes-Alsace Campaign, FUSA signal troops put lightweight SCR–300 infantry pack sets into the turrets of some lead tanks. This provided suitable communications, but at the cost of added discomfort to the tank crew, cooped up in a space already overcrowded.

Among the Signal Corps troops serving General Patton and the Third Army, morale was very high in spite of unusually difficult communications problems created by Third U.S. Army's (TUSA's) rapid sweep across France. Colonel Hammond, who had served Patton as his signal officer in North Africa and in the Sicily Campaign, was charged with maintaining Third Army's far-flung, ever-shifting, and complex communications network.[19]

Third Army began operations short of signal units, equipment, and suitable frequency assignments. The TUSA drive developed so rapidly that the planned wire system could not be used. Usually wire crews had time to install only one spiral-four circuit to each corps. A shortage of radios and radio operators forced Colonel Hammond to put more stations than was desirable into a single net. At times, when as many as five stations were netted, the net control station had found difficulty using special antennas in all

of the directions required. Moreover, the far-ranging units became widely separated—too far away for effective ground wave reception, yet too close for 24-hour sky wave operations.[20] Communications with VIII Corps in Brittany were almost impossible to maintain. By early September, VIII Corps, attacking Brest nearly four hundred miles from TUSA headquarters, became a part of Lt. Gen. William H. Simpson's Ninth U.S. Army, which had become operational on 5 September.[21]

In the first month of operations, the TUSA command post moved eight times for an average distance of 48 miles each move. In this situation Colonel Hammond's 100-mile radio relay systems became indispensable. The sets had arrived at the very last moment, the first one hurriedly installed in weapons carriers by the civilian engineers Waite and Colaguori, working with men from TUSA's 187th Signal Repair Company.[22] The equipment was used catch-as-catch-can, by men who had had time for only a few hours of instruction in its use, on TUSA's drive to the Moselle. All across France the two engineers kept moving the relay systems from hill to hill, patching the sets as best they could and praying that they would work. Fortunately they did, and the radio relay proved to be a very important factor in keeping General Patton in touch with other Allied forces in the drive across France.[23] Colonel Ham-

[18] (1) John J. Kelleher, "VHF and Microwave Military Communications," *Signals*, I, No. 4 (March–April, 1947), p. 47. (2) Williams, "First Army's ETO Signal Operations," *Signals*, II, No. 4, p. 10.

[19] (1) TUSA AAR, 1 Aug 44–9 May 45, pt. 22, p. 5. (2) "'Demon' Hammond . . . that chunky, insatiably curious West Pointer, was constantly being called on to perform miracles. He never failed." Robert S. Allen, *Lucky Forward* (New York: Vanguard Press, 1947), p. 55.

[20] TUSA AAR, p. 16.

[21] (1) Col. Elton F. Hammond, "Signals for Patton," *Signals*, II, No. 1, p. 10. (2) Blumenson, *Breakout and Pursuit*, pp. 636–37.

[22] See below, pp. 126ff.

[23] Interv, SigC Hist Sec with Col O'Connell, CO SCEL, 14 Apr 47. SigC Hist Sec file.

mond used the sets point-to-point over distances as great as 75 miles. All together, during August, his men installed 28 radio relay circuits, operating over distances totaling 1,175 miles.[24]

Colonel Hammond's scheme for advancing TUSA headquarters, more or less typical of all such operations, was a leapfrog arrangement. On arrival at a new command post, General Patton would select the location for the next command post forward. Hammond would extend his wire axis toward that point. An advance group, always in radio communication with the rear, went forward to select the actual site as soon as the area fell into Third Army's hands. Usually the advance party was headed by Hammond's efficient deputy, Col. Claude E. Haswell.[25] Within a few hours Waite, Colaguori, and their crews would set up the radio relay stations. The new location became LUCKY FORWARD (LUCKY being the code name for Patton's headquarters). When it was certain that full wire communication would be in service at this point, the forward echelon would move in and the process would be repeated. The previous command post then became LUCKY REAR. Since LUCKY REAR did not displace with each forward move, the lines of communication were often greatly extended, both to the front and to the rear.[26] At times during August as many as six or seven radio

relay stations trailed out behind Hammond all the way to Brest.[27]

Logistical considerations, most of all a shortage of gasoline, halted Third Army for a time west of the Moselle River at the end of August.[28] Gasoline shortages also hampered signal operations, particularly the work of the construction battalions. The TUSA signal units required nearly 5,000 gallons of gasoline daily.[29] Other shortages—signal supply and signal troops—plagued Hammond when operations resumed. The signalmen he now and then received as replacements always needed more training since the extremely abbreviated courses they had taken in the United States did not fit them to understand the complicated technical equipment they were expected to use. In combat, communications connections must be made very rapidly, and only skilled operators can make them. Hammond did praise the spirit of his men. "In spite of the almost impossible feats demanded of them," he said, their "ingenuity, loyalty, and persistence" overcame their lack of training and their few numbers.[30]

When TUSA was assigned a defensive role at the end of September, Hammond's signalmen were able to construct open wire lines to each corps and as far forward as possible. Wire crews rehabilitated existing commercial facilities of the PTT and for the first time were able to

[24] TUSA AAR, pt. 22, p. 6.

[25] Hammond said of Haswell, "Nobody ever had a more loyal conscientious and hard-working officer for his principle assistant. . . . the greatest credit for Third Army's successful communications should go to him." Ltr, Brig Gen Elton F. Hammond (Ret.), to Dr. Thompson, SigC Hist Div, 15 Jan 58. SigC Hist Div file.

[26] Col. Elton F. Hammond, "Signals for Patton," Signals, II, No. 1, pp. 5-11.

[27] MS Comment, Waite, Jul 59.

[28] For the detailed account of Third Army operations from August to mid-December, see H. M. Cole, The Lorraine Campaign, UNITED STATES ARMY IN WORLD WAR II (Washington, 1950).

[29] TUSA AAR, pt. 22, p. 7.

[30] (1) TUSA AAR, pt. 22, pp. 6, 22. (2) Hammond, "Signals for Patton," Signals, II, No. 1, p. 11. (3) Interv, SigC Hist Sec with Hammond, 16 Jan 58. SigC Hist Sec file.

recover and service some of the field wire they had laid during the advance. When TUSA resumed the attack on 8 November, Hammond could support the drive with the best wire network available since the campaign began in August. By mid-December TUSA possessed "practically perfect" communications to all its units, to higher headquarters, and to its proposed new command post at St. Avold.[31] This command post, however, was never occupied; the German counterattack of mid-December intervened.[32]

Air-Ground Communication Techniques

Probably the most significant development of the war in air-ground communications involving armored units occurred during the action at St. Lô. The 12th Army Group plans for the breakout depended heavily upon close air support by the IX Tactical Air Command (TAC). Close air support had generally been regarded by airmen as a bothersome diversion from their main task, but Maj. Gen. Elwood R. Quesada, the IX TAC commander, was a young, brilliant, and unorthodox officer willing to try new theories. Successful air support depended upon extremely careful control and co-ordination, and the crux of the matter was absolutely reliable communication between ground and air. General Quesada's signal officer, Colonel Garland, and FUSA's signal supply officer, Colonel Littell, solved the problem by putting Air Forces VHF command radios (SCR–522, the kind installed in fighter-bombers) into tanks, half-tracks, and jeeps. These radios, in the lead tanks of each armored column, could communicate with fighter-bombers immediately overhead as the advance took place. The tanks were literally led by the fighters, each move scouted by the planes. The speed and magnitude of the breakthrough—and its successful exploitation —depended in large measure upon the close air support made possible by this means of communication.[33]

Under General Quesada's direction, the fighter-tank team worked "with all the smoothness and precision of a well-oiled watch." This was how a War Department observer who arrived at IX TAC headquarters just as the breakout was getting under way put it. He went on to describe a typical mission:

German tanks and artillery had withdrawn from contact as [the American column] started off. The tank column was just coming up within range of the brow of a hill as they appeared on the scene. "Hello, Kismet Red, this is Bronco. Have you in sight overhead. We have no targets now. Is there anything in the woods off to the left or over the brow of the hill ahead?" Five minutes later the answer comes back, "Bronco, this is Kismet Red. . . . There are twelve Tiger tanks about four miles down the road retreating. Shall we bomb them?" "Yes, go ahead. . . ." So the P–47's go down and catch the tanks in a ravine. They blast the lead tank in the first pass and stall it. The others can't

---

[31] (1) TUSA AAR, pt. 22, pp. 7–11. (2) Hammond, "Signals for Patton," *Signals*, II, No. 1, pp. 10–11.

[32] See below, p. 163.

[33] (1) Williams, "First Army's ETO Signal Operations," *Signals*, II, No. 4, p. 10. (2) Bradley, *A Soldier's Story*, pp. 248–50, 337–38, 341, 345–49. (3) Ltr, Dr. David T. Griggs, Advisory Spec Gp, USSTAF, to Dr. Bowles, Expert Consultant to SW, 7 Aug 44. SCIA file, unnumbered, European Theater, 1–a. (4) Craven and Cate, eds, *Europe: ARGUMENT to V–E Day*, pp. 238–43. (5) Blumenson, *Breakout and Pursuit*, pp. 43, 44, 207–08, 334.

turn around and they are caught like eggs in a basket. Systematically the P–47's work them over from very low altitude and destroy them all. . . .

This is the kind of war they are fighting, and do the ground forces love it! The ground officers I talked to in many branches were uniform in their praise of the close support fighters.[34]

In the first six days, the AAF flew four hundred missions in support of the armored vehicles. Their targets for the most part were tanks, batteries, small troop concentrations, and motor transport. These they destroyed in large numbers, constantly worrying an enemy who was being forced to retreat in full daylight as well as at night. A German prisoner of war, who had served at length in Russia and elsewhere, later described the combined air-ground attack as the most devastating he had ever witnessed. This air-ground communications method served throughout the rest of the war with the same successful results.[35]

Improvisation and Flexibility

The eight weeks between mid-July and mid-September 1944 brought the spectacular sweep of the Allied armies across France to the German border. With the enemy's left flank pinned down by the U.S. First Army and his right by the British Second, the U.S. Third Army poured through the gap at Avranches, part bursting into Brittany, part swinging northeast on the Seine and outflanking Paris in the south. The British Second Army, the Canadian First Army, and the U.S. First and Third Armies crushed the German *Seventh Army* in the Falaise-Argentan pocket. Paris was liberated, Allied armor swept across northern France, the U.S. Seventh Army invaded southern France, and the Ninth Army took over the reduction of the bypassed Breton ports. Everywhere success attended the Allies.

In those weeks the Signal Corps precept, "Victory goes to the army with the best communications," was put to the test. Improvisation and flexibility, long emphasized in Signal Corps doctrine and training, became the mainstay of signal officers faced with "special situations" that developed all along the front. Slow hedgerow fighting, rapid pursuit, extended fronts, task forces, liaison with adjacent armies, defensive positions—no two situations were exactly alike. Signal Corps officers and troops took genuine pride in devising solutions to communications problems.[36]

Equipment that was useless in one situation might prove invaluable in another, as the 4th Signal Company of the 4th Infantry Division learned. During the slow Cherbourg campaign, the division turned in a ponderous, long-distance SCR–399 radio set, only to draw another frantically from army supply after the breakthrough and the pursuit to Paris and beyond.[37]

Signalmen of the 4th Division seldom fought the enemy—their job, as the signal

[34] Ltr, Griggs to Bowles, 7 Aug 44.

[35] (1) Williams, "First Army's ETO Signal Operations," *Signals,* II, No. 4, p. 10. (2) Bradley, *A Soldier's Story,* pp. 248–50, 337–38, 341, 345–49. (3) *SCAEF Rpt,* pp. 39–40. (4) Ltr, Griggs to Bowles, 7 Aug 44.
On air-ground communications (close support of infantry) in the Pacific, see below, pp. 230ff.

[36] For details of communications problems, see 99/12–31 (7661) Sig Sec 12th AGp AAR's for Aug-Nov 44, especially Daily Jnl entries for Aug.

[37] Hq ETOUSA OCSigO, Current Info Ltr (Nov 44), pp. 31–32. SigC Hist Sec file.

officer, Lt. Col. Sewell W. Crisman, Jr., saw it, was to lay wire and do it well, leaving the fighting to the infantry elements that had been trained for it. On the other hand, other division signal officers complained that the signal troops lacked "really protective" weapons and cited the need for armor on signal messenger vehicles. Lt. Col. William J. Given, signal officer of the 6th Armored Division, said that, in the action around Brest, the division signal company "has just received 17 bronze stars . . . but we'd like to trade them for a couple of wire teams, some armored cars and some machine guns." [38] Nonetheless, he summed up the feeling of almost every signal officer when he said, "Any modern outfit that doesn't improvise is not doing its job very well."

On D plus 9 the 30th Signal Company landed at OMAHA Beach, then moved near Isigny with the 30th Infantry Division. The company's first major test came on 9 July in the crossing of the Vire River. With four infantry and two armored divisions on the move in the area, the wire teams worked continuously for seventy-two hours to maintain their lines. Vehicular traffic along the congested roads snapped the wire on poles; heavy enemy shelling shattered it. Wire laid along the hedgerows suffered when armored vehicles plunged through old openings or made new ones as they moved into fields. Heavy rains created additional difficulties. [39] As the First Army advanced against fierce German resistance during August, battle losses among regimental communicators ran

high. The 30th Division signal officer, Lt. Col. E. M. Stevens, supplied replacements from the signal company. He also set up a signal school to train forty-one infantry replacements as wiremen and switchboard operators. [40] By mid-October the division was across France and Belgium into Germany. Aachen fell. Signal troops learned that lines laid in the gutters of paved streets were least vulnerable to shelling and bombing; antipersonnel bombs in particular spread myriads of fragments like flying razor blades and disrupted communications by damaging overhead wire lines.

At army level, the size and complexity of FUSA's communications system developed a need for two additional agencies not visualized in prewar or preinvasion planning. These were a communications control center and a locator agency.

The control center began with a large blackboard in an army tent and eventually filled a series of boards, in a hospital ward tent, manned twenty-four hours a day. Every circuit for which army signal troops were responsible was drawn on the board in schematic form. The officer in charge, from the signal operations battalion, wore a microphone combination headset and was connected over an intercom system with the operations officer of the army signal section, the chief telephone operator, the wire chief at the main frame, the NCO in charge of each carrier van in use, the teletypewriter switchboard operator, the radio relay stations, and the message center chief and the chief radio operator. A liaison officer from each signal construction bat-

---

[38] Hq ETOUSA OCSigO, Current Info Ltr (Dec 44), pp. 7–9. SigC Hist Sec file.

[39] 30th Sig Co AAR, Action Against Enemy Report (1945), Jul 44. SigC Hist Sec file.

[40] 30th Sig Co AAR, Action Against Enemy Rpt (1945), Aug 44.

talion on duty in the center had direct lines to his battalion command post. Commanding officers of the construction battalions had radio-equipped jeeps. The moment trouble developed on any circuit anywhere all responsible elements knew of it (because the intercom was a party line) and at once took the action necessary to clear it up. There was "nothing casual" about treatment of trouble anywhere in the FUSA army communications system.[41]

Any field army contains many units besides corps and divisions, units as diverse as artillery brigades and laundry or clothing repair units. At times FUSA's odd-lot units totaled nearly one thousand. To complicate matters such units were constantly being transferred from Advance Section (ADSEC) COMZ to armies, from one army to another, or attached or detached between corps and divisions. Keeping track of such units was exceedingly difficult, yet the Signal Corps had to deliver messages to them and get receipts. A FUSA message center lieutenant, who in civilian life had worked in the mail order department of Sears, Roebuck and Company, devised a solution that evolved into the FUSA locator agency.[42] The locator agency, in co-operation with the army adjutant general's office, established locator cards for each unit. A unit could not receive its mail unless it signed receipts for routine Signal Corps messages specially bagged and deposited at the designated pickup points. Eventually the system worked so well that staff sections came to depend on the Signal Corps to tell them what small, obscure units were assigned

to them at any given time, and where they were.[43]

Wire Communications

Of all the means of signal communication, the wire systems felt the greatest strain. The swift pace of the pursuit laid an almost impossible burden on wire. The armies used up nearly three thousand miles of wire each day. Surprisingly, even the armored division used a great deal of wire—more and more of it as the campaign progressed—until toward the end its wire consumption was virtually the same as that of the infantry division.[44] Wire units produced some amazing records. During the campaign on the Cotentin peninsula, for example, VII Corps' 50th Signal Battalion provided wire communications for six divisions, corps troops, and many other units not normally served. In one case, a single battalion wire team not only maintained the 82d Airborne Division line but also installed and maintained the division regimental lines when the division signal company suffered heavy losses. From 1 August to 15 September the 50th kept the wire system operating for the VII Corps through eleven moves, totaling six hundred miles. In forty-five days, the 50th laid a wire axis across France, Belgium, and into Germany.[45] The 50th was the first signal battalion to enter Belgium—on 6 September—and the first to enter Germany—on 15 September.[46]

---

[41] Ltr, Williams to Thompson, 31 Oct 57.
[42] *Ibid.*

[43] (1) *Ibid.* (2) Folder 11, Locator Sec, Basic Rcds of FUSA. SigC Hist Sec file.
[44] Williams, "First Army's ETO Signal Operations," *Signals*, II, No. 4, p. 9.
[45] FUSA Sig Sv, folder 16, Outstanding Achievements of SigC Orgns. SigC Hist Sec file.
[46] 50th Sig Bn, Hist, Sep 41–May 45.

SIGNAL COURIERS IN RUINED LUDWIGSHAFEN, GERMANY

In Brittany, signal units experienced the war of rapid movement across the peninsula and the relatively stable conditions around Brest. When VIII Corps was assigned the job of reducing the fortress of Brest, the 59th Signal Battalion became responsible for wire communications to three divisions, an extensive fire direction net, the radio co-ordination for naval bombardment of the city, and the maintenance of radio link contact to two armies, an army group, and a tactical air force. In addition, the battalion rehabilitated and placed in service 7,250 miles of existing open wire and underground cable in four weeks. Brest was strongly fortified with much long-range artillery and many antiair-craft and naval guns. Furthermore, the area was heavily mined. All signal units, among them the 2d, 8th, 29th, and 578th Signal Companies and the 310th Signal Operations Battalion, suffered their heaviest casualties to date.[47]

As the First Army drew near Germany's Siegfried Line, signal officers took especial pains that commercial cables terminating in German-held cities be disconnected in order to minimize the possibility of agents transmitting information to the enemy over commercial facilities. At the same time they connected certain other lines directly to American intelligence elements.

[47] (1) *Ibid.* (2) Opns Rpt folder, Brest Campaign, pp. 1–4. ETOUSA Sig Sec, Admin 572–E.

Friendly agents behind the German lines transmitted considerable valuable information over these lines.[48]

In the attack on the Siegfried Line, the men of the 143d Armored Signal Company (3d Armored Division) got a taste of fighting beyond their normal signal duties. On the night of 2 September the division command post near Mons, Belgium, was attacked by a German column trying to fight its way out of the trap 3d Armored Division was devising for it. Capt. John L. Wilson, Jr., commander of the signal company, described the next two days of action as "a type of Indian fighting." The command post became the focal point of the struggle, and in the numerous fire fights the signal company had its share of the action and took its share of the nine thousand prisoners that 3d Armored Division estimated it captured in two days.[49]

VHF Radio Relay

Despite the enormous consumption of wire, ETO's chief signal officer, General Rumbough, said that the only thing that saved communications was radio relay. It was not a lack of wire itself, although wire was in critical supply all through the campaign.[50] The forward rush of the Allied armies demanded something that could be installed more quickly than wire systems. Radio relay was the answer. It could be put into operation very quickly and needed few maintenance men to keep it operating. A single instal-

lation furnished several telephone and several telegraph circuits, each of which became a part of the whole communications system, quickly connected with any telephone or any teletypewriter in the system.[51]

The civilian engineers, Waite and Colaguori, stayed in the theater until mid-October to "introduce, install, and instruct" in the use of the radio relay.[52] The "introduction" part of their mission was easy, the engineers wrote later. The equipment sold itself; its inherent value was readily apparent once field signal officers saw it. "Installation and instruction" turned out to mean living and working in the battlefield areas under circumstances few civilians encounter. Colaguori and a small crew, after landing in Normandy with the assault forces, had stayed to help set up additional relay circuits for FUSA.[53] Waite remained at the St. Catherine's installation in control of cross-Channel operations until 14 July, when he flew to France. By then FUSA had six radio relay terminals in operation—one at VII Corps headquarters south of Carentan, one at V Corps near Trévières, one with XIX Corps moving toward St. Lô, and three at FUSA headquarters near Isigny.[54] Working in a hedgerow field near Isigny with two ETOUSA officers and crews from the 98oth Signal Service Company and the 175th Signal Repair Company, the civilian engineers by 2 August had assembled 14 additional terminals as

[48] 30th Sig Co AAR, Action Against Enemy Rpt (1945), Sep 44.

[49] (1) 143d Armored Sig Co AAR, Sep 44. (2) 143d Armored Sig Co AAR, Jul–Oct 44. (3) 143d Armored Sig Co AAR, Jan–Mar 45.

[50] See below, p. 153.

[51] Rumbough, "Radio Relay," Military Review, XXVI, No. 2, pp. 4–7.

[52] Waite-Colaguori Rpt.

[53] For D-day experiences of the two civilians, see above, p. 105.

[54] Waite-Colaguori Rpt, p. 35.

quickly as the components could be air-lifted to Normandy.[55]

Late in July an urgent call from VIII Corps sent the two civilians and a 6-man crew hurrying off toward Phillipe with AN/TRC–1 equipment. At corps head-quarters they learned that VIII Corps had made a breakthrough west of St. Lô, and both the 4th and the 6th Armored Division were heading toward Avran-ches. An antrac terminal was urgently needed to maintain corps communica-tions with 6th Armored Division head-quarters. Hurrying by back roads to a rendezvous point east of Coutances, where a division wire crew was to meet them with spiral-four, Waite and Colaguori set up their equip-ment and made contact with corps headquarters. Corps informed them that division headquarters had moved on to a point north of La Haye du Presnel in Brittany. Once more they set out, reached the designated point, and learned that 6th Armored Division head-quarters was now three miles south of the town. For several hours corps had been unable to keep in continuous con-tact with its fast-moving division. Wire was out because of the rapid advance, and even the normal radio communica-tions had proved sketchy.

By this time it was near midnight. Packing up in total darkness, the men encountered further delay when succes-sive groups of enemy bombers appeared and dropped bombs on American tank columns on a road paralleling the antrac position. Defending antiaircraft guns showered the ground near the radio sta-tion with shrapnel. Driving cautiously in darkness for twelve miles on roads lit-tered with wrecked enemy vehicles, past American crews filling shell craters in the road, the communications men ar-rived at their new location about 0300 and set up their station once more on listening watch. They congratulated themselves on the relative quiet of the spot; they could hear nothing more omi-nous than a few German machine gun and pistol volleys a few hundred yards away. At 0830 they got their first call from corps headquarters. But once more the division wire crew failed to appear. At noon the assistant signal officer of VIII Corps arrived at the station. He had no word of the wire crew, but he did have two pieces of news. American tanks had entered Avranches, and, in the dark-ness, Waite, Colaguori, and their crew had set up their station eight hours be-fore the infantry units followed the tanks through the area.[56]

As radio relay's virtues became known, everybody wanted it. Demands from signal officers of all armies, army groups, air forces, and forward sections of COMZ poured in. Tables of equipment had not caught up with it; as rapidly as sets could be seized from the production line they were shipped. General Rumbough di-rected that all requests for radio relay come to him personally, and he doled sets out as they were received.[57] Men of the 980th Signal Service Company, the only trained radio relay unit then in the theater, spread out all over France. Orig-

[55] (1) *Ibid.*, p. 37. (2) MS Comment, Waite, Jul 59.

[56] (1) Waite-Colaguori Rpt, pp. 41–42. (2) MS Comment, Waite, Jul 59.

For a detailed account of 4th and 6th Armored Division action in the entry into Avranches, see Blumenson, *Breakout and Pursuit*, pp. 309ff.

[57] Rumbough, "Radio Relay," *Military Review,* XXVI, No. 2, pp. 4–7.

inally the company was organized into a number of 6-man radio and carrier teams. Now the number of teams fell short of the demand for radio relay installations, and the experienced teams had to be split in half, then thinned again, the gaps being filled by men from the replacement pools. The 12th Army Group had one small detachment from the 980th, but, in order to keep in touch with the armies in the drive across France, it took radio repairmen from the Ground Force Reinforcement Command and gave them on-the-job training in radio relay.[58]

The two civilian engineers traveled from one headquarters to another. From the moment they arrived in Bristol until they left Paris in October they worked ceaselessly, giving on-the-spot instructions for unpacking and testing the equipment, installing it, siting it, operating it, and maintaining it. Finally, at a time when the calls for their services were coming in simultaneously from a half-dozen headquarters, ETOUSA set up a school in Paris. There, a first class of seventy officers and enlisted men representing all the interested organizations met for a week's instruction. It is a measure of the importance attached to radio relay that so many high-ranking field commanders engaged in decisive combat operations permitted men to be detached from the scenes of battle to travel to Paris for a training course. It would have been easy, the engineers wrote afterward, for commanders to have shrugged off the untried device, since including it meant deliberately upsetting signal plans that had been carefully worked out months earlier. From among the many they felt

deserved special credit, they particularly singled out Colonels Williams, Garland, Hammond, and Littell with high praise for their foresight and vigorous championship.[59] After the initial class, the Paris training school was maintained and conducted by officers of the Technical Liaison Division of the ETOUSA Signal Office. The school trained 25 officers and 450 enlisted men, more than half of them for the AAF, before December 1944.[60] Meanwhile, during September, October, and November, civilian technicians from Western Electric Company and officers from Camp Coles and the Technical Liaison Division, ETOUSA Signal Office, were busy introducing and setting up later antrac models, AN/TRC–6 and 8 sets. A British No. 10 (a 6-centimeter pulse set) was installed in the Eiffel Tower in Paris, with a second set on a high hill near Chantilly twenty-eight miles away.[61] By V–E Day there was enough relay equipment in the theater to provide 296 point-to-point installations, or 74 100-mile systems, each comprising two terminal stations with spares.[62]

The Invasion of Southern France

Meanwhile preparations had proceeded apace for the invasion of southern France by the U.S. Seventh Army under the command of Lt. Gen. Alexander M. Patch and by sizable French forces. The assault was to be mounted and supplied from the Mediterranean theater. Signal planning began early in 1944 from an

---

[58] 12th AGp AAR, XI, 193.

[59] Waite-Colaguori Rpt, passim.
[60] ETOUSA Rpt, II, 180.
[61] Ibid., II, 181.
[62] Rumbough, "Radio Relay," Military Review, XXVI, No. 2, p. 4.

AFHQ command post established on the island of Corsica. In control of the forces was 6th Army Group, with Colonel Lenzner as chief signal officer and Maj. Max R. Domras as signal supply officer. Col. George F. Wooley was Seventh Army's signal officer.[63]

Aboard the USS *Henrico* and the USS *Catoctin,* as the invasion fleet sailed from Naples, 1st Signal Battalion men handled communications afloat.[64] The command ship for this operation was unique in that it served as a joint Army–Navy–Air Forces control point. In the actual landings on 15 August, the airborne troops went first, communications men with them.[65] Since 8 June Signal Corps men who had been dropped in southern France had been taking part in guerrilla warfare assisting the partisans.[66]

Just before the amphibious assault, other Signal Corps troops emerged from their gliders with jeeps and trailers loaded with radio sets, telephone switchboards, field wire, and other communications supplies. They had networks operating when the amphibious landings took place. Some of these signalmen had been infantrymen, glidermen, and paratroopers before they had received training in communica

tions; others were Signal Corps soldiers who had volunteered for the hazardous and difficult work. However, the attachment of the 1st Special Service Force to the 1st Airborne Task Force created what was, in effect, a provisional division employed as infantry, and the 512th Signal Company, Airborne, was not equipped to function as a division signal company since it did not have enough vehicles, men, or communications apparatus. Other signal troops with the Seventh Army also would not have been adequate for their tasks, had they encountered stiff resistance. The 57th Signal Battalion lacked a complete radio intelligence platoon, and the 3151st SIAM Company was handicapped by a shortage of about seventy-five men, chiefly radio operators. A further complication lay in the failure of the naval task force to unload more than one platoon of one construction company before D plus five.[67]

As it turned out, the Seventh Army encountered heavy resistance only in the strikes against Marseille, which was taken on 23 August, and at the naval base at Toulon, which fell a few days later to French forces closing in from the north and west. By 28 August organized resistance at those two important ports had ended.

Landing with the assault troops were the signal supply troops of the 207th Signal Depot Company and the 177th

[63] (1) Sig Sec AFHQ, Hist, pp. 119ff. (2) Seventh U.S. Army, *Report of Operations in France and Germany, 1944–1945,* 3 vols. (Heidelberg, Germany: Aloys Gräf, 1946) (hereafter cited as Seventh Army, *Rpt of Opns, France and Germany*), vol. I, *passim.* (3) Opns Rpt folder, History of Operation DRAGOON (Invasion of Southern France). ETOUSA Sig Sec, Admin 572–E.

[64] Opns Rpt folder, History of Opn DRAGOON.

[65] For a complete story of signal communications in the assault, see Signals Report on Operation DRAGOON. SigC OP 370.2 Rpt folder 4 Gen, 16 Jul 45–7 Aug 45.

[66] (1) Seventh Army, *Rpt of Opns, France and Germany,* I, 68. (2) AFHQ, CSigO Monthly Bull, 1 Aug 45, sec. I, p. 1.

[67] (1) The Signal Corps Hits the Silk, Com folder. SigC Hist Sec file. (2) Rpt, Wooley, SigO Seventh Army, to CSigO, 21 Sep 44, sub: Preliminary Report, Seventh Army Signal Service Operations in Southern France, 15 August–20 September 1944. European–ETO folder, SigC Hist Sec file.

Regarding RCM in this campaign, see below, pp. 315, 318ff.

Signal Repair Company. Five enlisted men of the depot company working under Lt. Robert Miller got a taste of battle not ordinarily the lot of a depot crew. Coming ashore at H plus 1, much earlier than a depot unit would ordinarily disembark, they made their way to a designated rendezvous point through small arms fire and took thirteen German prisoners.[68]

Also among the initial assault forces were the signal operations personnel of the 71st, 72d, and 74th Signal Companies (Special) to work communications for the three division beach groups. The 163d Signal Photographic Company handled photographic coverage of both French and American units. A successful Seventh Army innovation was the use of SCR–300 radios in cub planes operating in a liaison net back to the command ship. The planes took to the air at H-hour plus 90 minutes from special flight decks on LST's. One plane reconnoitered in each division sector, sending back valuable information throughout the day.[69]

For men of the 57th Signal Battalion —veterans of Salerno and Anzio—the landing at Ste. Maxime on the Riviera was their third amphibious assault landing. H plus 2½ hours found the first wire teams ashore laying spiral-four cable for the VI Corps' three assault divisions, the 3d, 36th, and 45th. But the Signal Corps troops were to expend their greatest efforts in maintaining the swift pace of the advance. As fast as supplies were unloaded on the beaches, they disappeared to forward units. The assault moved ahead so fast that signal

supply was soon in difficulties. In particular, the troops needed field wire, batteries, and radio tubes. Railroad bridges at Grenoble and Besançon had been destroyed and could not be repaired immediately, and supplies therefore had to be moved forward by truck. There were so few trucks available to the Signal Corps that officers had to take communications vehicles to get the supplies off the beaches and had to arrange for special convoys of trucks to carry batteries and wire to the troops in the Besançon area. Despite all this, Colonel Wooley reported that there were no complaints on communications—the only request to the rear from the forward elements was, "Keep the wire and batteries coming." [70]

Throughout the campaign, a shortage of transportation plagued signal operations. As echelons of command spread apart, even high-speed wire construction methods such as rapid pole line (RPL) and multiairline (MAL) became inadequate and were no longer used. Instead, wire construction men of two battalions rehabilitated 1,716 miles of PTT open wire lines and strung 152 miles of spiral-four. Operations were handicapped, too, during the early phase of the campaign by delay in the arrival of signal units equipped with special-purpose vehicles for wire line construction. The 57th Signal Battalion used a captured German section car to follow open wire leads along the railroads through isolated stretches of country, and

---

[68] Opns Rpt folder, Hist of Opn DRAGOON, p. 5.
[69] Opns Rpt folder, Hist of Opn DRAGOON.

[70] (1) Sig Sec AFHQ, Hist, pp. 140–41, and app. D, pp. 11–12. (2) Rpt, Wooley, SigO Seventh Army, to CSigO, 21 Sep 44, sub: Preliminary Rpt, Seventh Army Sig Sv Opns in Southern France, 15 Aug–20 Sep 44. (3) Seventh Army, *Rpt of Opns, France and Germany*, I, 325. (4) Opns Rpt folder, Hist of Opn DRAGOON, *passim*.

four mobile radioteletypewriter installations built on 1½-ton cargo trucks to assure teletypewriter communications between corps command posts and divisions when wire circuits were cut off by shellfire or other interruptions. Insofar as communications were concerned, September was the Seventh Army's worst month. High-frequency, long-range radio took over where wire could not. Sky wave could be used almost exclusively to reach all commands. The majority of radio circuits covered distances of more than 100 miles.[71]

By 11 September, the Allied armies pushing up from the south made contact with those coming east from Normandy, and on 15 September SHAEF assumed command of the Franco-American forces.[72] Slowed by the barriers of the Vosges Mountains and the Moselle River, Seventh Army's communications altered, radio yielding largely to wire. By October, at army and corps level, radio was only an emergency means, although artillery, engineer, and infantry units constantly demanded more radios. Teletypewriter began to carry the bulk of army messages. Field wire became critical in November and had to be rationed. When three new division elements entered the Seventh Army without division signal companies, Colonel Wooley reported that only the close cooperation of corps and division signal officers and tactical good fortune prevented serious signal complications.

After the slow push through the mountains to St. Dié and Strasbourg, VI Corps speeded up and crossed the German border between Bitche and the Rhine River. Serving with the Seventh Army as it advanced into Germany were six signal companies—the 3d, 44th, 45th, 79th, 100th, and 103d. The veteran 36th Signal Company was with the French 1st Army. Three signal battalions, the 1st, 57th, and 92d, worked on the corps level.[73]

From D-day at Ste. Maxime to the German border and the Rhine, the 57th Signal Battalion laid 1,511 miles of spiral-four cable, 879 miles of W–110–B, and 451 miles of long-range W–143, recovering 75 percent of all the wire it laid except the W–143, and 26 percent of that. It also rehabilitated 2,614 miles of PTT open wire line; it transmitted 2,273,836 teletypewriter groups and 574,254 radio groups. Its messengers, traveling 129,867 miles, carried 91,749 messages.[74]

The Continental Communications System

The signal communications system in the ETO provided telephone, teletype-

---

[71] (1) Seventh Army, *Rpt of Opns, France and Germany*, I, 326. (2) 57th Sig Bn, SigC Tech Info Ltr 44 (Jul 45), p. 47. (3) Spiral-Four Construction, SigC Tech Info Ltr 41 (Apr 45), pp. 15–17. (4) Opns Rpt folder, Type Signal Bn (Consolidated), DRAGOON, *passim*. ETOUSA Sig Sec, Admin 572–F.

[72] *SCAEF Rpt*, p. 61.

[73] Opns Rpt folder, History of Opn DRAGOON. Other Seventh Army signal units included the 1st, 5th, and 7th Signal Center teams: the 226th and 250th Signal Operations Companies; the 117th Signal Radio Intelligence Company; the 152d and 154th Armored Signal Companies; the 28th Signal Construction Battalion; the 3253d Signal Service Company; the 53d, 59th, 60th, 101st, 286th, 287th, and 288th Radar Maintenance Units; a detachment of the 209th Signal Pigeon Company; the 3202d Signal Service Section; the 3151st Signal Information and Monitoring Company; and the 3201st Signal Intelligence Service Detachment. *Ibid.*, p. 10.

[74] 57th Sig Bn, SigC Tech Info Ltr 44 (Jul 45), pp. 47ff.

SWIMMING WIRE ACROSS THE MOSELLE RIVER

writer, and radio circuits serving over 70 major headquarters.[75] The British War Office, SHAEF, COMZ, ADSEC, SOLOC (Southern Line of Communications), CONAD (Continental Advance Section), the various army group headquarters, the 10 base section headquarters, the many Air Forces and Navy installations, the 7 army headquarters, the ports of Cherbourg, Marseille, Antwerp, and Le Havre, as well as UTAH Beach and OMAHA Beach—all required extensive communications systems. There were also the oil pipelines (2 main lines, with pumping stations with telephones every 10 miles, and main stations with telephone control every 50 miles). There were the railroads, which required two communications circuits along each right-of-way. And there were the redeployment centers, the hundreds of branch and general supply depots, and the many general and evacuation hospitals, all of which had to have extensive communications facilities.[76]

Wire carried the major portion of traffic, both tactical and administrative. Excluding air-ground traffic and traffic between highly mobile forward units, wire carried perhaps 98 percent of all messages transmitted by electrical means.[77] Planning, building, and controlling wire systems engaged the energies of a very large group of signal officers and men for many months before and after the invasion. In fact, even before strategical and tactical concepts

of OVERLORD jelled, the Signal Corps was hard at work evolving plans for an adequate outside wire plant. But equally early planning for the ETO allotment of signal troops fared badly. The theater general staff considered the requirements excessive and returned them for revision. So much time elapsed before the theater finally reached a decision that the War Department had already committed a large proportion of the available Signal Corps troops to other theaters. The ETO signal troop basis was fixed at a figure far too low. In spite of much frantic juggling of personnel figures later, there were never enough wire construction and maintenance men in the theater.[78]

Planning the Continental Wire System

Basic instructions for the combined main line system were laid down by SHAEF. In the U.S. zone, responsibility for the planning lay with the Joint Wire Group, composed of the signal officers of the First and Third Armies, Forward Echelon and Advanced Section, COMZ, and the Ninth Air Force, as well as of the 12th Army Group when it became operational. The group agreed upon two basic policies: pool all circuits in the main-line build, making them available to all organizations on a common user basis; and place all construction troops except those needed for specific missions under the control of the 12th Army Group signal officer. Each section of the main-line build, whether constructed by army, army group, or COMZ troops, would become a part of a co-ordinated,

---

[75] Maj Ted J. Palik, Signal Communications Problems in the European Theater of Operations (1949), Sig Sch Monograph, p. 13. The Sig Sch Libr, Ft. Monmouth.

[76] Ibid., app. A, Hq in the Theater Com Network, ETO.

[77] USFET Gen Bd Rpt, Study 111, p. 16.

[78] Ibid.

planned system. No French line or cable would be rehabilitated and put into service (except for immediate combat needs) unless it had an approved place in the over-all theater wire system. Thus the limited amounts of available wire plant materials and the limited numbers of construction troops could be utilized most efficiently.[79]

These policies were sound, but unfortunately the theater organization itself partially defeated their application. Because of the decentralization of control, a unified communications system had to be built upon co-operation rather than command action. As operations progressed and the combat zone moved forward, the rear areas divided into fixed-area base sections, each with its own headquarters command. Signal officers of the base sections were responsible to the base commanders rather than to the theater signal officer. Naturally, the primary interest of the base signal officers was to develop a good area system connecting the various depots, hospitals, and other service installations of their respective areas, rather than to extend or maintain portions of the main-line system that fell within the base section. They were also extremely reluctant to release any of their Signal Corps troops for theater requirements on trunk-line work. This led to many delays.[80]

It was also difficult to maintain the common-user principle. The air forces in particular made heavy demands for point-to-point operational circuits in the main-line system. As a matter of fact, several special systems were imposed upon the main-line system. There was,

for example, the Red Line system for key officers of SHAEF. Some Signal Corps officers contended that the priority system of handling trunk calls would have given staff officers the same rapid service as the Red Line without reducing the number of circuits available to common users.[81] General Lanahan, however, felt that in so large a theater the Red Line system was essential for rapid handling of high echelon calls. In addition, such a system "took the load of complaints off the back of the signal officer" and permitted him "to get on with the myriad of other duties" he had to perform.[82]

In their planning, the Joint Wire Group had decided that initially the continental main-line wire system must consist of new construction—open wire and spiral-four cable. The decision was a wise one. The French open wire system and the commercial cables were so damaged that for many weeks they could not be restored rapidly enough to supply military requirements.[83] Until the breakout, construction and rehabilitation troops had been bottled up in a fairly small area, unable to advance line communications forward. Once the Allied forces broke out of the beachhead, their advance was so rapid that new line construction could not keep up with the communications demands of higher headquarters. For a time, radio and messenger service had to take up the slack.[84]

In this period, 12th Army Group, the

---

[79] *Ibid.*, p. 18.
[80] *Ibid.*, pp. 18–19.

[81] *Ibid.*, p. 19.
[82] Ltr, Maj Gen Francis H. Lanahan, Jr. (Ret.), former CSigO SHAEF, to Huggins, CO SCIA, 31 Oct 57. SigC Hist Sec file.
[83] (1) 12th AGp AAR, p. 180. (2) USFET Gen Bd Rpt, Study 111, pp. 17–18.
[84] OVERLORD Rpt, IV, 861.

most forward headquarters having construction and rehabilitation troops, became responsible for extending the main-line system eastward. The rapid advance of the armies placed a desperate strain on the construction units. Two construction battalions per army and two for the army group were simply not enough in the period of rapid advance, even though 12th Army Group obtained all possible help from COMZ, ADSEC, and Air Forces sources.[85]

With new line construction temporarily unable to keep up with the advance, various military units began using the civil cable system on a help-yourself basis. Lines of the French government-owned long-distance cable system, the PTT, traversed normal military boundaries of control. Months before the invasion, the SHAEF Signal Division had worked out details of a control plan to be put into effect as soon as Paris was firmly in Allied hands. On 1 September SHAEF took over control and arranged for the establishment of the Paris Military Switchboard to provide trunk service by connecting military exchanges in other centers to the Paris exchange through the French PTT system.[86] On 10 September SHAEF established the operating medium, the Allied Expeditionary Force Long Lines Control Agency (AEFLLCA). Administered by the SHAEF Signal Division, it controlled policies, allocated routes and circuits to the army groups and to COMZ, and served as a central liaison office with the French civilian authorities.[87] Primarily intended to control the rehabilitation

and use of the PTT cables, AEFLLCA later took an active part in the whole main-line system. Actually, despite a certain amount of delay and friction, all organizations co-operated extremely well, considering the various pressures exerted.[88]

Rehabilitating Cable Systems

The prewar PTT system was quite extensive. During the German occupation PTT employees had managed to operate a clandestine smelting plant in suburban Paris and to construct new cables to serve secretly built transmitter and receiving radio stations. Meanwhile, the Germans also secretly built an extensive network of long-distance cables for their military needs.[89]

Allied bombings and the retreating Germans had heavily damaged both the liberated and the enemy facilities. Just before the Allied landings in Normandy, the French Forces of the Interior (FFI), in agreement with the Allied command, launched a systematic and successful program of sabotage. French technicians cut the cables at widely separated points, avoiding damage to hard-to-repair equipment such as loading pots and repeater stations. Within a few days after the landings there were widespread failures on existing systems in the Normandy

[85] 12th AGp AAR, p. 194.

[86] See below, pp. 140–41.

[87] OVERLORD Rpt, IV, 861–62, 883.

[88] Detailed accounts may be found in the signal division reports of the various headquarters. e.g., (1) 12th AGp Rpt of Opns, I, 72–73, and XI, 135–266. (2) ETOUSA Rpt, II, pp. 26–55b. (3) OVERLORD Rpt, III–VIII, *passim*.

[89] Extract from J. Mailly, "The Development and Organization of the Underground Long Lines Network," vol. 3, No. 1 of *Cables and Transmission*, published quarterly by Soltec, 16 Rue de la Baume, Paris 8, France. Reprinted in *Signals*, IV, No. 4 (March–April, 1950), 7ff., edited by Col. Howard W. Hunter.

area, and all efforts of the German wire crews to cope with them were to no avail. French cable splicers, when forced to work for the Germans, frequently made temporary splices wrapped with a bandage and then covered with a non-watertight sleeve. The splices held only until the first rain put them out of commission. This maneuver worked well against the Germans, but it caused the Allies a good deal of trouble later on when some of the splices became covered with the rubble of fallen buildings. Then it was the Allies who sweated and labored to locate and dig out the faulty cables.[90]

The Germans themselves, as they were driven back, wrecked the communications centers as thoroughly as possible, using destruction troops specially organized and trained for that purpose.[91] When time permitted, the demolition troops blew up or burned entire buildings, opened up buried cable and sawed or cut it in half and reburied it, cut single lengths of cable at successive manholes, and poured water over the severed ends. At some cable terminals, German signal troops created damage almost impossible to repair.[92]

Luckily, some installations were left to the ministrations of German troops inexperienced in signal matters and their "wreckage" was usually easy to repair. Luckier still, French technicians were able to save some of the vital communications centers. So hurriedly did

the enemy evacuate the Rhône Valley, along which the Dijon-Marseille cable ran, that at some points ingenious Frenchmen saved the communications installations for the Allies. At one repeater station the station chief convinced the German commander that a grenade exploded on top of the cable-run over the equipment bays would be most destructive. The resulting explosion, though satisfactorily loud, caused no real damage. At another repeater station the Germans, in a hurry to leave, accepted the promise of the French technician to blow up the station. As the Germans left the town, they heard explosions at the station and were satisfied. The technician had pulled the pins of the grenades and thrown them into an empty lot adjoining the station.[93]

French PTT employees gave the Allies one of the great breaks of the drive to liberate Paris. As Allied armies neared the outskirts of Paris, most of the Germans withdrew from the longline terminal plant on Rue Archives and wired the plant with time bombs that were intended to wreck it. The French employees seized the last few Germans remaining in the plant and informed them that everyone would stay in the plant. After several hours, the Germans, faced with the fact that they would be blown up along with the plant and their French captors, disconnected the time bombs. An important communications asset had been saved for the Allies.[94]

For every installation saved, however, two others had been destroyed. The big

[90] *Ibid.*

[91] (1) Palik, Sig Com Problems in ETO, pp. 21ff. and app. C, translated German field order, Preparation for Retreat. (2) Enemy Sig Demolitions, SigC Tech Info Ltr 38 (Jan 45), pp. 1–6.

[92] Williams, "First Army's ETO Signal Operations," *Signals*, II, No. 4, p. 9.

[93] Mailly, "The Development and Organization of the Underground Long Lines Network," *Signals*, IV, No. 4, pp. 7ff.

[94] Ltr, Lanahan to Huggins, 31 Oct 57.

repeater station at St. Lô, for example, was demolished by Allied bombings. Of the 130 principal repeater stations in the PTT system, 85 were destroyed or heavily damaged, as were 45 buildings housing them. The Signal Section, COMZ, had anticipated this contingency and had stockpiled all available repeaters. Special truck convoys rushed American repeater equipment to the front areas. When the supply was exhausted, captured enemy equipment and French-manufactured items were used. Though at first unfamiliar with foreign-built equipment, U.S. signal troops within a very short time were installing German, French, and Belgian equipment quite as easily and quickly as that of American manufacturers.[95]

General Lanahan, visiting a British-American signal crew working in the rubble of St. Lô shortly after its capture, noted that in addition to the destruction of the repeater station, artillery fire and bombs had broken the cables in numerous places. The British major in charge of the rehabilitation crew assured General Lanahan that he would have the cables repaired within five weeks. This promise he kept, although Lanahan had mentally calculated that if he succeeded within three months he would have done an outstanding job.[96] French civilian workers also provided valuable assistance on many cable rehabilitation projects, some crews working as much as ninety hours a week. Finally, from the United States came special volunteer crews of civilian cable splicers hurriedly recruited from telephone companies on the eastern coast and flown overseas to help restore civilian cables.[97]

Equipment and workers were not the only necessities. Coal to heat and dry out the buildings and equipment was another big item. For the shattered window panes, new glass—or temporary substitutes for glass—had to be found. The French had no diesel oil, engine oil, or gasoline to operate the power plants, and these items had to be furnished from Allied stores. The French civilian crews, though eager and able, lacked transportation, food, and blankets. The retreating Germans had commandeered all of the PTT vehicles, leaving only a few broken-down trucks, and from these the Germans had filched all the good tires.

The Allies' intensive efforts to rehabilitate the system quickly brought results. Five months after the liberation of Paris, almost 90 percent of the circuits in service in 1939 had been restored to service. By the end of the war, the long-distance network equaled that of the prewar system.[98] Throughout the campaign, the underground cable network was used almost entirely for military purposes. After the initial stages of the campaign, the cable system became the backbone of Allied communications. By V–E Day, COMZ had rehabilitated over 392,000 circuit miles of toll cable and had installed 1,907 new repeaters in fifty-five repeater stations in France, Belgium, the Netherlands, and Germany.[99]

The value of the rehabilitated civil system of long-distance telephone and

[95] ETOUSA Rpt, II, 35–36.
[96] Ltr, Lanahan to Huggins, 31 Oct. 57.

[97] CSigO Annual Rpt, FY 45, p. 642.
[98] Mailly, "The Development and Organization of the Underground Long Lines Network," Signals, IV, No. 4, pp. 7ff.
[99] ETOUSA Rpt, II, 35, 55–a.

telegraph facilities in the ETO was amply demonstrated. For example, during September and October 1944, the rehabilitated civil system yielded 3,076 circuits, totaling 205,845 circuit miles, compared to an estimated 100,000 circuit miles of new construction built by the combined efforts of the army groups, COMZ, and the tactical air forces. In other words, out of 300,000 circuit miles, only one-third were provided by new construction, even though all the military resources of the theater went into the effort.[100] If the Army had been forced to build lines equivalent in number to all those it used in the ETO during the course of the campaign, signal construction troops would still have been hard at work three years after the cessation of hostilities.[101]

The Paris Signal Center

Once liberated, Paris soon became the theater communications center. For a time, however, especially during late August and early September, communications facilities could not be installed fast enough to accommodate the rapid moves of large headquarters from England to the Continent. Communication between the War Department and the ETO suffered. Traffic to the United States was delayed as much as fourteen hours, and there were serious interruptions in the theater communications system.[102] The situation served well to illustrate the point that signal communications systems do not instantly come into being full-blown. They require much advance planning and a great deal of work, time, and trouble.

During August and September, traffic between the War Department and ETOUSA was extremely heavy—so heavy, indeed, that it put a strain on War Department facilities handling overseas business. A total of 356,669 messages containing more than ten million words flowed between the two points. Moreover there were 75 high-level secrecy telephone conversations and 95 teletypewriter conferences, not to mention 736 telephotographs transmitted.[103] This was more traffic than the amount carried across the Atlantic by all the existing prewar commercial facilities in any comparable period. Only extensive and complicated semiautomatic and automatic equipment of the most modern type could handle such loads. Furthermore, in the theater a telephone system to serve a large headquarters such as COMZ or SHAEF required as much equipment as that necessary to serve a city of 30,000 people in the United States.[104] Yet within two months' time SHAEF moved its main headquarters from London to Portsmouth to Granville to Versailles; Headquarters, COMZ, moved from London to Valognes to Paris; and Headquarters, 12th Army Group, moved four times.

---

[100] Overlord Rpt, V, 1573.

[101] 1st Lt Robert D. Strock, Signal Construction Troops Within the Theater Communications System (1948), Sig Sch Monograph, p. 13. The Sig Sch Libr, Ft. Monmouth.

[102] (1) Roland G. Ruppenthal, *Logistical Support of the Armies, Volume II*, UNITED STATES ARMY IN WORLD WAR II (Washington, 1959), p. 31. (2) Ingles, CSigo, Army-Navy Staff College Lecture, 19 Mar 45, Com folder. SigC Hist Sec file.

[103] Memo, CSigO for CofS Through CG ASF, 19 Oct 44, sub: Com Delays Occasioned by Frequent Moves of Large Hq in ETOUSA. Hq ASF file SigC, 1942–44, copy also in SigC EO CofS–Eisenhower, 1944.

[104] *Ibid.*

THE ETO: TO V-E DAY—I

Months earlier in London, plans had been set up for a phased, orderly move of COMZ to France as soon as two or more base sections had been established on the Continent.[105] But the tactical situation did not develop according to plan, and when COMZ moved to the Continent the phasing plan was disregarded. As a result, communications of the kind and in the quantity desired could not be provided immediately. A COMZ forward party arrived on the Continent on 14 July; requisitions for communications materials went forward to the United Kingdom on 20 July, and the troops and materials arrived on 29 July. When COMZ headquarters opened at Valognes on 7 August, the Signal Section had had only nine days to prepare for it. Working under the supervision of a single staff signal officer, Lt. Col. Percival A. Wakeman, the 3104th Signal Service Battalion and a small detachment of the 980th Signal Service Company selected sites, constructed buildings, installed a complete 15-kilowatt radioteletypewriter station, and established a cross-Channel radio relay circuit. On 25 August Paris was liberated. The next day an advance group from COMZ entered the city to search for housing and facilities. Within two weeks COMZ headquarters moved into Paris, bag and baggage.[106]

General Eisenhower considered the precipitate move of COMZ from Valognes to Paris to be ill-advised, particularly since COMZ used up precious air and motor transportation for the move at a time when there was a critical supply shortage at the front, a circumstance that resulted in a deluge of criticism from combat commanders.[107] General Eisenhower went so far as to tell the COMZ commander that he could not keep his headquarters in Paris.[108]

But from the communications standpoint, the move to Paris had been a logical one. Paris was the center of the cable, road, and railroad systems; it was "incomparably the most efficient" location for a communications zone headquarters and perhaps "the only entirely suitable location in France." [109] During the period when it seemed that COMZ would be forced to leave Paris, members of General Rumbough's staff, working with a reconnaissance group looking for new locations, considered the communications possibilities of Versailles, Reims, and Spa. They concluded that "any move of Hqs, COMZ, outside the greater Paris area would seriously cripple its present communications and hence its efficient operations." After a high-level meeting at SHAEF on 22 October, it was decided that COMZ need not move from Paris but must rigidly limit its personnel and the number of buildings it occupied.[110]

In spite of the potential advantages of Paris from a communications standpoint, the requisite facilities could not be pro-

[105] (1) Attachment 2, MS Comments, Brig Gen James S. Willis (Ret.) (former deputy for Telecommunications SHAEF and former Dir P&O Div SHAEF) to Ltr, Lanahan to Huggins, 31 Oct 57. (2) ETOUSA Rpt, II, 4-6. (3) Opns Rpt folder, CSigO Daily Jnl, 14-15 Jun 44, Movement of Hq ETOUSA. ETOUSA Sig Sec, Admin 298.
[106] ETOUSA Rpt, II, 38-39.

[107] Ruppenthal, Logistical Support of the Armies, II, 31-32.
[108] Bradley, A Soldier's Story, p. 406.
[109] (1) Hq ETOUSA, CSigO Daily Jnl, 22 Oct 44, item 2. SigC file, ETO Daily Jnl, Sep 44-Jun 45. (2) Lecture by Ingles, 19 Mar 45. (3) Ruppenthal, Logistical Support of the Armies, II, 31.
[110] Hq ETOUSA, CSigO Daily Jnl, 1 Oct 44, item 1, and 22 Oct 44, item 2. SigC file, ETO Daily Jnl, Sep 44-Jun 45.

vided immediately. General Rumbough described the signal facilities he was able to provide during the first few weeks as "the best possible, but not adequate." [111] The fact of the matter was that a large headquarters had displaced from one location to another without adequate consideration of the ability of the signal officer to provide service at the new location.[112]

Until wire lines could be brought into Paris and facilities rearranged, a single SCR–399 brought in with the advance group on 26 August provided the main communications channel between Paris and Valognes. On 10 September signal engineers set up a radio relay circuit, the terminal located on top of the Eiffel Tower. Rumbough's men brought landline printers and additional radio circuits into Paris when the major portion of Headquarters, COMZ, moved there. As quickly as possible during September the signalmen added new communications facilities. The fundamental difficulties in message handling during September lay in the shortage of reliable teletypewriter circuits between Valognes and Paris and between Paris and London. New direct VHF channels between London and Paris solved much of the difficulty. A major task, installing a 6-channel, long-range 40-kilowatt radio station, occupied scores of troops working in shifts twenty-four hours a day. The equipment for the station came packed in more than 1,000 individual boxes and crates, many of which had been severely damaged in shipment.[113]

Meanwhile, the various moves of SHAEF headquarters laid another heavy burden on the SHAEF Signal Section. SHAEF moved from Portsmouth, England, to the Continent at Granville on 1 September, despite a plea from General Vulliamy, the SHAEF chief signal officer, that the move be made no earlier than 15 September because of "signal considerations." [114] The signal center was set up at Jullouville, five miles south of Granville, in an area that had been heavily mined by the Germans. One signal officer was seriously injured and a truck loaded with equipment was destroyed by mines missed when the area was cleared. The signal offices were installed in portable huts; the thirty-two officers and thirty-nine enlisted men operating the facilities were housed in tents and trailers. The stay at Jullouville was short—on 20 September SHAEF Forward moved to Versailles.[115] General Vulliamy, hoping for enough time to provide adequate telephone facilities at Versailles, was told that SHAEF main headquarters also would move there immediately.[116] SHAEF was willing to accept a temporary reduction in communications facilities to gain political and tactical advantages by the move.[117]

On 5 October the main SHAEF headquarters moved officially. Actually, most of the staff officers had "infiltrated" Versailles during the two weeks the forward echelon had been located there. "The Signal Division . . . was not given enough advance information as to installations required," the historical re-

---

[111] ETOUSA Rpt, II, 41.

[112] Ltr, Lanahan to Huggins, 31 Oct 57.

[113] Hq ETOUSA, CSigO Daily Jnl, 16 Sep 44, item 6, and 23 Sep 44, item 1. SigC file, ETO Daily Jnl, Sep 44–Jun 45.

[114] OVERLORD Rpt, IV, 858.

[115] Ibid.

[116] Ibid., V, 1569.

[117] Ltr, Lanahan to Huggins, 31 Oct 57.

port of the division noted.[118] Most of the men from the signal units, who should have been at work maintaining existing communications, had to be diverted to the task of completing urgently required new installations.[119] Through the herculean efforts of Le Matériel Téléphonique a 3,000-line automatic exchange in the Petite Ecuries—Louis XIV's stables—was readied in the remarkable short time of five weeks.[120]

By mid-October communications matters at the Paris Signal Center were well in hand. The center and its associated military communications system were destined to become the largest ever established by any overseas theater. Within a year it rivaled the great signal center in Washington.[121]

Wire and radio, together with messenger service, were integrated into a smoothly functioning system—the sort of system that American commanders were wont to demand, wherever they were. In fact, it did not occur to them to expect anything less, accustomed as they were to the vast communications facilities available to them at home. By early 1945, most of the PTT cable systems in France and Belgium had been restored to service. Signal Corps troops had constructed many miles of open wire lines on important communication routes, while spiral-four and field wire served the forward areas. Approximately 1,660 wire circuits, incorporating an estimated 200,000 miles of wire facilities, operated in the COMZ.

VHF radio and manual radio telegraph systems supplemented and protected wire service. Paris was linked with WAR, the communications center of the War Department in Washington, by 2 complete multichannel and 2 single-channel radioteletypewriter systems, providing a total of 11 independent two-way radio circuits, and by 3 transatlantic cable circuits. The cable circuits had been established by restoring and diverting the German Horta-Emden cable. Before the war this cable had run from the United States through Horta in the Azores and Southampton, England, to Emden, Germany. British technicians severed the Southampton link. Specially trained Signal Corps crews terminated the cable and placed it in operation at Urville-Hague, near Cherbourg.[122] Communication between Paris and the other theaters was provided through radioteletypewriter channels to Caserta and Algiers, or by relay through WAR. Fifteen to 20 miles of teletypewriter tape sped through the automatic-packaged teletypewriter assemblies daily, carrying a traffic volume of approximately 7,500 messages—1,500,000 groups.[123]

To serve the 4,000 military stations in the Paris area, there were about 40 local switchboards, several of which were PTT automatic exchanges. Cables interconnecting the various exchanges permitted the routing of local traffic from one to another, handling 35,000 local calls daily. Long-distance calls, through the Paris Military Switchboard, averaged 19,000

---

[118] OVERLORD Rpt, IV, 886.

[119] Ibid.

[120] Ltr, Lanahan to Huggins, 31 Oct 57.

[121] For details of the first harried months in Paris, see ETOUSA Rpt, II, 56–61.

[122] MS Comment, U.S. Army Sig Bd, Ft. Monmouth, Jul 59.

[123] (1) App. B, Com in the ETO, to Memo, Code, ACSigO, for Ingles, CSigO, Reporting on Trip to ETO Beginning 29 Jan 45. SigC 370.2 ETO. (2) ETOUSA Rpt, II, 42ff.

PARIS SIGNAL CENTER *in German-built blockhouse.*

each day, 700 of them cross-Channel calls. Direct circuits from this board provided connections to each of the base sections on the Continent and in the United Kingdom, and to each of the army groups.[124]

The Signal Center had moved from the cramped, inadequate quarters in which it began operations in September to a new location. A 5-story concrete blockhouse built by the Germans a short distance from the Majestic Hotel offered suitable space. At the converted blockhouse, the Signal Corps installed tape relay and manual printer rooms, a radio operation room, crypto rooms, a message center, a radio control room, and con-

ference rooms.[125] Pneumatic tubes sped messages between this center and the classified message center in the Majestic Hotel. The radio control room was the first of its kind to be installed in the European theater. It was a technical center for controlling radio circuits and, in time, the entire tape relay network. All trouble shooting, distortion measurements, circuit rearrangements, and trouble analysis were controlled here by twenty-four highly trained men—nine officers and fifteen enlisted specialists. These men supervised the operation of the transatlantic radio, including the multichannel systems, VHF radio circuits, manual circuits, and high-speed circuits.[126]

The tape relay network was a part of ACAN, controlled by the Chief Signal Officer, Washington. The ACAN network consisted of the net control station in Washington, a network in the United States, and major trunk routes to overseas theater headquarters, where messages were relayed over the local networks of the individual theaters to their destination.[127] Stations in the ACAN net received messages by any means—messenger, pneumatic tube, private line teletypewriter, and so on—from the originator. These stations placed the messages on the network. Intermediate relay stations received the messages on a tape by means of typing reperforators, and fed them on to the next relay on the net by means of high-speed transmitter

---

[124] App. B, Com in the ETO, to Memo, Code for Ingles.

[125] Conference in this case meant teletypewriter conference (telecon) facilities by which overseas officers could confer with officers in Washington or other areas connected to the conference network.

[126] ETOUSA Rpt, II, 42.

[127] For a discussion of the development and expansion of ACAN, see Thompson, Harris, *et al., The Test,* pp. 427–90. See also below, pp. 580ff.

distributors. Relaying the messages by tape gave rise to the popular designation "tape relay network." Users found that this system provided a faster and more accurate means of handling messages. By February 1945, eight major relay stations in the ETO were tied into the ACAN network. They included: SHAEF; Headquarters, Communications Zone and ETO; Headquarters, 12th Army Group; Headquarters, U.S. Strategic Air Force; Headquarters, United Kingdom Base; Headquarters, Normandy Base Section; Atlantic Cablehead, Cherbourg; and SHAEF Forward. Each of these relay stations had direct communications to Washington and to each other. There were six relay tributaries and twenty tributary stations in the network.[128]

Two WAC officers and 180 WAC enlisted women were on duty in the Paris Signal Center by early 1945. Fifty-four Signal Corps women of the 3341st Signal Service Battalion in fact constituted the first WAC contingent on duty on the Continent. They had arrived at Valognes on 14 July for service in the signal center

there. Three WAC telephone operators took over the long-distance PTT board in Paris on the first day the French turned it over to the Allies. All together, five hundred Wacs served the Signal Corps in the COMZ as telephone operators, cryptographers, draftsmen, artists, clerks, and drivers of message center courier vehicles, releasing technically trained men for forward areas. The women operated their own messes and had their own administrative headquarters, the 3341st WAC Signal Service Battalion, activated in ETO, the first unit of its kind to be formed. These women on Signal Corps assignments represented 23.5 percent of all the WAC personnel in the Communications Zone, exclusive of the United Kingdom, approximately one Signal Corps woman to every 55 Signal Corps men in the area, as compared to one woman to every 234 men for the other services.[129]

---

[128] ETOUSA Rpt, II, 50–51.

[129] (1) Station List, COMZ ETO, 3 Mar 45. (2) Table, 3 Mar 45, Tab C to app. D, Orgn of Theater Pers, ETO, 1942–45. SigC 370.2 ETO. (3) Treadwell, *The Women's Army Corps*, pp. 318, 388, 408. (4) ETOUSA Rpt, II, 58. (5) Lt. Mary O. Kennedy, "Signal WAC," *Signals*, III, No. 2 (November–December, 1948), 28–29.

CHAPTER V

The Signal Corps in the ETO
to V–E Day—II

Signal Supply Problems in the ETO

Every officer assigned to supply in the European Theater of Operations is likely to wince at the memory of his tour of duty. His recollections usually bring bitter reminders of heartbreaking toil, endless confusion, interminable delays, and constant struggles against a vague antagonist known as *the system*, which often seemed to be no system at all. Signal supply throughout the campaign was seldom abundant; at times certain items became precariously scarce. These unavoidable periods of supply shortages resulted from the size of the operation and the inevitable consequences of the complexities thus introduced.[1] Even so, this was cold comfort for the using organizations that failed to receive wanted supplies and for COMZ, which had been unable to furnish them.[2]

In the months preceding D-day, England became a vast arsenal, crammed with military supplies of every sort. The Signal Corps had obtained War Department approval to establish a reserve for the First and Third Armies in excess of their authorized quantities of signal equipment. The authorized 75-day level of supply, based on replacement factors, assumed that organizations had a 45-day reserve level and a 30-day operational level, but Signal Corps stocks had not reached these goals. General Rumbough had accumulated a reserve stockpile of 80,000 tons of signal supplies, but the first days of fighting in Normandy ate into it at an alarming rate.[3] Furthermore, the tonnage figures did not tell the whole story, for the stock was not balanced—it contained more than needed in some categories, much less in others.

Replacement factors on certain items greatly exceeded the percentages established by the War Department. For example, in mid-1944 the replacement factor for the small hand-carried radios SCR–536 and SCR–300 stood at 15. But the mortality rates on these small radios carried by the front-line troops ran very high in the first weeks of the invasion.

---

[1] (1) USFET Gen Bd Rpt. Study 110. (2) FUSA, *Rpt of Opns, 20 Oct 43–1 Aug 44*, bk. VI, an. 12, *passim*, and *1 Aug 44–22 Feb 45*, bk. III, an. 8, *passim*. (3) TUSA AAR, pt. 22, *passim*. (4) ETO-USA Rpt, II, 66–95. AAR (5) OVERLORD Rpt, *passim*. (6) 12th AGp, Rpt of Opns, XI (Sig), 136–241. (7) Sup–ETO folder 12, SigC Hist Sec file. (8) Ruppenthal, *Logistical Support of the Armies, I, II, passim*. (9) Interv, SigC Hist Sec with Rumbough, 6 Jul 56.

[2] MS Comment, Shearer, Jul 59.

[3] (1) Interv, SigC Hist Sec with Rumbough, 20 Feb 45. SigC Hist Sec file. (2) ETOUSA Rpt, II, 65. (3) USFET Gen Bd Rpt, Study 110, app. 5, p. 1.

Many sets were lost in the landings or ruined by exposure to salt water. Some units reported losses of 50 to 100 percent. By 11 July Red Ball requisitions from First Army had exhausted the entire signal theater reserve, First Army was carefully editing combat requests for these items on a day-to-day basis, and the Signal Corps faced an emergency in the ETO.[4] COMZ sped a cable to Washington requesting air shipment of 1,111 SCR–300's and 5,914 SCR–536's. Within sixteen days, 45 tons of these sets alone had been flown to Normandy. Heavy combat losses in the drive across France kept SCR's–536 and 300 on the critical list of signal items the rest of the year, even though thousands of replacement sets poured in and the replacement factor moved up to 20. On 1 January, after still more losses in the Ardennes, the War Department increased the replacement factor to 22 for the SCR–300 and 26 for the SCR–536.[5] Experience with these sets confirmed that replacement factors cannot be established by simple arithmetical summations; the answers really depend on enemy operations and the fortunes of war.[6] Thus, logistical planning based on the best knowledge available sometimes missed the mark by a wide margin. The troublesome tale of replacements for tank antennas is a case in point.

Replacement allowances for tank antennas had been based on training requirements and experiences in maneuvers in the United States. As with all replacement allowances, signal supply planners tried to anticipate the worst possible conditions that might be encountered and then added a generous allowance for error. Nevertheless, as soon as tanks were ashore in numbers in Normandy, requests for replacement antennas far in excess of anticipated losses poured in from every tank unit. The reason was that the low-branched trees and thick hedges of Normandy ripped off antennas with fearful regularity. No American tank in training or maneuvers had ever encountered such terrain—probably the worst "tank country" that could be found. Local reserves of antennas were quickly exhausted, and soon COMZ was shipping from the fast-disappearing theater reserve. The need for antennas became desperate.

In the emergency, General Rumbough turned to the secret, direct radiotelephone channel to Washington. From London he talked directly to General Ingles, the Chief Signal Officer, urgently requesting the earliest possible shipment of more antennas. Within forty-eight hours the needed antennas were delivered by air.[7]

During the first weeks, as the troops slowly struggled forward from the beaches and new units poured in, poor weather conditions hindered supply operations, preventing the unloading of supply vessels and placing a further strain on signal supplies already on hand. Organizing the beaches and bringing up fresh supplies of men and equipment was a frighteningly difficult and complex

---

[4] (1) ETOUSA Rpt, II, 66. (2) Memo, Sig SupO FUSA for Plans and TngO Sig Sec FUSA, 11 Jul 44, sub: Rcd of Activities. Sup-ETO folder 12.

For the definition of *replacement factor*, see below pp. 358–59.

[5] ETOUSA Rpt, II, pp. 83, 86–d, 86–m.

[6] USFET Gen Bd Rpt, Study 110, p. 5. For similar figures on wire factors, see below, pp. 153–54.

[7] Ltr, Gen Rumbough to Mrs. Dixie R. Harris, 14 Aug 61.

task.[8] Miscalculations, mistakes of one sort and another, adversities and setbacks in tactical plans—all added to the initial logistical troubles.

The greatest Signal Corps problem during this period was lack of information as to which ships carried signal supplies. Even in England this information was seldom available to COMZ in time to be of any use. Ships arrived, were unloaded, and their cargoes sent to the nearest depot before the Signal Corps stock control section even received the manifest. Supplies desperately needed sometimes awaited discharge while other less necessary items were brought ashore. On at least one occasion, when berthing facilities at ports became critical, a vessel with urgently needed wire cargo aboard was not even unloaded. Because of its weight, wire was bottom loaded, with medical supplies loaded on top. Since casualties were fortunately running below estimates, the medical supplies were not needed, and the G–4 officer considered it "impractical to get at the wire."[9]

Meanwhile, as new units landed and became engaged in heavy fighting, their losses in signal equipment mounted. One division lost all of its SCR–610's to "snipers who seemed partial to artillery observers." Such items as radio tubes of all sorts, antenna mast sections, dynamotors, reel equipment, and mast bases were getting scarce.[10]

Wire had been requisitioned in tremendous quantities, but the supply melted away. Wire systems, once established, tended to become the principal means of communication except in front-line infantry companies. Signal construction companies were laying eight to fifteen miles per day in the congested area of operations, but they were hard put to it to keep the lines in operation. The immense traffic on the beaches was hard on wire. Trucks and tracked vehicles chewed up lines laid on the ground; bulldozers cut buried lines; cranes broke overhead wires; trucks knocked down poles.[11]

Preinvasion planning had assumed that ADSEC COMZ would take over full responsibility for supplying the armies on the Continent by D plus 15, and Forward Echelon, COMZ, by D plus 42. Actually, First Army retained control far beyond the dates originally planned. ADSEC, on D plus 55, was just beginning to control Class IV supplies, but First Army still controlled Class II supplies.[12]

Some signal personnel of ADSEC arrived on the Continent as early as D plus 1. Col. Pierson A. Anderson, director of the ADSEC Signal Supply Division, had served in a similar capacity at ETOUSA headquarters. Among his staff were twenty-two officers of a stock control team, newly arrived from the United States, where they had been specially trained in all phases of signal supply.[13] The first signal depot on the

[8] A particularly good account of the logistical problems on the beaches is contained in Ruppenthal, *Logistical Support of the Armies, Volume I,* Chapter X.

[9] MS Comment, Shearer, Jul 59.

[10] (1) Hq ETOUSA OCSigO, Current Info Ltr (Aug 44), I, 27–29. SigC Hist Sec file. (2) FUSA, *Rpt of Opns, 20 Oct 43–1 Aug 44,* bk. VI, an. 12, pp. 17–18. (3) VHF Cross Channel Circuit, SigC Tech Info Ltr 33 (Aug 44), pp. 3, 19–20. (4) Memos, Sig SupO FUSA for Sig Plans and TngO,

3 Jul and 11 Jul 44, sub: Rcd of Activities. Sup-ETO folder 12.

[11] VHF Cross Channel Circuit, SigC Tech Info Ltr 33 (Aug 44), pp. 3, 19–20.

[12] (1) Ruppenthal, *Logistical Support of the Armies, I,* 433–39. (2) ETOUSA Rpt, II, 4.

[13] ETOUSA Rpt, II, 4.

Continent was established near Femelle, between Carentan and Isigny, and was operated by the 216th Signal Depot Company. After the fall of Cherbourg, a second depot was located there, operated by the 208th and 221st Signal Depot Companies.[14] Others opened, closed, or were relocated as needs changed throughout the campaign.

During June and July there were no really serious signal supply shortages, though demands continued to be very heavy. Out of fairly substantial tonnages arriving over the beaches, First Army met its own needs, and those of the IX TAC, ADSEC, and additional units being formed on the Continent. Most of the new units arriving in July and August were intended for Third Army, and nearly all of them lacked most of their organizational equipment. During the planning phase in England, Third Army, like First Army, had prepared lists of signal equipment needed in excess of authorized tables of equipment. The lists were approved 1 June, five days before D-day, but could not be filled completely because First Army's heavy preinvasion needs had depleted signal stocks in England. Lt. Gen. John C. H. Lee, commanding general of ETOUSA SOS, had instructed his supply services: "Whatever First Army wants, you give them." [15] As the tactical situation devel-

oped following Third Army's activation, it was never possible to make up the deficit. Thus Third Army's needs were never as well cared for as they should have been.[16] TUSA remained in a supply squeeze throughout the campaign.

Possibly ADSEC suffered most in this period. Because of the critical shortage of port facilities and transportation, such shipments as arrived from England carrying the stores set up for initial stockage of the continental depots came unevenly, not in consecutive order as planned, and on an average thirty days behind schedule.[17] Since FUSA was providing virtually all signal equipment needs on the Continent, Colonel Littell, FUSA's signal supply officer, soon became alarmed at the shrinkage of his own stocks. In mid-July he complained that ADSEC could not even meet all the needs of its own troops and that the requisitions it extracted to FUSA were seriously depleting stores of replacement equipment and maintenance parts.[18]

ADSEC had problems of its own. All the while that the armies remained bottled up in the relatively narrow beachhead, supplies had to be moved in over the beaches and transported by trucks to the front line. Transportation was extremely tight. Early inauguration of an air transport service from England and the United States helped but had to

---

[14] *Ibid.*, p. 65.

[15] (1) USFET Gen Bd Rpt, Study 110, p. 11 and app. 3, p. 2. (2) Interv, SigC Hist Sec with Rumbough, 6 Jul 56.
Colonel Shearer, Deputy Chief Signal Officer, ETOUSA, commented, "It was bad enough to give First Army a blank check on the planned stock account, but to include the savings account as well was courting disaster." MS Comment, Shearer, Jul 59. Colonel Williams, FUSA signal officer, disagrees, feeling that FUSA's supply list was "very modest . . . I shudder to think what would have happened

if we had not had it." Ltr, Williams to Thompson, 14 Oct 57.

[16] Interv, SigC Hist Sec with Rumbough, 6 Jul 56.

[17] (1) ETOUSA Rpt, *passim.* (2) Ruppenthal, *Logistical Support of the Armies,* I, 463–74. (3) FUSA, *Rpt of Opns,* 20 Oct 43–1 Aug 44, bk. VI, an. 12, pp. 17-19. (4) TUSA, AAR, pt. 22 (Sig), p. 5. (5) 12th AGp, Rpt of Opns, XI (Sig), pp. 190–91.

[18] Memo, Sig SupO FUSA for Sig Plans and TngO, 29 Jul 44, sub: Rcd of Sig Activities. Sup-ETO folder 12.

be limited to items of high priority. Even so, the Signal Corps ranked second among the services in supply by air during the first twenty-five days.[19] There were too few service troops to handle the supplies, and their training left much to be desired. At the beach dumps signal supplies had to be sorted and put into an orderly arrangement before they could be issued to troops, and most of the depot troops had almost no training in this sort of work.

The manner of packing signal supplies created problems. Often the various components comprising a single heavy or bulky signal item came packed in several separate cases. Although standard procedures specified that no multi-packaged items would be shipped until all parts were together, in practice the procedure was seldom observed. The result, of course, was that items received lacking some of their component parts were useless.[20] Frequently, too, the outsides of packing boxes carried so many markings or were so plastered with mud as to defy identification of their contents. Yet if a box were opened to identify its contents, the equipment inside quickly deteriorated in open storage. Packing lists tacked to the boxes identified contents by catalog numbers, but there were no catalogs on the beach. Had there been, they would have been of little use because of their

bulk and their complicated format—much too complicated for field use.[21]

In July, the first group of men from Forward Echelon, COMZ, arrived on the Continent. They were joined on 7 August by a COMZ headquarters staff operations group that included the chief signal officer, General Rumbough, and the director of several of his divisions.[22] Rumbough lost no time in concluding arrangements to take over supply responsibilities. Since ADSEC beach dumps were practically barren of Class II supplies, FUSA turned over the signal supplies in its beach dumps to COMZ for stocking the continental depots. It was planned that each army would carry in its supply dumps only seven days' supply of rapidly moving items but would not attempt to carry all items. ADSEC's dumps would stock fourteen days' supply of the same items, plus additional items in frequent demand. In case ADSEC could not furnish the item requested by the armies, it would extract the requisition to COMZ. Only COMZ would maintain complete stock records.[23]

This plan seemed to be sound and workable. However, it was based upon the assumption that the tactical situation would develop according to existing plans, that ports and incoming tonnages would become available in a regularly increasing progression, and that COMZ would have enough time to develop an orderly system of depots. This was not the case. In late August and early September the "roof fell in" on supply officers. The tempting possibility of forcing an early end to the campaign

---

[19] USFET Gen Bd Rpt, Study 130, Supply and Maintenance on the European Continent, p. 34.

[20] An extreme example concerned radio sets SCR-694, waterproofed, fungus-proofed replacements for the short wave, portable infantry set SCR-284. The sets were received on the Continent without their essential power supply units, which had been loaded on a different cargo vessel. The power supply units did not catch up with the radio sets until close to V-E Day, so that very little use was ever made of the sets. USFET Gen Bd Rpt, Study 110, p. 11.

[21] USFET Gen Bd Rpt, No. 110, p. 11 and app. 3, p. 2.

[22] ETOUSA Rpt, II, 6.

[23] Ibid., p. 5.

led the Supreme Command to continue the pursuit despite existing logistical limitations. By mid-September virtually all of France, Belgium, and Luxembourg had been liberated, and the Allied front stretched in an almost unbroken line from the North Sea to Switzerland. On 25 July, the front lines were nearly 40 days behind the forecast phase lines. By 12 September (D plus 98) they had reached the line forecast to be reached by D plus 350. They had covered 260 phase-line days in 19 days of actual fighting.[24] This brilliant tactical advantage had been bought and bitterly paid for by the fighting men. The cost to the supply services was also very high.

The breakout and pursuit put an almost unbearable strain on supply. The lack of ports constituted the most limiting factor. Vessels that could not be unloaded because of lack of port capacity had to be held offshore, and this immediately created a shortage of shipping at the other end of the supply route, where supplies piled up. Transportation became a nightmare. Railroads thoroughly bombed and shot up by Allied airmen to deny their use to the enemy could not be repaired and put back into service quickly enough to be of much value in transporting supplies to the front. Every truck and every available relief driver was pressed into service, both within the Communications Zone and in the army areas, to augment the lift capacity of ADSEC's Motor Transport Brigade (MTB).

By the last week of August, SHAEF had decided to press the pursuit beyond the Seine. To meet the emergency, on 28 August COMZ and ADSEC pooled all their motor transportation and re-formed the Motor Transport Brigade into the Red Ball Express Motor Highway system. The trucks ran ceaselessly, day and night, over a giant loop of highway that fed one-way traffic from the western terminus at St. Lô on to the front lines and sent empty cargo trucks back to Normandy for reloading.

Along the highway the Signal Corps quickly installed a 6-station radio net, utilizing SCR–399 radio sets. The SCR–399 was well-suited to the job; it had a 100-mile range by key or voice, was mounted in a $2\frac{1}{2}$-ton truck, and hauled its own power plant in an attached trailer. The net control station operated at the headquarters of the MTB, which supervised the dispatching of the convoys, and controlled them all along the line. When a convoy departed from the regulating station at St. Lô, a message flashed to all the stations along the route describing what the convoy carried, its destinations, and how it was to be handled. Presumably this assured control of the convoy during its entire trip until it reached its destination. Actually, there were plenty of misroutings, unauthorized diversions of the convoys, and other mishaps. But without the radio network, and the regulating stations along the way, the whole system would have broken down in chaos within the first few days.[25]

---

[24] (1) T. Dodson Stamps and Vincent J. Esposito, *A Military History of World War II With Atlas* (West Point, N.Y., 1953), I, 461–63, Atlas Map 52. (2) Ruppenthal, *Logistical Support of the Armies, I*, 488.

[25] (1) Maj. A. A. Frederickson, Radio Off ADSEC, Rpt, Role of Signal Corps With the Red Ball Express Highway, Hq ETOUSA OCSigO, Current Info Ltr (Oct 44), p. 6. SigC Hist Sec file. (2) Red Ball Express, SigC Tech Info Ltr 37 (Dec 44), p. 15. (3) Interv, SigC Hist Sec with Rumbough, 20 Feb 45.

The logistical squeeze raised special problems for signal supply. Gasoline, rations, and ammunition for the armies held the highest priority. This meant that only a fraction of the signal tonnage requisitioned by the armies could actually be allocated for delivery to them, even when the supplies were available. And they were not always available because transportation difficulties kept the depots from achieving a balanced stock. For this reason ADSEC was never able adequately to fulfill its mission of giving direct support to the armies.[26] Under theater policy, ADSEC at first gave the armies whatever they asked for to the limit of the stocks on hand, and unrestrained requisitioning led to further difficulties. Army signal officers soon learned that the amount of supplies each received largely depended upon the ability to press one's demands vigorously and vocally. Thus the armies bid against each other; he who came first was served first and not necessarily on the basis of greatest need.[27] These generalities held true throughout the campaign, but undoubtedly their effect was most serious during August and September.

When it became evident that COMZ's supply capabilities could not possibly support all the combat requirements fully, the theater command instituted a strict rationing procedure based on tonnage allocations to each army in accord with its operational priorities. In the weeks between early September and mid-November all the armies operated on a hand-to-mouth supply basis. By 9 December the entire supply situation had brightened sufficiently to permit a return to normal requisitioning procedures.[28]

During the worst of the supply crisis, both FUSA and TUSA mobilized all available truck companies to help transport supplies. By 18 September, the Signal Section, FUSA, had two quartermaster truck companies assigned to it on a permanent basis, but Colonel Littell reported that "signal supplies received on a daily tonnage basis from COMZ are almost negligible to the point of complete supply failure."[29] At that time he was receiving about 10 percent of the tonnage ordered each day. On 3 October, Littell voiced a complaint echoed by other signal supply officers—that tonnage figures, on which G–4 based resupply to the Army signal depots, actually were deceptive. Of a hundred tons ordered, Littell had received eighty-five, but all of it was heavy, easy-to-handle items, neglecting equally important small, lightweight items such as antennas, handsets, cords, tubes, and resistors. Said Littell, "If this practice continues, there will be a critical shortage of spare parts . . . resupply can only be shipped on a basis of item for item, not a tonnage basis."[30] On a tonnage basis, Littell estimated he received in October as much as 20 percent of his requisitions; on an item basis, only 5 percent. Lt. Col. Louis V. Germain, Third Army's signal supply officer, agreed: "The emphasis on tonnage figures completely distorted the signal supply pic-

[26] USFET Gen Bd Rpt, Study 110, p. 19.
[27] Ibid., passim.

[28] For details consult Ruppenthal, Logistical Support of the Armies, II, 169–80.
[29] Memo, Sig SupO FUSA for Plans and TngO FUSA, 18 Sep 44. Sup–ETO folder 12.
[30] Memo, Sig SupO FUSA for Plans and TngO FUSA, 3 Oct 44. Sup–ETO folder 12.

ture—one ton of radio spare parts were on occasion worth 2,000 tons of pole line hardware." [31]

Third Army was accustomed to operating on a shoestring.[32] It took the field on 1 August with almost no signal equipment except the organizational equipment in the hands of its troops. The "reserve" stocks on hand consisted of one set each of radios SCR–300, 508, and 510; eight SCR–511's; and 6,000 miles of field wire. A lucky find of 30 miles of German spiral-four cable hidden in a cave near Chartres helped out. By dint of very close liaison with ADSEC, which Colonel Germain described as "very effective," he managed to build up his supplies to a 3,000-ton figure.[33] Half came direct from the United Kingdom, where a Third Army supply representative, Maj. Stephen C. Higinbotham, had been left behind to look after Third Army supply matters. In August Higinbotham sent Third Army four truck companies from the United Kingdom with signal supplies, including a considerable number of spare parts. In September, seven truck companies arrived at Third Army depots with enough supplies to offset the shortages existing at that time.[34]

Battle losses of the rapidly moving Third Army soon brought signal supply to a critical state. Spare parts were especially scarce. The 579th Signal Depot Company, which included two crystal-grinding teams, and the 187th Signal Repair Company arrived on the Continent with empty trucks. Third Army had been assured that, as fast as supplies arrived on the Continent, the army's needs would be met. But TUSA moved too fast for the supply replenishment system. All supplies for the first month's operations were picked up and moved by army trucks. Convoys operated twenty-four hours a day, and a hundred trucks were on the road constantly hauling supplies to Third Army depots. In the first eight weeks, ten depots opened, closed, and opened again a little closer to the front lines.

Each move meant a lengthening supply line back to the beaches, and the mistakes and difficulties that attend the operations of worn-out men and worn-out equipment began to appear. The signal depot company worked valiantly, but it was almost completely untrained in signal supply, unfamiliar with signal supply practices and procedures, and not even acquainted with Signal Corps nomenclature. The crystal-grinding teams felt completely frustrated. Their vehicles had been left behind in England, they could not operate their equipment in the open woods and fields, and there was no cover with suitable space or facilities. One team went to work handling radar supply, spare parts, and maintenance supervision. The other team finally got suitable quarters in mid-December and started grinding crystals, the work for which the men had been trained.[35]

Since the repair company had not been furnished any spare parts, the men set about obtaining them by salvage and cannibalization. No one could question too closely where one procedure left off and the other began, but in the

[31] TUSA AAR, pt. 22, pp. 1–11.

[32] Ibid., p. 179.

[33] (1) Ibid., p. 6. (2) TUSA, Of Sig SupO, Third Army Material History, p. 3. SigC Hist Sec file.

[34] TUSA, Third Army Material Hist, p. 3.

[35] Ibid., pp. 10–11.

first three months the repair company salvaged or cannibalized 335 pieces of German equipment and 183 pieces of American radio equipment, including two SCR–584 radars, to obtain spare parts. By October they had enough material to go to work as repair teams assigned to units.[36] Colonel Germain praised the repair companies highly for their ingenuity and ability to improvise. It was November before Third Army received its first issue of spare parts.

Taking parts from complete sets in order to repair other sets was an uneconomical procedure; in time it could lead to a complete breakdown of the supply system. By mid-August even those army units initially well supplied had exhausted their basic loads of spare parts. Spare parts stock coming into the Normandy beach dumps became intermingled with other supplies and often could not be found for issue. The 12th Army Group and COMZ decided to withdraw all repair parts from signal beach dumps and depots and concentrate them in a single location in Cherbourg. With the liberation of Paris the Signal Corps established a second and larger spare parts depot in that city. Signal Spare Parts Depot S–891, an enormous room fitted with steel frames holding many bins, provided the space necessary to segregate, identify, and issue spare parts quickly.[37]

Since signal repair parts, usually light in weight and small in bulk, often got lost in transit after shipments left the

spare parts depots, the 12th Army Group Signal Section instituted a special delivery system. Each of the armies designated a signal officer whose only duty was to handle spare and repair parts for his army. Once a week he made a delivery of parts to that army, stayed a day or two to find out what it needed, then went back to the Paris depot, loaded the material on trucks, and delivered it to the army. The system worked very well. Since the Paris depot also contained a large fifth echelon repair shop, it could handle any repairs that the armies could not. By the end of 1944, a large group of French civilians were employed in the depot and repair shop, in addition to a signal depot repair company of five hundred men.[38] The armies began segregating spare parts in bins in trailers; these in effect were mobile spare parts depots.

Some badly needed repair parts were not available in the United Kingdom, nor could they be obtained quickly enough from the United States. Local procurement frequently filled emergency needs but provided no substitute for large volume requirements. England's labor force was already fully occupied with Allied production needs. In France and Belgium, critically scarce raw materials, fuel, and electricity had to be furnished before workmen could make parts. Matching American designs proved difficult. The Signal Section of COMZ did successfully place orders with nearly a hundred French firms for

[36] (1) *Ibid.*, pp. 8–9. (2) TUSA AAR, pt. 22, pp. 7–10.

[37] (1) ETOUSA Rpt, II, 77, 80. (2) 12th AGp, Rpt of Opns, XI (Sig), 192. (3) USFET Gen Bd Rpt, Study 110, pp. 23–25, and app. 6, pp. 1–3.

[38] (1) Interv, SigC Hist Sec with Rumbough, 20 Feb 45. (2) 12th AGp, Rpt of Opns, XI (Sig), 192. (3) USFET Gen Bd Rpt, Study 110, pp. 24–25. (4) TUSA AAR, pt. 22, p. 13.

A second such depot was established later at Liège, Belgium, to assure close support to the First and Ninth Armies. ETOUSA Rpt, II, 86–h.

resistors, vacuum tubes, a pneumatic tube system for the Paris signal center, transformers, several types of meters and test equipment, antenna sections, and a few other small items.[39]

Of all the items on the chronically scarce list, probably wire was in short supply most consistently. There were a number of reasons, the principal one being that all the wire manufacturing facilities in the United States taken together could not produce enough.[40] The ETO was a "wire" theater. The War Department replacement factors of 44 for the standard field wire W–110–B and 38 for the assault wire W–130, based on experience in North Africa and Sicily, proved to be far too low for the ETO. After the War Department adopted the system of computing factors individually for each theater, factors for W–110–B and W–130 rose, eventually reaching 140 and 75 percent, respectively. Of all the wire manufactured for the Army, the amount allocated to the ETO steadily edged upward until it reached 65 percent.[41] Even this was not enough to fill the armies' needs.

In the first few months of operations, wire was strictly rationed to all the armies. Third Army was nearly always short of wire. In November COMZ issued 400 miles of field wire and 100 miles of assault wire to Third Army daily, but TUSA field units used up to 475 miles of field wire and 150 miles of assault wire per day, whenever that much was available.[42] As late as February 1945, though signal supply in general had improved greatly, Third Army was still so short of wire that it issued it only to units actually in combat. That month it issued 13,866 miles of wire; in March, 22,500 miles of W–110 alone.[43]

Except for wire, the worst of the signal supply problems were over by the end of November. Both FUSA and TUSA reported an "unusually good" flow of signal equipment in general during this period.[44] The assault in southern France had loosed the ports of Marseille and Toulon, relieving pressure on the Channel ports and beaches.[45] In late November the port of Antwerp was cleared for Allied use. Additional rehabilitated rail lines in western France came into service, and COMZ obtained more trucks. About this time the theater instituted several changes in supply procedures, partly because of the improvement in port and transportation facilities and partly as a result of recommendations made by top-ranking ASF visitors, including General Somervell himself, following inspection visits to the ETO in late 1944 and early 1945. The system of tonnage allocations to the armies gave way to a 10-day requisitioning procedure. Heavy consumption of fast-moving items in short supply created a list of 75 "critical signal items" that had to be controlled and allocated.

---

[39] (1) USFET Gen Bd Rpt, Study 110, pp. 12, 25, and app. 6, p. 2. (2) ETOUSA Rpt, II, 66–69. (3) Hq COMZ, Rpt of General Purchasing Agent, 30 Apr 45, *passim*.

[40] For a case history of reasons underlying the wire shortage, see below, pp. 378ff.

[41] (1) AG Ltr, SPX 411.7 (13 Feb 45) OB–S–SPDDM, 14 Feb 45, sub: Field Wire W–110–B and W–130. (2) CSigO, Annual Rpt, FY 45, p. 185.

[42] TUSA AAR, pt. 22, p. 11.

[43] *Ibid.*, pp. 16, 18.

[44] (1) FUSA Sig Sv, Signal Corps Technical Historical Report, 20 October 1943–28 February 1945, p. 36. (2) TUSA, Material Hist, pp. 3–4.

[45] For a discussion of port discharge and shipping problems, see Ruppenthal, *Logistical Support of the Armies, Volume II,* chs. III, IV, and XIV.

For these Colonel O'Connell of the Requirements Branch of the Signal Section, 12th Army Group, maintained a strict analysis of demands, status of supply, and shipments.[46]

It was difficult to achieve equity in the distribution of items on the critical list. The scarcer the article became, the greater the anxiety of the army signal officers to obtain as much of it as possible in order not to be caught short. In December the 12th Army Group's Signal Section stepped in and assumed the responsibility for allocating such items. From that time on until V–E Day, signal supply showed a gradual but steady improvement.[47] The armies, assured that each would receive a fair share, became more reasonable in their demands. While it could be argued that allocating supplies was not a proper function for an army group section, the signal supply officers who commented on the matter both during and after the war agreed that it was very helpful. The 12th Army Group was close enough to the tactical situation to be fully cognizant of the real needs of the armies, as COMZ was not. COMZ arranged for priority shipment of critical items by a special express train called "Toot Sweet" and gave the shipments special handling all the way to the forward ADSEC depots, from which point they were distributed to the armies. This system eliminated several requisitioning channels as well as the competition between the armies for scarce items.[48]

The improvement in supply at this time was most fortuitous, for the German counteroffensive in mid-December —the Battle of the Bulge—took a heavy toll of signal equipment. First Army lost the major portion of signal equipment in the hands of 6 infantry and 2 armored divisions.[49] For example, the Germans captured the 2d Infantry Division's radio repair and telephone equipment, spare parts, and all of its reserve signal supplies. Field wire consumption in First Army increased 500 percent. Third Army lost 90 percent of the signal equipment carried by its units and reported that during the period it supported and equipped 19 divisions in all, including 6 divisions rushed into the line.[50]

Emergency action in COMZ replaced signal supply losses fairly promptly. The Signal Supply Division, ETOUSA, rushed requisitions to the United States for some major items, including 20,000 miles of field wire consumed by FUSA during the Ardennes fighting. By the middle of January both armies reported that they had made up their losses.[51]

The German Ardennes offensive checked the movement of supplies forward to areas closer to the army fronts, clogged the transportation facilities,

[46] (1) 12th AGp Rpt of Opns, sec. IV (G–4), I, 24, and VI, 51. (2) Ruppenthal, *Logistical Support of the Armies, Volume II*, ch. XII, *passim*. (3) USFET Gen Bd Rpt, Study 110, pp. 19–21, and apps. 1, 2, 4, 5, and 7. (4) TUSA AAR, pt. 22, pp. 13, 14, 16, 18–19, 20, 23. (5) FUSA, *Rpt of Opns, 1 Aug 44–22 Feb 45*, bk. III, an., 8, pp. 181–82.

[47] USFET Gen Bd Rpt, Study 110, p. 21. Other factors such as improvement in port capacity and transportation, of course, share the credit.

[48] (1) USFET Gen Bd Rpt, Study 110, pp. 19–21, and apps. 1, 2, 4, 5, 7. (2) TUSA AAR, pt. 22, pp. 13, 14, 16, 18–19, 20, 23. (3) FUSA, *Rpt of Opns, 1 Aug 44–22 Feb 45*, bk. III, an. 8, pp. 181–82. (4) Ruppenthal, *Logistical Support of the Armies, Volume II*, ch. X, pp. 33–34.

[49] ETOUSA Rpt, II, 86–j.

[50] (1) FUSA, *Rpt of Opns, 1 Aug 44–22 Feb 45*, bk. III, an. 8, p. 181. (2) TUSA AAR, pt. 22, pp. 13, 16. (3) TUSA, Material Hist, pp. 3–4.

[51] ETOUSA Rpt, II, 86–j, 86–k.

and created backlogs of material held at Antwerp. A lack of depot space for temporary or in-transit storage added to the congestion. On 3 January 1945 a backlog of 14,900 tons of signal equipment waited at Antwerp, with only 1,000 to 1,500 tons moving out each day. A week later nearly 31,000 tons of signal items had piled up at Antwerp, on 21 February 16,000 tons still remained, and on 1 March, 17,000 tons. But by the end of March, with better transportation available and more depots established, nearly all of the backlog had disappeared.[52]

Despite significant improvement in signal supply matters in the closing months of the campaign, the armies in general were inclined to be critical of the amount of signal material they received. The combat forces, understandably exasperated by the restrictions that logistical considerations imposed on combat operations, were prone to dismiss them as the shortcomings of COMZ. Undeniably there were shortcomings in COMZ. But the armies displayed little understanding of COMZ's problems and difficulties. The manner in which Operation OVERLORD developed created a supply task out of all proportion to planned capabilities. The delay in clearing ports, the speed of advance in the breakout and pursuit that prevented the orderly development of a system of backup depots, roads, rail lines, and other facilities, and above all the unprecedented size of the operation presented problems on a scale never before encountered in a military operation.[53]

On the whole, Signal Corps supply operations compared favorably with those of the other technical services.[54] Not every Signal Corps customer received all the supplies he wanted at the time he wanted them, but all genuine crises were averted and reasonable demands were met as fully as possible.[55] No combat operation really suffered or was held up for want of signal equipment. That is as much as could have been expected under all the adverse circumstances.

Communications in the Ardennes Counteroffensive

By early December 1944, the Allied armies had advanced to the German border and across it at some points. Aachen, the first large German city to fall into Allied hands, yielded to the U.S. First Army late in October after three weeks of bloody fighting. From Arnhem in the north to the Belfort area in the south, Canadian, British, American, and French forces were poised, maneuvering for position, fighting their way forward in Alsace, and building up strength for the concerted advance that would carry them across the Rhine.

In the Ardennes sector, the American forces were stretched thin. Both Supreme Headquarters and 12th Army Group considered that a German attack in this area was possible, but rather

[52] (1) ETOUSA Rpt, II, 86-f, 86-g, 86-h, 90. (2) App. A, Orgn and Status of SSD, ETO 1945, Tab L, Memo, Brig Gen James A. Code, Jr., Actg CSigO, ETOUSA COMZ, for Maj Gen Thomas B. Larkin, DComdr COMZ, 24 Feb 45. SigC 370.2 ETO.

[53] For a penetrating discussion and evaluation of COMZ, see Ruppenthal, Logistical Support of the Armies, Volume II, especially pp. 348-63 and 503-11.

[54] 12th AGp, Rpt of Opns, VI (G-4), 24, 32, 38, 46, 50-1, 58, 62, 68, 76.

[55] USFET Gen Bd Rpt Study 110, p. 4.

unlikely.[56] Nonetheless the Germans did strike. In great secrecy Generalfeldmarschall Gerd von Rundstedt massed elements of three German armies, some twenty-four infantry and panzer divisions, and launched his attack on 16 December.

Army Group Communications

When the German attack began, General Bradley's 12th Army Group headquarters was located at Verdun and his tactical headquarters at Luxembourg City. To the north were General Simpson's Ninth Army headquarters at Maastricht and General Hodges' First Army headquarters at Spa. To the south, General Patton and the Third Army were at Nancy. Thus in a sense the enemy was between Bradley and the two northern armies. General Eisenhower feared that communications would be lost between Bradley, Simpson, and Hodges and therefore passed control of the First and Ninth U.S. Armies temporarily from 12th Army Group to 21 Army Group in a quick reshuffling of positions to meet Rundstedt's attack. According to General Bradley, SHAEF's fears were unwarranted, and so it turned out. Thanks to a flexible wire system, with alternate routes ready at hand, Bradley was never out of communication with either army at any time during the Ardennes action.[57]

Except for open wire links between Verdun and Aubange and between Verdun and Nancy, the 12th Army Group wire network consisted entirely of French underground cable circuits. With the onset of the winter rains, some splices in the underground cables had developed trouble. Colonel Black, 12th Army Group's signal officer, had provided alternate routing for important circuits by constructing an open wire lead between Verdun and Liège, with terminals at the Aubange and Jemelle repeater stations. This lead was equipped with four CF carrier systems operating on a 4-wire basis. "By having terminals at the cable repeater stations it was possible not only to split important trunk groups between the cable and open wire, but also to reroute circuits, by section, between the open wire and cable, in the event of failure of either."[58]

The enemy did indeed quickly overrun the 12th Army Group cable and wire routes in the vicinity of Bastogne and Jemelle. Colonel Black decided to abandon the repeater station at Jemelle without sabotage, once it became apparent that it could not be held.[59] Alternate circuits had already been cut in before the Germans reached Jemelle. To provide the necessary lateral communications, 12th Army Group rerouted all circuits to the west from Verdun through Reims and Paris, using circuits obtained from the underground cables under the allocational control of the Allied Expeditionary Force Long Lines

---

[56] (1) *SCAEF Rpt*, p. 75. (2) For a detailed account of the whole Ardennes campaign, including an analysis of "intelligence failures," see Hugh M. Cole, *The Ardennes: Battle of the Bulge*, UNITED STATES ARMY IN WORLD WAR II (Washington, 1965).

[57] (1) *SCAEF Rpt*, p. 76. (2) Bradley, *A Soldier's Story*, p. 476. (3) Interv, SigC Hist Sec with Rumbough, 20 Feb 45.

[58] 12th AGp, Rpt of Opns, XI (Sig), 202–03.

[59] The wisdom of this decision was confirmed later when American troops retook the station and found it intact except for blast and bomb damage. *Ibid.*, p. 203.

Control Agency. The AEFLLCA was in fact one of the major agencies responsible for providing communications facilities around the Bulge by circuits as far west as Paris. The rearrangement of circuits to provide wire communications from First and Ninth Armies and their associated air headquarters to 21 Army Group, between 12th Army Group and 21 Army Group, and between 12th Army Group and the First and Ninth Armies required setting up 2,000 circuit miles in seven days.[60] Except for very short intervals of interruption because of bomb damage, 12th Army Group was never without wire communications to 21 Army Group and to the First and Ninth Armies. In any event, HF radio circuits were maintained throughout the period. Two HF circuits were always available from Headquarters, 12th Army Group (Main), and one from Headquarters, 12th Army Group (TAC), to each army, including the First and Ninth even while they were temporarily under the control of 21 Army Group.[61]

General Bradley later called the telephone system "the most valued accessory of all." To blunt and then crush the German spearhead by attacking both flanks, it was necessary to bring up Allied divisions and shift them about very quickly. But it was unnecessary to resort to written orders; they were all oral, transmitted entirely by telephone.[62] Bradley said, "From my desk in Luxembourg I was never more than 30 seconds by phone from any of the Armies. If necessary, I could have called every division on the line. Signal Corps officers like to remind us that 'although Congress can make a general, it takes communications to make him a commander.' The maxim was never more brilliantly evidenced than in this battle for the Ardennes." [63]

The VHF (radio relay) stations serving 12th Army Group headquarters also stood directly in the path of the German advance. When the enemy threatened to overrun the sites, the men (an operating crew of eight Signal Corps men from the Signal Section, Headquarters, 12th Army Group, plus twelve men from the 825th Tank Destroyer Battalion, who had been assigned to guard the station) moved several times. Eventually they located two relays on Hill 561 near Jemelle, Belgium. On the day before Christmas the Germans took control of the area, and a German antiaircraft battery set up its guns only five hundred yards from the station. The relay station, itself, tucked away in its obscure site, remained unnoticed for some time.

The crewmen concealed a spare transmitter and receiver in the forest to save the equipment should the station have to be abandoned suddenly. During the daytime, with the sounds of battle and

---

[60] (1) *Ibid.* (2) OVERLORD Rpt, V, 175–76. (3) Ltr, Lanahan to Huggins, 31 Oct 57. SigC Hist Sec file.
[61] 12th AGp, Rpt of Opns, XI (Sig), p. 208.
Actually, "The Battle of the Bulge . . . offers an outstanding historical example of the flexibility of a grid communication system in providing alternate routes. . . . There seems to be practically no one . . . who knows that this is not a completely new thought." Attachment 2, MS Comment, Willis, to Ltr, Lanahan to Huggins, 31 Oct 57.

[62] Press Conf, Bradley, CG 12th AGp, reported in CSigO, Annual Rpt, FY 45, p. 7.
[63] Bradley, *A Soldier's Story*, p. 474.
For the similar experience of Maj. Gen. J. Lawton Collins using the Army's facile communications system in the Ruhr area to bottle up the enemy, see *Signals*, V, No. 4 (March–April, 1951), 46ff.

enemy troop movements around them
to mask the noise from the station's
power unit, the isolated signalmen continued to operate. They had an
important assignment. Their station was
a vital link in the only channel between
Headquarters, 12th Army Group, TAC,
at Luxembourg and Headquarters,
Ninth U.S. Army, at Maastricht, and
between 12th Army Group headquarters and the headquarters of First U.S.
Army at Spa. At night in the comparative stillness the men dared not transmit lest the noise from their power unit
reveal their presence. For three tense
days–the 24th, 25th, and 26th of December–they continued to pass along a
very heavy volume of traffic almost under the noses of the Germans. Then,
late on the afternoon of 26 December,
they spied a force of Germans only two
hundred yards away, headed straight
for their position. Hurriedly the men
closed the station and slipped into the
forest.[64] Of the 20 men at the station,
17 got through safely to the Allied lines.
Three, all members of the Signal Corps
crew, did not. One of the three eventually was returned as a repatriated
prisoner of war.

The time these signalmen bought was
not wasted. By the time the station was
forced off the air late on the afternoon
of 26 December, other Signal Corps
crews had succeeded in installing an alternate route on sites west of the
Meuse.[65]

Communications at Army and Corps Level

The full shock of the enemy December assault was borne by the
four divisions thinly deployed in the
Eifel-Ardennes sector–the 4th, 28th, and
106th Infantry Divisions and the 9th
Armored Division. Divided and bypassed, these forces slowed the enemy
drive but could not stop it. As the big
enemy gamble gained momentum all
along the First Army front, liaison teams,
isolated units, and convoys cut off from
the main bodies of Allied troops urgently sought information as to where to
go. Signal Corps message centers were
swamped with work. Locator sections
were set up to route individuals and units
to their proper destinations. Messengers,
forced many times to skirt or penetrate
enemy lines, completed scheduled runs
despite the confusion, and no messages
were lost during this phase of the operation. Cryptographic volume reached a
peak of 48,000 groups a day, the highest
since the invasion. On the fourth day of
the attack, First Army's front extended
for 181 miles, but neither then nor at
any time during the Ardennes reversal
was First Army headquarters out of communication with its major elements, or
the Air Forces, or the armies on its
flanks, or the rear. Either wire or radio
was always available, usually both. Except for short periods while cutovers to

---

[64] (1) 12th AGp, Rpt of Opns, XI (Sig), 203,
209. (2) Hq ETOUSA CSigO, Current Info Ltr
(Jul 45), pp. 27–28. SigC Hist Sec file.

[65] After the enemy retreat and as soon as the
snow melted, the Signal Corps men returned to the
station site. They found that the Germans had cut
down the antennas, searched the station thoroughly,
and had carried off the power units, operating

equipment, and vehicles. The spare receiver and
transmitter that had been hidden in the woods
were still there, intact, and in good condition.
Later, in Mainz, Germany, three each of the
station's six transmitters and receivers (identified
by their serial numbers) turned up in a captured
railway boxcar containing German equipment
packed for shipment to the German rear. ETOUSA,
Current Info Ltr (Jul 45), p. 28.

alternate routes were being made, wire and teletypewriter communications were continuous. Indeed, Colonel Williams reported that, while First Army had fourteen radio nets in operation, traffic was exceptionally light because of the amount of wire facilities available. He particularly praised the radio relay equipment, which he used between army and each corps throughout the period. With lines out, with ice and snow impeding rebuilding, this antrac equipment once again proved invaluable.[66]

The wiremen as usual had a busy and difficult time of it. The 97th Signal Operations Battalion, for example, had arrived in Europe for duty with the XVI Corps just in time to get into the Battle of the Bulge. Companies A and B went on duty with the hard-pressed 54th Signal Battalion serving the XVIII Airborne Corps in the areas around Stavelot, Houffalize, and Malmédy. The construction companies worked in the bitter cold, over icy roads, putting up poles and rolling out the wire as the Allies stood their ground against the Germans.[67]

The 50th Signal Battalion, which served the VII Corps, was located at Kornelimuenster. On the 21st of December VII Corps relinquished its area and divisions to XIX Corps and moved around the German Ardennes salient to a position directly across the path of the main enemy thrust northward. Long lines of communication to the shifting divisions, subzero temperatures, and rugged terrain severely taxed facilities. Tanks, gunfire, and skidding trucks repeatedly broke the wire lines. Mine fields sown liberally through the snow-covered area presented a deadly menace. Christmas, for the 50th, proved to be long on fireworks but short on celebration.[68]

Division Communication Experiences

Below corps headquarters the signalmen had a difficult time keeping the communications lines open. During heavy shelling on 16 December all wire communications were destroyed between 2d Infantry Division headquarters in Belgium and its subordinate units. In exposed positions, the 2d Signal Company's technicians reinstated the circuits in record time. Then the radio and telephone men, messengers, cooks, and clerks of the company took up arms and helped defend the installation and repel attacks by German armor and infantry. When the slashing German attack forced the division to withdraw on 19 December, a reliable wire system was available for use to co-ordinate the withdrawal. Last to leave the abandoned command post, which was under heavy shellfire and beset with infiltrating tanks and enemy infantry, were the communications technicians.[69]

The 30th Signal Company, an experienced outfit that had participated in many a hot action since its arrival in

---

[66] (1) Combat Operations Data, First Army in Europe, 1944-45. OCMH files. (2) FUSA, Rpt of Opns, 1 Aug 44–22 Feb 45, pp. 180–81. (3) *SCAEF Rpt*, p. 76. (4) Ltr, Williams to Thompson, 31 Dec 49. SigC Hist Sec file.

[67] "Spirit of the 97th Signal Operations Battalion," *Signal*, V, No. 6 (July-August, 1951), 9–11, 74, 80.

[68] History of the 50th Sig Bn, *passim.* SGBN-50-0(27904), Apr 41–May 45.

[69] (1) WD GO 26, 9 Apr 45. (2) Williams, "First Army's ETO Signal Operations," *Signals*, II, No. 4, pp. 5–11.

SIGNAL LINEMEN REPAIR WIRE IN THE ARDENNES

Normandy on 15 June, was readying itself for the planned crossing of the Roer River when the Germans struck in the Ardennes. The 30th hastily moved into Belgium, arriving at a location near Spa on 18 December. The heavy snow, the confusion of other units leaving the area, and the near misses of V–1 buzz bombs landing close to the signal area impressed the signalmen less, to judge by their after action report, than the unprecedented length of a coded wireless message the radio team in the corps net received during the period. The message ran to a massive 727 groups—it was far longer than the Bill of Rights.[70]

The 149th Armored Signal Company, which served the 9th Armored Division, was in Brouch, Luxembourg, when the Germans attacked. On its way to Arlon, Belgium, on 18 December, the signal company convoy was stopped in the village of Sauel (Luxembourg) and, except for the drivers, the signalmen were pressed into service for several days as security guards for the 9th Armored Division trains.[71]

In the series of hasty moves and regroupings that took place during the month, the 149th was busy. Throughout their offensive, the Germans jammed the VIII Corps command net, but the radio operators of the 149th were experienced and able to copy through the jamming. Many lower-echelon units also reported enemy jamming. The Germans had captured a considerable amount of American radio equipment in their ini-

tial thrust. Now they used it to confuse the American operators and to interfere with communications efficiency. First Army countered by routing administrative traffic through regular APO channels, leaving message centers free to expedite tactical combat traffic.[72] The messengers found the going rough. They traveled 15,500 miles during the month, often under fire. Their many attempts to reach the division's Combat Command R (which was encircled at Bastogne) failed—each time they were turned back.

From the beginning of the enemy drive, German artillery and infantry fire repeatedly destroyed wire communication facilities. One wire team of the 149th worked four days and nights without rest, repairing and installing wire lines. Once again radio relay saved the day. When wire lines went out, radio relay took over until the breaks could be repaired.[73]

The columns of the 147th Armored Signal Company moving south from Heerlerheide, Holland, toward St. Vith, Belgium, with the 7th Armored Division fell under fierce German attacks on the flanks on 17–18 December. In the resulting confusion each isolated section of the company made its own way. One group under 1st Lt. Woodrow Combs was cut off at Stavelot, where a quantity of signal supplies was housed. Lieutenant Combs commandeered all the available tank destroyers and AAA weapons and organized a defense against an approaching German amored column. The stand he and his men made stopped the Germans long enough for the signal-

[70] History of the 30th Signal Company. 330–SIG–o (27314) Hist 30th Sig Co, 1944–45.

[71] 149th Armd Sig Co AAR, 1–31 Dec 44. 609–41.2 (12648), 149th Armd Sig Co AAR, Oct–Dec 44, Jan–Feb 45.

[72] Ibid.

[73] Ibid.

IFF Antenna Used by the 217th Antiaircraft Battalion near Bastogne

men to remove their supplies from the threatened depots.[74]

At division headquarters, signal company officers stood guard at division roadblocks to warn of approaching enemy armor. Signal company personnel manned bazooka teams to defend a roadblock at Hotton and formed a half-track defense squad to establish a roadblock at Ortho.[75]

The sturdy defense of St. Vith by American forces denied the enemy that important area during the first critical days. Meanwhile, the 101st Airborne Division moved up from reserve to the vital road center of Bastogne. The 101st Airborne Signal Company was alerted to move to the Bastogne area on 17 December. A small advance detachment of the signal company moved out at once and started setting up communications at the division command post. It was soon joined by the rest of the signal company, well ahead of the division, but communications had to be devised piecemeal as the tactical situation developed. Wire communication to VIII Corps was established on 19 December.[76]

When it became apparent to the VIII Corps headquarters that the 101st would

---

[74] 147th Armd Sig Co AAR, Dec 44. L–374, 7th Armd Div 44, Misc.

[75] Ibid.

[76] 101st Airborne Sig Co, 101st Airborne Div AAR, Dec 44. Opns Rpt 3101–SIG–0.3 (22377)M, Dec 44–10 May 45.

soon be cut off from other American forces, signal officers hastily assembled a complete radio relay AN/TRC–3 installation in a truck and put a spare terminal set in a trailer to be towed behind the truck. They dispatched the equipment with the hope that it would arrive on time. Arrive it did, by the narrowest of margins, for it was the last vehicle to enter the town before the German encirclement was complete on 22 December.[77] Unfortunately, the trailer containing the spare terminal was destroyed by gunfire, but throughout the tense period that followed the radio relay equipment provided, in addition to radio net and wire lines, two radiotelephone and one radioteletype channel between division and corps. Capt. William J. Johnson, commanding the signal company, called it "a necessity in the situation, when we found ourselves surrounded with no other possible ground contact to higher headquarters, and later, especially to the units making the breakthrough."[78]

On that same day, 22 December, Johnson and his men put all movable signal equipment into the cellar of a building. Message center, switchboards, and radio stations all went into this underground shelter and were operated from that position during the siege. The large, long-distance SCR–299's, 399's, and 499's in their bulky trailers or vans were of course too big to be taken underground. These and the radio relay equipment remained outside. With wire lines under constant heavy enemy artillery fire and aerial bombardment, wire

teams of the 101st Signal Company were out repairing breaks continuously.[79]

On 22 December the 101st Airborne Division had withstood a violent attack from the northeast, possibly the first reaction of the enemy to the northward move of General Patton's Third Army. After weeks of work under the most trying weather and terrain conditions, Patton's signal officer, Colonel Hammond, had just completed an elaborate communications network and command post system in St. Avold in preparation for an offensive through the Palatinate and a move of army headquarters. The system had to be abandoned when Third Army stormed north to Luxembourg. In a matter of hours Colonel Hammond had set up an entirely new network under even worse handicaps,[80] though the initial expansion was made easier since he could take over and expand some existing 12th Army Group and PTT facilities.[81] On 26 December Patton succeeded in forcing a narrow corridor through the German tanks ringing Bastogne. It was only three hundred yards wide, but it opened the way to the American troops cut off there and punctured the German bulge, which began slowly to deflate under combined British and American pressure.[82]

RCM in the Ardennes

Now came the first and only battle test of Jackal, the high-powered airborne

[77] Rumbough, "Radio Relay," Military Review, XXVI, No. 2, p. 11.

[78] 101st Airborne Sig Co, 101st Airborne Div, AAR, Dec 44.

[79] (1) Ibid. (2) Rumbough, "Radio Relay," Military Review, XXVI, No. 2, p. 11.

[80] Allen, Lucky Forward, p. 169.

[81] TUSA AAR, I, 169, and pt. 22, pp. 11–12.

[82] (1) SCAEF Rpt, pp. 77–78. (2) George S. Patton, Jr., War As I Knew It (Boston: Houghton Mifflin Co., 1947), chs. 4 and 5, passim.

radio jammer AN/ART-3 developed by the Signal Corps for the AAF. The First and Third U.S. Armies had been reluctant to try Jackal jamming because a portion of the frequency band used by their tank radios overlapped into the German band to be jammed. Earlier tests in England had indicated somewhat inconclusively that little or no interference would be caused, since American radio for armored forces was FM while similar German sets and Jackal were AM.[83] Now that nearly the whole of the German *Sixth Panzer Army* was in the Ardennes fighting, it seemed a good opportunity to test Jackal.

Accordingly, beginning on 29 December and continuing through 7 January, Eighth Air Force B–24's, based in England and bearing the Jackal jammers blaring full blast, flew in relays over the battle area, coinciding with a Third Army counterthrust in the vicinity of Bastogne. The first results seemed inconclusive, but, according to later reports from German prisoners, Jackal effectively blanketed German armored communications during these crucial days. Nor were the American tankmen inconvenienced or made voiceless by the overlap in frequencies. The jammer effectively filled the German AM receivers with a meaningless blare, while the American FM sets heard nothing but the voices of their operators.[84]

---

[83] ETOUSA Rpt, II, 237–38.

[84] (1) CSigO, Annual Rpt, FY 45, pp. 235, 257. (2) 12th AGp, Rpt of Opns, XI (Sig), 232. This was the only employment of Jackal, for after Ardennes the remainder of the *Sixth Panzer Army* was transferred to the Eastern Front, and only a small amount of German armor remained on the Western Front. Thus, there were no further large-scale armored counterattacks by the enemy. *Ibid.*

The Closing Months of the Campaign

The Ardennes offensive was a bitter and bloody affair, but at best it served the Germans only as a delaying action. Although the losses in men and equipment made it necessary to regroup units and revise Allied plans, inevitably the Allies moved forward into the German homeland. The first phase of the spring offensive was aimed at clearing the German forces from the region west of the Rhine, a goal accomplished in January and February in a series of coordinated moves all along the Allied line. During the crossing of the Rhine in March, the envelopment of the German heartland in April, and the final, devastating days before the surrender on 7 May, the communications tasks confronting Signal Corps units continued to be diverse, as they had been throughout the campaign. A few examples serve to illustrate the point.

Signal Corps Participation in Technical Intelligence

As American troops drew near Germany, intelligence groups were alert to detect evidence of German progress in communications development and techniques. The Technical Industrial Intelligence Committee, organized in 1944 by the Joint Chiefs of Staff, watched for information on a German method of producing titanium dioxide capacitors in quantity for radio circuits, for German versions of field wire stranding machines, and for many other devices and processes of interest to the American Army. Teams of the Combined Intelligence Objectives Subcommitte (CIOS), representing the Combined Chiefs of Staff, sought information on infrared applications, remote control systems, new vacuum tubes, and a host of other intelligence targets. In these high-level technical intelligence activities the Signal Corps participated. As a matter of fact a Signal Corps officer, Maj. Neal D. Crane of the Technical Liaison Division, Office of the Chief Signal Officer, ETOUSA, had been named acting field team leader for the first CIOS field mission in the Paris area in October 1944. This first team of sixteen American and British military and civilian scientists represented the British Admiralty, War Office, and Air Ministry, and the U.S. Navy, Air Forces, Signal Corps, and Office of Scientific Research and Development (OSRD). Major Crane's reports to SHAEF on his 1944 mission helped establish the routines and administrative procedures used in later field missions.[85]

By this time five teams of the Signal Corps' own Enemy Equipment Intelligence Service were in the ETO. Their over-all activities were controlled by the Technical Liaison Division of the Office of the Chief Signal Officer, ETOUSA, but they were attached to the various armies and army groups.[86] The EEIS

teams were among the new types of signal units to serve in World War II. The first such team to operate in the ETO had arrived on 21 November 1943 and had been assigned to 1st Army Group.[87] The EEIS mission was several sided. For example, the highly trained technical experts of the teams were expected to cover the battle fronts, examining and analyzing captured enemy equipment to gain information on enemy developments and resources and on new ideas that could be exploited for Allied benefit or that could enable Allied laboratories to develop effective counterweapons and countertactics promptly.[88] Toward this end the EEIS teams studied and classified captured signal equipment, sending items of special interest to depots on the Continent, from where they were shipped to the Signal Corps laboratories in the zone of interior for study.

Captured enemy equipment not only produced tactical and technical intelligence but also bolstered supply.[89] Many items could be used at once without reworking. Others could be modified in the special laboratory of the Technical Liaison Division, Signal Division, ETOUSA. Captured equipment also yielded quantities of spare parts and accessories. Several U.S. armored divi-

---

[85] (1) ETOUSA Rpt, II, 175, 204–09. (2) Davis, "Technical Intelligence and the Signal Corps," *Signals*, III, No. 6 (July–August, 1949), 19ff. (3) SCIA files, Tech Intel Missions (CIOS) and TIIC/CIOS, Data Wanted, *passim*.

[86] (1) ETOUSA Rpt, II, 175–76. (2) Capt Chester A. Hall, Jr., Signal Corps Intelligence: A Brief History, 1940–1948 (1949), SCTC Monograph, Camp Gordon, Ga., *passim*. (3) Capt Robert W. Strunk, The Signal Corps Enemy Equipment Intelligence Service (1948), Sig Sch Monograph, *passim*. The Sig Sch Libr, Ft. Monmouth, copy also in SigC Hist Sec file.

[87] Ltr, Lt Col Herbert C. Taylor, CO EEIS Det 2 to CSigO, 2 Mar 44, sub: Rpt From SigC EEIS Team in ETO. SCIA file, EEIS Det 2, ETO.

[88] (1) FM 11–35, Signal Corps Intelligence, 2 Sep 42. (2) Hall, SigC Intel: A Brief Hist, 1940–48. (3) CSigO, Annual Rpt, FY 44, pp. 157–60.

[89] For example, the 84th Signal Company, 84th Infantry Division, used large quantities of signal material from captured enemy signal dumps in operations during April 1945. Of of the SigO Hq 84th Inf Div AAR, 1 May 45. L-670 84th Div Sig (34) Apr.

sions used captured German field wire, switchboards, telephones, and associated equipment to supplement their authorized wire allowances, enough of it to provide wire communication down to company and platoon level. French units captured German mine detectors in quantity, and the EEIS teams won French gratitude by demonstrating the use of the equipment.[90]

In the closing months of the campaign great caches of signal riches came to light in Germany.[91] So much valuable equipment was being shipped to the United States that in December the Signal Corps had established a special Captured Equipment Section in the Holabird Signal Depot in Baltimore, Maryland, in order to receive, sort, catalogue, and analyze the equipment returned from Europe and the other theaters and to speed the flow of items to the laboratories for further study. In the spring of 1945, EEIS teams attached to FUSA discovered, for example, "two car loads of commercial teletype and and dial telephone equipment found in the rail yard at Frankenburg, . . . two cars loaded with airborne radio equipment at Warburg railroad yard, . . . forced labor camp where a large quantity of electrical supplies were found . . . signal dump at Giflitz, found still intact . . . railroad yards at Wildungen where large store of signal

equipment found . . . radar-equipped aircraft still intact at airfield. . . ." [92] It is impossible to estimate the total tonnage of enemy signal equipment put into use by American armies, but it was large.

EEIS teams operated very close to the front, sometimes ahead of it. Though they posted signs or guards to protect their. finds from the ubiquitous G.I. souvenir hunters, troops of other branches untrained in signal matters often wrecked precious equipment in their search for mementoes. By 1 December 1944 the EEIS teams had sent back to the United States more than five hundred "hot items," so valuable that they warranted laboratory study, and had issued hundreds of technical reports.[93] Whenever the Signal Corps laboratories discovered information of value to the Navy or to the Air Forces, it was sent to them at once.[94]

Sigcircus and Sigcircus Junior

As the war progressed to the borders of Germany and beyond, the various headquarters began planning forward moves. By this time stable wire lines in the rear areas could carry the main communications load. Radio, however, would be needed for headquarters use in Germany and during the post-hostilities period, and COMZ signalmen set about reorganizing the rear networks and finding ways of augmenting forward coverage. Rapid moves and unpredictable day-to-day location of armies

[90] (1) Davis. "Technical Intelligence and the Signal Corps," Signals, III, No. 6, p. 22. (2) Hall, SigC Intel: A Brief Hist, 1940–48, app. 1.

[91] (1) See Daily Jnl Entries, CSigO ETOUSA, item 7, 14 Apr; items 6, 7, 22, 19 Apr; item 9, 21 Apr; items 8, 13, 22 Apr; items 10, 11, 25 Apr; items 6, 7, 8, 5 May 45. SCIA file ETO Daily Jnl folder 1. (2) Item 10, 8 May; items 12, 13, 9 May; items 7, 8, 14 May 45. SCIA file ETO Daily Jnl folder 2.

[92] (1) EEIS Det 10 Sig Sec, Weekly Det Hist, 1–7 and 8–14 Apr 45. FUSA Basic Rcds EEIS folder, SigC Hist Sec file. (2) SigC Tech Hist Rpt, 20 Oct 43–28 Feb 45, p. 46.

[93] ETOUSA Rpt, II, 203, 204.

[94] CSigO, Annual Rpt, FY 45, p. 391.

SIGCIRCUS, SHOWING TRANSMITTERS AND ANTENNAS. *Artist's conception of an installation, above. Below, Sigcircus unit in operation.*

made fixed station facilities impractical. Completely mobile radio stations would solve the problem, but earlier COMZ pleas for Dukws in which to mount such stations had been denied.[95] Engineers in the Communications Division, Office of the Chief Signal Officer, ETOUSA, took over an unfinished project originally commissioned from a French firm by the Luftwaffe during the German occupation. Under Signal Corps direction the firm, using American-made transmitters and radioteletypewriter equipment, built five completely mobile radio stations. These were dubbed, according to size, Sigcircus or Sigcircus, Junior.[96]

Sigcircus was completed in just three months and delivered early in 1945, when the Allies were closing the Colmar pocket and making their first crossings of the Rhine.[97] Sigcircus filled a communications need peculiar to the armed forces of the United States: to keep in constant touch with Washington as well as to intercommunicate with headquarters in the theater.

Sigcircus was a powerful, 60-kilowatt single sideband, multichannel, mobile radio station, the only one of its kind in the world. Completely self-sufficient, its elements were packed into seventeen huge, lumbering trailers, three of which carried the diesel power units and fuel supply. Sigcircus could do anything a fixed station of comparable power could do. Its radioteletypewriter channels provided simultaneous transmission and reception of as many as 300,000 words daily between the United States and

Europe. In addition, Sigcircus was equipped with all the paraphernalia of a modern broadcasting station—including a 300-watt transmitter for local broadcasts, up-to-date broadcast studio and control booths, facsimile equipment for transmitting and receiving photographs, and facilities for making recordings on wire, film, and disc.[98] It could also broadcast entertainment programs for troops. All these services Sigcircus could perform simultaneously, without interference. Sigcircus possessed its own signal center, complete with a conference room equipped with radioteletypewriter for sending and receiving messages between Europe and the United States simultaneously. There was also a crypto room, completely equipped.[99]

Once Sigcircus reached a destination, the Signal Corps team that proudly served this massive creation could set it up and put it into operation with remarkable speed. If commercial power was available at the site, a turn of a switch converted Sigcircus from diesel to commercial power operation. Within twenty-four hours, the station was ready.[100]

Sigcircus had four little brothers, each of them known as Sigcircus Junior. They were single-channel, radioteletypewriter mobile stations, two of them 1.2-kilowatt, two 300-watt in power. They traveled

---

[95] MS Comment, Shearer, Jul 59.

[96] (1) ETOUSA Rpt, II, 47–49. (2) Lt. Col. Loyd C. Sigmon, "Sigcircus," Signals, III, No. 6 (July–August, 1949), 27–28.

[97] Sigmon, "Sigcircus," Signals, III, No. 6, p. 28.

[98] One of its applications was its use in the SHAEF Public Relations Division broadcasting center in the Hotel Scribe in Paris. See Ltr, Lt Col Walter R. Brown, Com Br PRD SHAEF, to CSigO, n.d., sub: Press Com SHAEF. Press Com SHAEF folder, SigC Hist Sec file.

[99] (1) Ibid. (2) ETOUSA Rpt, II, 48–49.

[100] Actually the 24-hour time limit was conservative. In its very first operation under field conditions at Frankfurt, Germany, the team assembled the station in twelve hours and ten minutes. Sigmon, "Sigcircus," Signals, III, No. 6, p. 28.

in six 2½-ton trucks, which also carried the crews of two officers and 19 enlisted specialists from the 3104th Signal Service Battalion. Like their big brother, Sigcircus Juniors moved about from site to site very easily, and were ready for operation within twenty-four hours after arriving at a new location. They could transmit or receive 50,000 words daily. At Headquarters, ADSEC, and Headquarters, CONAD, Sigcircus Junior stations served well. They provided the principal communications, other than wire lines, back to Paris throughout various moves in France and Germany.[101]

Wire Spans Across the Rhine

Advancing wire communications into Germany meant putting wire spans, both heavy-duty submarine cable and open wire, across the Rhine River. Since the Rhine was wide and deep and had a swift current, this was no easy task.

On 7 March FUSA units had seized the Ludendorff bridge over the Rhine at Remagen, exploiting a "rare and fleeting opportunity" that promised to influence the whole future course of the war. The bridge was the only one the Germans were unable to destroy on the entire length of the river. The Allied high command rushed FUSA troop units across the bridge, hoping to build a striking force before the German Air Force could knock out the bridge.[102] Establishment of wire communications across the river at once became a matter of urgent necessity.

The assignment to bridge the Rhine with submarine cable fell to the men

of Company A, 32d Signal Construction Battalion, on 10 March. The 32d, along with the 35th Signal Construction Battalion, had already been singled out for praise by FUSA's signal officer, Colonel Williams, for the construction and maintenance of the vast wire network required by FUSA in its push across France.[103] The first phase of the bridging job was to prepare the heavy cable on reels. Arriving at the bridge the next day in the bustle and heavy traffic, the wire crew found only two boats in the vicinity, both being used on ferry duty. Since neither could be released for wire laying, the signalmen tied a 104-copperweld wire to one of the boats, paying the pull wire off the reel on shore by hand as the ferry crossed the river. On the opposite bank a K–43 winch took up the wire. Thus they pulled the 10-pair cable and a messenger strand across the river. The work of getting the cable across went on under a rain of antiaircraft artillery fire directed against persistent German air attacks on the Remagen bridge. By midnight the installation was completed, the terminals spliced in and tested. Following the successful laying of this link, five similar submarine cables were laid across the Rhine within the First Army's boundaries from Bonn to Andernach.[104]

[103] Williams called the work of the two battalions "most outstanding." Ltr, Williams, SigO FUSA, to CSigO ETOUSA, 6 Jan 45, sub: Rpt of Outstanding Achievements of SigC for Theater Historian. Basic FUSA Rcds folder 16, SigC Hist Sec file.

[104] (1) Incl 1, Rhine River Crossing, with Ltr, Lt Col Robert E. Conrath, ComO Hq FUSA Sig Sv, to SigO FUSA, 13 Mar 45, sub: Wkly Rpt of Wire Activities. FUSA Basic Rcds folder 14. (2) Ltr, Capt Joseph A. Beaurcgard, Hq 32d Sig Const Bn, to SigO FUSA, 10 Apr 45, sub: Major Incident for Month of Mar 45. FUSA Basic Rcds 32d Sig Const Bn folder 46. Both in SigC Hist Sec file.

[101] ETOUSA Rpt, II, 48–49.
[102] *SCAEF Rpt*, p. 91.

BURYING SPIRAL-FOUR NEAR THE RHINE WITH A CABLE PLOW

The 36th Signal Heavy Construction Battalion used much the same methods in laying a 1,600-foot open wire span across the Rhine between Urmitz and Engers in April, using four assault boats lashed together to pull the wire across after a barrage balloon employed in the manner of a fishing line had failed. The men used uncut timber found in a sawmill for poles and devised dead end and suspension fixtures from power insulators and clamps taken from a German trolley line. They completed this open wire span, one of the longest in the world, in eleven days. The men of the battalion christened it the Harry

C. Ingles Span in honor of the Chief Signal Officer.[105]

Climax in Europe

For the Signal Corps troops, the final weeks of the ETO campaign resembled the fast-moving events of the early summer of 1944. But the scent of victory was in the air; the faster the pace the better. During the rapid pursuit that followed the breakout of FUSA units

---

[105] (1) Hq ETOUSA OCSigO, Current Info Ltr (Jun 45), pp. 16–17. (2) Press Release, The Harry C. Ingles Wire Span Across the Rhine. Com folder, Hist P–4. Tab B. Both in SigC Hist Sec file.

from the Remagen bridgehead, VII Corps was spread over a 194-mile front. Wire lines that the 1st Signal Company laid for the 1st Infantry Division became so long that radio once more came into wide use.[106]

By early April the Third Army had passed Frankfurt and Hersfeld and had been diverted to attack from the vicinity of Erlangen, some 140 miles away. Because of the change in direction, the TUSA signalmen had to install an entirely new network and at the same time maintain the installation at Hersfeld until the First Army took over.[107] After the 3d Armored Division, closing in from the south, and the 2d Armored Division, from the north, opened a way through the Ruhr Valley in April, the 1st Division mopped up and held the territory passed over by TUSA. Armor and infantry, and the signal troops with them, sped along the smooth 4-lane highways into the heart of Germany.

To the rear Signal Corps men were strung out in detachments of varying size all the way back to Normandy, operating the communications systems of France, Belgium, and Germany. The 3188th Signal Service Battalion serves as an example. The battalion had survived the sinking of its troopship, H.M.S. *Empire Javelin,* in the English Channel on 28 December 1944. On the Continent, the men went to work on switchboard, teletypewriter, and repair and maintenance teams and detachments scattered throughout the theater. At one period teams of the 3188th were serving in seven

different sections of COMZ. Near the end of the war there were teams of the 3188th Battalion in four countries— France, Belgium, Germany, and Italy.[108]

Other signal units in many locations worked at the endless variety of signal tasks. The 926th Signal Battalion (Separate) linked air headquarters and fighter control stations with airfields as much as two hundred miles apart. The battalion's construction companies provided the wire links from fighter control to advance radar units, pressing cooks, clerks, supply men, and motor mechanics into service as linemen because they had too few specialists to do the job alone. Another Signal Corps air unit, the 555th Signal Aircraft Warning Battalion, operated communications lines that controlled some 3,500 aircraft missions. Maintenance men of a ground unit, the 143d Armored Signal Company, performed 10,000 repair jobs on more than 1,700 radio sets in less than a year, often almost in sight of the enemy, during the drive of the 3d Armored Division across Europe. For six weeks at Stolberg, Germany, nightly shelling forced the repair crews to work in dugouts.[109]

On 25 April the Allied armies cut Germany in two when the Soviet Army from the east and the 69th Division of FUSA met in the Torgau area on the Elbe, a highlight of the war recorded by a photographer of the 165th Signal Photographic Company.[110] By 4

[106] 1st Sig Co AAR, Jan–May 45. Opns Rpts SIG–0.3 (4873). (2) Combat Opns Data, First Army in Europe, 1944–45. OCMH files.

[107] Hammond, "Signals for Patton," *Signals,* II, No. 1, pp. 5ff.

[108] 3188th Sig Sv Bn History, 1945. SGBN–3188–0.1 (7906).

[109] Signal Activities, IX TAC, SigC Tech Info Ltr 43 (Jun 45) p. 8, and Trouble-shooting on the Fly, Sig C Tech Info Ltr 44 (Jul 45), p. 11. SigC Hist Sec file.

[110] FUSA, *Rpt of Opns, 23 Feb 44–8 May 45,* bk. III, an. 8, p. 222.

May Germany was cut off from Holland, Schleswig-Holstein, and Denmark to the northeast. On every side fleeing Germans surrendered by the thousands. On 5 May it was conceded that the principal objectives had been won in every sector of the European battlefield. At midnight 8–9 May the unconditional surrender of the German forces became official. Fighting ceased. But not so the work of the Signal Corps men. Teams with the Third Army at Regensburg went immediately to Munich to install a command post there. Insistent demands poured in for the perfection of the temporary networks laid during combat.[111]

Throughout the theater Signal Corps communications circuits had been carrying peak loads and expanding as the armies spread over greater areas. Volume continued to rise from September 1944 to the end of the fighting. Message traffic at the headquarters of the 12th Army Group increased from 523,755 teletypewriter groups, 136,566 radio groups, 338,721 cipher groups, 679 motor messenger deliveries, and 176 air courier deliveries for the week of 23 September to peaks of 2,813,026 teletypewriter groups for the week of 14 April; 344,593 radio groups for the week of 28 April; 739,390 cipher groups for the week of 21 April. The peak of 164,686 telephone calls came in the week of 7 April. Motor messengers carried their largest volume, 7,948 messages, during the week of 10 February. The heaviest air deliveries, 698, were made during the week of 12 May. Signal Corps photographers with the 12th

Army Group took 67,305 still pictures and exposed 1,121,467 feet of motion picture film between 1 December 1944 and the middle of June 1945, exclusive of pictures taken for technical and tactical purposes and processed in field laboratories.[112]

Message traffic was heavy also at all army headquarters in the ETO. Traffic volume reflected the tactical situation at any given time. Late in January 1945 the Third Army recorded the highest weekly volume: 898,054 teletypewriter groups, 47,154 radio groups, 250,968 cipher groups, an estimated 106,400 telephone calls, and 41,574 motor messenger deliveries. About a month later FUSA headquarters held the record with 1,054,486 teletypewriter groups, 74,378 radio groups, 357,471 cipher groups, about 104,300 telephone calls, 28,107 motor messenger deliveries, and 3,768 air messenger deliveries of registered matter alone. Within another month Third Army was again in the lead, but for the following few weeks Ninth Army's traffic topped the list, rising during the week of 14 April to 1,147,637 teletypewriter groups, 157,760 radio groups, 301,900 cipher groups, approximately 85,000 telephone calls, 32,340 motor messenger deliveries, and 877 air deliveries.[113]

During the eleven months of operations in the ETO, Signal Corps soldiers had laid over 900,000 miles of field wire, 105,000 miles during the last month before the surrender. Some 650,000 miles of wire and 35,000 miles of cable went into the more stable systems. Since the landings in Normandy, the Third Army

---

[111] (1) *SCAEF* Rpt, pp. 112–20. (2) Hammond, "Signals for Patton," *Signals*, II, No. 1, pp. 5ff.

[112] 12th AGp, Rpt of Opns, an. M, Traffic Load Data, XI (Sig), 259–66.

[113] *Ibid.*

alone had covered 81,500 square miles of territory with communications circuits; 32,763 square miles during the last campaign.[114]

The transfer of headquarters offices from the Paris-Versailles area to Frankfurt before adequate circuits had been established into Frankfurt placed a considerable strain on the existing systems, especially on the few telephone circuits to Paris. With the beginning of the occupation period emphasis shifted to the provision of a system of fixed radio installations for the entire theater in which Frankfurt-am-Main would be the key terminal. By mid-July teletypewriter circuits connected Frankfurt with Bremen, Berlin, Paris, Italy, and, of course, Washington. Soon Austria would be linked into the network. Units were being converted from tactical to occupational status. Although some carried well-known designations, they were in reality new units, made up entirely of new men who had replaced those with enough points to go home. As they deployed widely throughout the area of occupation, they required additional extensions of communications circuits.

The cessation of fighting meant no cessation of work for the Signal Corps men who remained in Europe, not even in the interim until they were deployed to the Pacific.[115]

The problems of a signal battalion commander in this period are reflected in the unit journal of the 3188th Signal Service Battalion. On 3 May he wrote:

Mussolini dead, Hitler dead, Goebbels a suicide, the link-up of Allied forces on the Western Front with Russian forces on the Eastern Front completed at many points, the Germans in Italy surrendered. It is, however, no holiday for this headquarters. Training schedules continue, communications duty continues and will increase as the new staging area expands for redevelopment operations and teams of other units filter in to replace our high-point men. . . . This headquarters struggles with stacks of paper work. . . . Reports are the biggest headaches. In the great hours of victory we are busy swabbing up other peoples' messes that accumulated in the past. We work here. Our own little triumph will come when we can get ahead of the job long enough to celebrate the triumph of the fellows who are much closer to the enemy than we are at this time.[116]

[114] Col. Brenton G. Wallace, *Patton and His Third Army* (Harrisburg, Pa.: Military Service Publishing Company, 1946).

[115] ETOUSA Rpt, II, *passim*.

[116] 3188th Sig Sv Bn, Unit Jnl, 1945. SGBN-3188-0.7 (28189), 1945.

The Signal Corps in the CBI

In the Orient the struggle with the Japanese sprawled over an immense and varied expanse of the globe, over continental land masses and ocean islands, from the eastern Pacific to India. This military scene contrasted sharply with the relatively compact homogeneous theaters of war in the west against Germany.

In the two halves of the globe signal officers and their Signal Corps troop units served within a similar organizational framework. The circumstances and problems, however, differed. The circumstances that characterized the west—in signal matters the massive supply of equipment, specialists, and communications services for large armies in relatively small land areas—were seldom approached in the eastern arenas of war. Instead, the theaters in the east received relatively small forces and little equipment, all widely dispersed. The diverse headquarters contended with problems of water and air movements over enormous distances, measured in the thousands of miles rather than in the hundreds. Co-operation and co-ordination with naval and air commands figured even larger here than they did in the west. There were times when Signal Corps men operated their circuits for the Army from stations afloat, or ashore jointly with naval communicators. Far more often than not

they operated in regions where there had existed previously no communications facilities. This circumstance differed distinctly from operations in Europe, where the Signal Corps regularly rehabilitated and then heavily used facilities that had long served the European nations. In most areas of the east, from Ledo to Nouméa, from Guadalcanal to Okinawa, signal units had to bring everything with them, all the radio and wire the Army required for both headquarters and field use. Signal Corps men also had to construct the buildings for the facilities, from the ground up—for example, at every base in the jungles of New Guinea and along the wilderness roadway over the Himalayan "Hump" between India and China.[1]

Of the theaters of war in the east, the most remote and diverse was China, Burma, India—the CBI. In fact, it was scarcely thought of as a theater at the beginning of the war. The War Department had approved the American Military Mission to China in mid-1941, particularly to handle lend-lease arrangements with that country. Brig. Gen.

---

[1] (1) Alvin P. Stauffer, *The Quartermaster Corps: Operations in the War Against Japan*, UNITED STATES ARMY IN WORLD WAR II (Washington, 1956), p. 96. (2) Maj Mandel N. Goldstein, A Type Theater Signal Office (Pacific), 23 Nov 48, Sig Sch Monograph, p. 1. The Sig Sch Libr, Ft. Monmouth.

John Magruder arrived in Chungking in October to head the mission. Two months later the plunge by the United States into the war necessitated a China Theater and an Army task force (already volunteers under Brig. Gen. Claire L. Chennault had been providing aviation assistance there). Early in 1942 the Japanese invasion of Burma drew Allied forces into that land—the Burma Corps led by British Lt. Gen. William J. Slim, and the Chinese Expeditionary Army under Lt. Gen. Joseph W. Stilwell. Meanwhile, to support American air and service troops in India, the War Department established a Services of Supply at Karachi under Brig. Gen. Raymond A. Wheeler. Not until after the fall of Burma in May 1942 did Stilwell consolidate a reasonably recognizable U.S. theater of operations in CBI.[2]

Signal Corps officers and men, notably elements of the 835th Signal Service Company (later, a battalion), from the very start served both Stilwell and Wheeler, the installations of the Tenth Air Force, and other Army troops that supported Allied operations widely dispersed across the CBI.[3]

CBI Signal Officers and Their Problems

The first signal officer to arrive in China was Lt. Col. Joseph E. Heinrich,

who reached Chungking with the American Military Mission under General Magruder some weeks before Pearl Harbor. Stilwell's party, arriving in March 1942, included Col. George L. Townsend, signal officer on Stilwell's staff. When Stilwell took command of the Chinese forces in Burma, Townsend served as the acting signal officer of the China Theater while Heinrich remained in the Chungking message center. Among the few American soldiers who shared with General Stilwell and his staff the bitter defeat in Burma were men of Team I of the 835th Signal Service Company who provided a difficult and tenuous, but vital, radio link with India and China.[4]

Later in 1942, as General Stilwell sought to train and equip the Chinese and as the Army Air Forces built up an airlift (replacing the severed ground route between China and India), Colonel Townsend left the theater. Col. Samuel S. Lamb, signal officer of the Tenth Air Force, became the acting signal officer on the CBI staff in the rear echelon headquarters in New Delhi, India. During these and many more months to come, until American production and Allied shipping improved and until priority demands in other more crucial areas of the global war relaxed, CBI signal officers and troops fared austerely in their operations and

[2] Charles F. Romanus and Riley Sunderland, *Stilwell's Mission to China,* UNITED STATES ARMY IN WORLD WAR II (Washington, 1953), p. 387. This volume and its two successors, by the same authors: *Stilwell's Command Problems* (Washington, 1955), and *Time Runs Out in CBI* (Washington, 1959), are basic to an understanding of the CBI and its involved organizational relationships.

[3] See Thompson, Harris, *et al., The Test,* pp. 114f., 279f., 305f., 460ff.

[4] (1) *Ibid.,* p. 115. (2) Intervs, SigC Hist Sec, with Capt Jerome R. Matherne, 4 Mar 44, and with Capt Harold E. Welsh, 8 Nov 44. SigC Hist Sec files. "This handful of radiomen and [Maj. Gen. Lewis H.] Brereton's few B–17's were the only American reinforcements to reach China, Burma, and India in time to play any part whatever in the lost campaign." Romanus and Sunderland, *Stilwell's Mission to China,* pp. 137–38.

support of the Allied effort in the CBI.[5]

Signal Corps support of the Army Air Forces figured especially large, as did assistance given to the training of Chinese troops toward the day when offensive action against the Japanese in Burma might be renewed. Signal Corps troops, serving in small detachments from Karachi on the western edge of the theater to Chungking on the eastern edge, built and operated communications facilities for ACAN and for Army Air Forces operations, which, during the two years the enemy sat astride the Burma Road, provided the vital Hump lifeline to China—the airlift over the mountains between Assam, India, and Yunnan, China.[6]

From the days early in 1942, when Signal Corps soldiers intended for Java found themselves, upon the fall of that island, destined to sail onward to India, until late 1943, Signal Corps men serving in the CBI theater continued to struggle with chronic communications exigencies and shortages.[7] Those who worked for the relatively big ACAN stations at Karachi and at theater headquarters in New Delhi were somewhat better provided for, as were also those serving some of the Air Forces activities such as the Hump airlift. But for many others—those serving with the Chinese and the teams that put in lonely months at remote AWS jungle sites in Assam and in northern Burma—the story was different.[8]

Among the latter were small teams serving as aircraft observers who radioed out their sightings of enemy planes amid most primitive wilderness environments. Their neighbors were sometimes head-hunters. Experiences with the tribesmen were often weird and occasionally hair raising. Such was an incident that befell members of a Signal Corps EEIS team who penetrated deep into the Naga Hills on the India-Burma border seeking the electronic equipment of a wrecked Japanese airplane. Spending a night near a Naga village, they found that the natives had placed a guard over them. Late in the night

[5] Intervs, SigC Hist Sec with Brig Gen Henry L. P. King, 5 Sep 44, and with Brig Gen Paul L. Neal, 6 Aug 57. SigC Hist Sec files.

[6] Donald O. Wagner, Army Command and Administrative Network, 1941–45, pt. II, China-Burma-India, SigC Hist Monograph E–6, pp. 57ff. SigC Hist Sec file.

A report that Col. Francis H. Lanahan, Jr., Planning Director in the Office of the Chief Signal Officer, prepared on 10 March 1943 for the Chief Signal Officer shows the preponderance of Signal Corps units serving the Army Air Forces. Memo, Lanahan for CSigO, 10 Mar 43, sub: Rpt on SigC Activities, China, Burma, and India. SigC OT 370.2 Rpts CBI, Tab. 3. In this report, Lanahan listed the units "now in, or under movement orders for, the China, Burma, and India Theater," as follows:

SOS	Air Forces
835th Sig Sv Bn	10th Com Squadron
2d "A" Platoon Sig	1036th Sig Co Sv Gp
Photomail Co	1043d Sig Co Sv Gp
Sig Det (Depot)	1083d Sig Co Sv Gp
	1086th Sig Co Sv Gp
	675th Sig AW Reporting Co
	679th Sig AW Reporting Co
	910th Sig Co, Depot, Avn
	955th Sig RI Co
	402d Sig Co, Avn
	430th Sig Co, Avn, Heavy Const

[7] Principally a detachment of the 52d Signal Battalion: 4 officers and 116 men.

(1) Memo, Maj Lamar D. Gaston for Rcd, 21 Jul 42. SigC OT 200.3 Pers ASF CBI, Tab O. (2) Thompson, Harris, et al., The Test, p. 113.

[8] (1) Intervs, SigC Hist Sec with T/4 John J. Wildman, 24 Nov 44, and with Sgt John E. Duffy, 16 Nov 44. SigC Hist Sec file. (2) History of Northern Combat Area Command, CBI and IB, 1943–45, I, 10. OCMH files.

awesome torch rites were performed close by, which the uncomprehending Americans feared were hostile. Not till morning did they learn that the guard and the ceremonies were intended to defend them from evil spirits.[9]

The Naga tribesmen prized not money but salt, and took it as pay for their occasional services to the Americans. Their chieftains hankered for red blankets, which Capt. John G. Haury of the 679th Signal Aircraft Warning Company judiciously gave out to win native allegiance. None of Haury's teams ever suffered violence at the hands of the natives, but at times they were worried, as evidenced by the following radio message Haury once received from one of his spotter groups: "Haury from Cranmer. Party Nagas went seven miles from here. Wiped out village of two hundred and fifty. Passed through with thirty heads. Have photos verifying this. Would like hand grenades. May need them." [10]

The lack of equipment, of the supplies that were badly needed, harrowed the spirits of many Signal Corps men, while other items that were not needed

might abound. "The soldier starts out young and full of hope," said a sergeant of the 835th Signal Service Battalion describing the CBI trooper. "Then he does not get equipment. At first, he thinks he will make up for the lack of material by putting in more effort. After a while he finds out that equipment just is not coming and that effort is not enough. He feels forgotten and discouraged." He added, "We got very little information, instruction books or the like. When we did get something, it was seven or eight months old." In the early days of the war, communications equipment, if it arrived at all, arrived in poor shape. "It almost broke our hearts to get a set in China and find two or three tubes out," CBI Signal Corps veterans recalled later. "We might just as well not get any set." [11]

There were other supply problems, summed up by a CBI signalman who said, "You have to revise your thinking about signal supplies when you are fighting in a part of the world where everything that doesn't rust quickly will corrode or rot away even faster, where batteries have less than half the normal expectancy, and insects do everything but march away with your poles bodily." [12]

Amid these harassments the Signal Corps men first on the CBI scene did as well as they could with what they had. In India they supplemented their meager supplies with odds and ends of British equipment. Everywhere they used whatever salvaged parts they could ob-

---

[9] (1) Signal Corps History, CBI, Mar–Oct 44, pp. 48ff., and chart of air warning sites. This history, in the Signal Corps History Section file, is in two bindings. The first contains the CBI account for April 1942 to March 1944, and for October 1944 to January 1945 (actually the India-Burma Theater then). The second contains the account for March 1944 to October 1944. Hereafter cited as SigC Hist, CBI, or IB, with dates. (2) Observations of Operational Forces in India-Burma, pp. 19-21. SigC 413.44 (R–400) India, Intel Br, OCSigO. (3) Interv, SigC Hist Sec with Lt Col Robert E. Meeds, EEIS Team CBI, 10 May 45, pp. 7f. SigC Hist Sec file.

[10] (1) Personal papers of Brig Gen Walter B. Larew (Ret.). (2) Interv, SigC Hist Sec with Larew, 16 Oct 57. Larew had served the Tenth Air Force as the signal officer of the 5320th Air Defense Wing (Provisional) from December 1943 to October 1944.

[11] Interv, SigC Hist Sec with Sgts Duffy and Lester Mansfield, 16 Nov 44, pp. 8, 11.

[12] Incl, Jungle Hazards of the Signal Corps, with ASF Transmittal Sheet, Comment 1, Maj Milton B. Herr to Chief Intel Br OCSigO, 4 May 45. SigC 000.7 Articles for Publication, vol. 2, Jan–Jun 45.

tain. Wire circuits were simple, often primitive, and radios, even ancient types, were few. The theater signal officer from mid-1943 to mid-1944, Brig. Gen. Henry L. P. King, stated that during the early months of the war "little more was provided than the minimum needed to support the activities of the Army Air Forces." General Stilwell recognized the Signal Corps plight, and he in fact took upon himself some of the onus for CBI communication inadequacies during the early months of the war, subsequently admitting that communications had been "handled very poorly, principally due to my own ignorance." [13]

A Signal Corps footnote to the Allied defeat in Burma in 1942 was put on record two years later: "It now seems apparent that the unsuccessful Anglo-Chinese defense of Burma in April and May 1942 can be attributed, in part, to a shortage of signal communication equipment and an inadequate co-ordination of the communication facilities which were available." [14]

By mid-1943 conditions in the theater were at last improving as General King arrived from Washington in June to become the CBI chief signal officer, bringing with him Col. Paul L. Neal who would become the SOS signal officer under Wheeler. [15]

By July 1943 the number of Signal Corps troops in the CBI had increased to several thousand. The majority of them, about 120 officers and 1,700 enlisted men, supported the major American effort there, the Army Air Forces. The remainder, under the theater chief signal officer's supervision, included the 955th Radio Intelligence Company, [16] a few V-mail personnel, and of course the 835th Signal Service Battalion, whose men operated in detachments scattered at key points in both China and India. General King would soon have many more troops. [17] By 30 June 1944 Signal Corps troops in CBI would number about 800 officers and warrant officers and nearly 13,000 enlisted men.

In consequence of plans drawn up by the CBI subsection of the Plans and Operations Division of the Office of the Chief Signal Officer in Washington, the CBI Signal Section in New Delhi in 1943 expanded to 56 officers, 4 warrant officers, and 196 enlisted men. The SOS headquarters Signal Section numbered nearly as many—35 and 184 officers and men, respectively. Entire new units soon appeared. Two signal operation companies, the 988th and 993d, were activated in mid-1943 to meet the needs of the Chinese forces who were readying to retake Burma. In October 1943, the 219th Signal Depot Company and the 181st Signal Repair Company arrived and received assignments in signal depots. In December the 96th Signal Battalion and half of the 31st Signal Construction Battalion reached the theater, the former to work on pole line con-

---

[13] (1) SigC Hist, CBI, Apr 42–Mar 44, p. 1. (2) Proceedings of Bd To Investigate Com, Tab B (Stilwell), cited above, p. 3, n. 2.

[14] SigC Tech Info Ltr 30 (May 44), p. 30.

[15] Interv, SigC Hist Div with Neal, 6 Aug 57. Flying in the same plane with King and Neal were Col. Edwin R. Petzing, designated signal officer of the Tenth Air Force (replacing Colonel Lamb), Lt. Col. Frank W. Bullock, King's supply officer, and Lt. Col. Paul A. Feyereisen, King's executive officer.

[16] By the autumn of 1943 the 955th RI Company and a detachment of the 2d Signal Service Battalion, under the Signal Intelligence Service (SIS), were having considerable success in radio intelligence work in the Burma area. SigC Hist, CBI, Apr 42–Mar 44, pp. 22ff.

[17] SigC Hist, CBI, Mar–Oct 44, p. 3.

struction along the Stilwell Road, the latter to build lines in India from Calcutta to Kharagpur and along the route to Assam. Not all the remaining half of the 31st arrived. Their transport, HMS *Rohna*, was sunk by enemy action in the eastern Mediterranean.[18]

There were still shortages of course—for example, the universal lack of spare parts and of maintenance facilities, as Colonel Heinrich, now signal officer of the Y-Force (Yunnan divisions, Chinese) lamented in December 1943. That same month, Colonel Neal urged that he, as the SOS signal officer, be enabled (despite War Department strictures) to stockpile pole line material and switchboards to meet needs presently unspecified but certain to arise. He cited needs for cable types, of which there were no supplies at all in India. And he added that nowhere in the country was a single set of cable splicer's equipment to be found. The following year, in September 1944, General King's successor as the Chief Signal Officer, CBI, Brig. Gen. William O. Reeder, explained: "We will work up a project for a 'stockpile' without using the word and make it modest enough to be defensible." [19]

But already, before the end of 1943, as Allied combat troops and the road builders of the Engineer Corps drove eastward from Ledo over the Naga Hills of the Indian border and down into the narrow valleys of northern Burma, troop and supply activities were definitely mounting and so were the enabling communications—both wire and radio.

Radio in fact preceded the wire. Along the Stilwell Road, for example, as bulldozers first broke the track into Burma in 1943, Signal Corps men at a 75-watt radio station in Ledo maintained communications with mobile radios at the advancing roadhead. By the time the workers pushed the track to Shingbwiyang in northern Burma, one hundred miles across the mountains from Ledo, the Signal Corps had six stations operating in the net, which primarily supported the road construction. Traffic over these radio channels alone reached 25,000 messages a week before wire service took over. By the spring of 1944, as signal troops erected the pole line along this stretch of the Stilwell Road, the radio net began to revert to a standby status in case the wire lines went dead. Radio continued to be needed, however, for initial communications along the advance sections of the road as it penetrated deeper into Burma, until wire lines could catch up. By August 1944 there were twelve stations

[18] (1) SigC History, CBI, Apr 42–Mar 44. p. 2. (2) Wagner, ACAN, 1941–45, pt. II, pp. 66–67. (3) Rpt, King to CG USAFCBI, 16 Dec 43, sub: Bimonthly Rpt of Sig SigC Corps Activities. SigC 307 OD 221 King Rpts.

[19] (1) Comments of Col Heinrich, SigO Y-Force, 1 Dec 43, and Comments of Col Neal to Lt Col Cox, 26 Dec 43. SigC OT 370.2 Rpts CBI, Tab 3. (2) Ltr, Gen Reeder to Brig Gen Frank C. Meade, 24 Sep 44. SigC OT 370.2 Rpts CBI, Tab 22. In a subsequent letter to General Ingles, 12 February 1945, page 2, same file, Reeder wrote: "We have carefully prepared and disguised stockpile project known at TIG–90 for theater reserve."

For some aspects of theater stockpiling, see Memo, Col Carter B. Magruder for Brig Gen John Elliott

Wood, 31 Mar 44, sub: Rpt on Sig Deficiencies in CBI. SigC OT 370.2 Rpts CBI, Tab 21. Magruder admitted that, because of the lack of stockpiles, signal supplies for such high priority projects as the B–29 bombing of Japan did not arrive in the theater until after the target date of the projected operations. See also Memo, Dr. Maurice E. Strieby, Expert Consultant, for Dr. Bowles, 28 Apr 44, sub: Results of Theater Survey Trip. SigC EO 370.2 Theaters of Opns, 1943–44.

in two nets serving the road. As the route reached China, the last radio stations the Signal Corps was to erect in this network opened at Wanting, on the China border, on 21 February 1945, and at Kunming on 5 March 1945.[20]

In addition to these local radio services, the Signal Corps was making progress in Army's long-range radio communications spanning the CBI. On 27 December 1943, for example, General King answered an inquiry from the Office of the Chief Signal Officer regarding the radio and radio circuits in use in CBI administrative nets. The radio sites at that time numbered 22, scattered over the 3,500 miles from Karachi, India, to Kweilin, China. Although many stations employed but one radio set maintaining manual hand-keyed circuits, the New Delhi station at the theater headquarters enjoyed no fewer than 10 transmitters including a Press Wireless radioteletype of 15 kilowatts and another transmitter of 10 kilowatts, a BC–340, that provided a high-speed Boehme circuit.[21]

The year 1944 would bring tremendous progress, as rapidly as the equipment could be obtained, toward faster, larger communications capacity with the increasing application of radioteletype and on-line automatic cipher sets.

General King, a fighter of uphill battles since the hectic days early in 1942 when, as chief of the Personnel Division of the Office of the Chief Signal Officer, he labored to build up Signal Corps allotments of officers and men,[22] was getting results as he worked to the breaking point to improve Army's signal service in the CBI. In January 1944, for example, he improved the administration of his sparse and far-flung signal activities by dividing the theater signal system into seven areas, each with its own signal officer, who served as the area representative of the theater chief signal officer.[23] In May 1944 General Ingles informed General King that, although many were jittery in Washington because of approaching European operations, more officers and men were becoming available to meet Signal Corps needs. The outlook was so favorable, he assured King, that "the majority of your Signal Corps personnel requirements should be filled by the end of 1944." [24]

More equipment was arriving, too. Much impetus toward good dependable communications arose during 1944 because of the MATTERHORN project, in which XX Bomber Command would attack Japan from B–29 bomber bases in Asia, specifically from Chengtu, north of Chungking, with support from India airfields. Operational control over the XX Bomber Command came from Twentieth Air Force headquarters in Washington, direct from the AAF commanding general himself, Lt. Gen. Henry H. Arnold, who acted as the

[20] Rpt, Maj Gen Lewis A. Pick, CG Hq ADSEC USFIBT, to Lt Gen Raymond A. Wheeler, CG USFIBT, Report on the Stilwell Road Overland Line of Communications India-Burma and China Theaters, 9 Aug 45, pp. 6of. OCMH files.

[21] Ltr, King to CSigO, 27 Dec 43, sub: Radio Transmitting Equipment, CBI Theater Admin Radio Net. SigC 307 OD 221 King Rpts.

[22] Thompson, Harris, et al., The Test, pp. 41, 47.

[23] The seven areas centered on Karachi, Delhi, Calcutta, Chabua, Kunming, Chungking, and Kweilin. (1) Organization Chart China-Burma-India. SigC History CBI, Mar–Oct 44, p. 1. (2) Wagner, ACAN, 1941–45, pt. II, pp. 91–92.

[24] Ltr, Ingles, CSigO, to King, Theater SigO CBI, 22 May 44. SigC OT 370.2 Rpts CBI, Tab 22.

HAND-GENERATED RADIO, *operated by men of the 988th Signal Battalion message center in Burma.*

executive director of the Twentieth Air Force for the JCS. It was the first time that military operations in an Army theater were commanded over such great distances, much in the manner in which the Navy Department in Washington operated its ships over the seven seas. Tremendous radioteletype facilities provided by the Signal Corps would give General Arnold the singular control that he desired.[25]

General King did not remain in New Delhi to reap the results of his efforts. Exhausted and broken in health, he could no longer carry on with his tasks and was replaced in June 1944 by General Reeder.[26] Riding the rising tide

---

[25] (1) **Romanus** and Sunderland, *Stilwell's Command Problems*, p. 114. (2) Wesley Frank Craven and James L. Cate, eds., "The Army Air Forces in World War II," *The Pacific: Matterhorn to Nagasaki, June 1944 to August, 1945,* vol. V (Chicago: University of Chicago Press, 1953), pp. 45–52, and *Men and Planes*, vol. VI (Chicago: University of Chicago Press, 1955), pp. 29 and 56. (3) Fleet Admiral William D. Leahy, *I Was There* (New York: McGraw-Hill Book Company, Inc., 1950) p. 261.

Later in the war, when the B-29 effort shifted from China to newly seized Pacific isles nearer to Japan, the AAF abandoned some of these large communications facilities in China and India. The Signal Corps then used them to alleviate equipment shortages elsewhere in the CBI. Interv, SigC Hist Sec with Neal, 6 Aug 57.

[26] Ltr, AG Hq USAFCBI to King, 9 Jun 44, sub: Travel Orders. SigC EO CSigO Diary, 21–23 Jun 44, Tab C.

of men and supplies, General Reeder with fresh energy attacked signal operations in the CBI. On 27 November 1944, General Ingles himself appraised the Signal Corps job in that theater:

In my opinion, General Reeder has the most difficult Signal job in any of the overseas theaters. I want all staff divisions and services of this office to give him all possible assistance. It is particularly desirable that the Plans and Operations Division do everything possible to fight his battles in the War Department and secure War Department approval of actions he desires to take.[27]

Soon after being assigned to the CBI, General Reeder visited his widely scattered installations and communicators. He noted variations in the local authority of the area signal officers, each somewhat differently representing the theater signal officer. In the sphere of road and pipeline construction under Maj. Gen. Lewis A. Pick of the Engineer Corps, SOS was the commanding authority, and the signal officer in the area reported directly to General Pick.[28] The signal officer serving the X–Force in the 1944 Burma campaign, Lt. Col. George F.

GENERAL REEDER

Moynahan, Jr., was on the staff of General Stilwell, who commanded both the Northern Combat Area Command (NCAC) and the CBI Theater. Regarding the ambiguous theater relationships in general, Reeder wrote on 24 September 1944:

There is an area of twilight between the combat authority of the X Force (commanded personally by Gen. Stilwell, a case of Grant fighting Meade's army) and the authority of Pick. This is occasioned by the fact that the X Force has no Army troops other than the Signal Corps troops we have assigned them. Therefore Pick builds their roads, bridges, runs their depots, handles their air dropping and a host of other things. For certain other reasons, the rear echelon of the X Force remains west of Ledo although the forward echelon is 160 miles further down the road and will soon be in Myitkyina. There results from this set-up a rather difficult problem for the theater signal officer.

---

[27] Ltr, Gen Ingles to Gen Code, Gen Harrison, Gen Matejka, Col Wesley T. Guest, and Col Edward L. Munson, Jr., 27 Nov 44, sub: Ltr From Reeder, Dated 15 Nov 44. SigC OT 370.2 Rpts CBI, Tab 22.

[28] It is worth noting that the Engineer Corps history of the Stilwell Road construction, submitted by General Pick in August 1945 to Lt. Gen. Raymond A. Wheeler, then the commanding general of the India-Burma Theater, devotes ten pages to signal communications and includes the subject under Engineering Data, following accounts of Roads, Airfields, and Pipelines. In other words, Pick regarded signal communications as an intrinsic part of his engineering responsibilities and accomplishments. Wheeler, Rpt on the Stilwell Road Overland Line of Com, IB and China Theaters, pp. 1, 6off.

Colonel Moynahan was inclined like the rest of the X staff, Reeder commented, to issue orders in the name of the theater commander. This could raise doubts as to just who might be General Stilwell's signal officer—the chief signal officer of the CBI theater, or the NCAC signal officer. Reeder, having raised the uncertainty, at once spiked it with the assertion "I have no doubt," and he set about doing his utmost to exert strong control over this most ambiguous and tortured of theaters.[29]

In visits over the area from Calcutta to Chungking, General Reeder probed all Signal Corps installations and organizations, finding in general great growth and improvement. In supply, for example, so much signal equipment was at last arriving that there now arose the problem of obtaining enough troops to handle it (in the China area, he found the signal depot at Kunming had but one officer and seven men to do the work).[30] He found his message centers prospering everywhere. The message center at the theater headquarters in New Delhi was moving as many as 400,000 groups of traffic a day; the load at Chabua reached 120,000 daily. "Compare the number of personnel doing it with what you have at big headquarters of other theaters and I think you will agree that the CBI is doing all right," he exulted in September.[31]

During the year 1944 a CBI attempt was made to combine the two signal sections, the one serving SOS, the other the CBI theater headquarters. Maj. Gen. William E. R. Covell, who had succeeded General Wheeler as Commanding General, SOS, made the suggestion seeking to reduce duplication and conserve men. Since SOS already handled the signal supply system (except that of the AAF and part of the Chinese signal supply), he believed SOS should set up a signal communications service to take over the construction, installation, operation, and maintenance of all permanent and semipermanent signal facilities in the theater, except those serving the AAF and combat troops. At the time he first made the proposal, early in 1944, the signal section of CBI headquarters contained about 60 officers and 200 enlisted men. The proposed service, Covell believed, would need only 30 of these officers and 110 of the men to do the job in co-operation with the existing SOS Signal Section. Though this looked like a fine conservation, the suggestion was rejected by theater headquarters, as far as signals

---

[29] Ltr, Reeder to Meade, OCSigO, 24 Sep 44, p. 2. SigC OT 370.2 Rpts CBI, Tab 22.

A reason for Stilwell's staff actions appears in a subsequent comment by Colonel Moynahan. The poor support that General Stilwell felt he received from the New Delhi headquarters—the rear area philosophy that he believed emphasized the buildup of rear supply areas leaving little for the combat in Burma—forced the CBI commander to take over some signal functions in early 1944. Stilwell, for example, removed the 96th Signal Battalion from SOS and put it under NCAC. He also took from the base signal officer the construction, operation, and control of open wire circuits, putting them under the signal officer of NCAC, although, Moynahan added, "this caused some repercussions." Memo, Col Moynahan, Dir Combat Developments, for Col Charles H. Burch, 14 Jul 59, sub: Draft MS, Thompson and Harris, The Signal Corps in CBI. SigC Hist Sec file.

[30] (1) Ltr, Reeder to Meade, 24 Sep 44, p. 2. (2) Ltr, Reeder to Ingles, 14 Oct 44, p. 5. Both in SigC OT 370.2 Rpts CBI, Tab 22.

[31] (1) Ltr, Reeder to Meade, 24 Sep 44, pp. 2, 4. Reeder pointed to the big ACAN station at Asmara, operated by three hundred men, whose "sole purpose seems to be relaying us." But Meade corrected him. Asmara had other, highly classified, tasks to do, in particular the transmission of heavy loads of SIS traffic. (2) Ltr, Meade to Reeder, 9 Oct 44, p. 2. SigC OT 370.2 Rpts CBI, Tab 22.

were concerned (consolidation in SOS was granted for transportation, engineers, and medical). Some months later, in November 1944, General Covell revived the proposal, but by then communications demands had so increased that the merger, if made, would release no one. There was no merger. It was evident that no surplus existed in the crescending business of Army communications. Furthermore, certain signal operations, such as the Signal Intelligence Service, were not suited to a supply organization.[32]

Hardly had General Reeder begun, during the late summer of 1944, consolidating and strengthening his signal responsibilities than he lost a third of his area of authority. In October 1944, the War Department separated the China portion of the theater from the India and Burma sections. General Reeder remained the chief signal officer in the New Delhi headquarters of the India-Burma Theater under Lt. Gen. Daniel I. Sultan. Just before the breakup, Reeder had traveled to China —to Kunming, headquarters of the SOS Advance Section 1, Y—Force Rear, Z—Force, and the Fourteenth Air Force —to strengthen Signal Corps support in that remote and difficult area. There had been much unhappiness in those quarters regarding theater signals. The Signal Section at New Delhi had tried to control Army communications in China through the three signal area officers assigned at Chungking, Kunming, and Kweilin, but the three officers had too few troops for

efficient operations. The Fourteenth Air Force had many more, and it was they who actually did most of the signal work in China. Consequently, the Fourteenth Air Force tended to regard the ineffective area signal officers as "rather a nuisance," and even proposed to take over all signal communications in China. General Reeder sought to placate the airmen, to establish better relations, and to convince them that he would provide them with better Signal Corps support in the future.[33]

Almost as General Reeder made the effort, high-level reorganizations sent his plans to build up his support of the China end of his mission aglimmering. The China Theater became ostensibly independent of Burma-India on 27 October 1944. Under the over-all command of Maj. Gen. Albert C. Wedemeyer, the new theater's signal responsibilities devolved upon Col. James H. Marsh. Marsh had been the China area officer in Chungking. Now he found himself the acting chief signal officer of the China Theater, with a total office force of exactly one enlisted man. Obviously, he was understaffed and had to ask Reeder and his organization in New Delhi "to continue to operate as the Theater Signal Section for both theaters." Wedemeyer rejected Reeder's offer to strengthen China headquarters signals in the person of either Colonel Neal, who had invaluably assisted the wire construction work from Calcutta to Kunming, or of Colonel Petzing, who now headed the planning activity in the New Delhi signal section of the India-Burma headquarters.[34]

[32] Hist Of, IBT, History of SOS, India-Burma Theater, 25 October 1944–23 June 1945, I, 32–35. OCMH files. See also History of SOS India-Burma Theater, 25 October 1944–23 June 1945, II, 209ff. OCMH files.

[33] Ltr, Reeder to Meade, 14 Oct 44, p. 4. SigC OT 370.2 Rpts CBI, Tab 22.

[34] Ltrs, Reeder to Ingles, 28 Nov 44, p. 2, and 12 Feb 45, p. 1. SigC OT 370.2 Rpts CBI, Tab 22.

As General Reeder saw it, the separate China Theater was a mistake. New people had been brought into China. He felt that accumulated experience built up in previous months had been swept away. And, as was expected, the India-Burma Theater, especially after the sudden collapse of the enemy in Burma late in 1944, became primarily a source of supply to China, which was being increasingly isolated by Japanese advances in the eastern areas of that country. For purposes of supply, the Office of the Chief Signal Officer in Washington, Col. Wesley T. Guest writing, informed Reeder, "we still would like to consider the two theaters as an entity and hope that there will be no attempt to set up separate stocks. . . . " That wish, Reeder replied, was "optimistic." And he added sardonically, "The War Department could have thought up other ways of further confusing our complicated situation, but I believe they have hit upon the best."

Actually, as matters turned out, General Reeder did manage to maintain close relations with Colonel Marsh and to provide men and material, in particular toward the completion of the China end of the Calcutta Kunming pole line, the dependable high-capacity communications facility that was essential if the expected quantities of supply by air, road, and pipeline were to reach their destination.[35]

The Calcutta-Kunming Pole Line

Among the major Signal Corps projects approved for the CBI in 1943 was the start of a pole line eventually to run nearly 2,000 miles from Calcutta through India's easternmost province, Assam, to Ledo, and on across northern Burma to Kunming in China. It would run beside the Ledo (Stilwell) Road, which was being constructed to join the Burma Road near the China border. The line was to be built in two major segments, the first traversing cultivated land from Calcutta to the Chabua-Ledo area, the second crossing wild mountain terrain from Ledo to Kunming.[36]

The logistical build-up for the war in Burma and the support of China required large-scale road building and such special supply facilities as pipelines. These in turn had to have communications, good dependable communications of high capacity, able to handle thousands of words day in and day out. "You can't pump oil," General Reeder wrote in October 1944 to the Washington headquarters, "without wire communications." [37]

The Assistant Chief Signal Officer in Washington, General Code, the very next month ordered his Personnel and Training Division to give priority handling to CBI requests for signal troops to support the road and pipeline projects of that theater. General Somervell, Chief of the Army Supply Forces, having just returned from a tour of the CBI, had

---

[35] (1) Ltr, Reeder to Ingles, 12 Feb 45, p. 1. (2) Ltr, Guest to Reeder, 15 Nov 44, p. 2. (3) Ltr, Reeder to Guest, 28 Nov 44, p. 2. All in SigC OT 370.2 Rpts CBI, Tab 22. (4) Hq USFCT, Signal Communication Under SOS and AAF, 1944-45, Report on Signal Communications in China Theater, 23 Oct 45.

[36] (1) CSigO, Annual Rpt, FY 44, p. 98. (2) An Unparalleled Construction Job, p. 1. Com folder, Hist P-4, Tab X, SigC Hist Sec file.

[37] (1) Ltr, Reeder to Ingles, 14 Oct 44, p. 4. (2) Wheeler, Rpt on the Stilwell Road Overland Line of Com, IB and China Theaters, p. 53.

put the road and pipeline at the top of the theater's needs.[38]

The needed wire communications facilities were planned and provided by the Signal Corps. The Corps had long before provided AAF radio communications between Chabua and Kunming. "The remarkable results being achieved over the Hump," General Reeder noted in September 1944, "are due in large part to excellent communications in the Chabua district." And he added an interesting remark touching a highly important but intentionally obscure facet of signaling that often tends to slow down radio communications. "In order not to impede rapidity of communications," he confessed, "we are doing some things here that violate crypto security. The onus is on me if anything ever happens and I will accept it." In this matter General Reeder accepted responsibility for a practice that Stilwell himself had authorized on the recommendation of his NCAC signal officer, Colonel Moynahan.[39]

Meanwhile, the reliable long-distance wire facilities that the Signal Corps had planned were becoming available also. Earlier, in January 1944, the Army Communications Service in Washington had completed the engineering of a long-distance high-capacity wire line system— C carrier—from Calcutta to the Chabua-Ledo area.[40] It also completed, by that spring, a complete circuit plan for the Chabua-Kunming stretch, that is, from the Chabua end of the Calcutta lines, on across rugged country into northern Burma, across still more rugged country and mighty river chasms, then over the Chinese border to Kunming. This plan, Project TIG–IB (one of many CBI signal projects coded TIG, for TIGER), involved 1,234 miles of 10-wire line, excluding poles, as follows:

10	C-type carrier telephone systems
16	carrier frequency telegraph systems
47	carrier repeaters
96	voice frequency repeaters
13	repeater stations
7	common battery exchanges [41]

[38] Action 1, Code to P&T Div, 1 Dec 43, on Memo, Meade for ACSigO, 30 Nov 43. SigC EO CSigO Diary, 1–22 Nov 43, Tab T. Also in SigC OP 371 CBI, Tab 1.

[39] (1) Ltr, Reeder to Meade, 24 Sep 44, p. 2. (2) MS Comment, Col. George F. Moynahan, Jul 59. SigC Hist Sec file.
There were others who agreed that communications security regulations were sometimes over-emphasized: "It is my considered opinion in many cases our security regulations do more harm than good to the war effort. The harm arises from the delays in messages and frequent garbles and from the man hours consumed in coding and decoding. In particular, relatively little use is made of automatic teletype coding equipment because of the many restrictions imposed by existing regulations." Memo, Strieby for Bowles, 28 Apr 44, sub: Results of Theater Survey Trip, p. 2. SigC EO 370.2 Theaters of Opn, 1943–44. Strieby's complaint about automatic teletypewriter cipher machines was be-

ing met by the installation of increasing numbers of the devices, Sigcums, as fast as they could be obtained.

[40] Memo, Stoner, Chief Army Com Sv, for Contl Div Program and Stat Br, 1 Feb 44, sub: Digest of Progress and Problems, 1–31 Jan, p. 2. SigC AC 319.1 Digest, 30 Jul 42–1 Dec 44. See also SigC OD 217 TIG–IB Chabua-Kunming Toll Line, 1944–45, passim.

[41] These facilities, together with associated equipment, added up to 3,270 tons. The final bill for the project was drawn up by 13 May 1944 (yet this was not all—at least five supplements to TIG–IB followed in later months). Memo, Stoner for Contl Div Program and Stat Br, 1 Jun 44, sub: Digest of Progress and Problems, p. 2. SigC AC 319.1 Digest, 30 Jul 42–1 Dec 44.
For accounts of some of the other TIG signal projects see SigC History, CBI, Mar–Oct 44, pp. 9–12. See also the TIG list in Hist, IBT, 25 Oct 44–23 Jun 45, I, pp. 201f.

ELEPHANT DRAWS WIRE TAUT *during pole line construction near Shampur, India. 31st Signal Construction Battalion.*

Construction of the Calcutta-Kunming pole line, comparable in length with that other great wire project, the Alcan Highway pole line in Canada and Alaska, began with the erection of the first 750-mile leg of the over-all project along the river valleys and rice paddies from Calcutta to Chabua. Signal Corps units completed this portion by December 1944. They also built a paralleling line from Parbatipur, some 200 miles north of Calcutta, to Ledo in the Chabua area, following the tracks of the Bengal-Assam railroad. This parallel line, started in August 1944, was also completed in December and provided 560 miles of supplementing wire facilities. It was built under most difficult conditions; the paddies were flooded at that time of year, vehicles could not be used, and men had to work

in deep mud or water all the time. Signal Corps men also built other lines in the Calcutta area, linking bomber bases at Chakulia and Kharagpur.[42]

Work on the Stilwell Road pole line had begun in mid-1943 in a small way when Maj. Clinton W. Janes, commanding a group of quartermaster troops and a few Indian Pioneers (for want of enough Signal Corps men), built the first thirty-seven miles of line out of Ledo using British materials. Later that year the 430th Signal Heavy Construction Company, Aviation, helped push the line eastward. The work proceeded slowly over the mountains, but upon the arrival of the 96th Signal Battalion at the year's end, progress became more rapid. The poles, bearing five circuits, reached Shingbwiyang in the Hukawng Valley of northern Burma by 7 April 1944.[43]

Throughout that year, as Signal Corps units and materials rapidly made their appearance, this pioneer line was pressed close behind the troops fighting their way down the narrow valleys of upper Burma to Myitkyina by August 1944 and, soon after, to Bhamo and juncture with

[42] (1) Wagner, ACAN, 1941–45, pt. II, p. 83. (2) Ltr, Reeder to Ingles, 24 Sep 44, pp. 1 and 3. SigC OT 370.2 Rpts CBI, Tab 22.

[43] (1) Hq USAFIBT, Publicity Release, 11 Jun 45, pp. 1–3. SigC OT 370.2 Rpts CBI, Tab 36. (2) Wheeler, Rpt on the Stilwell Road Overland Line of Com, IB and China Theaters, pp. 62ff. The 430th Signal Heavy Construction Company was a Negro unit, personnel of which were later transferred to the 445th Signal Construction Battalion. SigC History, CBI, Mar–Oct 44, p. 4. Early in 1945, General Reeder, returning Janes (by then a lieutenant colonel) to Washington after two years in CBI, described him as a capable man of action and a trouble shooter who should not be assigned a purely desk job. "He likes to jump in and get dirty while solving problems." "Don't keep him in the Pentagon," he added, "or he will blow up." Ltr, Reeder to Ingles, 12 Feb 45, p. 4.

the Burma Road, which the Japanese had closed in 1942.

Some of the earliest wire connections were made by spiral-four. The first shipment had just arrived at Calcutta when General Stilwell advanced into northern Burma shortly before the monsoon season of 1943, despite the engineers' warning that they could not get a roadway into the Hukawng Valley ahead of high water. Colonel Neal rushed quantities of the valuable field cable from Calcutta over the Naga Hills and strung it before the floods came. Though the water rose on schedule, Signal Corps men kept the lines serviced, using boats and elephants to do the job.[44]

Nor were monsoons and elephants the only oddities in CBI signal experience. There was, for instance, Colonel Janes's laconic and startling report of a temporary outage of communications: "Monkey in switchboard truck; operator fainted." Neal recalled the incident. Soon after Stilwell's descent into the Hukawng Valley and his first combat with the enemy in the vicinity of Shingbwiyang, a switchboard had been set up in a 2½-ton truck at his headquarters. When suddenly the wire service went dead, it was expected that a Japanese infiltrator had sabotaged the truck. Looking into it, investigators found a monkey fiddling with the board mechanism and the operator out cold. It seems that the latter, tense and tired, when he suddenly discovered his strange coworker, could take no more of the strains of the jungle and fainted dead away.[45]

Open wire lines were installed along the jungle road. All kinds of wire were used. "We even got 10,000 miles of wire from South Africa," recalled Colonel Neal, "every kind of wire except what the T/O&E called for." That the lines worked well was due to the skills of such signal engineers as Colonel Janes and Maj. Clarence D. Sheffield. The latter could make necessary calculations on the spot whenever unexpected developments occurred in the field, such as catenary suspensions across obstacles that desk engineers, plotting the first blueprints in New Delhi, could not foresee. Sheffield could determine at the site the correct transpositions needed to keep the lines electrically balanced. "He must have walked every foot of the Ledo-Muse stretch a dozen times," said Neal with pardonable exaggeration.[46]

Wire supply difficulties in CBI had at least one light moment. It occurred after a U.S. Senator had visited the theater. When he asked the troops what they most wanted, they answered "Beer." Some weeks later Colonel Neal received word that a ship was docking at Calcutta with urgently needed wire. When the holds were opened, they all contained nothing but beer. A recreation camp was set up in Calcutta, complete with beer, and troops were rotated there on rest leave from the jungles.[47]

---

[44] Unit Hist, 96th Sig Bn with NCAC, p. 10. SigC Hist Sec file.

[45] Interv, SigC Hist Sec with Neal, 6 Aug 57.

[46] Interv, SigC Hist Sec with Neal, 6 Aug 57. Credit for wire construction from Ledo to Bhamo, according to Colonel Moynahan, should go to Col. Robert Disney, Commanding Officer, 96th Signal Battalion. This unit built the 10-pin wire line that was used first to provide communications to the Chinese division headquarters in combat, after which the line was turned over to the base section. MS Comments, Moynahan, Jul 59.

[47] Interv, SigC Hist Sec with Neal, 6 Aug 57.

As the copper wires stretched on, carrying direct communications to the front from as far away as the theater headquarters in New Delhi, General Reeder commented to the Chief Signal Officer on 30 December 1944 that these tremendously long lines "bring forcibly to mind the fact that we of these theaters are definitely in the transcontinental telephone business." The opening of the Calcutta-Chabua circuit, making possible successful conversations between Delhi and Myitkyina, brought an immediate request from the Air Forces for a through circuit from Calcutta to Bhamo. The eventual wire plant in CBI would call for engineering and maintenance skills beyond the know-how of the usual Signal Corps wire units. General Reeder, urging that something be done about an organization for a long lines team, wrote, "Petzing and Borgeson who recently completed a painstaking tour from Calcutta to Myitkyina have evolved a special long lines team and have convinced me of the need for it. It is not to be found among any of the T of O&E 11–500 at the present time." Lt. Col. Carl A. Borgeson had pointed out that the main wire line traversing the India Burma and the China Theaters was "becoming rapidly the longest military wire network of all time." Borgeson buttressed his claim with a tabulation that showed the status of the enormous project as of 29 December 1944.[48] (*Table 1*)

Among the Signal Corps units that worked on the Calcutta-Kunming pole line were a number of signal battalions

TABLE 1—STATUS OF THE CBI POLE LINE, DECEMBER 1944

Section	Mileage	Status
Total	3,396	
New Delhi-Calcutta . . .	900	In service
Calcutta-Myitkyina . . .	1,175	In service
Myitkyina-Kunming . .	794	Work underway
Kunming-Chungking . .	527	Work underway

Source: Ltr, Reeder to Ingles, 30 Dec 44, with Incl, Memo, Borgeson for Deputy Theater CSigO USFIBT, 29 Dec 44. SigC OT 370.2 Rpts CBI, Tab 22.

—the 31st, the 96th, the 428th, the 432d, the 445th, Company B of the 3199th Signal Service Battalion, and a detachment of Company C of the 835th. The 432d helped complete the last link in China early in 1945, the linemen working both ways out of Yunnanyi—westward to Pao-shan and east to Kunming. Three Indian pioneer companies also helped: the 1296th, the 1297th, and the 1298th.[49]

The work was accomplished under most trying conditions. Besides the hazards of tropical jungles—diseases and pests, the monsoons, and the mountains—there were great rivers to cross, rivers subject to extreme flooding. Across the Brahmaputra on the way to Chabua, a group from the 31st Signal Construction

[48] Apparently nothing came of the long lines team proposal. Ltr, Reeder to Ingles, 12 Feb 45. SigC OT 370.2 Rpts CBI, Tab 22.

[49] (1) MS Comment, Maj Gen W. O. Reeder (Ret.), Jul 59. SigC Hist Sec file. (2) Wheeler, Rpt on the Stilwell Road Overland Line of Com, IB and China Theaters, p. 64. (3) Interv, SigC Hist Sec with Welsh, 8 Nov 44. SigC Hist Sec file. (4) Hq USAFIB, Publicity Release, 11 Jun 45, *passim.* The publicity release named three units that operated and maintained the line: the 3199th, the 3105th, and the 236th Signal Service Battalions. It also acknowledged the work of local Chinese and Burmese laborers, and the cooperation of the Indian Post and Telegraph System. The release cited some statistics as well: 60,000 poles, 95,000 cross arms, and more than 25,000 miles of wire.

Battalion laid a heavy 15-pair cable obtained through reverse lend-lease.[50]

Just east of Chabua on the road to Ledo in India lay the Burhi Dihing River, over which the men stretched 10 wires in a single 1,300-foot jump. Using flat-bottom boats, they made 18 attempts to pull the wires across the swift current before they finally succeeded. In Burma the Irrawaddy, athwart the Ledo Road near Myitkyina, presented the greatest challenge. At the narrowest point the river channel was 2,300 feet wide. Signal Corps men put up teakwood poles 65 feet high on either bank and stretched 32 strong copper-steel wires over the flood. Because the high water in monsoon season might reach and wreck these wires, the men erected a supplementing catenary suspension cable. Here they put up even taller teakwood poles —the two primary ones next to the river bank ran up to 76 feet. Two secondary poles standing behind them stood 65 feet tall. Each was guyed to teakwood anchors. Across the top from bank to bank a 26-pair cable was run, held taut and high by a messenger wire to which the cable itself was lashed—the messenger wire taking the weight of the suspension.[51]

---

[50] Vividly described in Signal Corps History, CBI, March–October 1944, app. M.

[51] An Unparalleled Construction Job, pp. 2–6, cited n. 36 (2), above.

The wires were not easily placed over the river. The swift current repeatedly broke the first line before it could be drawn taut and elevated above the water. Men of the 96th Signal Battalion made twenty attempts before they succeeded. (1) Wagner, ACAN, 1941–45, pt. II, pp. 85–86. (2) SigC Hist, CBI, Mar–Oct 44, app. H. This initial river crossing was made by the 96th Signal Battalion as a combat communications expedient, under the NCAC signal officer. MS Comment, Moynahan. See also Unit Hist, 96th Sig Bn, with NCAC, pp. 15f. SigC Hist Sec file.

The far-reaching pole line progressed section by section. Not every section was finished before work on the next one began. There were times when several were in various stages of completion. In October 1944, when the line was advancing through Burma, activity began in the eastern portion of the wire line in China. Equipment arrived first. Then in December near Pao-shan, China, Signal Corps men commenced stringing the wire. There were delays, especially affecting the construction of the first sections, occasioned by the monsoon season in mid-1944. In September the region around Mogaung in Burma was so flooded that the men could not place poles. They continued working nonetheless, trimming treetops and placing crossarms upon them. Elsewhere there were problems of clearing the line right of way and keeping it cleared. Engineer construction on the road and on the associated pipeline employed powerful equipment that often sideswiped poles and knocked over trees that then fell on the wires.

Progress was rapid through the last months of the war. The 5 wire-pairs that reached from Calcutta to Chabua and Ledo, thence over the Naga Hills into Burma and across that land to the China border at Muse, had been extended as of late 1944 by 4 pairs stretching on to Pao-shan. From there 2 pairs ran deeper into China, to Yunnanyi. Additional circuits were added to some sectors and the eastern terminus continued to be extended—to Kunming, the first major Chinese city linked by wire with India, then on 300 miles further east to Kweiyang, and, finally, by July 1945, another 100 miles to Tushan, some 2,300 miles from Calcutta.

The India-Burma Theater head-quarters, announcing in June 1945 that the Kunming-Calcutta link had been finished, gave the dates of some of the first long-distance calls over these wire lines: from Chabua and from Ledo via Calcutta to the theater head-quarters at New Delhi on 22 December 1944; from Myitkyina in Burma on Christmas Day, 1944; from Bhamo, also in Burma, on 1 February 1945; and from Muse, Pao-shan, and Yunnanyi (all in China) on 5 March, 20 April, and 1 May, respectively.[52]

"Over this vast communications sys-tem, men may now talk by telephone and send telegraphic messages over one of the most rugged and undeveloped regions of the earth's surface," concluded the India-Burma headquarters. That there was much talking over these lines, the list of big switchboards attests: one 8-position (requiring eight operators on duty at any one time) commercial board handling 800 lines and a 3-posi-tion commercial board. Army switch-boards included 1 of 6 positions (540 lines), 3 of 4 positions (360 lines), and 1 of 5 positions (450 lines). General Reeder, commenting bitterly on the War Department practice of editing his theater requisitions with an eye to re-ducing them, informed General Ingles in October 1944, "every switchboard along the route either has been rein-forced or will be, because of traffic." He had witnessed the operation of a 3-posi-tion board at Kunming, handling less than 200 phones. "I didn't believe it,"

he said, "when they told me they had pegged 1,600 calls in one hour so I stood behind the board for 15 minutes at 10 a.m. and now can readily believe they peg it." The size of the board must be doubled, he concluded, because three operators could not physically handle the traffic.[53]

Of this tremendous and remote mili-tary wire system General Reeder made a comparison in one of his letters to the Office of the Chief Signal Officer. Writing about the construction troubles, Reeder said, "My only comment has to be that the Alcan highway must have been a very quiet sector as compared with upper Assam." Jungle conditions, and especially overwhelming floods from the monsoons, whether in broad valleys or in narrow mountain cuts, pre-sented immense difficulties. At times Sig-nal Corps troops had kept the wire circuits in operation working on the overhead lines from boats. The signal supply officer of NCAC, Capt. George A. Weiss, obtained "through some undisclosed source," Moynahan subsequently recalled, "pontoons and outboard motors and employed them to set up a supply line which kept signal

---

[52] (1) Ltr, Reeder to CSigO, 27 Mar 45, p. 3. SigC OT 370.2 Rpts CBI, Tab 22. (2) Wagner, ACAN, 1941–45, pt. II, pp. 87f. (3) Hq USAFIB, Publicity Release, 11 Jun 45, pp. 5, 7.

[53] (1) Hq USAFIB, Publicity Release, 11 Jun 45, p. 7. (2) Ltr, Reeder to Ingles, 20 Oct 44, p. 2. SigC OT 370.2 Rpts CBI, Tab 22.

According to the unit history of the 835th Sig-nal Battalion, men of that outfit "installed and maintained twelve switchboards in the Kunming area in 1944: the Army Exchange board, with 1,000 subscribers; the Hospital Exchange board; the Signal board, with 60 subscribers; the OSS board, with 50 subscribers; the Branch board, with 400 subscribers; the ITC board, with 30 sub-scribers; the FATC board, with 30 subscribers; the CTC board, with 20 subscribers, and four Air Corps boards." Sgts John and Ward Hawkins, History of the 835th Signal Service Battalion, 1942–46, p. 82. SigC Hist Sec file.

construction elements in operation." [54]

Taking pride in these accomplishments, the Signal Corps men were understandably annoyed when a War Department publicity release bestowed credit on other CBI workers, especially the Engineers Corps, and overlooked such Army supporting troops as the wiremen. General Reeder, commenting on the *squib* as he termed the release, said: "as might have been expected in any statement, the source of which was either a SOS or an ASF installation, the word 'Engineers' appears prominently, and all others were included in the supporting cast." Reeder had already received a number of letters from his officers and men who had toiled in the forward areas of Burma. The release had "had an infuriating effect" upon them. "Guess I will have to put on my fighting clothes," Reeder wrote Ingles, "and go remind Billy Covell [the SOS CG in the India-Burma theater] that all last summer his bridges were out and his roads under water, while the Signal Corps rowed along and kept wire circuits in." [55]

Combat Communications

Communications for the Chinese troops who helped wrest northern Burma from the Japanese in 1944 were supplied by Signal Corps elements under Colonel Moynahan. Transferred in April 1944 from AFHQ in Caserta, Italy, to Shaduzup, Burma, to become Stilwell's signal officer in the Northern Combat Area Command, Moynahan found the Allied forces "attempting to carry out a tactical corps type effort with far fewer signal troops than are normally allocated to a U.S. Infantry Division." [56]

Teams of the 988th Signal Operations Company (Special) (later, a battalion), which had been constituted, activated, and briefly trained in 1943 from signal, air corps, ordnance, quartermaster, and medical troops in the Ramgarh and Ledo areas of India, provided and operated radio and wire facilities not only for NCAC headquarters but also for the Chinese divisions. These signalmen at first bore the full weight of all Chinese signal needs—from a radio team at Fort Hertz in the extreme north to elements serving all along the advance southward toward Myitkyina. Thus they were thinly distributed between NCAC headquarters and five divisions, as well as among intelligence and tank groups, until April 1944 when another Signal Corps unit, the 96th Signal Battalion, lent help. Together they installed, operated, and maintained the NCAC headquarters signal network and provided headquarters teams (radio, wire, and message center) to the Chinese 22d, 38th, and 50th Divisions. In addition they built and maintained open wire and spiral-four cable lines between Ledo and Shaduzup. Among other signal units serving in the Burma campaign were a repair team from the 181st Signal Repair Company and a 1-kilowatt radio team from the 835th Signal Service Battalion. [57]

---

[54] (1) Thompson, Harris, *et al., The Test,* pp. 482ff. (2) Ltr, Reeder to Ingles, 27 Mar 45, pp. 3ff. SigC OT 370.2 Rpts CBI, Tab 22.

[55] (1) Ltr, Reeder to Ingles, 27 Mar 45. (2) MS Comment, Moynahan, Jul 59.

[56] Moynahan, Memo for Burch, 14 Jul 59.

[57] (1) Moynahan, SigO, Sig Com in the Campaign of Northern Burma, pp. 6–11. CBI folder A46–160, drawer 14, SigC Hist Sec file. (2) SigC OT 200.3, Pers ASF CBI, 1942–44, Tab 17, *passim.*

The signal communications requirements in this campaign involved around-
the-clock telephone, teletype, radio, and
messenger service throughout the wide-
spread NCAC elements, often in areas
where only footpaths existed. They also
involved radio links with the British
Fourteenth Army, the Fort Hertz group,
the Y–Forces on the Salween River, and
the headquarters in Chungking to the
east and in New Delhi to the west.
The need to speed traffic to New Delhi
brought to the CBI radioteletypewriter
circuits—"probably the first time," wrote
Colonel Moynahan, "that such equipment had been employed by a mobile
field army over such a distance." He was
certainly right as to the distance. And
certainly the conditions were abnormal—unlike those the Signal Corps
experienced anywhere else, except in the
tropical islands of the Pacific. Moynahan
described the adversities: dense jungle
growth, high water along the rivers, and
the torrential rains of the monsoon
season, all of which severely handicapped the laying of wire and cable lines.
Low ground conductivity and the mask-
ing effect of heavy vegetation and high
mountain ridges adversely affected
radio communications, not to mention
the effect of dank heat and fungus
growths on the equipment itself. The
operation of FM radios in tanks also suffered from these circumstances. An effort
to use an L–5 liaison plane with its commercial radio set to work with an SCR–
245 on the ground was tried and found
not altogether successful. A better solution proved to be an SCR–528 in the
airplane, which could maintain good
communications over line-of-sight paths
with the sets in the tanks. Artillery fire
was directed by radios SCR–284, SCR–

300, and V–100. The SCR–300, when
employed in liaison aircraft, proved excellent for reporting artillery fire. This
set was also much used both in ground
combat and in communications with aircraft by the GALAHAD Force—the 5307th
Composite Unit (Provisional), or Merrill's Marauders—whose direction and
supply had to depend entirely upon
radio.[58]

Just as Signal Corps troops during
the early days of the CBI had improvised in every possible way to maintain
military communications, so likewise,
when they were confronted with shortages in Burma combat during 1944, they
continued to improvise as best they
could. Colonel Moynahan later recalled
with gratitude the technical skills of officers and men of his signal section of
NCAC, of the 96th and 988th Signal
Battalions, and of elements of the 835th
Signal Battalion. For example, during
the fight for Myitkyina the battery

---

[58] The V–100 was an American set (Pilot Corporation) resembling the SCR–284, but designed
for lend-lease. Under favorable conditions the sets
in Burma could work over distances up to 75
miles. The British No. 48 set was also much used
by the Chinese. (1) Moynahan, Sig Com in the
Campaign of Northern Burma, pp. 12–17. (2) Sig
Com—Burma, SigC Tech Info Ltr 30 (May 44),
p. 32. (3) Comments, Heinrich, 1 Dec 43. SigC
OT 370.2 Rpts CBI, Tab 3.
A brief account of the communications of the
5307th Composite Unit and its radios (SCR's–177,
284, and 300, and the AN/PRC–1) is contained in
Merrill's Marauders (February–May, 1944), AMER-
ICAN FORCES IN ACTION (Washington, 1945),
pp. 29f. Detailed accounts are given in Signal
Corps History, CBI, March–October 1944, pp.
22ff; in Hist of NCAC app. XII, pp. 85–IIIff.,
and in Ltrs, Capt Milton A. Pilcher, SigO Hq
5307th Composite Unit, to Theater SigO Hq
USAFCBI, 23 Jan 44, sub: Rpt on Sig Activities,
and 1 Mar 45, sub: Sig Com, 5307th Composite
Unit, A Reprint of Rpt Submitted 3 Aug 44.
SigC Hist Sec file.

supply for the SCR-300 walkie talkies ran out. Signal Corps men thereupon opened up hundred of batteries intended for SCR-195 sets and reconnected the cells so that they could be used to power the SCR-300's. When selenium rectifiers used in CF-1 and CF-2 carrier equipment (telephone and teletype) went bad, they improvised bridge rectifiers converted from vacuum tube units that they cannibalized from AM troop entertainment (Special Services) receivers. They built two complete radio teletype systems from repair kit parts. And they improvised a crystal-grinding facility that provided the crystals needed to maintain frequency stability in combat radios.[59]

Radio communications were of course absolutely necessary for the control and integration of a campaign in roadless jungles. Jungle warfare, almost more than any other sort of combat, compels the highest degree of dependence upon radio. And, ironically, the environment of jungle fighting presents conditions that are the most hostile to facile communications. Electromagnetic radiations are absorbed by the surrounding walls of foliage. Raising the antennas above the forest roof is difficult and time consuming. Vagaries of ionospheric reflection do not help matters. Yet radio had to serve. And it did, as troops moved in separate columns down isolated river valleys and in tunnellike trails through the vegetation tangle across mountain ravines and ridges.

Not only advance troop movements had to be co-ordinated by radio. Every man in such formations as the 5307th Composite Unit had to depend entirely upon air support for all his supplies—for every last item of food, ammunition, and medicine. Replacements could come only by air, and only airlift could remove the wounded and desperately ill to base hospitals over the mountains in India. The all-essential communications that could call for air support, and that guided the aircraft to the exact drop site, had to depend upon radio.

This dependence brought on difficulties and criticisms. Radio failures occurred, often not the fault of the operators or of the equipment, but of the physical laws of ionospheric reflection that could fail to reflect high-frequency radio waves after sunset, in effect blacking out vital radio communications. Night, on the other hand, was generally the only time the advancing troops halted and the radiomen had time to erect antennas, set up the transmitters, and establish a radio net.[60]

---

[59] Moynahan, Memo for Burch, 14 Jul 59. See also Hist, 96th Sig Bn, with NCAC, pp. 8f. SigC Hist Sec file.

Praising the extreme efforts of the few Signal Corps men to train and build up the communications competence of the NCAC forces, Moynahan gave credit to Lt. Col. Herbert N. Ostrom, Executive Officer, NCAC, Signal Section; Lt. Col. Woodrow Terry, Liaison Officer, New Sixth Army (Chinese); Lt. Col. LeRoy Trott, Liaison Officer, New First Army (Chinese); Maj. Floyd Rucy, Liaison Officer, 3d Chinese Signal Battalion; Colonel Disney, Commanding Officer, 96th Signal Battalion, and Lt. Col. Estill Thurston, Commanding Officer, 988th Signal Battalion. He also commended Col. Chen Yuen, signal officer first of the Chinese 38th Division and later of the New First Chinese Army, and Lt. Col. Peter Dewar, signal officer of the British 36th Division.

[60] (1) Romanus and Sunderland, *Stilwell's Command Problems*, pp. 150, 156, and 181. (2) Ltr,

Communications failures in the campaigning of Merrill's Marauder's caused some repercussions. General King, CBI theater signal officer, attributed the radio failures in this unit to inadequately trained communicators. He believed the radio needs of so unique a combat outfit could only be met by Signal Corps men well trained in radio, a point he persistently pressed. In May 1944 he went so far as to draft a message that he wanted General Sultan, deputy CBI commander, to send to the Chief of Staff, General Marshall. He wrote in draft:

Present Galahad organization has made a remarkable showing. Its communications, however, have been unsatisfactory. Failures in communications have caused constant concern. Units of this type which are on independent missions with radio the only practical communication between battalions, regimental hqs, higher hqs, and supporting airbase, . . . need radio personnel and equipment which is not normal in an infantry regiment. . . . constant repair of equipment is necessary. . . . recommend that radio personnel for Galahad replacements be made subject of special consideration and not treated as usual infantry replacement matter. Number of personnel should be twice that in original T/O. . . . Personnel who operate and maintain command net should receive special training in Signal Corps School.

To have granted General King's request would have violated the rule that Signal Corps troops should not operate in the Army below division level, below the division signal company. Officers in the CBI general staff headquarters hewed to the line. They upheld the decision the War Department had made in 1920 when it removed Signal Corps men from the front lines, where they had served in World War I.[61] They upheld the view that combat-trained and combat-minded communicators are better than Signal Corps specialists in battle units forward of division headquarters. Col. Francis Hill, on the staff in New Delhi, recommended no action on General King's request. He stated his reasons:

There is no evidence that Signal Corps personnel are essential. I have yet to see a radio set that can be packed on a mule that cannot be as well operated by a communications trained Infantryman, artilleryman, or LRPG man [long-range penetration group], as by a Sig Corps man. In fact the knowledge of such combat personnel of the procedures, terminology, and tactics of their branch makes them, in my opinion, superior to a Sig Corps man for combat units. WD practice seems to bear out the correctness of this contention.

The fact that our first Galahad arrived in this theater late, was hastily trained, had no Regtl Hq Btry, was filled with Sig Corps personnel carefully selected but not trained in LRP [long-range penetration] tactics and has had communication diffi-

---

King to Ingles, 5 May 44. SigC 307 OD 221 King Rpts. (3) Intel Rpt 413, JICA CBI, 5 Feb 44, Radio Communications, Burma Hukawng Valley, Signal Corps Activities, CBI, 1944. SigC Hist Sec file. (4) Charlton Ogburn, Jr., *The Marauders* (New York: Harper and Brothers, 1959), pp. 98, 130, 156, 159.

Communications failures were especially harassing in the advance on Shaduzup during an operation wherein the trouble stemmed from the fact that forced daytime marches precluded radio transmission during favorable daylight hours, and when the columns halted at night, ionospheric conditions blocked the signals. Interv, SigC Hist Div with Ogburn, Oakton, Va., 5 Aug 60. SigC Hist Sec file.

[61] (1) Memo, King for Deputy Theater Comdr USAFCBI, 13 May 44, sub: Com Pers for GALAHAD. (2) Routing Sheet, Rear Echelon Hq USAFCBI, Warner to CofS, with Draft Radio, Sultan to Marshall. (3) Terrett, *The Emergency*, pp. 23ff.

culties is no proof that Sig Corps personnel are essential. In fact, I consider it proof that Sig Corps personnel are undesirable and that better results can be obtained from key-clicking dough-boys who know their basic branch.[62]

General King's views had validity in this and in other theaters. In the Pacific, for example, Signal Corps men were being assigned to regimental combat teams, below division level, for the very reasons that King believed called for Signal Corps specialists in the regimental-sized GALAHAD.

A number of Signal Corps officers and men did serve in GALAHAD, as Colonel Hill stated, although the battalion communications platoons were hardly filled with them, nor were all of them the radio specialists that were needed. The signal officer serving Brig. Gen. Frank D. Merrill, commander of the 5307th Composite Unit, was a competent electrical engineer from the CBI Headquarters Signal Section. He was Capt. (soon to become a major) Milton A. Pilcher, who brought with him from New Delhi two more Signal Corps officers, 2d Lts. John W. Travis and William B. Filiak. Travis, a telephone man, assisted Pilcher in the unit headquarters. Filiak, a radio operator, commanded the communications platoon of the 3d Battalion. Still another Signal Corps officer and GALAHAD volunteer, 2d Lt. Alexander E. Glaves, a radio expert, commanded the 2d Battalion's communications platoon. The leader of the 1st Battalion's communications platoon was a Signal Corps officer, too, more by

chance than by intent. He was Lt. Charlton Ogburn, Jr., who had entered the Army as a Signal Corps photographer. When early in 1943 he volunteered for the mysterious long-range penetration group that became the famous Merrill's Marauders, he found himself assigned command of the 1st Battalion's communications platoon. This, in Burmese jungles, meant a radio platoon. He learned about military radio, as did so many other World War II communicators, the hard way.[63]

Major Pilcher, originally assigned to the CBI Signal Section to serve as one of General King's liaison officers with the Tenth Air Force in India, had volunteered for GALAHAD in the summer of 1943. After conferring with Colonel Fairweather, signal officer under Maj. Gen. Orde C. Wingate, the British originator of long-range penetration tactics, Pilcher proceeded to organize communications for GALAHAD. For one thing he requested and obtained thirty-three Signal Corps men to serve in the battalion communications platoons along with infantry communicators. He specifically asked for radio men, stating that "radio will be the 'life-line' for the unit," and, he emphasized, "it must be adequately manned." But not all the Signal Corps specialists whom he received were competent, though they learned with a will, and fast. Some of them completely lacked experience. Some came from fixed radio stations, some from antiaircraft units in the United States (prob-

[62] Routing Sheet, Hill, G–3, 13 May, sub: Com Pers for GALAHAD. SigC OT 370.2 Rpts CBI, Tab 26.

[63] (1) Intervs, SigC Hist Div with Col Milton A. Pilcher, 31 Aug, 21 Sep, and 2 Nov 60. SigC Hist Sec file. (2) Ogburn, *The Marauders*, pp. 33, 43f., and 54. A Signal Corps photo officer, Pilcher recalled, served in GALAHAD headquarters throughout the campaign. He was 2d Lt. David Lubin.

ably from Signal Aircraft Warning units). Because their experience was slight or ill-suited and because they were not hardened to the rigors of Burma campaigning, as were the infantrymen, Major Pilcher concluded after the GALAHAD action that infantry communicators were in general preferable to Signal Corps men (just as Colonel Hill in CBI headquarters had said earlier).[64]

Some of the infantry communicators proved outstanding, for example Lt. William T. Bright in Lieutenant Ogburn's platoon. But Signal Corps men, if they had all been adequately trained in the type of radio work employed in the campaign, would have been better, Major Pilcher later remarked. Specialized training and experience with the equipment, its use, and its maintenance are basically more crucial in communications tasks than whether the men are Signal Corps or other troops. Only Signal Corps specialists are likely to possess sufficient knowledge and experience in the intricate business of radio maintenance and repair.[65]

Despite all difficulties, radio communications in GALAHAD, Major Pilcher subsequently recalled, were reasonably good —both the circuits within the small combat units and the links between them and the Burma headquarters of Merrill and Stilwell. Long-range radio, however, between the 5307th and the rear base in the Ledo-Dinjan area to summon air supply, was more worrisome. The Washington planners had provided adequate radio for use in the battalions and Burma headquarters, but they had not sufficiently appreciated the more powerful radio requirements to cover the hundreds of miles back over the Naga Hills to India. In particular, Pilcher remembered with poignancy the labor involved simply in listening, not to mention transmitting, with the long-range AN/PRC-1. Since no batteries were designed to power the receiver component, its energy had to be cranked up on the hand generator, a tedious task for the communications platoon (the set's power demand, when transmitting, strained the arms and shoulders of the men still more). At GALAHAD headquarters, Pilcher often pressed the military police into the work of cranking the generator hour after hour. With the battalions on the trail, the communications platoon members, however weary from day-long marches, had to work the radio at night without much assistance. Major Pilcher gave

---

[64] (1) Ltr, Capt Pilcher to Theater SigO CBI, 17 Nov 43, sub: Com Plan, 5307th Provisional Unit, pp. 1 2. (2) Ltr, Maj Pilcher, SigO Hq 5332d Brig, 1 Mar 45, sub: Sig Com, 5307th Composite Unit, A Reprint of Rpt, 3 Aug 44, pp. 2 and 5. SigC Hist Sec file.

[65] (1) Intervs with Pilcher, 31 Aug, 21 Sep, and 2 Nov 60. (2) Ogburn, *The Marauders*, p. 54. Some of Pilcher's comments on repair and maintenance after the GALAHAD campaign read as follows: "Maintenance of equipment while on the march was difficult.... Changing tubes and repairing shorted or loose connnections were easily handled. It was necessary to cannibalize SCR–300 sets due to lack of spare parts. This work was done in the battalion repair sections when the unit stopped for more than two or three days. Hand generators caused considerable trouble.... Turnover of SCR–300's was approximately 100%... because extensive repairs could not be made in the

field and damaged [sets] could not be returned to the repair shops at the base. There was a high rate of loss due to enemy action and to rough treatment on rougher trails.... All batteries should be packed in wooden boxes as should tools and spare parts when mule carried." Ltr, Pilcher, 1 Mar 45. Reprint of Rpt, 3 Aug 44, p. 4.

GENERAL SUN LI-JEN USING SCR–300 NEAR THE STILWELL ROAD

them full credit in his after-action report:

However routine their jobs may be, the work of a communications man is as important and is as arduous as that of any man in the organization. Without communications, no unit can fight well, and without communications a long range penetration unit cannot fight. A communication man's work is never done. He walks all day with his unit and at night he "pulls his shift." If traffic is heavy or radio conditions poor, he works all night. In a fight he stands by his set clearing traffic until relieved.[66]

Actually, the radiomen and their radio sets served rather well everywhere in Burma. GALAHAD could not have accomplished its mission had this not been true. The failures tend to be remembered, however, and the successes forgot-

---

[66] Ltr, Pilcher, 1 Mar 45, Reprint of Rpt, 3 Aug 44, p. 2.

Another cranky problem often arises also in the

person of the staff officer who, if he does not understand communications, expects (as Pilcher worded it) "Wall Street" service in the field. The signal officer, Pilcher explained, must make commanders and officers aware of the capabilities and limitations of signal equipment and troops on hand lest too much be expected and fatal failures occur.

For a vivid description of the arduous work of cranking power into the AN/PRC–1 on the trails in Burma, see Ogburn, *The Marauders*, pp. 144f., 177.

ten—in a typically American manner that takes communications for granted, ignoring the amazing provision of any kind of adequate communications amid so primitive and unfavorable circumstances.[67]

That in general the radio communications of both the American and the Chinese forces in Burma succeeded is further attested by frequent mention of radio commands and control in the combat histories of GALAHAD and the Northern Combat Area Command. Air supply and air evacuation proved entirely successful in large-scale sustained operations. The 1944 campaign depended heavily upon the radios that first summoned the supporting aircraft, designated the drop or landing areas, and then communicated directly between the troops below, difficult to locate under tropical forest cover, and the planes overhead.[68]

Although, in general, little notice has hitherto been granted by American military students to radio communications, either to their essentiality or usual dependability in the wars that the United States has fought in this century, it is notable that this decisive element in the Allied recovery of Burma in 1944 was not overlooked by the Japanese. For,

in addition to granting that superior American air power and air support of ground troops were decisive in that struggle, the enemy acknowledged further that superior communications had made possible, in turn, the air support. To quote a Japanese officer:

With a *good signals system* and air supplies, the Allies were able to carry out their operations freely and unhindered whereas the Japanese without air supplies and with their only means of supply—ground transport—cut off, were in a paralyzed state. . . . The difference in ground-air cooperation between the Japanese Army and the Allies was the difference between victory and defeat.[69]

The essentiality of Army (including Army Air Forces) signal communications had not impressed the average CBI officer to the extent it had impressed leading ETO commanders and would impress men of the postwar era of supersonic vehicles and weapons—when communications would be elevated in Army doctrine to constitute one of a vital triad: fire power, mobility, and command control (signal communications).

Upon the capture of Myitkyina on 3 August 1944, the hard-fought northern Burma campaign came to an end. A forward thrust of special units—GALAHAD battalions with attached Chinese regiments—had, on 17 May, seized the airstrip and cleared it for limited use, amid continuing combat. Their communica-

---

[67] See above p. 13, n. 41, and comment of the Commanding General, 41st Division, in the South Pacific.

[68] Hist of NCAC, CBI, and IB, 1943–45, I, 47ff., and 92ff. See also Appendix XII of this history, entitled Growth, Development and Operating Procedure of Air Supply and Evacuation System, NCAC Front Burma Campaign 1943–45, sec. D, pp. 80–Vff. To quote from page 80–V: "Liberal use is made of telephone and radio operation. . . . The importance of the teletype system cannot be overemphasized. . . ." See also Ogburn, *The Marauders*, especially pp. 140, 144ff., 171, 177, 207ff., 229.

[69] Romanus and Sunderland, *Stilwell's Command Problems*, p. 90. Italics added. The words are those of Lt. Col. Iwaichi Fujiwara, on occasion G–2 and G–3 of the Japanese *15th Army*. Similar comments were attributed also to Lt. Gen. Takazo Numata, Chief of Staff, Headquarters, *Southern Army*.

tions were at first in dire straits—not enough wire and still less radio. Throughout the first week radio communications from the airstrip to the rear, totaling about a hundred messages a day, fell upon the shoulders of one officer and a skeletal section whose men had been salvaged from the already exhausted communications section of one of the composite regiments. Cipher work broke down because the regular cryptographers had all been flown out, incapacitated by wounds or diseases. The mule drivers and other troops who were pressed into this exacting work proved unable to handle it. For four days, Major Pilcher reported, "important traffic was delayed, garbled and confused," a grave situation, until rear headquarters was able to fly in desperately needed communications troops and equipment.[70]

Troops of the 835th, incorporated into the 988th Signal Battalion under the NCAC signal section, were among the Signal Corps men who came to the rescue of the Allied communicators on the Myitkyina airstrip. A team from Ledo landed by plane on 9 July, bringing in an SCR–188 and message center facilities. Under combat conditions, which frequently confined the men to foxholes, they managed to put their station on the air by 11 July. More members, wiremen, of the 835th arrived, and on the day after the city fell they installed a BD–98 in a tent in the town and strung field wire to the railhead, the airstrip, and combat headquarters. Later bulldozers, as they cleared roadways, ripped out lengths of wire, and natives, who prized the line as pack lashing, helped themselves. Even so, the operators kept the circuits open despite these and other interruptions. For example, late one night a call came into the switchboard in good English asking for a connection to Ledo. There was as yet no wire connection back to that distant base in India. Then the operator heard an unmistakable "banzai," and the Japanese, who had cut in on the line, cut the wire and the circuit as well.[71]

Throughout the Burma fighting the 96th Signal Battalion provided a variety of wire, radio, and message services, including message dispatch by liaison airplane. It provided these services with an exceptional variety of workers that included a Chinese engineer battalion, a provisional construction company from the 3d Chinese Signal Battalion, Kachin and Karen civilians (Burma hill tribesmen), and three Indian pioneer companies, all under command of the NCAC signal officer.

One of the 96th's technical sergeants rigged a mast and boom arrangement on a flatcar to rehabilitate wire lines along the railroad between Pinbaw and Hopin. Using this improvisation, which British soldiers dubbed the "wind-jammer," armed signalmen were able to

---

[70] Ltr, Pilcher, 1 Mar 45, Reprint of Rpt, 3 Aug 44, p. 6.
Lieutenant Travis, who had been in Merrill's rear headquarters, was brought forward during this action to supervise the installation of telephone lines serving the remnants of GALAHAD at the siege of Myitkyina. He received a Silver Star for heroism in laying the lines under fire. Intervs, SigC Hist Div with Col Pilcher, 31 Aug, 21 Sep, and 2 Nov 60.

[71] Hawkins and Hawkins, History of the 835th Sig Sv Bn, pp. 76–78.
Colonel Moynahan later commented that he also sent to the airfield, long before the fall of Myitkyina, a stripped-down SCR–399 mounted in a jeep and trailer, flown in by a C–47. MS Comments, Moynahan, Jul 59.

string eighteen to twenty miles a night, working after dark because supply trains crowded the rails during the daylight. They got illumination from landing lights salvaged from a C–47 aircraft and protection from 50-caliber machine guns that were mounted on the car. Before Bhamo was taken, the 96th skirted the town with spiral-four cable. Within a week after the town fell in December 1944, the battalion had a mobile signal center operating there— equipped with a switchboard mounted in a truck together with radio and teletype. The mobile radioteletypewriter link that they established with Myitkyina "proved to be a life saver," according to the battalion history, "whenever the wire line service was interrupted." Interruptions occurred. Three wiremen lost their lives along the lines; two were victims of an enemy shell, one fell under a rifleman's bullet.[72]

In the most unusual theater that was Burma, there occurred other instances, apart from GALAHAD experience, of Signal Corps officers doing combat communications work contrary to Army restrictions limiting the service of Signal Corps troops farther forward than the division signal company. The exception that General King had urged for GALAHAD became a necessity when the American artillery adviser for the 22d Division (Chinese), Lt. Col. Trevor N. Dupuy, who also commanded the Artillery Group (Chinese), was ordered to provide artillery support to two Chindit units in Burma in mid-1944. Among his essential needs in this last assignment

was an artillery communications section. No corps artillery communicators were available in the area. Colonel Moynahan therefore provided (in addition to the equipment) a Signal Corps team from the 988th Signal Battalion. The team commanding officer, as Moynahan recalled years later, was Lt. Louis Freiburg, a radio expert. As the young signal officer's plane arrived in the combat zone, the airstrip was under fire. Alighting nervous and shaken, he "pitched right in," in Dupuy's words, and quickly learned the duties normally required of a regular artillery battalion communications officer. This Signal Corps officer served through five months of heavy fighting down the railroad line to Indaw— —from early August, when the offensive in lower Burma began, to its conclusion in December 1944. One of his wiremen was killed in ambush. The Japanese, having broken the wire, lay in wait till the lineman came to make repairs.[73]

Whereas the enemy in Burma collapsed by the end of 1944, sooner than was expected, the enemy in China continued to succeed in his drives against Allied air bases there. Supply of China

---

[72] (1) MS Comments, Moynahan, Jul 59. (2) SigC Hist, CBI IB, Oct 44–Jan 45, p. 2. (3) Hist, 96th Signal Battalion, Supplement, Myitkyina to Lashio, 20 Dec 45, pp. 4, 8, 13–16.

[73] (1) Interv, SigC Hist Sec with Dupuy, 7 Feb 58, Washington, and Ltr, Dupuy to Thompson, 2 Aug 59. SigC Hist Sec file. (2) MS Comments, Moynahan, Jul 59.
Colonel Moynahan mentioned other Signal Corps officers who served in small units forward of the division, doing tasks normally assigned to infantry or artillery communicators.
Colonel Dupuy believed that it was not Lieutenant Freiburg, but a Lieutenant Forster who commanded the Signal Corps team sent to the Chindits. This was probably Lt. Louis J. Forster, Signal Corps, who received the Bronze Star for combat service in Burma in mid-1944 as communications officer for a corps artillery group. Ltr, Army Br Mil Pers Rcds Ctr, St. Louis, Mo., to Chief SigC Hist Div, 6 Sep 60. SigC Hist Sec file.

SIGNAL LINEMEN STRING WIRE BESIDE THE STILWELL ROAD

from seaports in India became more important than ever. Signal Corps tonnages arriving in Calcutta rose impressively in 1945. Motor convoys were by then moving the matériel over the newly opened Ledo, or Stilwell, Road to Kunming and beyond. "We began to get some of the supplies we'd been screaming for," recalled an officer of the 835th Signal Service Battalion in Kunming. "That made a hell of a difference," he added, "not only in the job we did but in the way the men felt about the work." It was quite a change from the isolation and discouragement of the early days in the CBI. Thus CBI signalmen, espe-

cially those of the 835th, had lived through tremendous changes since their arrival in 1942. "Many of them," reminisced the unit historians, "could remember a day when all Delhi code work was done in a hotel bathroom, when all messages were pounded out on a hand key, and when the available circuits numbered only two. Now a traffic load of half a million code groups a day was only normal." [74]

During early 1945 new Signal Corps units came into China, India, and Burma, and older units reorganized.

[74] Hawkins and Hawkins, Hist. 835th Sig Sv Bn, pp. 81, 93–95.

Units arriving in April and May 1945 included four signal service companies —the 3340th, the 3152d, 3182d, and 3183d.[75] In early April General Reeder, the India-Burma chief signal officer, transferred the 432d Signal Heavy Construction Battalion (Aviation) to the China Theater to help extend the long intertheater pole line eastward from Kunming to Tu-shan. By May the China Theater was asking General Reeder for the 96th and 988th Signal Battalions as well. Despite these transfers to China, the India-Burma Signal Corps troop strength at the end of the war stood at 687 officers and 11,980 enlisted men.[76] In May 1945, General Reeder was appointed G-4 on the staff of General Sultan, commander of the India-Burma Theater. Colonel Petzing was named chief signal officer of that theater, succeeding Reeder. The long pole line remained a major signal effort in those lands. Military demands upon its circuits continued to grow.

The demand upon the facilities of the Army Airways Communications System (AACS) "has now reached a point," General Reeder commented on 19 May, "where they cannot clear PX's over the hump by radio in time to beat the planes in." India, Burma, and China

theater commanders preferred wire line teletypewriter service, and Reeder intended they should have it. "The coordination of Hump Lift and Hump Allocations, and the supply services," he added, "literally demand fine communication between the depots of Calcutta and Chabua and the China SOS in Kunming." [77]

Suddenly in August the war ended. Allied effort in the CBI had kept the enemy out of India, driven him out of Burma, and maintained encouragement and assistance to China. In all this, General Reeder felt that the help to China in signal matters compared well with the work of others. "The splendid plans which were laid in the past (most of it due to [Henry L.] Page King, Neal, and Petzing)," he had written to General Ingles in February 1945, "are coming to fruition. As a result we are able to implement the Chinese plans better with troops than are most of the branches here."

General Reeder had foreseen that the pole line in China might never meet a war need, but he saw other values that it might have. "Any pole line construction will . . . be of service after the war to the Chinese government and to the Chinese people," he said. If these communications facilities provided by the Signal Corps helped strengthen good relations between the United States and the Chinese, he felt all the effort and cost were well spent.[78]

---

[75] SigC Hist, India-Burma Theater, Apr–Sep 45, p. 2.

For papers on the extensive reorganization of the 835th Signal Service Battalion in January 1945, see SigC OT 200.3 Pers ASF CHI, 1942–44, Tab O, and a second folder in this same file dated 1944–45, Tab 30.

[76] SigC, Hist, IBT, Apr–Sep 45, pp. 1–9. Of this total, as of 30 September 1945, 285 officers and 5,339 men were assigned to the AAF, the remainder to ground and service forces.

[77] Ltr, Reeder to Ingles, 19 May 45, pp. 2ff. SigC OT 370.2 Rpts CBI, Tab 22.

[78] Ltr, Reeder to Ingles, 12 Feb 45, p. 2, same file, Tab 22.

CHAPTER VII

The Signal Corps in the South and Central Pacific

Hardly less remote and diverse than the CBI theater, and even more vast, was the Pacific and the several areas into which the Allies divided it. The Pacific did not in fact constitute a theater at all in the sense that the ETO, for example, did. Its sea, continental (Australia), and island expanses, and the disposition of the relatively few, widely scattered armed forces therein required administration by "areas," specifically so designated rather than called "theaters." Some of the areas contained military elements of British, Australian, New Zealand, and Dutch origin, as well as American.

In March 1942, the U.S. Joint Chiefs of Staff had directed, effective by April, the organization of the Southwest Pacific Area (SWPA) and of the Pacific Ocean Areas (POA). SWPA remained a single unit under General Douglas MacArthur till well into 1945. It included Australia and the islands to the north, especially New Guinea (also the Netherlands Indies to the west, less Sumatra), and it encompassed regions further north and west, especially the Philippines.

The Pacific Ocean Areas were subdivided into three parts. One, the North Pacific, scene of Aleutian fighting early in 1943, lay far outside the main areas of conflict to the south. These latter areas constituted the Central Pacific and the South Pacific. The Central Pacific Area lay between the equator and latitude 42° north. The South Pacific Area, lying below the equator and east of longitude 159° east, by mid-1943 included major headquarters in New Caledonia and Guadalcanal, together with a scattering of lesser islands.

Over-all command of the Pacific Ocean Areas rested with the Commander in Chief, POA, Admiral Chester W. Nimitz. He directly commanded the North and Central Pacific. The South Pacific (SOPAC) he delegated to a subordinate who, after October 1942, was Admiral William F. Halsey, Jr., with headquarters in Nouméa, New Caledonia. These areas and commanders remained unchanged up to mid-1944.[1]

The South Pacific Area

Admiral Halsey's SOPAC staff was heavily naval and the armed forces he commanded were largely naval units and Marine troops. Army troops, first those of Task Force 6814, and AAF units were commanded by Maj. Gen.

[1] John Miller, jr., *Cartwheel: The Reduction of Rabaul*, UNITED STATES ARMY IN WORLD WAR II (Washington, 1959), pp. 2ff.

Millard F. Harmon. General Harmon, who had been senior AAF officer in the area, was made commanding general (COMGENSOPAC) with Navy's concurrence, on 14 July 1942, as the War Department organized the Army troops under him, designating them as the U.S. Army Forces in the South Pacific Area (USAFISPA).[2]

Offensive actions against the Japanese had begun in 1942 when SOPAC forces, the Marine Corps in August, then the Army in October, entered combat on Guadalcanal. Here, and in the simultaneous campaigns in SWPA on the southern end of New Guinea, Army troops were supported by Signal Corps installations and operators from the earliest days of the war with a limited variety of equipment and with the meager teams and units that accompanied the first task forces in those areas of the world. By mid-1943 the South Pacific Area was steadily accruing strength. U.S. forces had completed the capture of Guadalcanal early in the year and were, in co-operation with SWPA,

driving northwestward along the Solomons toward Rabaul.[3]

Army ground troops in the South Pacific generally found themselves fighting on islands, many of them small. This was a circumstance new to the U.S. military experience in the world wars of the 20th century. To those responsible for signal communications, the situation required an entirely different approach to the problem of establishing and maintaining military signals. It was an axiom, in the more familiar warfare on continental land masses, that the lines of communication which signalmen first set up be merely extended to accompany the progress of the troops. But among the Pacific islands the advance of communications presented a series of almost unrelated activities. Each isle constituted a self-contained entity that could be linked with other island entities by radio only, by powerful long-range circuits.[4] Signal

---

[2] (1) John Miller, jr., *Guadalcanal: The First Offensive*, UNITED STATES ARMY IN WORLD WAR II (Washington, 1949), pp. 22ff. (2) Samuel Eliot Morison, "History of United States Naval Operations in World War II," V, *The Struggle for Guadalcanal* (Boston: Little, Brown and Company, 1949), 185ff.

The USAFISPA signal officer described the SOPAC staff under Halsey as almost entirely Navy and Marine, with Army and Army-Air a separate headquarters under Harmon. The role of the Army command in this arrangement has been described by Army historian Maurice Matloff as "somewhat anomalous" since the troops Harmon commanded actually operated under the direct command of Halsey. See Incl. with Ltr, Maj. Gen. Francis L. Ankenbrandt, USAF (Ret.), Manager, Defense Projs, RCA, to Thompson, 24 Jan 58. SigC 314.7, Correspondence vols. II and III, Hist, 1958, SigC Hist Sec file; and Maurice Matloff, *Strategic Planning for Coalition Warfare, 1943-44*, UNITED STATES ARMY IN WORLD WAR II (Washington, 1959), p. 459.

[3] For Signal Corps activities in SOPAC before mid-1943, see Thompson, Harris, *et al.*, *The Test*, pp. 109ff, 468ff.

As to the meager forces in the desperate Pacific struggle in 1942, the Navy at the end of that year roughly estimated the entire Allied effort (not only in the Pacific but including also the CBI and the Indian Ocean) as constituting but 15 percent of all Allied resources—the remainder at that time being concentrated in the Atlantic and in the African and European theaters. Samuel Eliot Morison, "History of United States Naval Operations in World War II," VI, *Breaking the Bismarcks Barrier, 22 July 1942-1 May 1944* (Boston: Little, Brown and Company, 1950), 4. Within less than a year, by September 1943, U.S. Army forces operating against Japan had built up to over 771,000, compared to 1,032,000 deployed against Germany and Italy, a ratio of 3 to 4. Matloff, *Strategic Planning for Coalition Warfare, 1943-44*, page 319. See also Samuel Eliot Morison, *Strategy and Compromise* (Boston: Little, Brown and Company, 1958), p. 85.

[4] ". . . 60% to 75% of the [SOPAC] traffic was in radio message form," Col. Arvid B. Newhouse, "SOPAC Signals," *Signals*, II, No. 5 (May–June, 1948), 36.

Corps men in the South Pacific aptly compared the Army's island signals with Navy communications, each island being comparable to a ship, which requires two sorts of sharply different communications facilities—a limited system internal to the vessel and unlimited radio circuits extending from it to points hundreds and thousands of miles distant.[5]

As the campaign in the Pacific progressed, successive islands became the combat zone, while those to the rear generally converted to base commands —a base command in the Pacific being the equivalent of the communications zone in the continental warfare of Europe. Here were concentrated all depot, supply, troop training, and staging activities. Throughout the war much of the Pacific supply activity turned on Hawaii, which provided the hub of the Central Pacific Base Command, especially from mid-1944 on. In the general reorganization at that time the entire South Pacific Area converted to a base command with headquarters remaining in New Caledonia.[6]

Since 29 July 1942 Col. Francis L. Ankenbrandt had been serving as General Harmon's chief signal officer in the headquarters of USAFISPA at Nouméa,

New Caledonia. Aided at first by only one clerk and two typists, he served a somewhat uncertain organization— both Navy and Army. His skeletal headquarters signal section had to draw upon the Signal Corps troops who were on hand serving Army task forces on the various islands of the South Pacific area.[7] He had to depend upon the American Division, he reported in September 1942, for messengers, message center, communications and code people, and for telephone service. Not until late November did his headquarters outfit arrive, the 230th Signal Operations Company, "a godsend," he exclaimed.[8] He would have to wait many long months for other units he needed almost as badly, depot companies in particular.

Signal Relations With the AAF

Army airfields, their communications and navigational needs, and their radar to warn of enemy aircraft had from the

---

[5] (1) T/4 Walter D. Kunhart, Hq USAFISPA Sig Sec, Signal Corps Activities in the South Pacific Theater, December 1941–July 1944, p. 1. SOPAC folder, A46-160, drawer 16, SigC Hist Sec file. (2) History of U.S. Army Forces in the SOPAC Area During World War II, 30 March 1942–1 August 1944, pt. III, I, Army Administration and Supply, C, Sig (hereafter cited as USAFISPA Hist, pt. III, vol. I), 550. MS, OCMH files.

[6] Capt W. D. Gooley, Signal Supply in the Western Pacific Base Command, 1949, Sig Sch Monograph, p. 1. The Sig Sch Libr, Fort Monmouth. Base Commands in the Mediterranean were similar to those of the Pacific.

[7] In March 1942 Task Force 6814, later known as the Americal Division, had arrived. Its signal elements included the 26th Signal Company, the 175th Signal Repair Detachment, a detachment of the 162d Signal Photo Company, the 700th Signal AW Company, and a detachment of the 181st Signal Company. Kunhart, SigC Activities in SOPAC, pp. 2–3.

For U.S. communications in New Caledonia to mid-1942, see SigO, TF 6814, Report on Radio Situation, New Caledonia, 20 Jun 42. SOPAC folder, SigC Hist Sec file.

[8] (1) USAFISPA Hist, pt. III, I, 538f. (2) Ltr, Ankenbrandt, SigO USAFISPA, to Lanahan, OCSigO, 13 Sep 42, p. 1. (3) Ltr, Ankenbrandt to Lanahan, 6 Feb 43, p. 1. SigC OT 319.1 (111) Ankenbrandt Rpts.

According to the USAFISPA History, pages 526f., Ankenbrandt was served by a Provisional Signal Service Company, beginning in mid-October, which contained troops from several signal units already in New Caledonia.

beginning placed heavy demands upon the meager resources of the USAFISPA signal organization. It was months before even one signal officer could be assigned to serve the AAF full time. Meanwhile, AAF communications needs received priority over those of the growing Army ground establishment in SOPAC. At USAFISPA headquarters there had arrived by early 1943 no fewer than five signal companies to serve aviation needs. The 410th Signal Company (Aviation) had entirely taken over the airfield on Guadalcanal doing Army Airways Communications System work using SCR–188's, 197's, 299's, and a few Navy TBW sets. At Tontouta in New Caledonia the 905th Signal Depot Company (Aviation) was setting up supply for the Thirteenth Air Force. Men of the company were looking after radar repair—both for airborne radar and for the ground sets of the Aircraft Warning Service, serving not only Army AWS units but also the Army radar (SCR's–270 and 271) used by the Navy and the Marine Corps in the area. The company dispatched repair teams and spare parts by air transport, as needed, to the widely separated AWS sites in SOPAC. Incidentally, the theater Aircraft Warning Service, which in continental United States had long been primarily an AAF responsibility (though drawing on Signal Corps equipment and units), was entirely the South Pacific signal officer's concern until 1944.[9]

The Army in SOPAC was responsible for eight sizable air bases by March 1943. Each field required a signal detail of one officer and thirty-five men to install and operate telephone, tele-

graph, radio, and message center facilities.[10] The Signal Corps did the work and provided the operators until gradually the AAF supplied its own communications officers and men. When Colonel Ankenbrandt requested a signal service company (aviation) early in 1943, he was notified that the Air Forces was sending airdrome squadrons down to SOPAC, including a sufficient number of communicators to operate the local telephone, teletype, and radio service. He commented, with scepticism, "apparently they are putting in Air Corps personnel rather than Signal Corps. I have no idea how this will work and have 'tongue in cheek' about the whole matter."[11]

The Army Air Forces was in fact

---

[9] (1) Ltrs, Ankenbrandt to Lanahan, 2 Feb 43, p. 3, and 6 Feb 43, p. 1. (2) Ltr, Ankenbrandt to Lanahan, 8 Feb 43, p. 2. SCIA file 8, Ankenbrandt-Newhouse Rpts 1. (3) Thompson, Harris, et al., The Test, pp. 110, 475.

On the 410th Signal Company (Avn) at Guadalcanal, see: (1) History of the 410th Signal Company Aviation. AF Archives SIG–410–HI, Nov 42, 5728–10, USAF Archives, Maxwell Airfield. (2) Historical Record of the 20th Airways Communications Squadron, AACS, pp. 31–32. AF Archives SQ–A–COM–20–HI, Jan 43–Apr 44, 9666–50. (3) Hist Br Hq AACS AAF, The Army Airways Communications System, pp. 363ff. AF Archives 2690–1. (4) J. Bishop, "The Golden Sky Hook," Collier's, 113, No. 15 (April 8, 1944), pp. 22f.

[10] Ltr, Ankenbrandt to Lanahan, 3 Mar 43, p. 4. SigC OT 319.1 (111) Ankenbrandt Rpts.

[11] Ltr, Ankenbrandt to Lanahan, 1 Apr 43, p. 5.

The matter of Signal Corps versus AAF communications troops had evidently been a subject of discussion, with Brig. Gen. Frank C. Meade replying from the Office of the Chief Signal Officer. Having noted certain comments in a letter from General Meade on 19 March 1943, Colonel Ankenbrandt wrote Colonel Lanahan on 1 May, "I still have my 'tongue in cheek' until FM 1–45 is really changed back." He added, "It will be very interesting to watch the future in this respect. However, on his [Meade's] recommendation we are going right ahead as in the past so far as Signal Officers for our Air Force units are concerned." Ltr, Ankenbrandt to Lanahan, 1 May 43, pp. 8–9.

gradually taking to itself, here as elsewhere, the communications facilities and services that were a Signal Corps responsibility to provide to all the Army. Working together, Signal Corps men and AAF communications specialists speeded the installation of the better air navigational and communications facilities that were required along the vital heavily traveled airways serving the South Pacific islands. The AACS had set up its 20th Region in Tontouta under Capt. Cleo Lawrence with whom Colonel Ankenbrandt collaborated closely. During the early months of 1943, six AACS projects were under way, and in all of them Signal Corps specialists participated. They were on loan from Col. Carroll A. Powell's Central Pacific base in Hawaii, putting in improved radio ranges, radio teletypewriter circuits, separate channels for weather reporting, and so on.[12]

Signal Corps supply, long a weak spot in SOPAC signal activities, did not always please the airmen, who complained specifically that the 905th Signal Depot Company (Aviation) did not grant ready access to its supplies, kept no inventories, and even lacked the knowledge and understanding needed to judge the validity of AACS requirements. In May 1943 the commanding officer of the 20th Airways Communication Squadron, AACS, desperately seeking maintenance parts, sent requests everywhere he could think of, to the Signal Airways Service, SOS, to the Hawaiian Signal Depot, and to the Signal Section of the XIII Air Service Command, with unsatisfactory results.[13]

As the SOPAC forces grew and the campaign against the enemy gathered strength, the Thirteenth Air Force, based on Espíritu Santo, sent an advance echelon to Guadalcanal. To strengthen the signal section of the Thirteenth Air Force headquarters, Colonel Ankenbrandt assigned Lt. Col. Gus B. Hoffman, Signal Corps, as commanding officer of the section. Colonel Hoffman had been Army communications officer, first on Efate and then on New Caledonia.[14] As AAF control consolidated, the Air Service Command in SOPAC received responsibility for its supply matters. Under it were placed such units as the 905th Depot Company (Aviation). By August 1943 the XIII Air Service Command had taken over maintenance and spare parts responsibilities for all Army types of ground radars including 268's and also those Army types in the hands of the Navy and Marine forces. The USAFISPA signal officer was glad enough to be relieved of the burden and hoped that the change would "eliminate a lot of confusion and duplication of effort which existed previously."[15]

---

[12] (1) Ltrs, Ankenbrandt to Lanahan, 2 Feb 43, pp. 2ff., 1 Apr 43, pp. 3f. (2) Hist Subsec, G-2 HUSAFMIDPAC, U.S. Army Forces Middle Pacific and Predecessor Commands, History of Signal Section, 7 December 1941–2 September 1945 (hereafter cited as Hist, Sig Sec HUSAFMIDPAC, with section and page number), 1, 138 (sec. III, Radio Division, p. 12). OCMH files.

[13] Hist Rcd of the 20th Airways Com Squadron, AACS, pp. 18–20. However, the AAF spoke appreciatively of other Signal Corps assistance to the AACS work in SOPAC. See Thompson, Harris, et al., The Test, p. 288, n. 30.

[14] Ltr, Ankenbrandt to Meade, OCSigO, 30 Sep 43, no sub, p. 10. SigC OT 319.1 (111) Ankenbrandt Rpts.

[15] Ltr, Ankenbrandt to Meade, 31 Aug 43, p. 13. Colonel Ankenbrandt added that the XIII Air Service Command and the 905th Signal Depot Company (Aviation) were now doing a good job of radar maintenance and were overhauling SCR-270's that had been replaced by 271's on Bora Bora and Tongatabu. Ibid., pp. 13–14.

A few months later the USAFISPA signal officer was relieved of still another service to the AAF. Early in 1944, the XIII Fighter Command took over the Army's Aircraft Warning Service in the South Pacific. Brig. Gen. Dean C. Strother, previously charged with the fighter command, had hitherto left the AWS to the Army. But his successor, Brig. Gen. Earl W. Barnes, "agrees with me," Colonel Ankenbrandt wrote in January, "that running the AWS is one of the proper jobs of his command." [16]

Although the Signal Corps handed over much communications control to the AAF, supplying equipment and transferring men and units as well, there still remained considerable AAF work for which the USAFISPA signal officer was responsible. The Signal Corps continued to handle AAF administrative traffic, a load that steadily grew. After the move of the Thirteenth Air Force from Espíritu Santo to Guadalcanal, the traffic back to SOPAC headquarters required two circuits around the clock. Radioteletypewriter was needed to handle the load, and its installation was being rushed to completion in early 1944.[17]

By then, as the South Pacific fighting sputtered out in the northern Solomons and as the installations on New Caledonia, Guadalcanal, and Bougainville became bases of supply for operations further west and north, the Thirteenth Air Force transferred to the Southwest Pacific Area. Colonel Ankenbrandt left

SOPAC, too, when in mid-1944 the Signal Corps reassigned him as the AAF signal officer of the Pacific Ocean Areas. After the war he changed his branch of service altogether and became an AAF officer, exchanging the Signal Corps crossed flags for the propellers of the Army Air Forces. Ankenbrandt's career was a distinguished example of a course followed during World War II by many Signal Corps officers who began their career by serving the Air Forces and ended it by joining them. He transferred into the AAF on 2 February 1946 as a brigadier general.

Signal Relations With the Navy

Joint communications frequently characterized signal operations in the South Pacific Area, as in 1942 on Tongatabu, where a signal detachment of about fifty men, drawn largely from the 37th Division, set up a message center at Nukualofa. The Navy communications unit there not only handled cryptographic work for all interisland radio traffic, including Army signals, but even "reserved the right to delete or change any parts of messages which they did not consider necessary," commented the somewhat miffed signal officer on the island, Lt. Col. Dane O. Sprankle.[18] "In theory it is fine to consolidate," Colonel Ankenbrandt once said, speaking of joint communications. But the difficulties in joint practice sometimes clashed with the theory. "Tongatabu, Bora Bora, and Samoa-Ellice Islands," he wrote in January 1944, "are examples where such has been in operation and our operation (Army)

---

[16] The trend in SOPAC was catching up with the pattern of SigC–AAF relations elsewhere. Ltr, Ankenbrandt to Meade, 31 Jan 44, p. 11. SigC OT 319.1 (111.1), Ankenbrandt Rpts.

[17] Ibid., p. 2.

[18] Kunhart, SigC Activities in the SOPAC, pp. 22f.

gets 'balled up' or delayed unduly." He explained, "The Navy has minor differences in procedure and other rules and regulations contrary to our practice. Furthermore, the Navy is in practice now of ruling out practically all administrative traffic from their radio circuits, handling all of this stuff as 'Airmailgram.' Such procedure does not always suit our Army Commanders." [19]

At all the larger SOPAC bases, circumstances inevitably compelled generous co-operation, and truly joint Army-Navy communications facilities became the general practice. The theory that integrated communications best serve the interest of unity of command became a workable reality. In a situation where shipping space and ground room on a small island, as well as the troops and equipment that could be made available, were all at a minimum, it was natural that there should develop the single communications establishment called a joint communication center (JCC). The same equipment, the same circuits, the same codes and ciphers, the same message procedures, and the same operators served all units—

Army, Navy, and Marine—on the island.[20]

For example, there was a joint Army-Navy radio station and message center (NCS–WVHU) at Suva in the Fiji Islands. Its soldier and sailor operators carried on their work in caves until mid-1943, when the station moved into buildings above ground. The ACAN station in Nouméa, WVJN, was also operated jointly. Early in 1943 Signal Corps men were operating the big 15-kilowatt transmitter that had recently been installed, and they performed message center duties alongside naval communicators. Meanwhile the USAFISPA signal officer was busy selecting a location for a joint Army-Navy receiving station, eventually located in the Anse Vata section of Nouméa. "The entire responsibility," he reported, speaking of the receiving station, "will be ours [Army's]." [21]

A year later the last large joint communications facility in SOPAC was built on the island of Bougainville at Cape Torokina. Both the base radio station and the communications center were

[19] (1) Ltr, Ankenbrandt to Meade, 31 Jan 44, pp. 5f. SCIA file 8, Ankenbrandt-Newhouse Rpts 2. (2) Ltr, Ankenbrandt to Lanahan, 13 Sep 42, p. 5. SigC OT 319.1 (111) Ankenbrandt Rpts.

Improved joint procedures did develop as Army and Navy communicators had to work together of necessity. Late in 1942 a War Department General Staff observer, Col. Leonard H. Rodieck, reported on the message center in Nouméa, where an acute accumulation of military messages had developed, as follows: "The best set-up . . . was in Nouméa. . . . The Navy task force was in the harbor. General Harmon got all the Navy operators ashore to help out the Army, because the Navy was maintaining [radio] silence in the harbor. Nouméa finally got caught up to within four days, with the Navy's help, after being thousands of messages behind." USAFISPA Hist, pt. III, I, 525.

[20] (1) Maj Willis E. Kooken, The Island Command Signal Officer and the Joint Communication Center (1950), Sig Sch Monograph, Introduction and p. 1. The Sig Sch Libr, Fort Monmouth. (2) CSigO, Annual Rpt, FY 44, p. 41.

Reporting on his trip to the Pacific areas, General Somervell said in November 1943 that a primary problem in the SOPAC was developing arrangements that would remove the duplication of such facilities as communications systems. Min, Mtg of Staff Conf, ASF, 6 Nov 43, p. 2. SigC MP 337, Confs, 1942, 30 Apr 44.

[21] He added, too, ". . . the only real difficulty we had in going joint with the Navy is that their standard of living in the war zone is very much higher than the Army's." (1) Ltr, Ankenbrandt to Lanahan, 2 Feb 43, p. 2. SigC OT 319.1 (111), Ankenbrandt Rpts. (2) Newhouse, "SOPAC Signals," Signals, II, No. 5, p. 36. (3) USAFISPA Hist, pt. III, I, 529f, 537ff.

SIGNAL MESSAGE CENTER IN A CAVE, VELLA LAVELLA

constructed by the Army. The radio station was eventually operated by Navy communicators who served Army needs as well as their own. The communications center was operated jointly by Army and Navy personnel. In January 1944 Colonel Ankenbrandt shipped to Bougainville, as part of Army's contributions to joint communications there, a 300-watt station and a full team from the 842d Signal Service Company. Army circuits until then were provided by SCR–299's in the hands of the 233d Signal Operations Company.[22]

All the co-operation necessitated the development and use of joint radio frequencies, joint message-sending procedures, and joint conferences to co-ordinate these and other matters, not to mention the organization of new units such as the joint assault signal companies. An important element of the

[22] (1) Kunhart, SigC Activities in the SOPAC Theater, pp. 27ff. (2) Ltr, Ankenbrandt to Meade, 21 Jan 44, pp. 1–2. SigC OT 319.1 (111.1) Ankenbrandt Rpts.

The Joint Army-Navy station at Torokina is described in detail, with building layouts and photos, in Incl, XIV Corps, Bougainville Campaign Sig Rpt, 30 May 44, pp. 26–40, with Ltr, CG Hq XIV Corps to TAG, Attn: CSigO, 13 Jul 44, sub: Transmittal of Sig Rpts. SCIA file 125, Litz Rpts 2. See also sec. 2 of XIV Corps Sig Rpt. SigC Hist Sec file.

JASCO's was air liaison communications, whether with naval-marine planes or with AAF craft for close combat support. In October 1943 Ankenbrandt reported that five jeep installations, each containing an SCR–193 and a WE–233 VHF set, were ready for use in the next combat operations. These vehicular installations had proved very successful and were being widely used by Army, Navy, and Marine units.[23]

Signal Corps supply to the Navy of all sorts of communications equipment increased to such proportions by early 1944 that Colonel Ankenbrandt began to feel the pinch. SOS SOPAC (Brig. Gen. Robert C. Breene commanding) was seeking replacements and was unhappy about the situation. "Some of our rear area troops and our supply people do not like it but it just can't be helped," the USAFISPA signal officer acknowledged, adding "I do not have the slightest hesitation in transferring equipment around to the points where it will do the most good." [24]

Supply and Personnel Problems

Signal supply in the South Pacific was in general reasonably adequate except for telephone items. But there were severe difficulties in the shipping and manhandling. Often enough, the supplies were there but aboard ships moored offshore waiting to be unloaded.[25] Or, when at last discharged, signal boxes were frequently as good as lost in confused dumps ashore where, for lack of trained depot hands, inexperienced troops mislaid them. The effect upon Signal Corps operations was the same—bad. Yet evidently by the autumn of 1943 the shortages were not entirely real. "In all fairness," Colonel Ankenbrandt stated in October 1943, reacting to a statement by General Somervell of ASF on signal supply troubles, "I must say that there is no real critical shortage of signal supplies or equipment down here except for telephone equipment." [26]

Telephone equipment, the USAFISPA signal officer repeatedly emphasized, presented his chief supply

---

[23] Ltr, Ankenbrandt to Meade, 31 Oct 43, p. 3. SigC OT 319.1 (111.1), Ankenbrandt Rpts. Re JASCO's, see the discussion below, pages 231ff.

Earlier, in June 1943, there had been a hurried call from the Navy for 8 SCR–284's, installed in jeeps by the 230th Signal Company. At the same time Colonel Ankenbrandt diverted to Navy 20 SCR–511's from the Americal Division and 2 SCR–299's. The radio output of the 284's proved too weak. Ankenbrandt preferred to provide 193's and 299's. A little later the Navy found that Army's 600 series of FM sets were highly satisfactory. (1) Ltrs, Ankenbrandt to Lanahan, 5 Jun 43, p. 3, and 8 Jul 43, p. 4. SigC OT 319.1 (111), Ankenbrandt Rpts. (2) Ltrs, Ankenbrandt to Meade, 31 Oct 43, p. 3, and 31 Jan 44, p. 4. SigC OT 319.1 (111.1), Ankenbrandt Rpts.

[24] (1) Ltr, Ankenbrandt to Meade, 29 Feb 44, p. 3. SigC OT 319.1 (111.1), Ankenbrandt Rpts. (2) Stauffer, The Quartermaster Corps: Operations in the War Against Japan, pp. 75ff.

[25] Delay in unloading was especially acute in the period before mid-1943. (1) Thompson, Harris, et al., The Test, p. 471. (2) Joseph Bykofsky and Harold Larson, The Transportation Corps: Operations Overseas, UNITED STATES ARMY IN WORLD WAR II (Washington, 1957), pp. 497ff. (3) Richard M. Leighton and Robert W. Coakley, Global Logistics and Strategy, 1940–1943, UNITED STATES ARMY IN WORLD WAR II (Washington, 1955), pp. 398ff.

[26] (1) USAFISPA Hist, pt. III, I, 545ff. See also comment by General Ingles quoted in the SigC Tech Info Ltr 29 (Apr 44), p. 5. SigC Hist Sec file. (2) Ltr, Ankenbrandt to Meade, 31 Oct 43, p. 8. SigC OT 319.1 (111.1), Ankenbrandt Rpts. Ankenbrandt referred to a comment that Somervell had made to the effect that Signal Corps supply difficulties had exceeded those of the other supply services but that signal shortages were diminishing.

problem. The bases on New Caledonia badly needed better wire installations, carrier equipment, and switchboards of larger capacity. Guadalcanal, as it became an ever more important supply center, desperately needed such improvements too. It had been ready for good fixed plant installations since March 1943. It was still awaiting them seven months later. The requisitions had long been placed, but the sole switchboards at Henderson and Carney Fields, at Lunga Exchange, and at the Island Command headquarters continued to be such field expedients as BD-96's or commercial-type boards of insufficient capacity. "In this present day and age," Ankenbrandt exclaimed, "everybody wants to conduct their business by telephone (which is the American way of doing it) and there is no reason why we shouldn't give them the service they want." He shared with other theater signal officers the view that there was too much engineering of overseas projects by Washington desk officers who couldn't appreciate the distant needs. But the War Department suppliers, faced with more demands from more theaters than they could supply, were compelled to reduce the demands and to parcel out what they had as best they could—a hard fact not entirely appreciated by the theaters. "Please ask your folks to trust us and our judgment, . . ." the theater signal officer begged, "and just keep the stuff flowing down here." [27]

Colonel Ankenbrandt's request was quite impossible. Naturally, officers in distant theaters wanted to be abundantly supplied and wanted to decide what to use and how to use it, since they best knew their own theater needs. Take, for example, the words of Maj. Gen. Carl Spaatz in England late in 1942. When the War Department tried to trim the seemingly infinite variety of electronic airborne aids that were going to his Eighth Air Force, he exclaimed "send it all and let us decide what to use." [28] But there was not enough equipment in sight for such lavish practices. And if there had been, the theater depots would have become jammed with unused equipment. Stockpiling overseas had been forbidden by the War Department. The prohibition was deemed necessary precisely because the tendency to stockpile in rear area bases and depots was strong. General Somervell himself, after his visit to the Pacific theaters, expressed the view that there was too much build-up locally in bases that were falling further and further behind the island advance, that supplies were being wastefully accumulated far to the rear and service troops were being wasted on their care, that even combat troops were being used to handle supplies unnecessarily and wastefully. [29]

---

[27] Ltr, Ankenbrandt to Meade, 31 Oct 43, pp. 10-11. In an earlier letter Ankenbrandt did appreciate that "probably the bulk of these items [telephone equipment] is going East instead of West," and he frankly added, "however this does not make us feel any better about it down here." Ltr, Anken-

brandt to Lanahan, 6 Feb 43, pp. 4-5. SCIA file 8, Ankenbrandt-Newhouse Rpts. 1.
For a vivid description of Guadalcanal as a supply and communications (Navy) base, see Morison, *Breaking the Bismarcks Barrier*, pages 100ff.

[28] Thompson, Harris, *et al., The Test*, p. 246.
[29] John D. Millett, *The Organization and Role of the Army Service Forces*, UNITED STATES ARMY IN WORLD WAR II (Washington, 1954), pp. 74-75.
On stockpiling overseas, see above, p. 179.

But combat troops had to be so used wherever service troops were too few. By early summer of 1943 this shortage of service troops greatly troubled the USAFISPA signal officer. He had no trained men to handle the increasing inflow of signal supplies. No depot company had yet arrived. The need for its special skills pressed harder with each passing day. The lack of skilled hands would show up in adverse depot conditions for months to come. Meanwhile, the signal depot system remained haphazard, the actual work being done by details from whatever sources the men could be secured. Such was the handling of what was becoming a large signal section in the headquarters general depot, in fact the main USAFISPA signal supply point.[30]

By late summer two depot companies arrived (one was the 210th Signal Depot Company). "The results of the long delays in receiving our two Signal Depot Companies are now finally coming to light," Ankenbrandt noted on 31 August. "The enormous quantities of signal supplies we have been receiving had never been handled properly until just recently. All personnel engaged previously in this task were inexperienced and 'stolen' from any source we could put our hands on." Naturally the results were discouraging. Many needed signal items had disappeared in warehouse jumbles, unrecorded and as good as lost, until competent depot troops took over.[31]

What was true at the Nouméa supply depots was true also on Guadalcanal, which would soon equal Nouméa as a base of supply. The 217th Signal Depot Company had arrived there, badly needed, with much work cut out for it. Every day, boxes were turning up in the warehouses containing valuable equipment the Signal Corps men had long been seeking. The boxes were coming code marked, but no one knew what the markings meant. The signal officer implored his Washington headquarters to send information on all code shipments stating the exact meaning of the markings.

Signal supply inadequacies in the South Pacific—resulting not from a shortage of the supplies but of the right men to handle them—came to a climax early in 1944. The Signal Corps depot troops who had arrived recently were still too few to cope with an increasing flood of equipment as the Signal Corps supply machine and the nation's factories shifted into ever higher gear at home. The Chief Signal Officer, General Ingles, when he visited the South Pacific in February 1944, quickly put his finger on the weakest point—handling of supplies.[32]

An especially unfortunate incident had just occurred on Tenaru beach at Guadalcanal—AACS signal equipment had been hastily and roughly dumped ashore in a jumbled, 30-foot pyramid,

---

[30] (1) Ltr, Ankenbrandt to Lanahan, 5 Jun 43, p. 5. SigC OT 319.1 (111), Ankenbrandt Rpts. (2) Leighton and Coakley, *Global Logistics and Strategy, 1940–1943*, p. 418.

[31] (1) Ltr, Ankenbrandt to Meade, 31 Aug 43. SigC OT 319.1 (111), Ankenbrandt Rpts. "Our

troubles," Ankenbrandt summarized, "are far more lack of handling personnel and lack of transshipment facilities rather than actual lack of supplies." (2) USAFISPA Hist, pt. III, I, 544f.

[32] (1) Ltr, Ankenbrandt to Meade, 30 Sep 43, p. 8. SigC OT 319.1 (111), Ankenbrandt Rpts. (2) Ltr, Ankenbrandt to Meade, 29 Feb 44, p. 1. SigC OT 319.1 (111.1), Ankenbrandt Rpts.

with heavy generators on top and boxes of delicate teletypewriters and radio receivers underneath. A great deal of damage resulted; up to 30 percent of the equipment was ruined. It was but one of several such incidents. All were consequences of the long-standing supply situation in the area—the insufficiency of trained supply and depot personnel. "This particular shipment," Colonel Ankenbrandt wrote to General Meade, "was handled in cargo nets and in bad weather causing a large amount of damage. General Ingles got to see the pile and was very disturbed about it." Ankenbrandt added pointedly, "the 191st Signal Repair Company would certainly come in handy now down here." [33]

There were a few extenuating circumstances with respect to the Tenaru incident. Heavy rains had washed out bridges, preventing quick removal of the supplies to the signal depot. The shipment was one of the largest ever received, and the backlog to be landed was so great that this shipment was unloaded under great pressure—the speeding up under pressure being at the expense of careful handling. It was literally dumped as if by giant steam shovel. Yet General Ingles realized that rough handling could be expected, almost as a rule rather than an exception. He determined that as soon as he returned to the States he would improve the packing of signal equipment. [34]

The incident on Tenaru beach had its counterparts elsewhere, for example along White Beach on Leyte early in January 1945. With graphic pictures and equally expressive words, Lt. Col. Douglas O. Toft, an experienced Signal Corps supply officer, later set forth some of the supply officer's woes in combat areas. Heavy signal items such as wire and cable drums can easily be moved and stacked in the open by a few men with proper equipment (and the base commander is happy with the tonnage moved—the more moved, the better his efficiency record). But it is not so easy with smaller signal items of heterogeneous types. Toft wrote:

. . . if this incoming material is in the form of mixed boxes of signal supplies and equipment, it cannot be segregated as it is unloaded—time will not permit. The Transportation Corps would like to drop the boxes off the truck and have the trucks return to the docks. As a result your supplies will be thrown helter-skelter, with boxes lying on top of one another in total confusion. . . . These boxes contain valuable and delicate equipment and should not be handled in that manner . . . it involves extra labor later to segregate and stack this material . . . still worse, much of this equipment may be needed to fill requisitions that are on back order . . . for organizations already in action or going into action . . . and it is impossible to de-

---

[33] (1) Hist Rcd of the 20th Airways Com Squadron, AACS, pp. 18–20. (2) The Army Airways Communications System, II, 379. (3) Ltr, Ankenbrandt to Meade, 29 Feb 44, pp. 4–5. SigC OT 319.1 (111.1), Ankenbrandt Rpts. (4) Capt Lloyd B. Dodds, History of the Plant Engineering Agency, Army Communications Service, 1941–46, p. 390. SigC Hist Sec file. (5) Incl, Notes on Sig Sup Sv, Pac Theaters, with ASF Transmittal Sheet, Maj William E. Foltz, S&I Agency, to CSigO, 14 Apr 44, p. 11. SigC OT 370.2 Notes on SigC Sup Pac.
Twelve percent of the pile-up, Ankenbrandt later estimated, was a total loss; 70 percent needed repair. Repair work began and was still in progress in June 1944, five months after the damage was done. Ltrs, Ankenbrandt to Meade, 30 Apr 44, p. 8, and 2 Jun 44, p. 4. SigC OT 319.1 (111.1), Ankenbrandt Rpts.

[34] Ltr, Ankenbrandt to Meade, 5 Mar 44, p. 1. SigC OT 319.1 (111.1), Ankenbrandt Rpts.

SIGNAL SUPPLY DUMP, WHITE BEACH, LEYTE

termine what equipment you do have on hand.[35]

At best, supply operations in the Pacific fighting seem to have been difficult beyond most Signal Corps experience elsewhere. The worst was well exemplified by the Tenaru incident. Lt. Col. Arvid B. Newhouse, Colonel Ankenbrandt's assistant and executive, sympathized with the Signal Corps men who toiled in the Guadalcanal depot in seas of mud and who were handicapped at the shore by the lack of wharves. "Operating the Guadalcanal Signal Depot," he reminisced after the war, "was a really unpleasant task." [36]

Signal supply harassments were further aggravated early in 1944 by an administrative difficulty, specifically the assignment and control of three signal service platoons, which were on their way to the USAFISPA signal officer. Colonel Ankenbrandt was eager to receive them, anticipating that his supply

[35] Lt Col Douglas O. Toft, Some Signal Corps Supply Problems in the Southwest Pacific Area During World War II (1950), Sch Monograph, pp. 18–19. The Sig Sch Libr, Ft. Monmouth. See especially photos on pages ii, vi, and 23.

[36] Newhouse, "SOPAC Signals," Signals, II, No. 5, p. 39.

problems would improve when the platoons arrived. One, he planned, would clean up signal supply matters at Espíritu Santo; the second would put New Georgia signal supplies in order; and the third he expected to assign to the Bougainville area.[37]

Accordingly, General Meade in the Washington headquarters of the Signal Corps had asked that the platoons be absorbed in the existing signal service companies wherein they could work under SOPAC SOS serving the signal depots. But General Meade's request, however reasonable, could not be complied with in the field since the signal service company of the island worked for the island commander as an operating company, running the island communications for the commanding general and his headquarters. Therefore, this service company was entirely out of SOS control. On the other hand, signal supply and repair were SOS functions. They were handled by the SOS and the troops doing these tasks were necessarily under SOS command. As a result, the supply and repair platoon, which ought to be part of a signal service company, could not operate with the company in the SOPAC command setup. "It's the old story," remarked Colonel Ankenbrandt, "of splitting up one unit to work for two different Commanders, and the results have so far shown this undesirable."[38]

The USAFISPA signal chief experienced the usual personnel woes of a theater signal officer—never enough officers and men, especially never enough

that were competent or well trained. Similarly, Capt. Robert C. Danser, commanding the 806th Signal Service Company on Guadalcanal early in 1943, complained, " . . . our greatest problem at all times was a deficiency of personnel." In line maintenance and in building a pole line between Henderson and Carney Fields, Danser had had to employ heterogeneous crews, including untrained men borrowed from such sources as the Marine Corps, Coast Artillery, Field Artillery, and naval construction battalions.[39] In March 1943, Colonel Ankenbrandt regretted that his headquarters had to organize four signal service companies on a provisional basis and added, "like most units organized in that manner their quality is low, the personnel consisting generally of castoffs from other units. It is not a good way of building up Signal Service in a combat zone but there appears to be no other alternative, what with shortages of personnel back home, and shortages of shipping facilities to get new units down here." But it worked out well. A year later, in April 1944, Ankenbrandt was willing to concede that the units probably had accomplished "considerably more good to the South Pacific Signal Service than had we waited to get a like number of Service Companies activated, trained, and shipped from the States in those days."[40]

Although Ankenbrandt obtained au-

---

[37] Ltr, Ankenbrandt to Meade, 31 Jan 44, p. 8. SigC OT 319.1 (111.1), Ankenbrandt Rpts.

[38] Ltr, Ankenbrandt to Meade, 5 Mar 44, pp. 1–2. SigC OT 319.1 (111.1), Ankenbrandt Rpts.

[39] Interv, SigC Hist Sec, with Capt Robert C. Danser, 7 Oct 44. SigC Hist Sec file.

[40] Ltrs, Ankenbrandt to Meade, 3 Mar 43, p. 3, and 10 Apr 44, p. 1. SigC OT 370.1 (111 and 111.1), Ankenbrandt Rpts.

Seven signal service companies had been activated in SOPAC, according to Ankenbrandt. Only the 842d and 974th Signal Service Companies had come from the United States.

thority to organize these units locally, the War Department did not so readily grant his petitions for officer promotions. His officer allotments at one time compared so poorly with other services that he reviewed the allotments for the Office of the Chief Signal Officer—even fewer Signal Corps officers in SOPAC than Chemical Warfare Service officers. He sought promotions of some of his deserving lieutenant colonels, but was rebuffed. Writing in September 1943, he noted "with regret . . . the unfavorable action in the matter of authorizing three additional full Colonels, Signal Corps, for this theater," and added, "Only *two* Colonels out of 385 total authorized Signal Corps commissioned personnel in this theater doesn't look right to me." "What do you think?" he asked General Meade.[41] Signal Corps troops in the South Pacific Area totaled very nearly 7,000 in July 1943, distributed among a dozen islands. The number increased to almost 10,500 on 15 islands by February 1944.

The USAFISPA signal officer tried to obtain WAC units to perform message center and cryptographic duties in the larger well-established bases on New Caledonia and Fiji. But the War Department denied the request.[42]

Colonel Ankenbrandt strove to get electronic specialists for AACS installation work. The civilians whom OCSigO first sent out proved ill suited

for service under SOPAC conditions (factory representatives provided by the manufacturer were better) .[43] Adequate and competent cryptographers were hard to come by, as was the case in all overseas theaters. Ankenbrandt did obtain, after considerable effort, a number of American Indians whom the Navy wished to employ as code talkers in combat circuits, since their native tongue would be completely unintelligible to the enemy. But no sooner did he receive a group of 24 than he learned that the Navy was no longer interested. "We will keep the 24 we now have," he reported in March 1944. "Actually only five of the original 24 proved usable," he later added. "But they have been used steadily for several months, using voice codes which change frequently in order to aid in security."[44] Toward the end of the SOPAC campaign, as the Navy and Marine Corps

[41] (1) Ltr, Ankenbrandt to Lanahan, 19 May 43, p. 1. (2) Ltr, Ankenbrandt to Meade, 30 Sep 43, p. 1. Both in SigC OT 319.1 (111), Ankenbrandt Rpts.

[42] (1) Ltrs, Ankenbrandt to Lanahan, 1 May 43, p. 6, and 19 May 43, p. 1. (2) Ltr, Ankenbrandt to Meade, 30 Sep 43, p. 5. SigC OT 319.1 (111), Ankenbrandt Rpts. (3) Treadwell, *The Women's Army Corps*, p. 478.

[43] (1) Ltrs, Ankenbrandt to Lanahan, 2 Feb 43, p. 5, and 1 May 43, p. 3. SigC OT 319.1 (111), Ankenbrandt Rpts. (2) Ltr, Ankenbrandt to Meade, 31 Mar 44, pp. 6–7. SigC OT 319.1 (111.1), Ankenbrandt Rpts.

[44] Ltrs, Ankenbrandt to Meade, 31 Oct 43, pp. 6–7; 31 Jan 44, p. 7; 31 Mar 44, p. 5. SigC OT 319.1 (111.1), Ankenbrandt Rpts.
The Indians were needed "for telephone communications between COMAIRSOLS [Commander Air Solomons], COMAIR [Commander Aircraft], New Georgia, Russells, Segi, Munda, and certain other airfields," according to Lt. Col. John E. Watters, Report, New Projects. SigC OP 319.1 Daily Rpts, Jun 43–Oct 45.
According to Colonel Newhouse, they were Navajos who became "very useful members of the SOPAC team." Newhouse, "SOPAC Signals," *Signals*, II, No. 5, p. 39.
The Marine Corps employed "Navajo talkers," according to Samuel E. Morison, "History of United States Naval Operations in World War II," VIII, *New Guinea and The Marianas* (Boston: Little, Brown and Company, 1953), 376. See also "The Marines' Navajo Code Talkers," *Signals*, III, No. 1 (September–October, 1948), 22f.

withdrew from countermeasures work in the area, Colonel Ankenbrandt received both a radio intelligence company, the 112th, and an EEIS unit that sought, each in its own way, to ferret out the enemy's secrets.[45]

A unit that proved especially valuable to Colonel Ankenbrandt, one he successfully fought to retain against repeated efforts by the War Department to reassign it, was the 842d Signal Service Company. The company, composed of ten complete radio station teams, had been sent to the South Pacific in February 1943 to man the scattered island radio locations. An outstanding instance of the work of a team of this company occurred during the landing on Rendova in mid-1943. Communications were spotty. A Navy advance base radio station "had all sorts of trouble." A Marine Raider regiment on one flank was out of communications for five days. "Believe it or not," Colonel Ankenbrandt exclaimed, "the Army Administrative Station WVJU [Munda, in New Georgia] consisting of an SCR–299 and operators from a team of the 842d Signal Service Company provided the most reliable circuit." The team made the contact to USAFISPA headquarters and maintained the communications link from the first day of the landing, 30 June. "So far as I know," Ankenbrandt wrote

a month later, "they are still using the 299." He had meanwhile sent the team a 300-watt BC–447 fixed radio transmitter to replace the mobile truck-mounted SCR–299.[46]

Since not all the teams of the 842d Signal Service Company were continuously out on jobs, the remainder at New Caledonia headquarters built up a school. Erecting a building and gathering equipment, they created a radio school capable of handling sixty students at a time. The school supplied a steady flow of operators and technicians to support the South Pacific radio circuits. While providing task force teams to operate radio communications during the early occupation of newly captured islands, the members of the company who were temporarily assigned to USAFISPA headquarters trained inexperienced filler troops to become full-fledged radiomen. They even developed completely untrained men into competent Morse code operators and into radiomen able to install, tune, and operate such large long-range sets as the fixed BC–447 and the mobile SCR–299.[47]

Combat and Equipment

Signal Corps field radio and wire equipment in the South Pacific Area first went into combat under extreme tropical conditions on Guadalcanal. The

[45] (1) Kunhart, SigC Activities in the SOPAC Theater, p. 19. (2) Ltr, Ankenbrandt to Meade, 30 Apr 44, p. 11. SigC OT 319.1 (111.1), Ankenbrandt Rpts.

SOPAC had asked for an RCM company in mid-1943, a request first granted in Washington and then withheld. However, a team of forty-three RCM specialists was promised in January 1944. Watters, Rpt, New Projects.

The EEIS unit was team No. 3. EEIS 3 SOPAC–SWPA, Oct 43–Dec 44. SigC Hist Sec file.

[46] (1) Ltr, Ankenbrandt to Lanahan, 31 Jul 43, pp. 1–2. SigC OT 319.1 (111), Ankenbrandt Rpts. (2) History of the 842d Signal Service Company. SGCO 842–P 0.1 (44872).

[47] (1) Kunhart, SigC Activities in the SOPAC Theater, pp. 21–22. (2) Ltrs, Ankenbrandt to Meade, 19 Sep 43, p. 1, and 30 Sep 43, p. 2. SigC OT 319.1 (111), Ankenbrandt Rpts. (3) Ltr, Ankenbrandt to Meade, 19 Oct 43. SigC OT 319.1 (111.1), Ankenbrandt Rpts.

items originally used there, not having been waterproofed or protected by fungicides, suffered severely from dank heat and fungus growths. Metals corroded; insulating materials rotted or sprouted mold. Batteries were especially susceptible (the sound-powered telephone, which needed no batteries, at once proved its value). The heavy damp vegetation smothered radiations, reducing the weak output of small radios such as the old walkie-talkies SCR–194 and 195 to near uselessness in the jungle, which of course predominated in most areas. On open ground, however, these sets provided some service.[48]

Meanwhile, the USAFISPA signal officer had just received information of the forthcoming improved walkie-talkie, the SCR–300. The guidon set SCR–511 had so far seemed about as good a portable radio as the command could get. Speaking of the SCR–511, Colonel Ankenbrandt said in July 1943, "We received a report through Navy channels that this type set is no longer in production and is being replaced by the SCR–300." He added: "If such is the case, I would like to render a protest right now, because VHF sets (such as the SCR–300) do not work well in dense jungle operations and a set of the portability, frequency range, and power of the 511 is definitely required for this type operation."[49] Ankenbrandt would soon change his mind, however, as the new 300 type walkie-talkie arrived and proved out well, along with the 500 and 600 series of FM sets. For example, in the very next month, according to a 43d Division radio report from New Georgia, the men hardly ever used the 536's or 511's because of constant failure during heavy rains and high humidity. Nor did they use the 284 much because of its weight and lack of ruggedness. But they highly praised the SCR–193, 245, 299, and the new sets of the 600 series. SCR–193, old Army set that it was, proved a welcome replacement for a naval TBX radio with which Marine forces in the New Georgia–Rendova area in July 1943 had been unable to establish a good direct circuit with their base.[50]

Fighting in New Georgia during the summer of 1943 severely tested radio equipment. Around the Munda airfield, men fought and, as they did so, prayerfully worked their communication links with each other. Those links were vital, as one Private Billik appreciated. He was a radioman attached to the Marine Raiders using, instead of an Army set, a small Navy 9-watt transmitter, a TBX. "There we were, food and medical supplies running low, and our only means of communications was this TBX. . . . I'll never forget the way our Colonel paced back and forth," he recalled. "'Did you get 'em yet?' he kept on asking. I never realized the importance of radio communication until I got into this tight spot where the lives of men

[48] (1) Ltr, Ankenbrandt to CSigO, 15 Jan 43, sub: Tactical Ground Radio Sets. (2) Ltr, Ankenbrandt to Lanahan, 2 Feb 43, p. 4. SigC OT 319.1 (111), Ankenbrandt Rpts. (3) Sig Com in Jungle Warfare, SigC Tech Info Ltr 23 (Oct 43), p. 10. (4) Interv, SigC Hist Sec with Maj Edgar H. Felix, 16 Oct 44. (5) Miller, *Guadalcanal: The First Offensive*, p. 317.

[49] Ltr, Ankenbrandt to Lanahan, 31 Jul 43, p. 3. SigC OT 319.1 (111), Ankenbrandt Rpts.

[50] (1) Ltr, Ankenbrandt to Meade, 31 Aug 43, p. 4. SigC OT 319.1 (111), Ankenbrandt Rpts. (2) Miller, *Cartwheel: The Reduction of Rabaul*, pp. 127, 143.

. . . depended on me and my comrade." Billik babied the set and scrupulously kept a water-soaked record of his transmissions, receipts, and acknowledgements.

It was important that he did most carefully tend to his transmission procedure and security. In the same campaign, a Sergeant Rorick, operating a radio station on Rendova communicating with other division signal company stations, was waiting for the 43d Signal Company to report into the net. Suddenly a communication came through from the 43d, so it purported, with three priority messages. Rorick copied the enciphered texts and gave them to the code room, but the cryptographers could not get the text to "break," that is, to yield intelligible English text. Rechecking, they still could not break the enciphered gibberish. Meanwhile, Sergeant Rorick belatedly asked the station to identify itself. The reply yielded numbers that would not check with Rorick's authenticator chart. Obviously it was a Japanese station sending bogus messages. By posing as friendly and sending messages claimed to be urgent, the enemy operator was successfully delaying American traffic.[51] And obviously he also listened in on American traffic, ready to glean information that bad security or carelessness by the operators might yield.

Severe fighting on Bougainville followed the New Georgia campaign. The success of the XIV Corps mission, involving three airfields and their perimeter defense, rested heavily on a reliable communications system, the responsibility of the corps signal officer, Col. Raymond Strasburger.[52] Extensive wire nets were needed, one for the operation of the airfields, a second to serve the information center, a third to serve the antiaircraft artillery, a fourth for the general communications needs of the island, and a fifth for keying lines that ran to remotely located radio transmitters, putting them on the air. Alternate routes had to be provided for all the nets, so that traffic could be rerouted in case breaks occurred.

And occur they did. During the first hour of an enemy shelling on one occasion eight hundred circuits were blown out. Linemen had to work under fire on many occasions. For example, M/Sgt Edward J. Rounds of the 271st Signal Construction Company described the night of 18 March 1944, when he led a party of fifteen men to mend breaks in the lines between the Piva River bomber and fighter airstrips. The men had to endure heavy shelling while repairing wire breaks that day. At night matters were worse. Working in darkness, they found the wires badly broken up by the shelling. As they lay prone along the

[51] Ltr, CG Hq USAFISPA to CSigO, 23 Apr 44, sub: Experience of Radio Operators. SigC 319.1 (MT-249) Rpts, Combat Stories of Radio Operators. Private Billick was a member of the 842d Signal Service Company, according to Kunhart, SigC Activities in the SOPAC Theater, p. 36. For a detailed report of wire and radio installations in the New Georgia fighting, see Maj. Gen. Oscar W. Griswold, Signal Report, New Georgia Occupational Force, XIV Corps, 18 November 1943. SOPAC folder, SigC Hist Sec file.

[52] For reports of signals on Bougainville, see: (1) Ltr, Strasburger to CSigO, 9 Jan 44, sub: Sig Rpt. XIV Corps Sig Rpt, SigC Hist Sec file. (2) Incl, Hq XIV Corps, Bougainville Campaign Sig Rpt, 30 May 44, with Ltr, CG Hq XIV Corps to TAG, Attn: CSigO, 13 Jul 44, sub: Transmittal of Sig Rpts. SCIA File 125, Litz Rpts 2. (3) Signals on Bougainville, SigC Tech Info Ltr 32 (Jul 44), pp. 23f. SigC Hist Sec file.

lines under the slight protection of low scrub, they tended to keep their eyes on the shell fire. "I realize we weren't getting anywhere," Sergeant Rounds recalled. He therefore determined to do the watching for them while they worked. He stood up, saying "Well, fellows, I'll try and tell you when they are going and coming." Then he realized that he could not distinguish just which shells were approaching their position. "The men must have read my thoughts," he recalled, "because one of them looked up and inquired in a shaky voice, 'Are you sure, Sarge, that they aren't ricocheting?' After this I laughed and so did the other men." Their tension somewhat relieved, they finished their job and retired to safety just as the enemy detected the crew and began directing aimed fire at them.[53]

Close communications between infantrymen and tank crews were needed to co-ordinate attacks in the jungles. Sometimes an EE-8 telephone set was mounted externally at the rear of the tank, sometimes the hand-carried SCR-536 was used. Soldiers carrying 536's were special targets of enemy riflemen. According to Colonel Newhouse, two members of the 217th Signal Depot Company, 1st Lt. Gordon W. Cheeseman and T/3 James T. Hamilton, tried to make the SCR-536 less conspicuous. They worked out an arrangement by which a soldier's helmet could serve as the radio antenna, while a field telephone handset could be used as microphone and speaker, and the set itself, ordinarily carried conspicuously in the

hand, could be slipped out of sight in a field bag.[54]

By the end of 1943 the new SCR-300 had come to the combat troops in quantity. The men were pleased. "The SCR-300 sets," Colonel Ankenbrandt informed General Meade in January 1944, "have now been in action in the Torokina area, Bougainville, in the hands of the 37th and Americal Divisions and I have a preliminary report on them indicating that they are exactly what is needed for front line communications in this theater." The chief difficulty, from his point of view, was keeping them supplied with fresh batteries.[55]

From the point of view of the man who walked with this new walkie-talkie, one difficulty was the harness, which placed the load too low on the back, thus tiring the walker. Also, the belt carrier brackets had "a tendency to keep jabbing the man in the kidneys," reported 2d Lt. Joseph S. Dooley, communications officer of the 298th Infantry. Otherwise, the set proved excellent, transmitting for miles through jungle that muted other front-line sets such as SCR-195 and 536. Lieutenant Dooley called the radio "practically foolproof." On one 5-day patrol, "the dials did not have to be touched once," so stable was the frequency calibration. "My radio operators and I," Dooley concluded, "consider the

[53] Kunhart, SigC Activities in the SOPAC Theater, pp. 27f.

[54] Newhouse, "SOPAC Signals," *Signals*, II, No. 5, p. 38. Both Cheeseman and Hamilton received the Legion of Merit, awarded for outstanding service from 1 February 1944 to 9 March 1944. (1) Ltr, Maj R. N. Bond, CO 217th Sig Depot Co, to TAG, 1 Jan 45, sub: Hist of Orgn., SGCO 217-0.1 (28301) Hist 217th Sig Depot Co, 1944. (2) Kunhart, SigC Activities in the SOPAC Theater, p. 43.
[55] Ltr, Ankenbrandt to Meade, 31 Jan 44, p. 3. SigC OT 319.1 (111.1), Ankenbrandt Rpts.

SCR–300 an Infantry man's dream for better communication and control of troops by radio than ever before given us."[56]

Tropicalization became a meaningful term in the South Pacific. Having received a shipment of Signal Corps' newly tropicalized SCR–536's and 284's late in 1943, Colonel Ankenbrandt reported the sets were very much improved. SCR–536's, which before the treatment lasted only thirty-six hours in the jungle, were now holding up for a month or more.[57] By 1944 all Signal Corps radios were treated to resist tropical difficulties. Meanwhile kits were sent to the jungle theaters to treat the sets already on hand. The Office of the Chief Signal Officer sent men to help in the work. According to Colonel Newhouse, Capt. Robert G. Duffield and WO Stanley J. Garstka worked on the problem too, spraying sets with fungus-inhibiting shellac and baking it on. By December 1943 the Guadalcanal depot made it a practice to so treat all radios passing through its hands, stamping them with a TT (tropically treated) and the date. The treatment remained effective for about six months.[58]

Wire, having layers of insulation, endured the tropics better than untreated radios. Even the relatively lightly protected field wire W–110–B served well. Striking proof of this came from an incident on Tongatabu. To bypass a roundabout route of four miles, the men laid six hundred yards of the wire under the waters of a lagoon, an action that totally disregarded elemental wire laying instructions that the wire be kept high and dry. The line worked well for six months. New Zealand forces, when they happened to take up the wire a year later, were so amazed at its durability that they felt impelled to report the matter to General Ingles. They found the wire still serviceable for telephone operation. Although the outside insulation had rotted, the next coating of rubber remained intact and the inside wire (four steel and three copper strands) retained the appearance of new wire.[59]

Field cable—spiral-four with its heavier insulation and high communication capacity—was especially welcome in the tropics. In areas where poles quickly rotted or disappeared into the maws of termites, where insulators were hard to come by, where jungle paths were hard to clear for pole lines anyway, where jungle trees served as poles, and where basket-weave hitches often replaced insulator supports, spiral-four was a godsend. It could dispense with poles and insulators. It could be laid on the ground and through water, fresh or salt. After the snap joints had been heavily taped against seepage, spiral-four was often laid as undersea cable in areas where the jungle was so impenetrable it was easier for Signal Corps men to skirt the shore

[56] Incl, Ltr, Dooley to SigO, V Island Comd, AP 709, 13 Jul 44, sub: Rpt on SCR–300, with Ltr, Newhouse, Actg SigO USAFISPA, to Meade, OCSigO, 31 Jul 44. SigC 307 OD–218, 1944.

[57] Ltr, Ankenbrandt to Meade, 31 Jan 44, p. 4.

[58] Newhouse, "SOPAC Signals," Signals, II, No. 5, p. 37.

[59] (1) Kunhart, SigC Activities in the SOPAC Theater, pp. 24–25. (2) Incl, Hq 16 Brig Gp (New Zealand Forces) Tongatabu, 17 Aug 43, with Ltr, OCSigO Hq USAFISPA to CSigO, Washington, 1 Sep 43, sub: Wire W–110–B. SigC OT 319.1 (111), Ankenbrandt Rpts.

Manuals of later date did contain instructions for laying field wire under water. MS Comment, U.S. Army Sig Sup Agency, Jul 59.

and lay their spiral-four from a boat.[60]

What was needed above all else in these island operations to transmit high-capacity radio circuits over water or over jungle terrain so hostile to wire lines would have been that combination, so recently accomplished, of mobile radio and high-capacity wire techniques, producing radio relay. Radio relay equipment did come to the Pacific, but a little later than its appearance in North Africa, a little too late to help much in SOPAC. There had been a need for better high-capacity communications overwater between Henderson Field, Guadalcanal, and Tulagi, to co-ordinate defensive measures quickly in the early days when the enemy's attacks were too often devastating. "We asked for cable but that was not available," Colonel Ankenbrandt summarized the matter for the Office of the Chief Signal Officer in September 1943. "You then offered us radio teletype instead, which we gladly accepted." What OCSigO offered was the new radio relay. Before it arrived, the Guadalcanal-Tulagi area no longer needed it. The fighting had moved on to New Georgia. In October Colonel Ankenbrandt reported that the captain charged with the installation of the new equipment was in New Georgia, where he had set up two circuits, one from Munda to Segi Point, the other from Munda to the Barakoma airfield on Vella Lavella island.[61]

Colonel Ankenbrandt saw the AN/TRC-6 while on a visit to Washington late in 1943 and wanted it, calling it "the finest communications equipment I have ever seen." He added, "it is admirably adapted to jungle and island warfare." [62] AN/TRC-6 arrived in the ETO in time to serve well at the end of the war in 1945, but it got no further into the Pacific than Hawaii before the war ended. AN/TRC-1, 3, and 4 did get to the southwestern and western Pacific areas in time to be very valuable, especially in ship-to-shore operations at Hollandia, in the Philippines, and at Okinawa.

The South Pacific Area closed out 1 August 1944, except as a rear area supply base. Its name changed to the South Pacific Base Command, with the mission of holding the area to 158° west, of supplying Southwest Pacific Area operations and units in Bougainville, New Georgia, and other islands of the vicinity, and of rehabilitating combat units sent to the

---

[60] (1) Ltr, Memo, Hq USAFISPA OCSigO, 27 Aug 43, sub: Spiral-Four Cable as Under Water Cable, with photos. SigC OT 319.1 (111), Ankenbrandt Rpts. (2) Griswold, Sig Rpt, New Georgia Occupational Force, pp. 3ff. (3) Underwater Telephone Lines, SigC Tech Info Ltr 29 (Apr 44), pp. 29f. SigC Hist file. (4) CSigO, Annual Rpt, FY 44, p. 12.

The basket-weave wire hitch was developed in SOPAC. Wrapping wire around trees did not work since chafing in the wind wore through the insulation. The basket-weave hitch, using rope, plant fiber, or lengths of field wire, permitted the wire or cable to run straight and free, supported from tree trunks without chafing. (1) Kunhart, SigC Activities in the SOPAC Theater, p. 11. (2) Press Meets CSigO, SigC Tech Info Ltr 29 (Apr 44), p. 6. (3) Newhouse, "SOPAC Signals," *Signals*, II, No. 5, p. 37. (4) CSigO, Annual Rpt, FY 45, p. 196.

[61] (1) Ltr, Ankenbrandt to Meade, 30 Sep 43, p. 3. SigC OT 319.1 (111), Ankenbrandt Rpts. (2) Ltr, Ankenbrandt to Meade, 31 Oct 43, p. 2. SigC OT 319.1 (111.1), Ankenbrandt Rpts. (3) CSigO, Annual Rpt, FY 44, p. 96. (4) Memo, Stoner, ACS Div, for Progress and Stat Br, 11 Feb 43, sub: Digest of Progress and Problems, p. 3. SigC file, Digest of Progress, 14 Jan 43–10 Feb 43.

[62] Incl 1, Ltr, Ankenbrandt to Meade, 4 Apr 44, with Ltr, Meade to Ankenbrandt, 24 Apr 44. SigC OT 319.1 (111.1), Ankenbrandt Rpts.

Contrary to Colonel Ankenbrandt's view, the AN/TRC-6 was too complicated to have worked well in the jungle or in the moist tropics, according to Amory Waite. SigC R&D Draft MS Comment. SigC Hist Sec file.

South Pacific for rest. Colonel Newhouse remained as the signal officer of the South Pacific Base Command. Colonel Ankenbrandt transferred to Headquarters, Army Air Forces, Pacific Areas (AAFPOA), as the signal officer (director of communications). Many former SOPAC signal units and elements, such as the 230th Signal Operations Company, the 112th Radio Intelligence Company, Radio Team Detachment A, the EEIS team, and the radio relay experts, Capt. Forrest E. Crain and a Lieutenant Tracey, whom the Office of the Chief Signal Officer had dispatched with the new antrac sets, moved to the Southwest Pacific Area. The 701st, 702d, 578th, and 579th Aircraft Warning Battalions returned to the states.[63]

The Central Pacific Area

Flanking the South Pacific Area, north of its northern border (the equator) lay the Central Pacific Area. As in late 1943 the conflict with the Japanese made progress in the South and Southwest Pacific Areas, advancing up the island ladder that would lead to the Philippines, a second line of attack through the Central Pacific got under way. Here, around the turn of 1943–44, forces moving directly toward Japan, through the isles north of the equator, assaulted such small atolls and reefs as the enemy had occupied in the Gilbert and Marshall Islands. In mid-1944 the larger islands of the Mariana chain came under attack. These last objectives were sufficiently near the Japanese homeland to become suitable bomber bases. The new very-long-range

B–29 bombers of the AAF, under the direct command of General Arnold from his Washington headquarters, could better operate from the Marianas than from airfields in China.[64]

The Central Pacific Area came under the direct command, from his Hawaiian headquarters, of Admiral Nimitz, overall commander of the Pacific Ocean Areas. Admiral Nimitz' commander of Army troops in the Central Pacific was Lt. Gen. Robert C. Richardson, Jr., whose chief duty was to provide logistical support. Colonel Powell served as Richardson's signal officer. Colonel Powell, appointed late in 1941 as signal officer of the Hawaiian Department, remained in that feverish post throughout the war, as it became Headquarters, U.S. Army Forces Central Pacific Area, in mid-1943, and in June 1944, Headquarters, U.S. Army Forces Pacific Ocean Areas.[65]

---

[64] (1) Philip A. Crowl and Edmund G. Love, *Seizure of the Gilberts and Marshalls,* UNITED STATES ARMY IN WORLD WAR II (Washington, 1955), pp. 2–17. (2) Philip A. Crowl, *Campaign in the Marianas,* UNITED STATES ARMY IN WORLD WAR II (Washington, 1960), pp. 11f. (3) Matloff, *Strategic Planning for Coalition Warfare 1943–44,* pp. 33, 185ff., 328ff.
[65] (1) Miller, *Cartwheel: The Reduction of Rabaul,* p. 4. (2) Matloff, *Strategic Planning for Coalition Warfare, 1943–44,* pp. 89, 460.
Colonel Powell was promoted to brigadier general in November 1944. His signal office numbered about 90 in December 1941. It grew to 209 as of mid-1944. During the war its organization altered little, having about ten sections: administrative, personnel, radio, wire, signal center, supply, photographic, and so on. Only two new sections were added: plans and training in June 1942, and radio intelligence in August 1942. One section, aircraft warning, was eliminated in April 1942 when command of the signal aircraft warning function transferred to the AAF, the Signal Corps retaining only some radar installation and maintenance duties. Hist, SigC Sec, HUSAFMIDPAC, pp. iii, 2–7.

---

[63] Third Qtrly Rpt, 1 Jul–30 Sep 44, SOPAC. SigC OT 370.2 OD–111 Rpts SOPAC.

Signal Support of Amphibious
Assault Units

For the most part, the Central Pacific Area belonged to the Navy and the Marine Corps. Their troops greatly outnumbered those of the Army in operations in the area. The Army signal support operations, on the other hand, were much larger than the small size of the Army contingents might indicate, since both the Navy and the Marine Corps quickly appreciated that Army radios (especially the 500 and 600 series of FM sets) were superior for the needs of amphibious assault work. They demanded them in quantity. Colonel Powell and his signal office became the vortex of very heavy requirements for instructors and specialists and for the equipment to be used both in landing craft and in newly developed naval command ships.

Amphibious operations required special communications or command ships. Military authorities had learned from early assaults in Europe, at Dieppe and in the North African invasions, that warships were not suitable to direct and control the communications needed in the early stages of an amphibious attack. The shock of gunfire was apt to damage radio equipment.[66]

The Navy obtained in time for the Marshall Islands assaults specially equipped headquarters ships crammed with radio (much of it of Signal Corps types) and relieved of gunfire duties. Such ships, general communications vessels (1943) or amphibious force flagships (1945), AGC's in naval nomenclature, came into the Central Pacific by early 1944—two of them at first, the *Appalachian* and the *Rocky Mount,* and in later operations, the *Eldorado,* the *Estes,* and finally, from European waters in mid-1945, the *Ancon.*[67]

The application of Army radio equipment in Navy and Marine Corps amphibious operations resulted from troubles with small Navy sets in the Guadalcanal and Tarawa actions, no less than with the larger shipboard radios. The naval historian, Samuel Eliot Morison, took note of early amphibious communications failures, describing the battleship *Maryland's* radio, in the Tarawa action, as "primitive at best." He attributed these failures largely to imperfection in the equipment, complaining especially of the ra-

---

Morison, "History of the United States Naval Operations in World War II," VII, *Aleutians, Gilberts and Marshalls* (Boston: Little, Brown and Company, 1951), 153, 156, 207.

[67] Lt. Gen. Holland M. Smith, USMC, who understood radio communications problems, appreciated the "excellent communication facilities" of both the *Rocky Mount* in earlier campaigns, and the *Eldorado* at Okinawa. He mentioned that Secretary of the Navy James V. Forrestal was fascinated by the radio, teletype, and related equipment aboard the *Eldorado* (at Iwo Jima), adding his own comment that it was "indeed wondrous to behold." Holland M. Smith, *Coral and Brass* (New York: Charles Scribner's Sons, 1949), pp. 70, 143, 249, 252.

---

[66] The cruiser *Augusta* and the battleship *Maryland* had been employed as amphibious head quarters command ships with unfortunate results, the former off Casablanca, the latter at Tarawa. (1) Thompson, Harris, *et al., The Test,* p. 359. (2) Crowl and Love, *Seizure of the Gilberts and Marshalls,* pp. 145f., 161f., 172. (3) Jeter A. Isely and Philip A. Crowl, *The U.S. Marines and Amphibious War, Its Theory and Its Practice in the Pacific* (Princeton, N.J.: Princeton University Press, 1949), pp. 224f., 228, 252, 584. (4) Samuel Eliot

dios carried ashore in landing craft.[68]

Faced with a mounting flood of Navy and Marine demands, Colonel Powell's Supply Division in Hawaii had to revise sharply upward its needs for procurement, installation, and maintenance of Army radios. The amphibious forces of the Pacific areas continually discovered new uses for Army-type equipment in ship-to-air, air-to-ground, and ship-to-shore applications (for the last function, Signal Corps' radioteletypewriter and radio relay AN/TRC-1 came into heavy demand). In Hawaii, Colonel Powell's Signal Depot rushed installation of FM radios, of the 600 series in particular, on every sort of naval vessel—from small boats and landing barges to the battleship *Pennsylvania*.[69]

Not only were Colonel Powell and his staff called upon to equip every Marine and Army division (plus many naval elements) that went out from Hawaii, they also had to provide continuing signal support and replacement, usually in a hurry, throughout the Central Pacific Area. The list of signal

items used by the 1st Marine Division when it invaded the Palaus in September 1944 reads like any contemporary Army division signal table of equipment. There were SCR–300, 508, 528, 536, 608, 610, 694, and so on.

When the 1st Marine Division, staging in the Russell Islands for the assault, found that only 13 of 87 sets of SCR–610 on hand were serviceable, it hurriedly requisitioned additional radios from Pearl Harbor. Colonel Powell delivered them, 36 sets of SCR–694's, by air one day before the troops embarked for Peleliu and Angaur. The last-minute delivery was fortunate. Equipment losses were heavy in these assaults. The 4th Joint Amphibious Assault Company reported that over 50 portable radios were lost and that the last-minute delivery of the additional sets "proved invaluable in replacing the losses." [70]

The officers of Colonel Powell's Plans and Training Section in Hawaii conferred and co-operated closely with the signal officers of Army divisions and with the communications officers of many participating commands of the Navy, Marine Corps, and AAF before each campaign in the Central Pacific and in some other Pacific areas as well—the Gilberts in November 1943, the Marshalls in February 1944, the Marianas in June 1944, the Palaus in September

---

[68] Morison makes the comment that the Navy, following the North African invasion late in 1942, had complained of its radios as being inadequate for amphibious employment. But the Bureau of Ships, responsible for electronic development and supply, had not responded to these needs. Morison notes, however, that by 1944 the Fifth Fleet in the Pacific had made some communications improvements, replacing old ARC–5 sets with new superior VHF radios. These were Army-type voice radios employed to link airplane pilots, shore parties, and shipboard commanders. Morison, *New Guinea and the Marianas*, pp. 261f., and *Aleutians, Gilberts and Marshalls*, p. 183n. and 153. (4) Brig. Gen. P. C. Sandretto, "Radio VII, Sup, pp. 10–12). Besides supplying signal equipment to naval ships and four Marine divisions, the signal depot also equipped the 7th, 24th, 27th, 33d, 40th, and 77th Infantry Divisions and special units of artillery, armored, and garrison forces.

[70] (1) Incl, 1st Marine Div, Action Rpt, an. E, Com, 1 Dec 44, with ASF Transmittal Sheet, Action 1, Maj John S. Walter, Intel Br OCSigO, to Chief Logistics Plng Br, 9 Feb 45, sub: Distr of 1st Marine Action Rpt on Palau Opn. SigC OP 370.2 Gen Rpt, folder 1, 3 Jan–25 Apr 45, Tab 6. (2) Palau Com, SigC Tech Info Ltr 41 (Apr 45), pp. 13f. (3) Robert Ross Smith, *The Approach to the Philippines*, UNITED STATES ARMY IN WORLD WAR II (Washington, 1953), p. 497.

1944, Iwo Jima in February 1945, and Okinawa in April 1945. Readying for the first of these, the Gilberts, set a pattern for the rest. Frequent conferences with all the assaulting elements, and with representatives of the garrison forces who would take over the islands after the troops had secured them, preceded the determination of the signal units and equipment that would be provided and of the signal instructions and procedures that would be employed.

The planners quickly realized at the outset of the Gilberts campaign that the equipment needs of the assaulting elements of the 27th Infantry Division, supported by special joint communications parties of the 75th Signal Company (soon to become the provisional 75th JASCO), far exceeded the normal signal items and quantities of an Army division. Colonel Powell had to borrow communications items from other tactical units in the Central Pacific. He issued the following major items over and above the normal infantry division table of basic allowances and table of equipment:

1	SCR–188	Ship-to-shore communication
3	SCR–509	Control communication in LVT's
14	SCR–510	Control communication in LVT's
10	TG–97	Teletypewriter sets installed in headquarters ships
18	SCR–511	Supplementing normal infantry divisions T/BA
45	SCR–536	Supplementing normal infantry divisions T/BA
2	SCR–610	For division artillery fire control, supplementing normal T/BA
1	SCR–233	For air-ground liaison in 27th Division

Heavy training demands also arose. Navy and Marine communicators had to be instructed in the use of Army signal items. Beyond the technicalities in their use, there was the urgent need that all the several amphibious communications elements (Army, Navy, Marine—ground and air) receive combined training in amphibious exercises and simulated assaults. Colonel Powell provided Signal Corps instructors, for example, to work in joint staging exercises at the Marine staging area at Barber's Point in Hawaii.

Extensive joint training was never so thorough as might be desired. It was physically impossible to bring together all the military units to train as one big team because no base was large enough and because the conditions of the actual operation to come could not be reproduced.[71]

In the Gilbert Islands operations, among the first to land on Butaritari, Makin Atoll, in November 1943 were elements of the 27th Signal Company and of the 75th Signal Company (Special), supporting battalion landing teams. The radio contacts that they established between shore and higher headquarters still afloat were briefly interrupted, dampened by rain squalls plus some dousing received in the landing. These troubles were but intermittent and temporary. Amphibian tractors broke wire lines laid along the beach until the men resorted to stringing the wires in trees later that day. During the first day, communications for troops separated on two beaches, Red and Yellow, had to depend solely upon messenger service. The lack of direct

[71] (1) Hist, Sig Sec HUSAFMIDPAC, pp. 71ff. (sec. II, pp. 9ff.). (2) Morison, *Aleutians, Gilberts and Marshalls*, pp. 87f.

WIRES STRUNG ON A COCONUT PALM

radio contact between them that day seriously impeded the co-ordination and timing of the troop movements. By the morning of the second day all the required communications—wire, radio, and messenger—were functioning properly.

In communications procedures, however, there were some faults. Not all communicators, for example, were agreed upon a uniform time system. Both in the date-time groups of the messages and in the times employed in message content, there were variations —some message centers using local time; others, Greenwich civil time. Confusion inevitably developed from this failure

to co-ordinate and indoctrinate—a failure that was a direct consequence of hurried preparations and lack of sufficient joint training.

There were bright spots in the communications picture, nevertheless. The radios of the fire control parties served well for ship-to-shore circuits, and the air liaison parties were able to maintain good contact with the various headquarters. The radios of the field artillery batteries served dependably whenever wire lines were ripped out by tanks and other vehicles. The division commander found that whenever he could not obtain information from his landing teams through infantry channels he could generally get it through artillery circuits.[72]

Difficulty in communications between ground troops and support aircraft, calling for air strikes on specific ground targets, had been a problem early in South Pacific fighting. Although General Harmon and the Thirteenth Air Force had especially tried to give close air support in combat on New Georgia Island early in 1943, success had come seldom. Worse yet, the planes sometimes had bombed our own troops instead of the nearby enemy.[73] In subsequent amphibious actions in the Central Pacific, radio direction of aircraft closely supporting ground troops was improved in part because of better radio equipment. Close air support by the Navy carrier pilots proved the best to date in the Marshall Islands fighting.[74]

The control over air-ground liaison continued, however, to present problems that hampered air support effectiveness. Only exceptionally did air liaison parties attached to the infantry use their sets to call upon aircraft pilots (orbiting overhead) to strafe and bomb specific ground targets that confronted the troops. Notable exceptions occurred both in the Pacific, as on Luzon where Marine aviators supported the dash of 1st Cavalry Division troops into Manila, and in France during the St. Lô breakout when pilots of General Quesada's IX Tactical Air Command directly aided armored units.[75]

In general, neither Navy nor AAF commanders regarded air liaison parties or airplane pilots sufficiently skilled in the co-ordination of air-ground relationships. And in some crowded front-line situations, as on the island of Tinian, they feared that direct and indiscriminate infantry calls for air strikes might endanger friendly units in the vicinity.[76]

An AAF arrangement by the 308th Bomber Wing to support the Army assault upon Manila (the same action in which Captain Godolphin's radio jeep and his Marine pilots provided effective close support) proved cumbersome. The AAF liaison party was too large (twenty-nine officers and men, one Dukw, a weapons carrier, and a jeep) and unwieldy to keep up with the advancing troops, and the command channels were too involved, requiring that close support requests by the troops be forwarded and approved by division, corps, army,

---

[72] Crowl and Love, *Seizure of the Gilberts and Marshalls,* pp. 103–05.

One serious defect was lack of communications between tank crews and infantry teams. *Ibid.,* pp. 79, 93, 163. The defect was partly compensated for, in time for the Marshall assaults, by installing a telephone set on the exterior of each tank, and linking it into the crew's intercom system. *Ibid.,* pp. 183f.

[73] (1) Miller, *Cartwheel: the Reduction of Rabaul,* p. 142. (2) Robert Sherrod, *History of Marine Corps Aviation in World War II* (Washington: Combat Forces Press, 1952), pp. 150ff. Sherrod adds, pages 189ff., that SOPAC air-ground liaison made marked progress in the subsequent Bougainville combat.

[74] Sherrod, *History of Marine Corps Aviation in World War II,* pp. 293 and 296. Sherrod devotes all of Chapter 20 to a review of close air support, "close" meaning air strikes called by ground troops against enemy targets less than 200 yards away.

[75] (1) *Ibid.,* pp. 300ff. (2) See above, p. 121–22.

In the Philippines, Marine Capt. Francis R. B. Godolphin worked out close support tactics, involving direct communications between ground troops and Marine aircraft aloft, with full collaboration of 1st Cavalry Division G–2 Lt. Col. Robert F. Goheen (the two officers had been associated closely just before the war in the Classics Department of Princeton University, Godolphin as a professor, and Goheen as a student).

[76] Crowl, *Campaign in the Marianas,* p. 299.

and finally by the 308th Bomber Wing, before an air strike could be provided.[77]

On crowded Tinian requests for air support were radioed by the air liaison parties that served each regiment and battalion. The requests then filtered through division and corps headquarters. If not rejected, they then went for final decision and action to the naval aviation officer who was charged with support aircraft—Capt. Richard F. Whitehead, aboard Vice Adm. Richmond Kelly Turner's flagship, the *Rocky Mount*. Because of these circuitous channels (plus editing and consent at three levels of command), air support did not come as quickly as the infantry desired. Sometimes it came within thirty minutes, but often it was delayed an hour or more. Naval historian Morison states that the average time lag between ground request and the air strike in the Saipan campaign exceeded one hour "partly because there were 41 liaison parties competing for Whitehead's ear on one communication circuit."

Obviously, the naval air liaison circuit was overcrowded and the channel of command clogged. Marine troops and aviators were displeased with Navy's handling of close air support (an extreme case of delay between a ground request and air action was nineteen hours), so displeased in fact that Marine commanders demanded escort carriers for the sole use of Marine flyers in close support and were on the point of obtaining them by the war's end.[78]

Joint Assault Signal Companies

A notable Signal Corps contribution to the Central Pacific amphibious combat was its part in the JASCO (and in somewhat similar amphibious communications support provided in SWPA for three engineer special brigades which saw action in that area of the Pacific.)[79] A much larger unit than a normal signal company, the JASCO type company saw service in the Central Pacific, the Philippines, and on Iwo Jima and Okinawa, as well as in the ETO. JASCO's contained five or six hundred Army, AAF, and Navy communications specialists, trained in joint procedures, who provided the essential links between the land, sea, and air elements in operations against the enemy.

JASCO's were created in the Pacific in late 1943. They developed from the agglomeration of various communication teams, too small to remain independent units or too ineffective to operate alone. Take, for example, the problem of controlling effectively the fire of heavy naval

---

[77] Sherrod, *History of Marine Corps Aviation in World War II*, p. 301.

[78] (1) Crowl, *Campaign in the Marianas*, p. 132. (2) Isely and Crowl, *The U.S. Marines and Amphibious War*, pp. 334, 363, and 585f. (3) Morison, *New Guinea and the Marianas*, pp. 326ff.

Crowl, *Campaign in the Marianas*, page 286, details an instance of circuitous channels in radio control of naval gunfire at Saipan. An observation plane, controlling the fall of shot from the battleship *Colorado*, was not in direct communication with the ship but with an artillery post ashore. The post relayed the spotting data given by the observation plane by telephone to the Marine headquarters, also ashore. The headquarters then radioed the data to the ship. In this case, although the communications channels were thus roundabout, the data passed quickly enough so that there was no serious time lag.

[79] The brigade signal company, organized under TOE 11–537T, comprised 6 officers, 1 warrant officer, and 117 enlisted men. All the officers of the signal company of the 3d Engineer Special Brigade were Signal Corps. Maj James B. McNally, Signal Communications in Engineer Special Brigades, a research paper submitted to the Comdt, Engr Sch, Ft. Belvoir, Va., 1949, pp. 1–13, 36f. MS copy in Army Libr, Pentagon.

JASCO Team Using M-209 Cipher Converter, Lingayen Beach, Luzon

guns trying to soften up enemy beach defenses. This work required the co-operation and co-ordination of Navy and Marine (or Army) gunners, spotters, and radiomen. The Navy and Marines first developed in the Pacific a fire control party that included a naval officer, an artillery officer, radio personnel, and various equipment. This setup lasted only through Tarawa.

After that costly assault, the Joint Chiefs of Staff, following advice Maj. Gen. Alexander A. Vandergrift had given out of his Guadalcanal experience, directed that communications for air liaison, naval fire control, and shore parties all be pooled in one organization. The addition of shore fire control and air liaison parties to the special signal companies, which had been organized a year earlier, resulted in the JASCO.[80]

Two notable JASCO's supporting the Central Pacific forces were the 75th and the 295th. The 75th took form from a nucleus of 5 officers and 100 enlisted

---

[80] (1) Isely and Crowl, *The U.S. Marines and Amphibious War*, pp. 251f. (2) Maj Vincent W. Fox, The Role of the JASCO (1947), SigC Sch Monograph. The Sig Sch Libr, Ft. Monmouth. (3) AFSC Rpts, vol. 1, 1947–48, Conf L–26, Shore Parties. SigC OP 352.

men of the 75th Signal Company (Special), originally organized under TOE 11–517 into ten units, each intended to provide the communications for a battalion landing team.

Experiences of those elements of the company that served in the Gilberts led to considerable change before the assault upon the Marshall Islands. The company was much enlarged, reaching a total of 592 officers and men. Becoming the 75th JASCO, it provided twice the signal facilities of the parent special signal company. Shore fire control teams were doubled, from 5 to 10 officers and men. The air liaison parties were nearly doubled, from 3 to 5 members. Five were needed—to operate three radio sets (SCR–193, 542, and 284); to drive a jeep; to keep informed on the air support needs of the troops; and to maintain control over air-ground communications.[81]

The 295th JASCO, commanded by Maj. Irving R. Obenchain, Jr., received some training late in 1943 in Hawaii with the 106th RCT to which it had been assigned for the Marshall Islands campaign. After that action, the company trained further, again in Hawaii, with the 27th Infantry Division for

action in the Marianas beginning in mid-1944.[82]

One of the Signal Corps members of the 295th JASCO, T/4 Joseph A. Whitesell, received a Silver Star for gallantry in action on Guam. A radio operator serving with a naval gunfire team attached to an infantry battalion of the 27th Division, he was caught in an enemy counterattack, which killed many officers of the unit. Organizing a new defense line, he helped fight off the Japanese, looked after the wounded, and heartened the defenders. He refused to withdraw when he himself received a wound and fought on until fatally hit.[83]

Island Base Communications

Mobile or portable radios, radiomen, and communications training for the amphibious portion of assaults—for gaining and consolidating the beachheads—

---

[81] The 75th JASCO, as first organized under TOE 11–147S in the Marshall Islands campaign, contained:

a) 10 teams totaling 200 Army and 100 Navy officers and men for shore party communications (one to each battalion landing team, to establish and maintain communications on the beach, inland, laterally, and seaward).

b) 9 teams totaling 54 Army and 9 Navy personnel for shore fire control (one to each battalion landing team to control naval gunfire).

c) 13 parties totaling 52 AAF officers and men, for air liaison.

d) A headquarters of 72 Army and 5 Navy personnel.

[82] (1) Crowl and Love, *Seizure of the Gilberts and Marshalls*, pp. 178 and 185f. (2) Crowl, *Campaign in the Marianas*, pp. 45 and 130. (3) Hist, Sig Sec HUSAFMIDPAC, pp. 74f. and 82 (sec. II, pp. 12f. and 19). (4) McNally, Sig Com in the Engr Sp Brig, pp. 26f.

[83] Honoring him, the Signal Corps on 14 January 1955 named a new dial telephone exchange building at Fort George Meade, Maryland, the Whitesell Memorial Building. Joseph Anthony Whitesell, Biography folder, SigC Hist Sec File. See also: (1) WD PRO Release, Signalmen on Saipan, undated. Com folder, Tab 1, SigC Hist Sec file. (2) *Army Times* Editors, *A History of the U.S. Signal Corps* (New York: G. P. Putnam's Sons, 1961), pp. 161ff.

For Saipan signal reports, see (1) Incl, Lt Col George F. Hauck, SigO 27th Inf Div, Rpt of Sig Com Opn FORAGER (Phase 1), with ASF Transmittal Sheet, Action 1, Walter, Intel Br OCSigO, to Chief Logistics Plng Br, 25 Apr 45, sub: Battle for Saipan. SigC OP 370.2 Gen Rpt folder 1, 3 Jan–25 Apr 45, Tab 23. (2) Incl, Sig Rpt Saipan, with ASF Transmittal Sheet, Intel Br OCSigO to Chief Logistics Plng Br OCSigO, 26 Apr 45, sub: Battle for Saipan. SigC OP 370.2 Gen Rpt, folder 2, 26 Apr–2 Jun 45, Tab 2.

constituted only the first burdens upon General Powell and his Central Pacific Signal Office. After each island had been won, after the tactical commander secured the ground and its control passed to the island command, there next arose demands for communications to serve base developments. The communications included systems to link together the headquarters, airfields, harbor facilities, supply depots and defense installations, including radar stations, and they included fixed long-range radio (point- to-point) to link up the island signal center with other bases. These base developments continued to draw heavily upon the Central Pacific Signal Office.[84]

The plans for the signal detachment of the Army garrison force assigned to the first islands captured in the Central Pacific, the Gilberts, included provision of all telephone trunking and exchange facilities, long-range point-to-point administrative radio, and a base signal center. In September 1943 Colonel Powell organized a detachment of 5 officers and 42 men as a starter (more were later added). He drew them from various signal units under his command and gave them intensive training, including a week in the field with all their basic equipment. Assigned to the Amphibious Training Center in Hawaii for another week, the men of the detachment experienced along with their naval and Marine comrades the trials and troubles of transferring themselves and their equipment to landing boats and thence to the beaches, maintaining communications by visual methods if necessary.

Because of the training, the signal detachment that went ashore in the Gilberts in November 1943 to set up garrison or base facilities was relatively well trained. Its officers and men provided telephone services to all major echelons of the defense battalions, to AAF units, and to Army, Navy, and Marine establishments on the base. They installed and operated the island radio base station and maintained the signal center for the task force headquarters. Later, the signal center was converted, in the pattern common throughout the Pacific Ocean Areas, to a joint communication center where Army and Navy communicators worked together to serve all the armed forces in the area.

Thus a pattern was set for subsequent island base signal detachments which Colonel Powell's Central Pacific Signal Office provided again and again in the following months. The first detachment included a captain as commanding officer with 4 enlisted men to help with administrative chores, a message center section of 2 officers and 9 enlisted men (message center chiefs, clerks, and cryptographers), a wire section of one officer and 11 enlisted wire chiefs, plus linemen, switchboard operators, radio maintenance and powermen), and a radar section (2 radar repairmen). Their major equipment items included an SCR-399, a fixed radio transmitter BC-447 (with antenna, antenna mast, and power equipment), Hammarlund super-pro receivers, central office telephone sets TC-4, and TC-3 teletype switchboard and teletypewriter sets EE-97, together with 150 miles of W-110 wire and 10 miles of cable CC-345.

Adequate training was generally hard to attain. Army and Navy communica-

[84] Brig Gen. Carroll A. Powell, "Communications in Pacific Ocean Areas," *Military Review*, XXV, No. 10 (January, 1946), 30f.

tions men could rarely get together for sufficient joint practice, both because they were not organized sufficiently early, and because frequent changes in the over-all assault blueprints upset the signal plans. For these reasons the joint training of signalmen for the Marshall Islands in March 1944 was inadequate. Worse, during the ship loading, the men were separated from their equipment. Arriving at Kwajalein minus their signal facilities, they found the island commander demanding immediate signal services. Taking first things first, the signalmen looked for their equipment, which they found in a ship still loaded in the lagoon. The equipment lay buried under three hundred tons of steel air runway mat in the hold.[85]

The base build-up in the Marianas beginning in mid-1944 surpassed in size all previous Central Pacific efforts, after Hawaii itself. On the relatively large islands of the Marianas would be developed major military bases and airfields to support direct assaults upon the Japanese homeland. The sole interbase communications, necessarily all radio, had to become heavy duty. All circuits, both radio telephone and radioteletypewriter, had to convert to multichannel operation to carry the huge message loads necessary to supply, control, and direct thousands of air, ground, and sea units. For example, a multiplex radio circuit between Saipan and Guam, originally planned and installed to provide four channels, had to be enlarged to 12-channel operation, with relay with Hawaii, and thence with the United States and Washington so that General Arnold could freely control from the

Pentagon the tactics of his B-29 bombers in the far Pacific.

As the Pacific bases rapidly grew in size and scope through the last months of the war, on Kwajalein, in the Marianas, and finally in Okinawa, the joint communications centers mushroomed in operations and significance. All point-to-point overwater administration and operational circuits terminated in the JCC's at each base. All cryptographic facilities were concentrated there (except tactical troop and AAF crypto). All administrative and operational traffic within the base area passed through the JCC, to be distributed locally by land-line circuits or by messengers.

The JCC's in these Pacific bases were no temporary setup, as were Army communications centers in normal land operations, ready to accompany the command in the next troop movement. The JCC serving a Pacific island base had to stay there, and so it acquired the character of a permanent installation. Some items of normal Army signal center equipment, designed for the frequent moves of land armies, proved inadequate for the heavy load of long continued fixed operation. Hence General Powell had to provide quantities of such permanent type equipment as commercial automatic switchboards, permanent high-speed radioteletypewriters (as designed in World War II for Army ACAN stations), and cables of 600, 1,000 and even 2,000 pairs. Soon after the war, General Powell made some comparisons: the Kwajalein base communications system (telephone alone) became comparable in size to that of Lexington, Massachusetts. On Guam the Signal Corps developed an automatic exchange system larger than that of Cedar Rapids, Iowa;

[85] Hist, Sig Sec HUSAFMIDPAC, pp. 76–90 (sec. II, pp. 14–27).

the Okinawa system, largest of all, exceeded that of South Bend, Indiana.[86]

Outstanding among the radio sets provided for fixed point-to-point installations serving island garrisons and bases was the new VHF antrac or radio relay. These facilities Powell supplied, and teams from his office went to the mid-Pacific islands where they erected and maintained them along the island steppingstones to Japan, especially along the Mariana chain. The sets provided a dependable, high-capacity radio net over Saipan, Tinian, Rota, and Guam. They served primarily tactical command, weather information, and telephone and teletypewriter communications between several bomber wings and the headquarters of the XXI Bomber Command. Some of these VHF stations were erected by members of the 3116th Signal Service Battalion operating from Hawaii.[87] Radio construction teams of the 3116th put in stations all over the Pacific: Kwajalein, Majuro, Guam, Saipan, Angaur, Iwo Jima, Canton, Guadalcanal, Espíritu Santo, Funafuti, and New Zealand.[88]

Radar

Colonel Powell's Aircraft Warning Service Division provided large numbers of radar sets in the Central Pacific Area. Over seventy sets were installed in the Hawaiian Islands alone before the transfer to AAF, on 1 June 1943, of responsibility of all AWS (except for the maintenance of seacoast radar).[89]

Everywhere in the Pacific islands, Signal Corps search radars gave valuable warning of enemy planes, from the opening of hostilities on Guadalcanal to the end of the war.[90] The radars warned of approaching enemy planes and directed antiaircraft fire, with notable increase in accuracy after the arrival of SCR–584's in quantity by the second half of 1944. In AAF ground-controlled interception, Signal Corps ground and airborne radars worked together to help bring down en-

---

[86] (1) *Ibid.*, pp. 91ff. (2) Powell, "Communications in Pacific Ocean Areas," *Military Review*, XXV, No. 10 (January, 1946), pp. 31–34.

[87] Maj Robert F. Bowker, SigC, and E. M. Ostlund, Operational Research Sec, Hq USAFPOA, Incl, Rpt on Guam-Saipan-Interisland VHF Com, 14 Mar 45, with Ltr, CSigO to CG ASF, 25 Sep 45, sub: Rpt. SigC OD 218 PAC Theater, folder No. 4. Victor Colaguori of the Camp Coles Signal Laboratory, and H. E. Weppler of the Eatontown Signal Laboratory both worked on this project early in 1945. The distance between Tinian and Guam was a little too great to provide a dependable circuit until Colaguori remedied the situation by installing special rhombic antennas. MS Comment, Waite, Jul 59.

[88] Ltr, Hq 3116th Sig Sv Bn to CO Com Sv CPBC, 24 Aug 45, sub: Meritorious Sv Unit Plaque. Hist Sig Sec HUSAFMIDPAC, p. 144.

[89] Hist, Sig Sec, HUSAFMIDPAC, pp. 203 and 210 (sec. V, pp. 3 and 10). It had been under Colonel Powell that the first Army radars were placed in Hawaii in 1941 including the historic SCR–270, which detected the Japanese bombers 130 miles away on their way in to the attack on 7 December 1941. That the radar warning was overlooked was an unfortunate consequence of the almost universal ignorance of radar early in World War II—not only in the Army.

Shipboard radar, although soon to become indispensable in naval operations, was not well comprehended either in 1941 or in 1942. Morison remarked that in 1942 ignorance of radar capabilities in the U.S. Navy was "almost universal," and not till later, and then only gradually, did commanders fully appreciate radar and begin to study and analyze the information provided by radar screens (information that was eventually gathered into a sort of brain center, or command center, in large ships, the Combat Information Center). (1) Morison, *The Struggle for Guadalcanal*, pp. 170 and 282. (2) Thompson, Harris, *et al.*, *The Test*, pp. 4f.

[90] (1) Thompson, Harris, *et al.*, *The Test*, pp. 15f., 290f., 475ff. (2) Miller, *Cartwheel: the Reduction of Rabaul*, pp. 94, 248; and *Guadalcanal: The First Offensive*, pp. 107, 355.

emy craft—such ground radars as the SCR's–584 and 602, and the MEW (AN/CPS–1). A combination of SCR–602 on the ground and AI sets mounted in Black Widow fighter planes served well during the Philippine fighting in 1945. The first MEW to arrive in the Pacific—set No. 4 of the first five preproduction sets built by the Radiation Laboratory—was destined for Saipan late in 1944 to serve the XXI Bomber Command. The Japanese had been bombing the airfields and B–29's on Saipan with damaging effect, and General Arnold therefore ordered his AAF commander in the Pacific, Lt. Gen. Millard F. Harmon, to get the MEW into operation at once atop Mt. Tapochau.[91]

Radar was of very great value in the Okinawa fighting to warn of the deadly kamikazes. On Iwo Jima in the last months of the war, however, Signal Corps radars were indispensable not so much against the enemy as in support of our own aircraft. Working in conjunction with radio communications, weather facilities, and a variety of electronic landing aids, they helped to bring in many a damaged or wandering B–29, guiding it in from an uncertain return from Japan to a safe landing on the tiny island.[92]

---

[91] (1) Craven and Cate, eds., *The Pacific: Matterhorn to Nagasaki, June 1944 to August 1945*, pp. 582f. (2) History of Signal Corps Research and Development in World War II, IV, pt. 3, Proj 426–A, 14f. (Also recounted in "Hot Spot on Luzon," *Radar*, No. 10 (June 30, 1945), pp. 18f.) (3) Henry Guerlac, Radar MS, History of Radiation Laboratory, pp. 1411ff. and 1423ff. (B–VIII, 45ff). Photostat copy in SigC Hist Div.

[92] (1) Col. Henry R. Chamberlin, SigC, "Suribachi Sentinels," *Signals*, I, No. 2 (November–December, 1946), 35ff. (2) "The Radar at Iwo," and "Stop-gap on Saipan," *Radar*, No. 9 (April 30, 1945) 3–7 and 25ff. SigC Hist Sec file. (3) Lt. Col. Benjamin E. Lippincott, *From Fiji Through the Philippines With the Thirteenth Air Force* (New York: The Macmillan Company, 1948), pp. 69, 87, and 153. (4) Brig. Gen. P. C. Sandretto, "Radio Navigational Problems in the Central Pacific," *Signals*, V. No. 2 (November–December, 1950), 20ff. (5) Lincoln R. Thiesmeyer and John E. Burchard, *Combat Scientists* (Boston: Little, Brown and Company, 1947), p. 264.

CHAPTER VIII

Communications in the Southwest Pacific
to Mid-1944

Tropical combat in the Southwest Pacific placed Army communications and the Signal Corps in an environment similar to that of adjacent Pacific Ocean areas. Jungle conditions, excessive heat, and rain sorely strained Signal Corps men and their equipment. Great distances over water required sole dependence upon heavy-duty long-range radio. Actions under Allied and amphibious commands demanded close co-ordination of signalmen, signal procedures, and signal equipment in co-operation with the Navy, the Marine Corps, and often with British and Dominion forces. These circumstances of military operation were common to the South and Central Pacific as well as to SWPA, but in its organizational structure and manner of operation SWPA differed.

If the Pacific war was principally Navy's war, Army conforming therewith, SWPA provided an exception. The SWPA staff was definitely Army, not Navy. The naval commander of the Seventh Fleet that supported SWPA, in Morison's words, was "seldom admitted to General MacArthur's strategic staff discussions; he was simply told that the General intended to land at such a place on such a date, and the Navy must see that their movement to the

objective was properly covered." [1]

Whatever unified command there was in SWPA existed at the top only, in the commander in chief himself, General MacArthur, and in his staff relations. There was in SWPA no joint organization that reached down into the task forces and island commands, as it did in the South and Central Pacific. There were no joint communications centers in SWPA, and no joint units such as JASCO's, until the assaults upon the Philippines. Each participating service maintained its own communications centers and kept its own circuits separate for its own sole use. Co-ordination was accomplished, below MacArthur's GHQ, by co-operation and consent. [2]

[1] (1) Morison, *Strategy and Compromise*, p. 85, and *Breaking the Bismarcks Barrier*, p. 15. (2) Re SWPA organization in general, see Smith, *The Approach to the Philippines*, pp. 14f.

[2] Intervs, SigC Hist Div with Brig Gen Benjamin H. Pochyla, Chief, Plans, Progs, and Opns Div OCSigO (formerly ExecO Sig Sec GHQ SWPA), 15 and 18 Feb 60. In practice, GHQ SWPA produced the outline plan for each operation. MacArthur assigned the plan to a subordinate, usually Lt. Gen. Walter Krueger, who would co-ordinate all supporting tactical commands such as AAF SWPA, and ANF (Allied Naval Forces) SWPA, as well as SOS SWPA. Disagreements among these subordinates would be settled at GHQ, if necessary, and GHQ would review the final plans produced by such co-ordination. Draft MS, Comment, Robert Ross Smith. SigC Hist Sec file.

GHQ SWPA had taken form in MacArthur's hands during the spring of 1942 in Australia. Head of the Signal Section and the Chief Signal Officer, SWPA, was Brig. Gen. Spencer B. Akin. Akin had departed from Corregidor in March 1942 and accompanied MacArthur to Australia. He remained the chief signal officer for SWPA throughout the war and beyond, through all the subsequent moves and redesignations of MacArthur's command, from Australia to Tokyo and till his appointment in 1947 as the Chief Signal Officer of the Army in Washington, D.C.

The Unique Over-all Control of the SWPA Signal Officer

Signal officers in the theaters of war often yearned for greater control, for powers commensurate with the overriding, all-pervading requirements and circumstances of communications—in supply and equipment, in training and operation, in frequency control and radio intelligence. But in actual practice in World War II nowhere did a theater signal officer receive, delegated to him alone, all the authority needed to exercise integrated control over all major communications matters—nowhere, that is, except in SWPA.

General MacArthur gave General Akin more over-all control than any other theater chief signal officer possessed. Akin was the GHQ staff officer whom the commander in chief held responsible for all SWPA communications. MacArthur, petitioning the War Department in August 1943 to promote Akin, described him as:

. . . technically chief signal officer at this headquarters but who in effect exercises direct command over signal units in Australia including those of the American and Australian armies and of the civilian postmaster general's department . . . the excellent communication for all components in this area is entirely due to his own technical ability, foresight, energy, and tact although operating under the most difficult circumstances.[3]

Beyond these large responsibilities, which included supervision over all Army (and AAF), Navy, and Allied communications in SWPA, the commander in chief further gave Akin control over the Allied signal intelligence services, Allied radio and radar countermeasures, Allied signal supply, aircraft warning, and Allied research and development activity.[4]

Just as MacArthur operated with a relatively small staff for such a large command (this was necessary in part for reasons of manpower economy and was in part a consequence of MacArthur's

---

[3] Extract from Radiogram Q4143 Eighteenth, MacArthur to CofS WD, 18 Aug 43. Akin folder, SigC Hist Sec file.

[4] MacArthur spelled out these powers in a letter he wrote in 1947 to Under Secretary of War Kenneth C. Royall recommending Akin for the position of Chief Signal Officer of the Army: "This officer has been a member of my staff since October 1941. In that capacity he has, during the war, been the Chief Signal Officer for all Forces (Army, Naval and Air) under my command; Chief of the Allied Signal Intelligence Service; Chief of the Allied Signal Supply Service; Chief of the Allied Research and New Development Section; Director of Radio and Radar Counter-measures activities, and Supervisor and coordinator of Aircraft Warning Service. . . . I regard him as the best Signal Officer I have ever known. . . . Akin's experience in connection with the coordinated and cooperative integration of Army, Navy and Air Force signal communications renders him especially well qualified in this field at a time when unification of the Armed Forces is under consideration." Ltr, MacArthur to Royall, 14 Jan 47. Akin folder, SigC Hist Sec file.

GENERAL AKIN ARRIVES AT HOLLANDIA, *above.*   *Below, Signal Corps buildings on Hollandia, with General Akin's office on the right.*

insistence upon direct close relations), so Akin kept his signal section small, though it included Navy, AAF, and Australian liaison officers.

As a result of the economy of personnel and of the extreme flexibility with which Akin and his officers did their work, the SWPA chief signal officer himself ordered and distributed equipment and assigned personnel freely and directly in whatever manner a situation might require. The fixed units or organizations, even definite job titles that one expects to find in a large organization, scarcely existed in SWPA. What might have seemed a confused state of affairs was actually an ordered arrangement varying for each circumstance—an efficient employment of a minimum of men and equipment. General Akin's deputy was usually Lt. Col. Samuel S. Auchincloss, and his executive, Lt. Col. Benjamin H. Pochyla. Yet not always. Sometimes Akin alternated these officers, sending Auchincloss up to a forward assignment and bringing Pochyla back to GHQ as the deputy chief signal officer.

Unit organizations were likewise often rather vague, appearing on paper as coherent units, but containing elements that were actually separated far and wide. The so-called Central Bureau, Akin's signal intelligence organization (which included Allied elements as well as Signal Corps men), was not a single coherent centrally located unit as its name suggests. Its officers and men were scattered, some serving with AAF outfits, some aboard naval headquarters vessels.[5]

General Akin did not even organize a definite GHQ communications center, leaving that chore to his SOS signals. Yet at times Akin himself took temporary charge of the center which would, in this circumstance, become the GHQ communications center. Pochyla later recalled the good reasons against setting up a separate center serving GHQ. One was that Allied elements— Dutch and Australian Army and Royal Australian Air Force (RAAF)—used separate crypto systems and procedures and so had to operate their own message centers. Another reason was the scarcity both of communicators and of equipment.[6]

General Akin thus enjoyed a singular freedom of decision and action. He was expected by General MacArthur to exercise his powers in frequent visits throughout his command, especially in the forefront of each operation, after the pattern that MacArthur himself established and indomitably pursued. In his signal communications and other responsibilities General Akin sought in every way to insure the success of any operation, moving equipment and personnel as the immediate needs of the situation might require. Whenever he took direct action, he did so in conformity with the wishes of the local commander while informing the GHQ chief of staff. Akin's presence in forward combat areas, with authority to take im-

---

[5] When 2d Lt. John D. McKinney went to the Pacific in 1943 as commanding officer of a radio team of the 832d Signal Company, he found that

company personnel relations seemed "chaotic," because the officers and men were widely scattered in their assignments throughout SWPA. Interv, SigC Hist Div with Lt Col John D. McKinney, Washington, 8 Sep 60.

[6] Intervs, SigC Hist Div with Maj Gen Spencer B. Akin, Purcellville, Va., 12 Sep 60, and with Brig Gen Benjamin H. Pochyla, 15 and 18 Feb 60.

mediate action as needed, often nipped incipient difficulties and provided quick solutions. On one occasion, for example, he relieved on the spot a signal company that had proved ineffective in a forward combat area, and he then saw to it that a replacement unit was flown in at once.

An activity wherein direct control and quick action were peculiarly necessary was signal intelligence, one of the SWPA chief signal officer's large responsibilities. General Akin arranged for the direct and immediate provision of intercepted information to the commanders who were empowered to act thereon. To this end he attached signal intelligence elements to the commanders' headquarters or located them nearby. He assigned a signal intelligence detachment to Admiral Halsey's flagship, at the admiral's request. Vice Adm. Raymond A. Spruance, when he took command of the Fifth Fleet in SWPA, found this Army service so valuable that he continued to keep the signal specialists on duty with him. Similar units were likewise attached to AAF advanced headquarters as well as to ground force commands, and were always sufficiently close at hand so that information from their intercept sources could be acted upon immediately.

Intercept information often had to be put to use quickly, or its value would be lost. On one occasion Akin's intercept specialists learned from Japanese radio traffic that the enemy expected early Allied action against one of its large airfields and therefore had issued orders that all the airplanes be flown out the next morning to safer locations. The information was placed at once in the hands of the AAF commander, Lt. Gen. George C. Kenney, who saw to it that

his bombers got off the ground first. They destroyed large numbers of enemy aircraft still on the field at dawn.

In many cases of signal intelligence, any delay, such as sending the intercepts back to GHQ itself or even farther, to the War Department in the United States (as the War Department at one time in World War II advocated), and then relaying the decrypted information forward to the unit empowered to take action, would have nullified the value of the intercept.[7]

General Akin's sweeping control in command and operations was matched by his free scope in supply. He obtained and provided signal equipment from whatever sources he could and apportioned it to Army ground and air forces, to the Marines, and to Allied elements as the occasion might require. Much of the equipment came from Australia. Some equipment given to the AAF, for example, derived from RAAF contracts. Australian AT–20 radios were especially valuable and sought after; some thought them even better than comparable SCR–299's and 399's. Much radar equipment also came from Australian sources, and SWPA aviators were grateful, as Lt. Gen. Ennis C. Whitehead later attested (he had been deputy commanding general of the Fifth Air Force under General Kenney) :

. . . General Akin supported me 100% during the entire war and since. When we needed air warning [equipment] which had to be moved by airplane and none was available in the United States, he had it manufactured in Australia, how I do not know, but I know that we received the equipment.

---

[7] Interv, SigC Hist Div with Akin, 12 Sep 60.

As you know, the air out here was a wide-open fast moving affair . . . Akin's cooperation and drive in obtaining additional equipment for the Fifth Air Force was one of the principal reasons for whatever success we have had in this war.[8]

Although the SWPA chief signal officer through his relations with Allied and joint liaison officers in the GHQ accomplished a kind of joint control over SWPA signals, he did not direct that SWPA communications below his level be conducted jointly. He pursued the policy of MacArthur himself, allowing each service to operate separately but to co-operate at the same time. Each subordinate element down the line was thus expected to use its own communications equipment, personnel, and procedures in its own usual manner, while co-ordinating with participating forces. This was not a joint operation, and in signal matters duplication might be expected, but General Akin believed this method of operation was faster, more efficient, and entirely justifiable in wartime if it brought victory and brought it quicker.[9]

Task Force Communications by Co-ordination

By mid-1943 the Japanese had been driven from their deepest penetrations down under: from Buna, and from their assault on Port Moresby. General MacArthur established an advanced GHQ SWPA at Port Moresby itself, and the Allied advance up the northeast coast of New Guinea began with the dislodgment of the enemy from the Kakoda-Buna and Milne Bay areas and the seizure of Kiriwina and Woodlark Islands.[10]

In these and subsequent SWPA operations, the GHQ chief signal officer first arranged for and supervised the necessary signal co-ordination and co-operation of the several participating forces to the end that confusion, waste, and duplication might be minimized. General Akin gave the highest Army commander in combat areas the responsibility (while providing to him the needed equipment and troops) for the installation and maintenance of major communications facilities. The highest Army commander in most SWPA operations (apart from the conquest of the Lae-Salamaua area by the end of 1943 in which a large number of Australian forces bore the brunt of combat) was General Krueger, commander of the Sixth Army (sometimes called the ALAMO Force). Krueger's signal officer throughout the Pacific war was Col. Harry Reichelder fer.[11]

Colonel Reichelderfer provided communications for the task forces that took

---

[8] Ltr, Whitehead, CG FEAF, to S. Stuart Symington, ASW for Air, 21 Jan 47. Akin folder.

[9] Interv, SigC Hist Div with Akin, 12 Sep 60.

[10] For earlier Signal Corps participation in SWPA, see Thompson, Harris, et al., The Test, pp. 112f., 298ff., 467ff.

[11] Draft MS Comments, General Akin. SigC Hist Sec file. Other major forces under GHQ SWPA were Far East Air Forces (FEAF)—including the U.S. Fifth Air Force, and, later, the Thirteenth Air Force—the Seventh Fleet, the Third Fleet, and the Allied Land Forces.

For comments on Sixth Army command and relationships, see Charles A. Willoughby and John Chamberlain, MacArthur 1941–1951 (New York: McGraw-Hill Book Co., Inc., 1954), p. 124; and Courtney C. Whitney, MacArthur and His Rendezvous With History (New York: Alfred A. Knopf, Inc., 1956), pp. 94f.

over Kiriwina and Woodlark Islands on 30 June 1943. These islands off the tip of New Guinea were not occupied by the Japanese. To keep the enemy from suspecting such a landing, General Akin had seen to it that radio transmitters in Darwin and Perth, Australia, poured out deceptive radio traffic in order to cause enemy listeners to suppose that the Allies were planning moves out of north-western Australia, far from the actual assaults in the opposite direction off eastern New Guinea.[12]

With task force signals well under control, there were no communications problems at Kiriwina or Woodlark. Circuits were quickly established from the islands to headquarters at Milne Bay, to GHQ at Port Moresby, and to air and naval units. Colonel Reichelderfer's next move, to nearby Goodenough Island, also unoccupied by the enemy, was made in a single day in a mass transfer of men and equipment aboard two 38-foot boats. They arrived at Goodenough on 21 October 1943 and remained there till the year's end. "We didn't have a joint command in the true sense of the word," Colonel Reichelderfer later said in summarizing these and other SWPA signal experiences. Each element—Navy, Sixth Army, AAF, SOS—had certain missions, and each, he emphasized, used its own communications. The only joint circuits that they employed were limited to naval gunfire support and to air support communications during the landing phase of an operation. The SWPA command system "worked very well," Reichelderfer told an Armed Forces

Staff College audience in 1947, "and I liked the way we did it." [13]

Amphibious assaults, requiring the closest possible contact between air, sea, and ground forces, depended heavily upon radio, the only means of communicating under the circumstances, beyond the reach of ear or eye. The radio blueprints for each action were necessarily complex and extensive. The communications plans for the amphibious portion of an operation, Reichelderfer recalled, "always culminated in a conference prior to the issuance of the necessary field or operation orders which was attended by representatives of GHQ, SOS, Sixth Army, the Navy and the Air Force." Individual conferences for each of the many actions in New Guinea area took one or two days. Later on, preceding the large-scale Leyte and Luzon landings, the conferees took much more time. Every detail fell under scrutiny. Frequencies were assigned. Communications procedures and plans for co-ordination were formulated. The decisions at which the conferees arrived went into the signal annexes of the operation instructions and into the field orders of the troop units.[14]

At least such was the good intent. Sometimes the plans went awry and co-ordination fell short of the ideal. In the assault on Cape Gloucester, New Britain, for example, at the turn of 1943–44, the Navy failed to co-ordinate com-

---

[12] Willoughby and Chamberlain, *MacArthur 1941–1951*, p. 126.

[13] Reichelderfer, AFSC Lecture C–15, Communications SWPA, 29 May 47, Tab 24, pp. 2–3 and 12. SigC OP 352 AFSC Rpts, vol. 2, 1947–48.

[14] Col. Harry Reichelderfer, "Sixth Army Communications," *Signals*, III, No. 2 (November–December 1948), 5.

munications with the Army. Naval Task Force 76 radioed its reports directly to the Seventh Fleet commander. The commanding general of the assaulting troops (1st Marine Division) could not communicate with General Krueger in ALAMO headquarters until the marines were able to establish a headquarters ashore. General Krueger subsequently complained that he was not informed about the operation until midnight of the day of the assault when two Australian newsmen, who had witnessed the landings that morning, stopped off at ALAMO headquarters on their way back to Australia. In this instance, commercial news facilities carried the message to the Army commander before military channels did. Naturally General Krueger was annoyed. "My urgent representations to GHQ about this," he later wrote, "resulted in my headquarters not being overlooked at later operations." [15]

Another instance in which the operation fell short of the plans was described by Colonel Reichelderfer as occurring in a small-scale landing in the Admiralty Islands (on Los Negros, near Manus Island), early in 1944. During the first twenty-four hours of that action the participating Army elements had no communications back to the distant headquarters "except for what we got from the Navy ships." Colonel Reichelderfer, as soon as he learned of the deficiency, rushed SCR–399's and Signal Corps men into two LST's at Finschhafen. They reached the Manus area the next morning and established radio communica-

tions for the Army ground forces. The "failure" here had resulted from a last-minute change in the assault plan. Colonel Reichelderfer had participated in the initial plans, which did provide the communications he desired. But in the suddenly altered plan he had had no part, and his deputy had been unable to get adequate equipment sent in with the troops. "We couldn't take anything we couldn't carry on our backs," Reichelderfer explained, addressing an Armed Forces Staff College audience in 1947. [16]

General Ingles, the Chief Signal Officer in the Washington headquarters, cited this same incident in a talk to the same college, in order to illustrate the point that a commander must pay for his communications, that is, he must supply men and facilities, unless he decides his communications needs do not warrant the allotment of manpower and space. General Ingles told the audience that he happened to be present in General Krueger's headquarters at Cape Cretin, near Finschhafen, New Guinea, when the Manus operation occurred. General Krueger decided to leave out the long-range radio, the big truck-mounted SCR–399, because it would take up all the space in one landing craft. "He decided," Ingles said, "and in this case I think very wisely—that he was not willing to pay the price for his communications and dispensed with it,

---

[15] Walter Krueger, *From Down Under to Nippon* (Washington: Combat Forces Press, 1953), p. 39.

[16] AFSC Lecture C–15, 29 May 47, p. 6.
The large-scale assault as originally planned against Los Negros had been changed to a smaller effort, a reconnaissance-in-force, which General MacArthur ordered on short notice, allowing but five days for the readying of a few hundred troops. Miller, *CARTWHEEL: The Reduction of Rabaul,* pp. 321ff.

CAMOUFLAGED SCR-270 VANS NEAR FINSCHHAFEN

using the landing craft to land more combat troops." [17]

A major change of assault plans occurred late in the summer of 1944 as the Sixth Army at Hollandia made ready to invade the Philippines, intending origi-

nally to land on Mindanao in November and on Leyte in January. Suddenly in September came different instructions from the Joint Chiefs of Staff, who were conferring in Quebec. They approved a recommendation by Admiral Halsey that the landing on Leyte be launched much sooner, in October, and that Mindanao, Yap, and a number of other isles to the south be bypassed entirely. Many changes had to be made. This

[17] General Ingles, CSigO, Excerpts from Lecture before Army-Navy Staff College, 19 Mar 45, pp. 2-3. Com folder, Tab D, SigC Hist Sec file.

General Ingles explained that the actual landing operation was wholly in the hands of the local commander, and that General Krueger, miles distant in headquarters, however greatly he desired information over an Army circuit, could not do much about the assault anyway. Naval ships supporting the assault could of course radio back to Seventh Fleet headquarters, whence, no doubt, Krueger was able to learn how the assault was

progressing. Probably by this time, after his "urgent representations" in the Cape Gloucester incident some months earlier, Sixth Army headquarters was kept better informed of naval reports through GHQ.

was, in communications matters, "a rather ticklish job," Colonel Reichelderfer commented. "We got hold of the staff of the Twenty-fourth Corps," he recounted later, "brought them into headquarters for three or four days and went over the plans and orders and then revamped our plans to fit theirs . . . I had a little misgiving about how it would work." He was pleased with the results, however. Despite the fast and drastic changes, the Philippines effort turned out, he recalled, "as successful from a communications standpoint as we could hope for." [18]

The Signal Corps in Jungle Operations

Conditions under which Signal Corps men worked in SWPA were frequently wretched—wretched for the men, whether laying and maintaining wire or working in message centers, and wretched for the equipment also. The steaming heat often rendered life equally difficult indoors and out. "Imagine," Colonel Reichelderfer commented, "what the inside of a six-ton van, housing nine radio operators . . . felt like, completely closed up [under blackout conditions] with the temperature and humidity both in the nineties." Even at that, the communicators perhaps had it a bit better than some others. Describing the paltry

facilities of the Sixth Army, General Krueger himself noted that "priority was given to the message center." He thus underscored the vital importance of the communications links in the isolated circumstances of jungle warfare in the Pacific. He listed as next in priority cooking and eating arrangements, and, last, the shacks and tents for his own headquarters personnel.[19]

Wire-laying conditions in SWPA were worse even than those in the CBI, commented General Ingles on one occasion when he made the comparison to console the CBI signal officer.[20] Nowhere else did wire work compare with that in the Pacific jungles, where natural obstacles were compounded by lurking Japanese who found line parties especially vulnerable targets for ambush.

For example, not long before Colonel Reichelderfer arrived in SWPA, Lt. Gen. Robert L. Eichelberger, commanding troops in the swamps at Buna, noted the "outrageous conditions" under which his signal officer, Colonel Auchincloss (soon to be acquired by General Akin's GHQ Signal Section), and his signalmen maintained several hundred miles of field wire, laid along creek banks and in the mud of swamps. Enemy patrols repeatedly cut the lines. General Eichelberger recounted an incident that impressed him on his first night in the

[18] (1) Robert L. Eichelberger, *Our Jungle Road to Tokyo* (New York: Viking Press, 1950), pp. 167f. and 183. (2) AFSC Lecture C-15, 29 May 47, Tab 24, pp. 7f.
The XXIV Corps was a Central Pacific Area unit. It had been readying to assault Yap island, now bypassed, whereupon Admiral Nimitz loaned the troops to SWPA for employment in the initial Philippine assaults. Early in 1945 the corps was recalled to Central Pacific to prepare for the Okinawa campaign.

[19] (1) Reichelderfer, "Sixth Army Communications," *Signals*, III, No. 2, p. 8. (2) Krueger, *From Down Under to Nippon*, p. 134. (3) History, 99th Signal Battalion, p. 6. SGBN 99-0.1 (8212), 10 Mar 42-Jan 45.
[20] Ltr, Ingles to King, 17 Apr 44, no sub. SigC OT 370.2 Rpts, CBI, Tab 22. Ingles wrote: "I saw the film of your line construction . . . it reminds me of the line construction job on the north coast of New Guinea except that the New Guinea jungle is apparently much worse than that your crews are confronting."

Buna area. The signal officer of the 32d Division reported that the vital line to the Urbana front was dead. His men, he reported further, hesitated to check on the break because of enemy infiltration. Thereupon Colonel Auchincloss

. . . walked across the signal tent, glanced at the men assembled there, and then, with considerable care, selected a sharp knife and a pair of pliers and put them in his leather lineman's kit. As he started out of the tent he looked back over his shoulder at the silent signalmen. "I'm going out to fix that line," he said. "Any of you people want to come along?"

Every man followed, and soon the telephone connection to the other end of the American circuit was restored.[21]

In another incident in the Buna fighting Colonel Auchincloss, and General Akin as well, received decorations for bravery in action. American infantrymen were hesitating at a footbridge over the Buna swamps, believing that the Japanese were concentrated on the other side. General Akin, who was at the front that morning in the Mac-Arthur tradition, took the lead, together with Colonel Auchincloss, and crossed over without drawing fire. The infantrymen thereupon followed. No opposition was encountered at this point, although enemy fire did develop some distance beyond.[22]

Frequently during the New Guinea operations in 1942 and 1943, Signal Corps men worked closely with their Australian allies. They had trained together in Australia and had worked out differences in their communications policies and procedures, publishing a combined SOP to the advantage of both. A large contribution by the Australian signalmen was the wire line that they helped to build between 12 May and 5 July 1943 over the Owen Stanley Range along the Kokoda trail between Port Moresby and Dobodura. The line employed C carrier techniques, which increased the number of telegraph channels transversing its wires. Despite unusually heavy maintenance problems, the line "was well justified," in the words of the signal officer of the Base Section of Port Moresby, Maj. Dayton W. Eddy. That remarkable Allied wire line was soon extended through the jungles far beyond Dobodura, reaching northwestward along the coast to Finschhafen. The line branched inland also, up the Markham Valley, furnishing New Guinea, Eddy later commented with marked understatement, a "communication service far beyond its peacetime facilities."[23]

---

[21] Eichelberger, *Our Jungle Road to Tokyo*, pp. 36f.

For the Signal Report of the Buna Operation, see Incl D, an. 4, in Report of the Commanding General, Buna Forces, 1 December 1942–25 January 1943, pp. 100–103. SigC Hist Sec file. See also Incl, Sig Report with R&W Action 1, Maj Erwin E. Sullo to Opns Br OCSigO, 20 Aug 43, sub: Extracts From Hist of Buna Campaign. SigC OT 676 SWPA Gen 3, 1943–45, Tab 13.

[22] (1) Ltr, Whitehead to Symington, 21 Sep 47. (2) Interv, SigC Hist Div with Akin, 12 Sep 60.

[23] (1) Lt. Col. Dayton W. Eddy, "Melbourne to Tokyo," *Signals*, I, No. 4 (March–April, 1947), 31ff., and "Manila and the Capitulation," *Signals*, I, No. 5 (May–June, 1947), 42. (2) Experiences of a Division Signal Officer in the Southwest Pacific, SigC Tech Info Ltrs 26 (Jan 44), pt. I, pp. 7–8, and 27 (Feb 44), pt. II, p. 6. (3) Wesley Frank Craven and James Lea Cate, eds., "The Army Air Forces in World War II," vol. IV, *The Pacific: Guadalcanal to Saipan, August 1942 to July 1944* (Chicago: University of Chicago Press, 1950), p. 156.

Credit to Signal Corps men (attached to the Fifth Air Force) who helped the Australians is given in a history written by members of the Australian Army, AIS, 1939–45, Corps of Signals, *Signals* (Sydney: Halstead Press, 1949), p. 126.

Meanwhile, operations up the coast from Buna, especially in the Huon Gulf at Lae, the outlet of the Markham River, called for more wire construction than was usual in SWPA installations. Lae had been captured in mid-September 1943. While building airstrips and driving back the Japanese along the Markham River valley, the Allied forces had to have dependable high-capacity wire communications all along the 140 miles to Dumpu, deep in the New Guinea interior. Spiral-four provided the first, quickest means, and quantities of the cable had recently arrived. Its copper conductors, effectively protected beneath the heavy wrappings and rubber envelope, could withstand the corroding damp of the jungle. Spiral-four made possible the initial laying of the needed wire links.

General Akin had ordered the line construction in September 1943. One of the units assigned the task was the 440th Signal Construction Battalion (Aviation), attached to the Fifth Air Force. To get quickly from Port Moresby on the south side of New Guinea to the Markham River valley on the north, the unit made the trip by air. Two platoons squeezed themselves and their equipment into C-47 cargo planes (several 2½-ton trucks had to be cut apart). Landing at Nadzab part way up the valley, they hurried their equipment off the airstrip and under cover to avoid enemy air raids. After welding the truck segments back together again, they got to work. With native aid, they cleared a right of way where no road existed, and along it laid the temporary spiral-four line to Gusap (some miles short of their goal at Dumpu), using a farm plow to trench the cable. With im-

provised equipment and despite tropical illnesses (at times half the unit was sick), these and other Signal Corps troops did the job quickly, sometimes working in spots along the valley so isolated that their rations had to be dropped by parachute, from "biscuit bombers." [24]

To carry the spiral-four cable on to its eventual terminus at Dumpu, 2d Lt. Myron S. Myers and eighteen men of Company C, 99th Signal Battalion, came up the valley in a jeep convoy to Nadzab. They laid the last link in the line, after a wait at Nadzab until the enemy was sufficiently cleared out of the Dumpu area about mid-October. They and other workers on the line encountered trouble with the tributaries flowing into the Markham River. Some were wide streams of shifting sand over which the line had to be suspended. The longest crossings, over the Erap and the Leron Rivers, each stretched more than a thousand feet from H-towers on either bank. On one occasion the Signal Corps men had to turn engineers and build a bridge, without training in the art, using structural parts that the engineers had stored in the vicinity. The Lae-Nadzab section of the line was completed by 10 October 1943. On 7 November service was extended as far as Gusap.

<hr/>

[24] (1) U.S. Army Signal Corps SWPA, Spiral-Four in the Southwest Pacific Area, 23 May 44 (rev to 14 Jun 44), pp. 2, 16, 18–19. (2) The Markham River Valley Pole Line, An Official History of Project 1201–A. SigC USASOS SWPA, 16 Feb 44 (rev 13 May 44). Both in SigC Hist Sec file. This account of Company C, 60th Signal Battalion, reappeared, edited and condensed, with the same title in Signal Corps Technical Information Letter 29 (April 1944), pages 11ff.

Service all the way to Dumpu began on 15 December.[25]

The spiral-four cable line between Lae and Dumpu was an expedient, till it could be replaced by a more permanent heavy-duty pole line. The cable needed to be replaced both to accommodate heavier traffic requirements and to avoid maintenance troubles, the worrisome concern of the 928th Signal Battalion. Lightning bolts of severe storms tore out the cable. Ants ate the insulation. Natives found spiral-four provided the best belts they ever had. On one occasion an American field artillery officer cut out a piece to wire his tent. The worst worry to those responsible for wire line maintenance were the engineers. Maj. Gen. Hugh J. Casey, Chief Engineer, SWPA, recalls that General Akin "was always calling me to complain about our fellows tearing up his lines." Bulldozers building roads or clearing ground for airfields or buildings gouged out the buried cable. Replying to a query as to what could be done to keep wire lines free from vehicular interference, one officer sardonically answered "Use a phantom circuit." [26]

The pole line was a substantial one and required the labor of a number of units, both American and Australian. One of the Signal Corps units was Company C of the 60th Signal Battalion. The company's 6 officers and 256 men had landed at Lae in a downpour on 9 October 1943. Coming off an LST, one water-soaked Signal Corps man sloshing through the mud asked, "Are they sure we've landed yet?" At once they started a survey for the pole line and began building it. By April 1944 it was completed, carrying 32 wires from Lae to Nadzab and 16 from there to Gusap.[27]

The Markham River valley pole line was planned to carry four crossarms from Lae to Nadzab and two from Nadzab to Gusap, over a total distance of about a hundred miles. Stout poles were required by the hundreds. That meant, as so often in the experience of wire line units, that a number of Signal Corps men had to turn lumbermen. Men of Company C cut over a thousand poles in the valley.[28]

At the turn of 1943–44 elements of the 99th Signal Battalion and the 440th Signal Construction Battalion, which had remained in the Port Moresby area, engaged in a notable logging venture. The two battalions cut several thousand poles at a site named Uberi, high in the Owen Stanley Range, where a species of tree grew that was especially suitable for poles since the wood resisted tropical rot and termites. Of the members of the 2d Platoon, Company C, 99th Signal Battalion, reinforced by 20 men of the headquarters company

[25] (1) SigC SWPA, Spiral-Four in the SWPA, pp. 18–20. (2) The Markham River Valley Pole Line, pp. 4, 6–9. (3) History, 99th Signal Battalion, Company C, p. 3. SGBN 99–0.1 (44808), 31 Aug 42–20 Aug 44.

A second task force detachment of the 99th Signal Battalion, five men led by Sgt. James L. Smith, went to Nadzab to construct antennas for the AACS, Fifth Air Force. Their comment on conditions at Nadzab was a single word, "Rough!" Hist, 99th Sig Bn, p. 5. SGBN 99–0.1 (44809), 20 Jun 43–Apr 44.

[26] (1) SigC SWPA, Spiral-Four in the SWPA, pp. 26–27 and 33. (2) Experiences of a Division Signal Officer in the Southwest Pacific, SigC Tech Info Ltr 27 (Feb 44), pt. II, p. 10.

The so-called phantom circuit is an actual one. See definition in Thompson, Harris, et al., The Test, p. 583.

[27] The Markham River Valley Pole Line, pp. 2, 4, 9.

[28] (1) Ibid., pp. 3–4. (2) Interv, SigC Hist Sec with Lt Col George A. Kurkjian, OCSigO (formerly PersO, 60th Sig Bn), 7 Jul 59.

to a total of 133, only one officer and one enlisted man had ever had any woodsman experience before.[29]

As Australian troops reduced enemy positions at Finschhafen, fifty miles along the coast beyond Lae on the tip of the Huon Peninsula, they needed a wire link back to Lae. Again it was a job for spiral-four. The 928th Signal Battalion (Separate) got the task. First, Company B of the 60th Signal Battalion built a pole line eastward a few miles through an Australian base and on across the Rusu River. From here Company C of the 928th took it. Since any effort to cut a swath directly through the dense coastal jungle seemed hopeless, the men out-flanked it along the sea. Using eight barges, the construction parties landed equipment at intervals. Then they wriggled the line through the jungle, hacking their way from one landing point to the next. They completed the line to within six miles of Finschafen in thirteen days, by 8 December. They snaked through a second cable required by the Services of Supply in twelve days.[30]

Sixth Army headquarters communications remained on Goodenough Island till General Krueger's next big overwater jump, to Finschhafen. On 24 December 1943 Colonel Reichelderfer sent an advance command post communications detail to Cape Cretin in the Finschhafen area. The remainder of the communicators and their equipment arrived on 2 February 1944. "From my point of view," Reichelderfer later commented, "this was our first failure in communications although I set up two centers in Finschhafen with what we considered about twice the personnel and equipment we would need. . . . "

Actually, the operations did not turn out as expected. There were misunderstandings, and, after a conference with General Krueger, Colonel Reichelderfer at once set about providing a much larger communications setup. "It brought out to me one lesson that a communications officer or signal officer must always remember," Reichelderfer lectured his Staff College audience. "He should never let his operations officer out of his sight—his G–3. I think [Brig.] General [Clyde D.] Eddleman [who happened to be in the audience] can tell you I lived, slept, and ate with him from then on." [31]

Some of the troubles at Finschhafen were subsequently recounted by a young Signal Corps officer, Maj. Roger E. Dumas, who arrived at the communications center there in the first hectic days. " . . . the code room was stacked up with traffic," he recalled. "We did not have enough equipment or men." Seven planeloads of equipment were hurried in; a detachment of 40 men and 2 officers arrived from Port Moresby. Within three days eight transmitters were installed. "I had about 14 hours sleep in seven days," said Dumas.

After this troubled start, the communications center settled down and ran smoothly. About 80 percent of the traffic, Dumas estimated, dealt with air support missions. Many of the messages were

[29] (1) U.S. Army Signal Corps, SWPA, Timber, An Official History of a Signal Corps Pole Cutting Project, 25 Mar 44 (rev 5 May 44). SigC Hist Sec file. See also Timber, SigC Tech Info Ltr 32 (Jul 44), 17ff. (2) Hist, 99th Sig Bn, 20 Jun 43–Apr 44, p. 5.
[30] SigC SWPA, Spiral-Four in the SWPA, p. 22.

[31] (1) Reichelderfer, "Sixth Army Communications," Signals, III, No. 2, p. 6. (2) AFSC Lecture C–15, Com SWPA, 29 May 47, Tab 24, pp. 3–4.

urgent air support requests, "which came in and had to be gotten over to Air Force headquarters at Nadzab or next morning there would be bombers out bombing our own troops, a most unpopular procedure." Dumas added: "There had been some experience of this at Buna and we were out to see it did not happen again. . . ."[32]

In late 1943 and early 1944, three separate but strategically related amphibious operations presented signal problems that Colonel Reichelderfer believed were unique to SWPA. They involved landings at Arawe on the south coast of New Britain, at Cape Gloucester on the western end of that same island north of New Guinea, and at Saidor 120 miles up the New Guinea coast from Finschhafen. The command post for all three actions was at Finschhafen, which was linked with SWPA headquarters 1,500 miles away in Australia by radio and message center teams stationed at Milne and Oro Bays. There was also a radio and message center team at the headquarters advance post in Port Moresby and a rear echelon of the Finschhafen command post itself still on Goodenough Island, whence the main command post had just moved.

The region and its peculiarities directly affected communications. The assignment of radio frequencies that had succeeded farther south failed badly in the scene of these actions. Colonel Reichelderfer found that "frequencies which worked perfectly over the comparable distances at 10 degrees south latitude both day and night, would not function at all at night and were erratic in the

daytime in the vicinity of 6 degrees south latitude. A great deal more experience and data on radio propagation," he reported to the Washington headquarters, "will be necessary before the solution will be fully satisfactory." Even Safehand Airplane Courier Service suffered from the climate. Intended to operate on a daily schedule, it could not. Often the couriers and their message pouches had to sit out hours and even days of violent weather. "As this is being written," Reichelderfer commented, "no airplane has arrived or taken off from the airstrip serving this headquarters for three days, because of torrential rain storms."[33]

Despite transmission troubles, radio was succeeding in carrying Army's messages. Ten days after the last of the three landings, Colonel Reichelderfer reported, "the Army is operating a total of 24 high-powered radio circuits. Twelve of these circuits are at the rear echelon and seven are at the Command Post. . . ." Small radios worked well, within the recognized limitations imposed by the jungle (the dense vegetation absorbing radio waves, reducing the range of the sets).[34] "The SCR-300 radio sets," he reported further, "have proved to be a godsend in amphibious operations for ship-shore communications and shore party communications." Highly successful, too, was the big truck-

[33] Ltr, Reichelderfer to CSigO, 14 Jan 44, through CG Sixth Army, sub: Army Com, Recent Opns. SCIA file 94 Reichelderfer Rpts. (Also in SigC OT 310 Work Load Study, 1945.)
[34] Ibid.
For radio transmission problems in SWPA, see Radio Communications–New Guinea, SigC Tech Info Ltr 39 (Feb 45), p. 17.
Navy radio likewise suffered from propagation troubles in the Pacific. See Morison, New Guinea and the Marianas, p. 255.

[32] Interv, SigC Hist Sec with Dumas, 24 Nov 44, SigC Hist Sec file.

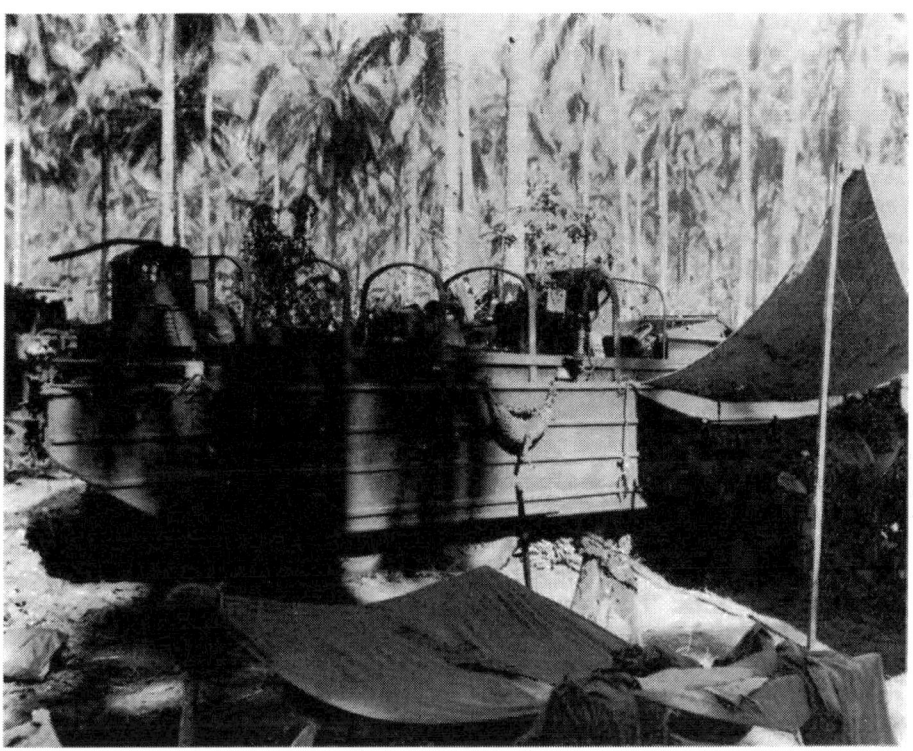

SCR-399 IN DUKW, NEW GUINEA

mounted SCR-399. Men of the 99th Signal Battalion took a 399 ashore in a Dukw at Aitape, New Guinea, on 22 April 1944. In one hour after the first landings they made radio contact with Sixth Army headquarters at Finschhafen 500 miles back. They broke that record on 17 May at Wakde, 250 miles farther along the jungle trail to Tokyo. There the signalmen landed and made radio contact with Finschhafen within 40 minutes after the first infantrymen had disembarked upon the beach.

Signal Corps men of the 99th also served as combat soldiers. At Aitape T/Sgt. David Armitage, Headquarters Company, located an enemy pillbox and killed one of five Japanese in it; the infantrymen took care of the others. On 27 May men of the battalion again closely supported combat operations during the invasion of Biak.[35]

---

[35] (1) Ltr, Reichelderfer to CSigO, 14 Jan 44, pp. 3-4. (2) Hist, 99th Sig Bn, pp. 4-6, SGBN 99-0.1 (8212), 10 Mar 42-Jan 45.

Regarding communications provided in the assault on Wakde in May 1944, the 99th Signal Battalion unit history states that "radio personnel operated 1 AT-20 transmitter, 2 BC-610 radios [the transmitter component of SCR-399], and 2 TW-12's. One SCR-193 worked PT boats on offshore patrol while 1 SCR-284 took care of the task force command net."

For highly successful use of these and other SCR sets in the Palau island assault, September-October 1944, see Palau Communications, SigC Tech Info Ltr 41 (Apr 45), p. 14.

New Guinea operations moved on to Hollandia, which would become a major port and base for future actions. The landing there began on 22 April 1944, pressed by the 24th and 41st Infantry Divisions of I Corps. The communications problem at Hollandia was characterized by its complexity and confusion, not least because of a diversity of headquarters. "We had the First Corps with us," the signal officer later commented, "the advance echelon of the GHQ, quite a large supply base of the SOS, the Naval command, and as a matter of fact, the whole Naval force before we got out; the Eighth Army came in and we conducted eleven operations by the time we got ready to leave there." [36]

The Hollandia landings were carried out on a large scale. The 58th Signal Battalion, serving I Corps, was the first signal battalion to function as an organic signal unit in SWPA combat. Personnel and equipment of this battalion aboard four LST's landed at Tanahmerah Bay within ninety minutes of H-hour on 22 April.[37] In setting up a message center ashore, the men laid wire to the 24th Division command post, put in BD-71 switchboards, and set up local radio circuits using SCR-300's. By the next

day contact was made with the Sixth Army headquarters at Finschhafen, using the 500-watt output of an Australian AT-20 transmitter. An SCR-299 simultaneously established a circuit with task forces at Aitape and Manus. But late that same day the battalion had to move from Tanahmerah to Humboldt Bay some 40 miles down the coast. Soon men of the 58th set up the I Corps communications center at Brinkman's Plantation. They also laid numerous landlines to the 41st Division command post, to various corps units, and to a distant radar warning station.[38]

The switchboards of two TC-12 telephone central office sets were in use by 26 April. Teletypewriter facilities also went in, only to be severely handicapped by troubles along the wire lines. According to the 58th Signal Battalion history, "the Engineers continued to keep the original two trunks (from the Corps message center to the 41st Division) torn out . . . so that the teletype was not able to function properly." Lt. Col. Charles H. Burch, I Corps signal officer, reported that three spiral-four cables to the Hollandia drome suddenly went dead on 22 May when a bulldozer knocked down a pole that stood well off the road, although there was plenty of room for the dozer to pass by on either side. Such examples of costly carelessness led the engineers to urge caution in their operations. "The Signal

---

[36] AFSC Lecture C-15, Com SWPA, 29 May 47, Tab 24, pp. 4-5.

By the time of subsequent moves, to Sarmi and Biak further along the New Guinea coast late in May, for example, communications ran more smoothly because, as Colonel Reichelderfer later reported, Signal Corps planned very carefully and took in communications that it knew would satisfy the every desire the commanding general might have.

[37] The communications cargo and Signal Corps personnel were so apportioned that "the loss of any one LST would not greatly affect signal operations." History, 58th Signal Battalion, SGBN 58-0.1 (7404), 22 Apr-6 Jun 44.

[38] Many Signal Corps radars were landed at Hollandia, not only aircraft warning (AW) sets for the AAF but also gun-laying (GL) radars. For example, 17 of the latter type had gone ashore by D plus 2: 13 SCR-268's and 4 SCR-584's. Memo, Capt Arthur J. Cornell, Asst AAO CAC, for SigO I Corps, 8 Jun 44, Sig Jnl, I Corps Staff, vol. 1, 29 May-12 Jun 44, RED VAULT.

PLOWING IN CABLE AT THE WATER'S EDGE, HOLLANDIA

Corps," the task force engineer informed his sector engineers, "is expending better than 50% of their time in reconstruction of lines damaged by Engineer units." [39]

By 30 April the operators of I Corps switchboards were maintaining 27 local

lines and 13 trunks in constant use, and linemen worked around the clock to maintain wire lines. By D plus 10 when the 41st Division moved to Hollekang, thirty men and an officer of the 442d Signal Construction Battalion (Aviation) were attached to the 58th for the task of laying ten miles of spiral-four from Brinkman's Plantation to the relocated division command post. Although the line ran through jungle swamps, well away from any engineer-beset roadway, it suffered from native depredations and even from the infantry who "thought it was Jap wire and opened the terminals." A second spiral-

[39] (1) Ltr, Lt Col Burch, I Corps SigO, to EngrO Hq U.S. Forces, APO 565, 22 May 44, Sig Jnl, Opn "G," vol. VI, 22–25 May 44. 98–TF7–31.1 (29228), 22–25 May 44. (2) Ltr, TF Engr to All Sector Engrs, sub: Damage to Sig Com, 17 May 44, Sig Jnl, Opn "G," vol. V, 17–21 May 44. 98–TF7–31.1 (29228), 17–21 May 44. See also Rpt, Plans and Opns Div, 16 Nov 44, p. 2, Daily Digest, Staff Divs OCSigO, 1 Jul–31 Dec 44, SigC Exec Of file.

four laid under water along the shore proved to be a more reliable circuit.[40]

Another large Signal Corps unit that landed early in the Hollandia action was the 16th Signal Operation Battalion. Among its accomplishments was the construction of one of the first large mobile communications assemblies in the Pacific, a type later known as an MCU (mobile communications unit). Six 10-ton vans were used: 2 for the message center (one housed the code room, the other the teletypewriter machines, files, supplies, and so on); 2 for radio operation; one for telephone operation; and the last for radio repair work. Landed from LST's they were set up in a coconut grove in shallow pits dug by bulldozers and sandbagged above ground nearly to the rooftop.[41] Within a month

of the first landings, communications operations in Hollandia became big business as traffic needs increased by leaps and bounds. "We had twenty-two long-range radio circuits out of Hollandia," Colonel Reichelderfer later remarked, "and handled as much as a hundred thousand code groups of traffic a day. To those of you who are not communicators," he told Staff College listeners in 1947, "that won't mean very much, but a hundred thousand code groups of traffic is really a lot of business." [42]

Following the first installations, much more wire, cable, and message center equipment was put into service—90 miles of spiral-four, for example, 240 miles of field wire, 25 miles of rubber cable, and 9 miles of pole line had been installed by the 58th Signal Battalion as of 6 June 1944.[43]

Messenger service received heavy use. Because of the distances and the difficult terrain, many messengers carried their rations and were out two or three days. Messenger service had to be amphibious, too. Waterways often provided the only practicable means of passage, especially

---

[40] (1) Hist, 58th Sig Bn. (2) Rpt, Hq USAFFE, 28 Jul 44, sub: Rpt 112, USAFFE Bd, Sig Communications During Hollandia Operations. SCIA file, unnumbered, Southwest Pac Theater folder 1, N through R. (3) Westward to Bataan, SigC Tech Info Ltr 36 (Nov 44), pp. 1ff. (4) Operations Report of the 442d Signal Construction Battalion. SGBN 442–0.3 (7856), 22 Apr–6 Jun 44.
The 58th Signal Battalion, besides employing Australian radio types, used a variety of SCR's ranging from the old SCR–177 to the newest SCR–300 and 399. The battalion history lists the following radio circuits in use by 1 May:
Two point-to-point circuits to Sixth Army with AT–20's, one of which was later changed to an SCR–399.
One linking the Task Force, the Admiralty Islands, and Aitape with an SCR–299 and later a TW–12.
Two command nets with an SCR–299 and an SCR–177, both later changed to TW–12's. This SCR–177 reached Sixth Army headquarters, about 600 miles back at Finschhafen, with a readability of three.
An aircraft warning net and a listening station on the Navy Dog circuit, both with SCR–193's.
Hist, 58th Sig Bn, pp. 4–5.
[41] Interv, SigC Hist Sec with 1st Lt Robert C. Osborne, 14 Nov 44. SigC Hist Sec file. Lieutenant Osborne had much to say about the unreadiness of the 16th Signal Operation Battalion: too little

technical training, especially in the operation of teletypewriters and cipher machines and in telephone and radio operation (but installation and maintenance men he admitted knew their business). The battalion had had too much combat training in his opinion. "We could march, drill with precision, fire a rifle, and creep and crawl like veterans, but we were not able to operate a Signal Center until we got our training overseas the hard way."
[42] AFSC Lecture C–15, Com SWPA, 29 May 47, Tab 24, p. 5.
[43] Hist, 58th Sig Bn, p. 14. As of 6 June, B Company had installed a TC–12 at Pancake and a BD–72 at the 58th Battalion headquarters. From these boards 100 EE–8 and 80 TP–6 telephones were operated. The company also operated and maintained a teletypewriter switchboard TC–3 and 5 EE–97 teletypewriters.

between scattered beaches separated ashore by impenetrable jungle. Messengers hitchhiked by boat from beach to beach until a Dukw became available (on 5 May at Pim jetty) specifically for message delivery. This was a happy innovation, supplementing by water the liaison aircraft service, which was also available to Signal Corps messengers.

The couriers provided a most valuable means of communication all along the coast of New Guinea. Since Signal Corps officers could not be spared, others were called upon to convey the pouches, usually officers who had returned to duty after injuries in other services. The loads for which they took full responsibility were not light, sometimes as many as twenty sacks of material, which they had to handle and move without help, shepherding them in whatever planes or boats, Army or Navy, they could board. And their trips were not joy rides. Often they averaged as many as eighteen hours a day in the air. An average of eight couriers served continually out of the Port Moresby message center. At Hollandia, the Safehand Courier Service was frequently performed by authorized enlisted men since officers were not always available.[44]

Messenger pigeons proved helpful, too, under the conditions imposed by tropical New Guinea. The tactical situation and the terrain were ideal for their use. The birds employed were Australian. They began to be used in mid-May after they had been settled at Joka, in the Hollandia area. By 25 May carrier pigeons were provided to patrols daily and often brought back important operational messages. As a result, infantrymen placed increasing confidence in this ancient mode of message sending.[45]

Granting the adverse effect of the tropical environment on all things electrical, Signal Corps men sometimes got unexpected service from their equipment. Thwarted ashore by the jungle impasse, Signal Corps men often laid wire in water, and found here, as in the South Pacific, that it worked, for a while at least—even the lightly insulated field wire W-110, which could resist fresh water penetration (and the resulting shorting of the circuit) for some time.[46] But spiral-four field cable, with its heavier insulation, proved quite effective even in salt water. Confronted with completely inadequate supplies of regular submarine cable, Signal Corps men time and again laid spiral-four

---

[44] Couriers sometimes broke under the strain, commented a Port Moresby message center officer, Capt. Earl G. Kline, who expressed regret that no recognition was ever granted them for their hard work. He added that the Pacific situation was such that a commanding officer did not have the time, could not literally find the paper, to sit down and write up commendations or recommendations for deserving officers and men. For these reasons—too much to do, too few to do it, primitive conditions, and sheer exhaustion—there was a paucity of medals and decorations given out in the Pacific war, he believed. Intervs, SigC Hist Sec with Lt Col Earl G. Kline, Deputy CO USASIA, 9 Jan and 19 Feb 59. See also Hist, 58th Sig Bn, pp. 5ff., and Westward to Bataan, SigC Info Ltr 36 (Nov 44), p. 5.

[45] (1) Hist, 58th Sig Bn, p. 12. (2) Westward to Bataan, SigC Info Ltr 36 (Nov 44), p. 7. (3) Ltr, 1st Lt. W. S. Curtis, SigC Hq 58th Sig Bn, to O/C, First Australian Pigeon Sec, 30 May 44, sub: Rpt on Employment of Pigeons in APO 565 Area, 24 Apr-30 May 44. Sig Jnl, I Corps, Staff, vol. I, 29 May-12 Jun 44, RED VAULT.

[46] The History, 58th Signal Battalion, mentions (page 8) a field wire line that was laid across Lake Sentani to the 163d Infantry regiment, and (page 13) describes W-110 as "very satisfactory through fresh water," adding that in salt water it would last "only three or four days on the average."

See also above, pp. 223-24.

lines in the sea. General Krueger, Sixth Army commander, praised the practice, especially mentioning the 99th Signal Battalion and the 273d Signal Construction Company at Biak and Noemfoor in the summer of 1944. General Krueger emphasized that the laying of rubber field cable in water had the valuable advantage of immunity from engineer and motor traffic on land.[47] It was also safe from enemy action.

Wire systems installed at Hollandia linked Army headquarters with I Corps and with the Cyclops airdrome. Part of the system lay under Lake Sentani—the lines in this case being spiral-four. Men of the 442d Signal Construction Battalion (Aviation) heavily taped and sealed the snap connectors against seepage and laid several cables, anchoring them at intervals with empty cable reels.[48] Spiral-

four, both in its normal employment as field cable and in its frequent emergency use as underwater cable, was as great a success in SWPA among wire equipment as was the short-range SCR-300 among radios.

The long-range radio of course remained the sole method of communication to distant points. Radio usage as usual raised problems of frequencies. There were not enough of them and interference often occurred between transmitters operating on similar frequencies. The Japanese would doubtless have liked to jam the American transmitters but did not, probably for fear of retaliation, for they, too, had to depend upon radio to communicate with their many island outposts.[49]

Enemy dependence upon radio provided an intelligence opportunity that General Akin never failed to exploit through the interception and analysis of Japanese radio messages. General MacArthur's G-2, Brig. Gen. Charles A. Willoughby, appreciated the presence on the SWPA staff of a chief signal officer who had had long experience and skill in this special, highly classified work. Willoughby attributed much of the Allied success in the New Guinea fighting, particularly in early 1944, to the knowledge thus obtained under General Akin's direction. The intelligence revealed enemy strongpoints to be avoided and weaknesses to be exploited. The information proved as decisive in the Pacific, General Willoughby believed, as it had in the World War I, when in 1914 German interception of Russian radio messages led to the over-

---

[47] Krueger, *From Down Under to Nippon*, pp. 103 and 112f. For similar line laying in the Central Pacific, see Crowl and Love, *Seizure of the Gilberts and Marshalls*, p. 329.

Even water traffic could cut wire lines, its seems, however. The 41st Signal Company at Biak reported that its Dukw laid a field wire line across the channel to Owi Island on 2 June 1944. Later that day, the report runs, "the line to Owi was cut by a Buffalo [LVT-A] running across it on the coral reef." Friendly shellfire, especially antiaircraft fragments, cut lines, too. Speaking of the latter, the 41st Signal Company report for 2 June 1944 added, "AA got 7 planes and 10 trunk lines." Hist Rcd, 41st Sig Co, p. 22.

[48] (1) SigC SWPA, Spiral-Four in SWPA, p. 24. (2) Opns Rpt, 442d Sig Const Bn, p. 3, 22 Apr–6 Jun 44.

Apparently, rubber cable could not long withstand the pressure of water at great depths (that is, rubber cable other than special submarine types). The 41st Signal Company replaced its field wire lines from Biak to Owi Island with cable. The channel extended nine hundred feet down. The men found that at this depth old cable (reconditioned for further use) shorted out at once, and new material lasted only a few weeks. The cable was described as 5-pair, rather than spiral-four. Hist Rcd, 41st Sig Co, p. 29.

[49] (1) Reichelderfer, "Sixth Army Communications," *Signals*, III, No. 2, p. 7. (2) Wagner, ACAN, 1941–45, pt. I, The Pacific, pp. 35f.

whelming victory at Tannenberg. Maj. Gen. Yoshiharu Tomochika, Chief of Staff, Japanese *35th Army*, later recognized that the American knack for landing at points weakly held by the Japanese was due to a superb intelligence system, a system that included both the relatively well-known guerrilla and coast watcher organizations, and the much less known intercept and analysis of radio signals.[50]

Radio Relay and Communications Ships to Hollandia

By June 1944 the Signal Corps men at Hollandia were doing a rushing business; message traffic would grow to a million groups a day by November.[51] The men were also hard at work on such communications innovations as radio relay (VHF antrac circuits) for mobile uses, the equipping of communications ships, and the outfitting of floating depots, installed in large seagoing barges—all for the amphibious operations looking toward the reconquest of the Philippines.

Radio relay equipment proved itself in the Pacific even more strikingly than in Europe during 1944. More often called VHF radio link in Pacific areas, in the form of AN/TRC-1, 3, and 4 (antrac for short), it was at first used in the South Pacific in several ways where quick, semipermanent circuits were needed, either in locations that forbade wire and cable, or for use until wire lines could be installed. "Temporary links" summarized the view

generally taken of antrac in 1943.[52] But antrac very quickly proved to be no temporary expedient. In its own right it was equal to wire lines, with some added advantages. And it was unsurpassed for maintaining communications with constantly moving tactical units, such as a division command post, or ships moving offshore or swinging at anchor. These amphibious uses were first perceived in the Pacific fighting.

The tactical possibilities of antrac began to appear at Hollandia, where rugged terrain and enemy infiltration, not to mention the ever-present menace of friendly engineer and artillery activity, made difficult the laying and maintenance of wire lines. At Humboldt Bay the 41st Signal Company had to depend entirely on radio the first two days after the 41st Division landed. And the radios which I Corps and its subordinate echelons employed were nothing elaborate—just ordinary radiotelegraph or radiotelephone types, recalled Colonel Burch, signal officer of I Corps in the Hollandia invasion. The 41st Signal Company used SCR-193, 284, and 300. I Corps headquarters at Humboldt Bay used an SCR-399 to reach the 24th Division during its first landing at Tanahmerah Bay.[53] Radio relay would have been ideal in such a situation to flash its circuits over jungle morasses where the installation and maintenance of wire lines would later use up weeks of painful and costly effort.

That more time was not actually expended on Hollandia pole lines resulted

[50] Willoughby and Chamberlain, *MacArthur 1941–51*, pp. 22, 180f., 240f.

[51] Wagner, ACAN, 1941–45, pt. I, The Pacific, pp. 43f.

[52] See above, p. 224.

[53] (1) Interv, SigC Hist Div with Burch, Chief P&P Div OCSigO, 13 Aug 57, SigC Hist Sec file. (2) Hist Rcd, 41st Sig Co. 341–SIG–0.1 (29070).

from the fortunate introduction of radio relay in New Guinea. Three teams, provided with this equipment and trained in its use, arrived in the theater for the limited mission of providing "remote keying facilities of the base radioteletype installation which was not scheduled for operation for some time after D plus 30." [54]

The limited mission at once yielded to a much larger assignment—the provision of primary communications circuits interconnecting segments of the great base now developing at Hollandia. The three teams arrived too late to take part in the tactical operations but their radio relay equipment speeded base operations, upon which the Philippine invasion awaited. Thereafter it figured very large indeed in all tactical operations as well.

The three teams (A, B, and C, elements of the 989th Signal Service Company) arrived at the SOS headquarters on D plus 30, that is, 22 May 1944. They were organized under the new cellular TOE 11–500. Each team of four officers and twenty-four men came equipped with two terminal sets of AN/TRC–3.[55] In less than a week the teams had set up and were operating

such high-capacity facilities as only many weeks of wire line installation would have provided. One section of Team C opened up at Hollekang, the other at the Cyclops Drome. Both sections of Team A installed their equipment at Leimok Hill, and both sections of Team B were at the communications center near Joka. Together they provided six voice and five teletypewriter circuits tying together I Corps, Base G, Sixth Army, and the 310th Bomber Group. Some of the circuits were actually carrying message traffic the day after the men began installing them. The remainder were in operation within two days. From then on the antracs gave excellent service. There were no major failures, and there was only occasional interference from radars on Leimok Hill and at the Cyclops Drome. It was inescapably evident to all, and to the commanding general in particular, that the equipment provided facilities that simply could not have been obtained so readily in any other way.[56]

Immediately, everyone wanted antracs. Higher headquarters got sets first, as the supply grew, and the specialists to operate them. The Fifth Air Force asked for antracs to use in the Biak area, and the Navy sought and obtained sets. Captain Crain, a Signal Corps officer who accompanied the new radios to instruct SWPA in their use, reported early in 1945 "each new operation brings to light additional uses of this highly flexible equipment . . . its possibilities are nowhere near exhausted." He listed four of the uses: (1) as a means of establishing immediate com-

---

[54] Rpt, Hq USAFFE, 22 Jul 44, sub: Rpt 119, USAFFE Bd SWPA, Employment of VHF Radio Link Equipment. SCIA file, unnumbered, Southwest Pac Theater folder 1, N through R. A condensed form of this report, Radio Relay at Hollandia, appeared in SigC Tech Infor Letter 36 (Nov 44), p. 8.

[55] Each set included 2 AN/TRC–1's, 2 carrier telephone terminals CF–1–A, and 4 carrier telegraph terminals CF–2–A, plus such accessories as power generators. The terminal equipment permitted C carrier operation of several telephone and telegraph (teletypewriter) circuits to be placed on the antrac radio beams, as on pole lines or spiral-four wire systems. See also CSigO, Annual Rpt, FY 44, pp. 94–95.

[56] Rpt, Hq USAFFE, 22 Jul 44, sub: Rpt 119. See also Rpt, P&O Div, 14 Sep 44, Daily Digest, Staff Divs OCSigO, 1 Jul–31 Dec 44.

munications with fast-moving tactical units, the equipment being mobile mounted; (2) as a means of communication along an axis where a pole line or submarine cable was planned but delayed; (3) as a means of handling ship-to-shore communications; and finally (4) as a link connecting beachheads to bases, reaching all tactical units and naval elements as well as furnishing Navy, press, and Army circuits. Radio relay blossomed into full flower in the Pacific. Island fighting placed a premium upon radio communications and so provided a rich soil in which antrac equipment quickly flourished. Amphibious warfare needs, involving myriads of ships offshore and many units and bases ashore, required the rapid, dependable, high-capacity radio interconnections, just what radio relay could provide. As a result, "a great deal of interest," Crain reported, "has now been aroused among U.S. Navy officials and Port Command officials of the U.S. Army." [57]

"Up to the month of August 1944," reported Crain, "a total of three 100-mile VHF Radio Link Systems and twenty-six VHF Radio Link Terminals were in operation." As he wrote his report in early 1945, he added, "At this writing in the Hollandia area alone there are a total of fourteen terminals supplying approximately sixty teletype trunks and twenty-six [telephone] trunks for both Army and Navy over an area of some three hundred square miles." [58]

Inevitably the flexible high-capacity VHF antracs replaced the single circuit radio sets previously used for ship-to-shore communications in amphibious work. Antrac gave ships the high traffic capacity of pole lines carrying the multiple circuits that carrier techniques make possible—without poles, wires, or the fixed position that wire equipment compels. Only a year or so earlier, naval ships had adopted for amphibious operations the Signal Corps FM radios of the 500 and 600 series, which offered superior facilities, but only single circuits. The Signal Corps FM radio relay, using carrier techniques that provided not one circuit but many (telephone and/or telegraph or teletypewriter), found immediate acceptance aboard Navy (and Army) communications ships. [59]

No overseas arena in World War II

---

[57] Capt Forrest E. Crain, Rpt to NEID, On the Use of VHF Radio Link and Associated Equipment in the South Pacific and Southwest Pacific Areas, AN/TRC-1, 3, and 4 (hereafter cited as Crain Rpt), pp. 1–4. SCIA file, unnumbered, Southwest Pac Theater folder 1. The report bears no date. Crain later identified the document as the last of a series of monthly reports he had sent from the Pacific, and the date of this last report he specified as 4 March 1945. Comments penciled on an MRS, Thompson, Chief SigC Hist Div, to Mr. Crain, OCSigO, 30 Jul 57, attached to the report cited above.
The NEID was activated in the Signal Corps Ground Signal Agency in September 1944. SigC Tech Infor Ltr 43 (Jun 45), p. 23.

[58] Crain Rpt, p. 4.
[59] The Signal Corps agreed to assign to the Navy in the month of December 1944 alone the following:

Radio set AN/TRC-1	22
Radio terminal set AN/TRC-3	28
Radio relay set AN/TRC-4	34
Amplifier equipment AN/TRA-1	6

Rpt, P&O Div, 24 Nov 44, Daily Digest, Staff Divs OCSigO, 1 Jul–31 Dec 44. SigC Exec Of file.
In mid-1945 at Manila the 16th Signal Battalion introduced a notable improvement in antrac use between ship and shore when it designed a hybrid coil that permitted the 2-wire telephone circuits of Navy ship systems to operate directly into Army's 4-wire (carrier type) antrac radio sets. Draft MS Comment, Waite, Jul 59.

required such varied movement as the far Pacific demanded. And General MacArthur could not have had on his staff a more mobile-minded signal officer than General Akin. Akin had experimented with truck- and trailer-mounted switchboards, teletypewriters, and message centers during Third Army maneuvers in Louisiana in 1941. The next year he exercised his mobile bent of mind in Australia, where he fitted a railroad car with communications equipment, including a 400-watt transmitter, to provide service wherever General MacArthur might travel within that continent.[60]

Before the end of 1942, as operations against the enemy began in the island and ocean areas northward from Australia, amphibious communications became necessary, and General Akin outfitted a Signal Corps fleet—a flotilla of small vessels equipped with radio. At first they served in a small way as relay ships from forward areas to headquarters in the rear. Their function soon expanded, however, till they took aboard the forward command post communications facilities. The little aggregation became the Army's CP fleet.[61]

The small communications ships proved so useful in amphibious actions that Army elements in SWPA operations continually competed to obtain their services. Army commanders preferred them to Navy communications ships, or AGC's. For one thing, Navy AGC's were hard to obtain for Army operations. For another, Navy AGC's tended to stay too far offshore, and they tended to depart from the vicinity of land combat as soon as possible. The naval commander of a large AGC was always mindful of enemy suicide boats and planes and he would generally, come darkness, move his ship out several miles from the beach, too far to provide the close communications support that Army elements ashore very much needed.[62]

The Navy had AGC's in the Central Pacific by the turn of 1943–44, but not in the Southwest Pacific Area at first, where General Akin turned to Australian sources for his CP fleet (until the Navy supplied in 1944 three specially equipped craft, known as PCE's (patrol vessels, escorts), for Army use). The first Australian vessels acquired by the SWPA chief signal officer were the *Harold*, an auxiliary ketch, and the *Argosy Lemal*, an auxiliary schooner. In their cramped spaces (neither ship exceeded 100 feet in length), General Akin installed Australian AWA radio sets built by Amalgamated Wireless of Australia. The vessels served at Port Moresby, at Woodlark, and in the Lae-Salamaua area through mid-1943. On 12 December 1943 the *Geoanna*, a 100-foot schooner, joined CP fleet.[63]

---

[60] (1) U.S. Army SigC SWPA, Seaborne CP's, An Official History of the SWPA SigC Command Post Fleet, 1 Jan 45 (rev 14 Jan 45), p. 1, 98–GHQ1–31 (12054), 14 Jan 45 (hereafter cited as Seaborne CP's). A condensed version of this history was printed under the title Signal Corps CP Fleet, in SigC Tech Infor Ltr 44 (Jul 45), 1ff. (2) Eddy, "Melbourne to Tokyo," *Signals*, I, No. 4, p. 33. (3) "Command Post Fleet," *Signals*, II No. 1 (September–October, 1947), p. 35.

[61] (1) Crain Rpt, pp. 4f. (2) Seaborne CP's, p. 2.

[62] Interv, SigC Hist Div with Pochyla, 15 and 18 Feb 60.

[63] (1) Seaborne CP's, pp. 2–3. (2) SigC CP Fleet, SigC Tech Info Ltr 44 (Jul 45), p. 1. See also above, p. 226, and below, pp. 275ff. re AGC's and PCE's. Still another SWPA CP vessel, the *Valador*, was equipped as a radio repair ship "to supply floating maintenance wherever most required." Seaborne CP's, p. 4.

Experience with these specialized vessels taught General Akin and his officers a good deal about the operation and possibilities of Army communications ships. Their operation at first presented problems, not least of which was divided control. The Navy crews, in some cases Australian civilians under Navy command, took their orders from naval authorities. Yet the entire purpose of such a ship was to serve Army needs.

A graphic account of some of the vicissitudes of the *Argosy Lemal* and its mixed crew came from S/Sgt. Arthur B. Dunning, Headquarters Company, 60th Signal Battalion. He and six other enlisted men of that unit were ordered aboard her on 9 September 1943, at Oro Bay, New Guinea, to handle Army radio traffic.[64] The commander of the ship reported to naval authorities, not to General Akin. After six months' service along the New Guinea coast, the skipper was removed for incompetence. His replacement was no better. Among other things, he obeyed to the letter Navy's order forbidding the use of unshielded radio receivers at sea. Since the Signal Corps receivers aboard the ship were unshielded and thus liable to radiate sufficiently to alert nearby enemy listeners, the men were forbidden to switch them

on in order to hear orders from Army headquarters ashore. As a consequence, during a trip in the spring of 1944 from Milne Bay to Cairns, Australia (on naval orders), the crew failed to hear frantic Signal Corps radio messages to the *Argosy Lemal* ordering her to return at once to Milne Bay to make ready for a forthcoming Army operation. On the way to Australia the skipper, after a series of mishaps attributable to bad navigation, grounded the *Argosy* hard on a reef. Most of the crew already desperately ill of tropical diseases, now had additional worries. The radio antennas were swept away along with the ship's rigging, and help could not be requested until the Signal Corps men strung up a makeshift antenna. Weak with fevers and in a ship on the verge of foundering, they pumped away at the water rising in the hold and wondered why rescue was delayed till they learned that the position of the ship that the skipper had given them to broadcast was ninety miles off their true position. As they threw excess cargo overboard, "some of the guys," recorded Dunning, "were all for jettisoning our skipper for getting us into all of this mess." Much later, too late for the need the Signal Corps had for the ship, the *Argosy Lemal* was rescued and towed to Port Moresby for repairs to the vessel and medical attention to the crew, many of whom were by then, according to Dunning, "psychoneurotic."[65]

[64] Besides Dunning, a radio operator, there were T/4 Jack Stanton, also a radio operator; T/Sgt. Harold Wooten, the senior noncommissioned officer; T/4 Finch and T/5 Burtness, maintenance men; and T/5 Ingram and Pfc. Devlin, code and message center clerks. Dunning described the *Argosy* as a 3-mast sailing vessel with a 110-horsepower auxiliary diesel engine. "She was the sixth vessel," he wrote, "to be taken over by the Small Ships Section of the U.S. Army . . . her primary purpose was handling [radio] traffic between forward areas and the main USASOS headquarters." Statement by Sergeant Dunning, contained in the History of the 60th Signal Battalion, SGBN 60-0.2 (27932), Jan–Dec 44. A copy is also in the Interv folder, SigC Hist Sec file.

[65] Dunning's "statement," a 6-page narrative account, vividly describes these and related incidents touching the *Argosy Lemal* (whose romantic name contrasted greatly with the battered little schooner) —describing them from the restricted viewpoint of one of the enlisted sufferers aboard her. It was the opinion of both General Akin and Captain McKinney that the navigating crewmen were civilians. Intervs, SigC Hist Div with Akin, 12 Sep 60, and with McKinney, 8 Sep 60.

Despite such snafus (Sergeant Dunning repeatedly used the term *fubar*),[66] the concept of a fleet of Army communications ships to serve as the signal section of a floating command post in amphibious operations proved sound. The CP fleet was needed, as Lt. Col. Dayton W. Eddy viewed the matter after the war, "to provide communications during assault phases," to continue providing them "during the period while fixed facilities were installed ashore," and, finally, "to function as standby or emergency facilities in case of difficulty ashore." The *Harold* was employed in the latter capacity by the Sixth Army in New Guinea waters. This was the chief use of the vessels after an assault had been completed and after fixed communications stations had been built ashore. Some Signal Corps officers felt that too much effort came to be lavished upon the equipping of later additions to the CP fleet.[67] But none could deny that these ships served the Army well. Their temporary use to insure communications so vital to over-all success, during the crucial hours and difficult first days of an amphibious action, entirely justified all the effort that went into them.

General Akin himself had no doubt of the value and necessity of Army communications ships in SWPA combat. On 21 March 1944, he set up in GHQ SWPA Signal Section a separate Sea-

borne Communications Branch to plan for extensive communications afloat and to provide a more adequate CP fleet. The first task was to obtain ships more suitable than the *Harold* or the *Argosy*.[68] Such a ship was the freighter-passenger, FP–47, acquired by Signal Corps in March 1944, at Sydney. The Army had built her in the United States in 1942, a sturdy, wooden, diesel-driven vessel only 114 feet long, but broad, of 370 tons, intended for use in the Aleutians. Instead she had sailed to Australia as a tug. The Signal Corps fitted her with Australian transmitters and receivers, also with an SCR–300 walkie-talkie, two SCR–808's, and an SCR–608, plus power equipment, antennas, and, finally, quarters for the Signal Corps operators. The Australian sets were intended for long-range CW signals operating in the high frequencies; the SCR's were short-range VHF FM radios for use in the fleet net and for ship-to-shore channels. Armed with antiaircraft weapons and machine guns (served by 12 enlisted men of the Army ship and gun crews), navigated by a crew of 6 Army Transport Service officers and the 12 men already mentioned, the FP–47 was ready for service in June. Her Signal Corps complement consisted of one officer and 12 men.

The facilities of FP–47 were needed immediately at Hollandia to supplement the heavily loaded signal nets that could hardly carry the message burden imposed by the invasion and the subsequent build-up there of a great base. Arriving

---

[66] Meaning, in one polite version, "fouled up beyond all repair."

[67] (1) Eddy, "Manila and the Capitulation," *Signals*, I, No. 5, pp. 42f. (2) Reichelderfer, "Sixth Army Communications," *Signals*, III, No. 2, pp. 7ff. (3) Intervs, SigC Hist Sec with Kline, 9 Jan and 19 Feb 59. (4) Intervs, SigC Hist Sec with Col Walter B. Bess, OCSigO (Com Chief Sig Sec Sixth Army in World War II), 16 and 20 Jan 59.

[68] (1) Seaborne CP's, pp. 2–3. (2) SigC CP Fleet, SigC Tech Info Ltr 44, pp. 1ff.

on 25 June, she anchored offshore and ran cables to the message centers on land. Her powerful transmitters opened new channels to SWPA headquarters in Brisbane and to the advance headquarters still at Port Moresby. At Hollandia, and at Biak, to which the FP–47 moved early in September, this one ship handled an average of 7,000 to 11,000 code groups a day.[69]

Before the Philippine invasion, the CP boats acquired shipboard antrac. Four Army communications ships, PCE–848, 849, and 850, and the *Apache* (primarily for use by news reporters), arrived at Hollandia on 2 October 1944, as the Southwest Pacific headquarters readied for the invasion of Leyte. They were "equipped with sufficient Signal Corps personnel and equipment to handle circuits for transmission, reception, and intercept as would normally be required in any established base," commented Crain. He added that the original plans expected the CP boat echelon to use single circuit SCR–284's or 188's for traffic to the beaches. For such use too many of the SCR's would be needed, and the VHF radio links aboard some ships in Humboldt Bay had already shown they could work well with shore stations. Consequently, within a week, by 11 October, all four CP ships received VHF radio relay sets. Their antennas went up as vertical single dipoles radiating in all directions so as to eliminate the fading that horizontal dipoles would cause as the ships swung at anchor. Tests proved that the arrangement would provide solid highly reliable circuits, each

set able to handle, by carrier techniques, several times the quantity of traffic of a single SCR of the 284 variety.[70] From then on, VHF was standard equipment on communications ships for shore circuits.

Signal Supply From Australia to Jungle Beaches

Such signal supplies as arrived in SWPA from the United States were meager in the early days of World War II. Australia had to provided very many signal items, some of them manufactured expressly for U.S. troops. Australian factories turned out much of the hardware for the pole lines that Signal Corps troops helped to build through northern Australia in 1942 and 1943, and in New Guinea, too. At Port Moresby Company C, 99th Signal Battalion, in 1943 built many miles of pole line, using Australian lead cable and finding Australian 1-piece steel poles "very satisfactory for cable runs and light wire construction where height is of no importance." [71] The Australians manufactured several thousand radio sets used by American troops, notably the 50-watt TW–12 and the much larger AT–20. The TW–12, patterned on a Signal Corps design, was built by the Amalgamated Wireless of Australia as a substitute for the SCR–188. Standard Telephones and Cable in Sydney manufactured the AT–20,

[69] (1) Seaborne CP's pp. 4–6. (2) "Command Post Fleet," *Signals*, II, No. 1, pp. 35ff.

[70] Crain Rpt, pp. 6–10.

[71] Hist, 99th Sig Bn, Co C, p. 2, 31 Aug 42–30 Apr 44. Colonel Reichelderfer commented on the "excellent" collapsible metal poles that the Australians provided his Sixth Army linemen. Reichelderfer, "Sixth Army Communications," *Signals*, III, No. 2, p. 7.

adapted by the Signal Corps from an RAAF 500-watt transmitter.[72]

Signal supply in the SWPA, as anywhere else, needed good planning and adequate training of the personnel. There was no time for either. "The Jap wasn't waiting for the trained men to arrive," said Colonel Toft, commanding officer of the 202d Signal Depot Company, "he was on the offensive in 1942. The problems were upon us and we had to use the people available."[73] Later, when some problems were solved, enough men trained, and depot buildings constructed, the front had moved hundreds of miles away up the island chain, leaving the depot far behind, a remote rear-area establishment. The problems reappeared in each new location at the scene of combat.

On 15 May 1943 Col. Hugh Mitchell arrived in Australia to become signal officer at Headquarters, USASOS SWPA, in the Grace Building on York Street in Sydney. On the 19th he took over from Col. Calvert H. Arnold, who had been the signal officer there since mid-1942.[74] As the fighting moved northwestward, so did the headquarters, still within Australia however. On 25 August 1943 the Signal Section (33 officers, 4 war-

rants, 55 enlisted men, and 23 civilians) moved to Brisbane. Until then the chief function of the Signal Section, USASOS SWPA, had been to organize the signal portion of the bases of supply that leap-frogged up New Guinea. After the move to Brisbane, the section acquired planning and technical supply activities as well. To meet the needs of SWPA growth, Colonel Mitchell expanded his Signal Section's four main divisions: administration, personnel, operations, and supply.[75]

Nowhere else did the signal depots serving overseas experience so many moves and vicissitudes as in SWPA over the thousands of miles of sea and jungle terrain that stretch from down under to Tokyo. Bad as were these unavoidable difficulties, there were exasperating moves of depot locations made within a single area. Such was the experience of the 202d Signal Depot Company at Milne Bay. Originally set up at Gilli Gilli, the depot was suddenly moved to Wagga Wagga, six miles away on the opposite shore of the bay. Then it moved back across the bay to a location about five miles east of the first site. The 202d overcame some of its headaches, in particular the one of packing and unpacking small bin stock items on each move, by using a shipping box with removable shelves and tops. The shelves could be inserted to form bin shelves when the boxes, without tops, were stacked after a move, and the contents were thus made available on the spot in the manner of

[72] (1) Eddy, "Melbourne to Tokyo," *Signals*, I, No. 4, pp. 34ff. (2) Intervs, SigC Hist Sec with Capt James A. Ferguson, 11 Oct 44, and with Maj Roger E. Dumas, 24 Nov 44. (3) Intervs, SigC Hist Sec with Frank W. Hogan, P&D Div OCSigO, 1 and 5 Jul 49 and 31 Mar 58. SigC Hist Sec file.

Both of these Australian-made radios were high-frequency, long-range sets, and heavy. The TW-12 weighed nearly 700 pounds packed, the AT-20, 8,000 pounds. Incl 1 to Rpt, Hq USAFFE, 28 Jul 44, sub: Rpt 112.

[73] Lt Col Douglas O. Toft, *Some Signal Corps Supply Problems in the Southwest Pacific Area During World War II* (1950), Sig Sch Monograph, p. iv. The Sig Sch Libr, Ft. Monmouth.

[74] Thompson, Harris, *et al*, *The Test*, pp. 299ff.

[75] (1) Hist Sec USASOS, Signal Corps U.S. Army Services of Supply, Jul 42–Dec 43, pp. 90ff. OCMH files. See also Hist Sec USASOS, Red Vault, Jul 42–Oct 44. (2) Sig Sup in the Pac Theater, SigC Tech Info Ltr 28 (Mar 44), 7ff.

LW Radar Mounted on LST, New Guinea

an orderly supply depot.[76] The 202d Signal Depot Company, along with other supply signal units of SWPA, operated under USASOS SWPA and its lettered bases that leapfrogged up the New Guinea coast, from Milne Bay, Sub-Base A, and Oro Bay, Sub-Base B, begun in April and December 1942, respectively. Later came the bases of Goodenough Island (C, in April 1943), Finschhafen (F, November 1943), Hollandia (G, June 1944), and so on.[77]

The Army's bases in New Guinea, Colonel Toft wrote, usually stretched along the beach for miles, since roads could best be built near the shore, and water transport was essential. In only a few locations did bases extend inland, as at Lae, where the Markham River valley provided flat plains into which roads were built. Each base was months in the building. Because engineers were too few, the depot personnel had to put up their own prefabricated warehouses, with a few engineer supervisors. Al-

[76] Toft, Some SigC Sup Problems in SWPA, pp. 16f.

[77] On these letter bases in general see: (1) Stauffer, The Quartermaster Corps: Operations in the War Against Japan, pp. 87ff; and (2) Hugh J.

Casey, U.S. Army Forces in the Pacific, Report of Operations, OCE, "Engineers of the Southwest Pacific, 1941–45," vol I, Engineers in Theater Operations (Washington, 1947), p. 120.

though the depot men could not properly care for their depot and supply duties, that was just when they had to perform such duties best, for it was just then that they were directly supporting the combat units. Later, Colonel Toft wrote:

By the time the base roads were in good condition, the telephone system operating satisfactorily, and a few warehouses standing, with some of the vital signal equipment under cover, the war had moved on four or five hundred miles. For example, by the time the Finschhafen Base was in fair operating condition, the war had moved on to Hollandia, where a new base was being madly constructed in the thick of the jungles and mountains.[78]

Supplies in the bases so rapidly left behind tended to pile up after the material was no longer of use in the immediate area but could not be readily moved to advance areas where it was needed. The only interbase transportation in the Pacific scene of sea and islands was necessarily either by water or by air, and ships could not be easily spared from the runs between the United States and the currently important bases in the combat areas. As a result, valuable equipment often sat unused at rear-island bases, however badly needed elsewhere. "My people are having a devil of a time with communications as they never roll the theater up from the rear," commented General Ingles after visiting Pacific areas in 1944. "They still have about the same installations in Australia," he explained, "as they had in the original build-up, though the headquarters in Brisbane is now about 3,000 miles in back of the front with dozens of installa-

tions in between." [79] "At one time," according to Colonel Toft, "there was a back-log of approximately 10,000 tons of signal supplies and equipment at Finschhafen waiting for transportation to Manila. It was easier," he explained, "although not cheaper to the taxpayer, to get supplies and equipment from the States than to move similar material at the rear bases forward." [80]

Signal supply at Hollandia experienced the usual vicissitudes of a large amphibious operation. On D plus 9 a signal dump set up for business at White Beach II. Signal equipment unloaded at random along the shore had to be located and put under cover, and, since there was little of it, issue was made only on emergency demands. Meanwhile a permanent base signal depot took form near Brinkman's Plantation. With difficulty because of inadequate transportation facilities, the dump supplies went to Brinkman's, and the dump at White Beach was finally closed down on D plus 30. As the airfields opened up, considerable signal supply came in by plane. Again, as happened at the beaches earlier, these supplies were rather haphazardly tossed out and lay around the airfields uncared for until men could be assigned to receive and move them to the signal depot.[81]

---

[79] Ltr, General Ingles, CSigO, to Lt Gen George H. Brett, Hq Panama Canal Dept, 15 Jun 44, SigC 676 Panama, 1944. SigC Hist Sec file.

[80] Toft, Some SigC Sup Problems in SWPA, p. 12.

A partial solution to this problem in SWPA was not to put some of the supplies ashore at all, but to stock them aboard a floating signal depot—a ship or barge serving this single purpose—that could move with the advance as needed. See below, p. 284.

[81] (1) Rpt, Hq USAFFE, 28 Jul 44, sub: Rpt 112, p. 11. (2) Westward to Bataan, SigC Tech Info Ltr 36 (Nov 44), p. 7.

---

[78] Toft, Some SigC Sup Problems in SWPA, pp. 11f.

There were sharp differences between the views and objectives of signal supply officers at a base and the signal officers at the front. The former, reported Colonel Strasburger, signal officer of the XIV Corps at Bougainville (SOPAC) in mid-1943, sought for his base large quantities of supplies, the need for which was not so much immediate as anticipatory. The signal officer of a tactical unit, however, wanted only a minimum of general supplies but a maximum of whatever was needed to meet immediate requirements.[82]

Another aspect of supply was that, whereas signal supply often seemed reasonably good at theater headquarters and in large rear-area bases (it seemed good to Ingles, who reported early in 1944 that "so far as the Pacific area is concerned . . . there is no critical shortage of signal equipment"), it seldom sufficed to please the using troops.[83] "For the first time in our lives we had all the equipment we needed," said Colonel Reichelderfer speaking of the Luzon landing in January 1945.[84] He had not been able to make such a remark earlier; his combat troops had chronically suffered from shortages through the New Guinea and Leyte fighting of 1943 and 1944. However much of the equipment may have been stored in the rear base depots, not enough of it got into the hands of the troops forward. Such was the complaint of the 162d Infantry regiment after its operations in the Salamaua area of New Guinea late in the summer of 1943. "At no time," the regiment complained, "was a sufficient supply of all signal items on hand." The thing the men wanted was an ideal that could never be realized—"a completely equipped signal dump and repair section . . . in operation as near to the action as deemed feasible." [85]

---

[82] Ltr, Strasburger, SigO, to CSigO, 9 Jan 44, sub: Sig Rpt, pt. II, p. 1. XIV Corps Sig Rpt. SigC Hist Sec file.

The tactical signal officer, Colonel Strasburger believed, should study his unit's table of basic allowances and eliminate items not needed at all (they did not have to be ordered simply because they were listed). Instead, he should use his time to get items that were not on the table of basic allowances but that he knew would nonetheless be badly needed.

[83] Press Meets the CSigO, SigC Tech Info Ltr 29 (Apr 44), p. 5.

[84] AFSC Lecture C-15, Com SWPA, 29 May 47, Tab 24, p. 15.

[85] Incl, Report of Operations of the 162d Infantry, p 4, with ASF MRS, Walter, Intel Br, to Com Coordinating Br OCSigO, 30 Jun 44, sub: Rpt of Opns of 162d Inf, 29 Jun–12 Sep 43 (extracts). SCIA file, unnumbered, Southwest Pac Theater folder 1, N through R, Tab 2.

CHAPTER IX

Communications in the Pacific
to V–J Day

Invasion of the Philippines became possible by the autumn of 1944. The first desperate fighting on Guadalcanal and in the Port Moresby–Buna area of New Guinea had given the impression that rolling back the enemy from a string of island strongholds might be equally difficult all along the advance. But the situation for the Japanese deteriorated. By late 1944 the Allies ruled the sea and the air. An arduous advance, followed by the slow building of bases, island by island—for the Signal Corps, the repeated installation of radio and of the extensive wire nets that every base required—could be accelerated, bypassing some enemy-held islands. The Allies could thus attack the larger objectives sooner than originally planned—first the Philippines, then the Ryukyus, then the islands of Japan itself.

The decision to hasten the invasion of the Philippines was made in September 1944 at a Quebec conference of the Combined Chiefs of Staff during a dramatic exchange of radioteletype messages with General MacArthur's headquarters in the Southwest Pacific. The ease and speed of this exchange underlined the efficient and facile world-wide communications system that the Signal Corps was building to serve the global needs of the war.[1] And the logistic capability of the bases and their supply lines down under the equator pointed up equally well the growing production, transportation, and construction strength of the Allies. By early 1944 all manner of manpower and materials were being concentrated in the Southwest Pacific. At midyear, impressive numbers of Signal Corps units began arriving. Meanwhile, other units already there were being augmented and still others were being activated locally.[2] Radio communications alone carried the orders and instructions, the plans and the

---

[1] (1) H. Hamlin Cannon, *Leyte: The Return to the Philippines,* UNITED STATES ARMY IN WORLD WAR II (Washington, 1954), pp. 9, 23. (2) Samuel Eliot Morison, "History of United States Naval Operations in World War II," vol. XII, *Leyte* (Boston: Little, Brown and Company, 1958), pp. 14ff. See also below, p. 590.

[2] (1) CSigO, Annual Rpt, FY 45, pp. 118ff. (2) Memo for Qtrly Rpt (3d Quarter) SWPA, unsigned, 6 Oct 44. SigC OT 310 Work Load Study, 1945. See also Sig Activities SWPA, Apr and May, same file.

There had been but 51 signal units in SWPA at the beginning of 1944 (18 serving the Army Ground Forces and Army Service Forces, 33 serving the Army Air Forces). There would be nearly 250 Signal Corps units in the area by March 1945. (1) Memo for CSigO, unsigned, 4 Jan 44, sub: Rpt on Sig Activities in the Central, South, and Southwest Pac Areas, p. 12. SigC OT 676 SWPA Gen 2, 1944, Tab 25. (2) Qtrly Rpt, Theaters Br, 1 Jan 45–31 Mar 45 (Pac Opns Sec–SWPA Subsec), p. 2. SigC OT 310 Work Load Study, 1945.

reports, for all interisland and interbase activity. And the necessarily close co-ordination of all elements—ground, sea, and air—either required the closest sort of co-operation of the communications services, as in SWPA, or developed a growing degree of joint operation, as in SOPAC, CENPAC, and in the Okinawa campaign.[3]

Before examining the large-scale communications of Army forces invading Leyte and Luzon, the Signal Corps account must take note of its unorthodox underground signals, which had been operating in and from the Philippines for two years and which would continue to operate during the invasion itself, contributing much to the successful conquest of the islands.

Underground in the Philippine Islands

Army communications did not entirely cease in the Philippines after the fall of Corregidor in May 1942. Remnants of the American and Filipino forces scattered, maintaining themselves as best they could. Their contact with the Allies depended on hidden radio sets and on furtive landings by American submarines. A network of small, long-range radio stations operated throughout the enemy occupation. The concealed and daring operators transmitted valuable military intelligence. They sent reports on Japanese shipping, and in many ways prepared the way for the eventual liberation. Thanks to these sources, General MacArthur obtained extensive in-formation concerning enemy troops and defenses in the islands, both before and during the fighting to regain the area. As coast watchers, these men sent reports of fleet movements and merchant shipping. The data they provided at the time of the Philippine naval actions were invaluable. And although few of the communicators were Signal Corps men, the equipment they used in the Philippines and the operation of their radio nets all deeply involved the U.S. Army Signal Corps.[4]

The collapse of American resistance in May 1942 had been too sudden to permit any arrangements for communications with the outside world by those units and individuals who took to the hills rather than surrender. SWPA headquarters in Australia anxiously awaited any friendly radio message that might be transmitted from the Philippines. Such a message, the first word from American survivors, came late in June 1942. Sent in the clear (that is, unciphered), it was heard by two U.S. Army radio intelligence stations, one in Townsville, Australia, the other in California. An RAAF station in Darwin also intercepted it.

Having established contact with the

---

[3] (1) Press Meets the CSigO, SigC Tech Intel Ltr 29 (Apr 44), pp. 5f. (2) Reichelderfer, "Sixth Army Communications," *Signals*, III, No. 2, pp. 7ff. See also Chapters VII and VIII above.

[4] (1) Cannon, *Leyte: The Return to the Philippines*, pp. 14ff. (2) Miller, *CARTWHEEL: Reduction of Rabaul*, pp. 24ff. (3) GHQ USAFPAC Mil Intel Sec, Intel Series, vol. I, The Guerrilla Resistance Movement in the Philippines. OCMH files. (4) Morison, *Leyte*, pp. 64f.

A reconnaissance group, known as the ALAMO Scouts, was organized early in the war by the Sixth Army and subsequently employed to infiltrate the Philippines and report observations by radio. See Sixth U.S. Army, Report of the Leyte Operation, 20 October 1944–25 December 1944, pp. 159ff.; also Sixth U.S. Army, Rpts of General and Special Staff Sections, Luzon Campaign, 9 Jan 45–30 Jun 45, III, 14f. See also Miller, *CARTWHEEL: Reduction of Rabaul*, pp. 277 and 322.

outside, the fugitive sender next designated a cipher system, specifying that he would use the old Signal Corps M–94 cipher disc. For the key word, he signaled that he would use the first name of the wife of Capt. Robert H. Arnold, Signal Corps. To establish his own identity, he gave his service number. He was himself Captain Arnold, a member of the Signal Company Aircraft Warning, Philippine Department, which had arrived late in 1941 to operate aircraft detecting radars. He and his detachment had taken an SCR–270 to Burgos Point in northern Luzon on the eve of the war, arriving there on the night of 7 December (6 December east of the international dateline). Now he was furtively making the first contact with the free world outside his guerrilla hiding place in Luzon, operating a radio transmitter built out of "junk." It was later learned that Arnold destroyed the SCR–270 radar, joined Col. Guillermo Z. Nakar's guerrillas, survived Nakar's subsequent capture and execution, played an important role in guerrilla activities thereafter, and then participated in softening up the Japanese early in 1945 when General MacArthur invaded Luzon.[5]

The radio stations of the Philippines resistance were operated by a variety of persons. A notable one, who first became a Signal Corps officer by way of a "bamboo commission," was Capt. Truman Heminway, Jr. A private first class, he had gone to the Philippines in September 1941 as an aerial photographer with the Army Air Forces. Sent to Mindanao after the Japanese wrecked Clark Field, he took to the hills and joined the guerrillas. When, somewhat later, a U.S. submarine secretly landed supplies including a small radio set, Heminway learned how to operate it. Eluding the enemy in repeated hairbreadth affrays, he maintained radio contact with SWPA. As the months passed, he learned by radio that he had been commissioned in fact a lieutenant in the Signal Corps, and later promoted to captain.[6] Heminway and 1st Lt. Joseph F. St. John, an AAF fugitive, operated their radio station on Leyte in the spring of 1944. Both were credited with the development of guerrilla radio communications on Leyte.[7]

Among Heminway's assignments, according to another account, was the maintenance of a coast watching station on Panaon Island, just south of Leyte along Surigao Strait. This station he operated from 10 April to 25 August 1943. His next station was on the southern end of Samar, from September to mid-November 1943. As the enemy sought to track him down, he shifted to other locations (on Dinagat Island), all overlooking the vital straits. By the time

[5] (1) Thompson, Harris, et al., The Test, p. 12. (2) History of Signal Corps Radar Units in the Philippine Islands, 1 August 1941–6 May 1942, pp. 1–2. Folder entitled Radar–Philippine–Capt C. J. Wimer, SigC Hist Sec file. (3) Col Russell W. Volckmann, We Remained (New York: W. W. Norton & Co., Inc., 1954), pp. 154 and 200–201. (4) Operations Report, 978th Signal Service Company, pp. 7–10. SGCO 978–0.3 (44684), 6 May 42–Aug 45. (5) U.S. Army SigC SWPA, Signal Achievement–Luzon, An Official Signal Corps History, 14 May 45, pp. 1–2. 98–GHQ1–31 (15229), 14 May 45.

[6] WD BPR Release, 11 Jun 45, Philippines Guerrilla Leader Tells of Experiences Eluding the Japs. Pers folder, Tab A, SigC Hist Sec file.
[7] WD BPR Release, 11 Jun 45, The Guerrilla Resistance Movement in the Philippines, pp. 3, 136.
St. John was orginally an AAF private first class with the 14th Bombardment Squadron at Clark Field. His guerrilla experiences were described by Cpl. Tom O'Brien, staff correspondent, in Yank (Far East Edition), 8 December 1944, vol. 2, No. 19, pp. 8–9.

American soldiers found him after the invasion of Leyte in October 1944, his radio had reported hundreds of enemy ships that had passed through the waters under his observation.[8]

Philippine guerrilla reports became so valuable that SWPA headquarters set up extensive radio nets and an intelligence apparatus to co-operate with the guerrilla forces. GHQ activated and trained the 978th Signal Service Company to handle the radio communications involved and to provide parties of men who were smuggled into the islands by submarine to augment the guerrilla activity, increase the flow of intelligence back to GHQ SWPA, and help in many ways to soften up the Japanese in the islands before MacArthur's return. The 978th was activated in Brisbane on 1 July 1943. Only about a fifth, principally cryptographic specialists, were non-Filipino. The rest were Filipino Americans who had been recruited in the United States and who had volunteered for this peculiarly hazardous duty. The men were trained to build, operate, and maintain radio stations; trained in weather forecasting and aircraft warning; taught to use cameras and to devise cryptographic systems in case those they carried in became compromised through capture by the enemy; and schooled in jungle living and guerrilla fighting.[9]

The work of the groups that infiltrated the Philippines was dangerous in the extreme. The first party—four men and an officer—secretly detached from the company in Australia in October 1943, was as secretly debarked from a submarine at Mindoro the following month. The group set up four radio stations on the island and operated them until the Japanese ferreted out the locations in March 1944. Maj. Lawrence H. Phillips, the commander, was killed. Two sergeants, Ramon Vittorio and Arcangel Baniares, were captured and tortured to death. WO Braynard L. Weiss, Phillips' radio operator, escaped, only to die on a later mission. Returning to Australia, he led another party on a mission in September 1944, but perished when the submarine *Seawolf* carrying the team to Samar was lost somewhere in the Celebes Sea.

All told, over one hundred men of the 978th Signal Service Company volunteered for Philippine missions. They brought in new equipment, such as specially built concealed radios, including two suitcase sets. One of the latter trapped the man carrying it when its obvious weight aroused the curiosity of a Japanese military policeman in Manila. Many of the men slipped into the islands during the months just before the invasion of Leyte and sent out invaluable reports. They created an effective guerrilla communications net that at one time included a dozen radio stations on Luzon that communicated directly with the 978th message center at GHQ SWPA and with some sixty subsidiary stations within the island net.[10]

[8] Guerrilla Coast Watcher, SigC Tech Info Ltr 45 (Aug 45), 7–9. SigC Hist Sec file.

[9] SigC SWPA, Sig Achievement—Luzon, pp. 3–4.

[10] (1) Opns Rpt, 978th Sig Sv Co, pp. 18ff. 116ff., 150. (2) SigC SWPA, Sig Achievement—Luzon, pp. 3–8. (3) Wagner, ACAN, 1941–45, pt. I, p. 48. (4) WD BPR Press Release, 11 Jun 45, The Guerrilla Resistance Movement in the Philippines, p. 6. (5) Col. Allison Ind, *Allied Intelligence Bureau* (New York: McKay Co., 1958), pp. 182ff. According to the operations report of the 978th Signal Service Company, pages 66–67, the Navy gave high praise to the radio reports received from the Philippines through the 978th's message center, especially touching the naval victories in the area during July 1944, ". . . Admiral Halsey giving 75 percent of the credit for the naval operations to the intelligence thus passed."

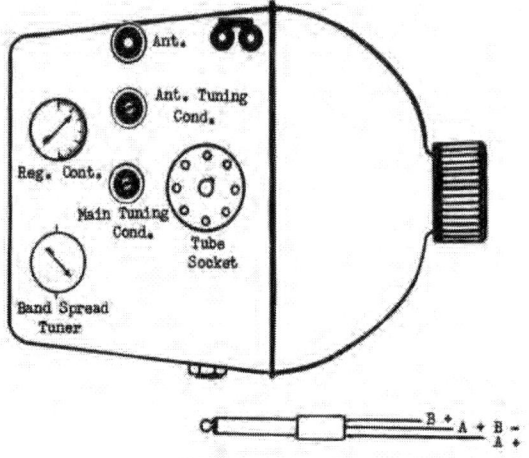

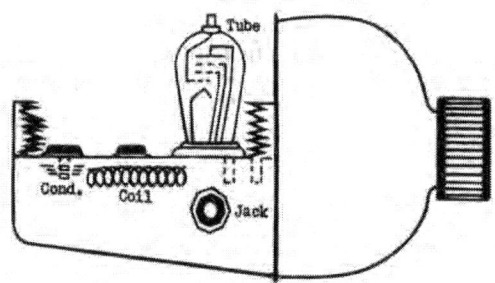

DRAWINGS OF A CANTEEN RADIO

Nor was concealed radio activity by Signal Corps men in the Philippines confined to the guerrillas. There was at least one incident of it in prison, involving a radioman, William D. Gibson, who had received his commission as a lieutenant in the Signal Corps only a few hours before the fall of Corregidor. A former U.S. "ham" working in Manila as a civilian radio technician, he had offered his services to the Army on Corregidor after the enemy invasion began. But his commission had been delayed till the last hours of his freedom because the medical officers busily treating wounded men had not given him the required physical examination. Subsequently, a prisoner in the Cabanatuan concentration camp, he came into the possession of a 1-tube regenerative radio receiver improvised by an officer of the Engineer Corps, Capt. Russell J. Hutchinson, who had built it of scrap parts and placed it inside a GI canteen. Hutchinson, on being shifted out of the prison, left it with Gibson. But the set no longer worked. Its single amplifying tube, a 12SK7, had burned out. Obtaining a different type of amplifier tube, a 6J7, stolen by an American sailor who had a prison job in a Japanese shop, Gibson rewired the set to accomodate the tube; a cauterizing iron from the prison hospital served as a soldering iron. Looking like any ordinary canteen, the radio was kept hanging at the lieutenant's bed. Japanese inspectors passed it by, suspecting nothing. Its antenna was a No. 22 wire woven inconspicuously into a rope clothesline. Only the headphones had to be secreted separately. The prisoners furtively operated the receiver in the evening, using battery power which was available in the prison hospital. The little set brought in radio programs emanating from Saigon, Tokyo, and San Francisco. Best of all was the Voice of Freedom broadcast by the *Apache* after the Leyte Campaign began.[11] This treasured radio receiver was left behind when the lieutenant, suddenly freed with the other prisoners, departed in the pell-mell of the daring Cabanatuan raid, 30 January 1945.[12]

The success of the heroic resistance in the Philippines was one small but important contribution to the impetus to drive the enemy out of the Philippines.[13] There were other factors, as the Allied organization and strength improved and the enemy's deteriorated. One was the implementation of the floating-base concept, now that the sea was becoming somewhat safer (apart from the new menace of kamikazes). Therefore the Signal Corps took to ships on a larger scale than in New Guinea. Message centers, radio stations, even supply depots—all became waterborne.

Afloat and Ashore at Leyte and Luzon

Long before the leap from Hollandia to Leyte, Signal Corps crews in Army radio ships had proved that Army communications facilities could be both marine and mobile. They had to be, in order to meet the special conditions of island fighting in the Pacific. By mid-1944 the *Harold, Argosy Lemal,* and *Geoanna,* three of the makeshift communications ships that had proved their value in the CP fleet along the New Guinea coast,[14] were required to be returned to the Transportation Corps. They were replaced, however, by much better vessels.

General Akin's Seaborne Communications Branch in the SWPA had already, early in 1944, asked the Navy for three ships outfitted specifically for use as Army communications shops. The re-

[11] (1) SigC SWPA, Sig Achievement–Luzon, pp. 49ff. (2) Ltr, Col Ray M. O'Day (Ret.) to Dr. Thompson, 19 Jul 60. SigC Hist Sec file. See also, Incl with Ltr, CSigO to Dir WD BPR OSW, 10 Oct 45, sub: Article for Publication, Signal Corps Man Makes Secret Radios in Jap Prison. SigC 000.7 Articles for Publication, vol. 4, Oct–Dec 45.

[12] U.S. Army SigC SWPA, Exposure Under Fire, Official History of Signal Corps Photography in the Luzon Operations, 25 Apr 45, p. 5. 98–GHQI-31 (15229).
The raiders comprised two ALAMO Scout teams and Company C, 6th Ranger Infantry Battalion, aided by guerrilla forces. A Signal Corps photographer, T/4 Frank Goetzheimer, a member of the raiding party, received a Bronze Star for his exploits. Sixth U.S. Army Rpt, Luzon Campaign, p. 16.

[13] (1) Willoughby and Chamberlain, *MacArthur 1941–51,* p 216. (2) Cannon, *Leyte: The Return to the Philippines,* p. 20. (3) Robert Ross Smith, *Triumph in the Philippines,* UNITED STATES ARMY IN WORLD WAR II (Washington, 1963), pp. 26–27.

[14] See above, pp. 262–63.

quest specified that they provide room for adequate radio facilities and that they carry some armament, too. The Navy, co-operating, looked to its very new PCE (R) 's (patrol craft escorts (rescue)). Designed for the protection of convoys against air and submarine attacks, these vessels were armed with a 3-inch gun, 40- and 20-milimeter anti-aircraft guns, machine guns, and depth charges. They contained extra space and berthing, intended to care for the survivors of stricken ships. The first three of these PCE's, being built in Chicago, were assigned to the Seventh Fleet, SWPA, for conversion to Army communications. Named merely PCE-848, 849, and 850, they were hurried down the Mississippi, commissioned at New Orleans, and rushed in the summer of 1944 to Brisbane.[15] There, under Signal Corps supervision, they were converted to their communications function. The new versatile high-capacity antracs (AN/TRC-1's) were installed in them, along with older single circuit radios SCR-284, 300, and 610. High-power Australian transmitters AT-20's and Australian receivers, AMR-100's, completed the conversion. The PCE-848 and 849, assigned to serve GHQ SWPA, each received 24 Signal Corps troops (2 officers and 22 enlisted men). The PCE-850, assigned to Sixth Army headquarters, got one warrant officer and 12 enlisted men. The Navy crews on each ship numbered about 100. Thus readied, the three communications ships sailed to Hollandia.[16]

The three PCE's constituted the CP fleet for the Leyte operation, along with two others, the FP-47 (the only holdover from Signal Corps' first communications ships in the New Guinea fighting) and the *Apache*. The *Apache* was something new in Signal Corps experience. It was a communications ship specifically and solely intended for public relations work. General Akin's Seaborne Communications Branch had gained enough experience in shipboard Army signals so that when the SWPA public relations officer asked for a correspondents' broadcast ship to send press copy to the United States (there had been difficulties getting press copy through Australian Postmaster General facilities), the Signal Corps men answered "Yes." They acquired the *Apache,* a 185-foot, 650-ton ship, which had served first as a revenue cutter, then as a Coast Guard vessel. Be-

---

[15] (1) Seaborne CP's pp. 3, 11ff. (2) See above, p. 262, n. 60.

The PCE-850 was the last and so rushed that crewmen working under pressure heard repeatedly over the ship's loud-speaker, "There will *be no* liberty tonight. . . . there will *be no* shore leave. . . ." They therefore dubbed her the *Beno.*

[16] (1) Seaborne CP's, pp. 13ff. (2) Capt Mike B. Davis, ExecO Hq Base Sec USASOS SWPA, History of the Signal Section, September 1944, 10 Oct 44, p. 2. Hist SigO Base, Jul 44–Jan 45.

Colonel Reichelderfer described his Sixth Army ship, the PCE-850, as fitted "with four 750-watt transmitters, four receiving positions, and a code room." Hit by a bomb and rammed too, off Leyte, it had to be returned to Hollandia for repairs by the end of its first week of Philippine service. Reichelderfer, "Sixth Army Communications," *Signals,* III, No. 2, 7f.

The armament desired for these ships might seem to run contrary to British and American experience in Europe and North Africa, teaching that a signal center afloat should never serve as a combat vessel as well. The PCE guns were light, for defensive use only. The one 3-inch gun was much smaller than the large guns on the heavy cruiser *Augusta,* whose shock of firing disrupted American communications in the assault phase on North Africa. See Thompson, Harris, *et al., The Test,* p. 359. The armament of the PCE's served well, destroying, or contributing to the destruction of, a number of enemy planes during the first days off Leyte.

ARMY RADIO SHIP PCE(R)–848 *in Humboldt Bay, Hollandia, above.   Below, radio operators of the PCE(R)–848 with equipment.*

cause of her age, fifty-five years, she had been sold for scrap just before World War II. Resurrected by the Maritime Commission, she was used for a while by the Navy. Then, in the somewhat sour words of her skipper, "Like everything else that nobody wants, she was turned over to the Army."

In July 1944 her conversion to the best known vessel of Signal Corps' CP fleet began in Sydney harbor. By dexterously combining various pieces of equipment, the Signal Corps installed a 10-kilowatt voice-modulated transmitter—a short-wave radiotelephone that could reach the United States directly. Radio relay, AN/TRC-1, was added to provide circuits to shore terminals. A variety of antenna rigs, a studio, and a control room completed the floating broadcast facility for war correspondents, who could now sail close into the theaters, pick up reports and news from shore over the VHF radio relay, and prepare and broadcast programs home quickly and directly. With a Signal Corps detachment of three officers and eleven enlisted men and with a ship and gun crew similar to that aboard the FP-47, the *Apache* was readied and sailed to Hollandia early in the autumn of 1944.[17]

Designated Task Unit 78.1.12 by the Navy, the five ships of the CP fleet were readied in October at Hollandia: the PCE-848, 849, and 850, the *Apache*, and the FP-47, which also served press needs. Aboard the PCE-848, General Akin occupied a cabin along with one of his staff officers who handled General MacArthur's messages (MacArthur him-

self sailed in the USS *Nashville*). Aboard the 848 also was a VHF team to operate radio relay equipment. The PCE-849 carried General Akin's assistant, more Signal Corps men, and an intercept team of the 978th Signal Service Company. The duty of the latter, a group of a dozen officers and men under Capt. Charles B. Ferguson, was to intercept enemy broadcasts and to receive messages from the guerrilla radios in the Philippines. The PCE-850 carried Colonel Reichelderfer and his Signal Corps assistants serving General Krueger's Sixth Army headquarters. Still other Signal Corps men worked communications circuits aboard the *Nashville* and the *Wasatch* serving Generals MacArthur and Krueger, respectively, using an assortment of radio relay and portable radio types.[18]

Such was the CP fleet as it arrived off Red Beach, Leyte Gulf, early on 21 October 1944, the day of the assault landing. As soon as radio silence was lifted, about 1100, Signal Corps operators switched on their equipment and began establishing radio contacts. While powerful long-range transmitters aboard FP-47 and the *Apache* broadcast to the world the news that the invasion had begun, local nets were established by smaller sets—both single circuit sets of older design and the latest multicircuit radio relay or VHF antrac.

Antrac now began to figure in a new highly significant application in the Pacific, in MCU's. On the day before the ships sailed from Hollandia, a mobile communications unit had been hurriedly

[17] (1) Seaborne CP's, pp. 7–10. (2) Davis, Hist of the Sig Sec. (3) Intervs, SigC Hist Sec with Hogan, 1 and 5 Jul 49, 31 Mar 58. (4) For similar ETO experience see above, pp. 107ff.

[18] (1) Seaborne CP's, pp. 15f. (2) SigC SWPA, Sig Achievement–Luzon, p. 8. (3) Opns Rpt, 978th Sig Sv Co, pp. 60, 69–70, 86.

assembled. Signal Corps men converted a 1½-ton truck into a radio relay terminal, complete with carrier equipment. The Navy supplied three LCM's (landing craft, mechanized) to carry all the facilities ashore. Arriving off Red Beach at Leyte, the CP fleet transferred the mobile equipment for the shore station into the LCM's, which headed for the beach at H plus 2. The communications truck landed amid mortar fire, which wounded some of the men but failed to damage the radio. Within twenty-five minutes, according to one account (fifteen minutes according to another), this shore-based antrac established circuits with the antrac in the CP fleet offshore. At once voice and teletype connections began supporting the complex movement of men and equipment to shore.

Meanwhile, General MacArthur's headquarters ship, the *Nashville*, established communications with the shore station as well as with other Army stations afloat. And at H plus 5 MacArthur himself went ashore, strode up to a microphone of the mobile communications unit there, and gave his "I Have Returned" speech. Signal Corps men aboard the *Nashville* repeated his words in a broadcast to the Philippine people. Other Signal Corps men on the *Apache* picked up the speech, recorded it, and rebroadcast it later to the United States using the ship's 10-kilowatt transmitter.[19]

The GHQ SWPA mobile unit was not unique in the Leyte landing. Colonel Reichelderfer had provided a similar one for his Sixth Army headquarters.

General Krueger noted that the establishment of his command post ashore "was materially facilitated by the foresight of Sixth Army's Signal Officer (Col. Harry Reichelderfer)." Krueger wrote, "He had mounted a complete army signal center on large vans which, together with the necessary Signal Corps men, was transported on LST's from Hollandia to Leyte."[20] The vans were seven in number, big 6-ton semitrailers—a message center van, a manual code van, a Sigaba (machine cipher) van, a telephone central van, a transmitter van, a receiver van, and a van equipped with carrier facilities.[21]

These assemblages of message center and high-capacity communications equipment, mobile-mounted in trucks, vans, and ships, were thus employed extensively at Leyte, serving both GHQ SWPA and the Sixth Army headquarters. Such mobile adaptations would soon be used on a still larger scale in the Luzon and Okinawa operations. In the words of one of the participating officers, "the Signal Corps set about providing personnel and equipment that could operate on the sea, as well as on land and yet be sufficiently mobile and flexible to cope with constantly changing tactical situations." They constituted provisional detachments that became known as the mobile and seaborne communications units.[22] Their high message capacity and flexibility were attributable largely to the use of VHF antrac. AN/TRC-1, 3,

---

[19] (1) Crain Rpt, pp. 6–7. (2) Seaborne CP's, pp. 16–17. (3) Radio Relay Equipment in the Philippine Operation, SigC Tech Info Ltr 43 (Jun 45), pp. 1ff.

[20] Krueger, *From Down to Nippon*, p. 163.

[21] Sixth Army Rpt, Leyte Opn, p. 247.

Besides the vans, nearly a score of truck-mounted radios were put ashore too—3 AT-20's, 4 SCR-399's, 2 SCR-299's, and 8 SCR-193's.

[22] Eddy, "Manila and the Capitulation," *Signals*, I, No. 5, 42.

and 4 sets came into the heaviest sort of demand. Within thirty days after the first landings, 18 VHF radio relay terminals were operating in the Leyte area, whereas the original plans had called for only 8–4 afloat and 4 ashore (to be installed and operated by Team K of the 989th Signal Service Company, attached to the CP fleet). By 18 December the number of these terminals totaled 22.[23]

During the first days when the CP fleet had to carry the bulk of the traffic load, Signal Corps men aboard the vessels moved heavy message flows. PCE–848 handled up to 10,000 words a day (PCE–849 serving as a monitor station and a stand-by for the 848). The PCE–850 worked even harder for Sixth Army nets, scoring a record load of 25,000 words in one day. The *Apache* and the FP–47 likewise handled heavy loads of press traffic.

Meanwhile, Japanese bombers did not overlook the communications ships. Both the 848 and the 850 were bombed and suffered casualties, including three Signal Corps men on the PCE–848, one killed and two wounded. The 849 narrowly escaped. Aboard all the CP vessels Signal Corps men experienced a new kind of combat, shipboard fighting. Speaking of a Signal Corps crew manning a 50-caliber machine gun on the 849, one of the ship's officers commented, "They are absolutely unflinching. I have seen them staying at their posts without showing a sign of fear when Jap planes were coming right at their guns."[24]

Japanese aviators continued to search out Army communications nerve centers ashore on Leyte. No sooner did the Signal Corps MCU's set up large-scale radio and message center operations on the land (first located in the town of Tacloban), than the planes came in. Repeated bombing attacks occurred into early 1945, until the Army Air Forces became well established in the area. The Signal Corps took no serious casualties, but the equipment was repeatedly damaged. Much time and labor had to go to the sandbagging of equipment items, particularly the big vital electric generators. Seeking to escape these troublesome hostile attentions, the Signal Corps remoted one of the transmitters some twenty miles down the coast, but the Japanese located and bombed it the very first time it went on the air.[25]

Communications at the Tacloban center had other troubles. Difficulties developed in transmitting back to GHQ SWPA at Hollandia, and message traffic on that circuit piled up. Capt. John D. McKinney, who had commanded the GHQ communications center at Hollandia since November 1944, was sent to Tacloban in January 1945 to solve the problem. He found that the transmitting antenna rhombic was improperly "aimed" at Hollandia, whose distant re-

[23] Crain Rpt, pp. 7–8.

Emphasizing the speed and message capacity that the combination of VHF radio relay and communications ships provided during the first days of the invasion, Captain Crain commented that ten days were subsequently consumed in setting up for operation ashore the same quantity of communications facilities that the CP fleet had been able to put into service in eight hours.

[24] Seaborne CP's, pp. 18–26.

Several Signal Corps men aboard one of Sixth Army's LST's carrying duplicate communications facilities ashore were killed and several injured when one of the ships approaching the beach early in the assault was struck by an enemy 75-mm. shell. Interv, SigC Hist Sec with Colonel Bess. Pers Div OCSigO, 20 Jan 58.

[25] Intervs, SigC Hist Sec with Kline, Deputy CO USASIA, 9 Jan and 19 Feb 59.

ceivers lay barely within the edge of the radio beam from Tacloban. The engineers in laying out the rhombic antenna masts had done so by map and compass right enough, but they had forgotten to allow for the considerable magnetic declination that exists in that part of the globe. The error was sufficient to throw the Tacloban-Hollandia beam badly off its target. This fault was remedied. When the whole communications center was moved from Tacloban to Tolosa later in January, communications improved perceptibly.[26]

During the fight for Leyte Signal Corps units and equipment experienced the usual vicissitudes of World War II combat. The pattern, long set in the Pacific, of heavy dependence on radio, applied on Leyte also. Radio sets had to carry the brunt of Army tactical communications because among other things, wire linemen were scarce and line work was sometimes almost prohibitively hazardous, so much so that at times half of the men assigned that duty had to stand guard for the other half as they strung the circuits. Infantrymen had to hand carry SCR–609's, which were normally transported in jeeps. To carry the sets over jeepless terrain, radiomen strapped the radio to one pack board, its batteries to another, and extra batteries and tubes to a third. Upon reaching a forward position, they slipped off the pack boards, connected the batteries, and were on the air. The walkie-talkie, SCR–300, designed for use on a soldier's back, was not so carried because Japanese riflemen singled the radios and their carriers out for special attention. Instead, the troops carried their 300's in jungle bags. Once,

when radio interference rendered an AM SCR–284 unusable, the men used an FM SCR–300, which they set up on high ground to serve as a relay station. Its operators were able to provide uninterrupted communications between a regiment and battalion, though the two units were twenty-five miles apart.[27]

The Americans invading the Philippines continued to receive information from the radio network operated by the guerrillas within enemy territory, but the guerrillas were now augmented by teams of ALAMO Scouts—one officer and five or six men to a team—specifically instructed to obtain intelligence within the combat areas. These teams, working closely together and supplied mainly by airdrop, sometimes provided the only sources of military intelligence during the advance. They provided, in Krueger's own words, "a considerable volume of extremely valuable information." At the height of the Philippine campaign more than seventy radio stations (guerrilla and ALAMO Scout) were in operation. The Scouts used chiefly SCR–300's and the newer 694's. The other sets, especially the ones used by the guerrilla forces, were a motley assortment: SCR's–284, 288, 300, Australian ATR 4–a, and a Dutch set having an electric generator driven by a bicycle-type treadle.[28]

The invasion of Luzon constituted the next and last heavy assignment for the Sixth Army. Meanwhile the Eighth Army under General Eichelberger (his signal officer was Col. Rex Corput) took

---

[26] Interv, SigC Hist Sec with McKinney, 8 Sep 60.

[27] Sig Notes–Pac, SigC Tech Info Ltr 44 (Jul 45), 24–25.

[28] (1) Sixth Army Rpt, Leyte Opn, p. .159. (2) Sixth Army Rpt, Luzon Campaign, III, 14–15. (3) Opns Rpt, 978th Sig Sv Co, pp. 164ff. (4) Krueger, *From Down Under to Nippon*, p. 189.

WALKIE-TALKIE SCR-300

over the combat tasks that remained in Leyte and adjacent islands. "We turned over to the Eighth Army all of our communications . . . lock, stock, and barrel. . . ." recalled Reichelderfer. "We actually transferred the equipment in the place together with what wire and frequencies we were using, and a good part of the personnel operating it." The PCE-850, for example, repaired after the damage it had received as Sixth Army communications ship at Leyte, reappeared early in 1945 serving Eighth Army's communications in the Mindanao operation.[29]

On Luzon the pattern of ground force communications was the same as on Leyte. Such signal developments as were unique in the Pacific fighting—the mobile sea and land adaptations—continued there. On 3 January 1945, the two GHQ PCE's, the 848 and 849, together with the *Apache* and the FP-47, had departed from Leyte for Lingayen Gulf. Lest the enemy, who listened to the daily broadcasts of the *Apache*, note that the origin of the *Apache* broadcasts had changed position and guess the reason, a similar transmitter ashore on Leyte continued to broadcast the recorded voices of the familiar announcers. General Akin sailed in the PCE-848. A number of Australian and Philippine signalmen accompanied him on the 848, while others sailed in the 849. On the day of the assault, 9

---

[29] (1) AFSC Lecture C-15, Com SWPA, 29 May 47, Tab 24, p. 7. (2) Report of the Commanding General Eighth Army on the Mindanao Operation, Signal Report, p. 130.

January 1945, a VHF circuit was put ashore. Within an hour it established communications with General MacArthur aboard the *Boise* and with the *Apache*, the PCE's, the *Wasatch,* and the *Tulsa* (a cruiser in the Seventh Fleet). A channel to the rear echelon of the Sixth Army was blocked for some hours because of transmitter trouble. The *Apache* made contact with the RCA station in San Francisco a few moments before 0800 on 10 January.[30]

During the Luzon Campaign General Akin's CP flotilla increased to such proportions that it became known as Signal Corps' Grand Fleet. Its floating accommodations had more than doubled in number and had increased severalfold in capacity. Some time before the invasion of Luzon, the SWPA Signal Section had planned additional vessels, able to carry larger installations afloat than the first small ships could accommodate. General Akin decided upon OL's (ocean-going lighters), more commonly called barges. Their spaciousness allowed the Signal Corps to carry upon the sea something of a shore-based ACAN station with separate transmitter and receiver locations, extensive message center accommodations, large antenna arrays, and so on. During April and May 1944, SWPA Signal Corps men acquired 7 OL's. By the year's end they had fitted out 4—2 for transmitter functions, 2 for receiving—and they gave them the designations CBT (communication barge transmitter) and CBR (communication barge receiver). A fifth vessel, which they had converted into barracks to accommodate operating personnel, they

dubbed CSQ (communications ship quarters).[31] Together, the vessels constituted a major radio station able to serve the GHQ afloat.

Some weeks later, as the American troops pressed into Manila, one of the first ships to enter Manila Bay, while fighting continued in the area, was PCE–849, on 27 February. It carried 25 tons of signal equipment, including 2½-ton transmitters for radioteletype channels intended to reach Brisbane and San Francisco. Then on 18 March the Grand Fleet arrived. Its big ocean-going lighters carried into Manila harbor a complete ACAN-type installation, outfitted with all the facilities of an Army communications station on land. There was a signal center, complete with tape relay equipment and antrac or radio relay (the latter to establish communications between barges). In each barge were terminal frames, which permitted ready connections between the barges and between shore and barge. There were 50-kilowatt diesel power units, two to each barge, and each engine unit was adapted for salt water cooling. Within forty-eight hours after the fleet anchored in Manila harbor to serve GHQ SWPA, the big SSB (single sideband) transmitters were communing with San Francisco, using a rhombic antenna ashore. The SSB's also provided radiotelephoto service both to the United States and to Australia. The floating Signal Corps station handled a heavy load of traffic for the press over a period of nearly two months. The press

---

[30] (1) SigC SWPA, Sig Achievement–Luzon, pp. 9–11. (2) Crain Rpt, pp. 8–11.

[31] (1) Seaborne CP's, p. 16. (2) SigC CP Fleet, SigC Tech Info Ltr 44 (Jul 45), p. 10. The CSQ was a former Australian steamer, the *Weeroona,* according to Signal Corps SWPA, Signal Achievement–Luzon, p. 16.

traffic alone averaged nearly 23,000 groups or words a day until Press Wireless opened a commercial station ashore and took over the load.[32]

The floating ACAN station was not the only Signal Corps seaborne innovation in Luzon waters. There were also signal supply vessels, floating Signal Corps depots equipped with all the appurtenances of a land depot such as hand trucks, monorail cranes, and shop facilities for extensive repair work (fifth echelon repair). Each floating depot was manned by a lieutenant and crew of 5 or 6 men from the 3168th Signal Service Battalion. They serviced invasion troops first; after that, they provided the initial signal supplies for new bases being built ashore. One of the floating depots, the BCL–3063 20,000-ton concrete barge known as the *Alcatraz*, was towed into Lingayen Gulf about S plus 10. It was a repair shop, and its stock included Class II material to supplement tactical supply, and also Class IV installation material. A similar depot barge was the BCL–3059, more commonly called the *Rock*. Still another was the concrete steamer, *François Henebequen*.[33]

"These ocean going barges," subsequently concluded Colonel Toft, "proved to be excellent for signal supply operations in amphibious operations, and for general work-horse duty in al-

leviating confused supply conditions in the early stages of development of the bases." A single barge, he explained, could support a corps in an amphibious operation. It could move the needed equipment (Toft considered signal supplies amounted to about 1 percent by weight of total Army supplies) right up to the scene of the assault. It could quickly send ashore, by Dukw, such equipment as might be safely stored in the open—bulk items such as wire and cable, and pole line hardware. Meanwhile, the barge could carry in its stock under cover items that required shelter. Finally, there was room in a large barge to house repair facilities.[34]

Late in the war the concept of a spare parts floating depot was discussed by the technical services, especially the Signal Corps, in War Department headquarters in Washington. A table of organization and equipment was authorized, and the 39th Signal Floating Spare Parts Depot was constituted in mid-1945. When the Chemical Warfare Service and the Medical Corps joined the venture, the unit became the 39th Composite Floating Spare Parts Depot. A ship, *Lock-Knot*, was readied in New York harbor. The depot unit went aboard in August, the hold and first and second decks were loaded, and the ship sailed on 22 August for the war in the east, scarcely ten days before the official surrender.[35]

[32] Press Wireless was one of several companies that served Manila before the war. It had been selected to help equip the Grand Fleet. CSigO, Annual Rpt, FY 45, pp. 149, 217.

[33] (1) SigC SWPA, Sig Achievement–Luzon, pp. 12–16. (2) Eddy, "Manila and the Capitulation," pp. 45f. (3) Bykofsky and Larson, *The Transportation Corps: Operations Overseas*, p. 451. Floating barge depots were also employed by Ordnance Corps. Draft MS Comment, Lida Mayo. SigC Hist Sec file.

[34] Toft, Some SigC Sup Problems in SWPA During World War II, p. 14.

[35] (1) Rpts, P&O Div, OCSigO, 12, 23, 25, 31 Jul, and 2, 13, and 30 Aug 45, Daily Digest, Staff Divs OCSigO, 1 Jul–31 Dec 45. SigC Exec Of file. (2) Rpts, P&O Div, 15 and 22 May and 12 and 26 Jun 45, Daily Digest, Staff Divs OCSigO, 1 Jan–30 Jun 45. SigC Exec Of file.

Ashore at Lingayen, General Akin's mobile communications unit serving GHQ SWPA pressed toward Manila as rapidly as had his communications vessels of the Grand Fleet. His mobile land setup compared in completeness with the seaborne facilities. Containing entire message centers with all the needed radio and power equipment, it totaled 100 vehicles: 38 trucks, 30 trailers, 20 jeeps, and 12 other conveyances.[36] Twenty of the trucks had first entered San Miguel, behind the Lingayen beachhead, and set up a GHQ signal center there as soon as the area was cleared of the enemy. Thereafter its advance became so rapid that when the Americans approached Manila, General Akin's mobile communications rushed into the city too soon to please Sixth Army troops who were doing the fighting. General Krueger, annoyed, characterized the Signal Corps men's zealous effort as a bit "premature." General Akin's men, Krueger later reminisced, "clogged Highway 3 with a long column of heavy Signal Corps vehicles." They got in the way of combat units and tanks that were still exchanging shots with the enemy. "It would have been a good idea," Krueger tartly commented, "for the chief signal officer [Akin] to have arranged for that movement with headquarters 6th Army, but unfortunately he had not done so." [37]

Actually, General Akin was but keeping up with his commander in chief, General MacArthur, who was so eager to get into Manila that he was in the fore-

front of the advance, in fact ahead of it at times.[38] During the advance through the central plains of Luzon en route to the capital city, MacArthur had been impatient with the rate of progress and had pressed at the head of the troops. At one point, Brig. Gen. Benjamin H. Pochyla later recalled, General MacArthur called a conference of his commanders at the forward position he happened to be occupying at that moment. It was probably the first time in history, Pochyla commented, that a theater commander in chief called his division, corps, and army commanders forward for a conference. As a consequence, the 1st Cavalry Division spearheaded an early breakthrough into Manila.

Throughout the advance Akin's mobile communications unit kept up with MacArthur. The Signal Corps men, using spiral-four cable, antrac radio relay, and some open wire lines they had rehabilitated along the railroad, maintained heavily used GHQ communications from their trucks and even at times from jeeps. General Krueger's complaint was somewhat uncalled for, since the communications vehicles were maintaining for General MacArthur the theater-level signal support that the commander in chief had to have. As for getting in the way of Krueger's Sixth Army combat elements, Signal Corps trucks and troops more than once, General Pochyla commented, fought with the enemy and cleared out resist-

---

[36] SigC SWPA, Sig Achievement–Luzon, pp. 22ff.
[37] Krueger, *From Down Under to Nippon*, p. 244.

[38] On one occasion in the Manila drive MacArthur's advance headquarters was "fifty miles closer to the front than that of his army commander." Whitney, *MacArthur, His Rendezvous with History*, p. 187.

ANTRAC (RADIO RELAY) TRUCK, LUZON

ance nests before the infantry arrived.[39]

To return to Sixth Army signals in the Luzon Campaign, the assault upon

[39] Interv, Sig Hist Sec, with Pochyla, 15 and 18 Feb 60.

The Foreword of Signal Corps, SWPA, Achievement–Luzon manuscript sums up the problem of keeping the impetuous MacArthur in communications: "When a CinC packs up and moves his hqs, the strain upon signal facilities is intense. When he keeps moving it, that strain is multiplied many times. And when he not only keeps moving, but keeps his hqs abreast of his advance elements, the ingenuity of communications soldiers is taxed to the very utmost. During the drive on Manila, Gen MacArthur's hqs were frequently in front of lower echelon command posts. The magnitude of the signal communications mission for a roving hqs the size of MacArthur's was enormous."

MacArthur's G–2, Maj. Gen. Charles A. Willoughby, repeatedly spoke of MacArthur's presence at the front line, especially during the approach to Manila. Willoughby, *MacArthur 1941–51*, pp. 267 and 280f.

the Lingayen beaches was again served by the *Wasatch* and the PCE–850, whose Signal Corps troops under Colonel Reichelderfer provided Sixth Army headquarters communications. These seaborne facilities were more than matched by large quantities of communications equipment that went ashore mounted in vehicles. Besides the familiar truck-mounted SCR–193's and 399's, there were trailers loaded with telephone and teletype switchboards and associated equipment. There were Dukw-mounted message centers, and still larger message centers housed in 6-ton vans. Other 6-ton vans carried radio sets of both American and Australian manufacture. To energize it all, there were sufficient power units, also on wheels. And of course there was radio relay with carrier facilities, landed in two trucks and a van.[40]

With the intent of establishing rapid high-capacity communications between Lingayen Gulf and Sixth Army troops fighting down the 130-mile corridor to Manila, Colonel Reichelderfer soon after the landing mounted the radio relay and carrier terminals in six 2½-ton trucks. Each truck included BD–71 and 91 switchboards for voice and teletype circuits. The BD–71 output wires were long enough so that the boards could be moved into foxholes if necessary. Some PE–75's mounted in trailers supplied the power, while other PE–75's stood by for emergency use. Men on detached duty from the 989th Signal Service Company operated the equipment: four VHF radio relay and carrier specialists to each truck, a switchboard operator and a power maintenance man to each truck, and an officer and two code clerks to every two trucks. Following close upon the advancing troops, they carried their radio relays forward in a series of twenty- to thirty-mile jumps: Dagupan, Camiling, Tarlac, San Fernando, Malolos, and finally Manila itself. Each location served in turn first as a forward terminal consisting of a receiver and a backward-looking transmitter, and then, when the troops progressed to the next site, as a back-to-back relay, with a forward-looking transmitter and receiver added, in order to communicate with the new advance terminal along the road to Manila.

By 10 March 1945 sixteen of the VHF radio relay sets handled three-quarters of all the voice and teletypwriter traffic that flowed in and out of the big city.

"VHF radio using AN/TRC–3 equipment," read the summarizing Sixth Army report, "proved itself to be a valuable supplement to wire communication and in certain cases formed the only possible means of voice and teletype communications."

Meanwhile, great though the use of radio was, the Sixth Army used also much more wire on Luzon than it had strung anywhere else in its Pacific campaigning. For example, about 15,000 miles of field wire W–110 were laid by tactical units. Over 9,000 miles of copper wire circuits were also built on the island by Sixth Army elements.[41]

On Luzon even more Signal Corps units toiled and struggled with their generally inconspicuous but essential tasks than had labored on Leyte.[42] Also on Luzon, as elsewhere, there were incidents of Signal Corps men pushing for-

[40] Sixth Army Rpt, Luzon Campaign, III, 134.

[41] (1) Ibid., p. 138. (2) Crain Rpt, pp. 8–11. (3) Radio Relay Equipment in the Philippine Opn, SigC Tech Info Ltr 43, pp. 2ff. (4) Reichelderfer, "Sixth Army Communications," p. 7. (5) SigC SWPA, Sig Achievement–Luzon, pp. 17, 42. General Krueger, appreciating such mobile communications facilities, wrote that the MCU's of his Sixth Army "proved indispensable in the landings and in the rapid advance to Manila."

[42] Signal Corps units serving the Sixth Army headquarters included the 16th Signal Operations Battalion, the 436th Signal Construction Battalion, nineteen teams of the 832d Signal Service Battalion, three carrier terminal teams of the 989th Signal Service Company, Company A of the 99th Signal Battalion, and a platoon of the 281st Signal Pigeon Company. SOS units included Company C of the 60th Signal Battalion, the 276th Signal Construction Company, the 442d Signal Construction Battalion, the 586th Signal Depot Company, the 3294th Signal Base Depot Company, and the 3292d Signal Base Maintenance Company. Sixth Army Rpt, Luzon Campaign, p. 134. Near the end of the Philippine campaign, OCSigO reported that the total number of signal units in SWPA, as of 31 March 1945, stood at 236. Qtrly Rpt, Theaters Br, 1 Jan 45–31 Mar 45, Pac Opns Sec–SWPA Subsec, p. 2.

WIRE CREW WITH WATER BUFFALO

ward their communications facilities amid combat, often exchanging their tools for weapons. A notable Signal Corps unit in the advance was the 52d Signal Battalion. It had originally been intended for the Philippines late in 1941, but was diverted by the events following Pearl Harbor to Australia and then fought up the island chain to the Philippines. On Luzon on one occasion fourteen wiremen of the 52d were cut off by a patrol of 100 enemy. They fought their way out, killing 20 Japanese, including the commanding officer, whose body yielded valuable papers. The 37th Signal Company wiremen had a similar experience when some 70 enemy troops came upon them from the rear as they were laying wire lines. The Signal Corps men turned upon the Japanese, routing them and killing six.[43]

Okinawa to Tokyo

Southwest Pacific forces, the Sixth Army under General Krueger and the Eighth Army under General Eichelberger, had won back the Philippines. Even as they completed that major operation,

---

[43] (1) Incl, Historical Summary of the 52d Signal Battalion, Jan 45, with Ltr, Maj Maurice F. Shepherd, Hq 52d Sig Bn, to SigO Hq Base G, 25 Jan 45. Opns Rpt SGBN 52-0.1 (44701). (2) SigC SWPA, Sig Achievement-Luzon, p. 40.

plans were being made to capture the last steppingstones on the way to Tokyo, the Ryukyu Islands, chief of which was Okinawa. The assault was to be made by American troops drawn from various concentrations of military forces in the Pacific. The Okinawa invasion constituted an extension of the island conquests of the Central Pacific and Pacific Ocean Areas in general, especially of the Marianas, such as Saipan and Guam, and most recently, of Iwo Jima.[44]

The over-all strategy, set by the Joint Chiefs of Staff, had called for landings on Okinawa forty days after the Iwo attack began on 19 February 1945. The JCS had directed Admiral Nimitz, Commander in Chief, POA, to plan and carry out the Okinawa campaign. Nearly two thousand ships were employed, including what were in fact complete self-contained floating bases, capable of self-support at sea for prolonged military operations. The Tenth Army was to grapple with the enemy on Okinawa. The Tenth Army included three Marine and four Army divisions. Its commanding general was Lt. Gen. Simon B. Buckner, whose signal officer was Col. Arthur Pulsifer.

The Okinawa invasion employed over half a million Navy and Army troops gathered from installations all over the Pacific Ocean areas. The signal support for the Tenth Army came principally from the central or mid-Pacific area, centered in the Hawaiian Islands. Such plans as had been made earlier for an invasion of Formosa and the China coast remained largely valid for the now altered pattern of attack, which bypassed Formosa for the Ryukyus. In Hawaii, Brig. Gen. Carroll A. Powell, Chief Signal Officer, U.S. Army Forces, Pacific Ocean Areas, co-ordinated communications plans and requirements in many a conference with representatives of the Tenth Army, Commander in Chief, POA, the Service Forces Pacific, and the Fleet Marine Force Pacific.

Some training was given in the Hawaiian area to key communications personnel designated for Okinawa, but it was limited because of a shortage of time. Equipment requests were reviewed, especially those in excess of the tables of equipment. As always in major campaigns, the plans were several times changed. At first, plans called for only eleven airfields to be built on Okinawa. Signal officers drew up communications for them. Then twenty-three airfields were decided on, and the communications planners had to redouble their efforts. The first plans contemplated communications only to cover the southern third of the island, with much subterranean cable and not very much wire line overhead. But then staff officers blueprinted large ports and naval bases, and huge warehouses over much of the island. As a result, more extensive circuits had to be planned, using carrier facilities in order to multiply their traffic capacity, and plans had to be made for supplementary submarine cable lines along the shore. Plans had to be drawn

---

[44] The marines took ashore at Iwo a considerable amount of Signal Corps equipment such as antracs and Dukws carrying SCR-299's and 399's. Marine tanks used SCR-300's and exterior telephones for communication with infantrymen. (1) Hq Amphibious Corps Landing Force, Iwo Jima Sp Staff Sec Rpts, app. I, Rpt by Signal Officer (CO Provisional Signal Group), pp. 21, 26. SigC OP 370.2 Gen Rpts, 4 Jul 45–23 Oct 45. (2) Incl, Sp Action Rpt, Iwo Jima, 23 Apr 45, with ASF Transmittal Sheet, Capt H. C. Viken, Intel Br OCSigO, to Chief Logistics Plng Br OCSigO, 4 Jul 45, same sub. SigC OP 370.2 Rpt folder 6 Gen Rpts, 17–31 Aug 45, Tab 17.

up for scores of Signal Corps units for the Army Ground Forces and the Army Service Forces—units of many sorts. Nearly all came from sources in the Central Pacific or from the United States (the Signal Corps units that had fought up the island ladder from the South and Southwest Pacific were granted a respite). Except for the JASCO's, most of the units were base development troops, yet they had to serve in a dual capacity. They first had to support the assault troops, then turn to their basic tasks.[45]

As the Tenth Army Signal Section (sixteen officers and fifty men) planned it, twenty-eight different types of signal units would be needed. Preparing both tactical and base communications for Okinawa, the planners labored over signal networks, seeking to reduce non-divisional nets to a minimum in order to reserve as many frequencies as possible for divisional nets. "When you realize that this plan," a Signal Corps officer lectured the Armed Forces Staff College in 1947, "included complete radio frequency assignments for fleet and task forces, for landing forces, shipboard aircraft, Central Pacific Forward Area

Island Bases, and land-based aircraft, as well as Army, Navy, and Marine Corps frequencies for fixed and mobile stations, you then realize the tremendous amount of effort expended for radio communications alone." [46]

Another large task for the planners were the MCU's, precursors of the joint communications center on Okinawa. These units used at first modified SCR–399's, augmented by SCR–608, 188, and naval sets TBS and TBW. The transmitters and receivers were separated, placed in separate shelters, HO–17's mounted in 2½-ton trucks. AN/TRC–3 and 4 radio relay was included, with carrier CF–1 and 2 equipment, all installed in ordnance small arms repair trucks, M30's. Being unable to obtain a TOE for radio intelligence (though it had been foreseen that Okinawa would be an ideal location for radio intelligence work), the Signal Section planners improvised a provisional radio intelligence company. They could not, however, get a photographic company, or cryptanalytic and countermeasures units. They therefore improvised several photographic teams and eventually obtained a SIAM company. Meanwhile, as Tenth Army signal units made ready on Oahu, twelve Signal Corps men were dispatched to Iwo Jima where they got valuable observer-operator experience. A last-minute jam developed when a SIAM platoon arrived three days before sailing, and a photographic team only the day before.[47]

The communications of this campaign

[45] Hist, Signal Section, HUSAFMIDPAC, pp. 105–15. (Sec. II, Plng and Tng, Sig Of Hist, pp. 41–50.) This history lists "required" and also "furnished" signal units, but they do not correspond because the furnished units fell short of the requirement. Nor do the furnished units compare perfectly with the units listed by Roy E. Appleman, James M. Burns, Russell A. Gugeler, and John Stevens, in *Okinawa: The Last Battle*, UNITED STATES ARMY IN WORLD WAR II (Washington, 1948), app. A.

For JASCO's in the Okinawa invasion, see AFSC Lecture C–13, Communications for Joint Overseas Operations, Army Assault, and Consolidation Phases, Tab 25, pp. 1ff. SigC OP 352 AFSC Rpts, vol. 2, 1947–48. See also, Rpts, P&O Div OCSigO, 10 Apr and 15 Jun 45. Daily Digest, Staff Divs OCSigO, 1 Jan–30 Jun 45, SigC Exec Of file.

[46] AFSC Lecture O–42, Okinawa, Tab 3, p. 7. SigC OP 352 AFSC Rpts, vol. 2, 1947–48.
[47] Tenth Army Action Rpt, Ryukyus Campaign, ch. 11, Staff Sec Rpts, sec. XII, Sig. Opns Rpts 110–33.4 (17865), 26 Mar–30 Jun 45.

achieved a consummation of all the joint concepts and the joint practices that Navy communicators and Army Signal Corps men had been developing and refining from the very outset of Central Pacific combat. This was true from the first blueprints of the circuits and message centers, which comprised "a truly over-all joint theater communications plan." The Signal Corps officer whose words these were, Col. Charles W. Baer, commanded the joint communications activities of the island command.[48]

[48] AFSC Lecture 0–42, Okinawa, Tab 3, p. 7.
Major Signal Corps units and elements of Colonel Baer's command, Task Unit 99.3.7, were:
81st Signal Heavy Construction Battalion
443d Signal Heavy Construction Battalion (Aviation)
3345th Signal Service Company
3180th Signal Service Battalion
3161st Signal Service Company
3181st Signal Service Battalion
241st Signal Operations Company
57th Signal Repair Company
213th Signal Depot Company
585th Signal Depot Company
75th JASCO, less air liaison and shore fire control parties
593d JASCO, less air liaison and shore fire control parties
Naval communications personnel of the JCC included:
Mobile Communications Unit 47B
Mobile Communications Unit 43D
Radio Installation Team No. 2
Public Information Mobile Communications Unit No. 1.
The total personnel figure of the Joint Communication Activities reached a peak of about 7,900 Army and 1,100 Navy troops. For a general account, see: (1) Incl, Hq ISCOM Okinawa, Jt Com Activities, to 30 Jun 45, with Ltr, Baer, CO Hq Jt Com Activities, to CSigO, 27 Aug 45, pp. 4–5, Joint Com Activities Okinawa, to 30 Jun 45 [SOPAC Action Rpt]. SigC Hist Sec file. (2) AFSC Lecture C–8, Communications for Joint Overseas Operations, Base Development Phase, 1949, Tab 51, p. 5. SigC OP 352 AFSC Rpts, vol 7, 1949. (3) AFSC Lectures C–13, Tab 25, pp. 6–7, and C–14, Communications for Joint Overseas Operations, Base Development Phase, Tab 29, pp. 3–10. SigC OP 352 AFSC Rpts, vol. 2, 1947–48.

The Navy's share was heaviest during the amphibious stage. All the communications ships were the Navy's. They were amphibious force flagships, or equivalents, such as the AGC *Eldorado* and *Estes*. Another ship, the LSV *Montauk*, carried an alternate staff for Tenth Army and a number of Army radio and message center operators. Signal Corps' CP fleet of SWPA renown did not participate at Okinawa. The Navy provided equivalent facilities in its AGC's, on which a considerable number of Signal Corps men served for the specific purpose of handling Army circuits during joint amphibious operations. They were organized in general as signal detachments, headquarters ships. One such organization, designated Type A detachment, was formalized on 18 March 1945 under T/D 11–1027. It included 35 officers and men, as follows: [49]

20 radio operators	(SSN–766)
5 cryptographers	(SSN–807)
4 message center clerks	(SSN–667)
1 first sergeant	(SSN–585)
1 teletypewriter repairman	(SSN–239)
4 commissioned officers	(SSN–0224)

When the Navy commissioned in 1944 two of its AGC's, the *Auburn* and the *Estes*, it requested 70 Signal Corps men (8 officers and 62 enlisted men, evidently

[49] (1) Rpt, P&O Div OCSigO, 10 May 45, p. 3. Daily Digest, Staff Divs OCSigO, 1 Jan–30 Jun 45. SigC Exec Of file. (2) CSigO, Annual Rpt, FY 44, pp. 87f., 115. (3) Maj Charles E Robertson, The Amphibious Headquarters Ship (1949), Sig Sch Monograph, The Sig Sch Libr, Ft. Monmouth.

comprising two Type A detachments) for duty on the two ships. There were other types of such detachments, and by the war's end, in September 1945, no fewer than 16 of the type called Army signal detachments, amphibious flagship (TOE 11-607), were serving aboard naval vessels.[50]

Signal Corps troops to the number of 3 officers and 32 enlisted men were required in 1945 to serve aboard a new press ship, the USS *Spindle-Eye*, described as a "news transmission ship" under naval command. So many Signal Corps men were now serving aboard naval communications ships of one sort or another that the problem of their administration went up to the War Department General Staff, which approved a plan in mid-1945 to designate the Commanding General, Army Ground Forces, as administrator for the signal detachments, headquarters ships.[51]

---

[50] (1) Ind, Maj Gen Idwal H. Edwards, ACofS G-3, 14 Sep 45, on Memo, Gen Thomas T. Handy, DCofS, for CINCUS and CNO, sub: Army Sig Dets for Amphibious Force Flagships (AGC). (2) Ltr, Lt Gen Joseph T. McNarney, DCofS, to CINCUS, 5 May 44, sub: Army SigC Pers for Assignment to Amphibious Force Flagships–1944 Const, with Ind, Gen Handy, 5 May 44. Both in WDGSA 210.31 sec. 1, case 50. General McNarney informed the Navy that trained Signal Corps troops with proper qualifications were "extremely scarce." Their assignment would be delayed, and they would have to complete their training on the ships.

[51] Rpt, P&O Div, 5, 6 and 7 Aug 45. Daily Digest, Staff Divs OCSigO, 1 Jul-31 Dec 45, SigC Exec Of file.

A "news transmission ship" under Army command for Pacific operations was briefly considered in mid-1945 by the Operations Division, the Signal Corps, and the Transportation Corps. Rpt, P&O Div, 20 Jun 45. Daily Digest, Staff Divs OCSigO, 1 Jan-30 Jun 45, SigC Exec Of file. Regarding *Spindle-Eye*, see Pauline M. Oakes, The Army Command and Administrative Communications System, pt. III, SigC Domestic Communications Network as Extended to Overseas Terminals During Demobilization, 14 August 1945-31 December

Thus it was Navy's ships that carried to Okinawa the Army commanders and the communications essential to their command. The Joint Expeditionary Force and troop commanders and the Command Air Support Control Unit sailed on the *Eldorado*. The second in command of the joint force and the commander of the amphibious force sailed on the *Estes*. The Tenth Army communications plan included command post locations afloat down to and including divisions, each commander receiving small patrol craft equipped with communications facilities. The core of communications, however, was still to be the mobile communications units,[52] whose vehicular radios moved quickly ashore and soon developed into the Joint Communication Center. The Okinawa JCC was to become the largest, most completely joint center in the Pacific, climaxing a practice that had grown up from the beginning of Army-Navy cooperation in amphibious island combat.

L-day, the invasion day for Okinawa, was 1 April 1945. Until the situation ashore stabilized, the JCC remained aboard the *Eldorado*, which handled all the long-range radio circuits to Guam and Saipan until these circuits could be turned over to the island commander. On 2 April all the Army radio operators and Signal Section clerks, who had been aboard the *Montauk*, transferred their work to the *Eldorado* to assist the JCC

1945 (1946), SigC Hist Monograph E-5C, pp. 59ff. SigC Hist Sec file.

[52] The Army furnished the primary MCU, the Navy furnished two secondary ones (MCU's 47-B and 43-D). Their function was "initially to provide all intra- and off-island radio communications for elements of the Tenth Army and the Island Command." Incl, Hq ISCOM Okinawa, Jt Com Activities, p. 10.

there, though they still had to live on the *Montauk*, becoming daily commuters, because of insufficient accommodations on the *Eldorado*.

Radio circuits worked well, though there was the usual trouble with frequency crowding and call-sign confusion. There was a considerable airplane message service, and also a boat message service between the several command ships. The JASCO's handled the control of naval gunfire against shore targets. Then, as shore conditions permitted, the MCU's, along with an operations company and a light construction battalion, climbed into two LST's. An important provision was that the LST's each carried a bulldozer, loaded last in order to be first ashore. These behemoths proved valuable in the work of getting communications vans and trailers in place and digging them in quickly.

By 11 April the mobile units ashore had radioteletype circuits in operation. By 6 May their radio circuits numbered eighteen, accompanied by many wire facilities on the island. In the message center, Army and Navy officers and men worked indiscriminately on all assignments for all arms and services.[53] The procedure manuals they used were mostly naval.

There were problems. In the early stages, the JCC (actually the primary and two subordinate MCU's) was overloaded with work; equipment was late in arriving; there was too much traffic that was too highly rated in urgency. On one day, for example, 17 percent of the traffic was urgent, 75 percent operational priority, 6 percent priority, only 2 percent routine, and none of it deferred. There were troubles with the automatic cipher equipment, essential to speed the transmission of enciphered radio traffic. Some of this equipment on hand early in July could not be used, complained Colonel Baer, "because many component parts have been echeloned at late dates." Some of the parts, he explained, had arrived in June, but "other component parts, necessary for operation, have been echeloned in as late as September." In plain language, they had not yet been sent, and were not scheduled for another three months. "Installation was made of the . . . equipment between Tenth Army and the JCC for transmission of Top Secret messages," Colonel Baer recorded on 7 July. "In order to do this," he added, "we had AFmidPAC send some of the parts . . . by air shipment." [54]

The chief problem that harassed the joint communications effort was the one that increasingly bedeviled an increasingly technological era calling for ever larger numbers of increasingly skilled men—personnel. Specifically it was the lack of enough qualified officers and men

[53] Compare this single purposiveness with the multiplicity (and duplication) of message centers that complicated SWPA communications two years earlier when the Sixth Army signal officer, Colonel Reichelderfer, had to provide communications not only with SWPA headquarters and with the message centers of various subordinate units, but with Naval air forces, and with the Australians as well. "I had seven different signal centers operating at one time," Reichelderfer later recalled. AFSC Lecture C–15, 29 May 47, Tab 24, p. 2.

[54] Baer, Hq Jt Com Activities, Jnl, 1 Apr–30 Jun 45 (with continuation to 31 Jul 45), entries under 5 and 7 Jul, pp. 127–28. Jt Com Activities Okinawa, to 30 Jun 45.

In an entry on page 96, dated 30 May 1945, Colonel Baer, speaking of radio communications, recorded that "the Temporary JCC went into operation at 270800, eliminating the Primary and Secondary MCU's." That is, the MCU's functioned as the JCC ashore until the morning of 27 May, nearly two months after L-day.

to staff and run well so large an operation. Tenth Army's communications,
which were handling 15,000 words of
radio traffic weekly by mid-April,
mounted to a peak of 475,000 words for
the week ending 2 June 1945. And the
complexity of the equipment was in-
tensifying. Colonel Baer summarized the
dilemma: " . . . if use is to be made
of all advancements in modern communications for command control, the
percentage of communications personnel
must rise or else use of these advancements will not materialize." [55]

Such success as the JCC and Joint
Communication Activities attained on
Okinawa, Colonel Baer attributed to the
outstanding efforts of those Army and
Navy personnel who were assigned to
communications. The many demands for
communications that developed during
the campaign often exceeded the limits
of the equipment and the men, "but
at no time," he declared, "was any activity without any communications." Colonel Pulsifer, speaking as the Tenth Army
signal officer, expressed equal pride. He
wrote on 28 May to General Ingles:

We have a condition out here "not in
the books." Our army is actually a small
theater though not officially so designated.
We have a tactical setup of two Corps and
a communication zone setup with a large

base development plan to be executed. We
top the whole affair. In addition we have
a local "Navy and Air Force" as members
of our command. Our regular Army Signal Section of 16 officers and 50 enlisted
men prepared the Base Plans as well as the
tactical plan. We did not get any staff
assistance until about February after all
our plans were made. Now as we see our
plan appearing on the ground instead of
on the map we are getting rather proud
of our signal setup.

Finally, that the joint communications
concept was wise and altogether desirable, Colonel Baer at least never
doubted. "Economy of equipment and
forces dictates that there must be only
one communication system serving all
agencies." Of the two ways in which a
joint system could be controlled—by
joint command or by joint committee—
Colonel Baer had doubt about which
was the better. Three months of operation on Okinawa proved conclusively to
him that "a joint command for co-ordinating communication activities [is]
sound and far superior to the committee
and board method." Boards and committees are prone to quibble or they fail
to compromise altogether, he explained,
whereas one officer responsible for
a joint system can exercise more
effective control.[56] Thus, in his opinion,
the unified command concept proved itself in a theater of war—whereas in the
Washington headquarters, where a conflict of unified command versus communications boards and committees had
flared early in 1943, the committee
system had won and continued to

[55] AFSC Lecture 0–42, Okinawa, Tab 3, p. 26.

Colonel Baer cited a shortage of some four
hundred telephone operators and the lack of professional communications engineers to lay out a
plant of the size and complexity required on
Okinawa.

On JCC matters in general, see: (1) Tenth Army
Action Rpt, Ryukyus Campaign, ch. 11, Staff Sec
Rpts, sec. XII, Sig, pp. 7, 10, and 20, Opns Rpts
110-33.4 (17865), 26 Mar–30 Jun 45; (2) Incl, Hq
ISCOM Okinawa, Jt Com Activities; (3) Donald
Becker, "One Voice of Command," Signals, III,
No. 5 (May–June 1949), 35ff.

[56] (1) Incl, Hq ISCOM Okinawa, Jt Com Activities, pp. 25–26. (2) Ltr, Pulsifer to Ingles, 28 May
45. SigC OP 370.2 Rpt folder 4, Gen Rpts Theater
of Opns, 30 May 45–11 Aug 45.

preside over Army communications to the war's end.[57]

Not all officers in combat theaters agreed with Colonel Baer. Both General Akin and Colonel Reichelderfer favored, out of their SWPA experience, separate communications systems for the several military services co-operating in task force operations. Likewise, the SOPAC signal officer, Colonel Ankenbrandt, had spoken in favor of separate circuits for each military arm. An officer who had served in the GHQ SWPA Signal Section, Lt. Col. Earl G. Kline, recalled years later that the JCC station on Okinawa had been difficult to communicate with because of confusion there, as communicators of the several services tried to work each other's radio circuits without sufficient training.[58] But the JCC idea had its points, and its operations improved as on-the-job experience accumulated.

Truly effective joint communications, commented a postwar lecturer addressing an Armed Forces Staff College audience, "calls for partial integration among the services themselves." It certainly requires a high degree of standardization of the signal equipment and the procedures and codes and ciphers that are employed. It was partly because of the varied equipment and the different procedures and systems of the several Allied participants that General Akin in SWPA operations let each service employ its own communications in its own way, co-ordinating with others but not operating jointly. To some World War II veterans, Rear Adm. John R. Redman quipped in 1952 (he was then Director of the Joint Communications-Electronics Committee), "Joint communications" meant that the Navy furnished the "joint" and the Army the "communications." [59]

In general, communications on and around Okinawa seem to have been among the best attained in the Pacific campaigning. This was well. Good communications were especially needed to warn of the enemy's air attacks and to destroy his kamikazes. The Navy singled out its VHF "flycatcher" circuit for praise in this regard. Good air support, "superior to that of any previous operation of the war," Tenth Army officers attributed to "the abundant communication facilities" in the landing force air support control units and to the tireless work of the air liaison parties. Besides the flycatcher circuit, the Navy spoke highly of its radio teletypewriter circuit from the *Eldorado* to Guam and praised its VHF teletypewriter service between the AGC communications ships and Tenth Army headquarters ashore.[60]

The introduction of Army's VHF radio relay to the Navy, however, was not effected without some of the opposition new devices always encounter. Colonel Pulsifer, Tenth Army signal

[57] Thompson, Harris, et al., The Test, pp. 552ff.
[58] (1) Thompson, Harris, et al., The Test, pp. 472–73. (2) Interv, SigC Hist Sec with Kline, 9 Jan and 19 Feb 58. See also above pp. 243ff.

[59] (1) AFSC Lecture, Tab 27. SigC OP 352 AFSC Rpts, vol. 9. (2) AFSC, Norfolk, Va., Communications for Joint Overseas Operations, 1947–48, pp. 1ff. (3) JCEC, What It Means—What It Does, Address by Rear Adm. John R. Redman, Signals, VI, No. 6 (July–August 1952), p. 23.
[60] (1) Tenth Army Action Rpt, Ryukyus Campaign, ch. 11, Staff Sec Rpts, sec. VII, Air, p. 5. Opns Rpts 110-33.4 (17865), 26 May–30 Jun 45. (2) AFSC Lecture 0-42, Okinawa, Tab 3, pp. 10, 24.

LW Radar Station, Tori Shima

officer, reported to General Ingles that the Army was using the equipment for ship-to-shore communications and "having success though some of the Navy bucked me very much." The antrac, AN/TRC–3, and 4, was of course foremost among the new technical developments and was put to use "with as great success out here as . . . in Europe," added Pulsifer, saying, "we are using it both tactically and administratively." [61]

Amid these communications developments, the use of pigeons on Okinawa

nearly faded away, but not quite. Pigeons could be employed, and they occasionally were, as an alternative to radio when the frequencies were clogged with too many transmissions. For example, Navy beachmasters at Buckner Bay had trouble getting prompt cargo information from incoming supply ships, data they needed to assign available anchorages. The Tenth Army Signal Section therefore gave the Navy baskets of pigeons. The birds were released from the convoys, bearing messages stating what each ship carried. Flying to their loft on the beach in a moment or two, they delivered their messages efficiently and quickly to the pleasure of the beachmasters and to

[61] Ltr, Pulsifer, SigO Hq Tenth Army, to Ingles, 23 May 45. SigC (OP) 370.2 Rpt Folder 4 Gen Rpts Theaters of Opns, 30 May 45–11 Aug 45.

the relief of harried radio communicators.[62]

Nonetheless, it was the opinion of
Colonel Pulsifer that pigeon services
were no longer needed. "I recommend
deletion of the pigeon company," he
urged Ingles, "because of recent technical developments and the ridicule by
staff officers." At the same time he
pressed for a radio relay company and
a full photo company, to augment the
six teams he had on hand on the island.
He also wanted a full radio intelligence
company rather than the provisional one
he had. "We have uncovered an SIS field
here that we have been told was unknown," and he needed more radio intelligence specialists to exploit the opportunity.

On one occasion in particular, in May
1945, the chief of the signal intelligence
division of Colonel Pulsifer's signal office, Lt. Col. Wallace M. Lauterbach,
and his provisional RI company brilliantly demonstrated to dubious Army
commanders (who had hitherto doubted
the RI potential) how valuable this service could be in tactical combat. Detachments of the provisional RI company on
Okinawa and adjacent islands in the
Kerama Retto had set up their inter
cept and DF (direction finding) facilities and were obtaining excellent fixes
on enemy transmitter locations. One location was on a hill, apparently
unoccupied, in the Shuri defense complex. Colonel Lauterbach induced the
reluctant artillery officer of the XXIV
Corps to test the indications obtained

by the RI unit. The heavy fire from all
division batteries in the area was placed
upon the seemingly abandoned hill in
a TOT (time on target) concentration.
It blew off the top, revealing a honey-
comb of installations. A Japanese division headquarters had been operating
completely concealed therein, except
that the radiations of visually unnoticed
radio antenna wires had been clearly
perceived and pinpointed by Colonel
Lauterbach's intercept and DF specialists.

Another specialized organization that
Colonel Pulsifer keenly desired was an
RCM unit. He had asked for one but
did not get it, and "now," he wrote in
May, "we find we could have used one
to good advantage. The Japs are starting
to jam us rather heavily, especially on
our ADCC circuits. They use lots of
window." [63]

Not all the jamming of U.S. equipment on Okinawa was done by the
enemy. Some of it was accidentally
caused by our own radiations. "The VT
[variable time] fuze, used with the
105 mm. howitzer," reported a staff college lecturer after the war, "burst all
along the trajectory, drawing howls from
our infantry." The artillerymen had to
stop using this highly specialized fuze

---

[62] Interv, Dr. Thompson, Sig Hist Off, with Col
Oscar C. Buser, CO U.S. Sig Com Security Agency,
Arlington, Va., 7 Nov 62. Buser, as lieutenant
colonel, was the Assistant Signal Officer, Tenth
Army, 1944–45.

[63] (1) Ltr, Pulsifer to Ingles, 23 May 45. SigC
OP 370.2 Rpt folder 4, Gen Rpts Theater of
Opns, 30 May 45–11 Aug 45. (2) Interv, Thompson,
SigC Hist Of, with Lauterbach, ExecO OCSigO, 26
Jul 61.
Months earlier the Office of the Chief Signal
Officer had been preparing two companies, the
3153d and 3155th Signal Service Companies, for
RCM work in the Pacific. Lt Col Frederic C.
Lough, New Projs, 30 Aug 44. SigC OP 319.1 Daily
Rpts, Jun 43–Oct 45.
Window, also called "Chaff," was, of course,
strips of tin foil dropped from planes to produce
false echoes, "blinding" aircraft search radars.

(so effective when all goes well), he added, since "it was determined that friendly destroyer radars were probably triggering them." This is a good example of the complexity of, and the absolute need of, adequate frequency control in any combat situation.[64]

Mopping up the Ryukyus proceeded through the early and midsummer amid plans to invade Japan's home islands. The Philippines now became the nucleus of feverish preparations, which included signals, the Sixth Army, and again the CP fleet.

The Sixth Army, while resting from the Philippine campaign, began readying for Operation OLYMPIC, the planned invasion of the Japanese home islands. No easy landing was anticipated. In the summer of 1945 Signal Corps men in the communications center serving MacArthur's GHQ in Manila—now changed in title from SWPA to AFPAC (U.S. Army Forces, Pacific)—organized a huge mobile communications unit intended to serve the advance echelon of army headquarters during the OLYMPIC operation. For its manpower, the unit drew principally upon the 232d Signal Operations Company, based at Manila, supplemented by teams from the 4025th Signal Service Group and from the Seaborne Communications Detachment (the CP fleet). Arrangements were made for all the normal multifarious activities of an army signal setup such as radio, wire, and signal center facilities, with details for plant and telephone, radio transmitter and receiver installation and operation, VHF and carrier, teletypewriter, message center facilities, crypto maintenance, and so on. And in particular, as everywhere else in the Pacific fighting, arrangements had to be made for communications ships and ship-to-shore signaling. The anticipated attack on the Japanese home islands was expected to repeat the pattern, requiring that Army signal centers be maintained afloat until the shore could be secured for dependable land installations.[65]

The big MCU was planned in three increments. The first, 100 percent vehicular mounted and manned by 150 to 200 officers and men, was to follow General MacArthur, wherever he might go ashore, to serve solely as his personal communications outfit. A second increment of about 600 men would go ashore, as soon as the beach was secure, and would set up heavy duty circuits with Manila, Honolulu, Hollandia, and other points. The third increment was to remain offshore as a reserve force, for ultimate employment ashore at Kagoshima.[66]

The expected ordeal never developed. Two atom bombs suddenly ended the war, and Tokyo announced its readiness to surrender. Meanwhile, American ships and men headed for Japan.

There was a variety of headquarters and of signal communications serving them. "Our last ship," said Colonel Reichelderfer, Chief Signal Officer, Sixth

---

[64] AFSC Lecture o-42, Okinawa, Tab 3, p. 9.

There was no serious jamming of communications circuits in the Okinawa campaign. "For reasons known only to the Japs," commented the same lecturer, page 25, "little interference of our radio communications was reported. . . . We were extremely fortunate . . . because some VHF circuits such as fleet common, small craft, and local command circuits were having from 60 to 125 stations per day using each of these circuits." *Ibid.*

[65] 1st Lt. Jacques Kunitz, "Sequel to Surrender on the Air," *Signals*, I, No. 2 (November–December, 1946), 47.

[66] Interv, SigC Hist Div with McKinney, 8 Sep 60.

Army, "was the LSV [landing ship, vehicle]-1 (USS *Katskill*) which operated under Navy control as an auxiliary command ship on our trip to Japan." It did not receive much use since the command ship of the Sixth Army, USS *Auburn*, sufficed.[67]

Sixth Army communications were not the first to reach the home islands. The *Teton*, a naval AGC command vessel completely equipped with communications facilities, left Okinawa on 18 August, along with the PCE boats of the old CP fleet. They arrived off Yokohama on 28 August.

Meanwhile, an advanced element of the MCU, organized in Manila, constituted the first communicator team to set foot on Japanese soil. Maj. John McKinney, who until that time had commanded the GHQ communications center in Manila, took the mobile communications unit to Okinawa, where he had only eleven days to test his mass of equipment and put it into good working condition. Arriving in Yokohama with the first load of his MCU's equipment (a score of planeloads brought in the rest of the MCU later on), McKinney and his small initial crew at once set up a communications center with much apprehension as hundreds of Japanese, their attitude unknown, looked on. Working around the clock, they pressed into service their initial, severely limited, facilities.

Not least of the communications demands were the insistent cries of the gentlemen of the press. Each sought priority for his own script, that it be radioed out first upon the formal surrender of Japan. Naturally, the first planeload of facilities had included no radio to satisfy press needs. Major McKinney turned to the big commercial transmitters of RCA, Mackay, and others, still intact from prewar days, but they were some thirty miles out of town, posing the problem of running a line to them through the rubble of Yokohama. This was solved, but then arose the question as to how to key the transmitters, which could handle only Boehme high-speed tape. The Army no longer employed such transmission, having long since converted to radioteletypewriter operation. No one knew the Boehme code. Some Japanese Boehme experts were available, though they could not read English. Major McKinney got them to transfer press articles, letter by letter, to tape, a task they could do without knowing the language.

Meanwhile, the newsmen brought in their reports in piles, each demanding priority for himself, putting his pages on top of the piles, hoping to win the next transmission. The signalmen, following strictly the just rule of first come, first served, quietly slipped each new offering underneath, at the bottom of the pile, to await its turn.[68]

[67] Reichelderfer, "Sixth Army Communications," *Signals*, III, No. 2, 8. The 16th Signal Operations Battalion, Sixth Army, landed at Wakayama in September and set up VHF communications on the beach to the *Auburn*. Later, the Sixth Army message center, radio and code rooms, and switchboards were set up in the Daiken Building in Kyoto. GHQ AFPAC communications centered in Tokyo. Krueger, *From Down Under to Nippon*, p. 366.

[68] Interv, SigC Hist Div with McKinney, 8 Sep 60.

Some Signal Corps officers, it was later recorded, "still recall the enormous pressure placed upon comcenters by name correspondents to get priority for their traffic." Draft MS Comment, Hq U.S. Army, Sig Sup Agency, 24 Sep 59, sub: Review of the Signal Corps: The Outcome, p. 6. Sig Hist Sec file.

Major McKinney and the advance elements of his MCU maintained message traffic from their post in the Custom House in Yokohama with the *Teton* in Tokyo Bay, with Manila, and with the battleship *Missouri* during the surrender ceremony on 2 September. On 8 September officers and men of this unit entered Tokyo itself with General MacArthur and the 1st Cavalry Division. They set up for business on the third floor of the Daiichi Building, MacArthur's GHQ, facing the Imperial Palace.[69] The war had come to an end in the city where, for the United States, it had started nearly four years earlier with the launching of the Japanese Imperial Fleet against Pearl Harbor.

---

[69] (1) Eddy, "Manila and the Capitulation," *Signals*, I, No. 5, 47. (2) Kunitz, "Sequel to Surrender on the Air," *Signals*, I, No. 2, 57ff. Sixth Army's last CP was at Kyoto, where it opened on 27 September 1945. It was the thirteenth of a long series of command posts that had begun in Australia at Camp Columbia, near Brisbane, on 16 February 1943. See the list given by Reichelderfer in, "Sixth Army Communications," *Signals*, III, No. 2, 5-7.

CHAPTER X

Electronic Combat: Countermeasures

The adversaries in World War II pitted more than men against each other. The struggle became one of increasingly ingenious and destructive mechanisms on land, on sea, and in the air. Permeating all these areas, a new type of conflict developed during the war—electronic combat.

Radar and Radio Countermeasures, a New Arena of Conflict

Nothing devised by man is perfect or foolproof. Combatants seek out every weakness in their opponents' tactics and in their equipment. In electronic radiations the foremost weakness is that, whether radio or radar, they travel through the ambient air or space, which nature has made common to all men. The same air or space that provides the medium through which an electromagnetic wave speeds, like its kindred light rays, also provides a path over which an opponent can transmit a counterradiation. As any radio listener knows, two transmissions at the same frequency interfere with each other, and neither is intelligible.

In matters of radio, nations and armies alike had long made every effort to regulate frequency assignments in order to prevent interference. In war no less than in peace, radio interference is a thing to be avoided. If you create interference over some of the frequency bands the enemy is using, that is, if you jam these frequencies, you deny the use of those areas of the radio spectrum to yourself as well. In addition, you might profit more by intercepting the enemy's signals and analyzing them for the intelligence they convey.[1]

Radio jamming, in World War II generally did not require, and did not receive, much attention. Everyone was far more concerned with listening in. However, when radar pulses burst into the realms of radio and when inhuman radio-guided missiles put in their terrifying appearance, the electromagnetic frequencies employed by the new military engines became suddenly too dangerous to neglect. The spectrum itself became a weapon that could be deadly. Its use by the enemy had to be combatted.

RCM combat quickly fell into a pattern of giddily circling cycles. First, one had to discover through radio and technical intelligence the details of the enemy's radio and radar systems, what frequencies he used and for what purposes. Secondly, one's research and development agencies had to devise equipment to counter the hostile system, generally at its weakest point (the countering device might be a particular

---

[1] Ltr, R. C. Raymond, Opns Analysis Sec MAAF Hq, to Dr. Frederick E. Terman, RRL, 21 Apr 44, no sub, p. 5. AAG 413.44–DV Radio.

electronic jammer able to interfere dis-
astrously with the enemy's radiotelephones, or with his gun-laying radars).
Thirdly, one had to use the countermeasure equipment suddenly and effectively in a planned action. Finally, the
enemy would then make changes, shifting to other frequencies, or developing
equipment to nullify the jammer. Then
the cycle would repeat. Victory in these
techniques would ultimately go to the
nation that best utilized its brains that
produced suddenly needed equipment
the faster, that played the game with the
greater ingenuity. It became a strange
combat of intelligence, of science, of production, of planned integrated tactics
behind the men who fired the guns, flew
the planes, and dropped the bombs.[2]

The forces engaged in this new form
of combat were marshaled under the
enigmatic letters RCM, which could
mean either radio or radar countermeasures. Deadly serious, it differed
much from all forms of fighting hitherto
known. It constituted something very
new in the military art, a thing entirely
characteristic of the ever more technical
twentieth century. It was fought by electronic engineers in the field and in the
laboratory and by crews of officers and
men who might be engineers in uniform.
Or if they were not, they were well on
their way to becoming skilled specialists.
Their equipment was often as not crash
built,[3] rather than mass produced, constructed on a sudden demand. Often the

scientists and engineers themselves had
to meet a dire and very specific situation,
one that would very likely never be repeated in quite the same form again. It
was special equipment, employed by
specialists in a special warfare.

The German radio-controlled glide
bomb used against naval targets presented just such a situation in 1943, and
the Allies rushed to jam its operating
frequencies. The Signal Corps, the AAF,
and the Navy all co-operated in this venture. Upon learning of the bomb, the
Signal Corps supplied the Navy with
search receivers and jammers to be installed in destroyer escorts that the
Navy hastily readied to meet the menace. The Signal Corps provided two
SCR–596 jammers, together with amplifiers and panoramic receivers, which the
Camp Coles Signal Laboratory had intended to use for AGF needs. Within
two days of the request, Camp Coles
sent the equipment (including an AN/
ARQ–5) and several men to install it.[4]

[2] (1) Col. Frederick C. Moore, "Radio Counter-
Measures," *Signals*, III, No. 2 (November–December, 1948), 25. (2) *Electronics Warfare*, pp. 1–3,
36–37.

[3] "Crash" construction originated in British usage,
when radio and radar researchers themselves
hastily built pieces of equipment. The Americans
borrowed the term along with the practice. The
civilian radar laboratories, Radiation Laboratory
(RL) and Radio Research Laboratory (RRL),
under the NDRC in Cambridge, Massachusetts,
set up a model shop specifically to turn out crash
items. This shop was named the Research Construction Company. By 1944 the Signal Corps
established a Research Division in the Aircraft
Radio Laboratory (ARL) somewhat similarly, to
specialize in airborne RCM devices, including
crash production of them. See also below, pp.
435ff.

[4] (1) CSigO, Annual Rpt. FY 44, p. 331. (2)
Memo, Col John J. Downing, Asst Chief E&T Sv,
for CSigO, 5 Oct 43, sub: Countermeasures Against
Guided Missiles. AAG 413.44–BP Radio. (3) Incl,
Hist Review of RCM Equip, pp. 15–17, with Ltr,
CO SCASA to CSigO, 24 Jan 44, sub: Hist Review
of RCM Equip. SigC 413.44 Radar, Hist (ET–
2627).
Effective jamming of the successful radio-controlled bomb was "considerably delayed" because
the Allies did not at first have suitable equipment
to analyze its signals. SCEL Postwar R&D Prog
(Tentative), 5 Dec 45, p. 106.

Conversely, the British airborne search radar, the early ASV-II, presented a similar problem to the enemy, as bombers so equipped hunted many a German sub to its destruction. Discovering the situation, the Germans developed a special receiver, the Biscay Cross, over which crewmen could hear the pulses of the probing radar aboard an approaching plane in time to dive their craft to safety. The Germans also used a receiver of French design, the Metox, to detect sufficiently in advance the radiations of the long-wave ASV-II radar. Soon, true to the pattern of RCM warfare, the Allies countered these measures with the new microwave ASV radars such as the SCR-517. The radiations of this set employed such shortwave lengths that the enemy's search receivers could not detect them. Nor did the Germans immediately devise suitable receivers since they did not imagine microwave radar to be possible. Thus it was a seesaw conflict, this RCM combat. For example, the very successful German air raid on the Allied port of Bari, Italy, in 1944, succeeded largely because the enemy blinded Allied radars in the area with metallic paper strips similar to British Window or American Chaff. They had first used this type of countermeasure with success at Bizerte, North Africa, in September 1943.[5]

RCM did not always succeed. The Allies, expecting that the dreaded buzz and rocket bombs, V-1 and V-2, might be radio controlled, amassed quantities of RCM equipment in England in 1944, but to no avail, since the enemy's V weapons (ballistic missiles) flew, after their first aiming, like gun projectiles, without guidance.

Already in mid-1942 the Communications Coordination Branch in the Office of the Chief Signal Officer had drawn up a summary of wartime jamming to that date. Late in 1941 the British had successfully jammed German tank radios during the Libyan campaign. The Japanese from the start of the Pacific fighting had at times interfered somewhat with Allied radio circuits. Then on 12 February 1943, the Allied world was shaken when it learned that the warships *Scharnhorst, Gneisenau,* and *Prinz Eugen* had eluded the British and escaped from Brest through the English Channel to German home bases. The world did not know at the time that the Germans on this occasion had effectively jammed British coastal radars, blinding them so that they did not detect the passing of the warships through the waters under their surveillance.[6]

---

[5] (1) Ltr, V. H. Fraenckel, Actg Dir ABL-15, to Terman, RRL, 29 Sep 43. SigC 413.44 RCM (RB-2070). (2) Incl, Capt Nathan L. Krisberg, Rpt, German RCM Activity in Connection With Raid on Bizerte the Night of September 6, with Ltr, CG AAF to Chairman, Countermeasures Cmte, JCB, 28 Sep 43, sub: Rpt on Enemy Use of Window. AAG 413.44-BN Radio.

[6] (1) Info Request Study No. S-6, Lt Col Sidney F. Mashbir, Stat and Reference Div, Com Coordination Br, 5 Jun 42, sub: Radio Jamming, SigC C&E Case No. 38, Study of U.S. Rqmts for Radio Jamming Equip, Tab E. (2) Baxter, *Scientists Against Time,* p. 158. (3) CSigO, Annual Rpts, FY 43, pp. 219-25, and FY 45, p. 412. SigC Hist Sec file. (4) Allan A. Michie, "The Greatest Hoax of the War," *Reader's Digest* (October, 1946), p. 118. (5) Capt. Helmuth Giessler, "The Breakthrough of the Scharnhorst—Some Radio Technical Details," *IRE Transactions of Military Electronics,* vol. Mil-5, No. 1 (January, 1961), pp. 2-7.

Sir Robert Watson-Watt subsequently re-evaluated this incident, concluding that the jamming did not entirely blind the radars, but that human error and confusion were chiefly responsible. Robert Watson-Watt, *The Pulse of Radar* (New York: Dial Press, 1959), pp. 358ff.

SKETCH SHOWING HOW CHAFF OPERATED

Radio and radar men knew what had happened in the English Channel. They knew, too, that, although radar was developing into a potent weapon, it could be rendered nearly useless unless they found effective antijamming (AJ) solutions, or unless they could build new radars less susceptible to jamming. The same applied to radio. Besides, what the enemy could do to the Allies in these matters, the Allies could do in retaliation, if they set about preparing. They did, at once.[7]

Organizing for RCM

The British were somewhat in the lead, as they had been with radar applications three years earlier. Already, Lt. Col. Marion Van Voorst, a Signal Corps officer and assistant military attaché in London, had reported on this subject.[8] In 1943 Dr. David B. Langmuir was in England studying the strange warfare of radio, radar, and countermeasures. He had been sent from the NDRC, where a special activity, organized as Division 15 under Dr. C. G. Suits, had taken form in 1942 to deal with RCM matters behind triple-barred secrecy. Division 15 even possessed its own laboratory, separately established apart from the Radiation Laboratory, but nearby at Harvard University. Called the Radio Research Laboratory (RRL), it operated under the direction of Dr. Frederick E. Terman.[9] This important RCM laboratory

at first rather overlooked the Signal Corps, which lacked representation therein, since it was the needs of the AAF that had instigated the establishment of RRL. But Maj. Gen. Lucius D. Clay, in ASF, when he heard that the Navy was sending two full-time liaison officers to the new RCM laboratory, determined that the Army, too, should send at least one officer since "our interest in . . . radio countermeasures is as vital as that of the Navy."[10]

For some time the Army—the Signal Corps in matters of this sort—had been working with RCM and had designed the search receiver SCR–587 and the jamming transmitter SCR–596. Both sets were the outcome of research projects that had begun at the Aircraft Radio Laboratory early in 1942.[11] Meanwhile, in the Office of the Chief Signal Officer the Army Communications and Equipment Coordination Board studied the entire subject. By November 1942

[7] *Electronics Warfare*, pp. 12ff.

[8] See papers in SigC 413.44 RCM Gen No. 1 (ET–2381).

[9] Baxter, *Scientists Against Time*, pp. 159–60. Subsequently Division 15 and its RRL created a British branch, the American-British Laboratory–15 (ABL–15), just as Division 14 and RL established in England in September 1943 the British Branch of the Radiation Laboratory (BBRL). (1) *Ibid.*, p. 408. (2) Dr. Henry E. Guerlac, Hist Div OSRD, Radar, 1945, pp. 1047ff., in consecutively numbered pages of photostat copy in SigC Hist Sec files. In original pagination these pages are sec, E, ch, III, pp. 1ff (3) Thiesmeyer and Burchard, *Combat Scientists*, p. 4.

The RCM activity in the ETO was headed by the Radio Countermeasures Division of the Signal Service ETOUSA till 23 August 1944, when it was subordinated as a branch under the Technical Liaison Division. ETOUSA Rpt, II, 170, 240.

[10] Martin P. Claussen, Development of Radio and Radar Equipment for Air Operations, 1939–44. p. 99, AAF Hist Monograph. Photostatic copy, SigC Hist Sec files.

[11] See Thompson, Harris, et al., *The Test*, p. 86. Interestingly enough, when two years earlier still, in 1940, the ARL had given some attention to jammers for use against enemy communications, the AAF had objected that time and effort were wasted on jamming. Claussen, Dev of Radio and Radar Equip for Air Opns, 1939–44, p. 97.

it concluded that the Chief Signal Officer should promote RCM research and should organize a group in his office solely to deal with it. The board recognized some of the implications. All the air space of earth and the entire radio and radar range of the frequency spectrum would become the arena of the new form of warfare. The control of this all-encompassing sphere could scarcely be the prerogative of any one arm, or any one service, or indeed of any one nation.

The subject by late 1942 had grown sharp enough to penetrate to the Joint Chiefs of Staff. So it was that Maj. Gen. Thomas T. Handy referred the matter to General Marshall, emphasizing the board's recommendation that high commands be provided with a special staff "whose function is to handle all phases of radio countermeasures. . . ." The staff was to include representatives from G–2, the Signal Corps (radio intelligence), AAF, the Navy, and others such as any Allied nations that might be concerned. General Handy added, "As approval of this recommendation would involve agencies not under War Department control, the Army Communications and Equipment Board recommends that the case be presented to the Joint Chiefs of Staff for consideration. The Operations Division, WDGS, and the Assistant Chief of Staff, G–2, have expressed concurrences." [12]

The War Department recognized that

the use of RCM, including radio deceptions as well as jamming, had become "a most important element in the conduct of successful operations." Advancement of the art, of its equipment and its procedures, "should be prosecuted with all dispatch." War Department authorities divided RCM responsibility between the Army Air Forces and the Signal Corps rather awkwardly. The chasm that had long split the Army's electronic development widened. For years, radio and radar progress had been hampered because airborne equipment fell to the Aircraft Radio Laboratory in Dayton, Ohio, while ground equipment, even Air Forces ground radios that functioned intimately with airborne counterparts, was developed in the Fort Monmouth laboratories in New Jersey. RCM activities conducted in aircraft were charged to the AAF, along with the responsibility for recommending the type, number, and assignment of AAF units engaged in RCM. Countermeasures other than those conducted in aircraft fell to the Signal Corps.[13] Soon this arbitrary division would prove troublesome. Would the Air Forces, for example, control the jamming of tank and infantry radio in combat simply

---

[12] (1) Ltr, Col Cedric W. Lewis, Exec Vice Chairman, Army Com and Equip Coordination Bd, to CSigO, 21 Nov 42, sub: Case No. 38, Study of U.S. Army Rqmts for Radio Jamming Equip. (2) Memo, Handy, ACofS, for CofS, 17 Dec 42, sub: Study of U.S. Army Rqmts for Radio Jamming Equip. OPD 413.44 (12–7–42) SigC file, C&E Case No. 38.

[13] Ltr, TAG to CG AAF and CSigO, 31 Oct 42. AG 676.3 (10–14–42). TAG assigned to the CSigO:

a. Preparation of policies, methods, procedures, training circulars, and field manuals.

b. Preparation of recommendations as to coordination and control.

c. Development of equipment, methods, and procedures for protection against enemy radio countermeasures activities.

d. Recommending the type, number, and assignment of units charged with conducting radio countermeasures activities, except Army Air Forces units. SigC 413.44 RCM Gen No. 1 (ET–2381).

because the jammers could be operated much more efficiently from the air?

While the Joint Chiefs of Staff mulled over the new problems presented by RCM, the Chief Signal Officer set up within his own bailiwick a Protective Security Branch under Maj. Lawrence C. Sheetz as part of the Army Communications Division, with the duty of establishing policies touching RCM.[14]

Months later, on 18 June 1943, joint and combined policy on the entire subject appeared. It laid down the procedures and co-ordination necessary lest haphazard jamming interfere with friendly operations. Even jamming the enemy's radio traffic might be unwise, if, for example, friendly radio intelligence were acquiring valuable information from that traffic. To conduct RCM operations, the Joint and Combined Chiefs of Staff recommended four new types of units: investigational, jamming, deception, and maintenance. Over the whole they drew tight blackout curtains: "Because of the necessity for extreme security . . . the number of individuals having access to operational information . . . will be kept to the absolute minimum."[15] Some thought the security so tight as to half strangle the entire program.

By mid-1943 RCM was getting into stride, both in development and production at home and in combat operations overseas. General Ingles wrote in July, "At the present time there is a very active program in the Signal Corps for providing special countermeasures equipment for interfering with the operation of enemy radar equipment."[16] In August, Col. John J. Downing, assistant chief under General Colton in the Engineering and Technical Services, asked the OSRD to lend Dr. Langmuir to the Signal Corps in order to help in RCM work, but Dr. Vannevar Bush felt he was too valuable in his British assignment.[17] No doubt he was. British and American bombers had begun to suffer grievously because of Wuerzburg radars, which the Germans were using as efficient GCI and GL sets. German flak in particular, directed accurately by the Wuerzburg, was taking ever-heavier toll[18] until the British developed Window, which was nothing more than aluminum foil strips that, when dropped from an airplane, sent back multitudinous radar echoes and blinded the enemy oscilloscopes, so that the aircraft's own echo became indistinguishable in the dazzle. The British were developing jamming transmitters, too, both radar and radio. Carpet, when tuned to the enemy's radar frequency, filled his scope with dancing light; and Jostle, a radio transmitter, could overpower with

---

[14] Co-ordinating equipment development, recommending the training of RCM experts and units, and so on. Memo, CSigO for Chief Sig Sup Sv, Chief Sig Opns Sv, and Dir Com Coordination Div, 17 Nov 42, sub: Radio Countermeasures. SigC 413.44 RCM Gen No. 1 (ET–2381).

[15] TAG Ltr, 18 Jun 43, sub: RCM Policy. (AG 311.23, 17 June 43, OB–S–B–M) SigC 413.44 RCM Gen No. 1 (ET–2381).

[16] Ltr, CSigO to CG AGF, Attn Lt Col Albert F. Cassevant, 19 Jul 43, sub: Recommended Countermeasures Equip Demonstration and Tests. SigC 413.44 RCM, Tng folder No. 1, 1943–45 (ET–2612).

[17] Ltr, Bush, Dir OSRD, to Downing, 21 Aug 43. SigC 413.44 RCM No. 7 (RB–2070).

[18] In the spring of 1944 flak damage and loss continued to exceed losses to enemy fighter planes by three to one. Unsigned sheet entitled Information, dated 22 May 44. AAG file 413.44–EG Radio.

meaningless noise the enemy's command radiotelephones.[19]

The impact of RCM first fell upon the Army Air Forces. The AAF had set up an electronics proving ground at Eglin Field in the Florida panhandle especially for RCM purposes. On 16 February 1943 the AAF asked the Signal Corps to provide permanent facilities there both for ARL and for Division 15 and its RRL. In the same month the Air Forces asked ARL to equip Ferret aircraft, the winged electronic laboratories outfitted to detect radar signals and to locate the ground stations.[20] By the summer of 1943 the Signal Corps was procuring Carpet jammers in the United States. Numbers of them went overseas in time to be used by the VIII Bomber Command over Bremen in October. In that raid sixty-eight American heavy bombers so equipped suffered substantially less from flak than did other planes that did not have Carpet to spread over the German gun-laying radars below.[21]

By the autumn of 1943, RCM developments in America were flourishing. They included antijamming and jamming sets, search receivers, radar direction finders, panoramic viewers, spot jammers, barrage jammers, and Tuba. The last was a roaring lion in the radiation spectrum, which General Colton urged upon the Air Forces in September.[22] In October, Dr. Suits, the chief of Division 15, NDRC, wrote prophetically to Dr. Edward L. Bowles, who circulated the letter to General Colton, Lt. Col. George F. Metcalf, and Lt. Col. James W. McRae in the Signal Corps: "We may expect to find that radio and radar countermeasures will become a full-fledged partner with radio communications and radar as a prime element of the planning of military and naval operations." Not only would this mean a tremendous increase in RCM sets, it would also mean a complete change in existing radar design. "I believe," Suits wrote further, "it is safe to conclude that the design of future sets will have to take

---

[19] It is fortunate that the Germans had not developed such measures as these in their 1940–41 assaults on England, for they could then have reduced or indeed canceled the efforts of those few fighter pilots to whom England owes so much. For this and many other similar cogitations, see Wilfrid Eggleston's discussion of the "see-saw football match" of scientific warfare in the great conflict in *Scientists at War* (Toronto: Oxford University Press, 1950), pp. 4–8.

[20] (1) Ltr, CG AAF to CSigO, 16 Feb 43, sub: AAF Electronics Proving Ground. AAG 413.44–Q Radio. (2) Ltr, CG AAF to CSigO, 25 Feb 43, sub: Equip for Ferret III. AAG 413.44–S Radio. (3) Claussen, Dev of Radio and Radar Equip for Air Opns, 1939–44, p. 101.

Capt. Donald E. Thomas, in the Electronics Branch, Office of the Chief Signal Officer, described the 1st Proving Ground Electronics Unit at Eglin Field as having been set up for the purpose of proving and service testing RCM equipment that the Signal Corps developed and procured for AAF operational use. ASF Transmittal sheet, Action 1, Thomas, O/C RCM Equip Sec Electronics Br, to Admin Staff Sec, Fiscal and Rpts Sec E&T Sv, 25 Feb 44, sub: Request for Rpts. SigC 413.44 RCM Rpts, Jan–Feb 44, No. 3 (RB–2075).

[21] (1) Baxter, *Scientists Against Time*, p. 167. (2) *Electronics Warfare*, pp. 14–15.

The use of Window, or Chaff, with electronic jammers, which Brig. Gen. Harold M. McClelland urged upon the Eighth Air Force in October, 1943, proved most fortunate. The Germans developed AJ means of listening for plane echoes through the confusion caused by Chaff, only to be foiled by the noise jammers. (1) Ltr, Gen McClelland to Maj Gen Ira C. Eaker, CG 8th AF, 4 Oct 43. AAG 413.44–GP Radio. (2) *Electronics Warfare*, pp. 16–17.

[22] Memo, Colton for Informal Army CM Bd, 11 Sep 43, sub: Rqmts for Tuba and Cigar. SigC 413.44 RCM No. 7 (RB–2070). (2) Baxter, *Scientists Against Time*, p. 162.

full cognizance of the possibility of jamming and deception. This will undoubtedly lead to more emphasis on narrow beam microwave gear and the inclusion of such features as variable RF, variable PRF, separate T and F, possibly FM detection and other features intended to minimize the susceptibility of jamming and deception." [23] RCM did become a "prime element" in operational plans, and the equipment itself became an indispensable weapon. "In recent months," an Air Forces record stated early in 1944, "it has become obvious that countermeasures are as effective and necessary as machine guns on the bombers." [24]

RCM Equipment and the Laboratories

While the ARL in Ohio and the RRL Division 15 in Massachusetts worked on airborne RCM, testing their products at Eglin Field, Florida, workers at the Camp Evans Signal Laboratory at Fort Monmouth occupied themselves with antijamming devices and procedures designed to render existing ground radars less subject to interference, such as they had suffered at Bizerte, Bari, and elsewhere in combat areas. Two AJ devices developed early in 1943 for the aircraft

search radars SCR's–270 and 271 were "Mary" and "George" boxes. The former, applying well-known electronic circuits, involved nothing new, but the "George" box was novel, "definitely a unique device," reported two electronic engineers who visited the laboratory in February 1943. Its circuit, which Camp Evans workers had developed without understanding why it worked, "could never have been arrived at by a conventionally trained engineer." The men who developed it deserved much credit, thought the visitors, who urged that the box next be sent to the highly theoretical physicists at RRL at Harvard to figure out why and how "George" worked. [25]

By mid-1943 members of the Camp Evans Signal Laboratory were co-operating with the Army Air Forces School of Applied Tactics (AAFSAT) at Orlando, Florida. Coast Artillery Corps men were also eager to learn AJ techniques in order to offset enemy jamming of their GL radars, particularly the SCR –268, which was very susceptible because of its low frequency long-wave lengths and diffused beams. [26] Neither were the microwave SCR's–545 and 584 completely immune. Together with the Signal Corps and the RRL, the Coast Artillery men produced motion pictures with which to train GL radar operators

---

[23] Ltr, Chief Div 15 NDRC to Bowles, 20 Oct 43. SigC 413.44 RCM No. 7 (RB–270). Suits complained that so far American progress in RCM had been delayed somewhat because of "supersecrecy."

[24] Incl, Memo, J. M. West for file, sub: Radio Countermeasures Prog USAAF, with AAF R&R, Action 2, Col George H. Sparhawk, Air ComO to AC of AS OCR, Rqmts Div, 19 May 44, sub: RCM Plng for Combat Theaters. AAG 413.44–EF Radio.

[25] Memo, J. H. DeWitt, Jr., Tech Consultant, for file, 19 Feb 43, sub: Countermeasures in Connection With the Use of Early Warning, GCI and Height Finding Sets. SigC 413.44 folder No. 1, AJ (ET–1978). ABL–15 was similarly occupied in England.

[26] SCR–268's could also interfere with each other. "When all the 268's in a small area went on the air, the signals from the main pulses marched up and down the base lines of the scopes in weird fashion." Dr. John Miller, jr., Draft MS Comment, Jul 59. SigC Hist Sec file.

in antijamming skills.[27] Excessive RCM secrecy had to yield. Getting AJ information to the radar operators in the field was becoming a most urgent need, as Colonel McRae in the Electronics Branch made emphatic: "There exists an ever growing need for antijamming methods for combatting the effects of enemy countermeasures attempting to neutralize our radar systems, and in particular for dissemination of information on this subject." [28] Operators had to recognize jamming interference on their scopes, or they were apt to call in repairmen, thinking their sets defective. Properly trained, the operators could often recognize target pips on their oscilloscopes despite interfering dazzles of light. By early 1944 the Fort Monmouth Signal Corps Publications Agency and the Dayton Signal Corps Publication Agency were incorporating AJ information and palliatives in the many radar and radio instruction manuals that the agencies prepared and issued with ground and airborne signal equipment.[29] Meanwhile scientists of the Operational Research Staff of OCSigO readied basic training publications outlining antijamming fundamentals.[30]

By 1944 field radarmen were receiving abundant experience in England as well as in North Africa and Italy. The Luftwaffe continued to send out forays during which the enemy aviators dropped Window in quantity. Capt. Donald E. Thomas, making observations in England in May 1944, concluded that the best AJ measures were training the operators to work through jamming and improving radar design, especially by the employment of higher frequencies.[31]

Antijamming was a major Axis concern. The Germans frantically sought AJ devices, especially for their Wuerzburg sets. The initiative in the skies lay with the Allies, who did most of the jamming. Signal Corps jammers for the Army Air Forces were multiplying prodigiously: Mandrel, Rug, Carpet, Dina, Jackal. The types of RCM airborne sets being delivered to the Air Forces in June 1943 had stood at only a half dozen, totaling only about one hundred

---

[27] (1) Ltr, Colton, Chief E&T Sv, to CG AAF, 3 Sep 43, sub: Tests Conducted at AAFSAT. (2) Ltr, Lt Col Carl W. Holcomb, AAA School, Camp Davis, N.C., to CG AGF, 13 Dec 43, sub: AJ Measures. (3) Ltr, CSigO to WD LnO with NDRC, 5 Feb 44, sub: Radar Jamming Tng Films. All in SigC 413.44 AJ No. 2 (ET–1979).
[28] Ltr, McRae, Actg Chief Electronics Br, to Suits, Chief Div 15 NDRC, 13 Mar 44. SigC 413.44 AJ No. 3 (ET–1980).
[29] (1) Ltr, Chief E&T to CO SCGSA, 28 Feb 44, sub: Preparation of AJ Literature. SigC 413.44 AJ No. 3. (2) CSigO Annual Rpt, FY 44, pp. 491–502. Regarding RCM training, see below, pp. 525ff.
[30] CSigO Annual Rpt, FY 45, pp. 75–77.
Two manuals, TB Sig–9 and TB Sig–16, were

most welcome and were "widely regarded with favor as excellent publications," wrote Lt. Col. Kirk Buchak in NATOUSA, who added that no radar operator could become skilled without full knowledge of the subject of jamming. Incl, Ltr, Buchak to CSigO, 16 Aug 44, sub: Radar AJ Techniques, with ASF Transmittal Sheet, Action 1, Chief ACS to E&T Sv, 7 Sep 44. SigC 413.44 AJ No. 4 (ET–2538). Dr. Lynne C. Smeby, of OCSigO's Research Branch, headed the preparation of AJ manuals. Baxter, Scientists Against Time, p. 168.
[31] Memo, Thomas for Chief Electronics Br, 11 May 44, sub: Radar AJ Observations of Capt Thomas While in England. SigC 413.44 AJ No. 3 (ET–1980).
Fortunately, thanks to British development of the cavity magnetron, Allied radar was already well advanced into the microwave region and new 10- and 3-centimeter sets were far less susceptible to jamming than were the older longwave radars. Fortunately, too, enemy radars continued to operate on long- or medium-wave lengths, which could be readily jammed.

sets. But a year later, the types on delivery had increased to a score or more and the quantities on order ran into the scores of thousands.[32] In the RRL alone the Signal Corps had some sixty-four RCM projects afoot (principally active or radiating jammers).

British and American bombers over Europe were dropping metal foil strips in astronomical amounts. British Window was being augmented by huge quantities of American Chaff, cut by machines that the NDRC had developed for the Signal Corps.[33] Chaff blinded German radar with greater efficiency than Window, one-fourth the weight of Chaff producing as much confusion in the enemy scopes as a given weight of Window. While the British hastened to secure American Chaff cutters,[34] facilities in the United States were pouring out two hundred tons a week, and workers at the ARL were devising better packaging of the aluminum strips for better dispersal after the packets slid down the bomber chutes and broke open in the airplane's slipstream into a shimmering cloud. Curtains of Chaff winking in the sky and the electronic roar of airborne jammers, such as Carpet, shielded and saved hundreds of Allied bombers and their crews over Europe from mid-1943 on, as the enemy's radars faltered and anti-aircraft gun crews cursed and fired blindly.[35]

As the time for the invasion of Normandy approached in 1944, the pressure for RCM equipment intensified. Officers in the Signals Liaison Office of the Air Ministry in London wrote frantically to Washington in February 1944, asking for a formidable number of special RCM items. "They understood," they wrote, "that the Signal Corps is more or less in control of the laboratories and model shops," and stated further that the Signal Corps "should be convinced that laboratories should be given the authority to expand such shops and make more experimental models for operational use." The London officers were asking for crash production.[36] If the Air Forces had to

---

[32] (1) Hist Of SCASA, Hist Rpt, ARL Development Projects, RCM Equipment, 1 July 1943–30 June 1944, p. 1. SigC Hist Sec file, A46–160, drawer 12. (2) CSigO, Annual Rpts, FY 44, p. 321, and FY 45, p. 414.

[33] Window was first used successfully by the British in a raid over Hamburg on 24 July 1943 and over Essen on the 25th. During the Essen raid, British intercept listeners heard German GCI operators exclaim in consternation "The British aircraft are reproducing!" Incl, Ltr, H. G. Stever, OSRD Scientific LnO, to Suits, Chief Div 15 NDRC, 30 Jul 43, with AAF R&R, Col Thurston H. Baxter, ACofAS Bombardment Br, 25 Aug 43, sub: Window. AAG 413.44–BF Radio.

[34] In August 1943, the RAF delegation in Washington asked the Signal Corps to obtain seventy-five window machines for them. Ltr, Air Commodore A. F. Lang to Gen Colton, 23 Aug 43. SigC 413.44 RCM (RB–2070).

The use of plain embossed foil instead of paper-backed saved two-thirds the weight and volume, while the production method of it as CHA–5 (RR–6/4) cut the packages to one-fifteenth of the original bulk. CSigO, Annual Rpt, FY 45, p. 415.

[35] (1) Hist Of SCASA, Hist Rpt, ARL Dev Projs, RCM Equip, 1 Jul 43–30 Jun 44, pp. 4–5. (2) Ltr, Terman, Dir RRL, to McRae, OCSigO, 27 Sep 43. AAG 413.44–BN Radio.

While operational needs for Chaff and RCM equipment grew by leaps and bounds, the British leaned heavily on American production. One officer, Air Commodore E. B. Addison, felt that "much of the Royal Air Force's program depends absolutely on American production." Ltr, Lt Col Robert L. Snider, CSigO Hq SOS ETOUSA, RCM Br, to Gen McClelland, 13 Nov 43. AAG 413.44–CL Radio.

[36] Ltr, CG AAF to CSigO, 4 Mar 44, sub: Request for RCM Equip, and Incl, Extract from Rpt for Week Ending 26 Feb 44. USAAF Signals Ln Of, Whitehall, London. AAG 413.44–DL Radio.

wait for service production models obtained in the usual manner of Signal Corps procurement, the sets would arrive too late. The officers in England urged that American laboratory engineers, after the manner of the British, take off their coats and do the work themselves. General Arnold passed the request on to General Ingles, adding, "since most of these items are under the control of your office, if they are available at all, we ask your assistance in meeting these requirements." [37] The special items thus desired, in small quantities, totaled forty-one.

The Eighth Air Force demanded huge quantities of the standard RCM sets. "This equipment is vitally needed," wrote a spokesman, asking that it be shipped "by the fastest available vessel as soon as production will permit." He wanted Carpet I (barrage jammer AN/APT-2, or RC-156)—enough of them so that every bomber might carry a set, with 75 percent spares. Of Carpet III (AN/APQ-9), he wanted 3,750 sets with complete A and B parts, plus 50 percent spares. He wanted hundreds of sets of Mandrel (AN/APT-3), or of RC-183, a spot jammer), Dina, and Rug jammers, search and intercept receivers, and much else. Some of this equipment was in production, some would begin to come off assembly lines in the weeks and months immediately ahead, but some would have to wait till summer, and some was still only under development.[38]

The many jammer types hitherto devised all put out relatively low power, at most no more than the 400 watts or so of an ordinary SCR-299.[39] Yet the effectiveness of a jamming transmitter depends upon its power output, on how loud it bellows, electrically speaking. Its bellow must reach the enemy's receiver with greater force than the radiation of the enemy's own transmitter, which is likely to be nearer the receiver and therefore able to reach it with a stronger signal than can the more distant jammer. For this reason, jammers had been more effective in aircraft because they could be flown close over the enemy's receivers and their interfering radiations might pour down overwhelmingly strong signals from nearby points of vantage aloft.

A jammer with tremendously powerful output would be most desired in this kind of warfare. Just such a set was developed, one so powerful that it could effectively jam the enemy's receivers from ground locations and from great distances. Dubbed Tuba, it was developed chiefly by the NDRC, with Signal Corps support, with a view to jamming from the ground a new type of German airborne radar, an AI set the enemy called *Lichtenstein*, or SN-2, with which German night fighters had begun harassing Allied planes.[40] Speak-

[37] *Ibid.*

[38] Ltr, CG Eighth Air Force Sv Comd to CG ASC Patterson Fld, Ohio, 23 Feb 44, sub: Requisition for Radio and Radar Countermeasures Equip and Summ of Previous Requisitions, with 2d Ind, CG AAF to CG ASC, 21 Apr 44. AAG 413.44-DV Radio.

[39] Except the AN/MRT-1, American Cigar, designed to jam with an output of several kilowatts the German air-ground radio FuG-16, up to 100 miles away. Ind, Military Characteristics for **High Power Ground-Based Com Jamming Transmitter AN/MRT-1**, with Ltr, Winter, Electronics Br, to Dir Camp Coles Sig Lab, sub: AN/MRT-1-Cigar. SigC ET 413.44 AN/MRT-1 folder No. 1, 1943-44.

[40] (1) Baxter, *Scientists Against Time*, p. 167. (2) *Electronics Warfare*, pp. 34-35.

ing of the new electronic innovation, an NDRC scientist said in mid-1944:

Tuba can most certainly be called a success. It has not been used in operations yet, but there is unmistakeable enthusiasm for it in the atmosphere. . . . It should also be pointed out that these high power ground jammers open up completely new fields of RCM activity. I cannot guess exactly what the uses may be, but certainly with three of the installations strategically placed around the continent of Europe, many possibilities might be opened up in support of various operations, and most certainly the enemy would get a blow between the eyes if he tried any new tricks at all within the available band.[41]

Some RCM Problems

As the war progressed, the applications and implications of RCM ramified endlessly. After its combat value had been demonstrated in the realms of antiaircraft radar and gun laying, everyone became interested in its further potentialities. The Army Ground Forces, for example, wanted to jam enemy tank radios. This raised questions such as who should co-ordinate and control the entire activity of monitoring and jamming in various situations, as this or that arm might desire, according to this or that tactical exigency. And it raised in a most intense form that long-standing bogey of radiations, the question of frequency control and assignment. This question is always most perplexing, even when it merely concerns the allocation of frequencies among the users who inevitably press for more communication channel allocations than there are frequencies available in the radiation spectrum. The perplexity would be compounded if a command wished to transmit a jamming signal that would drown out frequencies used by both friendly forces and the enemy.

RCM threw into sharper relief than ever the old question: Must not the control and assignment of frequencies be placed in the strong hands of an omnipotent and omniscient authority? Omniscient because the authority would have to have over-all knowledge of all aspects of the electronic warfare of modern combat. RCM was becoming linked not only with tactical combat and strategic planning, but with combat intelligence and with radio intelligence, too. Its associations with radio intelligence were to become especially close. Radio intelligence derives its benefits from listening uninterruptedly to enemy signals, analyzing them, and deducing many valuable items of information. The question thus arises as to whether it is more valuable to listen to the enemy's signals for the intelligence gained thereby or to jam them for some immediate tactical advantage in combat —the jamming of course cuts off the information sought by radio intelligence activities. Radio intelligence in the Army was the concern of the Signal Corps' Signal Intelligence Service (SIS), by 1944 the Signal Security Agency (SSA).[42]

A question arose as to whether RCM could best be lodged in the SIS, or in

---

[41] Ltr, Unsigned, to R. W. Larson, Chief Tech Aids, Div 15 NDRC, 12 Jul 44. SigC 413.44 RCM Gen No. 1 (ET–2381).

[42] Incl, Memo Capt S. T. Martin, Jr., for Lt Col Herbert G. Messer, 23 Aug 43, sub: Counter Measures Activities During Second Army Maneuvers at Lebanon, Tenn., with Memo, Martin for McRae, 14 Sep 43, sub: High Power Centimeter Com and Its Application to the Army. SigC 413.44 RCM No. 7 (RB–2070).

the General Staff under the Operations Planning Division or under the Military Intelligence Division (MID). The Chief Signal Officer early in 1943, General Olmstead, thought RCM ought to remain in the Signal Corps, assigned to the SIS. He further believed that centralized control over this new problem child of the electronics era would be stronger if lifted out of the Army Service Forces altogether and elevated in the General Staff of the Army. Colonel Guest, an officer in OCSigO, favored this view, regarding RCM as a foot in the door whereby the Signal Corps might some day itself enter the War Department General Staff. This did not happen in World War II.[43]

One of the largest problems raised by RCM involved crash procurement. How fast could the Signal Corps or the laboratories, whether ARL or RRL, rush special new equipment to the field? Rushed procurement was nothing new to the Signal Corps; it had been one of the most galling tasks with which the Corps had lived and slept since the day of Pearl Harbor. Crash procurement within the military household was new, however, borrowed from the British practice of hand building sets in almost a matter of hours, at most of days, to meet a particular exigency. And

in RCM exigencies had been the rule from the very start, as when, for instance, the British had to counter the German radio beams that guided streams of enemy bombers to the center of Coventry in the dark of night.[44] For purposes of crash production the Radiation Laboratory in Cambridge, Massachusetts, had already set up a civilian shop, the Research Construction Company. In consequence of RCM exigencies confronting Allied bomber fleets over Europe, General Ingles, in cooperation with the AAF, authorized at the turn of 1943–44 a crash production procedure in ARL and the associated Dayton Signal Corps Procurement District.[45]

Crash demands for RCM equipment and for certain radars became a new routine for the Signal Corps. On 10 April 1944, the AAF placed an "urgent" request for seven Mandrel spot jammers, AN/ART–3, asking that the Signal Corps waive any impeding specifications in order to rush the sets. On 27 July 1944 came a project of "extreme urgency" to crash-produce twelve AN/APG–15's, to be installed in B–29's—they were gun layers for blind fire against Japanese night fighter planes.[46] A flood of crash demands swept in with preparations to meet the long-dreaded plague of rockets which the Allies expected to be radio controlled, of which more will be mentioned later.

---

[43] OCSigO War Diary, 28 Jan and 25 Mar 43. DCSigO file.

Colonel Guest's comment was made in the spring of 1943, at a time when General Olmstead was planning an appeal to lift Signal Corps control out of the ASF and into the General Staff. See Thompson, Harris, et al., The Test, ch. XVI, passim. RCM did indeed go to the SSA. But then the SSA itself, both RCM and RI, was taken from the Signal Corps, late in 1945, and placed under the Military Intelligence Division. See below, pp. 348ff., 614ff.

[44] Michie, "The Greatest Hoax of the War," Reader's Digest (October, 1946), p. 118.

[45] See below, pp. 435ff.

[46] (1) Ltr, CG AAF to CSigO, 10 Apr 44, sub: AN/ART–3 Equip for Instal in B–26 Aircraft. AAG 413.44–DR Radio. (2) Ltr, CG AAF to CSigO, 27 July 44, sub: Crash Program for AN/APG–15. AAG 413.44–EZ Radio.

RCM Units on the Ground and Ferrets in the Air

The search aspect of RCM—locating enemy radar stations either to destroy or to counter them—became increasingly important during 1943 as the Allies probed the enemy's outposts. Since the Allies were planning to first invade the Aleutians and Sicily, later Italy and France, they had to know where enemy radars were located, so as to destroy them before invasion if possible. If the Allies could not destroy the sets, then they must learn their radiation characteristics, their frequencies, and their coverage in order to jam them effectively while Allied invading ships approached shore. In this work the Signal Corps and the AAF collaborated. By mid-1943 the Signal Corps had created the 1st Signal Service Platoon (Special) and dispatched it with its equipment to jam Japanese radars on Kiska, radars that the AAF had located by means of Ferret I. *Ferret* was the term applied to aircraft designed as electronic snoopers. Ferret I was a B-24 specially equipped to detect and hunt down radar signals, tracing them to their source and so discovering the station itself. As matters turned out in the Aleutians, jamming proved unnecessary at the time of the invasion of Kiska because the enemy suddenly withdrew and the radar signals vanished before the American forces moved into the island.[47]

By no means did this initial RCM effort go to waste. The 1st Signal Platoon (Special) gained valuable experience toward its next assignment, Corsica early in 1944. Digging in on a mountaintop, the men set up radar search sets, radar direction finders, and no fewer than fourteen transmitting antennas for Mandrel and Dina jammers. Throughout the spring and summer the signalmen co-operated with a British RCM team on Cap Corse and with Ferret aircraft, studying enemy radar beams that radiated from scores of sets spotted along the coasts of northern Italy and southern France. Identifying and locating eighty-seven radars, the platoon greatly helped Allied aircraft, which bombed or shot up many of the stations. The few that remained when the Allies invaded southern France in August 1944 were struck blind by the Signal Corps RCM unit in Corsica when it switched on its jammers.[48]

Meanwhile, the Signal Corps constituted two provisional signal service platoons for RCM in 1943 maneuvers in Louisiana and Tennessee. One unit disbanded after the maneuvers, but the

---

[47] (1) Hist Rcd, First Sig Sv Platoon (Sp), Operation BEAVER. SigC Hist Sec file. (The Aleutian RCM operation was coded as BEAVER I. A larger operation then followed in Corsica, BEAVER III. CSigO, Annual Rpt, FY 44, p. 333.) (2) *Electronics Warfare*, pp. 8–9. (3) Ltr, Brig Gen Alfred W. Marriner to CG ASC, 5 Aug 43, sub: Additional Equip for Ferret I. AAG 413.44-BC Radio. (4) Incl, Hist Review of RCM Equip, pp. 4–9, with Ltr, CO SCASA to CSigO, 24 Jan 44, sub: Hist Review of RCM Equip.

[48] (1) "Counter Radar in Southern France," *Coast Artillery Journal*, LXXXIX, No. 1 (January–February, 1946), 82–83. (2) Memo, 1st Lt Jack D. Reid for Lt Col Lawrence C. Sheetz, 28 Oct 44, sub: Informal Discussion of Tech and Operational Aspects of BEAVER III. SigC 413.44 RCM Gen No. 2 (ET-2382). (3) Memo, Dr. E. G. Fubini and H. Zeidler for Terman, 22 Jul 44, sub: Notes on Radar Ground Jamming (RGJ) Opns. AAG 413.44-EY Radio. (4) Incl, Rpt, 2d Lt R. C. Morris, RCM Liaison Activities in Corsica During the Period 4 June–4 July 1944, with Ltr, Marriner to Of of AGO Hq AAF, 8 Jul 44, sub: Transmittal of Rpt by Morris, RCMO Attached to 63d Fighter Wing. AAG 413.44-EU Radio. Lieutenant Morris spoke well of the work of the 1st Signal Service Platoon. WDMID and WDSS Hist Div, World War II: A Chronology, 15 Aug 44.

other, redesignated the 3144th Signal Service Platoon, shipped out to the Southwest Pacific. An entire battalion, the 3103d Signal Service Battalion, went to the ETO to engage in various countermeasures during the Normandy invasion. Also in the ETO were the 23d Headquarters and Headquarters Company Special Troops, all RCM specialists. The 3153d Signal Service Company was consigned to the Southwest Pacific for similar duty. Two more such units waiting to go overseas in February 1945 were the 3155th Signal Service Company at Camp Crowder and the 3191st Signal Service Company at Fort Monmouth.[49]

These were Signal Corps ground units, organized and trained in RCM, which was increasingly concerning the ground forces. The concern grew rapidly with spreading rumors of rocket weapons. Anxiety about the rumored V-1 and V-2 weapons became acute early in 1944. The AGF and its antiaircraft command made inquiries. They asked in March 1944 what RCM defenses were available to ground troops against these missiles or any other radio-controlled weapons. General Colton at once recommended the powerful jammer AN/MRT-1, first production sets of which the manufacturer was just now testing.[50] Simultaneously, General Ingles appointed a board of officers (Colonel Guest, Col. Floyd T. Gillespie, Col. W. Preston Corderman, Colonel McRae) to study Signal Corps responsibilities in radio countermeasures, other than those conducted in aircraft, both radio jamming and radio deception. Though the emphasis was on ground RCM, the Air Forces wanted to be included. Brig. Gen. Harold M. McClelland informed General Ingles in mid-April that "it would be helpful in the interest of coordination if I might be permitted to designate an officer to sit as an observer on this board." Having granted the permission, General Ingles opened the board to any who might be concerned, urging on 19 April that all interested ground force boards appoint RCM liaison officers to participate in a countermeasures educational program. The program would include conferences and field trips to laboratories engaged in RCM work, both in the Signal Corps and in the NDRC.[51]

---

[49] ((1) Memo, Unsigned, for CSigO, Feb 45, sub: Ground Radio Countermeasures Units. SigC 413.44 RCM Gen No. 2 (ET-2382). (2) Incl, Hist Review of RCM Equip, pp. 2-4.

[50] Ltr, CG AAC to CG AGF, 5 Mar 44, sub: Defense Against Radio or Radar Controlled Devices, with 1st Ind, CG AGF to CG ASF, 17 Mar, 44, and 3d Ind, CSigO to CG ASF, 19 Apr 44. SigC 413.44 RCM Gen No. 1 (ET-2381). The V-1 was a pilotless German aircraft with a large warhead—the buzz bomb. The V-2 was a long-range rocket.

[51] (1) Memo, McClelland, Air ComO, for Ingles, 16 Apr 44, sub: Radio Countermeasures, with Incls: (a) Memo, West, Tech Consultant for Air ComO, for McClelland, 7 Apr 44, sub: RCM Policy; (b) ASF OCSigO Of Order No. 64, 16 Mar 44. AAG 413.44-DT Radio. (2) Ltr, CSigO to CG ASF, 19 Apr 44, sub: Disclosure of RCM Info to AGF Bds. SigC 413.44 RCM Gen No. 1 (ET-2381).
The AAF did not overlook the part it might play in AGF interests in RCM—for example, assisting possible AGF needs for "air support countermeasures, such as jamming enemy tank and armored car communications." Accordingly, AAF requested the Chief Signal Officer to review possible AGF requirements of this nature. Ltr, CG AAF to CSigO, 19 May 44, sub: Radio Countermeasures Equip. AAG 413.44-EF Radio.
An important instance of air countermeasures supporting the ground forces occurred in the Battle of the Bulge, involving Jackal. (See above, pp. 163-164.) Jackal equipment had been tested and performance difficulties corrected during the summer of 1944 by the RCM Division of the Signal Service, ETOUSA, and by ABL-15 in England. ETOUSA Rpt, II, 237ff.

Meanwhile Ferrets were increasingly concerning the Air Forces and the Signal Corps. From 1943 on these big, highly specialized airplanes increased in number.[52] Three of the aircraft, Ferrets III, IV, and V, cruised unobtrusively around Sicily and Mediterranean coasts during 1943, their electronic specialist crews listening intently at search receivers and studying German radar signals with special pulse analyzers and direction finders. Meanwhile, news of this latest electronic art reached Pacific outposts, and General Akin, chief signal officer of the Southwest Pacific Area, asked for two Ferrets and an RCM laboratory for his sector of the world.[53]

Ferret operations called for a new kind of direction finder, a radar DF that could be carried aloft so that RCM flight specialists could readily determine the direction of intercepted radar rays. Signal Corps researchers developed the device as AN/APA–17, a radar DF assembly used with such airborne radar receivers as SCR–587 and AN/APR–4. On 17 December 1943 Col. Tom C. Rives, deputy air communications officer in AAF headquarters, asked the ASF for fifteen sets. Airmen needed them immediately for the eight Ferrets already in the field and for seven more

that were expected to be in operation by May 1944. Colonel Rives wanted the sets at once, although the AAF had not furnished the Signal Corps their military characteristics—the conventional preliminaries without which it was customarily impossible for the Signal Corps to proceed. In this case, Colonel Rives urged that "procurement should not be delayed pending classification proceedings." [54]

Wherever there were enemy radars, the American Ferrets saw service, sometimes co-operating with the British. It was mainly British Ferret crews who hunted down German radars along the invasion coast of France. In the Mediterranean, American Ferrets participated in the hunt, and in the Pacific the planes had the field to themselves. Ferrets VII and VIII worked over the South Pacific seas from December 1943 on. In six months they located nine Japanese radars in the northeast sector and seven in the eastern sector of their vast patrol area. From Darwin, Australia, to Balikpapan in Borneo, Ferrets swept the skies free of enemy radar detection and attack, so that slow Navy PBY's could safely lay mines in the Japanese shipping lanes.[55]

The Ferrets in the Pacific finally operated over the islands of Japan itself. There, Air Forces Ferret B–24 Liberators found, and in some cases attacked and destroyed, Japanese radar stations. One new type of Ferret had the very

[52] (1) "The Work of the Ferrets," *Radar*, No. 4 (August, 1944), pp. 21–27. (2) *Electronics Warfare*, pp. 10–12.

[53] (1) Ltr, Lenzner, APO 512, to CSigO, 3 Jul 43, sub: Rpt No. 6 on Flight No. 8 of Investigational Aircraft and Captured Enemy Ground Radar Equip. AAG 413.44–R, Radar. (2) 1st Ind, CG AAF to CG Fifth Air Force, 4 Aug 43, on Ltr, 1st Lt P. J. Rousculp to Dir of Com Hq, Washington, 26 May 43, sub: RCM in SWPA. AAG 413.44–P, Radar. (3) Ltr, Lt Col George C. Hale, Actg Com EquipO, to CG ASC, 15 Sep 43, sub: Raven Equip for Ferrets. AAG 413.44–BK Radio.

[54] Ltr, Rives, Deputy Air ComO, to CG ASF, 17 Dec 43, sub: Radar DF Assembly AN/APA–17. AAG 413.44–Y Radar.

[55] Incl, Oliver Whitby, Air Force Tech Observer, Rpt No. OWW–10, with Ltr, Maj H. U. Graham to Dr. Fubini, RRL, 19 Jul 44. AAG 413.44–EX Radio.

specialized job of detecting and destroying Japanese aircraft that carried radar. The B–24's were in fact flying laboratories, bristling with as many as a dozen types of antenna, while compartments and bomb bays were crammed with dozens of intricate Signal Corps electronic devices. A 1945 listing of electronic items in the B–24J Ferret enumerated forty-six different pieces of equipment.[56]

RCM in the Attack

Countermeasures to foil enemy radar detectors and gun directors became ever more important as the 1944 invasions of Europe approached, not only active jamming in the areas where Allied units were operating, but radio and radar deceptive measures in other areas to mislead the enemy into thinking the main attack was coming there. All the measures were invaluably effective during the Normandy invasion, in the "greatest hoax of the war." The Germans were deceived into believing that the main attack was coming on the Pas-de-Calais coast and that the Normandy landing was but a diversion. General Eisenhower subsequently wrote: "The German Fifteenth Army remained immobile in the Pas-de-Calais, contained until the latter part of July by what we now know from high-level interrogation was the threat of attack by our forces in the southeast of England."[57] Much of this RCM effort was British.

Rather similar to the RCM program for Normandy in June was the sister plan for the invasion of southern France in August. In that program American forces participated much more heavily, as they had done throughout the North African and Mediterranean operations. Countermeasures by the Allies and the enemy alike had increased rapidly in these theaters following the first use of Window by German raiders on Bizerte in September 1943. By the time of Anzio and the bitter fighting in Italy, RCM had become a major concern throughout the Mediterranean theater. An RCM board, attended by members from the U.S. and Royal Air Forces, from the U.S. and Royal Navies, and from the Antiaircraft and Coast Defense Sections of the Allied Forces Headquarters, took form under the Chief Signal Officer, AFHQ, to collect and disseminate RCM information and to control RCM activity.[58]

When Mediterranean forces invaded Elba, the island of Napoleon's first exile, on 16 June 1944, they laid extensive RCM plans. The actual landing on the south shore of the island was offset by RCM dodges on the north, which successfully diverted enemy gunfire. One measure was sonic—a few small craft, hidden by a protective smoke screen

[56] "The Search for Jap Radar," *Radar*, No. 10 (June 30, 1945), pp. 9–11. One of the Ferrets is said to have sprouted no fewer than thirty-six antennas. Baxter, *Scientists Against Time*, p. 163.

[57] (1) *SCAEF Rpt*, 6 Jun 44–8 May 45, p. 13. (2) Michie, "The Greatest Hoax of the War," *Reader's Digest* (October, 1946), pp. 117ff.

For RCM details during the invasion of Nor-
mandy see above, pp. 98ff., and for the Battle of the Bulge, pp. 163–64.

For communications deception in general see: Capt. H. V. Drinkard, Theater Cover Planning and Deception (25 Sep 50), and Capt. R. C. Doctor, Cover Plan and Signal Deception (Theater) World War II (18 Sep 50), Monograph, The Sig Sch Libr, Ft. Monmouth.

[58] Penciled account, unsigned and undated, Tab entitled Radar, in SigC 314.7 Orgn Chart and Hist of AFHQ.

close to the beaches, carried sound equipment, the powerful amplifiers and loud-speakers bellowing the recorded noise of "heavy chains rattling, motors running, etc., to create the impression of a large force of LCI's coming in through the smoke screen." [59]

Meanwhile, the RCM plan for the invasion of southern France profited from these experiences and from those derived in the Normandy invasion. Allied aircraft carried out some five hundred attacks upon the principal radar sites that Signal Corps and British units on Corsica had located, in cooperation with Air Forces Ferrets. Then, upon the invasion itself, there was jamming from Corsica, from fleet units and from aircraft, together with deception —the simulation of a large naval convoy approaching the west flank by a few vessels carrying jammers and towing reflector balloons. In addition, five C–47's carried out a dummy parachute drop over the east flank, and deceptive radio traffic was also broadcast. These dodges all proved effective. The enemy, confused, reported that attacks had been repulsed in areas where there had been none. His radar, beset by RCM, instead of helping, had hurt him. The actual landing progressed almost unopposed. [60]

RCM for CROSSBOW

The great European invasions of 1944 were not the only large RCM concerns that year. A countermeasures worry, peculiarly acute, pertained to CROSSBOW, Allied code name for the dreaded assault upon London by German V weapons and Allied countermeasures to defeat it. The weapons, it was anticipated, would be unmanned guided missiles of some sort. As early as February 1944 General Colton had written to a War Department liaison officer serving with the NDRC saying that the Army and the Navy laboratories and those of the NDRC had begun to work on possible countermeasures against guided missiles. Colton asked specifically that the NDRC work for the Army be assigned the project title SC–98.07, and that the work be carried out in cooperation with Signal Corps liaison officers Colonel McRae, Lt. Col. George Haller, and Captain Thomas. [61]

After the V–1's began buzzing over the Channel in mid-1944 and exploding in London with considerable efficiency and destructiveness, the mere threat of the V–2 gave the military an intense headache. [62] Bits of intelligence suggested the size and nature of the gargantuan rocket. The military rushed to counter it. The AAF pressed the Signal Corps

---

[59] Incl, Morris to Hq MAAF, 4 Jul 44, sub: Rpt of RCM Ln Activities in Corsica During Period 4 Jun–4 Jul 44, p. 5, with Ltr, Marriner, Hq USAAF MTO, to Office of Air ComO, Hq AAF, 8 Jul 44, sub as above.

[60] (1) Rpt No. JM/21, Rpt of Electronics Countermeasures in Operation DRAGOON, Aug 44, pp. 1–11. SCIA file, A–51–135. (2) "Jamming on D Day: How It Upset Jerry's Radar Front," Radar, No. 6 (November 15, 1944), pp. 10–11. (3) Electronics Warfare, p. 21. (4) Seventh U.S. Army, Report of Operations in France and Germany, 1944–45 (Heidelberg: 1946), I, 104.

[61] Ltr, Colton, Chief E&T Sv, to WD LnO with NDRC, 19 Feb 44, sub: Project on Countermeasures for Guided Missiles. SigC 413.44 RCM Guided Missiles No. 1 (ET–2623).

[62] The first V–1 came on 12 June 1944. The menace was reduced only by the most fortunate and timely combination of the microwave GL radars, such as the SCR–584, and the radio proximity fuze, during the summer of 1944. Baxter, Scientists Against Time, pp. 35, 235. See also below, pp. 477ff.

for RCM equipment with "overriding priority."[63] If the V–2 were radio controlled, if it followed a great arc through the stratosphere at speeds that surpassed a mile a second, obviously the time available for countermeasures, for detecting the guiding signal and for spotting a jammer on it, would be almost negligible, only fractions of a moment. Yet that fragment of time would be enough for the quick act of throwing the rocket out of control, so that it might crash wide of its target.

Special equipment had to be provided quickly to counter the V–2 control beams, if indeed the enemy could so control it, as the Allies believed they could. The powerful new Tuba, either the 15–kilowatt version AN/MRT–1, or a stronger 50-kilowatt version AN/GRQ–1, seemed to offer a suitable jammer. So far, a few sets had been built by Division 15, RRL. Eight sets of AN/MRT–1 were hurried to England, augmenting 6 sets already on hand there. The 14 sets, together with 15 modification kits to increase the frequency range of the jamming output, plus 4 AN/GRQ–1's, "are expected to be employed solely in the European Theater of Operations," wrote Lt. Col. Norman L. Winter, chief of the Electronics Branch of the Office of the Chief Signal Officer in September 1944. He added that these sets would be "operated and maintained by highly skilled technical personnel from the British Isles and/or U.S. technical aides." He surmised that their operation could be sporadic or could at times be sustained around the clock for several days.

The Signal Corps laboratories at Fort Monmouth constituted the Army's agency for handling the equipment, of which the GRQ–1 and the MRT–1 (mounted in seven trucks) comprised but two of a dozen complex items—receivers, recorders, cameras, other jammers, and numerous special kits for modifications and maintenance.[64]

The program rocketed. General Rumbough summarized it in the spring of 1945 as follows: "In the summer and fall of 1944, a concentrated countermeasures effort was made in preparation for the rockets. An extensive chain of listening stations, equipped with the latest American equipments, was set up along the English coast. Controlled from these listening stations were a considerable number of high powered jammers, including American Cigars, equipped for various types of modulation."[65] Suddenly the whole program came to an anticlimax. The V–2's were not radio controlled after all, and early in September the AAF canceled those portions of the program that could not be completed by the middle of the month.[66]

---

[63] Ltr, CG AAF to CSigO, 24 Jul 44, sub: Radio CM vs. "Big Ben," The German Large Radio Controlled Rocket. AAG 413.44–FJ Radio.

[64] (1) Ltr, Winter, Chief Electronics Br, to CO SCGSA, 4 Sep 44, sub: Radio Sets AN/GRQ–1 and AN/MRT–1 Maint. (2) Memo, Winter for ExecO E&T, 4 Aug 44, sub: Present Status of Activity by Electronics Br on Providing RCM for the New High Priority Army Air Force Rqmt, with ASF Transmittal Sheet, Action 1, E&T Sv to P&O Sv, 7 Aug 44. Both in SigC 413.44 RCM Guided Missiles No. 1 (ET–2623). (3) Memo, E. E. Combs, Engr, for File Proj 852–F, sub: Hist Review of Dev of Radio Set AN/MRT–1. SigC ET 413.44 AN/MRT–1 folder No. 2, 1944–45.

[65] Ltr, CSigO Hq ETOUSA to CSigO, 10 May 45, sub: Radio Control for V–2 Rockets. SigC 413.44 RCM Guided Missiles No. 1 (ET–2623). American Cigar included the AN/MRT–1 and GRQ–1 jammers.

[66] Ltr, CG AAF to CSigO, 7 Sep 44, sub: RCM vs. Crossbow (Modification of Prog). AAG 413.44–FO Radio.

Partially offsetting the unhappy circumstance that these rockets could not be jammed was the timely success of the Allies on the Continent, where their armies were already overrunning some of the German launching sites.

Meteorlike, the 14-ton V-2 first struck London on 12 September 1944, exploding volcanically, deep-driven by its impact, the sound of the ground explosion trailing off in the eerie scream of the mile-per-second plunge from the stratosphere.[67] Nothing could counter it, for the weapon was controlled mechanically and not by radio. RCM was of no avail. Nothing either known or imagined at the time could defeat this rocket once it had roared skyward from its launching site.

The RCM effort involved in CROSSBOW was not the less remarkable because fortune did not put it to use. Tuba, in particular, constituted a brilliant achievement, possessing the ability to radiate with all the power of the most potent broadcasting station, yet in microwaves at frequency rates hundreds of times greater than those of the AM broadcast band. Tuba would open up UHF (ultrahigh frequency) broadcasting, for one thing.[68] Finally, the RCM part of the CROSSBOW program had been a shining accomplishment in speed, improvisation, and co-operation. The Signal Corps received a bright bouquet for its efforts. "The response of the Signal Corps," read a letter from AAF headquarters, "and all the other agencies involved in this project has been magnificent."[69]

Shortly after this accolade, General Colton in turn congratulated Dr. James B. Conant and the NDRC, commenting that "the imminent danger to the British Isles from super-rocket bombs" anticipated in August was now receding as the Allies advanced deeper into Europe. He added, "I should like, however, to take this opportunity to express our appreciation of the splendid cooperation which Division 15 and its contractors have shown, and for the expeditious manner in which pressing delivery dates have been met. Delivery by Division 15 of equipment for this project has been prompt and most satisfying."[70]

RCM to the War's End

As Germany's resistance weakened, her coastal aircraft warning radar stations overrun, her aircraft knocked from the skies, RCM activity in Europe became limited to jamming German gun layers, the Wuerzburgs. Flak directed by these excellent gun layers had taken an almost prohibitive toll of Allied bombers until the Allies introduced large-scale jamming in the big raid on Hamburg in July 1943. Radar-aimed flak continued to bring down Allied bombers to the end of the war, but at a greatly reduced rate, thanks to Window, Chaff, and Carpet. The Signal Corps supply of Carpet jammers for the American planes never reached the demand of one to a bomber. The Eighth Air Force

[67] Baxter, *Scientists Against Time*, p. 36.

Since the rockets traveled far faster than the speed of sound, bystanders first heard the impact and explosion near at hand, while the sound of the rocket's passage through the sky came after, in the reverse of the order of events, exactly as when lightening strikes very close by.

[68] *Electronics Warfare*, pp. 34–35.

[69] Ltr, CG AAF to CSigO, 7 Sep 44.

[70] Ltr, Colton to Conant, Chairman, NDRC, 14 Sep 44. SigC 413.44 RCM Guided Missiles No. 1 (ET-2623).

could obtain only enough to outfit about 10 percent of its bombers until October 1944, when heavy shipments permitted the equipping of about 30 percent of the big planes. By year's end the percentage had climbed to at least 80 out of every hundred fitted with Carpet.[71]

The Germans had come to rely increasingly upon their radar defenses against Allied air attacks, though they suspected that the Allies might introduce countermeasures in air combat and had awaited the application with dread. Then it happened, at Hamburg. "The enemy has . . . delivered the long-awaited blow against our decimeter radar sets both on land and in the air," wrote a German officer. The success must be kept very secret, he emphasized. Every effort must be made, he wrote, to create the impression that radar jamming was not very effective.

But finding the Carpet jammers aboard those American bombers that were downed, Germans who understood the meaning of radar fell into ever deeper dismay. RCM was overwhelmingly effective and remained so, despite every effort by the Germans to counter it. The only real palliative, radar using microwave frequencies, was not immediately within grasp; the German research specialists had been ordered to abandon it.

That crucial raid, it later appeared, was for the Germans the Stalingrad of the air war.

The Germans' gloom deepened as

their electronic specialists found more and better jammers in the wreckage of the Eighth Air Force bombers, for example the AN/APT-2, the low-power American Carpet. By November 1944, the Germans noticed, too, that jamming signals were radiating much more strongly from USAAF formations than from those of the RAF. This was the consequence of the increased distribution by the Signal Corps of the new high-power airborne Carpets, AN/APQ-9.[72]

Japanese electronic defenses were never so formidable as the Germans'. Japan's radars were fewer and more easily dealt with. Yet they were improving, and the Americans were determined to keep well ahead of any new enemy radio or radar development. Some RCM equipment had been going to the Pacific all along. Much more followed, as the demand in Europe declined. To the Signal Corps this meant, above all, tropicalization. RCM equipment in Europe had not required it. The Pacific climate made it mandatory. General Ingles had assured the Air Forces in September 1944 that this precaution would be taken for all RCM gear intended for their use in the Pacific.[73]

With the equipment went RCM spe-

[71] Incl, Flak Radar Countermeasures in ETO—A Review and Evaluation of their Use by the Eighth Air Force, pp. 15 and 18–19, with Ltr, O. G. Villard, Jr., RRL, Cambridge, Mass., to OCSigO, Attn Capt R. J. Bowley, 11 Sep 45, no sub. SigC 413.44 RCM Gen No. 3 (ET–2757).

[72] Translated German documents (1) A Study of Present Window (Hamburg) Situation, *Anlage zo Chief NVW Abt., 4.IB–IIIB Nr 2170/43g Kdos,* pp. 1–3; (2) Jamming of Decimeter Communication Links by Enemy Airborn Jammers, 12 Dec 44, p. 9. These papers are contained in Electronics Intelligence Report No. 12/45, Hq, U.S. Strategic Air Forces in Europe (ACofS A–2), sub: German Views on the Effect of Allied Radar Countermeasures, inclosed with Ltr, CSigO Hq ETOUSA to OCSigO, 13 Jun 45, sub: Transmittal of Documents. SigC 413.44 RCM Gen No. 3 (ET–2757).

[73] 3d Ind, CSigO to CG AAF, 29 Sep 44, on Ltr, CG AAF to CSigO, 15 Aug 44, sub: Tropicalization of RCM Equip. AAG 413.44–FR Radio.

cialists. The commander of U.S. forces in the Central Pacific presented the War Depatment with his radio and radar countermeasures plan, asking for new RCM units—two radio deception teams, one radio deception company, and one radio jamming company. All of these became Signal Corps grist, especially for the Signal Security Agency, which already had numbers of radio intelligence units in the Orient.[74] By 1945, too, some 15 B–24 Ferrets were working above the Pacific, as were a number of B–29 Ferrets, flying out of the Marianas over the Japanese home islands.[75]

The Signal Corps Restricted to Ground RCM

At the turn of 1944–45, the entire RCM activity split in two when the AAF took over complete control of all its electronics, including research, development, and procurement. Hitherto the lion's share of RCM operations had gone to the Air Forces. Now that the AAF had taken over the development and procurement of all such equipment, it would seem that the Signal Corps might retain only such RCM activity as concerned the Army Ground Forces. Yet the dividing line between airborne and ground RCM, it would become increasingly evident, was anything but clear.

Meanwhile, having split into two parts what was essentially a single in-

tertwined effort, the Army now had to set up co-ordination. This was done, with channels extending to the General Staff, specifically to G–2, and to a new organization entitled the New Development Division. Henceforth, not only must the Signal Corps and the Air Forces keep each other informed on RCM progress, but G–2 as well. G–2 officers would reciprocate. Anticipating troubles sure to ensue after the split, the War Department told the Signal Corps and the Air Forces that if either became dissatisfied in matters of research and development, it should lodge its complaints with the New Development Division. "The employment of radio and radar countermeasures, including the jamming and the practice of radio and radar deception," the War Department acknowledged, "has become a most important element in the conduct of successful operations." Further, the War Department stated:

It is considered that the development of equipment and procedures for radio and radar countermeasures should be prosecuted with all dispatch. In order to cope with and rapidly counter new electronic development employed operationally, the Chief Signal Officer and the Army Air Forces are charged with the responsibility of soliciting the aid of the New Development Division, WDGS, in expediting delivery of small quantities of Radio and Radar Countermeasures equipment to theaters of operations even though this equipment had not fulfilled the requirements of AR–850–25.[76]

Not until well along in 1945 was the shift of all airborne RCM equipment,

---

[74] Msg No. R–23929, CG USAFCPA, Ft. Shafter, T. H., to WD, 28 Jul 44, ASF OPD (CM–IN–23942, 29 Jul 44) 037–Z. SigC 413.44 RCM Gen No. 1 (ET–2381).

[75] (1) CSigO, Annual Rpt, FY 45, p. 259. (2) "The Search for Jap Radar," Radar, No. 10 (June 30, 1945), pp. 9–11.

[76] (1) WD Cir 429, 3 Nov 44. (2) Unsigned, undated document (filed 1 Jan 45), sub: Policy Relations to the Development of Equipment for Radio and Radar Countermeasures. SigC 413.44 RCM Gen No. 2 (ET–2382).

laboratory facilities, engineers, and administrators carried out. In the meantime, the Signal Corps operations for the AAF—Mandrel and Carpet—continued to play a large part in the total RCM effort. The radio jammer Jackal actually blanketed German tank radio communications effectively during the Battle of the Bulge, according to the report of German prisoners.[77]

It was in the air, rather than on the ground, that Allied RCM in World War II bestowed the greater benefits, saving thousands of lives and hundreds of planes. Dr. James P. Baxter 3d summed up the Allied RCM accomplishment as follows:

The operational use of countermeasures equipment involved some of the most extraordinary duels of wits in the history of war, and it helped mightily to speed the day of victory. It has been estimated that radar countermeasures saved the U.S. Strategic Air Force based on England alone 450 planes and 4,500 casualties. But that is only part of the story. They played a major part in the masterly deception which covered our landings in Normandy and in Southern France. By blinding the eyes of our enemies while permitting our radars to scan with little or no interruption they struck from the hands of the Germans and Japanese new and potent weapons, while leaving us free to do our utmost.[78]

Reichsmarschall Hermann Goering, interviewed after the German surrender, ascribed much of the Allied success in the skies over Europe to RCM, which he admitted often reduced German radar and communications to uselessness.[79]

After the Air Forces took over their portion of Army RCM, a large remnant remained with the Army Ground Forces and continued to be a considerable responsibility for the Signal Corps. Electronics expanded so rapidly that abundant work remained for the Signal Corps. Ground countermeasures were growing in proportion to the increased use of guided missiles late in the war. Even the Japanese seemed likely to use them. There was also the new proximity fuze, the variable time (VT) fuze, which embodied a tiny electronic transmitter and receiver riding out a brief life span in the flight of a projectile. It also could be jammed, like any other radio or radar set. On 27 January 1945 the AGF asked the ASF to delve into all aspects of guided missile control and countermeasures. The AGF made it emphatic, labeling the program "essential," and calling for "a very high priority." [80]

RCM's Status in 1945

A variety of projects for ground countermeasures, of which Tuba was but one, already pressed upon the Signal Corps, but had not yet been drawn together

---

[77] See above p. 164.

[78] Baxter, *Scientists Against Time*, p. 169.

[79] Interrogation of Hermann Goering by General Carl Spaatz, Lt. Gen. Alexander M. Patch, Lt. Gen. Hoyt S. Vandenberg, Mr. Alexander P. de Seversky, and the historian of USSTAF, Dr. Bruce Hopper, 10 May 45, Air Intel Libr, quoted

in Reither, Use of Radio and Radar Equip by the AAF, 1939–45, p. 127.

This admission contrasts starkly with Goering's 1938 boast that "no enemy aircraft would ever get through to Berlin." That boast, it has been suggested, may have been based on his knowledge of radar, since the Germans possessed some air warning radar at that early date, as well as the rudiments of their excellent medium-wave Wuerzhurg range finder, later converted to a gun layer. Villard, Flak Radar Countermeasures in ETO—A Review . . . , p. 3.

[80] Incl, CG AGF to CG ASF, 27 Jan 45, sub: Countermeasures for Enemy Guided Missiles, with Ltr, Col Robert W. Raynsford, Asst Chief E&T Sv, to CO SCSGA, 8 Feb 45, sub: Establishment of Countermeasures Orgn at SCGSA. SigC 413.44 RCM Gen No. 2 (ET–2382).

in a tightly co-ordinated net. Early 1945 seemed the time to accomplish this. Col. Robert W. Raynsford, assistant chief of the Engineering and Technical Service, urged that the Signal Corps Ground Signal Agency, embracing the several laboratories in the Fort Monmouth area, speed up its efforts on search receivers. These were designed not only to detect proximity fuzes and guided missiles in flight but also to ferret out radio and radar stations. He urged, too, that the laboratories develop jammers for everything that radiates—for proximity fuzes and guided missiles as well as for ground radio and radar sets. He urged that they try to improve antijamming techniques and design, so as to protect friendly radio and radar devices from jamming by the enemy. More and better liaison would be needed since so many agencies and laboratories were involved, not the least the new agencies of the AAF. The technical control of the entire RCM program within the Signal Corps, Raynsford felt, ought to be concentrated in a special group or branch of the SCGSA at Fort Monmouth. "But," replied Col. Victor A. Conrad, the director of the laboratories there, "the needed men were lacking." Would the Signal Corps headquarters in Washington help him obtain qualified engineers and physicists for these very laboratories where severe personnel cuts had been ordered in mid-1943? Colonel Conrad pointed out that a countermeasures organization had in fact been set up at the Camp Evans Signal Laboratory to work part time on jammers and on deception and antijamming techniques and equipment. But as part time work, performed by men already employed in existing receiver and direction finder projects, this

was an inadequate and unsatisfactory arrangement.[81] A few months later a dispute arose over an important RCM report, which the laboratory workers had filed away unexamined and without action, and in May an engineer of the Office of the Chief Signal Officer investigated the situation, reporting that the laboratories suffered for want of manpower. "The RCM section," he specified in particular, "does not have sufficient personnel to review all the reports received." [82]

Ground RCM made progress, nonetheless, and in mid-1945 General Ingles brought General Somervell up to date on the subject. Military characteristics and projects had been established for ground jammers for use against airborne radar bombing sets, airborne radar navigation equipment, and guided missiles. The entire program was being conducted with a long-range view to extending research and development beyond the goals of the war, since Japan was the only Axis Power left.[83]

[81] Ltr, Raynsford to CO SCGSA, 8 Feb 45, with 1st Ind, Conrad, CO SCGSA, to CSigO, 23 Mar 45. SigC 413.44 RCM Gen No. 2 (ET-2382).
[82] Memo, M. F. Brosche, Engr Sig Equip OCSigO, for file, 23 May 45, sub: Rpt of Trip to Coles Sig Lab, 14-15 May 45. SigC 413.44 RCM Gen No. 2 (ET-2382).
[83] Ltr, CSigO to CG ASF, 11 Jul 45, sub: RCM for Guided Missiles, Radar Bomb Sights, and Airborne Radar Navigation Devices. SigC 413.44 RCM Gen No. 3 (ET-2757).
A summary of RCM projects in August listed two special investigations set up in the Signal Corps laboratories, one in the NDRC, and four more in NDRC for which approval had not yet been received. The Signal Corps noted that already there was duplication between the AAF program and that of the Signal Corps. The summary commented that AAF RCM activity included work "not within the scope of the AAF responsibilities." Memo, Capt L. M. Sundstrom, Com Coordinating Br RCM Sec, for Rcd, 17 Aug 45, sub: Countermeasures for Enemy Guided Missiles. SigC 413.44 RCM Gen No. 3 (ET-2757).

One Signal Corps engineer and RCM specialist, zealous in his subject and realizing that RCM was as yet a Hopalong Cassidy in the strange new world of Buck Rogers warfare, of which World War II might be but the prelude, wrote in September 1945 that the enemy in the future

. . . will make full usage of the principles of radio, and hence of the radio frequency spectrum up to the frontiers exploited at the time of such conflict. It is considered that the armed might of this nation should have access to the highest attainable level of technical equipment to counter an assumed attack by a highly technical enemy; and that such counter weapons as can be attained for prohibiting or interfering with the enemy utilization of radio waves should and must be designed and tested prior to such conflict; and that our protective forces must be equipped with such weapons. It is considered the duty of the Joint Countermeasures Committee, or any other organization which assumes the responsibilities of that Committee, to support an adequate research and development program such that our armed forces are not confronted with an enemy technical weapon utilizing waves of such a nature that no countermeasures weapon is in existence, or duly considered for procurement and issue.[84]

As every weapon spawns a counterweapon, so was the case with radar. The

parent weapons at first had seemed overwhelmingly complex to the Army, industry, and the nation of 1940–45. Afterward, the countermeasures equipment and its applications were bidding fair to surpass that original complexity. It is not enough, it is actually perilous, just to develop a new weapon. One must quickly develop a countermeasure for it, in case the enemy develops the same weapon also. Thus all weapon development tends to double itself.

This progression of military communications-electronics that began in World War II continued almost unabated in postwar years. Maj. Gen. Raymond C. Maude, a former Signal Corps officer, later the Director of Communications, U.S. Air Force, spoke in 1952 of the "humble beginning" of RCM during World War II. He described the progress attained by January 1952 as having so greatly advanced "that the field reaches across the entire communications-electronics spectrum." [85] There seemed to be no end to "What hath God wrought?" Morse's first message over the electric telegraph on 25 May 1844.

---

[84] Memo, C. K. Shultes, Radio Engr, CM Sec Radar Br, for file, 6 Sep 45, sub: Radio Countermeasures Policy. SigC 413.44 RCM Gen No. 3 (ET–2757).

[85] Speech, Gen Raymond C. Maude, New York chapter of the Armed Forces Communications Electronics Association, at Mitchel Air Force Base, Long Island, 30 Jan 52, reproduced in *Telecommunications Reports*, XVIII, No. 20 (February 4, 1952) 16.

CHAPTER XI

Signal Security and Intelligence

Every commander understands that his command control depends upon effective signal communications. Effective communications must be fast; they must be accurate; they must be secure. Under nearly all military circumstances security is the most important element of command control. A system that lacks good security is a disadvantage, and, worse, it is a threat to the user.[1]

Signal security is the safeguarding of the Army's own communications. It involves codes and ciphers, their safe distribution and correct use. Achieving signal security requires more than the best signal equipment systems that engineering ingenuity can devise. It demands large numbers of expertly trained and disciplined persons, both civilian and military, and strict adherence to policies and procedures in handling communications.

Along with signal security, signal intelligence contributes immeasurably to the successful conduct of military operations. Whereas signal security is the protection of one's own communications, signal intelligence is the penetration of the enemy's communications, and the valuable information thus acquired. Signal intelligence involves intercept of the enemy's messages; the analysis of his message traffic, from which much can be learned of his military dispositions and movements without reading the texts; and, finally, the breaking of his code and cipher systems so that his actual words, his plans, and his instructions, may be read.

Signal security and signal intelligence are, like Siamese twins, not easily separated. They are both entwined in military communications of all types. They use the same equipment, the same procedures, the same skills, the same training. They grew up together in the U.S. Army from the origin of the Signal Corps in the Civil War, when Maj. Albert J. Myer developed a cipher disc to speed rapid encipherment of messages.[2]

Throughout its existence the Signal Corps, as the Army's communications agency, has been charged with a large share of responsibility for these matters. The scope of the responsibilities and the extent to which they are shared by other staff and operating agencies have changed from time to time as expressed by Army Regulations. For nearly all of World War II the Signal Corps, under

[1] (1) Lecture, Maj Gen Frank E. Stoner, Communications Security, Comd and Gen Staff Sch, 1945. Copy in SigC AC 337 Conf and Lectures. (2) See also Maj. Gen Earle F. Cook, "Electronic Black Chamber," *Army*, XIII, No. 2 (September, 1962), 37ff.

[2] George Raynor Thompson, "Civil War Signals," *Military Affairs*, XVIII, No. 4 (Winter 1954), pp. 188ff.

Myer, the Army's first Chief Signal Officer, possessed a wide knowledge of this recondite specialty. See Albert J. Myer, *Manual of Signals*, in various editions, 1864 to 1879.

the staff supervision of G–2, was wholly responsible for all operating phases of the Army's signal security and intelligence activity, including code compilation; solution; interception; intelligence training; research and development; and printing, distribution, and accounting of intelligence materials. These activities it carried out through the Signal Security Agency and the 2d Signal Service Battalion, both with headquarters at Arlington Hall Station. Thousands were engaged in the highly secret, highly important, and highly difficult work.[3]

Evolution and Development of the Signal Security Intelligence Activity

World War I

Until World War I all Signal Corps officers shared in the security effort that was expended upon military communications, mostly a matter of enciphering and deciphering, using a simple cipher disc. The task was integral to the handling of message traffic and was familiar to every officer of the Corps. For some years before the war, the Signal Corps also prepared codes for the Army and the War Department.

World War I brought a heavy increase in the security and intelligence load. In Washington, the Military Intelligence Division, War Department General Staff, began compiling its own codes. The Adjutant General printed, distributed, stored, and accounted for Army codes and ciphers, a responsibility that

lasted until 1934.[4] The Signal Corps necessarily shared in the work, implementing the security systems in the Army message centers. Consequently, the work was split among these three organizations in the United States.

In the combat theater, in France, additional responsibility centered in the Signal Corps. Brig. Gen. Edgar Russel, Chief Signal Officer, American Expeditionary Forces (AEF), was charged with compiling American codes and ciphers and with the collection of all kinds of signal intelligence.[5] None of the existing codes at the disposal of the U.S. Army—the 1915 War Department Telegraph Code and the old Army cipher disc with running key, together with the official British Playfair Cipher—proved secure.[6] The Signal Corps' small but very efficient Code and Compilation Section in France produced a variety of codes for specialized purposes.[7] Of particular interest was a series of trench codes named after American rivers and lakes. They were designed to be changed frequently and rapidly. When the first, named the Potomac Code, fell into German hands a month after it was issued, it was replaced throughout the entire Army within two days.[8] The work was heavy.

---

[3] Except where otherwise noted, material in this chapter is based on historical documents made available to the authors by special arrangement with the Army Security Agency.

[4] ASA Lecture, The Origin and Development of the Army Security Agency, 1917–1947, (March 1948) (hereafter cited as ASA Lecture), p. 3.

[5] Hq AEF, GO 8, 5 Jul 17.

[6] ASA Lecture, p. 4.

[7] (1) Annual Report of the Chief Signal Officer, 1919 (hereafter cited as CSigO, Annual Rpt, 1919), pp. 536–38. (2) Capt. Garland Black, "The G–2 Signals Team," Signal Corps Bulletin 90 (May–June, 1936), pp. 24–42.

[8] History of the Signal Corps, American Expeditionary Forces (hereafter cited as AEF Hist, with volume, chapter, and pages noted), V, ch. XV, "Code Compilation Division," 124–28. SigC Hist Sec file. See Bibliographical Note for description of this 7-volume manuscript.

Within ten months the section compiled and printed more than 80,000 code books. They were sizable, too—a staff code intended primarily for field work contained about 30,000 words and phrases.[9] After the armistice the section took on its largest task during the war period, compiling a new War Department code.[10]

Intercept of enemy traffic and efforts to break the enemy's code and cipher systems began on a large scale in World War I. In Washington the Military Intelligence Division took over cryptological work. In the last few years before the war, the Army Signal School at Fort Leavenworth had begun instruction in cryptology. Still the Army could claim only five Signal Corps military code and cipher experts on enemy diplomatic systems when war came—Capt. Parker Hitt and 1st Lts. F. F. Black, Joseph O. Mauborgne, Frank Moorman, and Karl Truesdale.[11] None of these officers could be spared to work with MID in Washington.[12] MID hired a civilian, Herbert O. Yardley, commissioned him, and put him in charge of its cryptological activities.[13]

Securing competent personnel for intelligence staffs presented an enormous problem. In this emergency, Col. George Fabyan, a man of wealth who maintained a private research laboratory for cryptology and cryptanalysis at Riverbank in Geneva, Illinois, offered the War Department the use of his facilities to train a group of officers and enlisted men. Colonel Fabyan had an extensive library of older cryptographic literature. When the War Department accepted his offer, Fabyan sent a representative to the Signal School at Fort Leavenworth to learn all that the Army knew on the subject. Lieutenant Mauborgne, at that time an instructor at the school, gave Fabyan all the library materials, manuals, and information on Army methods, including a manual recently compiled by Parker Hitt. Using his own cryptographic resources and the material obtained from the school, Fabyan at his own expense set up a school at Riverbank for Army officers and men. He also obtained as instructors a number of civilian professors and scientists, among them the geneticist William F. Friedman. A number of these civilians, including Friedman, were later commissioned and sent to France for service in the Military Intelligence Division.[14]

Overseas, G-2's function of solution and interpretation received major support from the Signal Corps intercept stations. The Radio Section of the Signal Corps Radio Division, AEF, operated "all field stations pertaining to

[9] ASA Lecture, p. 4.

[10] AEF Hist, I, ch. V, "General," 81.

[11] (1) ASA Lecture, pp. 4–5. (2) Interv, SigC Hist Div with Maj Gen Joseph O. Mauborgne (Ret.), 2 Dec 60. (3) Interv, SigC Hist Sec with William F. Friedman, and MS Comment, 16 Feb 61.

[12] Colonel Hitt became the chief signal officer of First Army in France; Mauborgne, by then a lieutenant colonel, became the chief of the vitally important Engineering and Research Division in the OCSigO in Washington in World War I. Major Moorman was the chief of the Radio Intelligence Service, A-6 G-2, AEF. See (1) Hq AEF, GO 120, 24 Jul 18; (2) AEF Hist, vols. II and III, The Signal Corps in Combat, passim. (3) CSigO, Annual Rpt, 1919, passim, especially pp. 241–70.

[13] ASA Lecture, p. 5.

After the war, Yardley remained in cryptanalysis

work until 1929. See Herbert O. Yardley, The American Black Chamber (Indianapolis, Ind.: Bobbs-Merrill Co., 1931), passim.

[14] (1) Interv, SigC Hist Div with Mauborgne, 2 Dec 60. (2) Interv, SigC Hist Sec with Friedman, 16 Feb 61.

interception of messages of the enemy" and acquired "information concerning his communication system." [15]

There were listening posts close to the enemy lines, where German-speaking signalmen installed devices and eavesdropped on enemy telephone conversations and messages sent over the ground-telegraph system. There were signal intercept stations, whose operators meticulously recorded enemy air and ground radio messages. And there were goniometric (direction-finding) stations to ferret out and pinpoint the location of enemy stations.[16] Policing the American communications systems also went on constantly.

Organization Between the Two World Wars

After the end of World War I, the divided state of responsibility for the Army's cryptological work in Washington continued for a decade. All code and cipher compilation was consolidated under the Signal Corps in 1921. A significant event, full of future portent, occurred in January of that year when the Signal Corps hired the skilled cryptographer, William Friedman, who had returned to civilian employment after the war. Friedman, even in 1921 probably the nation's foremost authority on military codes and ciphers, became the chief of the tiny Code and Cipher Section in the Research and Development Division, Office of the Chief Signal Officer. Friedman's responsibilities were chiefly cryptographic—developing new systems and devices and improving security procedures in the handling of codes and ciphers in the Army. He carried on his tasks with the help of a single assistant until 1929.[17]

Cryptanalysis was not then a Signal Corps function. In peacetime, naturally, Army cryptanalysts have no enemy-enciphered traffic to work on. There are no messages of a hostile army to intercept, analyze, or decrypt. Military and civilian specialists can only practice with set exercises, prepare material for training purposes, and in general use analytic knowledge, skills, and insight toward detecting weaknesses in the Army's own systems and improving them in every possible way. "It is for these very reasons that those who have the responsibility of creating the Army's security systems should also be assigned cryptanalytic duties." [18]

Just such a consolidation of responsibility in the interest of effective operation came in May 1929. A change in Army Regulations placed all work connected with codes and ciphers under the Chief Signal Officer.[19] In so doing the War Department advanced the development of better security and intelligence in the Army. The Chief Signal Officer, Maj. Gen. George S. Gibbs, established in the War Plans and Training Division, Office of the Chief Signal Officer, a new section designated the Signal Intel-

[15] CSigO, Annual Rpt, 1919, p. 303.

[16] (1) Ibid., pp. 303–37. (2) AEF Hist, IV, ch. XI, Radio Section, Radio Division, 313–69. (3) Maj E. Alexander Powell, The Army Behind the Army (New York, N.Y.: C. Scribner's Sons, 1919), pp. 16–23.

[17] ASA Lecture, pp. 6–8.

[18] Intcrv, SigC Hist Sec (Thompson and Harris) with Maj Gen Earle F. Cook, DCSigO, 14 Jun 60, p. 1.

[19] AR 105–5, C–1, 10 May 29.

ligence Service.[20] William Friedman became its director. The duties assigned by the War Department to General Gibbs in 1929, and delegated by him to SIS, were preparation and revision of Army codes and ciphers and, in time of war, interception of enemy radio and wire traffic, the goniometric location of enemy radio stations, the solution of intercepted enemy code and cipher messages, and laboratory arrangements for the employment and detection of secret inks.[21]

Obviously Friedman needed more than his one assistant. General Gibbs succeeded in funding for and hiring a total of six. Until the approach of World War II, the staff remained small, but the potential under Friedman's competent care was enormous. Between 1930 and 1936 SIS's staff of seven persons established a training program for cryptanalysts and signal intelligence experts, sought to develop intercept facilities, and did valuable spadework toward emergency war planning.[22] By the outbreak of war in Europe in 1939, SIS had 19 persons on its staff; by the date of Pearl Harbor, 331. The tremendous expansion of World War II brought the figure to over 10,000 by V–J Day, not counting those signal intelligence specialists serving overseas under theater commanders.[23]

In the mid-1930's, crypto and crypto-related tasks were increasingly concentrated in the Signal Corps. When the War Department transferred TAG's responsibility for printing, storing, distributing, and accounting for Army's codes and ciphers to the Signal Corps in August 1934, all the crypto functions were at last united in the Signal Intelligence Service.[24] The intelligence product of this united activity began to be so major a concern of WDGS G–2 that G–2 took over complete control of it at the end of World War II. Until that time the Army's SIS, growing from a small nucleus of a few devoted officers and civilians to a huge, vital military service within the Signal Corps household, grappled successfully with the tightly controlled, well-integrated, highly secret operation.[25]

Until 1935, Mr. Friedman remained the civilian chief of the activity. The first military chief, Maj. Haskell O. Allison, was appointed in 1935. He was followed by Maj. William O. Reeder in 1938, Colonel Akin in April 1941, Colonel Minckler in June 1941, Colonel Bullock in April 1942, and Colonel Corderman in February 1943. Corderman remained in that position for the rest of World War II, becoming a brigadier general in June 1945.

Personnel Problems and Training

From the very beginning of SIS expansion, a most difficult problem was that of finding qualified people. Needed were persons temperamentally fitted to the painfully detailed work of cryptog-

---

[20] OCSigO Org Chart, 26 Dec 29, copy in SigC Hist Monograph E–5, Tab H. SigC Hist Sec file.
During World War I, Gibbs served as assistant chief signal officer, AEF. The Code and Ciphers Division was one of his direct responsibilities.
[21] AR 105–5, C–1, 10 May 29.
[22] Historical Research Notes, Signal Security Agency in World War II (hereafter cited as Hist, SSA in World War II), pp. 13–14.
[23] Ibid.

[24] AR 105–5, C–1, 21 Aug 34.
[25] ASA Lecture, pp. 9ff.

raphy, to the oftentimes maddeningly obstinate work of cryptanalysts adept at cipher breaking—men who were also able to keep secrets, who might continue for a lifetime in an activity that they could not reveal, in which they could expect no credit, whose skills would benefit them not one iota should they seek other employment.

It is not surprising that upon the creation of SIS, when Mr. Friedman was allowed six helpers (three junior cryptanalysts, one cryptanalyst aide, and two assistant cryptographic clerks), Civil Service could find no one with the required qualifications, certainly none trained in cryptanalysis and cryptography. It was obvious, as soon as a few intelligent, stable, and security-minded individuals were found, that SIS itself would have to train them in crypto duties.

SIS accordingly embarked on a vigorous training program, both to train new SIS civilian employees and to train officers and enlisted men of the Regular Army and the Reserves. Mr. Friedman turned teacher, writing a series of training manuals on cryptology and cryptanalysis to provide text material. To train Regular Army officers, the Signal Corps set up the Signal Intelligence School within the SIS. 1st Lt. Mark Rhoads became the first student in 1931 and Lieutenant Corderman the second in 1932. Although at first the plan was for each officer to receive a year's training, the difficulty of the subject soon demonstrated that two years should be spent in it, and that two officers should be in training at the same time.[26] Organized informally at first, the

school was officially constituted as a separate activity in 1934, with Lieutenant Corderman as instructor. Between 1930 and the attack on Pearl Harbor, the Signal Intelligence School trained nine Regular Army officers.[27]

But long before World War II began, the Signal Corps realized that many more officers would have to become acquainted with this specialized work if the SIS were to be ready to meet an emergency. A number of Reserve officers would have to receive training, both in the Signal Reserve and in the Military Intelligence Reserve. Beginning in 1930, special 2-week courses in military cryptography were given in the Office of the Chief Signal Officer.[28] Intending them as an introduction to the subject, to serve as a basis for further study, the SIS hoped to build up a nucleus of experienced cryptographers in the Reserves that could be called upon in event of an emergency. A start toward Reserve training in cryptography had been made in 1929 when five Reserve officers from each corps area attended a 2-week course. Eight from each area attended the 1930 courses. In 1931 there were no funds for the training and hence no students. In 1932 and 1933 only three Signal Reserve officers, plus two more from the Military Intelligence Reserve, received temporary training duty in the Signal Intelligence School.

In the autumn of 1936, Signal Corps mobilization plans called for 176 Signal Corps Reserve officers in the cryptographic classification. The number so assigned actually stood at 14. They were

---

[26] Memo, ACofS G–1 for CofS, 2 Oct 35. AG 319.12 (8–27–35).

[27] (1) Interv, SigC Hist Sec with Cook, 14 Jun 60. (2) ASA Lecture, *passim.*

[28] *Signal Corps Bulletin 56* (September–October, 1930), pp. 6ff.

civilian Reservists in the SIS, in other government and commercial code and cipher bureaus, and a few Reserve officers who had taken extension courses. Seeking another source for the crypto-trained Reservists who would be needed desperately should war come, the Signal Corps turned to the ROTC. At that time ROTC units turned out Reservists for combat classifications only. But by the end of January 1937, arrangements had been made with an ROTC unit at the University of Illinois to graduate Reservists in cryptography at the rate of about five a year.[29]

Ominous events in Europe in the late 1930's accelerated Army plans for emergency mobilization and expansion that soon overran SIS's training plans for Reservists. In the War Department in Washington, the first segment to benefit from an augmentation in personnel, space, and facilities was the Army's SIS.[30] Authorized increases in SIS between mid-1939 and 7 December 1941 brought the total actual strength of SIS to 331 officers, enlisted men, and civilians. Under Executive Order 8257, issued 21 September 1939, SIS could fill civilian positions without regard to Civil Service competitive requirements. SIS filled its first increment of 26 positions from a selected list of Signal Corps Reserve officers and enlisted men, together with a very few members of the American Cryptogram Association, the only civil-ian organization having a direct interest in codes and ciphers.

Rapid expansion brought changes in the SIS training program. The high standards of loyalty, character, and professional competence to be met resulted in clearance lags of several months between the dates of authorization and actual hiring. SIS resorted to pre-employment training. It also expanded its training courses, formerly given Reserve officers, to include specially selected civilians and enlisted men. By mid-1939, enrollments in these courses totaled 283.[31]

Troop Units: 2d Signal Service Company

Throughout the 1930's the dearth of intercept material posed a serious training problem for SIS. The agency had to depend upon such material as was available at Fort Monmouth, where the 1st Radio Intelligence Company was activated in 1938, plus material forwarded by the RI detachments of five signal companies. These were the Panama Signal Company at Quarry Heights in the Canal Zone and four numbered service companies—the 7th at Fort Sam Houston, Texas; the 8th at the Presidio, San Francisco; the 9th at Fort Shafter, Hawaii; and the 10th at Fort McKinley, Philippine Islands.[32] These detachments functioned under the signal officers of their various corps areas or departments.

Maj. Gen. Joseph O. Mauborgne, who became the Chief Signal Officer in October 1937, was one of the Army's top signal intelligence experts, long associ-

---

[29] (1) Memo, Capt Minckler for O/C WP&T Div OCSigO, 1 Oct 36. (2) R&W Actions No. 2, SIS to O/C WDMC, 1 Oct 36; No. 4, WDMC to WP&T Div, 2 Oct 36; No. 10, ExecO to CSigO, 9 Oct 36. (3) Ltr, CSigO to SigO 6th CA, 13 Oct 36. (4) Ltr, CSigO to SigO 6th CA, 28 Jan 37, sub: Sig Reserve Offs, Cryptographic Classification. All in SigC 352.11 Gen 1937.
[30] ASA Lecture, p. 20.

[31] Ibid., pp. 22–23.
[32] Hist, SSA in World War II, p. 31.

ated with the various cryptological specialities.[33] Well aware of the special needs of intelligence work and alert to the advantages of increased efficiency and security to be gained, he proposed late in 1938 that the several intelligence detachments be consolidated into a single organization.[34] General Mauborgne advanced cogent arguments. Such an organization would retain intercept specialists and cryptographers in the work that needed their skills so badly, forestalling the loss of the men to other assignments. The security of the activity could be better guarded and the morale and efficiency of the men improved with a single parent organization. On 1 January 1939 the 2d Signal Service Company was activated at Fort Monmouth, with a strength of 101 enlisted men and one officer. That single officer was 1st Lt. Earle F. Cook.[35] Thus was born a unique organization that served signal security and intelligence functions brilliantly in World War II. Eventually the officers, men, and women of the unit, which grew to a greatly oversized battalion during the war, implemented the signal security and intelligence function worldwide.

Men for the 2d Signal Service Company were carefully selected and painstakingly trained. They were too valuable to be regarded lightly. Policy for their selection, training, assignment, and transfer specified that they be "of excellent character . . . citizens preferably native born . . . whose loyalty, integrity, discretion, and trustworthiness are

unquestionable, whose financial status and/or habits . . . render them unlikely to succumb to any temptations arising from these sources, [who] have had at least one enlisted period, and who have indicated their willingness to spend about 40 percent of their service on foreign duty." [36]

With the activation of the 2d Signal Service Company, SIS, hitherto limited to a handful of people in the Office of the Chief Signal Officer, and a restricted War Department activity only, entered a new dimension of immense potential. Now SIS could and did assign overseas elements that would both enlarge the SIS sphere of activity and provide the valuable help of this specialized service to commanders where the company detachments were stationed.

Within the first year, the Fort Monmouth group divided several ways. On 22 March 1939 a detachment moved to Fort Hancock, New Jersey. In September the War Department directed that a new monitoring station be built at Fort Hunt, Virginia, and in October a detachment under 1st Lt. Robert E. Schukraft arrived to install and operate the station. Because of the need for close co-operation between SIS and the 2d Signal Service Company headquarters, the unit headquarters moved to Washington in mid-October to an area in the Munitions Building adjacent to SIS headquarters. Capt. George A. Bicher assumed command soon after the move. Thereafter throughout the war the two headquarters were always in the same location. A small detachment remained at Fort Monmouth to help

---

[33] See above p. 329.

[34] (1) Ltr, CSigO to TAG, 2 Sep 38, sub: Sig Intel. SigC 320.3 RID 1938. (2) AG 320.2 (9-2-38) SigC Misc (Ret) E-M, 15 Nov 38.

[35] Hist, SSA in World War II, p. 34.

[36] *Ibid.*

launch a new crytographic school.[37] By the end of 1939, the company was larger by two, one additional enlisted man and one officer. But it would grow to an authorized 150 men in 1941,[38] and to nearly 1,000 soon after Pearl Harbor.

Equipment Development

The Signal Corps mission had always included the provision of cipher and code equipment for Army communications. The simple cipher disc remained standard for many years—a quick facility for use in the field to convert the letters of a message to a meaningless scramble for transmission by wigwag, courier, or telegraph. Such a scrambled message was secure enough from the enemy, if by chance he intercepted a copy, unless a sufficient number of messages at the same cipher setting came into his hands. Should this occur, analysis of the messages could lead to a reconstruction of the key and the breaking of the system.

Although code books were widely used in World War I (requiring preliminary and prolonged compilation, printing, and distribution), ciphers were also employed. Colonel Mauborgne, who was deeply concerned with code and cipher matters throughout his Army career, developed a pocket-size field cipher device:

Several cipher bureaus have tried to break this cipher, but to date have been unsuccessful, notwithstanding the fact that they were given 25 messages in the same key. This device will replace the cipher disc which has been issued to the Army for many years.[39]

Colonel Mauborgne's device became the M–94, a cylinder having 25 rotating discs, which the Army adopted soon after World War I. Standardized in 1922, it long continued to be used by tactical units in some areas, notably in the China-Burma-India theater. It was not entirely replaced in that theater until midway through World War II by the small hand-held converter, the M–209.[40]

Whereas all other Army cipher devices and machines were developed by SIS itself, the M–209 was of commercial origin. SIS studied everything commercially available, including many inventors' proposals. This device alone had sufficient merit to warrant adoption. The little hand-operated cylinder and tape printer was improved and standardized late in the 1930's. Weighing but a few pounds, rugged, and operable by unskilled men, it became a popular device that Army and AAF troops employed in combat situations throughout World War II. The security of its encipherment, at the many settings it provided, gave enemy interceptors and cryptanalysts slim opportunity unless a considerable number of messages were intercepted at the same setting. Decipherment was of course accomplished by the same device at the receiving end.[41]

The M–209 always worked and was dependable under all field conditions, recalled Lieutenant Ogburn, communications officer of the 1st Battalion, 5307th Composite Unit—the Marauders—in Burma in 1944. His radio operators, with wistful thoughts of actress Greta

---

[37] (1) ASA Lecture, p. 24. (2) Hist, SSA in World War II, p. 35.

[38] AG 221 (2–16–41).

[39] CSigO, Annual Rpt, FY 1919, p. 240.

[40] Hist, SSA in World War II, p. 65.

[41] (1) Ibid., (2) ASA Lecture, pp. 17f., 25.

(the great) Garbo, affectionately dubbed the box "the Greater Garble." This was really libel, Ogburn explained, not of the lady but of the M–209. The encipherment and decipherment of the device were without fault. Any garbles rendering the message it processed unreadable were far more likely the fault of the radio operator who transmitted the enciphered letters from the M–209 tape.[42]

Modern military cipher machines probably began with the arrival of the typewriter in wide Army use early in the century, bringing with it the possibilities of mechanical encipherment by the time of World War I. Col. J. J. Carty (chief engineer of the American Telephone and Telegraph Company before his acceptance of a Signal Corps commission) and AT&T engineers, with the co-operation of Colonel Mauborgne, worked on this development:

> They conducted a series of experiments and finally devised apparatus whereby a message written in plain English could be quickly enciphered, printed in plain letters upon a page similar to the printing of a typewriter, and transmitted over a telegraph line and received at the distant end. The printed cipher telegram being copied upon the deciphering machine will finally appear in plain text.[43]

The machine developed by AT&T was the first successful electromechanical printing telegraph cipher machine. It did not get into production in time to be used overseas during World War I, but it was used daily between Washington, D.C., and ports of embarkation at Brooklyn, Hoboken, and Newport News.

Moreover, its development marked a turning point in the application of machine operations for communications security and intelligence.[44]

SIS began development early in the 1930's of one of the first of a series of the most basic machines making possible the transmission of massive flows of radio traffic over the communications channels of the Army during World War II. Secure rapid machine transmission by radioteletypewriter depended entirely on the cipher machine employed, which replaced the slow, tedious work of hand enciphering and deciphering of every classified communication in guarded crypto rooms at each message center.

Among the first and most significant of these machines was the Sigaba, a version of a series known technically as M–134's, to whose design the Navy made some contributions. The basic design was the Army's. The Army could not, during the financially depressed 1930's, however, produce the sets for want of funds. The Navy came to the financial rescue, and production began in the late 1930's. By Pearl Harbor the sets were already in use at major Army headquarters. From then on, they provided the nation's military forces with secure practical cipher machines essential to the prosecution of modern war. Army sets, thanks to stringent security regulations imposed by SIS, were never captured by the enemy. On one occasion, however, the ultra-security-minded Friedman, by then a lieutenant colonel in the Signal Corps, was badly worried

---

[42] (1) Interv, SigC Hist Div with Ogburn, 5 Aug 60. (2) Ogburn, *The Marauders*, p. 157.

[43] CSigO, Annual Rpt, FY 1919, p. 140.

[44] (1) *Ibid.* (2) Interv, SigC Hist Div with Mauborgne, 2 Dec 60. (3) A. L. Lavine, *Circuits of Victory* (New York, N. Y.: Doubleday, Page and Co. 1921), illustration opposite p. 402, and pp. 407ff.

when his colleagues told him that the Japanese had captured Sigaba in New Guinea. The report was true enough, but Sigaba was a village, not the cipher machine.[45]

Signal Security and Intelligence in World War II

Organization

By 7 December 1941, SIS was already expanding rapidly. War accelerated and stimulated SIS growth and channeled its activities in new directions. Now the military traffic, lacking in peacetime, flooded the activity with material of the utmost urgency.

When war struck, SIS consisted of the Signal Intelligence School, the 2d Signal Service Company, and four operating sections, A through D. In alphabetical sequence after Section A (for Administration) came B, the largest single activity—the analysts, cryptanalysts, and intelligence specialists, who fed their distilled findings to G–2, WDGS. Section B would grow to ever larger dimensions as its product came to constitute the chief source of G–2 information. This was the invaluable intelligence half of the Siamese twin. The other half constituted C Section—cryptographic and communications security. It too grew ever larger. D Section worked on secret inks, and was often called the Laboratory Section.

In the kaleidoscopic expansion of the Office of the Chief Signal Officer in the early months of war, SIS underwent a number of organizational redesignations. In one respect, its relation to the next higher echelon of the Office of the Chief Signal Officer, it remained stable. On 1 January 1942 it was placed under the Army communications activity (variously called a division, a branch, and a service), and there it remained throughout the war. SIS received the designation Signal Security Service in mid-1942, retaining that title for a year until a reorganization in mid-1943 settled on the name Signal Security Agency, by which it was known for the rest of the war.[46]

Meanwhile, in the Munitions Building SIS quickly became cramped for room. To provide the space and the security so vital to the agency's operations, the Signal Corps purchased the commodious and at that time sequestered domains of a private school for girls, Arlington Hall, in the Virginia suburbs across the Potomac. The move was completed in August 1942. "The Hall" became the home of SIS and the headquarters of the 2d Signal Service Company, the whole constituting a field activity of the Office, Chief Signal Officer.

SIS flourished in its new quarters, adding more and more sections and subsections as the workload grew ever greater. ASF cut red tape and administrative procedures in order to authorize the speedy construction of additional temporary buildings.[47] A Traffic Analysis

---

[45] Intervs (1) SigC Hist Div with Col Russell H. Horton, Deputy CO ASA, Arlington, Va., Oct 60, and (2) Gen Cook, 14 Jun 60. (3) See also Thomas M. Johnson, "Search for the Stolen Sigaba," *Army,* XII (February, 1962), pp. 50ff.

[46] (1) ASA Lecture, p. 2. (2) OCSigO Orgn Charts, 1942 through 1945, SigC Admin Log, 1939–45, *passim.* (3) Hist, SSA in World War II, pp. 15, 29.

Only the designations SIS and SSA will be used in this chapter.

[47] Interv, SigC Hist Div with Friedman, 16 Feb 61.

activity sprouted in B Section as Subsection B–6 in August 1942. In December F Section, Development, was created to carry on research and development work relating to SIS equipment, taking over from the Fort Monmouth laboratories the development of its own cryptographic devices. In March 1943 the sections became branches. By early 1944 two more branches had appeared—G, Machine Branch, and H, Information and Liaison Branch.[48] The final reorganization, in August 1944, established the eight branches under four divisions—Administration, Intelligence, Security, and Operating Service.[49]

Soon after the move to Arlington Hall, SIS acquired the first of its outlying stations, Vint Hill Farms Station, Virginia. It opened in mid-September 1942 and was operated by a detachment of the 2d Signal Service Battalion. Before the year was out, other stations were added in California and in Alaska. Before the end of the war a dozen more stations and detachments of the same battalion were serving in locations scattered around the world.[50]

In December 1944, G–2 assumed operational control of the Signal Security Agency, leaving administrative control and financial support with the Chief Signal Officer. On 15 September 1945 control passed completely from the Sig-

nal Corps. These organizational developments had important implications.[51]

Manpower and Training

With 181 people in the Washington headquarters on 7 December 1941, SIS already seemed large by prewar standards. Agency planners, estimating their manpower needs in the early months of the war, decided that a staff in Washington totaling 460 persons would probably be needed eventually.[52] But the needs of global war soon swallowed up this modest proposal. SSA eventually required the services of more than 7,000 people in the Washington headquarters.[53]

The keen competition for civilian and military manpower posed special hardships for SIS and SSA. Qualifications for positions were high, and the number of persons possessing the special skills and aptitudes was low. Linguists, statisticians, and engineers were especially scarce. The agency launched recruiting drives for civilians and for Wacs, but could not fully disclose the nature of the work to be performed. As a result a high rate of turnover among newer civilian employees persisted.[54] The problems of staffing and personnel control loomed large in the high-level staff decisions that after the war brought about the separation of signal security and intelligence activities from the Signal Corps. As matters stood during the war, SSA, though a part of the Office of the Chief Signal Officer, operated primarily to serve the War Department's Military

[48] Hist, SSA in World War II, p. 45.

[49] (1) Interv, SigC Hist Div with Maj Gen W. Preston Corderman (Ret.), and MS Comment, 29–30 Mar 61. (2) ASA Lecture, p. 35. (3) Hist, SSA in World War II, p. 29.

[50] (1) Progress and Problem Report Airways and Fixed Radio Br, Plant Div, 16 Sep 42. SigC 319.1 Digest of Prog and Problems No. 1, 1942, PEA. (2) Memo, Exec Contl Div OCSigO for Contl Div SOS, Attn: Col Joseph L. Battley, 28 Aug 42, sub: Field Instls, p. 7. (3) Hist, SSA in World War II, p. 50.

[51] See below, pp. 348ff.

[52] ASA Lecture, p. 32.

[53] Hist, SSA in World War II, p. 19.

[54] (1) ASA Lecture, p. 33. (2) Treadwell, The Women's Army Corps, pp. 319–20.

Intelligence Division. In personnel matters MID justified increases for SSA, which when approved went through awkward and time-delaying channels to ASF, which then increased the CSigO personnel ceiling, which in turn suballotted the increase to SSA.[55] More than once during the war MID suggested the establishment of SSA as an independent agency and the setting up of special manning tables. The Chief Signal Officer naturally opposed the loss of one of his most important agencies.[56]

Throughout the last three years of war, virtually all of the Army's signal intelligence training was centered in the SSA or controlled by it. Organized training of cryptographers and cryptanalysts got under way at Fort Monmouth in mid-1940.[57] A first course for enlisted men in July was followed by a second in October. Plans for activating a formal crytopgraphic school encountered administrative complications connected with the establishment of the Signal Corps' first Replacement Training Center (RTC) at Fort Monmouth in January 1941, and the school did not begin functioning until March. Under the competent tutelage of S/Sgt. Max Leighty, an expert cryptographer, 25 Regular Army men and 15 selective service trainees began the initial 48-week courses in cryptography, cryptanalysis, elementary foreign language studies, and IBM operations.[58]

The Cryptographic School was a part of the RTC, until that awkward administrative arrangement led to its transfer to the Signal Corps School in December 1941.[59] Leighty, by then a commissioned officer, became the officer in charge of the Cryptographic School. Shortages of housing and instructors and the rigors of explosive expansion that attended all training activities in the early months of the war plagued the school.[60] During the entire period at Fort Monmouth, the school produced no "graduates" in the usual sense of the word. Field needs for such specialists were so pressing that not a single student remained for the full 48-week course. Each month students in various stages of training left to take field assignments, to enter OCS, or were relieved because of inaptitude for the work. Actually, the curriculum permitted those who had already had training in some phase of the work to advance rapidly to more difficult applications. After the declaration of war, the school cut the training time and increased the intake of students. It soon became obvious that the best interests of the cryptographic training activity demanded a location entirely apart from either the RTC or the Signal Corps School. In October 1942, the Cryptographic School moved to Vint Hill Farms Station, where

---

[55] Rpt of Of Serv Div OCSigO, 19 Oct 43, pp. 2–3. SigC EO Daily Digests, Staff Divs OCSigO, 19 Jul–31 Dec 43.

[56] (1) Ltr, Maj Gen James A. Code (Ret.) to Thompson and Harris, 8 Aug 58. SigC Hist Sec file. (2) DCSigO file, pp. 96–100, passim. SigC Hist Sec file.

[57] See above, pp. 334–35.

[58] (1) 2d Lt Francis M. Taylor, History of Crypto-

graphic Training, Ft. Monmouth (1944), p. 3. SigC Hist Sec file. (2) Capt Frederick Reinstein, Signal Corps Training in World War II—Background and First Six Months of War, 1917–1942, SigC Hist Monograph C-1, pp. 66–69.

[59] Reinstein, SigC Tng in World War II—Background and First Six Months of War 1917–42, SigC Hist Monograph, C-1, p. 155.

[60] (1) Ibid. (2) Incl 1, Cryptographic Tng at Ft. Monmouth, to Ltr, Dir ESCTC Ft. Monmouth to Hist Sec Fld Of OCSigO, 23 Feb 44, sub: Hist of Cryptographic Sch at Ft. Monmouth. SigC Hist Sec file.

it remained for the rest of the war.[61]

The Vint Hill Farms School operated as a special training activity under the Chief Signal Officer. It trained Army men and women in cryptanalysis, traffic analysis, and cryptographic equipment maintenance. Much of this schooling was practical, on-the-job training. The SSA also operated a civilian training school for its own employees, an extension school (Signal Security School) that furnished lesson materials on cryptography and cryptanalysis, and an advance radio communications school that taught eleven specialities designed to produce a pool of trained officers for SSA needs.[62] A training branch within SSA controlled all training activities of SSA and collaborated with other training agencies in developing programs for units not wholly trained by SSA. Some units concerned with various intelligence aspects received unit training at the Eastern Signal Corps Unit Training Center at Fort Monmouth or the Central Signal Corps Unit Training Center at Camp Crowder. For these, the SSA training branch furnished training guidance and conducted technical inspections.[63]

The 2d Signal Service Battalion

With the outbreak of war, formidable tasks confronted the men of the 2d Signal Service Company. No longer was there a lack of intercept material or enemy traffic, but rather a great wealth of it. Col. Frank Bullock, the commanding officer of SIS, also commanded the 2d Signal Service Company, an assignment he held until 1 January 1943, when Colonel Corderman assumed command for the rest of the war.[64]

Detachments quickly moved overseas. Of an 18-man team already in the Philippines when the Japanese attacked, not all survived. As the end approached in the islands, Lt. Col. Joe R. Sherr, the acting officer in charge of the detachment, accompanied General MacArthur to Australia. Colonel Sherr became the executive officer for MacArthur's signal officer, General Akin, and organized Akin's Central Bureau (the intelligence activity) in Brisbane in August 1942.[65] Six enlisted men of the detachment were evacuated from Bataan by submarine; another group of six went from Corregidor to Australia to serve on intelligence missions. One man joined the guerrilla forces, became an officer, and survived the war; two others survived a Japanese prison camp; the remaining two perished one way or another.[66]

The imperative need for additional manpower soon brought a Signal Corps request to raise the company to battalion strength.[67] The War Department quickly agreed, and on 2 April 1942 the unit became the 2d Signal Service Battalion.[68] Throughout the next thirty-two months the battalion expanded enormously, at one time numbering 5,000

---

[61] (1) Taylor Hist of Cryptographic Tng, Ft. Monmouth, p. 11. (2) Thompson, Harris, et al., The Test, p. 139.

[62] Hist, SSA in World War II, pp. 52–53.

[63] History of Unit Training, Signal Corps Units, 7 December 1941–1 December 1945, pp. 3–4, 19. SigC Sec file.

[64] Hist, SSA in World War II, p. 38.

[65] Sherr was killed in an airplane accident in September 1942 while on special mission to India and China. Hist, SSA in World War II, p. 37.

[66] Hist, SSA in World War II, pp. 38ff.

[67] Memo, Minckler, OCSigO A-3, for O/C Mil Pers Div, 14 Feb 42, sub: Reorgn of the 2d Sig Sv Co. SigC 311.5 Gen 1942.

[68] AG Ltr, 320.2 (3-3-42) MR-M-SP, 14 Apr 42, sub: Reorgn of the 2d Sig Sv Co.

men.[69] Signal Corps efforts to redesignate it a regiment failed, principally because ASF, which controlled Signal Corps personnel matters, did not concur. Because of the strict wartime secrecy surrounding the activity, neither the Signal Corps nor G–2, although wanting more people for SSA, could explain why.[70]

Meanwhile, the demands for men to operate new intercept and monitoring stations multiplied. Midway in the war there were stations at various points in the United States, Alaska, the Aleutians, Hawaii, Australia, India, and Africa.[71] To conserve his valuable manpower, Colonel Corderman turned to womanpower. He asked for Wacs, primarily to perform duties at Arlington Hall, thus releasing enlisted men for overseas assignment. The first contingent of 800 women was approved in April 1943. Later authorized WAC strength stood at 1,500, but the actual strength never quite reached that figure.[72] The women of the 2d Signal Service Battalion performed their duties at all their stations with outstanding ability and devotion, despite the strain of the long hours, swing shifts, and the ever-present necessity for the most rigid and exacting security measures.[73] Colonel Corderman

was extremely proud of his Wacs. When they were first assigned, he attempted to give them lighter and less arduous duties than the men, but the women demanded "equal treatment" and the right to share the same duties as the men, including night-shift work. As Corderman put it, "We had no major problems with our Wac's. The work was hard, but they performed well, and never asked or wanted to be treated more considerately than the men." [74]

Thus the officer and enlisted strength, both male and female, steadily mounted as the war progressed. The number of stations these Signal Corps personnel operated around the world multiplied. Likewise, the number of messages intercepted and transmitted with utmost dispatch to The Hall for analysis and cryptanalysis increased to very great proportions. SSA pre-empted more and more circuits of the Army Command and Administrative Network for this work. The four radio circuits devoted to SSA use as of 7 December 1941 grew to forty-six full-time radioteletypewriter circuits by V–J Day.[75]

Not all detachments of the 2d Signal Service Battalion were engaged entirely in intercepting enemy traffic. There was also the matter of monitoring the radio traffic of Army stations in the United States. The stations at Bellmore on Long Island and at Tarzana in California, for example, limited their intercept activity to Army radio traffic in the United States.[76]

When operational control of the Signal Security Agency shifted to G–2 on 15 December 1944, the Signal Corps

---

[69] (1) Hist, SSA in World War II, p. 54. (2) ASA Lecture p. 36.

[70] Interv, SigC Hist Sec with Horton, Oct 60.

[71] Hist, SSA in World War II, *passim*.

[72] Treadwell, *The Women's Army Corps*, p. 316.

[73] Treadwell, *The Women's Army Corps*, pp. 318–21. The WAC historian comments on ". . . the ever-present strain of keeping security, and sometimes the knowledge that the operator, alone with a few of the Army's top authorities, shared secrets in which a slip of the tongue in public could cost the lives of hundreds of soldiers." *Ibid.*, p. 319. General Corderman has commented that Miss Treadwell's account made the SSA security problems sound "unreasonably difficult." Interv, SigC Hist Sec with Corderman, 29–30 Mar 61.

[74] *Ibid.*

[75] Hist, SSA in World War II, p. 20.

[76] *Ibid.*

no longer controlled personnel assignment within the 2d Signal Service Battalion, although it continued to be responsible for the technical control of equipment. G–2 thenceforth directed the shifts of Signal Corps personnel as necessary to facilitate the production of intelligence. The intelligence product dominated all other aspects of the activity. On 1 February the battalion was redesignated the 9420th Technical Service Unit, Signal Corps, the detachments receiving letter designations.[77] The unit reached its peak strength 1 April 1945. The 9420th Technical Service Unit became a part of the Army Security Agency in the postwar transfer of intelligence activities.

Wartime Operations at The Hall

Wartime operations of the Signal Security Agency headquarters at Arlington Hall centered around the twin objective, signal security and signal intelligence. Each division, branch, section, and subsection of SSA served to advance one or both of these objectives directly or indirectly. The means to gain these highly specialized objectives were out-of-the-ordinary personnel and equally extraordinary communications-electronics equipment.

Men and Machines—No one could deny that the extraordinary work at The Hall was likely to place upon the civilians (no less than upon the military) heavier demands, stricter discipline, and larger workloads than the government required of many of its employees elsewhere. For these reasons the turnover in

civilian positions was high, especially among persons more recently hired, a category that actually included the majority of civilians. Throughout the war, personnel shortages at SSA remained severe. In April 1944, for example, SSA and G–2 counted up a shortage of more than one thousand civilian positions in the agency.[78] To cope with an ever-increasing workload in the face of persistent personnel shortages, agency administrators made heavy use of machine labor in every possible sort of application.

The G, or Machine, Branch by itself became enormous. It controlled and directed the work of whole batteries of tabulating machines. As early as 1936, the Signal Corps had begun using Hollerith tabulating machines, which helped considerably in the labors of code compilation. These and the subsequent increasingly sophisticated IBM machines, data-processing and others, became more and more useful, indeed essential. Machines performed the onerous accounting and crypto tasks that otherwise would have required the hand labor of impossible numbers of clerks, running into the hundreds of thousands. There were 13 IBM machines, tended by 21 operators, at work on SIS projects on Pearl Harbor Day. By the spring of 1945, SSA's Machine Branch was employing 407 machines and 1,275 operators.[79]

In 1936 the then Chief Signal Officer, Maj. Gen. James B. Allison, noted that

---

[77] *Ibid.*, p. 54.

[78] Memo, Chief P&T Sv OCSigO for CG ASF, sub: Requested Allotment, . . . SigC Hist Sec file.

[79] (1) Supplement to CSigO, Annual Rpt, FY 36, p. 30 (contained in Supplements to CSigO, Annual Rpts, 1928–36). (2) Interv, SigC Hist Sec with Horton, Oct 60.

these machines were well adapted to certain types of cryptanalytic studies, enabling faster solution of certain code and cipher systems. This potentiality became a vital reality in the course of World War II.

R&D of Crypto Equipment—The large responsibility acquired by F Branch, SIS, at the end of 1942 was the development of crypto equipment — cipher machines and other communications security devices.[80] The transfer of crypto R&D from Fort Monmouth was not accomplished without considerable argument. In OCSigO, the Executive Control Division, debating the pros and cons of the transfer, argued in favor of the move. Security considerations overrode all others. Keeping to a minimum the number of persons with "need to know" about crypto equipment favored locating R&D within the security organization itself (too many people at the laboratories, about 100 of them, worked only part time on crypto R&D). It was logical also that the security requirement for maintaining and operating the devices in Army message centers the world over should rest in the organization responsible for over all communications security. Further, the organization that sought to break the encipherment of Army's own enemy devices (as well as those of enemy nations) could best put the lessons learned in cryptanalytic work to use in the design and improvement of Army's

current and future crypto equipment. Finally, the concentration of this kind of R&D within the agency that alone possessed full knowledge of this extremely recondite and specialized field would enable maximum speed in the development of new and better communications security paraphernalia.

There were reasons, too, of course, against the transfer, against removing the R&D of essential devices associated with Army communication systems from the R&D of the systems themselves. Col. Carroll O. Bickelhaupt, chief of the Control Division, OCSigO, tried to make some exceptions, pointing out that work on speech scrambling equipment and on devices for scrambling facsimile transmissions ought to be kept at the Fort Monmouth laboratories, along with the research and development on these basic telephone and facsimile communications systems. After all, security measures involving equipment to scramble the output of basic communications systems could not be easily separated from the over-all research and development of those systems.[81]

A year after the transfer, in November 1943, General Colton, chief of the Engineering and Technical Division, OCSigO, objected to the decision, arguing that SSA, operating in high secrecy and isolation from other Signal Corps R&D and communications systems developments, tended to design crypto equipment that was incompatible with standardized Army communications facilities. But from the point of view of

---

[80] The Fort Monmouth laboratories continued to develop a number of radio sets and special devices that were used for such signal intelligence purposes as direction finding by RI companies and by detachments of the 2d Signal Service Battalion. For details, consult the Signal Corps R&D Hist, *passim*.

[81] (1) Rpt, Duplication of Signal Security Service vs Signal Supply Service, inclosed with Memo, CSigO for Dir SCG SSS, 20 May 43. SigC EO 321 OCSigO Orgn 1942–44. (2) Interv, SigC Hist Sec with Cook, 14 Jun 60.

Arlington Hall, emphasizing security, the transfer was advantageous, and Colonel Corderman was pleased with the arrangement. No one could deny that security at least was well served.[82]

Upon the cipher machines of the M–134 series, beginning with the Sigaba, rested the safe transmission of the nation's military communications throughout World War II. Colonel Friedman held many of the patents. His contribution long remained, for reasons of security, little noted or rewarded until the U.S. Government years later bought his residual commercial rights for $100,000. Quantity production of the machines came to center especially upon an improved version with on-line features. These greatly increased the speed of enciphering at the transmitter and of deciphering at the receiver end of a circuit. The sets came into wide use. The Signal Corps installed them as fast as they came off the production lines in order to meet the avid demands of both the AAF and Army users.

The on-line features had a serious security disadvantage, however, in that the operator on the transmitting end sometimes forgot—when passing from unclassified traffic sent in the clear to classified—to flip the switch that would connect the on-line crypto equipment. At least twice this happened during the war. One message gave the travel route of General MacArthur during the New Guinea Campaign. The clear text, if intercepted, would have given the enemy a prize opportunity. Frantic corrections

were made to cover up the error, without MacArthur's ever knowing what happened. To prevent such errors, SIS later required that a monitor be assigned each channel, his full task being to listen and make sure that when classified traffic was being sent the on-line cipher machine was switched on.[83]

Security Operations—Communications security was the responsibility of C Branch. Although communications intelligence, Section B, the largest single branch of the SSA, produced intelligence of immense positive use in the successful conduct of the war, communications security was perhaps equally valuable, in a negative and less dramatic way, in keeping enemy cryptanalysts from learning as much about American moves as Americans learned about theirs.

Security monitored U.S. traffic, policing it in order to correct abuses that might enable the enemy to glean intelligence from messages or even to break them. Security monitors, listening to radio operators, had the onerous task of trying to catch errors in transmission methods and procedures so as to apply censure and render U.S. traffic more secure. Another, and possibly still more tedious task, with little use and less hope apparent to SSA cryptanalysts bedeviled with it, was the effort in The Hall at trying to break the code and cipher traffic of the U.S. Army. The purpose was of course the admirable one of seeking to detect weaknesses in American crypto systems before the enemy did, and to correct them. Although scores of people worked full time at The Hall trying to

[82] (1) Memo, Colton for CSigO, 20 Nov 43, sub: Proposed Reorgn to Handle Systems Engineering Work and to Centralize Contl of all SigC Dev. SigC EO 321 OCSigO Orgn, 1942–44. (2) Interv, SigC Hist Div with Corderman, 29–30 Mar 61.

[83] (1) Interv, SigC Hist Sec with Cook, 14 Jun 60. (2) Interv, SigC Hist Sec with Friedman, 16 Feb 61.

break the Army's radio enciphered traffic, the output of the cipher machines generally proved impregnable.[84]

Policing the U.S. Army's own traffic, crypto equipment, and communications procedures was only a secondary task of C Branch duty. The major job was to supply the code and cipher systems, the cipher machines, and other parapherphernalia that constituted the primary defense against enemy penetration of American military communications. After F Branch developed the machines, the production, distribution, and secure use of the machines devolved upon C Branch. Production was more difficult than for other Army equipment precisely because of the secrecy of the product. C Branch representatives had to struggle with innumerable military and federal priority people who allocated metals and rare materials in short supply. The struggle was compounded by the inability to tell allocation officers the full reasons and exigencies of SSA needs.[85]

Whether the code and cipher systems involved these machines, or more often, especially early in the war, code books and cipher systems (such as slide systems), key lists, and so on, the problem of getting enough systems into the hands of Army users was severe. Early in the war especially, the demand for many systems, in as many copies as there were burgeoning headquarters and message centers, put a tremendous strain on the growing but still inadequately staffed Signal Intelligence Service. There were times when no backup was available in case a particular system (of which there were several hundred) became compromised, as by capture by the enemy.[86]

The code and cipher systems of the Army were changed frequently, in a routine manner, to deny the enemy lasting advantages from any success he might win in breaking the systems. C Branch provided a large number of crypto systems to thousands of users. The mere printing of such a quantity, let alone the guarded distribution of every last copy of the highly classified documents (five million of them, some running to many pages each, for the 1940–44 period), constituted a task of stupendous proportions. A huge backlog piled up early in the war until SIS argued for and obtained its own printing plant. SSA representatives had to defend the plant to allocation and priority officials under the inevitable special harassment that security requirements forbade revealing the reasons for the desperate need.[87]

Communications security troubled C Branch not entirely for inherent reasons of control, wherein SSA had great authority, but because good security in the use of communications involved careful awareness on the part of all Army officers and users, not just signal officers. The former were sometimes not aware, or were careless of what constituted good secure procedure. As General Stoner continually emphasized, it was necessary for all to

. . . protect our communications by every means at our command. We of the Signal Corps are charged with the security of

---

[84] Interv, SigC Hist Sec with Cook, 14 Jun 60.
[85] Interv, SigC Hist Div with Horton, Oct 60.
[86] (1) Interv, SigC Hist Div with Horton, Oct 60. (2) Stoner, Lecture Com Security, p. 24.
[87] Interv, SigC Hist Div with Horton, Oct 60.

communications, but we need the full co-operation of everyone who comes in con-tact with those communications, either directly or indirectly. . . . Aside from the fact that one slip, one bit of carelessness, may endanger an entire operation, the compromise of a system invariably means the loss of hundreds, even thousands of manhours that went in the development of that system.[88]

Intelligence Production—By far the largest segment of SSA was B Branch, engaged in the production of signal in-telligence. G–2, naturally the major cus-tomer for this product, supervised the activity of B Section—indirectly until mid-December 1944, directly after that date.[89]

There were methods of gaining intel-ligence from message traffic short of breaking the actual security system used by the enemy, for example the methods of traffic analysis. Sometimes too, of course, an enemy code or cipher book was captured and put to good use if the system remained current in the enemy army, or until replaced in the periodic change-over practiced by all military security organizations. But the tech-niques of cryptanalysis provided most of the intelligence obtained and accounted for the bulk of SSA success.

Great credit is due to the pick-and-shovel work of the thousands of workers, both military and civilian, digging away at slow, ofttimes mentally exhausting tasks. To some in supervisory positions who knew a bit about the assembled

jigsaw puzzles and their value, the work could be exciting, however maddeningly intricate. For others having less "need to know," the business of extracting and processing the bits and pieces often re-quired endlessly repetitive and seem-ingly senseless calculations and routines, straining the mind and emotions alike. "You don't have to be crazy to work here, but it helps," was a common and rather realistic slogan in the highly secured, often tense, and hectic workrooms, fre-quently referred to as the salt mines.

In November 1942, the Protective Security Branch was set up in SSA. One of its missions was to devise methods to conceal traffic patterns over the immense radioteletypewriter links that the Signal Corps provided to the AAF, so that General Arnold could direct the strategy and tactics of the XX Bomber Command from his Washington headquarters. The work of radio deception was correlated closely with the Navy and the British. It came to involve active jamming too, both radio and radar, and RCM units were assigned to provide RCM services in the theaters. One such unit was the 3103d Signal Service Battalion activated at Fort Monmouth 20 December 1943; another was the 3153d Signal Service Company, which had 21 teams. Since very new techniques were applied, RCM activities required training manuals, and these the Protective Security Branch pre-pared.[90]

Signal Intelligence Units Overseas

The Signal intelligence organization in the overseas theaters varied according

[88] Stoner Lecture, Com Security, p. 9.

[89] Hist, SSA in World War II, *passim.* B Branch grew from 1,814 as of July 1943 to 2,574 in July 1944, by which time 82 percent of the workers were concentrating on Japanese Army message traffic.

[90] *Ibid.*, p. 47.

to the needs of the particular headquarters and the number and quality of the men available for the specialized duty.[91] In Europe, for example, a detachment of the ETOUSA division furnished signal intelligence for the 12th Army Group on the Continent.[92] As a practical matter, the signal intelligence service largely functioned as a part of G–2.[93]

Not all of the units bore the designation *signal intelligence*. Sometimes for security reasons, sometimes to outflank rigid tables of organization and set up essential but as yet unauthorized units, the innocuous and all-embracing word "service" was used to mask their real function. For example, there was the SSA's 2d Signal Service Battalion. There was also the 805th Signal Service Company of the Army Communications Service. The 805th was activated and trained for one specific purpose—to operate the equipment of one of the high-level secret conference facilities systems that the Signal Corps provided during the war.[94] Especially after 1943 when the Signal Corps cellular teams became available in flexible combinations tailored to specific needs, it became possible to place small units with desired skills at many points.[95]

The radio intelligence companies of World War II were the counterparts of the AEF's intercept signal units of World War I.[96] As organized under T/O 11–77 at the beginning of the war, RI companies formed an organic part of the army or GHQ signal service and were under the command of the appropriate army or theater signal officer.[97] There were radio intelligence platoons in the division signal companies. In October 1943, when the War Department introduced a number of changes into the organization of ground troops, the radio intelligence platoons were cut from the division signal company and their functions were taken over by the corps signal battalion.[98] Thereafter there were no organic signal intelligence troops at division level.[99]

Radio intelligence units, whatever their organizational composition, performed the dual functions of locating enemy stations and intercepting enemy traffic, and of monitoring friendly traffic to assure communications security.[100] Monitoring enemy transmissions became in most theaters the primary mission. The secondary mission, monitoring friendly traffic to detect security violations, suffered accordingly. After the war, staff officers studying signal operations concluded that inadequate provision had been made for security monitoring in the ETO. They recommended that special radio security monitoring

---

[91] For accounts of typical headquarters signal intelligence divisions, see, for example: (1) ETOUSA Rpt, II, 96–169; (2) History of Sub-Sec G–2, app., Sig Sec, I, HUSAFMIDPAC, 331–79.

[92] Hq ETOUSA, Technical Historical Report of Signal Security Detachment D, *passim*.

[93] 12th AG AAR, III, G–2 Sec, 157.

[94] Mary-louise Melia, Signal Corps Fixed Communications in World War II: Special Assignments and Techniques (1945), SigC Hist Monograph E–10, pp. 31–32. SigC Hist Sec file.

[95] For discussion of development of cellular type units, see above, pp. 22ff.

[96] See above, pp. 329–30.

[97] FM 11–20, 11 Nov 40, sec. V, *passim*.

[98] (1) WD Cir 256, 16 Oct 43, sub: Reorgn of Corps Hq and Organic Troops. (2) Greenfield, Palmer, and Wiley, *The Organization of Ground Combat Troops*, p. 310.

[99] FM 11–22, Jan 45, sec. 22, *passim*.

[100] (1) *Ibid.* (2) Reinstein, Study of SigC Unit Tng, 1942–44, p. 52.

companies be authorized, one for each field army. The sole mission of such units would be the monitoring of frequencies in use by that particular army.[101]

Late in the war intelligence officers, in Europe as elsewhere, were well satisfied with the RI companies' product. They called it "of material value . . . at times vital," and considered it one of the "most constantly profitable sources" of intelligence information.[102] In Washington in mid-1943, however, Maj. Gen. George V. Strong had expressed a different view. Arguing unsuccessfully for the establishment of a director of communications at the General Staff level, he also appeared to be arguing for centralized War Department control of radio intelligence companies. "At the present time," he said, "we have no adequate provision of equipment for RI companies, we have no Intelligence distribution of RI companies for world wide intercept coverage, and in consequence, Mr. John Q. Taxpayer as far as Military Intelligence is concerned, is getting, I suppose, ten cents worth of return out of every dollar he pays in taxes."[103] At the end of the war, General Staff control of the radio intelligence companies and other intelligence and security troops would in fact become a reality.

Signal Security and Intelligence Transferred to General Staff

The Signal Security Agency was administratively and functionally a vital part of the Signal Corps until mid-December 1944; from then until 15 September 1945, only administratively; after 15 September 1945, no longer a part of the Signal Corps at all.

When G–2 took over operational control in December 1944, leaving the thankless administrative housekeeping tasks to the Signal Corps, the step was a portent of things to come. At that time, it had been proposed that G–2 take over lock, stock, and barrel, but the possibility of upsetting a going activity in the midst of war forbade such action. Close co-operation continued, but the division of control in itself created problems. "This cleavage of control was by no means clear cut and sharply defined; the line was not straight. . . . "[104]

As the war drew to a close and it became clear that the theaters would soon cease to exist as active arenas of war, staff intelligence officers had become increasingly concerned over the possibility of adverse personnel actions that might choke off the flow of signal intelligence information. ASF personnel cuts in Washington during the war inevitably affected the Signal Corps. In late April 1944, for example, the SSA was understrength by more than 1,000 positions.[105] Maj. Gen. Earle Cook subsequently recalled how SSA within the Signal Corps was caught between two fires. One day late in the war the Assistant Chief of

---

[101] USFET Gen Bd Rpt 111, pp. 8–10.

[102] 12th AG AAR, III, G–2 Sec, 119–36.

[103] Proceedings of Bd to Investigate Com, Testimony of Gen Strong, ACofS G–2, 2 Jun 43, Tab U, p. 2.

The manning and equipping of tactical RI companies, General Cook subsequently explained, did not get well under way until late in World War II, whereas the strategic SIS function had been highly organized and effective from the very start of the war. Interv, SigC Hist Sec with Cook, 14 Jun 60.

[104] Hist, SSA in World War II, p. 19.

[105] Memo, Chief P&T Serv OCSigO for CG ASF, sub: Requested Allotment of Mil Pers for WD Sig Ctr, SigC Hist Sec file.

Staff, G–2, greatly praised the work SSA was doing and directed a personnel increase in order to take full advantage of cryptanalytic successes. On that very same day ASF cut Signal Corps personnel by 5 percent, the cut applying to SSA of course as well as to the rest of the Corps.[106]

War Department postwar planning on an over-all basis had begun quite early —in fact, midway in the war. It became the duty of SSA's commander, General Corderman, to begin implementing those plans as they affected SSA immediately after V–J Day. Early in August General Corderman created a postwar planning board to chart operations for the agency.[107] There were complex and perplexing problems, many arising from the "peculiar position of the Agency as a group within G–2 with resultant General Staff functions, and on the other hand, the responsibility for command and direction of units located in various areas throughout the world." [108] At the first and only board meeting, the members decided to reduce SSA civilian strength by about half—from 5,661 to 2,500. Within a few days, the matter became academic. The War Department decided to take over complete direction and sent out radiograms transferring all Army signal intelligence units, including the 2d Signal Service Battalion, to War Department control.[109] And on 6 September the War Department established the new Army Security Agency, effective 15 September.[110]

ASA contained all of the SSA elements, and more. It included all signal intelligence "establishments, units and personnel attached or assigned to major forces, commands or departments." [111] This gathered in ground and air units such as signal radio intelligence companies, signal intelligence service detachments, radio intelligence platoons of signal battalions, AAF mobile radio squadrons, and radio intelligence platoons of signal aviation companies.

The loss of the Signal Security Agency was a mighty blow both to Signal Corps operations and to Signal Corps aspirations.[112] Many senior Signal Corps officers had long cherished the conviction that all Army communications should be under Signal Corps control, through an organizational unit at General Staff level.[113] Communications security so intimately involved Army Signal Corps communications, message centers, and operators throughout the Army, the code and cipher distribution and implementation were so thoroughly a part of all Army Signal Corps activity, that dividing it caused much concern. Even so, the division was carried out, though not quickly or easily. Entanglement was too great.

The Deputy Chief Signal Officer, General Code, pointed out that the rather broad language of the 6 September directive left numerous responsibilities indefinite and areas of action unclear.[114] There was, for example, a

[106] Interv, SigC Hist Sec with Cook, 14 Jun 60.
[107] ASF SSA GO 49, 4 Aug 45.
[108] Hist, SSA in World War II, p. 55.
[109] CM–OUT 56718 and 53599, 22 and 28 Aug 45.
[110] AG 322 (4 Sep 45), OB–S–B–M, 6 Sep 45, sub: Establishment of the Army Security Agency.

[111] Ibid.
[112] See below, pp. 614ff.
[113] (1) Terrett, The Emergency, pp. 23–25, 133–35. (2) Thompson, Harris, et al., The Test, pp. 554–65.
[114] Memo, DCSigO for CSigO, 17 Sep 45, sub: Estimate of ASA. Sig EO, Estimate of ASA, 1942–45.

provision relating to procurement, storage, and issue of items peculiar to ASA. The same little word, "peculiar," had popped up to cause innumerable difficulties in the unscrambling of Army–Army Air Forces communications–electronics items in 1944, as General Code remembered only too well.[115] An ASA Signal Corps *ad hoc* committee, meeting on 21 September and using General Code's memorandum as a basis for discussion, cleared up most of the uncertainties.

An overriding circumstance, which the Signal Corps recognized no less than did other elements of the Army, lay in the relentless pressure of evolution. No one, in 1945, could be sure exactly what lay ahead for the nation in the coming decades. The one certainty was that new tasks and missions for the Army would inevitably involve new fields of specialization. The difficult and important field of signal intelligence could best be explored by an organization such as the Army Security Agency through the uncharted years of the future.

---

[115] Transmittal Sheet, Contl Div, OCSigO to ExecO, 13 Sep 45, sub: Estimate of ASA. For account of AAF assumption of electronic equipment responsibility, see below, pp. 437ff.

CHAPTER XII

Signal Corps Production at Full Tide

Supply operations at best are ponderous and complex. Every signal item the Army used during the war moved through the supply system in a steady progression of separate steps from placing contracts to distributing the manufactured product. Logistics specialists often spoke of the supply pipeline—that imaginary channel that stretched from the zone of interior to the overseas theaters. The first necessity was to fill the pipeline and the second was to keep it filled evenly, not clogged at one point and empty at another. By mid-1943 procurement of supplies—filling the pipeline—ceased to be a major worry. It became evident that American industry could produce enough material to fill all requirements. By May 1944 signal production, in size and scope, dwarfed all prewar estimates.

The Signal Corps by no means ranked first in production among the technical services. In terms of dollar values, its production totals stood somewhat below those of the Corps of Engineers, and far below those of the Quartermaster Corps and the Ordnance Department. The rate of Signal Corps expansion, measured against its prewar standards, was more impressive. The Signal Corps' monthly receipts of radio equipment were half again as great as the estimated yearly

output of the entire prewar industry.[1] The Signal Corps was using more fixed radio equipment in its global radio system than had existed in the whole world before the war. Purchases of friction tape to insulate wire splices in 1944 exceeded the $170,080 appropriated in 1934 for the entire Signal Corps research and development program. The 1944 cost of one radar set roughly equaled the $42,000 with which the Corps had started its radar development program in 1933.[2]

New developments had created sudden expansions in minor items—crystals, for example. The estimated prewar output of the crystal industry amounted to only 100,000 crystals annually. Industrial production rose from a monthly rate of 223,000 units in 1942 to 2,000,000 in 1943, and to 2,500,000 in 1944. The sixteen crystal-grinding teams that the

---

[1] For May 1944, monthly deliveries of air and ground radio and radar equipment, including miscellaneous equipment and depot spares of components such as power units and vacuum tubes, rose to $167 million per month. Memo, Maj F. W. Decker for Lt Col J. E. Gonseth, 15 Jul 44, sub: Valuation of Monthly Deliveries of Army Radio and Radar Equips. SigC C&E 300.4 Memo for Br Chiefs, Jul 1943-44.

[2] Brig. Gen. James A. Code, Jr., "Science in Signal Corps Development," The Scientific Monthly, LIX (July–December, 1944). (Reprinted from an address before the National Academy of Sciences, Washington, 24 April 1944.)

Signal Corps had sent into the theaters alone were turning out more crystals than the entire industry had produced a few years earlier.[3] Furthermore, the smaller, thinner crystals now used required much more precise grinding to closer tolerances, closely resembling the jewelers' art.

The proliferation of radio types furnished another index to Signal Corps supply expansion. Far from achieving the reduction of radio types that General Marshall had demanded of General Olmstead in 1941, the Signal Corps had developed many new special-purpose sets in response to demands from the using arms. The creation of new kinds of Army units required radio communications not contemplated in prewar planning. There were new tank destroyer, airborne, anti-aircraft, transportation, and military police units, for example. Since 1940 the Army had established 33 new types of units for the armored forces alone. The number of standard types of radio sets produced for the AGF more than doubled, from 18 to 40, between June 1940 and July 1943.[4] All together, in 1944 the Signal Corps was producing 81 types of radio sets and 22 types of radar sets for the Army.

Only a few of the radio sets that had been standardized, issued, and used be-fore 1939 were still considered useful enough to be included on 1944 tables of equipment. General Ingles, reacting coolly to a suggestion for a new field artillery radio, said, "We hesitate to start development of still another type of radio set, as the number of different types we now have is appalling. When the Office of the Chief Signal Officer was removed as a special staff section under the Chief of Staff and placed in the Army Service Forces, all control on the development of radio equipment was removed, and the various branches of the Army went wild." [5]

The Signal Corps was in fact supplying many services that would have been regarded as pure luxury by prewar standards. Moreover, the technical performance of Signal Corps equipment far exceeded the military concepts of a decade past. There were radio stations with power up to 40 kilowatts, for example; teletypewriter networks whose transmissions could be switched as readily as telephone calls; high-speed tape systems in which operation at a relay point consisted merely of pulling a piece of paper from a receiver and inserting it into an adjacent transmitter; carrier telephone systems down to and sometimes in advance of corps headquarters; and radio relay systems that could bridge wire gaps across streams, rivers, and even the English Channel, and that could rapidly extend circuits in giant leaps overland. Above all, radar, unknown before the war, had opened up entirely new concepts of communication and had necessitated the manufacture of whole systems

[3] (1) Mary-louise Melia, The Quartz Crystal Program of the Signal Corps, 1941-45 (1945), SigC Hist Monograph B-15, app. J. (2) Col Corput, Relations of the Signal Corps Ground Signal Agency to Monmouth Signal Corps Procurement District, training course lecture, MSCPD, Hist Rpt, MSCPD, Quarter Ending 1 Oct 44. Both in SigC Hist Sec file. (3) Annual Rpt, ASF, FY 43, p. 5.

[4] Incl, Rpt for Maj Gen Richard C. Moore, Chief Ground Rqmts Sec AGF, sub: Radio Equip for AGF, with Memo, Chief Rqmts Plng Sec OCSigO for ACSigO, 27 Jul 43, same sub. SigC-EO Equip, 1942-43.

[5] Ltr, Ingles, CSigO, to Tully, DCSigO AFHQ, 2 Nov 43. SCIA file 110, To CSO Washington.

For principal types of radio sets used in World War II, see below, Appendix.

of new equipment.[6] To procure and distribute this array of communications equipment the Signal Corps, in the fiscal year ending 30 June 1944, spent $3,417,600,000. It prepared 6,438 contractual instruments. Materials were counted in millions of pounds—120,860,000 pounds of copper and 27,826,000 pounds of aluminum, for example.[7]

The high rate of productivity that the Signal Corps had achieved by mid-1944 contrasted sharply with its generally unsatisfactory supply status a year earlier. The measures taken and methods used to accomplish the transformation constitute a valuable case history of one technical service's wartime experience.

Organizational Improvements

Undoubtedly much of the improved status of signal supply could be traced to the increased efficiency of Signal Corps operating agencies and of the communications industry, an efficiency sharpened by experience during thirty-one months of war work. Part of the improvement reflected the influence of ASF, which played a dominant role in co-ordinating and standardizing supply procedures among all the technical services. Part of it resulted also from the simple fact that it was much easier to maintain the momentum of the war machine than it had been to get it rolling. The vigorous and effective leadership of General Harrison as chief of the important Procurement and Distribution Service, Office of the Chief Signal Officer, was perhaps the most important factor of all. Harrison welded Signal Corps supply agencies and the communications industry into a team that produced gratifying results.[8]

The organizational soundness of the Signal Corps supply activities under General Harrison during the last year and a half of war is particularly noteworthy because in supply matters the Signal Corps had entered the war with a handicap. Its initial unreadiness resulted principally from the enormous difficulties inherent in developing and procuring radar, a totally new electronic weapon, and from the decision to gamble on new FM and crystal-controlled radios.[9] These ventures definitely paid off, but at the cost of extreme difficulties in procurement in the first half of the war period.

Administrative Organization in OCSigO

General Ingles' initial reorganization when he became Chief Signal Officer in mid-1943 included splitting off the research and engineering functions of the Signal Supply Service.[10] The supply or-

---

[6] Meade, Speech to Members of Army-Navy Staff College, Signal Communication Planning and Results in Joint and Combined Operations, 5 May 44. SigC Hist Sec file.

[7] CSigO, Annual Rpt, FY 44, pp. 367, 370.

[8] (1) Annual Rpts, ASF, FY 44 and FY 45, passim. (2) ASF MPR's, 1944–45, passim. (3) Min, ASF Staff Conf, 28 Jan 44, p. 1. (4) Ltr, Gen Ingles to Walter S. Gifford, President AT&T Co., 31 Aug 45. SigC 000.7 Publicity, 1945. (5) Interv, SigC Hist Sec with Col Eugene V. Elder, former CO PSCPD, 28 Sep 49.
"An outstanding man to serve under—a hard driver of himself and others, satisfied with nothing less than completing a job perfectly." MS Comment, Shearer, Jul 59.

[9] (1) Terrett, The Emergency, especially pp. 141–47, 155–59, 178–85. (2) Thompson, Harris, et al., The Test, especially pp. 58–102, 147–85, 218–76, 491–93.

[10] See above, pp. 6–7.

ganization, Procurement and Distribution Service, evolved gradually as General Harrison and his staff grouped functions that seemed logically to belong together.[11] By 1 January 1944 the organization chart showed four divisions —Procurement, Production, Requirements, and Distribution.[12] The statement of duties for the several branches of the divisions reflected the functional nature of the organization.[13] With minor changes the arrangement lasted throughout the war, although the Production Division became the Contract Analysis Division early in 1945, when the increasing emphasis on contract termination, cost analysis, and price adjustment made such action appropriate.[14]

Streamlining the Field Agencies

If enemy bombs had been aimed at the heart of Signal Corps supply, Philadelphia would have been the target. Installations grouped there included the largest procurement district; the most important depot; the busiest inspection zone; the most active Price Adjustment Field Office; the Storage and Issue Agency (S&I), central point of stock control; the Stock Numbering Agency, which furnished the means of identification of signal items; the Supply Survey Agency, which gathered data to control estimates of supplies needed; and the Cost Analysis Agency. All of these field

activities were under the staff supervision of the Procurement and Distribution Division in Washington. Other Philadelphia agencies not controlled by P&D but related to supply were the Plant Engineering Agency, which furnished the material, equipment, engineering, and installation service for Army fixed communications and AAF airways communications; the Philadelphia Regional Labor Office, which handled Signal Corps manpower and labor problems in the area; and the Philadelphia field office of the Legal Division, which furnished legal assistance on contractual and supply matters to all the Signal Corps agencies in the Philadelphia region.[15]

As the focal point of supply, the Philadelphia congeries presumably set the pattern for all other field activities. But in June 1943, such heavy backlogs of work existed at both the Philadelphia Signal Corps Procurement District (PSCPD) and the Storage and Issue Agency that officials feared production delays might result. Currently it took forty days to process an order through the PSCPD.[16]

The PSCPD was suffering at that time from the growing pains engendered by the sudden expansion of supply activity in the first eighteen months of war. The official War Department procurement policy, announced immediately after Pearl Harbor, established speed as the prime desideratum in sup-

---

[11] Misc Plng Papers contained in SigC DS (Harrison) Admin Pers, P&D Sv.

[12] SigC Admin Log, 1939–45, OCSigO, Orgn Chart 29, 1 Jan 44, p. 100. SigC Hist Sec file.

[13] Proposed Orgn, 8 Aug 43. SigC DS (Harrison) Admin Proc and Staff Mtg, 8 Aug 43.

[14] SigC Admin Log, 1939–45, Chart 31, 1 Jan 45, p. 122.

[15] (1) CSigO, Annual Rpt, FY 44, pp. 79–81, 367–454. (2) SigC Admin Log, 1939–45, Charts 29, 1 Jul 43, and 30, 16 May 44. (3) Hall, Dev of the OCSigO (1945), SigC Hist Monograph D–1, pp. 10–12. (4) ASF M–301, Army Service Forces Organization, 15 Aug 44. 305.00/23.

[16] Log entry, 17 Jun 43. DCSigO folder, 1942–45. SigC Hist Sec file.

ply matters.[17] The emphasis on speed in placing contracts, obtaining deliveries, and fulfilling schedules had tended to blur lines of authority at PSCPD and to disorganize methods of procedure. This administrative tangle Col. Eugene V. Elder started clearing away when he became the commanding officer of PSCPD in October 1943.

Over a period of months Colonel Elder converted the PSCPD from a horizontal functional basis to a vertical organization based on commodity specialization. A group of twenty-eight contracting officers was established, each officer in charge of a commodity section that was in effect a small procurement district within the periphery of the larger district. Each commodity section performed all functions in the procurement cycle on assigned items. The arrangement eliminated a mountain of interoffice correspondence and duplicate sets of records: 65 percent of the forms formerly used no longer were needed. Contracting speeded up. In the process of reorganizing PSCPD, Colonel Elder made no changes in the basic policies governing Signal Corps contracting procedures.[18] Their soundness was never in dispute. However, the new organization did provide the flexibility needed to apply the policies within the ever-changing pattern of procurement.[19]

The Storage and Issue Agency had a vital role in the distribution system. The agency, it should be emphasized, was a control point for stock and stock movements. S&I neither set the basic policies nor exercised operational control over the depots, yet the agency had the responsibility for seeing that shipments were made and that depots operated effectively.[20] In reality S&I was in the uncomfortable position of controlling without the authority to enforce control. Any failure reflected immediately and adversely upon "the Signal Corps as a whole, the Chief Signal Officer personally, and the S&I Agency directly." As one officer put it:

The Laboratories may get behind schedule on development; procurement may be delayed or omitted; plant plans may not be complete as of an estimated date, and no serious trouble will immediately develop as a result. Let Storage and Issue fail to have the necessary items at a port, or fail to provide training equipment for a newly-activated unit and the repercussions are loud and immediate, starting usually with the Chief of Staff.[21]

As matters stood in mid-1943, S&I had not been able to keep up effectively with the heavy demands placed upon it by the initial equipping of the expanding Army, and by the first offensives in North Africa and the South Pacific. It faced a staggering backlog of unprocessed requisitions, records, correspondence, and purchase requests. Clearly S&I needed an overhauling, but officials feared that a housecleaning would put

[17] Thompson, Harris, et al., The Test, p. 32 and n. 105.

[18] For detailed discussion of Signal Corps contracting policy and procedures and the supply problems inextricably woven into contract placement, see Thompson, Harris, et al., The Test, especially pp. 32–33, 147–85, 322–37, 491–535.

[19] (1) Hist, PSCPD, I, 83–87, 254–91. (2) Reorgn Rpt, PSCPD, 29 May 44. (3) Tng Manual, PSCPD, 4 Mar 44. All in SigC Hist Sec file.

[20] Gen Harrison's Opening Remarks, Depot Comdrs' Conf, Chicago, 14–15 Nov 43. SigC DS (Harrison) Depot Comdrs' Conf.

[21] OCSigO Staff Study, Examination of the Organization and Functions of the Storage and Issue Agency, OCSigO, 25 Mar 43. SigC file, Basic Orgn and Policy, S&I Agency, 1942–45, SigC Hist Sec file.

the agency even further behind in its work.[22]

In the next few months, through extraordinary efforts—a 7-day work week for all employees, as much as sixty-eight hours of overtime per employee per week, hiring high school pupils as typists and clerks on after-school hours—agency officials cleared out their paper-work backlog. Meanwhile, in a series of meetings with depot representatives, S&I chiefs discussed problem areas and arrived at solutions.[23] At the same time, S&I hurriedly pushed to completion the teletypewriter circuits that by August linked it with every depot in the supply system.[24]

In early 1944 the agency moved into a new building, which also housed the PSCPD and the Philadelphia office of the legal director, and assumed housekeeping duties for all three organizations. A new air of confidence pervaded S&I. It had streamlined its functions, added new sections, abolished others, and improved its bookkeeping and accountability records. It had also acquired more workers (by the end of the fiscal year the figure stood around 2,300) and seemed well able to handle the work for any offensive plans that might be afoot.[25]

Requirements

Introduction of the Supply Control System

During late 1943 and the first half of 1944, the Army introduced some important changes in the methods of calculating its requirements. Military planners estimated that the Army would reach its maximum strength early in 1944—about 7,700,000 men. Industrial conversion to a peak wartime footing was virtually complete; the broad strategic concepts for overwhelming Germany and Japan were generally established; the whole national economy was as fully mobilized as it was likely to be. In short, the most critical period had passed, but supply requirements had strained productive capacity to its limit. Obviously it was time to take a long, hard look at military procurement demands to review their validity.

The newly established Office of War Mobilization requested such a review in the summer of 1943. The War Department Procurement Review Board (the McCoy Board) and the War Department Special Committee for Restudy of Reserves (the so-called Richards Committee) were appointed.[26] As a result of their findings, a broad reduction in Army requirements took place. To im-

---

[22] (1) Thompson, Harris, et al., The Test, pp. 515–16, 520. (2) Log entry, 18 May 43. DCSigO folder, 1942–45, SigC Hist Sec file.

[23] The problems included deadline dates, controlled items, spare parts, packaging, waterproofing, stock identification, stock numbers, shipping documents, excess stock, substitute items, and use of tabulating equipment, to name but a few.

[24] (1) Morton H. Ullery, History of the Storage and Issue Agency (1946), I, 62–94. (2) S&I Agency Orgn and Functions, 26 Aug 43. Both in SigC Hist Sec file.

[25] (1) Ullery, Hist, S&I Agency, pp. 62–94, passim, and app. 8, Chart of Civilian Pers Strength. (2) Unsigned Memo, 4 Nov 43, sub: Sig Sup in

the Pacific, inclosed with Memo, Meade, Dir P&O Div, for Gen Code, 4 Nov 43, sub: Sig Com Extracts From Gen Somervell's Pacific Area Rpts. SCIA file, unnumbered Somervell Rpt.

[26] (1) Rpt, WD Proc Review Bd, 31 Aug 43. (2) Levels of Supply and Supply Procedure, 1 Jan 44, vols. I and II. Both in NARS World War II Rcds. The last-cited publication contains reports of both the board and the special committee, plus comments of the WDGS divisions and major commands and other pertinent data.

plement the reduction policy and to improve procedures used in estimating requirements, ASF instituted the Army Supply Control System (SCS), which gradually replaced the Army Supply Program (ASP) during the last year and a half of war.[27]

ASF Circular No. 67, which introduced the SCS, laid down procurement, inventory, and disposal policies and procedures and provided for co-ordination of requirements calculations, procurement scheduling, storage, issue, stock control at all levels, and the disposal of surpluses—in short the co-ordination of all phases of supply. The technical services were required to conduct "supply and demand studies," using calculating methods and procedures embodied in Circular 67. The resulting data were expected not only to determine requirements accurately but to spotlight supply areas in which corrective action was necessary. Thus shortages were to be overcome by increasing procurement schedules, and excesses were to be controlled by curtailing procurement or by instituting disposal actions.[28]

The new Supply Control System provided more detailed and comprehensive information than had the ASP. For example, whereas ASP set forth annual production targets, revised twice yearly, SCS's monthly and quarterly computations were recomputed, revised, and published monthly. This noteworthy advantage was partially offset by the terrific increase in workload resulting from the necessity of preparing the supply and demand studies. Preparation of each monthly report was a "major ordeal."[29] The Office of the Chief Signal Officer hastily reorganized the Requirements Branch as a division to serve as a control point and collecting agency for assembling the required information. Few sections of OCSigO remained entirely unaffected.[30] Since so many of the SCS reports required compilation from other published reports of the Office of the Chief Signal Officer, the number skyrocketed. In a single 3-month period, while the new system was being put into effect, the number of published reports rose from 701 to 2,194.[31]

The ASP and the SCS served the same purpose—they were published compilations of the consolidated needs of the Army, which not only guided the technical services in their procurement activities but also constituted their authority to contract and buy.[32] In this respect, the SCS was a great improvement over the ASP. Nevertheless the whole business of determining requirements was at best unbelievably complex. A really comprehensive discussion of requirements calculation in the Signal

[27] For detailed discussion of the Supply Control System and methods of computing Army requirements in general, see R. Elberton Smith, *The Army and Economic Mobilization*, UNITED STATES ARMY IN WORLD WAR II (Washington, 1959), ch. III.

[28] ASF Cir 67, 7 Mar 44, pp. 1–10, 12–24. Copy in SigC DS (Harrison) SCS.

[29] Smith, *The Army and Economic Mobilization*, p. 166.

[30] Memo, Dir Rqmts Div OCSigO for Chief ACS et al., 14 Apr 44, sub: Supply and Demand Studies. SigC DS (Harrison) SCS.

[31] André E. Gerard, The Story of Supply in the Signal Corps in World War II, pt. I, Rqmts (1945), SigC Hist Monograph B-1, p. 44. SigC Hist Sec file.

[32] Rpt, WD Proc Review Bd, p. 18. The board compared the ASP to a housewife's shopping list —a list, however, that ran into billions of dollars.

Corps alone would fill several volumes.[33]

Briefly, the five factors on which requirements were calculated were: (1) initial issue, (2) maintenance or replacement, (3) distribution, (4) overseas levels, and (5) shipping losses. Balancing them was supposed to produce the figures for total supply.

A deceptively simple formula determined initial issue. Signal tables of equipment showed in detail how many and what kinds of radios, telephones, and so on were allotted to each type of unit. The troop basis set forth the number of units. Therefore x number of soldiers should require y numbers of items. However, x and y were variables since changes in strategic concepts often altered the figures represented by x and y overnight. In the first two years of war the troop basis fluctuated most erratically.[34] Advances in electronic development brought forth new items such as radar for which there was no previous issue experience. Finally, there was the class of items that the Signal Corps called "project" material, such as the immensely important, costly, and complex equipment necessary to set up an entire area or theater communications system. The Signal Corps requirements for fixed communications systems for North Africa, for example, included such items as complete radio stations, telephone centrals large enough to service a great city, and thousands of miles of heavy-duty cable. Such items were difficult to manufacture and required at least eighteen months to produce. Project material could not be included on regular tables of allowances, yet it was vital to the Army, and the need for it had to be anticipated in figuring the total initial requirements.

The second factor, maintenance, was also often referred to as the *replacement factor,* the term the Signal Corps most often used. Obviously items once issued did not last forever; they started to wear out the first day of issue—sometimes, as in the case of batteries, before issue. Since some items wore out faster than others, the replacement factor had to be calculated for each individual item. Past experience furnished guides for calculating replacement of such things as food and shoes, but was less reliable for signal items, many of which were brand new. Differences in climate and terrain in the various areas of the world affected the consumption rate of signal items. Furthermore, men in the inactive areas or in training status used up equipment at quite a different rate from troops in active combat. The Signal Corps consistently argued that replacement factors should be figured on an individual theater basis, since needs in different theaters varied so greatly. The War Department eventually adopted this principle.[35]

The third factor, distribution, merely meant the quantity of items needed to keep the supply pipeline filled. It included stocks in transit within the United States in ZI depots, en route overseas, and in depots overseas.

The fourth factor, overseas levels, represented reserve stocks—insurance

[33] (1) An abbreviated discussion of the subject is contained in Gerard, Story of Sup in the SigC in World War II, pt. I. (2) See also the extensive files of the Requirements Section (later branch and division) in the 400 subseries of Dewey-decimal Signal Corps files.

[34] Thompson, Harris, et al., The Test, pp. 35–38, 188, 212, 321.

[35] See below, p. 359.

against unforeseen contingencies and sudden demands.

The fifth factor, shipping losses, also included such things as pilferage. For obvious reasons, distribution and shipping losses were factors of much more importance in the early days of the war.

From the beginning of hostilities, the Signal Corps procurement record in relation to ASP figures had looked worse than it was because of the rigidity of the calculations. The Signal Corps had fought hard to get a little flexibility into the estimation of its requirements. In early days, when the emphasis lay upon the initial equipping of the expanding Army, the ASP made no allowance for additional requirements for special tactical operations. Such additional requirements did occur frequently, with sudden demands for very large quantities of signal equipment. Running as high as several hundred percent above authorized table of allowance figures in some cases, these special issues had to be diverted from the units for which they were originally intended and the loss recouped later from production. In such cases the availability reports had to reflect "shortages" while the replacement equipment was being manufactured.[36]

In 1941 the War Department directed the Signal Corps to reduce its replacement factors, then considered too high. All through 1942 the Signal Corps sought a $500,000,000 increase in the ASP to cover signal equipment for the AAF, which had not yet expressed its requirements in concrete form. In the fall of 1942, ASF directed that replacement factors for items not issued in a designated period be reduced. The Chief Signal Officer reviewed recent demands from all sources and made up a list of items that he recommended be included in the ASP. The ASP included part of them in the February 1943 issue. In May 1943 the whole increase was finally approved. However, the procurement cycle being what it was, the effect of entering these requirements on the program would not be felt until 1944.[37] The War Department in 1944 adopted the use of separate replacement factors for the theaters, first grouping the theaters into two major areas and later into the six major theaters.[38]

The Signal Corps sent members of its Signal Supply Survey Agency, officers specially trained in all phases of supply and distribution, to the theaters in August 1943. Their specific mission was to help the theater commanders compile accurate data and complete reports on signal replacement factors.[39] Most Signal Corps replacement factors were found to

[36] Memo (writer unidentified), 8 Jun 43, sub: Review of SigC's Efforts To Increase Rqmts on the Sup Prog. DCSigO folder, 1942–45, p. 197, SigC Hist Sec file.

[37] (1) Memo, Meade, Dir Opns Div, for ACSigO, 19 Jul 43, sub: Proc Review. SigC–DS (Harrison) Proc. (2) AG Ltr, SPX–400 (13 Oct 43) OB–P–SPOPI–MBA, to Chiefs of Tech Svs, 27 Oct 43, sub: Procedure for Handling Rqmts of Spec Operational Sups. SigC 400.12 Proc No. 2, 1942–44. (3) Memo, 8 Jun 43, sub: Review of SigC's Efforts To Increase Rqmts on the Sup Prog. DCSigO folder, 1942–45, p. 197, SigC Hist Sec file.

[38] (1) Msg, TAG to COMINCH SWPA et al., 11 Jun 44, sub: Determination of Replacement Factors, Rates of Consumption and Expenditure. AG 400 (7 Jul 44) OB–S–D–M. (2) Msg, TAG to COMINCH SWPA et al., 9 Dec 44, same sub. AG 400 (28 Nov 44) OB–S–D–M.

[39] (1) Qtrly Rpt, SSA, 15 Jul 43–15 Oct 43, pp. 1–3. SigC Hist Sec file. (2) Qtrly Rpts, Distr Div OCSigO, Jul–Sep 43, pp. 7–8; Oct–Dec 43, p. 15; Jan–Mar 44, p. 13. SigC DB 319.1 Qtrly Rpts, 1943–45. (3) Smith, The Army and Economic Mobilization, p. 187.

SCR–300 IN HUERTGEN FOREST. *8th Infantry.*

be too low. For example, the replacement factor for the small back-packed radios, SCR–300, rose from 13 per 100 in August 1944 to 20 in December and to 28 in February 1945. Monthly shipments to the ETO rose steadily to a high of 2,500 each month in the period January through April 1945. The replacement factor for the SCR–536 rose from 13 to 20 in November 1944, to 26 in December, and to 32 in February 1945. The ETO received 6,000 sets each month from January to April 1945.[40]

Though Army requirements generally declined in 1944, requirements for all kinds of signal communications equipment rose sharply. The War Department calculations for ground radio require-

ments, for example, had been based upon the needs of tactical units, without providing adequate communications facilities between headquarters of theater and subordinate commands.[41]

Sudden emergencies also threw 1944 requirements planning out of phase. Less than a month before the Normandy invasion, on 7 May, ETO supply officers notified ASF via transatlantic telephone that two airborne divisions would have to be 100 percent re-equipped. The equipment list was received 10 May. It contained 214 items (327,272 individual pieces), of which the largest single category was 66 signal items, comprising 13,522 individual pieces. The gear had to be in port within four days. The equipment began to move to port on the night of 10 May by air, rail, and Army and commercial trucks. A small army of co-ordinators followed each step of the procedure. All Signal Corps items made the ship and arrived in England on 1 June.[42]

The foregoing examples of difficulties in realistic requirements planning serve to illustrate only a few of the problems the Signal Corps encountered. As late as February 1944, a high-ranking Signal Corps officer complained that the ASP was not a true statement of requirements —the Signal Corps could meet the ASP and still not meet actual requirements.[43]

The gradual change-over to the Supply Control System did improve matters somewhat, principally because it brought requirements and procurement groups into closer working relationships. The application of the SCS did not occur

[40] Annual Rpt, ASF, FY 44, p. 41.

[41] *Ibid.,* p. 95.
[42] *Ibid.,* p. 18.
[43] Log entry, 2 Feb 44. DCSigO folder, 1942–45, p. 186. SigC Hist Sec file.

overnight—rather it became operative by a process of infiltration, beginning in some of its aspects even before Circular 67 was issued. The last edition of the ASP was published in October 1944. Thereafter supply computations based entirely on supply and demand studies were published in monthly progress reports, MPR–20 series.[44]

Translating Requirements Into Production

In the opinion of many Army supply officers, one of the major deficiencies of ASP and MPR computations was their expression of "required production" in terms of dollar values. Arguments over the validity of this point of view are best left to the economists and statisticians.[45] Signal Corps officers pointed out that technical factors controlled the production of signal items. The multiplicity of types of equipment—each calling for its own particular components, each component itself comprising a complex, precise assembly of parts—was the major factor that created Signal Corps production problems.[46] It was especially difficult to translate Signal Corps production progress into terms of percentage gains in dollars when individual items such as radar sets were so disproportionately

costly. A single type of radar, for example, if behind schedule for lack of materials or machine tools could account for a high percentage of ASP "scheduled production" in dollars.[47] On the other hand, the ASP did not reflect lower price quotations, increased manufacturing skill and techniques, substitution of noncritical for critical materials, or simplifications of design. In April 1943, purchase plans for crystals were still being figured at a cost of $7.50 for crystals that actually cost $1.35 each. In October, a survey showed that the services actually purchased material for only 78 percent of the amounts used in planning and setting up the Army Supply Program.[48]

Thus it was one of the complexities of supply calculations that "official" figures might not reflect what they seemed to reflect and that all the careful attention to "yardsticks" might be ineffective if the scale of measurement was inaccurate. Nevertheless, the Signal Corps production figures for the last two years of the war were pleasantly acceptable to those in higher authority.

Balancing the production books for the calendar year 1943, results showed that the scheduled monthly production

[44] ASF Manual M–413, Supply Control System, superseded ASF Cir 67. M–413 was published in various editions dated 20 Jul 44, 22 Dec 44, and 10 Apr 45.

[45] There were in fact many acrimonious disputes over this point. Somervell was one who disliked the dollar-value technique. (1) Memo, Somervell for CofS, 30 Oct 42. ASF CofS GS (3) RG–200. (2) Smith, The Army and Economic Mobilization, pp. 155–57.

[46] MS Comment, Col Byron A. Falk (Ret.), in Memo for Col Leo J. Meyer, Deputy Chief Historian OCMH, 27 Mar 52. SigC Hist Sec file.

[47] See Thompson, Harris, et al., The Test, pp. 533–34, for the case of the SCR–584 in this connection.

[48] (1) Subcmte of House Cmte on Appropriations, 78th Cong., 2d Sess., Hearings on the Military Affairs Appropriations Bill for 1945, pp. 274ff. (2) OCSigO Fiscal Div, Appropriations, Signal Service of the Army. (3) OCSigO R&W, Chief Rqmt Br to Dir Materiel Div, 3 Jun 43, sub: Costs on RPR's. (4) Ltr, Dir P&D Sv to CO MSCPD et al., 18 Sep 43, sub: Obligation of 1944 Funds. (5) OCSigO R&W Action 1, Chief Purchasing Br to Dir Proc Div, 25 Sep 43, sub: Survey of Proc Results. (6) Memo, Dir Rqmt Div for Asst Chief P&D Sv, 8 Oct 43, sub: Status of SSA Funds. Last four in SigC 400.12 Proc No. 2, 1942–44.

rate had increased gratifyingly; it stood at 83 percent more at the end of the year than in January. In terms of dollar deliveries for the calendar year, that represented $1,913,000,000, or 97 percent of the required ASP's $1,971,000,-000 of selected items.[49] In terms of the entire Signal Corps procurement program, it meant about three billion dollars of items delivered during the year. Not all equipment groups gained equally. Airborne radar monthly production more than doubled during 1943, yet fell short of total requirements by nearly 18 percent. Aircraft equipment, exclusive of radar and ground radio and radar production, met or exceeded requirements. The doubled delivery rate for wire communications equipment during 1943 produced 94 percent of the requirements, an output barely equal to the going need.[50] On the whole, General Harrison and General Ingles could feel satisfied that actual deliveries of most types of Signal Corps items in the 1943 Army Supply Program were progressing reasonably well.

Early in 1944, when a new ASP was issued, General Harrison spelled out the general principles of procurement scheduling for the rest of the year in a letter to the procurement districts.[51] The Signal Corps at that time was one of the four technical services that had not yet attained the peak month delivery rates indicated by current forecasts. To attain 1944 production goals, the Corps had to increase deliveries of airborne radar by 103 percent, ground radar 14 percent, special ground radio equipment 32 percent, and wire communications equipment 15 percent.[52]

For a time it seemed that all these goals would be met with no worry at all. From January through June, procurement and deliveries proceeded with wonderful smoothness, these months constituting a period of heavy productivity. At the end of the fiscal year, 30 June, ASF reported that Signal Corps deliveries showed the greatest increase based on dollar value among all the technical services. Signal Corps supply items accounted for 13 percent of the Army Supply Program, approximately 95,000 separate items and 76,000 spare parts items. At the same time, prices paid for signal items declined 7.7 percent.[53] Suddenly in midsummer, at the very highest point of productivity, a serious lull in production confronted the supply services.

The Army Service Forces had expected all the technical services to achieve a peak month for deliveries early in the year, when most of the required production would be met. After that, ASF anticipated a gradual decline in Army requirements. The calculations rested on the assumption that industry would maintain its current high rate of production and deliveries. The rate of scheduled deliveries for the supply services as a whole, however, fell behind. ASF set the peak month first for April,

---

[49] These figures include airborne radar and radio equipment for the AAF, for which the Signal Corps had responsibility until 1945.

[50] (1) WD MPR, sec. 6, 31 Dec 43, pp. 52-53. ASF file. (2) SigC Preliminary Progress Rpt, Dec 43. SigC DS (Harrison) SigC Preliminary Proc Rpts.

[51] Ltr, Harrison, Chief P&D Div OCSigO, to CO's PSCPD, Dayton SigC Proc Dist and Depot, and MSCPD, 8 Mar 44, sub: Principles of Proc Scheduling for 1944. SigC 400.192 Prod Scheduling Policies, SigC Equip, 1944.

[52] WD MPR, sec. 6, 31 Jan 44, pp. 1-3. ASF file.

[53] ASF, Annual Rpt, FY 44, pp. 100, 109, 115, 119.

then May, then June, and later for October. By October it was necessary to roll back the forecasts of deliveries still further. This did not necessarily mean a lessening of the total requirements, but merely a postponement of the date when the material could be expected to be on hand.[54]

More and more often during the summer and early fall of 1944, contracting officers found manufacturers loath to accept new military orders. Deliveries on orders already placed were lagging badly. In August, a technical chief remarked at General Somervell's staff conference that "all manufacturers are pulling their punches and thinking about returning to civilian production." [55] The Chief Signal Officer warned General Rumbough in the European theater in August that the supply services were fighting a "very serious letdown" in the manufacturing plants.

In spite of everything the War and Navy Departments can do, the country is convinced that the European war at least is about over, and there is very much of a scramble to convert to post-war production. The Signal Corps still has 43 items, mostly airborne and ground radar, that are tight and on which we cannot get sufficient production. For the Army as a whole, dry batteries and wire are our outstanding headaches.[56]

From June to August 1944, Signal Corps procurement men desperately sought to halt a steady decline in procurement deliveries. The other technical services were equally hard hit. In August the decline was finally halted and deliveries started edging upward again. Of the total of 22.5 billions of dollars in ASF deliveries in fiscal year 1945 (ending 30 June 1945), 1.3 billions were in Signal Corps items.[57] Even so, the total Signal Corps deliveries were less than in fiscal year 1944. By the end of the calendar year 1945, the close supervision of supply planning and operations inherent in the supply control system had brought requirement calculation and production into balance. The Signal Corps was still refining and perfecting its statistical and reporting methods when the war ended.

The Effect of Overseas Procurement on Signal Corps Requirements

All the theaters regularly purchased supplies locally whenever possible. Australia in particular had provided the Signal Corps with many badly needed items, especially during the first two years of war.[58] Thus, in theory, overseas procurement within the theaters could reduce programed production requirements within the United States, but the volume of local purchasing of signal items had never risen high enough to warrant a reduction of signal items in the Army Supply Program.

Beginning in December 1943 the Signal Corps received regular quarterly reports and occasional special reports on local procurements of signal supplies from its signal officers in overseas thea-

---

[54] Min, ASF Staff Conf, 15 Aug 44, pp. 1–4. ASF file, NARS World War II Rcds.

[55] *Ibid.*, 15 Aug 44, p. 2.

[56] Ltr, Ingles to Rumbough, 11 Aug 44. SigC 475 SigC Equip (Rumbough), 1944–45.

For other factors that caused the let-down in production, see below, pp. 372, 378ff.

[57] Procurement, 9 Apr 52, prepared by Robert H. Crawford and Lindsley F. Cook, in Theodore Whiting, Statistics. Draft MS in OCMH files.

[58] See above, pp. 265–66.

ters.[59] In the ETO, for example, the Supply Division of the Office of the Chief Signal Officer, ETOUSA, sole agency authorized to procure signal supplies locally, maintained files of the names of manufacturing firms, with complete information as to their capacity and resources. Although a scarcity of fuel, electricity, and raw materials precluded any sizable production output from French and Belgian firms, about a hundred French firms had received orders for Signal Corps equipment, principally vacuum tubes, resistors, and other small parts, by October 1944.[60] British firms, though overloaded with Britain's own war orders, filled Signal Corps local procurement orders as often as possible. From June 1942 to March 1944 the Signal Corps bought the equivalent of 32,000 long tons of material in the United Kingdom.[61] The list of 1,521 items consisted mainly of packing materials, pigeons and pigeon equipment, and photographic materials, and a sprinkling of multiairline wire, radio sets, and other electronic signaling devices. An important exception was the purchase of 77,650 telephone poles varying in length from 20 to 40 feet.[62]

Lagging U.S. production in mid-1944 led military planners to examine the possibility of augmenting overseas supply by restoring factory facilities in liberated areas. In liberated Europe the two plants of the International Telephone and Telegraph Corporation, one in Paris and one in Belgium, seemed to offer the best possibilities for the Signal Corps. Officers with prewar knowledge of the plants were transferred to the Corps and certain civilians were lent to it by the parent company in the United States. The Civil Affairs Division of the War Department General Staff informed the Signal Corps that the whole matter lay within Civil Affairs jurisdiction, but General Ingles said, "Of course they cannot take care of it as they do not have the organization and know-how." Ingles suggested that the Civil Affairs Division retain jurisdiction —"who gets the credit is immaterial"— but that Signal Corps people in the theater do the work. Fortunately, within the theater, the Civil Affairs group welcomed Signal Corps assistance, and the rehabilitation plan had solid backing.[63]

In Algiers, both a wire-drawing factory and a lead-cable factory were operating for the Allies. Over 7,200 tons of copper-wire bar in North Africa had been secreted in a dozen different places to keep it from the Germans. When the Germans were expelled, the material came out of hiding and found its way back to the wire-drawing factory of

[59] Transmittal Sheet, Action 1, Contl Div OCSigO to CSigO, 1 Jan 45, sub: Staff Conf, 3 Jan 45, Proc in ETO. SigC 337 Confs Re Exped Prod and Manpower Shortages, 1944–45.

[60] ETOUSA Rpt, II, 67.

[61] Incl 3, Outline of the Highlights of Signal Supply in the ETO, with Transmittal Sheet, Action 1, Dir of Evaluation Div to CSigO, ETOUSA, 20 Dec 44, sub: Outstanding Achievements of SigC. 314.7 Mil Hists, vol. III.

[62] ETOUSA Rpt, II, 69.

All together, 294,964 poles weighing 29,000 tons without wire or insulators were shipped from the United Kingdom to Normandy. The problem of moving them across the English Channel was a difficult one, worked out by the Transportation Corps and the Corps of Engineers. After experi-

ments with rafting proved unsuccessful because of heavy seas and strong tides, barges moved the poles. (1) *Ibid.* (2) Signal Rafting, Admin 306.

[63] (1) Ltr, Ingles, CSigO, to Rumbough, Hq ETOUSA, 17 Jul 44. (2) Ltr, Rumbough to Ingles, 25 Jul 44. Both in SigC 475 Sig Equip (Rumbough), 1944–45.

Laminoires et Tréfilerie d'Afrique. Operating on a 3-shift basis, the factory could produce 125 to 150 tons of wire per month, enough for a lead-cable factory in Algiers, Lignes Télégraphiques et Téléphoniques. A quantity of lead for the cable operations was on hand, and more could be mined in Tunisia. The Signal Corps shipped about 600 tons of steel tape and quantities of insulating paper, jute, oil, and cellulose string to keep LTT in operation.[64]

Another factory in Casablanca built reasonably good glass insulators until late 1943, when a new and better glass factory in Naples came into Allied hands. Naples also supplied new cabling and wire-drawing machinery for the Algiers plants. The forests of northern Africa, central Africa, Portugal, and, at a later time, southern Italy produced thousands of telephone poles. Naples plants manufactured several items of pole line hardware. At Rome, beginning in September 1944, an Italian firm, Fatme, produced multiple telephone switchboards, multiple teletype switchboards, and other items for the U.S. Army.[65]

In general, Signal Corps equipment was ill adapted to foreign manufacture because of its highly technical nature and because it had to be interchangeable electrically, mechanically, and operationally with American-made equipment already in use. To translate procurement and manufacturing drawings and specifications, including changes of dimensions to the metric system, would require skilled translators and interpreters familiar with technical terms. To assure interchangeability, duplicate inspection equipment, such as test apparatus and gauges that were specially manufactured and ordinarily in critical supply at home, would have to be sent abroad. Finally, key personnel who knew American methods and manufacturing processes would be required as supervisors. These were the very people who were scarce in this country. The Signal Corps was already producing a substitute radio receiver for the R–100/URR in the European area, about one-third of the total 140,000 scheduled for production being made there. German repeaters for the use of the PTT French telephone system were also being produced in Antwerp factories.[66]

In April 1945, control of captured German industries was centered in the G–4 section of SHAEF, which established a Production Control Agency at Reims, with divisions in each of the services. The Production Control Division, Signal Service, was set up in Paris, pending a move of the SHAEF Control

[64] (1) Interv, SigC Hist Sec with Col Henry, 1944. (2) Sig Sec AFHQ, History of the Signal Section, Allied Force Headquarters, 24 July 1942–10 November 1945 (1945) (hereafter cited as Hist, Sig Sec AFHQ), app. D, pp. 3–4. SigC Hist Sec file.
[65] (1) Hist, Sig Sec AFHQ, app. D, pp. 4, 9, 15. (2) Ltr, Col Harrod G. Miller, Sig Sup Of NATOUSA, to Gen Ingles, 23 May 44, and Incl, Résumé of Local Proc of Sig Equip in NATO. SCIA file 110, To CSO Washington.

[66] (1) Memo, CofS ASF for Ingles et al., 30 Dec 44, sub: Conf on Dev of Prod for Essential Items on the Continent in ETO. (2) Transmittal Sheet, Action 1, Contl Div OCSigO to CSigO, 1 Jan 45, sub: Staff Conf of 3 Jan 45, Proc in ETO, and the following Incls: (a) Memo for Rcd, Prod of Sig Equip in ETO; (b) Incl 2, Short Sup Items Adapted for ETO; and (c) Incl 5, List of Manufacturers in ETO. Both in SigC 337 Confs Re Exped Prod and Manpower Shortages, 1944–45.

Agency to Frankfurt. Signal Corps responsibility included production control over German manufacturing of wire and cable; telephone, telegraph, radio, radar, television, photographic and meteorological equipment; dry batteries; electric bulbs; and tubes. The first step was to make a preliminary survey of German industries, and, for this duty, each of the armies was responsible for the industries within its territory. Lacking other suitable personnel, the job was turned over to the Enemy Equipment Intelligence Service teams assigned to each army. By 18 June, about 85 percent of the surveys covering some one hundred German firms had been completed. An analysis revealed that the signal service industries in the territory occupied by the U.S. forces were in most cases dependent for raw materials and components upon territories occupied by the British, the French, and the Russians. Thus, at least until an Allied council came into operation, it appeared that production of signal items in the territory occupied by the United States would be limited to the amount that could be manufactured with materials on hand.[67]

There were of course other benefits, social and political, involved in putting factories and workers in liberated countries into useful production, but the amount produced did not lessen materially the sum of the total requirements for Signal Corps items. In fact, the drain on materials and technicians tended to produce an opposite effect.

Developments in Production Control Measures, 1944–45

In 1942 placing contracts unquestionably constituted the most urgent supply matter. Under the intense pressure of the period, the procurement districts placed some contracts with manufacturers not qualified to produce. Other manufacturers misjudged their productive capacity and optimistically accepted too many contracts. Lack of raw materials held back some contractors; labor shortages delayed others. Whatever the reasons for delay might be, the responsibility of the contracting officers in the procurement districts continued until the articles contracted for had been delivered. By mid-1943 the most crucial problem confronting the Signal Corps supply organization was how to obtain deliveries on the contracts already placed.

The reorganization of the Philadelphia Signal Corps Procurement District on a commodity basis, already discussed, was the first step in an intensive drive to speed up deliveries. A second step created more effective tools to enable the contracting officers to discharge their responsibility for the whole procurement cycle. One of these tools was the development of more accurate methods of forecasting deliveries. Another was the return to the procurement districts of control over expediting activities. A third step that most contracting officers ardently desired—direct control of inspection—was not attained. The Signal Corps Inspection Agency remained a separate field agency directly responsible to P&D Service until the end of the war.[68] General Harrison had been

---

[67] Rpt, Col R. L. Hart, OCSigO, 30 Jun 45, Organizing German Production, Control Division of Signal Service, ETOUSA. SigC DS (Harrison) Critical Shortages, ETO.

[68] (1) Hist, PSCPD, I, 228ff. (2) SigC Admin Log, 1939–45, Chart 32, 1 May 45, p. 127.

favorably impressed with the agency on his first field visit and subsequently continued to feel that no useful purpose would be served by returning inspection activities to the control of the procurement districts.[69]

Forecast Method of Production Control

Without reasonably accurate forecasts of the quantities of specific items that would be delivered within a given period of time, the Army could make no sound estimate of its supply resources. Forecasts "controlled" production, in the sense that concentrated effort could be expended at any given period of time on most-needed items, while less critical items could be held back. To an extent, forecasts determined stock positions because delivery schedules of specific items could be accelerated or slowed according to need. Forecasts also aided manufacturers, who needed advance information in order to schedule work and maintain adequate stockpiles of materials.[70]

The Army compiled its supply estimates from many bits and pieces of information from all supply sources, of which the Signal Corps was only one. In 1943, Signal Corps forecasts were dishearteningly unreliable. Largely the work of plant expediters from the Army and Navy Electronics Production Agency (ANEPA), the forecasts tended to be overoptimistic.[71] The end result of such faulty forecasts was a decline in the Signal Corps' charged production rate.

Very soon after General Ingles became Chief Signal Officer in mid-1943, General Somervell expressed his displeasure with the 6-month decline in the Signal Corps' production rate. For May 1943 production fell 14 percent below the forecast and 8.8 percent below that of April. In January, forecasters had predicted a 41.4 percent increase by June; as late as May they believed it would be 24.9 percent. Actually, June production turned out to be only 4.3 percent above January. General Somervell pointed out that for several months Signal Corps forecasts had "shown no appreciable improvement [and] are now well below the average for the Technical Services."[72] General Ingles acknowledged that Signal Corps forecasting methods were "unquestionably defective."[73]

General Harrison recognized that the key to forecasting lay in providing the forecasters with more accurate sources of information. He therefore expanded and improved the supply system records. Forecasting became a joint responsibility of production specialists, including but not limited to ANEPA specialists. At the beginning of each month a forecast meeting in the procurement district brought together contracting officers, laboratory engineers, inspectors, expediters, storage and issue representatives, and staff officers of the P&D Serv-

---

[69] (1) Memo, Dir P&D Sv for CSigO, 1 Sep 43, sub: P&D. (2) Misc Plng Papers, 1944–45. Both in SigC DS (Harrison) Orgn P&D Sv.

[70] Hist, PSCPD, I, 251.

[71] Ralph H. Clark, Expediting Activities of the Office of the Chief Signal Officer, August 1941–June 1944 (1945), SigC Hist Monograph B–14, pp. 34–37. SigC Hist Sec file.

[72] (1) Memo, Somervell for CSigO, 17 Jul 43. (2) Memo, Somervell for CSigO, 13 Jun 43, sub: May Prod, Incl 4 to Memo, CSigO for CG ASF, 18 Jun 43, same sub. Both in SigC 400.12 Proc 1943.

[73] (1) Memo, Ingles for Somervell, 20 Jul 43, sub: SigC Proc Situation. SigC 400.12 Proc 1943. (2) Memo, CSigO to Chief P&D Sv, 27 Aug 43. SigC EO 400.12 Chief P&D Sv (Harrison), 1943–45.

ice, OCSigO. All participated in a review of the delivery results compared with the previous month's forecast. Then they fixed the schedules for the next month. After the forecast meeting, telegrams giving delivery schedules for the current month and two succeeding months went out to the manufacturers. Procurement district and field office personnel kept tabs on the manufacturers' progress during the month, ready to assist in any possible fashion.[74]

Almost at once the forecast figures improved, attaining by June 1944 an accuracy of 77 percent as to numbers of equipment items delivered, and 88 percent accuracy as to dollar value. Thereafter the summary data published by P&D Division each month showed a good correlation between percentage of deliveries forecast and received.

Pleased with the results, P&D set up a similar program to control production of newly developed items of equipment.[75] For each of the "hot" production items, one engineer from the developing laboratory and one production representative from the procurement district to which the item was assigned

constituted a development-production team (D-P team). The D-P teams acted as highly specialized nursemaids for the newborn items of equipment, coddling and shepherding their progress from the laboratory stage into the world of useful production. At the time, the Signal Corps had two hundred such items, the majority of them destined for the AAF, the most demanding of the Signal Corps' long list of customers. The D-P teams eventually were a resounding success. The closer collaboration between laboratory and procurement personnel insured prompt handling of technical and production problems.

Subsequently, in May 1945, the Signal Corps Ground Signal Agency inaugurated monthly development planning meetings. By this means production control reached back one step further in the supply chain. At the planning meetings, discussions centered around development projects about to be completed, facilities for placing development contracts, and ultimate plans for production quantities. Forewarned and armed with tracts and ultimate plans for production problems that might be encountered, the procurement representatives were able to avoid many a potential supply pitfall.[76]

Expediting

In its broadest sense, the expediting of deliveries involved many persons and agencies at headquarters, in field installations, and in contractors' plants.

[74] (1) Hist, PSCPD, I, 242-45. (2) Memo, Chief P&D Sv to Dir Prod Div ASF, 8 Sep 43, sub: Proc Status of SigC Items in MPR. SigC RP 400.12 Variations in Monthly Forecast. (3) ANEPA Wkly Prod Status Rpt for Week Ending 6 Aug 43. SigC DS 400.92 Prod Rpts, 1942 and 1943. (4) Memo, Actg CSigO for CG ASF, 18 Jun 43, sub: May Prod. SigC 400.12 Proc 1943. (5) Gerard, Story of Sup in the SigC in World War II, pt. III, Prod, SigC Hist Monograph B-1c, p. 53. (6) Review of Current Production Problems of the Signal Corps, presented by Gen Colton, Actg CSigO, at Staff Conf, ASF, 23 Mar 43. SigC DS (Harrison) Somervell Staff Mtgs.

[75] (1) Discussion of Dev-Prod Teams and Their Opn, 28 Feb 44, Incl 1, to Transmittal Sheet, Action 1, Asst Chief, P&D Sv, to Dir, Prod Div, 29 Feb 44. SigC DS (Harrison) Prod. (2) Hist, PSCPD, pp. 249-50.

[76] (1) Hist, PSCPD, p. 250. (2) Ltr, CO SCGSA Bradley Beach, N.J., to CSigO, 14 Jun 45, sub: Prod-Plng Mtg, and Incl 1, Notes on P-P Mtg, 24 May 45. SigC DS (Harrison) Prod.

With that view, any action that advanced the supply effort could be termed expediting. In the narrower sense, production expediting of electronic equipment was, until mid-1944, the special province of ANEPA.

The manifold problems attendant upon obtaining materials, expanding facilities, and in general operating the procurement machinery in the early days of conversion had brought the Signal Corps' Production Expediting Section into being in 1941.[77] The conflict of interests between the Army, the Navy, and the War Production Board had created the successor organization, the Army and Navy Communications Production Expediting Agency, in August 1942. ANCPEA was an agency of OCSigO, although its expediting responsibility extended also to communications equipment for the Navy. The Army and Navy Electronics Production Agency, a joint organization, was established on 28 October 1942 by agreement between the Commanding General, Army Service Forces, and the Chief of Procurement and Materiel, Navy Department.[78] A civilian director, it was

thought, could best enforce neutrality between Army and Navy demands. The ANEPA flourished, and soon there were regional offices at various procurement districts throughout the country and at several plants of the largest manufacturers of electronic equipment.[79]

The ANEPA served a valuable purpose, but from the Signal Corps point of view it was never entirely satisfactory as a production control tool. Confusion, duplication of effort, and a certain degree of friction persisted. Soon after the agency was activated, ANEPA, the Signal Corps, and the War Production Board signed an agreement covering field relationships.[80] The agreement did not please the contracting offices in the field. The ANEPA's regional officers, directed and controlled from Washington, worked far more closely with Washington than with the procurement districts they served. Signal Corps contracting officers felt frustrated because they were responsible for securing deliveries on contracts but the means for expediting deliveries was not theirs.

The creators of ANEPA had assumed that the agency would operate on a temporary basis only until industry got

---

[77] (1) For an account of the SigC Production Expediting Section activities in 1941 and of ANCPEA and ANEPA in 1942-43, see Thompson, Harris, et al., The Test, pp. 165-73. (2) A complete file of organizational papers for Production Expediting Section, ANCPEA, and ANEPA is contained in SigC 321 ANEPA Orgn, I, passim. (3) Detailed accounts of SigC expediting in general are contained in Clark, Expediting Activities of the Office of the Chief Signal Officer, August 1941-June 1944, and in History, PSCPD, pp. 185-233.
[78] (1) Incl 1, Tab B, Memo, CofS ASF for CSigO, 13 Aug 42, sub: ANCPEA, with Memo, Gen Marshall for Admiral Ernest J. King, CINCUS and CNO, 19 Oct 42, sub: Consideration of Your Memo, 17 Oct, sub: Electronics Precedence. (2) Memo, Colton, Dir Sig Sup Sv, for Somervell, CG ASF, 27 Oct 42, and Incl, Memo, CofS for CINCUS,

28 Oct 42. Both in ASF file, CofS Staff. (3) RG-200 files.
[79] Fred R. Lack of Western Electric Company was the first director, serving until 1 May 43 when Frank D. Tellwright of Bell Telephone Laboratories succeeded him. ANEPA's regional offices were located in Boston, New York, Philadelphia, Toledo, Chicago, and Los Angeles, and at plants of Western Electric in Chicago and Kearny, N.J., of General Electric in Schenectady, of RCA in Camden, and of Westinghouse in Baltimore. Address List ANEPA Regional Ofs, 15 Dec 43. SigC ANEPA Gen, 1944-45.
[80] Memo for Rcd (Lack), 1-10 Jan 43, sub: Duties and Responsibilities of ANEPA and Relation . . . to Radio and Radar Div of WPB. SigC 321 ANEPA Orgn, vol. I.

into full stride. Actually, in mid-1943, with the communications industry long since mobilized, ANEPA was still expanding. In June, its employees totaled over a thousand.[81] However, at the peak of expansion, by the latter half of 1943, industry was beginning to assume its own expediting work. The big five of the radio business—Radio Corporation of America, Western Electric, General Electric, Westinghouse, and Bendix—established their own expediting offices in late summer. Other manufacturers soon followed suit. With less work to do, particularly in the regional expediting offices, ANEPA began reducing its staff.

By January 1944, cutbacks in the Army program, plus better distribution and control measures and the cumulative effect of past conservation policies, eased the raw materials situation greatly. Copper, zinc, magnesium, and ferroalloys and alloy steel were in good supply. The technical services were encouraged to relax their conservation efforts, discontinue the use of substitutes, and reconvert to the use of original materials if such use would improve the military characteristics of an item, conserve labor or facilities, or result in lower costs. For example, there was now so much aluminum available that the services were urged to find new uses for it.[82]

Nevertheless, expediting activities could not stop overnight. Certain material shortages persisted; rubber substitutes, packaging materials, lumber, and chemicals were still in short supply.[83]

Signal Corps end items might be as simple as a $5 microphone or as costly and complex as a $160,000 radar.[84] There was never a time when there was not some sort of production bottleneck. Whatever the problem, Army expediters had to be on hand. The solution seemed to be to continue the function under new management.[85]

Over a period of several months in early 1944, functions and personnel were transferred back to the parent agencies.[86] To assimilate the Signal Corps' share, P&D set up a Production Field Branch in April 1944, and established field offices in New York, Boston, Philadelphia, Chicago, and Los Angeles staffed with 218 officers and civilians recruited almost entirely from among the 279 former ANEPA employees transferred to the Signal Corps.[87] In

[81] Clark, Exped Activities of the OCSigO, Aug 41– Jun 44, ex. 6, Number of ANEPA Pers.

[82] ASF Cir 3, 3 Jan 44, pt. III, sec. IX. ASF Contl Div file, 337 Staff Confs RG–200.02.

[83] CSigO Annual Rpt, FY 44, pp. 406, 418.

[84] For about the same amount of money that the Signal Corps spent for a single SCR–615 for the AAF, the Transportation Corps could buy a 100-foot tugboat, the Medical Department could purchase a 750-bed station hospital, or the Quartermaster Corps could get 1,000 storage tents.

[85] (1) OCSigO Engr and Tech Div, History of Signal Corps Research and Development in World War II (hereafter cited as SigC R&D History), vol. IV, pt. 4, Proj. 423–A. SigC Hist Sec file. (2) WD MPR, sec. 2–A, Distr, Storage & Issue, 30 Sep 43. ASF file. (3) Wkly Brief Summ of Prod Accomplishments and Difficulties Through 1943, passim. SigC DS 400.192.

[86] Memo, Mr. Tellwright, Dir ANEPA, for Rear Adm C. A. Jones, 24 May 44, sub: Disposition of ANEPA Pers. SigC 321 ANEPA Dissolution, vol II.

[87] (1) SigC 321 ANEPA Dissolution, vol. I and vol. II, passim. (2) Clark, Exped Activities of the OCSigO, Aug 41–Jun 44, passim. (3) Notes on Mtg of ANEPA SigCO and Certain Civilians with Hart and Prod Div Representatives, 29 Mar 44. (4) SigC, Prod Fld Of, Plng Memo, 3 Apr 44, sub: Establishment of SigC Prod Fld Ofs. (5) Memo for CC Dayton Proc Dist et al., 3 Apr 44, sub: Establishment of SigC Fld Prod Ofs. (6) SigC Prod Fld Br, Memo No. 2, 8 May 44, sub: Territorial Coverage of SigC Prod Fld Ofs. Last four in SigC IM 300.6 Fld Prod Memo, 1944–45.

the first three weeks of operation the offices handled 13,726 expediting cases, involving 440 items in 250 plants. Responsibility for more than 750 items remained to be transferred. Though ANEPA was dead, it left behind plenty of expediting work. From early 1944 on, however, the Signal Corps was entirely responsible for its own activities in that field.[88]

Manpower Control: The Signal Corps Labor Organization

One phase of production control—the amelioration of manpower shortages and labor problems—caused the Signal Corps relatively little concern. It was not that there were no manpower problems in the electronics industry, for they existed in abundant measure; rather the Signal Corps owed its relative freedom from manpower problems to the effectiveness of its own trouble-shooting labor organization.

Various civilian agencies, not the War Department, bore the principal responsibility for labor and manpower control. Yet undeniably the Army had a direct interest. The ASF, rent by internal disputes as to whether labor and manpower problems fell in the area of personnel or procurement, never developed a completely efficient labor organization.[89] Throughout the war the technical services played a vital role in the field of labor relations and manpower control. To the Signal Corps it seemed clear that manpower constituted a supply factor no less than did manufacturing facilities and raw materials. This was true even though the Signal Corps throughout the war kept its labor organization a part of the Legal Division.[90]

The Signal Corps was one of the first of the technical services to take forceful measures in labor control.[91] Apparently the Corps was also the only technical service to give special training to labor officers.[92] At the time the Signal Corps Labor Office was organized, ASF headquarters had not yet formally enunciated a policy on the handling of labor problems arising out of technical service procurement problems in the field.[93] In January 1943 ASF assigned control of such matters to the service commands on the theory that they were area problems. Events in late 1943 and early 1944 forced the ASF to appoint regional labor representatives who were also officers in charge of important technical service installations for the particular area involved. Thus, for example, Brig. Gen. Archie A. Farmer of the Phila-

---

[88] (1) CSigO, Annual Rpts, FY 44, pp. 433–34, and FY 45, pp. 568–74.

[89] For a complete discussion of ASF labor organization, see (1) H. M. Somers and John H. Ohly, War Department Organization for the Handling of Labor Problems in World War II, ASF-IPD Monograph 2, 1945, copy in OCMH files; (2) Byron Fairchild and Jonathan Grossman, *The Army and Industrial Manpower,* UNITED STATES ARMY IN WORLD WAR II (Washington, 1959), especially pp. 21–31; Millet, *Organization and Role of the Army Service Forces,* pp. 244–46, 329–31, 380–81.

[90] The Legal Division in fact was thought of primarily as an adjunct to procurement. See CSigO Annual Rpts, FY 42, pp. 16–24; FY 43, pp. 90–105; FY 44, pp. 61–83; FY 45, pp. 885–921.

[91] For accounts of activities, 1942 to mid-1943, see Thompson, Harris, et al., *The Test,* pp. 493–500.

[92] Log entry, 27 Jan 44, p. 85. DCSigO folder, 1942–45, SigC Hist Sec file.

[93] Lt Col James I. Heinz, Report of the Signal Corps Labor Office, 1945, p. 16. SigC Hist Sec file.

delphia Signal Depot served as the ASF regional director for Philadelphia.[94]

The slowdown in deliveries in mid-1944 could be blamed in part on overeager estimates of the end of the war,[95] but the developing manpower crisis was also a major factor. Throughout the late summer and autumn months, the labor situation remained exceedingly tight. The hard-pressed selective service culled many male workers, and WAC recruiting drives took many women employees. There was also labor unrest, many labor unions feeling that the time had come to abrogate their no-strike pledge. Absenteeism ran high, many women workers were quitting because of war fatigue, and on the west coast and in other tight labor areas many were leaving war industries to go back to their previous civilian employment. By December the situation was definitely bad; in early 1945 it was at its worst.

Equipment demands for the Army were very heavy in the last two months of 1944. Hard fighting and the severe winter weather drained off great amounts of material, which had to be replaced immediately. In addition, the Army was being called on to equip eight French divisions. Engagements in the Pacific had sent an unusually high proportion of naval vessels to repair docks, slowing down the construction of new ships on which the Army had counted. Civilian relief of liberated areas created additional material needs. Industry now estimated it would need

700,000 workers in the next six months if production demands were to be met. The United States Rubber Company at Lowell, Massachusetts, for example, needed 357 new workers each week to expand Signal Corps production of wire and cable; only 50 were obtainable. The military departments were convinced that the civilian agencies handling manpower problems were unable to solve a manpower shortage that was rapidly approaching the crisis stage.[96]

The Signal Corps weathered the manpower crisis without too much difficulty. Of the signal items on the critical list—field and assault wire, radar and radio tubes, and dry batteries—none was so far behind schedule as to endanger operations overseas. For another thing, the Signal Corps labor organization provided a substantial bulwark against the flood of anxious concern.

Labor supply officers and alternates had been appointed at all field offices in early 1943.[97] By mid-1944 there were 6 regional offices, Boston, New York, Philadelphia, Cleveland, Chicago, and San Francisco; 2 area offices, Buffalo and Los Angeles; and 3 labor liaison offices, at the 3 procurement districts in Dayton, Philadelphia, and Fort Monmouth. All reported to the Office of the Labor Counsel in OCSigO.[98] The labor officers concentrated their attention on wire and batteries, the signal items most

---

[94] (1) Millet, *Organization and Role of the Army Service Forces*, p. 331. (2) Heinz, Rpt of the SigC Labor Of, pp. 16–20.

[95] See above, p. 363.

[96] (1) Incl 1, Ltr, CofS and CNO to the President, 16 Jan 45, with Min of ASF Staff Conf, 17 Jan 45. (2) Memo, Dir IPD ASF for CG ASF, 12 Feb 45, sub: Dev in Manpower Situation . . . as of 12 Feb 45. Both in SigC 337 Confs Re Exped Prod and Manpower Shortages, 1944–45.

[97] CSigO Staff Conf, 5 Jan 44, Item 5. SigC EO 337 Staff Confs.

[98] (1) Heinz, Rpt of the SigC Labor Of, pp. 3–4. (2) CSigO, Annual Rpt, FY 44, pp. 69–73.

critically short. Wire manufacturers contended that they could not increase their production because of a labor shortage, but a survey undertaken jointly by the labor officer of the Office of the Chief Signal Officer and the Production Division showed the real problem to be the high turnover rate. Each of the regional labor offices in Boston, New York, Philadelphia, Chicago, and Buffalo then made a careful study of each wire plant in its respective area. Over a period of several months the labor offices introduced programs and methods to overcome absenteeism and thus increased wire production very substantially with only a minor increase in the number of employees.[99]

A similar survey of the battery industry revealed a true labor scarcity. Here labor recruiting drives brought outstanding success; in the fiscal year 1945 the labor offices conducted 158 such campaigns, most of them between September 1944 and March 1945, and most of them in the battery industry. The Chicago office staffed the Signal Battery Company of Milwaukee with 3,000 workers in less than four months. The Southeastern Regional Labor Office doubled employment—from 600 to 1,200 workers—at the National Carbon Company's plant in Charlotte, North Carolina, in less than three weeks. The industry adopted suggestions to improve morale that brought more efficient production. Labor officers obtained relaxation of wage structures under the "rare and unusual" rule of the War Labor Board (WLB) to correct inequities

in the low-paid battery field. The Signal Corps labor officers had become adept at getting favorable decisions in wage increase appeals. On a national average the WLB took 8 to 10 weeks to rule on a change. The Cleveland labor officer obtained a favorable decision for the General Dry Battery Company in 24 hours. The Southeastern Regional Labor officer obtained a proper wage structure for the National Carbon Company plant at Charlotte in 7 days.[100] In the summer of 1944 Signal Corps labor officers also obtained an exemption from the Department of Labor to permit female employees in the battery industry to work more than forty-eight hours a week. Apparently it was the only such exemption granted during the war.

In one case in 1945 the labor officers adopted the technique of bringing the mountain to Mohammed. The Burgess Battery Company in Freeport, Illinois, possessed more plant capacity than workers. All of the efforts of the War Production Board, the War Manpower Commission, and ASF headquarters to obtain more workers proved futile. So did a house-to-house canvass by the Signal Corps labor officers. But in Freeport the W. T. Rawleigh Company, manufacturers of patent medicines and home products, had excess plant space and workers. Since the Rawleigh employees would not transfer to Burgess, the labor officers brought part of Burgess to the workers. Over a weekend in early 1945 they transferred one Burgess production line to the Rawleigh plant. At the Burgess plant, employees who had previously worked a day shift on the

---

[99] (1) Heinz, Rpt of the SigC Labor Of, p. 47. (2) CSigO, Annual Rpts, FY 44, p. 72, and FY 45, p. 903.

[100] Heinz, Rpt of the SigC Labor Of, pp. 48–49.

transferred line manned a night shift on another line. Rawleigh operated the line transferred to it on a 2-shift basis. Thus the net gain amounted to two full production lines.[101]

The Signal Corps labor organization was not large—its peak strength, in 1945, amounted to 25 officers and 34 civilians.[102] But it was so successful that the ASF Labor Office called on it constantly for the loan of especially qualified men. For example, the chief labor officer, Col. Kenneth Johnson, spent 12 of the 20 months between September 1943 and May 1945 on duty with the ASF Labor Office working to increase tire production for the AAF and Ordnance. Other Signal Corps labor officers acted for ASF headquarters to spark recruiting drives in order to obtain various kinds of workers in New Jersey, railroad workers in the west, and electrical workers for the MANHATTAN Project.[103]

All through the early months of 1945 it was nip-and-tuck so far as labor supply was concerned, with the Signal Corps concentrating its greatest efforts in the wire and battery industries. By late April the situation was well in hand. A week or two later, the war in Europe ended, and the manpower shortage at home and in the armed services was over.[104] Redeployment and demobilization, however, would bring manpower problems of another sort.

Quality Control: The Signal Corps Inspection Agency

For most of the war years, inspection, like many another Signal Corps supply function, was organized on a "task force" basis.[105] This is to say that because the normal peacetime system of inspection would not at all fill the need for the vastly expanded duties of wartime, inspection became a self-contained, self-sufficient entity, not dependent upon any other segment of the supply system for support.[106]

The Signal Corps Inspection Agency had been activated in late summer 1942.[107] The agency headquarters was located in Dayton, Ohio, with five zone headquarters (activated on 5 October 1942) in San Francisco, Chicago, Newark, Philadelphia, and Dayton. Each zone headquarters was a Class IV installation that ran its own show in its designated territory. The zones issued the bills of lading required for transportation from point of inspection to destination, maintained direct communication with contractors and subcontractors on technical and inspection matters, handled their own personnel activities, maintained property accountability, and

---

[101] (1) *Ibid.*, pp. 49–50. (2) CSigO, Annual Rpt, FY 45, p. 906.

[102] CSigO, Annual Rpt, FY 45, p. 902.

[103] (1) Heinz, Rpt of the SigC Labor Of, pp. 56–58. (2) Log entry, 27 Jan 44, p. 85. DCSigO folder, 1942–45, SigC Hist Sec file.

[104] (1) Log entry, 27 Jan 44, p. 85. DCSigO folder, 1942–45, SigC Hist Sec file. (2) Rpts of the Regional Labor Ofs. SigC Hist Sec file.

[105] Address, Signal Corps Inspection, by Lt Col Eldon A. Koerner, former CO Dayton SigC Inspec Zone, and Dir SigC Inspec Agency, Sig Sup Mtg, Chicago, 26–28 Apr 46 (hereafter cited as Koerner Address). SigC 337 Sig Sup Mtg, Apr 46.

[106] For the transition from peacetime to wartime organization and activities of the Signal Corps Inspection Agency to mid-1943, see Thompson, Harris, *et al., The Test,* pp. 176–78, 324, 509–13. See also Gerard, Story of Sup in the SigC in World War II, pt. III, pp. 55–63.

[107] The letter establishing the agency was signed 4 September 1942, with an effective date of 26 August: Ltr, Dir SigC Sup Sv to CG PSCPD *et al.,* 4 Sep 42, sub: Establishing of the SigC Inspec Agency. SigC 400.163 Inspec 6, Sep 42.

displayed other manifestations of independence and self-sufficiency.

Through the period mid-1943 to mid-1945, the Inspection Agency employed an average of 6,200 civilians, whose payroll reached approximately $1,250,-000 a month. In addition, an average 217 military personnel, predominately officers, were assigned to the agency.[108] Agency inspectors accepted every month material worth nearly $200,000,000 and arranged for 25,000 shipments.[109] At more than 600 contractor plants, the agency maintained resident inspection groups, and in addition made many "roving" inspections.

Personnel remained the number one administrative problem during the life of the agency. The agency had absorbed a number of inspection organizations, each accustomed to a different set of administrative rules governing such matters as per diem, travel expenses, and salaries.[110] Gradually, uniform policies were established. Acquiring capable technical personnel posed no great problem but discovering or developing supervisory talent caused some headaches. Job management programs and a vigorous recruitment and training program solved this difficulty.[111] The effects

of selective service, which took many of the male inspectors, strengthened the trend toward employment of women in both technical and supervisory capacities.[112] In fact, the level of employment of women in the inspection field rose steadily until it reached approximately 65 percent, not counting headquarters office workers.[113] The Signal Corps' experience tended to dispel the myth that sex differences affect the capacity to absorb technical instruction. Said Lt. Col. Eldon A. Koerner, wartime commanding officer of the Dayton Signal Corps Inspection Zone, "These women demonstrated outstanding ability to absorb technical instruction and to perform capably as inspectors and supervisors on even the most complex types of radar and communications equipment." The agency also employed a high percentage of Negro workers.[114]

Accountability for government-furnished equipment (GFE) ranked as the number one operational problem. In the prewar emergency period and during the first months of rapid production expansion after Pearl Harbor, the goverment provided manufacturers with large amounts of scarce materials, components, and machinery in order to hasten conversion of factories to war production. Haste was the watchword; in June 1944 the War Department still had established no formal procedure to be followed.[115] Often a telephone call from an office in Washington started material from a Signal Corps depot to a manufacturer, without records or notification

---

[108] History of the Signal Corps Inspection Agency, 5 October 1942–2 September 1945 (hereafter cited as Hist, SigC Inspec Agency), Supplement A, Pers Stat, p. 2. SigC Hist Sec file.

[109] (1) *Ibid.*, Supplement B, Acceptances and Cost Statistics, p. 3. (2) Koerner Address, p. D-2.

[110] Specifically, inspection personnel from the Philadelphia Signal Corps Procurement District (which also performed inspection for the Chicago and San Francisco procurement districts) and from the Aircraft Radio Laboratory, the General Development Laboratory, and the Signal Corps Radar Laboratory were transferred to the Inspection Agency. Ltr, Dir SigC Sup Sv, 4 Sep 42.

[111] Hist, SigC Inspec Agency, Supplement R, Recruitment and Tng, pp. 1–3.

[112] Memo, Chief P&T Sv for CSigO, 20 Oct 43, sub: Retention of Key Pers of SigC Inspec Agency. SigC DS (Harrison) Inspec.

[113] Koerner Address, p. D-2.

[114] *Ibid.*

[115] TM 14–911, Jun 44.

to other Signal Corps agencies having a vital interest in the matter. The Signal Corps inspection zones felt a special concern because the property officer of the zone in which the contractor's plant was located was accountable for all GFE in that contractor's plant. The hapless property officer often found that involved GFE transactions had complicated his accounts almost beyond belief.[116]

Seven months before the War Department published its manual, the Signal Corps Inspection Agency had developed its own manual and standard procedures for GFE transactions. None of the controls proved entirely effective. With the end of the war, GFE transactions became insignificant, but the problem of settling wartime accounts lingered on. Eight months after V–J Day some 200 GFE accounts on terminated contracts still remained unsettled.[117]

Throughout the war, the Inspection Agency operated a laboratory that performed special inspection tests not possible in the field, made routine sample tests to check continuing quality on long-run procurement contracts, conducted research on specific new inspection problems arising in the field, prepared inspection procedures, developed new test methods and techniques, ran comparison tests on samples of items procured from more than one source, and accomplished a score of other important tasks.[118] In addition to all its other duties, the laboratory co-ordinated the work of the mobile calibration units of the Inspection Agency.

The first of the mobile calibration units was created in April 1944 to assure inspectors of the reliability and adequacy of test equipment used by manufacturers producing signal equipment. With the vast increase in amount and complexity of Signal Corps procurement, more and more small contractors with less previous production experience received contracts. Frequently they devised their own test equipment; naturally, not all of it was accurate. The Signal Corps Inspection Agency instituted a mobile testing program in 1943, on a limited basis confined to wire and cable plants near the Atlantic coast. Inspectors in a government car carrying calibration equipment visited the plants to check the manufacturers' testing equipment and facilities. The results were so valuable that the Inspection Agency expanded the program. The three inspection zones at Philadelphia, Chicago, and Newark each acquired ambulance-type 1½-ton trucks equipped with testing and calibrating instruments and operated by 3-man inspection engineer teams. Some manufacturers were at first inclined to be hostile, but all accepted the teams enthusiastically when the program demonstrated that it reduced the number of inspection rejections.[119]

The Signal Corps took the lead among the military procuring agencies in instituting inspection interchange agreements.[120] Under such arrangements in-

---

[116] Koerner Address, pp. D-3–D-5.

[117] (1) *Ibid.* (2) Hist, SigC Inspec Agency, Supplement N, Govt Owned Property, pp. 4–6.

[118] The Signal Corps Inspection Laboratory in fact predated the agency, having been established in July 1941 in the New York Signal Corps Procurement District in Brooklyn before that installation moved to Philadelphia. Hist, SigC Inspec Agency, Supplement J, The Inspec Lab, pp. 1, 4–6.

[119] *Ibid.,* Supplement K, The Mobile Calibration Units, pp. 2–5.

[120] Thompson, Harris, *et al., The Test,* p. 510.

spectors for one service performed inspection for both services in plants where both were procuring the same or substantially similar items or components. During the war, the Signal Corps placed single service inspection arrangements in operation at 119 plants throughout the country.[121] At 74 of these plants, the Signal Corps performed the inspections, while at 45 factories inspectors from another service did the work. Since the Navy purchased its own communications equipment while the Signal Corps had the procurement responsibility for all segments of the Army and, until late 1945, for the Air Forces also, the great majority of agreements were concluded between the Navy and the Signal Corps.

Assessing its experience with interchange inspection agreements at the end of the war, the Signal Corps concluded that a 10-percent saving in inspection manpower resulted. A much greater saving could have come from a firmer consolidation of procurement of like items by a single service.

The existing assignments of items to procuring services were based on the function of the using personnel in the field rather than on class of industry producing the item. For example, a canvas bag used by communications personnel . . . was assigned for procurement by the Signal Corps and a similar bag used in engineer operations to the Engineer Corps. In addition a number of common canvas items were procured by the Quartermaster Corps for common use. All this procurement involved one class of industry and potentially a single plant.[122]

In mid-1944, the inspection load in the southern California region justified a transfer of the San Francisco zone headquarters to Los Angeles. The move was made between 6 and 14 August, and the name was changed to the Los Angeles Signal Corps Inspection Zone.[123] Subsequently, the commanding officer of the Los Angeles zone became the head of a consolidated supply grouping that included, besides inspection, the field office of the Philadelphia Procurement District, the Western Regional Office of the Contract Settlement Agency, and a number of smaller organizations.

The high-level decision to transfer to the AAF all supply responsibility for communications equipment peculiar to its needs created grave problems for the Inspection Agency. Separating Air Forces and Army inspection operations was something like unscrambling an omelet. Inspection operations were thoroughly intermingled. Inspection Agency zones were organized geographically without regard to commodity, and a single inspection unit at each major plant handled both air and ground radios and other communications equipment. Segregating and transferring inspection of pertinent items to the Air Forces required a complete split in the inspection organization at all levels and much shuffling of personnel, not to speak of papers, files, and other paraphernalia. With much labor and a considerable amount of lost motion the separation was made, effective 1 April 1945.[124]

During its wartime existence, the Signal Corps Inspection Agency not only

---

[121] Hist, SigC Inspec Agency, Supplement I, Interchange of Inspec, p. 4.
[122] Ibid., p. 6.

[123] Hist, SigC Inspec Agency, p. 29.
[124] Ibid., pp. 30–31.

performed a supply function in an able and efficient manner but also introduced or extended a number of inspection practices that were to have wide application in the postwar years.[125] At the close of the war, the agency was inactivated, and the inspection function was once more assigned to the procurement districts.

The Crisis in Wire and
Batteries: A Case Study in Supply

Although the manifold supply problems that the Signal Corps faced during the war have been discussed at length throughout this volume and the two preceding it, the way in which the various supply factors interlocked and operated upon each other deserves a closer look. A recapitulation of events accounting for the critical shortages in field wire and dry batteries during 1944–45 provides a case study.[126]

Field Wire

The first weeks of fighting in France in 1944 quickly brought to a head the festering crisis in wire that had been building for a long time. It resulted

from a combination of many circumstances, some of them dating back to the procurement planning before the war. This is not to say that the planning was unsuccessful, because the wire plans of 1936, 1939, and 1941 contributed a great deal of very valuable information and pinpointed most of the production bottlenecks that could be expected. Together with the educational orders of 1939, they provided a solid working base for the great expansions to come.[127]

There were serious defects, however. Wire requirements estimates were much too low. Research for the 1936 plan brought to light a grave deficiency of stranding machine capacity but provided no plan for obtaining additional machines. The later plans, and the specifications for the educational orders, permitted either concentrically stranded or parallel-lay construction.[128] The plans did little to solve the stranding problem, but they did reveal manufacturing difficulties in insulating parallel lay, and what is more important, potential defects in the wire itself. Early in 1942 the Chief Signal Officer approved an engineering report recommending against parallel-lay construction.[129]

In mid-1941, when it began to suspect the bad news about parallel lay, the

---

[125] Details may be found in Hist, SigC Inspec Agency.

[126] The account is based on material drawn from the following sources unless otherwise indicated: (1) SigC 413.44 files, designated by equipment type, 1939 through 1945. (2) L. H. Drake and F. W. Thomas, Industrial Plng Br, PSCPD, Industrial Summary: Signal Corps Procurement of Wire and Cable, 1 Jun 46. SigC Hist Sec file. (3) Henry C. C. Shute, Prod Div PSCPD, Industrial Summary: Signal Corps Procurement of Dry Batteries, 15 Jan 46. SigC Hist Sec file. (4) CSigO, Annual Rpts, FY 44 and FY 45. (5) Hist, PSCPD, pp. 525–31. (6) SigC, R&D Hist, vol. V, especially Projs 512, pp. 2–6; 512–A and B; and 513–A. (7) SigC Bd Case 547, 26 Apr 44.

[127] (1) See Terrett, The Emergency, pp. 68 and 171; (2) Thompson, Harris, et al., The Test, p. 30. For summary of 1939–41 plans for W–110–B, see Drake and Thomas, Industrial Summ: SigC Proc of Wire and Cable, app. B.

[128] Concentrically stranded construction means using seven wires geometrically arranged and concentrically stranded together. For parallel lay, seven small steel or copper wires are fed concurrently into a vulcanizing machine, where the bunched parallel wires are covered by an extruded wall of rubber compound.

[129] Drake and Thomas, Industrial Summ: SigC Proc of Wire and Cable, pp. 13–31.

Signal Corps beat the bushes to flush out every company in the country that could possibly own any stranding equipment. It located 461 stranders, but less than 7 percent of them were suitable for manufacturing field wire W–110–B, the type that would be most needed. Pleas to the companies to accept government funds for expansion generally met a cold reception from the wire manufacturers, traditionally a group of ruggedly competitive individuals who felt that accepting government funds would lead to too much government interference with their businesses. On the other hand, manufacturers could not undertake expansion with their own funds unless they were assured of enough contracts to compensate for the expenditure, and no one could give such assurances. When war came on 7 December, only three companies (Anaconda, Okonite, and U.S. Rubber) had accepted Defense Plant Corporation funds under Signal Corps sponsorship for expansions amounting to $1,367,009, all of it for assault wire W–130.[130]

Meanwhile, after war began in Europe in late 1939, foreign orders poured in to American wire plants. Military concern that these orders would usurp plant capacity needed for domestic production soon gave way to the realization that the foreign orders were in fact providing experience to wire manufacturers and causing plant expansions. Lend-lease commitments to the British and the Russians helped to get new plant equipment quickly. A large commitment to the USSR for single conductor W–110–B carried an AA1 priority;

Signal Corps priorities for wire and wire-making machinery were lowest.[131]

The situation a month after Pearl Harbor was grave enough to set the most nerveless planners gibbering. The loss of natural rubber imports was expected, but the technical problems concerned with synthetic compounds were not yet known. Lend-lease demands for field wire W–110–B alone exceeded the highest over-all requirements anticipated during all the prewar planning years. As late as May 1941, military charts had indicated that 412,000 miles of W–110–B would be enough for the first year of war. Actual requirements stood at 832,000 miles by 1 January 1942. Requirements for 5-pair cables had multiplied thirteen times over 1940 planning estimates, and other types of wire and cable showed similar staggering increases.[132]

To production men the most maddening aspect of the whole problem was that no one could give them any firm idea of the probable requirements for any length of time. This lack of information continued to plague them until well into 1943, even while millions of dollars in government funds and more millions from the wire industry itself were being poured into plant expansions to provide for a production goal of 120,000 miles of field wire per month. Despite all the obstacles, production of W–110–B shot

---

[130] *Ibid.*, app. F, Chart 1.

[131] The Russians used single conductor wire, one of the wires of W–110–B, exclusively. The British received both single conductor and twisted pair wires. As late as the end of 1942, half of the year's production of 812,000 miles of W–110–B was single conductor, all of it for lend-lease, and almost all of it for the Soviet Union. Hist, PSCPD, pp. 543–44.

[132] See Thompson, Harris, *et al., The Test*, p. 30.

PREINVASION STOCKPILE OF TELEPHONE WIRE, THATCHAM, ENGLAND

upward throughout 1942, reaching 240,000 miles in the last quarter.[133]

But early in 1943 production rates took a dizzying nosedive. A major wire company was indicted for fraud;[134] a fire completely destroyed the Paranite Wire & Cable Company plant in Jamesboro, Indiana; Rome Cable Corporation had difficulty mastering the new, faster process for knitting the cotton covering instead of braiding it; Western Electric and several other companies were with-

drawn from production of W–110–B to work on spiral-four cable. Requirement planning lagged; the ASP of January 1943 stated quantities too low to keep the wire industry busy at the production rates already established. Production men in the Office of the Chief Signal Officer, convinced that the official program fell short of needs and that requirements would surely rise by midyear, scheduled the entire lot for completion in the first seven months of the year. Almost immediately the Controlled Materials Plan (CMP) went into effect, and its terms allotted only enough materials for officially approved requirements spread out over the entire

[133] Drake and Thomas, Industrial Summ: SigC Proc of Wire and Cable, app. D, Chart I, p. 3.

[134] (1) *Ibid.*, pp. 52–53. (2) Thompson, Harris, *et al., The Test,* pp. 511–13. Other prosecutions followed a few months later.

year. As a result, when requirements actually did go up sharply in June, many manufacturers had already committed their available capacity to other orders and the Signal Corps was helpless to recapture it.

Material shortages were pinching painfully. The CMP defined all wire mill products as "copper," though Signal Corps wire in its various finished forms used not only copper but rubber, cotton yarn, steel wire, vinyl resins, and nylon. Each became critically short at one time or another. Very early in the war, when it became evident that there would not be enough rubber for all needs, the Signal Corps turned to synthetics for wire insulation.[135] The development of synthetic rubber involved a truly gigantic industrial effort—designing new equipment and machinery for mass production, developing new manufacturing techniques, building new plants at a cost of $750,000,000. In two years, by the end of 1943, manufacturers were turning out 850,000 long tons of synthetic rubber of all types annually.[136]

The increasing shortage of labor hit hard at the wire industry in general, and the synthetics producers in particular. Each time selective service took a skilled vulcanizing machine operator or a man employed on a rubber compounding process, a crisis developed, for it took months or even years to train such specialized workers. The wire industry found it difficult to recruit labor because wages had been frozen at the relatively low peacetime rates.[137]

In the later months of 1943, though the downward trend in field wire production reversed itself and began crawling upward, requirements rose even faster. In the first three months of 1944, W–110–B production reached the same point it had attained in the last quarter of 1942, but requirements were two-and-a-half times greater. With the invasion of Normandy in June 1944, the situation quickly became critical.

The European theater was a "wire" theater. In the Pacific, the vast overwater reaches were inconsistent with complex administrative headquarter establishments, and the jungle raised formidable barriers against any extensive open wire construction. In contrast, in the heavily populated, urban areas of Europe, wire systems were essential. All this had been recognized, yet the seemingly tremendous quantities of wire requisitioned for the invasion of France soon proved to be insufficient.

The situation grew even worse following the breakthrough. The swift sweep across France to the Siegfried Line used up field wire lavishly and wastefully, because it left no time for wire recovery and rehabilitation.[138] In August the armies were using 75,000 miles of assault wire and 200,000 miles of field wire per month instead of the preinvasion estimates of 30,000 and 120,000 miles, respectively.[139] The War Department replacement factor for W–110–B, set at 50 percent in 1942 and lowered (against Signal Corps protests) to 44 percent in 1943, was increased to 75 percent for ETO in June 1944. Six months later the replacement factor jumped to 100 percent; by April 1945

[135] Thompson, Harris, et al., The Test, pp. 155–59.
[136] Drake and Thomas, Industrial Summ: SigC Proc of Wire and Cable, pp. 56–58.
[137] Ibid., pp. 58–59.

[138] See above, p. 124.
[139] Hist, PSCPD, p. 572.

the percent stood at 140.[140] By mid-August 1944 shipments of W–110–B had fallen behind theater requisitions by 230,000 miles, while shipments of assault wire W–130–A lagged by 100,000 miles.[141] There was only one thing to do —ration the theaters on a priority basis.[142]

The flood of requests for wire in Europe sharpened the worry at home. How could the Signal Corps increase production? Expanding the facilities was not the answer since it took two years, on the average, to build a factory and bring it to the point of useful production. The wire expansion projects of early 1942 were just now coming into full production. It seemed better to round out existing facilities to the maximum. Toward this end about $3,000,000 was authorized for stranding, braiding, twinning, and testing machinery. Getting the money did not necessarily mean getting the machines; it was very difficult to obtain wire machinery. Meeting in Philadelphia, worried Signal Corps, War Production Board, and industry representatives discussed ways and means of squeezing out increased production from machinery already in use. The manufacturers had a suggestion. Relax specifications, they said— Signal Corps performance standards were unnecessarily high; completely satisfactory wire could be produced under less rigid specifications. Rather reluctantly, Signal Corps agreed.[143]

Discouragingly, any increase in production of field wire soon brought about shortages of some of the materials used in its manufacture. Steel wire, especially in the 0.013″ size, soon became critically short. WPB assured Signal Corps that it would allocate enough steel to meet production schedules, but this was still not enough for a satisfactory inventory. Casting about for sources of supply, the Signal Corps discovered a quantity of steel wire originally intended for lend-lease and found that one strand of this wire could be combined with three strands of the regular steel to produce a satisfactory product. Using more than one strand gave a substandard W–110–B, but a product good enough for training purposes and even for combat use in Europe if plainly marked for one-time use only. Another discovery, a factory that could make a lightly coated galvanized 0.013″ wire, boosted W–110–B production another 2,000 miles per month. WPB helped by directing the yarn mills to produce specific quantities of cotton yarn for the wire-covering trade at the expense of other, less urgently required, production.[144]

Signal Corps and WPB sought to crack the labor bottleneck by putting the manufacturers of wire and cable on the National Urgency List for labor referrals in August 1944. Only a few weeks later, the insulating wire manufacturers who made the finished prod-

---

[140] (1) CSigO, Annual Rpt, FY 45, pp. 184–85. (2) Smith, *The Army and Economic Mobilization*, Table 23, Monthly Replacement Factors for Selected Items of Army Equip at Specified Dates, p. 190.

[141] OCSigO Prod Div, Qtrly Rpt, FY 45, p. 118. SigC Hist Sec file.

[142] (1) *Ibid.* (2) OCSigO, Annual Rpt, FY 45, p. 511.

[143] Drake and Thomas, Industrial Summ: SigC Proc of Wire and Cable, pp. 69–72.

[144] OCSigO Prod Div, Qtrly Rpt, 1st Quarter, FY 45, pp. 118, 155.

uct were taken off the list, and these plants failed to meet their production schedules. In December, they went back on the list. The November production schedules were sobering: only 81 percent of the required field wire W–110–B, 78 percent of the assault wire W–130, and 77 percent of W–143 could be provided, and these schedules did not take into account the amounts needed to provide a safe stock level. In desperation the Signal Corps appealed once more to the manufacturers, calling each in turn to Washington for conferences with ASF and WPB officials to plead for more wire. At the same time, the Signal Corps once more relaxed the specifications to permit a substitute design for W–110–B using plastic insulation without any braid at all, in order to take advantage of facilities released by the Navy. Additional relaxations from time to time permitted individual companies to utilize all possible facilities—a portion of low carbon steel or bronze wire instead of the scarce high-carbon steel strand; higher percentages of rayon instead of all-cotton braid. WPB used its directive power to set production schedules for the manufacturers, forcing them to defer less essential production.[145] By the end of 1944, W–110–B production reached 137,000 miles per month, and for the last quarter 391,000 miles.[146] In March 1945 it hit

an all-time monthly high of 185,000 miles.

Most of the concentrated supply effort in 1944–45 focused on the most needed field wire, W–110–B, and increased production of field wire took industrial capacity away from other types of wire. Although little has been said about it here, the problems of producing assault wire were in some ways even more complex.[147] One final factor affecting wire production arose from the ever-present necessity for introducing technological improvements, a process that inevitably slows production of any commodity.[148] Spiral-four and multiconductor cables, new packaging and dispensers, a new long-range field wire (W–143), and many other improvements were introduced during the war. There was, for example, AGF's urgent request for a new and improved general-purpose field wire. AGF wanted a stronger, more rugged, longer range wire than the standard assault wire W–130, yet very much lighter and smaller than field wire W–110–B. This wire, WD–1/TT, the Signal Corps began developing in 1943. WD–1/TT got into production in limited quantities late in the war. The Signal Corps thought so highly of it that it felt safe in saying "no other nation had a wire with comparable electrical and mechanical characteristics and with the minimum weight and volume."[149] Unfortunately the United States did not have much of it, either, in time for

[145] OCSigO Prod Div, Qtrly Rpt, 2d Quarter, FY 45, pp. 153–54.

[146] (1) Hist, PSCPD, p. 569. (2) Drake and Thomas, Industrial Summ: SigC Proc of Wire and Cable, app. E, Charts I–VII. Production figures for other types of wire in the last quarter of 1944 included 34,359 miles of long-range field wire W–143; 112,534 miles of assault wire W–130; and 82,201 quarter-mile units of spiral-four.

[147] See Drake and Thomas, Industrial Summ: SigC Proc of Wire and Cable, pp. 73–82.

[148] For a discussion of this point, see Thompson, Harris, et al., The Test, pp. 491–93.

[149] CSigO, Annual Rpt, FY 45, p. 242.

its use in battle.[150] That WD–1/TT appeared at all in the middle of the wire shortage is a tribute to American technology and American industry.

A further example concerns a new highspeed coil (wire dispenser) MX–301/G, which the Evans Signal Laboratory developed.[151] The laboratory built machines for the winding process, intending them only for depots in forward areas to repackage 2-mile reels of assault wire into shorter lengths. AGF received some wire packaged in the new dispenser and liked it so well that early in 1945 AGF demanded all assault wire to be so packaged. The new MX–301/G was indeed one answer to wiremen's prayers. With it they could lay wire silently, rapidly, and without rotating reels. Originated for laying wire from liaison aircraft at speeds up to 110 miles per hour, the MX–301/G could also be adapted to lay wire from manpack or from vehicles traveling 60 miles an hour. Crews could even shoot wire out by means of rifle grenades or bazooka rockets, and maintain continuous operation during the laying.[152] If all assault wire were to be so packaged, the Signal Corps had to provide more winding machines for the entire industry and teach the manufacturers the packaging process. The first Signal Corps machines were rather slow-winding, and the industry wanted no part of them. Eventually, the manufacturers spent a sizable amount of time and money developing better, faster-winding machines and improved packaging methods.[153]

Through the eleven months campaign in Europe, the Signal Corps was never in a comfortable supply position in regard to wire. The best that could be said was that there was never any really desperate shortage. In the last three months of 1944, General Eisenhower asked for field and assault wire on the basis of 500 miles per army per day, or a total of 67,000 miles a month. The Signal Corps, having shipped the general 72,705 miles in September, 85,800 in October, and 91,550 in December, was understandably surprised when an ASF labor officer stated publicly in January 1945 that Eisenhower had been receiving only 40,000 miles per month. This incorrect statement brought quick response from the wire manufacturers who were being pressed by the Signal Corps for even greater effort. One manufacturer, who alone produced 100,000 miles per month, asked heatedly what the Signal Corps was doing with all of its wire if that "horrible situation" actually existed.[154]

In January 1945 the Signal Corps shipped to the ETO 5,000 more miles of wire than asked for. By April it appeared that the expected cessation of hostilities in Europe would permit diversion of enough wire from the ETO to the Pacific to satisfy all demands. The ETO had consumed 900,000 miles of

---

[150] (1) *Ibid.*, p. 186. (2) Drake and Thomas, Industrial Summ: SigC Proc of Wire and Cable, pp. 76, 81–82.

[151] The project was transferred to Camp Coles Signal Laboratory late in 1944. R&D Hist, vol. V, pt. 1, Proj 512–B, p. 10. SigC Hist Sec file.

[152] (1) CSigO, Annual Rpt, FY 45, pp. 243–352. (2) R&D Hist, vol. V, pt. 1, Proj 512–B.

[153] Drake and Thomas, Industrial Summ: SigC Proc of Wire and Cable, pp. 80–81.

[154] Min, ASF Manpower Conf, 17 Jan 45. SigC 337 Conf Re Exped Prod and Manpower Shortages, 1944–45.

field wire in 11 months, 105,000 miles of it in the last month before V–E Day.[155]

Dry Batteries

Midway of the war, calls for dry batteries in astronomical quantities began to harry the Signal Corps. The dry cell battery was an indispensable item, for it was the power source for three hundred classes of military equipment. The Signal Corps alone used it in more than seven hundred items of equipment, either as a single cell, or in various combinations up to as many as ninety. Dry batteries powered flashlights, testing and maintenance equipment, field telephones, radiosonde units, direction finders, the small front-line radios—in short, any piece of portable equipment that did not require a large amount of power or that was used under conditions in which no other power source was available. Batteries were perishable; in commodity terms they were like fresh vegetables, which had to be rushed from producer to consumer because they deteriorated if stored for long periods of time. Thus under its prewar procurement methods, the Signal Corps calculated the number of batteries required annually and placed contracts for them as they were needed. Manufacturers supplied the batteries within a month's time after the orders were placed, sandwiching military orders in between civilian production. Once war was declared and civilian production greatly curtailed, the manufacturers

depended upon military orders for survival. It became necessary to schedule production in fairly even sequence in order to keep facilities in use and the industry labor force intact.

Prewar planning for battery production got bogged down before it even got started. Much of the important electronic equipment had not been produced, and some of it not even designed in 1940, so that it was manifestly impossible to schedule the kinds and quantities of batteries to be used in it. Hindsight suggests at least that it should have been apparent Signal Corps would have to change its method of figuring production in terms of battery types, while manufacturers were talking in terms of the cells that in various combinations make up batteries. Apparently no one realized a crisis was building until the end of 1942, when the Signal Corps sponsored the first expansions in the dry battery field.[156] Expansions were still being initiated in mid-1944.

Throughout the latter half of 1943 and all of 1944, battery problems received the concentrated attention of special Signal Corps "battery co-ordinators" and of a series of special "battery sections," which sprang up at one time or another in the supply organization of headquarters of the Office of the Chief Signal Officer, the procurement districts, the Chicago Signal Depot, and the Storage and Issue Agency. The strong centralized control that eventually solved the problem did not shape

[155] (1) CSigO Annual Rpt, FY 45, p. 5. (2) Wkly Prod Rpts, SigC DS (Harrison) Critical Shortages, ETO.

[156] A modest $892,300 to two plants of the National Carbon Company, 8 December 1942. These expansions tripled production at National, but not until March 1945. Shute, Industrial Summ: SigC Proc of Dry Batteries, pp. 18–19, 21, 28.

up firmly until the middle of 1944.[157]

Many problems needed attention. Though overseas users of American-made batteries preferred them above all others, American batteries still had shortcomings. There were too many varieties. This had come about partly because laboratory engineers, developing a piece of new equipment, very often designed a special type of battery instead of prescribing a standard battery. Men overseas reported that the batteries in the lightweight radio sets, notably the SCR–536, were inferior. Complaints of poor shelf life, of batteries that were either useless when received or that gave very limited service, persisted. If one cell, in a battery of several cells, failed, the entire battery became useless. In some instances as many as two hundred extra batteries had to be kept on hand to maintain one in use. This was partly a result of the procurement lag, partly the fault of poor packaging, and in part because the manufacturers who supplied some items of equipment furnished the batteries for them as well. This practice almost inevitably combined new equipment with time-exhausted batteries by the date the equipment reached the battlefields. Climatic conditions in some battle areas affected batteries adversely. The climate of the Southwest Pacific islands and to a lesser degree that of India and China could reduce a good dry battery to wet and moldy uselessness in no time.

From the day the first reports came back from the early Solomons operations, Signal Corps wrestled with the problem of tropicalization. In March 1943, the Storage and Issue Agency began working on packaging that could withstand immersion for forty-eight hours. Standards for tropicalization were announced on 1 July, but it was at least 1 November before they became very effective. Nevertheless, between April and September 1943 the Philadelphia Signal Depot packed twelve million dry batteries against moisture. One method covered the equipment with preservatives; an alternative method sealed the container with materials that absorb the moisture.

Battery manufacture required a dozen or so metals. Fortunately, except for copper and zinc, most of them were not scarce, but persistent bottlenecks cropped up in other necessary materials and items. At various times the shortage list included acetylene black, ammonium chloride, nails, nailing machines, extruding dies, presses, grommets, wire screen, paper slitters, mixers, steel cans, steel degreasers, molding powder, polystyrene, meters, conveyers, paper, foil, punches, granulators, heat treaters, and containers.[158]

---

[157] See: (1) Shute, Industrial Summ: SigC Proc of Dry Batteries; (2) Ullery, Hist, S&I Agency, I, 365–84; (3) Hist, PSCPD, III, 663–67; (4) OCSigO Prod Div, Qtrly and Annual Rpts; and (5) OCSigO P&O Div, Intel & Com Coordinating Br, Extracts From Operational and Inspection Reports Pertaining to Lessons Learned in Use of Signal Corps Equipment and Signal Corps Units, World War II, Microfilm No. 1, sec: Dry Batteries. All in SigC Hist Sec file. All information has been taken from these sources unless otherwise specified.

For discussion of dry battery problems to mid-1943, see Thompson, Harris, et al., The Test, pp. 497–98, 506, 516.

[158] Shute, Industrial Summ: SigC Proc of Dry Batteries, pp. 42–45.

In early 1945 lack of ammonium chloride would have stopped battery production had not the Chemical Warfare Service come to the rescue with 4,000 pounds it held. Ibid., p. 44.

Labor, too, constituted a limiting factor. The battery industry was concentrated in the heavily congested Chicago area, numerous new battery plants were coming into production, and the wage scale was low. Since the industry depended largely upon women workers, selective service demands were light, but on the other hand legislation restricting the hours of labor for female workers prevented overtime work and second shifts. The Signal Corps' Chicago Regional Labor Office did an especially good job of recruitment, moving into an area with a well-organized campaign of publicity and educational information. For example, at Freeport, Illinois, in October 1943, when the Burgess Battery Company lacked 600 of the 1,400 workers it needed to bring it up to capacity production, the labor officers put on a 3-day drive that recruited the 600, plus 175 applications that could be passed along to other plants.[159]

The situation reached an alarming climax in January 1944, when radio sets could not be shipped from depots because of the shortage of certain types of batteries.[160] Battery production was crawling upward, but too slowly to keep pace with the rising demands. The supply of acetylene black was dwindling fast; battery manufacturers were beginning to draw upon the stockpile reserve accumulated before the war began. It was touch-and-go whether the stockpile would last until the sole source of supply, a Canadian firm, Shawinigen Chemicals, Ltd., could expand its plant to capacity production.[161] Plainly the situation demanded a concentrated attack upon all elements holding back production.

The Office of the Chief Signal Officer had been gathering all the information it could lay hands on to assemble more accurate information on battery shelf life and operating characteristics. The information was essential in order to prepare more reliable estimates of maintenance factors, which in turn provided the basis for requirement planning. In December 1943 the laboratories had told their engineers to start using standard types of batteries whenever possible, rather than designing new types. Furthermore, after several weeks of negotiation, the Navy had turned over its battery procurement to the Signal Corps, in the interest of consolidating requirements. The two services then started work on joint Army-Navy specifications.

Until early 1944 all depots requisitioned batteries directly from the central repository, the Chicago Signal Depot, without regard to the total supply. If the batteries were in stock, Chicago shipped them, since it lacked any power to edit the requisitions. To center control in one organization the Storage and Issue Agency, on 25 January 1944, was given new powers, including that of stock control in the depots. In effect, the new arrangement made the S&I Agency responsible for co-ordinating and integrating all information regarding demand and capacity for filling it. Thereafter, the agency processed all requisitions for the most critical types

---

[159] History of Activities, Chicago Regional Labor Office, 14 December 1942–1 October 1945, pp. 29–30. SigC Hist Sec file.

[160] CSigO, Annual Rpt, FY 44, p. 113.

[161] OCSigO Prod Div, Qtrly Rpt, 1st Quarter, FY 45, p. 78.

of batteries. The procurement districts furnished S&I with monthly production figures for each battery manufacturer. With this information, the agency could allot the available supply to the points of greatest need. To pull all demands into one channel, the War Department, by Circular No. 175 dated 4 May 1944, radically changed the method of requisitioning within the theaters. Thereafter, all using organizations requisitioned their batteries through the Signal Corps channels within the theater, and each theater received batteries in bulk shipments based on the total theater demand.

These moves greatly simplified the problem of determining actual battery requirements. As a means of controlling production scheduling, delivery, and expediting functions, the Signal Corps divided the industrial area producing batteries into four sections and sent four picked officers from the Production Division of the Office of the Chief Signal Officer as "contact men" to the industry. This arrangement worked admirably. To shorten the supply lines and to assure fresh batteries for overseas operation, the S&I Agency worked out procedures under which the majority of batteries (and all of the overseas supply) were shipped directly from the manufacturers to the users or, in the case of overseas supply, to the ports of embarkation. The few batteries that went into storage at all were stocked in Philadelphia, Sacramento, and Chicago. Chicago, which had installed cold storage facilities in October 1943, stored the more perishable types.[162]

In June 1944 the battery industry produced 98,500,000 cells; in July, 114,-500,000; in August, 132,000,000; in September, 142,500,000. The Signal Corps shipped 30 percent more batteries to the ETO in August than in July, and 160 percent more of the most critical types such as BA–2, 38, 39, and 40. Still it was not enough. The Allied armies had liberated Paris and were sweeping across France; 6th Army Group forces were pushing up from the south in a second major invasion; and on the opposite side of the world Myitkyina was captured, Truk was bypassed in the landings at Saipan and Guam, and the Palaus operation raised the curtain for the recapture of the Philippines. In the year between October 1943 and September 1944, the number of troops on foreign duty tripled. In the same period the number of types of equipment in which batteries were used rose 247 percent. In the five months between March and August, consumption factors for batteries rose 176 percent, and the same period showed a 330-percent increase in requisitions over December 1943.[163]

Meeting in Chicago in July 1944, Signal Corps field production men mapped strategy to stem the rising flood of requisitions. They would curtail production of less critical types of batteries and concentrate on those most urgently needed. New packaging regulations, just issued, specified special construction of the containers, use of a varnish on steel jackets, and impregnation of the cardboard boxes with microcrystalline wax. These regulations, it was expected,

[162] Transmittal Sheet Action 2, S&I Agency to Chief Distr Div OCSigO, 1 Feb 44, sub: Rotation of Stock. SigC 400.211 Gen 1, Jan–Mar 44.

[163] (1) OCSigO Prod Div, Qtrly Rpt, 1st Quarter, FY 45. (2) Qtrly Rpt Distr Div Rpt, Jul–Sep 44, SigC 319.1.

would greatly reduce the number of batteries lost by shipping and moisture damage. (By this time, all batteries going to the tropics were tropically packed.) Expansion projects of 1943 and 1944 were adding useful quantities each month, but many of the plants had not yet reached their maximum capacity, and, if the labor supply grew more critical, would not do so. Stormy labor relations at the Ball Brothers Company in Muncie, Indiana, for example, kept labor officers tense. The company produced more than half of all the zinc cans for the entire battery industry. Two weeks before the invasion of France, a smouldering jurisdictional fight between competing labor unions at the plant had flared into "a state of civil war." The labor officers had persuaded the employees to go back to work, but trouble broke out again on 23 July, and the issues remained unsettled.[164] The labor office had conducted a successful recruiting campaign for new workers at the Marathon Battery Company plant in Wausau, Wisconsin, in May, and was currently engaged in its biggest order, 3,000 employees to staff the new Signal Battery Company in Milwaukee, slated to become the largest in the United States.[165] The labor officers were concentrating, too, on ways to increase production by stimulating employee morale and interest. Showing the

motion picture, "Objective Burma," brought good results. It emphasized that soldiers' lives depended on batteries for their front-line portable radios, a fact not always realized by workers on dull, routine jobs far from the battle fronts.

The best that could be said by the end of 1944 was that the gap between supply and demand had narrowed somewhat. In November blackout restrictions in the ETO were relaxed, and the BA–30 battery used in flashlights was no longer in such heavy demand. Facilities for the BA–30 converted to production of other types.[166] Dry-cell production reached 159,000,000 units in October and 165,000,000 in November. In December the Battle of the Bulge sent replacement figures upward once more. The ETO asked for 200,000 BA–40's alone in January 1945. The Signal Corps could supply only 160,000 and estimated that it would be April before it could reach the 200,000 figure.[167]

By February the Signal Battery Company in Milwaukee came into production, furnishing parts to the Battery Assembly Company at Billy Mitchell Field in Wisconsin, where prisoners of war assembled the finished product. January production totaled 184,892,000 cells; in February it climbed to 195,777,-000; in March it hit what was to be the all-time peak of 242,229,837.[168] By the last of March the backlog of requests

[164] Uneasy labor relations endured throughout the war in the ETO, with a third flare-up in April 1945. Despite this, the regional labor office so successfully calmed the warring factions that work interruption totaled less than four days, and the labor officers were commended for their efforts by both management and the union. Hist of Activities, Chicago Regional Labor Of, 14 Dec 42–1 Oct 45.

[165] Successfully, as noted above, p. 373.

[166] Transmittal Sheet, Capt C. H. Balfour, Jr., Redistribution and Disposal Br, to Capt L. E. Brockhart, Distr Div, 23 Nov 44. SigC 319.1 Monthly Digest of Prog and Problems.

[167] Min, ASF Manpower Conf, 17 Jan 45. SigC 337 Confs Re Exped Prod and Manpower Shortages, 1944–45.

[168] Shute, Industrial Summ: SigC Proc of Dry Batteries, Attachment 8, Dry Batteries Cell Prod and Dollar Value.

for batteries equaled fifteen days' production from all plants. General Ingles wanted a zero backlog and thought that he could get it by April.[169] And so he did, but whether it would have come about in the natural processes of production is open to question. By that time, production was up 125 percent over December, but requisitions from the ETO dropped off sharply in April. Almost without warning, the crisis was over.

Summary

The problems of producing field wire and dry batteries cannot of course be taken as typical of all Signal Corps supply experience in World War II. That so many of the possible deterrent factors were present in these two instances is precisely why it is useful to examine them. To some extent and in varying

number these same factors existed in other cases.

Undoubtedly the gravest deficiency lay in lack of requirements data. Prewar planning on a too-limited scale, the general lack of recognition by higher authority of the importance of the programs, capital equipment bottlenecks, conversion problems, and facility expansion were important factors. Shortages —of plant capacity, of labor, and of materials—caused grave difficulties. The Signal Corps' policy of maintaining rigid specifications, its lack of imagination in meeting changed supply conditions, and its generally inefficient reporting and expediting organizations in the early part of the war share part of the blame. Not the least of the limiting factors was the conflict between mass production and technological improvement.[170]

[169] Min, ASF Manpower Conf, 4 Apr 45, pp. 7–8. ASF file, NARS World War II Rcds.

[170] For recommended procedures compiled as a result of wartime experience in procuring important classes of Signal Corps equipment, see the series of Industrial Summaries listed in the Bibliographical Note.

CHAPTER XIII

Distributing Signal Supplies on a Worldwide Scale

With the initial equipping of the Army completed, replenishment became the principal supply task. The main stream of supply was directed toward Europe, with a smaller but steadily increasing flow to the Pacific. Deliveries had to be phased in such a manner that equipment came off the assembly line, was inspected, accepted, shipped to depots or directly to ports of embarkation, loaded on ships, and timed to arrive in the theaters as nearly as possible in perfect co-ordination with theater tactical needs. Both the ASF and the technical services bent their efforts toward perfecting the distribution system.

Within the Office of the Chief Signal Officer, distribution matters were principally (but not wholly) the concern of the Distribution Division from mid-1943 to the end of the war. The division provided staff supervision for operations relating to the receipt, storage, packing, marking, shipping, and issuing of signal supplies. Identification of items—stock numbering—was a part of its mission. So also were the repair of equipment for return to stock, and the disposal of surpluses. The vast depot system was its concern and, possibly the most important of all, stock control functions.[1]

Maintenance activities, however, were not a part of the P&D Service, belonging instead to the Engineering and Technical Service. Inspection was more nearly a distribution than a procurement function, although it concerned both. With spare parts, it seemed that everybody had a finger in the pie.

Storage Operations

In the early stages of the war, each of the technical service chiefs had exercised practically complete control over his own storage system. Soon after the March 1942 reorganization of the Army, ASF assumed staff supervision of storage operations of the technical services. By mid-1943, ASF had introduced some degree of uniformity into technical service practices. In the remaining war years, standardization accelerated. ASF shaped its policies toward developing efficient operation through use of modern production line methods, increased use of mechanized equipment, maximum utilization of space, and a functional type of depot organization.[2]

---

[1] CSigO, Annual Rpt, FY 44, p. 436.

[2] Capt Lyle D. Brundage, Storage Operations, December 1941–December 1945, ASF Storage Div Monograph, pp. 4–6, 12. Copy in OCMH files.

Reorganizing the Depots

Following an exhaustive study of all phases of depot operation, ASF's Control Division in March 1943 issued an important report, Depot Operations.[3] This document, popularly called Report 67, profoundly affected nearly every aspect of Army depot operations for the rest of the war.[4] Among many recommendations, Report 67 outlined a standard functional plan of organization for depots. ASF directed all the technical services to reorganize their depots in accordance with the plan by 1 July.[5] The resulting organizational structure in signal depots remained substantially the same for the rest of the war.

The chain of command extended from the depot commander through an executive officer and an executive control office. Each depot had seven divisions: Stock Control, Storage, Maintenance, Utilities, Transportation, Administration, and Personnel. The first three divisions carried out the basic depot mission, supported by the other four. The Stock Control Division could be thought of as the administrative mind of the operating divisions. Stock Control kept the records of stock receipt, storage, issue, and adjustments. The Storage Division, usually the largest of the three main divisions, cared for and stored all materials from the time they were received until final shipment was made. Its warehousing duties included proper packing and packaging, mechanization of warehouse equipment, identification procedures such as stock numbering, and so on. The Maintenance Division repaired all sorts of signal equipment returned from training areas in the United States, or from overseas. At times it also fabricated signal items.[6]

Late in 1944 a Property Disposal Division became a part of the depot organization structure. This division handled material returned from overseas and determined its disposition, whether to the civilian economy, to Signal Corps stock, or to salvage or scrap. Property disposal did not assume major importance until V–J Day.

In reality, the depot organization adopted in 1943 differed very little from that already in use at the principal Signal Corps installations such as the Philadelphia Signal Depot. The main effect at Philadelphia was to remove PSD from the jurisdiction of the Signal Corps Eastern Signal Service (SCESS), an administrative headquarters established in April 1943 to supervise eight separate organizations gathered together in Philadelphia. SCESS in its three months' existence interposed an additional administrative level between the Office of the Chief Signal Officer and the depot, a point about which the ASF Report 67 had complained.[7] SCESS was dissolved early in July and the PSD reorganized a few days later.[8]

[3] Contl Div, ASF, Rpt 67, Depot Operations, Mar 43.

[4] Brundage, Storage Opns, Dec 41–Dec 45, pp. 117–22.

[5] Memo, Maj Gen LeRoy Lutes, ASF, for Chiefs Tech Svs, 21 May 43, sub: Reorgn of Br Depots Under Rpt 67. SigC DS (Harrison) Depots.

[6] Novick, Story of Sup in the SigC in World War II, pt. IV, pp. 25–31.

[7] Summ of Conclusions and Recommendations, Rpt 67, Depot Opns, Contl Div SOS, Mar 43.

[8] (1) OCSigO Memos No. 72 and 73, 9 Jul 43. (2) History of the Philadelphia Signal Depot, 13 October 1941–31 December 1945 (hereafter referred to as Hist, PSD), pp. 219–47. SigC Hist Sec file.

Among the various signal depots, the lack of a standard pattern of organizational structure actually was less important than the lack of standarized operating procedures.[9] Foreseeing that if the technical services did not standardize their depot operating procedures, ASF would, the Signal Corps had been at work upon a publication, Standard Operating Procedure for Signal Corps Depots, since early summer of 1943. The first chapters were published in October 1943. ASF gave its blessing to the publication, but the depots were in no hurry to standardize.[10] Many depots had been writing their own instructions, based on their own extensive experience, but when ASF issued its own manual M–408, Depot Supply Procedures, making it mandatory that all depots follow it to the letter, all the signal depots put the Signal Corps SOP into effect without delay.[11] ASF accepted the Signal Corps publication in almost all respects as fulfilling the requirements set up by its own M–408.

Depot Facilities 1944–45

By early 1944 the Signal Corps was operating nine branch depots: Boston, Chicago, Dayton, Lexington, Los Angeles, Philadelphia, Sacramento, Seattle, and Holabird.[12] Holabird, in Baltimore,

had been taken over from the Ordnance Department in September 1943.[13] In addition, there were five Signal Sections of ASF depots—Atlanta, Belle Mead, New Cumberland, San Antonio, and Utah General Depots.[14]

The preinvasion build-up of stocks in late 1943 and early 1944 created definite warehousing problems for signal depots.[15] The bulk threatened to burst the walls of the one hundred or more buildings that housed the stocks. To accommodate their stores, the depots steadily increased their space and improved their facilities. Belle Mead, Chicago, Philadelphia, San Antonio, Sacramento, Los Angeles, and Utah added new space. At Dayton, where conditions had always been very bad because supplies were stored in a score of widely separated buildings, none of them well suited to warehousing, a huge, modern depot was rising. It was partially occupied by June 1944 despite a three months' setback from a fire in February that destroyed the original roof forms.

Statistics tell the story: in December 1943, Signal Corps warehouse and shed space totaled 8,543,000 square feet; in March 1944, 9,069,000; and in June 9,587,000. For the same periods hard-surfaced open-space totals were 4,329,000, 4,742,000, and 4,880,000 square feet, respectively. Gross open space

---

[9] Thompson, Harris, et al., The Test, p. 518.

[10] General Somervell wrote General Ingles complimenting the authors "both for the thoroughness of the job and the manner in which the material is presented." Memo, CG ASF for CSigO, 8 Jul 44. Hq ASF file, SigC 1942–44, RG–200 ASF Somervell, NARS World War II Rcds.

[11] (1) SOP, 1943, SigC 681, passim. (2) SOP, Instruction in Signal Corps Depots, 1944. SigC 681.

[12] CSigO, Annual Rpt, FY 44, p. 437.

[13] ASF Cir No. 75, 8 Sep 43.

[14] Previous volumes in this series have traced the development of the depot system to mid-1943. See Terrett, The Emergency, pp. 60, 100, 293–94; and Thompson, Harris, et al., The Test, pp. 28, 33, 174–83, 302, 514–20, 522–23.

[15] Memo, Capt M. T. Keil for Rcd, 9 May 44, sub: Accumulation of Depot Stocks. SigC OP 300.6 Memoranda for Rcd.

amounted in June to 7,039,000 square feet.[16]

In the last six months of war, the build-up of supplies for the expected invasion of Japan created another warehousing boom, especially in the west coast depots. Sacramento Signal Depot serves as an example. Sacramento had been designated a key depot for storage of radar, photographic, and teletype material to be shipped through the San Francisco, Los Angeles, and Seattle Ports of Embarkation.[17] To make more room, the Signal Corps moved supplies occupying 234,000 square feet of storage space from Sacramento into the Oakland annex in May 1944. Stocks in the annex soon overflowed the original 500,000 square feet of open space, filled up another 500,000, and, by September, pushed into still another 106,000 square feet. In the fifteen months between November 1943 and February 1945, booming Sacramento more than tripled the amount of tonnage it handled. It stocked 56,075 different items, 7 times the 1943 figure; processed 6 times as many line items; handled 5 times as many packages; and increased manhours of labor from 40,795 to 266,536. Total warehouse space occupied at Sacramento rose from 49,000 to 1,055,-000 square feet. Still, space was so critical that material that should have been stored inside had to be stacked in the open. Plans were drawn for a new

depot with 1,000,000 square feet of warehouse space, 1,250,000 square feet of open space, and housing facilities for 500 enlisted men and 500 prisoners of war.[18] This depot was about 30 percent completed when the war ended.

Although the expansion of facilities at western depots got top priority in 1945, other signal depots received their share of improvements, notably San Antonio, Chicago, Philadelphia, and Holabird. The Signal Corps finished the fine new building at Dayton, designed as an ideal depot, just in time to hand it over to the Army Air Forces in the transfer of responsibility for airborne items. Retaining its meteorological responsibilities, the Signal Corps established the Dayton Meteorological Depot as a subdepot of Lexington. As the war in Europe progressed, activities at Boston Signal Depot declined; it ceased to be of major importance and was designated a subdepot of Holabird Signal Depot on 1 March 1945.[19]

Depot Missions in the Chain of Supply

Each Signal Corps depot was charged with a specific supply mission, either as a key depot (the only depot stocking a particular kind of equipment), or as a distribution depot serving a segment of the zone of interior, or as a filler depot for a port of embarkation. Many

[16] (1) Qtrly Rpts, Storage Br OCSigO, for Jan–Mar 44 and 1 Apr 44–30 Jun 44. SigC DS 319.1 Digest of Progress and Problems, 1943–44. (2) CSigO, Annual Rpt, FY 44, p. 447. (3) Supplement to WD MPR, sec. 2–H, Storage Opns, 31 Jul 44, p. 5.

[17] (1) Ltr, Chief P&D Sv OCSigO to CG ASF, 31 May 44, sub: Depot Missions. (2) Ltr, Chief P&D Sv OCSigO to CG ASF, 11 Jul 44, sub: Depot Missions. Both in SigC 681 Gen (Depots) 1944–45.

[18] (1) OCSigO Qtrly Rpts, Distr Div, Jan 44 to Sep 45. SigC DB 319.1 Qtrly Rpts Distr Div, 1944–45. (2) 1st Ind, Actg Dir P&O Div ASF to CofEngrs, 9 Apr 45, on Ltr, CofEngrs to CG ASF, 6 Apr 45, sub: Acquisition of Land and Const of Buildings and Facilities for Sacramento Sig Depot. SigC DS (Harrison) Distr-Depots.

[19] Distr Div Digest of Progress and Problems, Mar 45 and Jun 45. DS 319.1 Digest of Progress and Problems, 1944–46.

depots performed several of these functions and at the same time fulfilled specific repair, assembly, and procurement duties.[20] Posts, camps, and stations within each of the nine service commands requisitioned signal supplies from a specifically designated distribution depot.[21] The geographic location of the depot in relation to the installations it serviced determined its designation as a distribution point. None was more than a few days' shipping time away from the stations it served.

The filler depots furnished the stocks for ports of embarkation to honor overseas requisitions. The earlier methods of correlating supply with demand in support of overseas operations had shifted between the alternatives of automatic supply, and supply by requisition. Automatic supply was favored for initially equipping units and for items such as rations and fuel that were consumed at a fairly uniform rate. Supply by requisition was the choice for equipment and items with fluctuating consumption rates. By the fall of 1943, experience had dictated an amended overseas plan recognizing that the method of supply for a given theater depended upon the stage of operations. Automatic supply was prescribed for the initial stages and, thereafter, a semiautomatic system that depended upon matériel status reports of critically short items which had to be apportioned among all the theaters. The ports of embarkation received these reports from the theater commanders, edited them to subtract quantities en route, then sent them along to the technical services, which parceled out the available stocks among the theaters according to established priorities. The European and Mediterranean theaters enjoyed first priority on most items, followed in order by the Pacific theaters and then the China-Burma-India theater.[22]

When a port commander received an overseas requisition, ordinarily he drew upon stocks from the one particular filler depot serving that port. If the item he needed was a key signal item, he had to go to the key signal depot stocking that item rather than to his filler depot. Thus in 1944 Dayton Signal Depot was the designated filler for meteorological equipment and maintenance parts for all ports. Other key depots were Chicago for teletypewriters, automatic central office switching equipment and parts, dry

---

[20] (1) Incl 1, Depot Missions, to Ltr, Chief P&D Sv OCSigO to CG ASF, 24 Feb 44, sub: Depot Missions. SigC-681, Depot Missions, 1944. (2) For discussion of key depot plan and designation of key items of Signal Corps equipment, see Thompson, Harris, et al., The Test, p. 519.

[21] In 1944 the depots serving the commands were:
1st Service Command—Boston Signal Depot
2d Service Command—Philadelphia Signal Depot
3d Service Command—Philadelphia Signal Depot
4th Service Command (except Tennessee)—Atlanta ASF Depot Signal Section
5th Service Command—Lexington Signal Depot
6th Service Command—Chicago Signal Depot
7th Service Command (except Wyoming and Colorado)—Chicago
8th Service Command—San Antonio ASF Depot Signal Section
9th Service Command—Los Angeles Signal Section (Southern Section of Service Command), Sacramento Signal Depot (Central Section), Seattle Signal Depot (Northern Section), and Utah ASF Depot Signal Section (Northern Section)
(1) Incl 1, Depot Missions, to Ltr, Chief P&D Sv OCSigO to CG ASF, 24 Feb 44, sub: Depot Missions. (2) CSigO, Annual Rpt, FY 43, p 55.

[22] (1) Logistics in World War II, Final Report of the Army Service Forces, 1 July 1947 (Washington, 1947) (hereafter cited as ASF Final Rpt), pp. 79–81. (2) WD Memo W700-8-42, 10 Oct 42, sub: Sup of Overseas Depts, Theaters, and Separate Bases. SigC OP 400 Sup Gen, Jan 42–Aug 45. (3) Memo, Actg Chief Rqmts Plng Br for Dir P&O Div, 1 Dec 43, no sub. SigC 300.6 Memoranda for Br Chief, Jul 43–Jul 44.

batteries, and certain manufacturers' telephones and parts; Holabird for photographic and fighter control equipment; Philadelphia for pigeon equipment; Belle Mead for fixed plant equipment, and so on.[23] Each port served a particular theater or group of theaters within a geographical area.[24] Days of sup-

ply varied from a minimum of thirty for some classes of supply in some areas to highs of three hundred for Nome, Bethel, Naknek, Ikatek, Søndre Strømfjord, and similar ice-locked areas. Weather stations in eastern and northern Canada were supplied annually as required.[25]

Depot Procedures and Problems

The Signal Corps' investment in depot stocks in early 1944 approached $1,500,-000,000, and its monthly transactions reached $350,000,000. Supplies in depots thus equaled roughly the total investment of the Standard Oil Company of New Jersey, or ten times the inventory of Sears, Roebuck and Company. Each month the Signal Corps depots handled as much stock as Sears, Roebuck and Company, Montgomery Ward, and the Atlantic and Pacific Tea Company combined. General Harrison reminded his depot commanders in April 1944 that they shouldered a tremendous public responsibility. Their first concern was to supply the Army adequately. At the same time, the depot commanders had to limit and control the quantity of stocks on the shelves and promptly and carefully dispose of supplies no longer needed. In other words, the commanders must discharge their trusteeship over the large expenditures in a sound and prudent manner.[26]

At the time General Harrison spoke,

---

[23] (1) Incl 1, Depot Missions, with Ltr, Chief P&D Sv OCSigO to CG ASF, 24 Feb 44, sub: Depot Missions. (2) Memo, Deputy Dir of Opns ASF for Chief of Transportation, 21 Jul 43, sub: Stocks at Ports of Embarkation. SigC 400.211 Maximum and Minimum List 1, Jan–Aug 43. (3) Incl, Schematic Diagram of Overseas Sup Plan for U.S. Forces, 25 Oct 43, with Memo, Dir of Sup ASF for Chiefs Tech Svs, 21 Jan 44, sub: Overseas Sup Plan. SigC OP 400 Sup Gen, Jan 42–Aug 45.

Except for the key items, the ports of embarkation drew signal supplies from the following depots:

New York and Hampton Roads Ports of Embarkation—Philadelphia Signal Depot and New Cumberland ASF Signal Section

Baltimore and Philadelphia Cargo Ports of Embarkation—Philadelphia Signal Depot

Boston Port of Embarkation—Boston Signal Depot

New Orleans Port of Embarkation—Chicago Signal Depot

Charleston Port of Embarkation—Atlanta ASF Signal Section

Los Angeles Port of Embarkation—Los Angeles Signal Depot

San Francisco Port of Embarkation—Sacramento Signal Depot

Seattle Port of Embarkation and Portland Sub-Port—Seattle Signal Depot

[24] In 1943–44, the ports supplied these areas:

New York Port of Embarkation—European Theater of Operations (except Iceland), and North Africa (except French West Africa and Senegal)

Boston Port of Embarkation—French West Africa

Charleston Port of Embarkation—Senegal and the African Middle East Theater (including Persian Gulf, Central African, and Middle East Commands)

San Francisco Port of Embarkation—Southwest Pacific, South Pacific, Central Pacific, and the Hawaiian Group

Los Angeles Port of Embarkation—China-Burma-India Theater

New Orleans Port of Embarkation—Latin American Theater

Seattle Port of Embarkation—Alaskan Theater

[25] Incl 1, Chart, Minimum and Operating Levels in Days of Sup, 1 Feb 44, with AG Ltr 400 (11 Jan 44) OB–S–E–M, 20 Jan 44, sub: Levels of Sup for Overseas Areas, Depts, Theaters, and Bases. SigC OP 400 Sup Gen, Jan 42–Aug 45.

[26] (1) Harrison, Opening Remarks, 16 Apr 44, Sig Sup Mtg, Chicago, 16–17 Apr 44. (2) Rpts, Sig Sup Mtgs, 14–15 Nov 43, 13–15 Feb 44, 16–17 Apr 44. SigC Hist Sec file.

the Signal Corps depots had in fact brought their operations to the highest state of efficiency achieved so far during the war. One of the more persistent problems, that of the number of back orders in the depots, had been eliminated. Diligent attention to finding substitutions for items requisitioned but not in stock and expediting actions to get certain urgently needed items delivered more quickly solved the problem.[27] Under the stimulus of critical attention, back orders decreased steadily. Of the 82,330 items stocked, the percentage on back order dropped in March 1944 to 4.2 percent and by April approached the vanishing point by reaching the "very minimum." [28]

To prevent a repetition of the backlog and to bring all the participating agencies into synchronization, the Signal Corps introduced new master procurement and issue control lists for all set assemblies and their components. The development laboratories—Fort Monmouth Signal Laboratory, Camp Evans Signal Laboratory, Aircraft Radio Laboratory—the Signal Corps Photographic Center, and the Plant Engineering Agency prepared the lists. Except at Fort Monmouth, a private engineering firm actually did the work and also wrote packaging specifications for the Storage and Issue Agency. Stock numbering experts studied each part to determine whether it was interchangeable electrically and mechanically with others produced by other manufacturers. If so, they assigned a single stock number, then cross-referenced duplicate and superseded stock numbers. Common components that were themselves subassemblies were grouped according to the highest common factor of parts for every piece of equipment in which they were used, to bring about the maximum flexibility of stocks and to provide complete "where used" information for each component. The engineers consolidated nearly 20,000 active stock numbers to about 6,000, thereby eliminating stock records at individual depots and at the S&I Agency on some 14,000 items.

Many benefits resulted. Depots conserved floor space as identical items stocked under different numbers were discovered and brought together. Subassemblies set up on the procurement-and-issue control lists could be assembled into sets without opening packages to add or remove items within the assembly. Set assembly schedules computed by electrical machines could use a limited number of components in various combinations to make a maximum number of sets. For almost the first time depots began to find their physical inventories in substantial agreement with their depot stock records. Contracting officers consolidated their procurement orders for components common to several types of equipment. By April 1944, 600 procurement-and-issue control lists with matching packaging specifications were available; the Stock Numbering Agency (SNA) was issuing corrected stock numbers, and teams of officers were in the field helping depots to convert their stock. The whole project was co-ordinated with the fungus-proofing, rust-

[27] Memo, O/C Inventory Contl Sec for ExecO Dist Div, 1 Dec 43, sub: Rpt of Progress. SigC FL 319.1 Progress Rpt, Inventory Contl Sec.

[28] (1) Ibid. (2) Memo, O/C Inventory Contl Sec for Capt J. D. Apolant, 1 Feb 44, sub: Rpts. (3) Memo, O/C Depot Ln Sec for Apolant, 29 Apr 44, sub: Digest of Progress and Problems of Depot Ln Sec for Period 25 Mar Through 25 Apr. Last two in SigC DS 319.1 Digest of Progress and Problems, 1943–44.

proofing, and repackaging programs.[29]

Manpower problems continually plagued the depots. Increasingly, all of them hired women workers, who performed dozens of jobs heretofore assigned exclusively to male employees.[30] Holabird Signal Depot used German prisoners of war very effectively. The first contingent, which arrived at Holabird on 20 May 1944, worked in the laundry, the warehouses, the mess, the post garage, and the automotive pool. On the salvage lot the POW's operated acetylene torches, power-driven saws, and cutting machines, preparing salvaged metals and lumber for sale or for further use in the depot. Under a policy of "fairness and firmness," the POW's proved to be excellent workers. No problems of discipline arose.[31] Philadelphia Signal Depot's first German prisoners of war arrived early in 1945.[32] In the opinion of the depot's commanding officer, the German POW's were considerably more productive than American civilian employees.[33]

Increased use of materials handling equipment helped alleviate manpower shortages. Since there was not enough of this type of equipment to meet the needs of all the military services at home and overseas and of the civilian economy as well, the War Department in 1942 had centralized all allocation and control of the equipment for the Army in the Storage Division, ASF.[34] All the signal depots continued installing mechanized equipment whenever they could lay hands on it. The number of fork-lift trucks in use tripled in the fiscal year ending 30 June 1944—from 115 to 345. In the same period the depots increased their pallets almost sevenfold—from 56,266 to 384,439.[35]

At Holabird the Signal Corps inaugurated many experiments in packing and warehousing. For example, Holabird developed better box pallets, designed to hold small items without crushing them, and without special packing or excessive handling. Holabird designed pallets with adjustable cornerposts that could be lengthened or shortened to conform to the size of the items to be stored. Depot officials set up scale models of storage areas, freight cars, handling equipment, and material to be stored. They estimated that a few minutes' study with the scale models resulted in better ways of storing every shipment, a saving of 10 to 25 percent of the floor area, and more economical use of vertical space. Holabird developed a new and superior method of bundling crossarms for telephone poles that reduced space requirements and handling time by 25 to 50 percent. The depot also fitted fork-

[29] (1) Memo, O/C Depot Ln Sec for Apolant, 29 Apr 44, sub: Digest of Progress and Problems of the Depot Ln Sec for the Period 25 Mar Through 25 Apr, SigC DS 319.1 Digest of Progress and Problems, 1943–44. (2) ASF Transmittal Sheet, Harrison to CG Air Tech Sv Comd, 20 Dec 44, sub: Pers for P&I Contl List Work. (3) OCSigO Memo, Ser 117, 11 Aug 44, sub: SigC Parts Contl Lists. Last two in SigC DS (Harrison) Distr.

[30] Qtrly Rpts, Storage Br OCSigO, 1 Apr 44–30 Jun 44. SigC DS 319.1 Digest of Progress and Problems, 1943–44.

[31] Historical Report of Activities, Holabird Signal Depot, vol. I, 8 September 1943–31 March 1944, and vol. II, 1 April 1944–30 June 1944 (hereafter referred to as Hist Rpt of Activities, Holabird Sig Depot). SigC Hist Sec file.

[32] The first contingent of 30 POW's from 250 requested by the Commanding General, PSD, arrived on 31 January 1945. History, PSD, pp. 438, 468.

[33] Interv, SigC Hist Div with Col Frank E. Eldredge, Mar 46. SigC Hist Sec file.

[34] For a complete history of materials handling equipment problems and operations in World War II, see Brundage, Storage Operations, pages 50–90.

[35] CSigO, Annual Rpt, FY 44, p. 447.

lift trucks with a special device that permitted the stacking of pallets and material in high ricks.[36]

Lexington usually paced the field in efficiency of operations.[37] By late 1944, improved operating methods and work simplification had brought all the depots in the Signal Corps system to a satisfying level of performance.[38]

In the fiscal year ending 30 June 1945, Signal Corps depots handled 1,554,000 shipments, 33 percent more than in 1944. Tonnage handled rose to 1,738,000 tons.[39]

Stock Control Measures
Mid-1943 to 1945

Stock control—the synchronization and bringing into balance of the various phases of receipt, storage, and issue of supplies—lay at the very heart of the distribution system. It was not a simple matter: in some degree or another stock control affected or was affected by most of the elements of supply. Moreover, each element was linked to another in a complex formula. Any disturbance of the formula was likely to set off chain reactions involving the whole procurement cycle as well as the diverse parts of the distribution system.

At the outset of war stock control practices among the various technical services varied widely. Each technical service chief operated under methods proved acceptable to the peculiar needs of his own organization by many years of experience under peacetime conditions. Within a few months it became clear that uniform stock control practices were an absolute necessity in order to deal with the multitude of administrative, technical, and physical problems resulting from the enormous increase of Army stocks.[40] The ASF undertook the difficult task of establishing a standard method of stock control among all the technical services.[41] ASF's first step was to inaugurate exhaustive studies of existing depot and stock control methods; its second was to issue a series of manuals setting forth mandatory systems to be used by all the technical services.[42]

Setting Stock Levels

As the central control point for all signal stock movements, the Storage and Issue Agency established stock levels in signal depots and signal sections of general depots.[43] S&I began setting levels in January 1935, while organizationally still a section within OCSigO headquarters.[44] At that time the process was simple—each depot sent in a list showing each signal item carried in stock, identified by stock number and nomenclature, and the recommended minimum and

---

[36] Hist Rpt, Activities, Holabird SD, 8 Sep 43–31 Mar 44, pp. 4–10.

[37] History of the Lexington Signal Depot, ch. 9 (Oct–Dec 43), charts 22, 23, and 24, and ch. 10 (Jan–Mar 44), charts 10, 11, and 12. SigC Hist Sec file. See also WD MPR, sec. 2–H, Storage Opns, for period cited.

[38] SigC 681, Depot Opns, Gen, 1944–45, passim.

[39] CSigO, Annual Rpt, FY 45, p. 948.

[40] ASF Distr Div Monograph, History of Stock Control, U.S. Army, pp. 1–50, passim. Copy in OCMH files. The monograph contains a complete account of the development and application of ASF stock control procedures.

[41] ASF Final Rpt, pp. 79–80.

[42] Thompson, Harris, et al., The Test, pp. 518–20.

[43] S&I Agency, Study of Stock Control, Supply and Stock Numbering, Jul 46, p. 1. SigC Hist Sec file. This publication, issued by the Training Staff, S&I, contains much valuable information on stock control methods and procedures.

[44] OCSigO Cir 1–7, 15 Jan 35.

maximum levels. S&I consolidated the information and set the final levels, basing its decisions on depot recommendations, previous years' issue experience, and number of organizations and equipment items in the field to be maintained. It revised the levels periodically to meet changing conditions. When stocks reached the minimum level (the reorder point), the depot placed a requisition on S&I, which then initiated replenishment procurement of the item.[45] This procedure served until July 1942, when the Office of the Chief Signal Officer took over the replenishment purchasing and instituted additional control records.[46]

A grave weakness in the Signal Corps system, according to an ASF study of September 1942, was that it based stock issue rates on the movement of merchandise from depots to the stations rather than on actual consumption by the user. The ASF also found duplications of stock numbers, a maldistribution of stock between depots, duplications of records, and a lack of co-ordination between OCSigO sections and branches.[47] The Chief Signal Officer at once began an intensive effort to correct these faults. One of his first moves decentralized the stock control functions and established S&I as a separate agency.[48] Further moves in general followed ASF directives. The ASF considered its stock control system "the most important single wartime improvement in distribution operations within the Zone of the Interior." [49]

Just before the ASF placed its system

of stock control into operation in mid-1943, the technical services undertook a complete physical inventory of all supplies available for issue at depots, posts, camps, and stations. The first eighteen months of war had left in these repositories a large amount of communications equipment that was unusable either because it was not completely identified or because the proper authorities did not know of its location. The inventories unearthed many carloads of equipment, which were sent to depots. Depot housekeeping was overhauled, stock redistributed upon a more equitable basis, and much rewarehousing accomplished.[50]

On 1 June 1943 ASF instituted its own procedures for establishing supply levels for all items of equipment carried at depots and reserve points. The system discarded depot minimums and maximums in favor of "reorder points" and "maximum distribution levels." ASF defined the maximum distribution level as the quantity of supply stock, on hand or due in, necessary to maintain enough working stock for issue to the depot's assigned area. It was calculated by a simplified method of multiplying the estimated monthly demand by a factor determined by the "procurement interval" for each item. The procurement interval was the time from initiation of procure-

[45] Ullery, Hist of the S&I Agency, I, 297.

[46] (1) *Ibid.*, p. 296. (2) OCSigO Cir 1–7, 30 Jul 42.

[47] ASF Dist Div Monograph, Hist, Stock Contl, U.S. Army, pp. 54–58.

[48] Thompson, Harris, *et al.*, *The Test*, pp. 514–15.

[49] *ASF Final Rpt*, p. 79.

[50] (1) Memo, Harrison for Ingles, 1 Sep 43, sub: P&D Sv. SigC DS (Harrison) Orgn P&D Sv. (2) Hist, PSD, III, 267. (3) Progress Rpt, Inventory Contl Sec, *passim.* (4) Ullery, Hist, S&I Agency, I, 66–75. (5) ASF Memo S700–18–43, 26 Mar 43, Determination of "On Hand" Figures as of 1 Jul 43, for Use in the Army Sup Prog. (6) Memo, unsigned, 27 Mar 43, Method of Taking Stock Inventory. (7) ASF Memo S700–23–43, 24 Apr 43, Method of Taking Stock Inventory. Last three in SigC 400.211 Maximum and Minimum List 1, Jan–Aug 43. (8) CSigO, Annual Rpt, FY 44, pp. 440–43. (9) ASF Dist Div Monograph, Hist, Stock Contl, U.S. Army, pp. 125–26, 139–41.

ment to delivery of an article. This might be 3, 4, 5, or 6 months—no item was considered to have a procurement interval of more than 6 months. Two factors determined the minimum level or reorder point for each depot—a basic "on hand" stock level not to exceed 60 days' supply and a replenishment stock level representing expected demand during the procurement interval for the item. In addition, there was to be a "utility reserve"—a quantity of stocks earmarked for a planned operation—and a "contingency reserve," to be set by the technical service concerned to cover demands for a period of time in case production were interrupted.[51] Such computations guided the Storage and Issue Agency in deciding whether to procure, cut back open procurement orders, or take no action.[52]

The ASF procedure was not entirely suited to Signal Corps operations. Based on the concept of depots as distribution depots only, it had the depots set their own maximum depot level on the basis of issue experience. The Signal Corps, however, had no depots whose sole function was distribution to posts, camps, and stations, and therefore used condition coding to identify the stock carried in various specialized categories within depots. Thus stock for nonrestricted issue might be carried on stock records in code condition 01, controlled items in 41, Plant Engineering Agency items in 04, set assembly reserve stock in 07, and so on. These code indicators permitted stock to be segregated, resulting

in much faster processing of paper work.[53]

On 21 December 1943, when the ASF issued a supply directive that called upon the technical services to classify their depots as filler, distribution, reserve, or key, and to determine the proper stockage of each major commodity according to the individual depot mission, Col. Frank E. Eldredge, commanding officer of S&I, anticipated that eventually the ASF system of determining stock levels would be extended to all depots. In the case of the Signal Corps that meant that there would have to be four stockpiles within the same depot for inventory purposes and four sets of stock cards listing almost the same items. Already, with only partial adoption of the program, the number of stock records had multiplied, increasing the paper work at both the depots and within the Storage and Issue Agency. Said Eldredge:

It is questionable whether or not we have gone so far with our present system that we cannot at this time turn our operation around and start over on a new basis. However, to compromise the situation . . . for the sole purpose of satisfying the Army Service Forces is multiplying by tenfold the amount of work required and the consequent chance of error. . . . Storage and Issue Agency is in the middle.[54]

[51] (1) Ullery, Hist, S&I Agency, I, 297–99. (2) Memo, Dir Opns ASF for CSigO, 13 Jul 43, sub: Depot Stock Levels. SigC 400.211 Maximum and Minimum List 1, Jan–Aug 43.

[52] Qtrly Rpt, Distr Div, Jul–Sep 43. SigC Fl 319.1, Progress Rpt, Inventory Contl Sec.

[53] (1) Transmittal Sheet, CO S&I Agency to Dir Distr Div OCSigO, 15 Dec 43, sub: Differences Between Current System of Stock Contl in the SigC and Recommended Procedures of ASF. SigC 400.211 Maximum and Minimum List 2, Sep–Dec 43. (2) Ullery, Hist, S&I Agency, I, 73–74. The Philadelphia Signal Depot was using 27 different condition codes in 1945. Hist, PSD, 31 Oct 41–31 Dec 45, pp. 442–44.

[54] Transmittal Sheet, CO S&I Agency to Dir Distr Div OCSigO, 15 Dec 43, sub: Differences Between Current System of Stock Contl in the SigC and Recommended Procedures of ASF. SigC 400.211 Maximum and Minimum List 2, Sep–Dec 43.

The point seemed to be that, although standardization is an excellent thing, flexibility, too, is not without merit. As a matter of fact ASF policies on stock levels—and stock control in general—were not altogether inflexible, and in any event were put into effect gradually. ASF made some concessions to meet the Signal Corps' special needs, and by the end of the war Signal Corps procedures were generally satisfactory to ASF. The Storage and Issue Agency continued to set depot stock levels and to initiate action to maintain such levels throughout the war.[55]

Stock Numbering

If an accurate means of item identification is lacking, any stock control system must fail. Each Signal Corps item, large or small, bore a distinctive nomenclature, a description of its physical and electrical properties or performance, a stock number, an IBM code number, and other descriptive data. Various sections of catalogs, parts lists, and other publications contained this information. If competently and completely described, a Signal Corps item would be at least as easy to identify as an individual whose full name, age, sex, residence, occupation, blood type, Social Security number, and fingerprints were known.

Unfortunately, midway in the war, part or all of the vital statistics of signal items were lacking in many cases. The stock number was the most important part of the item identification system.

The Signal Corps always assigned stock numbers to items and parts of items appearing on tables of basic allowances, tables of equipment, and tables of organization; to expendable supplies; to items used in development projects; to standard assemblies; and to each component of standard assemblies. Under the pressure of wartime procurement procedures, however, many items bore incomplete descriptions, not detailed enough to provide data on which to issue a stock number. Some bore manufacturers' part numbers instead of stock numbers. Others carried several stock numbers, particularly items used by more than one branch of the armed services.

At the beginning of the war, a small group of specialized engineers in the Nomenclature Section of the Engineering and Technical Service, OCSigO, performed the stock numbering function. The enormous increase in the number of signal items and parts and the pressure to issue items quickly created a corresponding increase in the workload. Delays in issuing stock numbers seemed to make it imperative to decentralize the stock numbering activity to the field, closer to the procurement and issue activities. In December 1942 a group of employees from the Nomenclature Section moved to Philadelphia to form the nucleus of a new field agency whose sole function would be stock numbering. The Signal Numbering Agency was formally activated in January 1943 as a Class IV activity under the staff supervision of the Research and Development Division, E&T Service.[56] SNA set up a headquar-

[55] Ullery, Hist, S&I Agency, I, 129, 135, 297–303. For detailed accounts of actions taken to comply with ASF procedures, see the quarterly reports of the OCSigO Distribution Division contained in Signal Corps Distribution Branch 319.1 Quarterly Reports, 1943–45.

[56] (1) CSigO, Annual Rpt, FY 43, pp. 50–51. (2) SigC Tech Info Ltr 15 (Feb 43), p. 52. (3) Novick, Story of Sup in the SigC in World War II, pt. IV, pp. 17–18, 28–29.

ters and a field branch in Philadelphia and branch offices in the Dayton, Monmouth, and Chicago Signal Corps Procurement Districts.

Although many of its functions were closely related to the research and development phase of supply, SNA actually occupied a pivotal place in the distribution system, and organizational control was soon transferred to the Distribution Division of P&D Service. The agency suffered the usual growing pains, perhaps more than ordinarily severe because of the intense pressure from ASF in 1943 to improve stock management procedures. By early 1944, the agency employed 549 people, and the Philadelphia group alone occupied six floors of a modern office building. Teletypewriter circuits linked the Dayton and Monmouth branches with the headquarters, whose files contained over 110,000 master stock number assignments arranged in alphabetical sequence, some 90,000 listings of manufacturers' part numbers, and a cross-reference file containing over 27,000 items of information organized to correlate official parts lists. Every month the agency processed 80,000 items of stock information, about 25 percent of them new stock number assignments. It edited parts and maintenance lists for procurement districts, contractors, the publication agencies, and the maintenance agencies.[57] A fifth field branch, established in mid-1944 at the Signal Corps Photographic Center on Long Island, served the Pictorial Engineering and Research Laboratory in its preparation of maintenance lists for items of photographic equipment.[58]

SNA edited, published, and distributed the manual of standard descriptions and the Signal Corps catalogs that set forth so much valuable information needed in procuring, issuing, requisitioning, storing, and maintaining items of equipment.[59] This work required the addition to the agency of a Catalog Division and a publications distribution staff in mid-1944.[60] The July issue of the Manual of Descriptions contained description requirements for 419 classes of items, plus an index listing 7,000 colloquial names by which Signal Corps items had been known in the past, cross-referenced to the 2,202 standard item names. For the first time it became possible to prepare a catalog in which an item could be located when only the name was known. Until then, all Signal Corps catalogs had been arranged ac-

---

[57] (1) Memo, CO SNA for CSigO, 5 Apr 44, sub: Qtrly Rpt, Jan–Mar 44. (2) Memo, CO SNA for CSigO, 10 Jul 44, sub: Qtrly Rpt, Apr–Jun 44. Both in SigC DS 319.1 Digest of Progress and Problems, 1943–44. (3) OCSigO Distr Div, Qtrly Rpts, Jul–Sep 43, pp. 8–9; Oct–Dec 43, p. 16; Jan–Mar 44, pp. 14–15. SigC DB 319.1 Qtrly Rpts, 1943–45.

[58] OSigO Distr Div, Qtrly Rpt, Jul–Sep 44, p. 26. SigC DB 319.1 Qtrly Rpts, 1943–45.

[59] During 1943–45 SNA prepared and issued various versions of the following sections of the Signal Corps catalog:

SIG–3, List of Items for Troop Issue
SIG–4–1, Allowances of Expendable Supplies
SIG–4–2, Special Allowances of Expendable Supplies for Schools, Training Centers, Boards and Fixed Installations
SIG–5, Stock List of All Items
SIG–5–1, Index to SIG–5 by Type Numbers
SIG–5–2, Index to SIG–5 by Manufacturers' Numbers
SIG–5–3, Alphabetical Index to SIG–5
SIG–5–4, List of Interchangeable and Substitute Items
SIG–7, Organizational Spare Parts
SIG–8, Higher Echelon Spare Parts
SIG–10, Fixed Plant Maintenance Parts

[60] (1) OCSigO Distr Div, Qtrly Rpt, Jul–Sep 44, p. 26. (2) OCSigO R&W, Action 1, Asst Chief P&D Sv to Contl Div, 17 Jul 44, sub: Establishment of New York Branch of SNA. SigC DS (Harrison) SNA.

cording to stock number sequence.[61] In many situations, particularly in the field, the earlier catalog was not much more useful than a telephone directory that listed the telephone numbers in sequence rather than by the subscribers' names.

The SNA stock-numbered all items that the Signal Corps procured, stored, and issued. This limitation automatically excluded experimental equipment procured in limited quantities for field tests; lend-lease items; spare parts groups intended to be broken down for stockage in depots as individual components; items procured by the Signal Corps but stored and issued by another service; and obsolete or salvage material. As time went on, there were fewer and fewer items that were without a stock number or bore the notation NSNR—no stock number required.[62]

SNA had always contended that really effective stock-numbering control must begin at the procurement source—that is, before parts left the manufacturers' plants. SNA argued that each item included in the purchase requests should be stock-numbered at the time the procurement districts placed the initial contracts. The procurement districts had stubbornly resisted any such arrangement because they believed it would unduly delay placing orders. The problem

hinged on the difficulty of getting sufficient information early enough in the procurement cycle to permit assignment of stock numbers.[63] SNA experimented with variations of the idea during the summer of 1944. In the autumn, General Harrison ordered the districts to try the system on an experimental basis.[64]

The procurement districts began stock-numbering their purchase requests in October.[65] Orders went out to the inspectors at manufacturing plants that, effective 1 November, no shipments would be released without stock numbers.[66] Both at home and overseas, depot personnel hailed the new procedure with enthusiasm, for it became possible to put stock numbers on the outside of packages. Depot personnel could tell what was in a package without opening it, thus saving an enormous amount of handling time. The Signal Corps was the only technical service to extend the use of

[61] (1) Memo, CO SNA for Dir P&D Sv OCSigO, 6 May 44, sub: Manual of Standard Descriptions. SigC DS (Harrison) SNA. (2) OCSigO Qtrly Rpt, Distr Div, Apr–Jun 44, p. 23. SigC DB 319.1 Qtrly Rpts, 1943–45.

[62] (1) Ltr, CO SNA to Asst Stock Controller OCSigO, 17 Apr 44, sub: What to Stock Number. (2) Ltr, Chief Plng Staff SNA to Chief P&D Sv OCSigO, 13 Apr 44, sub: What Should Be Stock Numbered. SigC 400.211 Gen 2, Apr–Jun 44. (3) SNA Policy Memo 19, 29 Apr 44, What to Stock Number. SigC 400.211 No. 2, Apr–Jun 44.

[63] 1st Ind, Asst Exec OCSigO to CG ASF, 25 Apr, on Memo, Dir Rqmts Div ASF for CSigO, 13 Apr 44, sub: Sup Item Identification. SigC 400.211 Gen 2, Apr–Jun 44.

[64] (1) OCSigO Distr Div, Qtrly Rpt, Jul–Sep 44, pp. 27–29. (2) OCSigO Memo 12, 10 May 44, sub: Processing Material for Stock Numbering. (3) Ltr, Asst Chief P&D Sv to CO PSCPD, 1 Aug 44, sub: Stock Numbering of SigC Items. (4) Ltr, Chief P&D Sv to Dir SigC Inspec Agency, 1 Aug 44, sub: Stock Numbering of SigC Items. Last three in SigC DS (Harrison) SNA.

[65] (1) Rpt, Agreement Between the Philadelphia Procurement District, Storage and Issue Agency, and the Stock Numbering Agency, 19 Sep 44. (2) Ltr, Chief Prod Fld Br OCSigO to O/C N.Y. SigC Prod Fld Of et al., 26 Sep 44, sub: Stock Numbering and Moisture Proof Packing. (3) Ltr, Dir Prod Div OCSigO to CO Dayton SigC Sup Agency, 2 Nov 44, sub: Contracts Lacking Stock Numbers. Last two in SigC 400.211 Gen 3, Jul–Dec 44. (4) OCSigO Distr Div, Qtrly Rpt, Jul–Sep 44, pp. 27–28. (5) OCSigO Distr Div, Qtrly Rpt, Oct–Dec 44, pp. 10–11.

[66] Ltr, Chief Prod Fld Br OCSigO to O/C N.Y. SigC Prod Fld Of et al., 26 Sep 44.

stock numbers to the packages shipped from manufacturers' plants.

As it turned out, only negligible delays in placing contracts occurred. By February 1945 SNA no longer found it necessary even to verify all stock numbers on purchase orders. The stock numbering system was working so well that malassignments had practically disappeared. Thereafter SNA processed only the new unnumbered items on the purchase requests.[67]

Stock Consolidation: The RIP Program

The most important element in the 1944 campaign to improve stock control procedures was the Reduction of Items Program (RIP), which reduced the number of individual items procured within given classes and purged depot stocks of obsolete items.

At that time a great many items stored in depots lacked sufficient descriptive data to be identified for practical use. The commanding officer of SNA, Col. William A. Kelley, called such items "Jones" cases, no more useful than the simple listing of the name Jones would be in a metropolitan telephone directory.[68] The depots also housed hundreds of spare parts "groups"—collections of parts intended for use with a particular radio set or end item. Originally intended to save time and money in field repair and maintenance, the spare parts groups actually failed in their purpose. Instead, they took out of supply chan-

nels individual parts that could have been used for repair of other sets.[69]

In September a special task force of 118 OCSigO engineers began examining and analyzing all stock-numbered signal items by classes to determine whether the number of items being procured could be reduced. Capacitors offered a likely starting point. From the thousands on the list, the engineers selected a certain number that could fill all needs. The rest they recommended for disposal, or put on a list of items not to be reordered when existing stocks were exhausted.[70]

In the first three months the engineers examined some thirty thousand items and completed work on all photographic items, on fixed capacitors, and on fixed and variable resistors. For these items alone, they listed 49 percent of the types either for disposal or to be used only until existing stocks were used up.[71]

The valuable results achieved in the first three months led General Harrison to increase the size of the task force to 450 people working full time in order to finish the entire project by 31 March.[72] During the next three months, the engineers scrutinized 188,843 items. All to-

---

[67] OCSigO Distr Div, Qtrly Rpt, Jan–Mar 45, p. 13.

[68] Ltr, CO SNA to Lt Col H. G. Wilde, P&D Sv OCSigO, 26 May 44, sub: Insufficient Info. SigC 400.211 Gen 2, Apr–Jun 44.

[69] MS Comment, Hq U.S. Army Sig Sch, 3 Aug 59.

[70] (1) Incl 1, Monthly Rpt of Progress and Problems, Sep 44, with Ltr, CO SNA to Asst Chief P&D Sv, 2 Oct 44, sub: MPR. SigC DS (Harrison) SNA. (2) OCSigO Distr Div, Qtrly Rpts, Jul–Sep 44, pp. 30–31, and Oct–Dec 44, pp. 11–12.

[71] (1) Ltr, CO SNA to Chief P&D Sv, 26 Oct 44, sub: RIP. SigC 475 RIP for 1944. (2) Incl 7, RIP, with Memo, Lloyd R. Hanlon, Proc Spec, for Col William M. Mack, 26 Dec 44, sub: Rpt on Trip to Philadelphia, 19–20 Dec 44. SigC 475 Spare Parts for SigC Equip, 1944–45.

[72] (1) Memo, Chief P&D Sv OCSigO for Chief Distr Div, 1 Jan 45. (2) Conf Notes, Reduction of SigC Stock Numbers, 3 Jan 45, and Incl, Pers Breakdown. Both in SigC DS (Harrison) SNA.

gether, they eliminated 45,516 items, or 24.5 percent, and classified them either as limited (in which case no more would be ordered), as superseded (to be combined with similar stocks and issued until used up), or as void (to be disposed of).[73]

When the blitz review ended in April 1945, the Signal Corps decided to continue the program on a permanent basis, but at a more leisurely pace.[74] From then on procurement agencies bought only selected items, equipment engineers used them whenever possible in development, and maintenance agencies designated selected components for maintaining equipment. In short, reduction of items was incorporated into the body of permanent Signal Corps policy.[75]

The Signal Corps derived manifold benefits from the Reduction of Items Program. The elimination of duplicate stocks simplified procurement, storage, and issue; reduced the number of stock numbers and increased the accuracy of those assigned; took most of the guesswork out of requisitioning in the field; and streamlined procedures all down the line. General Ingles considered the program "one of the many outstanding contributions of the [Procurement and Distribution] Service to the Signal Corps" and prophesied, "we will con-

tinue for many years to reap the benefits of it." [76]

Disposal of Excess Stocks

In theory the Army supply system operated in such a manner as to control overstockage. The authorized tables of equipment and the established stock levels at posts, camps, and stations theoretically determined the amount of material that should be in the hands of users of signal items; the responsible commanding officers at various levels reported overstockage to the issuing depots, which in turn redistributed returned stock to others who needed it or, if no need existed, disposed of the items as surplus or salvage. That was the theory. In practice it was extremely difficult to force material back into the supply stream even though machinery for doing so existed.[77]

No doubt some overstockage was inevitable. For one thing, the War Department policy toward approving special issues of equipment above the amounts authorized by tables was extremely liberal. For another, supply officers of all units tended to requisition more than they actually needed, particularly if the items sought were considered to be in

[73] (1) CSigO, Annual Rpt, FY 45, p. 458–59. (2) Memo, Dir Distr Div for Chief P&D Sv, 4 Apr 45, sub: RIP, with Incl, SNA Rpt on RIP. SigC 475 RIP 1, Jan–Apr 45.
[74] (1) Conf Notes, Transfer of Work of RIP into Procedure of SNA, 13 Mar 45. SigC 400.211 Gen 1, Jan–Apr 45. (2) Memo, Chief Prod Ln Br Maint Div OCSigO for Asst Chief E&T Sv, 19 May 45, sub: RIP. (3) Ltr, CO SNA to Advisory Cmte RIP, 15 May 45, sub: RIP, with Tabs A–E. Last two in SigC 475 RIP 2, May–Dec 45.
[75] SigC Tech Info Ltr 41 (Apr 45), pp. 31–32.

[76] 1st Ind, Ingles to Chief P&D Sv, 28 May 45, on Ltr, CO SNA to CSigO, 26 May 45, sub: Cooperative Action of All Svs to Establish Stock Numbering Procedures for Consolidation of Stock Items. SigC 475 RIP 2, May–Dec 45.
[77] (1) AG 475, 10 Jun 42. (2) AG Ltr, MO–SPPD–TS–M, 22 Jun 42. (3) AGO Memo W700–11–43, sub: Excess of Working Stocks. (4) Memo, TAG for Chiefs Sup Svs, 23 Dec 42, sub: Surplus and Obsolete Property. SPX 400.7 (12–12–42) OP–P–SPDDS–MP–R. (5) AGO Memo S5–140–43, 16 Jul 43, sub: Declaration of Mil Property as Surplus to WD. (6) Résumé of Pertinent Actions, Orders, Etc., Applying to Surplus Property. SigC 400.211 Gen 1, Jan–Mar 44.

critical supply. All the stern admonitions of the War Department that hoarding of supplies was unpatriotic and would not be permitted failed to stop the practice. Finally, overstockage at depots often resulted from the working of the Army Supply Program. Based on yearly, not monthly, calculations, the delivery schedules under ASP were weighted heavily toward end-of-the-year shipments. Depots could not refuse to accept deliveries, yet were forced to maintain minimum and maximum stock levels that bore no relationship to the incoming amounts of material on production schedules.

Actually, the general scarcity of signal equipment during the first eighteen months of war had prevented any sizable accumulation of excess or surplus stocks in depots or other repositories during that period.[78] By mid-1943, when ASF began implementing the new Supply Control System, the accumulation of excess and surplus signal supplies in depots and at posts, camps, and stations had begun to mount. Control of such supplies in depots rested largely upon control at the posts, camps, and stations. In 1943 the Signal Corps stepped up its inspections at the least controllable level —the stations.[79] Inspecting officers found that the stations had trouble in establishing realistic stock levels. Their stock control methods and record keeping varied greatly, and "signal property officers found it difficult to part with equipment in spite of the fact that they had not used it in long periods of time."[80] Nonetheless, quantities of excess and surplus items did begin moving back into the depots.

The depots were responsible for reviewing station stock records and for issuing instructions on the disposition of returned stocks.[81] Initially the depots, busy with more urgent matters, did relatively little to promote an aggressive program. In January 1944 ASF directed technical service depots to issue definite and detailed instructions concerning the return of excess material.[82] Many stations lacked classification and packing experts. Material returned from such stations arrived at depots poorly packed and not segregated as to degree of serviceability. When it was received, it had to be classified and sent to stock for reissue if it was serviceable, or disposed of, or repaired. Actually, had all the stations sent their excess stocks back to the depots religiously, the depots would have been engulfed. In early 1943 at the Philadelphia Signal Depot, for example, when only about 20 tons of excess stock were returned each week, a group of about 40 persons tallied in, classified, and identified the items. A year later Philadelphia was receiving 350 tons a week.

---

[78] Excess material was defined as any amount above the authorized amount—that is, above the maximum stock level authorized for a particular organization, supply point, or technical service. Surplus property was any amount declared by competent authority to be above the amount for which there was a need in the War Department. Memo, ACSigO for Chief P&D Sv, 7 Feb 44, sub: Excess and Surplus Property. SigC 400.211 Gen 1, Jan–Mar 44.

[79] For details, consult the voluminous reports of station inspections contained in the 400.211 files for 1943–44.

[80] Ltr, CO Boston Sig Depot to CSigO, 29 Jan 44, sub: Review and Revision of Sig Stock Levels at Ft. H. G. Wright Harbor Defenses of Long Island Sound. SigC 400.211 Gen 1, Jan–Mar 44.

[81] Memo, ACofS for Opns, ASF for CSigO and Others, 8 Jan 43, sub: Excess Stocks at Depots. SigC 400.211 Gen, 1942–43.

[82] ASF Cir 4, sec. III, 4 Jan 44, sub: Return of Station Excess Property to Depots.

It required 100 laborers, storekeepers, supervisors, and technicians just to process the Class C (unserviceable) equipment, which comprised only 14 percent of the returns.[83]

Several factors contributed to the increase in tonnage of returned stocks in 1944. Firmer control measures instituted by ASF, a downward revision of stock levels at posts, camps, and stations with a corresponding increase in excess stocks, a faster rate of troop movements overseas (outbound units invariably turned in quantities of equipment when they shipped out), and the introduction of the Supply Control System all tended to increase the flow of returned stocks to depots.[84] These developments led logically to the creation of the machinery and an organization to dispose of unneeded items of equipment.

Procurement Regulations provided the mechanism and authority for declaring excess stocks as surplus and for their sale under specified conditions.[85] If the items happened to be common to more than one technical service, transfers could be arranged. In the fall of 1943, the civilian disposal agencies began operating—the Procurement Division of the Treasury Department for consumers' goods, the Reconstruction Finance Corporation for capital and producers' goods, the U.S. Maritime Commission for ships and maritime property, and the War Food Administration for food and related products.[86] Use of these channels, particularly of the Treasury Department regional offices, relieved the technical services of many of the more time-consuming details of consummating sales and speeded the disposal processes.

Meanwhile, ASF had created a new branch to handle surplus and salvage material.[87] The Signal Corps followed suit, establishing the Redistribution and Salvage Branch within the P&D Service in August 1943.[88] Colonel Falk was named chief of the new branch and continued in that assignment to the end of the war. The branch was renamed the Redistribution and Disposal Branch in May 1944.[89]

A board of officers appointed within the Office of the Chief Signal Officer under the chairmanship of the Assistant Chief Signal Officer, General Code, mapped out a program co-ordinated with the continuing requirements for signal equipment.[90] During the next several months each of the depots organized redistribution and disposal divisions to handle surplus property, including units to assist local representatives of civilian disposal agencies.[91] The depots

[83] Hist, PSD, pp. 331–32.

[84] ASF Cir 51, sec. II, 17 Feb 44, sub: Station Excess Stocks, and ASF Cir 63, sec I, 2 Mar 44, same sub. See also ASF Manual M–416, Nov 44, sub: Stock Control Manual for Depots, and Signal Corps Standard Operation Procedure for Depots, 1943 and 1944 issues.

[85] (1) PR 7, 26 Jun 43, as amended 15 Oct 43. (2) WD Memo S5–140–43, 16 Jun 43, sub: Declaration of Mil Property as Surplus to WD. (3) Revision IV of SigC Proc Instrs Memo, 16 Jul 43, rev 10 Nov 43, sub: Disposition of Property. (4) SigC SOP, Redistribution and Salvage.

[86] ASF Cir 16, 13 Jan 45, sec. III, pt. 2.

[87] ASF Cir 25, 2 May 43, sub: Staff Supervision of Salvage and Surplus Property.

[88] SigC Admin Log, 1939–45, Orgn Chart 27, 15 Aug 43, p. 94.

[89] Ibid., Orgn Chart 30, 16 May 44, p. 108.

[90] (1) Memo, ACSigO for Chief P&D Sv, 7 Feb 44. (2) Of Orders 32, 8 Feb 44. SigC 400.211 Gen 1, Jan–Mar 44.

[91] (1) Ltr, Chief P&D Div to Comdrs All SigC Depots, 3 Jul 44, sub: Property Disposal Div in SigC Depots. SigC 400.703 Gen 10, Jul 44. (2) Ltr, Dir OCSigO Distr Div to CO's All Depots et al., 29 Dec 44, sub: Disposal of Excess and Surplus Sig Property in Depots. SigC 400.703 Gen 14, Dec 44. (3) Hist, PSCPD, pp. 379–82.

segregated surplus stock, set up display rooms to house samples of the items, and began submitting regular reports of amounts of material handled.[92]

In the nine months between September 1943 and June 1944, the Signal Corps disposed of $2,000,000 worth of unneeded material to other technical services and acquired some $600,000 worth of stocks, including 20,000 pounds of new, triple-distilled metallic mercury at less than market price, a real prize because mercury was badly needed at the time by the hard-pressed battery industry. The Corps also acquired a quantity of much needed wooden packing cases.[93] Between June 1944 and June 1945 the disposal figures rose to $50,000,000, representing vehicles, certain types of dry batteries, power units, panels, and tubes.

In the first six months of 1945, the depots devoted more and more time to disposal activities. Here again the Reduction of Items Program, which was going on simultaneously, helped tremendously.[94] RIP lists of obsolete items provided a ready means of identifying items that the depots could sort out and dispose of without any uncertainty. The second phase of RIP was completed by V–J Day, luckily, for the end of the war brought huge increases in disposal levels. Decreases in authorized stock levels produced more excess items, and the end of the fighting reduced the need for, and rendered surplus, many types of equipment. Disposal activities moved into high gear.[95]

Protecting and Maintaining Signal Equipment

Signal items are very precisely engineered. They vary enormously in kind, size, weight, and shape. Their weight may be measured in grams or tons, their size in fractions of a cubic inch or in thousands of cubic feet. A very large proportion of the items share a common characteristic—they embody electrical circuits. Many things electrical are fragile, most of them are relatively costly and complex, and all of them must be kept dry and free from dust and dirt if they are to perform their functions properly.

These characteristics of signal equipment created special problems of maintenance, repair, and packaging. In the first two years of war such matters got relatively little attention because procurement and production necessarily received the primary emphasis. Once the initial equipping of the Army was completed, maintenance and repair matters received a great deal more attention. From mid-1943 until the end of the war these hitherto neglected areas came very much into the spotlight. It was necessary to provide instructions for the proper care of signal equipment at all echelons, to train civilian specialists who could render service whenever called upon, and to establish facilities for equipment repair too difficult or too extensive to be accomplished by using organizations or forward depots.

Maintenance

Although a Maintenance Branch had existed in the OCSigO headquarters since 1941, its activities had consisted

---

[92] OCSigO Distr Div, Qtrly Rpts, Apr–Jun 44 and Jul–Sep 44.

[93] CSigO, Annual Rpt, FY 44, pp. 445–46.

[94] See above, pp. 405–06.

[95] For details, consult the Signal Corps files, 400.703 series, for late 1945 and for 1946.

largely of hit-and-run attacks on individual problems as they arose, rather than a grappling with broad basic policies. As a matter of fact, ASF itself was lax in dealing with this area of supply. It did not establish a Maintenance Division until April 1943. Meanwhile the Signal Corps, like the other technical services, took care of its own special needs, albeit somewhat haphazardly.

When General Ingles became the Chief Signal Officer he transferred the Maintenance Branch to General Colton's E&T Service and gave the branch the responsibility for all maintenance activities. This was a logical move. The laboratories had a strong proprietary interest in maintenance and spare parts and were in fact neck deep in the spare parts problem.[96] To round out the maintenance organization, Ingles formed the Signal Corps Ground Signal Maintenance Agency at Philadelphia and staffed it with personnel transferred from the Maintenance Engineering Branch of the old Research and Development Division, OCSigO. The SCGSMA devised maintenance procedures for ground signal equipment and trained men to service and repair it. The Signal Corps Aircraft Maintenance Agency at Wright Field performed similar duties for airborne signal equipment. Through several quick changes of name, the maintenance agencies settled down to become, respectively, the Ground Signal Maintenance Division and the Aircraft Radio Maintenance Division. One further or-

ganizational change near the end of the fiscal year brought staff supervision of fifth echelon repair shops back to the P&D Service and its newly activated Shops Branch. Other repair installations such as fourth echelon service command signal repair shops remained with the Ground Signal Maintenance Division.[97]

The Army maintenance organization was based on a 5-echelon system, backed up for supply by army and base depots.[98] The needs of each echelon of maintenance and supply varied for each individual type of equipment. Maintenance requirements for equipment being procured for the first time differed from those on subsequent procurements. The requirements of the zone of interior were unlike those of the theaters of operation. Other intricacies and deviations of procedure existed for equipment the Signal Corps bought for the Air Forces but that was maintained and distributed by the Air Forces; for equipment procured for the Navy, the British, and other Allies on special arrangements; and for the requirements of international aid.

[96] (1) CSigO, Annual Rpt, FY 44, pp. 345ff. (2) Thompson, Harris, et al., The Test, pp. 324-28, 525-32. (3) SigC Admin Log, 1939-45, OCSigO Orgn Chart 26, 1 Jul 43, and Chart 27, 15 Aug 43. (4) Hall, Dev of the OCSigO, SigC Hist Monograph D-1, pt. II, 1945, pp. 6-7.

[97] (1) CSigO, Annual Rpt, FY 44, pp. 443-45. (2) History of the Aircraft Radio Laboratory, 1 Oct 43, pp. 14, 18-19, 22-23, 34-36. SigC Hist Sec file. (3) Distr Div OCSigO, Qtrly Rpts, Jul-Sep 43, p. 7.

[98] First echelon maintenance: servicing or repairs that could be done by the operator, driver, or crew; second echelon maintenance: servicing or maintenance by the maintenance section of the unit that used the equipment; third echelon maintenance: maintenance, repairs, and unit replacement by mobile maintenance organizations; fourth echelon maintenance: general overhaul and reclamation of equipment, units, and parts, involving the use of heavy tools and the services of general and technical mechanics; fifth echelon maintenance: maintenance of equipment by personnel of maintenance and supply units located at fixed installations in the rear areas, including the reclamation or complete reconditioning of matériel, the limited manufacture of parts and equipment, and the supplying of equipment to lower echelons.

In May 1943, the Signal Corps published its General Maintenance Plan, which established broad maintenance policies and procedures.[99] The plan served as the keystone of the signal maintenance structure for the remainder of the war. It set forth policies for procuring, distributing, and using repair and maintenance parts, and assigned specific responsibilities to designated Signal Corps agencies.

A maintenance (spare parts) list for each major item of signal equipment showed the authorized allowances of parts permitted each user at each echelon. From these lists, using organizations determined what parts to buy and how many. As quickly as the maintenance engineers compiled a list, it was published and distributed to the field, and eventually republished in the ASF (Signal) catalogs.

As another aid to field users, the Signal Corps developed spare parts chests, packed with authorized quantities of spare parts required by second and third echelon tactical repair units. A constant flow of publications kept units in touch with the latest maintenance information. The Signal Corps published responsibility charts, which classified equipment into groups, and assigned responsibility for third, fourth, and fifth echelon maintenance within the continental United States. There were preventive maintenance letters, which outlined what must be done to keep equipment operating smoothly; lubrication orders designed to prolong the life of signal equipment through correct and timely lubrication; and modification work orders, which gave instructions for incorporating slight changes in signal equipment in the field for more efficient operation. The Maintenance Division trained civilian maintenance personnel and mechanics for work on signal equipment at service commands, ports of embarkation, and air service commands. Officer and civilian teams went to the overseas theaters to help commanders work out their maintenance problems.[100]

The maintenance activities of the Signal Corps during 1944 and 1945 helped materially to alleviate a Signal Corps problem that was never entirely solved—assuring an adequate supply of spare parts.

Spare Parts Supply

Throughout 1941–43 the Signal Corps, along with some of the other technical services, had lavished much anxious attention on the ubiquitous spare parts problem.[101] The Signal Corps was uneasily aware that this particular

[99] Memo, Chief Sig Supply Sv for All Concerned, 1 May 43, sub: Gen Maint Plan (for Equip Supplied by SigC), and the following Incls: (1) Gen Maint Plan, sec. I, (2) Gen Maint Plan, sec. II, and (3) Memo, sub: Maint Lists for SigC Equip. SigC BC 475 Spare Parts (Maint Equip, vol. I).

[100] (1) CSigO, Annual Rpts, FY 44, pp. 345–55, and 1945, pp. 379–88. (2) Report on Changes in Supply Procedure and Supply Levels, 1 Jan 44, bk. I, E&T, Questions 4, 5, and 6. SigC EC 400 Rpt on Changes in Sup Procedure and Sup Levels.

[101] Thompson, Harris, et al., The Test, pp. 324–28, 525–32.

For similar problems in other technical services, see, for example, Chester Wardlow, The Transportation Corps: Movements, Training, and Supply, UNITED STATES ARMY IN WORLD WAR II (Washington, 1956), pp. 499–502, 514–15, 522, and Harry C. Thomson and Lida Mayo, The Ordnance Department: Procurement and Supply, UNITED STATES ARMY IN WORLD WAR II (Washington, 1960), especially chs. XIII, XIX, and XXII.

CHECKING THE FREQUENCY OF A BC–779–A RECEIVER *at the signal repair section of General Stilwell's headquarters, Burma.*

headache was one that might very well be incurable, but the Corps nevertheless struggled unceasingly to bring about a lasting cure.[102]

Two major Signal Corps operating divisions shared the responsibility for spare parts supply. The Procurement and Distribution Service bought and distributed parts and administered stock control. The Engineering and Technical Service compiled the maintenance lists and spare parts annexes that served as the source of procurement information until such time as issue experience and usage gave better answers. A third division, Personnel and Training, published technical manuals containing much maintenance information. The constant stream of War Department and ASF circulars and memorandums, and the intraservice publications and correspondence by which the Signal Corps implemented them, attested to the enor-

---

[102] For details consult the following Signal Corps files: 413.4 Spare Parts 1, Jan–Feb 44; 413.44 Spare Parts 2, Mar–Jun 44; 475 Spare Parts, Jul–Dec 44; 475 Spare Parts 1, Jan–Apr 45; 475 Spare Parts 2, May–Jul 45; 475 Improvement of Spare Parts Sup in Pac Theaters, 1945; 475 Spare Parts for SigC Equip, 1944–45. All in SigC DS (Harrison) Spare Parts.

mous complications of the spare parts problem.[103]

In general, the basic principles governing spare parts supply were established by 1944.[104] Merely putting an item in the TOE's took care of first and second echelon needs, since the necessary technical manuals, maintenance parts and supplies, and tools and test equipment were either packed with the equipment or were issued automatically with it. Third, fourth, and fifth echelons had no specific authorization for spare parts, but sections 6, 7, and 8 of the supply catalog provided guides to initial issues of parts, tools, and test equipment until issue experience was available. After that, requisitions were based on usage. On the first procurement of a new item, the procurement district bought the equipment and the spare (maintenance) parts designated by the maintenance lists or spare parts annexes. The procurement districts notified the Storage and Issue Agency whenever subsequent procurements of the same equipment were about to be placed. The S&I Agency then initiated purchase requests for parts after reviewing the stock position, the issue experience data on all the parts, and the additional equipment being procured that must be serviced from depot stocks. The procurement districts and the S&I Agency tried to adjust the procurement schedules so that

spare parts would be produced concurrently with end equipment.[105]

Signal Corps distribution, filler, and key depots stocked and distributed spare parts in the same manner as end items.[106] The theaters received an initial bulk supply of spare parts issued automatically in quantities sufficient to set up base depot stocks, to cover necessary initial issues to organizations, and to provide for maintenance until the theaters could go on a requisition basis for replenishment. The theater commanders were responsible for establishing the necessary distribution facilities and stock control measures within the theater. Normally, the theaters could requisition only authorized items on spare parts lists, although, if unusual circumstances demanded unauthorized items or unusual quantities, stock could be requisitioned if adequately explained and defended. The supply services at home, however, had power to review and screen abnormally large requests.[107]

Even if the system had operated perfectly, it would still have been administratively complex and cumbersome. In practice, there were plenty of hitches, creaks, stresses, strains, slowdowns, and partial failures of the machinery. It seemed that, no matter how many spare parts were made and delivered, a shortage persisted. By 1944 all procurement officers were well indoctrinated with the

---

[103] See, for example, WD Cir 227, sec. IV, 1944; WD Cir 318, sec. IV, 1944; WD Cir 434, 9 Nov 44; WD Cir 69, sec. IV, 3 Mar 45; ASF Cir 19, 17 Jan 44; ASF Cir 2, 3 Jan 45; OCSigO P&D Sv Memo 18, 12 Jul 44.

[104] 1st Ind, Chief P&D Sv OCSigO, to CG ASF, 3 Mar 44, on Memo, ASF Stock Contl Div for Issue Br, 1 Mar 44, sub: Spare Parts Proc and Requisitions. SigC 413.44 Spare Parts 2, Mar–Jun 44.

[105] Except for spare parts for airborne radio sets for the AAF, which had a 90-day lead-in time while sets were installed in the airplanes and an additional 60-day testing period. Rpt on Changes in Sup Procedure and Sup Levels, bk. II, P&D Sv, par. 10, Question 3.

[106] See above, pp. 394ff.

[107] (1) WD Cir 434, 9 Nov 44. (2) Rpt on Changes in Sup Procedure and Sup Levels, bk. II, P&D Sv, par 10, Question 8.

TABLE 2—DOLLAR VALUE OF SPARE PARTS ACCEPTED JULY–DECEMBER 1943

Signal Corps Procurement District	November 1943	December 1943	Six Months Cumulative to December 1943
Total all districts			
All contracts....................	201,017,970.40	223,144,003.37	1,100,428,310.55
Spare parts.....................	15,410,242.10	14,804,006.92	68,908,007.14
Dayton			
All contracts............................	59,822,612.06	66,789,128.35	379,423,053.46
Spare parts................................	8,738,730.95	9,150,056.28	41,895,063.43
Monmouth			
All contracts............................	52,205,682.45	63,907,566.33	218,667,459.88
Spare parts................................	2,195,315.62	1,797,740.42	6,982,704.03
Philadelphia			
All contracts............................	88,989,675.89	92,447,308.69	502,337,797.21
Spare parts...............................	4,476,195.53	3,856,210.22	20,030,239.68

Source: Memo, Asst ExecO SigC Inspec Agency for CO SigC Inspec Agency Ln Sec OCSigO, 7 Jan 44. SigC 413.44 Spare Parts 1, Jan–Feb 44.

necessity of keeping spare parts rolling off the production lines along with the equipment. In the six months ending December 1943, the Signal Corps Inspection Agency had accepted $68,908,007.14 worth of spare parts on contracts for $1,100,428,310.55 worth of equipment at the three procurement districts.[108] (*Table 2*) By that time, as General Somervell noted, the technical services were filling the pipelines, but the overseas depot stocks had not yet reached approved levels and the demand remained large. Some overseas requisitions in fact seemed overlarge, up to ten times the amount needed according to issue experience tables. Ports of embarkation were expected to edit requisitions only if world-wide requirements were greater than the available supply. Sometimes the ports did query the theaters when the requisitions seemed excessive. Occasionally the theaters then reduced

the size of their requisitions, but more frequently defended them on the ground that the items were required "to win the war." [109]

In February and March 1944, during the final months of preparation for the Normandy invasion, General Colton and Major Marks of the E&T Service, toured the United Kingdom to check up on various supply matters. They found the general supply situation good, but the spare parts picture less bright. General Colton reported most ground units fairly well supplied with spare parts, but air units less well equipped, partly because many of the units had only recently arrived in the United Kingdom. At Cheltenham, the SOS field headquarters in the ETO for all U.S. depots in the United Kingdom, spare parts were not yet arriving in quantity. Of the first 600 items on a 100-page requisition from the V Corps posted to the stock records, 247 items showed a zero balance in stock. A 41-page requisition from the Eighth Air

[108] Memo, Asst ExecO SigC Inspec Agency for CO SigC Inspection Agency Ln Sec OCSigO, 7 Jan 44. SigC 413.44 Spare Parts 1, Jan–Feb 44.

[109] Min, ASF Staff Conf, 21 Dec 43, pp. 4–5.

Force asked for quantities exceeding the total maximum figure authorized for the theater. Major Marks reported that some of the officers in the Signal Supply Division, ETOUSA, felt that the maximum and minimum levels set for the theater were inadequate and that the receipt of parts through automatic shipment based on the monthly material status reports was too slow.[110]

Depots in the ETO had requisitioned a six-month quantity of spare parts, based on the number of troops then in the theater. Additions and cancellations of troop units to the theater made it difficult to keep depot stocks in balance. Also, troops arriving without their organizational equipment and therefore without third echelon spare parts had to be supplied from depot stock, leaving little on the shelves or in the bins. General Colton concluded regretfully, "It appears probable that spare parts will not at the present rate of shipment be in good supply for a long time." [111] He sent back lists of most critically needed spare parts and recommended special expediting action. "It will be time enough to argue about the theoretical correctness of the plan when reasonable quantities of spare parts are available," he said.[112]

The same factors that had held back an adequate supply of spare parts in the early days of the war were operating in 1944. As preparations for the invasion of Europe went forward, the pressure to get out great quantities of end items of equipment was very heavy. While shipments overseas accelerated, demands for equipping troops in the United States before movement overseas swallowed up masses of signal supplies. In most cases, the Signal Corps produced quantities greater than the forecasts. Component parts, however, were not flowing in sufficient quantity, and the choice had to be made between furnishing large quantities of end items or enough spare parts. The decision went to the end items, and spare parts production fell behind.[113]

To assure the most equitable distribution among all the users, the Signal Corps instituted a rationing system. It proved to be no more popular with those affected by it than any other rationing procedure.[114]

In the months following D-day in Normandy, component supply improved greatly, but the amount of fabricated spares failed to show a corresponding increase because the build-up for impending operations in the Philippines created a new accelerated cycle. On 9 June 1944, ASF published a procedure for rationing spare parts in short supply, based on assigned priorities of using agencies. The chiefs of technical services were to publish monthly lists of the spare parts to be rationed and the percentage

[110] Memo, Marks for CSigO, 14 Mar 44, sub: Visit to Sig Sup Div ETO, Cheltenham, 27 Feb–1 Mar 44, and Incl 1, Sup Memo, 29 Feb 44, contained in app. B, pp. 39–40 of Consolidated Report of Visit of Maj. Gen. Roger B. Colton and Maj. William S. Marks, Jr., to Signal Establishments in the United Kingdom, 8 Feb–28 Mar 44. SCIA file 74 Colton Rpts folder 1–b.

[111] Consolidated Rpt of Visit of Colton and Marks to Sig Establishments in the U.K., 8 Feb–28 Mar 44, app. B, p. 51.

[112] Ibid., app. B, p. 52.

[113] Ltr, Maj R. D. Lawlor, Chief Prod Contl Br OCSigO, to Maj G. J. Filberti, Jt Review Gp, 25 Oct 44, sub: Overseas Requisitions for Replacement Parts. SigC 475 Spare Parts, Jul–Dec 44.

[114] (1) Memo, Dir of Sup ASF for CSigO, 14 Feb 44, sub: Spare Parts Conf, 24 Jan to 2 Feb 44. (2) Memo, Dir Distr Div OCSigO for CG ASF, same sub, 19 Feb 44. Both in SigC 413.44 Spare Parts 1, Jan–Feb 44.

that would be furnished each agency. A Signal Corps officer, reviewing the circular, penciled an indignant comment, "Idiotic! If you publish the figure, say 50 percent, then Joe Supply Sergeant requisitions twice his needs." [115] The Signal Corps continued to use its own rationing system, which omitted published percentages.[116]

Rationing assured an equitable division of the available supply, but could not overcome the basic shortage. As operations proceeded and the armies moved faster over longer distances, equipment wore out more quickly. Frequent reports of cannibalization worried the supply officers since cannibalization of quantities of end items merely to obtain a few critically needed spare parts could soon lead to serious trouble. Indeed, by October 1944, theaters were reporting that equipment was failing and could not be repaired.[117] General Harrison, who in July had ordered an intensive campaign in all procurement districts to clear up shortages of critical spare parts on back order for the theaters, redoubled his efforts. Thousands of the requisitions were over sixty days old.

The problem could not be solved by a brilliant flash-of-genius method. Rather the solution depended upon dogged persistence and attention to detail, and at some points upon trial and error, improving a detail here and a procedure there. Spare parts supply improved after late 1944. Once the peak of effort toward initially equipping the Army and preparing for the Normandy invasion was past, manufacturers could produce both parts and end items more readily. The introduction of the Supply Control System tended to bring order into procurement processes by providing more accurate calculations of requirements and better records. Also as the war progressed, Signal Corps engineers responsible for providing maintenance factor data were able to substitute actual experience figures from the theaters for the educated guesses that in many cases had constituted the only guides early in the war. The practice of providing spare parts groups for particular sets in each maintenance echelon was modified. Breaking down spare parts kits and groups and placing the components in stock as individual items to be requisitioned as they were needed stretched the supply of parts because experience showed that many times not all parts provided in a group actually were used at the same rate. No engineer, however talented, could forecast with absolute accuracy at the time an item was being developed just what parts would wear out at a given time. Only prolonged field experience could provide such data.[118]

The attack on the spare parts problem necessitated the teamwork of many persons and organizations. ASF sent survey teams of technical service representatives to the active theaters to gather firsthand information. The theaters themselves forwarded helpful reports. The Signal Corps enlisted the co-operation of

---

[115] ASF Cir 174, 9 Jun 44, and Penciled Comment on p. 5, SigC 475 Spare Parts, Jul–Dec 44.

[116] (1) Memo, O/C Material & Rpts Sec for Col William L. Bayer, Chief Maint Br OCSigO, 20 Jul 44, sub: ASF Cir 174, pt. III, sec. VII, Jun 44. (2) SigC Distr Opns Ltr No. 21, 2 Aug 44. Both in SigC 475 Spare Parts, Jul–Dec 44.

[117] Ltr, Lawlor to Filberti, 25 Oct 44.

[118] (1) Gerard, Story of Sig Sup in the SigC in World War II, B–1b, pt. II, pp. 56–57. (2) Rpt on Changes in Sup Procedure and Sup Levels, bk. II, P&D Sv.

manufacturers, plugged everlastingly at preparation of maintenance lists, checked constantly on procurement actions, and followed up requisitions determinedly. Through intensive efforts all along the line, the spare parts situation had eased greatly by early 1945. Shipments still lagged behind deliveries of end items of equipment, however, and not all requisitions were filled promptly.[119]

The end of action in Europe failed to bring about a corresponding cessation in spare parts activity in that area. Spare parts excess to the needs of the ETO were being sorted, tropicalized, packed, and shipped to the Pacific when the war ended. It would be inaccurate to say that the spare parts problem was ever entirely solved. With the advent of V-J Day it merely ceased to be a burning issue. The intensive effort devoted to the matter had a carry-over value, however, for the experience gained in wartime provided extremely valuable documentation for postwar supply and maintenance activities.

Depot Repair Shops

The function of the fifth echelon repair shops in signal depots was to repair equipment for return to stock. Service command fourth echelon shops repaired equipment to be returned to the using organizations. At the outset of war, the distinction between the type and extent of repairs performed in fourth and fifth echelon shops was quite hazy. Depot repair shops did work for organizations at posts, camps, and stations almost inter-changeably with their service command counterparts. Gradually the Army drew a clearer line of demarcation, but official opinion shifted from time to time throughout the war.[120]

By 1944 the repair of unserviceable signal equipment for return to stock had become a major source of supply. In the earlier war years the output of the repair shops was meager, dependent largely on the initiative of individual shops, since there was then no centrally controlled system to co-ordinate repair facilities and output with over-all supply requirements. Repair and reissue of signal equipment remained an area of great potential supply value that was largely unexploited until the activation of the Shops Branch in the Distribution Division of OCSigO in August 1943.[121]

At that time the five shops in existence at the beginning of the war had increased to nine. They were located at the Atlanta, San Antonio, and Utah General Depot Signal Sections, and at the Chicago, Philadelphia, Lexington, and Dayton Signal Depots, the last having two branches—one in Wichita, and one in Buffalo. In December the Utah shop was closed and its equipment and personnel transferred to the newly activated Sacramento Signal Depot. Early in 1944 new shops were set up at the Los Angeles and Holabird Signal Depots.[122] The AAF took over the Dayton and Los

---

[119] SigC 475 Spare Parts 1, Jan–Apr 45, and 475 Spare Parts 2, May–Jul 45, *passim.*

[120] Unless otherwise indicated, this section is based on: Shops Br Distr Div OCSigO, History of Signal Corps Depot Repair Shops During World War II, 20 Sep 45 (hereafter cited as Hist, SigC Repair Shops), pp. 8–9. SigC Hist Sec file.

[121] (1) OCSigO Distr Div, Qtrly Rpt, Jul–Sep 43, p. 7. (2) Hist, SigC Repair Shops, pp. 1–9.

[122] (1) OCSigO Distr Div, Qtrly Rpt, Oct–Dec 43, SigC DS 319.1 Digest of Progress and Problems, 1943–44. (2) CSigO, Annual Rpt, FY 44, p. 445.

Angeles shops, which repaired only meteorological and airborne equipment, late in 1945.[123]

Each signal depot shop, virtually a small factory, could repair or fabricate almost any signal item, though not all could do it at the same rate or with the same degree of efficiency. Left pretty much to themselves until mid-1943, the shops' operating procedures, tool and test equipment, and physical layouts differed widely. A few months of close staff supervision from Washington resulted in a centrally controlled system that greatly improved both the quantity and the quality of the shops' output. Redesign of shop layouts, provision of more and better test equipment of standard design, and establishment of quality standards for repair and inspection of the product helped raise repair standards. A more equitable allocation of repair parts solved one difficulty, since the repair shops had previously been "low man on the totem pole" in regard to spare parts.[124]

Martin L. Cardwell, a signal equipment engineer in the OCSigO, developed and installed the first model repair line, an improvement later adopted by all Signal Corps fifth echelon shops.[125] Under the earlier method, a single workman performed all the various stages of work on a single complete item of equipment. The new method set up repair lines on a component basis that resulted in better use of space, more precise standards of workmanship, and increased capacity through mass-production tech-

niques. It also utilized the slower, less skilled workmen to better advantage and decreased the amount of test equipment needed. Another improvement concentrated repair of major items at one or two shops. Thus only Philadelphia worked on certain designated switchboards, transmitters, receivers, and various tuning units; Chicago on other designated receivers, rectifiers, remote control units, and so on. This relieved other shops from maintaining parts and test equipment for those special items. Moistureproofing and fungusproofing became routine for all items of repaired equipment.[126]

In the period January 1944 to August 1945, Signal Corps depot repair shops repaired and returned to stock $116,808,-000 worth of equipment. This represented 18.6 percent of the total supply. Between September 1944 and April 1945 the shops expended 2,158,000 manhours.[127] Besides the civilian employees, some shops used prisoner of war labor. The average output of individual items from the repair shops in early 1945 ran into the thousands—for example, 4,000 dynamotors, 1,000 small front-line radios, 5,000 headsets, 650 headsets, 650 reel units.[128]

As the load in depot repair shops increased, the load in service command shops declined, and depot shops began transferring a part of their "repair for

---

[123] Hist, SigC Repair Shops, p. 2.

[124] *Ibid.*, pp. 5–9.

[125] Meritorious Civilian Service Award, 22 Apr 46. SigC 200.6 Awards No. 9, 20–30 Apr 46.

[126] (1) Hist, SigC Repair Shops, pp. 11–12 and apps. B and F. (2) Novick, Story of Sup in the SigC in World War II, pp. 58–59.

[127] Maintenance, 16 Jan 50, prepared by George R. Powell, in Theodore Whiting, Statistics. Draft MS in OCMH files.

[128] (1) Hist, SigC Repair Shops, pp. 5–6. (2) Shops Br Distr Div OCSigO, MPR's, Jan Through Jul 44. SigC DS 319.1 Digest of Progress and Problems, 1943–44.

stock" burden to service command shops. By April 1945, twenty-two such shops in eight of the service commands were engaged in fifth echelon repair work.[129] The end of the war found the repair shops loaded with equipment and work. When hostilities ceased the need for repair ended abruptly, except for normal issue requirements. Large quantities of equipment on hand at the shops were placed in a deferred repair status and soon created a storage problem of major proportions. The emphasis shifted from repair to inspection and testing of returned material as repair production lines closed down and large numbers of workers were released. With the official decision that there was no basic difference between fourth and fifth echelon maintenance for the postwar Military Establishment, depot repair shops took over both kinds of work, and service command shops became third echelon.[130]

Packing and Packaging

Prewar planning had failed to recognize the necessity for special packaging of signal equipment to assure its delivery overseas in good condition.[131] Cogent reasons explained, if they did not excuse, the Signal Corps' tardiness in dealing with the packaging problem. Hardly anyone else had thought of it, either, before war came.[132] Peacetime maneuvers, which were supposed to reproduce the conditions of warfare realistically, had done nothing of the sort so far as equipment packaging was concerned. Under the restrictions that stringent economy imposed upon the prewar Army, very little signal equipment was available for maneuvers, and what there was of it had to be guarded and preserved jealously. Each signal officer was held accountable for equipment issued to him. If an item was damaged or lost, he paid for it out of his own pocket. Thus when the equipment was not in use, or during bad weather, the signal officer hustled it off the field and wrapped it up or stored it away very carefully. Obviously no sensible man would deliberately toss a packaged radio off a truck just to see whether the package broke open, or dump it in a creek just to test its vulnerability to water seepage.[133]

The extreme urgency of other supply matters in the first months of war delayed the packaging program. Measured against the vast problems of procurement, packaging the product seemed like a very minor detail indeed. At first there actually seemed to be no problem. The Army had a packing specification, which placed the responsibility for packaging upon the supplier of the goods. The manufacturers who held the great majority of Signal Corps contracts were the giants of the communications industry—Western Electric, General Electric, Westinghouse, Radio Corporation of

---

[129] (1) Transmittal Sheet, Comment No. 1, Shops Br Distr Div to Dir Maint Div, 2 Apr 45, sub: List of Sv Comd Sig Repair Shops. SigC 635 Gen 1, Jan–May 45. (2) SigC Depot Repair Shops Opns Ltr 14, 5 Mar 45, sub: Transfer of Repair for Stock Work to Sv Comd Sig Repair Shops. SigC 635 Gen 2, Jun–Dec 45.

[130] OCSigO Distr Div, Qtrly Rpts, Jul–Sep 45, Oct–Dec 45.

[131] Thompson, Harris, et al., The Test, pp. 521–24.

[132] See Erna Risch, The Quartermaster Corps: Organization, Supply, and Services, Volume I, UNITED STATES ARMY IN WORLD WAR II (Washington, 1953), pp. 201–02, 355.

[133] Novick, Story of Sup in the SigC in World War II, pt. IV, p. 37.

America, and Bendix. All of them did a large volume of foreign business and were quite familiar with the problems of export packing. The Signal Corps assumed that items of equipment from these contractors and from subcontractors trained by them would be adequately packaged for shipment to troops overseas. The fallacy in this reasoning was that the specification merely provided for packaging adequate for the point of first delivery, and in the first months of war the point of first delivery was the depot, which repackaged the items for delivery overseas. The depots possessed neither the personnel and equipment nor the specialized knowledge to handle the job. Furthermore, export packing under peacetime conditions was not at all adequate for the wartime demands of a global conflict stretching into areas no commercial company ever reached in the normal course of business. In peacetime, commercial companies could assume that their products would be handled carefully en route overseas, unloaded properly at commercial docks, and stored in protected warehouses at the end of the journey. In wartime, signal equipment was likely to be handled carelessly by inexperienced persons en route, doused with seawater in the exigencies of an amphibious landing under fire, and left in the open without shelter of any kind at some time during its journey to the front lines.[134]

In mid-1942, in an attempt to centralize and co-ordinate its packaging activities as directed by ASF, the Signal Corps organized a Packaging Section in the

Storage and Issue Agency.[135] The section found itself saddled with a mission much too broad for its capabilities. It soon became evident that the Packaging Section was merely floundering—it had far too few employees, and those it had knew too little about the work they were expected to do.[136]

Initially, the packaging engineers wrote packaging specifications for individual items of equipment on order or about to be put on order and then sent them to the contracting officers for incorporation in the contract. A reorganization of the packaging activity in March 1943 attempted to meet objections of contracting officers that packaging specifications did not arrive early enough in the supply cycle to be of much benefit. After March the Purchasing Division of OCSigO and the Stock Control Division of S&I Agency dutifully sent all purchase requests to the Packaging Section, which was supposed to incorporate packing and packaging information in the requests before the contracts were placed. But there were too many requests to process. Very often the requests covered the purchase of development equipment, and the Packaging Section engineers could not determine readily what the exact shape, size, or weight of the equipment would be, or

---

[134] Thompson, Harris, et al., The Test, pp. 521-23.

[135] Ibid., pp. 523-24.
The section was originally called the Equipment Protection Advisory Subsection. It became the Packaging Section on 25 March 1943. Ullery, Hist, S&I Agency, I, 387-88.

[136] Unless otherwise noted, the following is from: (1) Ullery, Hist, S&I Agency; (2) Novick, Story of Sup in the SigC in World War II, pt. IV, pp. 35-52; (3) Hist Notes on the Packaging Div, 19 Sep 45, S&I Agency Info file, Philadelphia; (4) Report of the Rapid Growth of the Packaging Section, SigC Hist Sec file; (5) Digest of Problems and Progress, 1944-46, SigC DS 319.1; (6) OCSigO Distr Div, Qtrly Rpts, 1943-45.

even the number of components in it. If the engineers wrote a specification without complete information, changes in the equipment during development often rendered the instructions obsolete. If the Packaging Section waited for complete information, the time lag was so great their work was of little value to the contracting officers, who wanted the information early enough to incorporate in the bid request so as to eliminate the time and money otherwise spent in renegotiating the contract after the detailed specifications became available. Either way was unsatisfactory, and the Packaging Section estimated that the contracting officers used no more than 5 percent of the specifications prepared for them.[137]

Three basic defects characterized the Signal Corps' packaging efforts during the period. The first lay in the method of attack: writing detailed specifications for individual pieces of equipment rather than providing broad, flexible instructions that could be applied to large classes of items. It was like using a fly swatter on an extermination problem that called for a DDT bomb. A second defect was the failure to grasp the real nature of the problem, which was one of training and indoctrination. Procurement officers, depot and inspection personnel, and manufacturers all had to be persuaded that good packaging was necessary. They also needed assistance in obtaining materials and working out procedures. The third deficiency concerned the limited scope of the program. The Packaging Section was altogether too small and weak to carry out its responsibilities. After a full year's

existence, the section had only nine qualified packaging technicians. Of this number five were awaiting early induction into the military service. General Ingles later said that, before August 1943, aside from specification writing, the section's activities consisted of "making sincere but ineffectual efforts to arouse a general consciousness of the need for good packaging." [138]

The personnel situation improved after a second reorganization in September 1943. By that time the Packaging Section had already supplied depots, manufacturers, and service commands with about 400 separate packaging specifications, but there was a considerable time lapse between corrective action at home and results in the theater.[139] For example, a division signal officer in New Georgia in the late summer of 1943 complained bitterly about the poor packaging of batteries, stating that losses from moisture deterioration alone ran as high as 50 percent.[140] Yet in April the Philadelphia Signal Depot had begun packaging all batteries in waterproof, moistureproof, and vaporproof wrappings and, by the time the New Georgia complaint arrived, had already sent overseas 12,000,000 batteries packed in this manner.[141]

Still intent upon turning out more and better detailed specifications faster, the Signal Corps early in 1944 engaged the

[137] Ullery, Hist, S&I Agency, I, 398.

[138] Memo, CSigO for ACofS G–4, 21 Nov 44, sub: Rpt of Packaging of Sups, SigC. SigC DS Packaging Rpt, SigC Hist Sec file.

[139] OCSigO R&W Action 1, Maj J. J. Healy, Chief Storage Br, to P&O Div, 15 Sep 43, sub: Matters Pertaining to Distr. SCIA file 84 Rives Rpt.

[140] Ltr, Col Ankenbrandt, SigO USAFISPA, to Gen Meade, Dir Opns Div OCSigO, 31 Aug 43. SCIA file 8 Ankenbrandt-Newhouse Rpts.

[141] OCSigO R&W Action 1, Chief Storage Br to P&D Div, 15 Sep 43.

services of a firm of architectural engineers who could provide expert knowledge of blocking, bracing, and design. Many of the earliest damage reports had emphasized equipment breakage caused by faulty bracing methods.[142] A number of engineers and technicians from the Packaging Section went on duty with the New York firm to receive training. This group became the New York Specification Section. During the next several months it turned out a sizable number of minutely detailed specifications for individual items of equipment. In fact, they were too detailed. Tailored to one procurement order, subsequent changes of dimension or components on following orders soon made the specifications obsolete. Furthermore, it developed that other factors besides blocking,

bracing, and design were equally important in packaging. The commercial contract was canceled in December.[143]

Meanwhile, beginning in late 1943, the Packaging Section broadened its scope of operations decisively. In a step toward general rather than specific instructions, it produced a publication (PE–100) that consisted of a series of numbered paragraphs of general instructions from which the packaging engineer could select standard clauses and provide contracting officers with instructions merely by referring to the numbers. This greatly speeded paper work but did not solve the initial difficulty of finding out the nature of the item, its dimensions, weight, and cubage. Next, packaging field sections were established in each of the inspection zones and in each signal depot or signal section. Thus, trained packaging experts became instantly available for visits to contractors' plants to expedite matters whenever a problem of material or interchangeability arose. The experts wrote "T-specs"—temporary specifications—often in longhand at the suppliers' plants; issued common specifications, covering more than one stock-numbered item, for such things as dry batteries, crystals, fuses, resistors, capacitors, and common tools; and wrote general specifications covering the packaging of small-piece parts, providing for standard-sized waterproof and moisture-vaporproof pouches, cartons, and containers.[144]

In December 1944 the Packaging Section set up a special testing and developing unit at Evans Signal Labora-

---

[142] See, for example, 1st Indorsement, Lt. Col. Thomas L. Clark, Officer in Charge, Signal Section Chicago Quartermaster Depot, to Chief Signal Officer, 4 February 1942, on letter, Chief Signal Officer to Signal Supply Officer Chicago Quartermaster Depot, 5 November 1941, sub: Automatic Telephone Unit, which states: "The equipment is beyond repair and cannot even be salvaged for repair parts on account of the manner in which the switchboard was roughly thrown into a packing container, and without any care or bracing was shipped to the Signal Section of the Chicago Depot. . . . This unit as received is a mass of junk. . . . The party who packed the unit made no effort to pack it securely, so it would reach destination intact, but merely threw it in a container; several spare parts were tossed in on top of that, and two heavy wooden mounting boards used for the base were heaved in on top of that. The result was that not a selector, line switch, or any part of the unit is fit for use." SigC 413.42 Gen 1, Jan–Jun 42.

In December 1941 a number of SCR–197 sets received identical damage to rear bumpers during shipment because of faulty bracing—a T-formation device strapped to the bumper with the bottom of the T secured to the end of the boxcar. Ltr, Div SigO 1st Armored Div to CSigO, 19 Dec 41, sub: Recommendation for Future Loading of Radio Sets (SCR–197). SigC 400.12 Controlled Items 14.

[143] Ullery, Hist, S&I Agency, I, 397.

[144] (1) Ullery, Hist, S&I Agency, p. 399. (2) SigC DS Packaging Rpt, Nov 44, passim. (3) Packing Sig Equip, SigC Info Ltr 43 (Jun 45), pp. 14–15.

tory to test the effectiveness of various types of packaging for items on development contracts. In its home quarters at Philadelphia, the section built a packaging workshop where it could make the simpler tests, store a stock of packaging materials to fabricate new types of packages, and keep models on display.[145]

Early in 1944 the Signal Corps turned toward the training aspects, which probably did more than anything else to solve the packaging problem. In a series of meetings with manufacturers, packaging techniques and problems were discussed. At the time, packing facilities at the depots were becoming overloaded because manufacturers actively resisted changes in packing specifications, believing the added work would retard production.[146] The field consultant system went into effect at about the same time. Such a program called for publications, and the Packaging Section determinedly pushed aside other work to write manuals of general instructions.[147]

With textbook material available, training courses became possible, and the Signal Corps engaged the services of the Forest Products Laboratory in Madison, Wisconsin. In June 1944, 87 officers and civilians, representing Signal Corps depots, inspection zones, procurement districts, and the S&I Agency, completed a very successful one-week intensive study of crating, boxing, and preserving signal material.[148] Other courses followed. By January 1945 Forest Products had trained 110 officers and 365 civilians. Then the Storage Branch, OCSigO, worked out its own program of training conferences for depot packing supervisors, conducted by Signal Corps training teams. At three special training centers—the Chicago Signal Depot, the Philadelphia Signal Depot, and the Signal Section of the Ogden ASF Depot—depot supervisors from the surrounding areas received intensive training in such subjects as corrosion prevention, packing, marking, and carloading. Armed with the latest joint Army-Navy specifications, literature, and manuals, the supervisors returned to their own depots to establish on-the-job training courses. Headquarters engineers visited each location to help set up the local training programs. All together, this phase of the training effort proved highly successful.[149]

While the Storage and Issue Agency fought the battle for better packaging on one front, other attacks were under way at other points. At the Holabird Signal Depot, packing and packaging engineers were developing new methods of amphibious packing.[150] Overseas reports had indicated that up to 90 percent of the failures in radios installed in vehi-

---

[145] (1) Ullery, Hist, S&I Agency, I, 401. (2) Hist Notes on the Packaging Div, 19 Sep 45. (3) Rpt of the Rapid Growth of the Packaging Section, pp. 4–5.

[146] OCSigO Storage Br, Progress Rpt, Feb 44. SigC DS 319.1 Digest of Progress and Problems, 1943–44.

[147] Signal Pack, Specification No. 72-0-6, and Signal Pack Guide, Specification No. 72-0-10, issued in 1944, summarized all the packaging principles developed to date, the application of materials to these principles, and standardized packaging processes for small items. A third manual, Standard Pack, issued in 1945, covered instructions for packing larger items.

[148] OCSigO Storage Br, Qtrly Progress Rpt, 1 Apr 44–30 Jun 44. SigC DS 319.1 Digest of Progress and Problems, 1943–44.

[149] Packaging and Packing Tng, SigC Tech Info Ltr 43 (Jun 45), p. 16.

[150] (1) Hist Rpt of Activities, Holabird Sig Depot, 8 Sep 43 to 31 Mar 44, pp. 4–10. SigC Hist Sec file. (2) CSigO, Annual Rpt, FY 44, p. 33.

cles resulted from moisture.[151] Holabird put the containers into moistureproof wrappers, which were then wax-impregnated, further waterproofed, sealed, and fitted into wooden boxes. The inner wrappings provided additional flexibility to the standard waterproof liners, which in the past had sometimes split and cracked during shipping. In addition the wrappings prevented water from seeping into the boxes when they were dropped overboard, thus making it possible to float the boxes from ship to shore.[152]

Early in December Holabird and Camp Evans, working independently but with an exchange of information, began processing the new gun-laying microwave radar, SCR–584, in its trailer for overseas shipment. Using specially manufactured asbestos grease or similar sealing material, the depots sealed joints and other crevices, with special attention to the protection of electrical connections at the bottom of each vehicle. To protect electrical connections, the engineers used a caulking compound that hardened on the surface but remained soft beneath. They covered open spaces with asphalt-saturated muslin, then sprayed the covering with sealing material. Finally, the men placed silica gel desiccant in each vehicle to make sure that the relative humidity of the vehicle interior would not exceed 20 percent for the next twelve months. The first twenty SCR–584 trailers so processed went to a port of embarkation late in December. Next the Holabird men went to work

on the SCR–399, developing a satisfactory method of packaging that set.[153] Holabird pioneered many of the more successful Signal Corps methods of overseas packing, but lack of space and facilities made it necessary to farm out packaging contracts to commercial firms, especially for the larger pieces of equipment such as the SCR–399 and power units.[154]

A frequent complaint from overseas concerned markings on equipment. Equipment was often not shipped with the using unit and when shipped with the unit sometimes became separated. In either case, identification on the outside packing of the equipment was essential. The Signal Corps Inspection Agency campaigned ceaselessly to compel manufacturers to use a strong, clear Signal Corps orange paint and stencils with large letters. Too often manufacturers used a weak yellow or an orange-red paint, unaware that both red and yellow indicated arms or services other than the Signal Corps.[155] During amphibious landings, Air Forces and Signal Corps equipment, especially, ended up in confused and intermingled heaps. Seeking a remedy, ASF introduced a new standard procedure of identification of separate shipments—a method of marking all cargo shipped overseas to identify shippers, receivers, and contents. The Signal Corps then used film strips, slides, posters, lectures, and other training material to familiarize all of its supply and

---

[151] Ltr, Col George I. Back, Dir Distr Div OCSigO, to CO S&I Agency, 16 Dec 43, sub: Protection of Signal Corps Equip on Overseas Shipment. SigC MA 400.258 Moisture and Fungus Proofing Prog.
[152] CSigO, Annual Rpt, FY 44, p. 33.

[153] Hist Rpt of Activities, Holabird Sig Depot, 8 Sep 43–31 Mar 44, pp. 68, 71.
[154] Hist Rpt of Activities, Holabird Sig Depot, 1 Apr 44–30 Jun 44, II, 159.
[155] Lt Col Eldon A. Koerner, Address, Signal Corps Inspection, Sig Sup Mtg, Chicago, 26–28 Apr 46. SigC 337 Sig Sup Mtg, Apr 46.

depot personnel with the procedure and the overseas markings.[156]

It was late 1944, three years after Pearl Harbor, before the campaign for better packaging reached its height. Indeed, packaging came in for so much critical attention throughout the military services in 1944 that severe shortages of packing materials developed. The technical services competed with each other, trying to corner the markets on various materials. The Signal Corps created a unit to approve substitutions and to calculate amounts needed. At the same time the Corps contributed its bit to the growing scarcity by accumulating stockpiles of certain critical materials such as desiccant and metal foil barrier, and locating them at strategic depots. By December, conflicts of interest between the Army and the Navy and the growing competition for packaging materials forced the formation of the Army Packaging Board, which soon became the Joint Army-Navy Packaging Board.[157] Thereafter all the services used standardized packaging. A contractor who furnished the same article for all three services packed the item in the same way whether for the Army, the AAF, or the Navy. Tests and packaging materials approved by one were approved for use by all. The Quartermaster Corps assumed purchasing responsibility for waterproof, greaseproof, and moisture-vaporproof materials for the ASF and the AAF. It then turned out that the duplication of orders and the separate stockpiling by the competing services had actually created an unnecessary shortage of materials in the first place.[158]

By early 1945 the Signal Corps' Packaging Section had succeeded in spreading the packaging gospel all along the supply chain. Laboratories consulted packaging experts when they began developing a new item of equipment. Manufacturers co-operated and gave valuable assistance. Well-indoctrinated inspectors kept a weather eye out for improper packaging. Looking toward redeployment problems, twenty-four 3-man packaging teams completed 5-week training courses at Holabird Signal Depot before shipping out to the ETO.[159] In short, the Signal Corps packaging program was finally in hand.

Evaluation and Summary

The two wartime Chief Signal Officers, Generals Olmstead and Ingles, acted promptly to establish administrative reorganization of Signal Corps distribution activities.[160] Even so, the size of

---

[156] (1) *ASF Final Rpt, I Jul 47*, app. 1, p. 253. (2) Maj. W. C. Frierson, Preparations for Torch, app. sec. K, an. E, SOS Memo, Lessons Learned From Recent Amphibious Opns in North Africa. OCMH files. (3) CSigO, Annual Rpt, FY 44, pp. 442–43. (4) Memo, Inventory Contl Sec for Apolant, 5 Apr 44, sub: Digest of Progress and Problems of Inventory Contl Sec for Period 31 Dec 43 Through 31 Mar 44. SigC DS 319.1 Digest of Progress and Problems, 1943–44.

[157] The Army Packaging Board was established 11 December 1944. The AAF joined the organization in February 1945. The Joint Army-Navy Packaging Board was established by Section II, War Department Circular 80, 1945. *ASF, Annual Rpt, FY 45*, p. 203.

[158] (1) *Logistics in World War II*, p. 78. (2) Packing Sig Equip, SigC Tech Info Ltr 43 (Jun 45), p. 15. (3) Novick, Story of Sup in the SigC in World War II, p. 45.

[159] (1) Rpt of the Rapid Growth of the Packaging Sec, pp. 4–5. SigC Hist Sec file. (2) OCSigO Distr Div, Digest of Progress and Problems, Jun 45. SigC 319.1 Digest of Progress and Problems, 1943–45.

[160] (1) Thompson, Harris, *et al., The Test*, pp. 177–83, 324–28, 513–32. (2) Novick, Story of Sup in the SigC in World War II, pt. IV, Distr, pp. 1–17.

the distribution task, which far exceeded anything envisioned in prewar planning, inevitably created difficulties. The initial emphasis on procurement and production problems in the first eighteen months of war permitted the distribution system to expand somewhat haphazardly. A very large proportion of signal items, such as radar and the FM series of radios, was brand new. The lack of issue experience on these and other new items created stock control and maintenance problems that only time could solve. Methods and procedures that had served well enough for many years in peacetime proved inadequate for the wartime task. After the Signal Corps and the ASF together introduced standardized procedures in 1943 matters improved rapidly. Within a few months the Signal Corps distribution system reached a high rate of efficiency.[161]

Standardization is the key word. It represents ASF's important contribution to distribution activities among all the technical services and their installations.[162] ASF's standardized depot and stock control procedures hastened improvements already begun by the Signal Corps itself. Without ASF control, for example, depot mechanical labor-saving devices such as forklifts could hardly have been obtained and distributed equitably according to the greatest need.

The best equipment in the world is worthless if it cannot be placed in the hands of the troops who need it and at the time required. Measured by this standard, the Signal Corps distribution system met the test, at first with some needless effort and lost motion, but eventually with a high degree of co-ordination and efficiency.

---

[161] In the last two years of war the Signal Corps distribution system performed more work with no increase in its labor force. In FY 1944, receipts and shipments totaled 1,162,000; in 1945, the figure increased 33.7 percent to 1,554,000. In the same period tonnage figures stood at 1,683,000 for FY 1944 and 1,738,000 for FY 1945. CSigO Annual Rpt, FY 45, p. 948.

[162] For details consult the series of monographs prepared by the ASF's Distribution, Storage, and Maintenance Divisions, especially Distribution Division monographs Storage Operations December 1941–December 1945, and History of Stock Control, U.S. Army.

CHAPTER XIV

Equipment: The Laboratories—AAF Items and Their Transfer

By the mid-point of World War II the pressure of immediate needs, especially for the forthcoming invasion of Europe, rendered academic in the several laboratories of the Signal Corps any question as to which—the immediate present or the more distant future—should receive the greater stress. In the Signal Corps, as everywhere else in the Army, research temporarily had to give way to a heavy program of practical assistance in readying equipment for the invasion of Normandy in 1944.[1]

The laboratory workers were needed to help maintain and improve the operation of the equipment that was already in, or on the way to, the field, and they could help in many ways. Lists of maintenance parts and procedures had to be compiled; modification kits must be engineered; some engineers and scientists were needed in the field to help troops use their equipment to its full potential—members of the laboratories went as members of teams whose function it was to introduce new equipment in oversea commands.[2]

Early in 1944 Dr. Maurice E. Strieby, a scientist consultant and adviser in the office of the Secretary of War, reported a significant observation after a field trip—enough research had already been done. His reactions were echoed by various Signal Corps people. Dr. Lynne C. Smeby, acting chief of the OCSigO's Office of Operational Research, wrote on 27 May 1944, "the peak development point for this war was reached several months ago." Army communications would be entirely adequate, Dr. Smeby thought, "if we could have full effective use of the equipment we now have in the field and of the equipment in immediate production."[3] The Chief Signal Officer agreed. Army's signaling devices, General Ingles noted in June 1944, "are now far ahead of training and they are changed with such rapidity that the personnel never reaches a stage

---

[1] See above, pp. 9–10. In Army R&D activity, the Signal Corps share was second only to that of the Ordnance Department. CSigO, Annual Rpt, FY 44, p. 2.

According to a postwar account of SCEL, most laboratory effort after Pearl Harbor, in wire, for example, went into such tasks as searching for substitutes for critical materials, design changes in order to improve the performance of existing equipment, and the moistureproofing and fungusproofing of equipment. Postwar R&D Program of the Signal Corps Engineering Laboratories (Tentative), 5 Dec 45 (hereafter cited as SCEL Postwar R&D Prog), p. 4.

[2] NEID teams. See above, p. 93, n. 87.

[3] (1) ASF Transmittal Sheet, Action 3, Smeby to Intel Br OCSigO, 27 May 44, sub: Results of Theater Survey Trip. SCIA file 127 Bowles Rpts. (2) Memo, Strieby for Bowles, 28 Apr 44, sub: Results of Theater Survey Trip, p. 3. Bowles folder, SigC Hist Sec file. See also Thiesmeyer and Burchard, *Combat Scientists*, p. 250.

of training which permits the development of more than 50% of the capabilities of the equipment." He added, "All development laboratories under my control are now directed entirely towards the improvement of existing equipment." [4]

Cutbacks in Laboratory Personnel and Projects

In war, as in every other human activity, there are contradictions and dilemmas. In laboratory work, for example, the question was whether to put money, material, and men into further long-range development, lack of which might at some later date prove crucial, or to use them on short-range projects that would affect the invasion effort. In 1943 there could be no doubt where the most manpower had to be expended. So pressing was the need to provide the invasion forces with massive manpower that personnel cuts applied even to the laboratories. In Signal Corps laboratories these reductions in the mid-course of the war cut deep, postponing basic research and considerably jolting much of the development progress. Necessity reduced, narrowed, and straightened the war programs. There were not enough materials or enough of that most vital resource—men. Men had to be taken from one task and shifted into another. The nation's leaders were all engaged in a jealous attempt to make ends meet. Much had to be taken from whatever was believed to be less impor-

tant and reassigned to whatever was judged to be most urgent.

The ASF commander, General Somervell, charged with the Army's biggest bookkeeping job, found himself obliged to curtail many research and development projects. He directed the technical services to determine the details of the lab reductions, reductions that the Army knew might be penny-wise and pound-foolish in an era of technological warfare. The Allied margin of technological superiority in World War II did in fact turn out to be uncomfortably narrow.[5] General Ingles, receiving the ASF instructions soon after he took control of the Signal Corps, passed the reduction order on to General Colton, upon whom devolved the difficult task of

---

[4] Memo, Ingles for Bowles, 27 Jun 44, sub: Comments on Strieby's Conclusions on Results of Theater Survey Trip. SigC EO 370.2 Theaters of Opn, 1943–44.

[5] The prize for mistaken R&D economies in the war goes to Hitler, especially for his radar research cuts. See James G. Crowther and Richard Whiddington, *Science at War* (New York: 1948), p. 87. In Great Britain close decisions involving radar development hung upon the conflicting views of Sir Henry Tizard, chairman of the Committee for the Scientific Survey of Air Defence, and Prime Minister Winston S. Churchill's science adviser, Frederick A. Lindemann (Lord Cherwell), who tended to favor other technologies over radar. Radar fortunately won out. See C. P. Snow, *Science and Government* (Cambridge, Mass.: Harvard University Press, 1961), and Earl of Birkenhead, *The Professor and The Prime Minister* (Boston: Houghton Mifflin Company, 1962).
One laboratory postwar summary stated it to be "increasingly apparent that the technological race with Germany was an extremely close one," and in the opinion of a leading Signal Corps scientist the fact "that the allies forged ahead of the Germans was only in part due to the fact that the allies expended greater funds and a greater amount of brain power on research on radar and electronics." Germany, expecting a short war, in 1939 terminated a great deal of its research work and transferred scientific personnel into its field armies. SCEL Postwar R&D Program, p. 1. See also Memo, Lt Col John J. Slattery for the CSigO, 9 Nov 45, sub: Trip to ETO, p. 42, Tab III, Slattery Rpt, 9 Nov 45. SigC Hist Sec file.

reviewing the laboratory projects in order to decide which would be canceled. Each project, no matter how long or how short a time it had been in the laboratories, no matter how broad or how detailed or how secret, came up for examination. Each was tested by two questions: Would its cancellation release critical materials to other projects still more vital? Would its cancellation tend to shorten the war and to lower the casualty lists? There was some leeway. If a project failed to meet either of these criteria, yet sought to forestall some technological advance of the enemy, the operation remained. And if a test had been going on so long that to bring it to an end would be economically unsound, work continued.

The order sounded drastic. Strictly applied, it would have been, but various circumstances helped to cushion the blow. The Army Air Forces, for example, eager to get projects begun by the Signal Corps for the AAF, did take over many. Expansion plans of the AAF benefited from the Signal Corps cut.[6] Again, while a few installations (notably the Toms River Signal Laboratory) were closed out, administrators found ways to reassign some of the people concerned rather than cut all from the lists. Officers were moved about. All together 3,800 civilians were dropped. A total of 90 projects were canceled, but 31 of them had in fact

been completed. The total cut in projects seems to have been about 17 percent, heavy but not drastic. Several projects were transferred to the Navy, for example the magnetic airborne detector and the sonic radio buoy for detecting submarines.[7]

Probably the cut was made as efficiently as possible in work that cried for more engineers, and more competent ones, if Signal Corps laboratories were to equal the standards of civilian laboratories or of the naval research establishments.[8] Perhaps it was not expected that the various laboratories should be equal in view of the policy that the Signal Corps should look outside the Army for advance theory and application.

The effect of the cuts may even have been beneficial to some degree. In the

---

[6] In at least one case in 1943, the AAF began independently to develop aircraft recording and ground playback devices. The Signal Corps objected, quoted chapter and verse of a 1942 agreement, and won for the moment—the AAF turning the project over to ARL. Ltr, CG AAF to CSigO, 27 Feb 43, sub: Proposed Aircraft Recorder and Ground Playback Equipment, with 6 Inds. AAG 413.44–AO Radio.

[7] Active projects as of 30 June 1943 stood at 362, as of 30 June 1944 at 289, a drop of 73 (not including NDRC projects). (1) CSigO, Annual Rpt, FY 44, p. 203. (2) Ltr, CG AAF to CSigO, 16 Aug 43, sub: Discontinuance of Dev of MAD and Sonic Equip. AAG 413.44–BC Radio.
An especially large project, the development of a better IFF system known as Mark V, was vigorously debated by the Signal Corps, the NDRC, and the British. In the end the Naval Research Laboratory received the assignment to develop the system. (1) Capt G. B. H. Hall, USN, British Radar Mission and U.S. Radar Working Cmte, Min of Conf, 10 Dec 43. SigC 413.44 Identification No. 12 (RB–2138). (2) CSigO, Annual Rpt, FY 45, pp. 310–13.
[8] In radar equipment the Navy was ahead of the Army, both in initiating development and in co-ordination with civilian research, according to an Air Corps spokesman in September 1943. Memo, Maj F. H. Richardson, Hq AAF, for Col Phillips, 14 Sep 43. AAG 413.44–Radar.
Army's Signal Corps liaison office at RL (5 officers and 2 secretaries) was likewise much smaller than Navy and AAF liaison offices. Newton, Peterson, and Perkins, Five Years at the Radiation Laboratory (Cambridge, 1946), p. 191. See also History of Signal Corps Liaison With the Cambridge Laboratory of NDRC, Radar folder Tab Y. SigC Hist Sec file.

case of the Camp Coles Signal Laboratory, according to one subsequent comment, the personnel build-up in the 1941–43 period had been too rapid, and many people of little ability had been hired. The 1943 layoff, while somewhat reducing the laboratory output, also pruned away much of the dead wood and led to a better, more responsive organization of experienced workers.[9]

The same was true in the Camp Evans Signal Laboratory, recalled Dr. Harold A. Zahl, Director of Research in the U.S. Army Signal R&D Lab, years later. "Early policy directives," Zahl commented, speaking of the first months of the war, "did not lean toward making the labs better as much as to . . . making them bigger. . . . We didn't ask for all these trainees in the first place," he recalled, "but it was understood that we had to take them . . . [otherwise] Selective Service would eventually take every able-bodied scientifically-trained man, on whom almost our entire program then hinged."

Then, after much time was spent training the unskilled workers, many were released in 1943. Dr. Zahl compared the Army's R&D personnel policy with the one enjoyed by the OSRD Radiation Laboratory and Radio Research Laboratory in Cambridge, Massachusetts. "Had we only been able to hire moderately," Zahl lamented, "and with some selection and then followed the same draft deferment policy under which the OSRD worked, we would not have had much of a scientific manpower problem in the laboratories."[10]

The directors of the several labs in the Fort Monmouth area tried to handle the imposed cuts and still maintain acceptable efficiency by purging wisely both the work force and the projects themselves. Some projects were cut back part of the way in some areas, and not at all in others. The directors continued work on about half of the air navigation projects and on all but one of the air communications projects; nearly half in ground radar and almost all in airborne radar; almost everything in wire communications, in radio direction finding, and in power and testing equipment. They made deep reductions only in sound and light and meteorological projects. Operations were continued until completion of the service tests of the item of equipment being devised, or until the item became standardized; and usually they went on until the first production model had been accepted. All together, 234 projects continued. The biggest cuts in personnel took place at the Camp Evans, Eatontown, and Fort Monmouth Laboratories. Evans closed its subordinate areas in New Jersey—at Fort Hancock, Twinlights, and Rumson. But its station at Clermont, Florida, where ground radar equipment was undergoing field testing, was enlarged. Many of the civilians who had been working in optics, acoustics, sound ranging, and meteorology at Eatontown were dismissed. The Toms River installation shut its doors. So did the Bethlehem and Detroit Field Sta-

---

[9] Draft MS Comment, Benjamin V. Blom, Tech Adviser Sig Com Dept AEPG, 6 Jul 59. SigC Hist Sec file.

[10] Draft MS Comment, Zahl, Jul 59. SigC Hist Sec file. See also Irwin Stewart, *Organizing Sci-entific Research for War, Administrative History, OSRD* (Boston: Little, Brown & Co., 1948), pp. 276ff.

In the 1943 cuts, Zahl's own branch in the radar laboratory at Camp Evans lost over 200 people, losing also the time spent to train them and the time required to plan their separation.

tions. Many employees transferred to the Signal Corps Ground Signal Agency at Fort Monmouth, along with the work of investigation into methods of suppressing radio interference.

General Ingles, however he may have felt about reduction in research efforts, unquestioningly acknowledged the frowns of higher authority on new equipment developments. "I am in complete concurrence with Mr. Strieby's observation relative to the development of new equipments," Ingles said in mid-1944, adding that Dr. O. E. Buckley and other communications experts had argued the same view, namely that further developments be eliminated.[11]

As a consequence, the laboratory organization achieved a certain symmetry, the agencies dividing and lining up behind either air signal or ground signal work. Wright Field at Dayton became the focus for the former, and the Fort Monmouth area for the latter. As constituted for the rest of 1943 and until the middle of October 1944, when the Air Forces took it over, the Signal Corps Aircraft Signal Agency contained such units as the ARL, the Aircraft Radio Maintenance Division, and the field laboratories at Indianapolis and at Boca Raton and Eglin Field, Florida. The Signal Corps Ground Signal Agency was composed of a number of laboratories—Evans, Eatontown, and Fort Monmouth—all located in a series of New Jersey towns near the main Signal Corps post of Fort Monmouth. A Ground Signal Maintenance Division was also included.[12]

Equipment Problems

Military R&D by Government vs. Private Institutions

Another question touching Signal Corps laboratory activity—how much research should the Corps itself conduct in addition to its testing and engineering obligations, and how far should it depend upon private institutions and industrial facilities—also became academic in mid-1943. Before the war there had been research-minded men in the laboratories, notably those who first developed Army radar, officers such as Colonel Blair and General Colton, at a time when there was no radar research to speak of outside the military. Army officers and civilian scientists in the Fort Monmouth laboratories undertook R&D on radar tubes, for example, when they set up the Thermionics Section late in the 1930's. Prewar private industry knew little of such tubes and would not attempt to manufacture them. Military research and development of this sort was unusual.

General Ingles, a few months after he became the Chief Signal Officer, reaffirmed the circumscribed laboratory program that the Army had been accustomed to pursue. Indeed the Congress and industry generally would permit no variations until the strange new world of military and governmental science during World War II began to alter the nation's attitudes in these matters. In October 1943 General Ingles wrote:

It has long been the policy of the Signal Corps to do development work on new

---

[11] Memo, Ingles to Bowles, 27 Jun 44, sub: Comments on Strieby's Conclusions. SigC EO 370.2 Theaters of Opns, 1943–44.

[12] (1) Review of SigC R&D Prog, 25 Aug 43. (2)

SigC Admin Log, 1939–45, pt. II, Fld Activities, pp. 138–143. Both in SigC Hist Sec file.

equipment by contract with civilian laboratories where one could be found which had the proper facilities. In my opinion this practice is sound and should be continued. Our own laboratories are principally engaged in testing equipment, in preparing technical specifications and in furnishing an engineering service for Signal Corps activities. Recent contracts we have made for research and development in new pieces of equipment have been in furtherance of a policy of long standing and have not been done with a view to personnel requirements. It has also been the Signal Corps policy for many years not to go into the manufacturing business but to procure the equipment on contract from industry built in accordance with specifications that we prescribe. There has been no extension of this practice because of recent personnel cuts.[13]

Other government laboratories in electronics and communications work entered the scene with a deeper feeling for basic research under pressure for new development, principally that required by the AAF. The requirements were not only pressuring the Signal Corps, whose AAF equipment added up to half of its total supply task, they also taxed the facilities of two great OSRD laboratories at Cambridge. There were no cuts in those civilian laboratories in mid-1943. They lay totally outside the military domain though they existed solely to serve it, and in general accomplished their purpose better under civilian control than they could have under the circumscribed conditions of military supervision in the World War II era. At the war's end, as the Cambridge laboratories closed out, Signal Corps Engineering Laboratories at Fort Monmouth continued to

look to private institutions, such as university research establishments. "The present laboratory policy of entering into contracts with capable scholastic organizations is a step in the right direction," Lt. Col. John J. Slattery stated in November 1945.[14]

Emphasis vs. De-emphasis of New Military Applications

The urgent demand for more soldiers in mid-1943 not only compelled the cuts in electronic laboratories but also lent emphasis to the opinion of many Army officers that electronic applications and gadgetry were running a bit wild, so wild that they dangerously complicated supply as well as personnel problems. Electronic equipment consumed too many materials and too many man-hours. Yet when this very objection had been raised by Under Secretary of War Robert P. Patterson in 1942 and the Signal Corps had obligingly proposed a reduction in AAF radio types, the AAF had responded most emphatically that not fewer but more types must be supplied.[15] The matter at issue did not rest there.

The question arose again in mid-1943. General Ingles wrote General Clay, Director of Materiel in ASF:

I can have a study made of the amount of radio equipment now authorized for units and submit the same to you. . . . [but] I

[13] Memo, Ingles, CSigO, for Dir, Purchases Div ASF, 12 Oct 43. SigC 200.3 Utilization, Code files 1943.

[14] Memo, Slattery for the CSigO, 9 Nov 45, sub: Trip to ETO, p. 45, Tab IV. See also below, pp. 623ff.

Scientific competency and creativeness require "a large measure of freedom." Baxter, *Scientists Against Time*, p. 7.

[15] Thompson, Harris, *et al.*, *The Test*, pp. 245–46.

do not desire to enter into a controversy with the AGF and AAF on the subject as I haven't the time at present to combat the uproar that will arise if an outside agency suggests that they are using far too much radio.

There is no doubt that the amount of radio equipment has been at least somewhat increased by the salesmanship efforts of Signal Corps and other radio enthusiastic personnel, particularly by the Army Communications Board and the "expert consultants" headed by Dr. Bowles directly under the Secretary of War. I have taken steps to put a stop to the salesmanship efforts of the Army Communications Board and have discussed the situation with Dr. Bowles and he has agreed to cease his own and the efforts of those under him in the direction of selling the Army radar equipment that they never thought of themselves.[16]

General Clay agreed with Ingles' views and replied: "we are prepared to support you to the full in this effort." Clay urged Ingles to discuss the problem with "the Ground and Air Forces with a view to obtaining their concurrence in the reduction of the number of types as well as in the reduction of quantities."[17] Obviously the exigencies of supply took precedence over research and development. And though such experts as Dr. Bowles and Dr. Strieby and their associates were specifically employed in Secretary of War Henry L. Stimson's office to analyze the needs of the Army and to recommend new applications and solutions, here was a countertrend seeking to cancel the purpose for which these scientists were employed. All in all, a good illustration was furnished of the conflicting viewpoints of supply on the one hand and of research and development on the other.

Improved Equipment vs. Better Training

Conflict also developed between R&D and training. As noted, General Ingles agreed with Dr. Strieby that the urgent need in 1944 was not better equipment but was how to enable troops in the field to use better the equipment they already had, how to train the users well enough to get more than 50 percent of the capabilities of, for example, the radar sets in the field. Yet it would be unfortunate if supply and training difficulties should lead the Army to suppress really significant new research and development advances. Something like this occurred in mid-1944, in the case of the GL radar SCR–584.

The SCR–584, after its first dramatic appearance in the field at Anzio early in 1944, rapidly proved its effectiveness in many ways other than in its intended function as a gun layer. It could detect targets on the ground such as distant bridges or armor concentrations and could direct air attacks against them, even in darkness. The radar operators, using radiotelephone, could direct an airplane over a ground target up to ten miles away with great precision.[18] General Bradley instructed General Quesada, commander of the IX Tactical Air Command, to so use the SCR–584 in ETO by mid-1944. Obviously, the radar could greatly help the ground forces too,

---

[16] Memo, CSigO for Clay, 5 Jul 43, no sub. SigC EO Ingles, 1943–45.

A few months later Ingles characterized the number of Army radio types as "appalling." See above, p. 352, and below, p. 468.

[17] Memo, Clay, Dir of Materiel ASF, for CSigO, 14 Jul 43. SigC EO Ingles, 1943–45.

[18] See below, pp. 475–76.

since its potential indicated a method whereby moving enemy equipment might be detected at night. It indicated a breakthrough in the difficult field of how to use radar in ground fighting. This seemed too important to overlook.

Dr. Bowles in Secretary Stimson's office did not overlook the matter. In fact he staged a demonstration of the SCR–584 at the River Entrance of the Pentagon Building. He set up the radar, a plotting board for controlling and positioning airplanes in flight, and proceeded on 12 and 13 July 1944 to demonstrate to high-ranking officers in the headquarters just what could be accomplished. Lt. Gen. Ben Lear, recently appointed Commanding General, Army Ground Forces, was among those who were impressed. But there was a block to such new AGF developments—the training problem. In his own account of the matter, Bowles recorded that he

. . . had on several occasions in the past attempted to arouse in the Ground Force Headquarters a greater interest in the application of radar and related devices, . . . had found them rather completely preoccupied with matters relating to the routine training and equipping of ground troops. Although it is hardly fair to criticize them for this attitude, in view of the magnitude of the job with which they were confronted and the superb way in which they met and dealt with it, it is reasonable to say that they had neglected many of the new weapons created during the war.[19]

The Chief of Staff, General Marshall, a month after the 584 demonstrations, wrote Dr. Bowles that it was most important at that date to find ways to interdict enemy movements of supplies,

armor, and men. He hoped radar techniques, something like aircraft control methods, might be developed "which would permit us to detect ground objects such as motor transport and tank columns and, if possible, concentrations of armor and supplies. . . ." After the demonstrations, Bowles wrote General Ingles, "I believe this will do much to stabilize thinking and effort both within the Army and outside on the development and adaptation of equipment and techniques for close support." But the reaction of the Chief Signal Officer was restrained, in accord with sentiments he had expressed earlier in 1944, namely that technical experts were putting too many ideas in the heads of troops and that the greater need was for better trained troops who could use well the equipment they already had. General Ingles replied to Bowles on 11 August:

At present the training of the operating and maintenance personnel is far behind the capabilities of the equipment we now have in use. This problem is not solved by sending small groups of experts to the theaters . . . unless we adequately train the military personnel who are to operate the equipment in combat, we will never carry out the Chief of Staff's desires in the matter no matter how much equipment we develop.[20]

Despite these counterefforts and trends, continuation of research and development in general won out. This was well, hindsight indicates. Highly advanced and specialized electronic countermeasures greatly aided the Nor-

---

[19] Bowles, MS, Office History, ch. V, pp. 72–73. Copy in Bowles folder, SigC Hist Sec file.

[20] Ltr, Marshall for Bowles, 18 Aug 44, attached to Memo, Bowles for Ingles, 19 Aug 44. SigC EO Bowles, 1943–45, SigC Hist Sec file.

mandy invasion. By deceiving the enemy into holding large forces in the Cap de Calais area for weeks after the real invasion had begun to the south, the Allies through countermeasure deception unquestionably saved themselves thousands of casualties. New electronic developments and applications promoted by Dr. Bowles and other scientists blunted German buzz bomb attacks and made possible blind bombing by radar techniques, employing such radars as the SCR–584 on the ground and the superlative airborne BTO (bombing through overcast) sets with which B–29's over Japan were weakening the enemy's resistance before atomic bombs exploded over Hiroshima and Nagasaki.[21]

Lab Cutbacks vs. Crash Production for the AAF

The 1943 project and personnel cuts in Signal Corps laboratories did hurt the Corps' ability to provide research and development services to the Army. When early in 1944 General Somervell asked the Chief Signal Officer to report on his problems, the one universal complaint voiced by all General Ingles' research and development sections related to the consequence of the 1943 personnel reduction.[22]

The AAF was also vocal on this score. Because aviation electronic development (as well as that of the rest of the Army) was set back by the personnel reductions, the airmen could cite an obvious

reason in support of their plaint that Signal Corps research and development of aviation equipment was unsatisfactory. They could point out that the chronic insufficiency of scientists and engineers engaged on AAF projects had been further aggravated by the laboratory cuts of 1943. This argument no doubt had a bearing on the transfer in 1944 of aircraft electronics from Signal Corps to the Air Forces.

Another factor in the transfer developed in mid-course of the war, a consequence of an urgent requirement, costly in manpower, which came upon the laboratories in the second half of 1943. Crash production, that is the construction of special equipment on sudden demand, provided the impetus.[23] The need for crash production, and the difficulty it entailed, at once became a bone of contention between the Signal Corps and the AAF.

For example, early in August 1943, the Air Forces asked the Chief Signal Officer to produce at once two dark trace consoles for experimental use with the MEW radar under test at AAF School of Applied Tactics. When the Signal Corps, replying, asked for a formal development requirement and request for two service test units—the prescribed routine—Air Forces answered, in effect: "No. We're in a hurry. We want two lab-built models and forget the red tape. . . ." The Signal Corps radar laboratory at Camp Evans replied that it could not hand-build two models. Director Paul E. Watson stated he was "unable to undertake the construction of the two subject

---

[21] See above, pp. 98ff., 115 and below, pp. 477ff., 483ff.

[22] Memo, Colton, Chief E&T, for CSigO, 18 Jan 44, sub: Current and Anticipated ASF Problems, with 5 Incls. SigC 319.1 EC Problems, 1944 (T–1105).

---

[23] See above, p. 302.

equipments, due to reduction of personnel." [24]

The Aircraft Radio Laboratory serving the AAF at Wright Field also suffered for the want of men. "The recent reduction of ARL personnel makes it imperative that the efforts of this laboratory be expended only on those items which have the highest priority," urged the commander of the 1st Proving Ground Electronics Unit of Eglin Field, Florida, where RCM equipment was put to test and where everyone had in mind the dire needs of the Eighth Air Force against the devastating German flak so accurately directed by enemy GCI and GL radars. Jammers were needed immediately, and in some quantity. [25]

The only way emergency items of equipment such as electronic transmitters to jam radars could be obtained quickly was to adopt the British practice of hand-building them. The Americans did so, successfully at the civilian Radiation Laboratory (in its Research Construction Company), less successfully in Army laboratories. Under AAF pressure the Signal Corps in late 1943 prepared a crash procurement procedure for RCM equipment, with representatives of AAF, ASF, the Navy, and the NDRC participating. [26] The plan was to handle "a limited number of truly urgently needed RCM equipments" in quantities not exceeding 100 sets or a value of $1,000,000. To cut corners and gain speed, the planners assigned operations to ARL and the Dayton Signal Corps Procurement District and Depot. General Ingles submitted the plan to the AAF on 3 January 1944. Three days later General McClelland replied, concurring with this crash procedure "in its entirety." He added: "It is hoped that you will adopt this procedure at the earliest practicable date." Accordingly, on 10 January General Ingles authorized the procedure, and ARL put it into operation by March. [27]

The plan did not prove very effective, possibly in part because of insufficient personnel at the ARL. Dr. Bowles noted that as of 15 April 1944 only three items had been procured by this effort by the Army to crash-produce Air Forces equipment. In his opinion, "the results to this date are not encouraging." [28]

So far were the laboratories of the Signal Corps from being able to build single sets of experimental equipment (after the manner in which they had once built the first SCR–268 and 270 radars), that the Air Forces ceased looking to the Signal Corps, even for modifications in these basic radars. For example, General McClelland early in

[24] Ltr, CG AAF to CSigO, 10 Aug 43, sub: Indicators for Radio Set AN/CPS–1 (MEW) and 4 Inds. AAG 413.44–BO Radio.

[25] Ltr, Col Charles B. Overacker, Jr., CO 1st Proving Ground Electronics Unit, AAF Proving Ground Comd, Eglin Field, Fla., to Hq AAF Air Com Of Equip Br, 12 Oct 43, sub: Countermeasures Equip Dev Prog. SigC 413.44 RCM folder 7, 1 Sep–14 Nov 43 (RB–2070).

[26] Memo, McRae, Tech Staff E&T, for file, 18 Oct 43, sub: Emergency Proc of Electronics Equip. SigC 413.44 RCM (RB–2070).

[27] (1) Incl, Proposed Detailed Crash Proc Procedure for RCM Equip, with Memo, CSigO for McClelland, Air ComO, 3 Jan 44. (2) Memo, McClelland for CSigO, 6 Jan 44. C–E Equip Transfer SigC to AAF, 1944. Tab F, Bowles papers. SigC Hist Sec file. (3) ASF Transmittal Sheet, Action 1, Dir Proc Div OCSigO to Asst Chief P&D Sv, 29 Mar 44, sub: Crash RCM Proc. AAG 413.44–DO Radio. (4) ASF Transmittal Sheet, Action 1, Col McRae, OCSigO, to Capt Bowley, 17 Mar 44, sub: Crash Proc Procedure, with Incl, SCASA, Rpt of Conf, 3 Mar 44. AAG 413.44–DK Radio. (5) CSigO, Annual Rpt, FY 44, pp. 203ff.

[28] Bowles papers, Tab H, p. 1.

1944 heard of urgent complaints that Air Forces SCR–268's in Mediterranean areas were being badly jammed by the enemy. Instead of looking to the Signal Corps for relief, he wrote directly to Dr. Terman, Director of RRL:

I understand that you have had your people working on possible "palliatives" for this radar set. Will you please inform us on the state of your study, and present outlook for a simple adaptor which will do some good? I would, also, like an estimate of what can be done on a "crash" basis in your laboratory to obtain a few sets of adaptors. . . . I consider this study to have a very high priority. Please let me hear from you soon since I would like to cable General [Maj. Gen. Ira C.] Eaker to inform him of possible corrective measures. I will, at that time, initiate appropriate action through the Signal Corps.[29]

Thus the Signal Corps appears to have played second fiddle in Air Forces electronic matters during the crucial months of late 1943 and early 1944 just when maximum effort was needed for the supreme effort against fortress Europe. To a considerable degree the Signal laboratories were prevented from meeting all needs. For example, Ingles' crash procurement program could not succeed without men to implement it. The Signals Liaison Office in the Air Ministry, London, pressing for countermeasures equipment early in 1944, urged that the Signal Corps expand its facilities and build "experimental models for operational use," but this was asking the impossible.[30] For the

Corps' laboratories, far from expanding, had been cut down. The ARL was still losing men as of May 1944; yet its workload was increasing. Air Forces officers tended to blame the Signal Corps "which controls the quantity of personnel at the Aircraft Radio Laboratory." Col. George C. Hale, communications equipment officer in the Air Communications Office, stated the matter on 16 May 1944 as follows:

It might be pointed out at this time that the Aircraft Radio Laboratory has on its books more mock-up and installation work than ever before and is seriously being handicapped by having its quota of personnel, which is not now adequate to perform all the work which they have, cut down even more by directives from the Office of the Chief Signal Officer which controls the quantity of personnel at the Aircraft Radio Laboratory. This situation is growing more serious every day since the draft is also pulling men from Aircraft Radio Laboratory who are vitally needed.[31]

Transfer of Communications Equipment Responsibilities to the AAF

In 1944 the Army transferred to the Air Forces all air electronics activity along with the Signal Corps installations and personnel that had so long served the AAF.

A Look Backward

A first long step toward the transfer had been taken in March 1942, with

[29] Ltr, McClelland, Air ComO, to Terman, Dir RRL, 3 Mar 44. AAG 413.44–DF Radio.

[30] Ltr, CG AAF to CSigO, 4 Mar 44, sub: Request for RCM Equip, with Incl, Extract From Rpt for Week Ending 26 Feb 44. USAAF Signals Ln Of, Whitehall, London. AAG 413.44–DL Radio. In urging this request upon the Signal Corps, the

Liaison Office looked to the Corps for leadership amid the U.S. Army's rather chaotic electronics activity, saying that it understood the Signal Corps was "more or less in control of the laboratories and model shops."

[31] AAF R&R, Hale, ACofAS MMD Com Equip, to Air ComO, 16 May 44, sub: Instal of AN/APS–1 Equip. AAG 413.44–EE Radio.

the reorganization of the Army. At that time, the Air Forces received control of many of the supply and service functions that ASF provided to the rest of the Army. The AAF set up its own Materiel Command and acquired many medical, quartermaster, and other services. Thus, certain AAF services, such as photography and training films, medical and hospital service in continental United States, storage and issue of common supplies, supply of air stations, and so on, duplicated the services to the rest of the Army, services that for the rest of the Army were gathered up after March 1942 in the ASF (SOS). The AAF considered that it had to have independent control over all items it deemed "peculiar" to its activity.[32]

From the reorganization of 1942 on, the AAF asserted that its radio and radar, especially airborne types, were "peculiar" to the Air Forces and that AAF ought to have complete control of the items. General Code, the Deputy Chief Signal Officer, led the opposition to this view, and General Somervell backed

---

[32] (1) *ASF, Final Rpt, 1 Jul 47,* pp. 197–98. (2) Millet, *Organization and Role of the Army Service Forces,* pp. 124ff. (3) Craven and Cate, eds., *Men and Planes,* p. 375. (4) Memo, J.A.C. [Code] for the CSigO, 10 Sep 42. DCSigO folder, 1942–45, p. 17. SigC Hist Sec file.
And in the words of a Signal Corps officer in 1947: ". . . Upon the formation of the Army Air Forces, the Air Force did not conceive of the Army Air Force as consisting of the Air Corps as the combatant arm, and other arms and services, such as Quartermaster, Signal, Ordnance, etc., supplying the combatant army, but a part of the Air Force. Regardless of the underlying reason, there appears to have been the feeling that unless personnel belonged to the Air Corps, they could not be a proper and integral part of the Air Force." Unsigned paper Sig ExecO, 30 Jul 47, Problem Presented: Status of the Signal Corps After Unification, Facts Bearing on the Problem, p. 3. Bowles papers, Tab H, SigC Hist Sec file.

him up. Code summed up the matter years later, as follows:

Immediately after the War Department reorganization at the beginning of World War II the Air Corps were given the procurement, research, and development of all items *peculiar to the Air Force.* General Arnold sent for me and requested that I arrange for such transfer at once. I demurred as General Olmstead was away in Panama. General Arnold was kind enough to suggest that we select an arbitrator before whom we would meet the next morning to present our cases. General Arnold was represented by General [B.] Meyers . . . and [Col. Alfred W.] Marriner and other staff officers. The Signal Corps was represented by Colton, Rives, Meade, and myself. We listened from 9 to 12 to the Air Corps present to General Somervell (his first day on the job) their reasons why the Signal Corps should turn over to them everything we were doing for the Air Corps. We adjourned for lunch and Colton said we were licked and was reluctant to return with us. I felt that such a move as the Air Force was suggesting would sabotage the war effort, so Meade and I conferred and when General Somervell asked what the Signal Corps had to say I spoke up and said, "I thought radio was radio whether under, upon or over the land or sea and could not be peculiar to the Air Corps." Somervell took a long time just looking at us and then said he agreed and everything would stay in the "status quo."[33]

Thus AAF effort in early 1942 to get control of its signal equipment failed. The Chief Signal Officer, at that time General Olmstead, put his finger on the real question involved, whether or not the AAF was to remain a part of the Army. Since in 1942 it did remain in the

---

[33] Ltr, Code to Thompson and Harris, 14 Aug 58, pp. 16–17. SigC Hist Sec file. See also papers in (1) SigC, 020–WD, Reorgn, of, 1942; (2) SigC 321 Transfer of Function, 1944–45; and (3) SigC 210.21 Assignment of Gen Off on Staff of AAF, 1943.

Army, the AAF had to look to those best qualified in the Army to provide signals. Obviously the qualification lay with the Signal Corps and would continue therein unless or until the AAF acquired qualified men (as it steadily did). The entire communications problem boiled down to co-operation and the Signal Corps won its point for the moment.[34]

For two more years the Signal Corps retained research and development, procurement, storage, and distribution of wire, radio, and radar required by the AAF. But friction remained frequent, particularly in interpretation of what items were "peculiar to the Air Forces." Again and again, the Air Forces claimed the right to take over activities that it felt were peculiarly its own in order to insure the success of the AAF mission. The Secretary of War himself had coined the phrase, according to Lt. Gen. Joseph L. McNarney, Deputy Chief of Staff, and the Secretary intended it to mean, McNarney believed, those items of equipment that the Air Forces had previously been accustomed to procure —aircraft, their motors, airframes, and so on.[35]

On the other hand, Col. Alfred W. Marriner (General Arnold's communications director) had no doubt that the phrase must include airborne electronic gear. "The existing division of responsibility," Marriner wrote in March 1942,

"for the development, procurement, supply, maintenance and operation of *communications and related radar equipment peculiar to the Army Air Forces,* which has proven completely illogical and unworkable, is one of the serious faults in the organization of the Army. This experience has definitely shown that the Signal Corps . . . has been wholly unsatisfactory, with disastrous effects upon the efficient functioning of the Air Corps." [36]

Despite Marriner's charges, Signal Corps–AAF relations were not "unworkable." Co-operation was not "disastrous." In fact, the radio and radar of the U.S. Army Air Forces ranked among the world's best. However, at AAF headquarters in Washington experience in communications was weak, particularly up to 1944. Marriner's office had often been shuffled about in AAF headquarters reorganizations, two moves in 1943 alone. After the first of these 1943 shifts Marriner's office was elevated in the hope that more could be accomplished thereby, as General McClelland, the Deputy Assistant Chief of Air Staff for Operations, Commitments, and Requirements, wrote hopefully:

. . . the inability of the Army, probably through the divided authority that exists between the Army Air Forces, the Signal Corps, and the Aircraft Radio Laboratory to come to decisions on development and production, is extremely embarrassing and certainly discouraging. I believe that there is a lot that you can do in your new position to improve the situation immeasur-

[34] Memo, Olmstead, CSigO, for file, 21 Mar 42, sub: Jurisdiction Over the Research, Dev, Proc, Storage, and Issue of Radio and Radar Equip for the Air Corps. SigC 020–WD, Reorgn of, 1942.

[35] Memo, Code, DCSigO, for CG SOS, 24 Mar 42, sub: Attached Memo of Dir of Com, AAF. SigC 020–WD, Reorgn of, 1942, Code file.

[36] Memo, Col Marriner, Dir Com AAF, for Gen M. H. Fairchild, 5 Mar 42, sub: Air Force Com, attached to Memo, Brig Gen Colton, 6 Mar 42, sub: Memo Concerning Proc, Storage, and Issue of Sig Equip. SigC 020–WD, Reorgn of, 1942. Italics in original.

ably. In fact, I think that this is one of your foremost responsibilities.[37]

Communications experience and knowledge in AAF headquarters were increasing, but they still remained insufficient in an activity as dependent upon electronics as air operation was becoming. Both the Signal Corps and Dr. Bowles had complained of the insufficiency, and by the autumn of 1943 General Arnold reorganized his electronics activity, elevating it another notch. He replaced the Communications Division with an Office of Air Communication in the Air Staff, and replaced Marriner with General McClelland, an air communications officer who knew his subject well.[38] The airmen would listen to McClelland because he was a pilot. Even General McClelland needed bolstering by a competent and experienced Signal Corps man, who might not be a pilot but who would be especially skilled in electronics development and communications activities. To this end, General Arnold sought and obtained from the Signal Corps one of its ablest officers, Colonel Rives, who had worked closely with air electronics since the early 1930's. Rives became McClelland's strong deputy, though he remained a Signal Corps officer until late 1945. Dr. Bowles, who promoted Rives's assignment, subsequently asserted that he was not being partial to the AAF. "They fell over their own

feet, too," he reminisced.[39] Air Forces desperately needed all the communications help obtainable at a time when air applications of radio and radar were far outpacing ground forces needs (ground communications—electronic applications would begin to step up more at the end of the war and especially in postwar years).

While Signal Corps officers and men were first working for, and then transferring to the AAF both in the headquarters and in such field activities as the Aircraft Warning Service and the Army Airways Communications Service, there were points of contact where relations became a chaffing, and the chaffing occasionally rubbed raw—for example, in the maintenance of ground radar sets, and again, in the matter of installing and maintaining stations for the AACS.

AACS and PEA

Throughout 1942 the building of radio, beacon, and direction-finding

---

[37] Memo, McClelland for Marriner, 8 Apr 43, sub: Radiation Lab Trainer Projs for Airborne Radar Equip. AAG 413.44-J Radar. See also, Thompson, Harris, et al., The Test, p. 548.

[38] (1) Thompson, Harris et al., The Test, p. 564. (2) Claussen, Development of Radio and Radar Equipment for Air Operations, 1939–44, ch. I, p. 13, AAF Hist Monograph. Photostatic copy in SigC Hist Sec file.

[39] Interv, SigC Hist Div with Dr. Bowles, 8 May 58. See also below, p. 450.

As Rives himself recalled the transfer years later:

"When General Ingles called me into his office and told me that General Arnold had asked for me as General McClelland's deputy, he advised me substantially as follows:

'Tom, when I detail an officer to another branch of the service, I expect that officer to do all possible to help that branch. About the only thing I want to tell you is not to ask for a number of Signal Corps officers to help you because I will not look with favor on the detail of others to the Air Forces.'

I followed General Ingles' instructions; I worked for the Air Force and I did not proselyte any Signal Corps personnel."

Ltr, Brig Gen Tom C. Rives, USAF (Ret.), to OCMH, 4 Aug 59. SigC Hist Sec file (Draft MS Comments).

facilities for Army airway stations over the world generated troubles. Sometimes the Signal Corps, upon whom the responsibility rested by War Department regulations, did the work. More often AACS men themselves put up the stations, using whatever equipment they could scrape together. This was an emergency improvisation. Late in the year, after much conferring and negotiation, the Signal Corps was confirmed in its responsibility. To accomplish it better the Chief Signal officer organized the Plant Engineering Agency and a Signal Airways Service (SAS), complete with dozens of teams whose sole job it was to install AACS facilities wherever they were needed throughout the world.[40]

The labors of the PEA and SAS teams provided essential support for the AACS. Relations had to be co-operative since the Signal Corps men came under one command, the AACS operators under another. Signal Corps control over installation teams centered in a few bases and sector headquarters such as Philadelphia, Miami, and San Francisco, which lay hundreds and thousands of miles from the actual sites of field station installations. It is not surprising that station engineering plans drawn up in the continental headquarters did not always correspond with conditions in the faraway sites. Naturally, troubles ensued. As a result, in the Near East the AACS wanted responsible SAS officers on the spot, at least as near as Cairo, so that the airmen would not have to deal with Signal Corps officials in distant Miami. Similarly in the South Pacific, com-

plaints arose that the island installations ought to be engineered in the area of operations and not in San Francisco. In Africa AACS men often had to put up their own equipment clumsily because the channels for getting SAS teams worked impossibly slow. Often AAF tactical needs were sudden and could not wait for the slow process through channels. Theater Air Forces commanders, suddenly needing AACS stations, ordered them to be completed on early deadlines. Also, as tactical air units advanced, the AACS stations serving them had to move forward without awaiting Signal Corps assistance.[41]

The problem of getting supplies and maintenance parts was a most discouraging aspect of Signal Corps–AACS relations. It loomed especially dark in the far Pacific. Possibly the need to supply the relatively small but highly specialized requirements of the Airways Communication Service tended to be overlooked because of the extreme pressure ASF put upon the Signal Corps to supply the rest of the Army (at least so it seemed to the AAF). Annalists of the 7th AACS Wing in the Pacific noted that AACS had no authority to supply its own technical equipment independent of the Signal Corps. Officers of the 71st AACS Group complained bitterly that they had no clear-cut authoritative channel for getting signal maintenance supplies. Di-

---

[40] Thompson, Harris, et al., The Test, pp. 277ff., especially 286–87.

[41] (1) Incl, Conf, 20 Aug 43, Cairo, Egypt, with 1st Ind, Maj H. Allen Carroll, Asst O/C Hq SE Sector SAS, to Chief SAS PEA, 30 Aug 43, on Ltr, Col Stuart K. Baker, SigC, to Chief SAS through SE Sector SAS, 21 Aug 43, sub: Rpt on Regions 13, 18, and 19. SigC 676.3 (CC CEB) East Africa. (2) Extract of Report From Hq USAFISPA, attached to OCSigO, R&W, Action 1, Maj Owen K. Brown, SPSOT–2, to PEA through ACS, 24 Jul 43, sub: Extract of Rpt From SigO, SOPAC Area. SigC 676.3 CC CEB SOPAC, 1942–31 Dec 43.

rectives did assign the storage and issue of AACS equipment to the 905th Signal Company in the South Pacific, but that company did not procure the equipment, the AACS charged. AACS charged further that the men of the 905th had no knowledge of the special fixed communications and air navigational equipment AACS required. The communications service hoped it could perhaps obtain what it needed directly from the SAS, but on trying, the AACS men found their hopes dashed. The Signal Airways Service was not designed to provide such service. General Stoner, chief of the Army Communications Service, admitted as much in November 1943 saying, "the creation of the Signal Airways Service did not contemplate the assumption of all maintenance associated with AACS equipment." [42]

This, the 71st AACS Group discovered when a requisition on SAS–PEA for sorely needed supplies came back seventy-six days later without comment, without indorsement, without action. When the frantic airmen sought action through the Services of Supply in the area, the local SOS authorities ruled their channel of supply improper. Finally, the 71st succeeded in getting AACS equipment directly from the Signal Depot in Hawaii, Colonel Powell, Signal Officer, U.S. Army Forces Pacific Ocean Areas, coming to the rescue. The 70th AACS Group annals likewise record thanks to Colonel Powell for improvised supply assistance. All the AACS supply frustrations in the Pacific came to a head

early in 1944 when half a million pounds of signal equipment was transferred from Nouméa to Guadalcanal and carelessly dumped, like so much lumber, on the beach in a pile thirty feet high. Heavy power generators on top crushed delicate radios and teletypewriters at the bottom, and most of the equipment was damaged or ruined. [43]

Amid these and other signal supply troubles, AACS men in the Pacific (and elsewhere too) continued to store, issue, and even install equipment as best they could. When at last signal equipment responsibilities were taken over from the Signal Corps, the AAF acquired the facilities it desired. [44]

Of the many essential services for the AACS that the Signal Corps did perform, one in particular the airmen thoroughly appreciated—the provision of radioteletypewriter facilities. Overtaxed communicators had worked frantically in AACS message centers and cryptographic rooms during the first two years of the war literally hand coding and hand keying increasingly heavy traffic loads. Beginning in 1943 Signal Corps men began installing radioteletypewriter service, which "saved the day," in the words of one AACS chronicler. [45] Teams working out of PEA as units of SAS began installations along the southeast airways in Central and South America. One of the first circuits went into

[42] 4th Ind, Stoner to CO PEA, 25 Nov 43, sub: Proposal Maint Plan for AACS Equip in Northeast Sector (basic, 16 Oct 43, missing). SigC CC 400 Gen, 1944–45. See also above, pp. 207–08.

[43] (1) Hist Data, AAF AACS 7th Wing 70th Gp, Jan 41–May 44, p. 7. (2) Hist Data, 7th Wing 71st Gp, pp. 19–20. Both in AAF Hist Archives. See also above, pp. 214–15.

[44] (1) Pacific Airways Com System Area, APO 953, Hist Rcd, Apr 44, p. 29. (2) Hist Data, 7th Wing, 1–30 Sep 44. Both in AAF Hist Archives.

[45] Hist Br, Hq AACS AAF, The Army Airways Communications System, II, 442ff. and 481. AAF Archives.

service in May 1943 between Miami and Borinquen Field, Puerto Rico. Another followed on 11 June between New Orleans and Albrook Field in the Canal Zone. Thereafter, the net spread along the island and coastal airfields of the Caribbean to the bulge of Brazil and thence to Ascension Island and Africa.[46]

In the North Atlantic area, Signal Corps men began in October 1943 to make radioteletypewriter installations linking Presque Isle in Maine with Gander and Goose Bay in Labrador, Narsarssuak in Greenland, Keflavík in Iceland, and Prestwick in Scotland. By 1944 AACS radioteletype circuits were installed from the United States across the Pacific to the China-Burma-India theater, especially to provide General Arnold in Washington with direct control over the fleets of heavy bombers he was readying for assaults on Japan. This was the first effort of a commander chaired in Washington to direct personally tactical operations in an overseas theater using the capabilities of the rapid, secure communications that the radioteletypewriter and accompanying teletype conference (telecon) system made possible.[47]

The communications had to be completely secure from enemy radio eavesdropping. And in that security lay another Signal Corps service the AACS, along with all other Army communicators, appreciated—the provision of automatic cipher machines. Even in the Southwest Pacific areas, the supply of cipher machines was good, markedly so on Biak, at Hollandia, and on Los Negros. The 68th AACS Group commented that the program introducing these efficient machines "progressed by leaps and bounds," and eliminated the tedious work of enciphering heavy loads of traffic by hand on the M-209 Haglin cipher cylinder box and on the hated "washboards" of the strip cipher systems. Writing in October 1944, the historian of the 68th AACS Group recorded: "The cooperation and expeditious handling by higher headquarters of the request for the above equipment made it possible to procure and install the equipment in record-breaking time."[48]

So much for some of the troubles and successes in Signal Corps–AAF relations in matters over which the Signal Corps possessed control under War Department regulations. This control, as it touched upon provision of supplies and of maintenance parts, was obviously not good in some sectors of the globe. Yet myriads of Army aircraft navigated, or as some would put it, "avigated," along world-circling airways in notable safety. That safety attests to over-all success of the combined AACS–Signal Corps effort. The venture was co-operative, just as was Signal Corps labor for the Ground Forces. Despite the bickering, the effort succeeded. "Communications generally are functioning quite well," reported a War Department expert consultant after a theater survey trip in the spring of 1944. "The South Atlantic route is definitely good," he added.[49]

[46] (1) Hist, 72d Group, 11 Dec 40–Sep 44, p. 7. AAF Archives, SQ–A–Com–152–HI, 11 Dec 44 (1896–12). (2) Hist Br, Hq AACS AAF, The Army Airways Communications System, pp. 481, 556.

[47] Hist Br, Hq AACS AAF, The Army Airways Communications System, pp. 166, 664, 673–74.

[48] 68th Gp AACS, Hist Data, 1–31 Oct 44, p. 10. AAF Hist Archives.

[49] Memo, Strieby for Bowles, 28 Apr 44, sub: Results of Theater Survey Trip, Bowles file. SigC Hist Sec file.

Problems of Ground Radar Installation, Maintenance, and Spare Parts

Another area wherein Signal Corps supply for the Air Forces suffered sharp attack concerned radar maintenance. The maintenance itself was no longer a Signal Corps chore. It had been, since late 1942, a responsibility of the Air Forces, specifically of the Air Service Command, but the Air Service Command received radar supplies and maintenance parts from Signal Corps procurement and depot activities, and that was the friction point.

It was one thing to develop and produce radar sets. It was quite another to maintain them—to keep them operating smoothly and continuously—in the field. The growing pains of radar harassed all the Army during the middle years of the war, and complaints continued to lash the Signal Corps, though the Corps had been stripped of its installation and maintenance obligations in ground radar since December 1942 when the ASC acquired these responsibilities. The ASC was even responsible for such coastal defense sets as SCR's–296, 582, and 682, which would seem to be no concern of the AAF.[50]

The AAF had its troubles efficiently maintaining ground radars. For one thing, AAF complained that it was unable to obtain parts and maintenance spares from Signal Corps supply channels. In North Africa, for example, LW radar such as the SCR–602's was badly needed but often inoperative for want of a tube or a power unit. Likewise, in Pacific theaters, officers reported that "the spare parts situation for all aircraft warning radar equipment is very unsatisfactory." Search radars were often off the air for days awaiting parts.[51] Meanwhile, the search areas lacked protection in locations where Japanese airplanes were strafing the Allies. Especially troublesome was the lack of spare fan belts and water pumps for the Le Roi power units employed with the SCR–270. Replacements were not to be had and the men had to use "every conceivable means of solving this problem."

Within the United States, the maintenance situation touching radar was also bad throughout 1943. For example, at the Aircraft Warning Unit Training Center (AWUTC) at Drew Field, Florida, fifteen radar sets were at one time out of operation for lack of spare parts. Parts had been stripped from forty-nine new SCR–270's that had arrived at the field for shipment overseas. Thus did the Chief of Air Staff, Maj. Gen. Barney M. Giles, draw up a bill of charges and hurl it at General Somervell in November 1943, saying "the spare parts situation is definitely critical . . . action must be taken."[52]

The Signal Corps, defending itself before General Somervell, rehearsed the

---

[50] Thompson, Harris, *et al.*, *The Test*, pp. 295ff. See also above, p. 208.

[51] For example, at the invasion of Hollandia in mid-1944, 13 sets of SCR–268's and 4 SCR–584's were landed in the first three days and set up for operation in an average of one and a half days. Soon all 584's became inoperative because of the failure of the T–214 transformer in the high voltage modulator. There was mass failure also of transformer T–531 in the high voltage supply for the oscilloscopes of the 268's. Memo, Cornell, Asst AAO CAC, for SigO Hq I Corps, 8 Jun 44. Sig Jnl, vol. I (29 May–12 Jun 44) I Corps, Rcd I Corps Staff Sigs, 29 May–12 Jun 44. See also above, p. 254, n. 38.

[52] Ltr, Giles, CofAS, to CG ASF, 8 Nov 43, sub: Spare Parts for AW Equip. AAG 413.44–AH Radar.

War Department letter of 26 December 1942, which had transferred to the Air Service Command the installation, maintenance, and supply responsibilities for all ground radar in overseas theaters.[53] Signal Corps concern ended with the filling of ASC radar requisitions. A substantial percentage of these, more than 80 percent, had in fact been met, according to Brig. Gen. John H. Gardner, Assistant Chief of OCSigO's P&D Service. Further, at the depots, "vigorous action is being taken," Gardner wrote, "to supply all unfilled items for which stock is available."[54]

A few weeks later Lt. Col. Haskell O. Allison, assistant adjutant general at ASC headquarters, Patterson Field, Ohio, commented that there had indeed been "a decided increase in recent shipments of material on back order from Lexington Signal Depot." But such spurts of activity, Allison added, were hardly the solution to the long-standing problem of ground radar maintenance. The Air Forces believed that, first, the Signal Corps must increase its procurement; and, secondly, that the channels of supply must be improved. There should be "emergency procurement facilities and methods so as to get emergency parts out of the routine

channels that have been established." Colonel Allison illustrated how sluggish the flow of supplies through routine channels could be. "It is an actual fact," he wrote, "that even today the spare parts for SCR–268 and SCR–270 equipments have not caught up with actual needs despite the fact that these sets have been used over two years."[55]

As for the SCR–602 LW radar, Allison added, "the only source of spare parts (other than from cannibalization of equipments) is the group of one hundred 'interim' set spares." These had been ordered at least as early as March 1943, but even by January 1944, he averred, "only 31 of these have been delivered, of which only three remain on hand." In addition to the inadequate interim spare part kits, the ASC had requested in August 1943 fifty complete depot spare part groups for the SCR–602, but "to this date," Allison complained, "not one group has been delivered nor can any definite information be obtained as to when any may be expected." "It can be seen," he concluded, "that the supply of maintenance parts for the world is at a dangerously low point and has been for some time."[56]

Allison added similar charges touch-

---

[53] AG 413.68 (24 Jun 42) OB–S–E–M, 26 Dec 42, sub: Maint of AGF Sig Equip.

The ASC in the Pacific reported adversely on power units PE–74, 75, and 84 and favorably on PE–52 and 95. Radar SCR–270 was characterized as "old reliable." Parts could not be obtained from Australia, the command complained, because "they can't make electronic equipment with the precision and small size to work in American sets." Memo, 1st Lt H. B. Phelps, SigC, for Capt J. E. Keely, 21 Mar 44, sub: Ground Radar in SWPA. SigC 413.44 Gen 18 (RB–2361).

[54] 2d Ind, Gardner to CG ASF, 20 Dec 43, on Ltr, Giles, 8 Nov 43.

[55] However, in certain SCR–268 items, the Lexington Signal Depot was tremendously overstocked, with more matériel pouring in. For example, the depot had on hand a half million vacuum tubes, type 127–A, with another quarter-million coming in from the factories, while the issue rate to the field was running at only five thousand a month. ASF Transmittal Sheet, Action 1, O'Connell, O/C Tech Staff SPSET, to Maint Br, Electronics Br, and Intel Security Subsec, 16 Feb 44, sub: Lexington Sig Depot Surplus Stocks. SigC 413.44 Gen 17 (RB–2360).

[56] 2d Wrapper Ind, Allison (writing for CG ASC) to CG AAF, 27 Jan 44, on Ltr, Giles to CG ASF, 8 Nov 43.

ing the SCR–588, saying that these sets had been in use for about a year and a half, but that not one depot spare parts group and not one complete ABC plan had been provided. There had been an interim XYZ plan, according to which the Signal Corps had sent a few parts but they were not enough. There was, incidentally, a story behind the lack of spares for the SCR–588. The set, like a number of other copies of British sets, was manufactured by a Canadian company, Research Enterprises Ltd. The company simply was not producing spares and refused to inform Signal Corps representatives of the status of production spares. Col. R. L. Hart, a Signal Corps production officer, recorded that whereas formerly production men in the plant had provided Signal Corps representatives with some information, even this source had been cut off since the manager of the radio division of the plant had ordered the production men not to talk. Colonel Hart reported that strenuous and repeated efforts had been made by the Monmouth Signal Corps Procurement District and by the resident Signal Corps officer at REL to discover the status of SCR–588 spare parts, but to the end of 1943, "none of these requests have produced satisfactory results." [57]

General Arnold read the entire sheaf of papers that Colonel Allison had prepared and then handed it over to General Somervell on 8 March 1944. The AAF chief asked that "all possible pressure be brought to bear in the effort to relieve this critical spare part shortage at the earliest possible date." Arnold added: "As will be seen, lack of same is seriously hampering the use of aircraft warning equipment in combat operations." Not very expeditiously, the ASF passed the complaints on to the Signal Corps nearly three weeks later in a fifth indorsement dated 25 March. Colonel Gardner again answered, on 10 April. All means of expediting had been taken. Gardner itemized them: reorder points had been set up; the responsible depot had been instructed to place orders on the procurement district without processing in the routine manner through the Storage and Issue Agency; special technical sections had been enlarged both at the S&I Agency and at the Camp Evans Signal Laboratory in order to hurry identification and substitution; the processing of stock number assignments had been speeded; maintenance lists, ABC plan, had been distributed, and so on. [58]

The problem of Signal Corps supply of radar parts displeased the Ground Forces, whose commanding general expressed annoyance over the situation in mid-1943. Lt. Gen. Lesley J. McNair urged that: "supply, maintenance and repair of Ground Forces radar equipment be handled through the channels normally employed for other signal equipment and not through the medium of the Air Service Command." His view was upheld in a conference with ASF and the Signal Corps on 27 July 1943. The conferees agreed that theater commanders should be free to organize the

[57] Ltr, Hart, Chief Prod Br, to Chief R&D Sv, Attn: Harrison, 16 Dec 43, sub: Spare Parts for Radio Set SCR–588–B. SigC 413.44 Gen 15 (RB–2135).

[58] 4th Ind, CG AAF to CG ASF, 8 Mar 44; 5th Ind, CG ASF to CSigO, 25 Mar 44; 6th Ind, Gardner to CG ASF, 10 Apr 44. All on Ltr, Giles to CG ASF, 8 Nov 43.

arrangements overseas as they wished, but "radar installation, supply, maintenance and repair for Ground Forces units in the continental United States should be a concern only of the Ground and Service Forces as is the case with other signal equipment." [59] This view won out, leading to a War Department order in October 1943. Previous arrangements issued 26 December 1942, "and all conflicting instructions pertaining to this subject" were rescinded by a new plan announced on 11 October 1943. It assigned to the Chief Signal Officer the storage and issue of all ground radar equipment, whether Air or Ground Forces, together with fifth echelon (or depot) maintenance of all ground radar within the continental United States. Maintenance of AGF radar at the third and fourth echelon levels would fall to the ASF, that is, to the Signal Corps. Signal Corps would also acquire responsibility for ground radar maintenance overseas, at fifth echelon level. This new distribution of responsibilities was to be completed and in full force by 1 April 1944. [60]

This directive laid upon both the ASF and the Signal Corps component thereof a large responsibility, more especially upon the Signal Corps, whose officers now became embroiled in much correspondence with the Air and Ground Forces. A plan, then an organization, would have to take form to permit Signal Corps maintenance of all ground radars. General Ingles, General Colton (who headed Ingles' Engineering and Technical Service), Col. William L. Bayer (who headed Colton's Maintenance Branch), and many others thus had to learn the details of the numerous stateside radar maintenance arrangements so that they could draw up plans, arrange conferences, and finally take over the new job, together with Air Service Command facilities and personnel, by 1 April 1944. While General Colton asked the AAF on 28 October 1943 to provide him with summaries of their ground radars, repair shop facilities, tool and test equipment, and personnel, General Ingles and Colonel Bayer addressed similar requests "by direction of Somervell," to each of the service commands within the United States. [61] Within his own headquarters, Ingles apportioned the radar responsibilities handed him. To Colton he assigned technical data; to Harrison, the supervision of fifth echelon shops; to Matejka and the Personnel and Training Service, the matter of technical instructions and technician training; and

---

[59] 5th Ind, Ingles to CG ASF, 3 Aug 43, on basic which is missing but noted as SPSET 413.44 Gen (4 Jun 43) sub: Instal and Maint of Airborne and Ground Sig Equip. SigC 413.44 Gen 16 (RB-2359).

[60] AG Ltr 413.68 (19 Aug 43) OB-S-D-M, 11 Oct 43, sub: Storage, Issue, Selection of Sites, Instal, and Maint of Ground Radar Equip. SigC 413.44 Gen 15 (RB-2135).
The Commanding General, AAF, was to transfer to the Commanding General, ASF, all ground radar, test equipment, and supplies used within the United States for radar repair, making arrangements directly with the Chief Signal Officer. General Arnold would also transfer personnel to the Commanding General, ASF. The Chief Signal Officer would train military and civilian specialists for installation and maintenance at the third, fourth, and fifth echelon levels.

[61] (1) Ltr, Colton to CG AAF, 28 Oct 43, sub: Transfer of Ground Radar Equip and Pers. AAF 413.44-X Radar. (2) Ltrs, CSigO to CG First Sv Comd, 6 Nov 43; to CG Second Sv Comd, 19 Nov 43: to CG Third Sv Comd, 17 Jan 44, et al., sub: Instal and Third and Fourth Echelon Maint of AGF Ground Radar Equip. SigC 413.44 Gen 16 (RB-2359).

to Meade and the Plans and Operations Division, the preparation of T/O's and TOE's for fifth echelon units, as well as the training requirements and assignments of third, fourth, and fifth echelon maintenance men.[62]

The October 1943 directive had been "intended to correct certain deficiencies reported from North Africa," according to Maj. Gen. Russell L. Maxwell, Assistant Chief of Staff G–4. In December General Maxwell asked General Somervell for a progress report. Ingles already had considerable for Somervell to include in his reply to Maxwell. Toward supplementing the fifth echelon ground radar maintenance shop at the Lexington Signal Depot, Ingles now had received authorization for fifth echelon radar repair facilities at the Holabird Signal Depot in Baltimore and at the Sacramento Signal Depot. On 23 November the War Department had approved a signal base maintenance company T/O and TOE 11–587, under which the four existing (214th, 216th, 221st, and 222d) signal base depot companies would be reorganized. General Ingles had asked also that three new signal base depot groups be constituted and activated. Meanwhile, he obtained from the Air Forces a summary of equipment, facilities, and men to be transferred into the new maintenance organization for which the Signal Corps was making plans. He had also begun training some eight hundred officers and men specifically for third and fourth echelon

maintenance of AGF radars within the United States.[63]

Unfortunately, all the War Department efforts to straighten out the radar maintenance maze failed. Perhaps conditions in the field, or perhaps human nature, made effective Signal Corps–Air Forces co-operation unworkable. On the west coast the ASC balked at transferring its ground radar maintenance to ASF and Signal Corps. In May 1944 General Arnold petitioned the Chief of Staff to modify his policy, indeed to reverse it, at least in west coast areas.[64] But for the moment, the General Staff stuck to its policy and ordered General Arnold to comply, adding "informal information indicates to the War Department that the transfer of personnel and equipment as required has not been consummated." [65]

The Air Forces bowed for the moment but its discontent with the War Department policy continued. Fourth Air Force headquarters complained in August 1944 that it received conflicting messages from General Arnold's headquar-

---

[62] Memo, CSigO for Chiefs E&T, P&D, and P&T Svs, and for Dirs Plans and Opns, and Contl Divs, 5 Feb 44, sub: Storage, Issue, Selection of Sites, Instal. and Maint of Ground Radar Equip. SigC 413.44 Gen 17 (RB–2360).

[63] Memo, Maxwell, ACofS G–4, for CG ASF, 20 Dec 43, sub: Maint of Ground Radar Equip, with 1st Ind, Somervell to ACofS G–4. SigC 413.44 Gen 15 (RB–2135).

[64] Memo, CG AAF to ACofS G–4, 26 May 44, sub: Responsibility for the Maint of Ground Radar Equip. AAG 413.44–AH Radar.
General Arnold wrote, "It is requested that the ASF be directed to return to the AAF all personnel, test equipment and supplies for maintenance of AGF radar equipment which were transferred to the Ninth Service Command, 1 April 1944. It is further requested that the AAF be authorized to provide the necessary repair and maintenance for all ground radar equipments employed by the Fourth Antiaircraft Command."

[65] Ltr, Maxwell, ACofS G–4, to CG AAF, 26 Jun 44, sub: Responsibility for the Maint of Ground Radar Equip (WDGS–14105). SigC 413.44 Gen 20 (RB–2363).

ters in Washington and from ASC in Ohio on the subject of who should store, issue, and maintain the ground radar of its AAA units.[66] The Third Air Force in Tampa plied General Arnold with bitter complaints against the Signal Corps system for supplying radar parts and urged that "a new method of supply of radar replacement parts be established at the earliest practicable date."[67] As the various air service commands over the world wrote to Washington, they expressed surprise and confusion at the change contemplated in ground radar maintenance. Always they claimed that they had been doing quite well providing maintenance facilities and men. The trouble, they generally agreed, lay in getting quickly (or at all) the items of equipment they requisitioned from the Signal Corps.[68]

When finally it came to implementing the War Department order that the Signal Corps take over fifth echelon maintenance of ground radars overseas, the ASC vigorously objected. "It appears . . ." the command wrote on 14 July 1944, "that an attempt is being made to effect a gradual change in the supply system for AAF types of ground radar equipment in overseas Air Service Com-

mands so that the overseas Signal Depots would be stocked by the Chief Signal Officer direct, and would then be the reissuing agency to the Air Force Service Command." "This is not the way we have been doing it," the command said in effect. It did not want to put the Signal Corps in business overseas supplying or maintaining Air Forces ground radar. The command recommended that Arnold "definitely and unquestionably establish the supply of maintenance parts for Army Air Forces types of ground radar equipments as an exclusive function of the Air Service Command."[69] Col. George C. Hale in the Washington headquarters, replying for General Arnold, sought to soothe the ruffled ASC, saying that of course "the correct channel for all ground radar equipment of exclusive interest to the AAF should be through AAF channels." Only ground radar sets and parts intended solely for the AGF would move through ASF channels. Then Colonel Hale added a significant statement touching the recommendation that the AAF take undisputed control over Air Forces ground radar supply. Consideration was currently being given, Hale wrote, to these very matters, and the ASC would be advised of the action taken.[70]

AAF Wins Control Over Its Communications-Electronics

The action was being taken. The decision had already been made. The Army

---

[66] Ltr, CG Hq Fourth AF to CG AAF, 22 Aug 44, sub: Responsibility for Storage, Issue, Maint of Ground Radar and Ground T/BA Com Equip for AAA Units under the Fourth AF. AAG 413.44–AM Radar.

[67] Ltr, CG Hq Third AF to CG AAF, 5 Apr 44, sub: Delays and Difficulties Experienced in Obtaining Replacement Parts Necessary to Maintain Radar Equip in Operative Condition. AAG 413.44–AH Radar.

[68] Yet a spokesman for the Twelfth Air Force remarked that Signal Corps supply was "very good," adding that most of the shortages of the past had been corrected. Memo, Col Dudley D. Hale, ComO, Twelfth AF, for Colton, 16 Apr 44. SigC 413.44 Gen 19 (RB-2362).

[69] Ltr, CG ASC to CG AAF, 14 Jul 44, sub: Sup Channels for AAF Types of Ground Radar. AAG 413.44–AM Radar.

[70] 1st Ind, CG AAF to CG ASC, 17 Aug 44, on Ltr, ASC to AAF, 14 Jul 44.

Air Forces had at last reached the point of gaining control over all electronic items and activities "peculiar to the AAF." Its radio and radar gear and applications had grown of course to tremendous proportions by 1944. Communications officers serving the AAF—McClelland, Rives, Maude, Ankenbrandt—had mended aviation's communications weakness of which Dr. Bowles had complained a year earlier. [71]

Dr. Bowles was, in fact, a considerable "power behind the throne" in all Army communications, an electronics scientist and college professor whose sympathy with the military and its problems and whose quick and keen appreciation had won him complete acceptance in the top military household since General Colton had induced him to leave the Massachusetts Institute of Technology early in 1942. Colton's intent that Bowles serve as adviser concerning Army communications-electronics in the ASF under Somervell failed when Bowles was "captured" by Secretary Stimson to work in the highest Army echelon, where in fact Bowles was more able to aid the Army over-all than he could have done in the ASF. Bowles served throughout the war as Stimson's expert consultant in communications and radar. Finding AAF needs especially pressing and receiving General Arnold's wholehearted welcome, Bowles received in September 1943 complete authority over AAF communications with power "to act for the Commanding General through the medium of the Chief of Air Staff, . . . and of the Air Communications Officer." Working with quiet efficiency and with the overriding authority that civilian status directly

under Stimson gave him, Dr. Bowles was able to cut across all Army commands. He played a large part in the transfer of communications-electronics to the AAF.

It was Dr. Bowles who induced General Arnold to appoint General McClelland director of AAF communications and then used influence in the transfer of one of the ablest Signal Corps officers, Colonel Rives, to the AAF. Bowles wrote to Robert A. Lovett, Assistant Secretary of War for Air, in June 1943:

. . . it seemed to me that McClelland was the outstanding man. At the same time, it was recognized that because of his characteristics it would be necessary to support him with a deputy whose characteristics were complementary. Universally it was felt that Colonel Tom Rives of the Signal Corps would be the man. In addition, the selection of Rives would make for a strategic combination of Air and Signal officers. [72]

By 1944 AAF radio and radar offspring felt well-weaned from the Signal Corps and sought to cast off all parental control. The beginnings of the final break, Colonel Rives subsequently recounted, took form during the last months of 1943, just when the Signal Corps, ironically enough, was expecting to recover ground radar maintenance. The break began as an AAF staff study launched in 1943 at the direction of General Giles. "The study was rewritten at least fifty times," reminisced Brig. Gen. Tom C. Rives (USAF, Ret.) in 1950,

---

[71] Thompson, Harris, et al., The Test, p. 540.

[72] (1) Ltr, Bowles to Lovett, ASW for Air, 26 Jun 43. OSC file, WDCSA-676 (28 Dec 43). (2) Interv, SigC Hist Div with Bowles, 8 May 58. (3) AAF Memo No. 20-11, WD Hq AAF, 2 Sep 43, Orgn, Com Consultant to CG. Bowles papers, Tab K. (4) Guerlac, Radar, pp. 991–1001 (sec. E, ch. I, pp. 9–19). Re Bowles's position and influence in general, see T. Burchard, *Q.E.D.,M.I.T. in World War II* (Cambridge, 1948) pp. 67ff.

P-61 Black Widow With AI Radar Antenna in the Nose Radome

"and was finally presented through Dr. Edward L. Bowles direct to General Marshall." [73]

The AAF study, completed in June 1944, attacked the problem rather differently from earlier onslaughts. It did not castigate the Signal Corps. In fact, the Signal Corps received praise. General Arnold wanted to avoid any criticism of the Signal Corps and emphasized that the Corps should be thanked for its invaluable aid. The problem was recognized as one of extreme complexity, and the Air Forces believed those complexities could best be solved if the AAF took over the responsibility for its own electronics.

The causes leading up to the transfer were many; not the least being the universal unhappiness caused when someone other than the operating organization obtained, delivered, and maintained one's operating equipment. A very definite cause, in the case of rapidly evolving airborne radar and communications-navigation electronics, was the Army supply routine. Quick, direct, tape-cutting procedures were necessary, but the Signal Corps had to conduct its development and supply service amid the Army routines under heavy (and as Sig-

[73] Rives added that if the study "had gone through regular channels, it would have died a quiet death." Ltr, Rives to Thompson, Hist Div Spec Staff, 8 Jan 50.

This is just what did happen to the Signal Corps efforts to improve top control of Army communications in the spring of 1943. Thompson, Harris, et al., The Test, pp. 536–65.

nal Corps officers felt, stifling) administrative layers of the ASF. Still another
very basic cause was that newly evolving
radar types required special aircraft
specially designed around the radars.
Airplane design was unquestionably an
AAF concern only. The first airplane so
designed was the P–61, the Black Widow,
which was engineered for the microwave
AI radar of the SCR–517 type, a radar
that enabled pilots to hunt down and
destroy enemy planes at night or in
clouds. Another airplane designed to
carry radar was the B–29, fitted with an
auxiliary wing to accommodate the antenna of that most efficient BTO radar,
the AN/APQ–7, or Eagle.[74]

All the arguments for the transfer that
could be thought of were contained in
the staff study General Giles had requested. Preparation of the study and of
its many supporting documents was directed by Dr. Lewis M. Hull, one of Dr.
Bowles's operational specialists. Bowles
passed the entire file on to the AAF
chief, General Arnold, on 9 May 1944,
urging the transfer on the grounds that
"the existing set-up represents a major
obstacle . . . prevents you from controlling one of the most vital of the
elements making up a combat aircraft
and ultimately a combat air force. Practically speaking, you have no actual control over the types, quantities, or deliveries of this type of equipment."
Bowles ascribed this communications-
electronics supply to "an archaic system
called upon to do that for which it was
never intended, to develop and procure
special instrumentalities for the Air
Forces as opposed to conventional

communications equipment common to
Air and Ground Forces." Bowles concluded, "I see no cure short of
transferring to the Air Forces complete
responsibility and authority for devel-
ment, procurement, and distribution of
communications equipment peculiar to
the Air Forces."

The accompanying study elaborated:
"Communications equipment has become an inseparable part of every military aircraft and Air Force operation.
Modern aerial tactics are based on maximum use of radar and radio navigation
bombing and fire control aids, aircraft
warning, ground-to-plane and plane-to-
plane communications." The study itemized 6 components for the P–61; for the
B–29, 14 items plus 8 countermeasures
components. The study determined that
"in military aircraft, modern communications equipment has of necessity become an integral part without which the
aircraft is useless in tactical and combat
flight." As for the difficulties of getting
supplied by a Signal Corps under layers
of ASF, the study concluded:

The critical delays in procurement do
not result from lack of effort or good will
within the military organization. They
stem primarily from:
  a. Huge quantities of war-stimulated
developmental sources, whose channeliza-
tion into the Army is immeasurably complicated by the necessity for access to a
procuring service which is independent of
the using arm.
  b. Sincere but non-essential contro-
versies between military participants whose
primary allegiance is necessarily to independent Forces.
  c. Absence of decisive co-ordinating
authority at any level which is readily
accessible to those agencies and individuals
who are charged with operating functions.
  d. Practical impossibility of effective

---

[74] Interv, SigC Hist Div (Thompson) with Bowles,
29 May 58. See below, pp. 486–87.

understanding and employment, by most personnel inside and outside of the two Army Forces in questions; of their complex organizational inter-relations.

Illustrative case histories of the procurement woes were added, for example, the receiver component of the SCR–521–A, the AN/APQ–13, the AN/APS–15, the AN/MPN–1.[75]

General Marshall, after receiving the staff study, agreed with the AAF recommendations. On 26 July 1944, Marshall informed Arnold and Somervell that he, too, believed "airborne radar and radio equipment, guided missiles and ground radar, and radio navigational aids should be considered as items of equipment peculiar to the Air Forces." Marshall sent drafts of the order he proposed to issue to the AAF and ASF.[76]

Much debate ensued. The director of the AAF communications directorate, General McClelland, itemized his reasons for seeking the transfer: the red-tape delay occasioned by the interposition of the Army Service Forces and the Signal Corps between the Army Air Forces and its electronic equipment; the division in responsibilities; the separation of the administrative offices; the increasing oneness of electronic devices and aircraft design, pro-

duction, and operation. The director added, too, "the vast majority of the research and development work on communication equipment is now done by either the National Defense Research Committee or the Navy Department and the Signal Corps acts as the agent and co-ordinator for the Army Air Forces."

General Ingles, rebutting, felt he successfully refuted every one of McClelland's points. As for the oneness of electronics with military machines and operation, this was no less true of all the Army than of aircraft. Administrative and red-tape troubles could be ironed out, but splitting up the essential oneness of all communications covering all the Army (and this included the Army Air Forces) would require the creation of a still higher signal organization, on General Staff level, that could arbitrate the electronic activities in both the AAF and the rest of the Army, which alone the Signal Corps would now serve. The higher over-all organization, Ingles believed, would be necessary to prevent chaos in frequency control and in duplicated effort and equipment. This would in turn increase, not simplify, administrative red tape. And as for AAF playing down the work of the ARL, Ingles attacked the assertion that the National Defense Research Committee and its laboratories, the RL and RRL, did the "vast majority of R&D work. . . ." All Radiation Laboratory work stopped far short of completion. The laboratory simply produced a breadboard model. And when it did crash-produce a handful of sets, "the Signal Corps has never yet seen two identical models." Thus an immense amount of necessary development work remained after the NDRC turned over its breadboard model. Such

[75] Memo, Bowles for Arnold, 9 May 44, sub: Air Forces Com with Incl, Memo for CofS, Responsibility for Dev, Proc, and Distr of Com Equip and Tabs D and E. Bowles papers.

[76] Item 1, Memo, CofS for Arnold and Somervell, 26 Jul 44, no sub. Transfer of Radar Communications Responsibilities to the AAF (hereafter referred to as SigC 321 Transfer of Functions) SigC 321 Transfer of Functions (Transfer of R&D Proc of Com and Radar Equip, etc.) 1944–45 DCSigO file. See also CofS papers bearing the notation 7, from Marshall's Memo, WDCSA: 413.44 (26 Jul 44) to Memo, Maxwell for CofS, 27 Oct 44. CofS file, RG 110.00–413.44, 1943–44.

work as bench engineering tests, flight tests, preparations of U.S. Army specifications, drawings, maintenance parts lists, technical descriptions for stock numbering, replacement factors, and co-ordination with the War Department Standardization Program on components still remained to be done. All this work had to be done by ARL before manufacture could start and before a set could be put into the hands of relatively unskilled men to use and to keep in operation in a theater of war.

General Ingles urged upon the Army Service Forces that the Marshall memo on the proposed transfer not be issued. The matter, Ingles believed, should be decided on the basis of efficiency in getting on with the war, and, Ingles asked pointedly, was it not obvious that things were succeeding, the AAF better equipped and more effectively operating than the air force of any other country? General Ingles reiterated his belief that any split in Army electronics would "introduce the necessity for an over-all adjudicating agency hitherto unnecessary." The split would break up research and development and would require more engineers in duplicated laboratories, where already there were too few talented men. Such talent was effectively applied in the Signal Corps laboratories as they existed in 1944, where skilled electronic engineers frequently worked on both air and ground items, concurrently or successively. Moreover, the proposed transfer would run counter to all tendencies to unite the military services. "The Secretary of War has advocated a union of Army and Navy to avoid duplication of operating agencies and to secure unity of action," Ingles reminded his superiors. "The

purpose of such advocacy is not furthered by dividing the science of the propagation and reception of radio waves between two independent Army groups, each with its own laboratories, scientists, and programs." Ingles concluded, quite as General Code had said in a similar debate with the AAF over a year earlier: "The principles of electronics is a single science with multifarious applications and all discoveries germane whether the equipment is to be used in the air, on the ground, or on or under the sea." [77]

This and much else were all to no avail as far as the Signal Corps was concerned.[78] General Marshall's decision became mandatory on 26 August 1944 when the Secretary of War ordered the Army Air Forces and the Army Service Forces to accomplish the transfer. He directed that a board (chaired by Maj. Gen. R. L. Maxwell) be set up to arbi-

---

[77] (1) Item 3, Ingles for CG ASF, 31 Jul 44, sub: Assumption by AAF of Responsibility for Research, Dev, and Proc of Airborne Radar and Radio Equip, Guided Missiles, and Ground Radar and Radio Navigational Aids. (2) Item 4, Memo, McClelland for Ingles, 6 Aug 44, sub: Responsibility for Research, Dev, and Proc of Com Equip Peculiar to the Army Air Forces. (3) Item 6, Memo, Ingles for CG ASF, 7 Aug 44, sub: Dev of Data for Memorandum to CG AAF Resulting from Conf, 5 Aug 44. All in SigC 321 Transfer of Functions. (4) Thompson, Harris, et al., The Test, pp. 548–49.

[78] General Marshall had at first specified that research and development only be transferred from the Signal Corps to the AAF. But General Ingles had refused, saying in effect "take all electronics responsibility or none," and at a conference in General Arnold's office (with Generals Somervell, Ingles, McClelland, Rives, and Dr. Bowles) it was agreed that all R&D, procurement, and distribution should go to the AAF. (1) Ltr, Rives to Thompson, 8 Jan 50, cited. (2) Ltr, General J. L. McNarney, USAF (Ret.), President, Convair, to Col. John V. Mills, CO SCIA, Attn: Hist Div, Thompson, 4 Nov 53, SigC Hist Sec file.

trate the details. The move would involve over half the value of all Signal Corps procurement, many Signal Corps establishments, about 1,000 officers and enlisted men, and more than 8,000 civilians.[79]

So huge a move could not be accomplished easily or completely at once since many AAF activities in the Signal Corps intimately concerned ground force interests too, for which the Signal Corps remained responsible. Some activities, offices, laboratories, and workers could be transferred easily, but many could not. Meanwhile, the progress of the war effort must not be unduly hampered by the change-overs. The transfer was in fact months in completing. In order to carry out the entire transfer smoothly, General McNarney instructed Generals Arnold and Somervell to set up a board of officers, to include three representatives from the AAF and three from the ASF, who would arbitrate and direct the undertaking. Disputed matters were to be referred to General McNarney himself for final arbitration.[80]

Of the heavy tasks this board encountered none was more tedious than the determination of just what items were peculiar to the Air Forces. Such matters as the transfer of the Aircraft Radio

Laboratory, and the assignment to AAF of Signal Corps' experienced R&D officer, General Colton (whom Arnold had requested), were relatively easy. But many things went hard for the Signal Corps. By October 1944, General Ingles felt that "the major difficulties occurring are the result of an attempt on the part of the representatives of the Commanding General, Army Air Forces, to expand the interpretation of the original intent of the Chief of Staff." [81]

On 21 October Ingles informed Somervell that transfer of the Aircraft Radio Laboratory posed no very great difficulty even though some few projects concerned the Army Ground Forces. "For purposes of continuity," said Ingles, "it was decided desirable to leave such projects under the control of the Aircraft Signal Agency with the expectation that minor adjustments between the Army Air Forces and Army Service Forces could be later made, if found necessary." But transfer could not so easily be accomplished at the Monmouth congeries. The Signal Corps would very much prefer to get the interests untangled and the transfer over with, since, General Ingles declared, "the details of the transfer are materially interfering with our operations." The completion of the move had to wait

[79] (1) Item 15, Memo, Raynsford, Asst Chief E&T Sv, for file, 6 Sep 44, sub: Transfer of Radar Com Responsibilities to the AAF. SigC 321, Transfer of Functions. (2) Memo, Ingles for ACofS, 17 Aug 45, sub: Items of Com and Radar Equip "Peculiar to the Army Air Forces." SigC 413.44, WD Cir R–429, 1944, DCSigO file. (3) Millet, *Organization and Role of the Army Services Forces*, pp. 128–29. (4) Craven and Cate, eds., *Men and Planes*, pp. 232, 374.

[80] Item 9, Ltr, SW to CG AAF and ASF, 26 Aug 44, sub: Transfer of Research, Dev, Proc of Com, and Radar Equip Peculiar to the AAF from the ASF to the AAF. SigC 321 Transfer of Functions.

[81] Item 115, Memo, Ingles for CG ASF, 17 Oct 44, sub: Transfer of Responsibility for Dev, Sup, and Maint of Items Peculiar to the AAF. SigC 321 Transfer of Functions. General Ingles agreed to the transfer on 20 August 44 of General Colton, who, he wrote, "was responsible in the emergency period prior to U.S. entry in the war and up until July 1943 for the *entire* Signal Corps program of research, development, procurement, and supply." Ingles underlined the word *entire*. Item 44, Memo, CSigO for CG ASF, 21 Oct 44, sub: Transfer of Responsibility . . . , p. 5. SigC 321 Transfer of Functions.

upon certain developments of important equipment needed by all three major forces.[82]

The ARL with all that pertained to it, such as field laboratories at Boca Raton and Eglin in Florida and at Indianapolis, went over to the AAF on 15 October 1944. This segment of the transfer took into the AAF about 300 Signal Corps officers and men and some 1,500 civilians.[83] Here, in the Signal Corps Aircraft Signal Agency, there were few Ground Forces interests to filter out. And there was no problem of physically moving men and plant. They were all already on or adjacent to AAF installations.

Much more difficult was the separation of AAF–AGF interests in the New Jersey laboratories of the Signal Corps Ground Signal Agency. For example, in the Eatontown lab segment, the Signal Corps worked on meteorological and DF equipment which concerned AGF as well as AAF interests. Likewise, at the radar labs at Camp Evans, some radar development concerned both forces—for example, the superb microwave gun director, the SCR–584. The 584 had been developed basically for antiaircraft artillery, but it could also be used to direct aircraft in bombing operations. Could the 584 be called an item peculiar to the Army Air Forces? General Ingles

pointed out, too, that the air search radar AN/TPS–3, though it had been developed for the AAF and seemed at first to qualify as "peculiar to the AAF," had been found in practice to be an efficient mortar locator, and so became very much a concern to the Army Ground Forces. Such were electronic intertwinings and developments that mocked all efforts to pigeonhole the equipment.

For a time the AAF wanted to operate the laboratories jointly with the Signal Corps. This action however, General Ingles refused to contemplate. He wished the transfer to be made when and as it became possible to sort out such mixed-up activities, even if in some cases the transfer might have to wait until the end of the war with Germany. The AAF, while refusing to wait that long, did agree to accept delay and accepted a target date of 1 April 1945 for completing the transfer of AAF interests in the New Jersey labs and at signal depots and in such agencies as the Plant Engineering Agency, the Storage and Issue Agency, and others (all these involving a transfer of 600 officers and enlisted men, and 5,776 civilians).[84] On 31 January 1945 the research and development of ground radar and ground communications equipment peculiar to the AAF were transferred, involving the Eatontown Signal Laboratory, recently

---

[82] Ltr, CSigO to CG ASF, 21 Oct 44, sub: Transfer of Responsibility, Radio and Radar Transfer to AAF (Bradley Beach). SigC Hist Sec file.

[83] Item 34, Ltr, CSigO to CO SCASA, 2 Oct 44, sub: Transfer of Responsibility for Dev, Sup, Maint of Items Peculiar to the AAF. SigC 321 Transfer of Functions. The AAF was to furnish engineering assistance for the completion of Signal Corps contracts, and the Signal Corps was to complete the development contracts then on the books. CSigO, Annual Rpt, FY 45, p. 227.

[84] (1) Item 51, Memo, Ingles for Brig Gen E. W. Timberlake, 3 Nov 44, sub: Transfer of Responsibility for Dev, Sup, Maint of Items Peculiar to the AAF. (2) Item 101, Incl, with Memo, CG ASF for ACofS, G–4, 21 Mar 45, sub: Transfer of Responsibility for Dev, Sup, Maint of Items Peculiar to the AAF. (3) Item 88, Ltr, Ingles to CG ASF, 15 Feb 45, sub: Rpt on Transfer of Eatontown Lab Area and Facilities to the AAF, with Incl. SigC 321 Transfer of Functions. (4) TAG to CG AAF, ASF SigC, CofEngrs, 10 Feb 45. SigC EO 321.

renamed Watson Laboratory,[85] and a field station in Clermont, Florida.

Haggling over what was "peculiar to the AAF" and what was not went on throughout the transfer. At a conference on 9 October 1944 a total of 392 items was declared "peculiar." But conferees on the 19th of that month deleted 21 items from the list and then added 202 more. The next day they added another 112. By 17 March 1945 it was agreed that these 685 items of electronic equipment that the Signal Corps had been developing and supplying were entirely of AAF concern and were so transferred.[86]

The AAF, which preferred, with the Navy, to split communications operations from communications development and supply, transferred the research and development and supply aspects of the former Signal Corps domain to the Air Forces matériel structure. Aircraft Radio Laboratory at Wright Field changed hands. Operational communications for the Air Transport Command became the sole and specific responsibility of the AACS. The Office of Air Communication under McClelland was consolidated in the special staff of AAF headquarters.[87] By then, however, World War II was nearing its end. The AAF went through the entire conflict with Signal Corps communications-electronic equipment. In the words of at least one postwar summary, "All Air Force material in this field that saw combat during World War II was developed under Signal Corps auspices." [88]

Signal Corps easily survived the loss of half its domain, a fact that shows how large a military effort electronics activity was becoming. The applications (of radar especially) to air power had been seen first and were fantastically implemented during World War II. The applications to ground fighting were less quickly recognized. But ground applications, such as mortar-locating radar, had begun to take form during the war and were increasing by the war's end on a scale that would soon fill the void left by the AAF transfer.

Signal Corps Research and Development at War's End

The center of Signal Corps research and development, the collection of lab-

---

[85] Named for Lt. Col. Paul E. Watson, SigC, who died in 1943. He had prominently assisted the development of Army radar at the Signal Corps labs before the war and was at his death director of the Camp Evans (Radar) Lab.

[86] CSigO, Annual Rpt, FY 45, pp. 228ff.
The following categories were determined to be AAF equipment:

a. Communications radio, radar, countermeasures, identification, and other electronic equipment used exclusively or preponderantly on aircraft.

b. Communications, radio, radar, and other electronic equipment used on the ground exclusively or preponderantly for detection or identification, location, control operation, or navigation of aircraft in accomplishment of the mission of the AAF.

c. Guided missiles equipment, launched from aircraft or dependent for sustenance primarily on the lift of aerodynamic forces.

d. Test equipment, training equipment, and other auxiliary equipment required for the successful use, operation, and maintenance of the classes of equipment specified above.

As of 1 April 1945 a total of 600 officers, 980 enlisted men, and 8,245 civilians employed by the Signal Corps had been transferred, virtually completing the shift.

[87] Memo, Bowles for Eisenhower, 10 Feb 47, sub: Mil Com, p. 18. Bowles folder.

[88] Staff Study on the Unification of Research and Development of Communications, Electronics, and Allied Material, prepared by E&T Div, OCSigO, 20 Feb 48, pp. 3–4. SigC EO R&D, 1946–48.

oratories in the Fort Monmouth area,[89] continued to flourish to the end of the war and beyond, in proportion to the rate at which electronic applications and communications developments within the Army Ground Forces continued to grow. New applications in the Army came harder than those for AAF. Yet there was no doubt even in the mid-course of the war that the many new uses would come eventually. "The Ground Forces problem," Bowles informed Secretary Stimson in August 1943, "though less ramified, is in some ways more difficult because it still demands the laborious exploitation of the full values of radar and other facilities in such applications as fire control and warning means to detect slow-moving ground objects. . . ."[90]

There remained much for the Coles Laboratory to accomplish in radio and wire communications equipment, for Camp Evans to do in radar applications (troop detectors, mortar locators, gun layers), and for the Squier Signal Laboratory[91] to achieve with electronic components, batteries, power equipment, and so on. But as 1945 wore on, especially after V–E Day, the pressure for engineering support of equipment in the field lessened. The practical work toward helping troops in the use of communications-electronics devices, to which the labs had devoted their efforts since 1943, now diminished.[92] It was

[89] A convenient chronology of the laboratories, their titles and headquarters, as given in the front of the Historical Report of SCEL, 11 Dec 45, copy in SigC Hist Sec file, is:
Signal Corps Radio Laboratory, Camp Alfred Vail, later Ft. Monmouth, May 1917–12 Aug 1929.
Signal Corps Laboratories, Ft. Monmouth, 12 Aug 1929–16 Mar 1942.
Signal Corps General Development Laboratories, Ft. Monmouth, 3 Feb–9 Dec 1942, and SigC Radar Lab, Ft. Hancock, N.J., later Camp Evans, Belmar, N.J., 17 Mar 1942–9 Dec 1942.
SigC Ground Signal Service, Camp Evans, later Bradley Beach, 9 Dec 1942–9 Jul 1945.
SigC Engineering Laboratories, Bradley Beach, 10 Jul 45.
[90] Memo, Bowles for SW, 23 Aug 43, sub: Résumé of Consultant Activity, p. 4. Bowles papers.
"During my work on ASW [antisubmarine warfare] I explored the possibilities of helping in the field of communications. The Signal Corps proved most difficult for me. Somehow I could not find a real way to participate. Much of this, perhaps as an admission of weakness on my part, I lay to the narrow or small view of people like Meade, Downing, and a few others who were in the headquarters. General Frank Stoner was most cooperative in his field, that of fixed point to point communications comprising the War Department net. I felt there were weaknesses in the ground forces communication—not so much in equipment as in systems. But here again the going

was hard. General McNair was firm in his policy of a small headquarters and his steadfastness of purpose that the function of the Ground Forces was training. In this they have done a marvelous job. There were also Ground Forces radar problems, but these were hard to define and attempt to solve without first insinuating oneself into the Ground Forces, that is, with their confidence. In the meantime, the Air Forces proved to be most tractable."
Pacific Trip, November–January 1944–45, Bowles, p. 3. Copy in SigC Hist Sec file.
[91] This had been in Fort Monmouth signal laboratories, renamed Squier Laboratory in honor of the World War I Chief Signal Officer, Maj. Gen. George O. Squier, the only chief who ever held a Ph.D. in electrical engineering. Squier Laboratory was so named on 28 June 1945. CSigO, Annual Rpt, FY 45, p. 57.
[92] Mention must be made of the field laboratory groups that the Army maintained in the ETO to work on special problems that grew out of combat applications. These were the British Branch of the Radiation Laboratory and the laboratory maintained by the Technical Liaison Division, OCSigO Signal Section, Headquarters ETOUSA. In the words of an eminently qualified Signal Corps scientist reporting at the war's end, "The services of these groups were so valuable that their counterparts were planned in the Pacific but these plans were terminated on the advent of V–J Day. The undersigned believes that such groups are here to stay since electronic equipment will become more rather than less complicated as time goes on." Memo, Slattery for CSigO, 9 Nov 45, sub: Trip to ETO, p. 43 (Tab III). Slattery Rpt to OCSigO, 9 Nov 45.

time to think of orienting research and development toward future military needs.

In spite of the loss of so much to the AAF late in 1944 and into 1945, overall activity at the Fort Monmouth labs remained high. Dr. Bowles, who had just returned from a visit to the laboratories, had spoken well of them, noting the fine spirit, co-operation, and enthusiasm among the laboratory workers, and commenting favorably on the projects under study, on the competence of the scientists, and on the very close co-operation between them and the industries engaged on the projects. "A very happy and constructive state of affairs," Bowles wrote General Ingles, "a healthy and enthusiastic atmosphere." The main problem, he noted, related to "the difficulties of retaining some of the very able civilian talent because of the inroads of the draft and the attractiveness of Navy commissions." [93]

The Chief Signal Officer did feel some disquiet about the laboratories in the late winter of 1944–45, and in March he informed Dr. Bowles that "neither [Maj.] General [George L.] Van Deusen [commanding the labs] nor myself are entirely satisfied with the organization of the Ft. Monmouth group of laboratories and have decided that it would be advantageous to have a survey made...." [94] General Ingles did not specify his worries.

The Signal Corps Engineering Laboratories were in fact more than holding their ground. Research and development projects in hand as of 30 June

numbered 258, only 31 less than the number reported at the close of the previous fiscal year, and 24 more than the 234 that remained after the transfers to the AAF. During the months that followed that transfer there was a gradual increase in the number of lab workers who were employed in the Squier Laboratory and in the Coles Signal Laboratory on seven groups of projects. [95]

As World War II ended, and plans for the future needs of the Army began to shape up, Signal Corps policy in R&D matters as set forth by the Engineering and Technical Division of OCSigO, looked to a wise peacetime program. Research and development, where reduced, was reduced with care lest necessary projects be struck out. As contracts with the NDRC were concluded, some R&D projects were transferred to the interested services. Other R&D was carried on under Signal Corps contracts. New contracts were undertaken in basic research toward integrated systems of radio and wire equipment (replacing the gamut of individual components that had characterized much of the war's hastily extemporized electronics), toward the eternal goals of lighter weight, smaller but more dependable equipment, and toward totally new ap-

[93] Ltr, Bowles to Ingles, 6 Mar 45. SigC EO Bowles, 1943–45.

[94] Ltr, Ingles to Bowles, 9 Mar 45. SigC EO Bowles, 1943–45.

[95] CSigO, Annual Rpt, FY 46, pp. 454ff., and 1944, p. 203.
A detailed study of the labs at the end of the war analyzed their activities under three main headings: (1) Systems; (2) Components; and (3) Research and Development. Systems was broken down into such topics as communications (wire, radio, television, facsimile, security); detection and fire control; intelligence and countermeasures; identification; proximity fuzes; meteorology; and photography. Subtopics under R&D included wave propagation, meteorology, antennas, thermionics, circuits, materials, and general physics. SCEL Postwar R&D Prog, 5 Dec 45, p. 7.

plications of electronics to ground warfare. These were matters that could not
be overlooked. They could not be neglected in peacetime, not after the lessons
of World War II had deeply impressed

upon the nation the vital character of
scientific contributions to war.[96]

---

[96] (1) CSigO, Annual Rpt, FY 46, pp. 154ff., and
pp. 224ff. (2) SCEL Postwar R&D Prog, 5 Dec 45,
passim.

CHAPTER XV

Equipment: Elaborations and Developments to V–J Day

Throughout the last two years of World War II the laboratories of the Signal Corps remained large and busy with many tasks, despite the heavy reductions in men and projects effected in 1943 and the transfer of half of their domain to the Army Air Forces in 1944 and 1945. Although the bulk of laboratory effort went into the improvement and engineering support of equipment already in the field, all research and development were not eclipsed.

General Colton, to whom fell the task of accomplishing the 1943 reductions, fended well for Signal Corps research and development activities, so basic to success in modern warfare. His order to the laboratories in December 1943, restricting research in favor of invasion preparations, was required by higher authority and was necessarily the consequence of overriding military operational needs. General Colton well knew that at the center of the laboratories lay a hard core of effort bearing upon future combat needs as well as upon the requirements of the moment. That hard core must not be lost. He therefore forbade any reduction in certain categories of projects: 17 of them at the Monmouth laboratories, 9 at Wright Field—a small percentage of the total sum of projects,

but a significant one. All RCM projects, for example, were continued without diminution. Further, in the New Jersey laboratories work continued unabated on radio relay equipment and on the SCR–694, the lightweight field radio intended to replace the SCR–284. General Colton also continued research on quartz crystals (efforts that would lead to synthetic quartz) ; new battery types, especially mercury batteries; and tool, test, and maintenance equipment. At the Aircraft Radio Laboratory nothing was to detract from research on the new, superlatively accurate BTO radars, the AN/APS–15 and APQ–7, or the test equipment under development for 10- and 3-centimeter microwave radars, or the radio guided bombs. All these developments greatly affected the progress of the war during its last months.[1]

---

[1] Ltrs, Colton, Chief E&T Div, to CO SCGSA, 8 Dec 43 and 29 Dec 43, and to CO SCASA, 18 Dec 43, sub: Rev Work Prog. SigC 413.44 Gen 15 (RB–2135).

War Department expert consultant on communications, Dr. Strieby, when urging in April 1944 that development be discontinued on most items (in favor of making "better use of what we have"), excepted multichannel VHF communications (i.e., radio relay), microwave telephone equipment, and the improved lip microphone. Memo, Strieby for Bowles, 28 Apr 44, sub: Results of Theater Survey Trip, p. 3. SCIA file 127 Bowles Rpts.

*A Few Examples—From Wire
Equipment to Electronic Fuzes*

Besides the large variety of RCM
equipment, the laboratories worked on
many new developments from mid-1943
on—some large, such as the new radio
relay AN/TRC-6 employing pulse modulation techniques and the packaged
carrier bays used in multichannel wire
and radio circuits; others small, but large
in significance, forerunners of a future
succession of items, ever smaller, but
better. Examples were the lip microphone, T-45; the small switchboards
such as the 12-pound SB-22/PT and the
still smaller SB 18/GT (composed of
six plastic adaptor plugs U-4/GT and
known as a "vest pocket" board) ; new
field wire WD-1/TT, plastic covered
(polyethelene), much smaller and better than W-110-B; the improved and
smaller sound-powered telephone TA-
1/TT to replace the TP-3, which had
proven so valuable in jungle fighting;
new methods of winding wire in the
high-speed dispenser coils (MX-301/G
for W-130, MX-302/G for W-110,
MX-306/G for WD-1/TT), which
eliminated the use of heavy steel spools
or reels and enabled such rapid unwind-
ing, without kinks, that the wire could
be run out from a speeding vehicle or
even from a low-flying airplane.[2]

Of great significance too was the small
mercury battery. Portable radio sets are
no better than their batteries, which
often fail. Dry batteries constituted a
never-ending problem to the Signal
Corps production and distribution services. Needed in the billions,[3] yet short-
lived, the batteries could not be stored
for long whether on supply shelves or
in unused equipment, least of all in
tropical heat. The typical sal ammoniac
paste dry cell remained a problem until
1943 brought relief with the appearance
of the RM (Rubin Mallory) cell, whose
virtue lay in a pellet of mercury oxide.
Though known before, the type was first
adapted for the military by the Signal
Corps, which built up huge production
facilities in order to manufacture the
cells in quantity. One-fourth the size and
weight of the older sal ammoniac type,
with much longer shelf life and several
times more electrical output, the RM
mercury battery became a large Signal
Corps contribution. Produced in the
hundreds of millions over the last two
years of the war, as BA-38-R, 49-R,
70-R, and 80-R, the batteries powered
the universally used "handie-talkies"
and walkie-talkies (SCR-536 and 300),
as well as the guidon set SCR-511 and
the new SCR-694.[4]

---

[2] (1) CSigO, Annual Rpts, FY 44, pp. 193ff.,
240ff., and 1945, pp. 352ff. (2) SigC Tech Info
Ltrs 33 (Apr 44), pp. 4f.; 38 (Jan 45), pp. 7f.;
40 (Mar 45), pp. 17f.; and 43 (Jun 45), p. 4. (3)
SigC R&D Hist, vol. V, pt. 1, Projs 512-A and B;
pt. 2, Proj 524-D; pt. 3, Proj 532-C; pt. 4, Proj
562-B; and vol. XI, pt. 3, Proj 2044-A.
Regarding the new general-purpose wire WD-
1/TT, replacing both W-130 and W-110-B, see
above, pp. 383-84.

[3] A War Department release dated 24 December
1945 stated that in 1945 2,100,000,000 dry cells had
been produced. Equip folder, Tab E, SigC Hist
Sec file. In the first quarter of 1945, 623,000,000
were produced, according to *ASF Final Rpt, 1 Jul
47*, p. 105.
[4] (1) CSigO, Annual Rpts, FY 44, pp. 248-50,
and FY 45, pp. 371-72. (2) S. L. Ackerman, "Bring
Them Back Alive," *Signals*, II, No. 6 (July-August, 1948), 10. (3) Shute, Industrial Summ: SigC
Proc of Dry Batteries, RM Cell, pp. 30ff.

Proximity fuzes, small, fist-sized, expendable radar (or doppler radio) sets of the type used for unrotated missiles such as rockets, bombs, and mortar shells were a concern of the Signal Corps.[5] The Aircraft Radio Laboratory developed for use in airborne rockets both a photoelectric fuse, MC–380, and a radar or radio fuze, MC–382. Work on the latter type adapted for bombs followed—AN/CPQ–1 and 2, designed to detonate above foxholes and exposed troops. The MC–382 and AN/CPQ fuzes contained miniature CW (doppler) radar sets, each complete with power supply, transmitter, receiver, amplifier, and an electric detonating circuit, all jammed into a package a few inches in size.[6]

Missile Controls

For decades, the rocket enthusiasts on both sides of the Atlantic had pored over their notions and hand-built models. Their conservative and conventional scientific brethren regarded the enthusiasts as hardly on the border of respectable science, if not beyond the pale altogether. Solid, sensible citizens ostracized them, but at least did not burn them for their black arts, as their ancestors would have done. But Adolf Hitler, who did almost no man a good turn, catapulted rocket enthusiasts to success and started a new era in the world of science when he gave state approval and, more especially, state funds, to the rocketeers' dreams.

Before the guided rocket, seeking a target above, came the guided bomb, dropping with the pull of gravity to a target below. The Germans introduced the glide bomb, radio-controlled, with some success in 1943,[7] whereupon the U.S. Signal Corps and the Navy undertook to develop similar weapons. Several modes of guidance were possible: (1) a radar in the bomb that would transmit signals and then detect echoes from a target and home on those echoes; (2) a television set in the bomb that would transmit a view of the target ahead to an operator in an airplane above, who in turn would steer the bomb by remote control; or (3) simply a radio control receiver in the bomb that would respond to guiding signals from an observer in an airplane above. The last method was the simplest and this the ARL quickly utilized in the Azon, a 1,000-pound bomb with movable fins that a receiver within could vary in response to signals radioed from the distant observer. Azon could be controlled in azimuth only but could be and was used very effectively against long narrow targets—against

[5] Baxter, *Scientists Against Time*, pp. 221–40. The type of proximity fuze used in rifled guns constituted a large dramatic task for the NDRC and the Navy; these fuzes rotated with the projectiles and suffered terrific shock, or setback, at the instant of firing.

The VT fuze program had begun before the war as an NDRC project at the National Bureau of Standards.

[6] (1) CSigO, Annual Rpts, FY 44, pp. 334–36, and FY 45, pp. 244, 308–10. (2) SigC R&D Hist, vol. IV, pt. 4, Projs 453–A, B, C, and D. (3) SCEL Postwar R&D Prog, pp. 124f. (4) Incl, Wind Driven Generator Developed for Proximity Fuzes, with Ltr, CSigO to Dir WD BPR OSW, 8 Oct 45, sub: Article for Publication. SigC 000.7 Articles for Publication, vol. 4, Oct–Dec 45.

[7] See above, p. 302.

railroad viaducts in Italy and bridges in Burma.[8]

Thus radio-guided bombs, introduced by the Germans, quickly proved practical. Next would come guided missiles, roaring up under their own power. The need for guided missiles was growing. The reach of antiaircraft guns had attained a maximum, the Army Ground Forces declared in February 1944, asserting that gun projectiles could not knock down stratospheric aircraft or high rockets such as the rumored German V's. Antiaircraft rockets were needed. The rockets themselves would be an Ordnance responsibility. Guided, they would become missiles, and their guidance would be electronic and therefore a concern to the Signal Corps. General Colton, however, gently braked the AGF appeal. He preferred not to begin work on such controls until Ordnance determined the type of missile and its flight characteristics. Maj. John J. Slattery, formerly a civilian engineer at the laboratories and currently a technical officer in the Washington headquarters, agreed, adding the

invariable lament of the laboratories since the 1943 cut—not enough manpower. "The project," he wrote in April 1944, "appears . . . to be desirable for a long range investigation, but one which the Signal Corps should not attempt at the present time due to the limitations of personnel." [9]

It should be noted here that the Germans had developed a successful antiaircraft rocket, the Schmetterling 8–117. They expected three hundred in August 1945, production increasing to three thousand a month by December. This missile, SCEL scientists commented late in 1945, "would have profoundly altered the aspect of air warfare, had the war lasted another half year." The consequences would have been "disastrous," as Lt. Gen. James M. Gavin put it years later.[10] The cavils against rockets and against government research in general were smothered by the eerie scream of Hitler's first V–2, which struck London with unheard of speed and impact on 12 September 1944.

Meteorology

Meteorology, though it took some of the deepest cuts at the laboratories in 1943, necessarily remained significant. Increasing employment of military aircraft the world over required more and better weather reports. "In more and more complex ways are we committed

---

[8] (1) CSigO, Annual Rpts, FY 44, p. 189, and FY 45, p. 419ff. (2) "Azon Does a Job in Burma," *Radar*, No. 8 (February 20, 1945), pp. 26–28. SigC Hist Sec file. (3) Baxter, *Scientists Against Time*, pp. 198f., 409. (4) Craven and Cate, eds., *The Pacific: Matterhorn to Nagasaki, June 1944–August 1945*, p. 238.

ARL developed also a similar bomb, Razon, which could be controlled in range as well as in azimuth. "Razon: Tests Reveal a Promising Tool," *Radar*, No. 10 (June 30, 1945), pp. 26–27. SigC Hist Sec file. The AAF early ordered considerable quantities of these bomb-guiding devices, in October 1943, placing requirements upon the Signal Corps for 10,000 Azons and 500 control transmitters and for 2,000 television transmitters and 100 receivers. Memo, C. S. Kleinau, Chief Aircraft Radio Br, for file, 20 Oct 43, sub: Conf on Guided Missile Prog, attached to OCSigO R&W Action 1, Kleinau to Tech Staff Sec and E&T, 21 Oct 43. SigC 413.44 RCM (RB–2070).

[9] Ltr, CG AGF to CG ASF, 9 Feb 44, sub: Dev of Antiaircraft Arty Material, with 3d Ind, Colton, E&T, to CG ASF, 3 Apr 44, the whole attached to ASF Transmittal Sheet, Action 1, Slattery, Tech ExecO, Electronics Br OCSigO, to Asst Chief of E&T, 3 Apr 44. SigC 413.44 Gen 19 (RB–2362).

[10] (1) SCEL Postwar R&D Program, pp. 85–86. (2) Lt. Gen. James M. Gavin, *War and Peace in the Space Age* (New York: Harper and Brothers, 1958), p. 86. See also below, p. 627.

now to operations on a worldwide basis," one authority would write soon after the war, "and more and more do all these techniques depend on precise knowledge of weather." [11] "Weather is a weapon," commented another. "If left to chance, it may help you and the enemy, hurt both of you, or aid one of you and hinder the other. If it is properly used, the weather can be . . . on your side most of the time." Ill understood and unappreciated, the meteorologists at the end of World War II stood nonetheless, like their fellow scientists and technicians in the communication-electronic discipline, on the threshold of a new era. [12]

The laboratories of the Signal Corps throughout the last years of the war continued to pursue a variety of meteorological projects. Eatontown Signal Laboratory made improvements in hydrogen gas generators and in the neoprene plastic balloons that the gas lifted aloft to indicate by their drift the direction and speed of the wind or, carrying the radiosonde, to detect other weather factors. On the ground the weather station crews no longer tracked the balloons with the telescopic viewer called a theodolite, but with the meteorological balloon radio direction finder, a device on which the laboratory completed development in 1943 (service test models reached the field by early 1944). The tracker was the SCR–658—sometimes called Rawin for radio wind—a meteorological direction finder whose operator,

hand-turning the antenna, could track up to 60,000 feet through darkness or cloud the signals of a radiosonde dangling beneath a soaring weather balloon. In addition to acquiring wind data, the SCR–658 garnered a variety of other weather information. The set included recording equipment, AN/FMQ–1. The recorder printed a continuous record of the weather data that the radiosonde perceived all along its upward course, and that a tiny battery-powered transmitter sent back to earth. The Signal Corps developed a variety of radiosondes. An improved FM version was the AN/AMT–2, able to measure continuously temperature, pressure, and humidity throughout the balloon's long ascent. [13]

For Rawin purposes, radar could be used in place of the radio direction finder. In fact, radar measurements of the balloon's wind drift were more accurate. The weather balloon itself did not return an echo, but metallized paper reflectors could be hung below the balloon. Folded so as to create angular pockets, these corner reflectors of aluminum foil returned very strong radar echoes. The Signal Corps developed not only such reflectors but also the SCR–525 and SCR 825, special meteorological radars, or direction finders, employing the pulse-echo principle of radar. [14]

[11] Memo, Bowles for Eisenhower, 10 Feb 47, sub: Mil Com, Related Svs, and Organizational Considerations, p. 2. Bowles Papers, Tab G.

[12] (1) AFSC Lecture I–27, The Weather Factor in Joint Operations, Tab 26, p. 1. SigC OP 352 AFSC Rpts, vol. 6, 1948-49. (2) SCEL Postwar R&D Prog, p. 127. See also John R. Deane, The Strange Alliance (New York: Viking Press, 1947), pp. 71ff.

[13] (1) SigC R&D Hist, vol. VII, pt. 2, Proj 732–I, and vol. IX, pt. 2, Proj 923–A. (2) CSigO, Annual Rpts, FY 44, pp. 201, 277f., and 288, and FY 45, pp. 331f.

The SCR–658 would eventually be replaced by the automatic tracking AN/CRD–1, under development in 1945. (1) SigC R&D Hist, vol. IX, pt. 2, Proj 923–E. (2) CSigO, Annual Rpt, FY 45, p. 333.

[14] (1) SigC R&D Hist, vol. IX, pt. 2, Proj 923–D, (2) Historical Report of the Signal Corps Engineering Laboratories, Ft. Monmouth, 1944, pp. 204f. SigC Hist Sec file.

SCR–658 Trained on Radiosonde AN/AMT–2 at Launching

Actually, almost any radar could be utilized for Rawin purposes, and all types of sets in the field came to be so used, including even the patriarch SCR–268.[15] Among the best, of course, were the SCR–584's, which troops employed as readily at night or through clouds as during the daylight hours in order to track a corner reflector hung upon a drifting balloon. The oscilloscope operator read off continuously the range, azimuth, and elevation of the soaring target while a crewman plotted the data on the standard Signal Corps plotting board ML–122 in order to compute wind direction and speed. By 1945 the Army Air Forces had allocated more than thirty SCR–584's to their weather service for Rawin use.[16]

Rawin would be the primary function of these SCR–584's, the Air Forces stipulated, but added that the sets would also play a secondary meteorological role—storm detection. Since the earliest use of microwave radars—the SCR–582 and 615 used in Panama in 1943—radar crewmen had noticed how clearly their sets could "see" dense storm clouds at great distances, because the

---

[15] Upon realizing this, the Signal Corps stopped the development of SCR–825. CSigO, Annual Rpt, FY 45, p. 288.

[16] (1) "Wind and Storms," Radar, No. 9 (April 30, 1945), pp. 45–46. SigC Hist Sec file. (2) WD Publicity Release, High Altitude Wind Direction, Velocity Determined by Radar, 31 Jul 46. Radar folder, Tab N, SigC Hist Sec file.

lofty thunderheads returned clear echoes. The sets were valuable in tropical lands where storms suddenly spring up, and useful wherever weather stations were absent, as over large waters areas, over enemy territory, or over mountain wastes.[17]

Radar ranges were limited, however, to one or two hundred miles. Something better was at hand, able to detect thunderstorms a thousand or more miles away—the technique called sferics, which makes use of lightning discharges. A flash of lightning is a very effective radio broadcast, as everyone knows who ever tried to listen to an AM radio program while a thunderstorm rumbled in the vicinity. Sferics (derived from atmospherics, or what the radio listener simply calls static) involves a system of two or more radio direction finders located some hundreds of miles apart but tightly linked by a communications net. The operators take delight in the crackles of static that the ordinary radio public abhors. The sferics DF men take bearings on the sounds of lightning discharges, co-ordinate their data, plot the bearings on maps, and locate storms at vast distances. The British were the first to use the technique. Learning of it, the Army Air Forces asked the Signal Corps for sferics equipment early in 1944. During that year the Eatontown Laboratory (later the Evans Signal Laboratory to which the project was transferred) developed a static or sferics DF, the AN/GRD-1. The Signal Corps obtained the first development models in October 1944 and in December provided the first complete American sferics system, four DF's, plotting equipment, and necessary supplies, enabling the AAF to establish a badly needed installation in the Pacific.[18]

Besides all the paraphernalia associated with Rawin and sferics, the Eatontown Signal Laboratory developed further a variety of meteorological sets, large assemblies of equipment mounted in trucks and trailers. The SCM-1 for the Army Air Forces became refined into the AN/TMQ-1; the SCM-9 and 10 for the field artillery became AN/TMQ-4. These complete weather stations, including radiosonde equipment able to determine weather conditions at all levels from the surface to the upper air, were for the benefit of aircraft operation and of artillerymen, who must know the conditions aloft through which large caliber shells pass in order to make ballistic allowances for wind and pressure. The complex sets required crews of several men each. But already the Air Forces was seeking automatic weather stations that could be placed in rigorous locations—on mountain peaks and ice-caps, for example—and that could, without a human caretaker, ascertain weather data and transmit the information (radioing it at predetermined intervals for weeks and months on end) to the nearest inhabited post, perhaps hundreds of miles distant. Accordingly, the laboratory developed robot sets

[17] (1) "Radar vs. Weather," *Radar* (unnumbered) (April, 1944), pp. 26–27. (2) "Storm Detection Is a Growing Job for Radar," *Radar*, No. 9 (April 30, 1945), pp. 47–51. Both in SigC Hist Sec file. (3) Thompson, Harris, *et al.*, *The Test*, p. 261n.

[18] (1) CSigO, Annual Rpt, FY 45, pp. 272–74. (2) SigC R&D Hist, vol. IX, pt. 2, Proj 924-A. (3) H. Berman, "Sferics," *Signals*, I, No. 6 (July–August, 1947), 37ff. For a generally informative article on World War II DF's and their many uses—meteorological, navigational, intelligence, and so on—see D. W. Wixon, "Friendly Agent," *Signals*, I, No. 5 (May–June, 1947), 23ff.

SCM–17, 18, and 19, forerunners of the automatic weather stations of the future.[19]

In the immediate future, too, the meteorological specialists at the Signal Corps Engineering Laboratories realized, rocketry would require better recording of data and better transmitting of it from greater distances in the sky —telemetering would become the name for these techniques. Weather balloons and their radiosondes would have to strain upwards to greater elevations. Indeed, there would be no end, no ceiling, upon the partnership of meteorology and communications-electronics, as man's curiosity continued to probe the upper atmosphere and beyond.[20]

Microwave Radars on the Ground, AN/CPS–1 and 6 and SCR–584

By the mid-course of the war radars were flooding out of the laboratories in an unbelievable variety of types and applications, not only aircraft sets (tail warning radars, airborne range finders, gun layers, Rebecca-Eurekas, and so on) but also ground sets. Among the latter were several versions of LW radars and height finders used to determine the elevation of aircraft.

The Chief Signal Officer strongly believed that there were too many types of ground radar. They had been engendered by extreme pressure and urgency early in the war, and by mid-1944 some of the sets constituted, General Ingles exclaimed, "outstanding examples of non-essential developments." He specifi-

cally mentioned several: in the LW category, "the development of the AN/TPS–10 when we already have in production four light-weight early warning radar equipments to perform the same task"; and in height-finding applications "the development of V-Beam equipment when we already have seven pieces of equipment to give us the height of an airplane, five of which are in good production." [21]

Microwave types of radar had replaced most long-wave radars in laboratory development by mid-1943, but microwave radar production by American industry had not yet offset the long lead enjoyed by the older long-wave sets. The latter therefore continued to outnumber microwave sets in the field, especially on the ground. Thus it was that the Army Air Forces, although they had decided by mid-1943 that they would need no more SCR–270's or 271's, nonetheless continued to operate the older radars in large numbers. In fact, the AAF estimated that through the fiscal year of 1945 it would keep 113 SCR–270's in operation and 61 SCR–271's. As late as

[19] SigC R&D Hist, vol. VII, pt. 3, Projs 792–A and –B; 794–A, –B, and –C.

[20] SCEL Postwar R&D Prog, pp. 136ff.

[21] Memo, Ingles for Bowles, 27 Jun 44, sub: Comments on Strieby's Conclusions on Results of Theater Survey Trip, p. 4. SigC EO 370.2 Theaters of Opn, 1943–44. See also Thompson, Harris, et al., The Test, pp. 261ff.

It had been noted early in 1943, in the Secretary of War's office, that the Army ground radar program was "chaotic," that "about a dozen early warning and height finding equipments were being worked on by different development labs," and that there was "tremendous duplication of effort and no immediate solution in sight." Dr. Bowles set up a committee to study the matter. Its report on 11 July 1943 led to curtailment of the Army program for these sets. See Henry E. Guerlac, Radar, 1945, page 664, in the consecutively numbered pages of the photostat copy in Signal Corps Historical Section files. In the original pagination, this is page 61, Section C, Chapter VII.

BASE OF SCR–270 RADAR, SHOWING AZIMUTH SCALE, VANUA LEVU, FIJI ISLANDS

October 1943 the Navy asked for 50 SCR–270's.[22]

By 1944 the oldest and most numerous of American radars, the ancestral SCR–268, was far down its decline. As of the middle of the year, 600 sets (issued for GL, an application for which this radar had never been intended but for which it was better than no radar) had been replaced by SCR–584's. Even

so, some 1,200 SCR–268's remained in use for searchlight control, the function

radars needed for fiscal year 1945, the SCR–270 and 271 far outnumbered other types:

Type	Number		Type	Number
Total				400
SCR–270	113		SCR–627	10
SCR–271	61		AN/CPS–1	23
SCR–527	50		AN/CPS–4	25
SCR–588	30		AN/CPS–5	40
SCR–615	40		TRU*	8
SCR–516	0		CH**	0

*Transportable radio unit (a type of British radar)
**Chain Home

A contributing factor to the long continued use of the older Army radars was a lag in microwave applications by the Radiation Laboratory to the radar needs of the Army. Guerlac, Radar, pp. 603ff. (sec. C, ch. VII, pp. 1ff.).

[22] (1) 1st Ind, CG AAF to CSigO, 24 Jun 43, on Ltr, CSigO to CG AAF, sub: Radio Set SCR–270 and 271. AAG 413.44–AQ Radio. (2) Ltr, CG AAF to CSigO, 3 Feb 44, sub: Estimate of AW Sets in Opn for FY 44–45. AAG 413.44–CV Radio. (3) Ltr, Keely, OCSigO, to Dir Camp Evans Sig Lab, 13 Oct 43, sub: Radio Sets SCR–270–DA–(A). SigC 413.44 SCR–270–12H No. 20 (RB–2015).

According to Air Forces' estimate of AWS ground

for which the sets had originally been designed. In this role the 268 served very well to the war's end, since its microwave successor, the AN/TPL–1, did not come into production in time to replace it in the field. The old 268's, even in discard, still had value, for in mid-1945 atomic researchers would ask for them in large numbers for postwar research in atomic energy.[23]

The old long-wave radars yielded to the new microwave types as fast as the latter reached the field. Allied researchers generally ignored the medium-wave types, in the 500-megacycle range wherein the Germans had very early attained their greatest success and wherein too they later bogged down (the Signal Corps produced one set in the medium range, the excellent SCR–602 type 8, or the AN/TPS–3, used late in the war as an LW radar).[24]

The microwave SCR–584 replaced the 268 in GL applications. The MEW, or AN/CPS–1, likewise began to replace the 270 and 271 in EW, but never

reached the field in anything like enough sets to put the older types of long-wave radar out of business before the war's end. This was especially true of the Pacific where priority for microwave radar equipment rated below that of the European theater and therefore was later arriving there. "The radar war in the Pacific was, as far as ground equipment went [except for SCR–584's], largely fought with long wave sets." The authority who made this statement also noted a greater lag of radar applications in the immense Pacific areas. This he attributed primarily to the difficult supply problems there, as well as to the fact that radar methods and equipment used effectively in Europe were impossible or impracticable in the Pacific. Finally he noted a lack of centralized control over Army operations in the Pacific as a whole.[25]

Foremost among new microwave ground radars was the microwave early warning pioneered by the Radiation Laboratory. Designed as the AN/CPS–1 to replace the old long-wave SCR's–270, 271, 527, and 588, this radar took a new departure with its novel antenna array, a long horizontal half cylinder.[26] The set at first impressed the Signal Corps variously. Some representatives viewed it apathetically because, for one thing, the radar in its prototype form could give only azimuth and range of a target and

---

[23] (1) Memo, Keil for Gonseth, 20 Jun 44, sub: Sup Status of Radio Set SCR–268. SigC OP 300.6 Memo for Rcd. (2) Ltr, L. W. Alvarez to Harrison, 23 Jun 45, and other papers (20 Sep 45). SigC EO 400.12 Chief P&D Sv (Harrison) 1943–45.
Even as late as the battle of Okinawa, SCR–268's were welcomed. A number of them arrived in May 1945 and were used at once in a radar surveillance net, 4 sets being installed on the western shore of the island, 5 on the eastern. GHQ USAF-PAC Anti-Aircraft Artillery Activities in the Pacific War, 1946, pp. 63, 135. OCMH files.
[24] This Army radar, like SCR's–268, 270, and 271, was entirely designed by the Signal Corps. Its transmitter tube was developed by Harold Zahl, then a major at the Evans Lab, and the group that perfected the set was headed by Capt. John Marchetti. Pushed by AAF and Signal Corps enthusiasm, the AN/TPS–3 became the best in the class of EW LW (early warning, lightweight) sets and saw service both in Europe and in the Pacific. Zahl, Draft MS Comment, Jul 59. See also Thompson, Harris, et al., The Test, pp. 263f.

[25] Guerlac, Radar, pp. 1380–83 (sec. E, ch. VIII, pp. 1–4) and p. 1410 (p. 31), also pp. 1529ff. (app. D, pp. 1ff.).
OSRD's field services, including radar assistance, were much later getting organized in the Pacific than in Europe. Baxter, Scientists Against Time, p. 411. See also Thiesmeyer and Burchard, Combat Scientists, Foreword, p. xi.
[26] (1) Thompson, Harris, et al., The Test, pp. 275f. (2) Guerlac, Radar, pp. 642ff. (sec. C, ch. VII, pp. 39ff.).

MICROWAVE EARLY WARNING ANTENNA, OKINAWA

not its altitude.[27] Others reacted with enthusiasm. Colonel Metcalf, chief of the Electronics Branch in OCSigO, asked the Air Forces to take action to determine the characteristics the AAF desired for the MEW. He urged conferences wherein representatives from the Office of Scientific Research and Development, the Air Forces, and the Signal Corps could co-ordinate MEW design, "so that procurement may be undertaken at the earliest possible date." He foresaw that MEW "may prove to be a definite improvement over our present equipment (SCR–270, 271, and 588); particularly, in its probable freedom from enemy jamming and in its improved performance in mountainous terrain."[28]

The Air Forces rushed the military characteristics. The Radiation Laboratory rushed a preproduction set for the Signal Corps to test at the AAF School of Applied Tactics, and General Colton

---

[27] One skeptic added to his criticism: "It is suggested to the Liaison Group that if the Radiation Laboratory persists in its efforts on the MEW that an attempt be made to direct these efforts towards producing a set giving altitude determination as well as azimuth and range."

This could be and was done, first by adding a second high horizontal beam to the AN/CPS–1 and then by creating a new set, AN/CPS–6, which employed a vertical antenna for height finding, in addition to the long horizontal search antenna. (1) Memo, N. A. Abbott, Radio Engr R&D Tech Staff, for file, 9 Dec 42, sub: Dev of SCR–682, SCR–598, and MEW. SigC 413.44 AN/CPS–1 No. 1, Dec 42–Jun 43 (MEW) (RB–2034). (2) Guerlac, Radar, pp. 668ff. (sec. C, ch. VII, pp. 65ff.).

[28] Ltr, Metcalf to CG Hq ASF, 21 Dec 42, sub: Prog for Dev and Proc of MEW Equip. AAG 413.44–1 Radio.

established a project for the AN/CPS–1 at the Camp Evans Signal Laboratory to supervise the activity.[29] Although it would be summer of 1943 before even the preproduction set was ready for testing, the Air Forces, overly hopeful, asked for twenty-five sets to be produced that year and another seventy-five in 1944. The AN/CPS–1 was a super giant in the realm of giant radio sets, which radars were. Weighing over sixty tons and as complicated as it was ponderous, it could not be hurried.

Men and papers scurried among the several agencies involved in its development, which was beset by changes of plan, changes of design, and changes of military characteristics.[30] Amid prolonged difficulties over the manufacture of the production set, the first laboratory-built MEW under test at AAFSAT in Florida proved itself to be far more than a mere long-range search radar.[31] "Preliminary experiments . . . " Colonel Rives stated in November 1943, "indicate that this set can be used for controlling friendly aircraft on bombing, photograph, and reconnaissance missions, as well as fighters on intercept missions." Prophetic words. More and larger oscilloscopes were needed to pre-

sent all the information which the long concave antenna gleaned, as it rotated, from the skies.[32] Five laboratory-built models known simply as MEW's went overseas in 1944, while production of the CPS–1 got under way at home, just as its successor, the prototype AN/CPS–6, began undergoing its tests at the AAF School of Applied Tactics. In this last set, microwave techniques would finally meet Air Forces' long-standing demand for a GCI radar that could determine with accuracy target height as well as range and azimuth.[33]

Just as the MEW provided the best solution of radar problems in EW and GCI, so the SCR–584 proved to be the answer to the antiaircraft artilleryman's prayer.[34] Army's SCR–584 became popular with the AAF, too, when it discovered that the set could alleviate problems

[29] (1) Ltr, CG AAF to CSigO, 2 Jan 43, sub: Mil Characteristics for MEW. (2) Ltr, L. A. DuBridge, Dir RL, to OCSigO, Attn: Colton, Chief Sig Sup Svs, 29 Dec 42. (3) Ltr, CSigO to Dir Camp Evans Sig Lab, 30 Dec 42, sub: MEW Type Equip. All in SigC 413.44 AN/CPS–1 No. 1 (MEW) (RB–2034). (4) SigC R&D Hist, vol. IV, pt. 3, Proj 422–A.

[30] (1) Ltr, CG AAF to CSigO, 17 Mar 43, sub: Proc of MEW Equip. (2) Ltr, Winter to ACofAS, Materiel, Maint, and Distr, 7 Apr 43, sub: Steering Cmte for MEW Set. Both in SigC 413.44 AN/CPS–1 No. 1 (MEW) (RB–2034). (3) Rpt, Wallace Clark & Co. to Gens Colton and Harrison, 16 Jul 43, sub: Microwave Early Warning Equipment AN/CPS–1 (hereafter cited as Wallace Clark Rpt). SigC 413.44 AN/CPS–1 No. 2 (MEW) (RB–2120).

[31] See Wallace Clark Rpt.

[32] Ltr, Rives, Deputy Air ComO, to CSigO, Attn: Keely, 17 Nov 43, sub: Radio Set AN/CPS–1. SigC 413.44 AN/CPS–1 No. 2 (MEW) (RB–2120).

[33] (1) CSigO, Annual Rpt, FY 44, pp. 284f. (2) "MEW: Its Shape and Look," Radar, No. 3 (June 30, 1944), pp. 4f. SigC Hist Sec file. (3) SigC R&D Hist, vol. IV, pt. 3, Proj 422–E. (4) MEW Becomes the Heart of the Radar Contl System, IX TAC booklet entitled Communications and The Tactical Air Commander, May 1945, pp. 21, 51. SigC 413.44 (ET–2744) Sets Gen 5, 1945.
The AN/CPS–6 combined the long horizontal antenna of the CPS–1 with a high half-moon-shaped vertical antenna, both mounted on a rotating platform comparable in size to a merry-go-round, and so dubbed.

[34] "You fair dinkum said that right, cobber," was the Australian flavored comment of Dr. Miller of OCMH who had served in the South Pacific with the 3d Marine Defense Battalion (renamed in mid-1944 the 3d Antiaircraft Battalion). The unit had been using SCR–268's and 270's in the Bougainville area when the new SCR–584's arrived, whose accuracy and smooth operation delighted the radarmen and gunners alike. Dr. Miller noted, too, the useful accuracy of the 584 in checking the calibration shots of 90-mm. guns. "You just set the antenna on the gun's angle of elevation, tracked the shell, and gave the range reading when it exploded." Dr. Miller, Draft MS Comment, Aug 59. SigC Hist Sec file.

of air interception. The AAA batteries, under air control, could be so accurately pointed by the microwave GL radars that they could shoot down enemy planes at night, relieving to some extent the demand for airborne interception radars in night fighter airplanes. Early in 1943 an Air Forces officer had informed Brig. Gen. Gordon P. Saville, charged with air defense, that the new 10-centimeter radars, employed with 90-mm. gun batteries, would "materially reduce hostile night bombardment." He therefore wished to secure the sets to supply to all 90-mm. gun batteries in the North African, South Pacific, and Southwest Pacific theaters, in order to "lessen the horrible scream for night fighters." [35] By mid-1943 the Signal Corps had completed the final design of the SCR–584 and was reducing the tremendous problems encountered in its production. [36] At the year's end microwave gun laying radar was ready to replace the long-wave SCR–268. At last the medium-wave German Wuerzburg, the best GL radar up to this time, would be outclassed.

A new factor that hastened the demise of the SCR–268 and promoted the SCR–584 was enemy RCM. After the raid on Hamburg in mid-1943, the Germans began retaliating very effectively against Allied long-wave radars. In November the Signal Corps informed the Air Forces that no amount of redesign could greatly improve the SCR–268 against jamming. All long-wave sets were susceptible "to the present form of enemy Window," General Ingles wrote, urging that "considerable effort should be directed toward the replacement of SCR–268 by SCR–584 for gun laying applications." [37]

Even as General Ingles wrote, the effort was beginning, with tryouts first in England and then in Italy. In England, the microwave SCR–584 immediately outperformed the British (Canadian-built) long-wave GL–3. Early in November came a report that the 584, feeding target data to a British predictor (or director, in U.S. terminology) that controlled the guns of an AA battery, had seen action against enemy raiders and had proved "very effective." Another report, comparing the 584 with the GL–3, stated that the SCR–584 located 80 targets where the Canadian set detected only 20. This particular 584, with an American crew, had been operating for three weeks, the report added, "without breakdown of any kind," under the British AA command on the Isle of Sheppey in the Thames River estuary. [38]

---

[35] Memo, Lt Col Robert Totten for Gen Saville, 27 Feb 43, sub: Gun Laying Radar Equip, bearing notations initialed M and A. AAG 413.44–G Radar. Someone (initial M—probably Marriner, then the AAF director of communications) penned a marginal note to the "Chief," presumably General Arnold, saying "a ball we should have picked up sometime ago—we didn't realize what the priority situation was." (The ground GL program had suffered throughout 1942 from a chronically low priority; see Thompson, Harris, et al., The Test, pp. 270f.) General Arnold, initial A, scrawled in red pencil "Good!" across Totten's words desiring that the Operations Division of the Commanding General, SOS, be influenced to supply all 90-mm. gun batteries in the theaters of war with the new microwave GL radars.

[36] Thompson, Harris, et al., The Test, pp. 265–74.

[37] Memo, CSigO for Maj Gen Homer R. Oldfield, 30 Nov 43, sub: Radar Interference. SigC 413.44 Gen 13 (RB-2133).

[38] Ltr, Warner, CAC RL, to CG AA Comd, Richmond, Va., 9 Nov 43, sub: SCR–584 Performance in U.K. SigC 413.44 SCR–584 No. 7 (RB-2094). This set was SCR–584B, Ser No. 2, which the British Ministry of Supply had obtained under lend-lease. It had first been set up and operated at the Air Research and Development Establishment at Malvern, England, on 7 October 1943. Performance of SCR–584B, Ser No. 2 in Great Britain, signed by Lee. L. Davenport, 26 Nov 43. SigC 413.44 SCR–584 No. 7 (RB-2094).

Generally used with the American computer M–9, the SCR–584 proved to be the best ground radar airplane killer of the war.[39]

In Italy the SCR–584 met the test of combat at Anzio, where older long-wave British and American radars were being reduced to ineffectiveness by German jamming. On 24 February 1944 the first 584's, together with an SCR–545, arrived on an LST from Naples.[40] One of the 584's was at once put to work supplementing a British 10-centimeter GCI radar, the Ames (Air Ministry experimental set) 14, which suffered from land echoes at ranges within twenty miles. The SCR–584, on the other hand, "gave automatic tracking on low flying aircraft out to 27 miles with an early warning range of 56 miles. Height accuracy up to 18 miles (away) was 200 feet and beyond this range the height readings were accurate within 1,000 feet. The two sets operating together gave an exceedingly effective GCI control, the SCR–584 taking care of interceptions from 0–20 miles and the British set from 20–60 miles." [41]

"When I first arrived at the Beachhead," wrote Maj. Harris T. Richards,

a Signal Corps radar officer from the Allied Force Headquarters, "the enemy was doing formation bombing of the Anzio-Nettuno Port Area. The SCR–268 was so effectively jammed by 'Window' and land jamming stations that the enemy had no worries from AA fire." But the 584's changed all that (by April the 68th and 216th AAA Battalions were completely equipped with 584's and the 108th AAA Battalion with 545's). "After three SCR–584's were put in action," Richards reported, "and five E/A [enemy airplanes] out of a formation of twelve were shot down, the enemy did no more formation flying over the area." [42]

Everyone wanted SCR–584's. The commanding general of the AAF in the North African theater complained that his 268's were being jammed and could not satisfactorily direct either searchlights or night fighter operations. He asked if better SLC radars would be furnished soon, or if 584's could be had. He explained that microwave radars,

---

[39] Or from the sea—"at no time did the Navy have in operation automatic tracking or a radar set comparable in performance to the Army's SCR–545 or SCR–584." Guerlac, Radar, p. 689 (sec. C, ch. VIII, p. 4).

[40] Baxter, *Scientists Against Time*, p. 115. See also above, p. 58.

[41] (1) CSigO, Annual Rpt, FY 44, pp. 191–92. (2) Incl, Operation of SCR–584 at Anzio, with Ltr, Warner, Air Defense Div SHAEF, APO 757, to Winter, OCSigO, 14 Jun 44. SigC 413.44 SCR–584 No. 13 (RB–2298). (3) "What Happened at the Anzio Beachhead," *Radar*, No. 4 (no date), pp. 29–34. (4) Guerlac, Radar, p. 708 (sec. C, ch. VIII, p. 23).

[42] Incl, Ltr, Richards, SigC Radar Off (AA Sec AFHQ), to M.G., AA&CD Sec AFHQ, 2 Apr 44, sub: Tech and Tactical Opn of the SCR–584 in the Anzio-Nettuno Bridgehead, with Ltr, Colton to CSigO, 7 Apr 44, same sub. SigC 413.44 SCR–584 No. 12 (RB–2297).

Richards explained that one 584 and one 545 were in operation at all times, the 545 furnishing IFF information to the 584 crew. Of the 8 operators sent with the sets, "only one could be considered as qualified," Richards asserted. The others had never had more than fifteen minutes each actual operating experience, and that long before, in their training school days. But numerous seasoned 268 operators were already in the area and were able to handle the new microwave sets very well. Actually the SCR–584 proved much easier to operate than the SCR–268. "A 268 operator could readily pick up the 584, which really operated like a dream. Using a 584 was fun." Miller, Draft MS Comment, Aug 59.

such as the SCR–584, performed very well despite enemy jamming. He soon learned, however, that he would have to continue using 268's for searchlight control since the first production of a microwave SLC set, AN/TPL–1, was at least a year in the future. But the 584's would fast become available for gun laying, chiefly for antiaircraft artillery batteries. Coast Artillery wanted the sets for sea targets, to direct their 155-mm. mobile guns, while awaiting production of new microwave CD (coast defense) radars, the AN/TPG–1 and the AN/MPG–1. For example, in the Pacific the Coast Artillery immediately demanded 28 SCR–584's and 56 qualified Signal Corps maintenance men, specifying 7 sets for Oahu alone and the rest for various advance bases.[43]

Strong demands also came from the Army Air Forces. Here was a radar that had been developed with the simple thought that it would serve as a gun layer for ground force use with AA guns. It was toward this end that the Signal Corps had taken over the prototype, XT–1, from the Radiation Laboratory and had militarized it, produced it, and was now distributing it for use by the Army Ground Forces and by AAA battalions.[44] But now, too, the set suddenly appeared to have special air applica-

tions, for example, for the control of aircraft in flight, a GCI radar, and so very much the Air Forces concern. In February 1944, General Ingles informed the Army Ground Forces that "the Army Air Forces will soon test a Radio Set SCR–584 to determine its suitability for use as an advanced stage GCI set," and he asked the Ground Forces to "make available to the Army Air Forces an experienced SCR–584 operating crew. . . . The Signal Corps," he added, "will provide maintenance personnel."[45] In mid-April, commanders in the European Theater of Operations requested twenty SCR–584's modified for use as emergency GCI radars. True, their relatively short range, designed for gun laying only, was a defect in GCI. The range could, however, be increased, and was.[46]

Within a month after the GCI request, AAF officers were contemplating using the set for another function, for directing fighter-bombers to ground targets. This radar could "see" both the planes above and targets on the ground below, miles away. When the bombers, coached by a controller using SCR–584 information, arrived over the target, their pilots could be told by radiotele-

---

[43] (1) Msg F–51904, CG USAF NATO to WD, 28 May 44. (2) Msg, WAR 44790, ASF CSO to CG USAF NATO, 1 Jun 44. SigC 413.44 SCR–584 No. 13 (RB–2298). (3) Ltr, Keely, O/C Ground Electronics Sec, Electronics Br, to Dir CESL, 3 Dec 43, sub: Modification of SCR–584 for Use Against Surface Targets. SigC 413.44 SCR–584 No. 7 (RB–2094). (4) Msg (CM–IN–3254, 5 Mar 44, 1405–Z), Ft. Shafter to WAR, 5 Mar 44. SigC 413.44 SCR–584 No. 7 (RB–2295).

[44] See Thompson, Harris, et al., The Test, pp. 265ff.

[45] Ltr, CSigO to CG AGF, 28 Feb 44, sub: Availability of Operating Pers. SigC 413.44 SCR–584 No. 10 (RB–2295).

[46] The 584 could determine the altitude of targets far better than older type radars. On this point, Dr. Miller commented: "The SCR–584 calculated altitude by a potentiometer which multiplied the sine of the angle of elevation by the range. The SCR–268 determined the angle of elevation fairly accurately, but its altitude readings were often wildly erratic. Its altitude computer was a 3-dimensional cam which received the data mechanically, and even the best of operators could not make it work really well." Miller, Draft MS Comment, Aug 59.

phone the exact instant at which to drop their bombs.[47]

This surprising use of a ground radar as a bombing aid would depend upon very accurate maps used in combination with precise plotting equipment at the radar site. Then the radar operator could track a friendly bomber in flight with such accuracy that he could precisely locate the plane in relation to the terrain below at any instant.[48]

[47] (1) Ltr, Colton, Chief E&T, to Army Electronics Tng Ctr, Harvard University, 17 Apr 44, sub: Transfer of SCR-584 Components. SigC 413.-44 SCR-584 No. 11 (RB-2296). (2) Ltr, Brig Gen Otto P. Weyland, President of Bd Hq XIX TAC, to CG Ninth AF, APO 696, 14 May 44, sub: Investigation and Rpt on SCR-584. SigC 413.44 SCR-584 No. 14 (RB-2366). (3) See also above, pp. 433-34.

[48] Bombing missions controlled by SCR-584's became frequent in the campaigns on the Continent after the Normandy invasion. See (1) "When and How the 584 Functions as a Controller," *Radar,* No. 5 (September 30, 1944), pp. 8-9; (2) "Close Control Bombing," *Radar,* No. 9 (April 30, 1945), pp. 8ff., SigC Hist Sec file; (3) Adaption of the SCR-584 for Close Support Contl, IX TAC, booklet entitled Com and The Tactical Air Comdr, May 1945, pp. 53f.

The Radiation Laboratory worked on the plotting system, described as follows: "The SCR-584 plotting table system is a device for studying radar bombing techniques. It consists of a standard SCR-584 whose range and azimuth outputs operate a plotting board that automatically records the ground track of an airplane on a sheet of paper 52 inches square, out to a maximum ground range of 20,000 yards from the SCR-584. When the airplane is at an altitude of 30,000 feet and at maximum range on the board, the airplane ground track is established to within plus or minus 100 feet. Information from the plotting table map determines bomb impact points corresponding to bomb release points. Using the reverse of the bombing procedure, the system has also been successfully employed for directing aircraft in maneuvers similar to those required for close ground support bombing. Tests have shown the system capable of 5 to 10 mil bombing at 20,000 feet to 30,000 feet." Incl 3, RL Rpt 595, 3 Jul 44, The SCR-584 Plotting Table System, with Ltr, Dir of RL, to Hq ASF, Attn: Electronics Br, OCSigO, 31 Jul 44. SigC 413.44 SCR-584 No. 15 (RB-2367).

Air Forces interest in the SCR-584 did not stop with this amazingly refined application of the radar. The AAF next wanted to employ the set for meteorological uses as well—to locate and track storm areas up to the maximum range, about forty-five miles. After allocating thirty-five sets for this special use, the AAF discovered that the British branch of the Radiation Laboratory had modified some of the 584's in the European Theater of Operations, increasing their range. Accordingly, the Air Forces asked the Signal Corps to provide kits to increase similarly the range of the thirty-five meteorological 584's, enabling them to detect storm clouds out to seventy-five miles.[49]

The SCR-584 thus became quite a versatile set. Conceived, developed, produced, and originally distributed solely as a gun layer, it became every kind of radar, from a basic GL to an SLC and CD, a GCI, a ground bomber controller and guide, and a meteorological set for Rawin and storm detection. Finally, when it was found possible to step up its range to 96,000 yards, the SCR-584 became a good medium-range warning radar as well. Such are the unpredictables that may arise in the research and development of military equipment.[50]

Equally unpredictable are the inclinations or disinclinations of men to employ the potentialities of such devices. The AAF generally tended to present an open mind to all possible uses. In general the AGF, swamped in

[49] 2d Ind, CG AAF to CG ASF, 31 Jul 44, on Ltr, Rives, Deputy Air ComO, to CSigO, 10 Jul 44, sub: Modification of Radio Set SCR-584 for Weather Use. SigC 413.44 SCR-584 No. 15 (RB-2367).

[50] Guerlac, Radar, pp. 710ff. (sec. C, ch. VIII, pp. 25ff.).

masses of men many of whom it was hard enough to train in the rudiments of warfare and simple equipment, was less perceptive. When radar specialists suggested in mid-1944 that the SCR–584 potentiality indicated possible uses by ground troops (to detect, for example, ground targets such as vehicular and tank traffic at night), certain ground force officers, headed by no less than General McNair, objected to such novel notions. These ideas, connoting more complex equipment, would complicate, they believed, the overwhelming training problem with which the Army was already confronted, the problem of how to teach the men to use with reasonable efficiency the equipment they already possessed.[51]

The SCR–584 Radar, VT Fuzes, and the Buzz Bomb

It was, of course, in its intended use as a gun layer that the SCR–584 stood unsurpassed, a fact abundantly attested from Anzio on. Its supremacy shone forth with high drama during June, July, and August 1944, during the defense against the invasion of England by pilotless buzz bombs. British intelligence had learned that such an attack would come. The situation seemed desperate. There had been a radar answer (CH) to the 1940 air raids by day; also a radar answer (GCI and AI) to subsequent air raids by night. But now the Germans were systematically and thoroughly flooding all the old British long-wave radars with jamming signals. For example, SLC radars were being so completely blinded that searchlight crews in England were falling back upon outmoded sound loca-

tors. Microwave gun layers, whose very short wave lengths and narrow beams of radiation rendered them much less susceptible to jamming, were now needed badly. Yet the British microwave GL radar program had not been pressed, in part because Professor Frederick L. Lindemann (Lord Cherwell), Churchill's own scientific adviser, had taken a dim view of radar antiaircraft fire control. Confronted early in 1944 with the threat of the flying bomb, the British commander of the Antiaircraft Command, General Sir Frederick A. Pile, turned to the American SCR–584. "It seemed to us," he wrote, "that the obvious answer to the robot target or the flying bomb (against which we were now being warned) was a robot defense, so I asked for an immediate supply of 134 of these amazing instruments. I wanted to get eventually at least 430 of them. . . ." He added:

As usual it was the Prime Minister who made this possible. I think it was at a Night Air Defense meeting at the end of February '44. . . . Fortunately for me Churchill was determined to hear what I had to say: "I want the General to tell us what equipment he wants," and so I did. The result was that the Prime Minister ordered the War Office to do everything they could to obtain the S.C.R. 584 and, indeed, everything that went with it.[52]

"Everything that went with it" involved first, RC–184, which was Mark

---

[51] See above, pp. 433–34.

[52] General Sir Frederick A. Pile, *Ack-Ack, Britain's Defense Against Air Attack During the Second World War* (London: Harrat, 1949) (hereafter cited as Pile, *Ack-Ack*), pp. 287, 313–14.

A Signal Corps record states that, in January 1944, the British first asked for 134 sets and by March increased the order to 310. OCSigO R&W Action 1, Dir of Plans & Opns Div, to Rqmts Plng Br, 9 Mar 44, sub: British Rqmts for SCR–584 and RC–184. SigC 413.44 SCR–584 No. 10 (RB–2295).

III IFF equipment, then maintenance and repair sets, and finally the complex electrical computer M–9. As General Pile had recommended, this was indeed a robot defense, all automatic (except that loading the guns was still done by hand) and superhumanly accurate, rendered still more so by the VT, or proximity fuzed, projectiles, which needed no human touch to set, but which exploded when the tiny radar (or doppler radio) built into the fuze sensed a target within a hundred feet. All this complex of American equipment was rushed to England along with artillerymen and technical experts from the Radiation Laboratory and the Signal Corps. One group, arriving on 10 February 1944, described its mission thus: "to prepare units as quickly as possible for using the SCR–584 radar, M–9 director, and 90-mm. guns for defense against a specific threat known as CROSSBOW, the projection of crewless, heavily loaded, jet-propelled planes from the coast of France towards the London and Bristol areas." When the group had completed its mission by 1 May, it had readied nearly 100 90-mm. batteries complete with the 584.[53]

The Allies were therefore prepared in June, when the V–1 robots first began coming from over the Channel bearing their deadly cargoes. The robot weapons, meeting a nearly automatic defense, uncannily accurate, exploded in the sky or crashed in open fields. Antiaircraft artillery guns, aided by the SCR–584, the M–9 computer, and the proximity-

fuzed shells, brought down most of the buzz bombs. On one day, for example, 68 were shot down by antiaircraft artillery; 14 by Royal Air Force pursuit planes; 16, which early warning radars detected, failed to reach the coast; 2 collided with barrage balloons, and only 4 buzz bombs out of a total of 104 the Germans had launched that day reached London.[54] All in all, the defeat of the buzz bomb was an extraordinary achievement of the new technological warfare. To the SCR–584 went the laurels. "Without this equipment," General Pile categorically asserted, "it would have been impossible to defeat the flying bomb." [55]

Successes and victories often hang on slender threads of effort and chance. In this instance they rested on the intertwining of certain research, production, and training efforts, combined with certain essential human relationships and confluence of events. General Pile recounts that he sent Maj. William M. Blair of his staff to Washington to ask for the 584's, hardly expecting he could get them. "Although, on his arrival, there was very little hope that his mission would prove successful, a 35-minute meeting with General Marshall, U.S. Army Chief of Staff, put a very different complexion on things," Pile wrote subsequently. "Largely due to the General's influence an immediate allocation of 165 S.C.R. 584's, together with all their ancillary equipment, was made, and they were

---

[53] Ltr, Capt William M. Blair to CG Frankford Arsenal, Philadelphia, 7 May 44, sub: Summ of Rpts No. 1 and 2 on Sp Mission to U.K. and Conclusions Reached. SigC 413.44 SCR–584 No. 12 (RB–2297).

The Signal Corps group contained three officers and one civilian, Hurach B. Abajian.

[54] (1) Baxter, *Scientists Against Time*, p. 235. (2) "The 584 Earns Its Keep," *Radar*, No. 5 (September 30, 1944), pp. 3–9; (3) "Postscript on Buzz Bombs," *Radar*, No. 6 (November 15, 1944), p. 35. (4) "One for V–1," *Radar*, No. 9 (April 30, 1945), p. 13. All in SigC Hist Sec file. (5) Guerlac, *Radar*, pp. 708f. (sec. C, ch. VIII, pp. 23f.).

[55] Pile, *Ack-Ack*, p. 314. See also Thiesmeyer and Burchard, *Combat Scientists*, pp. 252ff.

shipped to England on the very next boat." [56]

SCR-584 Modifications

By their very nature, research and development never stop. There is always room for improvement. So it was with the SCR-584. In mid-July 1944, a prominent British civilian physicist, J. D. Cockroft, wrote General Colton that he had been experiencing the buzz bomb attacks for several weeks. "We had to take some very active measures," he said, "to improve the shooting of light and heavy AA. The SCR-584 combined with the BTL Predictor is showing very great promise." But, he complained, when the 584 was employed against bombs flying especially low, it was "apt to lock onto ground clutter." When that happened, the oscilloscope operator would lose the reflection from the target in the mass of reflections from objects on the ground. On the margin of his note, Cockroft penned additionally, "Narrow strobes (N^2 gates) are therefore required." [57]

Gate was an antijamming device, devised by the Radiation Laboratory late in 1943 and sponsored by the Signal Corps. Named simply N^2, it had been developed as part of a program to render the set less susceptible to jamming. The N^2 had other advantages. For one thing, it greatly increased the minute accuracy of the radar. It reduced the length of the pulses to a fraction of a microsecond and it reduced the time between the pulses, when the receiver listens for the echo. The effect was that it eliminated many echoes, thus reducing ground clutter, and increased the capacity of the radar to discriminate between a target and other objects. For tracking the small low-flying buzz bomb, N^2 was an invaluable refinement. The Radiation Laboratory crash-built fifty N^2 kits for the European theater. The Army Ground Forces asked Signal Corps to equip all SCR-584's with N^2 Gate "at the earliest practicable date." [58]

---

[56] Pile, *Ack-Ack*, p. 339. General Pile wrote to General Marshall on 12 August, thanking him profusely both for the equipment and for "the great assistance Colonel [Arthur W.] Warner and these other officers have been to me." He even wished to thank the designers and factory workmen who turned out the radar and the VT fuze (so secret he could not name it, except by its British nickname, "Bonzo") with which "we have cut down the number of rounds per flying bomb destroyed to well under one hundred and the best batteries are actually getting one bomb for every forty rounds." Copy of Ltr, Pile to Marshall, 12 Aug 44, attached with Memo, Bowles for Ingles, 26 Aug 44. SigC (EO) Bowles, 1943-45. Dr. Bowles strongly supported General Pile in his quest for the 584's. Re Bowles's part in this matter, see Burchard, *Q.E.D., M.I.T. in World War II*, p. 68.

[57] Ltr, Cockroft, National Research Council, to Colton, 17 Jul 44, no sub. SigC 413.44 SCR-584 No. 15 (RB-2367).

[58] (1) Ltr, CG AGF to CG ASF, 28 Jul 44, sub: Rqmts for N^2 Gate-Radio Set SCR-584. SigC 413.-44 SCR-584 No. 15 (RB-2367). (2) "New Modifications Improve 584's Range, Tracking," *Radar*, No. 5 (September 30, 1944), p. 9. (3) "Countermeasures for the Mortar Menace," *Radar*, No. 11 (September 10, 1945), p. 4. Last two in SigC Hist Sec file. BBRL also made many modifications on the SCR-584. They did so, Colonel Warner, Air Defense Division SHAEF, wrote to Colonel Winter: ". . . in order to make it possible for the 9th A.F. to do close support work with fighters, photo planes and light bombers. The same mods [modifications] will also give a good G.C.I. . . . The N^2 gate is considered an absolute necessity for gunnery as well as close support and G.C.I. . . . The comfort and convenience of the present 584 will make any other design extremely hard to sell to people who know the 584. . . . The workmanship has aroused enthusiasm everywhere. The British are its most emphatic advocates and never cease marvelling at the amount of spares. . . . I had a chance to inspect a 584 that had been side-swiped and turned over on its side down an eight foot bank. The pins that hold the elevating screws down sheared in two cases and let the pedestal push out through the roof hatch, bending the parabola slightly. Everything else stayed in place." Ltr, Warner, Air Defense Div SHAEF, APO 757, to Winter, OCSigO, 14 Jun 44, no sub. SigC 431.-44 SCR-584 No. 13 (RB-2298).

The Signal Corps provided N² kits to modify existing SCR-584's under the designation MC-581. The kits were in demand everywhere. Hurach B. Abajian, a Radiation Laboratory engineer who had helped to develop the SCR-584 and who had been sent by the Army to solve 584 problems in the Pacific, wrote to Colonel Winter in midsummer 1944, "Since I put my only N² Gate on a unit at APO 709, I'd like nothing better than to put one to work in Northern New Guinea. Can you please have one sent to me in Brisbane?" He added as a postscript, "I'll take as many N² Gates as you can send." [59]

All these encomia and elaborations should not be taken to suggest that the progress of the SCR-584 in the U.S. Army was entirely free from trouble. There were the usual defects in the first factory productions: bad tubes, poor soldering, incorrect wiring. A number of complaints came from the Fifth Army in Italy, whither the first 584's had gone

early in 1944. Four sets put ashore at Hollandia in April 1944 soon broke down because of failure of the high-voltage modulator transformer T-214. Faulty workmanship in the factories received blame for breakdowns in electrical servomotors and in cable connectors. Errors in wiring explained units that could not possibly function and oscilloscope sweeps that rotated backwards. There was some complaint over the lack of spares. In general, however, the complaints were slight in proportion to the numbers and complexity of the sets, and spares were generally available—all of which contrasted favorably with the anguish of supply, maintenance, and spare parts bedeviling Signal Corps radar in 1942 and 1943. [60]

There was yet another problem—lack of trained SCR-584 operators. Too often field units did not know how to use the 584 when they got one. Major Richards, describing the 584 success at Anzio, was emphatic on one point. "operators and maintenance personnel must be thoroughly trained and know the equipment inside and out." [61] Yet competent operators were rarer than the proverbial hen's teeth, as is generally the case when new equipment reaches the field, unless

[59] Ltr, "Hank" [Abajian], APO 717, to Winter, 12 Aug 44. SigC 413.44 SCR-584 No. 15 (RB-2367).

Modification kits were items the Signal Corps supplied in considerable quantities and variety to vary and improve the performance of sets already in the field. The kits constituted a considerable R&D activity. Some of the kits for the SCR-584 were:

MC-607, an X-band kit, converting the wave length of the S-band (10 centimeter) to the X-band (3 centimeter).

MC-642, a moving target indicator kit, which enabled the 584 operators to discern moving aircraft through jamming interference and through echoes from the ground.

MC-546, a kit that converted the SCR-584 for CA fire control use, pending the production of the CD radar AN/MPG-1.

MC-544, a kit that provided remote indication —an oscilloscope employed at a distance from the radar site.

MC-577, a coupling modification kit.

RC-308, a plotting board for use with the 584 when employed as a mortar locator.

SigC R&D Hist, vol. IV, pt. 3, Proj 424, 12-15-1.

[60] (1) Msg W-5581/66785, NATO to CG USAF in ETO, 19 Mar 44. SigC 413.44 SCR-584 No. 10 (RB-2295). (2) Msg H-7298, CG USAF SOPAC, Nouméa, New Caledonia, to WD, 16 Apr 44. (3) Incl, Capt A. Haban, CAC Radar Off 45th AAA Brigade, Hq Fifth Army Firing Point, to CG Fifth Army AA Comd, 8 Apr 44, sub: Radar Conf, with Ltr, Colton to CSigO, 10 Apr 44. SigC 413.44 SCR-584 No. 12 (RB-2297). (4) Memo, Cornell, Asst AAO CAC for SigO Hq I Corps, 8 Jun 44. Sig Jnl, I Corps Staff, vol. I, 29 May–12 Jun 44, RED VAULT.

The manufacturers who produced the SCR-584's were Westinghouse, building SCR-584-B, and General Electric, building SCR-584-A.

[61] Incl, Ltr, Richards to M.G., AA&CD Sec AFHQ, 2 Apr 44.

special efforts have been made to repair the deficiency. For example, in the far Pacific SCR–584's had arrived as early as March 1944, but not everyone there knew how to employ them properly, at least not in General MacArthur's Southwest Pacific command. General Colton scurried to find someone whom he could send to advise and instruct. He wrote:

Radar Sets SCR–584 were received in the Southwest Pacific Area by 4 March 1944, but three secret radiograms received from that Headquarters and signed MacArthur indicate that they are not being used. The reason for this condition is because the operation of these sets is based upon radar techniques unknown in that theater and a man who is well trained on this set is needed. Mr. Abajian is such a man; however, he is not available, for he was sent to the European Theater of Operations in order to introduce the set there.[62]

When instruction books arrived in advance and when competent SCR–268 operators were able to study the 584, they could easily switch over to the new microwave radars, and they did so with zest, as did the radarmen of the 3d Marine Defense Battalion in the South Pacific Area.[63] But Army radar manuals, classified "secret," frequently never reached the troops precisely because the books were stamped "secret." Consequently, operators of the older long-wave radars often remained uninformed, if not apathetic.

So it appeared to Mr. Abajian when he was dispatched by the Signal Corps to the Pacific in July (after completing his ETO mission, setting up 584's for Cross-bow). By mid-1944 several scores of

SCR–584's had gone out to the South and Southwest Pacific. Of the units he visited Abajian found that "without exception every gun battalion is employing the SCR–584 almost exactly as it used the SCR–268. . . . This inexcusable failure to use the SCR–584 and M–9 combination to the fullest of their capabilities," Abajian wrote, "can be traced to the lack of instruction and information, to battalion and battery commanders, on the tactical use of the radar and on its characteristics." He said further:

Every battalion visited so far had been overseas long before the SCR–584 was delivered to them. None of the commanding officers had ever seen it perform against an aircraft. All practice firing had been executed with cloth sleeves, the signal from which is so poor that automatic tracking is almost impossible. Witnessing such performance served only to create doubt among the officers. The situation can be summed up with a direct quotation of one battery commander: "Hell, I've never seen shooting with it. You send me a new piece of equipment I never even heard of until shortly before I got it. I'm not going to accept anyone's word for it until I see it work.

Thus, for want of instruction, millions of dollars' worth of superlative new radar lay unused in an active theater of war. Abajian had a missionary job to do—demonstrate, teach, and spread the gospel to the doubting Thomases. He checked over the sets and asked each battalion to send an officer and two men to attend a course on the 584. He often got people who were not radarmen at all, these being needed to keep the 268's in operation. One battalion sent its S–2 officer. During his work with the 66th AAA Brigade, Abajian spent a week with each gun battalion, adusting their radars and instructing the operators. The commanding

[62] Ltr, Colton, Chief E&T, to Regional Labor Of, New York, c/o ANEPA, 28 Mar 44, sub: Draft Bd Release for Albert D. Paul. SigC 413.44 SCR–584 No. 10 (RB–2295).

[63] Miller, Draft MS Comment, Aug 59.

general of that unit, Brig. Gen. Charles A. French, was appreciative, saying that Abajian's work "has been of immense value to this brigade." [64]

Airborne Microwave Radars

Microwave radars had been mothered by the necessity for smaller sets to be used in aircraft. By the mid-point of the war airborne applications were multiplying amazingly. The Signal Corps was "more or less in charge," as certain officers aptly summarized its role.[65] The Radiation Laboratory and its civilian scientists under the OSRD carried the burden of research and development. The Signal Corps, through its Aircraft Radio Laboratory, helped adapt the initial laboratory creation to a militarily useful form. Then the Signal Corps shouldered its heaviest task, getting the manufacture of the equipment under way and procuring the sets. By that time, in mid-1943, airborne microwave techniques, microwave circuitry, tubes, and testing equipment were well established, after the success of the

first microwave AI's, such as SCR–520 and 720, against enemy night aircraft and after the victory of the microwave ASV's, SCR–517 and 717, and Navy's ASG (airborne search radar) over German submarines.[66]

As the Germans increasingly jammed Allied radar, microwave airborne sets acquired further value. In August 1943 the Royal Air Force, for example, asked for SCR–720's; Air Chief Marshal Sir Charles Portal explained that their microwave length rendered them far less vulnerable to Window countermeasures, which were reducing British long-wave AI–IV to uselessness. Fortunately, the production rate of the 720 enabled General Arnold to grant the request. Signal Corps procurement of the microwave ASV SCR–717, however, had encountered difficulties. The manufacturer, Western Electric, could not meet schedules and the Signal Corps had to turn to the Navy, ordering 2,450 ASG's.[67]

Along with the ASV microwave sets, the laboratories developed a bombing aid (it had been initiated in the Signal Corps in August 1942, for use with the SCR–517) that permitted accurate bombing from low altitudes. Known popularly as LAB (low altitude bombing), technically as AN/APQ–5, it helped to sink many ships in the Pacific. LAB had been developed as a stopgap technique until good BTO radars could

---

[64] (1) 1st Ind, French, CO 68th AAA Brigade, to CG 14th AA Comd, APO 501 (Through CG XIV Corps, APO 453), 22 Jul 44, on Ltr, Abajian, RL MIT (Army Tech Observer), to CG AAA Comd, Richmond, Va. (Through CG AAA Brigade, APO 706), 20 Jul 44, sub: The Use of the SCR–584 in the South and Southwest Pacific Theaters. SigC 413.44 SCR–584 No. 14 (RB–2366). (2) See also Guerlac, Radar, pp. 1414ff. (sec. E, ch. VIII, pp. 36ff.).

Abajian worked at a disadvantage because he was a civilian. Officer rank would have carried more weight and was necessary whenever tactical demonstrations might have been made. "The present situation," Abajian wrote back to Signal Corps headquarters, "still calls for a group of fire control teams, similar to the one sent to England . . . to give instructions in and demonstrations of the tactical use of the SCR–584 and M–9 combination." By 1945 the Signal Corps would send out just such groups, organized as NEID's.

[65] See above, p. 311.

[66] "War Against the U-boat," Radar, No. 5 (September 30, 1944), pp. 22–29. SigC Hist Sec file. See Thompson, Harris, et al., The Test, pp. 242–56.

[67] (1) Ltr, Portal to Arnold, 23 Aug 43, sub: SCR–720, and Ltr, Arnold to Portal, 28 Aug 43, same sub. AAG 413.44–R Radar. (2) OCSigO R&W Action, 2d Lt F. B. Gunter, Electronics Br SPSRD–3, to SPSCH–4, Attn: Maj Kamerson, 10 Mar 43, sub: Rpt on Budget Estimates. SigC 413.44 Airborne Radar Equip folder 1, Jan 42–Mar 43 (RB–1908).

be perfected. Rather than sending out the equipment with any expectation that uninitiated commanders in the theaters could readily put it into effective use, Dr. Bowles and the AAF set up a squadron of planes and pilots complete with radar operators and maintenance men, trained them as a unit in the States, and then sent the outfit to the Pacific to operate under the local combat commander, who welcomed them and was soon convinced of the value of their special skills. This was the way, Bowles believed, to introduce effectively specialized techniques and to win acceptance for them by the theater commander.[68]

Other notable 10-centimeter S-band radar aids included the ARO's (air range only), which were airborne range finders. The Signal Corps and Western Electric, beginning as early as November 1940, had worked on such a set, the SCR–523, but the models were too heavy. Next, the Radiation Laboratory at MIT, making use of a new microwave oscillator tube by General Electric—the lighthouse tube —developed an acceptable ARO. First named the SCR–726, then the AN/ APG–5, it came into production by the Galvin Corporation in 1944.[69] Another ARO was Falcon, or AN/APG–13, employed with 75-mm. cannon, which were specially mounted in B–25's for firing on Japanese shipping in Chinese waters.[70]

ARO quickly led to AGL (airborne gun layers), which would lock on a target and direct the turret guns of a bomber, doing in the air what an SCR–584 did on the ground. The Aircraft Radio Laboratory worked upon a variety of AGL's: SCR–580 and 702, becoming AN/APG– 1 and 2, which were 10-centimeter S-band sets; and AN/APG–3, a 3-centimeter or X-band radar.[71] Used only at the very end of the war in B–29's these radar gun sights were forerunners of sets that would prove effective against jet fighters of the Korean War. AN/APG –15 grew out of SCR–580, dating back to 1941 in ARL efforts, for use in experimental B–32's.[72]

Among the many radar projects at the Aircraft Radio Laboratory and at the Radiation Laboratory, none received higher priority or more lavish attention than radar for bombing through overcast,

[68] (1) Memo, Bowles for SW, 23 Aug 43, sub: Résumé of Consultant Activity, p. 8 (Radar Bombing), Bowles Papers, Tab J, p. 8. (2) Interv, SigC Hist Sec with Bowles, 8 May 58. (3) SigC R&D Hist, vol. II, pt. 5, Proj 209–B, partial. (4) "Low Altitude High Precision," *Radar* (unnumbered) (April, 1944), pp. 17–22. (5) "LAB vs. Jap Shipping," *Radar*, No. 6 (November 15, 1944), pp. 3–9. (6) "14th AF LAB Equipped B–24 Sinks 17,500-Ton Liner," *Radar*, No. 7 (January 1, 1945), p. 34. Last three in SigC Hist Sec file. (7) Guerlac, Radar, pp. 523ff. (sec. C, pt. V, pp. 4ff.) and pp. 1385ff. (sec. E, pt. VIII, pp. 6ff.).

Whereas in the Atlantic the Air Forces surrendered to the Navy all control over land-based bombers employed against enemy shipping, in the far Pacific AAF bombers continued to combat Japanese surface vessels, claiming hundreds of thousands of tons of enemy shipping.

[69] (1) SigC R&D Hist, vol. II, pt. 3, Proj 204–A. (2) Interv, SigC Hist Sec with Capt I. Paganelli, ARL, 17 Oct 44. SigC Hist Sec file.

[70] (1) SigC R&D Hist, vol. II, pt. 3, Proj 204–D. (2) "Falcon for Fire Control," *Radar*, No. 7 (January 1, 1945), pp. 14–18. (3) Guerlac, Radar, pp. 442ff. (sec. C, ch. II, pp. 18ff.).

[71] SigC R&D Hist, vol. II, pt. 3, Projs 205–F and 205–G.

[72] (1) *Ibid.*, Proj 205–K. (2) "Aid to the Turret Gunner," *Radar*, No. 8 (February 20, 1945), pp. 42–43. SigC Hist Sec file.

The AN/APG–15 had enjoyed highest priority at the Aircraft Radio Laboratory from April 1944 on. Interv, SigC Hist Sec with Col George E. Metcalf, ARL, 2 Oct 44, p. 4. SigC Hist Sec file.

AGL was not used in ETO, but was ready for use at the end of the Pacific fighting. CSigO, Annual Rpt, FY 45, p. 408.

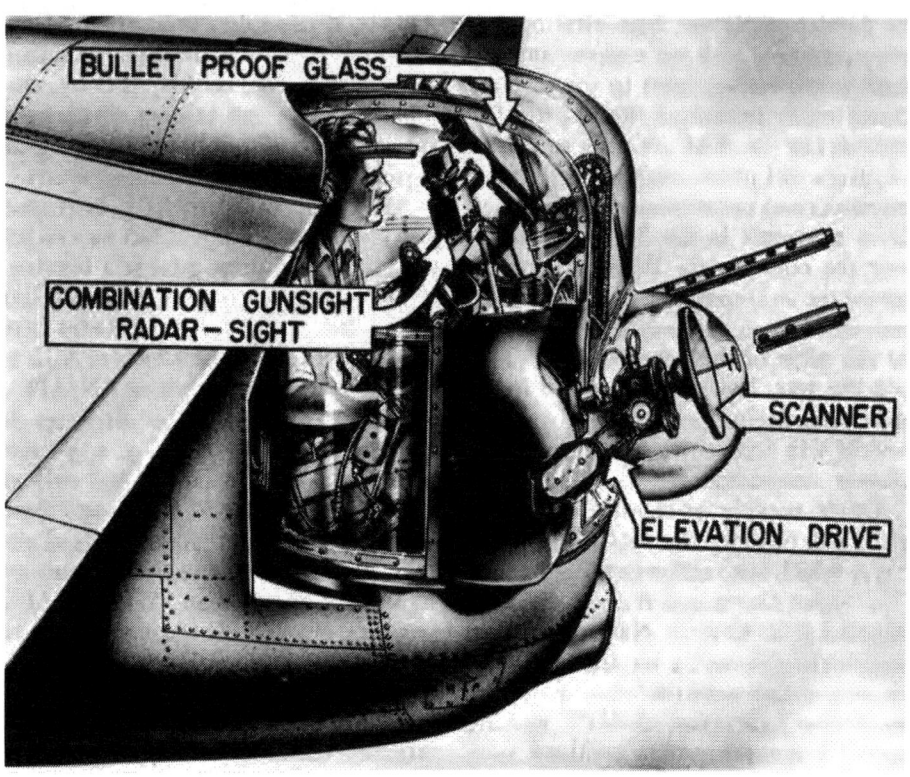

DRAWING OF AN AN/AGL TYPE RADAR *installed in the tail gun turret of a large bomber.*

that elusive objective the Air Forces had been pursuing since the late 1930's. Precision navigational systems had pointed to one solution, but a limited one. ASV radar had indicated a better method. Already ASV had proved so effective against sea targets that it had tipped the scales in submarine warfare. But the first ASV sets had not been quite good enough to "see" land targets well. Bombing German land targets was now the number one problem, especially in the German interior beyond the limited reach of Oboe, Gee, and Shoran navigational systems of blind bombing (the first two were British; Shoran was an ARL development,

originally SCR–297). These systems proved helpful in air attacks through 1943.[73]

For example, Oboe had enabled the first large-scale (1,000 planes) blind bombing of an area target, Cologne. Oboe was more than just helpful; it was absolutely necessary since clouds cover much of Europe much of the time, especially in winter. But the range of the

[73] (1) SigC R&D Hist, vol. II, pt. 4, Proj 208–A. (2) "Shoran: 5 Year Old Newcomer," *Radar*, No. 8 (February 20, 1945), pp. 16–23. (3) Guerlac, Radar, pp. 109ff. (sec. E, ch. IV, 1ff.).
Shoran was first employed effectively by the Mediterranean Tactical Air Force. CSigO, Annual Rpt, FY 45, p. 268.

system ran to only about 200 or 250 miles, far short of Berlin and industrial centers in east and south Germany. What was wanted was a radar that could "see" the ground well enough to drop bombs accurately anywhere, anytime. The demand grew. When, in December 1943, General Colton ordered stoppage of much research and instructed the laboratories to shift their engineers to preparations that would promote the invasion effort, he specifically exempted the BTO program at the Aircraft Radio Laboratory.[74]

He had to exempt it. Throughout the last half of 1943, the Air Forces had pressed hard for an American 3-centimeter, or X-band, BTO. The AAF wanted this set, called H$_2$X or Mickey, as an improvement on the British 10-centimeter, S-band, blind bombing aid that was sometimes called H$_2$S, sometimes Home Sweet Home, or even Stinky (since H$_2$S is the symbol for hydrogen sulphide, or rotten-egg gas, known to every high school chemistry student). Upon the Signal Corps rested the urgent demand for Mickey, AN/APQ–13. In August 1943, General Arnold had requested that thirty sets be delivered before the end of the year.[75] He did not

get them until January 1944, when the Signal Corps extracted mass production of an H$_2$X from Philco. Even the Philco product was not the desired AN/APQ–13 but a less acceptable variant, the AN/APS–15. Already in the late summer and autumn of 1943 the Radiation Laboratory had put together from components of the Navy ASG a number of APS–15's. These sets the civilian laboratory had mounted in B–17's of the 612th Bombardment Squadron of the 482d Heavy Bomber Group.[76]

The B–17's, so equipped, served as pathfinders, flying ahead of the main bomber force. Their radar operators, viewing the ground dimly in their oscilloscopes through any amount of cloud and overcast, located their targets and dropped smoke markers, over which the rest of the bomber fleet jettisoned their deadly cargoes, accurately enough for area bombing. Beginning in November, with Wilhelmshaven and Bremen as the victims, the Eighth Air Force bombers attacked again and again, "guided entirely by AN/APS–15 'X' band radar sets installed in leader aircraft." [77] They hit their targets with considerable accuracy, sufficient to bring inescapable destruction, despite cloud and night, upon German cities and large industries. German leaders and scientists knew it when they reconstructed a British H$_2$S radar in August 1943. With horror they recognized that the Allies had mastered microwave techniques they had thought impractical. With microwave radars the Allies had defeated the U-boats, the Nazis now realized, and they would next

[74] See above, p. 430.

[75] Ltr, CG AAF to CSigO, 23 Aug 43, sub: Urgent Rqmt for Radar Set AN/APQ–13. AAG 413.44–Q Radar.

The Air Forces gave the Signal Corps permission to divert components from the less critically needed ASV SCR–717 into production of the new BTO. Guerlac, Radar, pp. 530ff. (sec. C, ch. V, pp. 11ff.). See also pp. 1122ff. (sec. E, ch. IV, pp. 29ff.).

The R&D history describes APQ–13 as "one of the AAF's most valuable offensive weapons," adding that it was "a curious mixture of techniques, designs, and parts adapted from other developments." The Aircraft Radio Laboratory did a great deal of work on both H$_2$X versions, the APS–15 and APQ–13. SigC R&D Hist, vol. II, pt. 1, Proj 202–B.

[76] Ltr, CG AAF to CG Proving Ground Comd, Eglin Fld, Fla., 24 Aug 43, sub: Bombing Accuracy Tests of AN/APS–15 Radar. AAG 413.44–Q Radar.

[77] CSigO, Annual Rpt, FY 44, pp. 190, 304.

pound the fatherland itself—every target in it worth a fleet of bombers. And what the British 10-centimeter H_2S could do, the American 3-centimeter H_2X sets could do better, the first of which the Germans recognized and recovered from an American bomber shot down early in 1944 in Holland.[78] Lt. Gen. Carl Spaatz vigorously sought more and more Pathfinders—"the most critical need of the Strategic Air Forces," he wrote General Arnold in January 1944, "is for more Pathfinder aircraft. *A few H_2X airplanes now will profit our cause more than six hundred in six months.*" He continued:

"Results of the past two months' extensive use of Pathfinder (H_2X) aircraft in the Eighth Air Force has shown that the equipment offers enormous possibilities for further intensification of the bombing offensive against Germany. Because of the prevalent cloud cover over the targets, it has not been possible to photograph the damage from each mission. While complete assessment of the accuracy of H_2X bombing is therefore impossible, we do know that large concentrations of bombs hit precisely in the aiming point at Kiel, Wilhelmshaven and Bremen—the only targets where photographic interpretation was possible after a large H_2X operation. These strikes indicate that the potential accuracy of H_2X bombing justified the highest priority in providing this equipment on the scale recommended herein. The original twelve B-17's with experimental H_2X sets built

by hand in the Radiation Laboratory have led seventeen out of the twenty missions by the Eighth Air Force in the last two months. Cloud has prevented visual operations nine-tenths of the time.[79]

By the time production in the thousands got under way, however, the need for both the standard H_2X, AN/APQ–13 (built by Western Electric), and the stopgap Philco AN/APS–15 was lessening in the ETO. All through 1944 the bombers devastated their targets, railroad yards, dock areas, concentrations of factories, but "area bombing," a Signal Corps report in 1945 read, "was becoming less remunerative as large areas were destroyed and only isolated targets remained." Area targets did remain in Japan, and the AN/APQ–13 mounted in B–29 bombers proved their worth there during the last months of the war.[80]

Already the nemesis of the small isolated target was at hand—a remarkable 3-centimeter BTO called the Eagle (AN/APQ–7), which an Air Forces officer remarked in April 1944 was "the first blind bombing equipment which shows promise of meeting the M/C's." Even so, the Signal Corps had had occasion to complain that the lack of a suitable airplane to try out the new model was delaying the Eagle program (an old, familiar complaint at the Aircraft Radio Laboratory). The Air Forces had indeed assigned a B–24 for

[78] (1) Cajus Bekker (pen name of Hans D. Berenbrok), *Radar–Duell in Dunkel* (Hamburg: Oldenburg, 1958), pp. 251–80. (2) Curt Bley, *Geheimnis Radar: Eine Geschichte der Wissenschaftlichen Kriegfuerhrung* (Hamburg, Germany: Rowahlt, 1949) (hereafter cited as Bley, *Geheimnis Radar*), pp. 17ff. (3) Adolph Galland, *The First and Last, The Rise and Fall of the German Fighter Forces, 1938–45*, Translated by Mervyn Savill (New York: Henry Holt & Co., 1954), pp. 202ff. (4) Sir Robert A. Watson-Watt, *Three Steps to Victory* (London, 1957), pp. 451ff. (5) Churchill, *Closing the Ring*, p. 521.

[79] Ltr, Spaatz, Comdg USSAF in Europe, to CG AAF, 14 Jan 44, sub: H_2X Pathfinders for the Strategic AF. AAG 413.44–AC Radar. Italics original.

[80] (1) CSigO, Annual Rpt, FY 45, p. 32. (2) "More Hits, More Runs, Less Errors," *Radar*, No. 10 (June 30, 1945), p. 17. SigC Hist Sec file. (3) See also Guerlac, Radar, pp. 1446ff. (sec. E, ch. VIII, pp. 68ff.).

this purpose, but it had to be overhauled before it could fly. Moreover, the Air Forces had delayed contracting for a number of strictly Air Forces items that the Eagle's antenna would require—a special wing with struts and deicers. General Arnold summarily removed these difficulties when he ordered the Air Service Command to meet all Signal Corp requests touching Eagle, since "the program has the highest priority." [81]

Beginning with a flight test of the laboratory equipment as early as September 1943 over the Connecticut River valley, Eagle marked the peak of the long BTO effort. The set was remarkable in many ways—for instance, in its antenna. Eagle carried aloft the long narrow array (the Alvarez leaky wave guide, developed by the Radiation Laboratory) that had made the MEW a revolution among the revolutions that all military radars were. Entirely unlike the parabaloid bowl antenna that had characterized previous microwave airborne radars, this linear array of several hundred tiny dipoles totaling about sixteen feet in length had to be mounted in the leading edge of a wing, a special wing fastened beneath the bomber fuselage. And instead of yielding a round 360-degree PPI (planned position indicator) oscilloscope presentation, Eagle spread upon its scope a fanlike view of the radar scene below. There was no troublesome "eye" at the center, as in a round PPI picture. The resolu-

tion was better than anything attained hitherto—that is, the picture was clearer and showed more detail. Even in the first test over the Connecticut River the set had showed all the towns, rivers, and streams, the bridges over the rivers, and also the hills and their shapes, which could be determined by the radar shadows they cast. Eagle got into the war just in time to enable a few devastatingly destructive strikes against Japan.[82]

There were still other airborne radars—for example, tail warning (TW) sets. Developed by the Aircraft Radio Laboratory as AN/APS–13 for fighters and as AN/APS–16 for bombers, these radars were small, designed to scan a mile or so of space behind an airplane. Upon detecting any object in the area (most likely an enemy fighter closing in for a kill), the set automatically flashed a warning light in the cockpit.[83]

In addition a whole family of navigational radars or beacons sprang up, beginning with an airborne IFF interrogator-responsor, the SCR–729. IFF had originally been necessary for ground radar operators to challenge an

[81] (1) Ltr, CSigO to CG AAF, 23 Mar 44, sub: Radio Set AN/APQ–7 (Eagle). AAG 413.44–DU Radio. (2) Ltr, CSigO to Air ComO, 4 Apr 44, sub: Test Equip for AN/APQ–7, with 1st Ind, Lt Col George Hale (by Comd of Gen Arnold), Com EquipO, to Hq ASC, Patterson Fld, Ohio, 15 Apr 44. AAG 413.44–EL Radio. (3) Guerlac, Radar, pp. 538ff. (sec. C, ch. V, pp. 19ff.).

[82] (1) Memo, Maj Richardson for Brig Gen B. W. Chidley, AAF Hq, 24 Sep 43, sub: Flight Trial of "Eagle" Radar Bombing Device. AAG 413.44–S Radar. (2) "The Eagle Story: How It All Began," Radar, No. 10 (June 30, 1945), pp. 28–33, and No. 11 (September 10, 1945), pp. 36ff. (3) Guerlac, Radar, pp. 1458ff. (sec. E, ch. VIII, pp. 8off.).

[83] (1) SigC R&D Hist, vol. II, pt. 3, Projs 205–I and J. (2) Interv, SigC Hist Sec with Maj E. A. Massa, ARL, 9 Oct 44, pp. 5–7. SigC Hist Sec file.
TW radars were essentially altimeters, projecting their rays to the rear rather than downward. By October 1943, the AAF had placed urgent orders upon the Signal Corps for a total of 42,139 sets of the fighter plane TW type alone. Ltr, CG AAF to CG ASF, 28 Oct 43, sub: Radar Set AN/APS–13. AAG 413.44–U Radar.

aircraft and receive an identifying response. When aircraft themselves began carrying such radars as the ASV (SCR–521), it became necessary for the radar operators aloft to challenge ships or ground targets below and receive an identifying signal in reply, else the pilots assumed them hostile and attacked. The Aircraft Radio Laboratory, the Radiation Laboratory, and Philco developed and produced the SCR–729, an airborne interrogator-responsor, in 1943. It could challenge and receive responses from Mark III IFF sets in other airplanes, on ships, and at land installations. It acquired also another very valuable use: it could, for purposes of navigation, challenge, identify, and locate in azimuth and range special ground radar beacons. One such ground beacon was developed as AN/CPN–7, or BABS (blind approach beacon system). Another was a beacon developed for rescue at sea, the AN/CPT–2; it emitted signals that an aircraft equipped with an SCR–729 could pick up and on which it could home. The two beacons were developed by the Aircraft Radio Laboratory in 1943 and 1944, respectively, following British precedents.[84]

A group of navigational radars that became vitally important in parachute operations was the Rebecca-Eureka combination, British named for British prototypes. The Eureka was a portable ground beacon, which a soldier set up at a point where paratroopers were to land. Rebecca sets, aboard troop carrier aircraft, interrogated the ground set, whose responses enabled the pilots to fly directly over the drop area. The Aircraft Radio Laboratory developed Rebecca, AN/APN–2, which was similar to the SCR–729 but which operated on somewhat higher frequencies. As for the Eureka type, the Aircraft Radio Laboratory converted the Mark III IFF radar SCR–695 into AN/PPN–1 and 3. Subsequent Eureka development, however, AN/PPN–1 and 2, was transferred to the Camp Evans Signal Laboratory in New Jersey, since Eureka operated on the ground and so was a ground radar.[85] The Air Forces in mid-1943 requested that the Signal Corps procure 1,366 sets of AN/PPN–1 in 1943 and a like number of PPN–2's in 1944. Though the goal was not reached, nearly a thousand sets were delivered before mid-1944, just in time for D-day operations in Normandy.[86]

According to Colonel Metcalf, chief of the Electronics Division of the Office of the Chief Signal Officer, who was in

---

[84] (1) SigC R&D Hist, vol. II, pt. 2, Projs 203–D, E, and I. (2) Interv, SigC Hist Sec with L. B. Hallman, ARL, 3 Oct 44, pp. 8–9. SigC Hist Sec file.

These sets all employed long waves at about 200 megacycles. Microwave S- and X-band beacons were developed in 1944 and 1945: BUPS (AN/UPN–1 and 2) and BUPX (AN/UPN–3 and 4), whose signals could be received on microwave airborne radars.

[85] This is a fine example of the arbitrary splitting of sets of equipment that operationally formed a unit. The Rebeccas were retained at the Aircraft Radio Laboratory in Ohio because they were airborne radars; the Eurekas moved to the Signal Corps Engineering Laboratory in New Jersey because they functioned on the ground and because the Signal Corps Engineering Laboratory, under the Signal Corps Ground Signal Agency, had to control the development of ground equipment.

[86] (1) Interv, SigC Hist Sec with Hallman, 3 Oct 44. (2) SigC R&D Hist, vol. II, pt. 2, Projs 203–D, pp. 3 and 24–25; and vol. IV, pt. 5, Proj 463–A. (3) Ltr, CG AAF to CSigO, 4 Sep 43, sub: Rebecca-Eureka Equip. AAG 413.44–BI Radio. (4) CSigO, Annual Rpt, FY 44, p. 318. (5) "Rebecca and Eureka Do Their Jobs," *Radar*, No. 3 (June 30, 1944), pp. 26–29. SigC Hist Sec file. (6) See also above, p. 96, and Guerlac, Radar, pp. 122ff. (sec. E, ch. V, pp. 39ff.).

EUREKA GROUND BEACON GUIDING PLANES HOME

ETO at the time of the invasion, these beacons accomplished "the most outstanding use of airborne electronic devices in combat operations." He was speaking of the drop of 20,000 paratroopers by the IX Troop Carrier Command on 6 June 1944. Colonel Metcalf reported most favorably also on the BTO radar, AN/APS–15, of airborne gun layers, and of other aircraft radars that the British and Americans had crash-built. He had high words of praise for the hundred or so scientific and technical experts of BBRL. To these men and their counterparts in the Telecommunications Research Establishment—Britain's equivalent of RL—he attributed the radar successes. "It was the uniform opinion," he reported," of all Air Force and Signal Corps officers consulted that the successful operation of this equipment would have been impossible without this group of civilian specialists." [87]

---

[87] Memo, Metcalf, Dir ARL., 3 Jul 44, sub: Visit to ETO. SCIA file, unnumbered, European Theater, 1–a.

According to Colonel Metcalf in letter cited above, Brig. Gen. Paul L. Williams, commander of the Troop Carrier Command, asked that the highest commendation be given to officers and civilians of the Technical Liaison Section, Office of the Chief Signal Officer, ETO. One of these officers in particular, Maj. Lloyd H. Deary, was so helpful that General Williams sought his services for the AAF for the rest of the war.

THROAT MIKE WORN BY A TANK CREWMAN, LEFT, AND LIP MIKE, RIGHT. *Both could be used with radio or telephone.*

Radios

During the first years of the war Signal Corps had, of course, been under heavy pressure to develop and supply ground and vehicular radios for the Armored Force and for the Infantry.[88] By mid-1943 Army Ground Forces needs in this category were well in hand, thanks to full production of radios such as the "handie-talkie" SCR-536, the walkie-talkie SCR-300, the FM sets of the 500 and 600 series, and the SCR-299. Early in 1944 Colonel Williams, signal officer of the First Army in Europe, wrote enthusiastically to Gen-

eral Colton, saying "Armored Force sets SCR-508, 528, 538, and SCR-509 and 510 have become the backbone of communication within the armored division." The same was true of the 600 series (SCR-608, 628, 609, and 610) in artillery communications whenever wire was not used and to supplement it when wire lines were laid. The 600 series, Williams also noted, had come into universal use by naval fire-control parties, naval beach communicators, amphibious engineers, and assault infantry during amphibious landings. These were short-range radios whose special virtue Williams ascribed to "the inherent advantages of FM in overcoming static and ignition interference and in giving a clear voice signal of suffi-

---

[88] Thompson, Harris, *et al., The Test*, pp. 229ff.

SCR–193 RECEIVING AND TRANSMITTING RADIO, MOUNTED IN A JEEP

cient quality and volume to be heard over the noise of tank operation." [89]

The long-range SCR–299 and 399 had proved so dependable that they had become the standard for distant communications among the Allied nations. The medium-range vehicular SCR–193, long described as the work horse among infantry radios, Colonel Williams called the Springfield rifle of the Signal Corps radios, outmoded but reliable. He expected that the new SCR–506 would prove a superior set, but using troops, when they got the 506, concluded otherwise. "The comments we have received from units equipped with the SCR–506," General Ingles wrote in April 1944, "indicate that it is not nearly as well liked as the SCR–193 it is replacing." [90]

Combat troops, who had the best reasons to know, were exceedingly grateful for the advantages short-range Signal Corps radios of the FM types gave them. "One of the main reasons the American Army moved so fast against the Germans was that it had over-all information supplied by fast communications. In combat teams, that meant radio, and that radio meant FM." These were the words of an infantry battalion radio operator, Technician Zens. He explained:

---

[89] Ltr, Col Williams, SigO First U.S. Army, to Gen Colton, 18 Mar 44. SCIA file 74 Colton Rpts 1–b.

[90] (1) *Ibid.* (2) Ltr, CSigO to Gen King, CBI, 17 Apr 44, no sub. SigC OT 370.2 Rpts CBI, Tab 22.

One night, up in the Siegfried Line, when we needed more equipment than we had [FM radios], we got out an AM set. The loudspeaker crackled and roared with static. Twenty different stations came in at once with a noise like a platoon of tanks. I think we heard everybody in Europe on that AM receiver. I mean at the same time . . . English, French, Russian, German, . . . At least, we heard everybody except the station we were trying to reach.

The FM radios gave clear static-free communications. Zens illustrated with several detailed and graphic descriptions of close combat in which the FM sets in the hands of infantry company and battalion communicators and in tanks and artillery units brought the Americans success. "FM saved lives and won battles," he concluded, "because it speeded our communications and enabled us to move more quickly than the Germans, who had to depend on AM." [91]

Ground Radio Types for the AAF

All ground radio needs had not been so happily met, and at the turn of 1943–44 the loudest demands for ground sets came from the Army Air Forces. They even wanted, surprisingly since they had once resisted them, FM radio sets.[92] They had discovered that their requirements in ground equipment were growing— both for AM and for FM types in both the HF and the VHF ranges. They needed them in AWS nets and in fighter control (GCI) systems. They needed VHF sets for point-to-point use

in their tactical air forces. Available frequencies in the already congested high frequency bands were next to nil, forcing the airmen to use VHF, although VHF immediately hit a range ceiling, the short distance of travel within line-of-sight. The Air Forces pressed the Signal Corps for any and every suitable radio: Collins transmitters, Hallicrafter receivers, Motorola (Galvin) sets (FMTR–30 DW and 50 BW), FM sets built by Fred Link (types 1498 and 1505), marine service radio sets, forestry sets, and a set called the Jefferson-Travis, JT–350.[93]

All this was extracurricular equipment so to speak, over and above the old SCR–188 and 197 the Signal Corps had standardized for the Air Forces long before; over and above, also, the numerous VHF transmitters and receivers that comprised the SCS–2 and 3 VHF fighter control systems. In September 1943 General McClelland, air communications officer, informed the Signal Corps that he had an immediate requirement for a set such as the Link-type 1498, complaining that the SCR–624 (a recently developed VHF set for ground use) was not powerful enough, could not handle several channels simultaneously, and could not be transported by air. Colonel Rives, General McClel-

---

[91] Zens, "A GI's Report on Lower-Band FM— A Veteran Radio Operator's Experience With FM Under Battle Conditions," FM and Television, VI, No. 1, pp. 21, 74–75.

[92] Terrett, The Emergency, p. 184.

[93] (1) 1st Ind, CG AAF to CO AAF Ground Radio, AAF Com Fld Of SCGSA, Bradley Beach, N.J., 26 Jan 44, on Ltr, Lt Col M. L. Haselton, AC Proj LnO, to Air ComO Hq AAF, 14 Jan 44, sub: Commercial FM Transmitters-Receivers Standardization. AAG 413.44-CT Radio. (2) Ltr, CG AAF to CG Eleventh Air Force, 18 Jan 44, sub: Radio Equip for Ground Observer Posts. AAG 413.44-CZ Radio. (3) Ltr, Subcmte on Classification to SigC Tech Cmte, 3 Jan 44, sub: Classification of Radio Transmitter-Receiver Forest Service Type SPF as Limited Standard (Item 652, SCTC Mtg No. 296, 3 Jan 44). AAG 413.44-CT Radio. (4) Thompson, Harris, et al., The Test, pp. 234f.

land's deputy, informed General Ingles in December 1944 that the AAF was using the Link 1498 set as a stopgap and hoped to use the AN/TRC-1 similarly as soon as the AAF could get it. The AAF was also already using the Link-type 1505.[94]

In a desperate effort to get suitable ground sets (one officer characterized the ground radio situation in late 1943 as "extremely acute"),[95] the Air Forces seemed to have looked into available commercial radios quite on its own and in so doing it left the proper radio supplier for all the Army, the Signal Corps, in a considerable quandary. For example, one such commercial radio that the Air Forces sought on the Army Supply Program, 1 August 1943, was the Jefferson-Travis transmitter receiver. AAF wanted 500 sets in 1943, 600 in 1944. General Colton, head of the Engineering and Technical Service of the Signal Corps, asked if the Air Forces wanted this set as an "adopted type." AAF answered that it was wanted

as "limited procurement type," and explained:

Subject set was originally procured to fill an immediate requirement of a compact 50-75 watt HF radio set for mobile mounting in trucks to be used for radar reporting nets and for links in VHF systems where FM communication was not feasible. In this use it was intended to supplement SCR-188 Radio Set whose availability for this service was limited. Military characteristics closely approach those for SCR-188 with the exception that JT-350-A is designed to operate from 12, 24, 32, and 110V AC and for this reason is expected to be more flexible in operation.[96]

The Air Forces had evidently acted independently, somewhat disregarding the Army's established procedure. The Signal Corps had not been informed of just what the Air Forces wanted in the way of ground radio, nor in fact does it appear that the airmen themselves yet knew. The Signal Corps could not, General Colton made it clear, readily develop or provide what the Air Forces seemed to want until the airmen made up their minds as to just what they did in fact desire. "In order that the Signal Corps may adequately comprehend the communications requirement of the Army Air Forces, and develop equipment suitable for meeting requirements," General Colton wrote in August 1943, "it is essential that a knowledge of the proposed tactical use and desired performance characteristics be obtained." Colton appreciated that combat experience had influenced the requirements and it followed, he added,

---

[94] (1) Ltr, McClelland, Air ComO, to CSigO, 17 Sep 43, sub: 50-watt VHF Ground Radio Set. AAG 413.44-BL Radio. (2) Ltr, Rives, Deputy Air ComO, to CSigO, 31 Dec 43, sub: Point-to-Point VHF Radio Set. SigC 413.44 (ET-2375) Sets Gen.
In October 1943 the Air Forces ordered thirty sets of type 1505 to be shipped to the V Fighter Command, for use "for point-to-point communications in existing and contemplated Fighter Control and Aircraft Warning Services." A second lot of fifty sets was ordered in March 1944. (1) Ltr, CG AAF to CSigO, 13 Oct 43, sub: FM Radio Link Sets. AAG 413.44-BR Radio. (2) Ltr, CG AAF to CO PEA, 2 Mar 44, sub: FM Link Sets 1505. AAG 413.44-DF Radio.
See also, Vital Role of FM Radiotelephone, IX TAC booklet, entitled Communications and the Tactical Air Commander, May 1945, pp. 18f., 33ff. SigC 413.44 (ET-2744) Sets Gen 5, 1945.
[95] Memo, Col William F. McKee, ACofAS AAF Hq, for Air Com Div, 26 Aug 43, sub: SCR-527 Units. AAG 413.44-BF Radio.

[96] 1st Ind, CG AAF to CSigO, 22 Oct 43, on basic (missing), Colton to CG AAF, 24 Sep 43, sub: Radio Transmitter-Receiver, Jefferson-Travis Set, Model 350 Modified, 50-W (18-Q Type). AAG 413.44-CD Radio.

"that the Signal Corps personnel, whose responsibility it is to make such adaptations [as combat experience proved to be needed] must be fully informed of changes in requirements arising from such experience." He suggested a conference before the conclusion of tests that the laboratories were running on the Jefferson-Travis set and on a Signal Corps set, the SCR–237. He mentioned, too, an innovation that the laboratories had recently completed in order to meet the Air Forces' needs for an air-ground liaison radio, the AN/VRC–1. He called it an HF/VHF set, because it combined the old but very reliable HF SCR–193 with the VHF 12-volt version of the airborne command radio SCR–522, "but the intended use of this set in relation to Radio Set SCR–188–A and the Jefferson-Travis JT–350," he pointed out, "is not known." [97]

Radio Relay, From FM to Pulse Modulation

Out of the confusion attending Air Forces' acute need for ground radio developed a growing demand by the airmen for the radio relay concept. AN/TRC–1 equipment was coming into wide Army employment in every theater of the war, and in June 1944 General McClelland indicated that the AAF also intended to make extensive use of radio relay in ground nets. McClelland wrote:

The requirements of the Army Air Forces for point to point VHF equipment are increasing in all theaters. . . . Army Air Forces are issuing AN/TRC–1 sets to Fighter Control Squadrons for links within VHF systems and to Fighter Squadrons for inter-airdrome and squadron-to-group communications. In addition, AN/TRC–3 and AN/TRC–4 sets will be issued in many areas for multi-channel communications down to groups.[98]

Radio relay or antrac (often called VHF also, not to be confused with airborne VHF command radios such as the SCR–522) could well provide point-to-point communications for the AAF, as well as for AGF needs. Above all, in an era when ever more communications were wanted, it provided four voice channels and could be made to

[97] 1st Ind, Colton to CG AAF, 31 Aug 43, sub: Radio Set SCR–237 on basic (missing). AAG 413.-44–CD Radio.
The AN/VRC–1 was put on order in the thousands. Of this combination of the SCR–193 and the SCR–542, mounted in a jeep, the AAF ordered 1,692 to be delivered in 1943 and 338 in 1944. This order was placed on 27 October 1943. Some days later nearly 500 more went on order, to equip 12 new JASCO's, each company to include one air liaison section, each of which in turn would consist of 12 parties equipped with AN/VRC–1. However, since there was a dearth of the 12-volt 542's, regular 24-volt 522's would have to substitute. Ltr, Rives, Deputy Air ComO, to CG ASF, 5 Nov 43, sub: Additional Rqmts for Radio Set AN/VRC–1. AAG 413.44–BX Radio.
In January 1944, the AAF termed its requirements for VRC–1 "extremely critical" and added that "procurement . . . has already been unduly delayed." This in response to a Navy request for several hundred SCR–193's. AAF asked ASF to suspend Navy's request until AAF requirements had been met. Ltr, CG AAF to CG ASF, 25 Jan 44, sub: Navy Rqmts for SCR–193K. AAG 413.44–CU Radio.

[98] Ltr, McClelland to CSigO, 19 Jun 44, sub: Mil Characteristics for Point to Point VHF Radio Set. SigC 413.44 (Sets) Gen 1, Jan–Jun 44.
McClelland asked also for test sets of AN/TRC–8, an FM radio relay under development by the Signal Corps, operating on higher frequencies (around 250 megacycles) than the AN/TRC–1. A few sets went into use in Europe late in the war but suffered from range limitations in hilly terrain and from mutual interference when sets were operated too close together. (1) SigC R&D Hist, vol. VIII, pt. 3, Proj 824–D. (2) Draft MS Comment, Waite, Jul 59.

provide many more, whether voice, teletype, or facsimile. It was compact and readily transported.[99] From the first field improvisation (Motorola police radios in North Africa in early 1943) and from the first use in combat theaters a year later of production models of AN/TRC-1, 3, and 4, radio relay brilliantly proved its marked virtues.[100]

The radio relay concept, involving a revolutionary new kind of military communications facility, had taken form in the minds of officers and engineers in the Camp Coles Signal Laboratory before the concept was put to its first test in the field during the Tunisia Campaign in 1943. The concept had been developed on an "under the bench" basis at the laboratory since there was no specific authorization for such a project. When the value of the concept became recognized and demands for its implementation began to come from the field, the Signal Corps had equipment ready.[101]

The first order, for a small number of development sets of AN/TRC-1, had been placed by the Camp Coles Signal Laboratory with the Link Radio Corporation in New York City at the end of 1942. As of June 1943, the Air Forces requirement in the Army Supply Program stood at 1,116 sets to be delivered in FY 1943, at 1,632 sets in 1944. By August 1943, the need had so intensified that the 1944 requirement was increased to 4,372.[102] Very few sets were actually delivered in 1943, however.

While the Camp Coles Signal Laboratory and the Link Radio Corporation developed the AN/TRC-1, the Air Forces asked that 300 sets be delivered before the end of the calendar year (it expected six service test sets in September 1943), and it asked further that 150 of the new walkie-talkies, SCR-300, be modified for their ground radio needs. General Ingles at once replied that current production of the SCR-300's could not meet urgent ground force requirements. He added, "The delivery of 300 additional radio sets AN/TRC-1 during the current year will be even more difficult."[103]

Difficult was right, not least because no one agreed on just what the set

---

[99] A 100-mile system of 2 terminals and 3 relays could be installed by 44 men in 2 days. An equivalent wire-line facility normally required 4 battalions (nearly 2,000 men) working 10 days. The transport of AN/TRC-1 type relay equipment and vehicles required only 25 ship tons compared with 94 tons for the comparable wire system. (1) William S. Rumbough, "Radio Relay, The War's Great Development in Signal Communications," *Military Review*, XXVI, No. 2 (May, 1946), pp. 4f. (2) Ltr, Maj J. E. Keely, SigC Chief Radar Br, to Dir Com Equip, Dev Div, 26 Apr 45, sub: Recommendations for Modifications of AN/TRC-1 Radio Equip. SigC 413.33 CR RAD AJ (ET-2768).

[100] Thompson, Harris, *et al., The Test,* pp. 371ff. See also above, pp. 39, 59, 92ff., 104ff., 126ff., 259ff.

The British and Germans were also discovering the benefits of radio relay, the chief British equipment being the No. 10 pulse-modulated UHF system. The German sets were decimeter (500 megacycles) DMG-4K and 5K. (1) Ltr, Dir SCGSA Camp Cole Sig Lab to CSigO, 9 Sep 44, sub: Unusual Circuits and Components and Operating Instructions for the German Decimeter Radio Relay Set DMG-5K, with Incls. SigC 413.44 Point-to-Point Radio Relay No. 2, Jul-Dec 44. (2) Rpt, Plans and Opns Div, 27 Oct 43, Daily Digest, Staff Divs OCSigO, 19 Jul-31 Dec 43. SigC Exec Of file.

[101] Thompson, Harris, *et al., The Test,* pp. 236f.

[102] (1) SigC R&D Hist, vol. VIII, pt. 3, Proj 824-A. (2) Ltr, CG AAF to CSigO, 12 Aug 43, sub: Radio Transmitter and Receiver, 50 ACRR. AAF 413.44-BJ Radio.

[103] 2d Ind, CSigO to CG ASF, 27 Sep 43, on Ltr, Brig Gen David McL. Crawford, WDGS AGB, to CG ASF, n.d., sub: Radio Equip for AF in Theaters of Opns. AAG 413.44-BR Radio.

should be. In fact, the set had been developed in the early and midyears of the war without benefit of military characteristics, those essential requirements in normal Army development and procurement matters. Willard R. Clark, who had worked on the radio relay project at Camp Coles (along with other radio enthusiasts such as Maj. James D. O'Connell, Major Marks, Capt. Francis F. Uhrhane, Capt. K. S. Jackson, and Lt. Oliver D. Perkins),[104] later wrote that the Chief Signal Officer had authorized the project under his authority to provide communications of the most advanced type, without military characteristics. "The TRC-1 development was started as a laboratory investigation," Clark explained, "in anticipation of future military needs." Thus, the AN/TRC-1 was launched without the usual preparations. It had been promoted as a quickie, for needs that were likely to be immediate. A longer term research project was also under way at the same time in the Coles Laboratory for microwave radio relay, following the pattern of British pulse equipment. It would in 1945 yield the AN/TRC-6 and related radios, too late for much use in World War II. The TRC-1 sets, on the other hand, paid large dividends in the 1944 fighting.[105]

In April 1943 the Coles Signal Laboratory received delivery from the Link Corporation of eight models of AN/TRC-1. Modifying them as TRC-1, 3, and 4, the engineers and officers ran tests through the spring in the New Jersey countryside. They called the assembly a "100-mile radio relay system." The military characteristics followed, in a cart-before-the-horse reversal of usual Army procedures. The first military characteristics, adopted in July 1943, were of "limited procurement type." In September other tests of TRC-1 equipment were made over water along the coast of Maine, particularly atop Mt. Cadillac near Bar Harbor and on Cape Elizabeth near Portland, to duplicate conditions of communicating across the English Channel. The tests were successful and the system standardized.[106]

The Army Air Forces, which first sought quantity delivery of this equipment, kept making changes. Six service test sets built to its specifications were scheduled for delivery at the summer's end but were not ready by November. Then, when representatives of the Air Forces Board and the Tactical Air Force, lacking the service test sets, went to the Link radio factory to check up, they asked that immediate steps be taken to incorporate additions and substitutions in the 2,740 sets under procurement. The AAF wanted a dif-

[104] Clark was the section chief of the new Radio Relay Section. Most of the development was done by Jensen, Hines, Waite, Colaguori, and Russell A. Berg, with Clark's approval, under Jackson and Perkins. Draft MS Comment, Waite, Jul 59.

[105] Willard R. Clark, The Story of a Milestone, Radio Set AN/TRC-1 and Multichannel Radio Relay, pp. 4–10. Radio folder, Tab GG, SigC Hist Sec file. SCEL workers did not wage the "radio-relay blitz" alone, Clark added. The Engineering and Technical Division, OCSigO, "chopped red tape, promoted priorities, and did much to ex-

cite the growing interest in radio relay among the brass hats in the Pentagon." Clark also mentioned Lt. Col. V. A. Kamin, Maj. E. E. Boyer, L. Windmuller, R. F. Brady, and John J. Kelleher as being instrumental in developing the equipment.

[106] (1) Ibid., pp. 11ff. (2) SCTC Mtg 282, 27 Sep 43, sub: Classification as Standard of Radio Set AN/TRC-1. AAG 413.44–BW Radio.

ferent antenna, higher antenna masts, and remote control equipment.[107]

Meanwhile the Signal Corps took measures to expedite production. The Signal Corps labor officer in New York City deferred the induction of twelve of Link's key men and got emergency furloughs for three men who had already been inducted so that they could return to their jobs as supervisors in Link's metal shop and electrical assembly line. The Monmouth Procurement District had assigned two men to serve as co-ordinators at the Link plant, working full time there, expediting components. The New York office of ANEPA assigned one full-time expeditor to the Link plant and designated six people in the ANEPA office itself to give assistance on requests originating in the Link factory. The Production Branch of the Signal Corps Procurement and Distribution Division assigned an officer to co-ordinate the activities of the Monmouth Procurement District and of the New York ANEPA people. Also the Signal Corps helped the L. S. Branch Company, Newark, New Jersey, to get out sufficient antennas for the TRC–1.[108] Mr. Link himself wrote General Harrison, head of Signal Corps procurement, that his firm was "putting shoulder to the wheel in an unprece-dented manner in an effort to meet a technically impossible deadline. We still may not meet it in every sense of the word, but certainly will meet it in general or go down trying." He said that he had set all other work aside, had asked his employees to work a 70–75-hour, 7-day week and that they had gladly agreed.[109]

Still production lagged, chiefly because of further changes the military wanted made in the sets, although the military refused to recognize this as the cause of the delay. Late in December Mr. Link replied to a pressure note from General Harrison:

We feel that it was mutually understood between all parties concerned, including the Signal Corps officials, that final models could not be made available until all technical details relating to the equipment could be effectively frozen in the minds of Signal Corps Laboratory officials, the Contracting Officers and ourselves. I believe you will agree that it was not a case of our organization being unable to produce models as scheduled or of our lack of desire to make these models available as much as it is a situation where numerous changes of minor nature have been made in the new equipment at the request of Signal Corps engineering authorities that have made it impossible to supply the final models up to the present time.[110]

By the late winter of 1944 the Link Radio Company was turning out AN/TRC–1 in quantity. The sets proved excellent. One report stated that "all results of tests made on subject equipment had been thoroughly satisfactory . . . voice, teletype, and facsimile transmission had been put on the circuit hour

---

[107] (1) Ltr, Brig Gen Eugene L. Eubank (for AAF Bd) to CG AAF, 18 Nov 43, sub: Necessary Changes to AN/TRC–1 Radio Sets. AAG 413.44–CK Radio. (2) Ltr, Rives, Deputy Air ComO, to CSigO, 31 Dec 43, sub: Point to Point VHF Radio Set. SigC 413.44 (ET–2375) Sets Gen, 1944–45.

[108] Memo, 1st Lt D. F. Magner, SigC Prod Br, for Maj W. R. Herrlein, 24 Nov 43, sub: Fred M. Link Radio Co. SigC 413.44 (AN/TRC–1) No. 1 Radio Link Set, 1943.

The Navy also had in an order for 300 sets, which the Signal Corps sought to defer in favor of the Army order.

[109] Ltr, Link to Harrison, 10 Dec 43. SigC 413.44 (AN/TRC–1) No. 1 Radio Link Set, 1943.

[110] Ltr, Link to Harrison, 31 Dec 43. SigC 413.44 (AN/TRC–1) No. 1 Radio Link Set, 1943.

AN/TRC-6 ANTENNA ARRAY IS LOWERED FOR REMOVAL TO ANOTHER SITE

after hour without any interruption." General Colton in August 1944 warmly thanked Mr. Link. AN/TRC-1, 3, and 4 "have been most valuable additions to our military communication equipment . . . an invaluable means of communication comparing in efficiency, as a system, with regular long distance telephone pole lines." [111]

The production rate of the sets, how-ever, could not meet the rapidly growing need for military radio relay. "There was no question," Mr. Link recalled years later, "that Link Radio did not have the mass facilities required to produce the unprecedented requirement for AN/TRC-1, 3 & 4 systems." This fact, coupled with Army's desire to decentralize the manufacture of so vital an item, led the Signal Corps late in the summer of 1944 to assign further production contracts to the Rauland and Lear Avia Corporations, located in Grand Rapids and Chicago, respectively, in order to augment the output of the Link Radio Company in New York City.

---

[111] (1) Memo, O. C. Tallman, Actg Chief Tech Br Florida Fld Station, Clermont, Fla. (ASH SCGSA) for file, 10 Apr 44, sub: Further Investigation Info on Sv Tests of Radio Set AN/TRC-1. SigC 413.44 (AN/TRC-1) No. 3, Jul-Dec 44. (2) Incl, with Ltr, Colton, Chief E&T Sv, to Link, 19 Aug 44. SigC 413.44 (Sets) Gen 2, Jul-Dec 44.

At the same time, the Army granted to the antrac manufacturers higher precedence than Link had previously had to obtain materials and components.[112]

AN/TRC–1, 3, and 4 constituted 4-channel radio relay, operating in the very high frequencies, VHF, in the 70- to 100-megacycle band. Each channel could carry one voice circuit or four teletypewriter circuits. The Army needed even more radio channels than this form of relay could offer. It was becoming necessary to move to higher and higher frequencies in order to obtain the needed band width—in the hundreds and thousands of megacycles. Radar tubes had been evolved able to emit pulsed radiations in those ranges of the frequency spectrum, far beyond the capabilities of FM oscillators at that date. It would thus be possible to devise methods of communicating by pulse modulation at radar frequencies.

This very thing was first done by the British. Early in World War II information had been received in the United States concerning an 8-channel time-division multiplex pulse-modulated microwave (UHF) radio relay developed by the British as their wireless set No. X10A. In 1942 engineers from Signal Corps laboratories, Bell Telephone, and RCA laboratories had gone to England to examine the equipment. On returning they set about developing American versions, which became AN/TRC–5 and 6. About ninety sets of

AN/TRC–6 were produced in time to serve in World War II. Operating at much higher frequencies than the 70 to 100 megacycles of AN/TRC–1, with greater band width, providing the capacity to handle more channels of communications simultaneously, AN/TRC–6 opened up whole new realms of possibilities, quite as FM techniques had done a few years earlier.[113]

This new radio relay species was neither FM nor AM. It employed one signal in the microwave region (SHF, superhigh frequency) but it chopped that signal into eight pieces, one to a channel, providing eight channels simultaneously, twice the capacity of the TRC–1 equipment. The chopping progressed at lightning speed at the transmitter. The receiver put the pieces back together in perfect step with the transmitter. The technique, borrowing from radar and television, relied on precise time division of the signal in inconceivably minute bits, measurable in millionths of a second. This was a totally new method of communicating—radio pulse communications, pulse-modulated or pulse-position modulated, at the microwave frequencies of radar, at 4,300–4,900 megacycles. The almost infinitely minute bits of signal were, in a way, a return to the dits and dahs

---

[112] (1) Ltr, CO Monmouth SigC Proc Dist to Chief P&D Sv OCSigO, 19 Aug 44, sub: Higher Precedence Request for AN/TRC–1. SigC 413.44 (AN/TRC–1) No. 3, Jul–Dec 44. (2) Ltr, Link to Thompson, 18 Feb 62. SigC Hist Sec file. Mr. Link himself proposed Rauland and Lear as antrac suppliers (Lear had formerly worked in partnership with Link).

[113] (1) SCEL Postwar R&D Prog, pp. 27–29. (2) Memo, Windmuller for Messer, 20 Jan 44, sub: Dev of Pulse Modulated Radio Relay Equip. SigC 413.44 Point-to-Point Radio Relay No. 1, Jan–Jun 44. (3) J. J. Kelleher, "Pulse Modulated Radio Relay Equipment," Electronics, XIX (May, 1946), 124ff. (4) R. E. Lacy, Coles Sig Lab, Two Multichannel Microwave Radio Relay Equipments for the U.S. Army Communication Network, 30 Nov 45. SigC 000.7 Articles for Publication, vol. 4, Oct–Dec 45. (5) Lawrence G. Fobes, "Multichannel Radio Communication with the Army," IRE Transactions on Military Electronics, vol. MIL–4, No. 4 (October, 1960), 507f.

of Morse, hand-keyed. Only the hand that keyed the time-division signals was the electron itself, moving at the speed of light, with infallible precision.

The Bell Telephone Laboratories delivered several development models to the Camp Coles Signal Laboratory late in 1943. In January 1944, the Air Forces outlined a tactical requirement for the AN/TRC–6 and asked for four service test models. Meanwhile the Coles Laboratory worked not only on the AN/TRC–6 but also on two other antrac types, AN/TRC–5 and 8.[114]

In June 1944, the Air Forces, impatient, requested that the Signal Corps stage a demonstration of its several antrac types. General Ingles replied that it would be done, not only for the Air Forces but also for the benefit of all interested arms. The Signal Corps would parade at Camp Coles AN/TRC–3, 4, 5, 6, and 8. He added that the Signal Corps had already let development contracts for 48 sets of AN/TRC–6, and for 91 sets of AN/TRC–8. Ingles intended that the AN/TRC–6's be set up between the Aircraft Radio Laboratory in Ohio and the Signal Corps Ground Signal Agency in New Jersey, both to demonstrate a 600-mile radio relay line and to provide a good multicarrier communications link between these two widely separated halves of the Signal Corps research and development establishments.[115]

The Air Forces, close to accomplishing their intent to split the Aircraft Radio Laboratory away from the Signal Corps, were not interested in this unifying use of the new TRC–6. General Arnold wrote to General Somervell in July that the equipment could "better be used in active theaters." [116] And so it would be. AN/TRC–6 radio relay in the hands of the 3163d Signal Service Company reached the European theater in time to carry very heavy traffic loads during the last months of the war and established the pattern of microwave pulse-modulated communications systems of the future.[117]

Air-Ground Radio

Another ground radio problem that combat experience intensified was air-ground liaison, in order to communicate directly between aircraft and ground forces, whether infantry, tank forces, or paratroopers. All these ground elements had gone into action early in the war without VHF radios, which alone could communicate with the VHF command radios used by all Allied aircraft, the SCR–522.[118] "The history of air-ground

[114] (1) J. J. Kelleher, "VHF and Microwave Military Communication Systems," *Signals*, I, No. 5 (May–June, 1947), pp. 37–41. (2) H. S. Black, "AN/TRC–6, A Microwave Relay System," *Bell Laboratories Record*, XXIII (December, 1945), pp. 457–63. (3) SigC R&D Hist, vol. VIII, pt. 3, Proj 824–D and F.

[115] Ltr, CG AAF to CSigO, 26 Jun 44, sub: Radio Set AN/TRC–6, with 2d Ind, CSigO to CG ASF, 12 Jul 44. AAG 413.44–EY Radio.

[116] 4th Ind, CG AAF to CG ASF, 25 Jul 44, on basic cited in preceding note.

[117] (1) CSigO, Annual Rpt, FY 45, pp. 346f. (2) Ltr, Col Murray Harris, ExecO Hq USFET OCSigO, 10 Jul 45, sub: Opn of Radio Sets, AN/TRC–6 in ETO, 25 Apr 45–10 May 45, with 2 Incls. SCIA file, unnumbered, European Theater, 1945. (3) 12th AGp, Report of Operations, vol. XI (Signals), pp. 209ff. (4) Rpt, Plans and Opns Div, 28 Oct and 6 Nov 44. Daily Digest, Staff Divs OCSigO, 1 Jul–31 Dec 44. SigC Exec Of file. (5) Radio Relay, The AN/TRC–6. File in SigC Hist Sec.

[118] For the development of this radio set, see Thompson, Harris, *et al.*, *The Test*, pp. 78ff. and 39ff.).

liaison and equipment. . . ." wrote Lt. Col. William S. Marks, a former civilian radio engineer at the Fort Monmouth laboratories, "has not been a very happy one. What there is has been learned in the theaters the hard way and accomplished with improvised installations." [119]

Why had no provisions been made for such air-ground liaison? "The indicated policy," Colonel Marks explained, "has been that the Air Forces will furnish and operate the radio set." He traced the problem back to 1940 and the initiation of the Armored Force radio series. It was obvious even then that the German Stuka-tank teams coordinated their blows very successfully. Yet the SCR–506, Set II in Armored Force's 500 series, was at first planned to be a continuous wave radio only, although it would be the logical set for use between Armored Force units and aircraft. However, Marks went on, "No consideration was given for operation with the air since that was a responsibility of Air Forces." The need to communicate with aircraft repeatedly asserted itself, and, since aircraft command radios employed voice only, the design of the SCR–506 under development in 1941 was altered to include voice. It therefore provided a radiotelephone facility whose frequency range overlapped part of the high frequency range of the aircraft command set of that day, the SCR–274. This alteration delayed the SCR–506, and, when at last in 1943 production models

began to reach the Armored Force, they could not communicate with the newest Air Forces command radios, the VHF type. "Probably," Colonel Marks said in his 1945 review of the subject, the SCR–506 "has never talked with the air on a support mission." [120]

The reason was that by 1943 the old high frequency aircraft command radio SCR–274 had yielded to the VHF SCR–522, which leaped up to the 100- to 156-megacycle range, far above the reach of the 506, which remained only a high frequency radio. Despite this change in the aircraft command set, no ground arm had submitted characteristics for a companion radio to provide ground liaison in these very high ranges of VHF. Any proposal in that direction would have been an AAF prerogative, and no such proposal was forthcoming.

In the theaters, early combat tactics made it imperative that ground units be able to communicate directly with aircraft overhead. Combat troops had to improvise and they did. "The North African Theater," explained Colonel Marks, "sent back reports of what was called a 'Veep' set, an SCR–193 and an SCR–522 installed in a jeep." This became recognized in Signal Corps procurement and nomenclature; it became the AN/VRC–1, a hybrid development originating not with the laboratories but with field troops. General Colton called it the HF/VHF set. Thousands were ordered for infantry use and for joint assault signal companies.[121]

Thus at last the AN/VRC–1 impro-

---

[119] Memo, Marks, Ground Sig Sec Hq AGF, for Ground SigO, 30 Apr 45, sub: AGF Com. SigC 413.44 Integration of Radio and Wire Com (ET–2633).

[120] (1) *Ibid.* (2) SigC R&D Hist, vol. VIII, pt. 3, Proj (822) 11–9.2.
[121] See above, pp. 231ff., 494.

visation could provide air-ground liaison, but only for the infantry, not for the Armored Force, whose tank radios were FM and could not communicate with the SCR–193 component of the "Veep" hybrids, which were AM. American tanks and aircraft still could not communicate readily with each other. If there was to be any contact, the communication had to move in the "proper channels of command"— if a tank unit wished to call aircraft to bomb a specific target, the tank commander would have to call his ground headquarters on FM, and the headquarters in turn would have to call up an Air Forces control center employing wire lines, or AM radio such as the 193, the 506, or the 299. Air Forces controllers then could direct aircraft over their VHF command nets, using the ground VHF transmitter components of the SCS–2 or 3 systems or the SCR–624.

Stark necessity in Normandy cut through this rigmarole, and tankmen somehow mounted the SCR–522's in their juggernauts. "It is reported," Colonel Marks wrote, "that the SCR–522 is installed in some manner in tanks. By whom, in what tanks, and how many is not known." Colonel Williams, the First Army signal officer, subsequently explained in more detail that, when immediate fighter-bomber support was needed by ground forces at St. Lô, each armored battalion acquired an SCR–522. Before the St. Lô operation, he admitted, "communications for air support of ground troops were not very satisfactory. During the Normandy landings," he added, "no quick adequate means of obtaining close fighter-bomber support were available." At St. Lô, however, "each armored battalion was furnished with a VHF radio, SCR–522, the type installed in fighter bombers. This set was installed in the tanks which were to lead the armored columns. These tanks were in communication with fighter bombers immediately overhead as the advance took place." Williams concluded, "the speed and magnitude of the breakthrough at St. Lô and the successful exploitation were due greatly to this close air-ground communications." [122]

This was just what the Germans had done so successfully four years earlier. The lamentable fact that, despite the early example of the German tank-bomber team, American tanks and aircraft could not communicate directly till necessity forced an improvisation might seem on retrospect, a delinquency on someone's part. More likely the need was lost sight of in the fog of war preparations and organizational confusion.

In 1943 the Air Forces did rather belatedly request an air-ground liaison VHF radio, the AN/TRC–7, for the use of paratroopers. The Camp Coles Signal Laboratory developed it as a VHF set, with a range comparable to that of the SCR–522, broken into small packs the paratroopers could carry as they chuted to earth. The Air Forces tested the radio during the summer of 1944 and asked for 500 sets, crash-produced. "This is the first ground set developed specifically for ground-air liaison," wrote Colonel Marks, concluding his rather unhappy history of this category of equipment. From his review of air-ground liaison history he deduced "the serious need of the Ground Forces to maintain active

---

[122] Williams, "First Army's ETO Signal Operation," *Signals*, II, No. 4, p. 10.

liaison with the Air Forces on this sub-ject." Already both the Navy and the Air Forces were planning to develop another airplane set of higher fre-quency.[123]

Equipment Situation at the End of the War

Before World War II, Signal Corps equipment—wire and radio—had been designed to be rugged and simple, some-what to the detriment of portability, and for use in the latitudes of the United States. Suddenly World War II took U.S. troops to all parts of the globe. It put communications equipment to increased use under extreme climatic conditions. Radio received much greater use than ever before, all the way down to the smallest troop units, where untrained men had often to rely on small portable sets. It therefore became imperative that equipment be waterproofed and tropic-alized; that, while range and channel capacity be increased, weight be de-creased; and that items be kept rugged and simple to operate. Meanwhile, many World War II items had to be deve-loped by various commercial companies in order to hasten procurement. Specifi-cations, hastily prepared, stressed perfor-mance while keeping to a minimum limitations on components and mate-rials. As a result the Signal Corps could not achieve a high degree of standard-ization.[124]

So it was that the emergency character of Signal Corps research and develop-ment and supply in World War II spawned a sometimes unhappy mixture of equipment items, of individual com-ponents that, however excellent in themselves, were ill suited to work well in systems where effective co-ordination was needed. The "handie-talkie" SCR–536 infantry radio was AM and could not communicate with the walkie-talkie, which was FM. Tank radios were FM but their frequency range did not over-lap that of the walkie-talkie, so that tank-infantry teams could not radio to each other. These obvious defects, which resulted from headlong production with its accompanying lack of thoughtful planning, clearly indicated a need for communications systems containing inte-grated and co-ordinated wire and radio items that could communicate with each other. "I felt there were weaknesses in the ground forces communications—not so much in equipment as in systems," commented Dr. Bowles late in the war.[125]

One of Dr. Bowles' civilian consult-ants, Albert Tradup, looked into the ground force communications problems from September 1944 to the war's end. He studied in detail the many radio and wire nets of tactical troops. They were quite segregated—for example, a high frequency net from the infantry regi-ment headquarters to battalion head-quarters, a VHF net from battalion to company, an HF net within the com-pany, all three nets being entirely separate with no possibility of intercon-nection. To transfer a message from one

---

[123] (1) Memo, Marks for Ground SigO, 30 Apr 45, sub: Army Ground Forces Com. SigC 413.44 Integration of Radio and Wire Com (ET–2633). (2) SigC R&D Hist, vol. VIII, pt. 2, Proj 814–D.

[124] SCEL Postwar R&D Prog, Dec 45, p. 34.

[125] Dr. Edward L. Bowles Diary, Pacific Trip, Nov 44–Jan 45, p. 3. Folder of Bowles Diaries, Selections, SigC Hist Sec file.

net into another, radio operators had to repeat it. Tradup therefore urged that equipment be developed that could connect dissimilar radio channels to each other and to wire channels. He urged reassignment of frequency band widths so that the infantry radios might occupy a central place, with a frequency overlap with artillery radios on one side of the infantry band, and with armored force radios on the other. He noted the glaring lack of a common radio channel between infantry and tank radio sets. A start had been made to remedy this with the AN/VRC-3, a tank radio (40- to 48-megacycle, FM), which could communicate with the walkie-talkie SCR-300. For some time, too, the telephone set AN/VIA-1 had been in use, attached to the outside of a tank, over which an infantryman could reach the crew through the interior interphone system. But such solutions only created additional separate items of equipment, not ideal solutions.[126]

This confusion of Army's radio sets and types (and of wire components too), this array of individually good but collectively unrelated equipment items of World War II, pointed to the necessity that the Signal Corps must engineer the many sets and components to work together in a co-ordinated system wherein all might intercommunicate. This need was beginning to be formulated by such men as Tradup at the war's end.

Along with engineering of systems and integration of equipment, begun before the end of the war and certain to go on long afterwards, was miniaturization. Always in the military there is pressure to make equipment small, compact, light in weight. In communications electronics there was room for much improvement; small components enable smaller sets; tubes could be made smaller, and so on. Tradup mentioned the importance of this in his wartime reports. Nowhere were the possibilities more evident than in the case of field switchboards—in the excessively heavy regimental and battalion BD-71, for example. In the modulelike plastic units of the SB design was an omen of the form that future communications electronics equipment might take. And more communications would be needed. Tradup noted that the six drops of BD-71 were not enough for the growing communications needs of a battalion. He recommended 8 or 10. The subsequent SB-22 would have 12.[127]

FM had proved itself entirely in the tactical communications of close combat. Yet not all short-range combat radios were FM. For example, the "handie-talkie" was an AM set, SCR-536. So was the guidon set, SCR-511. Neither could talk with the walkie-talkie, SCR-300, an FM set. Before the war was over, work had begun on the FM successor to the SCR-536, the AN/PRC-6. The SCR-536 was a good example of the individual sort of set that was so often rushed into production during the war, without co-ordination with other sets. An-

[126] (1) Memo, Tradup, Expert Consultant OSW, 23 Nov 44. Folder of Bowles Papers, Tab E, SigC Hist Sec file. (2) See also Tradup's later study, Integrated Communications for Army Ground Forces, Preliminary Draft for Comments, 1 Feb 45. Folder of Bowles Papers, Preface, p. 4, SigC Hist Sec file.

[127] "From Scientist to Soldier," Signals, VII, No. 2 (November–December, 1952), 19.

other good example was the much used long-range SCR–299 (and 399 and 499). At war's end Signal Corps laboratory engineers were beginning to think of families of radio sets that could work together, and that could serve all arms, with such slight variations as frequency coverage; they began to think of radio and wire equipment that could work together, or interchangeably, through the same switchboards. Whether a message might travel partly by wire, partly by radio, did not matter so long as the operations of the equipment all meshed well. The first, and most likely line of action for the laboratories to follow in the future, a 1945 SCEL report stated, was "to improve existing standard equipments by designs which lead to integration of facilities, greater flexibility, and mobility, lower weight and bulk, interchangeability, and over-all standardization." [128]

In radar, the defects of early sets—insufficient accuracy, poor discrimination, poor height finding—were largely overcome by microwave developments that increased the range of reliable detection at all heights and gave accuracy comparable to optical methods in automatic tracking and gun laying. At the end of the war the Signal Corps Engineering Laboratories reported, "the present trend is towards the development of smaller and lighter-weight microwave radars using the same basic principles." [129] One innovation was doppler techniques. Radars had been harassed by ground clutter in

the detection of low-flying objects, and in fire control against them. By mid-1945 doppler techniques were being introduced in search sets but had not yet improved sufficiently for use in fire control.

The application of radar techniques to ground targets such as tanks and other vehicles was most difficult, indeed hardly possible till microwave radar arrived. Ground applications were badly needed in the last years of the war when the problem of locating enemy mortars became paramount, taking precedence over all other ground uses of radar. Mortar fire was causing a large percent of battle casualties. The problem began to be solved upon discovery that several types of existing radars, especially the SCR–584 and the AN/TPS–3, could locate enemy mortars by getting fixes, by means of radar reflections, on mortar shells at several points along their high arching trajectories. The Camp Evans Signal Laboratory first undertook in 1943 to adapt the TPS–3, altering it as the AN/TPQ–3. The Radiation Laboratory of OSRD would not accept the mortar location assignment, Dr. Zahl recalled years later, because of the belief that the problem could not be solved before the war ended. But the Signal Corps accepted the challenge to crash-build some sets. In Zahl's words:

The Laboratories took it up, worked hard for several months culminating in a show of unbelievable enthusiasm, when Captain Marchetti led his task force through 4 consecutive days of almost 24 hour effort, with occasional catnaps and food brought to them. Bleary-eyed, the bearded engineers . . . left building 20 at Camp Evans after almost 96 hours of continuous effort, almost ready to collapse but

[128] (1) SCEL Postwar R&D Prog, p. 3. (2) SigC R&D Hist, vol. VIII, pt. 2, Proj 814–G.
[129] SCEL Postwar R&D Prog, p. 75.

mortar locating radars were on their way to the Pacific.[130]

[130] Zahl, Draft MS Comment, Jul 59. See also Dr. Harold A. Zahl, "One Hundred Years of Research," *IRE Transactions on Military Electronics,* vol. MIL–4, No. 4 (October, 1960), p. 399.

Another Signal Corps gun locator device that came into use toward the end of World War II was the sound locator set GR–6. Developed by the Evans Laboratory, primarily for locating small arms fire, 10 sets reached the Pacific in time for use on Okinawa. In the hands of 5 teams of 8 men each, the GR–6 located 3 machine guns, 65 mortars, 13 antitank guns, 40 light or medium artillery pieces, and 16 heavy guns so accurately that in all but 6 cases the artillery was able to fire without previous adjustment, silencing the enemy weapons with the first shots. (1) SigC R&D Hist, vol. VI, pt. 1, Proj 612–H, pp. 13ff. (2) Appleman *et al., Okinawa, The Last Battle,* pp. 256f.

In 1944 the Camp Evans Signal Laboratory began the design of special mortar-locating radar, the AN/TPQ–2. Its sharp beams could also locate enemy troops and vehicles under favorable conditions. Preproduction models were just being completed as World War II came to a close.[131]

[131] (1) SCEL Postwar R&D Prog, p. 77. (2) Guerlac, Radar, pp. 1609ff. (sec. E, ch. VI, pp. 56ff.). (3) CSigO, Annual Rpt, FY 45, pp. 280ff. (4) SigC R&D History, vol, IV, pt. 1, pp. 4f. and pt. 4, Projs 435–B and C. (5) Anti-Aircraft Artillery Activities in the Pacific War, pp. 195 and 213. (6) Incl, Capt W. DeBlois, NEID, 11 Jun 45, sub: Summary of Counter-Mortar Radar Dev in ETO, with Ltr, Col Murray Harris, ExecO Hq ETO OCSigO, 15 Jun 45, sub: Counter Mortar Dev in ETO. SCIA file, unnumbered, European Theater, 1945.

CHAPTER XVI

Innovations in Signal Training

The Signal Corps' responsibility for procuring and training its portion of the Army's manpower remained one of its most important obligations throughout the war. The last two years of conflict brought significant changes in personnel and training objectives. Primarily the changes simply reflected shifts of emphasis in War Department policies and the necessary adjustments instituted as the war ran its course.

By mid-1943 moblization was virtually complete as the Army neared its authorized peak strength of 7,700,000 men. In the previous year, the Army's officer strength had increased two-and-a-half times, while its enlisted strength tripled.[1] The nation's military and civilian agencies began to feel the pinch as the manpower sources that once had seemed limitless shrank alarmingly. In the earlier years, when the great mass movement of selective service men from reception centers to replacement centers, schools, and units had met the first urgent call for bodies, the Army's expansion had taken place without much regard to troop basis ceilings.[2] In the last two years of war, the Army zealously conserved its manpower. Fixed personnel ceilings necessitated strict utilization of limited service personnel, Wacs, Negro troops, prisoners of war, and the use of civilians in lieu of military personnel whenever possible. Training quotas declined sharply; many training installations closed their doors. Improved assignment techniques assumed paramount importance in order to assure that every man was placed in the job best fitted to his capabilities. The Signal Corps had a lower rate of officer malassignments than any of the other technical services or any of the ASF staff divisions, according to an ASF survey late in 1943.[3]

The Army's initial requirements for cadres and fillers had constituted the primary consideration during the period of rapid expansion when many new combat units were being activated. By mid-1943 the greatest need was for more closely knit troop units, men drawn together in small groups and thoroughly instructed in teamwork. Thus the role of the Signal Corps replacement training centers declined in importance and that of its unit training centers (UTC's) correspondingly became more important.

The shift in emphasis brought the Signal Corps relief from hardships im-

---

[1] OCSigO R&W Action 1, Maj J. S. Vaughn, Mil Pers Br, to Gen King, 8 Jan 43, sub: Mil Pers Conf of ASF Pers Of. SigC MP 337 Confs, 1942 to 30 Apr 44.

[2] (1) Terrett, *The Emergency,* pp. 107, 203ff., 214–16, 245, 249. (2) Thompson, Harris, *et al., The Test,* pp. 34–57, 186–217, 316–22.

[3] Qtrly Rpt, OCSigO Mil Pers Br, 15 Oct 43–15 Jan 44, p. 46. SigC Hist Sec file.

posed by the cadre system during the early months of the war. No other arm or service required a greater number of different kinds of highly skilled technicians than the Signal Corps. Moreover, only men of high intelligence and special aptitudes could master electronics subjects, and real proficiency in some of the more complex specialties could be acquired only through many months of training.[4] When the commander of a signal unit lost some of his skilled men for a cadre withdrawn to form the nucleus of a new unit, he could not replace them readily. At the beginning of the war there were so few signal units in existence and so many new ones being organized that some units were almost "cadred out of existence." Within six months after Pearl Harbor, nearly every Regular Army Signal Corps organization had been stripped of trained men. Some had accompanied important missions overseas and others had departed for officer candidate schools, but the majority had simply been withdrawn to form cadres for new units.[5]

Gradual tightening of ASF control over training and personnel policies during the latter part of the war also introduced changes into Signal Corps procedures. ASF had wide authority in all technical service training matters, but the actual conduct of training was quite another matter. During the war the responsibility for actual conduct of training shifted between ASF staff divisions, technical service chiefs, and service commands.[6]

General Somervell, as commanding general of ASF, definitely wanted responsibility for technical training vested in the service commands.[7] The technical services chiefs felt just as definitely that they should have complete control over their own training programs. General Somervell never did obtain for the service commands all the powers he wished them to have, but neither did the technical services chiefs ever acquire the unhampered control they desired. Although the Chief Signal Officer in his annual report for the fiscal year 1943 pointedly remarked that "vast, sweeping changes" during the year had decentralized to the service commands "a sizeable portion of the personnel activities previously performed by the Office of the Chief Signal Officer," he was expressing a legalistic rather than a practical interpretation of the changes.[8] For example, ASF had promulgated a change in Army regulations that placed all Class I and II training installations (including all RTC's, UTC's, and schools) under the service commands.[9] Actually, the technical services chiefs continued to control the training staffs and faculties. Furthermore, certain training institutions were designated as Class IV, or "exempted" installations, entirely under technical services control. For the Signal Corps, these exempted installations included the important Fort Monmouth

---

[4] Capt Wilson G. Burden, OCSigO Mil Tng Br Study, Signal Corps Enlisted Administration (1945), pp. 19–21. SigC Hist Sec file.

For example, to name but a few, repeatermen, wire chiefs, automatic equipment installers, and intercept operators required at least nine to twelve months of training.

[5] Ibid., p. 3.

[6] History of Military Training, ASF, Training, Mission, and Organization of the ASF, pp. 1, 9. OCMH files.

[7] (1) Ibid., p. 12ff. (2) Millett, The Organization and Role of the Army Service Forces, pp. 326–28.

[8] CSigO, Annual Rpt, FY 43, p. 292.

[9] AR 170–10, Service Commands and Departments, 10 Aug 42.

TRAINEES OPERATE PORTABLE FIELD MESSAGE CENTER SWITCHBOARD, *Fort Monmouth, N.J.*

and Camp Murphy training installations. In May 1943 a change of more consequence took away the technical services' control over training programs and training staffs and faculties and gave it to the service commands.[10] However, in order to keep the experience and specialized knowledge of the technical services, ASF gave them inspection responsibilities for Class I and II installations.[11]

The trend toward greater flexibility constituted still another development of major importance to the Signal Corps and to the whole Army in 1944–45. This trend produced changes in the organization of signal units and also resulted in the establishment of pools of trained men ahead of the time when they were needed. The Signal Corps won its fight for flexibility of unit organization with its introduction of the cellular teams.[12] Through the medium of training battalions, it readied teams of specialists

---

[10] AR 170–10, 24 Dec 42, Change 5 (12 May 43).
[11] Hist, Mil Tng, ASF, pp. 12–26, *passim.*
[12] See above, pp. 22ff.

before receiving a formal request for them. This plan ASF later instituted for all the technical services as "preactivation" training.

Military Manpower

Throughout the war the War Department's manpower calculations amounted to *ad hoc* arrangements. Shifts in tactical situations resulted in frantic fluctuations in troop requirements. The Signal Corps operated on a feast-or-famine basis, now with an overstrength in officers and an understrength in enlisted men, now with substantial shortages or overages in both.

Requirements

As of 1 July 1943, the troop basis requirements for Signal Corps men were relatively small (6,000 each for the ASF and the AGF, 41,000 for the AAF), and personnel officers anticipated no difficulties in meeting the demands.[13] But a revision on 4 October sent ASF–AGF figures upward by 17,000; at the same time there was some decrease in the AAF troop basis. At that late date there was no possibility of furnishing all the troops required at the time they were needed.[14] Meanwhile the 1944 Troop Basis was evolving out of "rather thin air."[15] It picked up all the existing unfilled requirements from the augmented 1943 list and added a budget of troops for 1944. The total called for 2,539 officers

and 32,843 enlisted men for ASF units, 18,118 troops for AGF, and a minus quantity for AAF.[16]

The over-all 1944 Troop Basis included substantial increases in service troops. In that respect the earlier troop bases had ignored the facts of life. As a result, the Signal Corps had been called upon for large numbers of troops to be activated in excess of the troop basis. In 1942 it had furnished 18,000 signal troops over and above the authorized basis, and 33,000 in 1943.[17] The net effect of the 1944 authorizations so far as the Signal Corps was concerned represented a 50-percent increase in men in ASF units between December 1943 and the end of 1944. At the beginning of 1944, 60,000 signal troops were required for ASF units, and at the end of the year, 90,000.

Since the AGF troop basis contained mainly service support units, it became possible to transfer substantial numbers, mainly signal construction battalions, to the ASF during the early part of the calendar year. The AAF had a surplus of signal troops because of the contemplated disbandment of aircraft warning activities. But disbanding aircraft warning units did not mean transfer of either officers or enlisted men to the AGF or ASF. Instead the AAF kept them, building up its own communications units.[18]

As for Signal Corps officers, a surplus existed in the summer of 1943, and the War Department ordered the transfer of large blocks of officers to other arms and

[13] CSigO, Annual Rpt, FY 44, p. 458.

[14] Qtrly Rpt, OCSigO Mil Pers Br, 15 Jan–15 Apr 44, p. 1. SigC Hist Sec file.

[15] R&W Action 1, Gillespie, Chief Mil Tng Br, to Chief P&T Sv and Dir Opns Div OCSigO, 23 Aug 43, sub: Rqmts for Quota of Specialists. SigC 353 Gen, Aug 43, MT-174.

[16] (1) CSigO, Annual Rpt, FY 44, p. 457. (2) Qtrly Rpt, OCSigO Mil Pers Br, 15 Jan 44–15 Apr 44, p. 1.

[17] Qtrly Rpt, OCSigO Mil Pers Br, 15 Jan 44–15 Apr 44, p. 2.

[18] CSigO, Annual Rpt, FY 44, pp. 457, 459.

services. Between October and December 1943, 800 Signal Corps officers were transferred to the Corps of Engineers, 200 to the Corps of Military Police, and 20 to the Transportation Corps. During a 6-month period between December 1943 and June 1944, the AAF received each month 55 Signal Corps officers to be trained as pilots or as bombardiers and navigators, and another 20 each month for training in AAF intelligence schools. To shut off the production of new Signal Corps officers, the officer candidate school at Fort Monmouth took in only 75 new candidates every two months for an authorized capacity of 150.[19] When the increased requirements for 1944 became known, the ASF authorized an immediate increase in the Signal Corps' OCS to 1,500 capacity for the first four months of 1944.[20] By then it was impossible to produce the officers until late in 1944, since nearly all of the positions required additional technical school training of at least three months. The Signal Corps, which had begun the fiscal year with a plethora of officers, ended the period with far too few. In spite of a mad scramble to find the men and a resort to various temporary expedients, many requisitions for loss replacements of officers remained unfilled.

Strength

Notwithstanding the valiant attempts of the War Department to account for every last soldier on its rosters at any time, the exact statistics were often in doubt. It was particularly difficult for the Signal Corps to give exact figures on its soldiers, dispersed here, concentrated there, engaged in a multitude of communications duties all over the world. The wealth of detail necessary in strength reports partially defeated the purpose. Indeed, the War Department had recognized this fact when, in the summer of 1943, it authorized theater commanders to employ bulk allotments of men for overhead, that is, for administrative functions. In addition, the War Department had authorized the organization of provisional units to meet urgent combat needs.[21] Therefore, only the individual commanders in the theaters could know exactly what troops each theater had or how specialists were distributed within the theaters. The troop bases not only divided the Army into three main categories—AAF, AGF, and ASF—but added a fourth, Miscellaneous. That group contained trainees, including Army Specialized Training Program (ASTP) students, men assigned to War Department agencies, certain medical technicians, patients awaiting discharge, and an overseas overhead figure that covered everything not set up under a table of organization. For example, a bulk allotment of more than 3,000 men went to the North African theater for use in establishing a group of provisional signal organizations needed temporarily.[22]

As of June 1943, the Signal Corps estimated its enlisted strength at 287,000 and its officer strength at 27,004. From a

[19] Qtrly Rpt, OCSigO Mil Pers Br, 15 Oct 43–15 Jan 44.

[20] CSigO, Annual Rpt, FY 44, p. 459.

[21] AG Ltr, AG 322 (5–6–43) OB–I–SPMOU–M, 29 May 43, sub: Orgn of Units by Overseas Comdrs.

[22] OCSigO R&W Action 1, Chief Mil Pers Br to Chief P&T Sv, 21 Dec 44, sub: Overhead Allotments for Overseas Theaters. OCSigO Career Mgmt Br Card File, Units and Instals.

peak reached in August of that year, officer strength declined slightly during the next 12 months, while enlisted strength rose. On 1 May 1945 total strength reached 321,862. At that time the Signal Corps represented 3.9 percent of the Army.[23]

The ups and downs of the Signal Corp strength problems during World War II reflect the personnel expansion and contraction of the Army as a whole. But the Signal Corps percentage increase in strength in the period June 1940 to June 1944 was greater than that of the Army as a whole. While the Army increased 3,139 percent, the Signal Corps grew 5,422 percent. Or, expressed another way, the Signal Corps in 1944 was more than 54 times as large as it had been in 1940.[24]

Military Personnel Procurement, 1944–45

In the earlier war years, the Signal Corps had solved its manpower procurement problems in a variety of ways not available to it in 1944–45. The Affiliated Plan, the Electronics Training Group organization, the special Signal Corps use of the Enlisted Reserve Corps—these and other successful manpower procurement plans discussed in the two previous volumes of this subseries were either closed

or in the process of being closed by mid-1943.[25] Signal Corps personnel officers felt that had the Signal Corps depended entirely upon "normal" channels of manpower procurement, it "would have failed miserably in its wartime mission." [26] The special procurement programs initiated by General King, chief of the Military Personnel Branch of the Office of the Chief Signal Officer from October 1941 until January 1943, and his successor, Lt. Col. Duncan Hodges, tipped the balance. These programs enabled the Chief Signal Officer to fill both the commitments foreseen by the War Department and the very large unanticipated demands that arose. Evaluating their work, General Code remarked after the war that "King and Hodges did a truly wonderful job in staffing the military training activities. They were . . . always way ahead of the parade . . . thereafter all you had to do was coast on the training job and see that you received your proper quota of bodies." [27]

Officer Procurement

In August 1943 the Signal Corps reached its peak World War II officer

[23] (1) Qtrly Rpts, OCSigO Mil Pers Br, Jun 43 through Jun 45, passim, contained in Qtrly Rpts, 1 Jul 43–Oct 43, 15 Oct 43–15 Jan 44, and Annual Rpt, FY 45. (2) Strength of the Army (STM-30) Reports, 1 May 45.

[24] Capt Wilson G. Burden, OCSigO Mil Pers Br, Signal Corps Strength (1945), pp. 2–3. SigC Hist Sec file. Figures compiled from: (1) Annual Rpts, TAG, FY 40 and FY 41; (2) Strength of the Army Rpts (STM-30); and (3) SigC Mil Pers Br Strength Rcds.

[25] For discussion of these plans, 1941 to mid-1943, see Terrett, The Emergency, pp. 20, 21, 180, 207, 288–91, and Thompson, Harris, et al., The Test, pp. 39–45, 49, 57, 207, 209–12, 247, 312–18, 339.

Detailed accounts are contained in the following documents: (1) Ruth F. Sadler, History of the Signal Corps Affiliated Plan (1944), SigC Hist Monograph C-4; (2) Ruth F. Sadler, History of the Electronics Training Group in the United Kingdom (1944), SigC Hist Monograph C-5; and (3) Maj John F. Bullock, OCSigO Mil Pers Br Study, Direct Commissioning of Signal Corps Officers (1945). All in SigC Hist Sec file.

[26] Burden, SigC Strength, p. v.

[27] Ltr, Code to Harris, SigC Hist Div, 14 Aug 58. SigC Hist Sec file.

strength of 27,448.[28] This figure represented an increase of approximately 6,900 percent over the 1939 total of 400.[29] The prewar 400 (which old-time Regulars referred to as the Light Light Brigade) represented both Regular Army and Reserve officers; about 350 held RA commissions at that time, and only 30 more for a total of 380 in 1943.[30] The overwhelming majority of the officers who served the Signal Corps in World War II were commissioned during the war period. About 80 percent earned their commissions at officer candidate schools or in the Reserve Officers Training Corps (ROTC); less than 20 percent by direct commission.

The Signal Corps used the term *direct commissioning* to define the status of all officers who were not products of the OCS or ROTC. The 5,250 officers in this group included Electronics Training Group (ETG) officers, those secured under the Affiliated Plan, and those procured directly from civil life under the so-called Specialist Plan. They were more valuable than their numbers would suggest because they all possessed special, hard-to-get experience and knowledge.

By mid-1943 the sources for officers in the "rare bird" category had practically dried up. Selective service, various branches of the armed services, and essential industry had drained them. War Department moves to limit and centralize officer procurement culminated in the establishment of the Officer Procurement Service (OPS) late in 1942.[31] Further restrictions by redefinition to include only individuals who could not be secured through any available military training program and whose services were absolutely vital rang down the curtain on these programs. From that date on, OPS assumed sole responsibility for the commissioning of civilians in all branches of the Army.[32]

From early 1942, when the Signal Corps began putting its prewar Affiliated Plan into action, until the last request on 8 October 1943 for active duty orders on an enlisted man to be assigned to an affiliated unit, the plan brought in 1,281 officers and 4,146 enlisted men.[33] These men provided the nucleus for 404 affiliated Signal Corps units. Of the forty-five sponsoring companies, the overwhelming majority were from the telephone industry.[34] Such corporations and associations as the Western Electric Company, Inc., the Research Council of the Academy of Motion Picture Arts and Sciences, the Eastman Kodak Company, the International Federation of American Pigeon

---

[28] (1) Bullock, Direct Commissioning of SigCO's, p. vii. (2) CSigO, Annual Rpt, FY 44, Chart opposite p. 456, Growth, SigC vs. Total Army.

[29] Col. Floyd T. Gillespie and Robert H. Clearman, "Wartime Signal Training," *Signals*, II, No. 1 (September–October 1947), 21.

[30] Bullock, Direct Commissioning of SigCO's, p. vii.

[31] (1) WD Cir 367, Officer Procurement Service, 7 Nov 42. (2) AR 605–10 WD, Commissioned Officers, 30 Dec 42. (3) AG Memo S605-3-43, 15 Jan 43, sub: Off Proc. (4) Memo, CSigO for All Svs, Divs, and Brs, OCSigO and All SigC Exempted Acts, 20 Jan 43, sub: Limitations on Off Proc Effective 15 Jan 43. SigC SPSMP 210.1 Gen, 20 Jan 43.

[32] CSigO, Annual Rpt, FY 44, p. 293.

[33] Qtrly Rpt, OCSigO Mil Pers Br, 1 Jul 43–Oct 43, p. 7.

[34] Ltr, Gen Ingles, CSigO, to Dr. Buckley, President of Bell Telephone Labs, and Others, 12 Oct 43. SigC SPSMP Affiliated Units, 1943. Bell Telephone alone supplied 37.9 percent of the affiliated officer strength and the independent telephone companies 28.2 percent. CSigO, Annual Rpt, FY 44, Chart opposite p. 469.

Fanciers, and the American Racing Pigeon Union also gave valuable aid.

The ETG plan, from its inception in 1941 until its close in 1943, brought the Signal Corps 2,200 electrical engineers from a critically short labor market.[35] Of these men, 900 were trained in England. The ETG in London was disbanded late in 1943.[36] On 2 December, ETG headquarters issued its last order, General Order No. 7, closing out its own activities. Later ETG sections (19 and 20) had been sent to MIT, Harvard, and Camp Murphy for training.[37]

Enlisted Personnel

The October augmentation of the 1943 Troop Basis created a serious manpower problem for the Signal Corps. The Corps was obligated to secure and train 17,000 enlisted men in time to ship the units overseas for contemplated operations during 1944 in Italy, in the Pacific, and especially in the Normandy invasion. It could not look to the selective service, whose processes were bringing in altogether inadequate numbers of inductees. Moreover, the Assistant Chief of Staff for Training, G–3, had ruled that fillers for newly activated units must be drawn direct from reception centers, even though the priority for drawing such personnel was too low to permit the units to be activated in time for shipment.[38]

On the other hand, requisitions for loss replacements enjoyed the highest priority. Actually, this created a situation in which men could be pulled out of training battalions faster than they could be brought in. Heretofore, the RTC's had trained a large proportion of both fillers and loss replacements. When special units had to be formed—and the Signal Corps was forever being called on for special units not on the troop basis—they could be provided in less than six months by taking men from the RTC's, schools, and small training battalions, and by robbing existing units of specialists. With the RTC's restricted to loss replacements and with fewer qualified men available from existing signal units, the Signal Corps had to devise some plan to meet both the October augmentation of the troop basis and the yet unknown special demands sure to arise.[39]

The Signal Corps steadily maintained that RTC and school training were both essential if signal units were to perform effectively, especially in view of the varying lengths of time needed to teach different signal specialties. The ASF recognized the validity of this position. Early in 1943, when the Signal Corps converted its TOE units to more flexible cellular teams, it organized the 847th and 848th Training Battalions at Camp Crowder, Missouri.[40] A third, the 840th, had been activated in September 1943. Signal Corps training officers, casting about for some method of getting men they needed early enough to train them effectively, advanced an idea that the

[35] (1) Bullock, Direct Commissioning of SigCO's, pp. 63–64. (2) CSigO, Annual Rpt, FY 44, Chart opposite p. 470, ETG, Growth to 31 Dec 43.

[36] WD AGO 322, 4 Nov 43, PC–A, 15 Nov 43, Disbandment of Electronics Training Group.

[37] (1) Qtrly Rpt, OCSigO Mil Pers Br, 15 Oct–15 Jan 44. (2) See below, pp. 534–35.

[38] (1) CSigO, Annual Rpt, FY 44, pp. 460–61. (2) Qtrly Rpt, OCSigO Mil Pers Br, 15 Oct 43–15 Jan 44. (3) Burden, SigC Enlisted Admin, pp. 55–56.

[39] Qtrly Rpt, OCSigO Mil Pers Br, 15 Oct 43–15 Jan 44, p. 13.

[40] The cellular concept and the organization of the training battalions are discussed at greater length above, p. 509.

ASF adopted for the other technical services as soon as its virtues became apparent. The mission of the training battalions, with some modification, could serve as a basis for requisitioning personnel. The battalions were considered refillable, after units had received source personnel for them, to the limit of units on the troop basis.[41] The men could be given school, RTC, and cellular team training, then transferred fully trained to the ASF service units on the troop basis.

Hard on the heels of the October augmentation of the 1943 Troop Basis came the 1944 Troop Basis, which called for 23,966 new Signal Corps enlisted men. The training battalions furnished enough enlisted men for composite units during most of calendar year 1944.[42] The most critical shortage of men occurred during the early part of the year. At that time, the first-phase signal units slated for early shipment overseas did not even have cadre personnel. The Signal Corps therefore asked for the return of all Signal Corps troops provided for the Army Specialized Training Program, which had replaced the Army's Enlisted Reserve Corps program late in 1942.[43] The G-3 agreed to the return of 3,000 men in February 1944, and a few months later gave up another increment of over 3,000.

Among these men were advanced electrical engineers, including former Signal Corps personnel; about 600 civil and mechanical engineers originally scheduled for Fort Belvoir (Corps of Engineers); 1,175 miscellaneous ASTP students traded from the AGF in exchange for a like number of Signal Corps students from Camp Murphy; and about 1,400 linguists. These and other miscellaneous transfers accounted for nearly 10,000 ASTP students transferred to the Signal Corps by end of April 1944.[44] They greatly helped the hard-pressed Signal Corps to meet its commitments.

Training

During the last two years of war the organization of the Signal Corps' three large training centers shifted to keep pace with the changing needs of war.[45] During most of the period, several different training activities were gathered together at the Eastern Signal Corps Training Center at Fort Monmouth; the Central Signal Corps Training Center at Camp Crowder; and the Western Signal Corps Training Center at Camp Kohler, California. Each center contained a replacement training center or a unit training center, or both, to provide basic military and technical training for enlisted men, and one or more schools to provide advanced technical training.

Signal Corps training activities took a sharp turn of direction in the summer of 1943. The strength of the Army reached its anticipated crest, and the need for loss replacements, fillers, and

[41] (1) CSigO, Annual Rpt, FY 44, p. 461. (2) Qtrly Rpt, OCSigO Mil Pers Br, 15 Oct 43–15 Jan 44, pp. 14–16. (3) Memo for Rcd, OCSigO Mil Pers Br, 20 Sep 43, sub: Priority for Refilling the 840th, 847th, and 848th Sig Tng Bns. SigC MT 320.2 Strength of the Army, Jan 42–Dec 43 (MT-133).

[42] Qtrly Rpt, OCSigO Mil Pers Br, 15 Jan 44–15 Apr 44, p. 2.

[43] For a general discussion of ASTP, see History of Military Training, ASF, Army Specialized Training Program to 31 December 1944, and Supplement, Army Specialized Training Program, 1 Jan–30 Jun 45. OCMH files.

[44] Qtrly Rpt, OCSigO Mil Pers Br, 15 Jan 44–15 Apr 44, pp. 15–16.

[45] See above, pp. 11–12, for list of training facilities in mid-1943.

new activations declined. Moreover, the adoption of the cellular plan of organization for signal units required the molding of different types of specialists to work together as members of smooth-functioning teams and their consolidation into complete units for overseas shipment on short notice.[46] The net effect of these factors converted the replacement training centers into unit training centers, increased the degree of Signal Corps control over the units it trained for the ASF, and reoriented school programs.

Unit and Team Training

Unit training, as the ASF used the term, meant specialized training of the different elements of a unit to function in skilled teams as a part of the whole. This training was given at technical training centers. Specialists were readied in schools, RTC's, and UTC's; upon activation, a unit received specialists who had completed their individual and team training. In contrast, the AGF trained the bulk of its Signal Corps men within the unit and sent to service schools only those specialists requiring a high degree of technical skill.[47]

Unit training centers trained two types of units, generally referred to as "standard" and "service" type. For many years the Signal Corps had trained the standard units—signal construction battalions, signal depot companies, signal

port service companies, signal construction companies, and signal repair companies—that performed missions required in all combat areas. The service type companies were the relatively new units built up of cellular teams and tailored to perform such special missions as might be required in a particular theater or for a particular objective.[48]

In the earlier war years under the War Department doctrine that each service should have training responsibility for all tactical units assigned to it, in many cases both ASF and AGF had trained certain units common to both.[49] By 1944 the ASF and AGF had agreed that AGF would activate and train service troop units for divisions and corps while ASF would activate and train troop units required for the communications zone in theaters. An arbitrary distinction was drawn between the only type of signal units still common to both services, the construction units. For the AGF, they became known as light construction units; for the ASF, as heavy. In War Department theory there was a difference between the two. The light construction battalion was intended to construct wire lines rapidly, following closely on the heels of a fast-moving army. Its lines were not intended to be permanent; they would be converted to permanent open wire lines later on by the heavy construction battalions assigned to the army group. But in practice in both the ETO and the Pacific the two types of units were used interchangeably. ASF and AGF training methods were

---

[46] CSigO, Annual Rpt, FY 44, p. 472.
For discussion of the cellular plan of organization see above, pp. 22ff.

[47] (1) Gillespie and Clearman, "Wartime Signal Training," *Signals*, II, No. 1, pp. 21–27. (2) History of Unit Training, Signal Corps Units, 7 December 1941–December 1945, p. 1. SigC Hist Sec file.

[48] Unit Training, SigC Tech Info Ltr 27 (Feb 44), pp. 68–70, 75–79.

[49] (1) Annual Rpt of the ASF, FY 44, p. 281. (2) History of Military Training, ASF, Unit and Replacement Training, pp. 57–61. OCMH files.

practically identical, and little was gained by the artificial distinction.[50]

Until mid-1943, most of the troops the Signal Corps had trained were those destined for tasks in lower-echelon communications systems. It was evident that, as the Allies pushed the battle fronts farther and farther into enemy territory in ever-widening areas, more Signal Corps men would be needed for the so-called higher echelon systems. In other words, instead of division and corps communications facilities, men would be required to operate the infinitely more complex communications systems between army and other associated headquarters, from army to army groups, and from army groups to still higher headquarters.[51]

Development of the Signal Corps Unit Training Program—Realization of the ultimate need for highly skilled unit teams for such line of communications missions had led to the activation of the first unit training center on 15 September 1942, and the organization of the first signal training battalions (the 847th and 848th), at Camp Crowder early in 1943.[52] These battalions were the first to be rebuilt under the new blueprint provided by TOE 11-500. Their reorganization order also provided for the activation of a third training battalion, the 840th, at the Eastern Signal Corps Training Center at Fort Monmouth.[53] Most of the men required for the new battalion and for the reorganization of the two older ones were to be picked up by tapping the loss replacement stream at the RTC's.

In the summer of 1943 the War Department attempted to adjust trainee capacity of the AGF and ASF to an annual intake consistent with 1944 troop requirements, although as yet these requirements were not firm. It appeared that the replacement training centers, which had already outlived their originally allotted time, could be converted safely to unit training centers. Accordingly, all Signal Corps replacement training was consolidated at Camp Crowder, which thereafter supplied all loss replacements and such other individual technicians as were needed.[54] The Eastern Signal Corps Replacement Training Center at Fort Monmouth was officially inactivated and the Eastern Signal Corps Unit Training Center was established on 10 August 1943, while the Western Signal Corps Replacement Training Center at Camp Kohler closed 31 December 1943 and the Western Signal Corps Unit Training Center opened on 1 January 1944.[55] The new mission of the reorganized training battalions became an A to Z proposition,

---

[50] 1st Lt Robert D. Strock, Signal Construction Troops Within the Theater Communications System (16 Jun 48), Sig Sch Monograph, pp. 4-9. Ft. Monmouth.

[51] CSigO, Annual Rpt, FY 45, p. 631.

[52] Except where otherwise noted, material is from: (1) Burden, SigC Enlisted Admin, p. 48; (2) Reinstein, Study of SigC Unit Tng, 1942–44, pp. 2, 15–19; (3) Hist of Unit Tng, SigC Units, 7 Dec 41–1 Dec 45. All in SigC Hist Sec file.

[53] AG Ltr 322 (20 Sep 43), OB-I-SPMOU-M, 21 Sep 43, sub: Orgn of Certain Sig Tng Bns.

[54] (1) 1st Ind, CSigO to CG ASF, 31 Jul 43, sub: SigC RTC's, on Ltr, CG ASF to CSigO, 19 Jul 43, sub: ASF RTC's. (2) Memo, ACofS G-4 for CG's ASF and AGF, 7 Jul 43, sub: RTC's. Both in SigC 353.

[55] (1) Ltr, CSigO to CG ESCTC, 5 Aug 43, sub: Deactivation of ESCRTC and Activation of ESCUTC. SigC 352 Ft. Monmouth 4, Aug–Dec 43. (2) SO 30, Hq ESCTC, 10 Aug 43. (3) History of the Western SigC Tng Ctr, Sep 42–Sep 44, p. 57. SigC Hist Sec file. (4) CSigO, Annual Rpt, FY 44, p. 479.

taking in raw recruits and turning out fully trained teams of specialists.[56] That meant receiving and processing fillers from reception centers, conducting basic training and short-term specialist training, sending long-term specialists to special schools, and, after these preliminaries were finished, forming the specialists into cellular teams and conducting organized team training. In short, the metamorphosis of RTC's into UTC's did not involve an overnight change in function, but merely a rearrangement of assigned responsibilities.[57]

A newly inducted soldier arriving from a reception center was attached to one of the companies of a training battalion for six weeks of basic training. Another six weeks of team training in another company of the battalion followed. Unit training, the final phase, occupied about eleven weeks of the trainee's time, either in a unit organized under the battalion or in a tactical unit being trained at the center. In actual practice, especially in 1944 when many units were being shipped overseas, it was not always possible to provide a full six weeks of team training as a prerequisite to unit training. Under MTP-2, Mobilization

Training Program for Signal Corps Personnel, which became effective 1 July 1944, the six weeks of unit training began as soon as 75 percent of the men were qualified in their basic specialty and present with the unit for training.[58]

In the spring of 1944 the ASF introduced an important training reorganization, intended to unify and integrate training methods and procedures among all the technical services.[59] Under the new plan, all remaining branch RTC's of the various technical services and many of the UTC's were converted into ASF training centers. The ASFTC's were to act as personnel clearinghouses as well as training centers. Training center commanders took over assignment of personnel, previously an AG responsibility. All trainees received the same basic training for the first six weeks, after which they could be conconverted readily from one service to another, as requirements demanded, by undergoing instruction in the basic technical subjects of the new service.[60]

Since the new ASF training plan was practically identical with the unit and team training plan the Signal Corps had placed in effect more than a year earlier in its UTC's, the reorganization affected the Signal Corps very little. Camp Crowder became an ASFTC, but the unit training centers at Camp Kohler and Fort Monmouth continued as Class II, exempted installations, under the com-

---

[56] AG Ltr 322 (14 Dec 43), OB-I-SPMOU-M, 15 Dec 43, sub: Reorgn of 840th, 847th, 848th Sig Tng Bns.

[57] As formally stated, the mission of the UTC's was to form and train cellular teams organized under TOE 11-500 and to activate and train independent units in all phases, including preparation for overseas movement (POM) and shipment to ports of embarkation. In addition, the UTC's trained individual soldiers in Signal Corps specialties at the replacement training center level. (1) Hist of the Western SigC Tng Ctr, Sep 42-Sep 44, passim. (2) History of the Eastern Signal Corps Unit Training Center, Aug 43-Jan 45, passim. SigC Hist Sec file.

[58] MTP-2, 1 Jul 44.

[59] (1) ASF Cir 104, sec. III, 15 Apr 44, sub: Plan for Training Certain ASF Enlisted Men. (2) History of Mil Tng, ASF, Unit and Replacement Tng, p. 163.

[60] (1) Hist of Mil Tng, ASF, Unit and Replacement Tng, pp. 167-68. (2) Memo, Matejka, Chief P&T Sv OCSigO, for CSigO, 29 May 44. SigC MP 337 Confs, May 44-Nov 44.

mand of the Chief Signal Officer. At Crowder, although ASF scrutinized programs more closely, it approved them almost automatically. During the fiscal year 1944 Camp Crowder received 36,725 men for training and shipped out over 37,000. Of these, more than 12,000 went on to service and civilian schools for further instruction; 1,880 entered the ASTP courses; 810 became officer candidates; the remainder received various duty assignments.[61]

The ASF reorganization plan also introduced the preactivation training program. Essentially, this merely provided that all recruits were to be trained first as individuals before being assigned to units for unit training. This marked the abandonment of the old system, under which fillers for newly activated units often had been supplied directly from the reception centers, a practice the Signal Corps had resisted vigorously from the beginning. The preactivation training the ASF decreed was essentially what the Signal Corps gave its units in its signal training battalions. Recognizing this fact, the ASF readily agreed to exclude Fort Monmouth and Camp Kohler from designation as ASFTC's. Both the ASF director of training, Maj. Gen. Walter L. Weible, and officers in the ASF's Military Training Division and Military Personnel Division stated that they were well satisfied with Signal Corps training and did not wish to interrupt it.[62]

One training problem, never solved to the Signal Corps' satisfaction, concerned the length of time devoted to technical training. The War Department stressed basic training, to develop "a soldier first, a technician second." Actually, many Signal Corps troops, particularly those ASF units on duty in the communications area, served the Army best if they were, first of all, skilled technicians. Signal units were trained with a particular mission in mind and, as far as possible, for the probable terrain and climatic conditions under which they would work. Inspections to determine their state of readiness for the most part were confined to the scope of their technical tasks, and it was not expected that Signal Corps units should be highly proficient in front-line combat tactics.[63] Nonetheless, in most cases, basic training occupied more time than technical training and came first in the training cycle. If the training period had to be cut short, it was the technical training that suffered.

In the latter half of calendar year 1944, the overseas theaters began calling for signal units at an accelerated rate. For example, the 65th and 97th Signal Battalions had a scheduled readiness date of 20 October, but early in August requests came from the ETO asking that the two units be shipped immediately for Ninth Army operations.[64] The unexpectedly rapid advance of the Allied armies in Europe after the breakout from Normandy upset activation schedules. In the Pacific, operations scheduled to begin on 15 February 1945 actually started three months earlier, about 15 November 1944.

[61] Annual Report, ASF Training Center, 1944.

[62] OCSigO R&W Action 1, Matejka to CSigO, 4 May 44, sub: ASF Tng Ctr and Effect Upon SigC Tng Activities, Tab DD to Memo, Matejka for CSigO, 29 May 44, cited in n. 60(2).

[63] 2d Ind, Weible, Dir Mil Tng ASF, to CG 7th Sv Comd, 14 Jul 44, without basic Ltr. SigC 353 Gen, 1944 (MT-270).

[64] Memo, Col Joe J. Miller, SigO Ninth U.S. Army, for Gen Simpson, 8 Sep 44. SigC EO DCSigO, file C.

Both theaters demanded that units scheduled for later shipment be sent forthwith, in their "present state of training." Between June and December 1944, the Signal Corps shipped nearly 25,000 men in units overseas, a greater number than in any other 6-month period during the war. Shipments for the entire fiscal year, ending June 1945, stood at 32,451 men. Nearly half, 14,959, were shipped before completing their training.[65]

When these units arrived in the theater not all, of course, were able to perform their technical functions satisfactorily and rapidly. The ETO resorted to many improvisations and was forced into a considerable amount of unanticipated training because technical training in the United States had been cut short.[66] The Chief Signal Officer, anticipating criticism, in the summer of 1944 again asked that the ASFTC at Camp Crowder stress technical training "instead of putting all the emphasis on the basic training, which is now the case." He also suggested lengthening the training week to fifty-four hours, which was done.[67] However, his admonition that, "since we have a woefully insufficient over-all time, we must spend it on the technical phases of training," went unheeded.[68]

Although the Signal Corps remained dissatisfied with the length of time devoted to technical training, its training officers could take some satisfaction from the fact that the Signal Corps' early inauguration of the plan that the ASF later adopted as preactivation training made it possible for the units to be shipped at the time they were needed. The use of the special companies and signal training battalions for the training of cellular companies, particularly those requiring long-term training, proved to be an invaluable training contribution. Officers calculated that 14,940 enlisted men shipped during the fiscal year 1945 would have been delayed in shipment one to ten months if they had not been trained in the training battalions before their units were activated.[69]

Training Cellular Teams—At the unit training centers, the Signal Corps readied cellular teams in a great variety of specialties. Among them were small and medium depot teams; crystal-grinding teams; radio broadcast and radio repair teams; very high frequency installation and maintenance teams; 40 kilowatt multichannel multiplex radiotypewriter teams; cable repair, open wire, wire repair, and operations teams; inspection and maintenance teams; signal center teams; newsreel assignment teams; enemy equipment intelligence teams; still picture laboratory teams; film reel, reader, recorder, developing, paper processing, enlarger, and mail section teams.[70] In this

[65] (1) CSigO, Annual Rpt, FY 45, p. 624. (2) Hist of Unit Tng, SigC Units, 7 Dec 41-1 Dec 45, Tab A and Incls 1 Through 9.

[66] USFET Gen Bd Rpt, Study No. 112, Signal Corps Personnel, Training Command, and Administrative Structure, p. 3.

[67] (1) Ltr, Gen Ingles, CSigO, to Maj Gen Clarence H. Danielson, Hq 7th Sv Comd, 21 Sep 44. SigC EO DCSigO, file C. (2) Ltr, Matejka, Chief P&T Sv OCSigO, to Akin, USAF SWPA, 4 Dec 43. OCSigO Career Mgmt Br, Card file, Units and Instals.

[68] Ltr, Ingles, CSigO, to Danielson, Hq 7th Sv Comd, 15 Oct 44. SigC EO DCSigO, file D.

[69] Hist of Unit Tng, SigC Units, 7 Dec 41-1 Dec 45, p. 14.

[70] (1) Ltr, Matejka, Chief P&T Sv OCSigO, to CG ESCTC, 9 Dec 43, sub: Tng Progs for Cellular Type Teams. (2) OCSigO R&W Action 1, Lt Col Arthur A. McCrary, Com Coordinating Br, to Mil Tng Br OCSigO, 18 Dec 43, sub: Mission of Cellular Type Teams and Incl, Mission of Cellular Type Teams. Both in SigC 353 Gen 39, Dec 43.

multiplicity of designations were those such as the signal center teams with which line troops were thoroughly familiar, and others such as the enemy equipment intelligence teams of which they had scarcely heard. Yet even the signal center teams faced new skill requirements. Linguists were sought for them— men who spoke French, Russian, Dutch, Spanish, Norwegian, Polish, Turkish, Chinese, Portuguese, Greek, or Italian.[71] In 1944 Camp Crowder trained and shipped overseas 17 foreign language teams prepared to handle communications between U.S. armies and the armies of Allied nations. Six of the teams spoke Chinese; 4, Italian, 3, Russian, 2, French, and 1 team each was trained in the Dutch and Norwegian languages.[72]

Japanese language training in civilian institutions was one of the benefits the Signal Corps reaped from ASTP.[73] At the request of the Chief Signal Officer, the Army Specialized Training Division of ASF in September 1943 began training men in Georgetown University, Stanford, and the University of California. The 3-month course served as an introduction to further courses in reading and writing Japanese that the Signal Corps conducted at Arlington Hall, Virginia. The Signal Corps' standards for admission specified college graduates with considerable training in languages, preferably the classics, and a very high academic record. The ASTP, unable to select men on the same basis, required an Army General Classification Test score of 135 or better, and

at least two years of college training. Despite initial Signal Corps fears that such ASTP candidates could not master the work, a total of 206 out of 254 enrollees successfully completed the extremely intensive and very difficult course.[74]

The signal sections of the enemy equipment identification teams required basic intelligence instruction, which the Signal Corps was not prepared to give.[75] The teams therefore went to the Intelligence Training Center at Camp Ritchie, Maryland, where the Signal Corps' experimental and unused psychological warfare units had received their training earlier.[76] At Ritchie the EEIS teams studied the German and Japanese Army organization, particularly the disposition of enemy signal troops and signal equipment. Teams learned to interpret photographs with a view to pinpointing radar and other communications installations, to use maps and terrain intelligence, and studied wire surveillance and enemy wire-tapping methods. These subjects consumed seventy-two hours. If time permitted, an additional eight hours provided eminently practical instruction in hand-to-hand Judo training, "chamber of horrors" tests, firing with enemy weapons, and lectures on booby traps.[77]

EEIS teams, each composed of five officers and six enlisted men, were provided

---

[71] Memo, Capt Morton A. Rubin for Chief Mil Tng Br OCSigO, 13 Jul 43, sub: Status of Sig Ctr Teams. SigC 353 Gen, Aug 43 (MT-174).

[72] ASF, Annual Rpt, FY 45, p. 151.

[73] WD Memo, W615-72-42, 26 Dec 42, and WD Memo, W350-197-43, 17 Jul 43.

[74] Hist. of Mil Tng, ASTP, 1 Jan-30 Jun 45, inserted carbon copy, pp. 1-3.

[75] Memo, Deputy Dir Intel ASF for CSigO, 17 Feb 44, sub: Enemy Equip Intel Sv Teams. ASF file SPINT 210.684.

[76] Memo, Strong, ACofS, G-2, for ACofS G-3 WDGS, 3 Mar 43, and 1st Ind, CSigO to ACofS G-2, 25 Mar 43. SigC OR 320.3 Psychological Warfare Br, 011-S.

[77] (1) Memo, Chief P&T Sv OCSigO for CG ASF, 11 Mar 44, sub: Tng of EEIS Teams. SigC 353 Gen 3, Mar 44. (2) Ltr, CSigO to ACofS G-2 WDGS, 13 Apr 44, sub: Curricula of Sp Intel Course. SigC 353 Gen MT-270.

to each army.[78] All members had to be men of special qualifications, rated for general service, because immediately upon completion of training they would be sent overseas, as would the linguists with the signal center teams.[79] Another type of team used in intelligence operations, platoon traffic analysis units organized at the ESCUTC, underwent specialist training at Arlington Hall. These units operated in conjunction with radio intelligence companies, analyzing a tremendous bulk of intercepted traffic, and received training even beyond this phase in an active theater of operations.[80]

The development of on-the-job training became the most important technique used in readying cellular teams. The MT11–2, issued 1 July 1944, emphasized applicatory training methods for all line of communications troops. The Signal Corp had used such techniques since the beginning of the war. As early as 1942, teams from the 822d Signal Fixed Radio Station Company had been placed in operating installations of the ACAN throughout the United States. In succeeding months, units were assigned to locations wherever functional on-the-job training opportunities existed. Photographic units learned their trade on actual photo assignments at the Signal Corps Photographic Center at Astoria, Long Island; base depot companies, base maintenance companies, repair teams, and storage and issue teams trained at various Signal Corps depots;

40-kilowatt multichannel radioteletype teams worked on the transatlantic systems in the War Department Signal Center in Washington; and the intelligence teams were assigned variously to Arlington Hall, Vint Hill Farms station, Two Rock Ranch, and the Signal Security Agency.[81]

In February 1943 the Signal Corps had established the Plant Engineering Agency to supply, install, and maintain the fixed plant equipment for the vast and ever growing chain of navigational and communications stations of AACS.[82] The requirement for training many small teams of men needed to install and maintain the AACS equipment led to the opening of the Plant Assembly Center in Philadelphia in July. The Brookline Square Country Club at Upper Darby, Pennsylvania, near Philadelphia, provided housing and training space for the new center. At least one transmitter of each type installed by PEA was available at Brookline for study, and antenna erection courses included the study of those used for navigational aids.[83] Enlisted men received instruction in outside plant construction; weather station, airdrome control, loop range, Adcock range, and radio and teletype point-to-point installations; telephone switchboard installations; cable splicing; and diesel engine installation, operating, and maintenance. The Planetarium of the Benjamin Franklin Institute at Philadelphia conducted tours, lectures, and demonstrations for the weather station classes. Cable splicers from the Phila-

[78] Davis, "Technical Intelligence and the Signal Corps," *Signals*, III, No. 6 (July–August, 1949).

[79] Memo, CSigO for Dir AST Div ASF, 16 Apr 43, sub: Enlisted Linguists for Sig Ctr Teams. SigC 353 Gen 3, Mar 44.

[80] Ltr, Chief P&T Sv for CG ESCTC, 14 Apr 44, sub: Tng Directive for Traffic Analysis Units. SigC 353 Gen MT–270.

[81] Hist of Unit Tng, SigC Units, 7 Dec 41–1 Dec 45, pp. 18–21.

[82] Thompson, Harris, *et al.*, *The Test*, pp. 436–39.

[83] Memo, Lt Col R. R. Kilgore for Chief P&T Sv, 5 Jan 44, sub: PEA, Philadelphia. SigC 353 Gen 1, Jan 44.

delphia Electric Company demonstrated methods of power cable splicing, which was particularly helpful because the center had few power facilities available. Officers' courses were highly flexible, designed to take advantage of the individual's previous training and experience. After graduating from the center, many of the students received training in courses conducted at Fort Monmouth and elsewhere.[84] Even then, in many cases, months of field experience were necessary before the men could undertake some of the installations work PEA was called on to perform.

On-the-job-training offered many practical advantages, but operating installations could not assimilate all of the many units being trained during the latter part of the war. Instead, the Signal Corps set up whole simulated theater communications systems at the big unit training centers at Fort Monmouth, Camp Crowder, and Camp Kohler.[85]

The network system, signal facilities, and signal centers operated by cellular teams in training at Camp Kohler were representative of the others. By mid-1944 the Kohler Theater Headquarters Signal Center included a message center; teletypewriter, radio receiving and transmitting positions for remote operation; and a code room well equipped with cryptographic devices. From this signal center, trainees maintained communication with Kohler's simulated 20th Army Group headquarters, located

a half mile distant and equipped in the same way, and with the Camp Crowder simulated theater headquarters. There was also a base section headquarters, located at Davis, California. The signal centers were loaded with traffic, dummy messages prepared by typing students in training. All centers had telephone communication over the Camp Kohler training telephone system (the Cobra Exchange) and over leased commercial lines. The Cobra Exchange, though established primarily to train switchboard operators and maintenance men, became an important part of Kohler facilities when the post telephone system proved inadequate for the large number of students at the center.[86] Later, Kohler built the Rambler Exchange to provide an additional telephone training facility. A teletypewriter and telephone switchboard net of five simulated headquarters, pole line construction routes, a rhombic receiving area, and other refinements at Kohler helped to create a facsimile of the conditions that communications troops would encounter overseas.

Whenever possible, units were trained for the specific conditions of the theater area in which they would work. The 98th Signal Service Company, a tactical unit under training early in 1944 and destined for the ETO, would install, maintain, and operate a radio relay communications system. In training, the men of the company worked with the same equipment they would use in actual operations.[87] The 989th Signal Service

---

[84] (1) OCSigO R&W Action 1, Maj William A. Wood to P&T Sv and Mil Tng Br, n.d., sub: Tng Sch for Teletypewriter Mechanics, PEA. (2) Action 2, Chief ACS to P&T and Mil Tng Br, 18 Nov 43, same sub. Both in SigC 353 Gen CEB.

[85] CSigO, Annual Rpt, FY 44, p. 627.

[86] Hist, WSTC, sec. III, pp. 4–8.

[87] Ltr, Chief Mil Tng Br P&T Sv OCSigO to CG ESCTC, 1 Jan 44, sub: Tng Directive for the 98th Sig Sv Co. SigC 353 Gen, Jan–Feb 44 (MT-269).

Company, headed for the Pacific, was taught Melanesian pidgin English in addition to the usual subjects.[88] The 3184th Signal Service Battalion, activated at Camp Crowder in the spring of 1944, was trained to operate a signal center in a large headquarters.[89] Such a battalion might operate any kind of wire circuit (field wire, open wire, or spiral-four cable), large multiple switchboards that might have associated dial equipment, and associated switchboards at other locations. Its men would probably operate Sigaba or Sigcum equipment and be responsible for message center service. The maintenance and repair company was trained to maintain all wire and cable facilities within a limited radius of the headquarters, and to operate and maintain all vehicles in an emergency. Unit training, after completion of specialist and team training, concentrated on practice operations under difficult conditions involving frequent traffic overloads and shortages in teletypewriter and switchboard personnel. All members of the company were schooled in occasional continuous operation for 24-hour periods under the stresses and precautions of night operations.[90] Not all units would be so thoroughly trained, however.

Changing tactical situations sometimes altered or canceled the specific purpose for which a unit had been trained. The 998th Signal Service Company was activated and trained to operate one-kilowatt fixed radio stations at the terminals of a petroleum pipeline in an overseas theater, and the twelve 300-watt stations spaced along its length at airports. In such a network the traffic would be light and manual operation would suffice. Then ETO changed the route of the pipeline. Communications service already existed along the new line, and the teams of the 998th had to be retrained for work other than manual operation.[91]

Specialist School Training

While unit training was becoming firmly established, the training of individual specialists in Signal Corps schools continued largely within the original framework, which was inherently flexible enough to accept new methods, new requirements, and new trends.

On 11 January 1943 a third school augmented those at Fort Monmouth and Camp Crowder. The Western Signal Corps School was located at Davis, California, some twenty-eight miles away from the Western Signal Corps Training Center at Camp Kohler, of which it was a part administratively.[92] The new institution experienced few of the growing pains the older schools had felt.[93] The men sent there for communications training found no raw, bleak buildings set in muddy fields or sandy wastes. Instead, they moved into the

---

[88] Ltr, CSigO to CO 989th Sig Sv Co, 21 Aug 43, sub: Tng Prog for 989th Sig Sv Co. SigC 353 Gen, Aug 43 (MT–174).

[89] The 3184th was assigned to Headquarters, Western Base Section, when it went overseas.

[90] Ltr, CSigO ASF to CG 7th Sv Comd, 9 Mar 44, sub: Tng Directive for 3184th Sig Sv Bn. SigC 353 Gen 3, Mar 44.

[91] Memo, Chief Theaters Br OCSigO for Sig Unit Survey Br, 23 Oct 43, sub: 998th Sig Sv Co. SigC 353 Gen, Oct 43 (MT–176).

[92] The Western Signal Corps School was activated pursuant to Memo S105–22–42, Hq SOS, Nov 42.

[93] Lt. Col. Edward A. Allen was the first commander, followed by Lt. Col. James H. Ferrick on 4 March 1944. History of the ASF Western Signal Corps School, January 1943–October 1944. SigC Hist Sec file.

comfortable dormitories and classrooms of the University of California's College of Agriculture.[94] Despite conditioning on infiltration and obstacle courses and simulated combat in realistic dummy villages, living generally resembled life in college. It left the soldiers accustomed to hot and cold showers, soft bunks, and airy classrooms, not entirely ready for the physical hardships in theaters of war.[95]

Compared to the central and eastern schools, the authorized capacities of between 1,000 and 2,000 students at the Western Signal Corps School seemed low, but strength failed to reach even those figures. The school provided only radio and wire sections until July, when it added radar. Teaching followed the patterns established at Monmouth and Crowder. Except for students coming from non-Signal Corps sources, who had to be taught basic electricity and magnetism, the trainees were well qualified for the courses. Before the school was inactivated in October 1944, more than 95 percent of the 1,412 radio repair students and 1,730 operators enrolled had been graduated. The wire courses with a lower enrollment—1,212 in repeatermen courses and 405 in teletype maintenance—also graduated about the same proportion. Placement examinations contributed to the high average.[96]

Originally the radar school had been set up at the Presidio of San Francisco to train civilian mechanics as Signal Corps installation and maintenance crews. With its transfer to the Western Signal Corps School, the entire student quota was allotted to the Western Defense and Alaskan Commands, for training officers and enlisted men, not civilians, in radar repair. The courses were slanted specifically to meet the needs of the antiaircraft units of the two commands. Of the 85 officers, 555 enlisted men, and 6 civilians enrolled, more than 97 percent of those staying to the end of the courses were graduated.[97]

By this time the needs of the various theaters were better known than they had been earlier in the war. Combat tactics and equipment innovations were exerting a strong influence on training doctrine and practice at all Signal Corps schools. The issue to troops of the FM SCR–300 walkie-talkie in the summer of 1943, for example, inaugurated 144-hour courses in its use and care. Similarly, the introduction of radio and radar countermeasures opened up a new field of training activity.[98]

The National Defense Research Committee, the Navy, the Army Air Forces, and the Signal Corps were all engaged in projects designed to recognize and overcome the enemy's interfer-

---

[94] The University of California continued agricultural research in certain departments but put all its dormitories, classrooms, laboratories, gymnasiums, and athletic fields at the Army's disposal. Capt Frederick Reinstein, Study of Signal Corps Enlisted Schooling, 1939–44 (1945), SigC Hist Monograph C–8, p. 91. SigC Hist Sec file.

[95] Reinstein, Study of SigC Enlisted Schooling, 1939–44, p. 92.

[96] Hist of the ASF Western SigC Sch, Jan 43–Oct 44.

[97] Ibid.

[98] The Chief Signal Officer was assigned certain responsibilities for radio and radar countermeasures on 31 October 1942, but as late as August 1943 the responsibility for countermeasures operations in the theaters and for training specialists for the new service was still under study, still indefinite. (1) Ltr, TAG to CG AAF and CSigO, 31 Oct 42, sub: RCM. SigC EO 319.1 Rpts, 1944 (Code file). (2) Memo, Meade, Dir Opns Div OCSigO, for CSigO, sub: Special Pers and Tng Rqmts (Reporting on Conf, 10 Aug 43). SigC SPSOR 353 Gen.

ence in the ether lanes and to confound him by counterinterference. At the center of this activity was the radio operator, who had to learn to hear through the jamming, and the radar operator, who had to learn to distinguish between the genuine and the spurious signal on the oscilloscope.

The National Defense Research Committee devised a set of training aids, recordings embodying random noises and "bagpipe" sounds designed to be fed into the ear circuit. Other recordings combined jamming signals and speech by means of a mixing mechanism. The projects sounded simple, but it was not easy to rate student operators on the tests when students and instructors alike lacked experience in working through any sort of interference. Camp Coles Signal Laboratory prepared a "Listening Through Jamming" test record similar to a "Listening Through Noise" test record issued by the Psycho-Acoustic Laboratory of Harvard University. One side of the Signal Corps test record embodied random noises, the other "bagpipe" jamming signals.[99]

At best, radio jamming slowed up the speed of the fixed station operator, who used a typewriter to record the messages, or of the high-speed field operator who used a pencil. At worst, jamming could stop operations completely. Occasionally operators unfamiliar with jamming tore their sets apart looking for the source of the noise. Training radio operators to cope with enemy jamming greatly de-

layed their development of speed and accuracy, and therefore combat speed seldom equaled school speed until an operator had become accustomed to working under stress. Instructors learned that the higher a man's normal speed, the less jamming interference bothered him. An operator highly skilled in sending could practically annul the effects of deliberate interference with his transmissions, but this skill involved the use of tricks that were as individual as the operator. The enemy soon came to recognize them and was able to trace the movements of a unit by the transmissions of its radio operator.[100] Not all suspected enemy interference was real. For example, a station on Tontouta encountered interference on its air-ground frequencies nearly every day at the same time. Sleuthing eventually traced it to the cook's electric potato peeler.[101]

A radio net cast over a large part of the earth's surface, and serving all elements of the Army, required large numbers of operators of exceptional skill and ingenuity to cope with the many difficult situations into which they were plunged. In the early part of the war more criticism was leveled at radio operators than at any other product of Signal Corps training.

To improve the performance of radio operators in training, teams were assigned to the stations of the domestic radio network, which was being retained in a stand-by status for emergency use.

[99] The tests were administered according to the Harvard Laboratory's Manual of Instructions for Auditory Test, Series L, Type W, Ability to Listen to Noise. Ltr, Lt Col W. F. Atwell, Dir Camp Coles Sig Lab, to CSigO, 20 Mar 44, sub: "Listening Through Jamming" Test Rcd. SigC ET 413-44 RCM Tng folder 1.

[100] Notes on Conf, May 43, To Consider the Coordination of NDRC Projs, passim; Comments quoted: Maj F. E. Brady, p. 11; WO Masterson, p. 11. SigC ET 413.44 AJ folder 1.
[101] Capt Robert H. Kroepach, AC, Historical Data, 7th Army Airways Communications System Wing, 1944, p. 23. AAF Hq AACS, Ashville, N.C.

Members of the emergency staff served as instructors, and the students did not know that the presumably live traffic they were handling had been especially prepared for them by the Signal Security Agency with an eye to its possible interception by the enemy.[102] A system of monitoring student nets was instituted; more attention was given to the classification of operators as low speed, intermediate speed, and high speed, manual and automatic. When a new standard of code speed was adopted, students rated at twenty-five words per minute were found to be actually several words better than that. In brief, "so many weeks of instruction" became less impelling than "development of the specialist." [103] Radio security was stressed more. Nonetheless, General Somervell, aroused by reports from Pacific theaters, expressed dissatisfaction with radio operators produced in the Signal Corps' schools and suggested overtime use of the Fort Monmouth–Camp Crowder–Camp Kohler training network as a remedy.[104] But no one thing could turn a novice into an expert radio operator. Aptitude for the work, training, and combat experience all were needed to produce an expert, and jamming merely added another obstacle to becoming one.

Jamming multiplied the difficulties for the radarmen as well as for the radio operators. Radar was susceptible to interference by several types of emissions. A new technique by which moving pictures could be made of the cathode-ray indicators of radar equipment under conditions of jamming was put to use to produce training films for the AGF and AAF. Showing the films to general officers of the Army to acquaint them with the abilities of communications jamming units became "an essential part of radar countermeasures instruction." [105] The jamming course introduced at Camp Murphy cautioned that "every radar man must be able to recognize jamming, must know how to track in spite of it, and must be able to deal effectively with it." [106] A jamming signal generator for use in training with the SCR–296 radar set was ready for demonstration by July 1943 and was issued to the Coast Artillery School in September.[107] Somewhat later similar equipment went to the AAF.[108] In radar, as in radio, however, combat was the finishing school as well as the test.

Combat situations directed training projects into many new fields. Camp Crowder opened a malaria training area

[102] (1) Memo, Stoner, Chief Sig Opns Sv, for Chief Mil Tng Br OCSigO, 21 Jun 43, sub: Use of WD Domestic Radio-Telegraph Stations for Tng and Other Purposes and Their Maint for Emergency Use. (2) Ltr, CSigO to CG 5th Sv Comd, 21 Jun 43, same sub. Both in SigC 353 Gen, Jul 43 (MT–173).

[103] OCSigO R&W Action 1, Matejka, Chief P&T Sv OCSigO, to CSigO, 1 Apr 44, sub: Improvements in Radio Operator Tng. SigC 353 Gen 3 (Mar 44).

[104] Msg, CM–IN–5694, 14 Mar 44. SigC 353 Gen, 1944 (MT–270).

[105] (1) Ltr, CSigO to CG AAF, 7 Apr 43, sub: Radar Jamming. AAG 413.44–1 Radar 1943. (2) OCSigO R&W Action 1, Corderman, Chief Sig Sec Br, to P&T Sv, 2 May 44, sub: Motion Picture for Joint Chiefs of Staff. SigC 353 Gen, 1944 (MT–270).

[106] Southern Signal Corps School, Gun Laying Equipment Department, Jamming. SigC ET 413.44 RCM Tng folder 1.

[107] (1) Ltr, Winter, Chief Electronics Br OCSigO, to CG AGF, 19 Jul 43, sub: Recommended Countermeasures Equip Demonstration and Tactics. (2) Ltr, Brig Gen Lawrence B. Weeks, Comdt Coast Arty Sch, to Capt Donald E. Thomas, OCSigO, 2 Oct 43. Both in SigC ET 413.44 RCM Tng folder 1.

[108] Ltr, Col Winter to Dr. Suits, Chief Div 15 NDRC, 19 Oct 43. SigC ET 413.44 RCM Tng folder 1.

in August, one of the first in the country, as a result of reports from units such as the 835th Signal Service Battalion, which had gone to India in the early months of the war. The 835th suffered greatly from malaria and dysentery, and many of the men had to be invalided home for treatment.[109] Convalescent training, inaugurated in the summer of 1943, proved its worth as an aid to recovery as well as a means of developing skills.[110]

After the Navy Department was assigned cognizance over all antisubmarine activity and equipment, the Southern Signal Corps School and the Fort Monmouth School dropped their maintenance courses on magnetic airborne detectors and sonic buoy equipment, late in 1943.[111] On the other hand, the enemy's heavy use of land mines made it necessary to add mine detectors to linemen's TOE's, and courses in mine detection became part of the curriculum of the wire schools.[112] The advancing Army Airways Communications System called for greatly increased numbers of weather technicians. Meteorological equipment instruction, conducted initially at the Toms River Signal Laboratory and later transferred to the Eatontown Signal Laboratory in New Jersey, outgrew the laboratory facilities, which could provide training for no more than 2 classes of 20 men each in a 12-week course. In June

1944, when the AAF asked the Signal Corps to train 400 men as weather technicians, the Signal Corps was forced to propose that the Army Air Forces establish this type of training elsewhere.[113]

Photographic training took on new interest at Astoria with the introduction of color photography.[114] The Signal Corps quietly dropped its unrealistic requirement that a photographic officer must possess a degree in physics or engineering and substituted a requirement for journalistic experience.[115]

By mid-war, overseas theaters were operating a number of schools. The War Department kept them under close scrutiny, lest they mushroom and grow to rival the training centers in the zone of interior.[116] One such overseas training activity was the Signal Corps Training School in the Southwest Pacific Area. It had been organized at Fort Monmouth on 10 December 1943, under Lt. Col. Clayton Steele, and arrived in the theater on 29 March 1944. Its mission was to conduct short, intensive courses in Signal Corps specialties for selected replacements for overseas specialists. This overseas school had to build its facilities before it could teach. By July the structures were ready and the first 119 students had enrolled. By the end of the month, 547 men from SWPA were study-

---

[109] (1) Post Headquarters Diary, Camp Crowder, 19 Aug 44. (2) Signal Corps History, China-Burma-India, March–October 1944, *passim.* SigC Hist Sec file.

[110] Post Hq Diary, Camp Crowder, 27 Jan 44.

[111] Ltr, CG AAF to CSigO, 17 Aug 43, sub: Discontinuance of Tng on MAD and Sonic Equip. AAF 413.44-BC Radio.

[112] Ltr, CSigO to CO WSCTC, 14 Oct 43, sub: Extract From Monthly Ln Ltr. SigC 353 Gen, Oct 43 (MT-176).

[113] Memo, CSigO for CG ASF (probably 29 Jun 44), sub: Tng of Weather Equip Technicians. SigC 353 Gen 6, Jun 44.

[114] 1st Qtrly Rpt, Army Pictorial Service, 1945, p. 3. SigC Hist Sec file.

[115] TM 12–406, 30 Oct 43.

[116] (1) Ltr, Rumbough, CSigO ETO, to Meade, OCSigO, 22 Sep 43, sub: Tng of SigC Pers in This Theater. (2) Memo, Cansler, Asst Chief P&T Sv OCSigO, for Matejka, 30 Sep 43, sub: Tng of SigC Pers in Theaters. Both in SCIA file 4 Rumbough Rpts 1. (3) Ltr, Rumbough to Matejka, 9 Oct 43. SigC 353 Gen 36, 1943.

STUDENTS WATERPROOF BOXES *at the Processing and Packing School, New Caledonia.*

ing in eighteen courses.[117] Such training activities, bringing the school to the student rather than the student to the school, served a very useful purpose. They trained men in the specific specialties a theater needed, with no lost motion.

Especially in the last two years of war, combat theaters demanded that men be trained in a minimum of time. How to continue teaching the fundamentals, add new material made essential by combat experience, and still not extend the length of courses became a major problem. The Signal Corps steadfastly maintained that the quality of the end product, not the length of the training

course, should be the criterion for graduation.[118] Often the schools in the United States and overseas merged the training of officers and enlisted men in order to conserve time, facilities, and instructors, and because it was essential that officers be acquainted with what the enlisted technician had to know. Often, too, civilians were enrolled in the same classes with military men and women because of the close relationship of the functions for which each was responsible. This was true to a greater extent in the in-service or on-the-job courses conducted at Signal

---

[117] History, Signal Corps Training School, 1943–47. SigC Hist Sec file.

[118] (1) Ltr, Chief P&T Sv to CG ESCTC, 5 Apr 44, sub: Tng Time for SigC Specialist Tng in SigC Schs. SigC 353 Gen 4, Apr 44. (2) History, Eastern Signal Corps Training Corps, Quarterly Addendum, October 1943–June 1944. SigC Hist Sec file.

Corps depots and other administrative installations, however, than in the military schools.

Supply Training—Late in calendar year 1943, another specialized school, this one for supply training, opened at Camp Holabird, Maryland. Nothing in its prewar experience had prepared the Signal Corps for the size and complexity of the supply problems it encountered in World War II. It is not surprising that the number of officers well trained in supply procedures very quickly became insufficient, even though the depots began training courses for officers quite early, first at the Lexington Signal Depot in June 1942.[119] The Chief Signal Officer on 2 July 1942 directed the Philadelphia Signal Depot to establish a similar supply school for officers.[120] By the autumn of 1943, more than 2,100 officers had completed courses at these installations. Philadelphia had trained 851 officers in field supply. Another 736 had finished ground electronics supply courses at Lexington, where the number of students had exceeded the authorized capacity of the school by 74 percent during the summer. Still another 530 studying at the Dayton Signal Depot had completed courses emphasizing signal equipment for the Army Air Forces, particularly airborne equipment.

Although the Signal Corps specialist schools necessarily concentrated on courses designed to create graduates to fill operational assignments, they did not altogether neglect supply training. Fort Monmouth, for example, in July 1943 inaugurated a 60-day advanced course in signal supply subjects for field grade officers. Monmouth also injected problems covering supply under abnormal conditions into its field unit training.[121]

By summer 1943, enlisted men as well as officers were enrolled in depot supply schools, and on-the-job unit training at depots was assuming importance. The UTC at Camp Crowder sent wire repair sections of units in training to the Chicago Signal Depot, where the men spent eight weeks in practical work, repairing wire communications equipment in depot shops.[122] Parallel practical training went on in the simulated base camp at Crowder, where students repaired about 100 items of equipment weekly for the Chicago Signal Depot and shipped them back, ready for reissue to troops. Crowder sent the 212th Signal Depot Company to the Lexington Signal Depot to take an 8-week course. Two weeks were to be devoted to a paper problem into which tangled supply situations were injected; six weeks, to practical on-the-job repair work. Unhappily, the need for depot troops was so great at the time, in anticipation of the Italian campaign, that the entire course had to be compressed into two weeks' time so the company could be shipped overseas in mid-August.

---

[119] Ltr, CSigO to CO, Lexington Sig Depot, 4 Apr 42, sub: Tng School for Offs. SigC 352 Lexington Offs Tng Sch.

[120] (1) Ltr, Lt Col Raymond C. Hildreth, OCSigO, to CO PSD, 2 Jul 42. SigC 352 OCS No. 4, Jun–Aug 42. (2) Reinstein, Study of SigCO Schooling, 1939–44, pp. 184–86.

[121] (1) Ltr, CSigO to CG ESCTC, 4 Jun 43, sub: Sig SupO's Advanced Prog, and 1st Ind, ESCS to CSigO, 8 Jun 43. SigC 352 Ft. Monmouth 3, Mar–Jul 43. (2) Ltr, Actg Dir Sig Troops Div OCSigO to Comdt SigC Sch, 28 Jun 43, sub: Sig Sup Sv Offs Advanced Prog. SigC 353 Ft. Monmouth 3 (RTC), Jun–Jul 43.

[122] Ltr, CSigO to CO Chicago Sig Depot, 12 Jul 43, sub: Practical Tng for Wire Repair Secs of the 848th Sig Tng Bn. SigC 353 Gen 39, Dec 43.

These school and depot courses, together with other bits and pieces of specialized supply training such as special packaging courses given at other training locations, could not completely meet the need for supply officers and men. The Signal Corps recognized that supply training was quite as important as specialist training for operational assignments.[123] Thus when Camp Holabird became a Signal Corps installation, the Chief Signal Officer at once consolidated supply training there.[124] Holabird was one of the few military establishments that combined a post and a depot. It had "all the storage, packaging, and shipping facilities of a large military mail-order house," plus the classrooms, barracks, laundry, mess facilities, and other appurtenances necessary for housing, feeding, and training several thousand troops.[125]

The first class of 70 officers, arriving on 28 October 1943 before the depot was fully organized, found themselves acquiring practical experience in putting the depot's various activities into operation. A second class of 30 students reported on 16 December. The curriculum included requisitioning, receiving, warehousing and shipping, property accounting, and stock record procedures.[126]

Before the first officers arrived at Holabird, 144 enlisted men reported for enrollment in the frequency modulation radio school. The Signal Corps planned to use practical on-the-job training to qualify all radio repairmen as both FM and AM mechanics.[127] Frequency modulation repair training began in an open warehouse area, noisy and cold, lacking power outlets and storage and stockroom space. Although the FM school was classified as advanced training, as usual some of the students sent to take the course had no knowledge of radio, or even of electricity, and had to be given a preliminary course in basic radio.[128] Some 300 civilians, former employees of the ordnance depot previously housed on the post, were enrolled in supply classes to learn the differences between communications equipment and the ordnance items with which they had been working. By January 1944, Holabird's various courses accommodated 325 civilian and 500 military students.[129]

At Holabird, as elsewhere, new courses were added from time to time to meet changing needs. A course in crystal grinding was transferred from the Camp Coles Signal Laboratory to Holabird in November. Holabird initiated courses in nonelectrical instrument repair on the SCR-584 and in instructor guidance. Instruction included the AN/PRS-1, AN/TRC-2, and SCR-300 radio sets,

---

[123] Interv, SigC Hist Sec with Gen Tully, 2 Jun 45. SigC Hist Sec file.

[124] (1) ASF Cir 75, 8 Sep 43. (2) Ltr, Gardner, Asst Chief P&D Sv OCSigO, to CO Lexington Sig Depot, 27 Sep 43, sub: Tng of SigC SupO's. SigC 353 Gen 35, 1943. (3) Memo, Maj Mark L. Thompson for Dir Mil Tng ASF, 24 Dec 43, sub: Rpt of Tng Inspec of Holabird SigC Sch. SigC 353 Gen 1, Jan 44.

[125] Statement, George Schaun, Holabird Post Historian, 20 Jun 45, Min, P&D Conf, Jun 45. SigC Hist Sec file.

[126] Hist Rpt of Activities, Holabird Sig Depot, vols. I, II, and *passim.*

[127] (1) Hist Rpt of Activities, Holabird Sig Depot, I, 8. (2) Ltr, CSigO to CO Lexington Sig Depot, 23 Aug 43, sub: Radio Repair Secs. SigC 353 Gen 34, 1943.

[128] Hist Rpt of Activities, Holabird Sig Depot, I, 33.

[129] Memo Kilgore to Chief P&T Sv OCSigO, 5 Jan 44, sub: Holabird Sig Depot. SigC 353 Gen 1, Jan 44.

All activities at Holabird Signal Depot, including the school, were under the jurisdiction of the Procurement and Distribution Service, OCSigO, but military training matters were closely co-ordinated with the Personnel and Training Service.

about to be introduced in overseas theaters in the summer of 1944.[130] The Transportation Corps' railroad repair shop, which occupied part of the post, taught Signal Corps classes certain machine shop courses. The 1342d Service Unit, a Negro unit activated at Fort George G. Meade, moved to Holabird in October 1943 to continue training designed to give its members the equivalent of a third or fourth grade grammar school education before moving on to a replacement training center.[131] Supply officers of the 166th, 167th, and 168th Signal Photographic Companies received instruction in requisitioning, packaging, and storing photographic materials.[132] Military and civilian students qualified there for U.S. Army projection operators' permits, and still others learned maintenance and repair of photographic equipment.

A pressing need for frequency allocation officers overseas led the Signal Corps to establish an ionospheric utilization unit at Holabird. Collaborating closely with the Department of Terrestrial Magnetism of the Carnegie Institution of Washington and with the Psycho-Acoustic Laboratory at Harvard University, the Signal Corps training officers worked out a course that included instructions in the conversion of inonospheric data and the solution of actual problems. A hand-picked group of ASTP students, after an initial period of special training with the Interservice Radio Propagation Laboratory at the National Bureau of Standards, went to work immediately to produce information urgently needed by the AAF.[133]

In the 3-month period April through June 1944 Holabird graduated 269 officers, 847 enlisted men, and 288 civilians from the various courses. By then, Holabird's classes reflected the growing emphasis on team training and on-the-job techniques growing out of combat experience. Training of individual students in the standard supply courses declined. Only a handful of young officers were enrolled since most young officers were now being sent immediately to the overseas theaters. WAC and overage officers filled up the classes, which came to a close in midsummer. Crystal-grinding instruction ceased. Courses in the preservation and packing of equipment, tropicalization, personnel management and training, property disposal and salvage, and identification of equipment began.[134] The radar power school no longer maintained a regular schedule, its facilities being used for on-the-job training of civilians and signal units. The 221st and 222d Signal Depot Companies from Camp Charles Wood arrived in January; three signal

[130] The AN/PRS–1 mine detector for nonmetallic mines was a very ticklish piece of equipment to adjust and maintain. The device was analogous to a handmade laboratory instrument rather than a production item of equipment, and Holabird trained teams to introduce maintenance training into the theaters. (1) OCSigO R&W Action 1, Col Herbert G. Messer, Chief Ground Sig Equip Br, to Gen Colton, 9 May 44, sub: Maint of Mine Detector, AN/PRS–1. (2) Ltr, Actg Chief Mil Tng Br OCSigO to CG ESCTC, Ft. Monmouth, 18 May 44, sub: Tng of Radio Repairmen, SSN–648. Both in SigC 353 Gen, 1944, (MT–270).

[131] Hist Rpt of Activities, Holabird Sig Depot, I, 124.

[132] OCSigO R&W Action 1, Capt A. W. Seager, Equip Sec APS, to P&D Sv, 14 Dec 43, sub: Tng of Pers. SigC 353 Gen 39, Dec 43.

[133] (1) CSigO, Annual Rpt, FY 44, pp. 138, 141. (2) Hist Rpt of Activities, Holabird Sig Depot, I, 115.

[134] Unsigned Memo, 3 Apr 44. SigC OP 300.6 Memoranda for Br Chiefs, Jul 43–Jul 44.

repair companies were undergoing on-the-job training; other units followed.[135]

At Holabird, as at other training centers, it was difficult to get and hold a competent teaching staff. Urgent calls from combat theaters took away the younger military instructors. By January 1944, 120 of the instructors were civilians who had had to learn the subjects before they could teach them, and many of these men were subject to military call.[136]

The Lexington Signal Depot's unit training program began with the activation of the 216th Signal Depot Company at the depot on 16 January 1943. The 210th and 215th Signal Depot Companies supplied the cadre; Camp Crowder furnished fillers. The 8-week training course included practice in handling the paper work of the depot and in solving tangled situations purposely introduced, as well as practical on-the-job work.[137]

In August the 188th and the 189th Signal Repair Companies arrived for eight weeks' training in the repair of signal equipment. In the next two months the 185th and 186th Signal Repair Companies, two storage and issue sections of the 819th Signal Post Service Company, and several sections of the 825th Signal Repair Service Company received training at Lexington.

Aside from general supply training, the Signal Corps operated scores of specialized depot schools that trained men in desperately needed specialties throughout the war. The electronics power school, inaugurated at Lexington Signal Depot in May 1942 and later moved to Holabird Signal Depot in October 1943, is an example. This was the Army's first such school.[138] Many important types of electronic equipment depend on gasoline-powered or diesel-powered generators for their power source. Unless men were trained to operate and maintain these power sources, the most complex and important electronic equipment could be rendered impotent very quickly. The school encountered the full range of teaching difficulties—scarcity of qualified instructors, an almost complete lack of instructional literature, a lack of students competent enough or interested enough to train, and a shortage of equipment so severe that the units on which the students trained in 1942 could not be torn down for instructional purposes. Instead the equipment had to be maintained in a condition in which it could be shipped out, in operating condition, on eight hours' notice.[139] The Cummins Engine Company of Columbus, Indiana, helped tremendously by furnishing the school with equipment, textbooks, film strips, and other training aids.

The Lexington Supply School also trained numbers of special teams for urgent overseas assignments. Between December 1942 and November 1943 Lexington activated and trained twenty-four Signal Corps mobile technical crews composed of inspection and maintenance teams. Some were ground equipment specialists, others were especially trained for work on airborne signal items.

Aircraft Warning Training—By mid-1943 one of the most demanding of the

---

[135] Hist Rpt of Activities, Holabird Sig Depot, I, 47.

[136] Memo, Kilgore for Chief P&T Sv OCSigO, 5 Jan 44, sub: Holabird Sig Depot. SigC 353 Gen 1, Jan 44.

[137] Reinstein, Study of SigC Unit Tng, 1942–44, pp. 126–28.

[138] Lexington Signal Depot Schools, Tab A, Electronic Power School, p. 1. SigC Hist Sec file.

[139] *Ibid.*, p. 6.

Signal Corps training jobs was nearing its end. Aircraft warning duties had absorbed thousands of radar technicians, trained almost overnight in what was still an esoteric science. The Signal Corps and the Army Air Forces divided the training responsibility. The Southern Signal Corps School at Camp Murphy devoted itself to individual training, while the Air Forces' three unit training centers in Florida, California, and Virginia prepared Signal Corps ground radar units for field service with the Army Air Forces.[140]

Camp Murphy, following a pattern common to all military training centers during late 1943 and throughout 1944, reached its peak strength late in 1943 and then began a fairly rapid decline. In September and October 1943 more than 4,500 officers and enlisted men were enrolled in courses, 75 percent of them radar maintenance specialists for the AAF.[141] By May 1944 only about 1,500 were enrolled,[142] but the ratio of officer students to enlisted students rose sharply, reflecting a trend to qualify officers in technical subjects. In the fiscal year ending 30 June 1943, 10,226 enlisted men and 1,375 officers completed courses, but, in the following year, enlisted graduates dropped to 8,003 and officer graduates increased only slightly to 1,495.[143]

Two factors accounted for the economical concentration at Camp Murphy of a greater proportion of the Army's electronics training for officers in 1944. As pressure for enlisted radar specialists eased, it released facilities that could be utilized to train additional officers. Secondly, a War Department General Staff decision in late 1943 to discontinue training Electronics Training Group officers in British military schools provided a reservoir of officer students qualified to receive this type of instruction. The 19th and 20th ETG's, last of the second 500-student increment, had already been sent to Camp Murphy for preliminary instruction while they awaited transportation overseas. The men remained at the Florida school, and the overseas training was discontinued with the 18th ETG, then overseas.[144] With the exception of a few officers on research duty, all ETG students were returned to the United States for assignment. On 2 December 1943 the officer in command of the ETG in England officially disbanded the London headquarters, and all radar training was thenceforth concentrated in the United States.[145]

In general, aircraft warning officers followed a fixed training pattern. They learned the principles of radar at Harvard and their application at MIT. They moved next to Camp Murphy, where they supervised the installation and

---

[140] See above, p. 12, n. 38.

[141] Ltr, CSigO to CG ASF, 21 Sep 43, sub: Radar Tng AAF Pers. SigC 353 Gen, Sep 43 (MT–175).

[142] Capt Frederick Reinstein, History of Signal Corps Training, July 1944–December 1944 (1945), SigC Hist monograph C–12a, p. 37. SigC Hist Sec file.

[143] Reinstein, Study of SigCO Schooling, 1939–44, pp. 82–84.

[144] (1) Ltr, CSigO to CG ASF and CG AAF, 29 Mar 43, sub: Overseas ETG Prog. (2) WDGS DF, ACofS Opns Div WDGS to CG ASF, 22 Apr 43, sub: Overseas ETG, Jun 43–Oct 44. (3) Ltr, CSigO to CG ASF, 12 Oct 43, sub: Disbandment of ETG, ETOUSA. (4) AG Ltr to CG ETO, 22 Oct 43, sub: Disbandment of ETG. (5) Ltr, CSigO to CG ASF, 3 Nov 43, sub: Disbandment of ETG, ETOUSA. All in SigC 352.11 ETG, Jun 43–Oct 44.

[145] (1) AG Ltr to CG ETO, 15 Nov 43, sub: Disbandment of the ETG. AG 322 (4 Nov 43) PO–A. (2) GO 7, ETG Hq in London, 2 Dec 43.

maintenance of field sets. Then, along with the enlisted technicians, they received training in teamwork at the Aircraft Warning Unit Training Center at Drew Field. Officers trained in the ETG in the United Kingdom were the exception. Most of these men went directly to Drew Field, to aircraft warning units, or to the Army Air Forces School of Applied Tactics at Orlando, Florida.[146]

Out of every five radar officer students, one was a man educationally qualified to pursue advanced study to become an instructor, a design and research engineer, or a liaison officer in a plant manufacturing radar equipment. Since Signal Corps schools were not staffed or equipped to give this scientific instruction, such students, if not sent to the British military schools, enrolled at Harvard in the Cruft Laboratory course and at MIT. These institutions provided advanced courses in electronics and its applications to radar.[147]

About 80 percent of radar officers found themselves in a second category, men who would be assigned to field duty to supervise the installation, mainte-nance and repair of tactical radar equipment. Such assignments required less highly technical training. The Signal Corps trained these officers at Camp Murphy in a course whose subject matter approximated that conducted at the Cruft Laboratory, which was less advanced than the courses at MIT. The Signal Corps presentation relied heavily on graphics and word pictures instead of the mathematical analyses embodied in the Harvard course. A degree in electrical engineering, an essential prerequisite for the Harvard, MIT, and British courses, was a desirable but not mandatory prerequisite for the Camp Murphy training, for the practical reason that it was becoming increasingly difficult to fill the electronics quotas with men who possessed engineering degrees. At Camp Murphy the men devoted two months to the study of electronics principles and one month to radar, UHF, and microwave principles, and then went to aircraft warning units, the Antiaircraft Command, the Air Service Command, and possibly as many as one-third to Signal Corps depots and other headquarters.

Previously, officer students had entered the Southern Signal Corps School at three levels of preparation: directly from officer candidate school; OCS plus Harvard University's Cruft Laboratory course; and OCS plus Harvard, plus MIT. They had arrived in small numbers at indefinite and irregular intervals. Under the new plan, students arrived regularly. The existing Harvard and MIT courses financed by the U.S. Office of Education were discontinued on 21 December 1943, and new contracts were entered into for the training of the

---

[146] For the early history of the Electronics Training Group program, see: (1) Terrett, *The Emergency*, pp. 739-47; (2) Thompson, Harris, et al., *The Test*, pp. 24, 44, 45, 49, 57, 207, 209-12, 247, 312, 339; (3) Sadler, Hist of the ETG in the U.K., *passim*.

[147] The Army Electronics Training Center, organized to administer training at the Massachusetts Institute of Technology and Harvard, was activated 14 September 1942 by Section II, General Order 86, First Service Command, 2 October 1942, pursuant to authority contained in War Department Memo S950-5-42, 5 September 1942, as a Class I installation. On 26 July 1943 it became a Class IV installation under the jurisdiction of the Chief Signal Officer.

Insert, History, Training Activities, Army Electronics Training Center, p. 3 to History, Officers' Electronics Training Course, Harvard University, pt. I. SigC Hist Sec file.

better qualified 20 percent required for the more highly technical assignments.[148]

Between the inception of the program late in 1941 and the end of June 1944, 2,349 officers graduated from the Harvard course out of a final enrollment of 2,566. At the Massachusetts Institute of Technology, during the same period, 2,099 students received certificates out of an initial enrollment of 2,182. No comparison can be made between the Harvard and MIT instruction and radar courses given at other civilian institutions, because the former was more advanced than the instruction given anywhere else except in the United Kingdom. The practical training the ETG officers received in the United Kingdom with British troops in action makes comparisons there of little value.[149]

Despite all efforts to fill the electronics training program quotas, a shortage of men qualified to take the training persisted, and output did not equal estimated requirements for this type of officer specialist.[150] Moreover, of the electrical engineers obtained from the ROTC, not many could be spared for radar training because they were needed for technical assignments on radio and carrier transmission systems, particularly since the Signal Corps had scraped the bottom of the barrel by calling the last twenty-three officers provided by the Affiliated Plan to active duty during June, July, and August. The ASF had closed the door to further civilian pro-

curement, and without additional procurement from civil life the number of officers in prospect for radar duty by the end of 1944 would about equal estimated requirements at the end of 1943. Requisitions placed in 1942 for radar officers were still pending, unfilled, in mid-1943.[151]

Lacking Signal Corps students to fill the Camp Murphy school to capacity, quotas were assigned to the Navy and the Marine Corps and for the training of a limited number of officers of Allied armies. In the fall of 1943, twenty-one French officers, slated to take over operation of the American and British networks in North Africa, were studying the SCR–268 when it was learned that the newer SCR–584 would be used for gun laying in North Africa. Accordingly, instruction on that set was substituted for the original course.[152]

Meanwhile, as officer classes expanded during 1943 and 1944, Camp Murphy continued enlisted instruction largely along the lines originally planned. Until 1944, however, inadequate training facilities, especially a lack of equipment items, prevented the school from operating at maximum efficiency in all of its departments. For example, unlike Drew Field, Camp Murphy had no airplanes of its own. The Civil Air Patrol at Lantana Air Base, Lake Worth, Florida, and the Army Air Forces Technical School No. 5 at Boca Raton arranged informally to make a limited number of con-

[148] Memo, Chief Mil Tng Br for Chief P&T Sv OCSigO, 26 Aug 43, sub: Tng of Radar Offs. SigC 353 Gen, Aug 43 (MT–194).

[149] Hist, Offs' Electronics Tng Course, pt. I, p. 70.

[150] Ltr, CSigO to Mil Pers Div ASF, 22 Apr 43, sub: Proc of ETG Pers From Civil Life. SigC 352.11 ETG, Nov–Dec 42.

[151] (1) Ltr, OCSigO to ACofS G–1, Through Mil Pers Div ASF, 1 May 43, sub: Appointment of ETG Officers. (2) Ltr, TAG OSW to CSigO, 25 May 43, same sub, and 1st Ind, CSigO to TAG, 28 May 43. Both in SigC 352.11 ETG, Nov–Dec 42.

[152] OCSigO R&W Action 2, Sullo, Mil Tng Br, to Mil Tng Br, 22 Oct 43, sub: Tng of French Offs. SigC 353 Gen, Oct 43 (MT–176).

trolled flights for Camp Murphy. These provided some training in the calibration of radar sets, operator instruction on all types of ground radar equipment, use of radio recognition and identification equipment, and radar-controlled searchlight operation training.[153]

The AAF controlled all radar equipment and dictated training requirements, and the availability of equipment had a direct bearing on the curriculum. The Signal Corps, anxious to give more attention to jamming techniques, suggested in September 1943 that the Southern Signal Corps School and the Army Air Forces Technical Training Center at Boca Raton jointly conduct a series of problems. Such exercises could provide valuable practice for students at both institutions and for the crews in the aircraft warning networks within range and frequency of the jammers. ASF approved the proposal, but headquarters AAF tabled it because jamming equipment could not be provided.[154] Phonograph records had to be substituted for more realistic training in the increasingly important field of countermeasures.[155] At the request of AAF, Signal Corps planned to train half a class of airborne radio equipment repairmen on the new SCR-718 set, leaving the remainder to study the RC-24, on which all such specialists had previously learned their trade. Then the AAF decided that the new set was too simple to waste instruction time on it. Familiarity with the necessary maintenance literature and test equipment IE-45 would suffice. However, when the first IE-45's arrived from the manufacturer on 1 November, the Army Air Forces sent the entire lot overseas. It was mid-December before Camp Murphy got any IE-45's for school use, and until then the gap in SCR-718 enlisted instruction could not be closed.[156]

Camp Murphy undertook team and field training, but initially without a separate department set up for the purpose. Training did not progress smoothly. Double duty for facilities, training equipment, and instructors resulted in subordination of team training to individual instruction. When Camp Murphy acquired fifteen Civilian Conservation Corps buildings in March 1944, it organized a separate department for team training. The scarcity of instructors delayed the project until June, and by the time the new division started functioning, its days were already numbered since aircraft warning training was definitely declining. In October, the Southern Signal Corps School at Camp Murphy closed its doors. Aircraft warning training, with reduced student quotas, transferred back to Fort Mon-

[153] Ltr, Comdt SSCS to CSigO, 24 Apr 43, sub: Use of Aircraft in Tng, and 4th Ind, Comdt SigC Sch to CO Natl Hq Civil Air Patrol, 4 Nov 43. SigC 353 Gen, Oct 43 (MT-176).

[154] Ltr, Gillespie, Chief Mil Tng Br OCSigO, to Comdt SSCS, Camp Murphy, Fla., 7 Sep 43, sub: Recognition of Countermeasure Sigs, 3d Ind, CG ASF to CG AAF, 22 Sep 43, and 4th Ind, CG AAF to CG ASF, 23 Oct 43. SigC 353 Gen, Dec 43 (MT-178).

[155] OCSigO R&W Action 2, Sheetz, Protective Sec Br, to Mil Tng Br, 30 Dec 43, sub: Tng Rcd for Familiarization of Operators With Jamming Sigs. SigC 353 Gen, Dec 43 (MT-178).

[156] (1) Ltr, CSigO to CG AAF Through CG ASF, 16 Oct 43, sub: Tng of ASC Pers on Radio Set SCR-718; 3d Ind, CG AAF Hq ASC to CG AAF, 13 Nov 43; 4th Ind, CG AAF to CG ASF, 18 Nov 43; 6th Ind, ASF CSigO to Comdt SSCS, Camp Murphy, Fla., 3 Dec 43. (2) Ltr, CG ASC to CSigO, 2 Oct 43, sub: Addition of Radio Set SCR-718 to Tng of Radio Repairmen, Intercept, and Search. (3) OCSigO R&W Action 2, Capt M. J. Ogas to Fiscal & Equip Sec, 22 Oct 43. All in SigC 353 Gen, Oct 43 (MT-176).

mouth, the site of its beginning. Between the opening of the radar school at Riviera, Florida, in April 1942, before the completion of Camp Murphy, and its close in October 1944, 10,330 enlisted men received training and went to demanding assignments in every part of the world.[157]

Meanwhile, in March 1943, a Signal Corps officer, Brig. Gen. Stephen H. Sherrill, was transferred from the Western Signal Corps Training Center at Sacramento to take command of the Army Air Forces' largest training center, the Aircraft Warning Unit Training Center at Drew Field.[158] Up to this time the center had used the stage system of training, forming a unit in one stage and training it in another, with the result that responsibility was divided. General Sherrill instituted a system embodying a group of training battalions, each of which was responsible for the formation, training, and complete preparation for overseas movement of all units within a given category.[159]

Other circumstances contributed to a rise in training efficiency at Drew Field during the first months of General Sherrill's regime. AAF headquarters began regulating the flow of enlisted men into the center, providing about 6,000 each month, half of them fillers with previous training in service forces schools, a third qualified for specialist training, and no more than a sixth, basics. The AAF was able also to provide a more adequate supply of highly qualified instructors. Finally, training equipment, once very scarce, became available—both radar sets and airplanes. As conditions and techniques improved, AWUTC production of well-trained aircraft warning units mounted steadily. During the first nine months of 1943, Drew Field graduated 14,189 AWS specialists.

September 1943 brought instructions to the center to organize and prepare nine battalions to take part in the Normandy invasion and to gear its program to large-scale airborne and amphibious operations being planned for both Europe and the Pacific. Newer types of equipment arrived, necessitating new techniques and new types of training. Eleven new subcenters sprang into existence from Bradenton, Florida, to Hattiesburg, Mississippi, to house the overflow from Drew.

In the spring of 1944 Drew Field concentrated on exercises and field maneuvers. But, as at other training centers, the AWUTC's boom days were passing. By June 1944, the number of fixed station training sites had dwindled to nine, and all troops except those on field maneuvers were housed at Drew Field proper. More than 37,000 men had gone out in the preceding 16 months, and all the combat theaters had benefited from the training the radar units and crews had received at Drew Field. The next few

---

[157] (1) Ltr, Mitchell, Comdt SSCS, Camp Murphy, Fla., to CSigO, 22 Mar 43, sub: Grading System for SSCS, and 1st Ind, CSigO to Comdt SSCS, 5 Apr 43. SigC 352 Hobe Sound, MT-151. (2) Incl, Ltr, Maj Joseph A. Bulger, 1st Interceptor Comd, to Chief AC, 6 Jan 42, sub: Methods for Improvement of Results Obtained by the SCR-270's, to Memo, Maj Francis L. Ankenbrandt for Mitchell, OCSigO, 9 Jan 42. SigC file C&E Case Air Com Div.

[158] Memo, Brig Gen Miller G. White, ACofS G-1 WDGS, for CofS, 20 Feb 43, sub: Gen Officers. OCS file WDCSA 210.311-43.

[159] Except where other authority is cited, material on training at Drew Field is based on Brig Gen. Stephen H. Sherrill, "Signal Corps Training in the AAF," Signals, I, No. 2 (November–December, 1946), 26–30.

months witnessed the rapid decline of aircraft warning training. In the early winter of 1944–45 the AWUTC was inactivated, and its staff and equipment transferred to the AAF installation at Pinedale, California.[160]

Summary

Signal Corps personnel and training activities during the last two years of war benefited from the vigor and ingenuity that had characterized the efforts of the earlier years. Although much of the Chief Signal Officer's control of personnel procurement and training was taken over by ASF, the basic signal doctrine and techniques of training remained securely in his hands. Signal Corps organization and training innovations often set a pattern adopted by the ASF and applied to all the technical services. The cellular plan of organization of units and the plan for preactivation training represent the two most significant examples of Signal Corps training contributions.

The Signal Corps' tasks were so varied and its responsibilities so wide that training the large number of different kinds of units demanded an enormously complex curriculum. Lessons learned in combat continuously provided new material that was quickly reflected in Signal Corps training courses during the last

two years of war. Not all training methods succeeded equally well. The value of on-the-job training came to be recognized in 1944–45 as at least equal to that of classroom schooling.

The principal training deficiency from the Signal Corps point of view was the length of time available for technical training. For most of the war the Signal Corps was unable to establish its contention that electronics subjects are more difficult than any other Army specialty and that they require better students and a longer training period. By the end of the war in Europe, the Signal Corps' need for men in the higher intelligence brackets had been conceded, but unfortunately by then few such men were available.

In order to accommodate its heavy training load during the war, the Signal Corps required three replacement training centers, six service schools, four depot schools, two unit training centers, and dozens of technical vocational and industrial schools, colleges, and universities in the United States as well as technical schools in the United Kingdom. In addition, 268 civilian schools and colleges were utilized in a countrywide program of preservice training that produced about 50,000 Signal Corps enlisted reservists as well as a large number of trained civilian employees. Approximately 387,000 officers and men completed communications courses conducted by the Signal Corps.[161]

[160] (1) Interv, SigC Hist Div with Lt Col Frank E. Herrelko, AC, 11 Mar 47. SigC Hist Sec file. (2) History of the 2d Training Battalion (formerly the 588th Signal Aircraft Warning Battalion), Third Air Force, Oct 43, apps. I, II, III. AF Archives Sig-2-HI. (3) Sherrill, "Signal Corps Training in the AAF," *Signals*, I, No. 2, *passim*.

[161] OCSigO P&T Sv Mil Tng Br, Annual Report of Military Training, 1946, pp. 1–2. SigC 319.1 Annual Rpt of Mil Tng, 1946.

CHAPTER XVII

Army Photography at Home and Overseas

The Army's photographic service continued to create lively discussions at official levels throughout the last two years of war. The photographic service accounted for only 3 percent of the total of Signal Corps activity, yet General Ingles said in the late summer of 1944, "I get more kicks and commendations from the results of that service than from the results of all the rest of the Signal Corps activities put together." [1]

General Ingles might have added that the photographic service was the least understood of Signal Corps' responsibilities. Few persons outside of the Signal Corps had any knowledge of the capabilities or limitations of military photography, or any understanding of Army policies concerning its use. In fact, throughout the war years, War Department policies on Army photography tended to be contradictory and confusing. Photography was expected to be all things to all staff divisions. The War Department's Bureau of Public Relations was interested chiefly in dramatic, timely films and pictures for public viewing; training officers thought of photography in terms of mass teaching by visual methods; field commanders wanted tactical pictures for immediate strategic planning; a half-dozen War Department staff agencies gave Army

Pictorial Service directions and assigned projects with a blithe disregard for co-ordination with other agencies. All depended upon the provisions of AR 105–5, which placed the Army's photographic responsibilities with the Signal Corps except for work assigned by the Secretary of War to other agencies. [2]

The photographic activities of all the armed services suffered from "a fairly universal lack of full co-operation, and therefore of full use, from Washington to the fighting fronts," one high-ranking Signal Corps photographic officer remarked after the war, "Some few individuals saw the entire problem . . . but by and large, too often through all ranks and grades the photographic mission was an irritating gadfly—sometimes to be slapped down, more frequently to be brushed away, and often merely to be ignored." [3] The general lack of appreciation of photography perhaps was more apparent in the overseas theaters than in the zone of interior. But it is certainly true that not until the war was

---

[1] Ltr, Ingles, CSigO, to Tully, AFHQ, 17 Aug 44. SigC EO 312.1 Personal Ltrs.

[2] (1) OCSigO R&W Action 1, Gen Code for ACSigO, for Dir Contl Div, and for Dir P&O Div, 29 May 44, sub: Photo Responsibilities of the CSigO. SigC DCSigO file, Photo Coverage. (2) Incl, Outline of Photo Activities of the SigC Relationships With Mil Photography, with Memo, Secretary, Army Pictorial Board (Col Kirke B. Lawton), to ACofS, G–4, et al., 10 Apr 43. SigC 334 APB, pt. 1, 1943–44.

[3] Col Darryl F. Zanuck, Editorial in Signals, III, No. 3 (January–February, 1949), 12.

Prop Department of the Signal Corps Photographic Center, Astoria, L.I.

over did sober recalculation and assessment result in recognition of the real value of the Army's photographic service contributions.

The Army Pictorial Service Organization and Mission

The Army Pictorial Service (APS), the OCSigO staff agency for photographic matters, had weathered a Congressional inquiry into its training film activities early in 1943 with no ill effects.[4] For a 3-month period, the APS

had reported directly to ASF, bypassing the Chief Signal Officer, but early in July reverted to direct Signal Corps control.[5] Col. Kirke B. Lawton resumed his position as chief of APS, a job he held until Col. Edward L. Munson, Jr., became chief in July 1944.

Essentially, the APS mission remained unchanged during the last two years of war, though the volume of work performed nearly doubled. The APS continued to produce and procure training films, film bulletins, and film strips, including foreign language versions, and

---

[4] For an account see Thompson, Harris, et al., *The Test*, pp. 418–24.

[5] ASF Memo S–37, 30 Jun 43.

to make available training on scores of military subjects to the troops. The APS also produced information and historical films for military planning and analysis purposes, to orient troops to combat conditions, to document campaigns, and so on. An example of films in this category included the secret staff film reports compiled weekly from combat footage and shown only to the Chief of Staff and certain general officers. In a third category, morale and orientation films were shown to all members of the U.S. Armed Forces, Allied troops, war plant workers, and convalescent troops. Orientation films, the *Army and Navy Screen Maga-. zine, G.I. Movie Weekly*, industrial service films, educational reconditioning and recreational film, and special projects of many sorts came under this heading. APS also procured, but did not produce, entertainment films--the familiar Hollywood movies, so dear to the hearts of troops the world over.

For the use of all staff agencies, and all arms and services, and for other government agencies as well as commercial and private sources, the APS produced hundreds of thousands of still photographs. It processed V-Mail and Official Photo Mail; it operated the largest film distributing organization in the world and maintained one of the world's largest film libraries. With a view toward improving photographic equipment and processing techniques, APS conducted extensive research. Finally, it trained personnel to provide technicians for all photographic units of the Army except for the AAF.[6]

As wartime staff divisions went, the APS staff in Washington remained relatively small. APS activities centered around the Signal Corps Photographic Center (SCPC) at Astoria, Long Island. There the many film projects demanded the services of about 2,000 military and civilian writers, producers, cameramen, technicians, and photographic specialists of all sorts. At the peak of wartime operation, SCPC employed 287 officers, 610 enlisted men, and 1,361 civilians. At war's end, its activities were housed in 14 separate building locations, including the Western Division of SCPC in Beverly Hills, California.[7] The SCPC included the Signal Corps Photographic School (SCPS) for training combat photographers and the Pictorial Engineering and Research Laboratory (PERL), which performed the photographic research and development portion of the APS mission with notable success.

Another field agency, the Signal Corps Photographic Laboratory (SCPL), located at the Army War College in Washington, D.C., processed motion picture footage, including combat photography, completed film strips, and labored at a multitude of tedious, necessary chores such as the making of official

[6] (1) ASF Manual M-301, ASF Organization, 15 Aug 44, sec. 305.00/30–34. (2) CSigO Annual Rpt, FY 44, p. 593. (3) AR 105-255, 7 May 42. (4) James V. Clarke, Signal Corps Army Pictorial

Service in World War II, 1 September 1939–16 August 1945 (1945). SigC Hist Monograph, F-2a, *passim*. SigC Hist Sec file. (5) Lt Col Griffin L. Davis, History, Organization and Operation of the Army Pictorial Service (1952), Sig Sch Monograph, *passim*. The Sig Sch Libr, Ft. Monmouth. (6) *Business Screen*, VII, No. 1 (December, 1945), p. 34. This special issue of *Business Screen* is devoted entirely to the Army Pictorial Service.
[7] Capt Vernon G. Fleury, The Signal Corps Photographic Center (1949), Sig Sch Monograph, p. 6. The Sig Sch Libr, Ft. Monmouth.
The mission of the Western Division, SCPC, was procuring and supervising the production of training films from civilian studios.

portraits and identification photographs.

The SCPC could be thought of as a manufacturing plant, turning out one specific product, motion pictures, in a variety of forms for a fairly large group of diverse customers. The customers supplied the specifications for the product; the Signal Corps designed, engineered, and produced the specific item desired.[8] Thus the War Department Bureau of Public Relations decided upon the purpose and the message to be portrayed in the industrial service films it wanted for showing to war workers, while the SCPC wrote the scripts and produced the pictures.[9] Similarly, the Army Information Branch of the Information and Education (I&E) Division, ASF, planned and was responsible for the "content of, integration of . . . and final approval of" the biweekly *Army and Navy Screen Magazine* and the orientation films shown to troops.[10] Again the SCPC wrote the scripts and produced the films. In other words, the interpretation and presentation of the basic story idea was in general a Signal Corps responsibility. With so many films of various types being produced, it was not surprising that the public and the Military Establishment in general tended to think of the Signal Corps as the sole agency responsible for all phases of military motion pictures. The Signal Corps garnered the bouquets and the brickbats, whether it deserved them or not, as the Army Information Branch pointed out when it complained that the Bureau of Public Relations in its publicity on orientation films seemed to give sole credit to the Signal Corps, "without mention of the WD agency for whom the Signal Corps so expertly produced the film." [11]

Problems of Policy and Production Control

Although it was an assigned part of the Signal Corps' mission, providing photographic services for the Army obviously did not enjoy the same status and prestige as did the function of supplying electronic communications. Within and without the Signal Corps were many who would have been content to deposit photography on the doorstep of some other service.[12] The Chief Signal Officer himself told the Army Pictorial Board (APB) in 1944 that photographic work "could be assigned to another agency of the War Department without interference with the work of the Signal Corps, as there was very little connection between photographic work and other Signal Corps activities." He added that

---

[8] SigC 062.2 Policy (Motion Pictures), 1942–45, *passim*.

[9] (1) Ltr, Chief Pictorial Br BPR to CO SCPC, 21 Mar 44, sub: Revised SOP for Industrial Films. (2) Ltr, Chief Industrial Svs Div BPR to O/C Sp Coverage Div SCPC, 19 Apr 44, sub: Msg of Industrial Svs Film. Both in SigC 062.2 Prod, Policy–BPR, 1942–45.

[10] ASF Cir, 30 Nov 43.

[11] Memo, Asst ExecO Army Info Br ASF for Dir BPR, 2 May 44, sub: Suitable Accreditation of Army Info Br in Respect to War Info Films. SigC 062.2 Policy (Motion Pictures), 1942–45.

[12] Testifying in 1943 before a board investigating the desirability of establishing a director of communications at General Staff level, General Meade, SigC, said that if he were such a director, he would not wish to be bothered with photography, while Lt. Col. James McCormack, G–4, stated that photography "has no more to do with Signals than Donald Duck." Proceedings of a Bd to Investigate Com, Tab M, p. 13, and Tab D, p. 14. AG 311 (5–10–43) (1) Bulky Pkg, Army RG 207.03, Job A50–55.

any such transfer, however, should be delayed until after the war ended.[13]

In March 1943 the Secretary of War had created the Army Pictorial Board to co-ordinate Army motion picture activities.[14] The board's membership consisted of representatives of G–4, G–3, ASF, AGF, AAF, BPR, and the APS.[15] The board in fact did provide a channel for controlling certain aspects of film activities, especially in the matter of delineating responsibilities and relationships between the major arms. It did not, however, provide the strong centralized guidance that APS would have welcomed in the areas involving working relationships between APS and the various War Department agencies it served. When the board asked General Ingles in 1944 whether it could be of help to him, Ingles said that, although the board had not been of much help as yet, he considered it to be a high-level court of appeal. The very existence of the board, he said, helped to prevent problems from arising in the first place.[16]

A second War Department board concerned with photographic matters existed for a little over a year, during the period 1943–44. Beginning late in the North African campaign, a heavy volume of combat film of varying degrees of excellence began pouring into the SCPC. The center used the footage for many purposes, very often utilizing the same material in several different film series.

One important use was for the newsreels that kept the public informed of the progress of the war. To be sure, newsreels also incorporated AAF, Navy, and Allied film, but Signal Corps film comprised 30 percent to 50 percent of any newsreel.[17] The same combat footage used in a newsreel might be, and often was, used for War Department staff studies, for tactical purposes by field commanders, in film bulletins and other types of training films, for morale and indoctrination films, and to complete the historical film record of a campaign or a theater.

To assure the most effective utilization of combat film for staff study, G–3, on 3 March 1943, created the War Department Motion Picture Review Board.[18] The G–3 directed the three major commands to detail officers to the board to review combat film to determine its security classification within the Army, to select film for further staff study within the various commands, to recommend subjects for the preparation of film bulletins, and to advise APS as to specific activities on which photographic coverage was desired.[19] On the desk be-

[13] Min, 12th Mtg APB, 8 Aug 44. SigC 334 APB, pt. 2, 1944–45.

[14] (1) AG Memo, W210–4–43, 15 Mar 43. (2) Thompson, Harris, et al., The Test, p. 423.

[15] (1) AG 334 APB, 11 May 43. (2) Admin Memo, CofS ASF, Mar 43, sub: Army Pictorial Service (APS). SigC 334 APB, pt. 1, 1943–44.

[16] Min, 12th Mtg APB, 8 Aug 44.

[17] Memo, Chief Fld Activities Br APS for Chief Photo Utilization Br APS, 1 Sep 43, sub: Semi-Monthly Rpt. SigC AS 319.1 Digest of Progress and Problems, pt. 1, Aug 43 Through Dec 44.

[18] (1) WD Memo, WDGCT 413.53 (2–22–43), 5 Mar 43. AG 334 WD Motion Picture Review Bd. (2) Memo, CG AGF for ACofS G–3, 4 Mar 43, sub: Review of Combat Motion Picture Films. (3) Memo, ACofS G–3 for CG's ASF, AGF, and AAF, 5 Mar 43, sub: Review of Combat Motion Picture Films. (4) Memo, Chief APS for CG ASF, 7 May 43, sub: Review of Combat Motion Picture Film. Last three in SigC 062.2 Policy (Combat Photography), 1942–45.

[19] Memo, Deputy Chief APS for Members of WD Motion Picture Review Bd, 1 Jul 43, sub: Rev Procedure of Review Bd. SigC 062.2 Policy (Combat Photography), 1942–43.

fore each officer in the Pentagon auditorium, where the board met, APS installed a red light and a push button. The button controlled a device developed by APS especially to meet the needs of this unique audience. When a sequence of interest to any particular branch flashed on the screen, the representing officer pushed the button on his desk and the red light went on. As long as the light was on, a tape synchronized with the film made a notation of the fact that the portion of the film being shown at that time was of particular interest to that branch. After the showing, APS made up copies of the portions each officer had selected and sent them to his branch for detailed study.[20]

The board grew to number almost twenty members, including representatives of the Navy, the Coordinator of Inter-American Affairs, the OSS, and the BPR, as well as the ASF, AGF, and AAF. Each of the seven technical services had representatives, and so did the ASF's Morale Services Division, the Provost Marshal, and the Chief of Chaplains. The screenings proved to be very popular; by late 1943 APS had been directed to set up ten staff screenings each week, plus as many special screenings as could be accommodated, usually at least a dozen each week. The board attended screenings on Mondays; on Tuesdays and Fridays, G-2, G-3, and G-4 staffs saw the films their representatives had selected, as did the Joint Chiefs of Staff on Wednesdays and Fridays. On Thursdays the AGF staff at the Army War College viewed their selected films, which were shown also in Army War College classrooms on Thursdays and Fridays.[21]

Despite the popularity of the Motion Picture Review Board selections, ASF came to question the board's usefulness. Actually, although the board representatives generally held the rank of lieutenant colonel or higher, they customarily sent junior officers to meetings as alternates. In many cases these officers selected films for their general interest rather than for their training value. Many of the agencies chose substantially the same films and showed them weekly to relatively large groups of officers whose work had little connection with the material shown. In carrying out their classification function, board members passed upon the classification of the rough-cut film only for its uses in the Army. The BPR, functioning under joint security control, classified the same film in the original master print. Thus the board in large measure duplicated the classification function of the BPR. Furthermore, the same material that the board classified secret might be released by BPR for the public newsreels.[22] Finally, the weekly Staff Film Report, covering substantially the same material in a condensed and more carefully prepared form, was shown in Washington only three days after the combat films were shown to the board.

For all these reasons, the War Department General Staff decided in mid-1944 to abolish the War Department Motion

---

[20] Col Kirke B. Lawton, "Army Pictorial," *Radio News*, 31, No. 2 (February, 1944), 147.

[21] Memo, Chief Fld Activities Br APS for Chief Photo Utilization Br APS, 1 Sep 43, sub: Semi-Monthly Rpt.

[22] Memo, Brig Gen Clinton ·F. Robinson, Dir Contl Div ASF, for CofS ASF, 14 Jul 44, sub: Preparation and Use of Combat Films. AG 334 WD Motion Picture Review Bd.

Picture Review Board.[23] Instead, upon the recommendation of the Army Pictorial Board, the AGF, ASF, and AAF were directed to provide representatives for duty at the SCPC at Astoria to help select and distribute combat photography particularly useful to their commands. About the same time, the Army Pictorial Board took cognizance of the pressing priority problem that the APS had been unable to solve.

Each successful film that the SCPC produced immediately generated new demands for additional films from other sources. As one of the penalties SCPC paid for making a better product, its workload grew so heavy by 1944 that it threatened to engulf the entire film program. The center was chronically short of manpower and very often short of production facilities.[24] The difficulty arose chiefly because agencies dealt directly with the APS, and neither the APS nor the Chief Signal Officer had the authority to disapprove any film project or to refuse any pictorial request. Since the requests did not pass through any screening agency of the War Department, the APS was at a distinct disadvantage in obtaining funds or personnel to carry out the increased load.

Early in 1944, Colonel Lawton had attempted to establish work priorities for SCPC. He directed that, when demand

temporarily exceeded production facilities or personnel, work projects should be rated in the following order of importance: (1) combat films for staff review, (2) combat film reports for release to the public, (3) the *Army and Navy Screen Magazine*, (4) industrial service films, (5) orientation films, (6) training films, (7) combat bulletins for AGF and ASF training purposes, (8) French rescorings, (9) educational and vocational films, (10) *G.I. Movie Weekly*, and (11) Spanish and Portuguese rescorings.[25] But the ASF Military Training Branch objected immediately to the priority assigned to training films.[26] Recognizing that every other affected agency very likely would register similar complaints, Colonel Lawton rescinded his memorandum.[27]

When the Army Pictorial Board was created, one of the powers given to it was the "establishment of priorities of production." [28] Sitting in judgment on the merits of high-level staff agency requests for service was a touchy business, and the board had never exercised this function. Looking into APS's production troubles in mid-1944, the Control Division of OCSigO pointed out that actually "APB had never had the problems and recommendations of APS presented to it in such a way that it has been in a position to make recommendations on motion picture production to the Chief of Staff," and recommended that the matter be

---

[23] (1) Memo, ACofS, G–4, for TAG, 17 Aug 44, sub: WD Motion Picture Review Bd. (2) Ltr, TAG to CG's ASF, AGF, and AAF, 20 Aug 44, sub: WD Motion Picture Review Bd. Both in AG 334 WD Motion Picture Review Bd. (3) Min, APB 11th Mtg, 1 Aug 44, and 12th Mtg, 8 Aug 44. SigC 334 APB, pt. 2, 1944–45.

[24] (1) SigC MP 319.1 Gen folder on Pers Study, APS, Oct 43, *passim*. (2) SigC AS 319.1 Digest of Progress and Problems, pt. 1, Aug 43 Through Dec 44, and pt. 2, 1 Jan 45 Through 30 Sep 45, *passim*.

[25] Memo, Actg Chief APS for CO SCPC, 19 Jan 44, sub: Priorities of Prod. SigC 062.2 Policy (Motion Pictures), 1942–45.

[26] Memo, Dir Mil Tng Div ASF for CSigO, 1 Mar 44, sub: Prod Priority Assigned to Tng Films. SigC 062.2 Policy (Motion Pictures), 1942–45.

[27] Memo, Actg Chief APS for CO SCPC, 13 Mar 44, sub: Priority of Prod. SigC 062.2 Policy (Motion Picture), 1942–45.

[28] AG Memo, W210–4–43, 15 Mar 43, APB.

brought to the board's attention.[29] Meanwhile, General Ingles had suggested to Maj. Gen. Wilhelm D. Styer, General Somervell's chief of staff, that, if the APB was not going to handle priorities, the Signal Corps ought to be allowed to do so. Styer agreed.[30] As a result, G–4 expanded the membership of the Army Pictorial Board to include additional representatives who thereafter acted as a screening subcommittee, empowered to give final approval or disapproval to requests for the production of motion pictures other than training films.[31] The number of requests for motion pictures for which no real military need existed dropped sharply after the subcommittee had been in existence for a short time and the subcommittee was then dissolved.

Motion Picture Services

All Army motion pictures, for whatever purpose intended, were produced either by the Signal Corps itself or by the motion picture industry under Signal Corps contracts.[32] When APS received a request from a government agency to produce a motion picture, a script was written. After approval by the requesting agency, the Signal Corps decided whether it could translate the story on film in its own studios or whether commercial production would be advisable. Scripts to be produced commercially went to the Western Division of SCPC, which analyzed the production problems involved and requested the Hollywood studio best able to produce the picture to undertake production.[33] Almost without exception, the major Hollywood studios provided the pictures at cost, or at less than cost in those cases where no charge was made for overhead studio costs.

The Army owed much to Hollywood, quite aside from the films the industry supplied at low cost. Many of the great improvements in picture-making techniques at SCPC could be traced to a heavy infusion of industry-trained technicians in uniform. Training films in particular showed a dramatic change. The first training films the Army turned out were pretty dull. They sounded like photographed field manuals, which indeed many of them were. A disembodied voice off-stage "droned out such deathless lines as 'The occupant of the driver's seat makes a careful check with instruments to ascertain the accurate. . . .'" and so on.[34] Understandably such films failed to hold the interest of a generation of GI's weaned on exciting, fast-paced commercial movies. But by the time the heaviest film production load developed, the major portion of the SCPC staff consisted of men recruited from Hollywood studios. They brought with them the techniques and experience that had made Hollywood the undis-

---

[29] Transmittal Sheet, Action 1, OCSigO Contl Div to ACSigO, 25 Jul 44, sub: Study of APS Photo Prod Problems for Presentation to Subcomte, APB. SigC 062 Photographs, Photo Activities, 1944–45.

[30] (1) Transmittal Sheet, Action 1, Actg Chief APS to ExecO APS, 9 Jul 44. (2) Memo, CofS ASF for CofS G–4, 19 Jun 44, sub: Comte to Screen Requests for the Prod of Motion Pictures. Both in SigC 062.2 Policy (Motion Pictures), 1942–45.

[31] (1) Min, 10th Mtg APB, 27 Jun 44. (2) Memo, Chairman of APB (ACofS G–4), 30 Jun 44. Both in SigC 334 APB, pt. 2, 1944–45.

[32] Except those for AAF, which produced and distributed its own films.

[33] CSigO, Annual Rpt, FY 44, pp. 602–03.

[34] Col. Emanuel Cohen, "Film Is A Weapon," *Business Screen,* VII, No. 1 (December, 1945), 43.

puted world center of motion picture production. They revolutionized the SCPC.[35]

Training Films

The most numerous and by many standards the most important motion pictures that the Army produced were its training films. The training film, to use the term in its narrow sense, presented a course or a part of a course of instruction of a military school. For the AGF and the ASF, the Army Pictorial Service produced a total of 1,338 such training films during the course of World War II.[36] These figures do not include 88 adaptations of foreign training films, or 988 rescorings of training films into foreign languages. If these are added, plus some 100 revisions and reissues, the total reaches a figure well above 2,500.[37]

The APS had not been happy with its first training films. It worked hard to improve them. As more and better trained writers, cutters, cameramen, and producers became available, the quality of training films rose very quickly. By mid-1942, with training camps all over the country bulging with troops, films had become extremely useful training tools. Dressed up with animation and music, accompanied by dialogue written in lively GI style, they drove home the training lessons almost painlessly. A special division within APS furnished field co-ordinators to the using services to help prepare scripts and select subjects capable of visual presentation. In December 1942, at the request of the Commanding General, Army Ground Forces, the Chief Signal Officer began issuing quiz cards to enlisted men at military installations all over the country. The cards provided an accurate measure of the effectiveness of training films. An APS research service, also begun in late 1942, conducted studies of the extent of use and the value of films in training programs. By mid-1943 APS had acquired reasonably accurate statistics to guide its training film operations. Throughout the war, most reports indicated that training films cut training time by at least 30 percent, and many reports indicated a much higher percentage.[38]

It might have been expected that, after the peak of Army mobilization passed, fewer training films would be needed. Quite the opposite was true. As the need for films depicting basic training courses declined, new training requirements increased. The stream of new weapons pouring from the laboratories and production lines demanded a constant suc-

[35] Fleury, SCPC, pp. 7–8.

[36] Jacqueline M. Quadow, Training Films in the Second World War, Supplement, January 1944–August 1945 (1945), SigC Hist Monograph, F–1a, p. 6. SigC Hist Sec file.

[37] Final Report of ASF, p. 153.

These totals do not include 159 training films produced by the Air Forces, principally by the First Motion Picture Unit at Culver City, California, after the transfer of the Wright Field Training Film Production Laboratory to AF command, or 102 training films turned out at Wright Field, some of which had been started under Signal Corps control and with Signal Corps funds. Quadow, Tng Films in the Second World War, Supplement, Jan 44–Aug 45, p. 7 (Quadow figures from AAF Motion Picture Statistics Sec, 12 Dec 45).

[38] (1) APS Summary Report on Photo Activities of the Signal Corps, 4 August 1941–26 February 1943, pp. 371–73. SigC Hist Sec file. (2) Quadow, Tng Films in the Second World War (1944), pp. 113–20. (3) Col. Roland C. Barrett, "The Signal Corps Photographic Center," Business Screen, VII, No. 1 (December, 1945), 37.

cession of films showing troops how to use the new devices. Another important source of demand required films designed to show new techniques in the use of old weapons—techniques developed in battle in every overseas theater of operations.

Radar, for example, was a new weapon —so new that many troops lacked knowledge of its astonishing potentialities. Furthermore, scores of scientists in both enemy and Allied countries were rushing new and ever more complicated versions of radar devices to the battle fronts. The APS hurried into production a series of three films on radar designed to keep Allied troops posted on methods of German and Japanese interference by jamming. Three more pictures devoted exclusively to the astounding variety of uses of the microwave gun-laying radar SCR–584 won high praise and the grateful appreciation of a number of commanders. In the Pacific, some troops had been misusing the SCR–584 badly because, lacking information concerning it, they had been using it like the only other radar they had seen, the venerable long-wave SCR–268.[39] Three more films on the general uses of radar were readied in 1945 for all elements of the Army and for the Navy as well.[40]

The duller the subject, the greater the challenge to the SCPC crews. A Quartermaster Corps training film entitled *Conservation of Clothing and Equipage* might have become the film most likely to induce a heavy volume of classroom snoring. But the SCPC presented the subject in a novel and entertaining manner, obtained the services of Robert L.

Ripley to expound the marvels of GI equipment through statistics out of his *Believe It Or Not* newspaper feature, and turned out a hit.[41] For the Corps of Engineers, a 5-film series on map reading employed an informal, humorous tone to lighten a very technical subject. Other Corps of Engineer films pointed out how camouflage as practiced in training matched actual camouflage overseas, showed how to carry out port repair, and taught a score of other important engineer functions.

One of the most outstanding training films produced during the last two years of war was aimed at the misconceptions among Negro troops that prevailed about venereal disease. Training officers had found earlier films on the subject to be inadequate, or not wholly comprehensible. A great deal of careful research went into the preparation of *Easy To Get* in order to obtain the greatest possible authenticity of speech. *Easy To Get* used the colloquialisms most common among Negro soldiers. A whole street duplicating a section of a Negro quarter in a southern town was built on the SCPC stages.

Many a soldier laughed at the idea that he should change his socks when he got his feet wet. But on the western front in the winter of 1944 trench foot became a grave threat to the health and efficiency of the troops. At General Eisenhower's urgent request for a training film on the subject, combat cameramen in the field shot films concerning soldiers with bad cases of trench foot. The Medical Corps added instructions on prevention. *Trench Foot*, a useful example of a film

---

[39] See above, p. 481.
[40] CSigO, Annual Rpt, FY 45, p. 808.

[41] (1) *Ibid.*, p. 809. (2) Cohen, "Film Is A Weapon," *Business Screen*, VII, No. 1, p. 43.

bulletin, was rushed to completion in the record time of six weeks.[42]

Another valuable film bulletin produced quickly to serve a combat need grew out of operations on a Pacific island. AGF headquarters, seeking new methods of attack, asked to see every available foot of film showing the terrain and enemy defenses on the island. Within forty-eight hours camera crews covering the island action assembled four reels and rushed them to Washington. The film proved to be so valuable that AGF immediately ordered seven additional prints for study and analysis by other groups of experts.[43]

Other timely film bulletins included *DDT—Weapon Against Disease; Diary of a Sergeant,* the story of how amputees can make new lives for themselves with the aid of prosthesis; *Swinging Into Step,* dedicated to the rehabilitation of men who had lost their legs; and a whole series on more prosaic subjects such as packing equipment for redeployment, ordnance heavy tanks, and comparisons of German and American machine guns.

When American military equipment began flowing to Allied nations in quantity it became necessary to translate training literature into the language of the countries receiving the supplies.[44] In training films the volume of rescorings and adaptations became so great that APS set up the Foreign Language Division in SCPC to handle the work.[45] Rescoring had begun early in 1942, when

SCPC produced the first Chinese score for *The 60-mm. Mortar—Mechanical Training* at the Army War College, using lend-lease funds.[46] At the request of the State Department, the program was soon extended to the Latin American countries. The Inter-American Defense Board furnished the funds and selected the subjects.[47] In April 1943 SCPC began rescoring AAF training films into French for the use of French air cadets trained in this country, and in 1944 began rescorings in Italian for use in training Italian prisoners of war.[48] At the Western Division of SCPC in Hollywood, selected orientation films were also reanimated, retitled, renarrated, and redubbed into French, Spanish, Portuguese, and Chinese.[49]

Each of the programs—French, Italian, Chinese, Latin American—was undertaken by order of a different agency of the War Department. Totally unrelated War Department agencies prepared the directives and circulars and established the channels of authority independently. The APS was reluctant to refer the question to the ASF Control Division for a decision establishing a single channel of authority because of the high levels of the various staff agencies involved, but, by January 1945, the workload at SCPC had become so heavy and the pressure for priority from the various agencies "so nagging" that APS felt some review of the rescoring program

---

[42] CSigO, Annual Rpt, FY 45, p. 809.

[43] PTFB–103–180, a 4-reel silent film, with no release number or main title.

[44] WD Memo, W130–44, Translations of Tng and Tech Literature into Foreign Languages.

[45] Ltr, CO Foreign Language Div SCPC to Dir APS, 16 Feb 43. SigC 062.2 Rescoring–Policy, pt. 1, Apr 42–Dec 45.

[46] Thompson, Harris, *et al., The Test,* p. 391.

[47] Memo, Secy Gen Inter-American Defense Bd for CSigO, 1 Oct 42. SigC 062.2 Rescoring–Policy, pt. 1, Apr 42–Dec 45.

[48] CSigO, Annual Rpt, FY 44, p. 603.

[49] Incl 1, Rpt, Activities, Sp Coverage Br Western Div SCPC, for FY 44, 7 Jan 44, with Ltr, "Lee" (otherwise unidentified) to Maj Nelson, APS, 7 Jan 44. SigC 062.2 Policy (Motion Pictures), 1942–45.

had to be made.[50] The war ended before the matter was decided. The final tally showed 988 films rescored into foreign languages—353 into Spanish, 308 into Portuguese, 166 into Chinese, 128 into French, and 33 into Italian.[51]

In addition to the full-fledged training films, other types of visual training aids such as film bulletins, combat bulletins, film strips, and film slides served the Army's training program.[52] A film bulletin seldom exceeded twenty minutes running time (two reels) and dealt with a single topic. Since timeliness was all-important, film bulletins were produced as silent pictures in order to save the time of writing and recording narration. Training instructors and lecturers added their own commentary as the scenes were shown.[53] In September 1944 ASF authorized a new category, the technical film bulletin.[54] These new film bulletins were intended to make even greater use of the battle front information then flowing in from every theater in the form of excellent combat footage. *Front Line Chaplain*, *The Army Nurse*, *Flame Thrower Tactics*, *Combat Smoke Operations*—these titles suggest the topics depicted. By June 1945 more than 500,000 feet of combat film had been utilized to produce about 160 technical bulletins.[55]

The Army Pictorial Service furnished training agencies with still another useful visual training aid in the form of film strips. The originating agencies prepared the frame layouts and the accompanying lecture if the strip was to have sound accompaniment. APS produced and distributed the film strips. Between Pearl Harbor and the Japanese surrender, APS furnished more than 1,500 film strips on every conceivable subject— *Booby Traps*, *Intra and Extra Oral Splints*, *QM Battalion Baker*, *How to Fire a Furnace*, *Azimuth Determination by Solar Observation*, *Structure of the Horse and Mule*, and many others. Of the total, 41 had sound in the form of a record to be played as the film was projected on the screen. Many of the sound film strips were used in separation centers to provide information quickly to large groups of dischargees.[56]

Information and Historical Films

Combat coverage offered a rich source of immediate information for staff planning. To take advantage of it, the Chief of Staff early in 1944 ordered a weekly compilation of the most pertinent shots of tactical situations embodying employment of troops and equipment to be shown to a selected group of high-level staff officers and commanding generals in Washington and in all the theaters.

[50] Transmittal Sheet, O/C Domestic Prod Sec to Chief Mil Prod Sec APS, 11 Jan 45, sub: Rescoring Prog, and 5 Incls, on Spanish, Portuguese, French, Chinese, and Italian Rescoring. SigC 062.2 Rescoring Gen, pt. 1, May 43–Dec 45.

[51] Quadow, Tng Films in the Second World War, Supplement, Jan 44–Aug 45, p. 9.

[52] ASF Manual M–4, Military Training, Apr 45, pp. 31–41.

[53] (1) Outline of the Film Prod Prog of the SigC, 12 Dec 42. SigC 062.2 Policy (Motion Pictures), 1942–45. (2) Quadow, Tng Films in the Second World War, Supplement, Jan 44–Aug 45, pp. 9–10. (3) WD Memo, W105-2-43, 12 Mar 43.

[54] ASF Cir 311, 18 Sep 44.

[55] The technical film bulletins were subdivided into further categories depending upon subject matter and length. CSigO, Annual Rpt, FY 45, pp. 811–12.

[56] (1) Quadow, Tng Films in the Second World War, Supplement, Jan 44–Aug 45, p. 10. (2) FM 21-7, List of War Department Films, Film Strips, and Recognition Film Slides, Jan 46, pp. 81–157.

At high levels the *Staff Film Report* was rated the most valuable of all the film projects APS undertook during the war.

Editing the *Staff Film Report* was an exacting business. It meant reviewing more than 200,000 feet of combat film arriving each week from overseas theaters and selecting only the most pertinent material, enough for two to four reels. Editing, cutting, narrating, and recording all had to be done very quickly and with expert judgment. The General Staff in Washington and the commanders of the overseas theaters were unanimous in their approval of the films. Through the *Staff Film Report* they could view with their own eyes the details of operations in their own theaters and in other combat areas as well, studying details of terrain and climate, the operation of new weapons, the effect of innovations in doctrine, and so on. Prints were rushed overseas for showing at the same time that they were being shown in Washington, thus establishing liaison among all the theaters. The *Staff Film Report* was also made available to the Allies.[57] General Weible, Director of Military Training, ASF, rated the *Staff Film Report* "among the finest pictorial products of the war."

The restricted version of the *Staff Film Report,* with all secret or confidential material eliminated, became a combat bulletin and was issued to troops.[58] Prints were sent overseas as well as to all troop stations in the United States. Combat bulletins emphasized lessons learned in combat pertaining to teamwork, leadership, adaptation to battle conditions, the use of weapons and equipment, techniques, and local expedients, and were expected to point out both correct and incorrect practices.[59] Although the War Department circular announcing the new series stressed that combat bulletins would not be used as news releases, this came to be true only so far as public showings were concerned. The Chief of Staff pointed out that wounded soldiers in hospitals were eager to know how the campaigns were progressing, and in particular, what their own outfits were doing. From showings in hospitals, where The Surgeon General reported that the films had great therapeutic value, the use of combat bulletins spread quickly to other agencies. In effect, they became the Army's own newsreel. An average of 324 prints of a new bulletin went out to domestic and overseas users every week in 1944–45.[60] The Navy, too, wanted prints of all combat bulletins, since shots of Navy combat action were included regularly. Lt. Col. Emanuel Cohen, executive producer of SCPC, suggested that the combat bulletins ought to be a joint affair, similar to the *Army and Navy Screen Magazine,* in the interest of economy and efficiency.[61] The war ended before any such change could take place.

---

[57] (1) CSigO, Annual Rpt, FY 45, pp. 820–21. (2) Cohen, "Film Is A Weapon," *Business Screen,* VII, No. 1, p. 74.

[58] (1) Memo, Deputy Dir Mil Tng Div ASF for CSigO, 4 Jan 44, sub: Combat Bulls. (2) Ltr, Asst AG AGF to Chief APS Through Dir Mil Tng Div ASF, 4 Feb 44, sub: Combat Bulls, and 1st Ind, Dir Mil Tng Div ASF to CSigO, 11 Feb 44. Both in SigC 062.2 Policy (Combat Bulls), 1943–45. (3) WD Cir 86, sec. II, 26 Feb 44.

[59] (1) Ltrs, Chief APS to CG's NATO, USAFIME, *et al.,* 3 Apr 44, sub: Combat Bulls. SigC 062.2 Policy (Combat Bulls), 1943–45. (2) CSigO, Annual Rpt, FY 44, pp. 607–08.

[60] CSigO, Annual Rpt, FY 45, p. 821.

[61] Memo, Cohen, SCPC, for Chief APS, 1 Jan 45, sub: Combat Bulls. SigC 062.2 Policy (Combat Bulls), 1943–45.

Combat film also brought the front-line war to the industrial workers at home. Early in the war, SCPC began producing *Film Communiques* for the Bureau of Public Relations' Industrial Services Division. Thereafter *Film Communiques* appeared monthly until March 1945. Late in 1943, in an effort to solve some conflicts between the film information program of the Industrial Services Division of BPR and the film program of the Office of War Information, a special assistant to the Under Secretary of War met with representatives of both organizations to iron out difficulties. The Office of the Under Secretary of War had already sampled opinion among two hundred war manufacturers, asking them to evaluate the effectiveness of the Industrial Services films in boosting and maintaining output among war workers. Almost unanimously the manufacturers endorsed the films strongly and urged that the program be continued and expanded.[62]

The reorganized program called for the production of two short films per month, to be shown in manufacturing plants of 1,300 large manufacturers employing about 70 percent of all war workers. Prints to be furnished to OWI supplied the smaller war plants and other adult groups. Under Secretary of War Patterson felt keenly that the films would play a decisive part in war production. "We are in a difficult period," he wrote to the Chief Signal Officer, ". . . the feeling is wide-spread that the war is in its final phase and will soon be over . . . these films will counteract any

tendency . . . to take things easy."[63]

A typical film communiqué, *Little Detroit*, showed a truck assembly plant in North Africa. The *Price of Rendova* filmed the landing of invasion troops, establishment of a beachhead, and a Japanese bombing attack. Other films in the series showed the Air Transport Command landing supplies and evacuating wounded men in New Guinea. *Kill Or Be Killed, Channel Fortifications, The Battle of Midway, The Army Behind the Army*—these and other films brought a sense of participation to the industrial workers who produced the arms and equipment for the fighting men.[64]

Some specially tailored industrial service films showed particular categories of war workers how their own labors advanced the war effort. *Timber to Tokyo* for the lumber industry, *Life Line* for the medical supply industry, *Men of Fire* for foundry workers, *Attack Signal* for electronics workers, and *Cotton at War* for textile workers were of this type. At least 8,500,000 war workers in many industries as well as the general public saw the film called *The Birth of the B-29*. Toward the end of the war, a serious deterioration in the labor situation in the Detroit area led to a series of six 2-minute shorts to be shown to workers in that locality. The pictures pulled no punches; they exposed the horrors and brutalities of conflict in some of the most jolting combat pictures

---

[62] (1) Memo, John Hertz, Sp Adviser to USW, 29 Dec 43, sub: Industrial Sv Films. SigC 062.2 Policy (Motion Pictures), 1942–45.

[63] (1) Memo, USW Patterson for CSigO, 30 Dec 43, sub: Industrial Sv Film Prog. (2) Memo, CSigO for USW, 1 Jan 44, sub: Industrial Sv Film Prog. Both in SigC 062.2 Policy (Motion Pictures), 1942–45.

[64] Ltr, Chief APS to Dir SigC Inspec Agency, 4 Jan 44, sub: Army Motion Pictures Available for Showings to Industry, and Incls. WD Rpt folders, SigC 062.2 Tng Films 1, Jan–Mar 44.

shown during the war. The impact of such films as *Two-and-a-Half Minutes, The Line Is Busy, Hands, Silence,* and *Justice* was so great, the appeal so persuasive, that they were borrowed for use in the sixth war bond drive and later were used for manpower recruiting purposes in the Newark, New Jersey, area.[65] Another labor recruiting film, *What's Your Name?* played in 14,000 theaters. *This War Speeds Up* and *The Enemy Strikes,* the latter an authentic and harrowing account of the desperate Battle of the Bulge, also served their purposes with great effectiveness. The BPR arranged a system of national distribution, charging a nominal fee for handling and transportation costs only.[66]

In terms of public interest and audience reception, the combat footage used for the historical series of films—war campaign reports issued through BPR for public newsreels—ranked high. During the last two years of war, BPR demanded and got combat films for newsreel showing at the rate of one 2-reel subject each thirty days.[67] Since the importance of the pictures depended upon the speed with which they reached the screen, each had to be released within "30 days after the end of a campaign or portion thereof." [68] The BPR distributed 677 prints of each subject without

charge through the War Activities Committee of the motion picture industry and OWI.[69] Such pictures as *Eve of Battle,* the story of the Normandy invasion, *Tunisian Victory,* made jointly with the British Ministry of Information, and *Attack! The Battle for New Britain,* the story of the campaign at Cape Gloucester in the Southwest Pacific, reached enthusiastic home audiences while the events were still very much in the news.[70] BPR historical film bulletins included British, AAF, Marine, and Coast Guard film as well as Army footage.[71]

Making acceptable pictures for general viewing demanded both excellent combat footage as a source of film and great skill in cutting, editing, and putting together the finished picture. By 1944 the Signal Corps pictorial service was supplying both of these essential ingredients. But the War Department BPR, understandably anxious to assure wide distribution of popular subjects, sometimes tended to encroach on the time and facilities SCPC had to allot to other agencies. For example, in early 1945 an SCPC crew shot 3,000 feet of newsreel film for the BPR at Walter Reed Hospital, showing wounded men engaged in various activities. At the same time the crew shot some footage for a training film they were making for The Surgeon General as a follow-up to the rehabilitation film, *Meet Mr. McGonegal.* When BPR officials saw the

[65] CSigO, Annual Rpt, FY 45, pp. 818–19.

[66] Ltr, Chief of APS to Dir SigC Inspec Agency, 5 Jan 44, sub: Army Motion Pictures Available for Showing to Industry. SigC 062.2 Tng Films 1, Jan–Mar 44.

[67] (1) Memo, Maj Gen Alexander D. Surles, BPR, for Chief APS, 4 Jan 44, sub: Motion Picture Releases. (2) Memo, Chief APS for CO SCPC, 24 Jan 44. Both in SigC 062.2 Policy (Motion Pictures), 1942–45.

[68] Memo, Chief APS for CO SCPC, 24 Jan 44. SigC 062.2 Policy (Motion Pictures), 1942–45.

[69] Memo, Actg Chief APS for Asst Secy WDGS, 9 May 44, sub: Release of Two-Reel Campaign Pictures. SigC 062.2 Policy (Motion Pictures), 1942–45.

[70] CSigO, Annual Rpt, FY 44, p. 607.

[71] Memo, Chief Photo Prod Br APS for CO SCPC, 24 Mar 44, sub: BPR Hist Bulls. SigC 062.2 Policy (Motion Pictures), 1942–45.

film, they wanted all of it, including that for The Surgeon General, to be distributed immediately. The APS, considering that it had a responsibility to protect the other services for which it made pictures, refused to hand over The Surgeon General's film. Said SCPC's executive producer, "Sometimes I wonder whether it isn't advisable to stop all our operations and just work for the newsreels!" [72]

Throughout the war, the Historical Branch of SCPC collected and filed film sequences recounting American operations in the theaters for eventual use at war's end in compiling theater and campaign chronologies. Much of the material served other purposes during the war, but a continuing process of editing went on for the specific purpose of compiling the historical record. Editors selected more than 2,340,000 feet of combat film potentially useful for theater chronologies during fiscal year 1945 alone.[73] The Signal Corps regarded the historical chronologies as extremely important, even though obviously none could be completed until after combat ceased. The APS hoped to enlist the collaboration and advice of military historians in the War Department Historical Division in order to assure complete accuracy of scripts and presentation.[74]

Unfortunately, only a very small proportion of the chronologies were ever completed. The sharp postwar reduction in funds and in the number of writers, editors, and cutters assigned to APS all but halted the program in 1946 and eventually strangled it altogether. Only fourteen out of a projected fifty-nine films were ever completed.[75]

Morale-Building Films

Army commanders spoke often of morale, the hard-to-define intangible that weighed so heavily in the success or failure of a military unit. It could not be achieved by ukase, or memos of the "let there be morale" variety. On the other hand, the written word, the spoken word, and the art of the motion picture all helped to create the conditions under which high morale flourished. The Signal Corps produced motion pictures for the I&E Division, ASF, to help the individual soldier understand why he was in uniform and how his part in the global conflict was related to that of other soldiers and civilians. Films defined the enemy for him and acquainted him with his allies; films provided familiar entertainment for his off-duty hours; and films instilled in him a feeling of security about his postwar life.

Orientation films—pictorial presentations of the causes and events leading up to World War II—had been undertaken early in 1942 by a special motion picture production unit under the com-

---

[72] Memo, Exec Producer SCPC for Chief APS, 4 Jan 45, sub: Footage Shot at Walter Reed Hospital, with Routing Slip, Munson to Nelson, 8 Jan 45. SigC 062.2 Sp Coverage by APS, pt. 1, 1941–45.

[73] CSigO, Annual Rpt, FY 45, p. 848.

[74] (1) Memo for Rcd, W.L.W. (Dr. Walter L. Wright), Hist Div WDSS, 22 Feb 44, sub: Proposal for Co-operation With the APS. OCMH files. (2) Item h, Memo, Chief APS for Contl Div OCSigO, 1 Mar 44, sub: Digest of Progress and Problems. SigC AS 319.1 Digest of Progress and Problems, pt. 1, Aug 43 Through Dec 44.

[75] (1) Info obtained from Lt Col G. E. Popkess, Jr., APS, 10 Oct 46, and Lt Col J. S. Bardwell, APS, 20 Dec 58. (2) CSigO, Annual Rpt, FY 46, p. 585. (3) Daily Digest, Item 3, 8 Jan 46, SigC EO Daily Digest of Staff and Operating Divs, Jan 46. (4) DA Pamphlet 108–1, Jan 59, pp. 226–27.

mand of Maj. Frank Capra.[76] Originally placed in the I&E Division, ASF, and transferred to the Signal Corps' APS in the fall of 1943, Capra's unit undertook the orientation series of films as its principal task.[77] By early 1945 Capra had turned out seventeen remarkably effective films. The original seven in the *Why We Fight* series were generally regarded as unquestionably the films that contributed most to American understanding of the issues of World War II. During his basic training, every soldier saw these seven outstanding documentaries—*Prelude to War, The Nazis Strike, Divide and Conquer, Battle of Britain, Battle of Russia, Battle of China,* and *War Comes to America.* By popular demand, prints were shown to war workers and, ultimately, to the general public in movie theaters.

Originally, *War Comes to America* was to be produced in two parts. The first part covered the steps leading to America's involvement in the war; the second was to be a pictorial presentation of highlights during the war period. It became evident that no single picture could do justice to such a theme. In April 1945 the Army decided to drop all work on the second part of the film.[78] Capra returned to civilian life in June 1945.[79]

As the war ran its changing course, the subject matter of the orientation films kept pace. *Your Job in Germany* was readied especially for the occupation troops in that area. In the late summer of 1944, shortly before the Leyte Campaign got under way, General MacArthur's headquarters sent an urgent appeal for a film that would provide the soldiers of the invasion forces with the facts they needed concerning the Philippines. Little time remained; the film had to be ready within six weeks. The APS motion picture library held remarkably little footage depicting Philippine history, manners, customs, religion, and politics. Rounding up film from amateur photographers, lecturers, and commercial sources plus the Army footage, APS put together *This Is the Philippines* in time to be shown to all invasion forces. A second orientation film, *Westward Is Bataan,* was released jointly by MacArthur and the I&E Division, ASF.

One of the most important films produced during the entire war was made in great secrecy at the direction of the Chief of Staff. General Marshall feared that once Germany was defeated an uninformed and unreasoning clamor to "bring the boys back home" might play havoc with discipline and morale and greatly delay the defeat of Japan. It was important that the Army's plans for redeployment to the Pacific and the point system for Army discharge be explained to the military forces and to the public very soon after the defeat of Germany. Marshall decided to depend entirely upon a single motion picture to bring the information to all concerned practically simultaneously. That picture, produced months before the war in Europe actually ended and in anticipation of

[76] Thompson, Harris, *et al., The Test,* pp. 414–16.

[77] Memo, Brig Gen Edward L. Munson, Chief APS, for Col Robert Cutler, OSW, 18 Aug 45, sub: Statement on *Why We Fight* Series. SigC 062.2 Prod of Orientation Films, 1943–45.

[78] Ltr, Chief APS to Dir I&E Div ASF, 10 Apr 45, sub: Completion of *Why We Fight* Series. SigC 062.2 Prod of Orientation Films, 1943–45.

[79] The Chief of Staff, General Marshall, pinned the Distinguished Service Medal on Capra's blouse in recognition of his distinctive contribution to the war effort.

MAJOR CAPRA CUTTING ARMY FILM

V–E Day, was the orientation film *Two Down and One to Go.*[80]

Filmed in the summer of 1944, the picture received its official title on 8 September. In view of the great importance of the film, APS set up a special distribution procedure and the War Department issued special instructions to assure simultaneous showings in all overseas theaters and within the zone of interior.[81] Such thorough coverage, worldwide, presented a distribution problem unique in motion picture experience. Early in November, SCPC held a conference at Astoria with representatives of all the service commands in the United States to co-ordinate the details of the showings. Five photographic officers were dispatched overseas to visit all theaters, bases, and commands to which prints of the film had been shipped. For the commercial theaters in the United States, the BPR and the War Activities Committee of the motion picture industry acted in concert to arrange all details.[82]

By the end of December, 1,363 technicolor prints had been distributed to the various parts of the world. All was in readiness. As directed, showings of the film began simultaneously to military units and to civilian audiences in commercial theaters at 1200, Eastern war

---

[80] Cohen, "Film Is a Weapon," *Business Screen,* VII, No. 1 (APS Issue).

[81] WD Cir 428, 2 Nov 44.

[82] (1) Transmittal Sheet, Asst Chief APS for Contl Br OCSigO, 4 Jun 45, sub: Digest of Progress and Problems, APS. SigC AS 319.1 Digest of Progress and Problems, pt. 2, 1 Jan 45–30 Sep 45. (2) Clarke, SigC APS in World War II, pp. 200–201. (3) WD Memo 850–45, 31 Mar 45.

time, on 10 May 1945. Within five days, 95 percent of all troops in the zone of interior had seen the film. Overseas it took a little longer—about two weeks—to achieve a 97 percent showing. While some 7,000,000 troops at home and overseas were seeing the picture, their families were seeing it too, at approximately 800 first-run civilian movie theaters. The Army had relied on a single motion picture to spread the word on a matter in which more people were interested than any other single thing—discharge from the Army. It was an impressive demonstration of the value of film as an information medium.[83] A second film, *On to Tokyo*, released two weeks later, also reached the entire military audience and possibly an even larger civilian audience than did *Two Down and One to Go*.

A second category of films aimed at building and maintaining morale embraced a number of projects designed to inform, educate, and entertain. The *Army and Navy Screen Magazine* and the *G.I. Movie Weekly* presented the war in global terms, showed the integration of the various theaters and the relationship of the services to each other, and portrayed civilian activities at home in support of the war. Best of all from the soldiers' standpoint, they furnished good entertainment.

The APS produced the first issue of the biweekly *Army and Navy Screen Magazine* in April 1943. It included material filmed by the Navy, the AAF, and the Marine Corps as well as Army film and commercial features. This issue also introduced the war's best known film cartoon personality, Private Snafu. The prototype of all GI's who invariably do things the wrong way, Private Snafu struggled through a series of incredible adventures in every branch of the service and in every theater of war. Whatever the point to be made, Private Snafu taught it in his own cockeyed way. He got malaria and dysentery, was shot and stabbed, fell out of planes, and cracked up jeeps. Bumbling through ludicrous misadventures with equipment, falling prey to clip artists in bars and bazaars around the globe, exposing rumors and enemy propaganda techniques, humorously expressing the gripes and fears of soldiers, he served as teacher, morale builder, comrade-in-arms, and safety valve.

The *Army and Navy Screen Magazine* became a regular feature on the 45-minute program of *G.I. Movie Weekly*, which also included commercial releases, sports shorts, and newsreels. Content of the *Army and Navy Screen Magazine* and the *G.I. Movie Weekly* was the responsibility of the Morale Services Division of ASF. The APS provided the technical advice and mechanical facilities for translating the scripts onto the screen and distributed the finished product both at home and overseas.[84]

A three-way partnership between the Army Pictorial Service, the ASF's Special Services Division, and the motion picture industry assured American soldiers of a steady diet of their favorite enter-

---

[83] (1) CSigO, Annual Rpt, FY 45, p. 835. (2) 1st Ind, ACSigO to CG ASF, 21 Jul 45, on Ltr, AGO to all Comdrs, Depts, *et al.*, sub: SigC 062.2 Motion Picture, *Two Down and One to Go*, 29 Jun 45. SigC 062.2 Tng Film, 1945.

[84] (1) CSigO, Annual Rpt, FY 44, p. 605; FY 45, pp. 815–18. (2) Clarke, SigC APS in World War II, pp. 202–05. (3) Statement of APS Regarding Effect of Title V, PL 277, 17 Apr 44. SigC 062.2 Policy (Motion Pictures), 1942–45.

tainment films. The Army Motion Picture Service, a branch of Special Services Division, secured the films, most of which the film industry donated through its War Activities Committee of the Motion Picture Producers and Distributors of America, Inc.[85] The APS distributed the films overseas through a branch created especially for that purpose, the Overseas Motion Picture Service of the Distribution Division. OMPS also procured, distributed, and repaired the projectors used in showing the films.

OMPS sent three pictures each week to combat areas and four to noncombat areas. It operated twenty-one film exchanges in overseas areas; no theater of war was without one. Between 1943 and the end of the war, OMPS distributed 43,306 full-length copies of feature films and 33,236 of short subjects in co-operation with the motion picture industry. OMPS strove constantly to extend the range and speed of its services. In 1945 OMPS began supplying films to troop transports and hospital ships.[86] And in the Pacific, the Army and Navy jointly shared all entertainment films the Signal Corps distributed to that area.[87]

Undoubtedly the soldier audience constituted the largest and most appreciative group of viewers any entertainment film ever enjoyed. OMPS kept accurate records of the number of viewers and the audience reception to various types of films. For the night of 1 June 1945, in overseas theaters alone,

1,900,000 servicemen attended more than 6,000 separate showings of OMPS-distributed films. OMPS estimated that, at the rate of two shows per week, a minimum of 650,000,000 military personnel attended Army motion picture showings in overseas theaters alone during the war.[88] In the ETO, from May 1944 to June 1945 alone, attendance tallies showed that 145,000,000 troops saw the 600,000, separate film performances shown.[89]

Distribution of Films

The APS distributed the Army's films to troops everywhere through a system of film libraries, or film and equipment exchanges as they were called overseas. The entire distributing process became, at the peak of wartime operations, the largest in the world. OMPS alone distributed more entertainment films within a year than the four largest Hollywood producers combined had ever done.[90] OMPS, formed by the transfer of the Distribution Branch of ASF's Special Services Division to APS in November 1943, was one of three branches within the Distribution Division of SCPC, each of which performed a specialized distribution process.[91]

Films serving different purposes were distributed by different methods. Entertainment pictures and recurring subjects such as the *Army and Navy Screen Maga-*

[85] Ltr, Arthur L. Mayer, Asst Coordinator, War Activities Cmte, to Lawton, Chief APS, 23 Nov 43. SigC 062.2 Policy (Motion Pictures), 1942–45.

[86] CSigO, Annual Rpt, FY 45, p. 838.

[87] AG Ltr, AG-MT-N-413.53 (15 May 45), 16 May 45.

[88] "Through the A.P.S. Lens," *Signals,* I, No. 2 (November–December, 1946), 13.

[89] USFET Gen Bd Rpt 116, Motion Picture Sv, p. 1.

[90] Lt. Col. Orton H. Hicks, "Army Pictures Reach 'Round the World," *Business Screen,* VII, No. 1 (December, 1945), 53.

[91] (1) WD Memo S-90, 11 Nov 43 (effective 15 Nov). (2) Memo, ExecO APS for CO SCPC, 7 Dec 43. SigC 062.2 Policy (Motion Pictures), 1942–45.

MOBILE PHOTO LABORATORY IN NEW GUINEA, *above.* *Below, movie show in the field.*

zine required circuiting, in order to reach as many troops as possible in the shortest time. On the other hand, training films and special-purpose films had to be placed safely in film libraries at specific training installations in order to be on hand on the exact day when the particular subject covered in the film was reached in the training schedules. Thus, while OMPS circuited films through the twenty-one overseas Army exchanges as well as to the Navy and the Marine Corps, the Library Branch serviced the various training film libraries. Release Print Branch, the third organizational unit, stored, shipped, and received prints for both of the other branches.[92]

Control of the film libraries and exchanges lay with the service command or overseas theater in which they were located. The signal officer of the service command or theater supervised all film exchange operations through the visual aids officer on his staff. The visual aids officer was responsible for establishing and maintaining the library and any necessary sublibraries or exchanges distributing and exhibiting the films, providing the projector equipment and training the projector operators, and supplying information and various reports concerning the content of films and film utilization.[93] He was not responsible for the use made of the film, which was a training responsibility, or, in the case of entertainment film, a responsibility of Special Services.

Quite often the large Class A library or central film and equipment exchange located at a large headquarters provided fairly elaborate facilities—viewing rooms, classrooms, equipment maintenance and spare parts storage facilities, offices, film storage and inspection rooms, and so on. These central libraries or exchanges controlled the smaller sublibraries—the Class B installations, with facilities to serve from 30,000 to 50,000 troops, or Class C, serving the small units and isolated outposts. A service command central film library usually controlled twenty to thirty sublibraries, and a theater headquarters central film exchange an even larger number of subexchanges.[94]

Overseas exchanges, of course, were constantly in the process of closing at one location and opening at another as the troops they served moved on. Unquestionably the greatest source of comfort and relaxation for soldiers everywhere was the nightly movie. All theater commanders unhesitatingly granted air priority for shipment of films. On the grassy hillsides of Italy, in the mud of Germany, in the steamy heat of Pacific jungle outposts, wherever soldiers rested for the night the Army shows went on. Sometimes the screen went up in a half-ruined building, and quite often on the side of the mobile motion picture service van. Okinawa, Iwo Jima, Manila, and Saipan all had their own film exchanges within days after the beachheads were taken. The APS established a west coast liaison office in 1944 to help speed distribution of films to Pacific areas. The British, the AAF, and the Navy co-operated closely with the

[92] (1) Hicks, "Army Pictures Reach 'Round the World," *Business Screen*, VII, No. 1, 88. (2) CSigO, Annual Rpt, FY 45, pp. 824–32.

[93] Maj. Dennis R. Williams, "Right Time, Right Place, and Right Film," *Business Screen*, VII, No. 1 (December, 1945), 55–57, 97.

[94] Capt. William C. Ralke, "Operation of a Service Command Central Film Library," *Business Screen*, VII, No. 1 (December, 1945), 58.

APS. Navy and Marine Corps liaison officers were on duty in the SCPC's Distribution Division during the last eighteen months of war to co-ordinate policies and operations of the overseas motion picture distribution.[95]

For field use the Signal Corps bought standard commercial 16-mm. sound projectors, which possessed the essential characteristics of light weight, portability, and simplicity of operation. Equally important from the supply standpoint, they were low in cost and easy to manufacture. However, when the Army's requirements were added to those of the other services, the demand outran the supply. Critical shortages of projectors developed in several areas, notably in the ETO, resulting principally from a lack of maintenance and repair parts and facilities.[96]

Supply difficulties in projector equipment ran parallel to difficulties in communications equipment in general. In the earlier months of the war manufacturers of 16-mm. projectors were so busy with orders for complete assemblies that they neglected the timely delivery of maintenance and repair parts. Also, more repair parts were needed than had been anticipated. The 16-mm. projectors had been designed only for limited civilian use under controlled conditions; in the war they were abused, overused, and subjected to the most diverse climatic conditions. Actually, the equipment stood up remarkably well, all things considered.[97]

A complete maintenance list for a projector contained 138 individual parts, most of them very small. Frequently packages containing repair parts were lost in shipment, particularly since the projectors and repair parts did not enjoy the high shipping priority that the films themselves did. Hastily trained soldier operators proved to be unable to make even the simplest adjustments or to provide the most elementary maintenance such as cleaning or oiling. All these factors contributed to "deadlined" projectors much too often.[98]

Late in 1944 the APS moved to rectify the maintenance problem. It established its own depot facilities at the central overseas film and equipment exchanges and took over all major repairs. Matters improved greatly, but central exchanges of necessity had to be located at permanent headquarters locations. This meant that they could not serve the combat elements with the greatest effectiveness. For these outposts, APS distributed tool kits that provided the necessities for complete repair and adjustment of projector equipment. The kits included instruction literature and the American War Standard Test films.[99]

Still Pictures

Motion picture production tended to steal the limelight, but still picture production was no less important. Still pictures filled certain tactical and administrative needs that motion pictures could not. For identification, for de-

[95] CSigO, Annual Rpt, FY 45, pp. 826–31.

[96] (1) USFET Gen Bd Rpt 116, pp. 6–7. (2) Capt Everts R. Buchanan, Army Pictorial Service in a Theater of Operations, 10 Aug 50 (1950), Sig Sch Monograph, p. 15. The Sig Sch Libr, Ft. Monmouth.

[97] Capt. Edwin B. Levinson, "Operation and

Maintenance of Projectors in the Field," *Business Screen*, VII, No. 1 (December, 1945), 63.

[98] USFET, Gen Bd Rpt 116, pp. 6–7.

[99] Levinson, "Operation and Maintenance of Projectors in the Field," *Business Screen*, VII, No. 1, p. 64.

tailed study, for maintenance of permanent records, for publication in all manner of news media, still pictures were essential.

The Signal Corps provided the Army's still picture coverage through still picture units of the signal photographic companies and through other photographers in special teams working out of the SCPC in Astoria and the SCPL in Washington. In the combat zone, exposed negatives usually were developed at collecting points to the rear and then rushed to the United States. But in the earlier part of the war in some areas such as the Pacific and the Mediterranean, where few processing laboratories were available, the exposed negatives were flown directly to the United States for developing. Photographic officers were not altogether unhappy over the lack of forward processing laboratories overseas; they pointed out that under such conditions they were able "to avoid the countless requests for personal pictures masquerading under the guise of 'official.'"[100] Moreover, the possibility of contaminated water supply and the lack of temperature control under field processing conditions presented hazards to valuable film that could be avoided at base laboratories.

The Signal Corps Photographic Laboratory at the Army War College in Washington processed still picture negatives (as well as motion picture footage) until February 1943, when a branch of the still picture laboratory was opened in the Pentagon, where, in 1944, all still picture laboratory operations were consolidated.[101]

Each month during the last two years of war, more than 10,000 combat pictures flowed into the Still Picture Library that APS maintained in the Pentagon. In fiscal year 1945 alone, the library received 142,264 photographs.[102] The Still Picture Library provided a repository for still pictures comparable to the Central War Department Film Library for motion pictures at SCPC in Astoria. Cataloguing, indexing, filing, and cross-referencing the stills and servicing requests for prints kept a staff of about 30 civilians and 2 officers exceptionally busy. Late in 1943 the shortage of personnel reached a critical stage.[103] The officer in charge of the library stated that in his opinion "a large number of the photos received should never have been taken, and if they were taken, should never have been submitted to Washington." As a result, APS began rejecting those pictures it considered to be of no value for the War Department permanent files. After this editing procedure had been in effect a few months, the number of overseas pictures of only local interest dropped off to a mere trickle.[104]

From among the hundreds of thousands of pictures received, the Still Picture Library culled only the best. A picture selected for retention had to meet a high standard for its strategic, tactical,

---

[100] Robert L. Eichberg and Jacqueline M. Quadow, Combat Photography (1945), SigC Hist Monograph, F–2b, pp. 66, 79. SigC Hist Sec file.

[101] CSigO, Annual Rpt, FY 46, p. 583.

[102] CSigO, Annual Rpt, FY 45, p. 843.

[103] Incl 9, Memo, O/C Still Picture Sec for Chief APS, 2 Oct 43, with Transmittal Sheet, Action 1, Chief APS to Contl Div OCSigO, 18 Jan 44, sub: Current and Anticipated Problems. SigC AS 319.1 Digest of Progress and Problems, pt. 1, Aug 43 Through Dec 44.

[104] Transmittal Sheet, Action 1, Chief APS to Contl Div OCSigO, 1 Oct 44, sub: Digest of Progress and Problems for Sep 44. SigC AS 319.1 Digest of Progress and Problems, pt. 1, Aug 43 Through Dec 44.

training, intelligence, information, or historial value. By early 1945, there were 423,000 such photographs on file.[105] And by the end of the war, library holdings rose to more than 500,000 pictures, one-third of which had been received during the last year of war.[106]

The large number of requests for prints, many of which were not really essential, placed a heavy burden on the Still Picture Section. To the best of its ability, APS filled all requests labeled "official," but in 1945 when photographic paper and materials became critically scarce, it became necessary to edit all requests. In spite of this, the library furnished a total of 645,979 prints during fiscal year 1945.[107] The peak month came earlier, in September 1944, when APS furnished 71,316 prints.[108]

The Signal Corps had too few still picture cameramen to undertake all the desirable, though not essential, projects for which it received requests. In January 1945, the Adjutant General's Office advanced a plan to have all the graves of American Army dead photographed by Signal Corps photographers, with copies of the pictures furnished to the surviving relatives. AGO stated that the Marine Corps followed this custom, thereby building up much good will for its corps. General Ingles pointed out that the far greater size of the Army, and its much wider range of operations all over the world, made the cost of such a project simply prohibitive. He concluded that such a project would seriously curtail combat operations. The project was never undertaken.[109]

The APS strove earnestly to reduce the time interval between the taking of a picture and its arrival at its ultimate destination, whether in the public press or in the hands of a staff officer. Just before the Normandy invasion, the inauguration of a 24-hour air courier service from Europe greatly speeded the delivery of pictures to the Bureau of Public Relations and to the military services. The first D-day pictures were on General Marshall's desk within 24 hours.[110]

The introduction of radiophoto (telephoto) techniques for transmitting photographs by electronic means provided an even swifter method. The equipment developed for Army Communications Service by Acme Newspictures was ready for field testing by June 1942. The first operating installation was set up in Algiers early in 1943.[111] With the collaboration of BPR, a specially picked group of highly trained APS photographers and nationally known press photographers went to Algiers. They sent a single test photograph across the ocean one hundred times before the transmission quality proved technically satisfactory.[112]

The first radioed battle pictures on 18

---

[105] Logistics folder, 1945.

[106] CSigO, Annual Rpt, FY 45, pp. 599, 843.

[107] Ibid., p. 843.

[108] Maj. Frank Muto, "Still Pictures," Business Screen, VII, No. 1 (December, 1945), 82.

[109] Ltr, AGO to CSigO, 29 Jan 45, sub: Photos of Graves, with Incl, Ltr, AGO to ACofS G-1, same sub, 29 Jan 45, and 1st Ind, CSigO to AGO, 13 Feb 45. SigC 062.1 Sp Coverage by APS, pt. 1, Aug 44–Dec 45.

[110] Eichberg and Quadow, Combat Photography, p. 67.

[111] (1) Col. Carl H. Hatch, "Radiophotos," Radio News, 31, No. 2 (February, 1944), 218. (2) Hist, Sig Sec, AFHQ, app. B (Photo), p. 2. For description of technical operation of the equipment, see below, p. 605.

[112] Hatch, "Radiophotos," Radio News, 31, No. 2.

March 1943, showing the capture of Gafsa, found eager acceptance from staff officers and news media in Washington. As quickly as possible other radiophoto stations were installed—in Brisbane in July 1943; in Honolulu in February 1944; in Manila in January 1945.[113] Temporary stations operated along the battle fronts. One such station in Normandy sent 601 transmissions during the invasion. The special telephoto subsection of Army Communications Service in Washington delivered and processed 11,455 radiophoto prints of invasion scenes. From July 1944 through June 1945 other stations operated at various times at Cherbourg, Kharagpur, Port Moresby, Hollandia, in southern France, on Saipan, on Leyte, and at locations serving 6th Army Group and Seventh Army headquarters.[114] Each picture, map, or text required only seven minutes' transmission time.

In the closing days of the war, APS dispatched the first full color picture ever transmitted across the ocean. This picture of President Harry S. Truman, Prime Minister Clement R. Attlee, and Marshal Joseph Stalin at the Potsdam conference required a transmission time of 21 minutes, 7 minutes for each of the 3 separate color negatives necessary.[115]

As the war progressed, experience and better photographic training methods produced some of the finest pictorial coverage of the war.[116] Signal Corps

photographers shot 50 percent of all still pictures published in newspapers, magazines, and books in 1944.[117] Tactical pictures became more meaningful. Four cameramen in London assigned to photograph the first robot bombs produced valuable stills showing the trajectory, explosive intensity, and extent of damage.[118] Still pictures captured the great historical moments and recorded the important personalities for posterity. More than 400 excellent photographs of the first Quebec international conference brought requests for 5,000 prints.[119] The closing events of the war, the Potsdam conference, the surrender ceremonies, and so on, produced other records. President Truman chose a Signal Corps photograph for his official portrait, warmly congratulating the photographer for the excellence of his work. Another Signal Corps photograph was used for striking off the Presidential Medal.[120]

Photographic Equipment Supply and Research

As a result of the almost total lack of prewar procurement planning in the field of photographic supply, most of the photographic equipment used by the

[113] Eichberg and Quadow, Combat Photography, p. 67.

[114] CSigO, Annual Rpt, FY 45, pp. 728–29.

[115] (1) Ibid. (2) CSigO, Annual Rpt, FY 46, pp. 5, 597.

[116] For examples of excellent Signal Corps photographs see any of the volumes in the series UNITED STATES ARMY IN WORLD WAR II, es-

pecially the three volumes in the Pictorial Record subseries, The War Against Germany and Italy: Mediterranean and Adjacent Areas (Washington, 1951); The War Against Germany: Europe and Adjacent Areas (Washington, 1951); and The War Against Japan (Washington, 1952).

[117] CSigO, Annual Rpt, FY 44, p. 615–a.

[118] Muto, "Still Pictures," Business Screen, VII, No. 1, p. 47.

[119] Memo, Chief APS for Contl Div OCSigO, 2 Sep 43, sub: Digest of Progress and Problems for Aug 43. SigC AS 319.1 Digest of Progress and Problems, pt. 1, Aug 43 Through Dec 44.

[120] CSigO, Annual Rpt, FY 46, p. 597.

VARIETY OF CAMERAS USED BY 161ST SIGNAL PHOTO COMPANY *in the South Pacific*

Army's photographers throughout the war was of standard commercial design. The Signal Corps simply bought Speed Graphics, the stand-by of press photographers, assigned the nomenclature PH–47, and issued them to still photographers; Bell & Howell Eyemo motion picture cameras (PH–330); Eastman Kodak 35's (PH–324) in the miniature class; Leicas (AN/GFQ–1); Rolliflexes (AN/PFH–1); and so on. On the whole, such equipment served extremely well, but many a combat cameraman complained bitterly because his equipment could not stand up under rugged field conditions for which it had never been designed.[121]

The war was nearly over before complete and accurate statistics became available on which to base equipment requirements. Meanwhile, many of the industry leaders had shifted to war work in the electronics field, and industrial capacity became a serious bottleneck.[122] Shortages of film and of cameras developed late in 1942, and it was necessary to control rigidly the distribution and

[121] For a good discussion of types of photographic equipment used in World War II, see Eichberg and Quadow, Combat Photography, pp. 26–48.
[122] Clarke, SigC APS in World War II, pp. 79–81.

issue of these items. During most of the last two years of war, APS exercised supply control and procurement responsibility for film; approved requisitions for critical items of major equipment; was responsible for photographic research, development, and engineering; performed standardization actions; and reviewed and approved equipment tables.[123] The P&D Division, Office of the Chief Signal Officer, determined requirements and procured equipment other than film, while the Storage and Issue Agency edited requisitions and stored and issued the equipment.

In April 1943, using its technical branch as a nucleus, APS had organized PERL, assigning it the mission of redesigning, improving, and developing better photographic equipment.[124] PERL got off to a flying start, weathering the initial difficulties of insufficient funds, space, and personnel, to launch a full schedule of projects. By August 1944 a PERL staff of 154 officers, enlisted men, and civilians were hard at work on some 1,000 projects.[125] That was the peak of expansion; personnel cuts trimmed the staff to about 125 for the remainder of the war period.

Much of PERL's work involved the same sort of useful, unglamorous production and maintenance engineering for photographic equipment that the signal laboratories at Fort Monmouth performed for other types of signal equipment.[126] Such work included compiling production and issue control parts lists, standardization actions, stock numbering, reductions of items, preparation of equipment tables, writing moistureproofing specifications, lubrication orders, and repair specifications. PERL wrote, catalogued, and revised photographic technical manuals and instructional literature.[127] The laboratory also "provided the much needed source of technical information which had been woefully lacking during the earlier periods of the war and served to extend the available supply of specifications and technical data on which to base procurement."[128]

As it was, PERL entered the picture too late to change very radically a situation already shaped by the lack of sufficient planning data. The photographic industry suffered from material shortages throughout the war. Chemicals used in the manufacture of film became scarce very early. Labor pirating, loss of highly skilled technicians, lack of engineering data, and most of all the lack of firm requirements data and long-range facility planning combined to create an unhappy procurement record during the initial phases of the war. In the latter part of 1944 and the early part of 1945 the demands for photographic material rose sharply. In those months, within the zone of interior demands for photographic materials reached a peak. At the same time, theater requirements called for quantities far in excess of previous

[123] (1) I. D. Adams, Philadelphia SigC Proc Dist, Industrial Summary: Signal Corps Procurement of Photographic Equipment, 31 Jan 46, pp. 11–14. SigC Hist Sec file. (2) OCSigO Memo 139, 25 Sep 44, sub: Responsibilities for Photographic Items. SigC 475 Photo.

[124] Thompson, Harris, et al., The Test, pp. 410–11.

[125] Clarke, SigC APS in World War II, p. 184.

[126] See above, pp. 10, 427.

[127] (1) CSigO, Annual Rpt, FY 45, pp. 852–68. (2) Digest of Progress and Problems, Aug 43. SigC AS 319.1 Digest of Progress and Problems, pt. 1, Aug 43 Through Dec 44.

[128] Adams, Industrial Summ: SigC Proc of Photo Equip, p. 12.

estimates. Only the most stringent editing of all requirements and the institution of emergency purchases of equipment off the shelves of wholesalers and retailers saved the day.[129]

On the research and development side, PERL engineers succeeded remarkably well in providing better items of photographic equipment, considering the short time in which the laboratory existed. For the most part, PERL projects consisted of short-range modifications, improvements, or adaptations of existing items. The actual development work PERL accomplished either in its own laboratory, or through contracts with commercial concerns. Tool kits to enable cameramen in remote places to make camera adjustments and repairs, waterproof camera-carrying bags, a compact folding tripod that could be used while a cameraman lay prone on the ground, a photographic carrier for installing motion picture cameras in jeeps, an improved type of cameraman's helmet, with a cutaway section to accommodate sighting through a camera lens —all these projects made life easier for combat photographers.[130]

Tables of equipment for World War II photographic troops provided only the sketchiest sort of field processing facilities. PERL's first equipment project, undertaken in May 1943, was to develop a complete field processing laboratory that could be installed in a van. Even though many of the elements of a portable darkroom and processing laboratory were already in existence, putting them together in a practical item of field equipment was no easy task. The final result, laboratory darkroom AN/TFQ-7, was still being field tested when the war came to an end.[131]

Late in the war PERL undertook the development of a highly specialized camera for The Surgeon General, who wanted a foolproof clinical camera that medical personnel could use under varying light conditions to record surgical operations in color while they were in progress. By August of 1945 PERL had developed an experimental model that showed good results in tests at Walter Reed Hospital. The miniature camera, PH-562/TFQ-6, used a novel self-contained light source in the form of a gaseous vapor discharge tube. Since the light was flashed, through condenser discharge, for only about 1/25,000th of a second, it was possible to catch the fastest action. Moreover, the light was so brilliant that room lighting did not need to be considered in setting the proper exposure. The camera was simple to operate—the operator just focused on the subject through the reflex finder and pushed the release button, which automatically set the diaphragm, actuated the shutter, and closed the flash lamp circuit.[132]

In co-operation with the Signal Corps Engineering Laboratories at Fort Monmouth, PERL devised a combination motion picture camera, developing system, and viewing device that made it possible to photograph the traces on a

---

[129] *Ibid.,* pp. 13, 16.

For details concerning the critical shortage of 16-mm. and 35-mm. film stock in early 1944, see Transcript of Special Meeting, APB, 10 March 1944. SigC 334 APB, pt. 1, 1943-44.

[130] Details of these developments are contained in Signal Corps Research and Development History, Volume XV.

[131] (1) Clarke, SigC APS in World War II, pp. 167-73. (2) SigC R&D Hist, Vol XV, Proj 2772-A.

[132] SigC R&D Hist, vol. XV, Proj 2713-A.

cathode-ray oscilloscope and then view them after a 17-second development interval. This equipment became part of a static direction finder, used by the AAF to locate thunderstorms over distances of more than 1,000 miles.[133]

One of PERL's more important projects incorporated improvements in the Bell & Howell Eyemo motion picture camera, the work horse of the combat cameramen. PERL-designed modifications of the basic Eyemo design included a relieved aperture plate, a hand-triggered release, an improved winding key, behind-the-lens filter, and anti-reflection-coated lenses. Efforts to improve the spring drive in order that 100, rather than 50, feet of film could be run from a single winding added so much weight that it was not adopted. Either in its original design or as the improved and standardized version, this camera accounted for 90 percent of all motion picture film shot during the war.[134]

Among the developments undertaken by PERL but not completed in time for combat use were a number of items with promise for postwar military and industrial use. There was, for example, a lightweight, combat still camera, waterproof and dustproof, with interchangeable lenses, built-in film-cutting mechanism, combination viewfinder and coupled rangefinder. Although a version of the camera (PH–518/PF) saw limited action, it was not completely acceptable. Another war-born project, a photographic periscope to enable a cameraman to shoot pictures over the rim of a foxhole or a wall, ended when the war ended.[135]

Photographic Troops

Organization and Mission

For approximately the first half of the war period, there persisted considerable dissatisfaction with the manner in which combat photography was being handled. Photographic companies attached to field armies were furnishing thousands of feet of combat film and thousands of still pictures for a great variety of purposes. Cameramen all over the world were risking and sometimes losing their lives, yet the product of their labors brought little but criticism. In Washington, officials complained that combat pictures lacked reality and spectacular appeal; overseas, commanders objected that the combat photos did not do justice to the gallant deeds of the foot soldiers. The Signal Corps felt that commanders did not understand the photographic mission and therefore did not give their cameramen an opportunity to secure satisfactory combat footage. Many a commander was reluctant to have photographers at the front simply because, not understanding or appreciating what they could do for him, he did not want to be bothered. Furthermore, even in those instances in which the photographers were given an opportunity to record continuous battle action, it often proved disappointing. The truth was that the stark actuality of the battle front was seldom photogenic. Except for landings, the Chief Signal Officer pointed out, "the most striking

---

[133] *Ibid.*, vol. XV, Proj 2774–A.

[134] (1) Maj. Lloyd T. Goldsmith, "Pictorial Engineering and Research," *Business Screen*, VII, No. 1 (December, 1945), 66. (2) CSigO, Annual Rpt, FY 45, p. 852. (3) SigC R&D Hist, vol. XV, Introduction, p. 3, and Projs 2724–1 and 2724–2.

[135] SigC R&D Hist, vol XV, Projs 2712–A and 2712–B.

feature of the battlefield is its emptiness." [136]

Assignment of mission, probably the most important phase of military planning, was quite as necessary for photographic troops as for any other unit. But all too frequently, commanders failed to assign specific objectives, support, or zones of responsibility to the photographic officer. Division commanders who would not dream of telling their regimental commanders merely to "move forward" saw no impropriety in simply ordering the photographic officer to "cover the operation." A photographic officer had to be both tactful and tenacious to find out what his objective really was. [137]

Persistently, photographic officers found that the most poorly understood aspect of the photographic mission lay in its relationship to the public information office. Many tactical officers assumed that photographic troops were simply instruments of the PIO, and they bestowed on photographers the fighting man's general mistrust of all public information activities. [138] For their part, public relations officers deplored the fact that they did not control the operations of Army cameramen. The pictorial officer of the 12th Army Group Publicity Relations Branch paid tribute to the cooperation of APS personnel, but nonetheless recommended strongly that, in any future operation, public relations

should be given control of all pictorial assignments. [139]

Another source of Signal Corps dissatisfaction lay in the manner in which photographic troops were organized and trained. Photographic experience in North Africa had demonstrated very clearly the advantages of flexibility of organization for combat photo units. [140] But under AGF tables of organization, photographic troops were organized into companies, one for each field army. This arrangement was so unwieldy that commanders simply disregarded it. Actually, none of the companies operated as an entity. Small units, usually one officer and six enlisted men, were assigned to various corps, division, or other subsidiary units. In some cases detachments of a single photographic company might be scattered through more than one theater. Though this arrangement provided some degree of flexibility of operation, it also introduced grave problems of administration. Unless commanders all along the line understood photographic problems and used their photographic units intelligently, confusion, misdirection, and dissatisfaction followed. In May 1943 the War Department, acting upon urgent Signal Corps recommendations, directed the overseas theater commanders to designate photographic officers on their staffs to be charged specifically with all photographic functions. [141] This action went far toward solving the misunderstandings and difficulties that had handicapped

---

[136] Memo, Ingles, CSigO, for Patterson, USW, 1 Jan 44, sub: Films for the Industrial Sv Film Prog. SigC EO Ingles folder P.

[137] Capt Edwin T. Rhatigan, The Tactical Employment of Photographic Troops (n.d.), Sig Sch Monograph, pp. 1-2, 20-21. The Sig Sch Libr, Ft. Monmouth.

[138] Ibid., p. 9.

[139] 12th AGp Rpt of Opns, XIV (Publicity and POW), 56-58.

[140] Thompson, Harris, et al., The Test, pp. 400-402.

[141] (1) AG 210.31 (4-9-3) OB-S-D-M, 6 May 43, sub: Fld Photography. (2) Thompson, Harris, et al., The Test, pp. 403-04.

the operations of photographic troops, although the beneficial results did not become evident for some months. By the time of the Normandy invasion, a fairly satisfactory organization had evolved. Photographic matters were controlled through photographic officers on the staffs of the signal officers of each U.S. army group and army. The officer in charge of each assignment unit at corps or division headquarters also acted as the corps or division staff photographic officer. Thus a channel existed straight down from army group to the assignment units in the divisions.[142] Assignment units thus could be moved about very quickly if need be.

Meanwhile, in the latter part of 1943, the ASF approved the Signal Corps plan for cellular organization of many types of signal teams, among them several types of photographic teams.[143] Set up as ASF troops, flexible photographic detachments organized under TOE 11–500 were created for use in such numbers and at such places as they might be needed in any theater of war. Early in the war Col. Darryl Zanuck had recommended the formation of such units, and in North Africa he had organized his available manpower into just such teams.[144] Other Signal Corps photographic officers vigorously supported his views. Early in 1943, while General Olmstead was still the Chief Signal Officer, he had recommended such an organization.[145] Now his recommendation was being put into effect.

In the September 1944 revision of the tables of organization and equipment, 25 signal service detachments were authorized—10 photographic, 10 photographic production, and 5 newsreel detachments. These teams were intended to provide overseas photographic service wherever theater facilities were not adequate to fill the requirements of both the theater and the War Department. Temporary duty personnel already overseas formed the nucleus for 6 of the detachments; the remaining 19 were filled from personnel under the control of APS.[146] These special teams were permanently assigned to SCPC; the chief of APS exercised staff supervision for the Chief Signal Officer on all matters pertaining to War Department policy and could make recommendations to the theater commander on photographic policy and activities. Though the teams when overseas augmented the theater photographic missions and performed special assignments, their home station was always the SCPC. The signal photographic companies still served the AGF units, but coverage for headquarters installations and all ASF needs became the mission of the special teams.

At ETOUSA headquarters APS had been set up as a section on General Rumbough's staff, with operational photographic personnel attached. The highly qualified cameramen of the 162d Signal Photographic Company took care of the many special coverage assignments that fell to ETOUSA, and the 2d and 8th Signal Photographic Laboratory Units processed motion picture film and still picture negatives, made slides, copied charts, and disposed of a wealth of other photographic chores. This or-

---

[142] ETOUSA Rpt, II, 241.

[143] See above, pp. 22ff.

[144] Thompson, Harris, et al., The Test, pp. 398–401.

[145] Agenda for CSigoO Staff Conf, 12 Jan 43, Item 9. SigC 337 Staff Confs, OCSigO, 1942–43.

[146] CSigO, Annual Rpt, FY 45, p. 872.

COMBAT CAMERAMAN ON THE JOB DURING THE ARDENNES COUNTEROFFENSIVE

ganization worked well enough until the invasion, when the workload and scope of responsibilities increased so greatly that a reorganization became imperative. The resulting organization, approved in July but not activated until 17 August when COMZ headquarters moved to the Continent, separated staff and operating functions and created a unique operational organization. This was the 3120th Signal Service Battalion (Photo General Headquarters), to which the separate signal photographic companies then in the COMZ were assigned. Such an organization had never been tried before in any theater of operations, but from the start it worked with impressive smoothness. The bat-

talion provided centralized control of all COMZ photographic service and equipment; battalion headquarters and the 3265th Signal Service Company provided the personnel necessary to administer those units without organic administration, including the special coverage units arriving in the theater on specific missions.[147]

In the ETO, responsibility for photographic matters for the field forces lay with the Signal Section of the 12th Army Group—specifically with the Photographic Branch. Throughout the campaign on the Continent, the 12th Army Group shifted its available photographic

---

[147] ETOUSA Rpt, II, 242–43, 248.

PROCESSING PICTURES IN A PORTABLE LABORATORY *near the front lines in Italy*

units about to secure the most effective coverage. Footage of tactical interest was processed for immediate use by the laboratory unit of the company assigned to headquarters; all other material was forwarded to the COMZ laboratories for processing. At the end of March 1945 five signal photographic companies and one signal service company (photographic) were controlled by the 12th Army Group. At that time the 167th Signal Photographic Company and the 3264th Signal Service Company (Photographic) were assigned to the army group headquarters, while the 165th Signal Photographic Company was assigned to First Army, the 166th to Third Army, the 168th to Ninth Army, and the 198th to Fifteenth Army.[148]

The other theaters, less well supplied with photographic troops and equipment, followed the ETO pattern of organization to the extent possible. The special coverage units from the SCPC supplemented the regularly assigned field units. They furnished invaluable assistance in every theater, but especially in the Pacific. At the war's end, 15 of the detachments were overseas—6 in the ETO, 1 in the Mediterranean Theater of Operations, and 8 in the Pacific.[149]

Training Photographic Troops

The Army's photographic activities

---

[148] Until 4 October 1944, when it achieved branch

status, the unit was known as the Photographic Group of the Plans and Operations Branch. 12th AGp Rpt of Opns, XI (Sig), 149, 235, 239.
[149] CSigO, Annual Rpt, FY 45, p. 872.

required a great many specialists in addition to cameramen. Camera repairmen, maintenance men of various types, laboratory technicians, motion picture electricians, projectionists, draftsmen, animation artists, model makers, sound recorders, sound mixers, playwrights, editors of numerous sorts, darkroom assistants, film librarians—these and many others had to be taught their respective trades at the Signal Corps Photographic School at the SCPC.[150] Men inducted into the Army received their basic training in an RTC and then, if they showed aptitude or special interest in photographic work, were sent to the Signal Corps Photographic School for training. Not all of it was in formal classrooms. The twenty-two categories of so-called miscellaneous motion picture specialists were trained on the job in the various production activities of the center.[151] Upon satisfactory completion of the photographic training courses the graduates were assigned to photographic companies or to special units and teams, or were utilized as overseas replacements.[152]

As of early 1943, the school training cycle for combat photographers to be assigned to AGF's signal photographic companies varied from 6 to 8 weeks, depending on whether or not the trainee had had any previous civilian photographic experience. At the end of the school training period, AGF became responsible for continuing the training of Signal Corps photographic company personnel, including both mobilization training and additional technical training. Actually, the rigorous troop training schedules left little time for additional photographic training.[153] The Signal Corps felt strongly that the short time permitted for technical training at the school could not possibly turn out cameramen fitted to carry out their duties. An APS training officer in June 1943 warned that, unless the school could give at least 8 and perferably 13 weeks of specialist training, "this branch will not take the responsibility for the efficiency and operations of photographic companies." [154] He recommended that the matter be brought to the attention of all branches and services responsible for military training. Some instructors at the SCPC maintained that a man needed 8 months of specialized training to qualify as a competent motion picture combat photographer or sound recorder.[155]

As a matter of fact, a series of Signal Corps proposals to co-ordinate the specialist training the SCPC gave the men at Astoria with the AGF mobilization training did bring improvement eventually.[156] But the Signal Corps was never entirely happy with the degree of control it was permitted to exercise over the

[150] Categories compiled by Mil Tng Br P&T Div OCSigO, 8 Feb 45.

[151] CSigO, Annual Rpt, FY 44, p. 595.

[152] For details of training methods and techniques, see (1) Thompson, Harris, et al., The Test, pp. 394–96; and (2) Capt William A. Wood, Historical Background of the Training Division of the Signal Corps Photographic Center, Astoria, Long Island, 32 pp., passim. SigC Hist Sec file.

[153] (1) Eichberg and Quadow, Combat Photography, p. 21. (2) Interv, SigC Hist Sec with Sgt Bernard Liebman, 162d Sig Photo Co, Jan 45. SigC Hist Sec file.

[154] Memo, Capt Higgins for Maj H. G. Wilde, APS, 8 Jun 43. SigC 300.6 Office Memos (APS), 1943–44.

[155] Capt William A. Wood, History of Photographic Training, 1917–43, p. 34. SigC Hist Sec file.

[156] (1) Staff Study, Field Photography, prepared by APS, 22 Apr 43. SigC 062.2 Policy (Combat Photography), 1942–44. (2) Thompson, Harris, et al., The Test, pp. 404–05.

training of combat photographers. General Ingles felt that most of the criticism of combat photography resulted from the failure of combat commanders to recognize that insofar as the War Department was concerned, the primary mission of combat photographers was to secure combat pictures for release to the public, no matter what the regulations might say on the subject. AGF failed to "integrate the training of the photographic companies with the ultimate mission they are required to perform for the War Department." [157] General Ingles pointed out that the Signal Corps was responsible for updating and preparing pictorial material in a form suitable for release to the public, and he reasoned that the Signal Corps ought to be wholly responsible for selecting and training the cameramen who took the pictures. He said:

In view of the fact that the Chief Signal Officer is held responsible for the utilization of photographic results and . . . has the highly skilled instructors necessary both to insure the adequate training of these photographic companies and to integrate their activities with War Department requirements, it is recommended that he be given the authority and the responsibility for the training of Signal Photographic Companies.[158]

Unhappily (from the Signal Corps point of view), nothing came of the proposal. AGF successfully defended its contention that the primary mission of signal photographic companies was the taking of pictures for combat intelligence and that publicity and historical recordation were distinctly secondary.[159] Without question, Army regulations and statutory authority supported the AGF position. Official publications plainly stated that "when opportunities occur, combat photography is the first duty of all units." [160]

Unquestionably, combat photographers assigned to units performed a distinctly tactical mission.[161] On the other hand, the demands of the War Department bureaus for combat footage to be shown to the public greatly outweighed in quantity the tactical uses of combat pictures. The problem had to be dealt with less directly.

Appointment of staff photographic officers, already mentioned, solved some of the difficulties. For another, by agreement with the AGF, instructor teams from the SCPC traveled to training camps to give additional instruction to photographic companies during mobilization training.[162] Signal Corps also improved its own specialist training, adding more instructors and more and longer courses. In fiscal year 1944 the period of specialist training at Astoria in most cases covered seventeen weeks.[163] Finally, with the adoption of cellular TOE 11-500 and the organization of the new photographic detachments, the Signal Corps was able to augment tactical coverage as required. During the

---

[157] Memo, CSigO for CG ASF, 18 Jan 44, sub: Integration of Photo Tng With WD Pictorial Rqmts. SigC 062.2 Policy (Motion Pictures), 1942–45.

[158] Ibid.

[159] Palmer, Wiley, and Keast, The Procurement and Training of Ground Combat Troops, pp. 506–07. This source reports the facts correctly, but places the date one year later than it actually occurred, probably through a clerical error in recording the references.

[160] WD Pamphlet No. 11-2, 20 Apr 44, SOP for Signal Photographic Units in Theaters of Operations.

[161] Buchanan, APS in Theater of Opns, p. 6.

[162] CSigO, Annual Rpt, FY 45, p. 871.

[163] CSigO, Annual Rpt, FY 44, p. 595.

latter part of the war the combined effect of these measures produced a vast amount of excellent combat footage, enough to supply all needs.

With the formation of the special photographic detachments, training at the Signal Corps Photographic School intensified. The men received their basic military training at Fort Monmouth and their specialist and unit training at Astoria. Team training, as well as the specialist training previously given at the school, got under way in the late summer of 1944. Many of the instructors were photographic officers and enlisted men who had served in combat areas overseas. In October facilities at Pine Camp, New York, were made available to the photographic students for field training, including three consecutive days on bivouac under tentage. Beginning in February 1945, the school provided complete basic training for its special units, as well as advanced on-the-job training. The men and officers learned how to use the complete production and laboratory facilities of the center; were briefed thoroughly not only by APS officers but by liaison officers of the AAF, the Navy, the Coast Guard, OWI, BPR, and other organizations with which they might be working; spent hours at critiques of their work; and absorbed useful information from re-. turned combat cameramen as to work conditions overseas. In the period from June 1944 through June 1945, the school graduated its largest number of students—142 officers and 797 enlisted men and women.[164] In

addition, about 50 French Army students and smaller numbers from Canada and the Netherlands completed courses in production and laboratory techniques.

V-Mail Operations

One special category of Signal Corps photographic troops, not included in the regular combat camera teams or laboratory units, operated V-mail and Official Photo Mail stations in the zone of interior and in remote areas overseas. In 1942 the responsibility for V-mail was parceled out among the U.S. Post Office Department, the Signal Corps, the Navy Postal Service, and the Army Postal Service. The Signal Corps had been charged with "technical matters, involving equipment for filming, developing and reproducing, and the operation of such equipment" for the Army.[165] Translated into the practical mechanics of the function, the Signal Corps procured the microfilming, processing, and printing equipment necessary to turn a letter or document into microfilm at the transmitting end of the cycle and to develop, enlarge, and print it at the receiving end; contracted for the service at stations operated by the Eastman Kodak Company and its subsidiaries; and furnished and trained men to operate overseas stations where contract service was not available.[166] Throughout the war, a large slice of Signal Corps funds

---

[164] (1) Reinstein, Hist, SigC Tng, Jul 44–Dec 44, pp. 70–76. (2) Capt Frederick Reinstein, History of Signal Corps Training, January 1945–June 1945 (1945), SigC Hist Monograph C–12b, pp. 87–91. Both in SigC Hist Sec file.

[165] WD Cir 219, 7 Jul 42.
[166] (1) Mary E. Boswell, A Study of Signal Corps Contributions to V-Mail Through December 1943, SigC Hist Monograph F–4. (2) Boswell, A Study of Signal Corps Contributions to V-Mail Through 1943, Supplement, December 1943–August 1945 (1945), SigC Hist Monograph F–5, *passim*. Both in SigC Hist Sec file. Unless otherwise indicated, all material in this section is based upon these sources.

supported V-mail and Official Photo Mail activities.

Official Photo Mail was the name given to microfilmed official documents and communications between the War Department and U.S. Government activities overseas. It differed from V-mail only in that final reproductions were enlarged to 8 by 10-inch size instead of the 4½ by 5-inch reproduction of V-mail. For security reasons, the Signal Corps processed all OPM, even in V-mail stations that were contractor-operated. The first signal photo mail company was activated in July 1942, to furnish trained personnel for V-mail stations overseas and to operate the OPM station set up in the Pentagon.[167] Early in 1944 training activities moved from Fort Myer to Fort Monmouth, where better housing and laboratory facilities could be provided. At the height of the training program in 1944, four V-mail teams containing 14 officers and nearly 300 enlisted men were in training at Fort Monmouth.[168]

Contractor-operated stations handled the greatest volume of mail. It fell to the lot of Signal Corps detachments to take over operations in isolated military areas far from the main supply routes, where all manner of field expedients became necessary. Needless to say, these stations usually were located in unpleasant climates and in areas involving primitive working conditions. For example, the large contract station in Hawaii handled most of the processing for the South Pacific, but Signal Corps detachments operated on Guadalcanal, Saipan, Tontouta (New Caledonia), and at Suva, in the Fiji Islands. While the contract station at Brisbane handled much Southwest Pacific mail, the Signal Corps detachments processed it at Port Moresby and Leyte.[169] There were Signal Corps V-mail stations in Iceland; in the Persian Gulf area at Abadan, Iran; in the CBI at Karachi and Calcutta. The V-mail volume increased 400 percent in the six months between January and July 1943.[170] In mid-1944, there were 22 V-mail stations overseas and in the United States, handling about 63,500,000 letters per month. The total for the fiscal year 1945 reached 584,000,000 letters. The OPM stations run by Signal Corps detachments in Washington, Paris, Honolulu, and Brisbane established comparable records. In that same period, the Washington station alone microfilmed 475,498 documents and made 1,097,363 reproductions.[171]

It should be emphasized that over-all responsibility for V-mail operations lay with the AGO's Army Postal Service and that the Signal Corps was responsible only for the technical aspects of the program. As might be expected in any operation not wholly controlled by a single agency, some friction and a certain amount of duplication of effort existed. In mid-1944, the Army Pictorial Service and the Army Postal Service undertook a joint study of these factors in order to recommend such changes as might be helpful. It was found that no duplication existed in the United States, where

---

[167] Thompson, Harris, et al., The Test, p. 407.

[168] Boswell, Study of SigC Contributions to V-Mail Through 1943, Supplement, Dec 43–Aug 45, p. 2.

[169] Ibid., pp. 33, 38–40.

[170] Memo, Chief APS to Contl Div OCSigO, 2 Sep 43. SigC AS 319.1 Digest of Progress and Problems, pt. 1, Aug 43 Through Dec 44.

[171] CSigO, Annual Rpts, FY 44, p. 614, and FY 45, pp. 868–69.

ADJUSTING V-MAIL ENLARGER, ICELAND

all processing functions were carried out by Eastman Kodak under the technical supervision of the Signal Corps. Overseas, Army Postal Service personnel assigned to base post offices carried out the postal functions relating to V-mail, whereas signal photo mail detachments under the theater signal officers performed the photographic processes associated with V-mail.[172] Usually, the Army Postal Service and the Signal Corps detachments were housed in the same buildings but under separate commands. This arrangement necessitated the assignment of overhead administrative personnel to both services, and the preparation of duplicating reports.

As a result of the study, the War Department issued a new TOE combining the Army Postal Service and Signal Corps detachments into a single team operating under the officer in charge of the overseas base post office. A new War Department circular redefined specific areas of responsibility.[173]

---

[172] Except in SWPA, where the theater postal officer had responsibility for both.

[173] WD Cir 338, 18 Aug 44.

No doubt the importance of V-mail operations was worth any amount of time and trouble, but the Signal Corps officer in charge of the Signal Corps V-mail program for the last three years of the war recommended that, in the event of future use of such a method, the Army Postal Service be given complete responsibility, including all phases of technical operation.[174]

Summary

Like other services that the Signal Corps furnished for the Army, photographic service assumed a great variety of forms and was used for many purposes. Not always appreciated at the time, the prestige of APS increased steadily during the last two years of war and indeed in the postwar period. The mass training of millions of men in record time depended heavily on the training films and visual aids that APS produced; in fact, educational methods underwent a minor revolution in World War II. Combat photographers served as the eyes of the public as well as of the Army; millions of Americans at home would have had a very hazy idea of how and where the war was being waged if they had not had the benefit of the newsreels and still pictures that the combat cameramen furnished.

Clearer directives and a better defined War Department policy toward photography might have resulted in smoother relations between APS and its many customers, but by the latter part of the war other solutions had been found for most of the problems. In the field of procurement planning and equipment research, an earlier start would have accomplished more.

By the end of the war the Army Pictorial Service had earned the healthy respect with which it was regarded everywhere. Its record of accomplishment was impressive, both statistically and in terms of influence. Army photography had come of age.

---

[174] Memo, Lt Col Earle D. Snyder for Chief APS, n.d., quoted in Boswell, Study of SigC Contributions to V-Mail Through 1943, Supplement, Dec 43–Aug 45, p. 10.

CHAPTER XVIII

Signaling the World

The commodity dispatched overseas in greatest quantity during World War II, and at greatest speed, was neither munitions, nor rations, neither clothing nor supply items. It was words, billions of words, messages of strategy and command, plans of campaigns and reports of action, requests for troops and schedules of their movements, lists of supplies requisitioned and of supplies in shipment, administrative messages, casualty lists. All of this and much more, such as services for the press (news dispatches, telephotos) and services for the soldiers (expeditionary force messages), poured over far-flung wire, cable, and radio circuits and channels—routine and urgent, plain text and enciphered, on a scale unimagined before the war by any communications agency, military or commercial. All this was the work of the Signal Corps Army Communications Service. ACAN was actually moving some fifty million words a day (with a capacity of a hundred million daily) toward the end of World War II. Maj. Gen. Frank E. Stoner, chief of the Army Communications Service throughout the war, estimated that eight words were sent overseas for every bullet fired by Allied troops. "The pen is still mightier than the sword," he quipped.[1]

During the first half of the war, the many modes and agencies of communications within the continental United States were marshaled and reorganized to meet the needs of the armed services. The Army's domestic radio network was replaced by landline teletypewriter nets (a few Army radio circuits within the country were kept available, however, in stand-by status in case of emergency need). By 1943 both the internal networks and their overseas extensions comprised the expanding Army Communications Service, headed by an oper-

Employment of Communications in the Army, Tab 9, p. 4. SigC OP 352 AFSC Rpts, vol. 6, 1948-49. (3) Stoner, Army Communications, a Seminar Held at the Army Industrial College, Washington, 24 Sep 45, Com folder, Tab A-2. SigC Hist Sec file.

General Stoner estimated that Army's prewar radio net linking corps area headquarters and a few overseas department headquarters handled only about 5,000 messages a day (the 60,000 circuit miles of this net permitting a peak capacity of two million words a day, according to AFSC Lecture C-1, Employment of Communications in the Army, Tab 9, page 2). At the war's end all Signal Corps radio, telegraph, telephone, and submarine cable in the ACAN system totaled over 800,000 circuit miles. Stoner, Speech Before the Federal Communications Bar Association, 11 Jan 46, p. 1. Com folder, Tab A-1.

For accounts of the War Department radio net and other pre-World War II Army circuits see: (1) Terrett, *The Emergency*, pp. 48ff.; (2) Mary E. Boswell, The 17th Signal Service Company, A Component of the War Department Signal Center, World War I Through World War II (1945), SigC Hist Monograph E-5a, SigC Hist Sec file; (3) Karl Larew, draft MS, A History of the Army Command and Administrative Agency, 1899-1956; SigC Hist Sec file.

[1] (1) Mary-louise Melia, Signal Corps Fixed Communications in World War II: Special Assignments and Techniques (1945), SigC Hist Monograph E-10, p. 1. SigC Hist Sec file. (2) AFSC Lecture C-1,

ating agency in the Office of the Chief Signal Officer with three major branches: Traffic, Plant, and Security. Together with Philadelphia's large Plant Engineering Agency, which helped design, construct, and maintain installations, these several activities supported the Army's ever-extending networks.[2]

In mid-1943 the major ACAN stations outside the United States were in London, Algiers, Accra, Cairo, Asmara, Karachi, New Delhi, Brisbane, and Hawaii. Many lesser stations tied into the net wherever a local Army radio served local troops or commands, as at Reykjavík, Tehran, Nouméa, and on numerous Pacific isles and atolls.[3] From the major stations, which often served as relay points to outlying posts, lesser radio nets and wire lines radiated out to meet the needs of local Army installations. Control over this world-wide military communications system—ACAN—was vested in the Chief Signal Officer in the Washington headquarters, the location of the net control station WAR.[4]

The needs of America's world operations in World War II, together with the facilities and techniques the Signal Corps developed to meet the needs, opened up vistas of world communications on a scale and magnitude scarcely contemplated before. Or when contemplated by persons either in private enterprise or in government, the idea was not developed into a large-scale actuality until World War II provided the necessity, and the Signal Corps the men and the means.[5]

After the war, facile high-speed high-capacity world-wide communications, including such innovations as teleconferences conducted by teletype between conferees thousands of miles apart, became commonplace. Before World War II, the facilities to communicate overseas by commercial telegraph, whether via cable or radio, supplemented by high-frequency radiotelephone, were available, but slow and costly. Their use was not commonplace.

[2] Thompson, Harris, et al., The Test, pp. 435ff.

[3] "At the outbreak of the war only a few Signal Corps' officers had experience in international communication," General Stoner subsequently remarked. He added that the Signal Corps shaped its training in this field upon the efforts of such commercial communications leaders as Walter S. Gifford, David Sarnoff, Sosthenes Behn, and I. D. Hough. He commented further: "It was upon the teachings and guidance of these men and their staff that I leaned heavily for help in building the Army's system, and not the experts brought in by the Secretary's office and the Control Division of ASF." General Stoner also made much use throughout the war of a special advisory committee set up in the Army Communications Service to study and solve traffic problems. Among the committee members were M. F. Dull, R. W. Miller, and R. J. Anspach, all of AT&T, and B. E. Osgood of Michigan Bell. Stoner, Draft MS Comment, Jul 59.

[4] Pauline M. Oakes, The Army Command and Administrative Communications System, pt. II,

Signal Corps Domestic Communications Network as Extended to Overseas Terminals, FY 1941–15 August 1945, SigC Hist Monograph E–5b, pp. 13ff., 101. SigC Hist Sec file.

The Chief Signal Officer exerted direct control over ACAN in continental United States and technical control over the overseas portions.

One of the first occurrences of the phrase Army Command and Administrative Network in contemporary documents is in the CSigO Annual Report, Fiscal Year 1944, page 525.

[5] One man who had so contemplated was General Squier, Chief Signal Officer during World War I, who wrote: "The advances in radio telephony and telegraphy . . . portend the day which I believe is not far distant, when we can reach the ultimate goal so that any individual anywhere on earth will be able to communicate directly by the spoken word to any other individual wherever he may be." Pauline M. Oakes, The Army Command and Administrative Communications System, pt. I, War Department Radio Net Through Fiscal Years 1920–40, SigC Hist Monograph E–5, p. ii. SigC Hist Sec file.

Army communications before Pearl Harbor scarcely extended beyond the boundaries of the continental United States. "Our facilities," General Stoner recalled, "consisted primarily of radio communications, some wire and some cable to each one of the Corps Area Headquarters, and to some of the overseas commands, such as Puerto Rico, Panama, Hawaii, and the Philippines." Then suddenly the exigencies of the first year of war took the United States Army around the world, and with it went the Army's communications system. At the mid-point of the war, General Stoner could already say with pride, "We have got our net in, and it is the finest network in the world." [6]

ACAN Facilities and Techniques

Fiscal year 1944 saw the vigorous emergence of the Army Command and Administrative Network as a communications system unrivaled either in peacetime or in time of war. Its myriad circuits enmeshed the nation and reached out to bring into its web every overseas headquarters and every command, however remote. It transmitted securely, thanks to cipher machines.[7] And it transmitted fast, as signalized by the round-the-world passage on 24 May 1944 of a test message, completing the

trip in three and a half minutes (a similar test in 1945 cut the time to nine and a half seconds).[8] The ACAN system therefore met two of the most exacting requirements in military communications—security and speed. A third requirement was that traffic capacity be increased. The number of radio channels that the frequency spectrum permitted could not be multiplied. Laws of physics and the immutable spectrum itself forbade. Ways had to be found to provide greater traffic capacity over the same channels, using the same limited number of frequencies.

Thus, while the need for speed forced the abandonment of slow hand-keyed transmission and while the need for both speed and security urged the development of machine cipher devices, the necessity for greater traffic capacity compelled the Signal Corps to develop mechanical sending and receiving apparatus employing semiautomatic radio and carrier techniques, permitting the transmission of several communications simultaneously over circuits that handled only one channel before.[9]

The basic techniques that enabled these achievements were radioteletype-writer applications, coupled with carrier,

---

[6] Proceedings of Bd To Investigate Com, Tab O, pp. 1 and 12. AG 311 (10 May 43) (1) Bulky Pkg, Army RG 207.03, Job A50–55.

[7] The secrets of these devices were never compromised by enemy cryptanalysis, capture, or theft. Late in the war, in Europe (Colmar), a truck was stolen containing a Sigaba locked in a safe, but it was recovered unopened and uncompromised. (1) Harris, *Signal Venture*, p. 244. (2) Thomas M. Johnson, "Search for the Stolen Sigaba," *Army*, vol. 12, No. 7 (February, 1962), 50ff. See also above, p. 90.

[8] See also below, p. 607.

[9] For these developments, see (1) Thompson, Harris, *et al., The Test*, pp. 218ff; (2) Larew, Hist of the Army Comd and Admin Agency, 1899–1956, p. 31; (3) AFSC Lecture C–1, Employment of Com in the Army, Tab 9, pp. 3f.

Squier, a Ph.D. in electrical engineering as well as World War I Chief Signal Officer, had patented carrier techniques transmitting radio frequencies over wire lines in 1910. But successful application had to wait upon the development of improved components, especially electronic tubes. William Fraser, *Telecommunications* (London, 1957), Foreword, p. v.

multichannel and single sideband radio developments. The SSB technique was in itself a major innovation that provided several short-wave circuits using only one-half, or one sideband (suppressing the other sideband) of the usual spread of transmitter frequencies that extend out for several thousand cycles on each side of the center frequency. The technique, valuable for the conservation of frequencies in the severely congested short-wave portion of the spectrum, had been partly developed by AT&T. Early in 1942, W. G. Thompson of AT&T discussed with Stoner the possibility of further development and perfection of the technique for military use. SSB was needed at once (coupled with teletypewriter equipment and automatic ciphering) to speed and secure Army's growing traffic loads. SSB proved out well and quickly, and the first system, leased from commercial companies, opened successfully between Washington and London on 20 July 1942. Other big multichannel SSB systems followed, to Algiers, Brisbane, and elsewhere, until the technique became standard on all major radio circuits between the War Department and overseas ACAN stations.[10]

The conversion of numbers of Army circuits to RTTY (radioteletype) the world over constituted "perhaps the most important single Army Communications Service development during the year." This was the cautious estimate of an ASF report of fiscal year 1944. The author ventured to add that the development

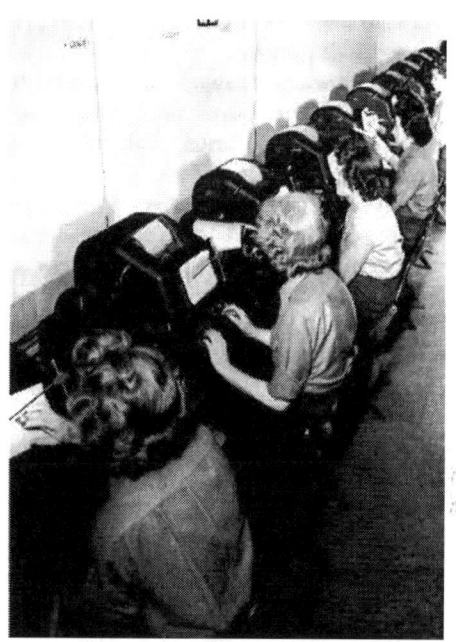

WACS OPERATE TELETYPEWRITERS *at ETOUSA Communications Center, Paris*

was "revolutionary." [11] For not only did radioteletype eliminate the slow transmission of Morse code by hand-keyed radio telegraph (accompanied by the still slower procedures of hand enciphering and deciphering) but it also enabled semiautomatic methods of transfer of traffic from wire to radio circuits, and vice-versa. In addition, it created a standard world-wide message transmission system, comparable to a single-gauge

---

[10] (1) Stoner, War Diary (p. 54 in his copy entitled Army Communications Service). Personal papers (Stoner). (2) See also Thompson, Harris, *et al.,* *The Test,* p. 312.

[11] Annual Rpt, ASF, FY 44, p. 188.
A single large SSB radio could provide six RTTY channels simultaneously, each operating at 60 words per minute, together with a two-way telephone or radio-photo channel, all within a single radio frequency band. Stoner, Speech to the Federal Com Bar Assn, 11 Jan 46, p. 4, Com folder, Tab A-1.

railroad system, over which any train can move to all points.

The standard "gauge" of the ACAN "track" was the 5-unit perforated tape, employing the five units of the standard teletypewriter code, which had been in general use for some years. This tape, with its 5-unit code perforations, was interchangeable between landline, radio, and overseas cable circuits. The resultant message in tape form could be routed by both types of circuits or a combination of circuits (wire and/or radio). After the creation of the tape at the point of origin, all the rest of its handling along the way, the relays and the transfers till the destination was reached, was automatic (except for reading or routing the tapes at relay points). The typing of the delivered text at the destination was automatic. The typing of whatever copies might be needed for information addressees along the way was likewise automatic. "A message could go from Keokuk, Iowa, around the world with drop-off copies at intermediate points, with manual typing necessary only at the point of origin," General Stoner told an Army Industrial College audience after the war. And, very important in military communications, the encipherment of the plain language text at the point of origin and its decipherment at every point of delivery were also automatic, accomplished by cipher machines working in conjunction with the teletypewriters.[12]

During 1944 and 1945 increasing numbers of ACAN signal centers completed conversion to semiautomatic operation, relieving the troubles engendered by greater traffic loads and smaller personnel forces to move them. For example, before conversion, the growing load at the Atlanta station (having increased by more than 15,000 words a day) compelled the rerouting of some of that traffic by way of Washington and Dallas. After the semiautomatic equipment went to work at Atlanta, the station handled the full load readily. Another alleviating technique was the conversion of some circuits from operation at 60 words per minute to 100. This speed-up relieved congestion on 16 transcontinental wire circuits, on 2 radioteletypewriter circuits extending overseas from Washington, the one to Caserta, Italy, the other to Honolulu, and on a third circuit, one between Manila and New Delhi.

Extensive use of "packaged" sets of the new equipment helped in the conversion. The semiautomatic packaged unit, teletypewriter set AN/TGC–1, was a streamlined militarized version of the first bulky product. It was compact, rugged, and easy to install, operate, and maintain. It was also tropicalized. The War Department Signal Center, where new ACAN equipment regularly met its first trials and tests, had designed and developed the packaged sets under the officer in charge in 1943, Maj. William S. Sparks, and his assistant, Capt. Ralph A. Scofield. On 15 January 1944 the radio semiautomatic section went to work in the signal center, encountering "little trouble." Its operations showed "immediate improvement," Stoner reported. The equipment enabled the center to handle its World War II peak

---

[12] (1) Speech [to Be] Made by Stoner to American SigC Assn, New York, 27 Feb 46, p. 9. Com folder, Tab A. (2) Stoner, Army Com, Seminar, Army Industrial College, 24 Sep 45, p. 3. (3) AFSC Lecture C–1, Employment of Com in the Army, Tab 9, p. 3.

TELETYPE CONFERENCE, AS VIEWED IN TELECOM ROOM OF THE PENTAGON. *Flashlight glare has obliterated the messages.*

load of almost 9,500,000 words on 8 August 1945.[13]

[13] (1) Memo, Stoner for Contl Div, Progress and Stat Br, 1 Feb 44, sub: Digest of Progress and Problems, 1 Jan–31 Jan 44, pp. 4ff. SigC AC 319.1 Digest, 30 Jul 42–1 Dec 44. (2) Melia, SigC Fixed Com in World War II: Sp Assignments and Techniques, pp. 21–26. (3) Oakes, The Army Comd and Admin Com System, pt. II, pp. 41ff. and 95. (4) CSigO, Annual Rpts, FY 44, pp. 542f., and FY 45, pp. 681ff., 703ff. (5) Stoner, War Diary, p. 182. The packaged carrier bays were built by Postal Telegraph and Western Union, which delivered the first sets to the signal center in December 1943.

Meanwhile much was done to streamline and improve ACAN operating efficiency, not all of it involving equipment, but rather procedures and methods— traffic engineering such as the juggling of circuits and traffic loads in various ways in order to secure maximum effectiveness and economy. One innovation toward a uniform intra-Army relay procedure took effect on 1 February 1945. It was a revised teletypewriter procedure, intended to simplify and reduce transmission time. It did eliminate the confusion that had previously hampered the relay of messages to combat zone stations.[14]

Telecommunication Group Conference (Telecon) Facilities

Radioteletype and automatic on-line encipher and decipher machines made conferences possible between various headquarters and men thousands of miles apart. The conferring parties needed but to assemble at the ends of an ACAN RTTY circuit and put questions that a teletype operator tapped out. The receiving party could answer and question in turn with only such delay as the typing time required, since both the transmission time and the encipher/decipher time were so nearly instantaneous as to be negligible. This was Sigtot.[15]

Thus, the instantaneous operation of the teletypewriters at the sending and receiving stations, however many thousands of miles apart, whether the connecting links were wire, radio, submarine cable, or all three, enabled men to confer with each other almost as over a telephone line. The use of a projection screen, which would display to a room full of persons the outgoing and incoming sentences, made possible teletypewriter conferences between groups

of men at the ends of the circuit. In addition the system provided a written record of the discussions. All this came to be called a telecon system and came to be used extensively and importantly, sometimes between more than two parties, by the use of several circuits, each with its own viewing screen. Just before the Normandy invasion, for example, General Marshall in effect brought together in conference General Eisenhower in the European theater and General MacArthur in the Southwest Pacific. He also brought in by means of a third circuit and screen Maj. Gen. John R. Deane, head of the U.S. military mission in Moscow. The remarkable, almost world-wide, conference lasted over an hour, and produced, Stoner stated, "an understanding between commands equal to one where all would be present in person." He exulted, "We carried three messages to Garcia today." This tremendous communications facility, he added, was "really one of the secret weapons of the war." [16]

Earlier developments in communications had, in time gone by (beginning with the Civil War), caused field officers to chafe under "control from Washington." Now, direct control was possible to the extent that a commander in the Washington headquarters could handle affairs in a distant theater almost as though he were physically there. For example, General Arnold, head of the Army Air Forces in Washington, directed from his office the operations of the XX

---

[14] (1) Oakes, The Army Comd and Admin Com System, pt. II, pp. 90ff. (2) CSigO, Annual Rpt, FY 45, p. 683.

[15] (1) Melia, SigC Fixed Com in World War II: Sp Assignments and Techniques, pp. 28–30. (2) Oakes, The Army Com and Admin Com System, pt. II, pp. 49a–50, 136–37.

By 1945 ACAN also provided Sigtot for the State Department in Washington, London, and Paris, and at the Army terminal in Moscow for joint use of the military attachés and State Department; also for the White House, the Presidential communications railroad car, the Presidential plane, the Presidential yacht, and after April 1945, President Truman's office in Kansas City.

[16] Stoner, Draft MS Comment, 1959.

A graphic description of State Department use of the telecon system during the Berlin crisis of 1948 in a four-way conference between Washington, London, Paris, and Berlin is given in AFSC Lecture C–1, Employment of Communications in the Army, Tab 9, page 1.

Bomber Command against Japan through the radio and wire teletype facilities that Signal Corps installed first in the CBI and later in the Pacific island bases from which that bomber command flew its planes. For General Arnold modern electronics was a boon. At least on one occasion, however, General Eisenhower thought otherwise. In July 1943 at the time Mussolini was divested of his power, General Eisenhower wanted to broadcast encouragement to the new Italian Government. Realizing that he must first get approval from Washington, Eisenhower lamented "that in the old days, before rapid communications, generals were free to do whatever they thought best; nowadays an opportunity could be lost while officers argued back and forth." [17]

At times the conferees had their bad moments since there were bugs in the system. "The teletype conference the other night," wrote General Reeder, CBI signal officer, on one occasion in 1944, "was not a howling success from the technical viewpoint. We sat around the machines for four hours and the total transmission (effective) could not have been more than a quarter of that." He complained to Brig. Gen. Frank C. Meade in the Washington headquarters that a "solid circuit" was needed, that is, good continuous transmission, uninterrupted by atmospheric interference and so on, and "a better operator than you had at your end." But the system had its

points. "From the agenda viewpoint," Reeder continued, "the conference was interesting in that it showed how nearly we are thinking alike." Its value was evident as a means of bringing field and headquarters commanders together and as a mode of working out their problems and coming to mutual understanding quickly.[18]

Its potential value as a means of direct command and control between headquarters thousands of miles apart had led General Arnold and the AAF to demand good conference facilities reaching the Far East. Some of the AAF plans for the system were so secret, it seems, that General Reeder did not know the details. This is evident from the following letter, which also throws further light on some of the early telecon difficulties:

What is prompting the tremendous urge for SIGTOT in Frank Stoner's outfit? We had the SIGTOT conference set-up here for months. No one ever used it, except the Signal Corps itself, for talk with Washington, and then on the occasions it was used, it was thoroughly unsatisfactory. It was unsatisfactory for two reasons: first, that a clearly written message or letter from the end originating the conference could have been written, read, and answered in the time spent fiddling over the conference circuit. The second reason for its undesirability is that it will operate successfully only when there is a solid circuit between the terminal points. This means that between us and WAR, we must have favorable conditions all the way, and such favorable conditions occur during only a

---

[17] (1) Robert Murphy, *Diplomat Among Warriors* (New York: Doubleday & Company, Inc., 1964), p. 186. (2) ASF Annual Rpt, FY 44, p. 198. The first conference terminal was Kharagpur, India. CSigO, Annual Rpt, FY 44, pp. 98, 531ff. (3) Lt. Col. F. H. Menagh, Use of Automatic Cipher Equipment in World War II, Sep 45. SigC AC 319.1.

[18] Ltr, "Bill Reeder BG," Hq Rear Echelon USAF CBI, APO 885, to Meade, Washington, 24 Sep 44, no sub. SigC OT 370.2 Rpts, CBI, Tab 22.

General Meade agreed that the conference was not "a howling success." He attributed the trouble not to the Washington operator, but to the relay station in Asmara, which lacked some needed equipment. Ltr, Meade to Reeder, 9 Oct 44. SigC OT 370.2 Rpts, CBI, Tab 22.

fraction of the day. While awaiting the favorable period, much time is spent lining up, resetting tapes, etc. The advantage which will be quoted by the lovers of SIGTOT is that the text comes through clear. To us that is unimportant. Most of the messages we receive here are multiple address, so that if we receive a message in clear, we must encipher it instead of decipher, as we would do if it came in code. All this may be gravy for Eddie French's outfit, but it is pure headache for us. Possibly there is some good reason behind this insane desire to force SIGTOT onto the field, and I will keep quiet in the hope that you will have one of Frank Stoner's boys explain to me just what is the object.[19]

Time and tireless effort remedied the initial difficulties of the teletype conference system. Before the end of 1944, scheduled conferences over ACAN circuits were averaging three a day, some of them running to as many as 20,000 words. By V–J Day Sigtot facilities were available at 19 overseas stations:

Algiers	Honolulu	Paris
Asmara	Kharagpur	Recife
Brisbane	Leyte	Tehran
Caserta	London	Valognes
Chungking	Manila	Versailles
Guam	Moscow	
Hollandia	New Delhi	

Special conference facilities were, moreover, extended to the military conclaves of Allied leaders at Quebec, Malta, Yalta, Berlin, and Potsdam, and

were heavily used by the President and by State Department members.[20]

Communications for VIP Conferences

As ACAN's efficient communications services became widely available and more efficient, they came to be demanded first and foremost by the heads of states. The meetings of these officials at the several highest level conferences during World War II repeatedly placed heavy pressure upon the Army Communications Service. The government heads and their civilian and military staffs had to have unlimited communications facilities, and the security of the messages they sent and received had, obviously, to be perfect. The circumstance that the VIP's frequently chose out-of-the-way places, normally not well provided with communications facilities, such as Casablanca, Tehran, and Yalta, did not make the task placed upon the Signal Corps any lighter. Signal Corps men had to create, on short notice, large-scale local facilities and effective connections with the world-wide ACAN so that the Big Three and their delegates might maintain unbroken contact with their advisers at home and with their military commanders the world over. The first such conference was held at Casablanca, in January 1943, where Colonel Hammond, then the signal officer of I Armored Corps, effectively installed and operated the required communications.[21]

---

[19] Ltr, unsigned carbon [Reeder] to Ingles, CSigO, 27 Mar 45, no sub. SigC OT 370.2 Rpts CBI, Tab 22.

These initial difficulties on the New Delhi circuit, General Stoner subsequently explained, arose from the distance and almost continuous atmospheric (ionospheric) disturbances on the Washington-Asmara relay to New Delhi. The trouble was soon corrected by increasing the output power of the radio transmitters and by selection of better operating frequencies. Stoner, Draft MS Comment, Jul 59.

[20] (1) Oakes, The Army Comd and Admin Com System, pt. II, p. 137. (2) Melia, SigC Fixed Com in World War II: Sp Assignments and Techniques, pp. 29ff. (3) Stoner, Draft MS Comment, Jul 59.

[21] Thompson, Harris, et al., The Test, pp. 454f.

Less remote was the site of an important conference the following summer. This was the first Quebec conference (QUADRANT, 12–14 August 1943). Though no great difficulties arose in communications, Quebec being well supplied with facilities, security requirements caused some trouble. The Signal Corps' chief problem in providing the facilities resulted from the fact that it was prevented for security reasons from beginning the work on installations till the last hours before the distinguished conferees arrived. No military preparations visible to the public were allowed until three days before Prime Minister Winston S. Churchill made his unheralded arrival. Then enough Signal Corps equipment and personnel drove into the city in a 15-vehicle convoy to get everything ready within the last two days. *Everything* included thirty-three items of teletypewriter and carrier equipment, a 320-line switchboard served by four operators, direct lines both to the White House and to the War Department Signal Center for relay to any point in the ACAN system.[22]

Conferences in November and December 1943 took place at Cairo (SEXTANT) and Tehran (EUREKA). For the Cairo conference the Signal Corps on short notice detoured some twenty tons of radioteletypewriter equipment that happened to be en route to Tehran. Landed in Cairo on 13 November, it helped to set up within four days a special radio channel reaching to Asmara. An efficient heavy-duty radioteletypewriter channel went into operation too, as well as a 4-position switchboard providing 300 telephone lines, not to mention a small single-position switchboard for the use of President Roosevelt and his party. Radio contact was maintained with the world around the clock by links from Cairo to the big Algiers station and to station WAR in Washington. At the Tehran conference, which immediately followed the Cairo conclave, the Signal Corps provided a local switchboard of 50 lines and radio circuits linking Tehran with the Asmara station in ACAN's round-the-world belt line.[23]

The second Quebec conference (OCTAGON, September 1944) made good use of the latest radioteletypewriter conference facilities. These tied in with the Sigtot facilities in the ACAN system extending to Washington and San Francisco and to such overseas points as New Delhi, Kharagpur, Brisbane, and Hollandia. The connection to General MacArthur's headquarters through Hollandia was importantly used, for it was at this conference that the Combined Chiefs of Staff sought to determine whether General MacArthur could attack Leyte earlier than 20 December, as then planned. In the course of the debate in the Château Frontenac, General Marshall requested General Handy to go to the signal control room adjacent and ask MacArthur in Hollandia, New Guinea, by radioteletypewriter if he could advance the attack date. Within five minutes Handy

---

[22] (1) Melia, SigC Fixed Com in World War II: Sp Assignments and Techniques, p. 44. (2) Stoner, Speech to the Federal Com Bar Assn, 11 Jan 46, p. 6. (3) Ray S. Cline, *Washington Command Post: The Operations Division*, UNITED STATES ARMY IN WORLD WAR II (Washington, 1951), p. 270.

[23] (1) Melia, SigC Fixed Com in World War II: Sp Assignments and Techniques, p. 43. (2) Cline, *Washington Command Post: The Operations Division*, pp. 226ff.

rejoined the conferees with the answer that MacArthur's headquarters had said he could invade on 20 October.[24] When the British, including the Prime Minister, could not believe Handy, they all went to the Signal Corps control room for a demonstration of these unheard of communications. They were convinced. President Roosevelt nudged the British Prime Minister, "Winnie, has your Army any communications like this?"[25]

A major effort was necessary to provide conference facilities in February 1945 at Yalta (ARGONAUT), where adverse weather and terrain and limited personnel added to the troubles engendered by the short notice. First word of the Yalta requirement arrived in the Mediterranean theater early in January 1945 and the deadline was 2 February. The equipment needed ran to 250 tons. It had to be assembled from the Mediterranean and European theaters, from the Persian Gulf Command, and from the United States, some of it by air transport. It included not only radios, teletypewriters, switchboards, power equipment, but even telephone poles. A floating radio relay station had to be provided. To this end the Navy provided the USS *Catoctin*, which was outfitted at Naples with one of the first long-range radioteletypewriter transmitters ever installed on a ship. Arriving off the Crimean Peninsula in the Black Sea, the Signal Corps men

found that the mine-infested harbor at Yalta could not be used. The ship had to anchor at Sevastopol, sixty-five miles away, and communications links had to be quickly provided across the mountainous peninsula to the Livadia Palace in Yalta. In the palace itself, site of the conferences, elaborate teletype and telephone installations had to be made. The wire lines to the *Catoctin* had to cross two mountain ranges. In case they should fail, a VHF radio relay circuit was provided also, paralleling the long wire line. At Sevastopol it was found that, when the *Catoctin* turned on its transmitter to signal to Algiers, the powerful signal interfered with the receivers on the ship. Therefore the transmitting antenna had to be removed to a hilltop ashore.

All together, the Yalta conference communications arrangements were strenuous, and the results were sufficiently remarkable to impress President Roosevelt. On returning and reporting to Congress, he mentioned the "modern miracle of communications," making it emphatic that "when we consider international relations, we must include international communications." When quoting these words of the President to the Federal Communications Bar Association early in 1946, General Stoner detailed some of the reasons for Roosevelt's enthusiasm:

While at Yalta the President had many teletype conferences with General Eisenhower—then at Rheims—with the White House and State Department in Washington, and even with Ambassador Hurley in Chungking. For the Chungking hook-up we used regenerative repeaters at Algiers, Washington, and Honolulu to create a single circuit over which the President and Mr. Hurley could exchange questions and

---

[24] Lt. Gen. Richard K. Sutherland, CofS, replying for General MacArthur who was at sea under radio silence.

[25] (1) AFSC Lecture C-1, Employment of Com in the Army, Tab 9, p. 5. (2) Melia, SigC Fixed Com in World War II: Sp Assignments and Techniques, p. 44. (3) Stoner, Speech to the Federal Com Bar Assn, 11 Jan 46, p. 7. (4) Cannon, *Leyte: The Return to the Philippines*, p. 9. See also above, p. 270.

answers immediately—with absolute security.[26]

The last of the World War II international conferences (TERMINAL) took place near Berlin at Potsdam, from 6 July to 3 August 1945. By early July over 200 tons of material and over 300 officers and men (also 27 Wacs) assembled at Halle, 80 miles southeast of Potsdam. Arriving in a convoy of 100 vehicles, the Signal Corps men installed at Potsdam a 6-position board to serve the President's party, about 500 telephones in some 100 separate buildings, and 70 miles of cable distribution, plus 2 radioteletypewriter systems, one to Washington, the other to Paris, and 2 VHF radio relay systems to SHAEF at Frankfurt, via Leipzig. The latter circuit utilized cable from Leipzig to Frankfurt, but, since the telephone repeater on that cable line had been bombed out, the Signal Corps had to install repeaters, ringers, and other equipment to permit the cable to work. A million and a half words flowed over the American facilities, with 100-percent continuity of teletype service.[27]

Expansion Through V–J Day

Midway through World War II the War Department Signal Center and station WAR were struggling to keep up with the flood of communications. By 1943 the 17th Signal Service Company, in charge of the station, was faced not only with heavier traffic loads but also with increasingly burdensome services such as larger training demands and the provision of special communications teams of various sorts.[28] As of April 1943 the company was authorized only 302 men. Actual needs compelled an overstrength, which stood at 530 at that date. There were never enough operators.

The general trend went something like this: as duties increased, overstrength increased, but not fast enough. As overstrength mounted, authorized strength was upped, but even slower.

In this connection, it should be noted that strength figures are very misleading, whether they show authorized or actual size. These numbers have to be carefully analyzed since they include transport radio operators and students along with everyone else. Counting these men would bring the overstrength into the thousands in some cases, and would not reflect the number working in the Signal center station, Property Office, Telephoto Section, and other jobs directly related to the traditional duties of the 17th.

The workloads rose. At the war's peak, the control station was handling 20 percent of the network's traffic. By mid-1944 Wacs were proving to be a great help (as of August 1944 authorized strength was 511 enlisted men and 27 Wacs). A very great help came from automation, in particular the conversion of the station's equipment to semiautomatic wire and radio and tape relay, completed in

[26] (1) Stoner, Speech to the Federal Com Bar Assn, 11 Jan 46, p. 7. (2) Melia, SigC Fixed Com in World War II: Sp Assignments and Techniques, pp. 35–40. (3) Sig Sec, AFHQ, Hist, 24 Jul 42–10 Nov 45, pp. 115–17 and 131f. (4) AFHQ, CSigO Monthly Bull, May–Jun 45, sec. V, Gen, Crimea Com. (5) Leahy, *I Was There*, pp. 274, 300.

[27] Melia, SigC Fixed Com in World War II: Sp Assignments and Techniques, pp. 40–42.

General Stoner accredited the outstanding communications at Yalta to Capt. Carl H. Hatch and his men, and at Potsdam to Col. Vernon B. Bagnall, assisted by Major Scofield and Capt. W. E. Ferrell. Stoner, Draft MS Comment, Jul 59, and War Diary, p. 153.

[28] Such as the team that installed the facilities for the conference in Quebec in September 1944. The following month another team went to ETO to help install the Paris signal center. CSigO, Annual Rpt, FY 45, p. 722.

January 1944. Mechanical ciphering increasingly replaced manual coding. By March 1945 the authorized strength, 920, began to catch up with the need. By then, too, the overgrown company acquired a new organization and designation, becoming on 1 February 1945 the 2506th Service Command Unit.[29]

Physical improvements in the Washington area outside the War Department Signal Center installations included by 1945 a UHF control system that linked station WAR with the receiver station in La Plata in nearby Maryland and with the transmitter stations at Fort Myer and Battery Cove, Virginia. This system provided a dependable line-of-sight radio service that was unhampered by wire line troubles or weather vagaries. As of June 1944 the Fort Myer and Battery Cove transmitter stations and the La Plata receiving station served as terminals for more than a score of major overseas ACAN circuits and stand-by continental circuits, accomplishing the task with an appropriate quantity of radios, up to 40 kilowatts in power.[30] (*Table 3*)

ACAN installations overseas expanded rapidly in 1944 following the Normandy invasion and accelerated successes in the Pacific. Major stations developed in France, principally in Paris and Reims,

at Hollandia in New Guinea, in Manila, and finally at the war's end, in Frankfurt, Germany, and in Tokyo.

ACAN in the European Theater

The ACAN facilities serving SHAEF and ETOUSA headquarters in England had become huge and well established during the months before the invasion of Normandy. The major radio transmitters had been converted to radioteletypewriter operation—JEAR serving ETOUSA, JEJE serving SHAEF, and JBJB serving the headquarters of the United Kingdom Base Command. By the spring of 1944 JEJE and JBJB had radio connections with JJJJ (AFHQ in Caserta, Italy), the Army Air Forces headquarters, and a number of tributary stations. Six of these tributaries as of February 1944 were JEHD, Headquarters, 6th Army Group; JECB, Headquarters, Continental Advance Section; JENY, Headquarters, Delta Base Section; JEOB, Headquarters, Advance Section; JBAF, Headquarters, Eighth Air Force; and JBAD, Headquarters, Base Air Depot Area, Air Service Command.[31]

Changes followed swiftly after the invasion in June 1944. Within hours of the first landings, station WAR came into communication with points on the French coast by radio circuits routed through London. A portion of the ACAN communications center serving SHAEF at Bushy Park, London, moved to the Portsmouth area, where an advanced command post took form by 1 July. General Ingles was unhappy with this move because "it required the installation of a large amount of equipment which was

---

[29] Larew, Hist of the Army Comd and Admin Agency, 1899–1956, pp. 29–37.

[30] CSigO, Annual Rpt, FY 44, pp. 543f.
By 1944 the Signal Corps was acquiring the entire output of Press Wireless production of 40-kilowatt SSB transmitters. The SSB systems the Army had employed earlier, as on the Washington-London circuit, had been leased from AT&T. By V-J Day the Signal Corps was operating a total of 12 SSB systems. (1) Oakes, The Army Comd and Admin Com System, pt. II, p. 39. (2) Melia, SigC Fixed Com in World War II: Sp Assignments and Techniques, p. 16. (3) CSigO, Annual Rpt, FY 45, p. 704. (4) Stoner, Draft MS Comment, Jul 59.

[31] ETOUSA Rpt, II, pp. 49ff.

TABLE 3—ACAN RADIO FACILITIES, JUNE 1944

Call Sign	Terminus	Xmtr Power	Call Sign	Terminus	Xmtr Power
Fort Myer Transmitting Station			*Battery Cove Transmitting Station*		
Circuits in Operation					
WTJ	Hawaii	15 kw	JDOA	Oran	15 kw
JJJJ	Caserta	15 kw	JBJB-G	London	15 kw
WVKF	Recife	15 kw	JBJB-Z	London	15 kw
JCYN	Cairo	15 kw	WVN	Puerto Rico	15 kw
JBHC	Rekyavík	10 kw	WVL	Panama	15 kw
WTE	White House officials	As required	WYTE	Trinidad	15 kw
			WZT·	Bermuda	1 kw
			WYQY	Azores	2½ kw
			JKZA	Accra	15 kw
Stand-by Circuits					
WVD	Seattle		WVT	Chicago	
WVV	Fort Omaha		WVY	San Francisco	
WVQ	Wright Field		WVR	Atlanta	
WVP	Governors Island		WVB	Fort Sam Houston	
Sets Installed					
	1 40 kw			1 40 kw	
	5 15 kw			5 15 kw	
	2 10 kw			2 2½ kw	
	1 SSB multichannel system, 40 kw			3 1 kw	

La Plata Receiving Station

Circuits in Operation

Same as transmitter circuits listed above

Sets Installed

36	Semi-pro receiving sets
12	Diversity equipment
1	Multichannel SSB receiver
12	Press Wireless frequency shift receivers
1	Hammarlund super-pro receiver
13	Western Electric radioteletype terminal equipment
4	UHF Transmitters (6 channels each)
4	Voice frequency channeling sets (6 channels each)

Source: CSigO, Annual Rpt, FY 44, pp. 545ff.

badly needed in France and which was thus immobilized for weeks in a location that was not as good as the former one." [32]

During the summer both the ACAN facilities serving SHAEF and those serv-

[32] (1) Excerpts from Lecture given by the CSigO before the Army-Navy Staff College, 19 Mar 45, p. 7. Com folder, Tab D, SigC Hist Sec file. (2) CSigO, Annual Rpt, FY 45, p. 678.
When General Ingles asked why SHAEF was

not kept at Bushy Park until it could be moved directly across the Channel, he was told, "The move was made in order to get the staff out into the field as they had never had any field training." Ingles believed the move "wasted a great deal of equipment and the efforts of large amounts of personnel."

ing ETOUSA moved to France, the former to Jullouville near Bayeux, the latter to the vicinity of Valognes, near Cherbourg. Neither move was brilliant, in part because of the lack of good local communications in these out-of-the-way provincial towns. The communications center of ETOUSA was by August jammed into the inadequate spaces afforded by a country château, circuits were dislocated, and traffic flow suffered considerable trouble for weeks until suitable and commodious facilities were eventually provided in Paris. On 1 September SHAEF communications moved across the Channel to a set of school buildings in Jullouville where the same unfavorable conditions prevailed as at Valognes. General Eisenhower had been eager to locate at Jullouville but had had to wait until some sort of communications could be assured back to England and among the forward echelons of air, naval, and French forces. Forward SHAEF communications closed out at Portsmouth on 1 September, opening in the main building of La Colonie Scolaire de St. Ouen at Jullouville, a location that proved as remote and unsuitable for the commanding generals as it did for the ACAN communications serving them.[33]

General Ingles believed that these ACAN moves to France before the capture of Paris were even a greater mistake than the shift to Portsmouth. He did not doubt but that ETOUSA communications should have remained in London until the entire setup could be moved bodily to Paris, the logical center in

France for the business of conducting the support needed on the immense scale required by the war in Europe. He cited these instances to demonstrate that future moves of any large Army headquarters and its communication nets must be planned weeks in advance. A single major ACAN radio station, he explained, required nearly a month to install.[34]

It was weeks before an ACAN station in France entered into direct communications with station WAR. Traffic passed via London until the first powerful ACAN radio station on the Continent was installed in mid-August at Valognes, a 15-kilowatt set providing multichannel radioteletypewriter direct to Washington. As the Paris location soon proved to be the best communications center in France, 40-kilowatt stations were erected there, and at the war's end in Frankfurt, Germany, also. For a while when the front was advancing from France into Germany, station WAR maintained a single channel radioteletypewriter circuit with SHAEF Forward at Reims. The Paris station went on the air in a remarkably short time, only ten days after the Germans had been driven out of the city, when high-frequency links direct to London were installed to replace such mobile radio connections as had been employed till then. In a few more weeks a powerful single sideband transmitter was in place and making direct contact with Washington, operating full time. The Signal Corps also restored for ACAN use the former German Horta-Emden cable, which provided two channels having a capacity of 110,000 words a day, a facility that proved especially val-

[33] (1) Capt Frederick Reinstein, Signal Corps Fixed Communications in the European and Africa–Middle Eastern Theaters (1945), SigC Hist Monograph E–7, pp. 115ff., 169f. SigC Hist Sec file. (2) Pogue, The Supreme Command, pp. 264, 276.

[34] (1) Excerpts from Lecture given by the CSigO before the Army-Navy Staff College, 19 Mar 45, pp. 7f. (2) See also above, pp. 139–40.

uable during the German counterattacks in December. Sigtot conference facilities between station WAR and Paris became available in November. An important special circuit inaugurated in France was the Redline net, serving exclusively General Eisenhower and his group commanders.[35]

On 5 October 1944 main SHAEF at Bushy Park closed, opening at Versailles and absorbing Forward SHAEF there. Rear SHAEF continued operating at Bushy Park for a few days and then moved to 31–39 Bryanston Square in London. As French, Belgian, and Dutch wire plants and circuits were rehabilitated on the Continent, much wire, cable, and carrier equipment was installed (no fewer than eleven cables were in use under the English Channel by February 1945). Forward SHAEF opened at Reims in February 1945, where an advance command post had moved in September 1944. As the European war drew to a close, plans were first made to make the last move of SHAEF to Frankfurt-am-Main in Germany, to the I. G. Farben Industrie building there. Forward SHAEF closed on 25 May and opened in Frankfurt the same day. Meanwhile, the large fixed installations in France, notably the former SHAEF automatic telephone system in Paris, were taken over by the Chief Signal Officer, COMZ.[36]

---

[35] (1) Reinstein, SigC Fixed Com in the European and Africa–Middle Eastern Theaters, pp. 116–18. (2) Oakes, The Army Comd and Admin Com System, pt. II, p. 131. (3) CSigO, Annual Rpt, FY 46, pp. 678f.

For details on the repair of the German cable, see Stoner, War Diary, 162.

[36] Reinstein, SigC Fixed Com in the European and Africa–Middle Eastern Theaters, pp. 123–36.

For details of ETOUSA COMZ communications

ACAN in Italy, Africa, the Middle East, and India

When AFHQ moved from Algiers to Italy in July 1944, the ACAN station serving it was installed in the Royal Palace at Caserta, near Naples, its radio answering to the call letters JJJJ. In February 1944, well before the main move of the headquarters, JJJJ had entered the ACAN system, employing Boehme high-speed transmission. This rapid but outmoded equipment gave way to multichannel radioteletype in March. JJJJ activity increased throughout the second half of 1944 as the Allies pressed the Germans northward through the Apennines. Although some of the station's circuits closed out (Seventh Army and 6th Army Group, which landed in southern France in August, moved north into the ETO sphere), other circuits such as weather circuits with Russia were added, swelling the total number of channels radiating out of Caserta to eleven. Through early 1945 traffic loads continued to mount, culminating in April when radio message groups handled by JJJJ averaged about half a million a month. Traffic thereafter began to diminish, the enemy in northern Italy surrendering on 2 May 1945. As spring became summer, and summer wore on, American personnel in the combined communications center of AFHQ declined, British allies taking over increasingly. By August, Signal Corps men numbered about 300 out of the total of 745 comprising the station. Following V–J Day the station's last radioteletypewriter circuit, Caserta-Algiers, was decommissioned, bringing to an end the

---

in France and the notable Sigcircus transportable radio, see above, pp. 166ff.

RADIO TEHRAN, IRAN

combined aspect of the AFHQ–ACAN operation, one of the oldest combined signal centers of the war.[37]

Aside from the radio stations that served the North African theater from late 1942 on, Casablanca, Oran, Accra, Cairo, notably Algiers (which remained an important relay ACAN station, JDJD, even after AFHQ removed to Caserta in mid-1944), there was the major station WVNT at Asmara in Eritrea, a site well south of NATO, and serving not so much that theater's operations as a major relay in the world belt line of the ACAN system. WVNT soon proved to be ideally located to pass radio transmissions east and west with minimum ionospheric interference. As the value of the station became increasingly apparent,

the Signal Corps installed more and ever better equipment there. One of the Army's first 40-kilowatt multichannel SSB sets was sent that way in 1942, only to be lost at sea in a ship torpedoed off Madagascar. A second set followed, to handle heavy loads of east-west traffic in the earth-circling ACAN belt line, and to pass large amounts of intercept traffic on a one-way journey to Washington. In 1944 the link between Asmara and New Delhi was greatly strengthened and its service speeded by the installation, at the New Delhi end, of radioteletypewriter equipment left in Cairo after the conference there late in 1943.[38]

In the Middle East Persian Gulf Command, the 833d Signal Service Company

[37] (1) Reinstein, SigC Fixed Com in the European and Africa–Middle Eastern Theaters, pp. 144–51. (2) Hist, Sig Sec, AFHQ, p. 176.

[38] (1) Oakes, The Army Comd and Admin Com System, pt. II. p. 123. (2) Reinstein, SigC Fixed Com in the European and Africa–Middle Eastern Theaters, p. 99. (3) Thompson, Harris, et al., The Test, pp. 115, 310, 455.

maintained wire lines and radio in Iraq and Iran. Aided by the 95th Signal Battalion, which arrived in March 1943, these troops and facilities assured communications along the railroad supplying Russia from the Persian Gulf. Ever larger quantities of wire and teletypewriter equipment were installed, and by 1 August 1944 four carrier wire systems were moving a traffic load that ran into millions of words a month.

Radio stations were installed at Basra, Iraq, and Andimeshk, Iran, in 1942. The Basra station, serving the theater command headquarters, was the net control station and also provided relay facilities for traffic moving eastward to India and southward to Asmara in Africa. A number of other radio stations were soon added, at Ahwaz and Tehran and at the ports of Bushire, Khorramshahr, Abadan, and Bandar Shahpur. Radio traffic rose to nearly a million and a half words a month, until late 1943 and 1944 when carrier wire teletypewriter began to take over up to two-thirds of the radio load.

The radio net in the Persian Gulf Command remained local during the first year and a half of its existence. In mid-1943 its circuits began to work directly into the ACAN world net when a 15-kilowatt Press Wireless transmitter was set up at Tehran (JFZA) in order to provide a direct channel to station WAR. It converted to radioteletypewriter operation in May 1944. Its direct contact with station WAR suffered, however, from fadeouts, just as the Karachi circuit had suffered earlier. As a result, the Tehran-Washington traffic was diverted by way of the dependable relay station at Asmara.[39]

At New Delhi, CBI headquarters, the ACAN station JGTA had grown slowly, for want of facilities, since the start of the war. The Karachi station served as the major relay point in India until high-power transmitters arrived in New Delhi in mid-1943. Not till August 1943 was JGTA ready to replace its manual radio link to Brisbane with Boehme. Much more equipment arrived in 1944, when the important Brisbane link was converted to radioteletypewriter. The equally important link westward in the equatorial belt line was also converted from Boehme to radioteletypewriter early in 1944 with the equipment that had provided the Cairo-Asmara circuit during the Cairo conference the previous December. In fact so many RTTY facilities arrived in India by mid-1944 that the theater was able to report, as of 1 August, that it enjoyed five additional RTTY circuits operating out of New Delhi: to Karachi, Chabua, Shaduzup, Calcutta, and Kunming.[40] In the spring of 1945 the India radio net, controlled from New Delhi, included, in addition

[39] (1) Reinstein, SigC Fixed Com in the European and Africa–Middle Eastern Theaters, pp. 84ff. (2) Capt Sidney L. Jackson, Theater Fixed Networks (1944), SigC Hist Monograph E–1d, ch. IV, Communications in the Persian Gulf Command, pp. 5ff. SigC Hist Sec file. (3) Thompson, Harris, et al., The Test, pp. 458ff.

The Signal Service in the Persian Corridor remained small throughout the war, attaining a peak of about 1,000 officers and men under Col. Samuel M. Thomas, an Engineer Corps officer who had had considerable Signal Corps technical training. T. H. Vail Motter, The Persian Corridor and Aid to Russia, UNITED STATES ARMY IN WORLD WAR II (Washington, 1952), pp. 232, 253–56.

[40] (1) Reinstein, SigC Fixed Com in the European and Africa–Middle Eastern Theaters, p. 99. (2) Memo, Stoner for Contl Div, Progress and Stat Br, 1 Sep 44, sub: Digest of Progress and Problems, 1–31 Aug 44, p. 2. SigC AC 319.1 Digest, 30 Jul 42–1 Dec 44. (3) Thompson, Harris, et al., The Test, pp. 114, 304.

to the RTTY circuits named above, circuits to Bombay, Ramgarh, Myitkyina, Ledo, Bhamo, Kandy in Ceylon, and Chungking. Meanwhile, the major beltline circuit to Brisbane closed out, and its replacement, New Delhi–Manila, opened up on 24 April 1945.[41]

Throughout the last two years of World War II, the New Delhi station served as a major link in the ACAN world-wide system. Station JGTA occupied an air-conditioned building, which also housed the theater signal section. By late 1944 the station equipment included a Federal BC–340 (10 kilowatts) working on the Asmara 2-tone duplex A and B circuits, a Federal BC–399 (one-kilowatt) used as a utility transmitter, a Federal BC–270 (300 watts) on the Ledo circuit, a Hallicrafter BC–610 (300 watts) on the Bombay circuit, a Federal BC–447 (300 watts) on the Ramgarh manual circuit, a Federal BC–325 (400 watts) on the Karachi 2-tone circuit, and a Federal BC–399 (one-kilowatt) working 2-tone on the Chabua circuit. There were 3 large Press Wireless sets. One of 15 kilowatts worked the circuit to Brisbane; a second, of 40 kilowatts, served the Asmara C circuit at reduced power; and a third, of 2.5 kilowatts, operated a Boehme circuit with Chungking. A Wilcox 96–C, 3 kilowatts, worked 2-tone on the Calcutta circuit, a Federal BC–399 1 kilowatt performed on the circuit with Myitkyina in Burma, and a Federal BC–399 was employed as a utility transmitter. Radio traffic over these New Delhi cir-

cuits exceeded 13,000,000 words during the month of March 1945. Power for the equipment came from seven 50-kilowatt and two 100-kilowatt diesel-engined generators. The New Delhi antenna system included 11 rhombics—2 directed on Asmara, one each to Washington, Brisbane, Kunming, Chungking, Calcutta, Chabua, Myitkyina, Kandy, and Hollandia. Three long wire antennas were directed on Ledo, Bombay, and Ramgarh.[42]

To Moscow and Back

Beyond the ETO and north of the ACAN round-the-world belt line through Asmara and New Delhi lay the USSR, quite beyond the ACAN system, till late in the war. Indeed, through the first years of the war, Moscow was almost as remote in communications matters as though located on another planet. Good direct communications had long been needed, but the United States had no means to this end except through a Mackay circuit, which was seldom usable, being unable to maintain contact with the Russians for more than a few minutes each day because of severe fading and auroral interference on the direct route to Moscow over the polar regions of the earth. There existed an indirect route passing through London, but it could not handle the load of military traffic. Messages were delayed for hours, even for as long as three days on occasions, until the United States offered to lend Signal Corps help.

By 1944 Army Communications Serv-

---

[41] (1) Signal Corps History of India-Burma Theater, April–September 1945, p. 25. SigC Hist Sec file. (2) Signal Corps History of India-Burma Theater, Jan–Mar 45, pp. 32f. SigC Hist Sec file.

The major landline teletype circuits by March 1945 were circuits to Agra, Bombay, Calcutta, Hastings Mill, and Karachi.

[42] Dr. Donald O. Wagner, Army Command and Administrative Network, 1941–45, pt. II, China-Burma–India (1945), SigC Hist Monograph E–6, pp. 103–05. SigC Hist Sec file.

ice plans for a good ACAN channel to the Soviet Union had made progress, despite Russian scepticism. The plans called for a circuitous route via automatic relay at the Algiers station. By April 1944 a 2½ kilowatt Press Wireless transmitter together with radioteletypewriter equipment had been shipped by air to Tehran. The shipment both of the equipment and of a small team of Signal Corps men under Maj. Raymond B. Jewett was delayed by Russian intransigence, especially opposition to certain of the personnel.[43] Radio frequencies and the Moscow call sign, JMRR, were not easily agreed upon either. It was late spring of 1944 when the equipment was ready and tests were completed.

The Moscow end of the WAR–JMRR circuit was unique in the ACAN system. Messages sent eastward from station WAR, relayed at Algiers to Moscow, flashed into the Soviet control center (SKWU), operated by Soviet personnel who had had some training in American communication methods. From this control center the Russians routed the messages to either of two destinations in Moscow—the U.S. military mission or a Soviet tributary. The Soviet tributary soon split into three terminals: the Foreign Office, the Foreign Trade Commissariat, and the War Office. This arrangement whereby a switching center routed traffic to either the American or Soviet message center permitted fairly independent operation. It offered both governments rapid and secure communications. Each message center remained largely independent, avoiding differences in language, custom, and operational procedures.

Special arrangements also had to be made at the Washington end of this circuit. Messages from Moscow arrived in the War Department Signal Center. Those intended for the Soviet Embassy were at first delivered by Western Union to the Embassy; then a tie line was installed between it and the Signal Center. There were difficulties. Time on the circuit had to be shared, United States messages traveling on even hours, Soviet Embassy traffic on the odd. Moreover, the circuit, though intended for 24-hour operation, was sometimes unusable. There was, for example, some interference from facsimile circuits. Since shared use of the single circuit was not altogether satisfactory, a second channel was desired, so that each nation could enjoy a circuit of its own full time. The second circuit was approved in January 1945 and began operating in April. These Washington-Moscow radioteletypewriter circuits, via Algiers relay, continued to operate until 6 May 1946. They were then replaced by a commercial route connecting New York and Moscow by way of Tangiers.[44]

ACAN in the Pacific

After the loss of WTA Manila upon the fall of the Philippines early in 1942,

---

[43] (1) Deane, *The Strange Alliance*, pp. 64ff. (2) Stoner, War Diary, p. 161.

[44] (1) Reinstein, SigC Fixed Com in the European and Africa–Middle Eastern Theaters, pp. 164ff. (2) Oakes, The Army Comd and Admin Com System, pt. II, p. 130. (3) CSigO, Annual Rpts, FY 45, p. 684, and FY 46, p. 473.
General Stoner reported in December 1944 that AAF needs for exchange of weather data had placed on this ACAN circuit with Moscow a load of about 8,000 words a day of operational priority weather traffic between the Washington weather central, WWI, and JMRR, Moscow. Memo, Stoner for Contl Div, Progress and Stat Br, 1 Dec 44, sub: Digest of Progress and Problems, 1–30 Nov 44, p. 9. SigC AC 319.1 Digest, 30 Jul 42–1 Dec 44.

Melbourne, Australia, first became the anchor of the ACAN system serving the South and Southwest Pacific areas. As the campaigns against the Japanese progressed, Brisbane (WVJJ, later WTO) replaced Melbourne as the ACAN station site. Equipped with powerful transmitters, the Brisbane station by mid-1943 was able to reach San Francisco directly and dependably, as well as stations in the CBI, thereby establishing a reliable round-the-world belt line of signals.

Brisbane traffic reached a million words a day as the campaigns advanced up through the islands of the south and southwest Pacific. Captured in April 1944, Hollandia by May became a major station, WVLH. In October, MacArthur's headquarters arrived and Hollandia became a communications center. The ACAN transmitters at Hollandia maintained connections with New Delhi and San Francisco, depending on radioteletypewriter supplemented by manual circuits to the many lesser stations among the islands. Traffic grew to a million words a day by mid-November 1944 and remained high even after GHQ moved to Leyte because supply headquarters USASOS remained for a time at the New Guinea base. Messages coming into the theater from outside continued to flow through Hollandia, where they were decoded, screened, and sent on to Leyte by courier or radio. The Hollandia ACAN station moved to Manila early in 1945, and the old station WTA, which had fallen to the Japanese on the capture of Corregidor in May 1942, arose from its ashes.[45]

The new WTA Manila used the 40-kilowatt transmitter that had gone in at Brisbane nearly two years earlier. It was set up at the Manila Country Club. The receiver installation went in the receiver station the Japanese had built. Code room, message center, and teleprinters were installed first at the Trade and Commerce Building, but later moved to the Municipal Waterworks Building. The USASOS at first used these ACAN facilities but later acquired parallel circuits of its own and removed to the Far Eastern University. A second multichannel SSB system was set up, beginning operations between Manila and San Francisco in June 1945. Manila ACAN thus became one of the largest overseas stations, with radioteletype circuits to Okinawa, San Francisco, Honolulu, Guam, Nouméa, Finschhafen, Brisbane, Hollandia, Leyte, Calcutta, New Delhi, and Chungking.[46]

At the war's end in mid-August ACAN stations in the Pacific participated in an extraordinary drama when the Allies sought to repair the communications links Japan had shattered on Pearl Harbor Day nearly four years earlier. Radio communications had to be re-established in order that surrender arrangements might be accomplished. Such links were neither easily nor quickly set up. Surrender on the air became a drama that consumed many hours on 15 August 1945.

First, Army radio operators in the ACAN system, then commercial stations the world over, became intensely concerned in establishing a radio contact whereby the Japanese might acknowledge the Allied peace terms and arrange to terminate the fighting, which meanwhile was continuing unabated.

---

[45] Wagner, Army Comd Admin Network, 1941–45, pt. I, The Pacific, pp. 20ff.

[46] Ibid., pp. 50–51.

It all began most unconventionally in the morning over a telecon channel to Manila, when a message in the clear arrived from Chief of Staff Marshall to General MacArthur giving notice of the Japanese capitulation and instructing MacArthur to proceed with surrender arrangements. A more formal instruction in top secret cipher came through a little later. By 1100 MacArthur had composed a message to the Japanese Emperor and the Imperial Command asking that they begin negotiations with him. He had to request that a radio station in Tokyo be designated to maintain communications with his Manila headquarters. Until he should receive this information, he arbitrarily designated a Japanese station (JUM) on a certain frequency to communicate with Manila WTA.

No Japanese station replied. None accepted the American call. Hour after hour, Army transmitters tried to break in on Japanese stations they could hear operating. MacArthur asked Washington to help. Finally near midnight on the 15th station JUM, while working Singapore, heeded the American intercession and asked the Singapore station to wait while the JUM operator listened to WTA. Army stations all over the western Pacific that had been anxiously listening for a Japanese response, swamped WTA with calls that JUM was answering. WTA sent the MacArthur messages, getting receipt for the first on 16 August at 0025. Another Japanese station (JNP) called WTA asking, "Do you want an answer to your message?" "Hell yes," shouted the officer in charge at WTA when he was shown the message. The American operator signaled back "Yes," and through the early hours of 16 August the exchange of messages on the sur-

render arrangements continued. The exchange went on through the 17th and into the 18th. Many stations the world over listened eagerly for the end. At one point, when there was some uncertainty as to whether Japan was receiving a certain important message, so many transmitters signaled the text that the Tokyo station after a few minutes desperately radioed, "Please send no more of message No. 5013. We have already receipted for over 500 copies." [47]

Special Services

Radioteletype for the AAF

By all odds the largest undertaking of the Army Communications Service, besides installing and operating the enormous world-wide communications system of the ACAN, was the rather special support given to the Army Airways Com-

[47] "Surrender on the Air, An Official Signal Corps History of Message Traffic on the Japanese Capitulation," *Military Review*, XXVI, No. 2 (May, 1946), 31ff. Reprinted in *Signals*, I, No. 1 (September–October, 1946), 30ff. A full version, the original, by Lt. Morton Sontheimer, SigC (USAF Pacific), complete to 19 August 1945, is "Surrender on the Air." SigC Sec file. See also AFSC Lecture C-1, Employment of Com in the Army, Tab q, p. 5. SigC OP 352 AFSC Rpts, vol. 6, 1948–49.

To quote General Stoner on the variety of radio stations that transmitted MacArthur's message to Tokyo: "Within a short time we lined up and brought into action the greatest concentration of radio power ever focused on one spot. The message was relayed to the FCC, the OWI, the Bureau of Public Relations, the Navy, RCA, Mackay, CBS, NBC, Mutual, the Vatican station, the Alaska Communication System, and to stations in Moscow, Chungking, Berne, Lisbon, and Stockholm. It was also sent on the distress frequencies. Soon General MacArthur's first orders were being beamed to Japan from many lands. It was a truly complete world-wide spectrum broadcast, taking precedence over everything else."

Stoner, Speech to the Federal Com Bar Assn, 11 Jan 46, p. 14.

munications Service. "We had one other huge task, which is not generally known to the public," remarked General Stoner speaking of the AACS. The AACS differed from ACAN in that it was strictly an AAF organization, manned and operated by the airmen, though Signal Corps men supplied the equipment, engineered and set up the installations, and in the early days of the war often operated the communications lines too, until the AAF could do so with AACS men, who very often merely transferred over from the Signal Corps.[48]

Pressure for radioteletypewriter service for the AACS developed early in World War II. Aircraft flights required swift communications between airfields. Weather conditions affecting air operations had to be transmitted quickly. When the AAF was harassed by the submarine war in the Atlantic during the first year and a half of the war, rapid communications were desperately needed to press antisubmarine combat. Army's communications and radar expert in Secretary Stimson's office, Dr. Bowles, studied the communications networks over the Atlantic and found them wanting. He noted on a chart of an antisubmarine net that he drew up early in 1943, "Telegraph communications of one kind or another now exist between all proposed stations on the antisubmarine net." But except for two radioteletypewriter circuits, one to London and one to Algiers, he noted that the communications facilities were "very slow because of the necessity for coding and decoding," slowed down still further "because of heavy traffic loads and

inexperienced telegraph operators." He concluded that the latest form of radioteletypewriter with automatic coding and decoding was essential. The Signal Corps was in fact already striving to provide this equipment for the AACS, with success. In August 1943, therefore, Bowles was able to inform Secretary Stimson that such a RTTY system, with automatic ciphering, "along the South Atlantic Ferry Route had been planned by the Signal Corps . . . installation is now in progress . . . the first few links being already in operation." [49]

The Signal Corps had developed radioteletypewriter, single channel, especially for AACS needs. To accomplish the major task of installing it in the hundreds of AACS stations that had mushroomed over the world, the Chief Signal Officer greatly expanded his plant activity, an engineering service of long standing in the Signal Corps, to design and lay out Army's communications stations. He expanded the activity into an agency, the Plant Engineering Agency, and located it in Philadelphia as a major field installation. Its Signal Airways Branch and Signal Airways Service divided up the world's AACS stations in four groups and tackled the huge job of providing not only radioteletypewriter facilities, but all the other communications, meteorology, and air navigation needs.[50]

It was the South Atlantic route to Africa and Europe that first got the single-channel RTTY net, along the

[48] (1) Thompson, Harris, *et al.*, *The Test*, pp. 278ff. (2) Stoner, Speech to the Federal Com Bar Assn, 11 Jan 46, pp. 5f.

[49] (1) Edward L. Bowles, Acute Problem of Ocean-Borne Transport and Supply, Apr 43, Tab XXII. Bowles papers, Tab T. (2) Memo, Bowles for SW, 23 Aug 43, sub: Significant Projects in Radar and Com. Bowles Papers, Tab I, p. 5.
[50] (1) Thompson, Harris, *et al.*, *The Test*, pp. 287, 437ff. (2) Dodds, Hist, PEA, 1941–46.

string of Caribbean islands to the bulge of Brazil, across the South Atlantic via Ascension Island, reaching Dakar by mid-1943. One of Dr. Bowles' expert consultants, Dr. Strieby, inspected the South Atlantic net in May 1943. Accompanied by Lt. Cols. Vernon B. Bagnall from the Office of the Chief Signal Officer and Stuart K. Baker from Signal Corps, and by two officers from the Air Transport Command, Strieby toured the South Atlantic route to study its military communications, in particular the radioteletypewriter facilities and the point-to-point and air-to-ground communications of the AACS. He found that despite considerable confusion and duplication, radioteletypewriter installations were making progress. When he made a second inspection a year later, amid a survey of AAF nets the world over early in 1944, he commented, "The South Atlantic route is definitely good, . . . a marked improvement over operations observed early last summer." By the early autumn of 1944 additional AACS radioteletypewriter circuits were in operation, reaching from the Atlantic to the Near East, as follows:

> Marrakech–Algiers
> Algiers–Naples
> Algiers–Tunis
> Tunis–Tripoli
> Tripoli–Benghazi
> Benghazi–Cairo
> Cairo–Abadan
> Tunis–Cairo

In the CBI theater, where pressure was mounting to provide the XX Bomber Command with such efficient communications that General Arnold could maintain control directly from Washington, there were troubles in the spring of 1944. One was that the require-

ments were mounting faster than the plans. Also, there were no stocks of matériel in the CBI to meet such sudden demands (ASF forbade theater stockpiling). Even so, the Signal Airways Service in the CBI Strieby found "well manned and functioning smoothly.[51]

By August 1944, Signal Corps had met the AACS needs in CBI, including the radioteletype control circuits and conference facilities Arnold needed all the way to Kharagpur. "The Kharagpur-Hsinching and Kharagpur-Honolulu circuits are in operation, for use by the Twentieth Air Force," General Stoner reported. He added that the following AACS radioteletypewriter circuits were also in operation in the CBI as of 1 August:[52]

> Karachi–Agra
> Agra–Barrackpore
> Barrackpore–Chabua
> Chabua–Kunming
> Kunming–Hsinching

Communications for the White House

A special service and a very important Signal Corps responsibility had long been the provision of communications for the President of the United States and his White House staff. In late 1941 Lt. Col.

[51] (1) Memo, Strieby for Bowles, 11 Jun 43, sub: Rpt on Instal of South Atlantic Com Facilities. Bowles papers, Tab A. (2) Memo, Strieby for Bowles, 28 Apr 44, sub: Results of Theater Survey Trip, pp. 1 and 5. SCIA File 127, Bowles papers. (3) Capt Sidney L. Jackson, Radnese "100", Chapter II of International Radio Circuits (1944), SigC Hist Monograph E–2b. SigC Hist Sec file. (4) Memo, Stoner for Contl Div, Progress and Stat Br, 2 Oct 44, sub: Digest of Progress and Problems 1–30 Sep. SigC AC 319.1 Digest, 30 Jul 42–1 Dec 44.

[52] Memo, Stoner, Chief of Army Com Sv, for Contl Div, Progress and Stat Br, 1 Sep 44, sub: Digest of Progress and Problems, 1–31 Aug 44, p. 3. SigC AC 319.1 Digest, 30 Jul 42–1 Dec 44.

William A. Beasely, assistant radio engineer at the Signal Corps laboratories, was ordered to the White House, where he took command of the White House Signal Detachment, a plain clothes unit of three Signal Corps officers and some forty enlisted specialists. The detachment was activated in early spring of 1942 under the direct control of the Chief Signal Officer.[53]

From then on the officers and men of this unit saw to it that the President and his staff were provided with rapid, efficient, and, above all, secure, communications not only in Washington but wherever the President might travel—by land, by sea, or by air. President Truman subsequently remarked, speaking of the conference of the Big Three in Potsdam, Germany, in mid-1945, "A President of the United States takes his office with him wherever he goes, and the number of details that require his attention never ends." [54] That of course means that all the flow of telephone and teletype that normally pours in and out of the White House must somehow be carried along at the President's elbow in the course of his rather frequent and sometimes very distant travels. The White House Signal Detachment accomplished the task without a failure throughout World War II, using all the military and commercial channels of the

nation, and in particular the ACAN global system.[55]

The provision of the VIP conference communications in World War II of course figured large in the task of the White House Signal Detachment. President Truman took particular interest in the facilities, even to the extent of sitting at the radioteletypewriter sets and pecking out his own messages on the keys.[56] Participation at the Potsdam conference in July 1945 initiated President Truman in the Signal Corps provisions that converted his quarters in the Berlin area into a "little White House." He was much impressed and congratulated the Secretary of War, writing, "The Signal Corps in providing communication facilities for the American Delegation at the Berlin Conference, and in particular at the 'Little White House,' allowed me to keep in almost instantaneous touch with my office in Washington and provided a steady flow of news and information which greatly assisted me during the conference." [57]

---

[53] (1) Thompson, Harris, et al., The Test, pp. 431ff. (2) History of the White House Signal Detachment. SigC Hist Sec file. (3) White House Signal Corps Detachment, Special Presidential Facility, copies of papers from SigC CE Br 013.2 White House Sig Det, Oakes Reference folder. SigC Hist Sec file.

Colonel Beasely remained the detachment's commanding officer until May 1943, when Maj. Dewitt Greer took command.

[54] Harry S. Truman, "Memoirs," Volume I, Year of Decision (New York: Doubleday and Co., Inc., 1955), p. 412.

[55] Maj. George J. McNally, Chief White House Sig Det, "White House Signal Team," Signals, II, No. 2 (November–December, 1947), pp. 43ff. A shorter version of this article was printed also, in Army Information Digest, vol. 2, No. 8 (August, 1947), 24ff.

[56] Lt. Col. George J. McNally, CO White House Army Sig Agency, "Communications for the President," Signals, XIV, No. 7 (March, 1960), 13.

[57] Extract from Ltr, Truman to SW, 8 Aug 45, quoted by Stoner, Draft MS Comment, Jul 59.

The President was pleased on the night of 18 July to be able to talk with his wife in Independence, Missouri, finding the connection surprisingly clear ("I learned later," he wrote, "that the calls were routed over Signal Corps circuits through Frankfurt and London to New York and from there to Independence"). Year of Decision, p. 354. The next morning he spoke proudly of the incident at breakfast with Admiral Leahy who recorded that Truman said, "He could hear her [Mrs. Truman] as plainly as if it had been merely a local call." Leahy, I Was There, p. 400.

Telephoto—Pictures by
Wire and Radio

Late in 1941, the Signal Corps, together with an engineer from Acme Newspictures, undertook to adapt equipment for wire telephoto work, and in June 1942 ACAN set up its first telephoto net, in consequence of the submarine warfare off the east coast of the United States. Daily submarine situation maps were distributed over the net, which extended from the first installations at New Orleans and New York City to each of the four defense commands and to the headquarters of the Alaska Communication System. Semiweekly weather charts were also transmitted, over a wire line network for the AAF. The technique, when applied to radio channels, became facsimile. It was first used on the Algiers multichannel single sideband transmitter when a special team flew there in February 1943 to ready the equipment, including a developing laboratory. The corresponding equipment at the Washington end, in the Munitions Building, was at first crammed into a converted broom closet presided over by Sgt. Joseph E. Dunn of the 17th Signal Service Company. Dunn operated the net control station of the entire telephoto system.

Over the Algiers facility news pictures from the North African theater traveled direct to station WAR. Similar radiophoto provisions followed in ACAN stations in London, Paris, Caserta, Honolulu, Brisbane, Manila, and, finally, Berlin. From processing a few dozen prints weekly beginning in June 1942, the operators of the radio telephoto facilities in station WAR reached a peak of 600 prints processed in the first week of the Normandy invasion. The pictures were all black and white, and each required about seven minutes to transmit and receive.

The picture or print to be sent was clamped to a drum at the transmitting station, and at the receiving end a similar drum was covered with sensitized paper. While both drums revolved at the same speed, one hundred revolutions a minute, synchronized, a beam of light scanned the transmitting drum laterally, covering a band about an inch wide a minute. The intensity of the beam, varying with the black, white, and gray tones of the picture, modulated the radio wave, which traveled to the receiver where the varying light was recreated, varying exactly in step with the pick-up beam at the transmitter end. As the beam at the receiver traveled over the sensitized paper on the drum, it reproduced the scene.

The methods and quality of this process improved steadily through the war. Then in August 1945, the first news color picture ever transmitted by radio (Sergeant Dunn receiving) arrived from Berlin on 3 August, picturing President Truman, Prime Minister Atlee, and Marshal Stalin at the Potsdam conference.[58]

By the end of 1945 there were six outlying stations of the facsimile net in operation: Manila, Honolulu, San Francisco, Paris, Tokyo, and Frankfurt. There had been at one time or another during the war 25 such stations. The peak year of facsimile traffic was 1944,

---

[58] See above, p. 565.

when 11,533 transmissions passed over the ACAN system.[59]

Expeditionary Force and Casualty Message Services

Messages from soldiers to relatives and friends back home were provided at reduced cost where communications facilities of American communications companies were available.[60] In areas where the British held control, there was difficulty over routing and financing such communications until mid-1942, when the Chief Signal Officer and the chairman of the Imperial Communications Advisory Committee in England worked out a satisfactory arrangement. Expeditionary force messages, chosen from some two hundred fixed texts, were sent at a flat rate of 60 cents a message, regardless of the land from which sent. The EFM's were approaching a million a month by the end of 1943. By that Christmas the commercial companies were overtaxed and it fell to ACAN to handle the overflow, some 111,000 messages. A similar overflow developed before the invasion of Normandy. ACAN sent about 8,000 EFM's between 5 and 8 May. Then on 8 May the Joint Chiefs of Staff suspended the service, fearing that the heavy increase in ACAN traffic would reveal to the listening enemy that something big was afoot. A year later, in May 1945, ACAN had to handle another, very different overflow of EFM's, beyond the capacity of commercial companies—some 6,000 messages from released prisoners of war. A tragic category of messages was the casualty message service. Western Union Telegraph Company, it had been agreed, would handle such messages after they had been received at station WAR over Army's communications system. The large number of these messages through the second half of 1944 required a special staff in the Pentagon, WAR, and the Adjutant General's Office.[61]

The Around-the-World Belt Line

The techniques of communications, also the air and sky through which radio waves speed, know no boundaries, no national or international restrictions. The air encompasses all nations of the world alike, and radio waves sweep as readily over one country as over another. But radio transmission and reception require land-based stations. The stations, the control of them, and the control of the communications passing through them, raise seemingly insolvable problems of international, diplomatic, and military complexity. To control communications is to control propaganda and to mold public opinion. Communications control implies access to much information and knowledge. And then there is the acute matter of security, concealing message texts, re-

---

[59] (1) Melia, SigC Fixed Com in World War II: Sp Assignments and Techniques, pp. 49–56. (2) Oakes, The Army Comd and Admin Com System, pt. II, pp. 135f., pt. III, pp. 26ff. (3) Boswell, The 17th Sig Sv Co, A Component of WD Sig Ctr, World War I Through World War II, pp. 78–80.

[60] These companies created such special telegram services as the casualty message procedure, the expeditionary force message, the homeward bound message, and the reduced rate telegraph money order. Telecommunications: A Program for Progress, A Report by the President's Communications Policy Board (Washington, 1951), p. 67.

[61] Oakes, The Army Comd and Admin Com System, pt. II, pp. 138–42, pt. III, pp. 61ff.

ports, and intelligence in cryptic form and preventing unauthorized persons from prying, copying, or seeking to learn the hidden meaning.

Before World War II, there had never been a unified international communications system under a single central control. Numerous wire and wireless companies of several nationalities offered wide, competing service, depending upon the location of their circuits and channels. The quality of the service varied much, and the expense was high. The messages they carried served chiefly business and the affairs of government. Inconvenience and cost precluded most people from wiring or telephoning to friends or relatives overseas.

The conditions of World War II made it imperative that the U.S. Army create and use a world-wide communications net, and Signal Corps ACAN became that net. Station locations around the world were obtained by conquest or by emergency agreement. Signal Corps operated and controlled the stations. Not all station sites were equally good and reliable since the vagaries of the ionosphere, by which long-distance high frequency radiations were directed over the earth, favored some sites and hampered others. By trial and error the better sites were discovered. The best routes, over which high frequency sky waves were most reliably transmitted with least disturbance, were found to lie around the equatorial regions. Stations in these areas—Asmara, Karachi, New Delhi, Manila, Honolulu—with their high capacity, multichannel radioteletypewriter equipment provided Signal Corps and the U.S. Army with dependable channels for any number of

messages, which could be relayed to other stations over the world efficiently, inexpensively, and rapidly, under a single integrated system. Private communications companies some years before the war had demonstrated that a message could be sent around the world in about nine minutes—but with some awkwardness of relaying and retransmitting through different facilities and companies.

On 24 May 1944 (the centennial of the first telegraph message that Samuel Morse sent from Washington to Baltimore) Signal Corps transmitted the same words that Morse had telegraphed in 1844: "What hath God wrought?" Station WAR transmitted the words both east and west around the world belt line. The two messages passed through four relay stations, San Francisco, Brisbane, New Delhi, and Asmara. The eastbound message made it first, returning to Station WAR in three and one-half minutes. The westbound message arrived a minute and a half later. Again on 28 April 1945, after the Signal Corps had installed faster radioteletypewriter equipment (semiautomatic tape relay), another message circled the world during a Sunday afternoon Army Hour radio program. "This is What God Hath Wrought, Army Communications Service," sped out of WAR, was automatically relayed by radioteletypewriter from Washington through San Francisco, Manila, New Delhi, and Asmara. Having covered 23,200 miles in five sky-wave hops by high frequency radio, it returned and was printed on a WAR receiving teletypewriter in nine and one-half seconds, those seconds representing the mechanical transmission time. The flight through the sky of course occurred

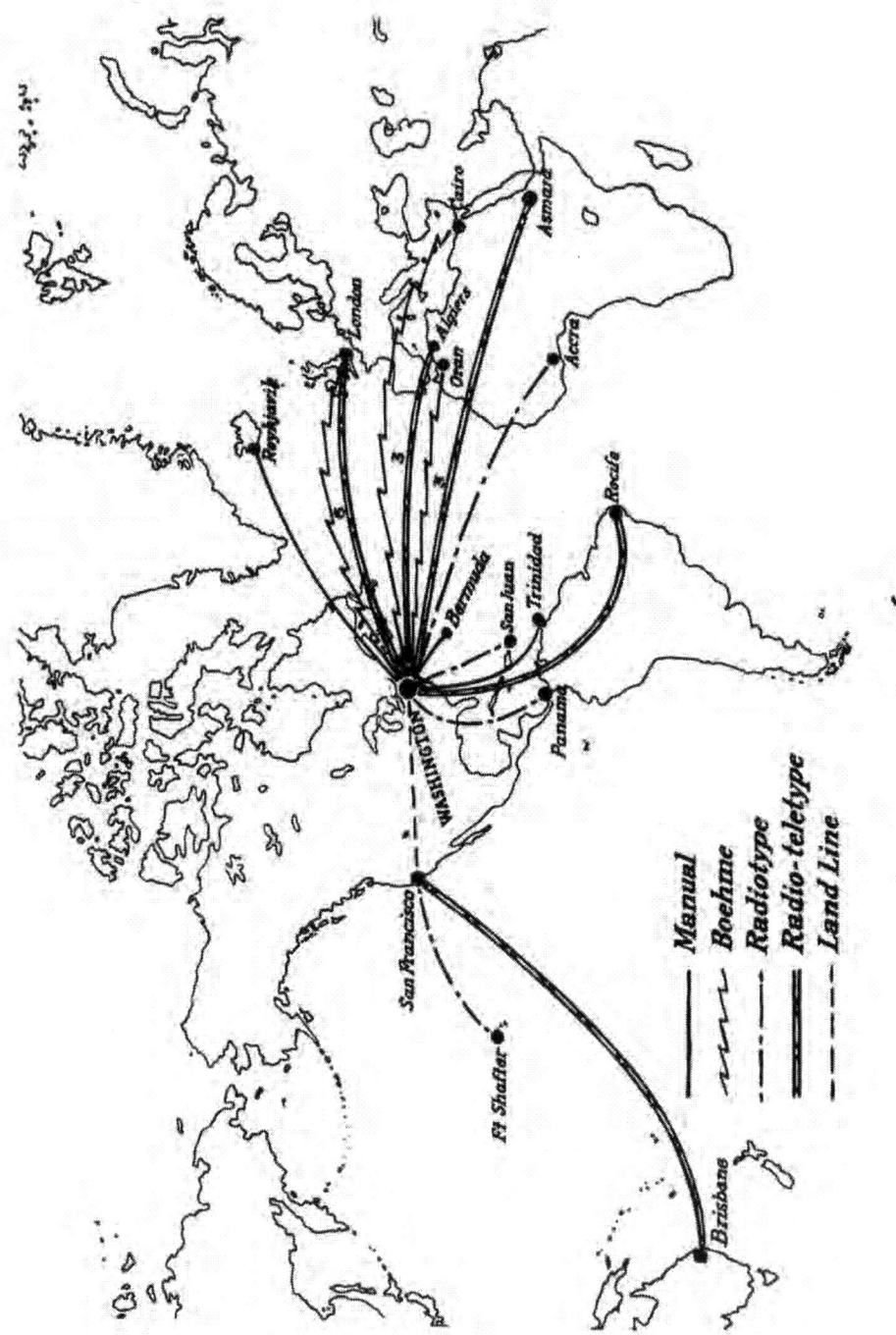

ARMY COMMAND AND ADMINISTRATIVE NETWORK OVERSEAS, DECEMBER 1943

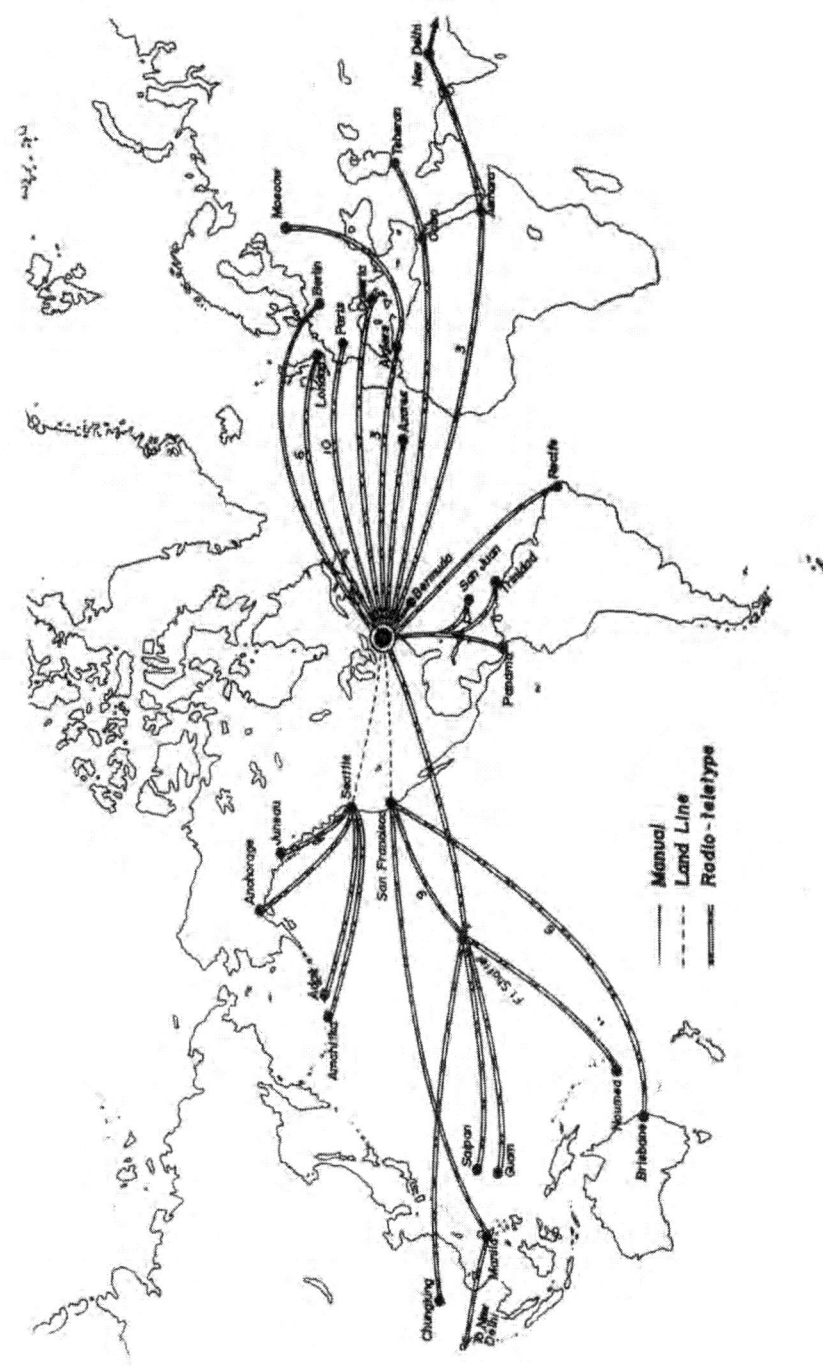

ARMY COMMAND AND ADMINISTRATIVE NETWORK OVERSEAS, JUNE 1945

at the speed of light—in one-eighth of a second.[62]

The Army Communications Service controlled at its peak about 3,000 officers and 21,000 enlisted men, Wacs, and civilians who built up and operated ACAN. General Stoner wrote to Lt. Gen. Matthew B. Ridgway early in 1947:

At no time during the war was the President of the United States, the Chief of Staff, the Joint Chiefs of Staff of the War Department without communication to any commander in the field. Nor was the international, rather the global service, which the Signal Corps provided limited just to military and government agency use. Considerable ACAN effort went into the needs of the press, into the transmission and circulation of news and information.[63]

ACAN, designed, installed, and operated by the Signal Corps Army Communications Service, had created the first world system of communications. True, it was intended to be temporary. It had been created despite international vexations, in the overriding need to win the war. And it served as but one tool of the U.S. Army. But it opened up areas that General Squier foresaw in World War I and that General Stoner now saw approaching in reality. There might someday exist for all men an equatorial communications belt line, dependable and free from electrical disturbances. It might be operated as a co-operative enterprise—belonging to no one nation alone—into which the people of every nation might feed messages addressed to any part of the world. It could be a communications system over which any man might communicate with his fellows in any other nation at a nominal cost. It could become, barring the perversities of politics and power, a powerful instrument toward building a better understanding among the peoples of the earth.

---

[62] *Ibid.*, pp. 87–88, 124.

Of this accomplishment, Brig. Gen. David Sarnoff, president of RCA, said in a letter to General Stoner, chief of the Army Communications Service: "I am glad to have lived long enough to see the remarkable developments of communications to a point where a message can go around the world in 9½ seconds. This surely must exceed the fondest dreams which Morse or Marconi could have entertained in their lifetimes." Ltr, Sarnoff to Stoner, 11 May 45. SigC 201.22 Commendations, No. 2.

[63] Stoner, Draft MS Comment with quote from Ltr, Stoner to Ridgway, Mil Staff Comm, United Nations, 7 Jan 47. Stoner added: "Approximately five million words of press and broadcasting information were carried daily over the Army Network for the Office of War Information."

For Signal Corps services to the press in the European theater, see above, pp. 107ff., and in the Pacific, pp. 276, 292, 299.

An ASF report early in 1944 divided the traffic load of the War Department Signal Center into two categories: (1) regular command and administrative messages; and (2) news digests. Although the second category constituted only about 4 percent of the total load, it remained a considerable quantity, containing news data that was broadcast overseas for distribution to troops abroad, news radioed to and from OWI. and State Department news digests. ASF–WD Analysis (MPR–31 Mar 44), sec. 6, p. 27.

CHAPTER XIX

The Army Signal Situation at War's End

OCSigO Organization in 1945

The seeming singleness of the Signal Corps mission—military communications and signaling—tended to dissolve into a bewildering variety of means and methods, not easily comprehended by most and looked askance by many, as if magical if not suspect. This circumstance made difficult a good understanding of Signal Corps activities. Historically, the mission of the Signal Corps had been since its Civil War origins a most varied one, serving as a catchall for many Army jobs, in general technical and specifically electrical. Dr. Bowles summed up the World War II signal situation for the Chief of Staff, General Eisenhower, early in 1947:

At the beginning of the recent war the tendency was to put almost everything of a mystical electrical character into the Signal Corps. This included responsibility for all aspects of communications, from research to the operation of our War Department world net. It embraced radar and complementary electronic devices. It embraced radio and radar applications to air navigation and landing, radar applications to fire control and to bombing. Meteorological equipment development, proximity fuzes, infra-red devices and identification equipment were not left out. Added to this

assortment, which had one thing in common—electron tubes—were others, including pigeons and photography.[1]

Throughout the last two years of the war the Signal Corps retained the same basic headquarters organization General Ingles had molded soon after taking office in mid-1943. By 1945 he and his assistant chief, General Code, aided by the Control Division together with several boards and committees, directed four staff activities—Operational Research, Plans and Operations, Fiscal, and Legal; and six operating services—Engineering and Technical, Procurement and Distribution, Personnel and Training, Army Communications, Army Pictorial, and the Office Service Division. The field activities directly under the OCSigO continued to number about sixty.

The variety and scope of Signal Corps responsibilities showed clearly in the organization charts over the years, steadily branching and extending both

---

[1] Memo, Bowles for Eisenhower, 10 Feb 47, sub: Mil Com, Related Svs, and Organizational Considerations, p. 17. Bowles papers, Tab C, SigC Hist Sec file. See also SCEL, A Guide to Post War Research and Development, 1946, p. 11. SCEL files, Ft. Monmouth.

TABLE 4—COMPARISON OF COMMERCIAL COMMUNICATIONS
ORGANIZATION WITH SIGNAL CORPS COMMUNICATIONS
ORGANIZATION

Private Industry	Army
AT&T Staff	OCSigO Staff
Bell Telephone Labs, under AT&T	Engineering and Technical
Western Electric Mfg. Co., under AT&T	Production and Distribution
Long Lines Dept of AT&T	Army Communications Service
AT&T Plant Schools	Personnel and Training and the Signal Schools

in the Office of the Chief Signal Officer and in its field installations. All the charts from 1933 through 1945 [2] revealed, amid the many ramifications and additions, a basic similarity disclosing a pattern fundamentally and functionally suited to Army communications activities. The same pattern could also be found in the organization of such a commercial communications empire as the American Telegraph and Telephone Company. (*Table 4*)

This comparison strengthened Signal Corps officers in their opinion that the Corps' organization was "probably the most desirable from the viewpoint of signal communication efficiency." They found further support for maintaining intact the Signal Corps organization in the high regard evinced by the signal communications officers and men of other nations. Universally the latter envied the unified control of the men, the matériel, and the communications that the Signal Corps enjoyed, enabling it to operate with greater speed and greater efficiency, especially in providing combat communications. Control over

its supply, while a source of difficulty in the Washington headquarters organization, was a decided boon to Signal Corps officers serving the troops in the field.[3]

During the war there were of course many changes in staffing, and a steady increase, too, as officers and civilians were added and shuffled about in organizational rearrangements in the Office of the Chief Signal Officer. These included such new functions as operational research, communications liaison, communications co-ordination, and numerous boards and committees. Committee work doubled and redoubled, not only between the several elements of the Army but also between the several armed services and between the United States military services and those of Allied nations. Committees such as the Army Communications Board, the Joint Communications Board, and the Combined Communications Committee all drew heavily upon the time and energy of Signal Corps representatives in high-level relations. Co-ordination and con-

---

[2] For the organizations of 1933 and 1943, see charts opposite page 72 in Terrett, *The Emergency*.

[3] (1) Unsigned paper originating in the OCSigO Exec Of (Sig ExecO), 30 Jul 47, sub: Status of the SigC After Unification, Facts Bearing on the Problem, p. 4. Bowles papers, Tab H. (2) Proceedings of Bd To Investigate Com, Tab J, Testimony of Col David E. Washburn, 19 May 43, pp. 27ff. (3) See above, pp. 19–20.

trol by boards and committees was a slow and sometimes painful process.[4]

Following the pattern that the new conditions of World War II partnership between military officers and civilian scientists everywhere presented,[5] the Signal Corps had created on 30 November 1942 an Operational Research Group under Dr. Everitt in the Plans and Operations Division.[6] Dr. Everitt and his assistants not only advised the Chief Signal Officer whenever the need arose, but also watched over the entire communications scene in the Army, using their own initiative as to what was required and where. They visited the theaters, making valuable suggestions and providing many services. Foremost among these were their studies of radio frequencies and the determination of the best ones to use. In short, these communications specialists served the Signal Corps after the manner in which operational researchers in the OSRD served the entire military effort at home and in the theaters overseas. It was all a part of the new technological combat of the 20th century. "I thought they did a very fine job," General Code said of Dr. Everitt and his staff.[7]

The specialists made studies and provided advice on problems of systems engineering, on training in the use of radar and air communications equipment, on the maintenance of such equipment, and on psychological factors in their use. They did much also to improve radar manuals and developed a master literature plan for the many equipment handbooks that the Signal Corps prepared, published, and distributed to all users of Army radar, radio, and wire.[8]

The operational research organization and activity in the Signal Corps was not confined to the Washington headquarters. It became necessary to extend its good works to overseas theaters also. Late in the war, General Rumbough, Chief Signal Officer, ETOUSA, set up in his Signal Section the Technical Liaison Division, first under Colonel Hessel, later under Col. Francis J. Uhrhane. By all accounts this division provided a most valuable technical service that was available on need to all directly, without passing through military channels. One report characterized this service as "vital and necessary," asserting:

[4] (1) CSigO, Annual Rpts, FY 44, pp. 19f.; FY 45, p. 29; FY 46, p. 23. (2) CSigO Rpt to SW, 1942, pp. 26–28, 45, 48–51. (3) Dr. Courtney R. Hall, Signal Corps Participation in Boards and Committees, SigC Hist Monograph D-2, passim. SigC Hist Sec file. (4) CCB Historical Record and Evaluation of Experiences as Guide to Future Planners. SSUSA file, SigC Hist Sec file. (5) Papers in SigC 334.7 Com Coordination Bd Charter. (6) Thompson, Harris, et al., The Test, pp. 55aff. (7) Maj. Gen. James A. Code, Jr., "Organization," Radio News, XXXI, No. 2 (February, 1944), 88ff. (8) See also in this issue of Radio News, Brig. Gen. Frank C. Meade, "Operations," pp. 123ff., on the Communications Liaison Branch and the Communications Coordination Branch.

[5] (1) Irvin Stewart, Organizing Scientific Research for War, Administrative History, OSRD (Boston: Little, Brown and Co., 1948), passim. (2) Guerlac, Radar, pp. 156iff. (sec. E, ch. VI, pp. 8ff.). (3) Baxter, Scientists Against Time, pp. 404ff. (4) Watson-Watt, Three Steps to Victory, pp. 203f., 408, and 444. (5) Crowther and Whiddington, Science at War, pp. 91ff. (6) Albert P. Rowe, One Story of Radar (Cambridge, England: University Press, 1948), pp. 51f.

[6] See above, pp. 5–6.

[7] Ltr, Code to Thompson and Harris, 14 Aug 58, pp. 13–14.

[8] (1) CSigO, Annual Rpts, FY 43, pp. 36f.; FY 44, pp. 126ff.; FY 45, pp. 46f. (2) Dr. William L. Everitt, "Operational Research," Radio News, XXXI, No. 2 (February, 1944), 161ff. (3) Dr. Courtney R. Hall, Staff Functions and Staff Agencies, OCSigO, pp. 91ff. (4) See above, p. 310, n. 30.

The foresight and initiative in setting up and the efficient administration of this division should be commended. Certainly in a war with the high degree of technical facilities as provided for this or any future war, experts with long training and experience should be available both in the military organization proper and when necessary called in from the communication industries to give technical advice, train, and otherwise help the using units to obtain the desired results.[9]

The Signal Corps organization in nearly all of its parts—personnel, training, E&T, P&D, and so on—was of course much affected by the loss of AAF equipment responsibilities late in 1944. The attendant reduction beginning in October of that year and continuing into the first half of 1945 did not, however, eliminate any major organizational elements in the OCSigO but did cut off a number of field installations such as the Aircraft Radio Laboratory at Wright Field, Ohio, and the Eatontown (Watson) Laboratory at Fort Monmouth.[10]

At the very end of World War II the Signal Corps suffered another loss that involved one of the larger activities of the Corps—signal intelligence. Variously called the radio, signal, or communications intelligence, or, more cryptically, a security service, this heavily veiled code

and cipher, intercept and cryptanalytic activity had been an integral part of the Signal Corps structure for many years, stemming in fact from Col. Albert J. Myer's cipher disc and *Manual of Signals* of Civil War days.[11]

In some respects the loss of this activity bit more deeply into the vitals of the Signal Corps than did the transfer of AAF communications support. The equipment and the procedures were those of the ACAN system. Signal Corps personnel operated the intercept receivers and channeled the intercepted traffic into processing and cryptanalytic centers, using Signal Corps wire and radio circuits. Radio intelligence companies in the field were Signal Corps units.[12]

Thus very many aspects of signal intelligence operation lay close to the heart of Army communications, and at many points signal intelligence operations were identical with those of the service that the Signal Corps provided to all the Army. Yet none denied that the intelligence product was a G–2 concern. On the other hand, most did not doubt that SIS operations should be performed by the Signal Corps. So thought General Stoner in mid-1943:

. . . because all of the means for collecting the raw material [intercept] is now in the

---

[9] (1) Tech Observers, Bell Telephone Labs, Rpt, Communications Problems in ETO, June 1944–August 1945. WD SigC Contract W–28–003–SC–1068, Task 5, Proj 4252–A, p. 3. Bowles papers, Tab U. (2) Ltr, Brig Gen Garland C. Black, SigO 12th AGp, to CSigO ETO, undated, sub: Ltr of Appreciation, attached to Memo, Bowles for Ingles, 9 Jun 45. SigC (EO) Bowles, 1943–45. (3) ETOUSA Rpt, II, 170–233. (4) See above, p. 458, n. 92. (5) Thiesmeyer and Burchard, *Combat Scientists*, p. 251.

[10] (1) CSigO, Annual Rpt, FY 45, pp. 48–55. (2) See above, pp. 449ff.

[11] See above, ch. XI, *passim*.

[12] Colonel Williams, First Army Signal officer, spoke highly of the combat intelligence provided by RI units, praising ". . . the assistance given G–2 in locating and following enemy troops, particularly armored units, by means of radio intercept direction finding methods and by breaking down enemy codes to inform G–2 of enemy radio traffic. I realize that at Pentagon level this job was taken from the Signal Corps by the Army Security Agency and War Dept. G–2 but at Army level it was my responsibility." Ltr, Williams to Thompson, 31 Oct 57, p. 14.

hands of the Signal Corps, I feel that our most efficient way to handle it would be not to separate the collection of the raw material and the actual operations of the circuits under the Signal Corps . . . The actual collecting, the intercept and actual exchanging of the raw material into intelligence should be a function of the Chief Signal Officer for the reason that we are charged with the compilation of all codes and ciphers, and some of the best information we get on the compilation of codes comes from our knowledge of things the enemy is doing that are wrong. I mean, take steps to see that our codes are free from those operational errors.[13]

A further complication, and a new addition as this "Wizard War"[14] of secret techniques and technologies progressed, was the matter of either radio or radar countermeasures or both, RCM, which bid fair to match or exceed the magnitude of signal intelligence and which was closely associated with it. Indeed, because RCM could be employed as a combat weapon and because control over it loomed so large, many thought that a stronger position of high-level authority, as in General Staff, seemed needed. Army scientists at the Signal Corps Engineering Laboratories regarded the technical problems of radio intelligence and radio countermeasures so closely linked that both might some

day become the function of a single field unit.[15]

The problem of how best to operate and control signal intelligence, whether by War Department G–2 or by the Signal Corps, remained acute throughout the war. When early in 1943 General Olmstead had tried to elevate the Corps into the General Staff with a view to winning stronger high-level control over the multifarious modes of Army communications, some officers believed that the importance of such radio intelligence matters as RCM and the obvious necessity for authoritative control over it might serve as a foot in the door whereby the Corps command could gain entrance into the General Staff.[16]

No drastic changes of organization were accomplished in these matters during the war, despite G–2 uneasiness over the awkwardness of the existing organizational arrangements.[17] General Code

---

[13] Testimony of Stoner, 24 May 43, p. 10. Proceedings of Bd to Investigate Com, Tab O.

The Director of Naval Communications, Rear Adm. Joseph R. Redman, testified similarly on 28 May. Ibid., Tab T, p. 6.

[14] Winston Churchill keenly perceived the wizard-like character of much of modern warfare, including the radio and radar part. He called it the "Wizard War" and even devoted a chapter to the subject in his monumental series of histories. Winston S. Churchill, "The Second World War," Their Finest Hour (Boston: Houghton Mifflin Company, 1949), p. 381ff.

[15] SCEL Postwar Prog, p. 103.

[16] DCSigO folder, 1942–45, pp. 2, 41. SigC Hist Sec file.

[17] Commenting on this subject, General Stoner in mid-1959 added the following statement: "The organizational awkwardness was due to the rapid growth of its importance as an intelligence agency. It was the strong documented opinion that only the Signal Corps could have handled the vast construction of highly specialized electronic plant required for this operation. It would have been impossible for G–2 to have provided this planning and construction along modern scientific principles. At no time during its operation by the Signal Corps was any requirement by G–2 unfilled and all initiative for new actions and pioneering came from the Signal Corps. The most awkward condition, if any, was caused by having to fight four rear guard actions with G–2 to preserve the general value to the war effort. At the end of the war its utility had been fully exploited to win the war, and our signal security had remained inviolate." MS Comment, Stoner, Jul 59. See also Memo, CSigO (Col Lanahan, Plng Dir) for CG ASF, 6 May 43, sub: Exceptions to Proposed Policies. AG 321.011 (4–28–43).

spearheaded Signal Corps resistance to all attempts to wrest intelligence control from Signal Corps as vigorously as some G–2 officers, including intelligence specialist Col. Carter W. Clarke, sought the control for G–2.[18]

Despite this tug of war, the signal intelligence function remained in the Signal Corps organization until after V–J Day. This highly classified activity accomplished a very successful share of the "Wizard War," but as a foot in the door, it failed to lever the Corps into a position of higher control in the War Department. Instead, the door was forcibly closed immediately after V–J Day when the entire Signal Security Agency was separated in mid-September 1945 from the parent Corps. However, the Corps continued to supply the Army Security Agency in G–2 with the majority of its military personnel and with all its vast communications support needs. Signal Corps relationships with its former signal intelligence function thus continued to be close and almost inextricably intertwined.[19]

---

[18] (1) DCSigO folder, 1942–45, p. 19. (2) Ltr, Code to Thompson and Harris, 8 Aug 58, pp. 11–12. Colonel Clarke was a Signal Corps officer assigned to G–2.

[19] It was on 15 September 1945 that the OCSigO staff activity, the Signal Security Branch of the Army Communications Service, was inactivated. This specialized headquarters activity and its field installation, the Signal Security Agency, were transferred to the War Department G–2 organization and redesignated the Army Security Agency. See above, pp. 348ff.

One of the last Signal Corps reports of this large enigmatic World War II organization described its functions as follows: "The Signal Security Branch, and the Signal Security Agency, a field installation responsible to the Chief Signal Officer, formulated doctrines and techniques for the protection of Army communications. These agencies initiated action and performed duties relating to signal security for which the Chief

Some Continuing Questions of Mission

Thus two large questions of mission—should the Signal Corps serve the AAF with communications support, and should the Corps operate the Army's signal intelligence activity—were resolved, it seemed, the former in the closing months of the war, the latter within two weeks of V–J Day. Only the future could tell how far resolved these problems actually were within the troubled area of military communications-electronics, which appeared on the one hand to require an over-all control to the extent that electromagnetic radiations are universal and cannot be confined to a single service. Yet on the other hand electronics communications were becoming so intimately a part of every military activity that each command wished to separate its portion and acquire full control over it. Toward the end of World War II a new Army contender in these arenas of conflict arose—the Ordnance Department. Electronics were becoming inseparable from new ordnance items such as the proximity fuzed projectile, the radar gun layer (replacing optical sighting equipment), and the guided missile, which might replace the big guns themselves and which was generally controlled in flight by electromagnetic radiations of one sort or another.

As early as mid-1943 there arose prob-

Signal Officer was responsible, and directed engineering and development of, and operated signal security facilities. In addition, they prepared, published, revised, stored, accounted for, and distributed all codes, ciphers, and cryptographic material for the Army." CSigO, Annual Rpt, FY 46, p. 39.

lems in the development of gun director T-38.[20] Colonel Downing, assistant chief of the E&T Service in OCSigO, described the T-38 effort as "a combined Ordnance Department–Signal Corps project with the Sperry Gyroscope Company for the production of a complete fire control system consisting of a combined radar-optical tracking head and a computer." Questions of how to apportion responsibility at once appeared. "The Ordnance Department is reluctant to release to the Signal Corps the degree of responsibility suggested," commented a Signal Corps officer. Should, then, ordnance officers become radar specialists? It was the Chief Signal Officer's impression, General Ingles wrote to the Chief of Ordnance on 29 October 1943, that the Ordnance Department

. . . has no desire to branch out into radar development for which the Signal Corps was made responsible by the 19th indorsement AGO Feb 29 1936 (AG 470.31 (6–4–34) Misc D). It is certain that the Signal Corps does not desire to undertake the development of any fire control equipment. . . . In order to make the specialized knowledge of both the Ordnance Department and the Signal Corps available in the development of the best possible type of equipment, I believe that director equipment that employs radar elements should be made the subject of joint development.[21]

By 1945 problems relating to the control of guided missiles were fast emerging, with a natural and growing desire on the part of Ordnance first to learn about and then to take over the techniques of missile guidance. According to a Signal Corps report in March of that year, "Although Signal Corps has the responsibility for radio and radar control systems, Ordnance Department is still interested in training their people in radio and radar control work so that such knowledge may be applied operationally." [22] The core of the problem, General Ingles said two months later, was whether the Signal Corps should retain or surrender responsibility for those electronic items used by the Ordnance Department.[23] It seemed likely that the same problem that had attended the separation of Signal Corps AAF equipment might arise in this connection—how to determine what electronic devices were peculiar to Ordnance.

1, Winter, Electronics Br, to E&T Sv, 29 Sep 43, sub: Ordnance Dirs. All in SigC ET 413.44 Gun Directors, 1943–45 (ET–2635).

General Ingles further suggested in his memorandum that military characteristics be processed through the technical committees of both Ordnance and Signal Corps, that liaison officers be appointed in each, that the Signal Corps review the contracts, that Ordnance service the production contract and expedite production, and that the Signal Corps furnish engineering service, inspection service, and so on.

[22] Memo, Lt Col C. S. Kleinau, Dir Electronics Equip Div OCSigO, for Chief E&T Sv, 1 Mar 45, sub: Tng in the Fld of Guided Jet Propelled Missiles. SigC 413.44 RCM Tng folder 1, 1943–45 (ET–2612).

[23] (1) Ltr, CSigO to Col Chester E. Davis, Ordnance Dept, 16 May 45. DCSigO folder, 1942–45, p. 25, (2) Ltr, Lt Gen Levin H. Campbell, Jr., to CSigO, 13 Jun 45, sub: Responsibility for Devs of Radio and Radar Equip. SigC OP 312.1 Policy 1945–46, Tab 1.

---

[20] Other ordnance items using radar as of 1 October 1943 included directors T–13, T–31, T–35, and height finder T–23. Two more by the end of the war were T–33 and T–41. CSigO, Annual Rpt, FY 46, p. 178.

[21] (1) Memo, Ingles for Chief of Ordnance, 29 Oct 43, sub: Dev of Radar Dirs for Fire Contl. (2) Ltr, Downing to WD LnO with NDRC, 15 Dec 43, sub: Appointment of Radiation Laboratory as Consultant to the SigC on Director T–38. (3) Memo, 2d Lt H. B. Phelps, Electronics Br OCSigO, for Col Winter, 1 Oct 43, sub: Ordnance Radar Components. (4) ASF Transmittal Sheet, Action

Problems of Supply vs. Operations,
Service vs. Arm

Whether the Signal Corps was primarily a supplier of equipment and services to the Army and so should be retained in a supply and service type of organization (such as the ASF through World War II), or whether the Corps was primarily an operating agency of the Army with authoritative control and command powers (needing an appropriate position of command within the military structure) remained a troublesome question. Actually the Signal Corps was both an arm and a service. In 1920 it had been officially recognized as an arm and was so designated—a combat arm of the line of the Army.[24]

Yet Signal Corps service and supply functions continued to eclipse its command and control duties, and even its operational tasks. In particular, the reorganization of the Army in March 1942 had placed the Chief Signal Officer under the Commanding General, ASF, which in effect left the U.S. Army Chief of Staff without a signal officer. "Eisenhower has *his* Chief Signal Officer. . . . MacArthur likewise has *his* . . . the commander of every field unit has *his* signal officer directly responsible to his orders and able to give orders in his name in matters pertaining to Signal Communications. Only in the War Department in Washington is the Chief Signal Officer of the Army removed from the General commanding the Army by several . . . echelons of staff officers." These were the words of the most eminent of retired Chief Signal Officers, General Gibbs, advising General Marshall in 1943.[25]

In actual practice during World War II General Somervell was bypassed in signal matters by the Chief of Staff and the War Department General Staff, who took communications problems directly to the Chief Signal Officer. "Most of the major directives I received during the war," commented the chief of the Signal Corps Army Communications Service, "came direct to me from General Marshall's office or the Operations Division of the General Staff." [26]

The ambiguity of such relationships was bound to cause difficulties and delay, and did. Acrimonious relations between the ASF, the AAF, and Signal Corps intensified. Communications committees galore and liaison officers had to arbitrate differences as best they could in order to get at least some things

---

[24] See authority cited above, p. 15, n. 46.

For a summary of supply versus control problems of the Signal Corps, see the findings of the board of officers appointed to investigate Army communications in 1943, inclosed with Memo, Col Arthur E. Burnap, President of Bd, for CofS, 22 Jun 43, sub: Transmittal of Bd Proceedings. AG 311 (5–10–43) (1) Bulky Pkg, Army RG 207.03, Job A 50–55.

[25] Incl 2, Gibbs to Marshall, 25 May 43, with Memo, Handy, 16 Jun 43, sub: Personal Ltr for CofS from Gibbs, re Com. OCS 210 G Open files (OPD-320, 5–23–42).

[26] "I do not recall a single operational order coming from ASF," Stoner reminisced. Once when ASF Control Division sent an officer to investigate the operations of ACS in May 1944, General Stoner complained to General Marshall, who personally told General Somervell there was no need of ASF Control Division interference. MS Comment, Stoner, Jul 59.

accomplished. Efficient control was conspicuously absent.[27]

Ever since World War I, Signal Corps officers had desired representation in the General Staff to the end that Army communications matters might be better appreciated in top-level planning and conduct of operations. Maj. Gen. George O. Squier, Chief Signal Officer, had recommended to Congress on 2 October 1919 that the Chief Signal Officer be made an ex officio member of the General Staff so that CSigO views might be heard in that body of officers.[28]

During World War II Signal Corps officers were occasionally assigned to the General Staff, but they were too few. So hard pressed was the Corps for competent officers of long experience that it could spare next to none to serve on that staff, however much their point of view and specialized knowledge might be needed there. After General Olmstead made his effort to place Signal Corps control in the General Staff in the spring of 1943, the Corps was firmly held in check by the Army Service Forces. Coordination and control had to be parceled out to various committees and boards, and control and operations of Army communications therefore suffered.[29] Signal Corps was not alone in its troubles. Throughout the government, both during the war and after it, coordination and control in these matters remained a tortured subject. The nation's leaders did not comprehend the scope and implications of communications-electronics, nor would they for years after the end of World War II, as more than one high-level study would point out.[30]

Yet during the war the Army was compelled to comprehend the involvements and requirements of effective communications control, at least with somewhat more understanding than was displayed in this sphere by the civilian nation at large. Early in the war the Chief of Staff, General Marshall, told his Chief Signal Officer, General Olmstead, that he presumed administrative communications in the Army would gain in efficiency if they were all under one directing head. He added that he believed communications constituted, to-

[27] Unsigned paper, Sig ExecO, 30 Jul 47, Status of the SigC After Unification, cited above, p. 612, n. 3 (1)

General Code had said at the time of the 1942 reorganization: "I am definitely of the opinion that failure to provide at least a Communications Coordination Division on the General Staff will operate most adversely to the accomplishment of Signal Communications in order to provide adequate combat communications throughout the Army." DCSigO folder, 1942–45, p. 5.

Co-ordination remained difficult. The defect continued to be felt to the end of World War II. For example, in July 1945: "The fact remains that there is no one agency staffed with competent technical personnel authorized to speak for the War Department on major policies with respect to communications. The need for such an agency is apparent. It would appear that the best interests of the War Department would be served by creating a group in the Operations Division of the War Department General Staff with full responsibility for performing the over-all policy and co-ordinating staff functions of the War Department with respect to all phases of communications. It is believed that the head of this group should be designated the Chief Signal Officer of the Army." Memo, unsigned, for CofS, 3 Jul 45, sub: WD Com Responsibilities, pp. 1–2. Bowles papers, Tab D.

[28] Otto O. Nelson, National Security and the General Staff (Washington: Infantry Journal Press, 1946), p. 275.

[29] Thompson, Harris, et al., The Test, pp. 541ff.

[30] (1) Telecommunications, A Program for Progress, A Report by the President's Communications Policy Board, Washington, 1951, pp. 11, 18, 30. (2) Senate, Report of the Ad Hoc Advisory Committee on Allocations to the Committee of Interstate and Foreign Commerce, Allocation of TV Channels, March 14, 1958, 85th Cong., 2d sess. passim.

gether with fire power and mobility, an attribute of command and should therefore remain under the direct control of commanders in the field.[31]

As the growing awareness of good communications increasingly pointed up the operation and control aspects of the Signal Corps mission, so did it also accentuate the fact that the Signal Corps was an arm, as well as a service. The Signal Corps had been restricted since World War I to the division level in the field army, the combat services it had provided up to the barbed wire in that war having been turned over, soon after the armistice, to regiment, battalion, and company communicators within the Infantry, Artillery, and so on. Yet in World War II combat, time and again Signal Corps officers and men served in units smaller than the division signal company. In the Pacific fighting particularly, Signal Corps detachments had served in regimental combat teams. It was already even then appearing that, the more vital the communications and the more complex the equipment's operation and maintenance, the greater was the need for skilled Signal Corps troops to provide communications to smaller combat units.[32] And among these troops the old Signal Corps catchwords, "Getting the message through," was often a matter of fighting it through.[33] By the end of

World War II the status of the Signal Corps as an arm seemed to be strengthening, tending to revert to its World War I responsibilities when Signal Corps men and the outpost companies of the signal field battalions served and fought in the front-line trenches.

Conduct of International Communications

What of Army communications in the way of over-all administrative signaling at headquarters, at the opposite end of the scale from front-line combat message service? Should the Signal Corps continue to develop special equipment, install it, and operate it in the world-wide ACAN system, or should it leave such global communications to the commercial companies already engaged in international message traffic and lease their facilities on need? Because the prewar facilities of these companies had been insufficient and inadequate for military needs, the Signal Corps had had to build the ACAN system. The Army might not find it necessary to rebuild such a system in the event of another war if American international communications facilities were highly developed, to the extent that the commercial companies could provide the traffic capacity, speed, and security that the military services would require.

These were matters for contemplation. Immediate problems that had to be settled at the close of World War II were posed by other questions. What, for example, would be done with ACAN after V–J Day? Should the Signal Corps continue to maintain its global circuits? Should it dismantle them? Should it turn them over to commercial interests?

There was in the Army a precedent

[31] Memo, Gen Olmstead for Brig Gen Charles M. Milliken, Chief Opns Br OCSigO, 31 Jan 42, sub: Co-ordination and Equip Div. SigC SPSTP–10 CSigO.

[32] Capt Robert C. Hawley, Employment of Signal Corps Officers as Battalion and Regimental Communication Officers (1953), Sig Sch Monograph. The Sig Sch Libr, Ft. Monmouth.

[33] CSigO, Annual Rpts, FY 43, pp. 9, 13; FY 44, pp. 8, 12ff.; FY 45, pp. 15ff. See also above, pp. 97, 126, 130, 159ff., 201, 253, 287–88.

for continued military maintenance of circuits that served undeveloped areas. The Signal Corps had handled all communications in Alaska throughout its territorial history, carrying traffic for civilians as well as for the military forces there. The Corps in doing this acted in the traditional pattern of government support and paternalism, installing facilities and providing services in frontier lands in order to assist their development until such time as the local population and local prosperity might permit private enterprise to take over the government services and operate them privately at a profit. Did world communications at the war's end need such assistance from the government in the form of Army Signal Corps support? Most thought not. Some even believed that commercial companies such as the AT&T should in the future take over entirely the services that the ACAN provided, relieving the Army of having to build and maintain such a system, so that the Signal Corps might better concentrate all its efforts on tactical communications-electronics services and operations for the Army.[34]

General Eisenhower as Chief of Staff seemed to acquiesce in this view. In a speech delivered in June 1946 he said:

There appears little reason for duplicating within the Army any commercial research or manufacturing organization, which by its experience is better qualified than the Army to carry out some of our tasks. A case in point is our world communications net which tied the theater commands to the War Department. Commercial communication interests make this type of communications their business and are organized to plan, engineer, and operate such a system. Peacetime co-operation would make possible the easy integration of these facilities in time of war as an organic part of the Armed Forces. In general, the more use we are able to make of outside resources, the more energy the Army will have to devote to strictly military problems for whose solution there are no outside facilities or which for special security reasons can only be handled by the military.[35]

Yet many Signal Corps officers during World War II and immediately after it inclined to the opinion that the Signal Corps should retain circuits serving Army installations wherever they might be over the world (whether Army, Navy, and Air should maintain separate, often parallel, systems or should consolidate them was a question that waited upon the future of unification of the armed services).[36] They generally inclined to the view also that there should be a consolidation of American world

---

[34] (1) Interv, SigC, Hist Div, with Bowles, 8 May 58, pp. 4f. (2) Sidney Sparks, Vice President RCA Communications, Inc., "The Role of International Telegraph Companies in Military Communications," *Telegraph and Telephone Age*, No. 4 (April, 1950), pp. 7ff.

[35] General of the Army Dwight D. Eisenhower, CofS, to Army Ordnance Assn., Detroit, Mich., 3 Jun 46, p. 3. Bowles papers, Tab O.

[36] "It is inconceivable that this nation could tolerate as a part of its over-all security structure individual global nets for the three primary branches of the armed forces," Dr. Bowles wrote Eisenhower early in 1947. "Coordination," he added, "is no substitute for authority, particularly when immediate action is vital." Memo, Bowles for Eisenhower, 10 Feb 47, sub: Mil Com, Related Svs, and Organizational Considerations, p. 1. Bowles papers, Tab G.

On the general subject of the merger of the communications of the several services, see Thompson, Harris, *et al.*, *The Test*, pp. 550ff., and also the following files: SigC (AY) 676 President's Com Cmte (1933), Army and Navy Cmte; SigC (OD) 676 Army-Navy Com System Merger, 1943; SigC (AC) 676 Army-Navy Merger, 1944; SigC (AC) 676 Army-Navy Merger, 1946 (includes Testimony, Ingles before the Manasco Cmte (House Cmte on Expenditures in the Exec Depts), Jan 46).

communications, perhaps with the nation's commercial companies merging into a single more efficient system under some degree of government supervision.

General Ingles had expressed at the end of 1943 his opinion that the Signal Corps should, as soon as the conflict ended, rid itself of international communications, except to overseas U.S. possessions, and that a single unified system should handle the international nets. He commented that the several American companies engaged in international message service operated in the disinterest of the nation because they competed with each other destructively. One result of this was that the British controlled the international field through their single unified (and therefore presumably more efficient) Cable and Wireless Ltd. General Ingles recommended that American international communications companies do likewise, operating under a board of representatives of the State Department, Army, Navy, Commerce, and the Post Office.[37]

General Stoner, chief of the Army Communications Service, likewise inclined to the view that a single federal system be maintained, at least for the handling of government traffic. He hoped that competing commercial companies would be merged into one organization. As for the existing ACAN system, he had no doubt, in September 1945, that such parts at least as remained in demand should be kept intact. The State Department at that time especially desired retention of the ACAN links with Moscow. The quantity of

messages exchanged with Moscow in fact increased 40 percent in the first six months after Japan surrendered. Stoner believed that ACAN would continue to provide secure telephone service to overseas points "because there will be many occasions when the President and the Prime Minister will want to talk to each other and when high officials of the State Department will want secure toll service in this postwar world." He hoped that commercial companies would agree to the standardized system that ACAN had created so that messages might pass quickly and cheaply between all points ice. Unless the commercial companies American international message carriers would help such standardization or service. Unless the commerical companies merged and constructed an integrated communications system over the world, which the military could lease on need, Stoner believed that the armed services would have to do again, in the event of another war, just what they had done in World War II—build their own world-wide system from the bottom up.[38]

It began to appear by 1946 that the

[37] Memo, CSigO for CofS, Through CG ASF, 31 Dec 43, sub: WD Policy Toward Merger of International Com Facilities. SigC (EO) CofS, 1944.

[38] Stoner, Army Com, Seminar at the Army Industrial College, 24 Sep 45, pp. 10–13. Com folder, Tab A–2, SigC Hist Sec file. See also Testimony, Stoner, 24 May 43, p. 12. Proceedings of Bd to Investigate Com, Tab O.

On 1 June 1945 General Stoner reported to a group of senators (Burton K. Wheeler, Ernest W. McFarland, Albert W. Hawkes, and Homer E. Capehart) inspecting Army Communications, Europe: "Our country must have a single integrated all purpose commercial communications system if we are to avoid the conditions we found at the beginning of World War II—one that can be taken over completely by the military together with the operating personnel. Otherwise we will have to build our own and we might not have the time. We must keep the Army's system operative until we get such a system." Quoted in MS Comment, Stoner, Jul 59.

international communications of the United States would not consolidate. Military nets would be cut back, each service maintaining only such circuits of its own in the World War II pattern as would continue to be needed in the oncoming cold war in order to operate its installations wherever located over the globe. The several commercial companies would return to the prewar pattern of competitive service (but co-operating more closely than ever with the nation's military services).[39] Some disintegration of the ACAN had begun, General Stoner complained in January 1946. "This plant is being dismantled," he said, "although we will retain some circuits to key points, particularly where we have bases or missions—Hawaii, with extensions to Manila and Tokyo; Panama, Puerto Rico, and Frankfurt. . . ." The around-the-world belt line was broken between Asmara and Manila. Army ACAN stations continued to operate at these two locations, but all intermediate relay points were abandoned. It would be a bad blunder, Stoner believed, if the nation reverted to the prewar situation and put aside the great world nets that the military forces had built up.[40]

The Pursuit of Research and Development

What of the Signal Corps' R&D responsibilities? These had increased along with the universal step-up of technological warfare. Should the Corps conduct more R&D, more research especially, in its own laboratories, as it had developed Army radar in the 1930's? Or should it contract for work of this sort at private institutions? Could Signal Corps officers competently and freely administer an effective R&D program from a subordinate place in the Army's supply structure? Scientists both in and out of the government pretty generally thought "No." The one eminent student of the subject, Dr. James P. Baxter 3d, historian of the OSRD, put it in no uncertain terms: "It is fatal to place a research organization under the production department." Similarly, Dr. Vannevar Bush himself testifying before Congress early in 1945 said "basically, research and procurement are incompatible."[41]

Yet it was important not only that able civilian scientists work in military laboratories but also that communications-electronics research matters be understood by officers competent to appreciate and judge them. Such personnel was especially needed by the Army. The Navy had for some years enjoyed the services of many such officers and scientists at the Naval Research Laboratory (NRL), where the naval

---

[39] For example, after the war ACAN was required to remove from French soil its important Algiers station. The location for purposes of relay to the Middle East and Moscow was especially valuable. The Army Communications Service at once negotiated at length with the State Department and the Federal Communications Commission toward obtaining a location in Tangiers, and then prevailed upon Mackay and RCA to build an all-purpose relay there, which ACAN could utilize after the loss of the Algiers station. MS Comment, Stoner, Jul 59.

[40] (1) Stoner, Speech before the Federal Com Bar Assn., Washington, 11 Jan 46, p. 10. (2) AFSC Lecture C-1, World-wide Armed Forces Communications Networks, Tab 10, pt. I, p. 7. SigC OP 352 AFSC Rpts, vol. 4, 1948–49.

[41] (1) Baxter, Scientists Against Time, p. 12. (2) Hearings Before the Select Cmte on Post-War Military Policy, Pursuant to House Resolution 465, 78th Cong., 2d sess., pp. 244f., Testimony, Bush, January 26, 1945.

implications of science and research were well understood. As early as 1915, no less an authority than Thomas A. Edison had urged the government to maintain a research laboratory jointly under Army, Navy, and civilian control. Only the Secretary of Navy, Josephus Daniels, showed interest. He set up the Naval Consulting Board, with Edison as chairman. In 1923, the board launched the Naval Research Laboratory, whose radio division was destined to go far in early naval radar developments. Civilian scientists of NRL were unfettered by military restraints. As one historian put it, "In contrast to Army laboratories where the atmosphere is likely to be that of a military establishment and where an officer is assigned to each project and the civilian investigator is subject to direct supervision, at the Naval Research Laboratory there is no participation in the scientific work by the assigned Naval officers." The latter served only as administrators who handled the naval business involved in the laboratory operation but who did not interfere in the research policy.[42]

Still freer was the civilian operation of the Radiation Laboratory under OSRD. When in 1940 British scientists brought over their resonant cavity magnetron, revolutionary generator of powerful microwave radar, asking American assistance in the development of microwave sets, Dr. Bush and the Microwave Section of Division D, OSRD, sought an American laboratory that could undertake microwave radar development. Nowhere in all the nation could a suitably equipped laboratory be found. Therefore a new laboratory had to be built. The OSRD created the Radiation Laboratory in 1941 specifically to conduct microwave R&D, just as the British had themselves a few years earlier set up their Telecommunications Radio Establishment, and as the Germans would belatedly do when, after recovering magnetrons in downed Allied bombers, they set up in 1943 the Rotterdam Commission to build German versions of microwave radars.[43]

Even at the Radiation Laboratory the relatively free scientists did not conduct much pure research. "Almost no work resembling the fundamental investigations of a peacetime physics laboratory was carried on," commented Dr. Henry E. Guerlac, the historian of RL. The most fundamental research pursued there was conducted by the theory group, composed of mathematicians and theoretical physicists. Their work however was not theoretical, but rather engineering research that sought to translate results as promptly as possible into principles of engineering design. All the rest of the effort of the hundreds of academic scientists at RL went into the practical development of new radar systems and the improvement of radar components. All of it was hurried short-term work since every

[42] (1) Guerlac, Radar, pp. 93ff. (sec. A, ch. IV, pp. 1 ff.). (2) Watson-Watt, Three Steps to Victory, p. 99. (3) A. Hunter Dupree, Science in the Federal Government (Cambridge, Mass.: Harvard University, Belknap Press, 1957), pp. 306, 333.

[43] (1) Stewart, Organizing Scientific Research for War, p. 24. (2) Rowe, One Story of Radar, p. 82. (3) Curt Bley, Geheimnis Radar, p. 24. (4) Bekker, Radar: Duell im Dunkel, pp. 266f.
    The first Germany copy of the H2S magnetron radar, the Berlin Geraet, required over fifteen months to reconstruct. Watson-Watt, Three Steps to Victory, p. 426.

man in RL knew that if a device could not be produced in time to be used, it was of little value to the war effort.[44]

The scientists in the laboratories of the Signal Corps pursued their tasks with considerably less freedom. Naturally, the rigors of field needs and of Army procurement pressures weighed heavily upon the laboratory workers. Their commanding officers, hard pressed by military practicalities and urgency, could give slight thought to new R&D projects consuming the time of their own people. Such propositions they preferred to assign to civilian organizations outside the Army structure. For example, when in 1940 the Signal Corps had received some $8,000,000 of R&D funds, far beyond all previous appropriations in this category, the Chief Signal Officer at that time, General Mauborgne, informed the Chief of Staff that he did not intend to expand the Signal Corps laboratories in order to meet this large R&D commitment. Rather, his policy

would be to place development contracts with commercial companies.

General Ingles reaffirmed this policy in 1943. Actually, the Corps did both—it depended heavily upon outside laboratories to pursue much of its World War II R&D work, and it enormously expanded its own laboratories as well. For the latter's heavy tasks of field testing, field support, and monitoring the Signal Corps R&D commitments continued to grow. "It is the fate of military laboratories to have an ever increasing burden of routine responsibilities thrust upon them during the war," Guerlac described the lot of laboratories within the Army household.[45] Yet at the same time, there were numerous research-minded Signal Corps officers, such as Colton, O'Connell, and Uhrhane, who saw to it that some forward-looking long-range R&D efforts continued in the Signal Corps laboratories.

By early 1945 it was obvious that military R&D would soon be directed toward the uncertain needs of future wars, since World War II was now rapidly drawing to its close. In the spring of 1945 the Signal Corps therefore re-examined its Engineering and Technical Service, its laboratories, and the headquarters organization as well. The Chief Signal Officer sought recommendations for improvement and in particular for such changes as might seem to be needed to accommodate the postwar period. A committee of leaders drawn from the electronics industry was

---

[44] Despite the sincere hardheaded purpose of this normally theory-minded group of physicists, there remained some scepticism among the military: "There was a certain amount of ill-concealed scepticism that a group of physics professors could produce anything useful. Even the more progressive service representatives felt, with some justice, that the Army and Navy knew their problems better than an inexperienced civilian group possibly could, and had accumulated a certain amount of radar experience, and certainly felt that to attempt to develop radar on a new frequency was a dubious enterprise when the full potentialities of long-wave radar had scarcely been tapped. There were even a few voices weighty in military councils in 1940–41 who said that research and development had necessarily to be curtailed, rather than expanded in wartime when the problems were those of production testing and training. This, it is true, did take place in the Army and Navy laboratories." Guerlac, Radar, pp. 409ff. (sec. C, ch. I, pp. 2–3).

[45] (1) Guerlac, Radar, p. 201 (sec. A, ch. V, p. 49). (2) Capt Harry M. Davis, History of the Signal Corps Development of U.S. Army Radar Equipment, pt. I, Revisions. SigC Hist Monograph A-1, pp. 2of. SigC Hist Sec file.

called in to make a survey.[46] After completing this task during late April and early May, the committee recommended that Signal Corps continue its policy of assigning certain types of research to industrial laboratories and other types, especially the development of equipment items and systems, to scientists in the Corps' own laboratories. These laboratories, several in number and scattered over the countryside around Fort Monmouth, should all be consolidated, the committeemen recommended, into one or two locations. They urged further that the detailed work of equipment design, engineering, and testing be placed entirely in the hands of civilian experts. The military staff, composed of officers whom they urged must be of "adequate technical competence," should see to over-all planning and should conduct relations with the using arms and with industrial laboratories. If these recommendations were followed, the committee members believed the Signal Corps laboratories would improve and would approximate the organization and operation of the nation's commercial laboratories that serve industry and engage in applied science.[47]

In October Maj. Gen. George L. Van Deusen, chief of the Signal Corps Engineering and Technical Service, made his comments on the committee report and passed it on to the Chief Signal Officer. The war was over, and the postwar period had by now arrived. Van Deusen accepted all the recommendations, at least in principle. As for the apportionment of R&D between industry and the Signal Corps, he agreed that the Corps laboratories should in general limit themselves to applied engineering, with a few exceptions.

In the especially difficult matter of personnel, putting the right men in the right jobs (an obvious need, yet one against which both Army personnel practices and civil service regulations often and most ironically conspire), General Van Deusen had more to say. Officers, for example, had to be assigned wherever familiarity with the organization and procedure peculiar to the Army was essential. He agreed that civilians who were qualified engineers and scientists should head research and development activities, but civil service salaries were too low. He intended to seek the establishment of salaries suitable to such top positions, and he explained some of the Signal Corps troubles during the war in these matters:

Supervision of research and development in our laboratories should be placed in the hands of qualified civilians. The war organization which placed Army officers (often civilian engineers in uniform) in charge of practically all phases of Laboratory activities was forced on us by personnel policies over which we had no control, especially the operation of the Selective Service Act.[48]

[46] The committee members were Dr. W. R. G. Baker, vice-president of General Electric Company; M. J. Kelly, executive vice-president of the Bell Telephone Laboratories; J. T. Tate, chief of Division 6 of the OSRD; C. W. Green, assistant to the vice-president of Bell Telephone Laboratories, and L. M. Leeds, manager of the Electronics Laboratory, General Electric Company.

[47] SigC Engineering Survey Cmte, Rpt to Gen Van Deusen, Chief E&T Sv. SigC 334 SigC Engineering Survey Cmte, 1945.

[48] *Ibid.,* with Comment 3, Van Deusen to CSigO, 15 Oct 45.

At the end of the war no one could doubt the immense importance of military R&D work, whether accomplished principally by commercial laboratories, or by Army, or by the two together. The lessons of World War II emphasized that R&D must be pursued with vigor no less before the shooting starts than afterward. Research must be depended upon to discover new weapons and new applications. Both research and development must see to it that the new weapons are well engineered for mass production and effective field use. The seesaw conflict with Germany in the air war, in the contest between radar and the submarine, in the "Wizard War" of countermeasures and counter-countermeasures, not to mention the late appearance of guided missiles and jet aircraft, was uncomfortably close. The Allied margin of success, it is well to remember, was definitely not wide, despite the dazzle of the atom bomb. Scientists at SCEL pointed to the German missile *Schmetterling*, which was scheduled for full production by the late summer of 1945. It was a ground-to-air rocket, developed by Dr. Wernher von Braun of V-2 and subsequent rocket fame. The scientists stated:

This weapon, had the war lasted another half year, would have profoundly altered the aspect of air warfare. In this connection it is important to note that an experimental model had been constructed in 1941 on the initiative of a few German scientists; but that subsequent development was not undertaken until two years later because of the obstinacy of the German High Command in concentrating all efforts on offensive weapons at the expense of long range research and development. This attitude was reflected in numerous other German developments, and the lessons implied in

its consequence should not be lost upon us.[49]

The SCEL scientists concluded that constant preparedness was henceforth necessary. The scope of what that preparedness would entail seemed a little unbelievable to a nation hastening after V-J Day to reduce, if not close out altogether, the military R&D establishments. The SCEL scientists believed that not only must the nation develop more advanced weapons than any other country but also that it must concurrently design counterweapons as well, and must do so continuously, "prior to any aggression, expected or remote." It seemed logical, then, that to keep technologically ahead of any potential enemy the nation must "pursue a vigorous program of research on which to base further developments." In the Signal Corps SCEL, civilian scientists proposed in December 1945 a program of what they called "absolutely imperative investigations . . . combining pure research and applied research and development" in fields of interest to the Signal Corps such as thermionics, prop-

[49] SCEL, Postwar R&D Prog, pp. 85f. See also (1) above, p. 464; (2) CSigO, Annual Rpt, FY 45, pp. 419ff.

In the words of Colonel Slattery, a SCEL scientist and Signal Corps officer who made an on-the-spot survey of German science late in 1945: "There is no doubt in the undersigned's mind that Germany was well ahead of the United States in the development of radar and electronic equipment at the beginning of the European phase of the war; that the Allies forged ahead of the Germans was only in part due to the fact that the Allies expended greater funds and a greater amount of brain power on radar and electronics." The Allies in large part got ahead of the Germans, he explained, because the Germans, expecting a short war, had canceled much of their R&D. Memo, Slattery for the CSigO, 9 Nov 45, sub: Trip to ETO, p. 42. Tab III, Slattery Rpt, 9 Nov 45.

agation, general physics, meteorology, circuits, antennas, communications techniques, power sources, and materials.[50]

All this seemed to be in virgin areas that would call for new dimensions in military thinking. The Signal Corps policy of keeping as much as possible of its R&D out of Army institutions and in private organizations by contract seemed headed for some alteration. Now that the war was over and the exigencies of immediate practical R&D for immediate field needs was past, it seemed likely that the Army would have to take a new approach to R&D matters, supporting basic research that looked to long-term developments, maintaining and supporting the work in an atmosphere conducive to good effort over long periods of time on a scale unknown in previous military peacetime experience.

Toward the Future: Shooting for the Moon

Whether or not SCEL's strong plea for basic research would be acted upon, and if so, whether items would be developed in the Corps' own laboratories or at outside institutions under contract, there was no doubt in 1945 that practical engineering of equipment would continue, as it always had, in Army laboratories in order to adapt matériel to field use, improving ruggedness, reliability, and ease of operation. In communications-electronics it was obvious that the laboratories would seek to miniaturize, systematize, and simplify. Yet, whereas some degree of simplification might be attained, the onward rush of electronics would introduce greater complexities, too. The rapid accumulation of new and better devices would make ever sharper the problem of the outmoding of the old, even if only a year or two old. "Galloping obsolescence," the scientists termed the problem. It was reaching such a point that the laboratories would make it a rule to begin development on new equipment as soon as the predecessor type had reached the service test stage, by which time it was already becoming obsolescent.[51]

By V-J Day whole new vistas were opening up in communications, such as the use of higher frequencies in FM and in pulse modulation employing the

[50] SCEL, Postwar R&D Prog, pp. 1–3. This comprehensive and detailed program was requested in August 1945 by Colonel O'Connell, director of SCEL Engineering Division, and led to a first tentative program issued on 5 December 1945 (reissued with some eliminations and additions in 1946 as A Guide to Postwar Research and Development). Capt Harry M. Davis, Signal Corps Research and Development Activities, 15 August–31 December 1945 (1946), SigC Hist Monograph A–5, pp. 29f. SigC Hist Sec file.

General Code, addressing the National Academy of Sciences in Washington, 24 April 1944, remarked that the Signal Corps had more and more tended to assign its R&D problems to scientists and engineers in industry and universities—a partnership that he believed should not be completely dissolved or demobilized after the war. Hardly indeed had the war ended when the Signal Corps set up the first direct postwar military-sponsored research contract with a university (Columbia) on radiation problems. In early 1946 the Signal Corps also participated in negotiations that led to an important joint service contract with the Massachusetts Institute of Technology toward maintaining laboratory work in the pattern set by the Radiation Laboratory of OSRD in World War II. MS Comments, Zahl, Jul 59.

[51] (1) Paper, C. B. Kinley, Radio Engr, Com Engineering Br OCSigO, entitled Post War Planning and Development Projects for Army Communications Service, attached to Memo Routing Slip, Kinley to Maj William J. Johnson, Col Kenneth D. Nichols, and Col Bagnall, 24 Aug 45. SigC 370.01 Materiel Demobilization Plng 3, Jun–Aug 45. (2) SCEL, Postwar R&D Prog, *passim.*

ever more powerful tube types that radar experience was bringing forth in ultrahigh and superhigh frequencies. There were new notions as to how to utilize radio relay, greatly extending its range beyond the line-of-sight limitations of the very high frequencies. It appeared that such radiations might be able to penetrate the ionosphere and outer space to immense distances. The moon, in short, might be put to use by earthlings as a giant reflector. "Some . . . already dream of bouncing a radar echo off the moon," announced a radar release in August 1945.[52]

This was no dream. Scientists in SCEL at Fort Monmouth were making calculations and concluded before the end of that year:

. . . a signal could be sent to the moon and the echo detected in a receiver, using equipment which can be built with present day techniques. A signal of this type would cover half the earth about half of each day. It is recommended that preliminary experiments be carried out immediately, and that specific applications be postponed, pending results of the experiments and a better evaluation of the problems involved.[53]

At the turn of 1945–46 preparations were under way, using radar of the SCR–271 type. A giant antenna, made of two SCR–271 antennas side by side, was raised on a 100-foot tower at the Camp Evans Signal Laboratory at Belmar, New Jersey. The radar employed components of an FM type that Maj. Edwin H. Armstrong had developed. Tremendous output power was needed in long pulses, one-half a second (ordinary radar, detecting targets up to one or two hundred miles distant, is restricted to very short pulses, a few microseconds long). And the pulse interval had to be sufficiently prolonged to allow the pulse to reach the moon, some 240,000 miles away, and for the echo to return—nearly 3 seconds for the round trip at the speed of light—before the next pulse could be sent out. The frequency employed was that of the SCR–271, about 112 megacycles.[54]

On 10 January 1946 the SCEL scientists received the first radar echoes from the moon. Man could communicate, it was for the first time proven, by electronic means through outer space. The moon, and artificial satellites of the future, could serve man's interests. The Signal Corps, using a radar type that it had pioneered for the Army just before World War II, now succeeded soon after the close of that war in opening up a new era of communications-electronics.

In Retrospect: A Summary

This chronicle of struggle, problems, and troubles with which the Signal Corps contended through World War II, must not conceal or darken the bright scene of the Corps' accomplishments and successes. The three volumes that constitute the record of the Signal Corps in World War II have been prepared in the belief that more can be

---

[52] *Time*, XLVI, No. 8 (August 20, 1945), 82.
[53] SCEL, Postwar R&D Prog, pp. 30–33.

[54] (1) CSigO, Annual Rpt, FY 46, pp. 13–15. (2) Orrin E. Dunlap, Jr., *Radar: What Radar Is and How It Works* (New York: Harper and Brothers, 1946), pp. 202ff. (3) Radar Echoes From the Moon, Official SigC Rpt on Project Diana; SigC Tells Tech Details of "Moon Radar"; WD Press Release, SigC Expands Radar Study of Moon, 29 Jan 46. Radar folder, Tabs K, L, and M, respectively. SigC Hist Sec file. (4) Davis, SigC R&D Activities, pp. 35ff.

Giant SCR–271 Antenna Beamed on the Moon at Camp Evans, N.J.

learned from the difficulties and the ways of surmounting them than can be obtained from a mere catalog of dates and accomplishments. It is hoped that this record and the manner of its presentation will prove useful and helpful to readers seeking specific assistance. But lest this treatment of problems leave the general reader with an impression that the Signal Corps served less well than other elements of the Army, or that its accomplishments compared less favorably, a brief summary of its remarkable achievements follows.

Beginning in 1941 with a paucity of officers and men, with a nearly empty storage cupboard, with a skeletal schooling organization, with an industrial support in the shape of a national industry that had next to no experience in mass production of precise military radio or radar, the Signal Corps in four years built up an enormous organization of skilled men, an Army plant of world communications, and mountains of equipment fabricated by an industry that the Signal Corps had helped to create. "We were walking on uncharted ground," the Assistant Chief Signal Officer wrote. "We had no pattern to follow either in organization or demands. When you consider that the job was well nigh impossible, for we needed more equipment than the entire industry had ever turned out, more trained men than were available or could be trained in the time allowed us, and had to fill demands for weapons unheard of, I believe a truly fantastic and wonderful job was done." [55]

The Signal Corps developed, supplied, installed, and maintained its specialized equipment not only for all the ground forces of the Army, but for that increasingly large element that was even more demanding of greater quantities of complex communications equipment than the Army Ground Forces, the Army Air Forces. Despite all the complaints of the airmen, the fact remains that the AAF enjoyed communications and radar that were at least the equal of any other air force in the world, at least for the later years of the war. Since the separation of AAF communications-electronics equipment from the Signal Corps did not begin until late 1944, practically all AAF facilities in this category throughout the war were provided by the Signal Corps, as well as AAF's voracious demands for AWS troops and for officers and men trained in every sort of communications specialty.

The radio equipment of the Army Ground Forces was clearly unsurpassed, the envy of all the Allies, who pressed to obtain for themselves such sets as the long-range mobile SCR's–299 and 399. Above all, the Signal Corps short-range vehicular FM radio sets gave American soldiers a facile voice communications facility, free from interference, beyond anything either the enemy or the other allied nations possessed. "I feel that every soldier that lived through the war with an Armored Unit owes a debt that he does not even realize to General Colton," exclaimed Colonel

---

[55] Ltr, Code to Thompson and Harris, 14 Aug 58, p. 3.
General Code felt that Signal Corps success rested on the "terrific work of the first two years" of the war under General Olmstead's explosively fighting drive. Some of the resultant upheavals were smoothed over by General Ingles in the last two years, during which, Code emphasized, "our production was meeting the schedules, our training was good, we met demands for personnel. . . ." Ibid., p. 13.

Williams after the war. Colton had promoted and pushed FM radio as well as radar in the early days of the conflict and before it, to the immense advantage of American troops. And the utmost efforts of Signal Corps production and distribution saw to it, Williams added, "that when we finally got into the decisive campaigns of the war we always had an adequate supply of signal equipment." [56]

The Signal Corps made many contributions to Army organization and efficiency, for example, in the concept of organizational control (the Control Division in the OCSigO set a new pattern and new standard for progress in administration). There were many contributions in that most difficult aspect of amassing a huge Army—the training of men—especially in intricate skills that had been unknown before World War II, such as radar.

Nor were Signal Corps achievements limited to the large vital assistance rendered to the Army itself, assuring the communications facilities that the commander must have in order to control his troops. The Signal Corps

achievement in World War II must include, in any over-all estimate, mention also of its contribution to the civilian nation. Its co-operation and assistance boosted the relatively slight prewar electronics industry of the United States to a foremost place in the nation's economy after V–J Day. The Corps helped build new factories and uncover new supplies of raw materials, so many of which were rare, hard to discover, or refine in quantities, such as quartz crystals. It was large-scale quarrying of these, and the techniques of fabricating millions of frequency control crystals (where only very small quantities had been laboriously produced before the war) that made possible the simple push-button tuning of tens of thousands of vehicular and aircraft radios in World War II. The Signal Corps contributed thousands of new developments and inventions to the electronics technology of the era, adding greatly to the scientific skills and experience of the United States. And at the war's end it returned to civilian life and employment many tens of thousands of men and women whom it had trained in communications-electronics and who would apply their new and specialized knowledge to the immeasurable benefit of the nation's future progress.

[56] (1) Ltr, Williams to Thompson, 31 Dec 49, p. 19. (2) See Harold A. Zahl, "Colton's Baby Comes Through," *Readers Digest*, 73, No. 436 (August, 1958), 178ff.

Signal Corps Equipment, World War II

The purpose of this appendix is to present a representative assembly of Signal Corps equipment, not only emphasizing the gear which was known in every wartime theater, but also including some items which, although under development or satisfactorily tested before the end of the war, never reached the field or even the production line. The grouping used is employed for convenience, in an effort to simplify the maze. It points out the principal but not necessarily the sole purpose of the equipment.

Military Communications

I. *Wire communication*

  A. Wire and cable

    1. Assault wire: very lightweight twisted pair (two conductors, each containing seven strands) which could be quickly laid over the ground

      a. W–130: weight 30 pounds a mile, talking range about 5 miles.

      b. WD–1/TT: weight 48 pounds a mile, talking range about 14 miles.

    2. Field wire: heavier and stronger, for use in long lines on the ground or on poles

      a. W–110–B: twisted pair, weight about 130 pounds a mile, talking range 12–20 miles.

      b. W–143: parallel pair, talking range up to 27 miles.

    3. Cable

      a. WC–548: spiral-four cable containing two conductor pairs spirally wound about a core. This most popular cable was used wherever possible in carrier systems. It was supplied in various lengths, or cable stubs, chief of which was CC–358, a quarter-mile length complete with snap couplings and built-in loading coils.

      b. Coaxial cable: hollow cable, or wave guide, for conducting VHF radio frequencies to and from the short VHF antennas (monopole whips, dipoles, etc.) and the associated transmitters and receivers.

  B. Line-laying equipment

    1. Reels for laying or recovering wire or cable

      a. DR–4 and 5: small drums or reels for wire.

      b. DR–7 and 15: larger reels for cable.

      c. CE–11: a reel unit carried by the operator, suspended from his neck for laying ¼-mile lengths of W–130.

d. RL–16: a two-wheeled handcart carrying two DR–4 drums; replaced during the war by the somewhat larger handcart, RL–35.

e. RL–31: a reel cradle for DR–4 and 5, carried by hand or in a vehicle.

f. RL–26: a heavy reel unit with gasoline engine drive, carried in a vehicle designed in 1932 for slow speed operation. Speedier versions were undertaken in 1945 as RL–108 and 118 ( ) /G.

g. RL–27: an axle or shaft carried between two men and bearing a wire reel, DR–4.

h. MX–301 and 302: cases holding coils of W–130 and W–110 (wound by special machines) for rapid laying of wire at speeds up to 60 miles per hour.

i. CY–196/ATC: container holding several MX–301 dispensers fitted beneath a liaison-type aircraft for laying W–130 from the air.

2. Plow for burying lines (especially spiral-four cable)

LC–61: towed by a truck; this device could plough wire or cable into the ground at 5 miles per hour to depths up to 18 inches.

C. Telephone equipment

1. Telephone sets (the telephones themselves are called handsets, *see below under* Accessories, *handsets*)

a. EE–8: standard field telephone set, hand-carried in a small case which included ringing equipment and batteries.

b. TP–9: a portable set including the generator and ringing components of EE–8 plus a vacuum-tube amplifier which extended the talking range of the wire line.

c. TP–3: a sound-powered field set, very lightweight, unencumbered by batteries, utilizing instead the energy of the speaker's voice to produce sufficient current in the wire for ranges of a few miles.

2. Telephone amplifiers to extend the talking range of wire lines

a. Loading coils: inserted at intervals in wire lines, they strengthen weak currents by induction

(1) C–114: used to extend the range of W–110.

(2) C–426: an improved coil for W–110 and W–143. Spaced at one-mile intervals in W–110, these coils extended its talking range to 20 miles. At 5/8-mile intervals in W–143, they could extend its range to over 80 miles.

b. Repeater sets: containing a power source and vacuum-tube amplifiers, repeater sets could boost wire ranges to scores and hundreds of miles

(1) For noncarrier lines, both two and four wires operating on voice frequencies only

(a) EE–89: a lightweight repeater for two-wire operation, weighing but 13 pounds including a dry battery.

(b) TP–14: also for a two-wire line but much heavier, 75

pounds, powered either by standard a–c or by 12-volt storage battery.

(c) TC–29: a portable repeater for four-wire operation. Its major component was repeater EE–99.

(2) For carrier systems (C-type), four (sometimes two) wires operating both on voice and on higher, or carrier, frequencies

(a) TC–23: a repeater set whose major component was CF–3, generally spaced at 25-mile intervals in spiral-four cable line.

(b) TC–37: a two-wire carrier repeater, whose major component was CF–5. CF–5, used in conjunction with converter CF–4 (part of TC–33) which converted four-wire carrier operation to two-wire, could extend the two-wire range to 150 miles.

(c) AN/TCC–5 and 6: small, lightweight carrier equipment developed for AAF. 5 was a miniature version of the four-wire repeater CF–3; 6 a miniature version of both the four-to-two-wire converter CF–4 and the two-wire repeater CF–5.

3. Telephone terminal sets: for four-wire carrier systems (C-type)
a. TC–21: this carrier terminal, whose major component was CF–1, could handle four telephone circuits on four bands between 200 and 12,000 cycles.

b. AN/TCC–3: a lightweight carrier terminal for AAF, a miniature version of CF–1 for use with either wire or radio relay systems.

4. Telephone switchboards
a. BD–71 and 72: portable switchboards of 6- and 12-line capacity respectively, yet quite heavy, about 45 and 75 pounds.

b. SB–5 and 22 ( )/PT: lightweight (about 12 pounds) 4- and 8-line field boards to replace BD's–71 and 72.

c. SB–18/GT: vestpocket five-pound 6-line emergency board composed of plastic adaptor plugs U–4/GT.

5. Telephone central office sets (telephone exchanges)
a. TC–1, 10, and 20: Army headquarters sets, TC–1 with a capacity of 100 to 300 lines was based on switchboard BD–80; TC–10 was similar but more rugged and more easily transported. TC–10 was built around switchboard BD–110 of 90-line capacity, but three to six of these boards could be used in series. TC–20 was built around switchboard BD–120.

b. TC–2 and 4: sets for corps and division headquarters respectively employing switchboards BD–89 and 96.

c. TC–12: a small lightweight telephone central office set for AAF, using BD–91 of 20-line capacity.

6. Interphone equipment, used in tanks, armored cars, and aircraft
a. For tanks
(1) RC–53, 61, 99, and 146: for tanks and armored cars.

(2) AN/VIA–1: an external phone at rear of a tank enabling an infantryman outside to talk with crewmen inside.

b. For aircraft

(1) RC–36, 45, and 51: for use in multiplace aircraft.

(2) AN/AIC–1, 2, and 3: developed for use in rarefied air at great altitudes.

D. Telegraph and teletype equipment, including radioteletype

1. Telegraph

a. TG–5: a portable six-pound field set or buzzer for manual keying and receiving.

b. Boehme equipment: high-speed keying and recording office equipment for automatically transmitting and receiving Morse code signals over radio circuits.

2. Teletypewriters and teletypewriter sets

a. TG–7: a page printer; a tape printer had been developed in the 1930's as TG–6. Late in the war a lightweight page printer suitable for a backpack was under development as AN/PGC–1 to replace TG–7, which weighed over 200 pounds. Several teletypewriter sets were also developed under nomenclature EE–97, 98, and 102. They included teletypewriters TG–7 and 37 and were capable of operation in the field on such portable power sources as PE–77.

b. TG–15: a heavy office set, 250 pounds, a page receiver and keyboard sender.

c. TC–16: reperforator teletypewriter set including a reperforator transmitter, TG–26. This set could produce from wire-line signals a perforated tape bearing both the message letter text and corresponding perforations in the five-unit teletype code. If the set were in a relay station, the message could be relayed automatically by running the tape through the reperforator transmitter. TC–17 (with TG–27) was identical with TC–16 and TG–26 except for its special keyboard designed for use in weather communications.

3. Teletype (and telegraph) repeaters and repeater sets

a. TG–9: designed to replace TG–4 to extend the wire range of two-way manual or printer telegraph.

b. TG–28 and 29: portable field repeaters to extend the normal telegraph range (60–90 miles) of W–110.

c. TC–18 and 19: repeater sets, terminal and intermediate respectively, for installation at the terminal or at an intermediate point along the wire line for boosting teletype signals. The chief components were repeaters TG–30 (terminal) and TG–31 (intermediate).

4. Teletype (telegraph) terminals

a. TC–22: a carrier terminal (of which the major component was CF–2) providing four teletypewriter circuits over a single telephone circuit, or twelve such circuits over spiral four since only the three upper voice frequency bands could be used for teletypewriter operation. Often telephone and teletype operation were combined, as one telephone and twelve teletype circuits. Such operation called for both TC-21 (telephone) and TC-22 (telegraph) equipment at the same terminal.

b. CF-6 (originally TC-28) : a teletype terminal, used in conjunction with TC-22, to provide additional teletype circuits on two- and four-wire systems.

c. TH-1 ( ) /TCC-1 (originally AN/TCC-1) : speech-plus-duplex (S+DX) terminal equipment which provided telegraph transmission over an existing telephone line—allowing a carrier telegraph circuit while retaining the voice circuit.

d. AN/TCC-4: a lightweight carrier terminal developed for AAF, a miniature version of CF-2 providing four telegraph or teletype circuits over a two-wire system or over radio relay equipment.

5. Teletype (and telegraph) switchboards

a. BD-100: providing facilities for 10 telegraph printer lines; a heavy board, weighing about 200 pounds.

b. SB-6 ( )/GG: a lightweight portable switchboard for four-line telegraph or teletype operation, replacing older telegraph boards, BD-50, 51, 52, and 53.

6. Teletype (and telegraph) central office sets

a. TC-3: a small central office set consisting of teletypewriter TG-7, switchboard BD-100, rectifier, and portable power unit.

b. AN/MRC-2: a mobile teletypewriter station providing two-way (duplex) operation over radio SCR-399, a vehicular long-range set.

7. Radioteletype equipment

Much of the foregoing wire teletype equipment could be, and was, used in radioteletype systems, wherein radio waves substituted for wire lines. Additional equipment designed specifically for radioteletype operation included the following:

a. O-5/FR: a signal shifter which, when attached to a transmitter radiating continuous-wave radioteletype mark and space signals, caused the transmitter to send out two different frequencies or tones —one for mark, the other for space.

b. AN/FRR-3: a frequency-diversity radio receiver (2.5–26 mc) designed to receive both mark and space radioteletype signals on two frequencies or tones.

c. AN/FGC-1: a radioteletype terminal set designed to convert the two-tone (or two-frequency) signals received by AN/FRR-3 into suitable impulses to operate a standard teletypewriter.

d. AN/TGC-1: a semiautomatic tape relay set— a reperforator at the receiver punched a tape, on which it overprinted the letter text for the convenience of personnel unable to read the perforation code.

The tape needed only to be manually inserted in the proper transmitter, according to the designation of the message it bore, to be hurried on its way over an outgoing circuit.

II. *Ground radio communication*

A. Short-range: up to 25 miles (usually five miles or less for radiotelephone sets)

  1. Portable sets

    a. SCR–194 and 195: one-man pack sets providing voice signals only on 27–65 mc; Army's first walkie-talkies.

    b. SCR–284: both portable and vehicular, providing both continuous wave and voice; rather heavy, weighing complete about 250 pounds.

    c. SCR–288: a stopgap set for SCR–284.

    d. SCR–300: the renowned walkie-talkie, an FM set, manually tuned over 40–48 mc. Signal Corps developed a version of this set for Field Artillery (FA) as SCR–619 (to substitute for SCR's 609 and 610) and a version of the 619 in turn for Armored Force as AN/GRC–12.

    e. SCR–509: AF–II, an 80-crystal (any two frequencies preset) push-button FM radio; version SCR–709 had fewer crystals.

    f. SCR–511: portable Cavalry guidon set, widely used by Infantry.

    g. SCR–609 and 809: FA equivalents of SCR–509 and 709.

    h. SCR–536: the handie-talkie, smallest of Signal Corps radio transmitter and receiver sets; a very popular AM set, followed by tropicalized and disguised versions, AN/PRC–4 and 6 respectively.

    i. SCR–694: both portable and vehicular, successor to SCR–284 to whose crystal control it added two preset frequencies. Its receiver used alone was SCR–714. A late and improved version with continuous-wave range up to 75 miles was AN/GRC–9.

    j. AN/PRC–3: a portable microwave transceiver developed for FA to replace signal lamps.

  2. Vehicular sets

    a. SCR–171 and 178: sets carried in a vehicle but operated on the ground; providing a 15-mile range on continuous wave only, 2–3 mc.

    b. SCR–179 and 203: cavalry saddle sets. SCR–179 was a saddle version of SCR–178.

    c. SCR–209 and 210: continuous-wave, tone, and voice sets for Armored Force.

    d. SCR–293 and 294: first FM sets for the Armored Force; crystal-controlled, providing voice communications only on 20–27 mc. A related FM set was SCR–298.

    e. SCR–508: AF III, an 80-crystal (any ten frequencies preset) push-button radio (transmitter and two receivers) with variations SCR–528 (transmitter and one receiver) and 538 (one receiver). SCR–708, 728, and 738 were crystal-saving versions. All provided voice only on 20–28 mc, FM.

f. SCR–510: similar to the portable SCR–509 but designed for vehicles only. SCR–710 had fewer crystals.

g. SCR–608, 628, and 610: similar to AF sets 508, 528, and 510 but designed for FA with 120 crystals on 27–39 mc. SCR–808, 828, and 810 were crystal-saving versions.

h. AN/VRC–3: an FM set designed for tanks on the same frequency band as SCR–300 to enable crew men to communicate with ground troops using the walkie-talkie.

B. Medium-range: 25 to 100 miles

1. Portable sets

a. SCR–177: carried in a vehicle but operated on the ground, providing continuous wave, tone, and voice.

b. SCR–543 and 593: vehicular and ground sets for CAC; SCR–593 was portable, being the receiver portion only.

c. AN/TRC–2: a version of SCR–694 designed for eight- to ten-man pack for jungle or mountain use providing a continuous-wave range up to 100 miles.

2. Vehicular sets

a. SCR–193: set which could be operated to provide continuous wave, tone, and voice, while vehicle was in motion.

b. SCR–245: popular mobile set providing four crystal-controlled frequencies, selected by switches.

c. SCR–506: AF II; standard medium-range vehicular set providing continuous wave and voice on four preset crystal frequencies.

d. SCR–583: a saddle or vehicular set designed to replace the short-range saddle set SCR–203.

3. Transportable radio relay equipment, both terminal and relay sets, employing directional beams in VHF, UHF, and SHF; FM or pulse-time modulated

a. AN/TRC–1, 3, and 4: VHF, on 70–100 mc, providing four circuits, FM.

b. AN/TRC–5: UHF, on 1500 mc, designed to provide seven radio circuits, employing pulse-time modulation.

c. AN/TRC–8, 11, and 12: VHF, on 230–250 mc, designed to provide four circuits, FM.

d. AN/TRC–16, 17, and 18: SHF, on 7000–8500 mc, designed as a very lightweight single circuit set for AAF.

e. AN/TRC–6: SHF, on 4300–4900 mc, a heavy duty eight-circuit set, employing pulse-time modulation.

C. Long-range: 100 miles and over

1. Portable sets

a. AN/PRC–1 and 5: suitcase continuous-wave sets designed for Military Intelligence Service (MIS).

b. AN/TRC–10: a larger, yet portable set, also for MIS.

2. Mobile sets: operated in trucks in motion or at rest and powered by large generators carried in trailers

a. SCR–197: powerful set but of poor mobility; on 1–18 mc with five preset crystal frequencies.

b. SCR–505 (AF I) and SCR–597: development of the former was supplanted by designs for the latter to provide 100 miles on voice, 350 on continuous wave (up to 5,000 miles from ground to aircraft) having three crystal push-button channels in range 2–20 mc.

c. SCR–299: excellent long-range set mounted in a panel truck and powered by the reliable PE–95 carried in a two-wheel trailer. The 299 replaced SCR–597 and became standard for all the Army. Version SCR–399 was housed in the standard shelter HO–17, mountable in any 2½-ton truck. An air transportable version, SCR–499, became standard for the AAF. These sets radiated about 350 watts of power, yielding dependable 100-mile range on voice while in motion, and many hundreds of miles on continuous wave, in Morse code.

3. Transportable sets

SCR–698: largest of SCR radio sets, a one-kilowatt broadcast transmitter, used (together with receiver and monitor set SCR–696) by MIS (Psychological Warfare Units) for broadcasting to enemy and conquered countries.

D. Radio remote-control devices

1. RM–7 and 14: used respectively with long-range SCR–197 and with short-range 194 and 195, permitting telegraph operation from a distance, or remote-voice operation over telephone set EE–8.

2. RC–47: used with the ground-air liaison set SCR–188 permitting transmission or reception, voice, tone, or continuous wave, over six to ten miles of wire.

3. RM–29 and RC–261, 289, and 290: remote-control units for a number of portable and vehicular short-range sets (SCR–300, 284, 608, etc.) permitting control at distances up to five miles.

4. AN/TRA–2: used with radio-relay sets AN/TRC–1,3, and 4 permitting control at distances up to two miles.

III. *Air radio communication*

A. Medium- and long-range command sets

1. Airborne component

a. SCR–183 and 283: HF sets (2–7 mc) operating on 12- and 24-volt airplane batteries respectively and providing continuous wave, tone, and voice for 10–45 miles between planes: 10–20 miles plane to ground.

b. SCR–264: first airborne VHF push-button set on 100–130 mc initiated by Signal Corps Laboratories in 1939, but use of the set was precluded by adoption of British VHF, SCR–522.

c. SCR–274: HF, up to 9 mc (VHF later added), 75 miles on voice, 150 miles on continuous wave.

d. SCR–522: a VHF set (100–156 mc) operating on 24-volt batteries with four preset crystal-controlled push-button channels. A version designed to operate on 12-volt batteries was SCR–542.

e. AN/ARC–3: an improved VHF set providing eight push-button channels.

f. AN/ARC–6: on still higher frequencies (225–285 mc) and especially designed to overcome jamming by the enemy.

2. Ground component

a. SCR–562, 563, 567, and 633: VHF transmitters and receivers used with fighter-control system SCS–2, semifixed.

b. SCR–573, 574, and 643: ditto, used with fighter-control system SCS–3, mobile.

c. SCR–643 and 644: fixed VHF transmitter and receiver stations.

d. SCR–624: an adaptation of SCR–522 for ground use, good for 130 miles line of sight ground to plane. A similar adaptation for parachute drop was AN/CRC–1.

e. AN/VRC–1: a jeep-mounted set combining the HF SCR–193 with the VHF airborne command set SCR–542 to provide both ground and air communication—continuous wave, tone, and voice—up to 60 miles.

B. Long-range liaison sets

1. Airborne component

a. SCR–187 and 287: for 12- and 24-volt operation respectively; manually tuned, continuous wave, tone, and voice on 1–12 mc range up to 2,000 miles.

b. AN/ARC–8: derived from SCR–287 but incorporating push-button tuning; composed of transmitter AN/ART–13 and receiver BC–348 or AN/ARR–11.

2. Ground component

a. SCR–188: provided continuous wave, tone, and voice on 1–12 mc, the continuous-wave range matching that of the airborne SCR–187 and 287.

b. SCR–237: developed with 10 preset crystal channels with intent to replace SCR–188.

c. SCR–499: a version of the long-range SCR–399, packaged for parachute drop in 200-pound bundles. The set became standard for AAF ground liaison. A lighter weight parachute version was developed as AN/CRC–5.

C. Short-range paratroop and glider sets

1. SCR–585: a modified handie-talkie for use in gliders, talking range up to one mile.

2. AN/ASC–1: having a range of but 500 feet, for talk between glider and tow plane.

3. AN/PRC–2: a VHF set for paratroop liaison.

4. AN/TRC–7: a heavier VHF paratroop liaison set weighing 100 pounds, parachuted in four packages including a hand generator and a 30-foot sectional mast.

IV. *Visual communication*

A. Flags

1. MC–44: semaphore, 18″ square, divided diagonally into red and white portions.

2. MC–113: semaphore flag kit containing two MC–44's.

3. M–238: set of colored flags for signaling between tanks.

B. Panels and panel sets: cotton cloth strips variously colored to identify ground areas and units for friendly planes

1. AL–119, 120, etc.: square or rectangular, for aerial liaison.

2. AP–30–A and C: in dark colors, for use on snow or light backgrounds.

3. AP–30–B and D: in light colors, for use on normal backgrounds.

C. Lamps, to transmit blinker code by night or day

1. Signal

a. EE–80–A: heavy (194 pounds) 12-inch lamp and tripod signaling by white, red, or green flashes using commercial 115-volt alternating current or direct current, range up to 12–14 miles.

b. EE–84: portable searchlight-type set (42 pounds) operating on dry cell batteries with range up to 5,000 yards in sunlight, far greater at night; white or red flashes.

c. SE–11: highly portable (7–8 pounds), flashlight-type, aimed like a gun with trigger key, daylight range 1,000–2,000 yards using red filter.

2. Identification: enabling planes to identify friendly ground vehicles and installations

a. AN/VVX–1: delivering intermittent flashes visible in bright sunlight three miles aloft or a mile or more along the ground.

b. AN/PVX–1: similar to above but portable, operating on self-contained battery to mark front lines, installations, etc. It could also serve as blinker signal lamp.

D. Optiphone (or photophone: *i.e.,* talk by light, by a steady modulated beam, not blinker light)

AN/TVC–1: formerly SE–10, involving a modulated light-beam transmitter and receiver, portable, with minimum range of 5,000 yards in sunlight and able to link telephone lines so as to span obstacles such as a river.

V. *Pigeon communication*

  A. Lofts, transportable, for housing large numbers of birds

    1. PG–46: prefabricated sectional housing for fixed use.

    2. PG–68/TB: a combat loft, collapsible and easily transported by a truck or trailer.

  B. Pigeon equipment including containers for carrying a few birds

    1. PG–60, 102/CB, 103/CB, and 105/CB: portable, carrying two to four birds, for combat troops.

    2. PG–100/CB and 101/CB: four- and eight-bird containers respectively, with parachutes for dropping to paratroops or isolated ground forces.

  C. Message holders to fasten to the legs of the birds

    1. PG–14: aluminum holders.

    2. PG–52, 53, 54, and 67: plastic substitutes for the PG–14.

  D. Pigeon vest, PG–106/CB, retaining a single bird, to be worn by paratrooper

VI. *Reproduced communication*

  A. Public address sets

    1. PA–1, 2, 3, 4, 5, and 6: sets varying from heavy systems powered by gasoline engine generators to simple portable microphones and amplifiers powered by batteries.

    2. AN/TIQ–1, 4, and 5: powerful outdoor sets with speaking ranges up to 7,000 yards.

    3. AN/PIQ–2, TIQ–2, and UIQ–1: portable battery sets.

  B. Recorders and reproducers of sound

    1. RC–17 and 169: recorders of speech or signals whether telephone, telegraph, or radio. RC–179 and 199 were used in radio intercept work to record any type of signal.

    2. MC–364: record player and amplifier.

    3. AN/ANQ–1 and 2 and GNQ–1 and 2: airborne voice recorders and ground playback equipment developed for air reconnaissance work.

  C. Facsimile

    1. RC–58: tape facsimile developed for use in AF vehicles to reproduce hand printed message texts received over vehicular radio sets.

    2. RC–120: a page transceiver, to send or receive a seven-inch square page—text, map, picture—transmission or reception requiring seven minutes to complete. A larger version for fixed station use was AN/TXC–1, which could handle a page 12 by 18 inches over voice communication channels.

    3. AN/GXC–2 and 3: transceivers for $4\frac{1}{2}$ by $5\frac{1}{4}$ and for 8 by $10\frac{1}{2}$ copy respectively.

Military Operations

I. *Radar*
  A. Searchlight control
    1. SCR–268: standard SLC set employing long waves, 1½ meters, on 205 mc.
    2. SCR–668 and 768: experimental SLC sets, the latter patterned after the British "Wigwam" radars enveloped in tents.
    3. AN/TPL–1: lightweight microwave set for use with 60-inch searchlights, developed from SCR–668.
  B. Early warning: for long-range detection of aircraft. EW radars merged into medium-range EW and GCI sets.
    1. SCR–270 and 271: respectively mobile and fixed long wave (3 meters, 109 mc) search sets, giving azimuth and range of aircraft up to 150 miles away. Versions designed to give elevation also were SCR–289, 530, and 531. SCR–539 was a PPI indicator developed for use with the 270 and 271.
    2. SCR–548 and 648: experimental outer harbor aircraft detectors, shipborne.
    3. SCR–602: copy of the British LW, lightweight warning radar, using long wavelengths at 200 mc.
    4. AN/TPS–3: an efficient lightweight radar developed from SCR–548, using medium wavelengths on 600 mc. Other transportable EW radars for use in mobile situations, such as invasions, were AN/TPS–1 and 2, the latter totaling less than 600 pounds.
    5. AN/TPS–10: a height finder and lightweight EW with narrow "beaver-tail" beam, for Air Forces use in hilly country; dubbed "Little Abner."
    6. AN/CPS–1: the powerful MEW, or microwave early warning radar, a huge set on 3,000 mc, radiating a 10-cm wave with range up to 200 miles.
    7. AN/CPS–2: a medium-range EW developed to employ variable frequencies between 510 and 725 mc in order to evade jamming.
    8. AN/CPS–4: a height finder only, to supplement MEW and SCR–270 and 271.
    9. AN/TRS–1: electronic fence, employing continuous-wave radiations; a beat-reflection-type radar developed to detect aircraft flying over hilly terrain where ground reflections handicap pulsed-type radar search sets.
  C. Ground-controlled interception
    1. SCR–516 and 527: the 516 was developed from the SCR–268; the 527 was copied from the British GCI.
    2. SCR–588: American copy, built in Canada, of the huge British CHL/GCI using long wavelengths.

3. SCR–615: a large transportable 10-cm microwave radar with range up to 90 miles.

4. AN/CPS–5 and 6: improved microwave sets for GCI applications.

D. Coastal defense and harbor surveillance: for long-range detection of surface craft.

1. SCR–296: a large fixed radar operating on medium waves, 700 mc.

2. SCR–582: a valuable microwave set, on 10-cm at 3,000 mc. Version SCR–682 was transportable.

E. Gun laying

1. For coast defense, against surface vessels

a. SCR–598: similar to SCR–296 but of shorter range and greater accuracy for fire control purposes, directing gunfire against such small craft as motor torpedo boats.

b. AN/FPG–1 and 2: fixed sets using very short wavelengths, 3-cm, at 10,000 mc which permit great accuracy.

c. AN/MPG–1 and TPG–1: respectively mobile and transportable 3-cm coastal gun layers, long range and very accurate.

2. For air defense and AA batteries, against airborne targets

a. SCR–547: a "radio height finder," replacing optical height finders supplying target range and elevation data. Known as "Mickey Mouse."

b. SCR–545: a gun layer using relatively a long wavelength for search and a microwavelength for tracking or following the target. It was a semiautomatic gun layer, requiring hand tracking.

c. SCR–584: an excellent 10-cm gun layer, completely automatic for fire on unseen targets, very accurate.

3. For aircraft, against airborne and surface targets

a. Aircraft range only, aiding fire on visual targets

(1) AN/APG–5: automatic range finder for turret gunners in B–17's and 24's, developed from experimental SCR–523 and 726.

(2) AN/APG–11: designed for toss bombing, from plane to plane.

(3) AN/APG–14: for B–29 gunners.

b. Aircraft gun sight radars, requiring hand tracking

(1) AN/APG–13: effectively used with the 75-mm nose cannon of B–25's, named "Falcon."

(2) AN/APG–15: an efficient radar gun sight for tail gunners of heavy bombers.

c. Aircraft gun laying, automatic, for blind firing

(1) AN/APG–1: (SCR–702) used in the Black Widow night fighter, P–61. Weighed 700 pounds.

(2) AN/APG–2: (SCR–580) a 10-cm AI and AGL for bomber gun turrets. A 3-cm version for B–32's was AN/APG–16.

(3) AN/APG–3: a smaller 3-cm AI and AGL for B–29's.

F. Tail warning

1. AN/APS–13: a small 20-pound radar for fighter planes; it flashed a red light and rang a bell in the cockpit to warn that another plane was approaching from the rear.

2. AN/APS–16 and 17: similar tail-warning indicators for bombers.

G. Air interception

1. SCR–540: patterned after the British AI Mark IV, which operated on a long wavelength, 1½ meters, at 200 mc.

2. SCR–520 and 720: AI–10, superior 10-cm, 3,000 mc, microwave sets, but heavy, 600 and 500 pounds respectively.

3. AN/APS–4 and 6: smaller improved AI's, operating on 3-cm wavelengths at 10,000 mc, developed in part from SCR–537.

H. Airborne search and bombing: early search types were called air-to-surface-vessel radars, ASV, which developed into low-altitude bombing types, LAB, and bombing-through-overcast, BTO, types.

1. SCR–521: a long wave (1½ meters) ASV, patterned after the British ASV Mark II.

2. SCR–517: ASV–10, a microwave 10-cm radar operating in the S-band at 3,000 mc. Weight 500 pounds. A smaller version for LAB, blind bombing at low altitudes, was SCR–717. Other SCR's in these categories were SCR–519, a 10-cm search and tracking set, and SCR–667, a 3-cm, X-band, set.

3. AN/APQ–5: an auxiliary bombsight much used in combination with the SCR–517 as a LAB set.

4. AN/APQ–11 and 12: (SCR–626) radar bombsights, designed especially for launching airborne torpedoes.

5. AN/APQ–13 and APS–15: superior BTO's, 3-cm sets (X-band), known to the Americans as "Mickey," to the British as H2X. They performed well at high altitudes and showed ground features in considerable detail.

6. AN/APQ–7 and 10: 3-cm BTO's of even greater clarity than "Mickey." APQ–7, dubbed "Eagle," weighed nearly 1,000 pounds.

I. Identification, friend or foe

1. Mark IV, American sets, involving equipment independent of any associated radars, giving instant response

   a. Ground interrogator-responsor

     SCR–532 and 533: for short and long ranges respectively.

   b. Airborne transponder

     SCR–515: 150-mile range.

2. Mark II, adopted from the British

   SCR–535: airborne transponder, which swept the frequency bands of the early EW radars, and caused its plane's echo in their scopes to appear large. No ground interrogator-responsor was needed.

3. Mark III, British IFF, standard for all the Allies; it depended upon associated radars for power and design; response was delayed

    a. Ground interrogator-responsors, differing for each radar type.
        RC–148, 150, 151, 127, 184, etc.: associated with SCR–268, 270, 271, 527, 584, etc.

    b. Airborne transponders
        SCR–595 and 695: on I-band, 157–187 mc. The 695 including also G–band, 200 mc, for benefit of long-wave GCI radars.

    c. Airborne interrogator-responsor
        SCR–729: enabling a plane to challenge the identification of other planes, which could answer if they carried SCR–595 or 695. SCR–729 was also much used in radar beaconry (*see under* Navigation, Radar).

4. Mark V/UNB: a universal identification and beacon system developed by U.S., British, and Canadian services, involving pulse sets in UHF.

J. Bomb proximity fuzing: fuzes operating on radar principles, emitting radio waves whose reflection from a nearby target served to explode the missile carrying such a fuze

    1. MC–382: designed for aerial rocket bombs.

    2. AN/CPQ–1, 2, 3, 5, and 6: designed to detonate bombs just above ground targets.

K. Glide-bomb control

    1. RC–171: radar homing bomb equipment, an S-band radar fitting into a winged bomb designed to seek, or home on, a target illuminated by a radar transmitter in the bombing aircraft.

    2. AN/APG–7: send-receive radar bomb, similar to RHB above, but containing its own radar transmitter.

L. Mortar location, enabled by radar tracking of the trajectory of the mortar shells

    1. AN/TPQ–2 and 4: microwave radars.

    2. AN/TPQ–3: a lighter weight medium-wave version, operating on 600 mc, modified from AN/TPS–3.

M. Personnel detection: radars of the continuous-wave, beat-reflection type

    1. AN/PPQ–1: a very short-range, hand-carried set, developed to serve as an aid to night patrols, or as a sensory aid for the blind.

    2. AN/PPS–1: a lightweight pack set to detect moving objects (tanks, trucks, men).

II. *Radio*

A. Mine detection: mine detectors bore Signal Corps designations, were produced and distributed by Signal Corps, but their development was a responsibility of the Engineer Corps

1. Portable: carried and operated by one man
   a. SCR–625: standard detector for metallic mines.
   b. AN/PRS–2, 3, and 4: portable detectors for nonmetallic mines.
2. Vehicular
   a. AN/VRS–2: detector designed to be mounted on a boom projecting ahead of a jeep and to stop the vehicle automatically upon
   detecting a mine ahead.
   b. AN/VRS–3: a similar set designed for use by tanks.

B. Remote mine detonation: remote-control system for detonating mines
   AN/TRT–1 and TRR–2: transmitter and receiver respectively, the
   latter designed to operate under water adjacent to a mine, which it
   could detonate upon receiving properly coded signals from the transmitter miles distant—up to 40 miles when the transmitter was carried
   by a plane.

C. Bomb control
   1. For glide bombs Azon and Razon
      a. RC–186 and AN/ARW–16: transmitters to control the bombs.
      b. RC–185 and AN/CRW–2 through 5, and 7 through 9: a group of
      receivers designed to fit within the bombs to receive the controlling
      impulses and transfer them to flight-control mechanisms.
   2. For power-driven bombs, such as rocket bombs and War Weary
   Willies, which were jalopy bombing planes loaded with explosives and
   directed by remote control against the enemy
      a. AN/ARW–18: transmitter, carried by the mother craft.
      b. AN/ARW–1: receiver carried by the missile.
   3. Automatic bomb release: whereby the bombardier in lead plane
   could release the bombs of all planes in his squadron simultaneously
      a. AN/ARW–9: controlling transmitter (also used with Azon and
      Razon) .
      b. AN/ARW–10: receiver, which actuated bomb release.
   4. Tracking of robot bombs: developed for projected use of American
   version of the V–1 buzz bomb (JB–2)
      a. AN/ART–19: transmitter carried by JB–2.
      b. AN/CRD–5: a direction finder to track signals from the above
      transmitter.

D. Direction finders (DF's) for fighter-control: VHF DF components of
fighter-control (or SCS) systems. The DF's took continuous bearings on
aircraft radio emissions, especially airborne pipsqueak (RC–96) , which
radiated a signal once a minute. The bearings, laid out on plotting boards
at control centers, served to track the planes in flight and enabled ground-
control officers to guide the planes by radio telephone.
   1. SCR–564, 565, and 566: fixed and mobile DF's, components of
   SCS–2 (see under Air radio communication, Ground component) .

2. SCR–575 and 634: mobile and air transportable respectively, components of SCS–3.

3. SCR–645: fixed VHF direction finder.

4. AN/CRA–1: a kit embodying an electric goniometer by which VHF sets (SCR–575 and 634) whose H-Adcock antennas had to be rotated by hand, could be converted so as to provide instantaneous indication of direction in a cathode-ray scope.

5. SCR–552: a VHF DF with unique antenna, a conicle or funnel-shaped dipole, which rotated constantly at 75 rpm.

III. *Wire*

A. The operators at SCS control centers and at information, filter, and operation centers for aircraft warning required rapid communication facilities. These were supplied by extensive wire nets, sometimes supplemented by radio also.

1. SCR–561 and 572: not radio sets but assemblies of telephones, switchboards, DF plotting equipment, filter and intercept tables, boards, etc. employed in co-ordinating fighter-control systems SCS–2 and 3.

2. SCS–5: an information center assembly, transported by six 2½-ton trucks.

3. SCS–6 and TC–15: mobile information center and filter center respectively, being successively smaller editions of SCS–5.

4. AN/TTQ–1 and 2: filter and operation centers transportable in two and one trucks respectively for plotting flights of aircraft. Still smaller versions for use with gun and searchlight battalions were AN/TSA–1 and 2.

B. Direction-finding and intercept centrals: transportable sets housed originally in K–35 trailers, later in HO–17 and in HO–27 shelters, and manned by radio intelligence units for locating enemy transmitters and for intercepting and recording their traffic

1. TC–8: a DF central set housed in two shelters and linked to associated DF radio sets by wire (or radio) nets.

2. TC–9: a RI (intercept) central housed in three shelters.

IV. *Sound, thermal, light*

A. Ranging equipment: for determining the range or distance to enemy artillery

1. Sound ranging: utilizing the different arrival times of a muzzle blast received by several spaced microphones to determine the direction and distance to an enemy gun

a. GR–3–C: utilizing a maximum of eight microphone listening posts.

b. GR–8: a lighter weight set using a maximum of six very sensitive microphones; a modified version became AN/TNS–2.

c. GR–6: an extremely accurate set using three microphones; a modification became AN/TND–1.

d. AN/TNS–1: designed to locate enemy mortars by sound ranging up to 5,000 yards.

2 Flash ranging: utilizing the data received by photoelectric cells from muzzle flashes

    a. GR–4: standard set in World War II; but it was too heavy and too delicate.

    b. AN/GTC–1: a lighter weight, yet more rugged, set.

3. Sound and flash ranging

    AN/TSS–1: combined both sound and flash reception at a single observation station. Flash reception was at first accomplished by a photoelectric cell, later by an infrared detector.

4. Hydrocoustic ranging: equipment utilizing underwater sound, developed for Coast Artillery Corps until it was transferred from the Signal Corps to the Navy in June, 1942

    GR–5: hydrocoustic tracking set, able to track vessels by their underwater sound to distances of 100,000 yards; a smaller version was GR–7.

B. Bomb-control (television, for remote control of flying bombs)

    1. AN/AXR–1: television receiver (formerly SCR–550) for installation in the controlling plane.

    2. AN/AXT–2 and 3: transmitters (formerly SCR–549) for installation in the controlled craft or flying bomb.

C. Photoelectric bomb fuze

    MC–380: a proximity fuze developed to fit into the nose of a bomb such as the airborne M8 rocket for use against aircraft. The fuze contained a photoelectric cell which, on detecting a reduction in light intensity as the missile came within 60 feet of its target, detonated the bomb.

D. Photoelectric and supersonic detectors, or sensory aids: carried in one hand, these devices (including the radar sensory aid AN/PPQ–1: under Operational radar, Personnel Detection), could aid blind men, or night patrolmen, to detect the direction and distance of nearby objects

    1. AN/PVQ–2: utilizing a pulsed beam of light which, when reflected from an object, impinged upon a photoelectric cell. This cell in turn modulated an audio signal, which the user detected in an earphone. The aid was unaffected by nonpulsed light, such as sunlight and ordinary electric light.

    2. AN/PNQ–1: utilizing a pulsed-supersonic tone (stealing the secret of the flight control of a bat). The tone, when reflected, was picked up by a microphone, supersonic like a bat's ear, and reduced to an audible tone in a hearing aid worn by the user.

E. Thermal detection

    Thermal equipment, utilizing infrared or heat radiations, largely occupied Signal Corps laboratories in the early 1930's at the beginning of radar development, which soon displaced infrared research. Yet infra-red equipment had proved useful in detection both of ships and aircraft, in searchlight directing and in early forms of the radar SCR–268. It had been tried in 1941, as the Thermopticon, aboard a B–18 bomber and had detected a second B–18 up to 1,200 feet away. Late in the war an infrared detector was incorporated in the sound- and flash-ranging set AN/TSS–1 to detect muzzle flashes, replacing a photoelectric cell which had first been used in this set. Also late in the war the Navy desired an infrared ship detector to be used during radar silence, and called upon Signal Corps for

AN/SSS–1: a shipborne heat-radiation detecting equipment to search for and detect ships up to ranges of 15,000 yards.

V. *Magnetic*

Magnetic airborne detector, or magnetometer

RC–132: an airborne device which, dangled beneath a low-flying plane, could detect a submerged submarine by its magnetic field, which extends from below the water up into the air. RC–132 became AN/ASQ–1, variations of which were designated ASQ–2 and 3.

Navigation

I. *Radio*

A. Compasses: airborne loop-antenna direction-finding receivers (DF's)

1. SCR–242: a LF–MF 12-volt set. A 24-volt version was SCR–282.

2. SCR–246: LF, 12 volts. A 24-volt version was SCR–276. Another version developed to home on much higher frequencies in VHF was SCR–256.

3. SCR–263, 273, and 280: dual remote-control compasses, operating in LF and MF.

4. SCR–269 and 279: standard automatic radio compasses for 24 and 12 volts respectively, LF and MF. Later versions of the standard SCR–269 were AN/ARN–6 and 7 (or SCR 599 and 639 respectively).

B. Beacons operating on radio-directional principles

1. Ground Forces homing equipment

a. Beacon attachments for radio transmitters

(1) RC–163: HF directional attachment, 25-mile range, for vehicular radios SCR–508, 510, 608, 610, etc.

(2) RC–302: attachment converting SCR–284 and 694 into beacons for guiding troops; similar to SCR–277.

(3) AN/TRA–3: all-directional, rotating antenna set, similar to RC–163 but lighter in weight.

b. DF attachments for radio receivers

(1) RC–300 and 303: for SCR–300 (walkie-talkie) and 511 respectively.

(2) BC–309: similar attachment for SCR–508, 608, and 619.

(3) MC–619: similar attachment for the handie-talkie SCR–536.

2. Ground radio range beacons for aircraft guidance

a. SCR–277: a military version of the commercial A–N quadrant type; fixed LF, 200–400 kc.

b. SCR–629: an E–T range, omnidirectional with rotating antenna operating in VHF on 100–156 mc.

c. AN/MRN–2 (formerly SCR–601) and AN/CRN–5: mobile and air transportable respectively, similar to SCR–277 but operating in VHF on 100–156 mc.

3. Air-sea-rescue beacon and receiver

a. SCR–578: an emergency transmitter, hand powered, for use by aviators downed at sea, nicknamed "Gibson Girl"; a modification became AN/CRT–3.

b. AN/ARR–6: an airborne receiver, preset to the frequency of the "Gibson Girl" and automatically giving an alarm upon receipt of the emergency beacon signal.

4. Buoy beacons, locator and sonic, parachuted into the sea

a. AN/CRN–1: a marker beacon, radiating a signal over a 50-mile range, received by aircraft radio compasses, SCR–263 or 269.

b. AN/CRT–1: sonic buoy, picking up submerged submarine sounds and transmitting them over a 10-mile range, received by a special airborne receiver AN/ARR–3.

5. Paratroop beacon

AN/CRN–4: a portable marker radio beacon supplementing Rebecca-Eureka radar types, sending a continuous-wave coded signal every 30 seconds for two hours over a 30-mile range.

C. Navigational direction finders

1. SCR–225 and 551: HF sets with H-Adcock antennas; used by RI units as well as by AAF to assist plane navigation.

2. SCR–291: a very large set developed for AAF from the RI set SCR–502 (see under Intelligence DF's) having fixed U-Adcock monopole antennas.

3. SCR–292: a smaller set employing rotating vertical-loop antennas.

4. AN/CRD–2: a transportable set, superior to, and much smaller than, SCR–551 and 291.

D. Instrument approach and landing systems: these comprised various ground and airborne components of SCS–51, formerly SCR–241 and 251 (all the ground components included SCR–610 for two-way communication with the airfield control tower)

1. Marker beacons and receivers (75 mc)

a. BC–302 and 902: small beacons employed with SCR–241.

b. AN/MRN–3: a jeep-mounted beacon.

c. RC–20, 39, 43, and 193: airborne receivers to detect the vertical

beams from marker beacons up to 16,000 feet; visual indication only
(flashing light on instrument panel as the plane passed over fan
marker, CAA beacon, etc.).

d. AN/ARN-12: an improved lightweight receiver, yielding both
visual and aural indication.

2. Localizer and glide-path sets

a. Localizer VHF transmitter and receiver (110 mc)

(1) AN/MRN-1: mobile ground transmitter (formerly SCR-591) to guide plane to runway. Air-transportable versions were
AN/CRN-7 and 10.

(2) RC-103: airborne receiver actuating a dial which showed the
alignment of approaching airplane in relation to the runway.

b. Glide-path UHF transmitter and receiver (330 mc)

(1) AN/CRN-2: mobile ground transmitter located along airstrip
(formerly SCR-592).

(2) AN/ARN-5: airborne receiver (formerly SCR-570).

(NOTE: The foregoing development culminated in SCS-51, an automatic
instrument-approach radio system, which involved an airborne localizer,
ground glide-path receivers, and a robot pilot.)

II. *Radar*

A. Altimeters (airborne absolute altimeters or terrain clearance indicators)

1. RC-24: a lightweight continuous-wave beat-reflection radar type
(FM), effective only up to 400 feet; renamed AN/ARN-1. An improved version known as AN/APN-1 gave readings up to 4,000 feet.

2. SCR-518 and 718: pulse-type radar altimeters effective up to about
40,000 feet.

B. Beacons

1. Ground

a. Locators developed for determining ground range and azimuth,
used to locate a forward observer for fire control purposes.

SCR-599: a portable 35-pound short-range set (interrogator and
responsor components were later designated AN/PPN-10 and 11
respectively).

b. Ground "navigation" system, employing fixed base stations which
emitted pulsed radiations as in the loran system, providing accurate
location for moving tactical units or for mapping purposes: SCR-560.

2. Ground-to-air

a. Portable beacons, having a 50-mile line-of-sight range, triggered
or interrogated by airborne radars such as AI, ASV, BTO, or IFF
types

(1) AN/UPN-1 and 2: portable S-band sets, operating on 3,000
mc, weighing respectively 115 and 80 pounds.

(2) AN/UPN–3, 4, and 11: X-band sets, 10,000 mc.
  b. Transportable beacons having a 100-mile line-of-sight range
    (1) SCR–621 and 640: heavy 350-pound sets responding to long wave radars SCR–521 ASV and 540 AI on 170–196 mc.
    (2) SCR–620: responding to microwave AI radar SCR–520 and to other 10-cm S-band sets on 3,000 mc; became AN/CPN–3, a bulky half-ton ground set. A similar set was AN/CPN–1.
    (3) AN/CPN–8: a much smaller S-band beacon.
    (4) AN/CPN–6: an X-band beacon on 10,000 mc responding to airborne X-band radars.
  3. Air-sea-rescue beacon
    AN/CPT–2: designed to transmit a continuous-pulse signal for 12 to 20 hours automatically. Called "Walter," it was of lighter weight than the "Gibson Girl" radio (SCR–578) and could be carried in fighter planes.
  4. Paratroop beacons ("Rebecca-Eureka") : portable, 25–100-mile-range sets
    a. AN/APN–2 (developed from SCR–729), 10, and 12: airborne interrogators.
    b. AN/PPN–1 and AN/TPN–1, 2, and 3: ground responders.
C. Loran and shoran
  1. Loran: long-range navigation (LRN)
    a. AN/APN–4 and 9: airborne receivers, originally SCR–622. A variant, SCR–722, derived from a NDRC development.
    b. AN/CPN–11 and 12: (formerly SCR–623) air-transportable slave and master beacon sets.
  2. Shoran: short-range precision navigation, aid in blind bombing (formerly SCR–297)
    a. AN/APN–3: airborne interrogator.
    b. AN/CPN–2: ground transponder station.
D. Blind approach systems
  1. AN/CPN–7: blind approach beacon system.
  2. AN/MPN–1: ground-controlled approach system, involving two mobile short-range microwave radars, in whose scopes the operators watched an approaching aircraft as they coached it to the landing strip, talking over radio telephones SCR–522 or 274. A small air transportable version of GCA was undertaken as AN/CPN–4.

Intelligence, Security, and Countermeasures

I. *Radio intelligence (RI) equipment*
  A. Radio monitoring sets
    1. SCR–243 and 244: low-, middle-, and high-frequency intercept receivers—100 kc to 20 mc.

2. SCR–607, 612, 613, 614, and 616: receivers for frequencies ranging from 15 kc to 600 mc and for continuous-wave, AM and FM types of signals.

B. Direction-finders, DF's: for locating radio transmitters

1. Short- and medium-range

a. SCR–206 and 503: small loop-antenna sets for MF and HF (up to 18 mc).

b. SCR–504: hand-carried, disguised as a suitcase.

c. SCR–555 and 556: heavy sets with rotatable H-Adcock antennas and extending from HF into VHF (18–145 mc).

d. SCR–700: set extending into UHF range on 140 to 600 mc; intended for use with RI intercept receiver SCR–616.

e. AN/TRD–2: an improved version of SCR–503 (incorporating an oscilloscope indicator for instantaneous indication of signal direction).

2. Long-range, semifixed, and transportable

a. SCR–255 and 551: HF sets having large rotatable H-Adcock antennas (dipoles 12 feet long) for taking bearings on sky waves. Also used by AAF for navigational purposes.

b. SCR–501 and 502: very large HF sets having fixed monopole, U-Adcock antennas, and instantaneous oscilloscope indicators. An air-transportable version of 502 was AN/CRD–2.

c. AN/CRD–3: a very large DF, like SCR–502, but designed for LF and MF reception and extremely sensitive to sky waves originating at very great distances.

C. Combined intercept and DF assemblies

1. SCR–558: consisting of DF's SCR–206 and SCR–504, intercept receiver SCR–612, and communication radio SCR–284, the whole assembled in one vehicle.

2. AN/VRD–1: a larger assembly, embracing DF SCR–503, intercept receivers SCR–612 and 613, and radio beacon RC–163, the whole mounted in two vehicles, each carrying an SCR–510 for communication with the other.

3. AN/GRA–2: a loop-antenna DF attachment for any HF or VHF intercept receiver in the range of 18 to 65 mc. A similar attachment was AS–4 (   )/GR to provide DF for any receiver in the range of 1.5 to 18 mc.

II. *Security equipment, for rendering communications unintelligible, scrambling them at the place of transmission and unscrambling them at the place of reception*

1. Cryptographic machines, enciphering and deciphering message texts mechanically

a. M–209: the Haglin converter, small, portable, hand-operated, converting letter by letter into or from a cipher equivalent, and slow.
b. M–134: automatic cipher machine.
2. RC–62: portable speech scrambler for voice communications by radio or wire.

III. *Countermeasures equipment*
  A. Radio
    1. Search receivers, airborne equivalents of ground RI sets
      a. AN/ARR–5 and 7: receivers covering from .55 to 143 mc. They could be used with radar scope indicators or with panoramic and photographic adapters.
      b. AN/ARQ–4 and 5: panoramic receivers for wide and narrow ranges respectively, used in jamming to counter the enemy's efforts to shift his signal from one frequency to another.

    2. Jammers, both ground and airborne, often used with search receivers
      a. AN/MRQ–1 and 2: powerful mobile ground jammers for LF, MF, and HF bands, modified respectively from SCR–698 and 399.
      b. AN/MRT–1: a very powerful 15-kw jammer developed for use against German ground-air communications in the 37–42 mc band, called "Cigar."
      c. AN/CRT–2 and PRT–1: small expendable jammers to be placed near enemy radios. CRT–2 was an airborne parachute set. PRT–1 was a portable hand-planted jammer, called "Chick."
      d. AN/ARQ–1 ("Sandy"), 7 ("Spotkie"), 8, and 9 (formerly SCR–596) were airborne HF and VHF spot jammers.
      e. AN/ARQ–11: a receiver to detect the frequencies of guided missiles and a transmitter to jam them.
      f. AN/ART–3, 5 through 11, and 14: a series of high-power barrage jammers called "Jackal," each set able to jam its entire frequency range continuously and unattended; used against enemy VHF and tank communications.

    3. Associated equipment
      a. AM–33 (   )/ART: a wide-band amplifier.
      b. AN/ARA–3: a device which converted liaison set SCR–287 into a spot jammer.
      c. AN/TRQ–1: a transportable radio-control intercept station developed for monitoring and controlling radio-jamming sets.

  B. Radar
    1. Search receivers
      a. SCR–587: earliest radar search receiver, 38–3,300 mc.
      b. AN/APR–2: autosearch receiver, which could automatically detect and record radar signals.

c. AN/APR–4, 5, 5A, 6, and 7: improved search receivers covering frequencies up to 6,000 mc.

2. Jammers

a. AN/TPT–1 and 2: ground radar jammers for frequencies from 70 mc to 1,450.

b. AN/APT–1 and 2: low-power radar jammers ("Dina" and "Carpet" respectively) for use in aircraft, able to jam frequencies between 70 mc and 710 mc.

c. AN/APT–3 ("Mandrel") and 5: respectively a spot jammer, 85–135 mc, and a semibarrage jammer, 350–1,400 mc.

d. AN/APT–4, 6, and 8: powerful magnetron jammers, 15–1,100 mc.

e. AN/APQ–2 ("Rug") and 9 ("Carpet III"): powerful barrage jammers.

3. Deception devices

a. AN/APQ–8 and 15: "Spoofer" sets which could throw back a strong echo, making one aircraft appear to be many.

b. "Chaff" or "Window" aluminum foil strips which, when dropped in quantity, threw back multiple reflections, blinding ground radar scopes. Chaff was also developed for large 60 and 81-mm. mortar shells as reflector RR–7/U, 10/U, 26 and 27 U.

4. Associated radar countermeasures equipment

a. Panoramic or oscilloscopic devices used with search receivers to enable operators to study and photograph the characteristics of enemy radar signals

(1) AN/APA–6 and 11: panoramic adapters or scopes.

(2) AN/APA–7: movie-camera photo set which provided a permanent record of oscilloscope presentation.

b. Radar DF's (AN/APA–17 and 24) for attachment to radar search receivers, giving instant cathode-ray indication of the direction of radar-beam source.

c. Automatic tape recorder AN/APA–23 developed to make a record of the frequency and reception time of signals picked up by radar search receivers AN/APR–4, 5, and 7.

d. Automatic tuning adapter (AN/APA–27) designed to detect enemy radar beams and to spot jam them without human assistance.

e. Alarm equipment AN/APR–3: warning to ferret-plane crewmen whenever their craft came dangerously within enemy GCI, AI, and GL radar waves. Dubbed "Boozer."

f. Monitor set AN/TPQ–1: assembly of broad-band receivers, 40–4,000 mc, both to analyze enemy radar waves and to direct friendly jammers.

Training, Testing, and Maintenance and Repair

I. *Training equipment*
A. Target control: radio transmitters and receivers for remote control of gun targets
    1. Water-target control
    SCR–586: receiver and transmitter, the receiver being carried in the target boat to control it on signals from the distant transmitter.
    2. Land-target control
        a. AN/VRW–1: vehicular receiver controlling motion of target car.
        b. AN/TRW–1: transmitter by which a distant operator controlled the receiver and the vehicle in which it was mounted.
    3. Air-target control
        a. RC–57, 64, and AN/ARW–26: airborne receivers.
        b. RC–56 and 65: ground transmitters.
        c. AN/ARW–8: airborne transmitter.
B. Firing error indicators
    1. For antiaircraft artillery training
        a. PH–32: shellburst spotter set including theodolites for observation of shellbursts and a camera to provide a motion-picture record.
        b. AN/TVQ–1: shellburst spotter set similar to PH–32.
        c. AN/ART–4 and GRR–1: airborne transmitter and ground receiver, the transmitter being carried in a target sleeve aloft, in order to note the projectile's shock waves and radio the extent of error to the receiver on the ground.
    2. For aerial gunnery training
    AN/ART–16 and ARR–10: airborne transmitter and airborne receiver.
C. Classroom training sets
    1. Trainers in the operation of ground and airborne radars
        a. BC–968 and BC–1070: trainers for SCR–268, 270, and 271. BC–1070 modified for PPI became AN/UPS–T2.
        b. RC–110, 225, and 253: AI trainers for SCR–540, 520, and 720.
        c. RC–111, 227, and AN/APS–T1, 1A, and 2: ASV trainers for SCR–517, 717, and 521.
        d. AN/APQ–T1: aircraft gun-laying trainer.
    2. Trainers in navigational aids
        a. RC–242 and 252: for instruction in loran usage.
        b. AN/APN–3 T1: for instruction in shoran usage.
    3. Countermeasure trainers
        a. AN/TPQ–T1 and 2: radar-jamming trainers to teach oscilloscope men to use their radars successfully despite jamming effects.
        b. AN/URA–T1: radio-jamming trainer to teach radiomen to copy messages amid jamming effects.

4. Code training sets

a. EE–81, 94, 95, and 96: classroom practice code and tape sets.

b. AN/GGQ–1 and GSC–T1: visual and audible code practice sets.

II. *Testing equipment*

(NOTE: for practically every new radio and radar set and for every new wire system it distributed, the Signal Corps had to provide suitable equipment for testing and maintenance. The items enumerated in categories II and III are selected from huge numbers of test, maintenance, and tool repair sets.)

A. Radio and radar

1. Testing sets for general and specific uses

a. I–56: a universal radio test set.

b. AN/GPM–1 and MPM–1: basic radar test sets.

c. IE–9 and 26: large sets for use by Signal Corps repair and service units.

d. IE–17 and 75: for testing handie-talkie SCR–536.

e. IE–30 and 57: for testing ASV and AI radars, such as SCR–517 and 520.

f. RC–68: for testing the radar SCR–268.

g. TS–20/APN–4: for testing airborne loran receiver.

h. AN/APM–28 and 29: for testing radars in L-band, 50 cm.

i. AN/APM–10, 33, 34, and 37: for testing S-band radars, 10 cm.

j. AN/APM–21, 22, 41, and 42: for testing K-band radars, 1 cm.

2. Frequency meters: for measuring and correcting the frequencies of radio and radar transmitters

a. SCR–211 and BC–221: for LF, MF, and HF to 20 mc.

b. TS–174/U: for VHF extending to 280 mc.

c. TS–175/U: for VHF and UHF, from 85 to 1,000 mc.

d. TS–213/U: for UHF and SHF, from 300 to 5,000 mc.

3. Phantom antennas, used in testing (or in practice sending) to suppress actual radiation and so keep the set "off the air"

a. A–55, 56, 57, and 58: for SCR–177, 183, 188, and 193.

b. A–31, 32, 33, 34, and 62: for vehicular radios in the "500" series.

B. Wire

1. General test sets

a. IE–10, 29, 53: for testing telegraph and telephone equipment, carrier terminals, repeaters, etc.

b. TS–2/TG: teletypewriter test set.

2. Specific test equipment

a. Telephone and telegraph test boards, to locate and clear wire circuit troubles

(1) BD–101: 120-circuit board for testing in a central office.

(2) BD–103: 20-circuit board for roadside testing in the field.

b. Fault locator, detecting short-circuits along wire lines TS–26 and 27/TSM: volt-ohm meters.

III. *Maintenance and repair equipment*

A. Radio and radar

　1. Maintenance and tool sets

　　a. ME–9, 13, 34, and 35: for general radio maintenance.

　　b. ME–104, 105, 108, etc.: maintenance and tool sets for specific radars, SCR–584, 545, 268, etc.

　　c. ME–53 and 67: for maintenance of walkie-talkie SCR–300.

　　d. TE–41, 46, 113, 114: tool sets for radio repair.

　2. Suppression of radio noise (vehicular interference) and static

　　a. AN/URM–3: radio-interference meter.

　　b. AN/ASA–1 and 3: discharge assemblies to drain static electricity from a plane in flight.

　3. Tropicalization: protecting electrical equipment against moisture and fungus

　　a. MK–2 and 1/GSM: kits containing infrared lamps, water-repellent and fungus–proofing varnishes, spray guns, etc.

　　b. 68–Q–4 and 5: kit developed to tropicalize radar SCR–268.

　4. Mobile repair stations: mounted in trucks and trailers, for third echelon maintenance

　　a. AN/MRM–1: for radio maintenance only.

　　b. AN/MSN–1: for both radio and wire.

B. Wire

　1. Construction and maintenance sets

　　a. ME–4, 11, and 30: for telephone centrals TC–1, 4, 10, and 12, of which these sets were usually component parts.

　　b. ME–22: for maintenance of field telephone set EE–8.

　　c. ME–10: for general maintenance and repair of telephone and telegraph equipment.

　　d. ME–7, 18, and 37: for teletypewriter maintenance.

　　e. TE–16: cable-splicing set.

　　f. ME–44, 47, 49, 75, 111, 112: tool sets for repair of wire equipment both telephone and telegraph.

　　g. TE–50: tool set for repair of teletypewriter equipment.

　　h. TE–27 and 58: for pole line construction.

　2. Mobile repair stations

　　a. AN/MTM–1: mounted in a truck and trailer to provide fourth echelon maintenance.

　　b. AN/MTM–2 and 3: similar mobile sets designed for third echelon maintenance.

Photography

I. *Cameras*
  A. Still pictures
    1. General use
      a. PH–120, 150, 195, and 205: portrait and view cameras taking large pictures, 8 by 10 inches.
      b. PH–47 and 324: taking average pictures, four by five inches, and small 33-mm. pictures respectively.
    2. Special use
      a. PH–518( ) /PF: camera especially developed for use in combat areas, stoutly constructed and tropicalized, taking 70-mm. film (pictures 2½ by 2¾ inches).
      b. AN/TFQ–6: a photoflash camera developed for recording surgical operations.
  B. Moving pictures
    1. PH–270 and 274: heavy newsreel-type 35-mm. cameras.
    2. PH–330: standard movie camera in World War II, 35-mm.
    3. PH–430 and 431: small, 16-mm. movie cameras.
II. *Projectors*
  A. PH–131 and 398: 16-mm. sound projectors.
  B. PH–331 and 405: 35-mm. sound projectors.
  C. PH–526/UF: projector for large audiences (up to 2,000).
  D. AN/TFQ–4: projector for small audiences (up to 600) ; rugged, for use under any conditions from arctic to tropical.
  E. PH–420–A: small portable projector screen for use in daylight.
  F. PH–222: small projector of film strip and slides.
III. *Other photographic equipment*
  A. Identification sets
    1. PH–385: for field use, including a 35-mm. camera, fingerprint set, lamps, etc.
    2. PH–261 and AN/TFQ–1: field sets including printing and enlarging equipment.
  B. V-mail equipment
    1. PH–512: rapid developer, machine-driven, for developing and drying 100-foot rolls of 16-mm. film or 50-foot rolls of 35-mm. film.
    2. PH–542: enlarger for 16 or 35-mm. film.
  C. Miscellaneous equipment
    1. PH–524/PF: low tripod, permitting the camera man to "shoot" while lying prone.
    2. PH–515/MF: photographic equipment pack for jeep transport, in cluding a tripod for operating a movie camera on the jeep.
    3. PH–253, 298, 406, 413: sets for processing and developing films of various sizes and types.

4. PH–13, 67, 129, 395: printers.
5. PH–275, 285, 511: enlargers.
6. PH–261, 383, 390, and 392: darkroom sets, housed in small tents.
7. S–11/GF and AN/TFQ–7: darkrooms housed in HO–27, the former a mobile shelter, the latter a transportable laboratory completely equipped for developing still and movie negatives in the field.

Meteorology

I. *Instruments of measurement*
  A. Barometers and barographs
    1. ML–2 and 330/FM: mercury barometers.
    2. MIL–9, 102, 331, 332, and 333/TM: aneroid barometers.
    3. ML–3: barograph with clock mechanism and ink-recording equipment.
  B. Thermometers and thermographs
    1. ML–4, 5, and 7: mercury and alcohol thermometers.
    2. ML–352/UM: thallium amalgam for use at temperatures below the minimum of mercury thermometers.
    3. ML–77 and 277: thermographs with ink recorder and clock-regulated mechanism.
  C. Psychrometers: for measuring humidity
    1. ML–24 and 224: relative humidity gauges, rotated by hand.
    2. ML–313/AM: automatic, for upper-air readings.
    3. ML–341/GM: for use in sub-zero temperatures.
  D. Anemometers
    1. ML–62 and 80: the former a small hand-carried set; the latter a standard wind speedometer with three cup-shaped wind scoops on a vertical axle.
    2. ML–107: portable set, including a wire transmitter, which noted wind direction and velocity as far away as 1,000 feet.
    3. AN/GMQ–1: similar to ML–107 but designed to operate with fixed ground or mobile weather stations.
  E. Helionephoscope and hygrometer
    1. ML–385 ( )/UM: helionephoscope, an illumination meter to measure intensity of sunlight.
    2. ML–342 ( )/GM: hygrometer to determine dew point at low temperatures.
  F. Cloud height indicators
    1. ML–121 and 318/TMQ–2: ceiling-light projectors, used only at night with clinometer ML–119.
    2. AN/GMQ–2: projector, detector, and recorder; capable of continuous operation unattended.

3. AN/AMQ-4: optical device for use from a moving airplane.

G. Theodolites and plotting equipment: telescopes, plotting boards, etc., for visually tracking ascending pilot balloons to determine wind direction and velocity

  1. ML-47 and 247: telescopes mounted on tripods.

  2. ML-120 and 122: lightweight wood and plastic plotting boards.

II. *Data-gathering instruments*

A. Radiosonde equipment

  . 1. Airborne radiosondes, transmitters which were carried aloft by balloons or planes

    a. ML-141: standard audio-modulated transmitter and associated weather instruments; became AN/AMQ-1.

    b. AN/AMT-1, 2, 3, and 4: balloon and parachute sets.

  2. Ground receivers and DF's, the function of the latter being to track the emissions of the drifting radiosonde so as to determine wind direction and velocity at all levels through which the transmitter may pass.

    a. SCR-658: both a DF and a receiver of the radiosonde transmissions; developed from SCR-258, originally designed as a radiosonde DF only.

    b. AN/CRD-1: lightweight DF and receiver on UHF developed for postwar radiosondes.

  3. Ground receivers and recorders.

    a. AN/TMR-1 (AN/TMQ-5) and 2: transportable receivers and recorders used in conjunction with SCR-658.

    b. AN/FMQ-1: device automatically recording radiosonde data on a printed graph.

B. Wire sonde equipment

AN/UMQ 4: instruments held aloft by a captive balloon and transmitting data to ground over wires running along the balloon cable.

C. Aerographs: automatic weather recorders

  1. ML-175 and 195: attached to exterior of airplane and transmitting data to recording equipment inside.

  2. AN/AMQ-2 and 3: comparable instruments, but attached to interior of plane and automatically recording pressure, temperature, and relative humidity for four hours to elevations of 23,000 feet.

D. Spherics equipment

AN/GRD-1: semifixed direction finder designed to take bearings on static, or lightning flashes, at distances up to 1,500 miles.

E. Ionospheric equipment

AN/CPQ-7: set developed to measure, by means of radar reflections, the height of the ionosphere and obtain data valuable to HF (skywave) radio transmission.

F. Radar trackers: radar sets to track special radar reflectors which were carried either by balloons or by parachutes released from rockets

    1. SCR–525: massive radar with large triple antenna array, the whole weighing 15,000 pounds.

    2. SCR–825: much lighter set, air transportable.

III. *Weather station sets*

  A. Mobile, attended stations

    1. SCM–1: mounted on a truck and trailer; designed for the AAF.

    2. SCM–9 and 10: respectively, radiosonde and ballistic wind sta-. tions, developed for Field Artillery. The sets were subsequently combined and became AN/TMQ–4.

    3. SCM–13: radiosonde and wind station developed for Coast Artillery.

    4. AN/TMQ–1: air-transportable station with complete meteorological station equipment; for the AAF. AN/TMQ–4 was a meteorological station for the Field Artillery.

  B. Automatic unattended stations, including telemetering devices

    1. SCM–17: a station developed to transmit, by radio pressure, temperature and relative humidity data up to 300 miles over a month; controlled by clock mechanism and powered by batteries.

    2. SCM–18: parachute set designed to begin operation upon reaching ground and to transmit its data up to 100 miles for a week.

    3. SCM–19: large semipermanent set powered by a gasoline engine and able to collect pressure, temperature, humidity, wind, rainfall, and sunlight data and to transmit it over distances up to 500 miles for a three-month period.

IV. *Other meteorological equipment*

  A. Balloons

    1. Pilot balloons: small, for revealing winds aloft

      a. ML–50, 51, 64, 155, 156, 157, 158: of various colors and composition; all for observing low-level wind conditions.

      b. ML–159, 160, and 161: larger, 100-gram rapid ascent balloons for observation (by theodolites) of high-level winds.

    2. Sounding balloons: large, for carrying radiosondes to the stratosphere

      a. ML–131: 350-gram balloon (14 feet in diameter when fully inflated) .

      b. ML–162: a still larger balloon, 700 grams.

  B. Hydrogen generators

    1. ML–165 and 185: heavy generators for field use.

    2. ML–303, 304A, and 305A/TM: one- or two-pound can of calcium hydride, each capable of inflating a small balloon.

    3. AN/TMQ–3: portable generator for inflating 350-gram balloons.

Accessories

I. *Power equipment*

A. Electric generators, powered by

  1. Gasoline

    a. PE–49 and 210: lightweight one-cylinder engined d–c generators for powering SCR–177 and 188 and for charging batteries.

    b. PE–77: a portable 70-pound one-cylinder unit for field teletypewriter set EE–97.

    c. PE–201: a 300-pound one-cylinder unit which powered telephone and telegraph carrier equipment.

    d. PE–75 and 95: respectively a 300-pound one-cylinder unit and a 1,500-pound four-cylinder unit both widely used with many Signal Corps sets to supply standard 120-volt 60-cycle alternating current.

    e. PE–74, 84, and 85: heavy (2½-tons) four-cylinder-engined generators used with radars such as SCR–268, 270, and 271.

    f. PU–6/TPS–1: a compact 130-pound unit used with LW radars such as AN/TPS–1 and 3.

    (NOTE: by 1945 the Signal Corps had many other gasoline engine generators in the PU category under development to replace the PE types which served throughout the war.)

  2. Wind

    AN/CSQ–1: an air-transportable generator with a wind-driven propeller mounted atop a 60-foot tower designed to charge storage batteries, which in turn powered automatic weather stations developed for the AAF.

  3. Hand: the electric generator, laboriously hand-cranked during the operation of the radio, yielded sufficient current for small portable sets

    a. GN–35: used with SCR–131, 161, and 171.

    b. GN–45 and 58: used respectively with SCR–284 and 694.

  4. Heat: thermoelectric power units PP–19, 107, 131–133, were experimental generators of low power (20 watts or less) which converted heat (derived from burning gasoline) to electric current. These generators were not adopted in the field because of the weight of fuel which they required and because of the smoke they produced.

B. Electric power converters

  1. Dynamotors and vibrators: devices which draw direct current from storage batteries of low voltages (usually vehicular) and convert it to the various high voltages required by the multiple needs of radio transmitter and receiver components

    a. Dynamotors

      (1) DM–34 and 35: used to power vehicular radios SCR–508 and

608 from 12-volt storage batteries. DM–36 and 37 were similar but operated from 24-volt vehicular batteries.

(2) PE–55: drawing current from a 12-volt vehicular battery to operate the SCR–245.

(3) PE–194: used to convert energy from an airplane battery to operate the command VHF radio SCR–522.

b. Vibrators

(1) PE–157, which provided power for the SCR–511 when used in vehicles, drawing energy from the storage battery.

(2) PE–212: power pack developed for use with the walkie-talkie SCR–300. It included a small storage battery and a vibrator to convert the battery energy to the voltage requirements of the radio set.

2. Rectifiers: devices which convert standard commercial alternating current to direct current as required

a. RA–43 and 120: used to power the teletypewriter central TC–3 and portable radios SCR–510 and 610, drawing on standard power lines, when available.

b. RA–36 and 87: used to recharge storage batteries.

C. Batteries

1. Dry (primary) batteries

a. Single and multiple units or cells containing an activating paste, usually sal-ammoniac, and weighing from a few ounces to several pounds

(1) BA–23, 30, 65: $1\frac{1}{2}$-volt single cells.

(2) BA–1, 205/U, 209/U: 3-volt cells.

(3) BA–9, 216/U: $4\frac{1}{2}$-volt cells.

(4) BA–203/U and 207/U: 6 and 9-volt cells respectively.

(5) BA–2, 8, 219/U: $22\frac{1}{2}$-volt cells.

(6) BA–56, 59: 45-volt cells.

(7) BA–27, 39, 40: multiple-unit batteries consisting of a number of cells and having an increased power output.

(8) BA–102, 127, 130, 140: similar to BA–2, 27, 30, 39, and 40 but especially designed to operate efficiently in cold climates.

b. Special batteries activated by mercury compounds or by sea water

(1) BA–38, 49, 70, and 80: mercury dry-cell batteries used late in the war in SCR–300, 511, 536, and 694.

(2) BA–229 ( ) /CRN: battery intended to be immersed in sea water, which activated its silver-chloride and magnesium electrodes; developed for use with radio buoy beacon AN/CRN–1.

2. Wet (storage or secondary) batteries

a. BB–54, 205/U: 2-volt batteries.

b. BB–29 and 213/U: 4-volt batteries.

c. BB–49, 51, 55: 6-volt batteries, similar to automobile 6-volt storage batteries except for the BB–51 which weighed only a few ounces.

d. BB–46, 50, 201/U: heavy 12- and 14-volt batteries (BB–46 weighed 120 pounds).

e. BB–52: a 36-volt battery, tiny like the 6-volt BB–51 and the 2-volt BB–54, each of which weighed only about one third of a pound, used to power radiosondes when borne aloft by meteorological balloons.

II. *Radio antennas and antenna masts*

(NOTE: in general, antennas were furnished as integral parts of radio sets, such as radio relay antenna AS–19/TRC–1, the 3-element horizontal dipole and 40-foot tube steel mast used with AN/TRC–1, 3, and 4.)

A. AN–29: fishpole antenna used with the short-range radios SCR–609 and 610.

B. AN–130 and 131: short and long whip antennas, for walkie-talkie SCR–300.

C. RC–63: a lightweight 32-foot mast (of fir wood in four sections) and wire providing a vertical half-rhombic (inverted V) antenna for the short-range radios SCR–194, 195, and 609.

D. RC–291 and 296: special antennas designed to extend the range of the walkie-talkie SCR–300 by elevating its radiations above jungle tree tops. RC–291 consisted of a vertical whip from whose base radiated four horizontal whips, the whole elevated upon a pole or tree top. RC–296 was a single vertical whip mounted upon a lightweight sectional mast 30 feet high.

E. RC–292: somewhat similar to RC–291 but accompanied by 30-foot mast and designed to extend the short ranges of SCR–608 and 628.

F. AN/GRA–4: equipment which permitted the construction of several types of antennas for use with short and medium range sets such as SCR–177, 193, 245, and 284.

G. MS–49 through 56: lightweight tubular steel sections comprising a 25-foot mast for SCR–178, 179, 203, and 284. Some of these sections were also commonly used to form a 15-foot vehicular whip antenna (fishpole), set into mast bases MP–37 or 57. Similar sections MS–116, 117, and 118 were used with mast bases MP–48, and AB–15/GR to provide six- and nine-foot whips.

H. MS–65 through 73: aluminum sections providing a 45-foot mast for the long-range mobile radio SCR–197.

I. MA–6 and 7: heavy sectional masts supporting the antennas of the Air Forces VHF ground radios SCR–573, 574, and 624. MA–6 was a 90-foot mast assembled from 11 three-inch steel tube sections. MA–7 was a 50-foot plywood mast.

III. *Headphones, microphones, handsets, and chest sets*

A. Headphones (or double receiver headsets)

1. P–11, 16, 18, 20: radio headphones.

2. HS–18, 23, 33, 38: headphones used with airplane radio and inter-

phone sets, adapted for use within helmets and at high altitudes.

3. HS–30: very lightweight headset widely used by ground forces, having ear inserts patterned after the phones of hearing aids.

B. Microphones

1. T–17: standard radio microphone, held in the hand, switched on for talking.

2. T–30: throat microphone leaving the user's hands free.

3. T–45: lip microphone, attaching to the upper lip of the speaker and used when the surrounding noise was high, because it does not reproduce "ambient" sound as hand-held microphones usually did.

C. Handsets: both radio and telephone, being the hand-held receiver-transmitter unit only

1. TS–9: standard telephone handset (carbon type), part of the battery-powered telephone set EE–8.

2. TS–10: special telephone handset (magnetic type) used with the sound-powered telephone set TP–3.

3. TS–13: standard radio handset incorporating a switch button which the operator pushed when he wished to transfer from reception to transmission.

4. TS–15: handset which combined parts of TS–9 and 13, and which was used with the walkie-talkie SCR–300.

D. Chest sets: transmitter attached to the speaker's chest, with press-to-talk switch mounted on the chest plate (receivers were of headphone type).

1. TD–1 and 2: radio chest sets replacing HS–19.

2. TD–3: chest set designed for use with a gas mask, employing a lip or throat microphone.

3. TD–4 and 5: improved chest sets for use by vehicular or aircraft radio operators.

IV. *Trucks, trailers, and shelters*

A. Trucks and trailers

1. For wire line construction work

a. K–43: telephone maintenance and construction truck with a tripod derrick for raising and setting poles.

b. K–44: truck mounting (1) an earth borer to drill holes and (2) a single derrick mast to set poles.

c. K–36, 37, and 38: trailers, the first and second for hauling poles, cable reels, etc., the third for transporting cable splicing set TE–56.

2. For transporting and housing large radio and radar sets, communication centrals, meteorological station sets, etc.

a. K–18 and 19: truck and trailer for transporting and housing the long-range SCR–197. Trailer K–19 was developed into a 4-wheel house trailer, K–35, for mobile telephone, telegraph, RI, DF, and message centrals.

b. K–51: a panel truck used with the long-range radio SCR–299.

c. K–53: a special van body mounted on a standard 2½-ton 6 x 6 truck.

d. K–55: a semitrailer, lighter weight than K–35, used similarly to house central office sets. It was also used for meteorological (SCM) and fighter-control (SCS) components. It was usually hauled by trucks K–53 or K–60.

e. K–56 and 60: trucks with van bodies to house and transport large radar sets.

f. K–75 and 78: large van trailers, the former for SCR–545; the latter for SCR–584.

B. Shelters

1. HO–17: a plywood shelter similar to a van truck body but an independent unit. It could be carried by any standard 2½-ton truck and could be removed and placed on the ground. Its plywood walls included built-in wire screening to provide electrical shielding. Its dimensions were approximately 11 by 6 by 5 feet. It was widely used for housing large sets, for wire and message centrals, intercept units, and so on.

HO–27: a transportable shelter similar to HO–17 but lacking the wire screen shielding.

Bibliographical Note

The sources detailed in the Bibliographical Notes of the two preceding volumes of the Signal Corps subseries (*The Emergency*, to 7 December 1941, and *The Test*, to mid-1943) also provide the bulk of data the authors employed for this final volume of the subseries. These materials were heavily used as they applied to the period from mid-1943 to V–J Day for it is those last two years of the war that constitute the time frame of *The Outcome*, in keeping with the chronological treatment of the Signal Corps subseries of the UNITED STATES ARMY IN WORLD WAR II histories.

These sources—containing the voluminous files of the many elements of the Office of the Chief Signal Officer (including also records of the Office of the Chief of Staff, the Army Air Forces, and the Army Service Forces, such as the ASF training monographs) —were located at the time of their use in the Departmental Records Branch of The Adjutant General's Office. In 1958 that organization, with its record holdings, was transferred to the Federal Records Center, General Services Administration, in Alexandria, Virginia. Notable among the materials used in *The Outcome* were the Signal Corps annual reports for fiscal years 1943, 1944, 1945, and 1946 (all in manuscript form), the History of Signal Corps Research and Development, the industrial summaries and related procurement and supply histories, the Signal Corps Information Letters, the Digest of Progress and Problems, Signal Corps Intelligence Agency

(SCIA) files, and the many Signal Corps historical monographs prepared by the Historical Section of the OCSigO during the war and immediately after it. All these sources are described in the Bibliographical Note of *The Signal Corps: The Test*.

A number of additional sources, some of which the authors employed for the first time in *The Outcome*, require detailing here. Foremost were those files and accounts that deal with Signal Corps activities in the overseas theaters. Since the files of overseas commands were concentrated in the Army's Kansas City Research Center, in Kansas City, Missouri, searches were made among the organizational records in that center, which yielded quantities of useful material. Greater use, however, was made of copies of overseas reports that were located in the SCIA files, in the files of the Plans and Operations Division, OCSigO, and in the files of the Chief Signal Officer and his deputy (the Code files) described in the Bibliographical Note of *The Test*.

Another useful source of theater materials is the collection compiled in the World War II Historical Section of the Signal Corps. These files, entitled simply Italy, Sicily, North Africa, and so on, include copies, or extracts of copies, of official Army operations reports, after action reports, observers' reports, and other documents concerned with a particular campaign or geographical area.

Especially valuable among the histories of the signal sections of theater commands were the 6-volume history of the signal elements of SHAEF (Report of the Signal Division, Supreme Headquarters, Allied Expeditionary Force, Operation OVERLORD), and the 2-volume manuscript history of the Signal Service, Headquarters, ETOUSA (Historical Report of ETOUSA OCSigO, Admin. File No. 574). Equally helpful were the reports of the signal sections of field armies, as follows: the First United States Army (FUSA), *Report of Operations, 20 October 1943–1 August 1944*, Book VI, Annex No. 12 (in a sequel FUSA *Report of Operations, 1 August 1944–22 February 1945*, the Signal Section portion is Annex No. 8 in Book III); the Third United States Army (TUSA), After Action Report 1 August 1944–9 May 1945, Part 22; and the 12th Army Group After Action Report, or Report of Operations 19 October 1943–12 May 1945, Volume XI, Section 5 (Signal). For the Mediterranean theater, the History of the Signal Section, Allied Force Headquarters, was a most useful document in the period July 1942 through November 1945. The same headquarters also published the AFHQ CSigO Monthly Bulletin, which proved equally useful. Copies of all these documents are located in the World War II Records Division, National Archives, and also in the Signal Corps Historical Section file.

Contrasting disadvantageously with these rather comprehensive accounts of Signal Corps activities in the theaters of the west, are the sketchy, incomplete accounts of the signal sections of the CBI and of some of the Pacific commands. The CBI Signal Section history is fragmentary. A poor carbon copy of several portions of both the CBI and successor IB Theaters, but not of the China Theater, is in the Signal Corps Historical Section file. The same file also contains a partial manuscript history of the Signal Section of the U.S. Army Forces in the South Pacific Area (USAFISPA). Data derived from this South Pacific account was supplemented by the signal portion of an over-all manuscript history entitled History of the U.S. Army Forces in the SOPAC Area During World War II, 30 March 1942–1 August 1944, on file in the Office of the Chief of Military History. The signal portion constitutes Segment C of Part III of Volume I, subtitled Army Administration and Supply. Still another imperfect manuscript account is the signal portion of the History of the U.S. Army Forces Mid-Pacific (HUSAFMIDPAC), also filed in OCMH. Of Signal Corps activities in the Southwest Pacific Area, no single inclusive history was ever prepared. Instead, a number of accounts were written in the Signal Section, GHQ SWPA. These manuscripts describe limited areas of activities, only a scant half-dozen at that, bearing titles such as Seaborne CP's, or History of the SWPA Signal Corps Command Post Fleet; Signal Achievement, Luzon; The Markham River Valley Pole Line; and Spiral-Four in the SWPA. All are on file in the Federal Records Center.

In order to supplement the theater signal record, especially in the Pacific areas, the authors made considerable use of those Armed Forces Staff College lectures (delivered in the 1945–49 era) that dealt with communications subjects. These accounts were prepared by former theater signal officers, giving their recollections and opinions, recounting the lessons of their World War II experience in signal matters. Copies of transcripts of the lectures are in the files of the Plans and Operations Division, Office of the Chief Signal Officer, in the Alexandria Federal Records Center. The authors also made much use of a set of Signal School monograph studies written by students at the Advanced Officers School at Fort Monmouth, in the 1948–52 era. In these topical studies the student officers drew heavily upon their World War II experience, thus making the monographs a valuable historical source. The monographs are on file in the Signal School Library at Fort Monmouth.

Interviews and manuscript comments received greater use in this volume than in the preceding two, again especially in the Pacific and CBI chapters. Many of the interviews are of late date and are therefore susceptible, as are the manuscript comments, to the usual infirmities of remembrance well after the event. The manuscript comments comprise a quantity of materials contributed by the many readers who received the first draft of *The Outcome* in 1959.

Numbers of special collections of papers were studied and put to use, such as the personal account compiled by Maj. Gen. Frank E. Stoner, who was chief of the Army Communications Service throughout the war. General Stoner loaned the copy to the authors

for use in their revision of the first draft of *The Outcome*. A valuable collection of pertinent papers and studies was made available by Dr. Edward L. Bowles, who was consultant to the Secretary of War on communications-electronic matters. A file of excerpts and notes from these Bowles papers is reserved in the Signal Corps Historical Section file.

A special collection of source materials, available only in the Army Security Agency, and then only on extraordinary permission of that Agency, was utilized in the chapter on signal security and intelligence. In the World War I background account of that activity the authors used the extensive manuscript prepared in the Signal Corps in 1918 and 1919, an account entitled History of the Signal Corps, American Expeditionary Forces. The account totals seven volumes. Volume I bears the subtitle General History; Volumes II and III, History of the Signal Corps in Combat; Volumes IV and V, Technical and Administrative Services; Volume VI, Miscellaneous; and Volume VII, Recognition of Services. Copies of the monograph are in the Signal Corps Historical Section file in the Federal Records Center, Alexandria, and in the SHAEF records in the World War II Records Division, National Archives.

List of Abbreviations

AA	Antiaircraft
AAA	Antiaircraft artillery
AACS	Army Airways Communications Service
AAF	Army Air Forces
AAFPOA	Army Air Forces, Pacific Ocean Areas
AAFSAT	Army Air Forces School of Applied Tactics
AAG	Air Adjutant General
AAO	Antiaircraft officer
AAR	After action report
ABL	American-British Laboratory
AC	Air Corps
ACAN	Army Command and Administrative Network
ACofAS	Assistant Chief of Air Staff
ACofS	Assistant Chief of Staff
ACS	Army Communications Service
ACSigO	Assistant Chief Signal Officer
Actg	Acting
Admin	Administrative
ADSEC	Advance Section, Communications Zone
AEAF	Allied Expeditionary Air Force
AEF	Allied Expeditionary Force (World War II); American Expeditionary Forces (World War I)
AEFLLCA	American Expeditionary Force Long Lines Control Agency
AFHQ	Allied Force Headquarters
AFPAC	Army Forces in the Pacific
AFSC	Armed Forces Staff College
AG	Adjutant General
AGC	General communications vessel (1943) or amphibious force flagship equipped with special communications facilities (1945)
AGF	Army Ground Forces
AGL	Airborne gun layers
AGO	Adjutant General's Office
AGp	Army group
AI	Airborne interception (radar)
AJ	Antijamming
AM	Amplitude modulation (radio)
An.	Annex
ANCPEA	Army and Navy Communications Production Expediting Agency
ANEPA	Army and Navy Electronics Production Agency
ANF	Allied Naval Forces
APB	Army Pictorial Board
APO	Army Post Office

App.	Appendix
APS	Army Pictorial Service
AR	Army Regulations
ARL	Aircraft Radio Laboratory
ARO	Air range only
ASA	Army Security Agency
ASC	Air Service Command
ASF	Army Service Forces
ASFTC	Army Service Forces Training Center
ASG	Naval sets related to ASV
ASP	Army Supply Program
Asst	Assistant
ASTP	Army Specialized Training Program
ASV	Air-to-surface vessel (radar)
ASW	Assistant Secretary of War
AT&T	American Telephone and Telegraph (Company)
Avn	Aviation
AW	Aircraft warning
AWS	Aircraft Warning Service
AWUTC	Aircraft Warning Unit Training Center
BABS	Blind approach beacon system
BBRL	British Branch of the Radiation Laboratory
Bd	Board
Bk.	Book
Bn	Battalion
BPR	Bureau of Public Relations
Br	Branch
BTO	Bombing-through-overcast (radar)
Bull	Bulletin
CA	Coast artillery; corps area
CAC	Coast Artillery Corps
CBI	China-Burma-India (Theater)
CBR	Communication barge receiver
CBT	Communication barge transmitter
CD	Coast defense
C&E	Communications/co-ordination and equipment
CENPAC	Central Pacific
CG	Commanding general
CH	Chain Home (British radar)
CINC	Commander in Chief
CINCUS	Commander in Chief, U.S. Fleet
CINCPOA	Commander in Chief, Pacific Ocean Areas
CIOS	Combined Intelligence Objectives Subcommittee
Cir	Circular
Cmte	Committee
CNO	Chief of Naval Operations
CO	Commanding officer
Co	Company

CofAS	Chief of Air Staff
CofS	Chief of Staff (U.S. Army)
Com	Communication or communications
	Com is used throughout this volume as the abbreviation for both *communication* and *communications* in accordance with Army practice during the war period, although Signal Corps men used the abbreviation *Comm.*
Comd	Command
Comdg	Commanding
Comdr	Commander
Comdt	Commandant
COMGENSOPAC	Commanding General, South Pacific
COMINCH	Commander in Chief
COMNAVEU	Commander of Naval Forces in Europe
COMZ	Communications Zone
CONAD	Continental Advance Section, Communications Zone
Conf	Conference
Cong.	Congress
Const	Construction
Contl	Control
CP	Command post
CSB	Combined Signal Board
CSigO	Chief Signal Officer
CSQ	Communication ship quarters
CTC	Corps training center
Ctr	Center
CW	Continuous wave
DComdr	Deputy commander
DCSigO	Deputy Chief Signal Officer
Dept	Department
Det	Detachment
Dev	Development
DF	Direction finding (radio) or direction finder
Dir	Director
Dist	District
Distr	Distribution
Div	Division
DSCIZ	Dayton Signal Corps Inspection Zone
DTN	Defense Telecommunications Network (British)
Dukw	Amphibious truck, 2½-ton, 6 x 6
EEIS	Enemy Equipment Intelligence Service
EFM	Expeditionary Force Message
Engr	Engineer
Equip	Equipment
ESCRTC	Eastern Signal Corps Replacement Training Center
ESCS	Enlisted Signal Corps School
ESCTC	Eastern Signal Corps Training Center
E&T	Engineering and Technical

ETG	Electronics Training Group
ETO	European Theater of Operations
ETOUSA	European Theater of Operations, U.S. Army
EW	Early warning
EWLW	Early warning, lightweight
Ex.	Exhibit
Exec	Executive
ExecO	Executive officer
Exped	Expediting
FEAF	Far East Air Forces
Fld	Field
FM	Frequency modulation (radio); Field Manual
FO	Field order
FP	Freight-passenger ship
Ft.	Fort
FUSA	First U.S. Army
FUSAG	First U.S. Army Group
FY	Fiscal year
G–1	Personnel section of the War Department General Staff, or of any other headquarters on the division or higher level.
G–2	Military intelligence section of the War Department General Staff, or of any other headquarters on the division or higher level.
G–3	Operations and training section of the War Department General Staff, or of any other headquarters on the division or higher level.
G–4	Supply section of the War Department General Staff, or of any other headquarters on the division or higher level.
GCI	Ground-controlled interception (radar)
GFE	Government-furnished equipment
GHQ	General headquarters
GL	Gun laying (radar)
GO	General order
Gp	Group
GPO	General Post Office (British)
GS	General Staff
HF	High frequency
Hist	Historical
Hq	Headquarters
HUSAFMIDPAC	Headquarters, U.S. Army Forces, Middle Pacific
IB	India-Burma
IBM	International Business Machine (Corp.)
IBT	India-Burma Theater
I&E	Information and education
IFF	Identification, friend or foe (radar)
Incl	Inclosure
Ind	Indorsement
Inf	Infantry

Info	Information
Inspec	Inspection
Instal	Installation
Instr	Instruction
Intel	Intelligence
IntelO	Intelligence officer
Interv	Interview
IPD	Industrial Personnel Division
IRE	Institute of Radio Engineers
J	Radio intercept service designed to monitor radio traffic between front-line units and to report to headquarters (British). *See* SIAM.
JASCO	Joint Assault Signal Company
JCC	Joint Communication Center
JCS	Joint Chiefs of Staff
jnl	Journal
Jt	Joint
LAB	Low altitude bombing (AN/APQ–5)
Lab	Laboratory
LCM	Landing craft, mechanized
LCT	Landing craft, tank
LCVP	Landing craft, vehicle and personnel
LnO	Liaison officer
Libr	Library
LRP	Long-range penetration
LRPG	Long-range penetration group
LST	Landing ship, tank
LSV	Landing ship, vehicle
LVT	Landing vehicle, tracked
LVT–A	Landing vehicle, tracked (armored)
LW	Light warning (radar)
MAAF	Mediterranean Allied Air Force
MAD	Magnetic airborne detector
Maint	Maintenance
MAL	Multiairline (a type of British pole line construction)
MCU	Mobile communication unit
MEW	Microwave early warning (radar)
Mgmt	Management
MID	Military Intelligence Division
Mil	Military
Min	Minutes
MIT	Massachusetts Institute of Technology
MPR	Monthly progress report
MRS	Memo Routing Slip
MSCPD	Monmouth Signal Corps Procurement District
Msg	Message
MTB	Motor transport brigade
Mtg	Meeting

MTO	Mediterranean Theater of Operations
MTOUSA	Mediterranean Theater of Operations, U.S. Army
Narr	Narrative
NARS	National Archives and Records Service
NATO	North African Theater of Operations
NATOUSA	North African Theater of Operations, U.S. Army
NCAC	Northern Combat Area Command
NCO	Noncommissioned officer
NCS	Net Control Station
N.d.	No date
NDRC	National Defense Research Committee
NEID	New Equipment Introductory Detachment
OCS	Officer candidate school
OCSigO	Office of the Chief Signal Officer
Of	Office
Off	Officer
O/C	Officer in charge
OL	Ocean-going lighter
OMPS	Overseas Motion Picture Service
OPD	Operations Division
Opn	Operation
Orgn	Organization
OSRD	Office of Scientific Research and Development
OSS	Office of Strategic Services
OSW	Office of the Secretary of War
OWI	Office of War Information
Pac	Pacific
PBY	"Catalina"; twin-engine Navy patrol-bomber
PCE	Patrol craft, escort
PCE (R)	Patrol craft, escort (rescue)
P&D	Procurement and distribution
PEA	Plant Engineering Agency
PERL	Pictorial Engineering and Research Laboratory
Pers	Personnel
P&I	Procurement and issue
Plng	Planning
P&O	Plans and operations
POA	Pacific Ocean Areas
POM	Preparation for overseas movement
POW	Prisoner of war
P&P	Plans and programs
PPI	Plan position indicator
PR	Procurement Regulations
Proc	Procurement
Prod	Production
Prog	Program
Proj	Project
PSCPD	Philadelphia Signal Corps Procurement District

PSD	Philadelphia Signal Depot
P&T	Personnel and Training
PTT	Postes Télégraphes et Téléphones
Qtrly	Quarterly
RA	Regular Army
RAAF	Royal Australian Air Force
RAF	Royal Air Force
RCA	Radio Corporation of America
Rcd	Record
RCM	Radio/radar countermeasures
RCT	Regimental combat team
R&D	Research and development
RDF	Radio direction finding (a term for radar before early 1942) or radio direction finder
Reorgn	Reorganization
RI	Radio intelligence
RIP	Reduction of Items Program
RL	Radiation Laboratory
RM	Rubin Mallory (cell)
RN	Royal Navy
ROTC	Reserve Officers Training Corps
RPL	Rapid pole line
RPR	Radio position finding; radio position finder
Rpt	Report
Rqmt	Requirement
R&R	Routing and Reference
RRL	Radiation Research Laboratory
RTC	Replacement Training Center
RTTY	Radioteletype
R&W	Routing and work sheet
S–2	Intelligence section of a unit not having a general staff
S–3	Operations and training section of a unit not having a general staff
SAS	Signal Airways Service
SCAEF	Supreme Commander, Allied Expeditionary Force
SCASA	Signal Corps Aircraft Signal Agency
SCEL	Signal Corps Engineering Laboratories
SCGSA	Signal Corps Ground Signal Agency
Sch	School
SCIA	Signal Corps Intelligence Agency
SCPC	Signal Corps Photographic Center
SCPD	Signal Corps Procurement Depot
SCPL	Signal Corps Photographic Laboratory
SCPS	Signal Corps Photographic School
SCR	Set complete radio
SCS	Supply Control System (Army)
SCTC	Signal Corps training center
SD	Signal Depot

Sec	Section (an office)
Sec.	Section (part of a document)
Secy	Secretary
Sep	Separate
Ser	Serial
SHAEF	Supreme Headquarters Allied Expeditionary Force
SHF	Superhigh frequency
S&I	Storage & Issue
SIAM	Signal Information and Monitoring
Sig	Signal
SigC	Signal Corps
SigCO	Signal Corps officer
SigO	Signal officer
SIS	Signal Intelligence Service
SLC	Searchlight control (radar)
SNA	Stock Numbering Agency
SOLOC	Southern Line of Communications
SOP	Standing operating procedures
SOPAC	South Pacific Area
SOS	Services of Supply
Sp	Special
Spec	Specification
SPOBS	Special Observer Group
SSA	Signal Security Agency
SSB	Single sideband
SSCS	Southern Signal Corps School
Stat	Statistical
Summ	Summary
Sup	Supply
SupO	Supply officer
Sv	Service
SW	Secretary of War
SWPA	South West Pacific Area
TAC	Tactical Air Command
TAG	The Adjutant General
T/BA	Table of basic allowances
TBX	Semiportable radio equipment of low power (Navy)
T/E	Table of equipment
Tech	Technical
TF	Task force
TIG	CBI signal projects coded TIG, for TIGER
Tng	Training
TngO	Training officer
T/O	Table of organization
TOE	Table of organization and equipment
TUSA	Third U.S. Army
TW	Tail warning
UHF	Ultrahigh frequency

U.K.	United Kingdom
USAAF	U.S. Army Air Forces
USAFCBI	U.S. Army Forces, China-Burma-India
USAFFE	U.S. Army Forces in the Far East
USAFIB	U.S. Army Forces, India-Burma
USAFISPA	U.S. Army Forces, South Pacific Area
USAFPOA	U.S. Army Forces, Pacific Ocean Areas
USAR	U.S. Army Reserve
USASOS	U.S. Army Services of Supply
USASRDL	U.S. Army Signal Research and Development Laboratories
USFCT	U.S. Forces, China Theater
USFET	U.S. Forces, European Theater
USFIBT	U.S. Forces, India-Burma Theater
USMC	U.S. Marine Corps
USSTAF	U.S. Strategic Air Force
USW	Under Secretary of War
UTC	Unit training center
V–1	A pilotless German aircraft with a large warhead—the buzz bomb
V–2	German long-range rocket
VF	Voice frequency
VHF	Very high frequency
VIP	Very important person
VT	Variable time; vacuum tube
WAC	Women's Army Corps
Wac	Member of Women's Army Corps
WAR	Communications center of the War Department in Washington
WD	War Department
WDCSA	War Department Chief of Staff, Army
WDGS	War Department General Staff
WDMC	War Department Message Center
WDSS	War Department Special Staff
Wkly	Weekly
WO	Warrant officer
WPB	War Production Board
WP&T	War plans and training
Xmtr	Transmitter
ZI	Zone of interior

Glossary

Altimeter	An aircraft device for measuring altitude.
Alvarez leaky wave guide	A long narrow linear array antenna of several hundred tiny dipoles totaling about sixteen feet in length that enabled the Eagle (*q.v.*) to spread upon its scope a fanlike radar view.
Antrac	A term often used for radio relay equipment. It is derived from the nomenclature AN/TRC—Army-Navy Transportable Radio Communications—assigned to several types of radio relay and other radio sets.
Azimuth	Direction, in terms of horizontal angle, measured clockwise from north.
Azon	A 1,000-pound bomb, controlled in azimuth only, with movable fins containing a receiver that could vary in response to signals radioed from an observer in an airplane above. It was effective against long, narrow targets.
Biscay Cross	A special receiver (German) over which a submarine could hear probing radar pulses on approaching plane.
Black Widow	An airplane (P–61) designed for microwave airborne interception SCR–517 type radar.
Boehme	High-speed radio transmission of Morse code signals by means of perforated tape that can mechanically key a transmitter at speeds up to 400 words a minute.
Breadboard model	A display of electronic equipment assembly in which the wiring and components are spread out over a horizontal surface for ease in making changes in the circuitry; employed both in development laboratories for experimental work and in school instruction.
Carpet	A jamming device, airborne (British).
Carrier	Carrier method, whether involving wire or radio, is a technique that permits many messages, many separate signals, to travel simultaneously without mutual interference over a single circuit.
Cathode ray tube	A vacuum tube with a picture screen, on which the electron beam emitted from the cathode produces a visual indication. *See also* Oscilloscope.
Chaff	Strips of aluminum foil dropped from plane to produce false echoes, "blinding" aircraft search radars; an American device. *See also* Window.
Chain Home	British long-range aircraft detecting radar.
Chain Home Low	British radar able to detect aircraft flying at low elevations.
Chindit	Refers to Brigadier Wingate's 77th Indian Infantry Brigade, nicknamed after the legendary guardian of the

	Burman shrines.
Cigar	A jamming device, ground or airborne. *See also* Tuba.
Cipher	A method of secret writing that retains the letters but transposes them, or replaces them with substituted letters, according to a plan or key.
Code	A method of communication in which predetermined symbols or terms are substituted for the words of the message text.
Common battery switchboard	A switchboard that provides, from a central power supply located at the board, the current needed to operate the telephones connected to the board. Opposite to local battery switchboard (*q.v.*).
Continuous wave	A method of radio communications employing radio waves in which successive cycles are of constant amplitude. The method of transmission may be by hand key or by machine signals.
Crash	Rapid hand construction of equipment by laboratory and engineer personnel.
Cryptanalyst	One who recovers an original message text from an encoded or enciphered cryptogram, without knowing the key; also one who reconstructs such a key.
Cryptography	The process of putting message texts into meaningless letters or symbols by means of code and/or cipher systems.
Dah-dit	The dash-dot, or long and short, signals of Morse code, variously grouped to spell out letters of the alphabet.
Diana	A project using radar to the SCR–271 type (about 112 megacycles) that employed FM-type components to send long pulses to the moon.
Dielectric	An insulating material placed between the plates of a capacitor.
Dina	A Signal Corps jamming device (airborne) employed by the Army Air Forces.
Dipole	A T-shaped antenna, such as the familiar television antenna, used with VHF radiations.
Direction finding	Determining, by means of a radio receiver and special antennas, the direction and location of a transmitter to whose radiations the receiver is tuned. *See also* Goniometry (radio).
Dynamotor	An electrical rotary device usually employed in the power supply of a vehicular storage battery to convert the battery voltage into the higher voltages required by radio operation.
Eagle	A 3-centimeter bombing-through-overcast radar aid (AN/APQ–7), remarkable for its antenna (the Alvarez leaky wave guide, *q.v.*).
E-boat	Small German torpedo boat (S-boat).

Electromagnetic wave	A radio or radar radiation traveling in space at 186,293 miles per second; also heat, light, X-, gamma, and cosmic rays, which are all alike except in frequency and wave length.
Eureka	Ground-based beacon (AN/PPN–1) that sent pulsed responses to Rebecca beacons. The Eurekas were carried by paratroopers aboard Pathfinders. *See* Rebecca and Pathfinder.
Falcon	A 10-centimeter S-band radar aid, air range only (AN/APG–13) employed with 75-milimeter cannon that were specially mounted on B–25's, for firing on Japanese shipping.
Ferret	An airplane, equipped with Signal Corps electronic devices, developed for radar warfare.
Festung Europa	Fortress of Europe, a German term.
Frequency	The number of cycles per second that characterizes any electromagnetic wave or radiation.
Freya	German long-range search (radar direction finding) device.
Gate	An antijamming device (N^2), developed to render the SCR–584 set less susceptible to jamming in the microwave sector of the frequency spectrum.
Gee	A "blind" bombing navigational system (British).
"George" box	An antijamming device developed for the aircraft search radar SCR–271.
Goniometry (radio)	Measuring or taking angles, by means of radio receivers, and directional antennas, on radio/radar radiations so as to determine the location of the transmitter. *See also* Direction finding.
Gun laying	The process of aiming a gun, often at a target which cannot be seen or which is moving, requiring complex calculations.
"Handie-talkie"	A hand-carried infantry radio transceiver, the SCR–536 during World War II.
Hand-key	In manual radiotelegraph sending, the key (operated by the hand or fingers) is a kind of switch capable of being opened or closed rapidly in order to form the dots and dashes of Morse code signals.
High frequency	3–30 megacycles.
High-speed radio	*See* Boehme.
Home Sweet Home	Nickname for H_2S. A British bombing-through-overcast radar, 10-centimeter S-band. Also known as Stinky. *See also* Mickey.
Interrogator	A pulsed transmitter whose signals challenge and automatically elicit an identifying reply from a transponder in a distant craft; part of the identification, friend or foe (radar) system.
Ionosphere	The outer layer of the earth's atmosphere, which reflects

the sky wave component of radio waves of the high-frequency band, enabling long-distance signals.

Jackal	High-powered airborne radio jammer (AN/ART–3).
Jam, to	To cause interference in radio/radar signals by sending out messages in an interfering manner; to make a radio/radar apparatus ineffective by jamming radio or radar signals or by causing reflection of radar waves from a special device.
Jostle	A radio transmitter jamming device (British) that could overpower the enemy's command radio telephones with meaningless noise.
Kamikaze	A suicidal attack by an air attack corps plane containing explosives to be flown in a crash on a target.
Key	*See* Hand-key.
Kilocycle	One thousand cycles per second.
Kilowatt	One thousand watts.
Lichtenstein	Enemy's name for a type of German airborne radar, an airborne interception set. Also known as SN–2.
Link-Sign procedure	A British method by which radio operators could identify each other with scant likelihood of revealing their identification to enemy listeners.
Local battery switchboard	A switchboard which interconnects telephone sets, each having its own dry batteries to provide the talking current. Opposite to common battery switchboard (*q.v.*).
Loran	Long-range aid to navigation: a highly accurate system employing beacons and aircraft or ship receivers, the receivers determining the position of the beacons from their radiations.
Low frequency	30–300 kilocycles.
Luftwaffe	German Air Force.
Magnetron	An electronic tube in which the electron flow is controlled by an externally applied magnet and which is capable of producing powerful oscillations at microwave frequencies.
Mandrel	A spot jamming device (AN/APT–3).
Manual radio	Transmitting Morse code dah-dits by hand key.
Maquis	A French guerrilla fighter resisting the Germans in World War II.
"Mary" box	An antijamming device developed for the aircraft search radar SCR–270.
Merrill's Marauders	The 5307th Composite Unit (GALAHAD).
Metox	A receiver (French design) used by the Germans to detect the radiations of the long-wave ASV–II radar.
Mickey	A U.S. bombing-through-overcast radar, 3-centimeter, X-band (AN/APQ–13). Also known as H$_2$X. *See also* Home Sweet Home.

Microwave	Radio waves that radiate at frequencies above 300 megacycles with a wave length of 50 centimeters (20 inches) or less.
Moonshine	British metal foil kitelike reflectors that (towed or released by a few aircraft) gave radar picture or swarms of invading warplanes.
Morse	Morse code: communications according to the code, employing combinations of dashes and dots (dah-dits) to spell out the letters, as in radio or wire telegraphy.
Oboe	A "blind" bombing navigational system (British).
Open wire line	A pole line carrying bare wires, usually galvanized iron or bare copper, for telephone and/or telegraph communications.
Oscilloscope	A cathode ray tube (q.v.) used, like a television picture tube, in a radar receiver to display visually target echoes.
Pathfinder	A British airplane using special navigational devices to guide "blind" bombing missions.
Phantom circuit	An additional channel of communications which can be superimposed upon two physical pairs, that is, two pairs of telephone wires already carrying two channels of communications.
Photo Mail	Used to describe microfilming of official documents and communications between the War Department and U.S. Government activities overseas. The filmed messages were enlarged at destination. *See also* V–mail.
Piezoelectric effect	The effect of producing an electrical voltage in a crystal by compressing or twisting it.
Point-to-point	A term used of radio operation between two stations (generally fixed, with directional antenna arrays) signaling between each other only. Compare with radio broadcast operation, when a transmitting station signals to all receivers in its net, which are tuned to the frequency employed by the transmitting station.
Radio compass	A receiver that determines the direction of received radio waves and registers the direction visually on a meter or compass scale.
Radio range beacon	A radio transmitter radiating a narrow directional guide beam on which craft may "home."
Range	The distance from a gun or an observer to the target.
Rawin	Radio Wind, that is, determination of wind speed and direction at different altitudes by means of radio.
Razon	A bomb similar to Azon (q.v.). The Razon could be controlled in range and azimuth.
Rebecca	Beacon (AN/APN–2), carried by Troop Carrier Command for the purpose of interrogating and receiving pulsed responses from ground-based Eurekas (q.v.).

Rectifier	An item of equipment which converts, or rectifies, alternating current (AC) to produce a desired direct current (DC).
Responsor	The receiver of an identification, friend or foe (radar) system, used with an interrogator (q.v.).
Rhombic antenna	A large transmitting antenna utilized by fixed long-range radio stations. The antenna wires, extended between four poles or towers, form a diamond-shaped or rhombic pattern, capable of directing powerful electromagnetic waves in a definite direction.
Rug	A jamming device, airborne (AN/APQ-2).
Schmetterling 8-117	Antiaircraft rocket (German).
Sferics	Derived from atmospherics, or what the radio listener simply calls static technique that makes use of lightning discharges.
Shoran	A short-range navigation system employing electronic methods similar to Loran (q.v.).
Sigaba	A cipher machine requiring separate operators and separate processing at both transmitting and receiving stations to encipher and decipher messages.
Sigcircus	A completely self-sufficient 60-kilowatt single sideband, multichannel, mobile radio station that could perform simultaneously radio teletypewriter operation, local broadcast, photograph facsimile, and shortwave broadcasts. The radioteletypewriter channels provided for simultaneous transmission and reception of as many as 300,000 words daily.
Sigcircus Junior	There were four of these single-channel radioteletypewriter mobile radio stations, two of them 1.2 kilowatts, two 300 watts in power. These stations could transmit or receive 50,000 words daily.
Sigcum	An on-line cipher machine, automatically insured that the output of the transmitting teletypewriter was made secure, that is, enciphered and rendered unbreakable to enemy intercept and analysis effort. The Sigcum at the originating station jumbled the text and the Sigcum at the receiving end deciphered the transmission automatically.
Sky wave	That portion of a radio wave transmitted from an antenna that travels upward and is reflected down to earth by the ionosphere (q.v.). Used in the high-frequency band by long-range military radios, the sky wave under favorable conditions enables communications over very long distances.
Specialist Plan	A plan for direct recruitment of specialists from civil life.
Spiral-four	A rubber-covered field cable of four conductors especially constructed for the transmission of multiple telephone

	and/or telegraph signals by means of wire carrier techniques.
Stinky	*See* Home Sweet Home.
Stuka	A German airplane, the JU–87.
Theodolite	A telescope, similar to the tripod-mounted transit of a surveyor, by which an observer can follow moving objects, such as a weather balloon, reading its elevation and azimuth from moment to moment.
Traffic	Passing of messages over wire circuits or radio channels.
Transceiver	A radio transmitter and receiver combined in one unit, portions of its circuits being used for both functions.
Transponder	A combined receiver-transmitter employed in the identification, friend or foe (radar) system. The receiver on being challenged by a distant interrogator, stimulates the transmitter to send back coded identification signals. *See also* Interrogator *and* Responsor.
Tuba	A jamming device (British ground-based Cigar) with a 38–42-megacycle band capacity, that had sufficient power to jam German aircraft communications across the Channel.
Ultrahigh frequency	300–3,000 magacycles.
V–mail	A method by which personal mail was microphotographed on 16-millimeter film for ease and economy of transportation. At the destination the filmed messages were enlarged and reproduced for delivery.
Very high frequency	30–300 megacycles.
Violet Plan	A plan under which French Forces of the Interior in agreement with Allied command launched systematic sabotage program just before Normandy landings.
Walkie-talkie	A portable radio set adapted for carrying on a soldier's back, having a longer range than the smaller "handie-talkie." The standard walkie-talkie during World War II was the infantry's SCR–300, replacing the original walkie-talkies, the SCR's–194 and 195.
Window	Strips of tin foil dropped from plane to produce false echoes, "blinding" aircraft search radars, a British device. *See also* Chaff.
Wuerzburg	A German gun director (radar), the Wuerzburg, *Flakmessgerat* 39–T, radiating on medium-length waves at about 500 megacycles.
( )	"Bowlegs" in Signal Corps nomenclature system; indicates that it applies to all models of the set.

Code Names

ALAMO	Code for U.S. Sixth Army while operating as a special ground task force headquarters directly under GHQ SWPA
ANVIL	Plan for Allied invasion of southern France in the Toulon-Marseille area
AVALANCHE	Invasion of Italy at Salerno
BEAVER I	Aleutian radio/radar countermeasures operations
BEAVER III	Corsica radio/radar countermeasures operations
CENT	Task force for Sicily assault landing
CROSSBOW	General term used by the Allies to refer to the German long-range weapons program and to Allied countermeasures against it
DIME	Task force for Sicily assault landing
DRAGOON	Allied invasion of southern coast of France, 15 August 1944, planned under the code name ANVIL
EUREKA	International conference at Tehran, November 1943
FORAGER	Operations in the Marianas
GALAHAD	American Long-range penetration groups (Burma)
GOLD	Normandy beach assaulted by troops of British 30 Corps, 6 June 1944
HUSKY	Allied invasion of Sicily, July 1943
JOSS	Task force for Sicily assault landing
JUNO	Normandy beach assaulted by troops of Canadian 3d Division, 6 June 1944
KOOL	Task force (floating reserve) for Sicily assault landing
LUCKY	General Patton's headquarters in ETO
MATTERHORN	Plan for operating B-29's from Cheng-tu against Japan
NEPTUNE	Actual 1944 operations within OVERLORD. Used for security reasons after September 1943 on all OVERLORD planning papers that referred to target area and date.
OCTAGON	Second Quebec conference (U.S.-British), September 1944
OLYMPIC	Plan for March 1946 invasion of Kyushu, Japan
OMAHA	Normandy beach assaulted by troops of U.S. V Corps, 6 June 1944
OVERLORD	Allied cross-Channel invasion of northwest Europe, June 1944
QUADRANT	First Quebec conference (U.S.-British), 12–14 August 1943
SEXTANT	International conference at Cairo, 22–26 November, 2–7 December 1943
SHARK	Task force for Sicily assault landing
SHINGLE	Amphibious operation at Anzio, Italy
SWORD	Normandy beach assaulted by troops of British 3d Division, 6 June 1944

TIGER	A code name for various Chinese-Burma-India signal projects
TORCH	Allied invasion of northwest Africa.
UTAH	Beach assaulted by troops of U.S. VII Corps, 6 June 1944
WIDEWING	Code name for U.S. Eighth Air Force switchboard at Bushy Park, Teddington, London (SHAEF headquarters)
X–Force	Force under General Stilwell's Command in Burma campaign, 1944
Y–Force	30 U.S.-sponsored Chinese divisions in Yunnan
Z–Force	30 Chinese divisions the United States once hoped to reorganize in East China

UNITED STATES ARMY IN WORLD WAR II

The following volumes have been published or are in press:

The War Department
  Chief of Staff: Prewar Plans and Preparations
  Washington Command Post: The Operations Division
  Strategic Planning for Coalition Warfare: 1941–1942
  Strategic Planning for Coalition Warfare: 1943–1944
  Global Logistics and Strategy: 1940–1943
  Global Logistics and Strategy: 1943–1945
  The Army and Economic Mobilization
  The Army and Industrial Manpower

The Army Ground Forces
  The Organization of Ground Combat Troops
  The Procurement and Training of Ground Combat Troops

The Army Service Forces
  The Organization and Role of the Army Service Forces

The Western Hemisphere
  The Framework of Hemisphere Defense
  Guarding the United States and Its Outposts

The War in the Pacific
  The Fall of the Philippines
  Guadalcanal: The First Offensive
  Victory in Papua
  CARTWHEEL: The Reduction of Rabaul
  Seizure of the Gilberts and Marshalls
  Campaign in the Marianas
  The Approach to the Philippines
  Leyte: The Return to the Philippines
  Triumph in the Philippines
  Okinawa: The Last Battle
  Strategy and Command: The First Two Years

The Mediterranean Theater of Operations
  Northwest Africa: Seizing the Initiative in the West
  Sicily and the Surrender of Italy
  Salerno to Cassino
  Cassino to the Alps

The European Theater of Operations
  Cross-Channel Attack
  Breakout and Pursuit
  The Lorraine Campaign
  The Siegfried Line Campaign
  The Ardennes: Battle of the Bulge
  The Last Offensive

Index

Made in the USA
Middletown, DE
25 July 2020